Lecture Notes in Computer Science 9204

Commenced Publication in 1973
Founding and Former Series Editors:
Gerhard Goos, Juris Hartmanis, and Jan van Leeuwen

More information about this series at http://www.springer.com/series/7407

Kuai Xu · Haojin Zhu (Eds.)

Wireless Algorithms, Systems, and Applications

10th International Conference, WASA 2015
Qufu, China, August 10–12, 2015
Proceedings

 Springer

Editors
Kuai Xu
Arizona State University
Phoenix, AZ
USA

Haojin Zhu
Shanghai Jiao Tong University
Shanghai
China

ISSN 0302-9743   ISSN 1611-3349   (electronic)
Lecture Notes in Computer Science
ISBN 978-3-319-21836-6   ISBN 978-3-319-21837-3   (eBook)
DOI 10.1007/978-3-319-21837-3

Library of Congress Control Number: 2015944437

LNCS Sublibrary: SL1 – Theoretical Computer Science and General Issues

Springer Cham Heidelberg New York Dordrecht London

Printed on acid-free paper

Springer International Publishing AG Switzerland is part of Springer Science+Business Media
(www.springer.com)

Preface

The 10th edition of the International Conference on Wireless Algorithms, Systems, and Applications (WASA 2015) was held during August 10–12, 2015, at Qufu, Shandong, China.

The conference is motivated by the recent advances in cutting-edge electronic and computer technologies that have paved the way for the proliferation of ubiquitous infrastructure and infrastructureless wireless networks.

WASA is designed to be a forum for theoreticians, system and application designers, protocol developers and practitioners to discuss and express their views on the current trends, challenges, and state-of-the-art solutions related to various issues in wireless networks.

The technical program of the conference included 36 contributed papers together with 42 invited papers, selected by the Program Committee from a number of 133 full submissions received in response to the call for papers.

The papers of WASA 2015 cover various topics, including cognitive radio networks, cyber-physical systems, distributed and localized algorithm design and analysis, information and coding theory for wireless networks, localization, topology control and coverage, underwater and underground networks, vehicular networks, PHY/MAC/routing protocols, information processing and data management. Emerging topics were also discussed at WASA 2015, including: mobile cloud computing, security and privacy, radar and sonar networks, programmable service interfaces, energy-efficient algorithms, systems and protocol design, operating system and middleware support, and experimental testbeds, models, and case studies.

We would like to thank the Program Committee members and external reviewers for volunteering their time to review and discuss conference papers.

We would like to extend special thanks to the Steering Committee and general chairs of the conference for their leadership, and to the finance, publication, publicity, Web, and local organization chairs for their hard work in making WASA 2015 a successful event.

Last but not least we would like to thank all authors for presenting their work at the conference.

June 2015

Kuai Xu
Haojin Zhu
Jiguo Yu

Conference Organization

Steering Committees

Xiuzhen Cheng	The George Washington University, USA (Chair)
Yingshu Li	Georgia State University, USA (Chair)
Jiannong Cao	Hong Kong Polytechnic University, Hong Kong, SAR China
Ness Shroff	The Ohio State University, USA
Wei Zhao	University of Macau, SAR China
PengJun Wan	Illinois Institute of Technology, USA
Ty Znati	University of Pittsburgh, USA
Xinbing Wang	Shanghai Jiao Tong University, China

Honorary General Chair

Wanxue Qi	Qufu Normal University, China

General Chair

Jiguo Yu	Qufu Normal University, China

Program Chairs

Kuai Xu	Arizona State University, USA
Haojin Zhu	Shanghai Jiao Tong University, China

Publication Chairs

Linwei Niu	West Virginia State University, USA
Anu Bourgeois	Georgia State University, USA
Hang Liu	The Catholic University of America, USA

Publicity Chairs

Peixiang Liu	Nova Southeastern University, USA
Xiang Lu	Chinese Academy of Sciences, China
Selcuk Uluagac	Florida International University, USA

Web Chairs

Zhipeng Cai	Georgia State University, USA
Guangshun Li	Qufu Normal University, China
Yuan Zhang	Jinan University, China

Finance Chair

Linzi Ma	Qufu Normal University, China

Local Organization Chair

Shudong Zhang	Qufu Normal University, China

Program Committee

Abdulrahman Alhothaily	The George Washington University, USA
Habib M. Ammari	University of Michigan-Dearborn, USA
Zhipeng Cai	Georgia State University, USA
Bin Cao	Harbin Institute of Technology, China
Ionut Cardei	Florida Atlantic University, USA
Mihaela Cardei	Florida Atlantic University, USA
Cailian Chen	Shanghai Jiao Tong University, China
Siyao Cheng	Harbin Institute of Technology, China
Wei Cheng	Virginia Commonwealth University, USA
Xiuzhen Cheng	George Washington University, USA
Mianxiong Dong	National Institute of Information and Communications Technology, Japan
Yingfei Dong	University of Hawaii, USA
Hongwei Du	Harbin Institute of Technology, China
Zhenhai Duan	Florida State University, USA
Xiaofeng Gao	Shanghai Jiao Tong University, China
Zhongwen Guo	Ocean University of China
Fen Hou	University of Macau, SAR China
Xiaoxia Huang	Chinese Academy of Sciences, China
Donghyun Kim	North Carolina Central University, USA
Hwangnam Kim	Korea University, South Korea
Sanghwan Lee	Kookmin University, Korea
Deying Li	Renmin University of China
Fan Li	Beijing Institute of Technology, China
Ming Li	Utah State University, USA
Minming Li	City University of Hong Kong, SAR China
Qun Li	College of William and Mary, USA

Xinfeng Li	The Ohio State University, USA
Yanhua Li	University of Minnesota, USA
Yingshu Li	Georgia State University, USA
Zhenhua Li	Tsinghua University, China
Hongbin Liang	Sun Yat-Sen University, China
Bin Lin	Dalian Maritime University, China
Peixiang Liu	Nova Southeastern University, USA
Xiang Lu	Chinese Academy of Science, China
Manki Min	South Dakota State University, USA
Aziz Mohaisen	Verisign Labs
Linwei Niu	West Virginia State University, USA
Wenzhuo Ouyang	Rice University, USA
Na Ruan	Shanghai Jiaotong University, China
Sushmita Ruj	Indian Statistical Institute, Kolkata, India
Zhiguo Shi	Zhejiang University, China
Ashwin Sridharan	AT&T
Zhou Su	Waseda University, Japan
Yipin Sun	National University of Defense Technology, China
Jin Teng	Cisco
Xiaohua Tian	Shanghai Jiao Tong University, China
Chao Wang	Beijing Institute of Technology, China
Chaokun Wang	Tsinghua University, China
Li Wang	Beijing University of Posts and Telecommunications, China
Licheng Wang	Beijing University of Posts and Telecommunications, China
Yu Wang	University of North Carolina at Charlotte, USA
Yuexuan Wang	The University of Hong Kong, SAR China
Lifei Wei	Shanghai Ocean University, China
Xiaofu Wu	Nanjing University of Posts and Telecommunications, China
Kai Xing	University of Science and Technology of China
Kuai Xu	Arizona State University, USA
Dong Xuan	Ohio State University, USA
Minhui Xue	East China Normal University, China
Qinshui Xue	Shanghai Jiao Tong University, China
Dejun Yang	Colorado School of Mines, USA
Jianguo Yao	Shanghai Jiao Tong University
Dongxiao Yu	The University of Hong Kong, SAR China
Jiguo Yu	Qufu Normal University, China
Wei Yu	Towson University, USA
Lichen Zhang	Shaanxi Normal University, China
Haojin Zhu	Shanghai Jiao Tong University, China
Hongzi Zhu	Shanghai Jiao Tong University, China
Ting Zhu	The University of Maryland, Baltimore County, USA

Additional Reviewers

Gong, Shimin	Kumrai, Teerawat	Zhang, Chaofeng
Hu, Chunqiang	Li, Hong	Zhang, Xiang
Huo, Yan	Li, Hongjuan	Zhang, Yunjun
Hussain, Rasheed	Shen, Yanyan	Zhu, Haojin
Kim, Hyunbum	Wu, Yueshi	Zhu, Hongsong

Contents

Privacy-Preserving Public Auditing Together with Efficient User Revocation in the Mobile Environments

Feng Chen[1]($\boxtimes$), Hong Zhou[2], Yuchuan Luo[3], and Yingwen Chen[3]

[1] School of Information System and Management,
National University of Defense Technology, Changsha 410073, China
chenfeng@nudt.edu.cn
[2] Guangzhou General Hospital of Command, Guangzhou 510010, China
zhouhong2015@163.com
[3] College of Computer, National University of Defense Technology,
Changsha 410073, China
{lychuan.cs,csywchen}@gmail.com

Abstract. Cloud platforms can provide elastic infrastructure for mobile users. Therefore, publicly auditing the integrity of shared data outsourced on the cloud is very important since the cloud may be untrusted. However, existing remote integrity checking protocols can not preserve owner's privacy nor provide efficient user revocation. In this paper, we analyze a previous work, and improve the protocol to get better user revocation efficiency and preserve the users' privacy against the untrusted cloud platform and the auditor.

Keywords: Mobile computing · Cloud Computing · Data integrity · Public auditing · User revocation · Privacy-preserving

1 Introduction

Utilizing the data storage and sharing services provided by cloud, mobile users can easily share data with each other as a group. More narrowly, users in a group can create data and share it with others. The others in the same group are able to not only access and modify the data, but also share the version he modified. Although the providers of cloud commit a reliable and secure environment to users, the integrity of data might still be damaged due to the carelessness of humans and the failures of hardware or software [2].

A number of protocols [5–11,13,14,16] have been proposed to protect the integrity of data in cloud. Most of them focus on *personal data* except the protocol designed by B. Wang *et al.* [3], which provides a way to publicly audit the shared data in the cloud with efficient user revocation. In this paper, we'll analyze the protocol they proposed and improve it for better efficiency and security.

© Springer International Publishing Switzerland 2015
K. Xu and J. Zhu (Eds.): WASA 2015, LNCS 9204, pp. 1–8, 2015.
DOI: 10.1007/978-3-319-21837-3_1

Review Protocol of B. Wang [3]. They supposed that once a user modifies a block of shared data, he needs to compute a new signature for the modified block. In addition, when a user is revoked from the group for some reasons, he should no longer be able to access or modify the shared data, and the signatures from this revoked user should not be valid to the group anymore. As a result, the blocks previously signed by this revoked user must be re-signed by an existing user in the group, so that the integrity of the data can still be verified with the public keys of the existing users.

Utilizing *Proxy Re-signatures* [4], they designed a public auditing mechanism for shared data with efficient user revocation. In their protocol, every time a user is revoked, the cloud will re-sign the blocks that were previously signed by this revoked user, which means the untrusted cloud must know the signer of each block. However, this information may be privacy for the group. What's more, the cloud itself is able to arbitrarily convert signatures from one user into ones from another user with the given re-signature keys, which makes it no sense to distinguish the signers of different data blocks. Besides that, their protocol may leak the data content to the auditor since it requires the cloud to send linear combinations of data blocks to the auditor during the auditing.

Our Work. In this paper, we propose an efficient and privacy-preserving public auditing protocol, which can solve the problem mentioned above. To get better user revocation, we introduce a system administrator(SA) into the system, which is in charge of the keys for the group. Every time a user of the group modifies a block, the modifier must send a request to the SA, which will generate and send a signing key to the modifier to sign the data block he modified and a corresponding re-signing key to the cloud to re-sign the data block. Thus, user revocation is becoming a simple thing that just needs to remove the revoked user from the group since there is no need to do re-signings anymore. With this improvement, the cloud do not need to know the signers of the data blocks, which protects the privacy of the users. On the other hand, we adopt a technique called random masking [12] to ensure the data privacy, which guarantees that the auditor could not learn any knowledge about the data content during the efficient public auditing process.

The rest of this paper is organized as follows: In Sect. 2, we present the detailed design of our mechanism, followed by the evaluation of our protocol in Sect. 3. Finally, we conclude this paper in Sect. 4.

2 The Improved Protocol

In this section, we'll give an improved protocol that can solve the problems mentioned above.

2.1 Overview

System and Threat Model. There are four entities in our system: the cloud, the third party auditor(TPA), the users who share data as a group and the

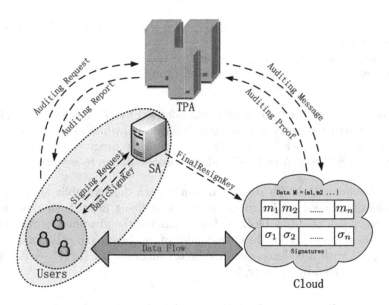

Fig. 1. The system model includes four entities: The cloud, the TPA, the users and the SA.

system administrator(SA)(as illustrated in Fig. 1). The cloud not only provide storage and sharing services to the users, but also act as proxy. The TPA publicly audits the integrity of the shared data for the group. The *SA* maintains the users list(UL) and is in charge of generating signing keys and the corresponding re-signing keys. Since there must be one to maintain the users list, the existing of the SA is reasonable.

Design Goals. There are three goals for our improved protocol.

First, *Correctness:* The TPA is able to check the integrity of shared data without retrieving the entire data, even if some users are revoked from this group.

Second, *Efficiency:* The user revocation should be efficient.

Third, *Privacy-Preserving:* Preserving the privacy of users against the cloud and preventing the auditor from knowing the data content during the efficient public auditing.

2.2   Preliminaries

In order to present the detailed design of our protocol, we'll introduce some preliminaries as follows.

Bilinear Maps. Let $G_1, \hat{G}_1$ and G_2 be groups of the same prime order q. We say a map e: $G_1 \times \hat{G}_1 \to G_2$ is a Bilinear map if:

(1) for all $a, b \in \mathbb{Z}_q, g \in G_1$, and $h \in \hat{G}_1$, then $e(g^a, h^b) = e(g, h)^{ab}$ is efficiently computable;
(2) the map is non-degenerate;
(3) there exists a computable isomorphism from $\hat{G}_1$ to G_1.

Proxy Re-signature. Proxy re-signatures, redefined by G. Ateniese *et al.* [4], in which a semi-trusted proxy is given some information which allows it to convert A's signature on a block into B's signature, but the proxy can't generate any signatures on behalf of A or B. We call the process above *re-signing.*

Support Dynamic Data. To support dynamic data during public auditing, the block identifiers need to design carefully. By utilizing index hash table in ref [13,15], users can modify a block without changing the identifiers of the others. More specifically, $v_i \in \mathbb{N}^*$ be the virtual index of this block, and r_i be a hash value of $H'(m_i \| v_i)$ with a collision-resistance hash function $H' : \{0, 1\}^* \to \mathbb{Z}_q$. Thus a block is identified by $id_i = \{v_i \| r_i\}$.

2.3 Privacy-Preserving Public Auditing for Shared Data with Efficient User Revocation

Our privacy-preserving public auditing protocol consists of six stages, namely **Setup, KeyGen, BasicSign, FinalReSign, ProofGen, ProofVerify**. In **Setup**, the SA generates the *cpk* and the *csk* of the group. In **KeyGen**, every time the SA receives a valid request, it generates a new pair of keys: $< BasicSignKey, FinalReSignKey >$, where the $BasicSignKey$ is for the user to compute a basic signature on blocks in **BasicSign** and the $FinalReSignKey$ is for the cloud to re-sign the block to the common public key in **FinalReSign**. When a user is revoked from the group, he will be removed from the users list(UL) and the request from him is not valid for the SA anymore. In **ProofGen** the cloud is able to generate a proof of possession of the shared data. Using the *cpk*, a public verifier is able to check the correctness of a proof in **ProofVerify**.

Symbol Definition: The global parameters are $(e, p, G_1, G_2, g, w, H, h)$, where G_1 and G_2 are two groups of the same prime order p, e is a bilinear map: $G_1 \times G_1 \to G_2$, g is a generator of G_1, w is a random element of G_1, H is a hash function with $H : \{0, 1\}^* \to G_1$, h is a hash function with $h : \{0, 1\}^* \to \mathbb{Z}_q$. $M = (m_1, m_2, \ldots, m_n)$ denotes the shared data, where n is the total number of blocks in shared data. d is the total number of users in the group.

Setup. The SA generates a random $s \in \mathbb{Z}_p$ as the common private key *csk* and computes the common public key $cpk = g^{csk}$. And the SA maintains a users list(UL), which contains ids of all existing users in the group and is public and signed by the SA with the *csk*. The SA only responds to users in the UL.

KeyGen. Every time received request from users of the group, the SA generates a random $x \in \mathbb{Z}_p$ as the BasicSignKey *bk* and computes the FinalReSignKey $fk = csk/bk$, then sends the *bk* to the user and the *fk* to the cloud.

BasicSign. Once a user created or modified a block m_k with block identifier id_k, he/she must compute a new signature on it as follows: First the user sends a request to the SA and waits for the response. Second, the user computes a new signature $\sigma'_k = (H(id_k)w^{m_k})^{bk} \in G_1$ with the *BasicSignKey* from the SA's response. Third, the user sends block m_k along with the basic signature σ'_k to the cloud for *FinalReSign*.

FinalReSign. Following the *BasicSign*, the cloud will re-sign the block using the *FinalReSignKey* fk from the SA as follows:

$$\sigma_k = (\sigma'_k)^{fk} = (H(id_k)w^{m_k})^{bk \cdot csk/bk} = (H(id_k)w^{m_k})^{csk}.$$

Up to now, a valid signature on the block is finally generated.

ProofGen. To check the integrity of the shared data, an auditing message $\{(l, y_l) | l \in L\}$ is generated by the TPA , where $y_l \in Z_q$ is a random and L is a c-element subset of set $[1, n]$, which locates the c selected blocks that will be checked in this auditing task.

Receiving the auditing message, the cloud generates a proof of possession of shared data as follows:

1. First, the cloud computes the linear combinations $\alpha' = \sum_{l \in L} y_l m_l \in Z_p$, then it chooses a random $r \in Z_p$ and calculates $R = e(w, cpk)^r$. After that, the cloud computes $\alpha = r + \mu\alpha'$ to blind α' with r, where $\mu = h(R)$.
2. Second, the cloud computes an aggregated authenticator $\beta = \prod_{l \in L} \sigma_l^{y_l} \in G_1$.
3. Third, the cloud outputs an auditing proof $\{\alpha, \beta, R, \{id_l\}_{l \in L}\}$ and sends it to the verifier.

ProofVerify. With the auditing message $\{(l, y_l) | l \in L\}$, an auditing proof $\{\alpha, \beta, R, \{id_l\}_{l \in L}\}$, and the cpk, the TPA checks the correctness of this auditing proof by verifying whether:

$$R \cdot e(\beta^\mu, g) = e((\prod_{l \in L} H(id_l)^{y_l})^\mu \cdot w^\alpha, cpk) \qquad (*)$$

3 Evaluation

In this section we'll prove the correctness of our improved protocol and discuss the efficiency it has gained and how it preserves the privacy of users against the cloud and the privacy of data content against the TPA.

3.1 Correctness

The correctness of out improved privacy-preserving public auditing protocol with efficient user revocation lies in Equation (*). Based on the properties of bilinear map, the correctness of Equation (*) is presented as follows:

$$R \cdot e(\beta^{\mu}, g) = e(w, cpk)^{r} \cdot e((\prod_{l \in L} (H(id_{l}) \cdot w^{m_{l}})^{csk \cdot y_{l}})^{\mu}, g)$$
$$= e(w^{r}, cpk) \cdot e((\prod_{l \in L} (H(id_{l})^{y_{l}} \cdot w^{y_{l} m_{l}}))^{\mu}, g^{csk})$$
$$= e(w^{r}, cpk) \cdot e((\prod_{l \in L} H(id_{l})^{y_{l}})^{\mu} \cdot w^{\mu \alpha'}, cpk)$$
$$= e((\prod_{l \in L} H(id_{l})^{y_{l}})^{\mu} \cdot w^{r+\mu \alpha'}, cpk)$$
$$= e((\prod_{l \in L} H(id_{l})^{y_{l}})^{\mu} \cdot w^{\alpha}, cpk)$$

What's more, the revoked users, who have been removed from the UL, will not get response from the SA, which means the revoked users are not able to get the pair of keys to complete the process of generating a valid signature in our mechanism. As for *repaly attack* problem, it can be easily be solved by attaching a time stamp to the key pairs that the SA sends to the users and the cloud.

3.2 Efficiency

We argue that our protocol is efficient during user revocation, because when a user is revoked from the group, what needs to do is only to remove this revoked user from the UL. Since all the shared data on the cloud are with signatures from the common key, there is no need to re-sign blocks when user revocations, which greatly improved the efficiency of user revocation.

3.3 Privacy-Preserving

Utilizing of the SA, the cloud don't need to re-sign blocks previously signed by revoked users, which means the cloud don't have to know the signers of the blocks anymore in our protocol. That is important, because it will prevent the untrusted cloud from identifying the key member of the group.

More than that, our improved privacy-preserving protocol guarantees that the TPA can not derive the data content from the linear combination during the auditing process.

Proof: We supposed that the TPA can produce a valid signature without knowing α', Now the TPA is assumed as an adversary, on received an auditing message, it firstly randomly picks μ, α from $\mathbb{Z}$, and let $R = e((\prod_{l \in L} H(id_{l})^{y_{l}})^{\mu} \cdot w^{\alpha}, cpk)/e(\beta^{\mu}, g)$. Then it backpatches $\mu = h(R)$. The proof of this backpatching technique lies in the [17], which has proved this backpatching technique is not feasible with all the restricts.

4 Conclusions

In this paper, we have analyzed the public auditing protocol proposed by B. Wang *et al.* and proposed an improved public auditing mechanism based on theirs. By adding a system administrator, we allow a mobile user to basically sign a block using a *BasicSignKey* and then the cloud to re-sign the block into the common key with the corresponding *FinalReSignKey*, thus the TPA is able to audit the integrity of shared data with only the common key, which improves the efficiency of user revocation and preserves the users' privacy from the cloud and makes it no sense for the cloud to arbitrarily re-sign blocks. Besides that, with the random masking technique, we guarantee that the TPA can't get any knowledge of the data content during the auditing, which preserves the data privacy against the TPA.

References

1. Ren, K., Wang, C., Wang, Q.: Security challenges for the public cloud. Internet Comput. **16**(1), 69–73 (2012)
2. Armbrust, M., Fox, A., Griffith, R., Joseph, A.D., Katz, R.H., Konwinski, A., Lee, G., Patterson, D.A., Rabkin, A., Stoica, I., Zaharia, M.: A view of cloud computing. Commun. ACM **53**(4), 50–58 (2010)
3. Wang, B., Li, B., Li, H.: Public auditing for shared data with efficient user revocation in the cloud. Infocom **2013**, 2904–2912 (2013)
4. Ateniese, G., Hohenberger, S.: Proxy re-signature: new definitions, algorithm and applications. In: Proceedings of ACM CCS, pp. 310–319 (2005)
5. Ateniese, G., Burns, R., Curtmola, R., Herring, J., Kissner, L., Peterson, Z., Song, D.: Provable data possession at untrusted stores. In: CCS 2007: ACM Conference on Computer and Communications Security, pp. 598–609 (2007)
6. Deswarte, Y., Quisquater, J.J., Saidane, A.: Remote integrity checking. In: Proceedings of the 6th Working Conference on Integrity and Internal Control in Information Systems, pp. 1–11, Lausanne, Switzerland (2003)
7. Erway, C., Kupcu. A, Papamanthou, C. et al.: Dynamic provable data possession. In: Proceedings of the 2009 ACM Workshop on Cloud Computing Security, pp. 213–222, Chicago, USA (2009)
8. Sebe, F., Domingo, J., Martinez, A., Deswarte, Y., Quisquater, J.: Efficient remote data possession checking in critical information infrastructures. IEEE Trans. Knowl. Data Eng. **20**(8), 1034–1038 (2008)
9. Hao, Z., Zhong, Z., Yu, N.: A privacypreserving remote data integrity checking protocol with data dynamics and public verifiability. IEEE Trans. Knowl. Data Eng. **23**(9), 1432–1437 (2011)
10. Wang, Q., Wang, C., Li, J., Ren, K., Lou, W.: Ensuring data storage security in cloud computing. In: Proceedings of ACM/IEEE IWQoS 2009, pp. 1–9 (2009)
11. Wang, C., Wang, Q., Ren, K., Lou, W.: Privacy-preserving public auditing for data storage security in cloud computing. In: Proceedings of InfoCom 2010. IEEE, March 2010
12. Wang, C., Chow, S.S.M., Wang, Q., Ren, K., Lou, W.: Privacy-preserving public auditing for secure cloud storage. IEEE Trans. Comput. **62**(2), 362–375 (2013)

13. Wang, Q., Wang, C., Li, J., et al.: Enabling public auditability and data dynamics for storage security in cloud computing. IEEE Trans. Parall. Distrib. Syst. **22**(5), 847–859 (2011)
14. Wang, B., Li, B., Li, H.: Knox: privacy-preserving auditing for shared data with large groups in the cloud. In: Bao, F., Samarati, P., Zhou, J. (eds.) ACNS 2012. LNCS, vol. 7341, pp. 507–525. Springer, Heidelberg (2012)
15. Zhu, Y., Wang, H., Hu, Z., Ahn, G.-J., Hu, H., Yau, S.S.: Dynamic audit services for integrity verification of outsourced storage in clouds. In: Proceedings of ACM SAC 2011, pp. 1550–1557 (2011)
16. Chen, L.: Using algebraic signatures to check data possession in cloud storage. Future Gener. Comput. Syst. **29**(7), 1709–1715 (2013)
17. Shacham, H., Waters, B.: Compact proofs of retrievability. In: Pieprzyk, J. (ed.) ASIACRYPT 2008. LNCS, vol. 5350, pp. 90–107. Springer, Heidelberg (2008)

Multi-proxy Multi-signature Binding Positioning Protocol

Huafeng Chen[1], Qingshui Xue[1 (✉)], Fengying Li[2], Huajun Zhang[1], Zhenfu Cao[1], and Jianwen Hou[3]

[1] Department of Computer Science and Engineering,
Shanghai Jiao Tong University, Shanghai 200240, China
chenhuafeng@sjtu.edu.cn, {xue-qsh,zfcao}@cs.sjtu.edu.cn,
zhanghuajun.cn@gmail.com
[2] School of Continuous Education,
Shanghai Jiao Tong University, Shanghai 201101, China
fyli@sjtu.edu.cn
[3] Shanghai Academy of Spaceflight Technology, Shanghai 201109, China
houjianwen0707@gmail.com

Abstract. Position-based cryptography has attracted lots of researchers' attentions. In mobile Internet, there are many position-based security applications. For the first time, one new conception, multi-proxy multi-signature (MPMS) binding positioning protocol is proposed. Based on one secure positioning protocol, one model of MPMS binding positioning protocol is proposed. In the model, positioning protocol is bound to MPMS tightly, not loosely. Further, we propose one scheme of MPMS binding positioning protocol. As far as we know, it is the first scheme of MPMS binding positioning protocol.

Keywords: Positioning protocol · Proxy signature · Multi-proxy multi-signature · Model · Scheme

1 Introduction

In the setting of mobile Internet, position services and position-binding security applications become one key requirement, especially the latter. Position services include position inquiring, secure positioning and so forth. Position inquiring consists of inquiring your own position and positioning of other entities. The technology of inquiring your own position has GPS (Global Positioning System) and other satellite service system. The technology of positioning of other entities has radar and so on [2–6]. As we all know, the positioning of other entities is more challenging one. Position-binding security applications such as position-based encryption and position-based signature and authentication are increasingly necessary for us. Take one application about position-based signature and authentication as an example. One mobile or fixed user signs messages at one place and sends them to another mobile user. The receiver can verify

© Springer International Publishing Switzerland 2015
K. Xu and J. Zhu (Eds.): WASA 2015, LNCS 9204, pp. 9–18, 2015.
DOI: 10.1007/978-3-319-21837-3_2

whether or not the received message is indeed signed at the place by the signer. Even if the signer moves to another address, it will not affect the receiving and verification of signed messages. On March 8, 2014, the missing Malaysian Airline MH370 can't be found till now, as reminds us of the significance of positioning and related security applications.

Currently, the research on position-based cryptography focuses on secure positioning about which some work had been proposed [1]. These positioning protocols are based on one-dimension, two-dimension or three-dimension spaces, including traditional wireless network settings [1], as well as quantum setting [7,8]. It seems to us that position-based cryptography should integrate secure positioning with cryptographic primitives. If only or too much concentrating on positioning protocols, perhaps we will be far away from position-based cryptography. In other words, nowadays positioning is bound loosely with related security applications, not tightly, as results in the slow progress of position-based cryptography and applications.

The proxy signature scheme [9], a variation of ordinary digital signature schemes, enables a proxy signer to sign messages on behalf of the original signer. Proxy signature schemes are very useful in many applications such as electronics transaction and mobile agent environment. Since the conception of the proxy signature was brought forward, a lot of proxy signature schemes have been proposed [10–12]. In 2001, Hwang et al. first proposed a MPMS scheme [13]. Till now, there is not any publication about MPMS scheme binding positioning protocol.

Relying on the thoughts, in the paper, our main contributions are as follows.

(1) We propose one model of MPMS binding positioning protocol. MPMS binding positioning protocol is one kind of MPMS, but a novel one. The definition is given and its model is constructed. In the meantime, we define its security properties.
(2) To realize the kind of MPMS, one secure-positioning-protocol-based MPMS scheme is proposed and its security is analyzed as well.

We organized the rest of the paper as follows. In Sect. 2, we introduced function of positioning and one secure positioning protocol. In Sect. 3, the model and definition of MPMS binding positioning protocol are given. We proposed one scheme of MPMS binding positioning protocol in Sect. 4. Finally, the conclusion is given.

2   Positioning Protocol

In the section, we will introduce the function of positioning protocols and one secure positioning protocol.

2.1   Function of Positioning Protocols

The goal of positioning protocol is to check whether one position claimer is really at the position claimed by it. Generally speaking, in the positioning protocol, there are at least two participants including position claimers and verifiers, where the verifiers may be regarded as position infrastructure. According to destination of the positioning, there are two kinds of positioning protocol, i.e., your own position positioning protocol and others' position positioning protocol. As of now, lots of works on your own position positioning protocol have been done [2–6]. Nevertheless, research on others' positions positioning protocol is far less and there are still many open questions to resolve. In our model and scheme, we will make full use of the two varieties of positioning protocol.

2.2   One Secure Positioning Protocol [1]

Here, we will introduce one others' positions secure positioning protocol.

In the section, we will review N. Chandran et al.s secure positioning protocol in 3-dimensions [1], which can be used in mobile Internet.

In the protocol, 4 verifiers denoted by $V_1, \ldots, V_4$, which can output string X_i are used. The prover claims his/her position which is enclosed in the tetrahedron defined by the four verifiers. Let $t_1, \ldots, t_4$ be the time taken for radio waves to arrive at the point P from verifier $V_1, \ldots, V_4$ respectively. When we say that $V_1, \ldots, V_4$ broadcast messages such that they "meet" at P, we mean that they broadcast the messages at time $T - t_1, T - t_2, T - t_3$ and $T - t_4$ and respectively so that at time T all the messages are at position P in space. The protocol uses a pseudorandom generator namely an ε-secure $PRG : \{0,1\}^n \times \{0,1\}^m \to \{0,1\}^m$. They select the parameters such that $\varepsilon + 2^{-m}$ is negligible in the security parameters. X_i denotes a string chosen randomly from a reverse block entropy source. The protocol is given as follows:

Step 1. $V_1, \ldots, V_4$ pick keys $K_1, \ldots, K_4$ selected randomly from $\{0,1\}^n$ and broadcast them through their private channel.

Step 2. For the purpose of enabling the device at P to calculate K_i for $1 \leqslant i \leqslant 4$, the verifiers do as follows. V_1 broadcasts key K_1 at time $T - t_1$. V_2 broadcasts X_1 at time $T - t_2$ and meanwhile broadcasts $K_2' = PRG(X_1, K_1) \oplus K_2$. Similarly, at time $T - t_3$, V_3 broadcasts $(X_2, K_3' = PRG(X_2, K_2) \oplus K_3)$, and V_4 broadcasts $(X_3, K_4' = PRG(X_3, K_3) \oplus K_4$ at time $T - t_4$.

Step 3. At time T, the prover at position P calculates messages $K_{i+1} = PRG(X_i, K_i) \oplus K_{i+1}'$ for $1 \leqslant i \leqslant 3$. Then it sends K_4 to all verifiers.

Step 4. All verifiers check that the string K_4 is received at time $(T + t_i)$ and that it equals K_4 that they pre-picked. If the verifications hold, the position claim of the prover is accepted. Otherwise, the position claim is invalid.

3   The Model of MPMS Binding Positioning Protocol

3.1   The Model

In the model, there are four kinds of participants including the original signer group (OSG) which consists of n original signers $OS_1, OS_2, \ldots, OS_n$, the proxy signer group (PSG) which consists of m proxy signers $PS_1, PS_2, \ldots, PS_m$, the verifier (V) and position infrastructure (PI). All original signers (OSs) at individual positions cooperate to delegate their signing power to all proxy signers (PSs) at individual positions. All of PSs cooperate to sign one message at positions after their positions are confirmed by PI. V checks that the MPMS is generated by all of PSs at individual positions on behalf of all of OSs at the specified positions. PI, which is reckoned as one trusted third party, provides position services for all OSs and PSs.

3.2 Definition

MPMS Binding Positioning Protocol. Simply speaking, the kind of MPMS combines traditional MPMS and positioning protocols as one single scheme. It is mainly composed of three modules of multi-proxy multi-signing power delegation, multi-proxy multi-signing and multi-proxy multi-signature verifying. In the module of multi-proxy multi-signing power delegation, each of OSs first sends one request to PI for the purpose of cooperatively delegating signing power of theirs to all PSs. Then PI runs one positioning protocol to confirm the positions of all OSs and PSs. If all of their positions are valid, PI sends individual proxy delegation key package (*pdkp*) to each OS, and sends individual proxy signing key package (*pskp*) to each of PSs. Then all of OSs cooperates to produce multi-proxy multi-signing delegation warrant to all of PSs. In the module of multi-proxy multi-signing, each of PSs has to first check that his/her position is indeed at the designated position, which is specified in the multi-proxy multi-signing delegation warrant. If it holds, each of PSs can use his/her *pskp* to sign the message for only once and sends corresponding individual MPMS to signature collector. The signature collector checks the validity of individual MPMSs. If all are valid, the signature collector can generate the integrated signature, called MPMS binding position protocol, and sends it to V. In the module of MPMS verifying, V uses the identities and positions of all OSs and all PSs to check the validity of the MPMS binding positioning protocol.

Remark 1. During the module of multi-proxy multi-signing power delegation, if neither any OS nor PS can confirm its position, the OSG can't fulfill their delegation of signing power. In the module of multi-proxy multi-signing, each PSs have to confirm its position, before he/she is able to cooperate to generate the MPMS. During the module of MPMS verifying, it is unnecessary for the verifier to confirm the positions of all original signers and proxy signers.

In the model, it will be seen that we regard the three modules as three primitives. Therefore, the positioning protocol is bound tightly with the delegation of signing power and generation of the MPMS, instead loosely.

The MPMS binding positioning protocol is composed of four primitives: Initialization, PropMProxyMDelegate, PropMProxyMSign and PropMProxyMVerify. The model is illustrated in Fig. 1.

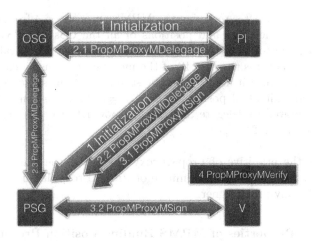

Fig. 1. Model of MPMS binding positioning protocol.

Initialization. PI takes as input secure parameter 1^k, generates system master key mk and outputs system public parameter pp, in the meantime, the system distributes users' identity ID_i for user i .

PropMProxyMDelegate. Each of OSs first sends his/her request to PI. PI confirms the positions $Pos_{OS_1}, Pos_{OS_2}, \ldots, Pos_{OS_n}$ of all OSs by running positioning protocol with each OS, and checks the validity of positions of all PSs. If all OSs is indeed at their position, and all PSs' positions are valid, PI generates and sends the acknowledgement along with $pdkp_{OS_i}(i = 1, 2, \ldots, n)$ to individual OSs by one public or safe channel. $pdkp_{OS_i}$ encapsulates positioning protocol, delegation key, the OS's identity ID_{OS_i} and position Pos_{OS_i}, delegation algorithm, etc. According to the acknowledgement fromPI, all of OSs cooperate to generate proxy delegation warrant dw and send it to each of PSs. PI generates the $pdkp_{PS_i}$ and sends it to $PS_i(i = 1, 2, \ldots, m)$. dw contains identities and positions of all OSs and PSs, message types to sign, expiry date and so on. $pskp_{PS_i}$ encapsulates positioning protocol, proxy signing key, the PS's identity ID_{PS_i} and position Pos_{PS_i}, signing algorithm, etc.

PropMProxyMSign. Each $PS_i(i = 1, 2, \ldots, m)$ first executes his/her $pskp_{PS_i}$ toconfirm his/her position Pos_{PS_i} with PI and check whether it is identical to the one in the proxy delegation warrant dw. If it holds,then he/she is able to use $pskp_{PS_i}$ to sign the message m for only once and sends corresponding individual proxy signature (m, s_i, dw, pp) to the signature collector which checks the validity of individual proxy signature s_i by using the identity ID_{PS_i} and position Pos_{PS_i} of PS_i and corresponding verification algorithm. If all the s_i are valid, the collector generates the final MPMS (m, s, dw, pp) and sends it to V.

PropMProxyMVerify. After receiving the MPMS (m, s, dw, pp) from the PSs, V takes as input the identities and positions of all the OSs and PSs as well as pp to check whether or not the proxy delegation warrant dw is valid, then V check whether or not s is the MPMS of the message m by using corresponding verification algorithm. If it holds, V can be sure that the message m was signed by all of PSs at individual position $Pos_{PS_i}(i = 1, 2, \ldots, m)$ on behalf of the OSG who cooperated to delegate their signing power to the PSG at individual position $Pos_{OS_i}(i = 1, 2, \ldots, n)$.

Remark 2. In the primitive of PropMProxyMDelegate, the Clerk can be any original signer. Similarly, in the primitive of PropMProxyMSign, the signature collector can be any proxy signer.

3.3 Security Properties of MPMS Binding Position Protocol

Positioning Protocol Binding. Besides security properties of MPMS, this kind of MPMS needs the security property of positioning-protocol-binding. In the module of PropMProxyMDelegate, the OSG is unable to finish their delegation of signing power without confirming of positions of all OSs and PSs with PI. In addition, the individual $pskp$ of each PS generated by PI is tightly bound with positioning protocol. In the module of PropMProxyMSign, if the PSG need sign one message on behalf of the OSG, each PS has to make use of its $pskp$ to run the positioning protocol with PI before he/she is able to sign one message.

Remark 3. One maybe think we should make use of one-time digital signing algorithm or one-time signing private key. Actually, in the model, using one-time signing key is optional. Since position-based applications are closely related with position instant authentication or confirmation, it seems to us that position-based cryptography should be deeply researched regarding online cryptography, which focuses on instant cryptographic algorithms and security processing.

3.4 Proxy Delegation Key Package (pdkg)

In the model, we make use of *pdkp* to fulfill the proxy delegation. *pdkp* is one type of executive modules such as .exe or .dll. It consists of delegation key, position localizing protocol, delegation generation algorithm, identities and positions of both OS and PS, and so on. Its structure is showed in Fig. 2.

3.5 Proxy Signing Key Package (pskg)

In the model, *pskp*s is also one kind of executive modules. It is composed of one position localizing protocol, one proxy signing algorithm, proxy signing private key and so forth. Its structure is showed in Fig. 3.

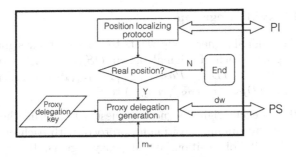

Fig. 2. Structure of proxy delegation key package.

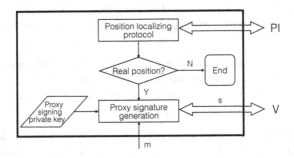

Fig. 3. Structure of proxy signing key package.

4   One MPMS Scheme Binding Secure Position Protocol

In this section, we proposed one MPMS scheme binding secure positioning protocol, in which there exist n original signers and m proxy signers. The scheme mainly includes four kinds of participants: the OSG which consists of $OS_1, OS_2, \ldots, OS_n$, the PSG which consists of $PS_1, PS_2, \ldots, PS_m$, the verifier (V) and PI. PI will make use of the secure positioning protocol mentioned in Sect. 2.2 to provide services of position for n OSs and m PSs. In addition, PI will be regarded as the trusted third party and system authority. The scheme is composed of four primitives: *Initialization*, *PropMProxyMDelegate*, *PropMProxyMSign* and *PropMProxyMVerify*. As primitives, they mean that they either fully run or do nothing. We will detail the four primitives as follows.

4.1   Initialization

PI takes as input secure parameter 1^k and outputs system master key mk and public parameter pp, at the same time, PI distributes user identity ID_i for user i. We can rewrite the primitive as Initialization (k, mk, pp) .

4.2 PropMProxyMDelegation

Step 1. When the original signer group wants to delegate their signing power to the proxy signer group, each of original signers $OS_i (i = 1, 2, \ldots, n)$ first sends requests $(ID_{OS_1}, Pos_{OS_1}, ID_{OS_2}, Pos_{OS_2}, \ldots, ID_{OS_n}, Pos_{OS_n}, ID_{PS_1}, Pos_{PS_1}, ID_{PS_2}, Pos_{PS_2}, \ldots, ID_{PS_m}, Pos_{PS_m}, res_{dele})$ to PI.

Step 2. After PI gets each original signer's request, PI confirms the positions of each original signer by running positioning protocol with each original signer, and checks the validity of positions of all proxy signers. If each of original signers OS_i is indeed at its position $Pos_{OS_i} (i = 1, 2, \ldots, n)$, and all proxy signers' positions $Pos_{PS_i} (i = 1, 2, \ldots, m)$ are valid, PI sends the acknowledgement $(ID_{OS_1}, Pos_{OS_1}, ID_{OS_2}, Pos_{OS_2}, \ldots, ID_{OS_n}, Pos_{OS_n}, ID_{PS_1}, Pos_{PS_1}, ID_{PS_2}, Pos_{PS_2}, \ldots, ID_{PS_m}, Pos_{PS_m}, ack_{dele})$ to each original signer, or the scheme fails to stop.

Step 3. PI generates and sends proxy delegation key packages $pdkp_{OS_i} (i = 1, 2, \ldots, n)$ to individual original signers OS_i by one public or safe channel. $pdkp_{OS_i}$ encapsulates positioning protocol, delegation key, and the original signer's identity ID_{OS_i} and position Pos_{OS_i}.

Step 4. Each of original signers OS_i uses its proxy delegation key packages $pdkp_{OS_i}$ to confirm the validity of its position and generates its individual proxy delegation $(ID_{OS_1}, Pos_{OS_1}, ID_{OS_2}, Pos_{OS_2}, \ldots, ID_{OS_n}, Pos_{OS_n}, ID_{PS_1}, Pos_{PS_1}, ID_{PS_2}, Pos_{PS_2}, \ldots, ID_{PS_m}, Pos_{PS_m}, dw_i)$. OS_i sends it to the Clerk. dw_i is the signature generated by proxy delegation key packages $pdkp_{OS_i}$.

Step 5. The Clerk checks the individual proxy delegation dw_i is produced by OS_i, if the verification of all $dw_i (i = 1, 2, \ldots, n)$ holds, the Clerk generates the final proxy delegation warrant $(ID_{OS_1}, Pos_{OS_1}, ID_{OS_2}, Pos_{OS_2}, \ldots, ID_{OS_n}, Pos_{OS_n}, ID_{PS_1}, Pos_{PS_1}, ID_{PS_2}, Pos_{PS_2}, \ldots, ID_{PS_m}, Pos_{PS_m}, dw)$. Here we can simply denote dw by $dw = \prod_{i=1}^{n} dw_i$

Step 6. The Clerk sends the final proxy delegation warrant to each of proxy signers. dw contains the identities and positions of all original signers and proxy signers, message types to sign, expiry date and so forth.

Step 7. PI generates the proxy signing key package $pskp_{PS_i} (i = 1, 2, \ldots, m)$ and sends it to each proxy signer. $pskp_{PS_i}$ encapsulates positioning protocol, individual proxy signing key, the proxy signer's identity ID_{PS_i} and position Pos_{PS_i}, signing algorithm, etc.

4.3 PropMProxyMSign

Step 1. When the proxy signer group wants to sign the message m on behalf of all original signers, each of proxy signers $PS_1, PS_2, \ldots, PS_m (i = 1, 2, \ldots, m)$ runs individual proxy signing key package $pskp_i$ for executing positioning protocol to confirm the validity of theposition Pos_{PS_i} withPI.

Step 2. If $PS_i's(i = 1, 2, \ldots, m)$ current position Pos_{PS_i} is identical to the one in the delegation warrant dw, proxy signing key package $pskp_i$ prompts PS_i to input the message m to $pskp_i$. Thus proxy signing key package $pskp_i$ produces the individual proxy signature s_i and sends it to the signature collector; if PS's current position Pos_{PS_i} is not identical to the one in the delegation warrant dw, PS_i is unable to perform the function of proxy signing and stops.

Step 3. After the signature collector receives the individual proxy signature $s_i(i = 1, 2, \ldots, m)$, he/she check s_i is the individual proxy signature by using verification algorithm,the identity and position of PS_i.

Step 4. if all $s_i's$ verification hold, the signature collector generates the final MPMS s by processing all individual proxy signature $s_i(i = 1, 2, \ldots, m)$. Here we can simply denote s as $s = \prod_{i=1}^{m} s_i$.

Step 5. The signature collector sends (m, s, dw, pp) to the proxy signature verifier V.

4.4 PropMProxyMVerify

Step1. After receiving the MPMS (m, s, dw, pp) from the proxy signers, V takes as input the identities $ID_{OS_1}, ID_{OS_2}, \ldots, ID_{OS_n}, ID_{PS_1}, ID_{PS_2}, \ldots, ID_{PS_m}$, positions $Pos_{OS_1}, Pos_{OS_2}, \ldots, Pos_{OS_n}, , Pos_{PS_1}, Pos_{PS_2}, \ldots, Pos_{PS_m}$, and pp to check whether or not dw is valid. If it is valid, the scheme continues, or fails to stop.

Step 2. V takes the same input as Step 1 to check whether or not s is the MPMS on the message m by using corresponding MPMS verification algorithm. If it holds, V can be sure that the message m was signed by all proxy signers at the position $Pos_{PS_i}(i = 1, 2, \ldots, m)$ on behalf of the original signer group who cooperated to delegate their signing power to all proxy signers at the individual position $Pos_{OS_i}(i = 1, 2, \ldots, n)$.

Remark 4. In the scheme, the signing algorithms which all original signers and proxy signers use for the sake of proxy delegation and multi-proxy multi-signing, can be any digital signature algorithms based on identity or attribute. As to the generation of the proxy signers' proxy signing key packages, in the scheme, it is produced by PI. Thus, the scheme is proxy-protected.

Due to the page constraints, we will detail correctness and security analysis of the proposed scheme in the full version.

5 Conclusions

In the paper, we construct a model of MPMS binding positioning protocol. Its definition, security properties and construction are given. As far as we know, it is the first model of combining positioning protocol, proxy signature and MPMS.

In the meantime, we also propose one secure-positioning-protocol-based MPMS scheme. We will further improve relevant models and schemes. We believed that the research on positioning-protocol-based cryptographic models or schemes will become one focus in the setting of mobile Internet.

Acknowledgments. This paper is supported by NSFC under Grant No. 61170227 and 61411146001, 973 Project under Grant No. 2012CB723401, Ministry of Education Fund under Grant No. 14YJA880033, and Shanghai Projects under Grant No. 2013BTQ001, XZ201301 and 2013001.

References

1. Chandran, N., Goyal, V., Moriarty, R., Ostrovsky, R.: Position based cryptography. In: Halevi, S. (ed.) CRYPTO 2009. LNCS, vol. 5677, pp. 391–407. Springer, Heidelberg (2009)
2. Naveen, S., Umesh, S., David, W.: Secure verification of location claims. In: Proceedings of the 2nd ACM Workshop on Wireless Security, pp. 1–10. ACM (2003)
3. Dave, S., Bart, P.: Location verification using secure distance bounding protocols. In: 2005 IEEE International Conference on Mobile Adhoc and Sensor Systems Conference, p. 7. IEEE (2005)
4. Laurent, B.: Trust Establishment Protocols for Communicating Devices. Ph.D. thesis, Eurecom-ENST (2004)
5. Capkun, S., Hubaux, J.-P.: Secure positioning of wireless devices with application to sensor networks. In: Proceedings of IEEE INFOCOM 2005, 24th Annual Joint Conference of the IEEE Computer and Communications Societies, vol. 3, pp. 1917–1928. IEEE (2005)
6. Capkun, S., Srivastava, M., Cagalj, M.: Secure localization with hidden and mobile base stations. In: IEEE Conference on Computer Communications (INFOCOM) (2006)
7. Buhrman, H., Chandran, N., Fehr, S., Gelles, R., Goyal, V., Ostrovsky, R., Schaffner, C.: Position-based quantum cryptography: impossibility and constructions. In: Rogaway, P. (ed.) CRYPTO 2011. LNCS, vol. 6841, pp. 429–446. Springer, Heidelberg (2011)
8. Harry, B., Serge, F., Christian, S., Florian, S.: The Garden-Hose Game: A New Model of Computation, and Application to Position-Based Quantum Cryptography (2011). arXiv: 1109.2563
9. Mambo, M., Usuda, K., Okamoto, E.: Proxy signature for delegating signing operation. In: Proceedings of the 3rd ACM Conference on Computer and Communications Security, New Dehli, pp. 48–57. ACM, New York (1996)
10. Li, J.G., Cao, Z.F., Zhang, Y.C.: Nonrepudiable proxy multi-signature scheme. J. Comput. Sci. Technol. **18**(3), 399–402 (2003)
11. Hwang, S.J., Chen, C.C.: Cryptanalysis of nonrepudiable threshold proxy signature scheme with known signers. Informatica **14**(2), 205–212 (2003)
12. Tsai, C.S., Tzeng, S.F., Hwang, M.S.: Improved nonrepudiable threshold proxy signature scheme with known signers. Informatica **14**(3), 393–402 (2003)
13. Hwang, S.J., Chen, C.C.: A new multi-proxy multi-signature scheme. In: 2001 National Computer Symposium on Information Security, pp. F019–F026, Taipei, Taiwan, ROC (2001)

Efficient Network Structure of 5G Mobile Communications

Kwang-Cheng Chen[1]([✉]), Whai-En Chen[2], Wu-Chun Chung[3],
Yeh-Ching Chung[3], Qimei Cui[4], Cheng-Hsin Hsu[3], Shao-Yu Lien[5],
Zhisheng Niu[6], Zhigang Tian[6], Jing Wang[6], and Liqiang Zhao[7]

[1] National Taiwan University, Taipei, Taiwan
ckc@ntu.edu.tw
[2] National Ilan University, Yilan City, Taiwan
wechen@niu.edu.tw
[3] National Tsing Hua University, Hsinchu, Taiwan
wcchung@sslab.cs.nthu.edu.tw, {ychung,chsu}@cs.nthu.edu.tw
[4] Beijing University of Post and Telecommunications, Beijing, China
cuiqimei@bupt.edu.cn
[5] National Formosa University, Huwei, Taiwan
sylien@nfu.edu.tw
[6] Tsing Hua University, Beijing, China
{niuzhs,zgtian,wangj}@tsinghua.edu.cn
[7] Xidian University, Xi'an, China
lqzhao@mail.xidian.edu.cn

Abstract. 5G mobile communications requires system and network considerations from many aspects. Instead of high spectral efficient physical layer communication, We introduce efficient network structure supplying a new design paradigm to meet user experience, spectral efficiency, and energy efficiency, under wide range of services and applications on top of 5G mobile communication networks, with virtual networking over software defined networking facilitating.

1 Introduction

5G mobile communications and subsequent issues on wireless communication systems and wireless networks emerge as the most important technology challenge at this time. It is widely addressed regarding 1,000 times of data rate [11]. However, in this paper, we wish to supply a different view on efficient network structure to facilitate 5G mobile communications as a paradigm shift.

Tradition network design considers efficiency to satisfy quality of services (QoS) based on connection-oriented traffic like voice and video. However, the traffic has significantly changed in 5G and actually also for 4G. Internet traffic like web browsing dominates in mobile communication networks, particularly social media. In this paper, instead of common targets on aggregated data rate and quality of service (QoS) metrics, we would like to focus on the efficient network structure of 5G mobile communications, in particular the quality of user experience (QoE), spectrum efficiency, and energy efficiency that is

© Springer International Publishing Switzerland 2015
K. Xu and J. Zhu (Eds.): WASA 2015, LNCS 9204, pp. 19–28, 2015.
DOI: 10.1007/978-3-319-21837-3_3

related to battery at any specific user equipment (UE) or any device/machine [3]. Researchers have focused on the spectrum efficiency at physical layer, while the aggregated data rate can not really reflect user's demand. We consider more important to satisfy network throughput for a specific user equipment or a machine. In other words, to satisfy quality of user experience (QoE) is more important in the 5G systems and networks. As Internet traffic dominates in 5G networks, latency is a critical factor of users' QoE, working together with cloud computing. These considerations form a unique view to design the efficient network structure of 5G mobile communications.

The efficient network structure is even more complicated by considering another extreme of traffic from Internet of Things (IoT) that is usually composed of small packets from tremendous number of devices and machines, as the foundation of cyber-physical-socio systems. In this paper, we are indicating the approach by information-centric processing to establish spectral and energy efficient network structure for 5G.

2   Cloud Based Service Architecture

Although the heterogeneous cloud radio access networks (H-CRAN) have shown the potentials in spectrum efficiency and energy efficiency enhancements to support emerging applications, the second characteristic of providing ultralow latency services is still a huge challenge. To enhance the end-to-end latency performance, a proper resource scheduling/allocation scheme is to reduce the transmission delay in the air interface. Adopting an access control policy is also effective to reduce latency in wired/wireless backhaul. However, the unacceptable signaling overheads in the air interface still impose large data exchange delay to existing mobile networks. In addition to latency resulted from signaling overheads, the H-CRAN further induces two new sorts of latency that may be severer than that in the air interface. The first one is latency in resource optimization. Radio resource optimization is a widely discussed issue, and the existing results reveal that the computational complexity is increased along with the number of available radio resources, the number of devices, and the number of eNBs. Unfortunately, it is projected that the number of devices will exponentially increase in the following decade. To support the increasing number of devices, the number of available radio resources should be increased as well as the number of eNBs in the H-CRAN. This growing computational complexity may eventually obstruct the latency performance. The second one is latency in the routing/paging procedures to forward data to a mobile device in the H-CRAN. In the existing mobile network design, the routing and paging procedures assume that each mobile device may communicate with any other mobile devices and servers. Therefore, fixed routing/paging information with a hierarchical information inquiry scheme is adopted. However, this design fully ignores the fact that a mobile device may frequently communicate with the mobile devices or web servers within its social network, while rarely exchange data with terminals/servers outside its social network. The existing routing/paging procedures

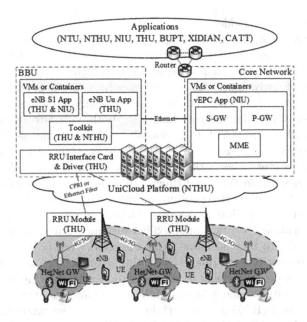

Fig. 1. Could services and applications on top of 5G mobile communication networks

may therefore result in a severer delay than that in the air interface. We can thus obtain the design paradigm of low-latency network architecture [1].

Figure 1 depicts an illustration of the integration in which mainly consists of five parts: IoT devices and machines, UniCloud platform, Cloud-RAN, core network and applications. In the device domain, M2M devices are able to communicate with each other via heterogeneous wireless techniques like WiFi and Bluetooth; or even communicate with application servers via 4G LTE and next 5G communications. We attempt to not only propose efficient algorithms to approach green M2M communications, but also introduce a HetNet GW to leverage multiple wireless communications for legacy devices that might not be equipped with a 4G/5G module. With mature techniques in cloud computing, both CRAN and core network are desired to be hosted on UniCloud to sustain more flexible and scale-out communication services. The baseband unit of an eNB is able to be deployed on a set of virtualized resources of UniCloud based on the separation design of RRU and BBU in Cloud-RAN. Moreover, virtualized core components of a vEPC are able to be deployed on UniCloud with the techniques of network function virtualization. Accordingly, 5G communications and data transmissions between radio access network and backhaul data network could be processing on the cooperative 5G cloud platform.

3 New Domain/Layer Network Structure

The objective of this network architecture is to explore the sustainable development model for future mobile communication network. The sustainability could be expressed in 3 dimensions:

1. Sustainable business model

   As we known, telecommunication operator is facing the scissor effect of floor revenue growth and explosive traffic (then cost) growth. To seek for a healthier situation, the telecommunication industry has to change the business model in two sides. Firstly, more valuable services have to be provided to mobile internet industry for new revenue resource; Secondly, we want to leverage the Moore's Law of IT infrastructure (including both hardware and software) to lower the OPEX and CAPEX. Previously, mobile internet service provider stay in one end of mobile network and users stay in the other end of mobile network, so the mobile network is saw as pipe or connectivity. With the competition pressure from WiFi and Bluetooth, mobile networks value (revenue) can not be valued more. However current mobile internet service provider are building their own application network (cloud computing) to serve more and more users, mobile network should sell networking services to mobile internet service provider to be paid more. With the effort from IC vendor like Intel, the hardware cost or performance obey the Moore's Law, so we can use not so many hardware deployment to support exponential growing users/services. Actually, the software obeys Moore's Law also. Open source or cloud computing make the cost (R&D investment) does not follow the exponential growing of users/services. Comparing to OPEX, CAPEX in telecommunication industry does not occupy remarkable ratio in revenue. Therefore OPEX should also leverage the Moore's Law of IT software infrastructure.

2. Sustainable network architecture

   According to cooper's law, mobile network throughput per unit area (bps/m2) increased 1000000 times for past 45 years, it says, mobile network throughput per unit area doubled every 27 months. For past 45 years, we used 25X spectrum and improve the spectral efficiency 25X, and the cellular density increase 1600X. However, for next 1000X traffic increasing in next 10 years, we have only 3X more spectrum and 6X spectral efficiency, so the cellular density have to be increased 56X. That means the focus for technical development of mobile network has to change from improving the spectral efficiency to refine the architecture to accommodate exponential scale increasing.

3. Sustainable evolution mode

   Because of the objective of business model shift and the CAPEX saving, the evolution mode of one generation per 10 years has to a changed to smoother and smarter one. The network architecture should encourage such evolutional mode.

All these requirements lead to a kind of open network architecture. Open network services to mobile internet service providers; Open network virtualization interface to COTS IT infrastructure; Open network protocol architecture to different player (operator, system vendor, mobile virtual network operator (MVNO), network optimization service provider, third-party innovational developer etc.) who concern different aspects of network and operating, different RAT, different vertical industry scenario, different region, different technical trial, etc. We therefore can organize the entire mobile network into 4 domains and 4 layers as Fig. 2.

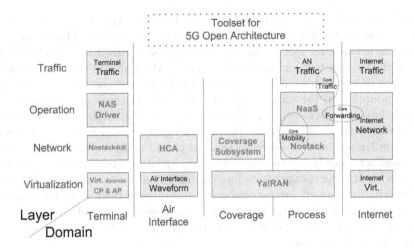

Fig. 2. Domain and layer structure of 5G mobile communications.

For different cross points of domains and layers, corresponding schemes can be developed with the same goal of open network architecture:

- Open Operation & Business : Networking/Operation as a Service
- Open Cellular Networking : HCA (Hyper Cellular Architecture)
- Open FrontHaul : Coverage Subsystem
- Open Infrastructure :YaRAN (Yet another RAN)
- Open Network Protocol : NoStack (Not only Stack)
- Open Terminal Architecture : Nostack4UE & YaRAN4UE
- Open Air Interface Waveform : Soft Defined Air Interface

Here, our focuses are HCA, YaRAN and NoStack. These technical solutions are mapped in to various system components of a 5G mobile network. Hypercellular network suggests a network concept in which signaling and data are decoupled at the air interface to mitigate the signaling overhead. Consequently, the need to rely on cellular operation can be alleviated and control overhead could be subsequently reduced to allow energy efficient operation of base stations.

4   Information Centric Wireless Network Design

Due to the booming of Internet application, social media and data generated by IoT has become the major portion of modern communication networks [4,5]. Consequently, the attractive network design of 5G mobile communication relies on interaction of cyber-social systems, to fully utilize the spectrum and to smooth hybrid heterogeneous networks (multi-band systems, cellular-WiFi, macro-micro-femto cell networks, etc.). On the other hand, to provide a compatible wireless system, one fundamental concept of a cyber-physical-social network can be implemented by introducing a new information processing network between physical network and application/social network. The information processing network focuses on how to match wireless resource to most popular or needed social content and increase the total performance of the whole system. It consists of two main function: information cache and content-based (social-based) grouping. In the part of information cache, the information processing network determines what content should be cached. Due to limited cached space and efficiency issue, the information processing network can only cache those most popular contents to decrease the end-to-end delay between cloud server and consumer. Another issue is how to group social network into a sub-network to form a file sharing network to reduce the burden of the core-network. By forming a file sharing network among consumers according to their social relationship, core network need not to transfer data to consumers separately. Instead, only those key consumers access core network to retrieve information and share them among their social networks.

Consequently, 5G networking actually has a kind of cyber-physical-socio scenario that is illustrated as Fig. 3. To achieve the goal of information-sharing among tens or thousands of devices, such as machine-to-machine network [2], network grouping according to their social relationship is necessary. That is, information processor should focus on how to match wireless resource to most popular or needed social content and increase the total performance of the whole

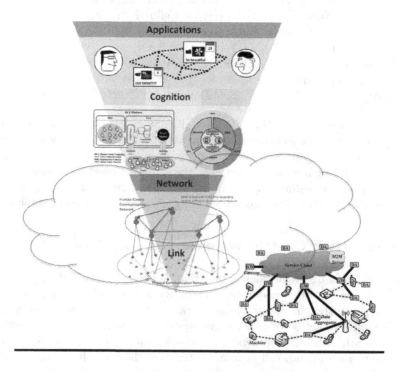

Fig. 3. The cyber-physical-social networking scenario in 5G

system. To find the balance between overhead of inferring and performance, Least Absolute Shrinkage and Selection Operator (LASSO) is an immediate tool to determine community members associated with different users, instead of finding the exact isolated social structure. Ideally, we can group sensors into almost disjoint clusters to simplify the algorithms for efficient transmission and device management. In practice, this situation does not always arise, and the algorithm to solve such problems is NP-hard. Instead, we choose the most dependent nodes of a given sensor to form its community and control the size of the community and accuracy of data recovery by l_1-norm optimization. A fraction of the sensor measurement can thus be eliminated to save transmission energy. A LASSO problem can be formulated as

$$\min \tau |\mathbf{u}_i|_1 + \frac{1}{2} ||\mathbf{x}_{[-i]}\mathbf{u}_i - \mathbf{x}_i||_2^2 \tag{1}$$

where $\mathbf{x}_i$ is the observation signal and $\mathbf{x}_{[-i]}$ is the sensing matrix which does not include ith community. The nodes corresponding to non-zero entries of u_i are collected together to form the community structure. Here, we focus on minimize mean square error. $E(||\mathbf{x}_{[-i]}\mathbf{u}_i - \mathbf{x}_i||_2^2)$ and minimize the community to reduce feedback overhead simultaneously. With the proper setting, which indicates the weighting of community size, we can form a small community of nodes with expected error less than pre-defined error level. Of course, leveraging sparse signal processing [2,5] is another plausible approach to tackle general ultra dense networks.

An important characteristics of Internet is that most of transferring data flows are generated by seldom file sources. However, in the current communication architecture, these popular data flows are processed separately. Such large amount of data suffer from severe end-to-end delay while passing through core network of communication system. Here, we propose tomography and in-network computations to find the most popular information flows in the mobile communication systems [6,7]. The tomography is a tool that we can predict the structure of the whole system by observing the feedback of stimulation. We successfully apply this technology into cognitive radio network (CRN). CRN tomography is shown in Fig. 4. The message flow originally exists in CRN, θ is the unknown information of interests, and $\mathbf{y}$ represents observation taking values in an observation set Γ which may be a set of vectors. The purpose of CRN tomography is to infer θ according to $\mathbf{y}$ and full/partial information about $\mathbf{s}$. There are two strategies to infer the value of θ: passive inference and active inference. For passive monitoring, we can obtain the inference result of $\hat{\theta}$ by

$$\hat{\theta} = \Phi_p(\mathbf{y}, \Upsilon[\mathbf{s}]), \tag{2}$$

where $\Upsilon(.,.)$ is the passive inference. For active monitoring, the probing signal is transmitted to induce or enhance the correlation between target information and observation. The probing signal p may be completely or partially known beforehand, and we use the information extraction function $\Lambda[\mathbf{p}]$ to characterize

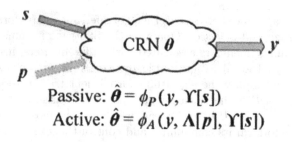

Passive: $\hat{\boldsymbol{\theta}} = \phi_P(y, \Upsilon[s])$

Active: $\hat{\boldsymbol{\theta}} = \phi_A(y, \Lambda[p], \Upsilon[s])$

Fig. 4. Scheme of radio network tomography.

a priori knowledges of **p**. Therefore, we can formulate the active tomography problem as

$$\hat{\theta} = \Phi_A(\mathbf{y}, \Gamma[\mathbf{p}], \Upsilon[\mathbf{s}]). \tag{3}$$

By stimulating the system with probing signal **p** and the resulting signal **y**, we can know the parameters of the system.

After understanding the structure of the system, we can easily identify those popular information in the network. Based on earlier study on social network properties of mobile communication networks and through in-network computations and cache [8] these information in suitable routers or devices via information from social relationship, we can significantly reduce the end-to-end delay. This step actually involves tradeoff between computing/storage and communication/networking, which is another frontier in communication networking to facilitate IoT traffic of small packets and massive social media delivery in an efficient way.

5   Virtual Network Realization over Software Defined Networking Platform

Building up a platform that can integrate the social information and the resource in physical network is the key technology for future communication networks. SDN has been proposed as a possible solution to integrate network resource in different network layers. The main features of SDN include: separation of control and data planes; centralized and programmable control planes of network equipment; support of multiple, isolated virtual networks. The SDN provides a programmable framework to facilitate network configuration of more flexibility. In other words, via the SDN structure, the network is not only for data transmission but also for information flows of different applications. That is, SDN converts a realistic network into a virtual network and therefore more flexibility than before.

To serve 5G traffic of both IoT and social media, we propose new architecture of SDN in following. Figure 5 illustrates the architecture of 5G wireless communications, from which, we can find that there are two main data flows: social

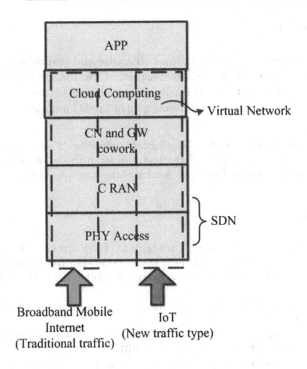

Fig. 5. Implementation of virtual network by software-defined network.

media data flow and IoT data flow, have been integrated into SDN. With the help of SDN, we can build up two virtual networks to serve video and IoT traffic flow separately and reach the optimal performance. In this section, we firstly focus on how the property of complex network can influence the implementation of realistic communication systems. Second, we aim to develop the communication theoretical breakthroughs and new networking design paradigm through the networking research of information centric networking among this architecture, and hence reach the effective information delivery so as to greatly enhance the spectral-efficient and energy-efficient in communication systems and networks. For example, we have successfully developed an algorithm to control the information over a network. How to implement such a successful control scheme into our platform is a promising research direction. All in all, the research results shall serve as helpful tool in networked data processing problems in different scientific areas, thus to facilitate the information-centric processing for communication and social networks.

Consequently, we can fully take advantage of the concepts developed with system examples in [9], to revolutionize the system design to accommodate totally different traffic types, via the effective management of radio resource to PHY, and thus to facilitate CRAN compatible with cloud computing applications and services. This task is further fertilized by implementation of CRAN protocol stack on cloud computing and on top of software radio implementation for both core network and hyper-cellular access network [10].

6   Conclusion

This paper suggests the efficient network structure and realization of 5G mobile communications by considering different aspects. Cloud services and applications are therefore possible on top of this efficient network structure. We expect such an approach to generally meet the diverse goal of the 5G mobile communications.

Acknowledgement. This study is conducted under the "Energy-Efficient Mobile Communication Systems Project" of the Institute for Information Industry which is subsidized by the Ministry of Economic Affairs of the Republic of China.

References

1. Lien, S.Y., Hung, S.C., Chen, K.C., Liang, Y.C.: Ultra-low latency ubiquitous connections in heterogeneous cloud radio access networks. To appear in the Special Issue on Heterogeneous Cloud Radio Access Networks, IEEE Wireless Communications
2. Chen, K.C., Lien, S.Y.: Machine-to-machine communications: technologies and challenges. Ad Hoc Netw. **18**, 3–23 (2014)
3. Han, N.D., Chung, Y., Jo, M.: Green data centers for cloud-assisted mobile ad hoc networks in 5G. IEEE Netw. **29**, 70–76 (2015)
4. Condoluci, M., Dohler, M., Araniti, G., Molinaro, A., Zheng, K.: Toward 5G densenets: architectural advances for effective machine-type communications over femtocells. IEEE Commun. Mag. **53**, 135–141 (2015)
5. Wunder, C., Boche, H., Strohmer, T., Jung, P.: Sparse signal processing concepts for efficient 5G system design. IEEE Access **3**, 195–208 (2015)
6. Lien, S.Y., Cheng, S.M., Shih, S.Y., Chen, K.C.: Radio resource management for QoS guarantees in cyber-physical systems. IEEE Trans. Parall. Distrib. Syst. **23**(9), 1752–1761 (2012)
7. Yu, C.K., Cheng, S.M., Chen, K.C.: Cognitive radio network tomography. IEEE Trans. Veh. Technol. **59**(4), 1980–1997 (2010)
8. Niesen, U., Shah, D., Wornell, G.W.: Caching in wireless networks. IEEE Trans. Inf. Theory **58**(10), 6525–6540 (2012)
9. Lien, S.Y., Chen, K.C., Liang, Y.C., Lin, Y.H.: Cognitive radio resource management for future cellular networks. IEEE Wirel. Commun. **21**(1), 70–79 (2014)
10. Zhao, T., Yang, P., Pan, H., Deng, R., Zhou, S., Niu, Z.: Software defined radio implementation of signaling splitting in hyper-cellular network. In: SIRF. ACM (2013)
11. Andrews, J.G., Buzzi, S., Choi, W., Hanly, S.V., Lozano, A., Soong, A.C.K., Zhang, J.C.: What will 5G be? IEEE J. Sel. Areas. Commun. **32**(6), 1065–1082 (2014)

Optimal Channel Assignment Schemes in Underlay CRNs with Multi-PU and Multi-SU Transmission Pairs

Long Chen[1,2]($\boxtimes$), Liusheng Huang[1,2], Hongli Xu[1,2], Hou Deng[1,2], and Zehao Sun[1,2]

[1] School of Computer Science and Technology,
University of Science and Technology of China, Hefei 230027, Anhui, China
[2] Suzhou Institute for Advanced Study,
University of Science and Technology of China, Suzhou 215123, Jiangsu, China
{lonchen,dengh,luciola}@mail.ustc.edu.cn, {lshuang,xuhongli}@ustc.edu.cn

Abstract. In underlay spectrum sharing scheme, both channel assignment and power allocation will affect network performance such as throughput, etc. This paper first defines the joint channel and power control problem, which aims to optimize the max-total and max-min throughput of SUs, with interference constraints on primary receivers. For the max-total problem, we formulate the problem as a bipartite matching and derive a maximum weighted matching based algorithm STMA to solve this problem. For the max-min problem, on the basis of the ORA algorithm, we derive a polynomial time algorithm OCAA to iteratively assign the channels to each SU pair under the power constraint. Simulation demonstrates, the throughput of SU network grows with the maximum transmission power of SUs below the interference power of PUs. STMA algorithm achieves an average of 46.67 % performance gain when path loss component $\alpha = 2$ and 13.08 % enhancement when $\alpha = 3$ compared with random algorithm. The OCAA algorithm effectively ensures the max-min fairness of the capacity among SU pairs in finite iterations and achieves at least 97 % performance gain than the random method under most cases.

Keywords: Cognitive radio · Underlay · Channel assignment · Multiple pairs · Max-min fairness

1 Introduction

In cognitive radio networks (CRNs), secondary users (SUs) or cognitive radio (CR) users opportunistically sense channels that are not occupied by primary users (PUs) and make good use of the spectrum to enhance spectrum efficiency. In general, there are three different types of cognitive spectrum utilization methods: overlay [6], interweave [13] and underlay approaches [9,12,19]. For underlay approach CR users are permitted to use the same spectrum occupied by PUs

© Springer International Publishing Switzerland 2015
K. Xu and J. Zhu (Eds.): WASA 2015, LNCS 9204, pp. 29–39, 2015.
DOI: 10.1007/978-3-319-21837-3_4

provided the interferences to PUs are within a threshold that PUs could tolerate. In this approach, both the communications among PUs and SUs could be guaranteed. Underlay approach is used in various areas. For example, by deploying femtocells underlying macro-cells, it is beneficial for enhancing the coverage of indoor communications as well as increasing system capacity [2]. On the battle field, when bandwidths are constraint, soldiers who act as PUs and static surveillance sensors in the filed act as SUs coexist, improved underlay CRN scheme may guarantee the resource demands of PUs and meanwhile alleviate performance degradation of the SU network. In this work, we focus on the underlay approach mainly for three reasons. First, it is easier to implement. Second, time critical communication is permitted in the SU network. Third, it is energy efficient by introducing a central control station to save the individual node's sensing power.

With the underlay scheme, both channel assignment and power control will affect network performance, such as system throughput etc. If the transmission powers of SU transmission nodes are too high, interferences received at the primary receivers may surpass the thresholds that they can tolerate. Hence the communication of PU pairs will be disturbed. Otherwise, the throughput of SU pairs will suffer. Since users in the CR network are randomly distributed, channel assignment to the SU pairs can directly affect the calculation of interferences to the corresponding primary receivers. Therefore, power control and channel assignment should be jointly studied.

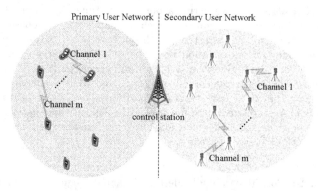

Fig. 1. Architecture of the underlay CRN

As shown in Fig. 1, dual-hop relaying is adopted for the benefit of lowering the interference to PUs. Previous works either focus on analyzing the outage probability of SU network or on relay selection methods to maximize the throughput of SU network which is consisted of *only one transmission pair*. In reality, multiple transmission pairs in both PU network and SU network coexist, how to assign each of the channels used by PUs to SUs efficiently is a challenge. This is different from wireless ad hoc networks, due to the spectrum diversity and changing characters introduced by cognitive radios. Although relay selection will also affect the performance of SU network, it is not considered here by assuming relay nodes have been selected by each of the SU transmission pairs. This is reasonable because if there is not a relay node in the link between a secondary sender-receiver, through the procedure of topology discovery with a common control channel (CCC) [5] between the nodes in SU network, a proper relay could be found and linked to the secondary sender-receiver. Hence a triple transmission pair is formed. Here we concentrate on the joint channel and power control problem without considering competing relays among SU pairs.

The main contributions of this paper can be summarized as follows:

- We firstly define the STMP problem, which aims to optimize the max-total throughput of SUs with the constraints of interferences on primary receivers.
- The problem is formulated as a bipartite matching problem in a bipartite graph and we derive a maximum weighted matching based algorithm to solve this problem.
- Secondly, motivated by the max-min fairness of resource allocation, we formulate the FCAP problem that maximize the minimum transmission rate of SU transmission pairs.
- Then, on the basis of the ORA Algorithm [16], we derive a polynomial time algorithm OCAA to iteratively assign channels to each SU pair thus maximizing the minimum throughput among all SU pairs.
- Simulation results show, the throughput of SU network grows with the maximum transmission power of SUs below the interference power of PUs. Both the STMA algorithm and the OCAA algorithm outperform the random method under most cases.

The remainder of this paper is organized as follows: Section 2 presents an overview of related works for relay aided underlay CR network. Section 3 presents the network model. Problem formulation is described in Sect. 4. We solve the proposed problems in Sect. 5. Simulation results are provided in Sect. 6, followed by concluding remarks in Sect. 7.

2   Related Works

Previous works [8,12] either considered the channel assignment and power control problem to optimize the throughput or to minimize the outage probability in CRNs. However, they only considered on a single SU pair and failed to consider the problem from the perspective of a whole system. Although existing works [4,11] jointly considered the power and channel allocation, they do not suit for the underlay scenario and relay influence was not considered by [4]. Authors in [7] adopted a similar scenario as this paper. But the main goal of [7] was to efficiently assign SUs to PUs during primary time slots to optimize transmission rates of PUs. In this paper, we optimize both max-total and max-min throughput of SUs, with interference constraints on primary receivers.

Authors in [18] studied the outage performance of SUs, subjected to the outage constraint of the PU and the peak transmission power constraint of the SU. They also considered the interferences between PUs and SUs, but not the throughput of the SU network. In [15], authors jointly presented relay selection and SU network outage performance analysis. [3] derived both single and multiple relays selection schemes for the SU network with only one source node and one destination node. Only a few works [9,14,17] have studied the throughput performance of SU network, *all of these papers have adopted the single transmission pair model to derive either the outage probability or capacity of the single communication pair in SU network.*

3   Network Model

As shown in Fig. 1, we consider a CR network where there are both multiple PU and multiple SU pairs in the network system. A central control station [7] is deployed to sense the spectrum used by PUs and assign channels to SU pairs in the SU network without interrupting the communication of primary transmission pairs. Each one of the primary transmission pairs works on an identical channel orthogonal to the other channels which will not cause interferences between different primary pairs.

3.1   Network System Description

As shown in Fig. 2, PU network (PUN) is consisted of a transmission node S_{p_i} as well as a receive node D_{p_i}, where $i \in \{1, 2, \cdots, m + h\}$. Accordingly, SU network (SUN) is constituted of transmitter S_{s_j}, relay R_{s_j} and destination D_{s_j} where $j \in \{1, 2, \cdots, m\}$. The variable h is a non-negative integer $h \in \mathbb{N}$ and is used to vary the number of channels.

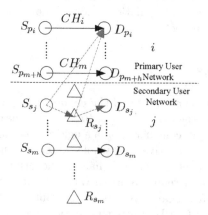

Fig. 2. Network model in underlay CRNs

3.2   Channel Model

Let h_{ij} denote the channel coefficient between sender node i and receiver node j, $h_{ij} = x_{ij}(d_{ij})^{-\alpha/2}$ [10]. Where x_{ij}, α and d_{ij} each denotes the fading coefficient, the path loss exponent and the Euclidean distance between sender i and receiver j respectively. Channel gain can be expressed as $G_{ij} = x_{ij}^2(d_{ij})^{-\alpha}$. For SUs, Amplify-and-Forward (AF) dual-hop relaying is adopted. Assume each one of the nodes in the network is equipped with a half duplex antenna so that one node could not perform both transmission and receiving works at the same time. The signal to interference plus noise ratio (SINR) between sender i and receiver j can be $\gamma_{ij} = (P_i G_{ij})/(\sum_{k \neq i} P_{kj} G_{kj} + N_0)$, where N_0 is noise power constant of surroundings at the receiver and P_i is the transmission power of node i. Usually, signal to noise ratio (SNR) can be used instead of SINR to model the channel conditions. For ease of illustration, here SNR is used to calculate channel capacity between one source node and one destination node.

4   Problem Formulations

Based on the network model proposed in Sect. 3, we firstly give some basic notations of the network system, and then define the resource allocation problem as two sub problems: max-total throughput of user pairs in the SUN and max-min capacity among all pairs in the SUN.

Let X_{ij} be a binary variable and is defined as:

$$X_{ij} = \begin{cases} 1, & \text{channel } i \text{ is allocated to pair } j \text{ in SUN} \\ 0, & \text{otherwise} \end{cases} \tag{1}$$

Define ω_i as the bandwidth of the ith channel, which is primarily used by PU pair i and can be allocated to the SU pairs by the control station. The sum of ω_i equals to Ω, which is the total bandwidth of all the channels. With the underlay CRN, the interferences caused by transmissions of SUs in channel i to the ith primary receiver D_{p_i} is denoted as I_i [12]. When all the primary receivers are homogeneous, all values of I_i could be the same. P is the maximum transmission power of users in the SUN, with which both the sender and relay node in the SUN must conform for the sake of nodes in the SUN are usually static and energy constrained. C_{ij} is the channel capacity of SU pair SP_j who transmits through the ith channel. According to Shannon's theorem, channel capacity C_{ij} can be defined as:

$$C_{ij} = \omega_i \log_2[1 + \min\{(\frac{P_{s_j}|h_{s_j r_j}|^2}{\sigma_{r_j}^2}), (\frac{P_{r_j}|h_{r_j d_j}|^2}{\sigma_{d_j}^2})\}] \tag{2}$$

where $\sigma_{r_j}^2, \sigma_{d_j}^2$ each denotes the signal noise of surroundings at receiver node R_{s_j} and D_{s_j} respectively. Firstly, we define Problem I, the Sum Throughput Maximizing Problem (STMP). Since there are multiple channels available in a multi-PU and multi-SU transmission pairs environment. An improper way to allocate the channels of PUs could lead to a degradation of SU performance in the SUN. This is because the interference to the primary receiver caused by the transmission of a SU through the channel may surpass the threshold that the PU could bear. Problem I is formulated as Sum Throughput Maximizing Problem (STMP) of the SUN. The main aim of this problem is to solve such problem: how to assign each of the primary channels to communication pairs in the SUN considering the interferences of SUs to receivers in the PUN, so that the sum rate of the communication pairs in the SUN is maximized. The STMP problem can be formulated as:

$$(\mathcal{OPT}-1) \qquad Obj: \ Max \ \sum_{i=1}^{m+h}\sum_{j=1}^{m} X_{ij}C_{ij}$$

$$S.t. \qquad (C1): \sum_{i=1}^{m+h} X_{ij} \leq 1$$

$$(C2): \sum_{j=1}^{m} X_{ij} \leq 1$$

$$(C3): \sum_{i=1}^{m+h}\sum_{j=1}^{m} w_i X_{ij} \leq \Omega$$

$$(C4): P_0 \leq P_{s_j} \leq min\{\frac{I_i}{|h_{s_j p_i}|^2}, P\}$$

$$(C5): P_0 \leq P_{r_j} \leq min\{\frac{I_i}{|h_{r_j p_i}|^2}, P\}$$

$$and \quad (1)(2)$$

(3)

where C1 ensures for each SP_j, only one of the communication channels can be assigned to them by the control station. C2 means each one of the channels can only be assigned to one SU pair. C3 is the sum bandwidth constraint. Finally, C4 and C5 are used to bind the communication powers of the secondary sender and the secondary relay in the SUN. The upper bounds of C4 and C5 refer to the transmission powers without interrupting the primary receiver [12,17].

Next, we define Problem II, the Fair Channel Assignment Problem (FCAP). For multiple transmission pairs in the SUN, after assigning each of the channels for the transmission pairs, each source-relay-destination pair will have a different capacity after we apply a channel assignment algorithm. Then we want to find out how to optimally assign channels to the SU pairs so as to maximize the minimum capacity among all SU pairs. Max-min fairness though has been addressed by literatures in ad hoc networks; the methods they used cannot be directly employed in channel assignment problem of underlay CRNs. This is because in ad hoc networks, max-min fairness can be achieved through network flow analysis. Here, channel allocation problem is no longer a data flow problem, thus new methods should be derived to solve the FCAP problem. By introducing a channel capacity demand R for each secondary transmission pair in the SUN, the FCAP problem can be formulated as:

$$(\mathcal{OPT}-2) \quad Obj: \quad Max \ R$$

$$S.t. \qquad (C6): \sum_{i=1}^{m+h} \sum_{j=1}^{m} X_{ij} C_{ij} \geq R \qquad (4)$$

$$(1) \sim (2) \ and \ (C1) \sim (C5)$$

5 Problem Solving

5.1 Solving STMP Problem

In first step, the related parameters or variables will be initialized. Then the distances between secondary senders and primary receivers as well as between secondary relays and primary receivers are calculated. Since the main procedure of this algorithm is to assign each channel i to each SU pair SP_j in the SUN and allocate powers for the secondary senders and secondary relays. In the second step, during the probe procedure, there might be multiple potential channels which could be assigned to a SU pair. Then a many-to-one match will be the result of running completion of the procedure. Where, "many" refers to multiple channels and "one" means a single SU pair. Then using KM algorithm the optional matching could be derived in the final step. It should be noted that when using channel i, SU pair SP_j should maximize the transmission power to get a higher transmission rate. So the upper bounds of both C4 and C5 should be adopted as the assigned transmission power. The detail of the algorithm is shown as Algorithm 1.

The assignment result of STMA algorithm can optimize the throughput of the SUN. The time complexity of the STMA algorithm is about $O(m^2(m+h)))$. Due to limited space, proofs are omitted.

5.2 Solving FCAP Problem

First of all, for each SU pair SP_j, considers each channel c_i in the cognitive radio environment and computes the capacity C_{ij} by (2) and with power constraints C4 and C5. In this way, for each SU pair, the list of channels that can increase the capacity compared with zero could be obtained. Since the target of this initialization is to acquire an initial feasible solution for the OCAA algorithm to start the iteration procedure, without loss of generality, the channel from the list could be assigned to the SU pair in random. When the channel has been assigned to one SU pair, the channel could not be reassigned to other SU pair. When this procedure ends, each SU pair will maintain a channel and have a capacity larger than zero. The second step of OCAA algorithm is to iteratively find a nicer assignment. This is the main procedure of the algorithm. In the beginning of this sub-procedure, the algorithm will find out the smallest capacity among all the SU pairs and denoted as R_{min}. The OCAA algorithm will increase the R_{min}

Algorithm 1. Formal description of the STMA algorithm

1: Step 1: Algorithm initialization
2: **for** $j = 1$ to m **do**
3:    **for** $i = 1$ to $m + h$ **do**
4:       //Calculate the distances between SUs and primary receivers
5:       $d_{s_{s_j} d_{p_i}} = \sqrt{(x_{ss}[j] - x_{dp}[i])^2 + (y_{ss}[j] - y_{dp}[i])^2}$
6:       $d_{r_{s_j} d_{p_i}} = \sqrt{(x_{rs}[j] - x_{dp}[i])^2 + (y_{rs}[j] - y_{dp}[i])^2}$
7:       $A[j][i] \leftarrow 0; C[j][i] \leftarrow 0$ // array initialization
8:       $|h_{s_j p_i}|^2 = d_{s_{s_j} d_{p_i}}^{-\alpha}, |h_{r_j p_i}|^2 = d_{r_{s_j} d_{p_i}}^{-\alpha}$
9:    **end for**
10: **end for**
11: Step 2:Probe to get the potential channels
12: **for** $j = 1$ to m **do**
13:    **for** $i = 1$ to $m + h$ **do**
14:       **if** $\frac{I_i}{|h_{s_j p_i}|^2} = I_i d_{s_j p_i}^{\alpha} \geq P_0$ and $\frac{I_i}{|h_{r_j p_i}|^2} = I_i d_{r_j p_i}^{\alpha} \geq P_0$ **then**
15:          $P_s[j] = \min\{\frac{I_i}{|h_{s_j p_i}|^2}, P\}$ and $A[j][i] \leftarrow 1$ //c_i to SP_j
16:          $P_r[j] \leftarrow \min\{\frac{I_i}{|h_{r_j p_i}|^2}, P\}$ // power of secondary relay
17:          $C[j][i] = \omega[i] \log_2[1 + \min\{(\frac{P_s[j]|h_{s_j r_j}|^2}{\sigma_{r_j}^2}), (\frac{P_r[j]|h_{r_j d_j}|^2}{\sigma_{d_j}^2})\}]$//channel capacity
             of SP_j using channel c_i
18:       **end if**
19:    **end for**
20: **end for**
21: Step 3:Bipartite graph based matching procedure
22: Construct bipartite graph G
23: Adopt KM algorithm and Hungary method to find a saturated matching

---

value for the corresponding SU pair and at the same time keep the capacity of the other pairs in the SUN stay not below $R_{\min}$. Due to limited space, the detail of the algorithm can be found at the technical report [1].

6   Simulation Results

In this paper, Matlab 7.1 is used for all the simulations. An example of simulation topology is shown in Fig. 3(a), where the circles and squares represent secondary users in the network and the lines are used to link each of the secondary user pairs. Each triangular in the figure denotes a primary receiver node. To express neatly, primary senders are omitted in the figure. In our simulation, each of the experiments is repeated for 100 times and the average values are acquired. Path loss component $\alpha = 2$ to 3. The maximum power levels of SUs range from -10 dB to 20 dB. The total bandwidth $\Omega = 1000$.

Figure 3(b) demonstrates the relationship between maximum transmission power of SUs and the throughput of the SUN. When the maximum transmission power P increases, the throughput of SUN grows accordingly. This is because the system throughput is in positive correlation with the transmission power of SUs. The throughput starts to grow rapidly when P is larger than 5 dB. Moreover, when the environmental noise at the SU $\sigma_{r_j} = \sigma_{d_j} = \sigma$ decreases from 5 to 0.1, the throughput of the SU system achieves a great enhancement. This can be easily explained because when each of the interferences to the SU pairs decreases, the channel capacity can enjoy a high enhancement according to (2).

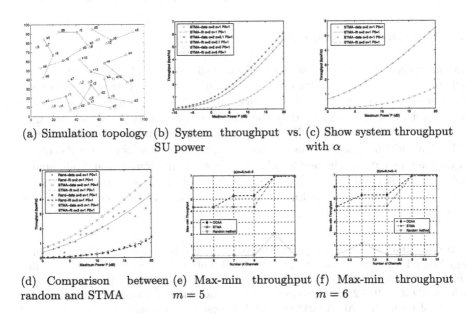

(a) Simulation topology (b) System throughput vs. (c) Show system throughput
                             SU power   with α

(d) Comparison between (e) Max-min throughput (f) Max-min throughput
random and STMA $m = 5$ $m = 6$

Fig. 3. Simulation topology and results

The relationship between path loss component and the throughput of SUN is shown in Fig. 3(c). A high path loss component will greatly degrade the throughput performance of SUN. The throughput can achieve almost 5.5 bps/Hz when the path loss component is $\alpha = 2$ whereas the maximum throughput is only 1.43 bps/Hz when $\alpha = 3$.

In order to evaluate the performance of the STMA algorithm better, we also derive and implement a random scheme. The results are illustrated in Fig. 3(d). The random algorithm also follows the constraints of C1 and C2. It can be seen in Fig. 3(d), STMA outperforms the random method in all situations. The STMA algorithm achieves an average of about 46.67 % performance gain when $\alpha = 2$ and 13.08 % enhancement when $\alpha = 3$ compared with random algorithm. Hence, STMA algorithm is better than random algorithm.

Figures 3(e) and 3(f) depicts the max-min throughput $R_{\min}$ performance in comparisons with OCAA, STMA as well as random method. From Figures 3(e) and 3(f), it is obvious that OCAA out-performs both the STMA algorithm and random method in all situations. For the random method, the algorithm executes for 1000 times in Matlab and selects the average number of the minimum throughput among all the transmission pairs in the SUN. On average, OCAA achieves a maximum of 21.9 % performance gain than the STMA algorithm on the max-min fairness. Random method is the poorest method to ensure the max-min fairness in all situations, which suggests that it should not be used when trying to maximize the minimal throughput in the SUN, since in the best case of the random method, OCAA is still 97 % better than the random method.

7   Concluding Remarks

In this paper, we present the optimal channel assignment and power control scheme with multiple PU transmission pairs and multiple SU transmission pairs in underlay CRNs. Since previous works mostly focus on single pairs in both PUN and SUN, the schemes they use could not be directly used in a multiple transmission pairs scenario. We derive a bipartite matching based algorithm STMA algorithm to achieve the maximum throughput of SUN and we also derive a channel allocation scheme OCAA, to ensure the minimal throughput among all SU pairs is maximized, which is called max-min fairness. Simulation results show both of the two algorithms are effective when compared with the random method.

Acknowledgement. This paper is supported by the National Science and Technology Major Project under No. 2012ZX03005-009, National Science Foundation of China under No. U1301256, 61170058, 61272133, and 51274202, Special Project on IoT of China NDRC (2012-2766), Research Fund for the Doctoral Program of Higher Education of China No. 20123402110019, and Jiangsu industry-university-research Fund (No.BY2012127).

References

1. Chen, L., Huang, L., Xu, H.: Technical report: Optimal resource allocation for multi-pu and multi-su transmission pairs in underlay cognitive radio networks. http://home.ustc.edu.cn/lonchen/tech_MPMS.pdf
2. Cheng, S.M., Lien, S.Y., Chu, F.S., Chen, K.C.: On exploiting cognitive radio to mitigate interference in macro/femto heterogeneous networks. Wirel. Commun. **18**(3), 40–47 (2011)
3. da Costa, D.B., Elkashlan, M., Yeoh, P.L., Yang, N., Yacoub, M.D.: Dual-hop cooperative spectrum sharing systems with multi-primary users and multi-secondary destinations over nakagami-m fading. In: 2012 IEEE 23rd International Symposium on Personal Indoor and Mobile Radio Communications (PIMRC), pp. 1577–1581. IEEE (2012)
4. Digham, F.F.: Joint power and channel allocation for cognitive radios. In: Wireless Communications and Networking Conference (WCNC), pp. 882–887. IEEE (2008)
5. Gao, C., Chu, S., Wang, X.: Distributed scheduling in mimo empowered cognitive radio ad hoc networks. IEEE Trans. Mob. Comput. **13**(7), 1456–1468 (2014)

6. Goldsmith, A., Jafar, S.A., Maric, I., Srinivasa, S.: Breaking spectrum gridlock with cognitive radios: an information theoretic perspective. Proc. IEEE **97**(5), 894–914 (2009)
7. He, S., Jiang, L., He, C.: A novel secondary user assisted relay mechanism in cognitive radio networks with multiple primary users. In: Global Communications Conference (GLOBECOM), pp. 1254–1259. IEEE (2012)
8. Laneman, J.N., Tse, D.N., Wornell, G.W.: Cooperative diversity in wireless networks: efficient protocols and outage behavior. IEEE Trans. Inf. theory **50**(12), 3062–3080 (2004)
9. Li, L., Zhou, X., Xu, H., Li, G.Y., Wang, D., Soong, A.: Simplified relay selection and power allocation in cooperative cognitive radio systems. IEEE Trans. Wirel. Commun. **10**(1), 33–36 (2011)
10. Liu, S., Wang, Y., Zhu, Y., Yang, H., Pan, L.: Analysis of outage performance in cognitive radio networks. Int. J. Mach. Learn. Comput. **3**(6), 503–507 (2013)
11. Liu, Y., Tao, M.: Optimal channel and relay assignment in ofdm-based multi-relay multi-pair two-way communication networks. IEEE Trans. Commun. **60**(2), 317–321 (2012)
12. Luo, L., Zhang, P., Zhang, G., Qin, J.: Outage performance for cognitive relay networks with underlay spectrum sharing. IEEE Commun. Lett. **15**(7), 710–712 (2011)
13. Ma, L., Shen, C.C., Xin, C.: Coni: credit-based overlay and interweave dynamic spectrum access protocol for multi-hop cognitive radio networks. In: Global Telecommunications Conference (GLOBECOM), pp. 1–6. IEEE (2011)
14. Bao, V.N.Q., Duong, T.Q., da Costa, D.B., Alexandropoulos, G.C., Nallanathan, A.: Cognitive amplify-and-forward relaying with best relay selection in non-identical rayleigh fading. IEEE Commun. Lett. **17**(3), 475–478 (2013)
15. Seyfi, M., Muhaidat, S., Liang, J.: Relay selection in cognitive radio networks with interference constraints. IET Commun. **7**(10), 922–930 (2013)
16. Shi, Y., Sharma, S., Hou, Y.T., Kompella, S.: Optimal relay assignment for cooperative communications. In: Proceedings of the 9th ACM International Symposium on Mobile ad hoc Networking and Computing, pp. 3–12. ACM (2008)
17. Sidhu, G.A.S., Gao, F., Wang, W., Chen, W.: Resource allocation in relay-aided ofdm cognitive radio networks. IEEE Trans. Veh. Technol. **62**(8), 3700–3710 (2013)
18. Tran, H., Zepernick, H.J., Phan, H.: Cognitive proactive and reactive df relaying schemes under joint outage and peak transmit power constraints. IEEE Commun. Lett. **17**(8), 1548–1551 (2013)
19. Xu, W., Zhang, J., Zhang, P., Tellambura, C.: Outage probability of decode-and-forward cognitive relay in presence of primary user's interference. IEEE Commun. Lett. **16**(8), 1252–1255 (2012)

A Group Bandwidth Reservation Scheme for the Control Channel in IEEE 802.11p/1609 Networks

Yen-Hung Chen[1], Ching-Neng Lai[2], Yuan-Cheng Lai[3(✉)], and Yang-Chi Li[4]

[1] CyberTrust Technology Institute, Institute for Information Industry,
5F, No. 106, Sec. 2, Heping E. Rd, Taipei 106, Taiwan
pplong@gmail.com
[2] Department of Information Technology, Hsing Wu University,
No. 101, Sec.1, Fenliao Road, Taipei 24452, Taiwan
093062@mail.hwu.edu.tw
[3] Department of Information Management,
National Taiwan University of Science and Technology,
No. 43, Sec. 4, Keelung Road, Taipei, Taiwan
laiyc@cs.ntust.edu.tw
[4] OTTO Software Partner Taipei Co., LTD,
4F, No. 299, Min Sheng W. Road, Taipei 103, Taiwan
Vicky@osp.com.tw

Abstract. IEEE 802.11p/1609 standards divide the radio spectrum into one control channel (CCH) and six service channels (SCH) for emergent/management frame exchange and service dissemination, respectively. Previous schemes, however, still suffer from enormous collisions of emergency messages or the large overhead of control messages in CCH, leading toward poor bandwidth usage. This paper develops group reservation MAC (GRMAC) to minimize the number of collisions in CCH to increase its overall goodput. GRMAC allows vehicles to reserve the CCH bandwidth while they stay in SCHs in order to reduce the number of collisions in CCH. Also, GRMAC migrates the CCH bandwidth scheduling mechanism from CCH to SCHs to reduce the burden on CCH bandwidth resources. The simulation results under heavy load reveal that GRMAC achieves two times the goodput achieved by the conventional IEEE 802.11p/1609 mechanism.

Keywords: WAVE · IEEE 802.11p · IEEE 1609 · Bandwidth reservation

1 Introduction

The intelligent transportation system (ITS) was proposed to integrate information and communication technologies into vehicles and transport infrastructure to improve vehicular safety. To accelerate the commercialization of ITS, the IEEE Standards Association (IEEE-SA) developed the IEEE 802.11p and IEEE 1609 standards for wireless access in vehicular environments (WAVE) to improve vehicular safety [1–5]. These standards allow drivers to obtain useful and up-to-date information about traffic on the road from

© Springer International Publishing Switzerland 2015
K. Xu and J. Zhu (Eds.): WASA 2015, LNCS 9204, pp. 40–49, 2015.
DOI: 10.1007/978-3-319-21837-3_5

other vehicles or roadside infrastructure in a limited contact time. The IEEE 802.11p/ 1609 standards simplify the time-consuming IEEE 802.11 carrier sense multiple access (CSMA) scheme by modifying it in three ways. First, the radio spectrum is divided into one control channel (CCH) and six service channels (SCHs) for emergent/management frames exchange and conventional application service dissemination, respectively. The otherwise very long channel scanning time of vehicles is reduced simply by monitoring the CCH to receive emergent safety messages or connection setup information for the dissemination of services over SCH. Second, the channel time is divided into the CCH interval (CCHI) and the SCH interval (SCHI), enabling vehicles to monitor the emergent data in CCH in a common time interval (CCHI) and to receive service in SCH during another common time interval (SCHI). Third, multiple handshaking procedures - namely association, authentication, RTS/CTS, and ACK functionalities - are not used to shorten the connection setup time.

Trading multiple handshaking procedures for instantaneous data exchange would result in serious collisions and, therefore, cannot effectively handle a sudden burst of WSM traffic when a series of emergent events occur. On the other hand, IEEE 802.11p/ 1609 standards do not regulate traffic transmitted over CCH, which are the emergent traffic that concerns safety and traffic that carries connection setup information. To be more specific, the traffic that carries connection setup information would encounter a long delay and become overdue if the emergent safety traffic consumes all of the CCH bandwidth. In this situation, vehicles would not be able to determine on which SCHs the application services are to be disseminated, and the transmission of service data will therefore be in vain.

In light of the above concerns, this work proposes group reservation MAC (GRMAC) to minimize the number of collisions in CCH and thereby to improve the CCH bandwidth efficiency. GRMAC reduces the number of collisions in CCH by enabling vehicles to coordinate and reserve the CCH bandwidth in SCHs during SCHI. GRMAC also separates the connection setup traffic from the emergent safety-related traffic to prevent the connection setup information from becoming overdue owing to interference by the emergent safety-related traffic. To solve the problem that vehicles on different channels cannot exchange messages, GRMAC divides the vehicles into groups, each of which comprises a set of vehicles using the same SCH. Each group sequentially (according to the channel number) uses its reserved bandwidth in next CCHI. The vehicles therefore do not have to negotiate over CCH transmission opportunities with other vehicles that are on different SCHs. The CCH transmission sequence of the vehicles in a group is simply the sequence in which these vehicles disseminate their own service data over SCH. Accordingly, the overhead of GRMAC in terms of SCH bandwidth resources is minimized.

This paper is organized as follows. Section 2 reviews the literature on the IEEE 802.11p/1609 standards and the problems associated with the IEEE 802.11p/1609 CCH channel access scheme. Section 3 formally introduces the design of GRMAC. Section 4 demonstrates the superior performance of GRMAC over that of the IEEE 802.11p/1609 standards by simulation. Finally, Sect. 5 draws conclusions.

2   Background

2.1   IEEE 802.11p/1609 Standards

The IEEE 802.11p and 1609 draft standards were proposed to support seamless wireless access to interoperable services in vehicular environments (WAVE). These standards use multi-channel cooperation to handle the unique characteristics of a vehicular network, such as its highly dynamic nature and rapid topological changes.

Multi-channel cooperation involves two mechanisms, which are displayed in Fig. 1. First, the radio spectrum is divided into one control channel (CCH) and six service channels (SCHs). CCH is used to management frames and emergent data, while SCH is used specifically for the transmission of service data. Vehicles can establish communications and exchange emergent messages over CCH to reduce the enormous setup time that is required, for example, in channel scanning [6].

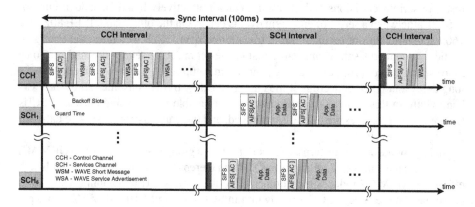

Fig. 1. WAVE channel coordination

The second mechanism is the division of the channel time into sync intervals, each one of which comprises one CCH interval (CCHI) and one SCH interval (SCHI). This division enables a vehicle that is equipped with a single antenna to monitor CCH in a common time interval, CCHI, to communicate management frames and emergent data. After the CCHI, the vehicle can hop to the chosen SCH to exchange service data during SCHI.

The IEEE 802.11p/1609 network accommodates two protocol stacks - the WAVE short message protocol (WSMP) and the conventional TCP/IP protocol suit (such as IPv6 and TCP/UDP) - to optimize the operation of different applications in WAVE. WSMP is designed for applications that require the exchange of time-sensitive data, such as emergent safety and traffic information. To increase transmission efficiency, WSMP requires none of the multiple handshakes that are defined by the IEEE 802.11 standard, such as association, authentication, RTS/CTS, and ACK functionalities. Accordingly, WSMP composes the application data as a WAVE short message (WSM); addresses it to the broadcast MAC address, and transmits it directly over CCH without establishing any connection. The receiving vehicle accepts the frame and passes it to the upper protocol stack.

Applications that require non-time-sensitive data still depend on an efficient connection setup because contact time between vehicles and roadside units is limited. The IEEE 802.11p/1609 standards therefore modified the IEEE 802.11 channel access scheme for compatibility with the conventional TCP/IP protocol: a service provider broadcasts a WAVE service advertisement (WSA) frame over CCH during CCHI to announce the availability of the service. This WSA contains detailed information about the service, including the IP and MAC addresses of the service provider, the port number of the application, and the SCH number of the channel on which the provider is offering the service. If other vehicles receive this WSA and choose to acquire the service, they can hop to the designated SCH during SCHI to receive the service data. This mechanism enables vehicles simply to monitor the CCH to receive the service setup information without channel scanning or other handshake procedures, which could results in an intolerable connection establishment delay in WAVE.

2.2 Problems Associated with CCH Channel Access

Two problems are encountered when CCH uses the IEEE 802.11p/1609 CSMA scheme for WSM and WSA transmission. First, trading multiple handshake procedures for the ability of exchange data instantaneously would result in serious collisions and, therefore, low CCH bandwidth usage. Two reliable reservation-Aloha (RR-Aloha)-based schemes, called DMMAC and DR-MMAC, were developed to reduce the number of collisions in CCH and SCH [7, 8]. However, RR-Aloha requires a vehicle to broadcast the previous CCH bandwidth usage over CCH during CCHI, consuming a large fraction, 25 %, of the CCH bandwidth [9]. Furthermore, DMMAC and DR-MMAC allow each vehicle to use only a single slot in CCH in a CCHI, and this strategy does not effectively exploit the CCH bandwidth to transmit a sudden burst of WSM traffic when an emergent event occurs.

The second problem is that the IEEE 802.11p/1609 CSMA mechanism does not regulate the WSM and WSA traffics because these traffics share CCH and compete with each other. The WSA traffic experiences high delay and becomes overdue if the WSM traffic consumes all of the CCH bandwidth. In this situation, vehicles cannot determine on which SCHs the application services will be provided so the service providers would distribute the service data in vain. Accordingly, VMESH and VCI-MAC were both developed to divide the CCH interval into a management interval and a safety interval, of which the former is used for exchanging management traffic and the latter is used for transmitting safety data traffic [10, 11]. However, contention-based schemes are used to schedule both traffics, leading to serious collisions.

3 Group Reservation MAC

This section formally introduces the proposed bandwidth reservation protocol, which is called the group reservation MAC (GRMAC), for solving the problems associated with IEEE 802.11p/1609 standards, which were described in the preceding sections. GRMAC allows vehicles to exchange their CCH bandwidth requirement and reserve the CCH bandwidth in SCHs during SCHI. This strategy can reduce the number of collisions in

CCH and regulate the WSM and WSA traffics. It can also lighten the burden of CCH bandwidth scheduling. Below we present the concept of GRMAC. Table 1 provides the notation that is used in this work.

Table 1. Used notation

Notation	Definition
RG_i	The reservation group located in the i-th channel
V_i^j	The j-th vehicle belongs to the RGi
BRN	The bandwidth reservation notification applied for reserving the CCH bandwidth
GRI	The reserved CCH interval for WSM/WSA traffic
CI	The contention interval for unreserved WSM/WSA traffic
MTI	The time interval to separate the traffics between members within the same RG
GTI	The time interval to separate the traffics between RGs
GRI_{wsm}	The GRI period applied for WSM transmission
GRI_{wsa}	The GRI period applied for WSA transmission
$GRI_{wsm}^{\max}$	The maximum GRI_{wsm} interval
$GRI_{wsa}^{\max}$	The maximum GRI_{wsa} interval

3.1 GRMAC: An Overview

As displayed in Fig. 2, GRMAC provides three main modifications to IEEE 802.11p/ 1609 standards, which are reservation group (RG), bandwidth reservation notification (BRN), and the division of CCHI into group reservation interval (GRI) and contention interval (CI).

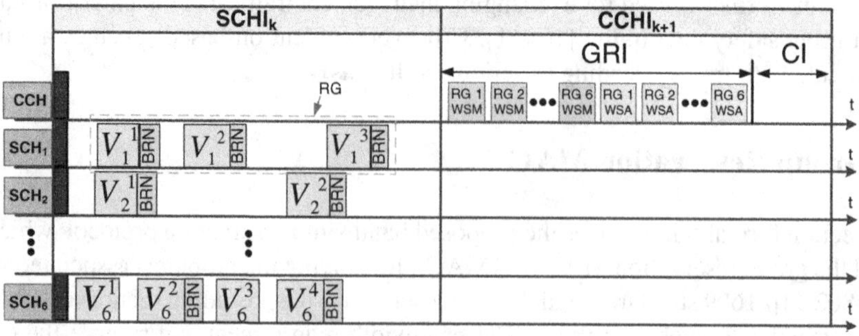

Fig. 2. Overview of GRMAC

First, as presented in Fig. 2, GRMAC divides vehicles into reservation groups (RGs). An RG is a set of vehicles that use the same SCH during a SCHI and require CCH to transmit data. The RGs sequentially (based on their SCH number) reserve the CCH bandwidth and transmit data over CCH during CCHI. This grouping strategy therefore solves the problem that vehicles cannot negotiate over CCH transmission opportunities with other vehicles on different SCHs.

Second, to reserve the bandwidth of CCH, a vehicle must attach a piggyback, which is two bits data, onto the service data when the service data is disseminated over SCH. This piggyback is called the bandwidth reservation notification (BRN) and it is used by the vehicle to notify other vehicles of its demand to transmit WSM/WSA traffics in CCH in the following CCHI. The CCH transmission sequence of vehicles in a single group can also be the sequence in which these vehicles disseminate their service data with BRN. Accordingly, the vehicles do not have to perform an additional bandwidth contention procedure in SCHs to schedule CCH data transmission, so bandwidth efficiency is increased.

A BRN contains two one-bit fields; these are the WSM and WSA fields, as displayed in Fig. 3. Each field is used to declare the need to make a reservation. If the WSM field is set to one, then the vehicle has reserved the CCH bandwidth for its WSM traffic, and if the WSA field is set to one, then the vehicle has reserved the CCH bandwidth for its WSA message. For example, if the two one-bit fields are set to (0,1), then the vehicle intends to reserve CCH bandwidth for its WSA message but does not need to reserve CCH bandwidth for its WSM traffic. This vehicle then attaches this BRN to the service data frame that is scheduled to be disseminated over SCH during SCHI. The CCH bandwidth will be reserved when other vehicles receive this BRN-attached service frame.

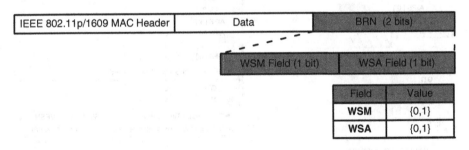

Fig. 3. BRN data structure

Third, GRMAC divides the CCHI into a group reservation interval (GRI) and a contention interval (CI) for the reserved CCH bandwidth and the newly incoming WSM/WSA traffics, respectively, as displayed in Fig. 4. Therefore, the incoming traffic, which did not reserve CCH bandwidth in SCH during the preceding SCHI, can still have opportunities to transmit during a CI using the conventional IEEE 802.11p/1609 CSMA scheme.

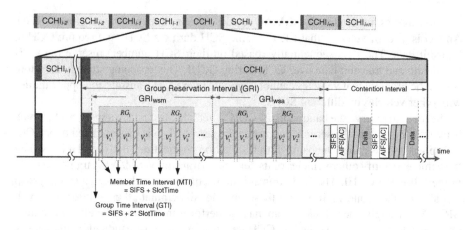

Fig. 4. GRI and CI

With respect to the GRI, GRMAC divides the GRI into GRI_{wsm} and GRI_{wsa} for WSM and WSA traffics, respectively. All vehicles transmit frames sequentially during both GRI_{wsm} and GRI_{wsa}. Both GRI_{wsm} and GRI_{wsa} have an upper bound (GRI_{wsm}^{max} and GRI_{wsa}^{max}) that prevents one of these two traffics from consuming all of the CCH bandwidth. This strategy regulates the ratio of the bandwidth consumed by WSM traffic to that consumed by WSA traffic, and can prevent the WSA traffic from encountering high delay and becoming overdue.

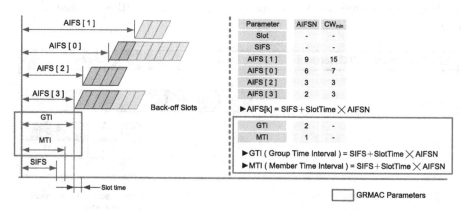

Fig. 5. Inter frame space parameter set used over the CCH

Figure 5 also presents two new intervals, the member time interval (MTI) and the group time interval (GTI), which are defined to separate the traffics within a single RG and between RGs, respectively. After detecting an MTI, which means a vehicle V_i^j has completed its transmission, the next vehicle V_i^{j+1} in the same group can begin to transmit data. After detecting a GTI, which means the current RG_i has completed its WSM/WSA transmission, the next group RG_{i+1} can begin to transmit. The first group RG1 can begin transmitting WSM data when all of the RGs have finished WSA transmission, as shown in Fig. 4.

Figure 6 displays an example transmission sequence of RGs and new-comers in CCH. First, each RG sequentially transmits WSMs and then transmits WSAs during GRI. If a new-comer wants to disseminate frames over CCH, it must wait until all RGs have completed transmitting during GRI, and then use the CSMA scheme to access the channel.

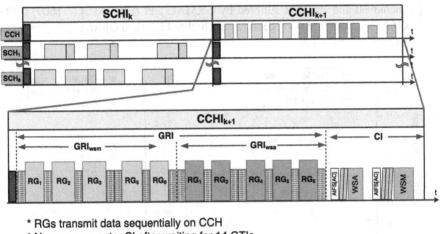

* RGs transmit data sequentially on CCH
* New comers enter CI after waiting for 14 GTIs

Fig. 6. RGs' and new comer's transmission sequence in CCH

Based on the above descriptions, the CCH bandwidth reservation procedure can be summarized as follows. First, a vehicle on the i-th SCH joins the i-th RG (RGi) after notifying this vehicle's demand for CCH bandwidth reservation through its BRN. Second, the RGs then sequentially transmit data over CCH during the next CCHI, in an order determined by the RG numbers. Third, the transmission sequence of the members of an RG on CCH in the next CCHI is the order in which the members transmit their BRN over SCH during SCHI.

4   Simulation Results

To evaluate the performance of GRMAC, some comparisons between GRMAC, IEEE 802.11p/1609 is made in terms of system goodput and frame error rate (FER). The system goodput is the goodput of all WSM traffics that can be received by a vehicle in CCH during CCHI. The FER is the ratio of the number of frames received with errors to the total number of frames received.

The simulation environment is an IEEE 802.11p/1609 OFDM system with a 10 MHz frequency band. The traffic that arrives through each connection follows a Poisson distribution. To simplify the simulated scenarios, each vehicle has one application service and the corresponding traffic to which the WSM protocol is applied (called WSM traffic herein). The former is transmitted on one SCH during SCHI and the latter is transmitted over CCH during CCHI. The default arrival rate of the application service is 100 Kbps, and that of the WSM traffic is 300 Kbps.

To compare the effects of total WSM traffic load on system goodput and FER, the number of vehicles is increased from 2 to 16, so the overall WSM traffic load is varied from 0.6 Mbps (300 bps × 2) to 4.8 Mbps (300 bps × 16). Figure 7 compares the system goodput achieved and the FER suffered by GRMAC and IEEE 802.11p/1609. IEEE 802.11p/1609 has poorer system goodput and higher FER than GRMAC, as presented in Fig. 7(a), (b), respectively.

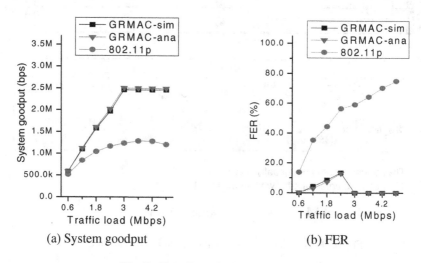

(a) System goodput   (b) FER

Fig. 7. The effect of WSM traffic load

Figure 7(a) demonstrates that the system goodput of GRMAC reaches 2.46 Mbps and GRMAC outperforms IEEE 802.11p/1609 by a factor of two when the overall WSM traffic load exceeds 3 Mbps. GRMAC has the highest system goodput for three reasons. First, GRMAC transfers some of the traffic load associated with the CCH bandwidth coordination mechanism from CCH to SCH, reducing the consumption of the CCH bandwidth during CCHI. Second, the number of collisions between frames that are transmitted in CCH during CCHI is reduced since the CCH bandwidth for the WSM/WSA traffic in SCHs is reserved during SCHI according to a schedule. Third, GRMAC separates the WSM and WSA traffics to eliminate the interference between them, reducing the number of collisions, and thereby improving goodput.

Figure 7(b) demonstrates that the FER experienced using GRMAC increases with the total WSM traffic load increases from 0.6 Mbps to 2.4 Mbps, and then drops to zero as the traffic increases above 2.4 Mbps. When the traffic load is low (0.6 Mbps–2.4 Mbps), only a short GRI is required to transmit the frames that are queued in the buffer of each vehicle, so the data traffic that arrives after GRI will be transmitted during CI and undergo some collisions. However, when the overall WSM traffic load exceeds 2.4 Mbps, enough data frames are queued in the buffer of each vehicle to require the reservation of the entire CCHI. Consequently, the duration of GRI equals the duration of CCHI and all of the frames are transmitted in during GRI, so no frame collides with any other.

5 Conclusion

The proposed GRMAC method enables vehicles to coordinate and reserve CCH bandwidth in SCHs during SCHI, maximizing the system goodput for CCH during CCHI. GRMAC not only reduces the number of collisions in CCH but also reduces the consumption of CCH bandwidth resource for scheduling WSM/WSA traffic. Accordingly, GRMAC uses only a little SCH bandwidth to schedule WSM/WSA traffics. The simulation results verify that GRMAC provides a higher goodput than the IEEE 802.11p/1609 standard. With a large WSM traffic load of 3 Mbps, GRMAC provides two times of the goodput that is achieved using IEEE 802.11p/1609.

References

1. IEEE 802.11p: Part 11: wireless LAN medium access control (MAC) and physical layer (PHY) specifications amendment 6: wireless access in vehicular environments, July 2010
2. IEEE Std. 1609.1TM-2006: IEEE trial-use standard for wireless access in vehicular environments (WAVE) – resource manager, Oct 2006
3. IEEE Std. 1609.2TM-2006: IEEE trial-use standard for wireless access in vehicular environments (WAVE) – security services for applications and management messages, July 2006
4. IEEE Std. 1609.3TM-2006: IEEE trial-use standard for wireless access in vehicular environments (WAVE) – networking services, April 2006
5. IEEE Std. 1609.4TM-2006: IEEE trial-use standard for wireless access in vehicular environments (WAVE) – multi-channel operation, Nov 2006
6. Jiang, D., Delgrossi, L.: IEEE 802.11p: towards an international standard for wireless access in vehicular environments. In: Proceedings of IEEE Vehicular Technology Conference, pp. 2036–2040 (2008)
7. Lu, N., Wang, X., Wang, P., Lai, P., Liu, F.: A distributed reliable multi-channel MAC protocol for vehicular ad hoc networks. In: Proceedings of Intelligent Vehicles Symposium, pp. 1078–1082 (2009)
8. Lu, N., Ji, Y., Lin, F., Wang, X.: A dedicated multi-channel MAC protocol design for VANET with adaptive broadcasting. In: Proceedings of Wireless Communications and Networking Conference, pp. 1–6 (2010)
9. Borgonovo, F., Capone, A., Cesana, M., Fratta, L.: ADHOC MAC: new MAC architecture for ad hoc networks providing efficient and reliable point-to-point and broadcast services. J. Wireless Netw. 10(4), 359–366 (2004)
10. Zang, Y., Stibor, L., Walke, B., Reumerman, H.J., Barroso, A.: A novel MAC protocol for throughput sensitive applications in vehicular environments. In: Proceedings of Vehicular Technology Conference, pp. 2580–2584 (2007)
11. Wang, Q., Leng, S., Fu, H., Zhang, Y., Weerasinghe, H.: An enhanced multi-channel MAC for the IEEE 1609.4 based vehicular ad hoc networks. In: Proceedings of INFOCOM IEEE Conference on Computer Communications Workshops, pp. 1–2 (2010)

k-Perimeter Coverage Evaluation and Deployment in Wireless Sensor Networks

Ying Chen[1], Changying Li[2], Jiguo Yu[1(✉)], Hongsong Zhu[3], and Yuyan Sun[3]

[1] School of Information Science and Engineering, Qufu Normal University, Ri-zhao 276826, Shandong, People's Republic of China
jiguoyu@sina.com
[2] Southern Shandong Academy of Engineering Technology Managements Center, Ji-ning 272000, Shandong, China
[3] Beijing Key Laboratory IOT Information Security Technology, Institute of Information Engineering, CAS, Beijing 100093, China

Abstract. Coverage is a fundamental issue in wireless sensor networks (WSNs). Degree of coverage is often used as a measurement of the quality of service (QoS) of WSNs. In this paper, we consider two problems: coverage evaluation and deployment. The former aims to evaluate the coverage degree of the monitored area, while the latter aims to deploy new sensors inside the monitored area to meet the application requirements without affecting the initial deployment. For the k-perimeter coverage evaluation problem, a k-perimeter coverage evaluation scheme (k-PCE) is proposed. Based on our k-perimeter coverage evaluation scheme, a greedy k-perimeter coverage rate deployment scheme (k-PCRD) is proposed, while is shown that the time complexity is lower than existing studies. Simulation shows the superiority of the proposed algorithms.

Keywords: Wireless sensor networks · Perimeter coverage · Perimeter coverage evaluation

1 Introduction

Recent advance in the sensor technology, wireless communication technology, embedded and micro-electro-mechanical systems have greatly promoted the emergence and development of WSNs. WSNs are used extensively in many fields, such as military applications, environment monitoring and disaster prevention and so on [1]. Coverage is one of the most fundamental problems in WSNs. The basic coverage issue reflects how well the sensor observes the physical space. That is, each position in the physical space is at least one sensor within the sensing range. In this paper, we study k coverage problem such that each location inside the monitored area is covered by at least k sensors.

Jiguo Yu—This work was partially supported by the NNSF of China for contract 61373027, 61472418 and NSF of Shandong Province for contract ZR2012FM023.

K. Xu and J. Zhu (Eds.): WASA 2015, LNCS 9204, pp. 50–59, 2015.
DOI: 10.1007/978-3-319-21837-3_6

Depending on the application and the environment, node deployment can be realized either in a predefined way or randomly. In this paper, we adopt the random deployment, which is more suitable for practical application. k-coverage is that each point in the area is within the sensing range of at least k sensors. Sensors have limited battery life. It may not be feasible to recharge or replace failure sensors, especially when sensors are deployed in harsh areas. A variety of reasons will lead to failure of the sensor. This also causes a change in the initial deployment. Therefore, many applications require $k > 1$ to tolerate sensor failure.

Coverage problems have attracted widespread attentions in recent two decades. Roughly Speaking, k-coverage includes two problems: k-coverage evaluation and deployment. k-coverage evaluation aims to evaluate whether the monitored area is k-covered. Deployment problem aims to deploy new sensors in the monitored area to meet the application requirements. For the k-coverage evaluation problem, most of the existing studies just give a yes or no answer to the coverage degree of the whole monitored area. In practical applications, most of the answer is negative. We may want to know the percentage of the monitored area that is not k-covered in order to evaluate the cost of redeployment. Therefore, it is essential to propose a scheme to solve the problem.

The main contribution of the paper is summarized as follows. For the k-coverage evaluation and deployment, we propose k-perimeter coverage evaluation (k-PCE) and k-perimeter coverage rate deployment (k-PCRD). Different from the existing work, k-PCE and k-PCRD have the following advantages.

1. We propose a novel scheme to determine the coverage degree of the monitored area and introduce new concepts.
2. Based on k-PCE, we propose a k-perimeter coverage rate deployment scheme (k-PCRD). k-PCRD does not involve the division of monitored area such that we do not consider the size of the grid.
3. The time complexity of k-PCE and k-PCRD are lower than Grid Scan [8] and k-coverage contour evaluation and deployment [13].
4. k-PCE and k-PCRD can be directly applied to irregular monitored area.

The rest of the paper is organized as follows. Section 2 reviews the related work. Section 3 describes the problem studied, k-perimeter coverage evaluation scheme is proposed. In Sect. 4, based on k-perimeter coverage evaluation scheme, k-perimeter coverage rate deployment scheme is proposed. Simulation results are presented in Sect. 5. Section 6 concludes the paper.

2   Related Works

Due to the limited lifetime of sensors and the importance of the monitoring area, many applications require $k > 1$ to tolerate sensor failure. It may not be feasible to recharge energy depletion or replace failure sensors in many situations. k-coverage has attracted lots of attentions during the past few years, which has been extensively studied in the literature.

In [2], Huang and Tseng formulated coverage problem as a decision problem, whose goal is to determine whether every point in the monitored area of the sensor networks is covered by at least k sensors. In [3], Zou and Chakrabarty introduced a virtual force model for coverage evaluation. In [4], Shakkottai et al. proposed a one-coverage evaluation scheme for grid deployments. In [5], Meguerdichian et al. studied a Voronoi diagram-based, worst-case k-coverage evaluation. In [6], Deng et al. discussed the energy efficient area coverage problem considering boundary effects in a new perspective. That is, transforming the area coverage problem to the target coverage problem and then achieving full area coverage by covering all the targets in the converted target coverage problem. In [7], Xu and Song studied three restricted coverage problems, that is, the linear k-coverage, k-road coverage and minimum strong dominating set.

In [8], Shen et al. proposed a scheme named Grid Scan. The basic idea is to partition the monitoring area into uniform-sizes grids and then evaluate the coverage degree of each grid. In [9], Pi and Yu formulated the redeployment problem as a 0-1 programming model and propose some heuristics to solve the problem. In [10], Lazos et al. addressed the problem of stochastic coverage in heterogeneous sensor networks. In [11], Hefeeda and Bagheri proposed new algorithms to achieve k-coverage in dense sensor networks. In [12], Ammari and Giudici extended the problem to connected k-coverage.

In [13], Sheu et al. proposed k-coverage contour evaluation and deployment. The monitored area is divided into nonuniform-sized grids. Each grid is further divided into subgrids, if grid can obtain more precise coverage information. A sensor can be deployed in the highest coverage-weight points. In [14], Lee et al. addressed the path-based coverage of the wireless sensor network. In [15], Khoufi et al. proposed a projection-based method that tends to minimize the number of sensor nodes needed to fully cover such an area. In [16], Li and Zhang proposed an algorithm using the properties of empty circles to evaluate whether coverage holes exist or not in WSNs and identify the exact nodes on the boundaries of holes.

3 k-Perimeter Coverage Evaluation Scheme(k-PCE)

3.1   Problem Description

Given a set of sensors, $S=\{s_1,s_2,...,s_n\}$, in a 2-D area. Suppose that no two sensors are located in the same location. Sensors are to be static after deployment and have the same sensing radii. Sensors are aware of their own location through either the global positioning system (GPS) or other the location techniques. We also assume the transmission range of a sensor is at least twice the sensing range of a sensor so that connectivity is also guaranteed [17].

Let S be the set of Pre-deployed sensors and n is the total number of sensor nodes. S_i is the ith sensor in S. S_d is the set of sensors deployed. S_{id} is the perimeter coverage degree of sensor. N_i is the set of neighbors of sensor S_i. Each neighbor, $S_j \in N_i$, can contribute any coverage to S_i's perimeter, i.e., $\forall S_j \in N_i, |S_i - S_j| \leq 2R, N_i \subseteq S$. Where $|S_i - S_j|$ denotes the distance between S_i and S_j. the angle of S_i's arch, denoted by $[l_j, r_j]$, is perimeter-covered by S_j. $flag$ is a boolean variable. If l_i has emerged, $flag_i=1$, otherwise, $flag_i =0$.

Definition 1. *Perimeter coverage.* Sensor S_i is perimeter coverage if each point on the perimeter of S_i is within the sensing range of at least a sensor other than S_i itself.

Definition 2. *k-perimeter coverage.* Sensor S_i is k-perimeter coverage if all points on the perimeter of S_i is covered by at least k sensors other than S_i itself.

Definition 3. *Partially perimeter coverage.* Sensor S_i is partially perimeter coverage if some point on the perimeter of S_i is uncovered by k sensors other than S_i itself.

Definition 4. *k-perimeter coverage rate (k-PCR)* is the ratio of the number of k-perimeter coverage relative to the total number of sensor nodes.

Definition 5. *k-coverage rate* is the ratio of the area of k-covered grid relative to the whole monitored area.

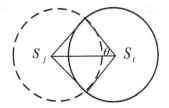

Fig. 1. The angle of S_i's arch covered by S_j

We determine whether a sensor S_i is k-perimeter coverage or not. Sensor S_i and sensor S_j are located in positions (x_i, y_i) and (x_j, y_j), respectively. The distance between S_i and S_j is denoted by $d(S_i, S_j) = \sqrt{(x_i - x_j)^2 + (y_i - y_j)^2}$. If $d(S_i, S_j) > 2R$, then, S_j does not cover the perimeter of S_i. Otherwise, S_j can cover the perimeter of S_i. The range of perimeter of S_i covered by S_j is calculated as follows. Without loss of generality, as shown in Fig. 1, S_i is located on the right S_j, $x_i > x_j$, $y_i = y_j$. Arch corresponding angle is 2θ, where $\theta = \arccos \frac{d(S_i, S_j)}{2R}$. Therefore, the range of angle perimeter-covered by S_j is $[\pi - \theta, \pi + \theta]$.

3.2   A k-Perimeter Coverage Evaluation Scheme(k-PCE)

In this section, we determine the coverage degree of the monitored area. The main ides is to determine perimeter coverage degree of each sensor and then calculate perimeter coverage rate. For all the neighbors of a sensor S_i, $S_j \in N_i$, the range of angle perimeter-covered by S_j is denoted by $[l_j, r_j]$. For each sensor in the N_i, we place intersection points on the line $[0, 2\pi]$ and sort the whole points in an ascending order into a list L. We traverse the line segment $[0, 2\pi]$ by visiting each element in the sorted list L from the left to right and determine the perimeter coverage degree of S_i. k-perimeter coverage sensor should be placed into the set K. Partial perimeter coverage sensor should be placed into the set P.

Finally, the k-PCE algorithm returns two sets K and P. The pseudo-codes of k-PCE are as follows.

The k-PCE algorithm returns two sets K and P. P is the set of partially-perimeter coverage sensors. P contains partially-perimeter coverage sensor and the minimum degree of partially-perimeter coverage sensor. K is k-perimeter coverage sensor. By the aid of K, we can calculate k-perimeter coverage rate of the monitored area.

Algorithm 1. k-Perimeter Coverage Evaluation Algorithm(k-PCE)

---

   1. For each $S_i \in S$ **do**
   2.   **For** each $S_j \in N_i$ **do**
   3.   Determine the range of angle perimeter-covered by S_j, denoted by $[l_j, r_j]$;
   4.   Place point l_j and r_j in the line segment $[0, 2\pi]$;
   5.   **End For**
   6.   Sort all these points in an ascending order into a list L;
   7.   Traverse the line segment $[0, 2\pi]$ by visiting each point in sorted L from left to right;
   8.   **If** $S_{id} > k$ **then**
   9.   Add S_i to K;
   10. **else**
   11.   Add S_i to P;
   12.   Add S_{id} to P;
   13. **End If**
   14. End For
   15. Return K and P

Theorem 1. k-PCE can determine the coverage degree of the monitored area.

Proof. Based on k-perimeter coverage evaluation algorithm, the perimeter coverage degree of each sensor is calculated. k-perimeter coverage of sensor should be placed into the set K. Partially-perimeter coverage of sensor should be placed into the set P. Assume that there is a sensor S_i that is m-perimeter coverage and $m < k$, where m is a constant. According to k-PCE, S_i is restored in P, since S_i is not k-perimeter coverage. Degree of the monitored area cannot be k. Assume that each sensor is k-perimeter coverage. According to k-PCE, we can determine that the coverage degree of the monitored area is k. Therefore, our proposed algorithm is correct and can determine the coverage degree of the monitored area.

Theorem 2. The time complexity of k-perimeter coverage evaluation algorithm is $O(nd \log d)$.

Proof. For any one sensor S_i, d_i is the number of neighbors of S_i, i.e., $d_i = |N_i|$. The time cost of step 2–5 and 6 are $O(d_i)$ and $O(d_i \log d_i)$, respectively. Finally the complexity of traversing each element in the sorted list from left to right is $O(d_i)$. We determine whether a sensor is k-perimeter coverage or not, which takes $O(d_i \log d_i)$. We determine whether each sensor is k-perimeter coverage or not, which takes $O(nd \log d)$, where, $d = \max\{d_1, d_2, ..., d_n\}$. Therefore, the time complexity of k-PCE is $O(nd \log d)$.

4 k-Perimeter Coverage Rate Deployment(k-PCRD)

In general, there are two purposes for the deployment of sensors. First, the same number of sensor is deployed in the same monitored area to achieve high coverage. The other is to deploy fewer sensors to achieve the same coverage. In the paper, our aim is the latter. We want to deploy fewer sensors to achieve the same coverage in the monitored area.

In the k-PCRD, we first executes k-PCE to return the set P and then calculate k-PCR. Sensors should be deployed in the largest perimeter coverage degree, if k-PCR cannot reach the application requirements. We select the maximum number of sensors that are neighboring to a sensor, if the largest perimeter coverage degree is more than one. The step is repeated until satisfying the needs of the application or no other sensors for deployment. The pseudo-codes of Algorithm 2 are as follows.

Since partially perimeter of sensor are uncovered, it is possible that there exist some redundant sensors. Therefore, after deployment, we need to remove those redundant sensors and add them back to the set of sensor deployed so that they are still to deploy. After removing redundancy still meet the needs of application. The pseudo-codes of checking redundancy are Algorithm 3.

Algorithm 2. k-Perimeter Coverage Rate Deployment Scheme (k-PCRD)

D; a set of deployment monitored area sensors
1. Execute k-PCE and determine P from its return values;
2. Calculate k_{rate};
3. **While** (required k_{rate} is not satisfied) and ($S_d \neq \phi$) **do**
4. $S_{selected} = max(P)$;
5.   **If** (the number of $S_{selected}$)> 1 **then**
6. $S_i = max(S_{selected})$;
7.   **else**
8. $S_i = S_{selected}$;
9.   **End If**
10.   Deploy $3 \times (k\text{-}S_{id})$ sensors;
11.   Add deployment sensors to D;
12.   Remove deployment sensors from S_d;
13.   Execute k-PCE algorithm return P and K;
14.   Calculate k_{rate};
15. **End While**
16. Call Prune Redundant Deployment(S_d,D);

Algorithm 3. Prune Redundant Deployment(S_d,D)

---

1. For i=1 to $|D|$ **do**
2. S_i is the ith sensor in D;
3.   Remove S_i from D ;
4.   Execute k-PCE and calculate k_{rate};
5.   **If** $k_{rate} < 1$ **then**
6.   Add S_i to D;
7.   **else**
8.   Add S_i to S_d;
9.   **End If**
10. End For

Theorem 3. k-perimeter coverage rate deployment can k-cover the whole area.

Proof. Assume that there is a sensor S_i that is m-perimeter coverage and $m < k$, where m is a constant. According to k-PCRD, the largest perimeter coverage degree of sensor needs to be deployed new sensors. S_i will be k-perimeter coverage after several loops, which is against the hypothesis. Thus, k-PCRD can achieve the k-cover of the monitored area.

Theorem 4. The time complexity of k-perimeter coverage rate deployment algorithm is $O(Nd \log d)$.

Proof. n is the number of Pre-deployed sensors in the monitored area. $N(N > n)$ is eventually the number of sensor deployment. d ($d < n$) is the maximum number of sensors that are neighboring to a sensor. We know the time complexity of k-PCE is $O(nd \log d)$ in the Sect. 3. Therefore, the time complexity of k-PCRD is $O(Nd \log d)$.

5   Simulation

In this section, we evaluate the performance of our scheme by simulation. Pre-deployed sensors are randomly and uniformly deployed in a $100*100m$ monitored area. Once deployed, sensors are static. The sensing radius is 15 meters for all sensors. We consider only coverage and redeployment issues. Therefore, the MAC protocol and routing protocol are ignored in our simulation. Each experiment is at least repeated 30 times with distinct sensor pre-deployments.

5.1   Simulation of k-Perimeter Coverage Evaluation

Obviously, in the k-perimeter coverage evaluation experiment, the number of sensor is a basic metric for computation of cost estimation. The radius of sensor is also a metric for judging the performance of the k-PCE scheme. We analyzed

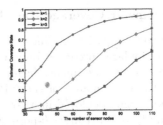

Fig. 2. Number of sensors versus PCR under different coverage degree

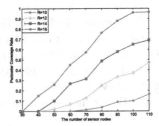

Fig. 3. Number of sensors versus PCR under different radius for k=2

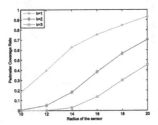

Fig. 4. Radius of the sensor versus PCR under different coverage degree

the influence of the number of sensors and sensing radius, respectively. All data are averages from 30 times experiment.

The number of sensor has impact on the k-perimeter coverage evaluation. Figures 2 and 3 show perimeter coverage rate varies with the number of sensor deployed. From Fig. 2, we can see the perimeter coverage rate increases as the number of sensor increases under different coverage degree. From Fig. 3, we can see the perimeter coverage rate varies with distinct sensing radii. Generally speaking, the perimeter coverage rate increases as radius of sensor increases, if the same number of sensor is deployed in the monitored area.

Radii of sensors have impact on the k-perimeter coverage evaluation. Figure 4 shows the perimeter coverage rate is related to the radius of sensor. From Fig. 4, k-PCR increases as the radius of sensors increases under different coverage degree. k-PCR is different under different k. k-PCR increases as k decreases.

5.2   Simulation of k-Perimeter Coverage Rate Deployment

In this section, we discuss our simulation finding and show how the proposed algorithm compares to other similar approaches found in the literature. In the k-perimeter coverage rate deployment experiment, the number of redeployed sensor is main metric for judging the performance of the k-PCRD scheme. Similarly, sensors are randomly and uniformly deployed in a $100 * 100m$ monitored area.

From the simulation result below, we can see k-perimeter coverage rate deployment is superior to Grid Scan [7] and coverage rate deployment (CRD) [12]. The Grid Scan can achieve the redeployment. However, the main drawback of Grid Scan is that the grid size is hard to be decided and has coverage holes. k-coverage rate deployment scheme in [12], improves Grid Scan. However, CRD divides the monitored area into grids. Our schemes do not consider region partition and consider sensors inside the monitored area. The whole monitored area is k-covered if each sensor is k-perimeter covered. The time complexity of PCRD and the number of sensor are lower than the above two schemes. From the Figs. 5 and 6, we can see PCRD is smaller than CRD for the number of redeployed sensor.

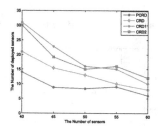

Fig. 5. Number of sensors versus number of deployed sensors for k=2

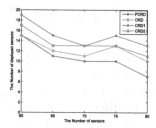

Fig. 6. Number of sensors versus number of deployed sensors for k=3

6   Conclusion

In the paper, we propose two schemes: k-perimeter coverage evaluation (k-PCE) and k-perimeter coverage rate deployment (k-PCRD). In the k-PCE, we can determine whether a sensor is k-perimeter coverage or not. Based on k-PCE, k-PCRD is proposed. k-PCRD can increase k-perimeter coverage rate. k-PCRD is to deploy sensors for the largest perimeter coverage degree.

Note that, the proposed schemes need to know the location of each sensor. It is hard implemented in large-scale wireless sensor networks. In the future, our goal is to relax the assumptions, such as the location of sensors, the radii of sensors and connectivity. In addition, a distributed algorithm is also necessary to efficient execution.

References

1. Cheng, S., Cai, Z., Li, J.: Curve query processing in wireless sensor networks. IEEE Transactions on Vehicular Technology (2013)
2. Huang, C., Tseng, Y.: The coverage problem in a wireless sensor network. J. Mob. Netw. Appl. **10**(4), 519–528 (2005)
3. Zou, Y., Chakrabarty, K.: Sensor deployment and target localization based on virtual forces. In: Proceedings of ICC2003, pp. 1293–1303 (2003)
4. Shakkottai, S., Srikant, R., Shroff, N.: Unreliable sensor grids: Coverage, connectivity and diameter. J. Ad Hoc Netw. **3**(6), 702–716 (2005)
5. Meguerdichian, S., Koushanfar, F., Potkonjak, M., Srivastava, B.: Coverage problems in wireless ad-hoc sensor networks. In: Proceedings of ICC 2002, pp. 1380–1387 (2002)
6. Deng, X., Yu, J., Yu, D., Chen, C.: Transforming area coverage to target coverage to maintain coverage and connectivity for wireless sensor networks. Int. J. Distrib. Sens. Netw. **2012**(254318), 12 (2012)
7. Xu, X., Song, M.: Restricted coverage in wireless networks. In: Proceedings of IEEE INFCOM, pp. 558–564 (2014)
8. Shen, X., Chen, J., Sun, Y.: Grid scan: A simple and effective approach for coverage issue in wireless sensor networks. In: Proceedings of ICC 2006, pp. 3480–3484 (2006)
9. Pi, X., Yu, H.: Redeployment problem for wireless sensor networks. In: Proceedings of ICC 2006, pp. 1–4 (2006)
10. Lazos, L., Poovendran, R.: Stochastic coverage in heterogeneous sensor networks. Proc. ACM Trans. Sens. Netw. **2**(3), 325–358 (2006)
11. Hefeeda, M., Bagheri, M.: Randomized *k*-coverage algorithms for dense sensor networks. In: Proceedings of IEEE INFOCOM, pp. 2376–2380 (2007)
12. Ammari, H., Giudici, J.: On the connected *k*-coverage problem in heterogeneous sensor nets: the curse of randomness and heterogeneity. In: Proceedings of IEEE ICDCS 2009, pp. 265–272 (2009)
13. Sheu, J., Chang, G., Wu, S., Chen, Y.: Adaptive *k*-coverage contour evaluation and deployment in wireless sensor networks. Proc. ACM Trans. Sens. Netw. **9**(4), 40 (2013)
14. Lee, C., Shin, D., Bae, S., Choi, S.: Best and worst-case coverage problems for arbitrary paths in wireless sensor networks. In: Proceedings of IEEE MASS 2010, pp. 1699–1714 (2013)
15. Khoufi, I., Minet, P., Laouiti, A.: Asimple method for the deployment of wireless sensors to ensure full coverage of an irregular area with obstacles. In: Proceedings of ACM MSWiM 2014, pp. 21–26 (2014)
16. Li, W., Zhang, W.: Coverage hole and boundary nodes detection in wireless sensor networks. J. Netw. Comput. Appl. **48**, 35–43 (2015)
17. Wang, X., Xing, G., Zhang, Y., Lu, C., Pless, R., Gill, C.: Integrated coverage and connectivity configuration in wireless sensor networks. In: Proceedings of ACM SenSys 2003 (2003)

Modeling Flu Trends with Real-Time Geo-tagged Twitter Data Streams

Jaime Chon, Ross Raymond, Haiyan Wang, and Feng Wang[✉]

School of Mathematical and Natural Sciences,
Arizona State University, Tempe, USA
fwang25@asu.edu

Abstract. The rich data generated and read by millions of users on social media tells what is happening in the real world in a rapid and accurate fashion. In recent years many researchers have explored real-time streaming data from Twitter for a broad range of applications, including predicting stock markets and public health trend. In this paper we design, implement, and evaluate a prototype system to collect and analyze influenza statuses over different geographical locations with real-time tweet streams. To evaluate the accuracy of the influenza estimation based on tweet streams, we correlate the results with official statistics from Center for Disease Control and Prevention (CDC). Our preliminary results have demonstrated that real-time tweet streams capture the dynamics of influenza at national level, and could potentially serve as an early warning system of influenza epidemics or flu trends.

Keywords: Influenza · Mathematical modeling · Geo-tagged twitter stream

1 Introduction

Recent years have witnessed tremendous growth of online social media such as Facebook and Twitter which offer people innovative platforms for sharing news stories, exchanging information and reporting latest statuses such as flu and epidemics. Although government agencies such as CDC (Centers for Disease Control and Prevention) of United States regularly report official and aggregated statistics on the trends of influenza or outbreaks such as SARS and Ebloa, these statistics often fail to reflect the latest development and progress since there is delay caused by manual data collections and complicated reporting processes.

The rising popularity of social media has led people to share their flu statuses and symptoms online, thus allowing an alternative channel to collect, analyze and monitor the latest trends of influenza development. Towards building a flu-surveillance system and studying whether Twitter data can be used as a robust indicator of influenza, this paper designs, implements, and evaluates a prototype system which automatically collects, analyzes and models geo-based flu tweets from real-time Twitter data streams for characterizing and modeling flu trends.

© Springer International Publishing Switzerland 2015
K. Xu and J. Zhu (Eds.): WASA 2015, LNCS 9204, pp. 60–69, 2015.
DOI: 10.1007/978-3-319-21837-3_7

Specifically, we extract flu tweets from real-time data streams and tag each tweet with geographical locations based on three information sources: (i) the geographical locations of the user who tweeted the message, (ii) the physical location where the user sent the tweet and enabled their geographical location tracking in the Twitter App, or (iii) the geographical location mentioned in the content of the tweets. The availability of geo-tagged flu tweets allows us to characterize and model flu trends at different geographical locations in real-time, which could serve as early warning signals before CDC releases official statistics, typically a few days or weeks later.

To verify the relevance of flu trends modeled by our system, we correlate geo-tagged flu tweets with the reported flu cases releasee from CDC official statistics. Our experimental results reveal a strong temporal correlation between these two metrics at coarse-grained geographical levels such as countries, but show little correlations between these metrics at fine-grained geographical levels such as cities, states or regions. The strong correlation between flu tweets and CDC statistics at national level demonstrates the potential application of our system for providing early prediction and warning of flu trends.

The contributions of this paper are two-fold as follows:

- We explore geo-tagged flu tweets from real-time Twitter data streams to characterize, analyze and model the trends and statuses of influenza and epidemic over different geographical locations.
- We develop a prototype framework for geo-based Twitter flu data analysis and modeling, correlate flu tweets with CDC statistics on the reported flu cases, and demonstrate the potential application of our system for providing early prediction and warning of flu trends.

The remainder of this paper is organized as follows. Section 2 describes the architecture of the real-time system we have developed for collecting, processing, analyzing and modeling influenza statuses with tweet data streams. In Sect. 3, we present the preliminary results with real-world tweets and characterize the correlation between flu tweets and reported flu cases at CDC. Section 4 describes related work of modeling influenza with social media data, while Sect. 5 concludes this paper and outlines our future work.

2 System Framework for Tweet Data Collection, Processing and Analysis, and Mathematical Modeling

Figure 1 illustrates our proposed framework to collect, analysis, and modeling Twitter data with mathematical models.

2.1 Twitter Data Collection

Twitter provides two mechanisms for programmatic access to their data encoded in JSON format: REST API and Stream API. The REST API provides access to user profile and follower data. This data allows the generation of a user following

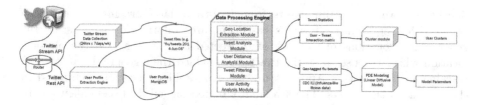

Fig. 1. Twitter data collection, Analysis, and Modeling Framework

topology, which captures who follows whom in Twitter and is critical to study the influence between Twitter users. The Streaming API continuously delivers real-time stream of Tweets matching a given search query over a persistent HTTP connection. The stream API offers two endpoints: Sample and Filter. The Sample endpoint delivers a small random sample (typically 1 %) of all public statuses (Tweets). The Filter endpoint delivers all Tweets that match a given query, which can include keywords, locations, and users, up to 1 % of all public Tweets. The aggregate Tweet information can be used as an indicator of what happens in real life.

We collect both Twitter user and Tweets information. Since it is hard to have a complete view of the whole Twitter user topology due to the large scale and dynamics of Twitter network, we start our collection with tweets associated with a specific topic or event, such as flu, Ebola, earthquake, etc., then collect the user profiles of users actively interact with these tweets and further build the topology of these active users.

Twitter Stream Data Collection module handles establishing and maintaining the connection with Twitter servers to retrieve tweets based on chosen keywords and/or tweets with a particular user as a source. Tweets are saved in JSON format in flat files with collection dates as file name. JSON format is chosen to eliminate encoding/decoding errors, efficiency, and flexibility. Flat file is chosen to remove the overhead of a traditional database;

User Profile Extraction module handles the collection of user data, including user profile and user's follower ids for every user observed in the Tweet data stream. The fetched data are stored in a MongoDB database [1], which is a document-based non-SQL database which provides fast and scalable storage. MongoDB is chosen due to its ability to handle the complex random reads needed by our user processing algorithms.

2.2 Twitter Data Processing

Data processing can be further divided into data cleaning and data analysis.

Tweet Filtering Module carries out the cleaning of the raw tweet stream from Twitter. The main functions of the module are: filtering and handling of messages (notifications), removing extraneous fields from Tweets and user profiles, and reordering user's Tweets.

The raw Tweet stream contains not only Tweets matching the given query, but additional messages (notifications) from Twitter. These messages need to be filtered from the Tweet Stream. Two examples of notifications are: a tweet matching the query has been deleted, or the backlog for the stream is filling up. The latter example occurs when the tweet processing algorithm is not fast enough to process the tweets as fast as Twitter sends them.

We also remove all extraneous fields for each tweet to conserve disk space. This filter can be safely applied since a tweet contains a number of fields not relevant to our processing needs, the removed fields are only relevant in the case of displaying a tweet to a user. For example, the tweet will contain a url for a CSS file containing custom formatting information for a particular tweet.

The last component of this module reorders the tweets on disk to ensure tweets are in order of their timestamp. This needs to be done because Twitter doesn't guarantee that tweets will arrive in order, users are in different time zones, and most importantly all of the tweet processing algorithms depend on processing tweets in order for the simplicity/efficiency of the algorithms.

Geo-location Extraction Module. Based on [2], 84.2 % of twitter users have specified location in their twitter profiles and 10.3 % of twitter users have geo-location enabled Tweet. However, there are still challenges as follows: only a very small percentage of Twitter users add gps information to their tweets,; a significant number of users attempt to thwart automated systems by using bogus locations in their profile or by using valid locations with non-standard spelling or characters ("a" would be replace by "@"); all geocoding services have api limits that would be easily reached, and currently all geocoding services rely on input being as close to a location as possible and not on random text that may contain a location. We implement our module based on the "carmen" library [7] for geocoding tweets. This library provides us with a framework to resolve Tweet locations, and a small database of known locations.The included database contains names of states, abbreviations, cities, and common misspellings. We have expanded the database to include a lot more of the previously mentioned entities, as well as zip codes, airport codes, monuments, etc. We add enhancement to the Carmen library by adding a new resolver to process the Tweet text. The four fields we use to geo-tag a tweet are coordinates, place, profile.location, and text.

Tweet Analysis Module. Besides generating statistics of collected tweets, a major functionality of this module is to discover the retweet relationship, which is a mapping from a source (original) tweet to all its recursive retweets/replies. Discovering which tweets are retweet, reply, or contain the same content as the source tweet is important since when the flu tweet count is calculated, only source tweets instead of all tweets mentioning flu are considered. This is because for source tweets with tens of thousands of retweets/replies, most of the retweets are just simple "take care" or "get well" which does not reflect whether the person who retweets the source tweet has flu symptoms or not. The flu cases are majorly captured in the source tweets.

There are three ways that a tweet can be retweeted. User clicks the "retweet" button, or "reply" button, or directly retweets a Tweet by typing RT at the beginning of a Tweet to indicate they are re-posting someone else's content.

To identify the source tweets and count the number of retweets, we go through each tweet and check if it is a reply (checks if the "in_reply_to_status_id" has a value) or a retweet (checks the "retweeted" field and if the pattern "RT @" occurs within the text), then increments a counter if the tweet belongs to an already identified source tweet. If the tweet is not categorized as reply or a retweet, the tweet id and text is stored as a source tweet.

In the case where the "retweeted" field is missing and the tweet contains the "RT @¡user name¿" pattern in the text, the algorithm will employ various techniques to compare the text to the text of already discovered tweets. One key item to note is that the retweet pattern can occur several times. The algorithm will loop through each "RT @" pattern from the outermost to the innermost and check if the user name belongs to any observed tweet. If this check passes, the algorithm will now attempt to match the text to the already observed texts. This means taking into account truncated text, as well as user added messages in the beginning and in the end of the text.

User Activity Analysis Module is used to measure a user's level of engagement by extracting the interaction between users and tweets and produces the user-tweet interaction matrix. The matrix records which users are involved in which source tweets and can be used to further cluster users into groups based on their tweeting behavior and cluster tweets into groups based on the users that are interested in them.

User Distance Analysis Module is used to measure how far a user is from the source by calculating the distance metrics for all the users actively participating in the discussion of a specific topic. Our definition of distance is a function of user activity, user profile, and their distance to the source user. The definition can be extended to add graph metrics such as the k-shell value of each user. User distance is an input to the PDE modeling module which can characterize and predict the spreading of a specific topic.

2.3 Mathematical Modeling

After data is collected, cleaned, and analyzed, the last component in our prototype is the mathematical modeling. This component includes two modules: (1) User/Tweet Clustering. We apply existing clustering algorithms such as spectrum clustering, k-mean algorithm to cluster users and tweets. We can verify our clusters using the collected user and tweet information. (2) PDE model design. PDE models are used to describe temporal and spatial diffusion of flu related topics and predict flu trend in real life.

3   Preliminary Results

3.1   Statistics of Collected Tweets

We have collected raw Twitter data covering several dimensions and categories as described below: (1) Any tweet that contains the keyword *flu*. This is one of the most common illnesses that CDC tracks closely. (2) Tweets containing the keyword *Ebola*. Investigating this dataset can help identify the spreading pattern for an actual outbreak of an unexpected disease, therefore increases the accuracy and speed of the predictive model in identifying new outbreaks. (3) Tweets related to the Malaysian Airlines flight disappearance. Tracking an event with high media coverage gives insight into the unique communication fluctuations due to such event.

Table 1 gives a brief summary of the scale of the collected data.

Table 1. Summary of collected data

Category	Amount
Total Size of Data	150GB
Total Number of Tweets	121,556,931
Total Number of Source Tweets	40,518,977
Total Number of Unique Users	19,083,164
Data Collection Start	October 11, 2013
Data Collection End	March 17, 2015

3.2   Correlation Between Twitter Flu Tweet Trend and CDC Reported ILI Case Trend

To verify the relevance of flu trends modeled by our system, we correlate geo-tagged flu tweets with the reported flu cases released from CDC official statistics. We adopt the flu data collected between January 3 and March 26, 2014, which is a subset of all the collected flu data that align with the flu season.

Figure 2 shows the number of weekly new flu tweets in Twitter and the number of weekly reported ILI cases provided by CDC. It shows strong linear correlation between the lines. In order to measure the linear correlation, we adopt Pearson's product-moment correlation coefficient $\rho_{X,Y} = \frac{cov(X,Y)}{\sigma_X \sigma_Y}$, where $cov(X,Y)$ is the covariance between variablex X and Y, and σ_X is the standard deviation of X. The result shows that the correlation coefficient between Twitter weekly new flu tweets count and the newly reported ILI is as high as 0.9297.

We further divide the tweet counts by regions and investigate the correlation between regional tweet counts and regional CDC regional ILI cases to investigate whether Twitter tweet data can be used to indicate the flu trend as the level of region. Figure 3 [6] illustrates the 10 regions defined by CDC. Figure 4 shows no obvious correlation. For example, during week 2 of our data collection, region 5 has the highest number of tweet flu count while region 6 has the highest number

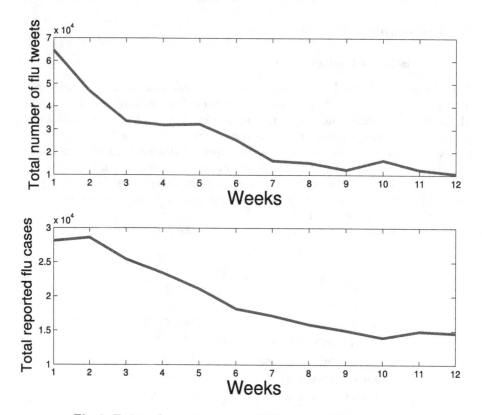

Fig. 2. Twitter flu tweet trend vs. CDC reported ILI case trend

Fig. 3. CDC region

of CDC ILI cases. The lack of correlation between twitter flu count and CDC ILI cases at regional level might be caused by noises in the tweet text and needs further investigation.

In summary, our preliminary results reveal a strong temporal correlation between these two metrics at coarse-grained geographical levels such as countries, but show little correlations between these metrics at fine-grained geographical

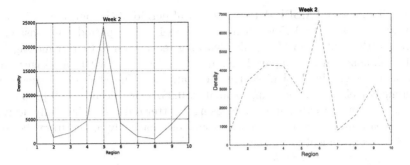

Fig. 4. Regional Twitter flu tweet trend vs. CDC reported regional ILI case trend

levels such as cities, states or regions. The strong correlation between flu tweets and CDC statistics at national level demonstrates the potential application of our system for providing early prediction and warning of flu trends.

4 Related Work

Many works have used Twitter and other types of social media data to assess and categorize the kind of information for measuring the spread of a disease in a population. For example, [8] looked at three web based biosecurity intelligence systems they pointed out the importance of social media, namely Twitter, recognizing how fast the information is passed and also seeing that many issues or messages were not altered through other means. Reference [9] suggested a complementary infoveillance approach during the 2009 H1N1 pandemic, using Twitter. They used content and sentiment analysis to 2 million tweets containing the keywords swine flu, swineflu, or H1N1. For this, they created a range of queries related to different content categories, and showed that the results of these queries correlated well with the results of manual coding, which suggests that near real time content and sentiment analysis could be achieved, allowing monitoring of large amounts of textual data over time. Reference [10] collected tweets matching a set of 15 previously chosen search terms including flu, vaccine, tamiflu, and h1n1 and applied content analysis and regression models to measure and monitor public concern and levels of disease during the H1N1 pandemic in the United States. Using a regression model trained on 1 million influenza related tweets and using the incidence rates reported by the Centers for Disease Control (CDC) as reference, the authors reported errors ranging from 0.04 % to 0.93 % for the estimation of influenza like illness levels. Reference [11] also analyzed cholera related tweets published during the first 100 days of the 2010 Haitian cholera outbreak. For this, all tweets published in this period and containing the word cholera or the hashtag #cholera were considered, and these data were compared to data from two sources: Health Map, an automated surveillance platform, and the Haitian Ministry of Public Health (MSPP). They showed good correlation between Twitter and Health Map data, and showed a good correlation (0.83) between Twitter and MSPP data in the initial period of the outbreak, although this value decreased to 0.25 when the complete 100 days period was considered. Reference [12] applied SVM machine learning techniques to twitter messages to predict influenza rates in Japan. Reference [13] analyzed Twitter messages using regression models, in the United Kingdom and the United States respectively, obtaining correlation rates of approximately 0.95. More recently, [14] proposed a tool for real-time disease surveillance using Twitter data, showing daily activity of the disease and corresponding symptoms automatically mined from the text, as well as geographical incidence.

5   Conclusions and Future Work

Twitter, a popular online social media with hundreds of millions of users, provides a simple and robust platform for users to post their latest statuses including influenza symptoms. Rather than waiting for CDC to release the official statistics on the aggregated flu trends, this popular online social media offers an alternative channel to continuously monitor, collect and model influenza trends via flu tweets from real-time Twitter data streams. In this paper, we develop a prototype system to automatically collect, analyze and model flu trends via Twitter data streams. More importantly, we explore the geographical locations from user profiles, tweet location feature that attaches the current user location to a tweet, and the geographical information in the content of the tweets to tag flu tweets with coarse-grained and fine-grained locations. These geo-tagged flu tweets provide an accurate view of the latest flu trends at different regions. In our experiments, we correlate geo-tagged flu tweets with CDC statistics on the reported flu cases, and find the potential application of our system for providing early prediction and warning of flu trends. Our future work lies in developing more accurate geo-tagging mechanism and extending this framework to characterize and model flu trends from national, regional, and state level.

Acknowledgments. This project is supported by NSF grant CNS #1218212.

References

1. https://www.mongodb.org
2. http://www.beevolve.com
3. https://dev.twitter.com/
4. http://www.json.org/
5. https://www.openstreetmap.org/
6. http://www.cdc.gov/flu/weekly/regions2008-2009/hhssenusmap.htm
7. Dredze, M., Paul, M., Bergsma, S., Tran, H.: Carmen: a twitter geolocation system with applications to public health. In: AAAI Workshop on Expanding the Boundaries of Health Informatics Using AI (HIAI) (2012)
8. Lyon, A., Nunn, M., Grossel, G., Burgman, M.: Comparison of web-based biosecurity intelligence systems: biocaster, epispider and healthmap. Transboundary Emerg. Dis. **59**(3), 223–232 (2012)

9. Chew, C., Eysenbach, G.: Pandemics in the age of twitter: content analysis of tweets during the 2009 H1N1 outbreak. PLoS ONE 5(11), e14118 (2012)
10. Signorini, A., Segre, A.M., Polgreen, P.M.: The use of twitter to track levels of disease activity and public concern in the u.s. during the influenza a h1n1 pandemic. PLoS ONE 6(5), e19467 (2011)
11. Chunara, R., Andrews, J.R., Brownstein, J.S.: Social and news media enable estimation of epidemiological patterns early in the 2010 haitian cholera outbreak. Am. J. Trop. Med. Hyg. 86(1), 39–45 (2012)
12. Aramaki, E., Maskawa, S., Morita, M.: Twitter catches the flu: detecting influenza epidemics using Twitter. In: Proceedings of the Conference on Empirical Methods in Natural Language Processing Association for Computational Linguistics, pp. 1568–1576 (2011)
13. Lampos, V., Cristianini, N.: Tracking the flu pandemic by monitoring the social web. In: Proceedings of the 2nd International Workshop on Cognitive Information Processing (CIP), pp. 411–416 (2010)
14. Lee, K., Agrawal, A., Choudhary, A.: Real-time disease surveillance using twitter data: demonstration on flu and cancer. In: Proceedings of the 19th ACM SIGKDD Conference on Knowledge Discovery and Data Mining (KDD), 11–14 August 2013 Chicago, IL, pp. 1474–1477. ACM (2013)

Radio Signal Based Device-Free Velocity Recognition

Mingwei Dai and Xiaoxia Huang[✉]

Shenzhen Institutes of Advanced Technology,
Chinese Academy of Sciences, Shenzhen, China
{mw.dai,xx.huang}@siat.ac.cn

Abstract. Existing work on RF-based movement recognition focus on analyzing the received signal strength (RSS) in the physical layer. Most of the approaches require the Line-of-Sight signal which limits the application in the Non-Line-of-Sight (NLOS) environment. More importantly, how to distinguish the velocity of human is still an open problem. In this paper, we present an approach for device-free velocity recognition leveraging the radio-frequency (RF) signal in the NLOS environment which is a great challenge for activity recognition. We extract features from the information of received packets to classify different velocities. The classification of human speed can achieve high accuracy in the experiment.

Keywords: Activity recognition · Radio frequency (RF) signal · Device-free motion detection · Non-line-of-sight

1 Introduction

Human activity recognition and estimation have received many attention due to the development of the Internet of things. Activity recognition is used to detect the intrusion event from a series of observations on the subject actions and the environment. In the monitoring system, the velocity of the subject is a noteworthy part for activity recognition.

Traditional velocity recognition is based on vision-based detection or sensors carried by the subject. Vision-based detection generates large volumes of video data to detect human existence and moving speed, but it is subject to varying lighting condition. Moreover, the overhead of infrastructure installation is considerable in many scenarios. Sensor-based recognition takes advantage of the inexpensive sensors to collect different types of data. The accelerometer is commonly used to monitor the velocity [1]. The accuracy of accelerometer based detection highly depends on the placement of sensors on the body. Sensor-based method is limited by on-board battery. Moreover, it is not applicable to the scenario without wearing sensors on the subject. So device-free approach is preferred for velocity recognition in many scenarios, such as intrusion detection.

As the RF signal is highly sensitive to the change in the environment, the radio signal could be used for velocity recognition. Since we are constantly

© Springer International Publishing Switzerland 2015
K. Xu and J. Zhu (Eds.): WASA 2015, LNCS 9204, pp. 70–82, 2015.
DOI: 10.1007/978-3-319-21837-3_8

exposed to electromagnetic radiation on various radio frequency originating from a variety of sources [14], it is convenient to utilize the wireless transceiver to sense the motion in a specific region. The human body selectively absorbs, scatters or reflects RF signals, resulting fluctuation of delay spread and time dispersion of a signal at the receiver. The variation of signal quality is harmful to communication, but might enrich the available signal characteristics and cause information burst for activity recognition on the other hand.

This motivates our research on the radio based device-free velocity recognition. In this work, we present a new approach for human velocity recognition using the link state information in the NLOS scenario. The signals are blocked or reflected by a person moving in the monitoring area, resulting in slow fading and channel quality fluctuation. The rate of slow fading depends on the speed of the subject. Different moving speed causes dynamic change of signal propagation path. Consequently, packet transmission is subject to the moving speed. The packet delivery ratio and the time interval of received packet vary with moving speed in the environment. By analyzing the collected time series of the received packet, we are able to detect different human speed in the monitoring area. The result shows that our mechanism achieves relatively high accuracy in the NLOS environment with negligible deployment cost. The packet detection beacon could be modulated onto wireless carrier and deployed in the real indoor environment with off-the-shelf devices for movement and velocity recognition. The main contributions of this work are as follows.

- Realize active device-free activity recognition by exploring packet state relevant characteristics.
- Classify different level of speed by analyzing the new metrics of time interval characteristics of received packet. Our method achieves higher classification accuracy than the fixed sampling RSSI method.

2   Related Works

A broad range of methods can be utilized to sense the human movement. Movement recognition based on wireless signal can be classified into device-bound and device-free approaches [2].

In device-bound movement recognition, wireless signals such as GSM [3] and FM radio [4] have been utilized to detect human activity. The target carrying the device collects wireless signal variation as the feature for recognition. The daily GSM trace could be monitored to detect daily motion speed of three levels [13]. As human body is an effective antenna for ambient electromagnetic noise [5], the body would change the electromagnetic environment and the signal quality. The EMI (Electromagnetic Interference) has been collected for electrical event sensing [16].

Human movement with different speed causes different Doppler shift which has been used in device-free movement recognition. The Doppler-based radar can detect movement and eliminate the stationary noises in the environment conveniently [10]. Many previous works have extracted the Doppler signature to estimate and analyze the human activity-related features [11,12]. Since the Doppler effect is highly correlated with the motion speed and direction of the target, it can indicate the human activity by extracting the features in the frequency and time domain. The wivi [18] captures the reflections of its own transmitted signals off moving objects behind a wall in order to track moving humans through walls.

The average magnitude of each signal subcarrier, RSSI (Received Signal Strength Indication), indicates the fluctuation of the signal. It has been proved that the variance of RSSI might help identify the type of movement [6]. But RSSI is sensitive to the shadowing effect and multipath. The inherent fluctuation of RSSI becomes more serious in the NLOS indoor environment and leads to significant uncertainty for activity and velocity recognition. The estimate of velocity based on RSSI [2,6,7,15] with the fixed interval sampling rate are not accurate enough to classify different walking speed. The distinction of walking speeds in [6] is conducted in the circle with 3 meters in diameter. It is hard for a continuous signal-based system to accurately distinguish the speed of an individual [8]. In this paper, we use the packet transmission state and the time interval of received packet as the features to measure the different speed instead, which are new metrics for the radio signal based activity recognition.

3   RF-Based Movement Recognition

As the presence and motion of human in an wireless environment affect the signal strength and SNR, the state of the received packet changes with the quality of the signal. To achieve device-free velocity recognition with the packet information, we need to address the following challenges.

The first challenge for RF-based velocity recognition is to promptly distinguish the presence of human in the monitoring area. The wireless signal is volatile and the link condition varies even in empty period, we need to eliminate the signal variation caused by clutter environment in empty period, and extract the features in the motion period to capture the movement accurately.

Another challenge is to distinguish the velocity of subject with high resolution. Unlike the sensor based method recording the speed with accelerometer, the high speed moving event is easily missed in RF based device-free recognition. The dramatic fluctuation of RSSI might happen both during high speed and low speed movement which makes it hard to distinguish the corresponding speed level. So more signal characteristics should be studied to measure the speed accurately.

3.1   Motivation

The packet receiving situation is classified into three states according to the quality of signal, including decoded successfully, failed to be decoded and packet loss, i.e. packet cannot be sensed by the receiving node.

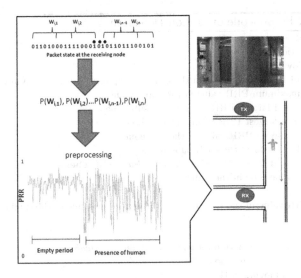

Fig. 1. The packet stream at the receiving node. The 1-0 series indicate the packet state in time.

We use the packet receive rate (PRR) to evaluate the transmission. The packet state $s(i)$ is marked "1" if the packet is decoded successfully. It is "0" if the packet is lost or undecoded. Figure 1 shows the basic process of human presence detection based on the received packet state series. The packet receive rate $P(W_{i,n})$ is the proportion of decoded packet among all the transmission packets in window of size w_n collected at the receiving node.

$$P(W_{i,n}) = \frac{1}{w_n} \sum_{i=1}^{w_n} s(i) \tag{1}$$

Classified by the packet receive rate, there are three scenarios in presence of human movement.

1. Degradation case. The communication performance is moderate without human presence. When a person appears, he/she might block or absorb the signal, resulting in the degradation of PRR during movement.
2. Enhancement case. The original communication environment is so poor that the RX node could only receive corrupted packets. Once a person enters the monitoring area, the packet transmission could be enhanced by the signal path from the target. So the PRR could be improved by the human activity during movement.
3. Idle case. PRR is not sensitive to the motion. This case is not ideal for movement recognition. The situation could be calibrated by rotating the receiving antenna, thus turning into the degradation case.

In cases (1) and (2), the communication performance is subject to the human appearance and movement, resulting in varying PRR. Moreover, the degradation

---

Algorithm 1. Pseudocode of Motion Detection

Input: The PRR sequence
Output: The motion period
  Initialize WindowSize
  for every pair of PRR readings defined as the subsequence within the WindowSize **do**
      Max = the maximum PRR value in the subsequence
      Sec = the second largest PRR value in the subsequence
      Trd = the third largest PRR value in the subsequence
      Min = the minimum PRR value in the subsequence
      Thd = the Threshold of the PRR subsequence
      if $Max\text{-}Min > Thd$ & $Sec\text{-}Min > Thd$ & $Trd\text{-}Min > Thd$ **then**
        The PRR value remain the same
      else
        all the PRR value in the subsequence = the average value of the original subsequence
      end if
  end for
  Compute the standard deviation for each subsequence($Stdvalue$)
  if $Stdvalue$ > detection Threshold **then**
    return human moving in the area
  else
    return the area is empty
  end if

---

case is more general in real communication environment. Therefore, we choose case (1) for the identification of human activities in our experiment.

3.2 Human Presence Detection

In velocity recognition system, it is necessary to distinguish whether there is any subject in the monitoring area first. In order to recognize different human states, we should eliminate the static clutter in empty period and extract the motion period from the sequence.

We use the mean filter to eliminate the fluctuation in the empty period and track the standard deviation of packet receive rate using a sliding window of PRR readings. Since the fluctuation of PRR in motion period is more dramatic than in the empty period, we use the gaps between the peak values and minimum value in each window as the index to evaluate the fluctuation. Once the gaps are smaller than the threshold, the status of this window could be regarded as empty. Then the PRR values in this window take the average PRR of the original window that the static clutter is eliminated. During the motion period, the PRR fluctuates intensely, so the standard deviation increases accordingly. The motion period can be identified by evaluating the standard deviation of each subsequence. The procedure to distinguish the motion period in the PRR sequence is detailed in Algorithm 1.

One packet receive rate sequence collected both in empty and motion period in which one subject moves in the monitoring area at different speed is shown in Fig. 2(a). PRR is high and remains stable during empty period. In presence

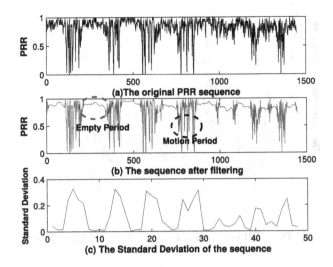

Fig. 2. The PRR sequence and the corresponding standard deviation series for data collected during both empty period and human movement period. The fluctuation corresponds to the movement at different speed.

of human, apparent fluctuation of PRR can be observed. The decreased of PRR at different degrees corresponds to different motion traces at different speed. Figure 2(b) shows the PRR sequence after filtering, the fluctuation of PRR in empty period is eliminated. The standard deviation of PRR is shown in Fig. 2(c), the motion event is declared by setting threshold to the standard deviation of each subsequence.

3.3 Limitation of PRR

When a person runs through the monitoring area within a short period, human body may impact the transmission slightly, so only a few small peaks could be observed during high speed movement. PRR records the variation of link quality when the subject passes through the monitoring area, but it loses many subtle characteristics related to the moving speed. As a result, the fluctuation of PRR may not capture the velocity very well. Figure 3 shows the correlation coefficient of the PRR series from different speed traces. Classifying moving speed with PRR feature achieves poor resolution because the PRR series of different speeds do not show great distinction in terms of the correlation coefficient. Although PRR could be used to distinguish the movement and empty period in NLOS environment, it is not suitable to classify different moving speed with PRR only. More sophisticated features are necessary to classify the human speed.

3.4 Features for Velocity Classification

Besides measuring PRR with normal statistical method, more packet transmission relevant features could be extracted for the classification of motion speed.

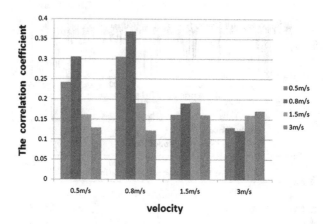

Fig. 3. The PRR correlation between different speed traces.

As human move in the monitoring area, the channel quality fluctuates accordingly, resulting in the change of packet receive rate and the time interval of adjacent received packets. The arrival time of each received packet varies with the human motion and could be used to measure the speed.

We define several parameters to measure human velocity through the time interval of received packet.

i. *acf*, Auto-Correlation Function. *acf* is a good indicator of dependency of time interval [9].

$$acf_l = \frac{\sum_{i=1}^{n-l} (t_i - \bar{t})(t_{i+l} - \bar{t})}{\sum_{i=1}^{n} (t_i - \bar{t})^2} \tag{2}$$

Let t_i denote the time interval between packet i and packet $i - 1$ (i.e. the delay between successive packets). l is the correlation lag. $\bar{t}$ is the average delay. If packet i experiences large delay, packet $i + l$ would also experience large delay with high probability. Human with different moving speed affects the interval, so *acf* of the time interval of received packet changes accordingly.

ii. R_n, rate budget. R_n is correlated with the time interval of the decoded packet and the transmission rate.

$$R_n = \frac{F_{out}}{F_{in}}(t_n - t_{lt}) \tag{3}$$

F_{out} is the transmitting rate. F_{in} is the receiving rate. $\frac{F_{in}}{F_{out}}$ could be regarded as the reception ratio. t_n is the arrival time of the current decoded packet and t_{lt} is the arrival time of the previous decoded packet in the series. To evaluate the channel quality with time delay, we define $(t_n - t_{lt})$ as the time interval between adjacent decoded packets. During the empty period, the interval between decoded packets and the reception ratio are almost constant. Different speed causes different data rate and impacts the probability of successfully

decoded packets disparately. Larger value of $(t_n - t_{lt})$ means that human movement causes degradation of channel quality.

iii. L_{oc}, the interval with the packet position information.

$$Loc_n = \frac{d_n}{p_n} \tag{4}$$

The transmission time interval between the received packets (include decoded
and undecoded) is t_n on average in our experiment. Let d_n denotes the time
interval of two adjacent received packets larger than the normal received packet
time interval, which is an abnormal time interval at the receiving node. p_n measure the position distance between two adjacent received packets.

$$p_n = \frac{b_{i+1} - b_i}{l_n} \tag{5}$$

l_n is the total number of received packet of the trace, and b_i is the serial number
of the corresponding packet. Large value of d_n with small p_n means that there
are many lost packets in the abnormal interval. This indicates dynamic change of
channel quality happens during the motion period, which can be used to evaluate
different speed level.

In order to detect the time interval, each packet is stamped with the packet
arrival time at the receiving node. Besides the received packet state sequence in
which each packet is assigned a unique packet number, we also collect the time
series of the received packet with the arrival time of each packet for analysing.

$$u_i = \alpha^{\sum_{i=1}^{l} acf_i / \max(\mathbb{A})} + \beta * \frac{\sum_{j=1}^{m} R_j}{\max(\mathbb{R})} + \gamma * \frac{mean(loc_i)}{\max(\mathbb{C})} \tag{6}$$

Given the packet arrival time series corresponding to the motion period, we
define a function which is the weighted sum of the three features in (6). α, β
and γ are the weights for the ratio of three features to their reference trace
which is defined as the trace with the maximum value of the feature in the
collected data. $\mathbb{A}$, $\mathbb{R}$ and $\mathbb{C}$ are the set of all the n traces of three features for
the collected data that $\mathbb{A} = \{\sum acf_1, ..., \sum acf_n\}$, $\mathbb{R} = \{\sum R_1, ..., \sum R_n\}$ and
$\mathbb{C} = \{mean(loc)_1, ..., mean(loc)_n\}$. To determine the weight value, we count the
occurrence of every training trace that conform to the range of every speed level
in each feature. For example, if R_n in the training data has been found 14 times in
20 traces conform to the group range, β could be 0.7. We determine the weights
through the training data in the experiment. The three attributes in (6) describe
the likelihood of the test traces, which are similar for the same speed level. The
utility function u_i is used to classify different speed. Faster speed causes lower
value of u_i. Algorithm 2 shows the procedure to classify different speed.

4   Experiment

Based on the preliminary analyse in Sect. 3, we evaluate the detection of human
velocity with the proposed method.

Algorithm 2. Pseudocode of Velocity Recognition

Input: The arrival time of received packet sequence for each motion period
Output: The different speed level
 for every pair of packet arrival time sequence **do**
  for the subsequence with the decoded packets **do**

$$\text{Calculate the corresponding } R_n = \frac{F_{out}}{F_{in}}(t_n - t_{lt}) \text{ and } acf_l = \frac{\sum\limits_{i=1}^{n-l}(t_i-\bar{t})(t_{i+l}-\bar{t})}{\sum\limits_{i=1}^{n}(t_i-\bar{t})^2}$$

  with different lags in each sequence
  end for
  for the subsequence consisting of received packet with the abnormal time interval d_n **do**
   Calculate the corresponding $Loc_n = \frac{d_n}{p_n}$
  end for
 end for
 Collect $\mathbb{A}$, $\mathbb{R}$ and $\mathbb{C}$ to calculate u_i of each trace in

$$u_i = \alpha \frac{\sum\limits_{i=1}^{l} acf_i/\max(\mathbb{A})}{} + \beta * \frac{\sum\limits_{j=1}^{m} R_j}{\max(\mathbb{R})} + \gamma * \frac{mean(loc_i)}{\max(\mathbb{C})}$$

 and evaluate different speed by map the value to the training data, classify different speed level by the sequential minimal optimization (SMO) of the support vector machine (SVM) with 10-fold cross-validation.

4.1 Experiment Setting

The experiment is performed in four corridors. Only one person is monitored at one time. We choose the aisle in the experiment because the route is basically fixed. The transmitting USRP node is arranged in each end of the aisles with the -14 dBi gain antenna placed at around 5.5 in. height shown in Fig. 1. Since the fixed position of transmitting and receiving antenna, the transmission power is -20dbm which covers the experiment area. In our test, the receiving USRP node only operates in one given frequency and communicates with the corresponding transmitting USRP node, so that the effective detection area is one aisle (13m x1.5m) in each test.

4.2 Classification of State

We first evaluate different states of subject in the monitoring area by the packet receive rate. Four states of human presence are considered, empty, standing, walking and running, each state is repeated for 20 times. The directional and omnidirectional antenna are used at the transmitting node for comparison. We collect packet state series in the experiment and distinguish different states by calculating PRR for each trace. The k-Nearest Neighbors algorithm (K-NN) and sequential minimal optimization (SMO) of the support vector machine (SVM) could be used for offline classification with the Weka machine learning toolkit [17]. We perform 10-fold cross-validation on our collected data. The result of the classification is shown in Fig. 4.

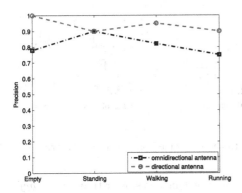

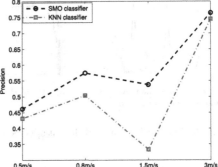

Fig. 4. The classification accuracy with directional and omnidirectional antenna at transmitting node.

Fig. 5. The SMO and KNN classification accuracy of different speeds with PRR attribute.

It can be concluded that the classification based on directional antenna outperforms the omnidirectional antenna in terms of accuracy, since the directional antenna concentrates the signal strength in the monitoring area. As standing and empty are two static states, the PRR sequences of the two states exhibit relatively steady pattern. The average classification precision of empty and standing reach 95 % when using directional antenna. Figure 5 shows the classification of four levels of speed by the PRR attribute with KNN and SMO classifier for comparison. According to the low precision, it is difficult to classify different moving speed with PRR only.

4.3 Classification of Velocity

In the classification of the velocity, we perform experiment at four speeds, 0.5m/s, 0.8m/s, 1.5m/s and 3 m/s in the corridors. The experiment of each speed is repeated for 40 times. For comparison, the RSSI-based detection is set up in the same environment with our received packet interval based detection. The sampling rate of RSSI at the receiving node is fixed. To compare with the device-bound method, we utilize the accelerometer in the cellphone and use the three-axis accelerometer data to detect four levels of speed. The cellphone is held in hand and kept relatively stationary to the body.

In our approach, the speed detection is based on packet state sequence. From the original time interval of the received packet sequence, *acf* is calculated and compared to that of the empty period. Faster speed incurs rapid change of the transmission state. So the time interval of adjacent decoded packets could be similar with high probability. To discriminate the different velocity, *acf* of different speed is divided by the corresponding *acf* in the empty period at the same span. Figure 6(a) shows when human pass through the monitoring area at speed over 1.5 m/s, *acf* of the movement period is greater than that of the

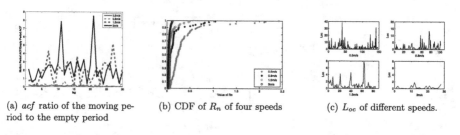

(a) *acf* ratio of the moving period to the empty period

(b) CDF of R_n of four speeds

(c) L_{oc} of different speeds.

Fig. 6. The distinction of different speeds with three received packet interval attributes

corresponding empty period. When the human velocity is slower than 1m/s, *acf* becomes lower than that of the empty period.

We randomly choose 20 test traces at four speeds and calculate the top 20 value of R_n for each trace. CDF of 100 R_n values for each speed is shown in Fig. 6(b). Longer dwelling time in the monitoring area leads to signal blocked by the human body for longer duration, and causes longer time interval of the decoded packet with higher probability. Moreover, the transmission rate decreases when the signal is blocked by human body. Therefore, R_n is large when it takes long time for one person to pass through the aisle. Figure 6(c) shows L_{oc} at different speed. Slower speed leads to longer interruption of transmission packet, so L_{oc} is high due to long time interval of received packets within a short position distance.

With three attributes, we calculate u_i for every trace. The distribution of u_i of four speeds is shown in Fig. 7, each speed contains 40 traces. The plus sign indicates the outlier of u_i in each speed. The horizontal line in each box shows the median of u_i. Obviously, u_i is disparate with respect to the moving speed, it decreases when the speed increases and can be used to classify different velocity.

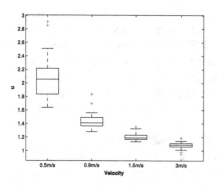

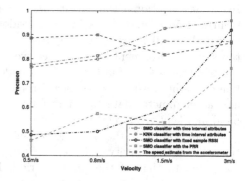

Fig. 7. Distribution of u_i.

Fig. 8. F-measure of the classification accuracy of different detection methods.

Figure 8 shows the classification accuracy with our received packet interval based detection compared to the fixed-sample RSSI [6,8] and accelerometer-based methods using F-measure evaluation criterion. The F-measure considers both the precision and the recall of the test in computing the score. The RSSI-based method achieves low accuracy when the speed is lower than 1.5m/s, with average accuracy of 65 % in the fixed-sample RSSI detection. The average accuracy of our method is 86.6 % and 82.8 % with SMO and KNN classifier which is improved by 24.4 % on average compared to the fixed-sample RSSI method. The packet receive rate based velocity recognition achieves similar accuracy to the RSSI based method.

Since the cellphone is kept horizontal to the moving direction, we collect the peak-valley value of the Z-axis accelerometer data to model the stride of the subject [19,20]. The velocity is estimated by the step length divided by the span between the peak and valley. But the gait might be misjudged due to the noise of the accelerometer data caused by the shaking of the cellphone during high speed moevment. The average estimation accuracy is 88.6 % which is close to our received packet interval based detection. According to Fig. 8, accerelometer based approach achieves better estimation accuracy at speed below 1.5m/s. However, due to the effect of accumulated error, it is inferior to our approach at moving speed of 1.5 m/s and 3m/s.

5 Conclusion

In this paper, we present a new method to recognize indoor human presence and motion speed. Wireless signal is suitable for device-free movement recognition, especially in the NLOS scenario. The PRR and packet time interval based features proposed in the paper can be used to measure the human moving speed. The classification accuracy of walking speed of the proposed method is improved by 24.4 % on average compared to the fixed-sample RSSI based method. Our approach can be deployed in the indoor space covered by WLAN for activity recognition in the indoor space. Open challenges remain for future work. We will further study the impact of the size of person on speed detection, and investigate the movement recognition in presence of multiple persons.

References

1. Ravi, N., Dandekar, N., Mysore, P., Littman, M.L.: Activity recognition from accelerometer data. In: Proceedings of the 17th Conference on Innovative Applications of Artificial Intelligence, Pennsylvania, USA (2005)
2. Scholz, M., Riedel, T., Hock, M., Beigl, M.: Device-free and device-bound activity recognition using radio signal strength. In: Proceedings of the 4th International Conference on Augmented Human, Germany (2013)
3. Varshavsky, A., Lara, E., Hightower, J., LaMarca, A., Otsason, V.: GSM indoor localization. Pervasive Mob. Comput. 3(4), 907–920 (2007)

4. Youssef, A., Krumm, J., Miller, E., Cermak, G., Horvitz, E.: Computing location from ambient FM radio signals. In: Proceedings of the IEEE Wireless Communications and Networking Conference, LA, USA (2005)

5. Cohn, G., Morris, D., Patel, S.N., Tan, D.S.: Sensing gestures using the body as an antenna. In: Proceedings of ACM CHI, Vancouver BC (2011)

6. Sigg, S., Shi, S., Bsching, F., Ji, Y., Wolf, L.: Leveraging RF-channel fluctuation for activity recognition: active and passive systems, continuous and RSSI-based signal features. In: Proceedings of MoMM, Austria (2013)

7. Woyach, K., Puccinelli, D., Haenggi, M.: Sensorless sensing in wireless networks: implementation and measurements. In: Proceedings of the Second International Workshop on Wireless Network Measurement, Boston, Massachusetts, USA (2006)

8. Sigg, S., Scholz, M., Shi, S., Ji, Y., Beigl, M.: RF-sensing of activities from non-cooperative subjects in device-free recognition systems using ambient and local signals. IEEE Trans. Mob. Comput. 13(6), 698–720 (2013)

9. Jiang, W., Schulzrinne, H.: Modeling of packet loss and delay and their effect on real-time multimedia service quality. In: Proceedings of International Workshop on Network and Operating System Support for Digital Audio and Video, USA (2000)

10. Chetty, K., Smith, G., Woodbridge, K.: Through-the-wall sensing of personnel using passive bistatic WiFi radar at standoff distances. IEEE Trans. Geosci. Remote Sens. 50(4), 1218–1226 (2012)

11. Pu, Q., Gupta, S., Gollakota, S., Patel, S.: Whole-home gesture recognition using wireless signals. In: The 19th Annual International Conference on Mobile Computing and Networking (Mobicom 2013), Florida, USA (2013)

12. Kim, Y., Ling, H.: Human activity classification based on micro-Doppler signatures using a support vector machine. IEEE Trans. Geosci. Remote Sens. 57(5), 1328–1337 (2012)

13. Sohn, T., Varshavsky, A., LaMarca, A., de Lara, E.: Mobility detection using everyday gsm traces. In: Proceedings of the 8th International Conference on Ubiquitous Computing, California, USA (2006)

14. Scholz, M., Sigg, S., Schmidtke, H.R., Beigl, M.: device-free radio-based recognition. In: Proceedings of the 4th workshop on Context Systems, Design, Evaluation and Optimisation (CoSDEO 2013), Zurich (2013)

15. Youssef, M., Mah, M., Agrawala, A.: Challenges: Device-free passive localization for wireless environments. In: Proceedings of the 13th Annual ACM International Conference on Mobile Computing and Networking, Canada (2007)

16. Gupta, S., Reynolds, M.S., Patel, S.N.: Electrisense: singlepoint sensing using emi for electrical event detection and classification in the home. In: Proceedings of the 13th International Conference on Ubiquitous Computing, Beijing, China (2010)

17. Hall, M., Frank, E., Holmes, G., Pfahringer, B., Reutemann, P., Witten, I.H.: The WEKA data mining software: an update. SIGKDD Explorations (2009)

18. Adib, F., Katabi, D.: See through walls with WiFi. In: Proceedings of the 2013 ACM Special Interest Group on Data Communication, Hong Kong, China (2013)

19. Welk, G., Differding, J.: The utility of the digi-walker step counter to assess daily physical activity patterns. Med. Sci. Sports Exerc. 32(9), 481–488 (2000)

20. Mladenov, M., Mock, M.: A step counter service for Java-enabled devices using a built-in accelerometer. In: Proceedings of the 1st International Workshop on Context-Aware Middleware and Services: affiliated with the 4th International Conference on Communication System Software and Middleware, Dublin (2009)

Minimum-Cost Information Dissemination in Social Networks

Dongping Deng[1], Hongwei Du[1(✉)], Xiaohua Jia[2], and Qiang Ye[3]

[1] Department of Computer Science and Technology, Harbin Institute of Technology
Shenzhen Graduate School, Shenzhen, China
ddp9110hit@gmail.com, hwdu@hitsz.edu.cn
[2] Department of Computer Science, City University of Hong Kong,
Kowloon Tong, Hong Kong, China
csjia@cityu.edu.hk
[3] Department of Computer Science and Information Technology,
University of Prince Edward Island,
Charlottetown, PE C1A 4P3, Canada
qye@upei.ca

Abstract. In a social network, when the number of users discussing a topic exceeds a critical threshold, the topic will have a serious impact on the corresponding community. In this paper, we consider the problem of finding the minimum set of initial users of a topic to propagate a message so that, with a given guaranteed probability, the number of users discussing the topic would reach the critical threshold. This study is formally called the *Minimum-Cost Information Dissemination* (*MCID*) problem in our research. Different from the influence maximization problem, the MCID problem attempts to achieve influence maximization from the minimum cost perspective. To tackle the problem, we proposed a novel method based on h-hop independent set, HISS. Based on the independent set, HISS guarantees that the source nodes are sparsely distributed in the network. In addition, since HISS utilizes h-hop graph transformation, it can reduce the number of source nodes and avoid the scenarios in which the source nodes have common neighbors. The proposed method was evaluated with two real networks. The experimental results indicate that our proposed algorithm outperforms the state-of-the-art algorithms.

Keywords: Influence maximization · Social networks · Independent set

1 Introduction

Social network systems, such as Facebook and Twitter, enable a completely different method to express personal opinions and share useful informations. Typically, when a user of a social network system publishes a message, it can be seen by his followers. These followers may provide their comments or forward it to their own followers. In this manner, if a message is appealing, the number of

© Springer International Publishing Switzerland 2015
K. Xu and J. Zhu (Eds.): WASA 2015, LNCS 9204, pp. 83–93, 2015.
DOI: 10.1007/978-3-319-21837-3_9

people that have viewed the message will grow exponentially. When the number exceeds a preset threshold, the message will be listed as one of the hottest topics in the social system and attract a tremendous amount of attentions.

From the perspective of promoting a specific message, it is therefore important to choose an appropriate group of people (called source nodes [1]) to publish messages so that the number of viewers can reach the threshold. In our research, we attempt to find the least number of people who need to publish the message in order for the number of viewers to exceed the threshold. The problem we focus on is different from the influence maximization problem proposed by Domingos and Richardson [2] in the sense that the influence maximization problem tries to maximize the number of viewers for a given number of publishers.

In our research, the problem to be tackled is formulated as an optimization problem called *Minimum-Cost Information Dissemination (MCID)*. It is aimed at achieving a given influence maximization at the minimum cost. We proposed a novel method called the *h-hop Independent Set Scheme (HISS)*. The main contributions of this paper are summarized as follows:

- We define the MCID problem in social networks, which is a very realistic problem that needs to be tackled.
- We propose a novel method based on the h-hop independent set, HISS, which is different from the general greedy algorithm proposed by Kempe [1].
- We demonstrate the effectiveness of the proposed method using two real-world datasets. Our experimental results indicate that our algorithm outperforms the existing methods.

The rest of the paper is organized as follows. Section 2 includes the related work. The research problem is formulated in Sect. 3. The proposed method is presented in Sect. 4 and the experimental results are summarized in Sect. 5. Finally, Sect. 6 concludes this paper.

2   Related Work

Many studies have attempted to solve the influence maximization problem by finding a seed set with k nodes in order to maximize the influence coverage of the seed set. Domingos and Richardson [2] consider the influence maximization issue first in order to help companies determine to market valuable customers. Then Kempe et al. [1] prove this problem is NP hard and present a greedy algorithm which guarantees a (1-1/e) approximation of the optimal solution. However, the algorithm is based on Monte Carlo simulations. It is time-consuming. Later, many studies propose many improved methods (e.g. [6,7,9,11]). In [9], it proposes the CELF algorithm by simplifying the computations of selecting seed nodes during simulations. Chen et al. [6] proposes the NewGreedyIC algorithm which the time complexity is $O(kRm)$. Its main idea is to delete the useless edges and then to get a smaller graph to model the information propagation. In [3], Xu et al. recast the problem of influence maximization to a weighted maximum cut problem and use a semidefinite program-based (GW) algorithm.

Seed minimization problem is to realize influence maximization from a minimum cost perspective. In [5], Zhang et al. propose the *seed minimization with probabilistic coverage guarantee* (*SM-PCG*) problem. They use Monte Carlo simulations to estimate the probability that the influence coverage of seed set reaches the given threshold. In this paper, we focus on the MCID problem and present a novel approach HISS which is based on h-hop independent set.

3   Minimum-Cost Information Dissemination Problem

In this section, we formulate the problem to be tackled. The details of the problem formulation are presented as follows.

A social network is modeled as a directed social graph $G = (V, E)$, where V is the set of nodes representing users in a social network, and E is the set of directed edges representing friends relationship between pairs of users. There exists a directed edge from node u to node v if node v follows node u. For example, in MicroBlog social network graph, nodes are the users in MicroBlog and two nodes have a directed edge if there is a relationship of following, such as v follows u, then there is a directed edge (u, v). Each edge $(u, v) \in E$ is associated with a forwarding probability $p_{(u,v)}$. Hence, $p_{(u,v)}$ is the probability that node v forwards the message received from node u. The formal definition of *Minimum-Cost Information Dissemination (MCID)* problem is given as follows:

Problem Definition: Given a directed social network graph $G = (V, E)$ and a percentage P of users that should receive the message. Our problem is to find the minimum set of source nodes S to spread a message such that at least a percentage P of users will be likely to forward the message.

Note: A user is likely to forward a message is defined as the probability of the user to receive the message from the set of source nodes S is equal or greater than a given threshold θ.

4   HISS: A Three-Step Scheme

Most existing solutions to the influence maximization problem are based on the greedy algorithm proposed by Kempe [1]. It selects source nodes one by one through computing the gain of nodes' influence spread. There are some problems in the selection of source nodes. For example, some source nodes with great gain are neighbors or source nodes might have many common neighbors. Thus, the whole set of the source nodes achieves inefficient while the influence coverage is overlapped between the source nodes. For information dissemination with multiple sources, we need to consider the combined spreading power of the set of source nodes as a whole, not simply considering the spreading power of each source node individually. The better idea is to choose the source nodes that are sparsely distributed in the network. Once a node is selected as a source, all its neighbors within certain hops cannot be source nodes. We should maximize the combined spreading power of the whole set of source nodes. In our research, we will solve the MCID problem by using the h-hop independent set. We call the proposed method the *h-hop Independent Set Scheme (HISS)*.

HISS solves the MCID problem by carrying out the following three steps:

Step 1. Transform the graph G to h-hop graph G'. The nodes reachable within h hops are all neighbors. This step need to combine with Step 2. Step 2 to find the candidates of source nodes will use the independent set method. If we only do Step 2 without Step 1, some source nodes may have many common neighbors. Combined with the independent set, the graph transformation can reduce the number of common neighbors between source nodes. If $h=2$, the source nodes may not have common neighbors. Choosing a suitable h can reduce the number of source nodes in some degree and keep the performance of our method more efficient.

Step 2. Find the candidates of source nodes. We use independent set approach to choose the candidates of source nodes, which avoid source nodes are neighbors. Combined with Step 1, source nodes are sparsely distributed in the network.

Step 3. Obtain the source nodes. We will compute the probability $p(S,v)$ of a node received the message from the set of source nodes S. When $p(S, v) \geq \theta$, we will think node v is likely to receive the message. If the given threshold θ is bigger, node v is more likely to receive the message. According to the required percentage P, we will obtain the final source nodes.

The details of these steps are described as follows.

4.1   Transform the Graph G to h-hop graph G'

Definition 1 (*h*-hop Graph Transformation). *We define* $G' = (V', E')$ *where* $V' = V$ *and there exists an edge* $(a, b) \in E'$ *if the number of hops of the shortest path from a to b in G is less than or equal to h. The newly added edge is associated with a probability* $p_{(a,b)}$. *The probability* $p_{(a,b)}$ *of node b to receive the message from node a is the sum of probability from multiple paths which the number of hops from a to b is less than or equal to h.*

Graph transformation is based on the *Dijkstra* algorithm. Figure 1(a) is the original graph $G = (V, E)$. Figure 1(b) is the graph $G' = (V', E')$ which is 2 hops transformed from original graph G.

(a) Graph G (b) Graph G'

Fig. 1. Graph transformation when $h=2$.

4.2 Find the Candidates of Source Nodes

We will use the independent set method to find the candidates of source nodes. The nodes in an independent set are not adjacent with each other. However, the independent set concept is used in undirected graph. Our problem is based on directed social networks. The source nodes chosen are able to influence their followers. Thus we just need to consider nodes which have outgoing edges. In order to get the suitable independent set, we use the graph decomposition method. All of the graphs can be simplified until its *order* = 0 when iteratively using the formula (1). *order* is the number of nodes whose out-degree is not equal to 0.

$$I(G) = \begin{cases} v_i \cup I(G * v_i), & \text{if } d_{out}(v_i) \geq d \\ I(G - v_i), & \text{if } d_{out}(v_i) < d \end{cases} \tag{1}$$

v_i is the ith node in graph G. $I(G)$ is the independent set of graph G. $I(G*v_i)$ is the independent set of graph $G * v_i$. $G * v_i$ is the graph after done $RS(v_i, *)$ *transformation*. $I(G - v_i)$ is the independent set of graph $G - v_i$. $G - v_i$ is the graph after done $RM(v_i, -)$ *transformation*. $d_{out}(v_i)$ is the out-degree of v_i.

Definition 2 ($RS(v_i, *)$ transformation). *Remove edges started from the nodes which have an edge with v_i, and then delete the edges joined with v_i. After applying these operations to graph G, we get the graph $G*v_i$.*

Definition 3 ($RM(v_i, -)$ transformation). *Remove edges started from v_i in graph G, and then get the graph G-v_i.*

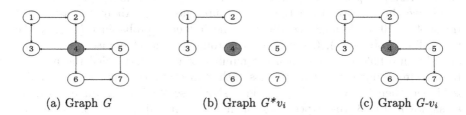

(a) Graph G (b) Graph $G*v_i$ (c) Graph G-v_i

Fig. 2. $RS(v_i, *)$ transformation and $RM(v_i, -)$ transformation when v_i=4.

The selection of node v_i in the formula (1) can be chosen according to the node's weight. The weight of node v_i is computed by the sum of probability of its neighbors forwarded the message from node v_i. The parameter d and $RM(v_i, -)$ transformation are used to control the quantity of candidates of source nodes. We put forward an algorithm called *Candidates Of Source Nodes (COSN)*.

4.3 Obtain the Source Nodes

According to the required percentage P of nodes that should receive the message from the set of source nodes S, we will choose source nodes from the candidates.

Algorithm 1. COSN Algorithm.

Input: $G' = (V', E'), \{p_{(a,b)}\}_{(a,b)\in E'}$
Output: A set I contained the candidates of source nodes
1: $I = \emptyset$.
2: calculate the weight and out-degree of each node in V'.
3: **while** *order* > 0 **do**
4:    select node v_i with the maximum weight.
5:    **if** $d_{out}(v_i) \geq d$ **then**
6:      $I = I \bigcup v_i$.
7:      do $RS(v_i, *)$ transformation.
8:    **else**
9:      do $RM(v_i, -)$ transformation.
10:   **end if**
11: **end while**
12: **return** I;

$p(S, v)$ is the probability of node v received the message from S. If the node v is the source node, then $p(S, v) = 1$. Otherwise,

$$p(S, v) = 1 - \prod_{\forall w \in S} (1 - p(w, v)) . \qquad (2)$$

We define $p(w, v)$ is the probability of node v received the message from source node w. Here the value of $p(w, v)$ is the sum of probability from multiple paths from node w to node v, which can be obtained by running Breadth First Search (*BFS*) or *pruned BFS*. When $p(S, v) \geq \theta$, we will think node v is likely to receive the message from the set of source nodes S. About the setting of threshold θ, it is decided according to the influence probability (namely the forwarding probability). If the influence probability is set unified $p_{(u,v)} = 0.1$ and the threshold $\theta = 0.9$, then the number of nodes forwarded the message received from source nodes may be less. If the expectation of influence probability is higher, then the value of threshold θ should set higher. In our experiment as shown in Fig. 3, the expectation of influence probability is 0.5, we set the threshold $\theta = 0.8$. Through computing the probability of nodes received the message from the set of source nodes S, we can estimate the number of nodes need to choose. We assume the nodes in set I are enough to achieve the percentage P. If the percentage of nodes which is likely to receive the message reaches the required percentage P, we will stop choosing the nodes. Algorithm 2 shows the procedure of seed selection for this task.

5   Experimental Results

The details of our experimental results are summarized in this section. Specifically, our experiments were carried out using real social network traces. The experimental results include two components: the impact of different h-hop graph transformations and the performance of the proposed scheme HISS.

Algorithm 2. MaxWeightIS Algorithm.

Input: $G = (V, E), I, P, \theta$
Output: The set of source nodes $S \subseteq V$
1: $S = \emptyset$.
2: Initialize $prob = 0$ and $seedSize = 0$.
3: **while** $prob < P$ **do**
4:     $num = 0$.
5:     $seedSize$++. // the size of the set of source nodes
6:     $S = \{w|w$ is the kth node in $I, k \leq seedSize \& k \in N\}$
7:     **for** $\forall v \in V$ **do**
8:         calculate the probability of node v received the message from source nodes S
            using Eq. (2).
9:         **if** $p(S, v) \geq \theta$ **then**
10:             num++.
11:         **end if**
12:     **end for**
13:     $prob = num/nodeSize$. // nodeSize is the number of nodes in V
14: **end while**
15: **return** S.

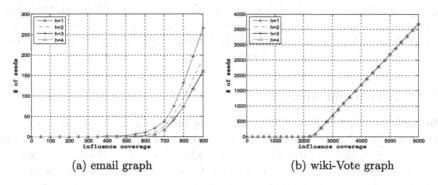

(a) email graph   (b) wiki-Vote graph

Fig. 3. Performance of h-hop graph transformations under a fixed probability threshold $\theta = 0.8$.

5.1   Experiment Setup

Datasets. In our experiments, we conduct them on two real social networks. The first one is *Arenas/email*, which is a network relationship graph from University of Rovira i Virgili, Tarragona. It represents a relationship of email interchange between users. The second network is wiki-Vote, published by Leskovec [10]. It is a network from Wikipedia community, representing the voting relationship between Wikipedia users. The features of these two datasets are presented in Table 1.

Experiment Methods. The experiments contain two tasks. Our first task is to test the performance with different h-hop graph transformations. To do so, we will use the two datasets to do the experiment. Using the IC model, the influence

Table 1. Features of datasets

Features	Nodes	Edges	Average Degree	Average Path Length
Email	1133	5452	4.812	3.932
Wiki-vote	7115	103689	14.573	3.341

(namely forwarding) probability $p_{(u,v)}$ between nodes is randomly generated by using (0,1) uniform distribution. According to the Six-degree theory, we should choose h smaller than 6. Meanwhile, considering the higher average degree of datasets and to keep our algorithm performance efficiently, the number of some nodes' neighbors may beyond the number of nodes in graphs when $h = 5$. Thus we will test the $h = 1$ to 4. Through estimation in theory, we will choose a suitable h to do the next experiment. Our second task is to verify the performance of our algorithm using the h-hop graph transformation. We will use IC model and WC model to do the experiment separately. The greedy algorithms (e.g. [1,6, 9]) which generate the seed set sequence through Monte Carlo simulations are very time-consuming. Thus we will compare the performance with two baseline algorithms: Max Degree algorithm and Random algorithm. Although these two approaches can not get the source nodes according to the required percentage P, we get the detailed information of the influence spread with the growth seed size. Then we can compare them with our proposed approach.

5.2   Experimental Analysis

The Selection of h. Figure 3 demonstrates the performance of our algorithm after h-hop graph transformations. We can observe in email graph, compared with h=1 or 2, the performance is better when h=3 or 4. When h=1, source nodes may have many common neighbors. Compared with other values of h, it will need more source nodes with the same influence coverage. When h=2, source nodes may not have common neighbors. When h=3, source nodes are sparsely. However, when h=4, source nodes are too sparsely and the out-degree of the node with max weight is big which may lead to small influence coverage of the other source nodes. Different social networks have different structure features, such as average degree. In the wiki-Vote graph, the differences from h=1 to 4 are not obvious. It may be caused by its high average degree and using the independent set guarantees the source nodes are sparsely distributed in the network. From Fig. 3, we will do the next experiment with 3 hops graph transformation.

Performance of Our Algorithm Compared with Baseline Algorithms. We conduct two datasets of tests for this purpose. We use IC model and WC model to compare the size of the seed set selected by various algorithms. For IC model, it has two different setups of forwarding probability. One is generated by random using (0,1) uniform distribution, another is set unified $p_{(u,v)} = 0.1$. Figure 4 and 5 are the result of datasets under WC model and IC model separately. It shows our algorithm has a better performance than other algorithms.

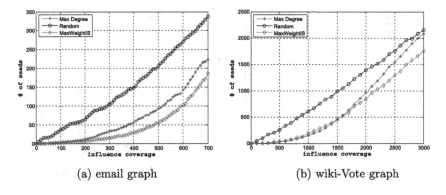

(a) email graph   (b) wiki-Vote graph

Fig. 4. Size of selected seed sets vs influence coverage η under WC model.

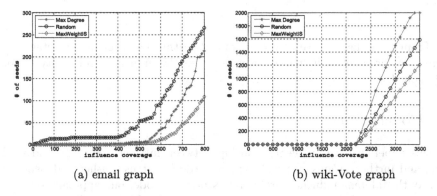

(a) email graph   (b) wiki-Vote graph

Fig. 5. Size of selected seed sets vs influence coverage η under IC model with $p_{(u,v)}$ using (0,1) uniform distribution.

In particular, for datasets under WC model (Fig. 4(a) and (b)), on average our algorithm selects seed sets with size 15.5 % less than those selected by Max Degree algorithm in these two graphs, 44.1 % less than Random algorithm in email graph and 20.2 % less than Random algorithm in wiki-Vote graph. Under IC model (Fig. 5(a) and (b)), our algorithm is 50.2 % less than Max Degree algorithm in these two graphs, 72.2 % less than Random algorithm in email graph and 28.8 % less than Random algorithm in wiki-Vote graph. Figure 6 demonstrates the result for IC model with $p_{(u,v)} = 0.1$. The performance of our algorithm in the email graph (Fig. 6(a)) is only 16.3 % higher than Max Degree algorithm. If the forwarding probability is small, it will reduce the probability of node being activated with source nodes sparsely. While the source nodes obtained with Max Degree algorithm may be neighbors or have many common neighbors. Source nodes obtained with Max Degree may be better than our algorithm, such as Fig. 6(a).

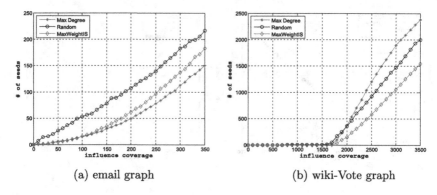

(a) email graph   (b) wiki-Vote graph

Fig. 6. Size of selected seed sets vs influence coverage η under IC model with $p_{(u,v)}=0.1$.

From these figures, we can know our algorithm has a great advantages in higher requirement of influence coverage when the influence probability is not set unified.

6   Conclusion

In this paper, we study the relationship between influence coverage and seed size, and further propose a novel approach HISS that uses h-hop independent set. With different influence probabilities of each node, our approach outperforms the state-of-the-art algorithms. It is more applicable in practice than other approaches. In conclusion, if only one or two seeds are needed, the Max Degree algorithm leads to satisfactory performance. If the goal is to achieve high influence coverage with less seeds, HISS should be used. The experimental results based on real-world datasets indicate that the proposed method outperforms the state-of-the-art algorithms.

References

1. Kempe, D., Kleinberg, J., Tardos, E.: Maximizing the spread of influence through a social network. In: KDD 2003, pp. 137–146 (2003)
2. Domingos, P., Richardson, M.: Mining the network value of customers. In: KDD 2001 pp. 61–70 (2001)
3. Xu, W., Lu, Z., Wu, W., Chen, Z.: A novel approach to online social influence maximization. Soc. Netw. Anal. Min. **4**, 153 (2014)
4. Goyal, A., Bonchi, F., Lakshmanan, L.V., Venkatasubramanian, S.: On minimizing budget and time in influence propagation over social networks. In: Social Network Analysis and Mining, pp. 1–14 (2012)
5. Zhang, P., Chen, W., Sun, X., Wang, Y., Zhang, J.: Minimizing Seed Set Selection with Probabilistic Coverage Guarantee in a Social Network. In: KDD 2014, pp. 1306–1315 (2014)

6. Chen, W., Wang, Y., Yang, S.: Efficient influence maximization in social networks. In: KDD 2009, pp.199–208 (2009)
7. Li, S., Zhu, Y., Li, D., Kim, D., Ma, H., Huang, H.: Influence maximization in social networks with user attitude modification. In: IEEE ICC, pp. 3913–3918 (2014)
8. Nguyen, D.T., Das,S., Thai, M.T.: Influence maximization in multiple online social networks. In: Global Communications Conference (GLOBECOM), pp. 3060–3065 (2013)
9. Leskovec, J., Krause, A., Guestrin, C., Faloutsos, C., Van Briesen, J., Glance, N.: Cost-effective outbreak detection in networks. In: KDD 2007, pp. 420–429 (2007)
10. Leskovec, J.: Wiki-vote social network. http://snap.stanford.edu/data/wi-ki-Vote.html
11. Zhang, Y., Gu, Q., Zheng, J.: Estimate on expectation for influence maximization in social networks. In: PAKDD 2010, pp. 99–106 (2010)

Finding Overlapping Communities with Random Walks on Line Graph and Attraction Intensity

Xiaoheng Deng[1][(✉)], Genghao Li[1], and Mianxiong Dong[2]

[1] School of Information Science and Engineering, Central South University,
Changsha 410083, China
dxh@csu.edu.cn
[2] Department of Information and Electronic Engineering,
Muroran Institute of Technology, Muroran 050-8585, Japan

Abstract. Since community structure is an important feature of complex network, community detection has attracted more and more attention in recent years. Most early researchers focus on identifying disjoint communities, whereas communities in many real networks are overlapped. In this paper, we propose a novel algorithm MCLC with random walks on line graph and attraction intensity to discover overlapping communities. MCLC algorithm first generates a weighted line graph from a undirected network, then divides links into "link communities" through random walks on the line graph. Finally, it transforms the "link communities" to "node communities" using the function of attraction intensity. The "node communities" are permitted overlapped, and the overlapping size is controlled by the threshold of attraction intensity. Experiments on some real world networks validate the effectiveness and efficiency of the proposed algorithm. Comparing overlapping modularity Q_{ov} with other related algorithms, the results of this algorithm is satisfactory.

Keywords: Community detection · Random walks · Link community · Overlapping community

1 Introduction

Including social, biological, and technological systems, many systems in world can be described as complex networks whose elements are neither purely regular nor purely random. One of the most relevant features of complex networks is community or modular structure, which often refers to groups or clusters having more internal than external connection [1]. Finding and analyzing community structure often provides invaluable help in deeply understanding the structure and function of a network, as widely demonstrated by several case studies in social science, biology, ecology, economics etc. [2–5].

A large quantity of approaches for detecting community have been proposed over the years. Most early approaches focus on identifying disjoint communities [7]. This type of detection put each node into one and only one community.

© Springer International Publishing Switzerland 2015
K. Xu and J. Zhu (Eds.): WASA 2015, LNCS 9204, pp. 94–103, 2015.
DOI: 10.1007/978-3-319-21837-3_10

However, communities are nested and overlapped in most real world networks. For example, in a social network where each vertex represents a person, and the communities represent the different groups of friends: one community for family, another community for co-workers, still one for friends in the same sports club.

In the paper, we propose a overlapping communities detection algorithm MCLC with random walks on line graph and attraction intensity. First we generate a weighted line graph from the original graph. Next, we compute the similarity(distance) between links through random walking on this line graph. The similarity is larger(the distance is smaller), the edges are more likely to be assigned into a same community. Then we get a hierarchical tree derived from the links distance, and "link communities" output by cutting the tree. Finally, we define the function of attention intensity and the "link communities" can be converted to "node communities" by setting a appropriate threshold of attention intensity.

2   Related Work

2.1   The Weighted Line Graph Model of Network

Generally, a network is simply regarded as a graph $G(V, E)$, where $|V| = N$ represents vertices and $|E| = M$ represents edges. In the most instances case the network is directed and weighted, and we denote by $W = [w_{ij}]$ the $N \times N$ weight matrix, where $w_{ij} \geq 0$ is the weight of the link $i \to j$. The graph adjacency matrix $A = [a_{ij}]$ is the $N \times N$ binary matrix, where $a_{ij} = 1$ if $w_{ij} > 0$, and $a_{ij} = 0$ otherwise. In the paper, we consider the undirected networks, namely $w_{ij} = w_{ji}$. If the network also unweighted, then $W = A$, all weights equal to 1.

Evans et al. [8] proposed the definition of "line graph". The incidence matrix $B = [b_{i\alpha}]$ is a $N \times M$ matrix, which is a important bandage between node graph and line graph. The elements $b_{i\alpha}$ can be obtained by

$$b_{i\alpha} = \begin{cases} w_{ij}, & \text{node } i \text{ and } j \text{ are two ends of edge } \alpha; \\ 0, & \text{otherwise.} \end{cases} \tag{1}$$

The line graph $L = [l_{\alpha\beta}]$ is a $M \times M$ adjacency matrix, where $l_{\alpha\beta} = 1$ if link α and link β have a common node, otherwise $l_{\alpha\beta} = 0$. Random walks in line graph should depend on an weighted link matrix $H = [h_{\alpha\beta}]$, it can be obtained by matrix B:

$$H_{\alpha\beta} = \sum_i \frac{b_{i\alpha} b_{j\alpha}}{s_i}. \tag{2}$$

where s_i is the strength of node i and $s_i = \sum_j w_{ij} = \sum_\alpha b_{i\alpha}$. As seen in Fig. 1, it has displayed four different matrices and illustrated the transformation of a graph adjacency matrix A into a weighted matrix H.

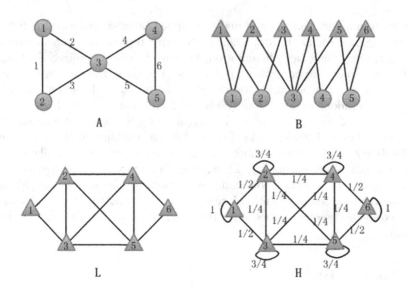

Fig. 1. Four different matrices

2.2   The Distance Between Links

The $M \times M$ link weighted matrix H can be associated to a M-state Markov chain, the transition matrix $P = [P_{\alpha\beta}]$ is defined by

$$p_{\alpha\beta} = \frac{h_{\alpha\beta}}{\sum_{\beta} h_{\alpha\beta}} \tag{3}$$

Consider a large number of repetitions of a random walk start from link α. $[P^t]_{\alpha\beta}$ is the probability that the walker start from α and stay in β after t steps. Thus, if random walks of length T are performed from α, the excepted probability of visits to β is $\sum_{t=1}^{T} [P^t]_{\alpha\beta}$ $(1 \leq t \leq T)$. Cluster analysis can be used to group "similar links" into candidate link communities. We propose a (symmetric) similarity $\phi_{\alpha\beta}$ defined by

$$\phi_{\alpha\beta} = \phi_{\beta\alpha} = \sum_{t=1}^{T} \left([P^t]_{\alpha\beta} + [P^t]_{\beta\alpha} \right) \tag{4}$$

Then the distance $d_{\alpha\beta}$ between link α and β can be obtained by complementing the similarity and normalizing the results from 0 to 1,

$$d_{\alpha\beta} = d_{\beta\alpha} = 1 - \frac{\phi_{\alpha\beta} - min\ \phi}{max\ \phi - min\ \phi} \tag{5}$$

2.3   The Function of Attractive Intensity

Suppose a network with M links, $C_L = \{P_1, P_2, \ldots, P_q\}$ is a partition of the links into q link communities, with $\bigcup_c P_c = E$ and $P_c \cap P_d = \emptyset$ for all c, d. In order to transform link communities into node communities, we propose an effective function of attractive intensity $I_i^{P_c}$, which is defined as

$$I_i^{P_c} = \frac{\sum_{(i,j)\in P_c} w_{ij}}{\sum_j w_{ij}} = \frac{s_i^{in}(P_c)}{s_i} \tag{6}$$

where (i,j) represent a link with two end nodes i and j, s_i is the strength of node i, $s_i^{in}(P_c)$ is the sum weight of i connected links in link community P_c.

The value of $I_i^{P_c}$ is belong to $[0,1]$, which indicates the attraction intensity form link community P_c to node i. When $I_i^{P_c} = 1$, node i is attracted by link community P_c completely, namely i is contained by P_c; when $I_i^{P_c} = 0$, link community P_c has no attraction to node i, namely i is out of P_c. So we only need consider attractive intensity on the edge nodes between link communities. These edge nodes can be expressed by:

$$edge\_node = \{u | (u,v) \in P_c, (u,w) \in P_d, c \neq d\} \tag{7}$$

All the edge nodes can be regard as overlapping nodes, but the number of overlapping nodes is often large in this case. Here we set a threshold δ of the attractive intensity to control the overlapping size: if the maximal attractive intensity I_{max} to an edge node u satisfied

$$I_{max} = \max_{1 \leq c \leq q} \{I_u^{P_c}\} = I_u^{P_m} > \delta \tag{8}$$

and the link community P_m is unique, then the edge node u can be entirely absorbed into the link community P_m; otherwise the edge node u is an overlapping node. At a result, some of the edge nodes can be bring into appropriate link communities, the rest of edge nodes are still overlapping nodes.

3   The Algorithm

According to the three main idea given above, our MCLC algorithm can be summarized as three main stage as follows:

1. Given a undirected network $G(V,E)$, number each link, then compute the incidence matrix B and the weighted link matrix H, the pseudo-code of H generating can be shown in Algorithm 1;
2. Calculate the distance(similarity) between links by random walks of length T on the weighted line graph. We describe the pseudo-code of link distance calculating in Algorithm 2. Then we use average-linkage clustering method to divide network into q link communities $C_L = \{P_1, P_2, \ldots, P_q\}$;
3. For nodes which are inside of a link community, bring the node into the link community; for edge node which are between link communities, set a proper attraction intensity threshold δ, then assign the edge nodes into appropriate link communities. As a result, the link community change to node community allowed overlap.

Algorithm 1. Atrans2H

1: Input: graph $G(V, E)$
2: $G(V, E) \rightarrow$ graph weigthted matrix W
3: Sort each edge in G and save in matrix LG
4: $n = size(W, 1)$
5: $m = length(LG)$
6: $B = sparse(n, m)$;
7: **for** α in 1 to m **do**
8:     **if** node i connect to edge α in LG **then**
9:         $B(i, \alpha) = W(i, j)$
10:     **end if**
11: **end for**
12: Compute the strength of each node and save in vector S
13: $M = dig(1/S_1, 1/S_2, , 1/S_n)$
14: $H = B * M * B^T$
15: Output: H

Algorithm 2. LinkDistance

1: Input: H,T
2: $m = size(H, 1)$
3: $P = sparse(m, m)$;
4: **for** i in 1 to m **do**
5:     **for** j in 1 to m **do**
6:         $P(i, j) = H(i, j)/\sum_j H(i, j)$
7:     **end for**
8: **end for**
9: $D = sparse(m, m)$
10: **for** t_1 in 1 to T **do**
11:     $Ptot = P$
12:     $Pcurr = P$
13:     **for** t_2 in 2 to t_1 **do**
14:         $Pcurr = P * Pcurr$
15:         $Ptot = Ptot + Pcurr$
16:     **end for**
17:     $S = (Ptot + Ptot^T)/T$
18: **end for**
19: $S(i, i) = 0$
20: $D = 1 - \frac{S - minS}{maxS - minS}$
21: Output: D

Note that the choice of the time horizon T is potentially critical. Cluster analysis yields a different hierarchical tree (dendrogram) for each time horizon T, whose choice is thus nontrivial. At the two extremes, setting $T = 1$ restricts the pairs of nodes which are candidate to nonzero similarity to neighboring pairs only, whereas larger and larger values of T tend to make any link equally similar to any other.

Average-linkage hierarchical clustering builds a link dendrogram from the links distance. If you want to get a partition of q communities, cutting this dendrogram at the maximal q cluster. We give the pseudo-code of our MCLC algorithm in Algorithm 3.

Algorithm 3. MCLC

1: Input: graph $G(V, E), T, q$
2: $H \leftarrow Atrans2H(G)$
3: $D \leftarrow LinkDistance(H, T)$
4: $Cluster(D, q) \rightarrow C_L = \{P_1, P_2, \ldots, P_q\}$
5: Find the edge nodes between C_L and save in set U
6: **for** i in U **do**
7:     **for** P_c in C_L **do**
8:         calculate attraction intensity $I_i^{P_c}$
9:     **end for**
10:     **if** $I_{max} = I_i^{P_m} > \delta$ and P_m is unique **then**
11:         node i only belong to P_m
12:     **end if**
13: **end for**
14: Update C_L to $C_N = \{P_1, P_2, \ldots, P_q\}$
15: Output: C_N

The attraction intensity threshold δ is belong to $[0, 1]$. The lager δ, the more difficult to meet the condition, in other words, the more edge nodes are overlapping nodes. Generally we set $\delta = 0.5$ in accordance with the notion of "community in a strong sense" put forward by Radicchi et al. [9], or simply: in a undirected and unweighted network, if the most and more than a half of u connected links are in a unique link community, then node u can be absorbed into the link community.

Analyzing the complexity of MCLC algorithm , the first steps run in time $O(k_{max}^2 n)$. In the second step, it takes (tm^2) to calculate the similarity between links. In the third step, it take $O(n)$ to put nodes into link community. Finally the total computing time is $O(k_{max}^2 n + tm^2 + n)$, the worst computing time is upper bound at most $O(m^2 n)$.

4   Experiments and Results

To evaluate the performance of MCLC, we implement our method and design experiments in Matlab platform, running on a PC with 2.94 GHz, 4 GB memory and Win7 operating system. we will consider the algorithm in some real word networks.

4.1   Zacharys Karate Club Network

Zacharys karate club network [10] is a real social network, which is a widely used network for testing communitys algorithm. There are 34 individuals and 78 links in the network, and the links represent friendships between individuals in the karate club. Later, the club split in two as a result of the contradiction between the administrator and the instructor. When we apply the MCLC algorithm to this network, the results can be shown in Fig. 2.

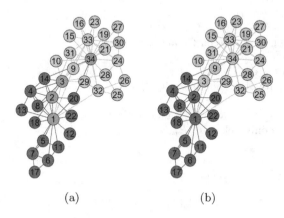

(a)   (b)

Fig. 2. Zacharys karate club network. (a) Two communities generated by MCLC method when $\delta = 1$, which colored with red and blue respectively, and the green nodes represent the overlapping parts; (b) Two communities generated by MCLC method when $\delta < 0.6$.

We divide the karate network into two communities using our MCLC algorithm with $T = 1$. First we set $\delta = 1$, all the edge nodes (number 1,2,3, and 34) are overlapping nodes, the remain nodes are absorbed into two link communities, as seen in Fig. 2(a). The maximal attractive intensity of the four edge nodes are 0.8125, 0.8889, 0.6000 and 0.8824 respectively. So if we set $\delta < 0.6$, all edge nodes can be absorbed into the related link communities, the result can be seen in Fig. 2(b). Except the node 3 is assigned error, other nodes are consistent with the real nodes partitions.

4.2   Dolphins Network

Dolphins network [11] is an undirected social network of frequent associations between 62 dolphins in a community living off Doubtful Sound, New Zealand, as compiled by Lusseau et al. (2003). In the 7-years observation, the original community naturally divided two big group, then the larger group separated into four small group later.

From Fig. 3, the network is divided to two large group by our method with $T = 1$. Figure 3(a) indicate the two link community using MCLC algorithm, and

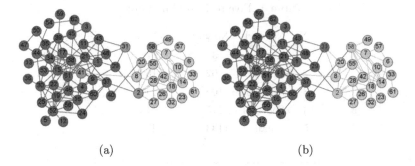

$$(a) \qquad\qquad\qquad\qquad\qquad (b)$$

Fig. 3. Dolphins network. (a)Two communities generated by MCLC method, the red and the blue edges represent the two link communities respectively, the green nodes represent the edge nodes; (b) When $\delta < 0.6$, every edge node between link communities reassign to node community respectively.

the green nodes (number 2,31,41,58) are edge nodes. The maximal attractive intensity of the four edge nodes are 0.7500, 0.6000, 0.8750, 0.8889 respectively. If we set $\delta < 0.6$, all edge nodes can be absorbed into one neighbor community, as seen in the Fig. 3(b). Fortunately, the modified partition of dolphins is consist with the natural partition completely.

4.3   Comparison with Other Community Detection Methods

In this section, we compare our MCLC algorithm with CPM [12], Link [13] and UEOC [14] algorithm on the five real-world networks listed in Table 1. Here we choose the overlapping modularity Q_{ov} [15], an extension of modularity Q [16], to testing community structure. It is defined as following:

$$Q_{ov} = \frac{1}{2m} \sum_{l} \sum_{\{i,j\} \in C_l} \frac{1}{O_i O_j} \left[a_{ij} - \frac{k_i k_j}{2m} \right] \qquad (9)$$

where m represents the number of edges in the network, $O_i(O_j)$ represents the number of communities to which vertex $i(j)$ belongs, a_{ij} is the element of adjacency of the network $k_i(k_j)$ is the degree of vertex $i(j)$.

Overlapping modularity Q_{ov} is the fraction of the edges that fall within the given groups minus the expected such fraction if edges were distributed at random, which also consider the influence of overlapping nodes. If each vertex i satisfied $O_i = 1$, namely each vertex only belong to one community, then Q_{ov} will reduce to Q.

We have made many experiments on these real networks, and compared the maximum Q_{ov} with different algorithm. To reduce the time cost, we set $T = 1$ and $\delta = 0.5$. From Fig. 4, the result of MCLC is very good among those methods, and it is the best on the four real world network except Football.

Table 1. Five real-world networks

No	Network	No.vertices	No.edges
1	Karate	34	78
2	Dolphins	62	159
3	Polbooks	105	441
4	Football	115	613
5	Email	1133	5451

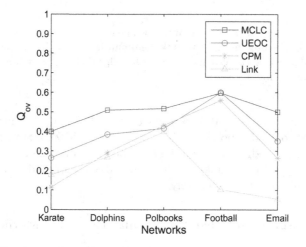

Fig. 4. Comparing Q_{ov} with different methods on networks

5   Conclusion

The MCLC algorithm, which can detect the overlapping community structure of complex networks, is proposed in this paper. Unlike traditional random walks starting at nodes, our random walks are at links. First, it generate the weighted line graph from the original network graph. Next, suppose M members walk on the line graph randomly. After walk T steps, calculating the similarities and distance between members. Then the average-linkage method is adopted for producing the partition of link communities. At last, we reassign the edge nodes between link communities to neighbor community by setting the threshold of attraction intensity. The experiment results on the real-world networks are as good as or even better than those of the existing methods, validating the efficiency of the proposed algorithm. However, we have not down the experiments on the lager scale networks due to the limitation of devices, and the time complexity is higher than expected, which may be improved in the future.

Acknowledgements. The author gratefully acknowledges support from National Natural Science Foundation of China projects of grant No. 61272149, 61379058, 61379057, 61350011 and JSPS A3 Foresight Program of JSPS KAKENHI Grant Number 26730056, 15K15976.

References

1. Rosvall, M., Bergstrom, C.T.: Maps of random walks on complex networks reveal community structure. Proc. Nat. Acad. Sci. **105**(4), 1118–1123 (2008)
2. Deng, X.H., Liu, Y., Chen, Z.G.: Memory-based evolutionary game on small-world network with tunable heterogeneity. Physica A: Stat. Mech. Appl. **389**(22), 5173–5181 (2010)
3. Dong, M., Kimata, T., Sugiura, K., Zettsu, K.: Quality-of-Experience (QoE) in emerging mobile social networks. IEICE Trans. **97**–**D**(10), 2606–2612 (2014)
4. Ping, Y., Cao, Z., Zhu, H.: Sybil-aware least cost rumor blocking in social networks. GLOBECOM **2014**, 692–697 (2014)
5. Li, M., Zhu, H., Gao, Z., Chen, S., Yu, L., Hu, S., Ren, K.: All your location are belong to us: breaking mobile social networks for automated user location tracking. MobiHoc **2014**, 43–52 (2014)
6. Piccardi, C., Calatroni, L., Bertoni, F.: Communities in italian corporate networks. Physica A: Stat. Mech. Appl. **389**(22), 5247–5258 (2010)
7. Fortunato, S.: Community detection in graphs. Phys. Rep. **486**(3), 75–174 (2010)
8. Evans, T., Lambiotte, R.: Line graphs, link partitions, and overlapping communities. Phys. Rev. E **80**(1), 016105 (2009)
9. Radicchi, F., Castellano, C., Cecconi, F., Loreto, V., Parisi, D.: Defining and identifying communities in networks. Proc. Nat. Acad. Sci. U.S.A. **101**(9), 2658–2663 (2004)
10. Zachary, W.W.: An information flow model for conflict and fission in small groups. J. Anthropol. Res. **33**, 452–473 (1977)
11. Lusseau, D., Schneider, K., Boisseau, O.J., Haase, P., Slooten, E., Dawson, S.M.: The bottlenose dolphin community of doubtful sound features a large proportion of long-lasting associations. Behav. Ecol. Sociobiol. **54**(4), 396–405 (2003)
12. Palla, G., Derényi, I., Farkas, I., Vicsek, T.: Uncovering the overlapping community structure of complex networks in nature and society. Nature **435**(7043), 814–818 (2005)
13. Ahn, Y.Y., Bagrow, J.P., Lehmann, S.: Link communities reveal multiscale complexity in networks. Nature **466**(7307), 761–764 (2010)
14. Jin, D., Yang, B., Baquero, C., Liu, D., He, D., Liu, J.: A Markov random walk under constraint for discovering overlapping communities in complex networks. J. Stat. Mech: Theory Exp. **2011**(05), P05031 (2011)
15. Shen, H., Cheng, X., Cai, K., Hu, M.B.: Detect overlapping and hierarchical community structure in networks. Physica A: Stat. Mech. Appl. **388**(8), 1706–1712 (2009)
16. Newman, M.E.: Fast algorithm for detecting community structure in networks. Phys. Rev. E **69**(6), 066133 (2004)

Computing an Optimal Path with the Minimum Number of Distinct Sensors

Chenglin Fan, Qing Yang, and Binhai Zhu[⊠]

Department of Computer Science, Montana State University,
Bozeman, MT 59717-3880, USA
chenglin.fan@msu.montana.edu, {qing.yang,bhz}@cs.montana.edu

Abstract. Wireless sensors can be deployed in boundary regions to replace human in intruder detection. Given a deployment of such a wireless sensor network, we present a method to compute a path crossing the minimum number of distinct sensors from a source to a destination.Then, we propose the selfish path problem, in which the intruder is always getting more closer to the destination, and we design a greedy algorithm for this problem. We implement these algorithms and compare the number of sensors crossed by a random path, a line segment path, a selfish path, and two paths generated by Dijkstra's algorithm and an adapted Bellman-Ford algorithm. Some important empirical results are obtained.

1 Introduction

With the development of technology, wireless sensor networks are more and more widely used in gathering important parameters of our environment, such as temperature, sound, pressure, etc. One of the fundamental issues that arises in wireless sensor networks is coverage [13]. From this perspective, the quality of service in wireless sensor networks can be measured by k-coverage together with connectivity and barrier coverage, *etc.* When a given region needs to be fully covered, we usually want the region to be k-covered (meaning that each point is covered by at least k sensors). These problems have been covered in [8,9].

In many situations, however, one only needs to detect whether there is an intruder penetrating a boundary region. Then, the whole region does not have to be fully covered; instead, we can guard the boundary of some important or sensitive parts of a region using a wireless sensor network — *barrier coverage*. See an example in Fig. 1. We review the important researches on barrier coverage.

Arora *et al.* deployed wireless sensors in a one-kilometer-long region, to verify the ability of using wireless sensors to detect the intruders [1]. Kumar *et al.* gave the definition of k-barrier coverage as follows: if a wireless sensor network guarantees that an intruder is detected by k distinct sensors before it reaches the destination, then the sensors form a *k-barrier coverage* [10]. They presented an algorithm to determine whether a given belt region is k-barrier covered in polynomial time.

Given a wireless sensor network, Kumar *et al.* designed optimal algorithms to determine the sleep schedules to maximize the network lifetime while satisfying

© Springer International Publishing Switzerland 2015
K. Xu and J. Zhu (Eds.): WASA 2015, LNCS 9204, pp. 104–113, 2015.
DOI: 10.1007/978-3-319-21837-3_11

Fig. 1. An example of barrier coverage, the arrow shows the trajectory of an intruder.

the k-barrier coverage condition in a belt region [11,12]. Yang *et al.* considered how to maintain k-barrier coverage using the minimum amount of energy [16]. The sensors discussed above are undirected sensors (omnidrectional sensors), which means that a sensing region is a disk. Directed sensors, where the sensing region is a circular sector, have also been considered, on k-barrier coverage in a belt region [14] and on extending the network lifetime [15].

An important problem in barrier coverage is when the k-coverage requirement is not satisfied. Chen *et al.* [5] introduced the concept of local barrier coverage. Their motivation is to track the trajectory of an intruder in a small part of the belt region, they proposed a Localized Barrier Coverage Protocol (LBCP) algorithm for the local barrier coverage problem. Later, Chen *et al.* [6] also introduced a new barrier coverage model called *one-way* barrier coverage: for two sides A and B of a belt region, it is legal to cross the belt region from side A to side B, but not the other way around. This model has some applications in practice. For example, it is legal for people to exit an office but illegal to enter the office without an official approval.

Motivated by this, the following problem was proposed from the intruder's perspective: as each sensor usually works with certain probability, if a intruder wants to be most likely undetected, he/she should avoid crossing many sensors. Formally, given a wireless sensor network, the problem is to find a path from the source s to the destination t crossing the minimum number of distinct sensors. Chan and Kirkpatrick [4] showed that the minimum number of sensors is at most twice of the minimum number of distinct sensors, and the optimal path in G crosses the same sensor at most twice when all sensors have the same radius, where G is the dual graph of the arrangement of sensors. No constant approximation is known when sensors have different sizes. On the other hand, no implementation was done in [4].

In this paper, we follow Chan and Kirkpatrick to solve the problem of computing a path crossing the minimum number of (distinct) sensors. We present a list of practical algorithms and implement all of them. Summarizing, the problems we want to solve in this paper are as follows:

- For a given deployment of wireless sensor network, how to compute the minimum number of distinct sensors from a source to a destination?
- How to determine the number of distinct sensors in a greedy selfish path?

2   Problem Definitions

We formally define the problem to be studied in this paper as follows. Throughout this paper, all of our theoretical results are for arbitrary wireless sensor networks (WSNs), i.e., the senors do not have to be uniform. But our empirical results are on uniform sensors.

Definition 1. (Minimum Number of Sensors Between a Source s and a Destination t) *Given the deployment of a WSN, we try to count the number of sensors intersecting a path from a source s to a destination t. If a sensor appears more than once in the path, e.g., m times, then this sensor contributes a value m to the total number of sensors. The minimum number of sensors between a source t and a destination t is the minimum number of sensors in all possible paths between s and t.*

Definition 2. (Minimum Number of Distinct Sensors Between a Source s and a Destination t) *Given the deployment of a WSN, the minimum number of distinct sensors between a source s and a destination t is the minimum number of distinct sensors in all possible paths between s and t. Here, if a sensor appears $m \geq 1$ times on a path, it will only contribute a value one to the total number of sensors.*

Definition 3. (Selfish Path Between a Source s and a Destination t) *Given the deployment of a WSN, a path from s to t is called selfish if for any two points p_1, p_2, where p_1 precedes p_2 on the path, satisfy that $d(p_1, t) \geq d(p_2, t)$.*

3   The Minimum Number of Distinct Sensors Problem

In this section, we consider the core problem of this paper — the minimum number of distinct sensors problem. We slightly abuse the terminology of 'sensor' and 'sensing region', when the context is clear.

3.1   A General Property for a Special Wireless Sensor Network

It is proven that the optimal path from s to t crosses each sensor at most twice, when all the sensors have exact the same size [4]. Here we show that if no three sensors intersect then this bound can be improved. The theorem is as follows.

Theorem 1. *Given a WSN, if no three sensors intersect at the same point, then there is an optimal path P from s to t (crossing the minimum number of distinct sensors) which crosses any sensor at most once.*

Proof. Suppose the optimal path from s to t has to cross the same sensor twice, with loss of generality, let P_e be such a path from s to t which crosses the sensor S_e twice. Let p_1 be the point where P_e leaves S_e for the first time. Let p_2 be the point where P enters S_e for the second time. (See Fig. 2.) We ignore other sensors covering p_1 and p_2 except the sensor S_e. As no three sensors intersect at the same point, among the remaining sensors, no two intersect inside S_e. Then, one can find a path $P_{1,2}$ from p_1 to p_2 which is inside S_e and avoids any remaining sensor. Hence, we obtain a path P'_e from P_e, by replacing the part from p_1 to p_2 using $P_{1,2}$, which crosses S_e once.   □

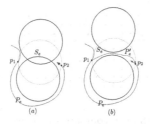

Fig. 2. Illustration for the proof of Theorem 1.

3.2 A Discrete Method to Compute the Arrangement

The above theorem, while interesting, is very limited in practice — to achieve a good coverage, we must use a lot of sensors such that a point should be covered by several sensors at the same time. So we have to cover the general case.

For a belt region, Kumar *et al.* [10] converted the deployment of sensors into a graph, where each sensor corresponds to a node in the graph, there is an edge between two nodes if their corresponding sensing regions intersect each other. Let u and v be two nodes located on the leftmost and rightmost side of the belt region. Then the belt region is *k-barrier covered* if there are k vertex-disjoint paths from u to v. (Then, crossing each path, the intruder must be detected at least once.) The setup for the general case is similar, except that a path does not necessarily form a barrier.

Formally, the framework for the general case is follows. Each sensor corresponds to a disk (bounded by a circle) with a center and certain radius. These circles form an arrangement. We then design a discrete method to compute the arrangement. Finally, we convert the arrangement into a directed (dual) graph $G = (V(G), E(G))$, where each cell corresponds to a node, and there is an edge between two nodes if their corresponding two cells are adjacent to each other. The weight of an edge $e = (A, B) \in E(G)$ is defined as: if node A corresponds to cell c_a, node B corresponds to cell c_b, S_a is the set of sensors cover c_a, and S_b is the set of cells cover c_b, then the weight of edge e, e_w, is the number of sensors in $S_b - S_a$ (or, $|S_b - S_a|$).

A naive way to solve the problem is to run a standard shortest path algorithm from s to t on G. But this method counts a sensor appearing on the path multiple times. Therefore, we make some changes to the Bellman-Ford algorithm, and use the modified Bellman-Ford algorithm to compute the minimum number of distinct sensors on a path from s to t. We next present more technical details.

In computational geometry, the sweep-line Algorithm [3] can be used to compute the arrangement of circles. However, it needs a complex data structure to implement. In fact, it needs a balanced binary tree to store the status of the sweep-line, and a priority queue to store the events. Moreover, it needs to deal with some complex conditions when an event occurred. Besides, the shape of a single cell could be quite complex. Here, we present a simple discrete method to compute the arrangement. See Fig. 3 for an example.

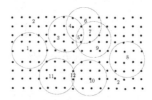

Fig. 3. Discrete method to compute the arrangement of sensors.

The algorithm is as follows:

(1) Using a set of grid points in the plane (which form a standard rectilinear grid graph). For each grid point p, use $set(p)$ to denote the set of sensors that cover point p. For each sensor c_i, add c_i to $set(p)$ if p is covered by sensor c_i.

(2) Let p be any grid point, perform a depth-first search on the grid graph starting at p. Let point q be adjacent to p, the point that has just been visited. If $set(p) = set(q)$, then put p and q in the same cluster $C(p)$.

(3) For a point $r \notin C(p)$, if r is adjacent to a point q in $C(p)$, and $r \in C(r)$, then cluster $C(r)$ is a neighbor of $C(p)$.

(4) Each cluster $C(p)$ corresponds to a cell of the arrangement, or, to a node in the graph G. The neighbors of $C(p)$ correspond to the neighboring cells in arrangement, or, the adjacent nodes of $C(p)$ in the graph G.

Hence we construct the (dual) graph G after the above steps. As it is easy to locate s (resp. t) in a cell of the arrangement (whose dual is a node of G), the problem is really to find a 'good' path in G.

3.3   Dijkstra's Algorithm

Dijkstra's algorithm is a benchmark for our empirical comparisons. With Dijkstra's algorithm, we can obtain the shortest path between s and t, which crosses the minimum number of sensors. However, the algorithm does not necessarily give the minimum number of distinct sensors. In Fig. 4, Dijkstra's algorithm returns a path crossing two distinct sensors, but there exists a path which only crosses one (distinct) sensor twice.

It is proven that the optimal path from s to t crosses each sensor at most twice, when all the sensors have exact the same size [4]. That naturally gives a factor-2 approximation for the problem when all the sensors have the same size. (No approximation is known when the sensors have different sizes.) We will show how to compute the exact minimum number of distinct sensors in the next subsection.

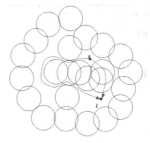

Fig. 4. Dijkstra'a algorithm returns a path crossing two sensors, but the optimal path crosses only one sensor twice.

3.4   Adapted Bellman-Ford Algorithm

We make some changes to the Bellman-Ford Algorithm [2,7] to have a new method to compute the optimal shortest path with the minimum number of distinct sensors.

The idea is as follows. We record the actual path (not just weights) from the source s to a node u, and when a path continues and crosses a sensor v, we check whether v has been crossed or not. That information might give us a better path from s to v, possibly crossing few distinct sensors.

The adapted Bellman-Ford algorithm needs k loops. In each loop, we run the $relax(u,v)$ operation for each edge (u,v) of G. The difference between our algorithm and the traditional Bellman-Ford algorithm is in the details of the relaxation operations.

In the initialization step, we set $list[s]$ to be empty, where s is the source. We use $list[v]$ to record all possible paths from s to v, and $list[u,v]$ to denote the set of sensors in $S_v \setminus S_u$. The detail of the Relax operation is shown in Algorithm 1. The operation $+$, and comparison operation $>, <, =$ between two paths is shown in Fig. 5. (These operations really correspond to the set operations $\cup, \supset, \subset$, and $=$.) Our operation $+$ can guarantee that any path does not have duplicate sensors.

Define a *non-trivial* path as a path P_1 in $list[v]$ such that for any other path P_2 stored in $list[v]$, neither $P_1 < P_2$ nor $P_2 < P_1$ holds. We have the following theorem.

$$
\begin{array}{ccccc}
list[u] & & & & \\
P & + & list[u,v] & & = P_t \\
c_1, c_3, c_5 & & & & c_1, c_3, c_5 \\
c_2 & & c_3 & & c_2, c_3 \\
c_6 & & & & c_3, c_6 \\
\end{array}
$$

$$
\begin{array}{lll}
 & list[v] & \\
c_1, c_3, c_5 > c_1, c_3 & & \text{do nothing} \\
c_2, c_3 < c_2, c_3, c_4 & & \text{replace} \\
c_3, c_6 \ - > & & \text{add} \\
\end{array}
$$

Fig. 5. The detail of relaxation for edge (u,v).

Algorithm 1. Relax(u,v,list[u,v])

---

for each path P in $list[u]$ do
  $P_t = P + list[u, v]$.
  flag=0;
  for each path P_v in $list[v]$ do
    if $P_t > P_v$ then
      flag =1;break;
    else if $P_t \leq P_v$ then
      flag=-1;break;
    end if
  end for
  if $flag > 0$ then
    $P_v = P_t$;
  else if $flag = 0$ then
    $list[v]$.insert(P_t).
  end if
end for

Theorem 2. *For any node v, all possible non-trivial paths that pass through at most k nodes (excluding the source s) are already recorded in $list[v]$ after k loops of relaxation.*

Proof. We prove this theorem by an induction on k.

(1) Basis: when $k = 1$, the path $P = list[s, v]$ is recorded in $list[v]$, where v is adjacent to s, after one loop of relaxation.
(2) Inductive hypothesis: we assume the statement is true when $k = i$. This means that we obtain all possible non-trivial paths that pass at most i nodes in $list[u]$, for any node u, after i loops of relaxation.
(3) We now consider the case when $k = i + 1$.

The path P passing $i + 1$ nodes from s to v is composed of a path passing i nodes from s to some u and a path from u to v, where u is a neighboring node of v, and the path from s to some u is already recorded in $list[u]$ after k loops of relaxation. By the inductive hypothesis, for any node u, the possible non-trivial paths that pass at most i nodes are already be recorded in $list[u]$ after i loops of relaxation. Hence the non-trivial path $P = list[u] + list[u, v]$ is recorded after the $(i + 1)$-th loop. □

We comment that the running time of this algorithm could be exponential if k is large. But in practice k should be relatively small. In the next section, we consider a special kind of path — selfish path.

4   The Greedy Selfish Path Problem

We first consider the optimal selfish path problem in this section. Recall that the optimal selfish path is the selfish path crossing the minimum number of distinct sensors. A selfish path does not have to be unique. The optimal selfish path P from s to t crossing the minimum number of distinct sensors could cross the same sensor twice. (It is not hard to construct such an example.) The optimal selfish path problem is still open, even when all sensors are uniform.

Due to that an optimal selfish path could cross a sensor twice, here we propose a greedy selfish path algorithm as follows.

1. Discrete the plane into grid points.
2. For two adjacent grid points p_1, p_2, there exists an edge from p_1 to p_2 if $d(p_1, t) \geq d(p_2, t)$.
3. In the resulting graph, use Dijkstra's algorithm to compute the path from s to t crossing the minimum number of sensors.

Note that this algorithm does not necessarily cross the minimum number of (distinct) sensors. In the next section, we will compare this algorithm along with some others through some simulations.

5 Empirical Results

In this section, the comparison of five kinds of paths between the source s and destination t are done as follows.

1. The random path, which is path from s to t passing through several random points in the plane. It is easy to check the number of distinct sensors of a random path from s to t.
2. The line segment path, which is the segment $\overline{st}$. It is obvious that the line segment path never cross the same sensor twice.
3. The greedy selfish path, which never crosses the same sensor twice (but is not necessarily a global shortest path).
4. The shortest path computed by Dijkstra's algorithm in the dual graph, which crosses the same sensor at most twice when all the sensors has the same radius.
5. The shortest path computed by the Adapted Bellman-Ford algorithm. We also call it the optimal path, crossing the minimum number of distinct sensors.

The setup for the simulations is as follows. The sensors are of certain radius and are deployed in the 10×10 square. The center of each sensor is randomly distributed in the square. The random route is obtained by producing some random points in the square, and then connecting them together in a random order. In Fig. 6 and Fig. 7, we show the the average number of sensors detected for over 1000 random (s, t) pairs where the sensor radii are 2 and 1 respectively.

From Fig. 6 and Fig. 7, it can be seen that: (1) The average number of sensors crossed in random path is the highest, while the Adapted Bellman-Ford algorithm gives the smallest number (though only marginally lower than that of Dijkstra's algorithm). (2) The average number of sensors crossed by the line segment path is higher than the ones crossed by the greedy selfish path, which are both higher than that of Dijkstra's algorithm. (3) When the sensors are uniform and randomly distributed, the scenario that the optimal path crossing the

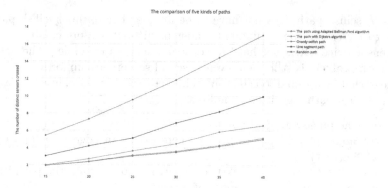

Fig. 6. The comparison of five kinds of paths between the source and destination. The radius of each sensor is 2, and the sensors are randomly distributed in a 10×10 square.

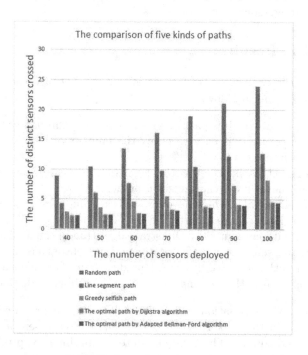

Fig. 7. The comparison of five kinds path between the source and destination. The radius of each sensor is 1, and the sensors are randomly distributed in a 10×10 square.

same sensor twice rarely happens — as the difference is very small between number of sensors crossed by the Adapted Bellman-Ford algorithm and Dijkstra's algorithm.

In the future, we will focus on the problem when each sensor works with a probability p.

References

1. Arora, A., Ramnath, R., Ertin, E. et al.: ExScal: Elements of an extreme scale wireless sensor network. In: Proceedings of the 11th IEEE International Conference on Real-Time Computing Systems and Applications, HongKong (2005)
2. Bellman, R.: On a routing problem. Q. Appl. Math. **16**(1), 87–90 (1958)
3. de Berg, M., Choeng, O., van Kreveld, M.: Computational Geometry: Algorithm and Application, 3rd edn. Springer, Heidelberg (2008)
4. Chan, D.Y.C., Kirkpatrick, D.: Approximating barrier resilience for arrangements of non-identical disk sensors. In: Bar-Noy, A., Halldórsson, M.M. (eds.) ALGO-SENSORS 2012. LNCS, vol. 7718, pp. 42–53. Springer, Heidelberg (2013)
5. Chen, A., Kumar, S., Lai, T.-H.: Local barrier coverage in wireless sensor networks. Ieee trans. mobile comput. **9**(4), 491–504 (2010)
6. Chen, A., Li, Z., Lai, T.-H., Liu, C.: One-way barrier coverage with wireless sensors. In: Proceedings of IEEE INFOCOM 2011, pp. 626–630 (2011)
7. Ford, L.R., Fulkerson, D.R.: Flows in Networks. Princeton University Press, Princeton (1962)
8. Huang, C.-F., Tseng, Y.-C.: The coverage problem in a wireless sensor network. In: Proceedings of WSNA 2003, pp. 115–121 (2003)
9. Kumar, S., Lai, T.H., Balogh, J.: On k-coverage in a mostly sleeping sensor network. In: Proceedings of MobiCom 2004, pp. 144–158 (2004)
10. Kumar, S., Lai, T.-H., Arora, A.: Barrier coverage with wireless sensors. J. Wireless Netw. **13**, 817–834 (2007)
11. Kumar, S., Lai, T.-H., Posner, M.E., Sinha, P.: Optimal sleep-wakeup algorithms for barriers of wireless sensors. In: Proceedings of BROADNETS 2007, pp. 327–336 (2007)
12. Kumar, S., Lai, T.-H., Balogh, J.: On k-coverage in a mostly sleeping sensor network. J. Wireless Netw. **14**(3), 277–294 (2008)
13. Meguerdichian, S., Koushanfar, F., Potkonjak, M., Srivastava, M.B.: Coverage problems in wireless ad-hoc sensor networks. In: Proceedings of IEEE INFOCOM 2001, vol. 3, pp. 1380–1387 (2001)
14. Ssu, K.-F., Wang, W.-T., Feng-Kuang, W., Tzu-Ting, W.: K-barrier coverage with a directional sensing model. Int. J.Smart Sens. and Intell. Syst. **2**(1), 79–93 (2009)
15. Tang, J., Zhu, B., Zhang, L., Hincapie, R.: Wakeup scheduling in roadside directional sensor networks. In: Proceedings of IEEE GLOBECOM 2011, pp. 1–6 (2011)
16. Yang, H., Li, D., Zhu, Q., Chen, W., Hong, Y.: Minimum energy cost k-barrier coverage in wireless sensor networks. In: Pandurangan, G., Anil Kumar, V.S., Ming, G., Liu, Y., Li, Y. (eds.) WASA 2010. LNCS, vol. 6221, pp. 80–89. Springer, Heidelberg (2010)

ULRAS: Ultra-Lightweight RFID Authentication Scheme for Mobile Device

Kai Fan[1(✉)], Nan Ge[1], Yuanyuan Gong[1], Hui Li[1], Ruidan Su[2], and Yintang Yang[3]

[1] State Key Laboratory of Integrated Service Networks,
Xidian University, Xi'an 710071, China
{kfan, lihui}@mail.xidian.edu.cn, lbxxgn@126.com,
gyy890922@qq.com
[2] School of Computer Science and Technology,
Xidian University, Xi'an 710071, China
surd007@163.com
[3] Key Lab. of Minist. of Educ. for Wide Band-Gap Semicon.
Materials and Devices, Xidian University, Xi'an 710071, China
ytyang@xidian.edu.cn

Abstract. RFID is widely used on mobile devices and makes it possible to take advantage of RFID system to complete mobile payment or merchandise information reading. However, the widespread use of RFID tags brings the possibility for various security risks and privacy problems. In addition, the storage space, processing capability and power supply of RFID tags are limited. In this paper, in order to reduce the computational cost we present an ultra-lightweight RFID authentication scheme, named ULRAS. ULRAS only uses Bit and XOR operations to prevent the DDOS attack. ULRAS uses sub-key and sub-index number into its key update process to achieve the forward security. Compared to the SASI protocol and the Gossamer protocol, ULRAS cost less computation and communication resources and have stronger security.

Keywords: Ultra-lightweight · RFID · Authentication · Sub-key · Timestamp

1 Introduction

With the development of mobile devices and the growing popularity of mobile devices, people want to meet people's requirements of daily life through apply mobile devices. For example, people can use the mobile device to identify a product, animal or person through radio signals [1]. RFID (Radio Frequency Identification) is one of the most important technologies of mobile devices, which could make the mobile device meet above mentioned requirements. RFID is an Automatic Identification and Data Capture (AIDC) technology, which can provide read/write capability (barcodes are read only) and does not require line-of-sight contact with reader. Although RFID has many advantages, but the wireless channel between readers and tags are not secure and fixed which make RFID system face many security threats, such as anyone can read RFID information and the attacker can spoof a legitimate tag reader to obtain information of

© Springer International Publishing Switzerland 2015
K. Xu and J. Zhu (Eds.): WASA 2015, LNCS 9204, pp. 114–122, 2015.
DOI: 10.1007/978-3-319-21837-3_12

tags. Therefore, the security has become one of the key issues to be addressed for RFID to be widely used.

So far, some security authentication schemes for RFID are presented. For example, a key sharing mechanism based zero-knowledge authentication protocol proposed by Engberg et al. [2], a challenge-response authentication protocol presented by Keunwoo et al. [3], a security layer authentication protocol based on the AES algorithm designed by Feldhofer et al. [4] and re-encryption mechanism based authentication protocol presented by Junichiro et al. [5]. While these schemes mentioned above to a certain extent can resolve some security issues, but because of the low-cost tags have limited storage space and computing capability which make the traditional encryption algorithm and authentication mechanism cannot be applied directly in RFID systems. Therefore, these schemes are not good for widespread using of low-cost RFID systems which used on mobile devices.

Currently there is a class authentication protocol designed for low-cost RFID sys-tem, namely ultra-lightweight RFID authentication protocol, which uses some of the more simple logic bit operation to replace the more complex hash computation and other cryptographic operations, thereby greatly reducing the computational complexity of the protocol. These logical bit operations include: AND, OR, NOT, XOR and shift operation. Typical ultra-lightweight protocol includes SASI protocol [6] and Gossamer protocol [7]. The SASI protocol satisfy the requirement of mutual authentication, data integrity, tags anonymous and forward security requirements, but do not very well resisting unsynchronized attacks and do not have any ability to resist DOS attacks [8]. The Gossamer protocol can effectively prevent replay and forgery attack, and could provide a good anonymous functions. However, the Gossamer protocol cannot resist the unsynchronized attack effectively and have little anti-Dos ability [9]. So these protocols cannot meet the security requirements of the RFID scheme.

To resolve the above problems, we present a new ultra-lightweight RFID scheme, named ULRAS, in this paper which consume less computing and storage resources and could meet requirements of forward security, mutual authentication, synchronization and non-denial of service. ULRAS makes use of sub-key [10] and timestamp to achieve the forward security and resist replay attack [11].

The rest of the paper is organized as follows. In Sect. 2, security requirements of RFID authentication are provided. In Sect. 3, ULRAS is proposed and describe the scheme process in detail. In Sect. 4, the performance of ULRAS is evaluated in terms of security and efficiency. Finally, concluding remarks are provided in Sect. 5.

2 Security Requirements of RFID Authentication

When we were designing a secure RFID authentication protocol, we need to consider a wide range of security requirements, which include data confidentiality, integrity, availability, authenticity, privacy etc. In addition, a secure RFID protocol also needs as much as possible to meet the following security requirements:

1. Non-Tracking.

If we want to protect the tag owner's personal privacy and other sensitive information, you need to ensure that the output data for each tag is indistinguishable, and the attacker cannot gain any useful information to distinguish from the interactive data of tags between the two sides. And the attacker cannot speculate the information about the next session according the data obtained from this session. Successfully tracking tags will make the privacy and the personal location information of the label holders are disclosed to the attacker, which is not conducive to the protection of personal privacy and security. Therefore, the protocol should ensure that the tag cannot be tracked.

2. Distinguishability.

For multi-tag RFID systems, the responses of different tag should be distinguishable for the licensing server at the same time, which means the legitimate servers can distinguish the output corresponding to which tag exactly after the successful certification. But it need to ensure that the output information of the tag to the attacker should be indistinguishable, which means that the attacker cannot use this information to identify the corresponding tag successfully.

3. Forward Security.

The transmitted information should be protected. Furthermore, even if the system is attacked, the messages transmitted in the past are still secure. For RFID systems, it is particularly important that ensuring forward security and it is conducive to the protection of personal privacy and national secrets.

4. Backward Security.

Even if the attacker get all the information of before session in some way that he cannot infer the next communication information according to the obtained information. The requirement of backward security can resist replay attack effetely.

5. Synchronization.

The protocol should ensure the system synchronization by updating the shared information between the database and the tag, in order to ensure the legal tag's authentication in the next session.

3 Ultra-Lightweight RFID Authentication Scheme for Mobile Device

In this section, we will propose ULRAS and basic ideas are as follows: the scheme only with a simple shift and XOR operations, greatly reducing the cost of operations. And it uses the concept of timestamp, thus improving the system of forward security. And the scheme uses the concept of sub-keys, making the key update only needs to update some parts of the keys.

3.1   Initialization

The explanations of symbols are as follows:

IDS_{old}: The index number used last time.

IDS_{new}: The index number of the successful use this time.

K: The key of the tag, which is divided into four parts and each part indexed by i_{sub}.

K_{old}: The key of the tag that successful used in the last round session.

K_{new}: The key of the tag used in this session.

$K(i_{sub})$: The old sub-key indexed by i_{sub}.

i_{sub}: The sub-index number.

T_R: The random time-stamp generated by the reader.

T_t: The last time time-stamp.

R_t: The random number generated tag.

$Rot(x, y)$: Shift operation $H(ID_i)$, which the K_i^{old} is the hamming weight of y.

In this scheme, the necessary information (IDS, ID, K, T_t) should be stored in each tag, in the same $(ID, (IDS_{old}, K_{old}), (IDS_{new}, K_{new}))$ should be stored in the server corresponding each tag.

3.2   The Authentication Process

The authentication process of ULRAS is shown as Fig. 1.

The authentication process of ULRAS is as follows:

Step1: The reader generates the random time-stamp T_R, and sends authentication query $Query$ and T_R to the tag.

Step2: The tag judges whether $T_R > T_t$, if T_R is not larger than T_t, the authentication is failed. Otherwise, the tag generates the random number R_t, and calculates $M_1 = Rot(Rot(ID \oplus K \oplus R_t \oplus T_R, ID + R_t), K \oplus R_t)$, and then sends IDS, M_1 and R_t to the reader.

Step3: The reader will find the equal value in database according to IDS firstly, if it can find the corresponding value in the database, the database will calculate M_1' through $M_1' = Rot(Rot(ID \oplus K \oplus R_t \oplus T_R, ID \oplus R_t), K \oplus R_t)$ which using the founded value $IDS = IDS_{old}$ or $IDS = IDS_{new}$, and judge whether $M_1 = M_1'$. If the equation is equivalent, the authentication is successful.

Step4: The database calculates $M_2 = Rot(Rot(ID \oplus R_t \oplus T_R, ID \oplus R_t), K + R_t)$ and generates the random index number $i_{sub} \in \{1, 2, 3, 4\}$, and calculates M_3 according to $M_3 = Rot(i_{sub} \oplus K, K \oplus R_t \oplus T_R)$ by $i_{sub} \in \{1, 2, 3, 4\}$.

Step5: M_2 and M_3 will be sent to the tag. At the same time, the database performs the refresh operation. In this operation, the entity will generate a new sub-key by $subkey = Rot(K(i_{sub}), K \oplus R_t \oplus T_R)$. If $IDS = IDS_{old}$, then the entity just need to update K_{new} and IDS_{new} where $IDS_{new} = Rot(IDS \oplus R_t, K \oplus R_t \oplus T_R)$, and K_{new} should be updated to the new key K which can be generated by replacing $K(i_{sub})$ with the sub-key. If it was found that $IDS = IDS_{new}$ before, it should update $IDS_{old} = IDS_{new}$ and $K_{old} = K_{new}$ firstly, and then performs IDS_{new} and K_{new} with the same operation as described above.

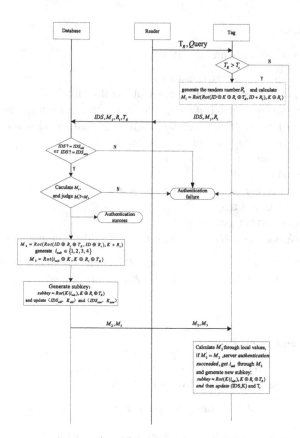

Fig. 1. Authentication process of ULRAS

Step6: After the tag receives M_2 and M_3, the tag should calculate M'_2 using its stored value, and judge $M'_2 = M_2$. If $M'_2 = M_2$, the database authentication is successful, and then get i_{sub} from M_3 and calculates sub-key by $subkey = Rot(K(i_{sub}), K \oplus R_t \oplus T_R)$.
Step7: The K will be updated to the new value which can be generated by replacing $K(i_{sub})$ with the sub-key, and let $T_t = T_R$.

4 Evaluation

4.1 Security Analysis

ULRAS is able to resist the common RFID attacks effectively. Especially,through introduce the thought of the sub-key and the sub-index number into the key update process that further improve the scheme forward security. And it makes the scheme have the anti-DOS attack capability through using the timestamp.

1. Mutual Authentication.

ULRAS could make the database authenticates the tag by M_1, and make the tag authenticates the database by M_1. In this way, we can achieve mutual authentication.

2. Non-eavesdropping.

For each query of reader the tag's response message is different, so that the attacker is not able to track the tag according to a specific output. ULRAS has the ability to resist an attacker to track.

3. Non-spoofing.

To the attacker who want to counterfeit the tag, even if he could get message (IDS, M_1, R_t) before but each of (IDS, M_1, R_t) is different. Furthermore, the generation of M_1 each time is different which need to rely on the private information (ID, K) of the tag. The attacker does not know this private information, so it is hard for him to disguise a message which could pass the authentication by the database. Likewise, the tracker cannot disguise valid M_2 which could pass the authentication by the tag. For this reason, ULRAS can against disguising attack effectively.

4. Non-replaying.

Although the attacker can obtain all the exchanging information which generated before. However, due to is the function about the time-stamp and the random number R_t, so that the value of is different on each session. Therefore, the attacker cannot disguise information before to achieve legality certification.

5. Forward Security.

After each successful session, the key value should be updated using different and R_t each time in both the tag and the database. So even if the attacker achieves some information used, he cannot base on this information to trace back to the communication before. In addition, ULRAS makes the sub-key and the sub-index number throughout the entire update process. A part of the k should be updated randomly in each time, which makes the entire update process have stronger stochastic properties. So ULRAS is forward security.

6. Non-denial of Service (Non-DoS).

When the reader start to a new query, the tag will judge whether $T_R > T_t$ firstly. If, the authentication is failed. Only if the operation used for authentication will continue. Compared with most schemes which responding to all the query, ULRAS can reduce the number of denial of service attacks to a certain extent and prevent unauthorized reader continue to send queries consumed lots of resources of tag. Therefore, this scheme can effective against denial of service attacks in some cases.

The comparison between ULRAS, SASI and Gossamer in security is shown in Table 1.

From Table 1, we can find that neither of SASI and Gossamer can prevent synchronicity attacks and Dos attacks. However, ULRAS can prevent synchronicity

Table 1. The security comparsion

Scheme	SASI	Gossamer	ULRAS
Mutual authentication.	√	√	√
Non-eavesdropping.	√	√	√
Non-spoofing.	√	√	√
Non-replaying	√	√	√
Forward security	√	√	√
Synchronization	×	×	√
Non-DoS	×	×	*

(×: not secure, √: secure)

attacks effectively and prevent Dos attacks to some extent. Conclusively, ULRAS improves the safety.

7. Synchronization.

In a normal session, if the tracker head off the last message which sends to the tag, the database cannot be successfully verified. In this case, the database has been updated successfully, but the tag cannot be updated. So the tag and the database will lose the synchronization. However, the (IDS, K) used in the last session is stored in (IDS_{old}, K_{old}) in the database, so that this tag is still able to pass the certification and get the synchronization.

4.2   Performance Analysis

We will compare ULRAS with SASI and Gossamer in performance. In order to compare easily, assumes there are m tags in the system and the length of data is L.

1. The Cost of Storage.

To SASI, $(ID, (IDS_{new}, K_{1new}, K_{2new})(IDS_{old}, K_{1old}, K_{2old}))$ are stored in tag, therefore the cost of storage space in the tag is 7L. (ID, IDS, K_1, K_2) are stored in the database. The cost of storage space it needs in the database is 4 mL. By the same method, we can get the cost of storage space in the tag is 7L and the cost of storage space in the database is 4 mL in Gossamer. But in ULRAS, the cost of storage space in the tag is 4L and the cost of storage space in the database is 5 mL.

Comparing these three schemes in storage in Table 2, the source of the reader and of the database is unlimited usually. Compare to the tag, the reader and the database have enough storage capacity, but the storage capacity of tag is limited. Thus we pay more attention to the cost of storage space in the tag. From Table 2, we can find the tag need smaller storage space in ULRAS, reduce the cost of storage space in the tag and increase little cost of storage space in the database. Therefore, this scheme is more suitable for low-cost RFID system.

Table 2. Storage overhead comparsion

Scheme	SASI	Gossamer	ULRAS
Database	4 mL	4 mL	5 mL
Reader	0	0	0
Tag	7L	7L	4L

2. The Cost of Computation Time.

Here + is the number of and operation, Rot is the number of displacement operation, Rot^2 is the number of displacement operation of twice, MIXBITS is the number of MIXBITS operation. Because of these three schemes use displacement operation, the computation cost of these three schemes is similar, and the computing capability is stronger both in database and reader. Therefore, we only should care about the computational overhead of resource-constrained tag.

From Table 3, one random number generation in the tag is needed in ULRAS. There are some displacement operation in the tag is needed in SASI and Gossamer, therefore ULRAS need more computation cost in the tag compared to SASI and Gossamer. But ULRAS just add a random number generation, so the computation is also very effective.

4.3 The Cost of Communication

The cost of communication include the number of communication times and the length of the communication data. When we designed ULRAS, as long as one of these two kinds of communication cost could be reduced that can be seen as reducing the communication overhead.

From Table 4, we can see that the protocol just need communication three times to complete the authenticate process between the tag and the server. Therefore, ULRAS has a relatively low communication overhead.

Table 3. Computation cost comparison

Scheme	SASI	Gossamer	ULRAS
Cost	$\oplus, +, \wedge, \vee, Rot$	$\oplus, +, Rot^2, MIXBITS$	$T_R, \oplus, +, Rot^2$

Table 4. Communication cost comparison

Scheme	SASI	Gossamer	ULRAS
Times	4	4	3
Cost	6L	6L	6L

5   Conclusions

ULRAS combines the simple logical cryptographic operations with the time stamp, so it can resist on Dos-attack. ULRAS uses sub-key and sub-index in entire key update process. To each update process, ULRAS just need to randomly update the part of the key K, which makes the update process have stronger random characteristics. This approach significantly increases the difficulty for the attacker to associate with two sessions, so that ULRAS can effectively improve the forward security. Comparing to SASI and Gossamer, ULRAS ensure that increased computational overhead in tag is not too much, and reduces the storage costs and communication costs, and provide the higher security. Therefore, ULRAS is more suitable for low-cost RFID systems in mobile devices.

Acknowledgment. This work has been financially supported by the National Natural Science Foundation of China (No. 61303216 and No. 61373172), the China Postdoctoral Science Foundation funded project (No.2013M542328), and National 111 Program of China B08038.

References

1. Juels, A.: RFID security and privacy: a research survey. IEEE J. Sel. Areas Commun. **24**(2), 381–394 (2006)
2. Engberg, S.J., Harning, M.B., Jensen, C.D.: Zero-knowledge device authentication: privacy and security enhanced RFID preserving business value and consumer convenience. In: Proceedings of PST 2004, pp. 89–101 2004
3. Rhee, K., Kwak, J., Kim, S., Won, D.H.: Challenge-Response based rfid authentication protocol for distributed database environment. In: Hutter, D., Ullmann, M. (eds.) SPC 2005. LNCS, vol. 3450, pp. 70–84. Springer, Heidelberg (2005)
4. Feldhofer, M.: An authentication protocol in a security layer for RFID smart tags. In: Proceedings of MEC 2004, pp. 59–762 (2004)
5. Saito, J., Sakurai, K.: Grouping proof for RFID tags. Adv. Inf. Networking Appl. **2**, 621–624 (2005)
6. Chien, H.Y.: SASI: a new ultralightweight RFID authentication protocol providing strong authentication and strong integrity. IEEE Trans. Dependable Secure Comput. **4**, 337–340 (2007)
7. Peris-Lopez, P., Hernandez-Castro, J.C., Tapiador, J.M., Ribagorda, A.: Advances in ultralightweight cryptography for low-cost RFID tags: gossamer protocol. In: Chung, K.-I., Sohn, K., Yung, M. (eds.) WISA 2008. LNCS, vol. 5379, pp. 56–68. Springer, Heidelberg (2009)
8. Cao, T., Bertino, E., Lei, H.: Security analysis of the SASI protocol. Dependable Secure Comput. **6**(1), 73–77 (2009)
9. Bilal, Z., Masood, A., Kausar, F.: Security analysis of ultra-lightweight cryptographic protocol for low-cost RFID tags: gossamer protocol. In: Proceedings of NIS 2009, pp. 260–267 (2009)
10. YA-TRAP, T.G.: Yet another trivial RFID authentication protocol. In: Proceedings of PerCom 2006, pp. 632–643 (2006)
11. Khan, G.N., Zhu, G.: Secure RFID authentication protocol with key updating technique. In: Proceedings of ICCCN 2013, pp. 1–5 (2013)

Soft Reservation Based Prioritized Access: Towards Performance Enhancement for VoIP over WLANs

Bing Feng[1]([✉]), Zhen Wang[1], Chi Zhang[1], Nenghai Yu[1], and Yuguang Fang[2]

[1] Key Laboratory of Electromagnetic Space Information,
Chinese Academy of Sciences, University of Science and Technology of China,
Hefei, China
{fengice,wang1992}@mail.ustc.edu.cn, {chizhang,ynh}@ustc.edu.cn
[2] Department of Electrical and Computer Engineering, University of Florida,
Gainesville, FL, USA
fang@ece.ufl.edu

Abstract. In this paper, we propose a novel scheme for VoIP over WLANs, referred to as SRPA (Soft Reservation based Prioritized Access). To fully exploit the on/off characteristics of conversational speech to improve the VoIP capacity, SRPA adopts soft reservation where the reserved channel resources of voice users in silence periods can be released to support more backlogged voice users in talking periods. SRPA completely separates admitted voice users from new voice users, and the admitted voice users are given higher priority access to the channel, based on the fact that maintaining the QoS requirements of admitted voice calls is more important than admitting new voice calls. The dedicated contention period for admitted voice users is contention backoff window whose size is dynamically adjusted on the basis of estimation of the number of contending voice users. In addition, a two-state Markov model is derived for the proposed scheme to analyze the VoIP capacity. Both analysis and simulation results demonstrate that SRPA significantly improves the VoIP capacity while guaranteeing the strict QoS requirements of admitted voice calls in WLANs.

Keywords: Soft reservation · Hybrid MAC · QoS · VoIP · WLANs

1 Introduction

The real-time Voice over WLAN (VoWLAN) services need strict QoS requirements. The Medium Access Control (MAC) schemes play a significant role in

This work was supported in part by the Program for New Century Excellent Talents in University of China under Grant NCET-13-0548, by the Innovation Foundation of the Chinese Academy of Sciences under Grand CXJJ-14-S132, by the Fundamental Research Funds for the Central Universities of China, and by the Natural Science Foundation of China (NSFC) under Grants 61202140 and 61328208. The work of Y. Fang was partially supported by US National Science Foundation under Grant CNS-1343356.

K. Xu and J. Zhu (Eds.): WASA 2015, LNCS 9204, pp. 123–133, 2015.
DOI: 10.1007/978-3-319-21837-3_13

supporting QoS, and most of them can be divided into either contention-free or contention-based approach. In legacy IEEE 802.11 standard that is originally designed to support best-effort traffic, there are two access mechanisms including Distributed Coordinate Function (DCF) and Point Coordination Function (PCF). To enhance the support of QoS in WALNs, the Hybrid Coordination Function (HCF) for MAC is introduced in the new IEEE 802.11e standard including Enhanced Distributed Channel Access (EDCA) and HCF Controlled Channel Access (HCCA). However, due to the contention nature, the contention-based schemes such as DCF and EDCA have limited VoIP capacity [1,2]. When the traffic load of voice users increases, the QoS cannot be guaranteed due to the frequent collisions.

On the other hand, the contention-free protocols such as polling-based PCF and HCCA can provide collision-free transmissions and do support strict QoS for real-time services. The HCCA is an extension of PCF with QoS mechanisms. However, the HCCA adopts hard reservation. It is assumed that the polled user still has packets to transmit. Thus, once a voice user is added to the polling list, the Access Point (AP) will poll it in subsequent cycles until the whole call ends [3]. It is noted that the VoIP service is different from other real-time services. Usually, In normal conversation, when one voice user is talking, the other one is silent. Thus, a voice user does not keep talking in the whole call. Generally, voice traffic is modelled as a two-state Markov process with alternating talkspurt (on) and silence (off) states [4]. The existence of voice user with no packets to transmit during silence periods leads to the null-polling overhead that decreases the utilization of channel resources. Thus, the challenge that still needs to be tackled is how to increase the VoIP capacity in HCCA.

In this paper, with minor modifications to the IEEE 802.11e, we propose SRPA (Soft Reservation based Prioritized Access) scheme. The contributions of the proposed SRPA scheme are listed as follows. First, SRPA adopts soft reservation where the channel resources not used by silence voice users can be used by other active voice users. When admitted voice users change state from silence to talkspurt, the first voice packet of a talkspurt needs to contend for the channel. Once the transmission is successful, the AP will poll this admitted voice user in subsequent cycles for the transmission of the whole talkspurt. Then when the current talkspurt ends, the admitted voice user is removed from the polling list. Thus, SRPA exploits silence suppression to increase VoIP capacity by statistical multiplexing among on/off voice calls. Second, different from previously proposed schemes [5–7] that mainly focus on how to protect real-time voice traffic from best-effort data traffic so that the admitted voice users are mixed up with new voice users to contend for the channel with same access priority during the same contention period, SRPA differentiates admitted voice calls from new voice calls based on the fact that, from the voice users perspective, degrading the QoS of admitted voice users is more annoying than blocking of new voice calls. In previous schemes [5–7], under heavy traffic of new voice users, the voice packet collision probability increases and admitted voice users encounter delay in gaining access to channel. The real-time voice services discard the delayed packets, which degrades the QoS of VoIP and even leads to user quitting the ongoing voice call. In SRPA, we provide deterministically prioritized access to admitted voice users and only statistically prioritized access to new (unadmitted) voice users. To guarantee the deterministic priority, a contention period that is contention backoff window is exclusively used by the admitted voice users, and to keep the collision probability for contending admitted voice users below a certain threshold, the contention window size is dynamically adjusted based on the estimation of the number of contending voice users.

The rest of this paper is organized as follows. In Sect. 2, we present the proposed MAC scheme and the performance analysis is provided in Sect. 3. Section 4 presents the numerical and simulation results, followed by the conclusions in Sect. 5.

2   Protocol Design of SRPA

2.1   Basic Description of SRPA

The centralized MAC scheme SRPA adopts the basic structure of the IEEE 802.11e HCF. The beacon frames transmitted by the AP divide time into repeating Service Intervals (SI) including a contention-period (CP) where a contention-based scheme is used, and a contention-free period (CFP) where the contention-free transmissions can be provided by the polling-based HCCA. During CP, a novel structure is used in SRPA while the IEEE 802.11e HCF adopts EDCA.

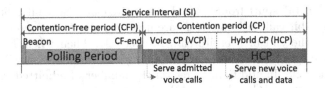

Fig. 1. The structure of a service interval in SRPA.

As shown in Fig. 1, during the CP, the dedicated voice contention period (VCP) is used to serve admitted voice users. The VCP is ahead of hybrid contention period (HCP), which guarantees deterministic priority to admitted voice users. During HCP, both new (unadmitted) voice users and best-effort data traffic are served. A complete separation between admitted voice users and other services guarantees that the performance of admitted voice users will not be affected by new voice users and best-effort datat traffic. Note that only after some voice users are admitted into the network, the VCP exists. In other words, initially, CP only contains the HCP. The 802.11e EDCA is used during HCP. As in EDCA, the new voice service and data traffic have different values for the channel access parameters. Thus, the new voice users only get statistical priority access to the channel during HCP, which guarantees that the voice traffic does not occupy the entire bandwidth. It is emphasized that the voice contention period VCP is backoff contention window whose size is variable in every cycle, and contending admitted voice users choose backoff counters from the dedicated backoff contention window.

In a SI, The broadcast CF-end frame piggybacks voice contention window size CW_v for VCP. When admitted voice users in silence state begin talkspurts, they need to access the channel by contention and they should defer their access until the arrival of the CF-end frame to get the latest CW_v to execute contention backoff using backoff counters randomly selected within $[0, CW_v - 1]$ during VCP. The other services utilize the residual bandwidth left by admitted voice users. Thus, after receiving the broadcast CF-end frame, both unadmitted voice users and best-effort data users first need to set their backoff counters to CW_v so that they do not access to the channel during VCP. Then when the backoff counters reach zero due to the backoff counter count-down procedure, they enter the hybrid contention period and contend for the channel by the legacy EDCA with new backoff counters and binary exponential backoff scheme. As in 802.11e, to avoid the stretch of SI, if the end of a transmission is behind of the nominal start of the next beacon frame, the user does not transmit during HCP.

In SRPA, the standard CSMA/CA scheme is used during VCP, and every contending admitted voice uer executes the backoff procedure. The binary exponential backoff scheme used in 802.11 standard is not used for contending admitted voice users during the VCP. Every contending admitted voice user only accesses to channel once during every cycle. After its access, it will wait for the next broadcast CF-end frame to start the next channel access.

The MAC header of a frame includes two indicators that differentiate the end of a current talkspurt from the end of a entire call. The 1-bit talk indicator (TI) and the 1-bit call indicator (CI) are used to indicate the end of a current talkspurt and the end of a entire call, respectively. Then when $TI = 1$, the admitted voice user is removed from the polling list. Otherwise, it will be polled again in next cycle. In addition, to record the number of admitted voice users, a admission counter (AC) is kept in AP. Then when the AP admits a new voice user, it increases AC by one. When a admitted voice user ends its entire call, i.e., $CI = 1$, the AC is decreased by one.

2.2   Dynamic Adjustment of Contention Window for Admitted Voice Calls

In SRPA, the dedicated voice contention window size for admitted voice users during VCP should be adaptively adjusted based on the current estimation of the number of contending admitted voice users in the network.

Based on the speech activity dector, it is found that a conversation speech follows an alternating pattern of silence and talkspurt periods. In SRPA, we adopt the two-state voice traffic model presented in [10]. During the model, the alternating talkspurt (on) and silence (off) periods are exponentially distributed. Let t_1 and t_2 denote the mean duration of a silence period and a talkspurt period, respectively. After duration T, the probability that a admitted voice user transits from silence state to talkspurt state is $\alpha = 1 - e^{-T/t_1}$, and the probability that a admitted voice user in talkspurt state transmits to silence state is $\beta = 1 - e^{-T/t_2}$.

There are three types of states for a admitted voice user: silence state, reservation state, and contention state. Initially, a admitted voice user is in reservation state. If it does not complete the current talkspurt, it remains in reservation state to transmit the rest voice packets of current talkspurt (transition $T_{r,r}$). Otherwise, it turns to silence state due to the end of current talkspurt (transition $T_{r,s}$). Then when a admitted voice user in silence state has no voice packets to transmit, it remains in silence state (transition $T_{s,s}$). Otherwise, if it begins a new talkspurt, it enters contention state (transition $T_{s,c}$). When its contention transmission is successful, it passes into reservation state and is added to the polling list (transition $T_{c,r}$). However, if the new talkspurt ends before a successful transmission that is served as a reservation for the rest of voice packets, the contention voice user returns to silence state (transition $T_{c,s}$). If the new talkspurt does not end and the reservation has not been made successfully, it remains in contention state (transition $T_{c,c}$).

At the beginning of cycle k, the number of admitted voice users is N_k. Let S_k, C_k, and R_k be the number of admitted voice users in silence, contention, and reservation state during cycle k, respectively. Clearly, $N_k = S_k + C_k + R_k$. Then, at the beginning of cycle $k + 1$ and just after the end of cycle k, we have $N_{k+1} = N_k - D_k + A_k$, where D_k is the number of admitted voice users whose calls terminate during cycle k, and A_k is the number of voice users that are newly admitted through admission control scheme during cycle k. Note that the value N_{k+1} is know to the AP due to the defined admission counter AC.

Let $N_{c,s}^k$, $N_{c,r}^k$, $N_{r,s}^k$, and $N_{s,c}^k$ denote the number of admitted voice users corresponding to the transitions $T_{c,s}$, $T_{c,r}$, $T_{r,s}$, and $T_{s,c}$ during cycle k, respectively. Then we have

$$S_{k+1} = S_k + N_{c,s}^k + N_{r,s}^k - N_{s,c}^k$$
$$C_{k+1} = C_k - N_{c,s}^k - N_{c,r}^k + N_{s,c}^k. \tag{1}$$

Note that the values S_k and C_k are estimated values, but R_k is the actual value that is equal to the number of admitted voice users in the polling list. Based on the estimated values C_{k+1} and S_{k+1}, the AP estimates $\hat{C}_{k+1}$ that the number of admitted voice users that will access to the channel by contention during VCP in cycle $k + 1$, and $\hat{C}_{k+1} = C_{k+1} - N_{c,s}^{k+1} + N_{s,c}^{k+1}$, where $N_{c,s}^{k+1}$ and $N_{s,c}^{k+1}$ should be estimated at the beginning of cycle $k+1$. According to the voice traffic model, when there are C_{k+1} admitted voice users in contention state and S_{k+1} admitted voice users in silence state, the AP can get $N_{c,s}^{k+1}$ and $N_{s,c}^{k+1}$ by $C_{k+1} \cdot \beta$ and $S_{k+1} \cdot \alpha$, respectively.

During cycle $k + 1$, the failure probability of channel access is defined as the ratio of the total number of unsuccessful transmissions to the number of admitted voice users that contend for the channel during VCP, i.e.,

$$P_f = \frac{\hat{C}_{k+1} - CW_v[k+1] \cdot P_{suc}}{\hat{C}_{k+1}} \tag{2}$$

where $CW_v[k+1] \cdot P_{suc}$ represents the number of successful transmissions, $CW_v[k+1]$ is the optimal contention window size for VCP during cycle $k+1$, and the probability P_{suc} is that a backoff counter within $[0, CW_v[k+1]-1]$ is selected by exactly one contending admitted voice user, i.e.,

$$P_{suc} = \binom{\hat{C}_{k+1}}{1} \left(\frac{1}{CW_v[k+1]}\right) \left(1 - \frac{1}{CW_v[k+1]}\right)^{\hat{C}_{k+1}-1}. \tag{3}$$

To keep the P_f below a target value, the equation $P_f = P_{tra}$ should be satisfied, where the targeted value of failure probability is P_{tra}. Then the approximate value of $CW_v[k+1]$ for VCP during cycle $k+1$ is obtained by

$$CW_v[k+1] = \left\lceil \frac{1}{1 - e^{\frac{\ln(1-P_{tra})}{\hat{C}_{k+1}-1}}} \right\rceil. \tag{4}$$

3   Performance Analysis

3.1   Analytical Model

In this part, we use a discrete Markov chain to describe the voice system with N_v admitted voice users. The system states can be obtained by observing the state changes at the beginning of every cycle. In this paper, the analytic model proposed in [8] for cellular systems is developed to analyze the performance of SRPA in WLANs. As $N_v = S_i + C_i + R_i$, the system state in cycle i can be denoted by $Z_i = (R_i, C_i)$. Then the system can be modeled as a two-dimensional Markov process $\{Z_i\}$. When the system is in steady-state Z_i, there are S_i, R_i, C_i admitted voice users in silence state, reservation state, and contention state, respectively. When the probability that the system enters the steady-state Z_i is π_i, we can get the stationary probability vector $\boldsymbol{\pi} = [\pi_0, \pi_1, ..., \pi_w]$. Note that the number of system states is finite, and the dimension of the system state space Ω is $w = |\{Z_i\}| = \sum_{l=0}^{N_v} N_v - l + 1 = \frac{1}{2}(N_v + 2)(N_v + 1)$, and the Ω is $\Omega = \{R_i, C_i | 0 \le R_i, C_i \le N_v, \text{and} \quad R_i + C_i \le N_v\}$.

According to $p_{i,j}$ that the probability of state transition from Z_i to Z_j, the state transition probability matrix is $\boldsymbol{P} = [p_{i,j}]_{w \times w}$. Then we need to construct the matrix $\boldsymbol{P}$. Based on (1), the $p_{i,j}$ is obtained by the distribution of $N_{s,c}$, $N_{c,r}$, $N_{r,s}$, and $N_{c,s}$. Then the $p_{i,j}$ is

$$\begin{aligned}
p_{i,j} =& Pr\{R_j = r_j, C_j = c_j | R_i = r_i, C_i = c_i\} \\
=& \sum_{u=0}^{c_i} \sum_{v=0}^{N_v - r_i - c_i} Pr\{N_{s,c} = v\} \cdot Pr\{N_{c,r} = u\} \\
& \cdot Pr\{N_{r,s} = r_i + u - r_j\} \\
& \cdot Pr\{N_{c,s} = c_i - u + v - c_j\}.
\end{aligned} \tag{5}$$

To simplify the notation, the binomial distribution probability is defined as

$$B(X, x, p) = \binom{X}{x}(p)^x(1 - p)^{X-x} \tag{6}$$

and the probability that N voice users randomly select backoff counters from M backoff counters and exactly r backoff counters are selected only by one voice users, is

$$\Gamma_M^N(r) = \sum_{z=r}^{N}(-1)^{z-r}\binom{N}{z}\binom{z}{r} \cdot \frac{(M)!(M-z)^{N-z}}{(M-z)!(M)^N}. \tag{7}$$

The different terms in (5) are obtained based on the voice traffic model. The probability that v among $N_v - r_i - c_i$ silence voice users begin talkspurts is $Pr\{N_{s,c} = v\} = B(N_v - r_i - c_i, v, \alpha)$ and the probability that c_i admitted voice users in contention state select random backoff counters from $CW_v[i]$ obtained by Eq. (4) backoff counters, and yield u backoff counters selected only by one voice users, is $Pr\{N_{c,r} = u\} = \Gamma_{CW_v[i]}^{c_i}(u)$, and the probability that $r_i + u - r_j$ among r_i reservation voice users return to silence state is $Pr\{N_{r,s} = r_i + u - r_j\} = B(r_i, r_i + u - r_j, \beta)$, as well as the probability that $c_i - u + v - c_j$ among $c_i - u$ contention voice users return to silence state is $Pr\{N_{c,s} = c_i - u + v - c_j\} = B(c_i - u, c_i - u + v - c_j, \beta)$.

After obtaining the matrix $\boldsymbol{P}$, we can get $\boldsymbol{\pi}$ based on the normalization equation $\sum_{m=0}^{w-1}\pi_m = 1$ and the matrix equation $\boldsymbol{\pi} = \boldsymbol{\pi P}$. In addition, the stationary distribution for the system variables C and R can be get by $p_C(l) = Pr\{C = l\} = \sum_{(c_m, r_m)\in\Omega, c_m = l}\pi_m$ and $p_R(l) = Pr\{R = l\} = \sum_{(c_m, r_m)\in\Omega, r_m = l}\pi_m$, respectively. Then we can obtain the expected values by $E[C] = \sum_{l=0}^{N_v}l \cdot p_C(l)$ and $E[R] = \sum_{l=0}^{N_v}l \cdot p_R(l)$.

3.2   System Performance

Give the service interval T_{SI}, the VoIP capacity, i.e., the maximum number of admitted voice users that can be supported in SRPA, is obtained.

The mean duration of the time for admitted voice users is $\overline{T}_{\text{ad-voice}}$. According to the $E[C]$ and $E[R]$, we get the following results:

$$\overline{T}_{\text{ad-voice}} = PIFS + T_B + E[R] \cdot \overline{T}_t + PIFS + T_{CF-end} + \overline{T}_{\text{VCP}} \tag{8}$$

where T_{CF-end} and T_B are the mean duration of a CF-end frame and a beacon frame, respectively. A mean polling transmission time is

$$\overline{T}_t = PIFS + T_{polling} + SIFS + T_H + T_{E[P]} + SIFS + ACK \tag{9}$$

where the mean duration of a voice packet payload is $T_{E[P]}$, the mean duration of a polling frame is $T_{polling}$, and the average duration of a frame header including MAC header and PHY header is T_H. The mean duration of VCP is

$$\overline{T}_{\text{VCP}} = CW_v \cdot (P_c \cdot T_c + P_s \cdot T_s + P_i \cdot \sigma) \tag{10}$$

where T_c and T_s denote the mean duration of a frame collision and a successful frame transmission during VCP, respectively. An idle time slot is σ and the mean air propagation delay is δ. Then we have

$$T_c = T_H + T_{E[P]} + DIFS + \delta$$
$$T_s = DIFS + T_H + T_{E[P]} + \delta + SIFS + ACK + \delta. \tag{11}$$

Based on Eq. (6), we obtain the success probability, idle probability, and collision probability by $P_s = B(E[C], 1, \tau)$, $P_i = B(E[C], 0, \tau)$, and $P_c = 1 - P_s - P_i$, respectively. Note that the probability that a contending admitted voice user randomly selects a backoff counter from CW_v backoff counters during VCP is $\tau = \frac{1}{CW_v}$.

Since the mean duration of $\overline{T}_{\text{ad-voice}}$ is limited by the T_{SI}, we obtain the VoIP capacity for SRPA scheme through the equality $\overline{T}_{\text{ad-voice}} = T_{SI}$.

Table 1. System parameters

Parameters	Value	Parameters	Value
SIFS	10 μs	DIFS	50 μs
PIFS	30 μs	Idle slot	20 μs
MAC header	34 bytes	PHY header	192 μs
Beacon frame	40 bytes	CF-end frame	20 bytes
Polling frame	36 bytes	ACK	14 bytes
Data frame rate	11 Mbps	Service interval	80 ms

4 Performance Evaluation

In this section, both analysis and simulation results are presented. The numerical result of VoIP capacity for proposed SRPA scheme is given based on a set of typical system parameters. Through the network simulator OPNET (version 14.5), we also get the simulation results to evaluate the system performances. The system parameters are summarized in Table 1. In our performance evaluations, we only consider about the uplink voice users, and the international standard for telephone audio [9] is used for voice source code. For the two-state voice traffic model, the mean durations of exponentially distributed silence period and exponentially distributed talkspurt period are 1.35 s and 1 s, respectively.

4.1 Numerical Results

Under the provided system parameters, the numerical result of the VoIP capacity for G.711 voice codec with different T_{sp} is shown in Table 2. In addition, we also show the corresponding results of HCCA scheme and HCCA+EDCF scheme (i.e., HCCA with multiplexing). From Table 2, it can be seen that, compared with other schemes, the proposed scheme SRPA significantly increases VoIP capacity. The performance improvement from statistical multiplexing is evaluated by comparison between HCCA and HCCA+EDCF. The performance improvement from the proposed adaptive voice contention window that is dedicated for contending admitted voice users is evaluated by comparison between SRPA and HCCA+EDCF. In addition, Table 2 also shows that more voice users can be supported when the sample period is enlarged.

Table 2. Comparison of the maximum number of VoIP connections.

Sample periods	10 ms	20 ms	30 ms	40 ms	50 ms
SRPA	34	63	94	116	143
HCCA+EDCF	29	51	76	95	118
HCCA (no multiplexing)	23	38	56	71	86

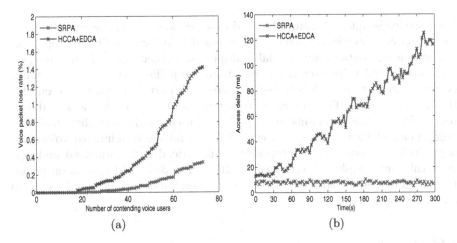

(a)   (b)

Fig. 2. Simulation results. (a) Voice packet loss rate versus the number of contending voice users. (b) Access delay of admitted voice users versus the simulation time.

4.2   Simulation Results

Figure 2(a) shows the simulation results of the voice packet loss rate. In the simulation, voice packets are considered as lost only when reaching the maximum delay bound. As we can see from Fig. 2(a), the voice packet loss rate increases with the number of contending voice users during VCP. When the number of contending voice user exceeds a certain value, the voice packet loss probability increases sharply. Since in HCCA+EDCF scheme, the EDCF only provides statical priority to admitted voice users, the contending admitted voice users need to take more time to access the channel, and the packet loss rate increases more quickly than SRPA. The proposed scheme SRPA guarantees the QoS of admitted voice users by adaptively adjusting the contention period so that the SRPA can support more voice users while satisfying the QoS requirement of voice packet loss probability.

To evaluate how new voice users and best-effort data traffic influence the performance of ongoing voice users, we conduct this simulation where the traffic arrival in the network are listed as follows: there are 10 best-effort data users in the network during the whole simulation time, and for every 30 seconds, 4 new voice users are added into the network. The simulation runs 300 seconds. Figure 2(b) shows the access delay of admitted voice users for both HCCA+EDCF and SRPA schemes. In SRPA, since the admitted voice users have the highest priority access to the channel, other services do not affect the access delay whose value is steady. But in HCCA+EDCF scheme, for admitted voice users, the access delay increases sharply and the fluctuation is large.

5 Conclusion

VoIP service is different from other real-time services due to the on/off characteristics of conversational speech. The proposed MAC scheme SRPA adopts soft reservation and obtains substantial multiplexing capacity gain. In soft reservation, a admitted voice user is removed from the polling list due to the end of current talkspurt, and when it begins a new talkspurt, it needs to contend for the channel and the first successful transmission of voice packet is served as a reservation for the remaining voice packets. Based on the fact that, from the user's point of view, degrading the QoS in the middle of admitted voice calls is generally not considered acceptable or user-friendly, the admitted and new voice calls are completely separated in SRPA. The dedicated contention period for contending admitted voice users is contention backoff window and its size is adaptively adjusted.

References

1. Shin, S., Schulzrinne, H.: Measurement and analysis of the voip capacity in IEEE 802.11 wlan. IEEE Trans. Mob. Comput. 8(9), 1265–1279 (2009)
2. Gao, D., Cai, J., Foh, C.H., Lau, C.T., Ngan, K.N.: Improving wlan voip capacity through service differentiation. IEEE Trans. Veh. Technol. 57(1), 465–474 (2008)
3. Stoeckigt, K.O., Vu, H.L.: Voip capacity analysis, improvements, and limits in IEEE 802.11 wireless LAN. IEEE Trans. Veh. Technol. 59(9), 4553–4563 (2010)
4. Wang, W., Liew, S.C., Li, V.O.: Solutions to performance problems in voip over a 802.11 wireless LAN. IEEE Trans. Veh. Technol. 54(1), 366–384 (2005)
5. Kawata, T., Shin, S., Forte, A.G., Schulzrinne, H.: Using dynamic pcf to improve the capacity for voip traffic in ieee 802.11 networks. In: Proc. IEEE International Conference on Wireless Communications and Networking Conference (WCNC 05). vol. 3, pp. 1589–1595 (2005)

6. Lam, R.Y., Leung, V.C., Chan, H.C.: Polling-based protocols for packet voice transport over ieee 802.11 wireless local area networks. Wireless Communications, IEEE 13(1), 22–29 (2006)
7. Wang, P., Jiang, H., Zhuang, W.: Ieee 802.11 e enhancement for voice service. Wireless Communications, IEEE 13(1), 30–35 (2006)
8. Jiang, S., Rao, J., He, D., Ling, X., Ko, C.C.: A simple distributed prma for manets. IEEE Trans. Veh. Technol. 51(2), 293–305 (2002)
9. Cai, L.X., Shen, X., Mark, J.W., Cai, L., Xiao, Y.: Voice capacity analysis of wlan with unbalanced traffic. IEEE Trans. Veh. Technol. 55(3), 752–761 (2006)
10. Narasimhan, P., Yates, R.D.: A new protocol for the integration of voice and data over prma. IEEE J. Sel. Areas Commun. 14(4), 623–631 (1996)

Impact of a Deterministic
Delay in the DCA Protocol

Li Feng[1], Jiguo Yu[2]$^{(\boxtimes)}$, Xiuzhen Cheng[3], and Shengling Wang[4]

[1] Faculty of Information Technology,
Macau University of Science and Technology, Macau, China
lfeng@must.edu.mo
[2] School of Information Science and Engineering,
Qufu Normal University, Rizhao 276826, Shandong, China
jiguoyu@sina.com
[3] Department of Computer Science,
The George Washington University, Washington, D.C., USA
cheng@gwu.edu
[4] College of Information Science and Technology,
Beijing Normal University, Beijing 100875, China
wangshengling@bnu.edu.cn

Abstract. The delayed channel access (DCA) protocol is an improved version of IEEE 802.11 DCF. In DCA, a node first waits for an extra delay before it enters the normal DCF procedure, so that more packets can be backlogged and transmitted upon each transmission opportunity. Therefore, DCA is of great practical importance in improving channel utilization. However, how the extra delay affects the performance of DCA has never been theoretically investigated. In this paper, we propose a theoretical model to characterize the impact of a deterministic extra delay on collision probability, throughput, and MAC delay. We find that the system performance is significantly affected by the relationship between the deterministic delay and the number of nodes and can be well predicted by our model. The extensive ns2 simulations verify that our model is very accurate.

Keywords: Wireless LAN · Delayed channel access · DCA · Performance

1 Introduction

IEEE 802.11-based wireless LANs (WLANs) [1] have been widely deployed. In 802.11 distributed coordination function (DCF), each node is limited to send at most one data packet upon each transmission opportunity. This limitation will badly lower channel utilization.Therefore, the delayed channel access (DCA)

This work is partially supported by the NNSF of China for contract 61373027 and NSF of Shandong Province for contract ZR2012FM023, Macao Science and Technology Development Fund under Grant (No. 013/2014/A1 and No. 104/2014/A3).

© Springer International Publishing Switzerland 2015
K. Xu and J. Zhu (Eds.): WASA 2015, LNCS 9204, pp. 134–144, 2015.
DOI: 10.1007/978-3-319-21837-3_14

protocol is proposed in [4]; the basic idea is that a node first waits for an extra random delay before it enters the normal DCF procedure so that more packets can be aggregated and transmitted upon each transmission opportunity, thereby improving channel utilization. The aggregation technology (i.e., many packets are packaged into a super-frame for one transmission) is a very promising technology and has been adopted by the latest 802.11ac [5,9]. The DCA protocol, which tries to answer how and when to aggregate these packets, is therefore worth studying further. However, to the best of our knowledge, all existing papers (such as [10]) investigated the performance of DCA only via simulation. In this paper, we first propose a theoretical model to study the impact of the extra random delay on the system performance.

To better understand the DCA protocol, this paper studies a special case of DCA (i.e., when the random delay is a deterministic constant) and we call it the delayed-DCF protocol. In the delayed-DCF, a node must wait for an extra deterministic delay before it enters the normal DCF procedure and transmits at most one packet upon each transmission opportunity. If the deterministic delay is set to zero, the delayed-DCF becomes the legacy DCF. Note that there is a distinct difference between the deterministic delay and the backoff time in the legacy DCF procedure: the former is independent of the channel status, while in the later, its timer may be suspended and resumed, depending on the channel status. This paper is devoted to proposing a theoretical model to characterize the impact of the non-zero deterministic delay on the collision probability, throughput, MAC delay mean, and MAC delay variance.

In this paper, we investigate the saturation performance of the delayed-DCF network, where each station always has a packet to transmit. We find that the system performance is significantly affected by the relationship between the deterministic delay d in microseconds (ms) and the number of nodes n. For example, the mean MAC access delay of each packet is almost equal to d ms when $d > n$, and is $O(n)$ ms otherwise. Our model well characterizes the impact of this relationship on the system performance. The extensive simulations verify that the proposed theoretical model is very accurate.

The rest of this paper is organized as follows. Section 2 outlines the DCF and delayed-DCF protocols. Section 3 proposes a theoretical model to evaluate the performance of the delayed-DCF protocol. Section 4 verifies the proposed theoretical model via ns2 simulation. Finally, Sect. 5 concludes this paper.

2   DCF and Delayed-DCF

2.1   IEEE 802.11 DCF Protocol

The IEEE 802.11 DCF [1] is based on carrier sense multiple access with collision avoidance (CSMA/CA). DCF has two channel access mechanisms: the mandatory basic access mechanism and the optional request to send/clear to send (RTS/CTS) access mechanism.

In this paper, we consider the basic access mode only. With the help of Fig. 1 (a), we now describe the main procedure used in the basic access mode.

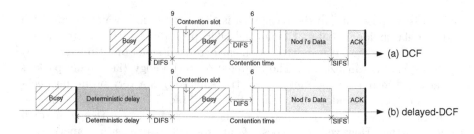

Fig. 1. Illustration of access modes for (a) DCF and (b) delayed-DCF.

Before transmitting a packet, a node must sense the channel for at least a DCF interframe space (DIFS). During the DIFS time, if the channel is sensed idle, the node may begin the transmission process; if the channel is sensed busy, the node will defer access and enter a contention period.

During the contention period, the node employs the binary exponential backoff (BEB) algorithm to resolve collisions. In the BEB algorithm, a node initially generates a random backoff time uniformly distributed in $[0, CW_{min} - 1]$, where CW_{min} is a given minimum CW size. Thereafter, the backoff counter decreases by one for each idle time slot and is suspended for each busy slot. The suspended backoff counter resumes after the channel is sensed idle for a DIFS period. When the backoff counter reaches zero, the node starts transmitting the head of line (HOL) packet at the beginning of the next time slot. For example, in Fig. 1 (a), node i first chooses a backoff time equal to 9 and starts counting down. When the backoff counter reduces to 6, node i suspends the counter because the channel is sensed busy and resumes the counter later after the channel is sensed idle for a DIFS period.

For each successful transmission, the sender will receive an acknowledgement (ACK) frame after a short interframe space (SIFS). If the node does not receive the ACK within a certain time (i.e., ACK timeout), it assumes that the data packet was not successfully received at the destination node and doubles the CW and repeats the above procedure. Doubling of the CW stops after the maximum window size CW_{max} is reached. When a retransmission limit is reached, the sender discards the data packet. Note that according to the 802.11 DCF protocol, two consecutive data packet transmissions of a node is separated by at least a random time uniformly distributed in $[0, CW_{min} - 1]$.

2.2 Delayed-DCF

Figure 1(b) illustrates the delayed-DCF. Like DCF, a node in delayed-DCF transmits at most one packet upon each transmission opportunity. However, unlike DCF, a node in delayed-DCF always waits for a deterministic delay (denoted by d in this paper) before entering the subsequent DCF procedure. A special case is that when the deterministic delay, d, is equal to 0, the delayed-DCF protocol becomes the legacy DCF protocol.

The delayed-DCF protocol actually adopts a mixed-type contention resolution method. One is the deterministic delay, which is independent of the channel status, and its counter is never suspended and will keep counting down once the counter is installed. The deterministic delay postpones the time that nodes contend for channel. Another is the backoff time, which is greatly affected by the channel status and therefore its counter will be suspended for a busy slot and resumed for subsequent idle slots. The backoff time increases as the contention becomes more intensive. The two types of delays objectively alleviate contention intensity.

This paper concerns the impact of the deterministic delay d on the performance of the subsequent DCF procedure, which is never investigated before.

3   Performance Analysis

In this section, we propose a theoretical model to evaluate the performance of the delayed-DCF protocol. We first analyze the collision probability that governs all other other performance metrics and then compute the throughput and the mean and variance of the MAC access delay.

We now introduce the terminologies and assumptions that we will use in our analysis: a packet transmission is said to be *finished* when the packet is either successfully received at the destination node or dropped due to reaching a retransmission limit; time is measured in MAC time slots unless explicitly indicated. Similar to [6], we assume that (1) all nodes are in saturation operation and reside in a single-cell network (i.e., all stations are in the sensing range of each other); (2) the collision processes of the nodes can be decoupled; and (3) channel conditions are ideal so that transmission errors are a result of packet collision only.

3.1   Analysis of the Collision Probability

This section characterizes the collision probability and the attempt rate, which are governed by a fixed-point system described below.

Let γ denote the collision probability experienced by a tagged node on the condition that the buffer is not empty. Let β denote the attempt rate of each node (i.e., the ratio of the number of attempts in a generic slot) on the condition that the buffer is not empty, where the generic slot represents the time elapsed for one decrement of the backoff counter. According to the decoupling assumption 2), the tagged node will experience a collision if at least one of the remaining $n - 1$ nodes transmits, where n ($n \geq 2$) is the number of contending nodes. Therefore, we can express γ in terms of β as follows:

$$\gamma = 1 - (1 - \beta)^{n-1}. \tag{1}$$

We now express β in terms of γ, following the approach in [6]. According to the BEB algorithm, a packet can undergo a maximum of M attempts, where each attempt is preceded by a backoff stage with a randomly selected backoff count η_k at stage k. The probability of $j + 1$ attempts, where $j = 0, \ldots, M - 1$, is given by

$$\delta(\gamma, j) = \begin{cases} (1 - \gamma)\gamma^j, & j = 0, \cdots, M - 2 \\ \gamma^{M-1}, & j = M - 1, \end{cases} \tag{2}$$

where the upper term on the right is the probability that the packet suffers j collisions before success, and the lower term is the probability of either $M - 1$ collisions before success or M collisions.

Let R and X be the number of attempts and the time (in generic slots) excluding DIFS, respectively, incurred by a packet transmission of the tagged node between when the node starts decreasing its deterministic delay and when its targeted packet transmission is finished. Then X includes two components: one is the number of the generic slots (denoted by ξ) elapsed during the deterministic delay d and another is the number of the generic slots elapsed after the deterministic delay and before the targeted packet transmission of the tagged node is finished. From (2), we have

$$R = j + 1, \text{ w.p. } \delta(\gamma, j), \, 0 \leq j \leq M - 1, \tag{3}$$

$$X - \xi = \sum_{k=0}^{j} \eta_k, \text{ w.p. } \delta(\gamma, j), \, 0 \leq j \leq M - 1,$$

where 'w.p.' means 'with probability'. In (3), η_k is uniformly distributed in $[0, CW_k - 1]$ with mean $\bar{\eta}_k \triangleq b_k = (CW_k - 1)/2$, where $CW_k = 2^k CW_0$ for $0 \leq k \leq m - 1$ and $CW_k = 2^m CW_0$ for $m \leq k \leq M - 1$; m determines the maximum backoff window size $CW_{\max}$ (i.e., $CW_{\max} = 2^m CW_0$) and CW_0 is the minimum window size. Let $\bar{R}$, $\bar{X}$ and $\bar{\xi}$ denote the mean of R, X and ξ, respectively. We have

$$\bar{R} = \sum_{j=0}^{M-1} (j + 1)\delta(\gamma, j) = 1 + \gamma + \cdots + \gamma^{M-1}, \tag{4}$$

$$\bar{X} = \bar{\xi} + \sum_{j=0}^{M-1} \sum_{k=0}^{j} b_k \delta(\gamma, j)$$

$$= \bar{\xi} + b_0 \delta(\gamma, 0) + \sum_{k=0}^{1} b_k \delta(\gamma, 1) + \cdots$$

$$= \bar{\xi} + b_0 + \gamma b_1 + \gamma^2 b_2 + \cdots + \gamma^{M-1} b_{M-1}.$$

We now calculate $\bar{\xi}$. Let Ω be the length of a generic slot and $\bar{\Omega}$ be the mean of Ω. According to the definition of ξ, we have

$$\bar{\xi} = \frac{d}{\bar{\Omega}} \tag{5}$$

and hence we only need to calculate $\bar{\Omega}$. The generic slot duration Ω depends on whether a slot is idle or interrupted by a successful transmission or a collision.

We then define Ω as

$$\Omega = \begin{cases} \sigma & w.p.\ 1 - P_b, \\ T_s + \sigma & w.p.\ P_s, \\ T_{\bar{s}} + \sigma & w.p.\ P_{\bar{s}}, \end{cases} \tag{6}$$

where

$$P_b = 1 - (1 - \beta)^n = 1 - (1 - \gamma)^{\frac{n}{n-1}}, \tag{7}$$

$$P_s = n\beta(1 - \beta)^{n-1} = n(1 - (1 - \gamma)^{\frac{1}{n-1}})(1 - \gamma),$$

$$P_{\bar{s}} = P_b - P_s,$$

denote the probability of a busy slot, the probability of a successful transmission from any of the n contending nodes, and the probability of an unsuccessful transmission from any of the n contending nodes, respectively; $\sigma = 1$ slot $= 20\ \mu s$; and T_s and $T_{\bar{s}}$ are the mean time for a successful transmission and an unsuccessful transmission, respectively. The parameters T_s and $T_{\bar{s}}$ depend on packet payload length, SIFS, DIFS, and other protocol parameters. Note that since the backoff counter must decrease one slot before the next decrease, to be strictly correct, we add one slot in each of the last two terms of Ω. From (6), we can calculate $\overline{\Omega}$ by

$$\overline{\Omega} = \sigma + P_s T_s + P_{\bar{s}} T_{\bar{s}}. \tag{8}$$

Now applying the renewal reward theory, we have $\beta = \frac{\overline{R}}{\overline{X}}$. From (4) and (5), β is given by

$$\beta = \frac{1 + \gamma + \cdots + \gamma^{M-1}}{\frac{d}{\overline{\Omega}} + b_0 + \gamma b_1 + \gamma^2 b_2 + \cdots + \gamma^{M-1} b_{M-1}}. \tag{9}$$

Note that when $d = 0$ in (9), β reduces to (1) in [6].

So far, we have expressed β in terms of γ in (9). Substituting β in (9) into (1), and solving the fixed-point equation with respect to γ, we can calculate the collision probability γ and then the attempt rate β.

3.2   Computation of Throughput and Delay

This section presents formulae for the throughput, and the mean and variance of the MAC access delay.

Throughput: For the per-node throughput, Γ, we adopt the expression derived in [3,6], namely

$$\Gamma = \frac{P_s}{n} \frac{L}{\overline{\Omega}}, \tag{10}$$

where L is the packet size in bits, $\frac{P_s}{n}$ is the per-node probability of a successful packet transmission.

Mean and variance of MAC access delay: We define the MAC access delay as the interval between when a packet enters the head-of-the-line of its queue and when the packet is successfully received at the destination node. Let D denote the MAC access delay and it consists of (1) the deterministic delay d, and (2) the random time interval D_1 between when the deterministic delay ends and when the packet is successfully received at the destination node.

Let $\overline{D}$ and $\overline{D}_1$ denote the mean of D and D_1, respectively. We have

$$\overline{D} = d + \overline{D}_1. \tag{11}$$

$\overline{D}_1$ can be calculated by (18) in [8] and is given as follows:

$$\overline{D}_1 = A_1 + B_1,$$
$$\text{where } A_1 = \frac{1 - \gamma}{(1 - \gamma^M)} \sum_{i=0}^{M-1} \gamma^i \{\theta_1 \sum_{k=0}^{i} \overline{\eta}_k + iT_{\overline{s}}\},$$
$$B_1 = T_s - T_{ACK},$$
$$T_{ACK} = \text{the transmission time of an ACK packet,}$$

where θ_1 is defined in (13).

Let $Var(D)$ denote the variance of D. We have

$$Var(D) = Var(D_1). \tag{12}$$

$Var(D_1)$ can be calculated by (19) in [8] and is given as follows:

$$Var(D_1) = \frac{1 - \gamma}{(1 - \gamma^M)} \sum_{i=0}^{M-1} \gamma^i \{A_2^i + B_2^i\},$$
$$\text{where } A_2^i = \sum_{k=0}^{i} (\overline{\eta}_k \theta_3 + (\theta_1)^2 Var(\eta_k)),$$
$$B_2^i = (\theta_1 \sum_{k=0}^{i} \overline{\eta}_k + iT_{\overline{s}} - A_1)^2,$$

where θ_1 and θ_3 are defined in (13).

$$q = (n-1)\beta(1-\beta)^{n-2}, \tag{13}$$
$$\theta_1 = \sigma + \theta_2,$$
$$\theta_2 = (qT_s + (\gamma - q)T_{\overline{s}})(1 - \beta),$$
$$\theta_3 = (q(T_s - \theta_2)^2 + (\gamma - q)(T_{\overline{s}} - \theta_2)^2)(1 - \beta)$$
$$+ (1 - \gamma(1 - \beta))(\theta_2)^2.$$

4   Model Verification

This section verifies our model and illustrates the performance of the delayed-DCF protocol. We use the 802.11 simulator in ns2 version 2.28 [2] with some modifications. The purpose of these modifications is to add a deterministic delay

Table 1. Default parameter settings used in this paper.

CW_0	32	Header	241 µs	=	Mheader + Pheader + RouteHeader
m/M	5/7	T_s	940 µs	=	Header + L_{tm} + SIFS + δ + ACK + δ + DIFS
σ	20 µs	$T_{\bar{s}}$		=	T_s
δ	0 µs	L_{tm}	335 µs	=	460 bytes @ R_{data}
SIFS	10 µs	ACK	304 µs	=	24 bytes @ R_{basic} + 14 bytes @ R_{basic}
DIFS	50 µs	Mheader	20 µs	=	24 bytes @ R_{data} + 4 bytes @ R_{data}
R_{data}	11 Mbps	Pheader	192 µs	=	24 bytes @ R_{basic}
R_{basic}	1 Mbps	RouteHeader	29 µs	=	40 bytes @ R_{data}

d into the traditional DCF so as to be consistent with the delayed-DCF protocol. In our simulation, we use the DumbAgent routing protocol and set the simulation time to 100 seconds. The default parameter values shown in Table 1 are set in accordance with 802.11b. We consider a one-hop star network with an AP and n saturated nodes, where the AP only acts as the receiver of data packets from all nodes. We present the theoretical results under the assumption of $T_s = T_{\bar{s}}$. For practical networks, this assumption does not necessarily hold. However, many analytical studies, including [3,7] and [6], adopt this assumption, and it has also been adopted by the developers of the ns2 simulation tool [2]. The assumption is equivalent to assuming that ACK packets are transmitted at the basic rate and the ACK timeout after a collision matches the guard time observed by non-colliding nodes.

In our simulations, we study the impact of d on the throughput, the collision probability, the mean and standard deviation of the MAC access delay when the number of nodes n varies from 4 to 30, where $d = 5, 10$ ms. It has been proved in [8] that for a one-hop WLAN with n contending nodes and $d = 0$ ms, the mean MAC delay of a packet is $O(n)$ ms. We will show that the system performance of the delayed-DCF protocol varies significantly, relying on the relationship between d and n. The main reason is that the dominant component of the MAC access delay is the deterministic delay of d ms when $d > n$, and is the random delay in DCF of $O(n)$ ms otherwise.

Figure 2 plots the collision probability versus the number of nodes, where the theoretical results are calculated by (9) and (1). From this figure, we can see that the collision probability increases as n increases when $d = 5, 10$ ms. However, for each n, the collision probability when $d = 5$ ms is obviously larger than that when $d = 10$ ms. The reason is that the larger d greatly alleviates the contention intensity, leading to a lower collision probability. Particularly, when n increases from 4 to 10, the simulated collision probability when $d = 5$ ms increases from 0.02 to 0.22, whereas it is zero when $d = 10$ ms.

Figure 3 plots the per-node throughput versus the number of nodes, where the theoretical results are calculated by (10). From this figure, as n increases from 10 to 30, we can see that the per-node throughput decreases and is almost equal for each n when $d = 5, 10$ ms. However, for each $n < 10$, the per-node throughput when $d = 10$ ms keeps unchanged and is obviously less than that

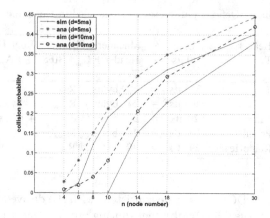

Fig. 2. The collision probability versus the number of nodes.

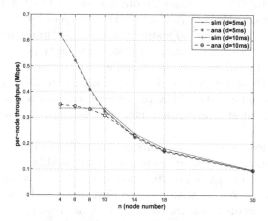

Fig. 3. The per-node throughput versus the number of nodes.

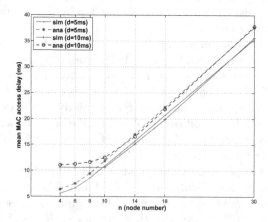

Fig. 4. The mean MAC access delay versus the number of nodes.

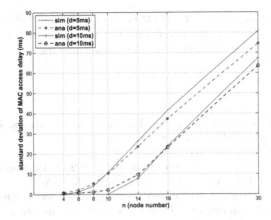

Fig. 5. The standard deviation of the MAC access delay versus the number of nodes.

when $d = 5$ ms. The reason is that when $d > n$, the MAC access delay and hence the per-node throughput is governed by d, and the larger d often makes the system idle, thereby lowering the channel utilization.

Figure 4 plots the mean MAC access delay versus the number of nodes, where the theoretical results are calculated by (11). From this figure, the MAC access delay when $d = 10$ ms is almost equal to 10 ms and is obviously less than that when $d = 5$ ms for $n < 10$, however, it is almost equal and is $O(n)$ ms for each $n > 10$ when $d = 5, 10$ ms. This manifests that the dominant component of the MAC access delay is the deterministic delay d ms when $d > n$, and is the random delay in DCF of $O(n)$ ms otherwise.

Figure 5 plots the standard deviation of the MAC access delay versus the number of nodes, where the theoretical results are calculated by (12). From this figure, we can see that the standard deviation increases as n increases when $d = 5, 10$ ms. However, the standard deviation when $d = 5$ ms is obviously larger that when $d = 10$ ms for each n. Particularly, the standard deviation when $d = 10$ ms for $n < 10$ is almost zero since the MAC access delay is almost a constant and is equal to 10 ms under this case.

Finally, from all these figures, we can see that all theoretical results, except the theoretical collision probability which slightly deviates from the simulated value, can well match the corresponding simulated results, indicating that our model is very accurate.

5   Conclusion

This paper proposes a theoretical model to evaluate the performance of the delayed-DCF protocol. Our model accurately characterizes the impact of the deterministic delay in the protocol on the system performance. The delayed-DCF protocol is a special case of the DCA protocol, whose idea is to introduce an extra random delay before a node enters the normal DCF procedure so that more packets can be backlogged and transmitted upon each transmission opportunity. The study in this paper is very helpful for further modeling the DCA protocol and suitably designing its configurable system parameters.

References

1. IEEE Std. 802.11-2007, Part 11: Wireless LAN Medium Access Control (MAC) and Physical Layer (PHY) Specifications, June 2007
2. http://www.isi.edu/nsnam/ns/ns-build.html
3. Bianchi, G.: Performance analysis of the IEEE 802.11 distributed coordination function. IEEE J. Sel. Areas Commun. 18(3), 535–547 (2000)
4. Changwen, L., Stephens, A.: Delayed channel access for IEEE 802.11e based WLAN. In: IEEE International Conference on Communication, pp. 4811–4817, June 2006
5. Gong, M., Hart, B., Mao, S.: Advanced wireless lan technologies: IEEE 802.11ac and beyond. ACM Mob. Comput. Commun. Rev. (MC2R) 18(4), 48–52 (2014)
6. Kumar, A., Altman, E., Miorandi, D., Goyal, M.: New insights from a fixed point analysis of single cell IEEE 802.11 WLANs. IEEE/ACM Trans. Netw. 15(3), 588–601 (2007)
7. Malone, D., Duffy, K., Leith, D.: Modeling the 802.11 distributed coordination function in non-saturated heterogeneous conditions. IEEE/ACM Trans. Netw. 15(1), 159–172 (2007)
8. Sakurai, T., Vu, H.L.: Access delay of the IEEE 802.11 mac protocol under saturation. IEEE Trans. Wirel. Commun. 6(5), 1702–1710 (2007)
9. Siddiqui, F., Zeadally, S., Salah, K.: Gigabit wireless networking with IEEE 802.11ac:technical overview and challenges. J. Netw. 10(3), 164–171 (2015)
10. Zhao, Q., Ma, Z., Dai, H.: Performance evaluation of the delayed-dcf scheme in wireless LANs. Int. J. Future Comput. Commun. 2(5), 391–394 (2013)

EBRS: Event Based Reputation System for Defensing Multi-source Sybil Attacks in VANET

Xia Feng[1], Chun-yan Li[2]($\boxtimes$), De-xin Chen[3], and Jin Tang[1]

[1] Co-Innovation Center for Information Supply and Assurance Technology,
Anhui University, Hefei 230601, People's Republic of China
fengx.ahu@foxmail.com, ahhftang@qq.com

[2] School of Computer Science and Communication Engineering, Jiangsu University,
Zhenjiang 212013, People's Republic of China
lcy20110416@163.com

[3] College of Computer Science, Sichuang University,
Chengdu 610065, People's Republic of China
lhy5154@163.com

Abstract. Sybil attack can counterfeit traffic scenario by sending false messages with multiple identities, which often cause traffic jams and even lead to vehicular accidents in vehicular ad hoc network (VANET). It is very difficult to be defended and detected, especially when it is launched by some conspired attackers using their legitimate identities. In this paper, we propose an event based reputation system(EBRS), in which dynamic reputation and trusted value for each event are employed to suppress the spread of false messages. EBRS can detect Sybil attack with fabricated identities and stolen identities in the process of communication, it also defends against the conspired Sybil attack since each event has a unique reputation value and trusted value. Meanwhile, we keep the vehicle identity in privacy. Simulation results show that EBRS is able to defend and detect multi-source Sybil attacks with high performances.

Keywords: Vehicular ad hoc network · Multi-source Sybil attacks ·
Event reputation value · Event trusted value

1 Introduction

As an important part of Intelligent Transportation System (ITS), VANET has been developed rapidly in the past twenty years. It purports to promote traffic management, improve road safety and the quality of people's travel experience [1]. In VANET, there are two communication models: vehicle-to-vehicle (V2V) communication and vehicle-to-infrastructure (V2I) communication, as described in Fig. 1. However, the characteristics of dynamic topology, autonomous movement and the influence of traffic rules, road and weather conditions bring many security threats to VANET [2,3]. To deal with these threats, many applications

© Springer International Publishing Switzerland 2015
K. Xu and J. Zhu (Eds.): WASA 2015, LNCS 9204, pp. 145–154, 2015.
DOI: 10.1007/978-3-319-21837-3_15

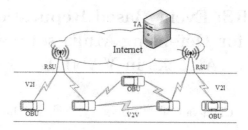

Fig. 1. Architecture of VANET

of VANET give each vehicle a unique identity, and take some security rules and methods with these identities.

A legitimate identity gives a license for vehicle to act as an internal node in VANET, but the identity-based security is vulnerable to Sybil attack. Sybil attack was first proposed by Douceur [4]. A Sybil attacker will hold many identities by forgery, theft or conspired sharing, and these false identities will help the attacker to cheat the other vehicles, or destroy the security rules. For example, sending false messages and fabricating traffic scenarios affect the normal travel [5]. In addition, Sybil attackers can destroy some vote-based routing protocols and even lead to DOS attacks with the multiple identities. In a word, Sybil attack will give the attackers many legitimate identities to do bad things, such as blackhole attack, wormhole attack and selective forwarding attack, etc.

Currently, Sybil attack detection is an emerging research area in VANET. Many methods are proposed, such as RSSI-based (Received Signal Strength Indicator) detection method [6,7], vehicle movement trajectory based method [8,9] and neighbors information based method [10]. But there are two things make the existing methods cannot work well: one is conspired Sybil attack, in which the attackers have legitimate identities and they share their identities with the accomplices; the other is privacy requirement of anonymous [11,12], that makes the impostors more difficult to be found. In this paper we present an event based reputation system to defense Sybil attack, and we take multi-sources of false identity into account. In order to protect privacy, vehicle sends message with pseudonym instead of its real identity. Through verifying the local certificate of vehicle, EBRS can detect Sybil attack with forgery or theft identities. Moreover, in order to defense conspired Sybil attack, EBRS establishes a dynamic reputation value and trusted value for the event in VANET. If the reputation value and trusted value are below its corresponding threshold, the message about the event can't be spread, thus suppressing the propagation of false information. The rest of paper is organized as follows. In Sect. 2, a survey of existing Sybil attack detection methods is given. The models and design goals are given in Sect. 3. We propose EBRS in Sect. 4 and system evaluation in Sect. 5. Finally in Sect. 6, we conclude the paper and outline the future work.

2   Related Work

As each vehicle has only one identity and one identity can't be located at two positions, each relatively accurate position has only one vehicle. Based on this idea, many researchers proposed the method of estimating a node's position using RSSI to detect Sybil attack. If two messages have the same estimated position, we conclude that they are from the same node which is the Sybil attacker [6,7]. However, the message signal strength may be influenced by complex road conditions, so the detection accuracy is limited. What's more, this method can't defend against conspired Sybil attack. As vehicles move autonomously in VANET, no vehicles will always pass by the same road side unit (RSU) at the same time in a certain period of time. Therefore, taking RSUs as references, the vehicles generate their movement trajectories. Through computing and comparing vehicles' movement trajectories, Sybil attack can be detected. Vehicles with the same or similar motion trajectory are defined as Sybil attackers [8,9] (also named as timestamp series approach, TSA). However, this method has the risk of leaking out vehicle's motion information and location privacy. Without consideration of traffic jam and vehicle fleet, different vehicles will not always have the same neighbors in a certain time. Grover. [10] put forward a method to detect Sybil attack using the similarity of neighboring information (SNI). Although this method doesn't need the help of RSU, the reality of neighboring information depends on the loyalty of neighbors. This can be used by the Sybil attackers to launch a new Sybil attack.

In summary, RSSI-based method has difficulty in distinguishing Sybil nodes and normal nodes which are located near to each other. Vehicle movement trajectory based method has the risk of revealing vehicles location privacy. Neighbors information based method has an assumption that the majority of neighbors are normal nodes which is a detection paradox itself. According to the false identity sources in Sybil attack and the characteristics of VANET, EBRS can protect vehicle privacy and defense against Sybil attack with multi-sources.

3   Models and Design Goals

3.1   System Model

Figure 1 illustrates the hierarchical architecture of VANET, which consists of three interoperating components. In VANET, an on board unit (OBU) is installed on every vehicle. It is used for real-time traffic information collection, traffic event perception, and warning messages acceptance. There is an event table (ET) to store different events and a tamper-proof device in OBU. RSU generates local certificates for vehicles in its communication range with an agreed session key. Trusted authority (TA) takes charge of distributing and storing the nodes information in VANET. In this paper, we make the following assumptions. TA and RSU can never be compromised by any attackers and they are always trusted. The drivers can't tamper OBU information arbitrarily. The overlap area of RSUs is out of consideration of our work.

3.2   Attack Model

To launch a Sybil attack successfully, a malicious node must try to present as multiple independent identities. It can fabricate traffic scenarios by sending false messages. Figure 2 shows the faked smooth traffic scenario launched by a Sybil attacker. Normally, vehicle will send warning message to notify other vehicles slow down or detour to another road when it runs into a traffic jam. However, Sybil attacker A might create the illusion of a vehicle S passing the traffic congestion area smoothly which will impact the judgment of other drivers. They may make wrong decisions, leading the congestion area more congested or even vehicles pile-up. This is a great threat to the lives and properties of drivers and passengers. Similarly, in order to use the road itself, Sybil attackers can send false information in the situation of smooth traffic. In this work, we are intend to solve this Sybil attack related with sending false messages.

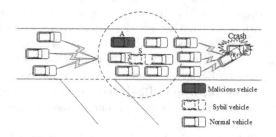

Fig. 2. Faked smooth traffic scenario by Sybil attack

3.3   Design Goals

To deal with the problems in existing Sybil attack detection methods and above attack model, we present an event based reputation system. Its design goals are:

1. Conditional privacy preserving: vehicles use time-limited pseudonyms in the V2V and V2I communications which preserves the identity privacy of vehicles. But when a malicious vehicle is detected, TA has the ability to retrieve the vehicle's real identity from its pseudo identity. Therefore, EBRS can prevent the malicious node from repudiating its message.
2. Independent detection: the essence of Sybil attack is collaboration of multiple Sybil nodes. To prevent the potential Sybil attack happened again, the Sybil attack detection method should be carried by vehicles independently.
3. Defense against Sybil attack with multiple false identity sources: Sybil attacker can get multiple false identities using the method of forgery, theft and conspiracy, EBRS is capable of defensing and detecting all theses Sybil attacks.

4   Event Based Reputation System

4.1   Initialization and Notation

TA takes charge of the task of system initialization. According to the definition of bilinear maps, let G_1 be a cyclic additive group which is generated by P and

G_2 be a cyclic multiplicative group. G_1 and G_2 have the same prime order q. P is the generator and $P \in G_1$. TA chooses a random number s as its prime secret key and it will update this key periodically. TA pre-distributes a unique ID, secret key, hash function $h : \{0,1\}^* \longrightarrow Z_q^*$ and s to the vehicle who wants to join in VANET. TA assigns a secret key and certificate to each RSU. The main notations throughout this paper are shown in Table 1.

Table 1. Notations

Notations	Descriptions
PID_v	pseudonym of vehicle v
PK_v/sk_v	public/secret key of vehicle v
PK_r/sk_r	public/secret key of RSU r
$Lcert_{rv}/Lcert_{vr}$	local certificate of vehicle v in the range of RSU r
$Cert_r$	certificate of RSU r
T	fresh time of local certificate
RV_E	reputation value of event E
TV_E	trusted value of event E
T_E	time of event E
L_E	location of event E
$Type(E)$	type of event E

4.2 EBRS Process

EBRS establishes a local certificate for every vehicle and dynamic reputation value and trusted value for every event in VANET.

1. Process of local certificate generation. According to elliptic curve cryptography algorithm, vehicle V_i obtains its public key PK_i and pseudonym PID_i through computing $PK_i = sk_i \cdot P \bmod n$ and $PID_i = hash(PK_i \parallel s)$. Then it sends PK_i and PID_i to its local RSU r. After receiving the information, local RSU r will send a message to TA to validate PK_i and PID_i. If PK_i or PID_i is not in VANET, RSU r will break off the process of local certificate generation forcibly. Otherwise, RSU r will compute its public key PK_r, session key SK_{ri} with V_i and $V_i's$ local certificate $Lcert_{ri}$ using the following formulas. After that, it will send $(PK_r, Cert_r, T)$ to V_i and put $(PID_i, SK_{ri}, Lcert_{ri}, T)$ into its certificate list (CL).

$$PK_r = sk_r \cdot P \bmod n, \ SK_{ri} = PK_r \oplus PK_i \bmod n, \tag{1}$$

$$HV_{ri} = hash(PID_i\|Cert_r), \ Lcert_{ri} = HV_{ri} \times SK_{ri} \bmod n. \tag{2}$$

After receiving the message from RSU r, A will compute its session key SK_{ir} with RSU r, HV_{ir} and its local certificate $Lcert_{ir}$ using the following formulas.

Under normal circumstances, $SK_{ir} = SK_{ri}, HV_{ir} = HV_{ri}, Lcert_{ir} = Lcert_{ri}$. The aforementioned process can be formalized as Fig. 3.

$$SK_{ir} = PK_i \oplus PK_r \bmod n, \ HV_{ir} = hash(PID_i \| Cert_r), \tag{3}$$

$$Lcert_{ir} = HV_{ir} \times SK_{ir} \bmod n. \tag{4}$$

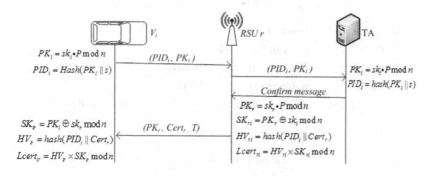

Fig. 3. Process of local certificate generation

2. **Process of local certificate validation.** Assumed that there is a traffic accident in front of V_i, it will broadcast a warning message to its neighbors. The format of this message is $(PID_i, E_{SK_{ir}}(Lcert_{ir}), M, HM_i)$, where $M = (L_E, T_E, Type(E), RV_E, TV_E)$, HM_i is the hash value of M. After vehicle V_j (supposing it is in the range of V_i) receiving the warning message from V_i, it will send a message to its local RSU r to authenticate the certificate of V_i. RSU r will search its CL to get the session key with V_i. If formula 5 is satisfied and the certificate is within its fresh time T, the pseudonym and local certificate of V_i is being proved to be correct. RSU r will send the confirm message to V_j. Once receiving the confirmation message, V_j will authenticate the integrity of message using formula 6. If it is holds, V_j will record RV_E and TV_E. Otherwise, it will ignore the message from V_i. There may be three reasons for the warning message not passing the validation of RSU. (1) V_i attempts to use both expired pseudonym/certificate and pseudonym/certificate in hand to communicate with other vehicles which leads to a Sybil attack; (2) a malicious node attempts to use the pseudonym stealing from V_i to launch a Sybil attack; (3) a malicious vehicle attempts to launch Sybil attack by forging a pseudonym and session key. In this case, RSU r will issue a warning message about Sybil attack and report to TA who can trace the malicious vehicle's real identity.

$$D_{SK_{ri}}(E_{SK_{ir}}(Lcert_{ir})) = Lcert_{ir} = Lcert_{ri}, \tag{5}$$

$$HM_j = hash(M) = HM_i. \tag{6}$$

3. **Process of setting event reputation value and trusted value.** To deal with Sybil attack sending false messages, EBRS is enlightened by [13] to build a dynamic reputation value and trusted value for every event in VANET. Event reputation value is defined as the times of a vehicle sensing the event and the event trusted value is the number of distinct vehicles who have sensed the event. If vehicle V_i senses an event E_j for the first time, it will build an event entry for this event in its ET. At the same time, V_i will broadcast a warning message to its neighbors. After receiving this warning message, V_k (supposing it is in the range of V_i) will establish an event entry in its ET for this event if it hasn't sensed this event before. Otherwise, it will update the reputation value and trusted value of this event. When the reputation value and trusted value of this event both reach its corresponding threshold, V_k will notify its driver through the user interface in OBU. The driver will take some actions about this event. Meanwhile, V_k will broadcast a warning message about this event to its neighbors. If V_i is a Sybil attacker who sends false message, its subsequent vehicles will not sense the event as it doesn't happen. Therefore, RV_E and TV_E will not reach their thresholds. Thus inhibit the dissemination of false message. Supposing that V_j is an accomplice of V_i, they plan to launch a Sybil attack. As they can't change RV_E, the event reputation value can't reach its threshold. Thus the false message will not be spread any longer, EBRS defends against the conspired Sybil attack. In order to respond and transmit the message quickly which is very perilous and urgent, we can define different threshold for different type of event.

5   System Evaluation

In this section, we analyze and evaluate the performance of EBRS. In our simulation, vehicles move according to the street map in the Houston area based on a Tiger database file. In this map, there are 383 points and 1,188 road segments in total. We have evaluated our method in 2 Km road segment area obtained from these realistic traces with variation the number of vehicles.

5.1   Simulation Results Analysis

Figure 4 is the communication delay of EBRS and TSA, from which we can conclude that the communication delay of EBRS is much less than TSA. With the increase of vehicle density, the communication delay will increase. This is because that too many vehicles on the road will cause intense competition of wireless channel in the process of communication. In addition, the bigger the packet is, the higher will be the communication delay. The delivery ratio of EBRS and TSA is shown by Fig. 5. It indicates that when the vehicle density is small, the message delivery ratio is small, too. The reason is that when the number of vehicles on the road is little, the distance between vehicles will be too far to receive the message. With the increase of node density, the delivery ratio will increase, too. But when the number of vehicles is above 100, the delivery ratio will be decrease. As more vehicles on the road, they will send message at the same time which leads to the

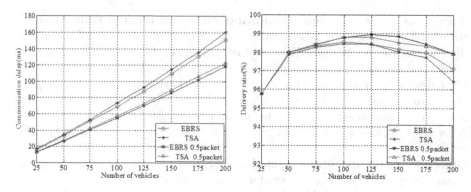

Fig. 4. Communication delay   **Fig. 5.** Delivery ratio

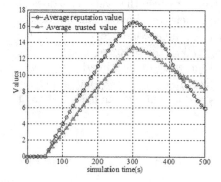   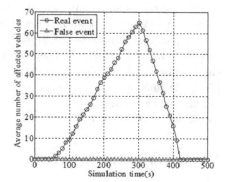

Fig. 6. Average event reputation value   **Fig. 7.** Average number of affected
and event trusted value   vehicles by false event and real event

increase of packets loss. From these figures, we can conclude that our method is much better than TSA.

To study the impact of event reputation value and event trusted value on EBRS, Fig. 6 shows the event reputation value and trusted value with the increase of simulation time. We suppose that the sampling interval of OBU is 1 s and range of sensor is $20m$. The event of traffic jam is happened at the $50th$ s. If the event reputation value doesn't change in 10 s, it will be decreased 1 per 20 s. When the event reputation value is 0, it will be deleted from the event table. As is shown in Fig. 6, the event reputation value and trusted value increases with the simulation time from the $50th$ s to the $300th$ s. When the event is resolved at the $300th$ s, the corresponding values will decrease. We set the reputation threshold to 10 and trust value threshold to 4 of traffic jam. A vehicle trusting the existence of an event is defined as an affected vehicle. If there is a conspired Sybil attack in VANET, the malicious node will send false event to its neighbors. From Fig. 7, we can conclude that EBRS can prevent the spread of false event successfully. On the contrary, the real event can be spread quickly to many vehicles. As a result, EBRS defends against the conspired Sybil attack sending false message.

5.2 Performance Evaluation

Table 2 gives the comparison of EBRS and other methods in Sect. 2. In Table 2, $\sqrt{}$ indicates the method can detect the corresponding Sybil attack, × means that the method can't meet corresponding requirement and △ means the method didn't consider that requirement. It indicates that EBRS can not only preserve vehicle privacy, guarantee message integrity, but also can defense against Sybil attack with multiple false identity sources.

Table 2. Comparison of EBRS and other methods

Detection methods	Sybil attack with faked identities	Sybil attack with stolen identities	Conspired Sybil attack	Message integrity	Privacy protection
RSSI [6]	$\sqrt{}$	$\sqrt{}$	×	△	△
TSA [9]	$\sqrt{}$	×	×	$\sqrt{}$	×
SNI [10]	$\sqrt{}$	$\sqrt{}$	$\sqrt{}$	△	×
EBRS	$\sqrt{}$	$\sqrt{}$	$\sqrt{}$	$\sqrt{}$	$\sqrt{}$

V2V and V2I communication overheads of TSA and EBRS are given in Fig. 8. As TSA needs transmit message, the latest timestamp certificate and RSU certificate, its communication overhead is much bigger than EBRS.

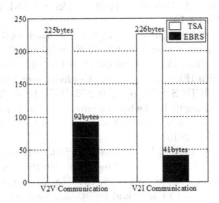

Fig. 8. Comparison of communication overheads

6 Conclusion and Future Work

Compared to existing methods, EBRS can defense against multi-source Sybil attacks, ensure the integrity of message and preserve the privacy of vehicles. By establishing a reputation threshold and trust threshold for each event message, the dissemination of false message is restricted no matter it is from forgery identities or legitimate identities. In EBRS, a trusted RSU is used to issue the certificate of vehicles in its communication range. Our further work will loosen the strong security assumption of RSU, and try to find an automatic mode to establish the trust relationship among the participant vehicles.

Acknowledgments. This research was financially supported by National Natural Science Foundation of China under Grant An No.61472001 and No.U1405255.

References

1. Al-Sultan, S., Al-Doori, M.M., Al-Bayatti, A.H.: A comprehensive survey on vehicular Ad Hoc network. J. Netw. Comput. Appl. **37**, 380–392 (2014)
2. Sumra, I.A., Hasbullah, H.B., AbManan, J.B.: Attacks on security goals (confidentiality, integrity, availability) in VANET: a survey. In: Laouiti, A., Qayyum, A., Mohamad, S., Mohamad, N. (eds.) Vehicular Ad-Hoc Networks for Smart Cities, pp. 51–61. Springer, Singapore (2015)
3. Wang, L.M., Li, X.J., Zhong, H.: A revocable group batch verification scheme for VANET. Sci. China: Inf. Sci. **43**, 1307–1325 (2013)
4. Douceur, J.R.: The Sybil attack. In: Proceeding of International Workshop on Peer-to-Peer Systems, pp. 251–260, Cambridge (2002)
5. Bissmeyer, N., Stresing, C., Bayarou K.M.: Intrusion detection in VANETs through verification of vehicle movement data. In: Vehicular Networking Conference (VNC), pp. 166–173. IEEE press, New Jersey (2010)
6. Yu, B., Xu, C.Z., Xiao, B.: Detecting Sybil attacks in VANETs. J. Parall. Distrib. Comput. **73**, 746–756 (2013)
7. Bouassida, M.S., Guette, G., Shawky, M.: Sybil nodes detection based on received signal strength variations within VANET. IJ Netw. Secur. **9**, 22–33 (2009)
8. Chen, C., Wang, X., Han, W.L.: A robust detection of the Sybil attack in urban VANETs. In: The 29th IEEE International Conference on Distributed Computing Systems Workshops, ICDCS 2009, pp. 270–276. IEEE press, Montreal (2009)
9. Park, S., Aslam, B., Turgut, D.: Defense against Sybil attack in the initial deployment stage of vehicular ad hoc network based on roadside unit support. Secur. Commun. Netw. **6**, 523–538 (2013)
10. Grover, J., Gaur, M.S., Laxmi, V.: A Sybil attack detection approach using neighboring vehicles in VANET. In: Proceeding of the 4th International Conference on Security of Information and Networks, pp. 151–158. ACM press, Sydney (2011)
11. Li, Z., Chigan, C.: On joint privacy and reputation assurance for vehicular ad hoc networks. IEEE Trans. Mob. Comput. **13**, 2334–2344 (2014)
12. Chim, T.W., Yiu, S.M., Hui, L.C.K.: VSPN: VANET-based secure and privacy-preserving navigation. IEEE Trans. Comput. **63**, 510–524 (2014)
13. Lo, N.W., Tsai, H.C.: A reputation system for traffic safety event on vehicular ad hoc networks. EURASIP J. Wirel. Commun. Netw. **2009**, 1–10 (2009)

iSound: A Smartphone Based Intelligent Sound Fusion System for the Hearing Impaired

Kathryn Grebel[1], Duy Dang[1], Liran Ma[1($\boxtimes$)], Donnell Payne[1], and Brent Cooper[2]

[1] Department of Computer Science, Texas Christian University,
Fort Worth, TX, USA
`i.ma@tcu.edu`
[2] Department of Psychology, Texas Christian University,
Fort Worth, TX, USA

Abstract. High quality hearing aids can come with a premium price tag. As a result, it can be challenging for a hearing impaired individual to obtain a hearing aid. Without such a device, the individual may struggle to communicate with others. To address this challenge, we aim to develop a smartphone-based hearing aid application (termed as iSound) that can serve as an alternative option for hearing impaired individuals. The iSound app is designed to have the capability to adapt to various scenarios with different requirements. Specifically, iSound can utilize both gain (volume) increases and frequency compression techniques as required. We implement iSound on an off-the-shelf Android-based smartphone. The current implementation of iSound is demonstrated to be able to compress signals to a desired range of frequencies as specified, with some distortions and delays. We believe iSound can be a viable alternative for hearing impaired individuals.

1 Introduction

Successful communication depends on all participating parties having the ability to hear as well as speak. This is not always the case because approximately 8.6 % of the US population is classified as hearing impaired and in need of a hearing assistance device [1]. In addition, our auditory systems begin to deteriorate as we age, making it difficult to hear sounds at higher frequencies. Hearing aids are traditionally adopted to reduce the impact of hearing impairments.

Recently, there have been multiple techniques proposed to increase hearing aid functionality. Examples of these techniques include frequency compression, amplification, and the ability to adapt to different environments. Research shows that hearing aids utilizing frequency compression techniques generally increase the perception of speech better than the devices that do not [2]. The implementation of these techniques can produce a higher quality hearing aid.

However, these higher quality hearing aids can be cost prohibitive. As a result, many hearing impaired individuals might still struggle to obtain an effective hearing aid. The lack of affordable options motivates us to develop an alternative solution of comparable quality. Smartphones have become ubiquitous and a vital part

© Springer International Publishing Switzerland 2015
K. Xu and J. Zhu (Eds.): WASA 2015, LNCS 9204, pp. 155–164, 2015.
DOI: 10.1007/978-3-319-21837-3_16

of people's daily lives. Today's smartphones have the capabilities to process and transform sound signals. We aim to develop an app (termed as iSound) that utilizes these capabilities to function as a hearing aid. The benefit of this approach is that a smartphone app can be easily acquired and is relatively inexpensive.

This paper discusses the design and implementation of iSound on an off-the-shelf Android-based smartphone. With the individual users needs in mind, we develop a smartphone app that determines the bandwidth of frequencies where his/her hearing capabilities are maximized. During conversations, audio signals are received and modulated to within the aforementioned bandwidth and amplified when necessary. This could afford hearing impaired individuals the ability to fully partake in communication.

The remainder of the paper is organized as follows. We start by discussing the related work in Sect. 2. Next, we review our design in Sect. 3. We then explain our current system implementation in Sect. 4. Following that, we report our evaluation results in Sect. 5 and finally, we consider future improvements to the design and conclude the paper in Sect. 6.

2   Related Work

The related information necessary to develop and implement the hearing aid app consists of three basic parts: frequency compression techniques, digital signals, and pitch shifting. Frequency compression refers to reducing all of the frequencies in a bandwidth (i.e. range of frequencies) into a compressed, target bandwidth. A digital signal is a representation of a continuous sound wave consisting of discrete sample points. Pitch shifting refers to manipulating the signal to adjust its pitch for the purpose of frequency compression.

2.1   Frequency Compression Techniques

Modulating the frequencies requires that they are reduced so that all are within the desired range. This is accomplished by using either frequency transposition, linear frequency compression, or nonlinear frequency compression. Frequency transposition reduces every frequency value outside of the user's range by the same quantity in Hertz (Hz). When a frequency is reduced using transposition it can overlap a value already present in the target range. This overlap can cause distortions.

Linear frequency compression reduces every frequency value by a set ratio. We call this ratio the frequency scaling ratio, r, and calculate it as follows:

$$r = \frac{c}{4000\,\text{Hz}}. \tag{1}$$

The variable c is the cutoff frequency for the user's bandwidth of hearing capability (i.e., the maximum frequency that the user can hear with relative clarity), and 4000 Hz is the maximum frequency of the Human Voice Frequency Range (HVFR). Thus, for every input frequency value, f_0, the output frequency value, f_1, is given by:

$$f_1 = r f_0. \tag{2}$$

Nonlinear frequency compression is similar to linear frequency compression in that they both utilize a frequency scaling ratio. However, nonlinear compression is predicated on the notion that hearing loss tends to be more prevalent in higher frequency bandwidths and less likely to effect lower frequency bandwidths. Certain bandwidths do not require the same amount of compression as do others, thus the same frequency scaling ratio should not be applied to every bandwidth. The HVFR is broken into the different sub-bandwidths based on the frequency regions found in an audiogram, and a scaling ratio is calculated for each. The ratio for the highest sub-band is calculated in the same manner as the ratio used for linear frequency compression. The remaining ratios are derived using a combination of the initial ratio value and the level of hearing loss for each sub-band.

2.2 Digital Signals

A digital signal is a sequence of discrete values/sample points representative of a sound wave. The number of samples used to represent one second of a sound wave is determined by the sampling rate. For example, using a sampling rate of 44,100 Hz means that 44,100 sample points are used to represent one second of sound. When the sampling rate is 22,050 Hz the same number of samples represent two seconds of sound. Thus, given a sampling rate, a signals duration is measured by the number of its representative sample points.

2.3 Pitch Shifting

François discusses a pitch shifting method in [3]. Pitch shifting is the process of adjusting the frequency of a signal without affecting its duration. The method detailed in the article is mainly focused on pitch shifting for electric guitar signals which behave differently than vocal signals. The method utilizes Fourier transforms and inverse Fourier transforms which can be difficult to code and computationally inefficient. Nevertheless, the algorithm introduces the idea for effectively pitch shifting an audio signal.

3 Design

Our primary objective is to compress the frequency bandwidth of the input audio signals to within a target bandwidth. In addition, we want to maintain an acceptable latency period between input and output audio signals of less than $50 ms$ and incur as few distortions as possible created by the frequency compression process. Because iSound is primarily for communication purposes, our main concern is with speech signals. We develop our design for the Human Voice Frequency Range (HVFR) 85 Hz–4000 Hz, i.e., the maximum frequency that we are concerned with is 4000 Hz.

3.1   Frequency Compression Parameter

We want to incorporate the user's specific hearing capabilities in order to adapt
the app to fit his/her individual requirements. We utilize techniques similar to
those that audiologists use to fit a patient's hearing aid. A person's hearing is
evaluated with an audiogram (i.e., a logarithmic plot of frequency (Hz) vs hearing
threshold (dB)). A sample audiogram is depicted in Fig. 1. The hearing threshold
is the minimum sound level, measured in dB, required to hear a given frequency.
Depending on the hearing threshold, a person's hearing ability for that frequency
region is classified as normal hearing, mild loss, moderate loss, moderately-severe
loss, severe loss, or profound loss. The app uses the information in the audiogram
to establish a target bandwidth of frequencies corresponding to the user's hearing
capabilities. This is accomplished by choosing the frequency regions that are
classified as normal hearing or minimal loss.

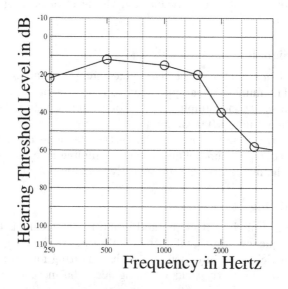

Fig. 1. Sample audiogram

3.2   Frequency Compression Scheme

We utilize a frequency compression technique to condense all of the frequencies
in the HVFR to within the target bandwidth previously discussed. In particular,
linear frequency compression is employed in our design because of the relative
ease in implementation and the desire to maintain acceptable latency values. A
signal's frequency is inversely related to the length of its period, T, i.e., $f = \frac{1}{T}$.
Thus, a simple way to reduce the frequency of the input signal is to increase the
length of its period by an amount proportional to the frequency scaling ratio

discussed in Sect. 2.1. Unfortunately, this results in an output signal that has a longer duration than the input signal, which can cause the audio to be visually out of sync.

Thus, the linear frequency compression is carried out using a process known as pitch shifting [3]. Pitch shifting is based on the concept of increasing the length of a signal's period as mentioned above. However, steps are taken to preserve the duration of the signal. Since we are working with digital signals, preserving the duration means preserving the number of representative sample points as discussed in Sect. 2.2.

We know that increasing the length of a signal's period reduces its frequency, but also causes an increase in its duration. In order to preserve the signal's duration, an intermediary signal is created so that it has a duration equal to the product of the frequency scaling ratio and the duration of the input signal. The length of the period of the intermediary signal can then be increased by an amount proportional to 1 minus the scaling ratio (i.e., $1 - r$). This produces an output signal equal in duration to the input signal that also has a reduced frequency.

The pitch shifting process involves two principal steps: time scaling and up-sampling. A major benefit of utilizing pitch shifting in the design is that it is easily customizable. That is, there is more than one way for implementation. This provides us with the ability to choose an implementation that best meets our stated goals.

Time Scaling. The intermediary signal is created by utilizing a time scaling technique (i.e., the method of adjusting the duration, or number of sample points, of a signal without affecting its frequency). In general, the number of sample points in (i.e., the length of) the intermediary signal, l_1, is given by multiplying the length of the input signal, l_0, by the scaling ratio r:

$$l_1 = rl_0. \tag{3}$$

The intermediary signal can be created with one of the following three time scaling techniques:

- The first technique is to directly collect the first l_1 sample points of the input signal as the intermediary signal. The rest of the input signal is discarded. This technique requires the least computation among the three techniques;
- The second technique is Pitch Synchronous Overlap and Add (PSOLA) where a signal of a single frequency is divided into a sequence of overlapping, periodic segments. Each segment is one period in length and is partially shared with its neighboring segments. Because the segments overlap each other by the exact same amount, adding or removing a segment does not affect the frequency of the overall signal. The duration of a signal is decreased by removing one or more of these overlapping segments. Since PSOLA is a time-domain-based approach, the computations are relatively simple and efficient [4];

– The third technique is phase vocoder. It is a frequency-domain-based technique that utilizes an overlap-add approach like PSOLA. Instead of using pitch synchronization, this technique modifies the signal's phases in its short-time Fourier Transform to achieve synchronization between the overlapping segments. The phase vocoder can compute more complex signals than PSOLA, but it is not as computationally efficient as PSOLA [5].

Up-sampling. The signal is then up-sampled (i.e., the process of inserting additional sample points to increase the duration of the signal and lower its frequency) to produce the output signal. Up-sampling can be accomplished using one of the following three techniques:

– Point insertion by averaging is the process of inserting a new point every m points in the intermediary signal, where m is calculated as follows

$$m = \frac{r}{1-r}. \tag{4}$$

The value of the inserted point is calculated by averaging the two points adjacent to it.
– Cubic spline interpolation derives a piecewise-defined function, consisting of 3rd degree polynomials, where each piecewise function corresponds to a pair of points, e.g.,

$$f(x) = \begin{cases} g_1(x) & 0 \le x \le 1 \\ g_2(x) & 1 \le x \le 2 \\ \vdots & \\ g_n(x) & n-1 \le x \le n \end{cases} \tag{5}$$

– Lagrange interpolation derives an nth degree polynomial using the formula

$$P_n(x) = \sum_{j=0}^{n} y_j \prod_{k \ne j} \frac{(x - x_k)}{(x_j - x_k)}. \tag{6}$$

In both cubic spline and Lagrange interpolation, the output signal is created by using the derived formulas to calculate the desired number of evenly space representative sample points.

4   Implementation

The current implementation is based on the Android 4.4.2 operating system (Kit Kat). To be specific, our implementation of iSound is on the Samsung Galaxy S5 that has a 2.5 GHz Quad-Core Processor and 2GB of RAMs. The sampling rate is set at 44.1 kHz, which is equivalent to CD quality audio. The bluetooth headset utilized for the app is the Logitech Wireless Headset H800. The app's implementation can be broken down into two main parts: front end and back end. The front end (i.e., user interface) is where the user enters his/her specific hearing requirements. The back end is where the actual signal processing occurs.

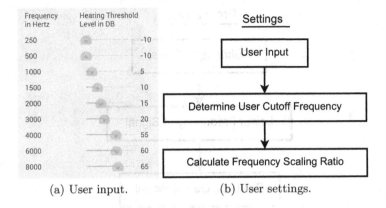

| (a) User input. | (b) User settings. |

Fig. 2. Front end.

4.1 Front End

When the app is launched for the first time, the user is prompted to enter his/her specific hearing prescription given by the audiologist. Specifically, the app's interface has eight separate input fields as shown in Fig. 2(a), one for every frequency level found on an audiogram. Each level has a corresponding SeekBar for the user to specify their hearing threshold in decibels (dB). The possible settings for the SeekBar range from −10 to 110, mirroring an audiogram as shown in Fig. 1. The app then uses that prescription information to calculate the user's settings needed for future signal processing in the back end as shown in Fig. 2(b). Specifically, the user's cutoff frequency (i.e., the maximum frequency of the user's hearing capability) is determined by evaluating each frequency level's class of hearing loss. The lowest frequency level classified as minimal hearing loss is designated as the user's cutoff frequency. For example, in Fig. 2(a) the user's cutoff frequency is 3,000 Hz. The frequency scaling ratio is calculated using Eq. 1. Specifically, the scaling ration for Fig. 2(a) is 0.75.

4.2 Back End

When the user runs the app, the back end starts processing the incoming audio signals as shown in Fig. 3. Sound is picked up by the phone's microphone and converted to a digital signal consisting of discrete sample points. These digital sample points are sent to the app. The app then creates a buffered input signal by creating an array containing a finite number of sample points. The length of the array is determined by the minimum number of sample points that the Android OS requires for a chosen sampling rate. For example, this implementation of the app buffers input signals as arrays containing 1,024 sample points because it is the required minimum for the sampling rate 44.1 kHz.

Next, the frequency of the signal is lowered by creating an intermediary signal and up-sampling it. Specifically, the intermediary signal is obtained by

Processing

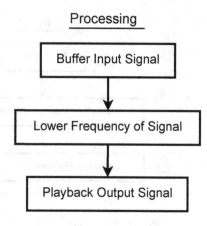

Fig. 3. Back end.

creating an array consisting of the first l_1 points from the input signal, where l_1 is calculated using Eq. 3. This method of time scaling is utilized because it is the simplest to implement and most computationally efficient of the three methods discussed. Up-sampling the intermediary signal creates the output signal. The up-sampling is accomplished using either the point insertion by averaging technique, cubic spline interpolation, or Lagrange sinterpolation as detailed in Sect. 3.2.

Finally, the Android AudioTrack class buffers the output signal in preparation for playback. The streaming mode of the class pushes each element of the buffered output signal one-by-one to a queue in the phone's AudioSink hardware. The hardware then plays the processed sound for the user.

5   Evaluation

We assess the application's performance with the following criteria: (i) the accuracy of the shifted input frequencies; (ii) latency periods between input and output audio signals; (iii) distortions created by the compression process. The testing environment is setup such that the user's maximum cutoff frequency is $c = 3000\,\mathrm{Hz}$ and the frequency scaling ratio is $r = \frac{3000\,\mathrm{Hz}}{4000\,\mathrm{Hz}} = 0.75$.

We test the application's performance in regards to the first criterion using a Samsung Galaxy S5, Echo Capture (an Android app that plays and graphs sound) [6], an online tone generator [7], and an online tuner [8]. The tone generator produces various, specified frequencies within the HVFR. The phone's microphone is held near the computer's speaker for the purpose of capturing the generated frequency. After processing the input signal, the app stores the output signal in a public file on the phone. Echo Capture then plays the contents of the public file as the input for the online tuner, which gives the frequency of the output signal. We then compute the actual frequency scaling ratio by dividing the output frequency by the input frequency (note: the ideal scaling ratio is given above as r), i.e.,

$$r_A = \frac{f_1}{f_0}. \tag{7}$$

This process is repeated until we obtain 30 pairs of ideal and actual frequency scaling ratios. We then use the mean absolute error method to evaluate the app's performance in producing the expected output frequency. The test data collected is displayed in Table 1. The calculated mean absolute error is 0.05. We also found that the actual ratios were very consistent; in 28 of the 30 cases the actual ratio is 0.80, i.e., 0.05 greater than the ideal ratio of 0.75. Further evaluation is necessary to determine the reason for the discrepancies in the output frequencies as we are currently unsure of the cause.

Table 1. Frequency shifting test data

Input frequency (Hz)	Ideal ratio (r_I)	Detected frequency (Hz)	Actual ratio (r_A)	Absolute difference $(|r_A - r_I|)$
1000	0.75	805.47	0.81	0.06
1500	0.75	1205.94	0.80	0.05
2000	0.75	1597.52	0.80	0.05
2500	0.75	1994.69	0.80	0.05
3000	0.75	2402.92	0.80	0.05
3500	0.75	2799.64	0.80	0.05
4000	0.75	3196.05	0.80	0.05
4500	0.75	3604.25	0.80	0.05
5000	0.75	4000.68	0.80	0.05
5500	0.75	4397.31	0.80	0.05
6000	0.75	4805.35	0.80	0.05
6500	0.75	5202.18	0.80	0.05
7000	0.75	5598.88	0.80	0.05
7500	0.75	5995.12	0.80	0.05
8000	0.75	6403.51	0.80	0.05
			SUM	0.76
			MEAN	0.05

Furthermore, people with no known hearing impairments tested the app during a face-to-face conversation. All agree that i) there are distortions present in the output signal; ii) the latency period between the input and output signal is noticeable and almost certainly longer than $50ms$. The majority of the distortions in the output signal are most likely a result of the time scaling method utilized. Because a portion of the tail end of each input signal is discarded, consecutive output signals do not match up perfectly. That is, the consecutive signals are no longer smoothly connected. The result is the periodic clicking sound heard in the output. The too large latency values are a result of audio processing issues that are inherent to the Android operating system.

We also observed that cubic spline interpolation can take up to 20 min and Lagrange interpolation can take at least 10 minutes to accomplish the up-sampling of an intermediary signal that is less than $23ms$ in length. This currently makes the point insertion by averaging technique the better choice for up-sampling the intermediary signal.

6   Conclusion

In this paper, we discuss the design and implementation of a smartphone-based hearing aid app. Specifically, our app applies user input to tailor its parameters by calculating an individualized target bandwidth and utilizing frequency compression techniques to increase speech intelligibility. Input audio is shifted to within the target bandwidth using linear frequency compression. The scheme is implemented as an app on an off-the-shelf Android-based smartphone. Our preliminary results show that the app does lower the frequencies of input signals, but there are distortions in the output audio and the latency exceeds the desired limit, which might require moving development to another platform entirely. We intend to improve this scheme by exploring the means for further reducing latency periods and distortions. Additionally, we plan to devise a method to introduce scenario adaptability to the app.

References

1. Holt, J.A., Hotto, S., Cole, K.: Demographic Aspects of Hearing Impairment: Questions and Answers. Center for Assessment & Demographic Studies, Gallaudet University (1994)
2. Simpson, A., Hersbach, A.A., McDermott, H.J.: Improvements in speech perception with an experimental nonlinear frequency compression hearing device. Int. J. Audiol. 44(5), 281–292 (2005)
3. François, G.: Guitar pitch shifter. Matlab Code and Mathematic Equations. http://www.guitarpitchshifter.com/matlab.html (2012)
4. Charpentier, F., Stella, M.: Diphone synthesis using an overlap-add technique for speech waveforms concatenation. In: IEEE International Conference on Acoustics, Speech, and Signal Processing, ICASSP 1986, vol. 11, pp. 2015–2018. IEEE (1986)
5. Laroche, J., Dolson, M.: Improved phase vocoder time-scale modification of audio. IEEE Trans. Speech Audio Process. 7(3), 323–332 (1999)
6. Capurso: Echo Capture
7. Tone Generator: Online Tone Generator. http://www.onlinetonegenerator.com
8. Seventh String Software: The Seventh String Tuner. http://www.seventhstring.com/tuner/tuner.html

Estimation Based Adaptive ACB Scheme
for M2M Communications

Hongliang He, Pinyi Ren$^{(\boxtimes)}$, Qinghe Du, and Li Sun

School of Electronic and Information Engineering,
Xi'an Jiaotong University, Xi'an, China
hehongliang@stu.xjtu.edu.cn
{pyren,duqinghe,lisun}@mail.xjtu.edu.cn

Abstract. It is a critical challenge to support massive access of devices
in a short period in machine-to-machine (M2M) communications. In this
paper, we propose a estimation based adaptive Access Class Barring
(ACB) scheme to improve the scalability of M2M networks. First, we
propose a simple estimation scheme to estimate the network loads. Then
we obtain two functions which are the relationship of ACB's *barring factor* (the parameter of access probability) and network loads to maximize
the system throughput. According to the estimation and the obtained
functions, eNB changes ACB barring factor dynamically to adapt to the
network load conditions. At the same time, we summarize the boundedness of the adaptive scheme. Finally, simulation results illustrate that
our scheme can increase the system throughput and reduce access delay
obviously.

Keywords: M2M · Adaptive ACB · Throughput · Delay

1 Introduction

The Internet of Things (IoT) is expected to provide ubiquitous connectivity among
machines and it recognized as a revolution in our daily life [1]. Machine-to-machine
communication, also called machine-type communication (MTC) in the Third
Generation Partnership (3GPP) standards, is one of the most important applications of IoT [2,6]. For M2M communication, generally a large number of devices
need to transmit small data and they will access the physical random access channel (PRACH) randomly [7], it is a difficult task to enable M2M communications
when a huge number of devices access the network simultaneously for it will results
in heavy congestion and delay [8], which is different from the traditional human-
to-human (H2H) communications and other communications [3,4].

The M2M overload problem is considered as a foremost problem. One of solutions is the scheduling which eNB can allocate the resources, such as preambles,

The research reported in this paper was supported by the National Natural Science
Foundation of China (NSFC) under Grant No. 61461136001.

K. Xu and J. Zhu (Eds.): WASA 2015, LNCS 9204, pp. 165–174, 2015.
DOI: 10.1007/978-3-319-21837-3_17

to the specified devices. But it involves a large signaling overhead [5]. Other solutions are random access oriented. In 3GPP [9], a network coordinated random access scheme called as the Access Class Barring (ACB) is adopted. However, ACB cannot adjust the access probability (one of parameters of ACB) adaptively in each slot. According to the delay characteristic of different M2M devices, Extended Access Barring (EAB) is proposed to enhance the ACB scheme. In [14], authors proposed a cooperative ACB scheme to balance the traffic of different cells. In [10], a fast adaptive slotted ALOHA scheme is studied. In [11], the authors studied the group based massive access management. In [12], an adaptive medium access control mechanism for cellular based machine-to-machine (M2M) communication is proposed. Similarly, dynamic Access Class Barring for M2M communications in LTE networks is considered in [13].

One of the reasons that M2M networks occur congestion is the eNB (the base station of LTE) cannot know the network traffic exactly. In this paper, first, we propose a simple estimation scheme to estimate the network loads. Then we get two dynamic adjustment functions, which are the relationship of ACB's access probability and network loads, to maximize the system throughput. Simulation results illustrate that two functions can achieve the same performance and it shows that our scheme significantly outperforms the traditional ACB scheme in terms of not only throughput but also average delay. Finally, we summarize the boundedness of the adaptive ACB scheme.

The remainder of the paper is organized as follow. In Sect. 2, we present the system model. Section 3 describes the estimation scheme. In Sect. 4, we analysis the metrics of adaptive ACB scheme. In Sect. 5, simulation results are presented to evaluate the performance of the proposed scheme. The paper is concluded in Sect. 6.

2   System Model

Consider a random access M2M communication scenario, which is shown in Fig. 1. One eNB and a great quantity of M2M devices in the cell. We assume the M2M devices are uniformly distributed. There are two status to every M2M device, idle or active.

2.1   Access Class Barring

In each slot i $(i = 0, 1, 2, \ldots, L)$, the eNB broadcasts an ACB barring factor p $(0 \leq p \leq 1)$, the M2M device which is activated generates a random number q $(0 \leq q \leq 1)$. If q is less than p, the active device pass through the ACB check, and it will apply for the preamble. Otherwise, the device will be barred for a period of random time [15]

$$T_{barring} = (\theta + \alpha \times rand) \times T, \tag{1}$$

and it need to repeat the ACB check in next slot, where $rand$ is a random number uniformly range from interval $[0, 1)$, T is another parameter of ACB scheme (it is a constant in this paper), $\theta = 0.7$, $\alpha = 0.6$.

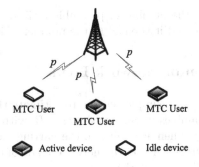

Fig. 1. Random access scenario

2.2   Random Access Procedure

The contention-based random access (RA) procedure is consisted by a four-message handshake [2]. After an active M2M device passed the ACB check, it randomly selects a preamble to transmit an access requests in message-1. Then the eNB transmits a Random Access Response (RAR) in message-2. In message-3, when the M2M device receives a response to the selected preamble, if more than one devices select the same preamble in the same RA slot, a collision will occur and the collision devices will retransmit in the next slot. In message-4, based on the reception of a Connection Request, the eNB transmits a Connection Resolution message as an answer to message-3. Noticing that in this process the eNB can obtain the number of preamble collisions and successes, but it does not know how many devices ask for the preambles. So it does not know the situation of congestion.

2.3   The Device Activation Model

In proposal [16], we know the model that the devices arrive in a period of time denoted as T_s with probability $g(t)$ and follow a beta distribution with parameters $x = 3, y = 4$

$$g(t) = \frac{t^{x-1}(T_s - t)^{y-1}}{T_s^{x+y-1}\mathcal{B}(x,y)}, \tag{2}$$

where $\mathcal{B}(x,y)$ is the beta function.

Define A_i is the number of device arrivals (i.e. network loads) in slot i, it is the sum of three-type devices: the number of active devices in slot i, it obeys beta distribution as described in formula (2); the number of devices collided in last slot $i - 1$, which will re-access the network in slot i; the number of devices did not pass the ACB check in some previous slots, which need to re-access the network in slot i. The number of devices which apply for the preambles as B_i and it is by A_i after ACB check. In each slot, the available preambles are K. Denote G as the preambles that only one device to apply and it is equal to the number of preamble successes; C as the preambles that two or more than two devices to apply and it is equal to the number of preamble collisions; I as the preambles that no devices to apply and it is equal to the number of idle preambles.

3   The Estimation of Network Loads

In this section, we propose a simple scheme to estimate the number of devices which apply for the preambles in current slot (i.e. B, without loss of generality, we omit the subscript i). Then according to the barring factor, we can estimate the number of device arrivals A (i.e. the network loads of current slot), because of A and B have the following relationship

$$B = Ap. \tag{3}$$

According to A, the eNB can change the ACB barring factor dynamically and it will be described in next section.

If B devices request to K preambles with equal probability $1/K$. The probability that one preamble is selected by exactly one device is

$$P_s = \binom{B}{1} \frac{1}{K} \left(1 - \frac{1}{K}\right)^{B-1}, \tag{4}$$

where K is the number of preambles in one slot, P_s is the probability of one preamble success. So we can get the distribution of the number of preamble successes G as

$$P(G = g) = \binom{K}{g} (P_s)^g (1 - P_s)^{K-g}. \tag{5}$$

This is a binomial distribution, so the expectation is

$$\bar{G} = E(G) = KP_s = B\left(1 - \frac{1}{K}\right)^{B-1}. \tag{6}$$

The probability that one preamble is selected by none of devices is

$$P_{none} = \left(1 - \frac{1}{K}\right)^{B}. \tag{7}$$

So we can get the distribution of the number of idle preambles I as

$$P(I = e) = \binom{K}{e} (P_{none})^e (1 - P_{none})^{K-e}. \tag{8}$$

This is also a binomial distribution, so the expectation is

$$\bar{I} = E(I) = KP_{none} = K\left(1 - \frac{1}{K}\right)^{B}. \tag{9}$$

So we can know that

$$\frac{\bar{I}}{\bar{G}} = \frac{K-1}{B}, \tag{10}$$

and

$$B = \frac{(K-1)\bar{G}}{\bar{I}}.\tag{11}$$

From Sect. 2 we have known that eNB can obtain the number of preamble collisions and successes, so we can estimate B as

$$\hat{B} = \frac{(K-1)G}{I}.\tag{12}$$

Then

$$\hat{A} = \frac{\hat{B}}{p}.\tag{13}$$

where p is the ACB barring factor. Estimate the traffic load is to adjust the network parameters (e.g. p) dynamically and the next work in our paper is to find the optimal adaptive function.

4   Parameters Analysis

4.1   Analysis of the Adaptive ACB Scheme

There are A_i devices arrive in slot i, so we can get the probability

$$\Pr\left(B_i = b_i \middle| A_i = a_i\right) = \binom{a_i}{b_i} p_i^{b_i}(1-p_i)^{a_i-b_i}.\tag{14}$$

where p_i is the ACB barring factor in slot i. We only consider that $A_i \geq 1$, and the expectation of B_i is

$$E_{B_i}\left(B_i \middle| A_i\right) = A_i \cdot p_i.\tag{15}$$

From the law of total expectation, we can obtain that

$$E_{B_i}(B_i) = E_{A_i}\left(E_{B_i}\left(B_i \middle| A_i\right)\right) = E_{A_i}(A_i \cdot p_i).\tag{16}$$

Devices which arrive in slot i, select all K preambles with equal probability p_i/K. So the probability that one preamble is selected by exactly one device as

$$P_{one} = \binom{a_i}{1}\frac{p_i}{K}\left(1 - \frac{p_i}{K}\right)^{a_i-1}\Bigg|_{A_i=a_i}.\tag{17}$$

So if there are G_i preambles to succeed, the probability of G_i is

$$\Pr\left(G_i = g_i \middle| A_i = a_i\right) = \binom{K}{g_i}P_{one}^{g_i}(1-P_{one})^{K-g_i}.\tag{18}$$

Obviously, this is a binomial distribution, the conditional expectation is

$$E_{G_i}\left(G_i \middle| A_i\right) = K \cdot P_{one}\big|_{a_i=A_i}.\tag{19}$$

According to the law of total expectation,

$$E_{G_i}(G_i) = E_{A_i}\left(E_{G_i}\left(G_i\middle|A_i\right)\right) = E_{A_i}\left(A_i \cdot p_i \left(1 - \frac{p_i}{K}\right)^{A_i-1}\right). \tag{20}$$

We know that the number of device successes are equal to the number of preamble successes, so the number of device collisions can be described as $F_i = B_i - G_i$,

$$E_{F_i}(F_i) = E_{B_i}(B_i) - E_{G_i}(G_i) = E_{A_i}\left(A_i \cdot p_i \left(1 - \left(1 - \frac{p_i}{K}\right)^{A_i-1}\right)\right). \tag{21}$$

4.2   Analysis of Metrics

In this paper, we consider the following two performance metrics:

- **Throughput ratio:** Throughput is defined as the expected number of M2M devices which access the network successfully in a period of time T_s, which is equal to the total number of preamble successes. In this paper, we prefer to consider the ratio of throughput and the total number of active devices in T_s, and we call it throughput ratio or access success probability.
- **Average access delay:** The delay of one device is the time from device sending the request to preamble until access to the M2M network successfully. So the average access delay can be defined as the ratio that the sum of each active device's delay to the total number of active devices in time T_s.

Equation (20) shows the number of device successes in each slot, so the throughput ratio can be formulated as

$$\lambda = P_{\text{suc}} = \frac{1}{N}\sum_{i=1}^{L}E_{G_i}(G_i), \tag{22}$$

L is the total number of slots, N is total number of active devices in T_s. In adaptive ACB scheme, the delay is caused by two reasons, the ACB barring and the collision. From formula (21), we obtain the collision devices' number in slot i as $E_{F_i}(F_i) = E_{B_i}(B_i) - E_{G_i}(G_i)$ which will repeat the ACB check in slot $i+1$, so the delay caused by collision in slot i can be denoted as

$$\tau_{1,i} = \left(E_{B_i}(B_i) - E_{G_i}(G_i)\right)l, \tag{23}$$

l is the length of each slot. So the total delay caused by collision is

$$\tau_1 = \sum_{i=1}^{\infty}\tau_{1,i} = \sum_{i=1}^{\infty}\left(E_{B_i}(B_i) - E_{G_i}(G_i)\right)l. \tag{24}$$

From formula (1), we know that devices locate in slot i can only go to the slot $[i + \theta T/l, i + (\alpha + \theta)T/l)$ after ACB check ($rand = 0$, $rand = 1$ respectively).

The average number of devices from slot i go to the slot $[i + \theta T/l, i + (\alpha + \theta)T/l)$ is $E_{A_i}(A_i) - E_{B_i}(B_i)$ (the number that devices pass through ACB are B_i, so the number that devices do not pass through are $A_i - B_i$), devices that uniformly drop in each slot in $[i + \theta T/l, i + (\alpha + \theta)T/l)$ are $(l/\alpha T)\left(E_{A_i}(A_i) - E_{B_i}(B_i)\right)$. so the delay brought by ACB check in slot i is

$$\tau_{2,i} = \sum_{v=i+\theta T/l}^{i+(\alpha+\theta)T/l} \frac{l}{\alpha T}\left(E_{A_v}(A_v) - E_{B_v}(B_v)\right)(v - i)l. \tag{25}$$

Then the total delay brought by ACB check is

$$\tau_2 = \sum_{i=1}^{\infty} \tau_{2,i} = \sum_{i=1}^{\infty} \sum_{v=i+\theta T/l}^{i+(\alpha+\theta)T/l} \frac{l}{\alpha T}\left(E_{A_v}(A_v) - E_{B_v}(B_v)\right)(v - i)l. \tag{26}$$

so we can obtain the average delay as $\tau = (\tau_1 + \tau_2)/N$.

4.3   The Proposed Adaptive Scheme

From formulas (20) and (22), we know that the throughput ratio is related with A_i and p_i. We hope that if eNB broadcasts a constant p_i, the loads A_i in the network is optimal or if eNB knows the network loads A_i it can broadcast a optimal barring factor p_i. We should notice that if the throughput in each slot is maximum, the system throughput will be maximized. So we can consider the maximal throughput from two aspects.

First, taking the derivative of λ with respect to A_i,

$$\frac{\partial \lambda}{\partial A_i} = p_i\left(1 - \frac{p_i}{K}\right)^{A_i - 1}\left(1 + A_i \cdot \log\left(1 - \frac{p_i}{K}\right)\right), \tag{27}$$

the base of logarithm is e. It can prove that when $A_i \leq -1/\log(1 - p_i/K)$, $\partial \lambda/\partial A_i \geq 0$, so A_i is the bigger the better and the maximum A_i is K when $p_i = 1$ under this condition. When $A_i > K$, the maximum of throughput ratio is got when $\partial \lambda/\partial A_i = 0$ and we can obtain that

$$A_i = \frac{-1}{\left(1 - \frac{p_i}{K}\right)}, \tag{28}$$

and

$$p_i = K(1 - e^{-\frac{1}{A_i}}). \tag{29}$$

So the control function is

$$p_{i1}^\star = \begin{cases} 1 & A_i < K \\ p_i & A_i \geq K. \end{cases} \tag{30}$$

and we call it method 1. Second, taking the derivative of λ with respect to p_i,

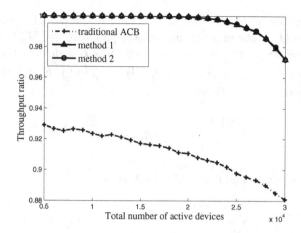

Fig. 2. The comparison of throughput ratio

we can get that

$$\frac{\partial \lambda}{\partial p_i} = A_i \left(1 - \frac{p_i}{K}\right)^{A_i-1} \left(1 - \frac{p_i}{K}(A_i - 1)\left(1 - \frac{p_i}{K}\right)^{-1}\right). \tag{31}$$

It can prove that when $A_i < K$, $\partial \lambda / \partial A_i \geq 0$, and the optimal p_i is 1. When $A_i > K$, the maximum of throughput ratio is got when $\partial \lambda / \partial p_i = 0$ and we can obtain that

$$p_i = \frac{K}{A_i}. \tag{32}$$

So the control function is

$$p_{i2}{}^\star = \begin{cases} 1 & A_i < K \\ p_i & A_i \geq K. \end{cases} \tag{33}$$

and we call it method 2.

Intuitively, if A_i and p_i exist strong corresponding relationship, the two different methods will bring similar effect. In fact, it can be proved that when $0 \leq p_i \leq 1$, the two optimal functions is almost the same, and our simulation results also show it.

4.4 The Boundedness of the Adaptive ACB Scheme

First, it is hard to change the network parameters in current slot, so the eNB can just change the parameters in next slot. It brings some errors. Second, the estimation will brings errors too. These two type of errors will affect the performance of the adaptive scheme. Third, from the formula (30) and (33), we can find that the dynamic scheme can only adjust the traffic when $A_i > K$, when $A_i < K$ it can not help and the access depends on the random access. It maybe brings the waste of preambles, and it can be further improved, which is our future work.

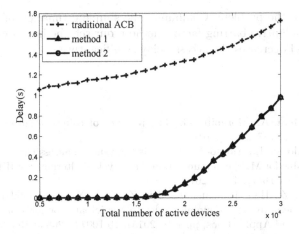

Fig. 3. The comparison of delay

5   Simulation Results

To evaluate the performance of the proposed scheme, we adopt simulation parameters in [16]. Consider a $T_s = 10\,$s randomization period and the RACH be configured to occur every 5 ms (PRACH configuration index is 6, a slot is 5 ms), there are 54 preambles in each slot. This means there are 200 RACH opportunities per second and a total of 10800 preambles per second. N range from 5000 to 30000. The mitigation of congestion can be measured by two main metrics, the system throughput and the access delay, we analysis the metrics by simulation and they are showed as follow. In order to compare, we set the traditional ACB's barring factor as 0.8 and the barring is 4, it can be proved by simulation which can obtain the best throughput.

From Fig. 2, we can know that the throughput ratio of two optimal adaptive functions are almost the same and they are higher than the traditional ACB obviously.

From Fig. 3, we can observe that the delay improvement achieved by two optimal functions as compared to the traditional ACB. In addition, the delay also illustrate two optimal adaptive functions have the same performance.

It shows that the system throughput and the access delay improved obviously by using the adaptive ACB scheme, which benefits from the combine of estimation scheme and the optimal adaptive functions. Simulation results illustrate the proposed scheme can really alleviate the congestion of M2M network.

6   Conclusion

The ability of traditional ACB to alleviate the congestion problem of M2M network is limited. In this paper, we propose an estimation based adaptive ACB scheme to solve the problem. Combining the simple estimation of the network loads and the adaptive barring factor method, our scheme improves the system throughput and decreases the access delay significantly.

References

1. Atzori, L., Iera, A., Morabito, G.: The internet of things: a survey. J. Comput. Netw. **54**(15), 2787–2805 (2010)
2. Laya, A., Alonso, L., Alonso-Zarate, J.: Is the random access channel of LTE and LTE-a suitable for M2M communications? a survey of alternatives. IEEE Commun. Surv. Tutorials **16**(1), 4–16 (2014)
3. Xu, Q., Su, Z., Han, B., Fang, D., Xu, Z., Gan, X.: Analytical model with a novel selfishness division of mobile nodes to participate cooperation. Peer-to-Peer Networking and Applications, pp.1–9 (2015). 10.1007/s12083-015-0330-6
4. Su, Z., Xu, Q., Zhu, H., Wang, Y.: A novel design for content delivery over software defined mobile social networks. IEEE Network **29**(4) (2015)
5. Gotsis, A.G., Lioumpas, A.S., Alexiou, A.: M2M scheduling over LTE: challenges and new perspectives. IEEE Veh. Technol. **7**(3), 34–39 (2012)
6. Wu, G., Talwar, S., Johnsson, K., Himayat, N., Johnson, K.: M2M: From mobile to embedded Internet. IEEE Commun. Mag. **49**(4), 4936–4943 (2011)
7. Wiriaatmadja, D.T., Choi, K.W.: Hybrid random access and data transmission protocol for machine-to-machine communications in cellular networks. Ieee trans. wirel. commun. **14**(1), 33–46 (2015)
8. Cheng, M., Lin, G., Wei, H., Hsu, A.: Overload control for machinetype-communications in LTE-advanced system. IEEE Commun. Mag. **50**(6), 38–45 (2012)
9. 3GPP TR 23.898 V7.0.0: Access class barring and overload protection (2005)
10. Wu, H., Zhu, C., La, R., Liu, X., Zhang, Y.: FASA: accelerated S-ALOHA using access history for event-driven M2M communications. IEEE/ACM Trans. Netw. **21**(6), 1904–1917 (2013)
11. Lien, S., Chen, K.: Massive access management for QoS guarantees in 3GPP machine-to-machine communications. IEEE. Commun. Lett. **15**(3), 311–313 (2011)
12. Wang, G., Zhong, X., Mei, S., Wang, J.: An adaptive medium access control mechanism for cellular based machine to machine (M2M) communication. In: Proceedings of IEEE International Conference on Wireless Information Technology and Systems (ICWITS), pp. 1–4. IEEE Press, New York (2010)
13. Duan, S., Shah-Mansouri, V., Wong, V.W.S.: Dynamic access class barring for M2M communications in LTE networks. In: IEEE Global Communications Conference (GLOBECOM), pp. 4747–4752. IEEE Press, New York (2013)
14. Lien, S.Y., Liau, T.H., Kao, C.Y., Chen, K.C.: Cooperative access class barring for machine-to-machine communications. IEEE Trans. Wirel. Commun. **11**(1), 27–32 (2012)
15. Phuyal, U., Koc, A.T., Fong, M., Vannithamby, R.: Controlling access overload and signaling congestion in M2M networks. Proceedings Conference Record of the Forty Sixth Asilomar Conference on Signals. Systems and Computers (ASILOMAR) 2012, pp. 591–595. IEEE Press, New York (2010)
16. 3GPP TSG RAN WG2 #71 R2-104663, [70bis#11] LTE: MTC LTE simulations (2010)

Optimal Power Allocations for Two-Users Spectrum Sharing Cognitive Radio with Interference Limit

Yanfei He[1(✉)], Yuan Wu[1(✉)], Jiachao Chen[1], Qinglin Zhao[2], and Weidang Lu[1]

[1] College of Information Engineering, Zhejiang University of Technology,
Hangzhou, China
{yfh_zjut,jason_chen09}@163.com
{iewuy,luweid}@zjut.edu.cn
[2] Faculty of Information Technology, Macau University of Science and Technology,
Macau, China
zqlict@hotmail.com

Abstract. In this paper, we analytically quantify the optimal power allocations for two-users spectrum sharing cognitive radio, in which two secondary users (SUs) share the licensed spectrum resource of a primary user (PU) for data transmissions. Specifically, the SUs aim at maximizing their total throughput while taking into account both their respective throughput requirements and more particularly, an interference limit constraint imposed by the PU. To derive the optimal power allocations, we categorize the feasible region of proposed problem into three different cases, and for each case, we derive the optimal power allocations in analytical expressions. Different from previous works showing that the optimal power allocations only resided on one of the vertexes of the feasible region, our results reveal that the optimal power allocations might reside on the boundary of the feasible region that corresponds to the PU's interference limit constraint. Numerical results are performed to validate our analytical results.

Keywords: Power allocations · Spectrum sharing cognitive radio · Interference limit

1 Introduction

With a rapid growth of wireless services in the past decades, the issue of *spectrum congestion* has attracted a lot of research interest. Spectrum sharing via cognitive radio (CR), in which unlicensed users (also called as secondary users, i.e., the SUs) are eligible to share the spectrum with the licensed users (also called as the primary users, i.e., the PUs), has been considered as a promising

This work is supported in part by the National Natural Science Foundation of China (61303235 and 61402416), ZJNSF-LQ13F010006, and the Macau Science and Technology Development Fund under Grant 104/2014/A3.

K. Xu and J. Zhu (Eds.): WASA 2015, LNCS 9204, pp. 175–189, 2015.
DOI: 10.1007/978-3-319-21837-3_18

approach to improve the spectrum utilization and to relieve the spectrum congestion problem [1,2]. The premise of the spectrum sharing via CR lies in that the transmissions of SUs cannot cause a harmful influence to the PU, which consequently necessitates a careful design of power control such that (i) each SU can obtain a satisfactory throughput, and (ii) the aggregate interference caused by the SUs' transmissions does not exceed a tolerable threshold set by the PU. Our work aims to analytically derive such optimal power allocations for maximizing the SUs' total throughput while taking into account each SU's individual throughput requirement and the PU's interference limit constraint.

To analytically derive the optimal power allocations, we focus on the case of two SUs sharing the spectrum of a PU. In particular, the problem is similar to the two-users transmit power control problem in wireless interference channel, which has been studied in [3–6] but without taking into account the PU's interference limit. Specifically, reference [3] investigated the power allocations for two mobile users in two different cells but only considered each user's peak transmit power constraint. As an extension of [3], reference [4] further considered each user's minimum throughput requirement. Both [3] and [4] showed that the optimal power allocations exhibited a so-called *binary* property. Reference [5] formulated a *rise-over-thermal* constraint (which can be treated as the interference limit at each mobile user) and revealed that the optimal power allocations only resided on one of the vertexes of the feasible region. Reference [6] investigated the power allocations for two interfering device-to-device users with both having the maximum and minimum rate constraints. Again, the optimal power allocations were found only at the vertexes of the feasible region.

To the best of the authors' knowledge, it is still an open topic to analytically derive the SUs' optimal power allocations when the PU's interference limit, a critical property for spectrum sharing cognitive radio, is taken into account. We notice that there exist previous works investigating the power allocations for multiple SUs subject to the PUs' interference limit constraints by using the algorithmic approaches [7–9]. They, however, seldom can derive the optimal power allocations analytically. This is our objective here. Specifically, different from the aforementioned previous works, we find that besides the vertexes of the feasible region, the SUs' optimal power allocations might also reside on the boundary of the feasible region that corresponds to the PU's interference limit (which thus are more general than the previous works). We validate this result via extensive numerical simulations and also show how the PU's interference limit influences the derived optimal power allocations.

2   System Model and Problem Formulation

2.1   System Model and Problem Formulation

We consider a scenario of two SUs sharing the licensed spectrum of one PU. Each SU is comprised of a transmitter and a receiver, and the PU performs the uplink transmission to the base station (BS). Let p_1 and p_2 denote transmit powers of

SU1 and SU2, respectively. We consider the two-users throughput maximization problem as follows:

(P1): $\max F(p_1, p_2) = W \log_2 \left(1 + \dfrac{p_1 g_{11}}{n_1 + p_2 g_{21}} \right) + W \log_2 \left(1 + \dfrac{p_2 g_{22}}{n_2 + p_1 g_{12}} \right)$

subject to: $p_1 g_{1B} + p_2 g_{2B} \leq \Gamma,$ (1)

$$\dfrac{p_1 g_{11}}{n_1 + p_2 g_{21}} \geq \gamma_1,$$ (2)

$$\dfrac{p_2 g_{22}}{n_2 + p_1 g_{12}} \geq \gamma_2,$$ (3)

$$0 \leq p_1 \leq p_1^{\max}, \text{ and } 0 \leq p_2 \leq p_2^{\max}.$$ (4)

Specifically, g_{ii} denotes the channel power gain from the transmitter of SU i to its receiver, g_{ij} denotes the channel power gain from the transmitter of SU i to the receiver of SU j, and g_{iB} denotes the channel power gain from the transmitter of SU i to the BS. Besides, n_i denotes the power of the background noise experienced by the receiver of SU i (Notice that n_i can also incorporate the interference from the PU to SU i), and W denotes the bandwidth of the PU's channel. We assume W to be unit (i.e., $W = 1$) in the rest of this work for easy presentation. Constraint (1) ensures that the total interference from the two SUs cannot exceed the PU's interference limit, which is denoted by Γ. Constraints (2) and (3) ensure that each SU i achieves its required signal to interference plus noise ratio denoted by γ_i (or equivalently, each SU i achieves its required throughput $\log_2(1 + \gamma_i)$ measured by the channel capacity formula). Finally, constraint (4) ensures that each SU i's transmit power cannot exceed the upper bound $p_i^{\max}$. In the rest of this work, we use (p_1^*, p_2^*) to denote the optimal power allocations of the two SUs of Problem (P1).

2.2 Feasible Region and Feasibility of Problem (P1)

It is apparent that (p_1^*, p_2^*) strongly depends on the feasible region comprised of (1)–(4). To geographically characterize the feasible region of (P1), we first define the following five lines:

$$\text{Line } l_0 : p_2 = f_{l_0}(p_1) = -\dfrac{g_{1B}}{g_{2B}} p_1 + \dfrac{\Gamma}{g_{2B}},$$ (5)

$$\text{Line } l_1 : p_2 = f_{l_1}(p_1) = \dfrac{g_{11}}{\gamma_1 g_{21}} p_1 - \dfrac{n_1}{g_{21}},$$ (6)

$$\text{Line } l_2 : p_2 = f_{l_2}(p_1) = \dfrac{\gamma_2 g_{12}}{g_{22}} p_1 + \dfrac{\gamma_2 n_2}{g_{22}},$$ (7)

$$\text{Line } l_{m1} : p_1 = p_1^{\max}, \text{ and Line } l_{m2} : p_2 = p_2^{\max},$$ (8)

where lines l_0, l_1, and l_2 are obtained by making constraints (1), (2), and (3) strictly binding, and lines l_{m1} and l_{m2} are obtained by fixing $p_1 = p_1^{\max}$ and $p_2 = p_2^{\max}$, respectively.

The above five lines together constrain the feasible region of Problem (P1) as shown in Fig. 1. Using the five lines, we further provide *a set of critical points*

Table 1. List of critical points

Critical points and their coordinates	Lines
$Q = \left(p_1^{\max}, p_2^{\max}\right)$	l_{m1}, l_{m2}
$X_0 = \left(\dfrac{\Gamma - g_{2B} p_2^{\max}}{g_{1B}}, p_2^{\max}\right)$	l_0, l_{m2}
$X_1 = \left(\dfrac{\gamma_1 n_1 + g_{21}\gamma_1 p_2^{\max}}{g_{11}}, p_2^{\max}\right)$	l_1, l_{m2}
$X_2 = \left(\dfrac{g_{22} p_2^{\max} - \gamma_2 n_2}{\gamma_2 g_{12}}, p_2^{\max}\right)$	l_2, l_{m2}
$Y_0 = \left(p_1^{\max}, \dfrac{\Gamma - g_{1B} p_1^{\max}}{g_{2B}}\right)$	l_0, l_{m1}
$Y_1 = \left(p_1^{\max}, \dfrac{g_{11} p_1^{\max} - \gamma_1 n_1}{\gamma_1 g_{21}}\right)$	l_1, l_{m1}
$Y_2 = \left(p_1^{\max}, \dfrac{n_2 \gamma_2 + g_{12}\gamma_2 p_1^{\max}}{g_{22}}\right)$	l_2, l_{m1}
$Z_0 = \left(\dfrac{\gamma_1\gamma_2 g_{21} n_2 + \gamma_1 n_1 g_{22}}{g_{11} g_{22} - \gamma_1\gamma_2 g_{12} g_{21}}, \dfrac{n_2 \gamma_2 g_{11} + \gamma_1\gamma_2 g_{12} n_1}{g_{11} g_{22} - \gamma_1\gamma_2 g_{12} g_{21}}\right)$	l_1, l_2
$Z_1 = \left(\dfrac{g_{21}\gamma_1 \Gamma + g_{2B} n_1 \gamma_1}{g_{11} g_{2B} + g_{1B} g_{21}\gamma_1}, \dfrac{g_{11}\Gamma - g_{1B} n_1 \gamma_1}{g_{11} g_{2B} + g_{1B} g_{21}\gamma_1}\right)$	l_0, l_1
$Z_2 = \left(\dfrac{g_{22}\Gamma - g_{2B} n_2 \gamma_2}{g_{22} g_{1B} + g_{2B} g_{12}\gamma_2}, \dfrac{g_{12}\gamma_2 \Gamma + g_{1B} n_2 \gamma_2}{g_{22} g_{1B} + g_{2B} g_{12}\gamma_2}\right)$	l_0, l_2

to be used in the rest of this work in Table 1. Specifically, Table 1 shows the coordinates of each critical point (in the first column) and the two lines whose intersection point corresponds this critical point (in the second column). For instance, point Z_0 in Table 1 represents the pair of *minimum* power allocations $(\hat{p}_1, \hat{p}_2) = ((Z_0)_h, (Z_0)_v)$ such that the SUs meet constraints (2) and (3) together exactly, **where we use $(Z_0)_h$ (or $(Z_0)_v$) to denote the horizontal-coordinate (or the vertical-coordinate) of point Z_0, with the subscript h representing "horizontal" and subscript v representing "*vertical*". We will use the same notations in the rest of this paper.**

Using point Z_0, we can characterize the feasibility of Problem (P1) as follows.

Proposition 1. *Problem (P1) is feasible if both conditions (C1) and (C2) below are met:*

$$(C1): 0 \leq Z_0 \leq Q, \ \text{and} \ (C2): (Z_0)_v \leq f_{l_0}((Z_0)_h).$$

Proof. Condition (C1) means that Z_0 is feasible to the transmit power capacities of the SUs in constraint (4), and condition (C2) means that Z_0 is feasible to the

PU's interference limit in constraint (1). In this work, we use $Z_0 \leq Q$ to represent *element-wise no greater than*, i.e., $(Z_0)_h \leq (Q)_h$ and $(Z_0)_v \leq (Q)_v$. Recall that function $f_{l_0}(\cdot)$ has been defined in Eq. (5).   □

Remark 1. Condition (C1) in Proposition 1 is equivalent to

$$g_{11}g_{22} - \gamma_1\gamma_2 g_{12}g_{21} > 0, \tag{9}$$

i.e., the interference channel power gains should be weaker enough to accommodate the throughput requirements of both SUs. In particular, constraint (9) means that the slope of line l_1 in Eq. (6) should be greater than that of l_2 in Eq. (7) such that their intersection (i.e., point Z_0) exists.   □

3   Optimal Power Allocations of Problem (P1)

In this section, we focus on solving Problem (P1) analytically, supposing that (P1) is feasible (i.e., conditions (C1) and (C2) are met). In particular, to account for the most general case of the feasible region, we assume that $f_{l_0}((Q)_h) \leq (Q)_v$ holds. Otherwise, the PU's interference limit will not influence the feasible region of Problem (P1) at all. In this case, the optimal power allocations had been given in [4]. Graphically, it means that point Q is above line l_0 (i.e., points X_0 and Y_0 always exist as shown in Figs. 1 and 2), and the interference limit Γ in constraint (1) indeed influences the feasible region.

A deep look at Problem (P1) shows that its feasible region can take the following three different cases (depending on the different positions of point Q relative to line l_1 and line l_2).

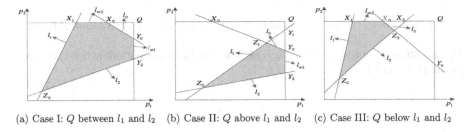

(a) Case I: Q between l_1 and l_2 (b) Case II: Q above l_1 and l_2 (c) Case III: Q below l_1 and l_2

Fig. 1. Different cases of the feasible region of Problem (P1) according to the different locations of Q relative to lines l_1 and l_2.

Case I: $f_{l_1}((Q)_h) \geq (Q)_v$ and $f_{l_2}((Q)_h) \leq (Q)_v$ hold, meaning that point Q is between lines l_1 and l_2, and points X_1 and Y_2 appear, as shown in Fig. 1(a). Note that functions $f_{l_1}(\cdot)$ and $f_{l_2}(\cdot)$ have been defined in Eq. (6) and Eq. (7), respectively.
Case II: $f_{l_1}((Q)_h) \leq (Q)_v$ and $f_{l_2}((Q)_h) \leq (Q)_v$ hold, meaning that point Q is above lines l_1 and l_2, and points Y_1 and Y_2 appear, as shown in Fig. 1(b).

Case III: $f_{l_1}((Q)_h) \geq (Q)_v$ and $f_{l_2}((Q)_h) \geq (Q)_v$ hold, meaning that point Q is below lines l_1 and l_2, and points X_1 and X_2 appear, as shown in Fig. 1(c).

We next provide the optimal power allocations of Problem (P1) for each of the above three cases. However, even we suppose that Case I happens, it is still difficult to derive the optimal power allocations analytically, since it strongly depends on the location of l_0 representing the PU's interference limit. To categorize the impact of l_0, we further consider *the following four different subcases of Case I*, depending on how line l_0 locates with respect to points X_1 and Y_2.

Subcase I.1 $f_{l_0}((X_1)_h) \geq (X_1)_v$ and $f_{l_0}((Y_2)_h) \geq (Y_2)_v$, meaning that both points X_1 and Y_2 are below line l_0, and points X_0 and Y_0 appear as shown in Fig. 2(a).

Subcase I.2 $f_{l_0}((X_1)_h) \leq (X_1)_v$ and $f_{l_0}((Y_2)_h) \leq (Y_2)_v$, meaning that both points X_1 and Y_2 are above line l_0, and points Z_1 and Z_2 appear as shown in Fig. 2(b).

Subcase I.3 $f_{l_0}((X_1)_h) \geq (X_1)_v$ and $f_{l_0}((Y_2)_h) \leq (Y_2)_v$, meaning that point X_1 is below line l_0, and point Y_2 is above line l_0, and points X_0 and Z_2 appear as shown in Fig. 2(c).

Subcase I.4 $f_{l_0}((X_1)_h) \leq (X_1)_v$ and $f_{l_0}((Y_2)_h) \geq (Y_2)_v$, meaning that point X_1 is above line l_0, and point Y_2 is below line l_0, and points Z_1 and Y_0 appear as shown in Fig. 2(d).

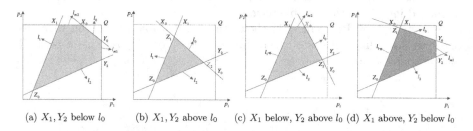

(a) X_1, Y_2 below l_0 (b) X_1, Y_2 above l_0 (c) X_1 below, Y_2 above l_0 (d) X_1 above, Y_2 below l_0

Fig. 2. Different subcases in Case I according to the different locations of line l_0 relative to points X_1 and Y_2.

3.1   Optimal Power Allocations for Subcase I.1

In this subsection, we focus on analytically deriving the optimal power allocations for Subcase I.1. We first present the following result.

Lemma 1. *The optimal power allocations* (p_1^*, p_2^*) *of Problem (P1) for Subcase I.1 (shown in Fig. 2(a)) reside within the vertexes* X_0, X_1, Y_0, *and* Y_2, *or on the line segment of* l_0 *between points* X_0 *and* Y_0.

Proof. Please refer to Appendix I.   □

To further characterize (p_1^*, p_2^*) that might appear on the line segment of l_0 between points X_0 and Y_0, we use (1) to substitute p_2 by p_1 and equivalently transform the objective function $F(p_1, p_2)$ as:

$$\hat{F}(p_1) = \log_2 \left(\frac{g_{21}\Gamma + g_{2B}n_1 - g_{21}g_{1B}p_1 + g_{11}g_{2B}p_1}{g_{21}\Gamma + g_{2B}n_1 - g_{21}g_{1B}p_1} \right)$$

$$+ \log_2 \left(\frac{g_{2B}n_2 + g_{12}g_{2B}p_1 + g_{22}\Gamma - g_{22}g_{1B}p_1}{g_{2B}n_2 + g_{12}g_{2B}p_1} \right). \tag{10}$$

Moreover, the following result holds for the above $\hat{F}(p_1)$.

Lemma 2. *Function $\hat{F}(p_1)$ has three different extremal points, which can be expressed as follows:*

$$p_1^{o_1} = \frac{-B + \sqrt{B^2 - 4AC}}{2A}, \quad \text{and } p_1^{o_2} = \frac{-B - \sqrt{B^2 - 4AC}}{2A}, \quad \text{if } A \neq 0;$$

$$p_1^{o_3} = -\frac{C}{B}, \quad \text{if } A = 0,$$

where parameters A, B, and C are given in Eqs. (11), (12) and (13), respectively, in the middle of the next page. The superscripts $o_1, o_2,$ and o_3 represent the three different cases of the extremal points.

$$A = \frac{g_{2B}}{\ln 2} \left[g_{11}g_{12}g_{2B} (n_1 g_{2B} + g_{21}\Gamma)(g_{12}g_{2B} - g_{22}g_{1B}) \right. \tag{11}$$

$$\left. - g_{22}g_{21}g_{1B} (g_{1B}n_2 + g_{12}\Gamma)(g_{21}g_{1B} - g_{11}g_{2B}) \right]$$

$$B = \frac{g_{2B}(n_1 g_{2B} + g_{21}\Gamma)}{\ln 2} \times \left[g_{11}g_{2B} (2g_{12}g_{2B}n_2 + g_{12}g_{22}\Gamma - g_{22}g_{1B}n_2) \right. \tag{12}$$

$$\left. - g_{22}(g_{1B}n_2 + g_{12}\Gamma)(g_{11}g_{2B} - 2g_{21}g_{1B}) \right]$$

$$C = \frac{g_{2B}(n_1 g_{2B} + g_{21}\Gamma)}{\ln 2} \left[g_{11}g_{2B}n_2 (n_2 g_{2B} + g_{22}\Gamma) - g_{22}(g_{1B}n_2 + g_{12}\Gamma)(n_1 g_{2B} + g_{21}\Gamma) \right]$$
$$\tag{13}$$

Proof. Please refer to Appendix II.   □

Lemma 2 and the equivalence between $\hat{F}(p_1)$ and $F(p_1, p_2)$ imply that the derived extremal points $p_1^{o_1}$, $p_1^{o_2}$, and $p_1^{o_3}$ could also possibly maximize $F(p_1, p_2)$, depending on whether they fall within the line segment of l_0 between points X_0 and Y_0 (i.e., $[\frac{\Gamma - g_{2B}p_2^{max}}{g_{1B}}, p_1^{max}]$ according to Table 1). Based on this deduction, we define the three new points, bounded by points X_0 and Y_0, as follows:

$$O_1^{I.1} = \begin{cases} (p_1^{o_1}, f_{l_0}(p_1^{o_1})), & \text{if } (X_0)_h < p_1^{o_1} < (Y_0)_h; \\ \varnothing, & \text{otherwise,} \end{cases}$$

$$O_2^{I.1} = \begin{cases} (p_1^{o_2}, f_{l_0}(p_1^{o_2})), & \text{if } (X_0)_h < p_1^{o_2} < (Y_0)_h; \\ \varnothing, & \text{otherwise,} \end{cases}$$

$$O_3^{I.1} = \begin{cases} (p_1^{o_3}, f_{l_0}(p_1^{o_3})), & \text{if } (X_0)_h < p_1^{o_3} < (Y_0)_h; \\ \varnothing, & \text{otherwise.} \end{cases}$$

Note that points X_0 and Y_0 have been provided in Table 1, and $p_1^{o_1}$, $p_1^{o_2}$, and $p_1^{o_3}$ have been given in Lemma 2.

Using Lemmas 1 and 2, we can derive (p_1^*, p_2^*) of Problem (P1) under Subcase I.1 as follows.

Theorem 1. *(Optimal Power Allocations for Subcase I.1): The optimal power allocations (p_1^*, p_2^*) of Problem (P1) under Subcase I.1 are:*

$$(p_1^*, p_2^*) = \arg \max_{(p_1,p_2) \in \{X_0, X_1, Y_0, Y_2, O_1^{I.1}, O_2^{I.1}\}} F(p_1, p_2), \text{ if } A \neq 0;$$

$$(p_1^*, p_2^*) = \arg \max_{(p_1,p_2) \in \{X_0, X_1, Y_0, Y_2, O_3^{I.1}\}} F(p_1, p_2), \quad \text{ if } A = 0.$$

Proof. Please refer to Appendix III. □

3.2   Optimal Power Allocations for Subcase I.2

Similar to Subcase I.1, we can also characterize the optimal power allocations of Problem (P1) under Subcase I.2. Specifically, we also define the following three points, which are bounded by points Z_1 and Z_2:

$$O_1^{I.2} = \begin{cases} (p_1^{o_1}, f_{l_0}(p_1^{o_1})), & \text{if } (Z_1)_h < p_1^{o_1} < (Z_2)_h; \\ \varnothing, & \text{otherwise,} \end{cases}$$

$$O_2^{I.2} = \begin{cases} (p_1^{o_2}, f_{l_0}(p_1^{o_2})), & \text{if } (Z_1)_h < p_1^{o_2} < (Z_2)_h; \\ \varnothing, & \text{otherwise,} \end{cases}$$

$$O_3^{I.2} = \begin{cases} (p_1^{o_3}, f_{l_0}(p_1^{o_3})), & \text{if } (Z_1)_h < p_1^{o_3} < (Z_2)_h; \\ \varnothing, & \text{otherwise.} \end{cases}$$

Note that $p_1^{o_1}$, $p_1^{o_2}$, and $p_1^{o_3}$ have been given in Lemma 2. However, different from Subcase I.1, in Subcase I.2 (as shown in Fig. 2(b)), the line segment l_0 is constrained by points Z_1 and Z_2 (given in Table 1). Hence, the optimal power allocations of Problem (P1) under Subcase I.2 are as follows.

Theorem 2. *(Optimal Power Allocations for Subcase I.2): The optimal power allocations (p_1^*, p_2^*) of Problem (P1) under Subcase I.2 are:*

$$(p_1^*, p_2^*) = \arg \max_{(p_1,p_2) \in \{Z_1, Z_2, O_1^{I.2}, O_2^{I.2}\}} F(p_1, p_2), \text{ if } A \neq 0;$$

$$(p_1^*, p_2^*) = \arg \max_{(p_1,p_2) \in \{Z_1, Z_2, O_3^{I.2}\}} F(p_1, p_2), \quad \text{ if } A = 0.$$

Proof. The proof is similar to that for Theorem 1 in Appendix III. We thus skip the details here due to space limitation. □

3.3   Optimal Power Allocations for Subcase I.3

Similar to Subcase I.1 and Subcase I.2, we define the following three points, which are bounded by points X_0 and Z_2 in Subcase I.3:

$$O_1^{I.3} = \begin{cases} (p_1^{o_1}, f_{l_0}(p_1^{o_1})), & \text{if } (X_0)_h < p_1^{o_1} < (Z_2)_h; \\ \varnothing, & \text{otherwise}, \end{cases}$$

$$O_2^{I.3} = \begin{cases} (p_1^{o_2}, f_{l_0}(p_1^{o_2})), & \text{if } (X_0)_h < p_1^{o_2} < (Z_2)_h; \\ \varnothing, & \text{otherwise}, \end{cases}$$

$$O_3^{I.3} = \begin{cases} (p_1^{o_3}, f_{l_0}(p_1^{o_3})), & \text{if } (X_0)_h < p_1^{o_3} < (Z_2)_h; \\ \varnothing, & \text{otherwise}. \end{cases}$$

Using the above $O_1^{I.3}$, $O_2^{I.3}$, and $O_3^{I.3}$, we can derive the optimal power allocations of Problem (P1) under Subcase I.3 as follows.

Theorem 3. *(Optimal Power Allocations for Subcase I.3): The optimal power allocations (p_1^*, p_2^*) of Problem (P1) under Subcase I.3 are:*

$$(p_1^*, p_2^*) = \arg \max_{(p_1, p_2) \in \{X_0, X_1, Z_2, O_1^{I.3}, O_2^{I.3}\}} F(p_1, p_2), \ \text{if } A \neq 0;$$

$$(p_1^*, p_2^*) = \arg \max_{(p_1, p_2) \in \{X_0, X_1, Z_2, O_3^{I.3}\}} F(p_1, p_2), \quad \text{if } A = 0.$$

Proof. The proof is similar to that for Theorem 1 given in Appendix III.   □

3.4   Optimal Power Allocations for Subcase I.4

Similar to Subcases I.1, I.2, and I.3, we define the following three points, which are now bounded by points Z_1 and Y_0 in Subcase I.4:

$$O_1^{I.4} = \begin{cases} (p_1^{o_1}, f_{l_0}(p_1^{o_1})), & \text{if } (Z_1)_h < p_1^{o_1} < (Y_0)_h; \\ \varnothing, & \text{otherwise}, \end{cases}$$

$$O_2^{I.4} = \begin{cases} (p_1^{o_2}, f_{l_0}(p_1^{o_2})), & \text{if } (Z_1)_h < p_1^{o_2} < (Y_0)_h; \\ \varnothing, & \text{otherwise}, \end{cases}$$

$$O_3^{I.4} = \begin{cases} (p_1^{o_3}, f_{l_0}(p_1^{o_3})), & \text{if } (Z_1)_h < p_1^{o_3} < (Y_0)_h; \\ \varnothing, & \text{otherwise}. \end{cases}$$

Using points $O_1^{I.4}$, $O_2^{I.4}$ and $O_3^{I.4}$ defined above, we provide the following Theorem 4.

Theorem 4. *(Optimal Power Allocations for Subcase I.4): The optimal power allocations (p_1^*, p_2^*) of Problem (P1) under Subcase I.4 are:*

$$(p_1^*, p_2^*) = \arg \max_{(p_1, p_2) \in \{Y_0, Y_2, Z_1, O_1^{I.4}, O_2^{I.4}\}} F(p_1, p_2), \ \text{if } A \neq 0;$$

$$(p_1^*, p_2^*) = \arg \max_{(p_1, p_2) \in \{Y_0, Y_2, Z_1, O_3^{I.4}\}} F(p_1, p_2), \quad \text{if } A = 0.$$

Proof. The proof is also similar to that for Theorem 1.   □

Summarizing the above four subcases, we finish deriving the optimal power allocations for Problem (P1) under Case I.

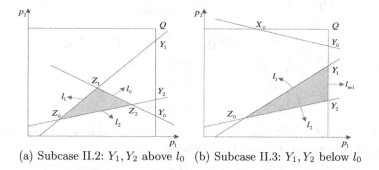

(a) Subcase II.2: Y_1, Y_2 above l_0 (b) Subcase II.3: Y_1, Y_2 below l_0

Fig. 3. Subcase II. 2 and Subcase II.3 in Case II according to the different locations of line l_0 relative to points Y_1 and Y_2. Notice that Subcase II.1 has been given in Fig. 1(b)

3.5   Optimal Power Allocations for Case II and Case III

We next derive the optimal power allocations under Case II and Case III by using the similar approach as that for Case I, i.e., categorizing different subcases that differentiate the location of l_0. In particular, we will show that each subcase of Case II (or Case III) is equivalent to one subcase of Case I, and thus the analytical optimal power allocations provided before in the previous Subsections A, B, C, and D are also applicable to the subcases of Case II and Case III.

Specifically, we first consider Case II, which includes three subcases[1], i.e., Subcase II.1 as shown in Fig. 1(b), Subcase II.2 in Fig. 3(a), and Subcase II.3 in Fig. 3(b), depending on how line l_0 locates with respect to points Y_1 and Y_2. In particular, A deep look at Subcase II.1 shows that it is in fact similar to Subcase I.4 (as shown in Fig. 2(d)), and the optimal power allocations in Theorem 4 is applicable. Subcase II.2 is similar to Subcase I.2 (in Fig. 2(b)), and thus the optimal power allocations in Theorem 2 is applicable. Finally, the optimal power allocations under Subcase II.3 are given by $(p_1^*, p_2^*) = \arg\max_{(p_1,p_2)\in\{Y_1,Y_2\}} F(p_1, p_2)$ according to Lemma 1. We thus finish deriving the optimal power allocations for Case II. Using the same approach as for Case II, we can also derive the optimal power allocations for Case III (which in fact also has three different subcases). Due to space limitation, we skip the details for the derivations for Case III in this paper.

---

[1] Different from that for Case I, the two points Y_1 and Y_2 in Case II have the same horizontal-coordinate, and thus there only exist three (instead of four) subcases in Case II.

4   Numerical Results

In this section, we perform numerical simulations to validate our analytical results in Theorems 1, 2, 3, and 4. In particular, due to space limitation, we focus on presenting the results that the optimal power allocations (p_1^*, p_2^*) occur on line l_0 when the PU's interference limit is binding, i.e., one of the extremal points given in Lemma 2 turns out to be the optimal power allocations, which is a key advance we have made in this work in comparison with the previous ones. We set the background noise $n_i = 0.01\,W$ and set the SUs' maximum transmit powers $p_1^{\max} = 1.0\,W$ and $p_2^{\max} = 1.5\,W$.

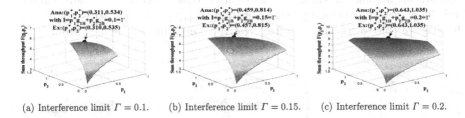

(a) Interference limit $\Gamma = 0.1$.   (b) Interference limit $\Gamma = 0.15$.   (c) Interference limit $\Gamma = 0.2$.

Fig. 4. Sum throughput $F(p_1, p_2)$ with different interference limits (i,e, Γ) of the PU for the case of $A \neq 0$. The channel power gains are $g_{11} = 0.2$, $g_{22} = 0.4$, $g_{12} = g_{21} = 0.01$, $g_{1B} = 0.15$, and $g_{2B} = 0.1$, and the SUs' minimum SINR requirements are $\gamma_1 = \gamma_2 = 2$.

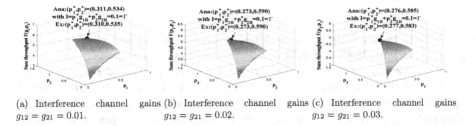

(a) Interference channel gains (b) Interference channel gains (c) Interference channel gains
$g_{12} = g_{21} = 0.01$. $g_{12} = g_{21} = 0.02$. $g_{12} = g_{21} = 0.03$.

Fig. 5. Sum throughput $F(p_1, p_2)$ with different levels of cross interference (i,e, g_{12} and g_{21}) for the case of $A \neq 0$. The rest of the channel gains are $g_{11} = 0.2$, $g_{22} = 0.4$, $g_{1B} = 0.15$, and $g_{2B} = 0.1$, and the SUs' minimum SINR requirements are $\gamma_1 = \gamma_2 = 2$. The PU's interference limit is $\Gamma = 0.1$.

Figure 4 shows the values of $F(p_1, p_2)$ by enumerating different (p_1, p_2) for three cases of the PU's interference limit Γ (i,e, $\Gamma = 0.1, 0.15$, and 0.2). In this figure, we set $g_{11} = 0.2$, $g_{22} = 0.4$, $g_{12} = g_{21} = 0.01$, $g_{1B} = 0.15$, $g_{2B} = 0.1$, and $\gamma_1 = \gamma_2 = 2$, which yield $A \neq 0$ according to (11). In each subfigure, we mark out the optimal power allocations (p_1^*, p_2^*) (denoted by "Ana:"), which are analytically derived according to one of Theorems 1, 2, 3, and 4. In particular, only one theorem is applicable to derive (p_1^*, p_2^*), depending on which of the specific cases (i.e., Subcases I.1, I.2, I.3, and I.4) occurs. For instance, Subcase I.2 occurs in Fig. 3(a), and we thus use Theorem 2 to derive (p_1^*, p_2^*) accordingly. To validate this result, we also use exhaustive search to find the optimal power allocations (in a brute-force manner) and mark out the corresponding result which is denoted by "Ex:". The comparisons between the two sets of the results show that the analytically derived (p_1^*, p_2^*) match those obtained by exhaustive search very well, thus validating Theorems 1, 2, 3, and 4. Besides, in each subfigure, we also mark out the SUs' total interference, i.e., $I = p_1^* g_{1B} + p_2^* g_{2B}$, which matches with Γ well, meaning that the optimal power allocations (p_1^*, p_2^*) indeed occur on line l_0 (i.e., the PU's interference limit constraint is strictly binding). Moreover, the comparisons among the three subfigures show that when the PU's interference limit increases, the optimal power allocations (p_1^*, p_2^*) increase accordingly, i.e., the SUs are able to transmit more aggressively and achieve a higher throughput.

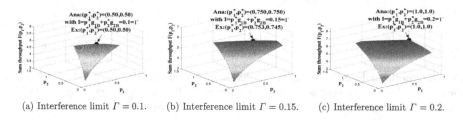

(a) Interference limit $\Gamma = 0.1$.   (b) Interference limit $\Gamma = 0.15$.   (c) Interference limit $\Gamma = 0.2$.

Fig. 6. Sum throughput $F(p_1, p_2)$ with different interference limits (i,e, Γ) of the PU for the case of $A = 0$. The channel power gains are $g_{11} = g_{22} = 0.2$, $g_{12} = g_{21} = 0.02$, and $g_{1B} = g_{2B} = 0.1$. The SUs' minimum SINR requirements are $\gamma_1 = \gamma_2 = 2$.

Figure 5 shows $F(p_1, p_2)$ with different levels of the cross interference (i.e., $g_{12} = g_{21} = 0.01, 0.02$, and 0.03 in the three subfigures, respectively). Here, we set $g_{11} = 0.2$, $g_{22} = 0.4$, $g_{1B} = 0.15$, $g_{2B} = 0.1$, $\gamma_1 = \gamma_2 = 2$, and $\Gamma = 0.1$, which again yield $A \neq 0$ according to (11). Similar to Fig. 4, the analytically derived optimal power allocations (p_1^*, p_2^*) based on Theorems 1, 2, 3, and 4 match those obtained by exhaustive search very well. Besides, the optimal power allocations (p_1^*, p_2^*) indeed occur when the the PU's interference limit constraint is binding. In particular, the comparison among the three subfigures shows that when the cross interference is weak, both SUs can transmit simultaneously (i.e., sharing the PU's spectrum) for maximizing their total throughput. In comparison, when the cross interference becomes greater, only one favorable SU will be selected to transmit (to avoid excessive interference between the SUs) for maximizing their total throughput. This in fact turns back to the results in the previous work, i.e., the optimal power allocations occur on one of the vertices of the feasible region.

Finally, Fig. 6 also shows $F(p_1, p_2)$ for the case of $A = 0$ (in particular, we set a symmetric case that $g_{11} = g_{22} = 0.2$, $g_{12} = g_{21} = 0.02$, $g_{1B} = g_{2B} = 0.1$, and $\gamma_1 = \gamma_2 = 2$, which yield $A = 0$ according to (11)). And we vary $\Gamma = 0.1, 0.15$, and 0.2 in the three subfigures. Again, in all the tested cases, the analytically derived optimal power allocations match those obtained by exhaustive search, thus validating Theorems 1, 2, 3, and 4 for the case of $A = 0$.

5 Conclusion

In this paper, we have derived the optimal power allocations for two SUs sharing the licensed spectrum of a PU in spectrum sharing cognitive radio. Specifically, the two SUs aim at maximizing their total throughput, while taking into account both their respective throughput requirements and the PU's interference limit constraint. We categorized the feasible region into different cases and then analytically derived the optimal power allocations for each case. Different from previous works showing that the optimal power allocations only resided on one of the vertices of the feasible region, our results reveal that the optimal power allocations might reside on the boundary of the feasible region that corresponds to the PU's interference limit constraint, and thus are more general. We have performed extensive numerical results to validate our analytical results and show how the PU's interference limit and the cross interference among the SUs influence the optimal power allocations.

Appendix I: Proof of Lemma 1

The proof is similar to that in [4], which considered the feasible region comprised of each user's peak transmit power constraint, but without considering the PU's interference limit constraint (represented by line segment l_0 between points X_0 and Y_0 as shown in Fig. 2(a)). Thus, using the similar technique as in [4], we can prove that X_0, X_1, Y_0, and Y_2 are the candidates for the optimal power allocations of Problem (P1). Moreover, since (i) for some $\lambda > 1$, there exists

$$F(\lambda p_1, \lambda p_2) = \log_2(1 + \frac{\lambda g_{11} p_1}{n_1 + \lambda g_{21} p_2}) + \log_2(1 + \frac{\lambda g_{22} p_2}{n_2 + \lambda g_{12} p_1})$$
$$= \log_2(1 + \frac{g_{11} p_1}{\frac{n_1}{\lambda} + g_{21} p_2}) + \log_2(1 + \frac{g_{22} p_2}{\frac{n_2}{\lambda} + g_{12} p_1}) > F(p_1, p_2),$$

i.e., the total throughput of the two SUs increases when the power allocation pair (p_1, p_2) increases, and (ii) p_1 and p_2 are coupled by function $g_{1B} p_1 + g_{2B} p_2 = \Gamma$ on line l_0. Therefore, the points on the line segment of l_0 between X_0 and Y_0 are also the possible candidates for the optimal power allocations.

Thus, the optimal power allocations of Problem (P1) under Subcase I.1 must reside within the vertexes X_0, X_1, Y_0, and Y_2, or on the line segment of l_0 between points X_0 and Y_0.

Appendix II: Proof of Lemma 2

To derive the possible extremal points on line segment l_0 between points X_0 and Y_0, we calculate the first order derivative of $\hat{F}(p_1)$ as follows:

$$\frac{d\hat{F}(p_1)}{dp_1} = \frac{A p_1^2 + B p_1 + C}{D},$$

where parameters A, B, and C have given in Eqs. (11), (12) and (13), respectively. Meanwhile, parameter D is given by:

$$D = \left(n_1 g_{2B} + g_{21}\Gamma + g_{11}g_{2B}p_1 - g_{21}g_{1B}p_1\right) \times \left(n_1 g_{2B} + g_{21}\Gamma - g_{21}g_{1B}p_1\right) \times$$
$$\left(n_2 g_{2B} + g_{22}\Gamma + g_{12}g_{2B}p_1 - g_{22}g_{1B}p_1\right) \times \left(n_2 g_{2B} + g_{12}g_{2B}p_1\right).$$

In particular, $D > 0$ always holds, since the four items (in the product form) in D correspond to the numerators and denominators in the $\log(\cdot)$ expression in Eq. (10). By imposing $\frac{d\hat{F}(p_1)}{dp_1} = 0$, we obtain a quadratic equation $Ap_1^2 + Bp_1 + C = 0$, whose roots can be analytically given by

$$p_1^{o_1} = \frac{-B + \sqrt{B^2 - 4AC}}{2A}, \text{ and } p_1^{o_2} = \frac{-B - \sqrt{B^2 - 4AC}}{2A}, \text{ if } A \neq 0;$$
$$p_1^{o_3} = -\frac{C}{B}, \qquad \text{if } A = 0,$$

which correspond to the extremal points on line segment l_0 that might maximize $\hat{F}(p_1)$ (or equivalently, $F(p_1, p_2)$).

Appendix III: Proof of Theorem 1

For the case of $A \neq 0$, there exist two extremal points $O_1^{I.1} = (p_1^{o_1}, f_{l_0}(p_1^{o_1}))$, $O_2^{I.1} = (p_1^{o_2}, f_{l_0}(p_1^{o_2}))$ on the line segment of l_0 according to Lemma 2. In companion with the previous four points $X_0, X_1, Y_0,$ and Y_2 (which have been proved in Lemma 1), the optimal power allocations (p_1^*, p_2^*) of Problem (P1) under Subcase I.1 can thus be given by

$$(p_1^*, p_2^*) = \arg \max_{(p_1, p_2) \in \{X_0, X_1, Y_0, Y_2, O_1^{I.1}, O_2^{I.1}\}} F(p_1, p_2).$$

Similarly, for the case of $A = 0$, there exists one extremal point $O_3^{I.1} = (p_1^{o_3}, f_{l_0}(p_1^{o_3}))$ on the line segment of l_0. Again, in companion with the previous four points $X_0, X_1, Y_0,$ and Y_2, the optimal power allocations (p_1^*, p_2^*) under Subcase I.1 can thus be given by

$$(p_1^*, p_2^*) = \arg \max_{(p_1, p_2) \in \{X_0, X_1, Y_0, Y_2, O_3^{I.1}\}} F(p_1, p_2).$$

References

1. Liang, Y.C., Chen, K.C., Li, G.Y., Mahonen, P.: Cognitive radio networking and communications: an overview. IEEE Trans. Veh. Technol **60**(7), 3386–3407 (2011)
2. Liu, Y., Cai, L.X., Luo, H., Shen, X.: Deploying cognitive cellular networks under dynamic resource management. IEEE Wirel. Commun. **20**(2), 82–88 (2013)
3. Gjendemsio, A., Gesbert, D., Oien, G.E., Kiani, S.G.: Optimal power allocation and scheduling for two-cell capacity maximization. In: Proceedings of International Symposium on Modeling and Optimization in Mobile, Ad Hoc and Wireless Networks (2006)

4. Chen, C.S., Oien, G.E.: Optimal power allocation for two-cell sum rate maximuzation under minimum rate constraints. In: Proceedings of IEEE International Symposium on Wireless Communication Systems (2008)
5. Chandrasekhar, V., Shen, Z.K.: Optimal uplink power control in two-cell systems with rise-over-thermal constraints. IEEE Commun. Lett. **12**(3), 173–175 (2008)
6. Yu, C.H., Doppler, K., Ribeiro, C.B., Tirkkonen, O.: Resource sharing optimization for device-to-device communication underlaying cellular networks. IEEE Trans. Wireless Commun. **10**(8), 2752–2763 (2011)
7. Wu, Y., Zhang, T.Y., Tsang, D.H.K.: Joint pricing and power allocation for dynamic spectrum access networks with stackelberg game model. IEEE Trans. Wireless Commun. **10**(1), 12–19 (2011)
8. Wu, Y., Zhu, Q.H., Huang, J.W., Tsang, D.H.K.: Revenue sharing based resource allocation for dynamic spectrum access networks. IEEE J. Sel. Areas Commun. **32**(11), 2280–2297 (2014)
9. Huang, J.W., Berry, R., Honig, M.L.: Auction-based spectrum sharing. ACM MONET **11**(3), 405–418 (2006)

Adaptive Resource Allocation for Anti-money Laundering Based on SMDP

Xintao Hong[1], Hongbin Liang[2]([✉]), and Zengan Gao[1]

[1] School of Economics and Management,
Southwest Jiaotong University, Chengdu, China
xintao.hong@gmail.com, gaozengan133@163.com
[2] School of Transportation and Logistics,
Southwest Jiaotong University, Chengdu, China
hbliang@swjtu.edu.cn

Abstract. Anti-money laundering(AML) compliance is having deeply effects on the culture, organization, and technology of Fiancial institutions(FIs). One of the most critical research issues in AML is how to efficiently and adaptively allocate limited AML resource to analyze suspicious transactions to achieve maximal AML rewards. In this paper, a novel Adaptive AML Resource Allocation Model(AAMLRAM) based on Semi-Markov Decision Process (SMDP) is proposed to allocate AML resources optimally in AML resource allocation domain to analyze the suspicious transaction report sent from FIs. Based on our proposed AAMLRAM, AML resource allocation domain can achieve maximal AML rewards, taking into account not only the incomes of identifying the suspicious transaction but also the cost resulted from AML resource occupation as well. Extensive simulations are conducted to demonstrate that our proposed model can achieve higher AML resource allocation domain system reward compared to traditional approach based on the Greedy resource allocation algorithms. Performance comparisons with various AML resource allocation schemes are also provided.

Keywords: Anti-money laundering(AML) · Semi-Markov Decision Process(SMDP) · Adaptive AML resource allocation model(AAMLRAM)

1 Introduction

Financial institutions (FIs) such as banks are legally obliged to compliance with statutory and regulatory requirement for monitoring, analyzing and reporting suspicious activities that may be connected with criminal activities. Tremendous quantities of suspicious transaction reports have submitted to the financial intelligence units(FIU) which carried out its mission by receiving and maintaining financial transaction's data; analyzing and disseminating that data for law enforcement purposes, but only a few transactions are deemed suspicious within a given amount. The poor quality of intelligence, together with the false negatives, the false positives and missing detected, leads to a gradual increasing in

K. Xu and J. Zhu (Eds.): WASA 2015, LNCS 9204, pp. 190–200, 2015.
DOI: 10.1007/978-3-319-21837-3_19

the inferior quality of the suspicious transaction reporting system that greatly affected the monitoring/analyzing of suspicious transactions and transferring of suspected criminal information and significantly negative impact on these data's utilization.

To improve the effectiveness of suspicious transaction reporting system and the information analysis capacity of FIs, it requires FIs to spent more effort and resources (such as human, computation, communication, storage resource, etc.) to identify and report these suspicious transactions. Utilizing these AML resources in preventing of money laundering, of course, come at a large sum of compliance costs, and it is highly burdensome to the FIs [1]. Years of research by KPMG shows, the rapid growth of AML compliance costs has become a sustained phenomenon in the development of international financial industry. The rationality of the FIs is reflected in the desire to maximize the difference between compliance cost and expected benefit that accrue as the result of AML activity. Thus not all of these FIs are willing to commit more AML resource and to bear the increasingly significant AML compliance cost [2].

Furthermore, AML compliance is having deeply effects on the culture, organization, and technology of FIs. The key driver for implementing a solid AML program is reputation risk. Non-compliance that implies reputation risk may trigger current and potential customers away and result in loss of business. According to Harvey [2]: "loss of reputation can result in direct costs (loss of income), indirect costs (client withdrawal and possible legal costs) and opportunity costs (foregone business opportunities) all of which will reduce the overall profitability of the firm." It may be surmised that in order to avoid these cost, FIs will spend effort and resources to prevent, control and insulate the institution from losses due reputation risk [3].

Therefore, in order to make the best use of AML resources to analyze these financial data and information with the considerations of the increasing AML resource's consumptions and compliance cost to archive maximal AML rewards, it is of critical importance to allocate the AML resources adaptively according to diverse requirements of the identification of AML suspicious transaction report, which has become a major problem in the effective resource management of AML.

In fact, there are a number of papers in the literature that intends to give more view on the economic analysis of AML compliance in FIs and the effectiveness of the suspicious transaction reporting system. Jackie Harvey [4] draws attention to compare the probable costs and benefits of AML compliance and found that costs of compliance are significant, and that there is a need to understand more clearly both the objectives of regulation and the amount of money-laundering activity coming about. Milind Sathye [5] attempted to estimate the cost of AML compliance to help realize the regulatory burden of the legislation. Furthermore, some of the AML approaches on the basis of data mining techniques have been proposed and applied in literature. Most of these approaches have been widely used for financial modeling, which tries to identify money-laundering patterns by different techniques such as support vector machine [6], correlation analysis [7], neural network [8], etc. It is known that the Markov model is extensively used in wireless communication and cloud computing [9–11], but none of these works addressed AML resource's allocation issue based on a reward model, considering prioritized suspicious transaction reports.

In this paper, we present an adaptive AML resource allocation model based on Semi-Markov Decision Process (SMDP) to achieve the objective mentioned above. Our proposed Adaptive AML Resource Allocation Model(AAMLRAM) considers not only the incomes of identifying the suspicious transaction, but also the cost resulted from AML resource occupation in the AML domain. Thus, the overall economic gain is determined by a comprehensive approach which considers all the factors mentioned above.

The rest of this paper is organized as follows. In Sect. 2, the basic system model is described. The Semi-Markov Decision Process Model for AML system is presented in Section. We evaluate the performance of the proposed economic model in Sect. 4 and conclude this paper and discuss the future work in Sect. 5.

2   System Model

In AML resource allocation system, an Anti-Money Laundering Resource Allocation Units (AMLRAUs in our following discussion) can handle a portion of AML resources (human, computation, communication, storage resource, etc.) that can satisfy the minimal resource requirement to process a suspicious transaction report in the AML domain. Each AMLRAU has the capacity to process one suspicious transaction report at a time, and two types of suspicious transaction reports are defined to be handled by an AMLRAU: (i) *Higher-Risk Operation* (HRO), which is include higher-risk of product and service, customer and entities, transactions and geographic locations; (ii) *Lower or Moderate Risk Operation* (L/MRO)[12]. Comparing with L/MRO, HRO indicates the transactions that potentially expose the FI to financial loss, increased expenses, or reputation risk and it also involve the more possibilities to attempt launder money, finance terrorism, or conduct other illegal activities through the FI. Thus, suspicious transaction report at HRO level needs to be processed immediately with higher priority.

2.1   System Description

In this paper, we consider an AML resource allocation domain with K AMLRAUs. The maximum number of AMLRAUs that can be allocated to a suspicious transaction report is c AMLRAUs (we denote as c allocation scheme), where $c \in \{1, 2, ...C\}$, $C \leq K$. Generally, the duration for processing a suspicious transaction report in the AML domain depends on the number of AMLRAUs allocated to that report. The relationship between the processing time of a suspicious transaction report and the number of allocated AMLRAUs in the AML domain can be expressed as a function denoted as $\xi(c)$. Assume the time to process a suspicious transaction report by using one AMLRAU in an AML resource allocation domain is θ_s, therefore the time to handle the report is $\xi(c)\theta_s$ if c AMLRAUs are allocated to that report. The higher processing speed for a suspicious transaction report in an AML resource allocation domain means more suspicious transaction reports can be processed by the AML resource allocation domain, which can increase the whole AML domain system reward significantly. Thus, in order to improve the whole system reward of an AML resource allocation domain by speeding the processing time of a suspicious transaction report, the traditional Greedy algorithm [13] always decide to allocate maximal AMLRAUs to the report. But on the other hand, if the AML resources (denoted by the number of AMLRAUs) allocated to the current report by the AML resource allocation domain are too high, then the following several arrival suspicious transaction reports may be postponed by the AML resource allocation domain because of insufficient available AML resources. As a result, the system rewards of that AML resource allocation domain degrade as well.

To model this complex dynamic AML resource allocation process, without loss of generality, we assume the arrival rates of both *HRO* and *L/MRO* suspicious transaction reports follow Poisson distributions with mean rate of λ_h and λ_l, respectively. The life time of reports follows exponential distributions. The mean processing time of a suspicious transaction report which is allocated only one AMLRAU in the AML resource allocation domain is $1/\mu$. Thus the processing time of the suspicious transaction report allocated c VMs in the AML domain is $\frac{\xi(c)}{\mu}$, which implies the mean processing rate of suspicious transaction report is $\frac{\mu}{\xi(c)}$.

Since the decision making epoch is randomly generated in the AML domain, we use Semi-Markov Decision Process (SMDP) to model the dynamic AML resource allocation process based on the system description we presented above. SMDP is a stochastic dynamic programming method, which can be used to model and solve optimal dynamic decision making problems. There are six following elements in the SMDP model: (a) *system states*; (b) *action sets*; (c) *the events that cause the decisions* ; (d) *decision epoches*; (e) *transition probabilities*; and (f) *reward*. In the following, we first present the system states, the actions, the events and the reward model for the AML resource allocation domain.

2.2 System States

According to the assumption, there are total K AMLRAUs in AML resource allocation domain, and c AMLRAUs can be allocated to a suspicious transaction report, which is from 1 to C, where $C \leq K$. However, the arrival of *HRO* suspicious transaction report and *L/MRO* suspicious transaction report, and the finish of processing that suspicious transaction report are distinct events. Thus the system states can be described by the number of the suspicious transaction reports processed by AML domain which occupy the same number of AML-RAUs, and the events (including both arrival of suspicious transaction report and completing to process a suspicious transaction report) in the AML resource allocation domain. Here, we use c to indicate the number of AMLRAUs allocated to one suspicious transaction report (denoted as c allocation scheme as presented in Sect. 2.1), $c \in \{1, 2, ...C\}$. Therefore, the number of the suspicious transaction reports being processed by AML domain which occupy c AMLRAUs in the AML resource allocation domain can be denoted as s_c.

In the AML resource allocation domain, we can define two types of report events: (1) a *HRO* or *L/MRO* suspicious transaction report arrives from a FI, denoted by A_h and A_l, respectively; and (2) the completing to process a suspicious transaction report occupying c AMLRAUs in the AML resource allocation domain, denoted by F_c. Thus, the event e in the AML resource allocation domain can be described as $e \in \{A_h, A_l, F_1, F_2, ..., F_C\}$. Therefore, the system state can be expressed as

$$S = \{s | s = \langle s_1, s_2, ..., s_C, e \rangle\}.$$

where $\sum_{c=1}^{C} (s_c * c) \leq K$

2.3 Actions

For a system state of the AML resource allocation domain with an incoming suspicious transaction report from a FI (i.e., A_h or A_l), the AML resource allocation domain needs to make a decision on whether to accept the suspicious transaction report and what is the allocation scheme (i.e., how many AMLRAUs to allocate to the report) if the decision is acceptance. If the decision is acceptance, then the c allocation scheme is assigned to the arriving suspicious transaction report, thus the action to assign the c allocation scheme can be denoted as $a(s) = c$. While if the decision is postponement based on the whole system reward, which means no AMLRAU will be assigned, thus the *HRO* or *L/MRO* suspicious transaction report will be postponed. Then the action to postpone the suspicious transaction report can be denoted as $a(s) = 0$.

And for the completing to process a suspicious transaction report in the AML resource allocation domain (i.e., $e = F_c$), the action for this event can be considered as to calculate the current available AML resources and denoted as $a(s) = -1$. Therefore, the action space can be defined as $a(s) \subseteq Act_s$, where

$$a(s) = \begin{cases} \{0, 1, ...C\}, & e \in \{A_h, A_l\} \\ -1, & e \in \{F_1, F_2, ..., F_C\} \end{cases} \tag{1}$$

2.4 Reward Model

Based on the system state and its corresponding action, we can evaluate the whole AML resource allocation domain system reward (denoted by $r(s, a)$), which is computed based on the income and the cost as follows:

$$r(s, a) = w(s, a) - g(s, a), \quad e \in \{A_h, A_l, F_1, F_2, ..., F_C\}, \tag{2}$$

where $w(s,a)$ is the net lump sum income for the AML resource allocation domain, and $g(s,a)$ denotes the system cost of AML resource allocation domain.

The net lump sum income are the benefits from avoidance of the cost of reputation risk (direct costs, indirect costs and opportunity costs) plus the cost of financial penalty, which can be computed as:

$$w(s,a) = \begin{cases} 0, & a(s) = -1, e \in \{F_1, F_2, ..., F_C\} \\ 0, & a(s) = 0, e \in \{A_h, A_l\} \\ E_h - \xi(c)\theta_s\beta, & a(s) = c, e = A_h \\ E_l - \xi(c)\theta_s\beta, & a(s) = c, e = A_l. \end{cases} \quad (3)$$

In the Eq. (3), E_h and E_l are the incomes of the AML resource allocation domain obtained by accepting a *HRO* suspicious transaction report or a *L/MRO* suspicious transaction report from the FI, respectively. β denotes the price per unit time, which has the same measurement unit as the income. Thus, $\theta_s\beta$ denotes the expense measured by the time consumed to process the suspicious transaction report using one AMLRAU in an AML resource allocation domain. Therefore, $\xi(c)\theta_s\beta$ denotes the expense measured by the time consumed to process the suspicious transaction report using c AMLRAUs in an AML resource allocation domain.

In (2), $g(s,a)$ is given by:

$$g(s,a) = \tau(s,a)o(s,a), \quad a(s) \in Act_s. \quad (4)$$

In (4), $\tau(s,a)$ is the average expected processing time when the system state transfers from current state s to the next potential state j and the decision a is made; $o(s,a)$ is the cost rate of the processing time, it is defined as the number of all occupied AMLRAUs, thus it can be computed as

$$o(s,a) = \sum_{c=1}^{C}(s_c * c). \quad (5)$$

3   SMDP Based Adaptive AML Resource Allocation Model

There are three types of events in the AML resource allocation domain (i.e., an arrival of a *HRO* suspicious transaction report, an arrival of a *L/MRO* suspicious transaction report, and the completing of a processed suspicious transaction report). The next decision epoch occurs when any of the three types of events takes place. Based on our assumption, the arrival of suspicious transaction report follows poisson distribution and the completing of a processed suspicious transaction report follows exponential distribution. Thus, the expected time duration between two decision epochs (i.e., $\tau(s,a)$) follows exponential distribution as well. Then, the mean rate (denoted as $\gamma(s,a)$) of expected time can be represented as

$$\gamma(s,a) = \tau(s,a)^{-1} = \begin{cases} \lambda_h + \lambda_l + \sum_{c=1}^{C} \frac{s_c \mu}{\xi(c)}, & \begin{aligned} & e \subseteq \{F_1, F_2, ..., F_C\} \\ & \text{or } e \subseteq \{A_h, A_l\}, a = 0; \end{aligned} \\ \lambda_h + \lambda_l + \sum_{c=1}^{C} \frac{s_c \mu}{\xi(c)} + \frac{\mu}{\xi(c)}, & e \subseteq \{A_h, A_l\}, a = c. \end{cases} \tag{6}$$

Thus the expected discounted reward (denoted as $r(s,a)$) during $\tau(s,a)$ can be obtained,

$$r(s,a) = w(s,a) - o(s,a)E_s^a \left\{ \int_0^\tau e^{-\alpha t} dt \right\} = w(s,a) - o(s,a)E_s \left\{ \frac{[1 - e^{-\alpha \tau}]}{\alpha} \right\}$$

$$= w(s,a) - \frac{o(s,a)}{\alpha + \gamma(s,a)} \tag{7}$$

where α is a continuous-time discounting factor, and $w(s,a)$, $o(s,a)$ and $\gamma(s,a)$ are defined in (3), (5) and (6) respectively.

Then the only element left to be calculated is the transition probabilities. Let $q(j|s,a)$ denote the state transition probability from the current state s to the next state j when action a is chosen. Then the transition probability $q(j|s,a)$ can be expressed as following.

For the state $s = \langle s_1, s_2, .., s_c, .., s_C, A_h \rangle$, $q(j|s,a)$ can be obtained as

$$q(j|s,a) = \begin{cases} \frac{\lambda_h}{\gamma(s,a)}, & j = \langle s_1, s_2, ..., s_C, A_h \rangle, a = 0 \\ \frac{\lambda_l}{\gamma(s,a)}, & j = \langle s_1, s_2, ..., s_C, A_l \rangle, a = 0 \\ \frac{s_c \mu}{\xi(c)\gamma(s,a)}, & j = \langle s_1, s_2, .., s_c - 1, .., s_C, F_c \rangle, s_c \geq 1, a = 0 \\ \frac{(s_c+1)\mu}{\xi(c)\gamma(s,a)}, & j = \langle s_1, s_2, .., s_c, .., s_C, F_c \rangle, a = c \\ \frac{s_m \mu}{\xi(m)\gamma(s,a)}, & j = \langle s_1, s_2, .., s_m - 1, .., s_c + 1, .., s_C, F_m \rangle, s_m \geq 1, m \neq c, a = c \\ \frac{\lambda_h}{\gamma(s,a)}, & j = \langle s_1, s_2, .., s_c + 1, .., s_C, A_h \rangle, s_c \leq C - 1, a = c \\ \frac{\lambda_l}{\gamma(s,a)}, & j = \langle s_1, s_2, .., s_c + 1, .., s_C, A_l \rangle, s_c \leq C - 1, a = c. \end{cases} \tag{8}$$

where $c \subseteq \{1, 2, .., C\}, m \subseteq \{1, 2, .., C\}, m \neq c$.

For the states $s = \langle s_1, s_2, .., s_c, .., s_C, A_l \rangle$, $q(j|s,a)$ can be obtained as

$$q(j|s,a) = \begin{cases} \frac{\lambda_h}{\gamma(s,a)}, & j = \langle s_1, s_2, ..., s_C, A_h \rangle, a = 0 \\ \frac{\lambda_l}{\gamma(s,a)}, & j = \langle s_1, s_2, ..., s_C, A_l \rangle, a = 0 \\ \frac{s_c \mu}{\xi(c)\gamma(s,a)}, & j = \langle s_1, s_2, .., s_c - 1, .., s_C, F_c \rangle, s_c \geq 1, a = 0 \\ \frac{(s_c+1)\mu}{\xi(c)\gamma(s,a)}, & j = \langle s_1, s_2, .., s_c, .., s_C, F_c \rangle, a = c \\ \frac{s_m \mu}{\xi(m)\gamma(s,a)}, & j = \langle s_1, s_2, .., s_m - 1, .., s_c + 1, .., s_C, F_m \rangle, s_m \geq 1, m \neq c, a = c \\ \frac{\lambda_h}{\gamma(s,a)}, & j = \langle s_1, s_2, .., s_c + 1, .., s_C, A_h \rangle, s_c \leq C - 1, a = c \\ \frac{\lambda_l}{\gamma(s,a)}, & j = \langle s_1, s_2, .., s_c + 1, .., s_C, A_l \rangle, s_c \leq C - 1, a = c. \end{cases} \tag{9}$$

where $c \subseteq \{1, 2, .., C\}, m \subseteq \{1, 2, .., C\}, m \neq c$.

For the states $s = \langle s_1, s_2, .., s_c, .., s_C, F_c \rangle$, the action for this departure state is always -1 which means $a = -1$, then the transition probability $q(j|s,a)$ can be obtained as

$$
q(j|s,a) = \begin{cases} \frac{\lambda_h}{\gamma(s,a)}, & j = \langle s_1, s_2, ..., s_C, A_h \rangle \\ \frac{\lambda_l}{\gamma(s,a)}, & j = \langle s_1, s_2, ..., s_C, A_l \rangle \\ \frac{s_c \mu}{\xi(c)\gamma(s,a)}, & j = \langle s_1, s_2, .., s_c - 1, .., s_C, F_c \rangle, s_c \geq 1. \end{cases} \tag{10}
$$

where $c \subseteq \{1, 2, .., C\}$.

Then the maximal long-term discounted reward is obtained and can be denoted as

$$
\nu(s) = \max_{a \in Act_s} \left\{ r(s,a) + \lambda \sum_{j \in S} q(j|s,a)\nu(j) \right\} \tag{11}
$$

where $\lambda = \frac{\gamma(s,a)}{\alpha+\gamma(s,a)}$, and $r(s,a)$ and $q(j|s,a)$ can be obtained in the Eqs. (7), (8), (9) and (10).

4   Performance Evaluation

In this section, we evaluate the performance of the proposed economic AAML-RAM based on SMDP by using an event driven simulator compiled by Matlab, and compare our proposed model with the traditional greedy algorithm. Since the HRO suspicious transaction report demands a higher QoS level compared with L/MRO suspicious transaction report, thus our simulation mainly focuses on the performance of HRO suspicious transaction report.

In our simulation, the maximal number of AMLRAUs can be allocated is $C = 3$, and the scheme that allocates $c_1 = 1$, $c_2 = 2$, $c_3 = 3$ AMLRAUs to a suspicious transaction report is denoted as allocation scheme c_i. The time to process a suspicious transaction report by the AML resource allocation domain is assumed as a linear function of the number of AMLRAUs allocated to the suspicious transaction report, which can be denoted as $\xi(c) = \frac{1}{c}$. Thus, the value of $\xi(c_1)$, $\xi(c_2)$ and $\xi(c_3)$ can be obtained as $\xi(c_1) = 1$, $\xi(c_2) = \frac{1}{2}$ and $\xi(c_3) = \frac{1}{3}$. The total resource capability of the AML resource allocation domain is up to $K = 10$ AMLRAUs. Unless otherwise specified, the arrival rates of the HRO and L/MRO suspicious transaction report are $\lambda_h = 7.2$ and $\lambda_l = 2.4$ respectively, and the completing rate of processed suspicious transaction report occupying one AMLRAU is $\mu = 6.6$. Since the time to process the suspicious transaction report occupying one AMLRAUs is $\frac{1}{\mu}$, then the completing rate of processed suspicious transaction report occupying multiple AMLRAUs is $\frac{\mu}{\xi(c)}$ which is described in Sect. 2. Thus, the completing rates of processed suspicious transaction report occupying one, two and three AMLRAUs are $\mu_{c_1} = 6.6$, $\mu_{c_2} = 13.2$ and $\mu_{c_3} = 19.8$, respectively. To assure reward computation convergence, the continuous-time discounting factor α is set to be 0.1. The simulation results are collected with each experiment running 18000 s, and each experiment runs 1000 rounds. The other parameters used in this simulation are listed in Table 1.

Table 1. Simulation parameters

Parameter	E_d	δ_d	β	γ_d	U_d	θ_d	θ_s
Value	50	30	1	1	10	60	12

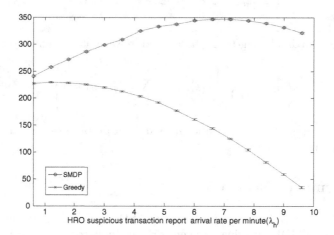

Fig. 1. System reward of *HRO* suspicious transaction report compared between SMDP model and Greedy method, varying with the arrival rate of *HRO* suspicious transaction reports($\lambda_l = 2.4$, $\mu = 6.6$, $K = 6$)

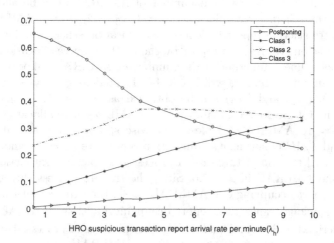

Fig. 2. Probabilities for each action of *HRO* suspicious transaction report using SMDP model, varying with the arrival rate of *HRO* suspicious transaction reports($\lambda_l = 2.4$, $\mu = 6.6$, $K = 6$)

To evaluate the performance of the proposed dynamic resource allocation model, we compare the long-term reward and postponing probability of the *HRO* suspicious transaction report between our model and greedy method in Figs. 1 and 2. In Fig. 1, the reward of *HRO* suspicious transaction report of our model increases at the beginning, then falls down with the increase of the arrival rate of *HRO* suspicious transaction reports (λ_h), while the reward of *HRO* suspicious transaction report using the greedy method declines always. It can be seen in this figure that the reward of the *HRO* suspicious transaction report of our proposed model performs much better than that of greedy method. In Fig. 2, with the increase of the arrival rate of the *HRO* suspicious transaction reports, our model would rather to allocate more c_1 and c_2 AMLRAUs to the *HRO* suspicious transaction report other than c_3 AMLRAUs, thus the dropping probability of our model is lower than that of the greedy method. As the postponement has more impact on the system lump income compared with acceptance (in our simulation, the lump income $w(s, a)$ or fine of postponement is -70, while the corresponding lump incomes $w(s, a)$ for c_1, c_2 and c_3 are 8, 14 and 16, respectively), thus the lower postponing probability of our model gains more rewards of *HRO* suspicious transaction report than the greedy method. We can also see in Fig. 2, when the arrival rate of the *HRO* suspicious transaction reports is over 7, the probabilities to allocate c_1 and c_2 AMLRAUs (especially the probability of c_1 AMLRAU) exceed the probability to allocate c_3 AMLRAUs, which explains the reason why the reward of *HRO* service of our proposed model falls down when the arrival rate of *HRO* suspicious transaction reports exceeds 7 shown in Fig. 1. In a word, our model can achieve higher reward of *HRO* suspicious transaction report while keeping lower postponing probability of *HRO* suspicious transaction reports at the same time comparing with the greedy method, which are shown in Figs. 1 and 2, respectively. Thus, our model outperforms the greedy method with the increase of arrival rate of *HRO* suspicious transaction reports.

5   Conclusion

In this paper, we have proposed an SMDP-based model to allocate AML resources adaptively in terms of AMLRAUs based on suspicious transaction reports from FIs. By considering both benefits and expenses of AML resource allocation domain, the proposed model is able to allocate different numbers of AMLRAUs to suspicious transaction reports dynamically based on the AML resource status and system performance, thus to obtain the maximal system rewards. Simulation results show that the model can achieve a higher system reward and a lower suspicious transaction report postponing probability compared with the traditional greedy-based resource allocation algorithm. In the future, we will study a more complex decision-making model with different types of suspicious transactions. We will also investigate the optimal AML resource planning by determining the minimal AML resources to achieve the maximal system rewards under a given postponing probability constraint.

Acknowledgement. This work was supported in part by the National High Technology Research and Development Program of China(863 Program, Grant No: 2015AA01A705), the National Social Science Foundation of China (Grant NO. 12XJY028) and China Postdoctoral Science Foundation (Grant No. 2013M541014). Hongbin Liang is the corresponding author.

References

1. Geiger, H., Wuensch, O.: The fight against moneylaundering: an economic analysis of a cost-benefit paradoxon. J. Money Laund. Control **10**(1), 91–105 (2007)
2. Harvey, J.: Compliance and reporting issues arising for financial institutions from money laundering regulations: a preliminary cost benefit study. J. Money Laund. Control **7**, 333–346 (2004)
3. Saunders, A., Cornett, M.M.: Financial Institutions Management: A Risk Management Approach, 6th edn. McGraw-Hill, New York (2008)
4. Harvey, J.: An evaluation of money laundering policies. J. Money Laund. Control **8**, 339–345 (2005)
5. Sathye, M.: Estimating the cost of compliance of AMLCTF for financial institutions in Australia. J. Financ. Crime **15**, 347–363 (2008)
6. Tang, J., Yin, J.: Developing an intelligent data discriminating system of anti-money laundering based on SVM. In: International Conference on Machine Learning and Cybernetics (2005)
7. Salerno, J.J., Yu, P.S.: Applying data mining in investigating money laundering crimes. In: Conference: Knowledge Discovery and Data Mining, pp. 747–752 (2003)
8. Kaboudan, M.A.: Biologically inspired algorithms for financial modelling. Genet. Program. Evolvable Mach. **7**, 285–286 (2006)
9. Zhu, H., Du, S., Gao, Z., Dong, M., Cao, Z.: A probabilistic misbehavior detection scheme toward efficient trust establishment in delay-tolerant networks. IEEE Trans. Parall. Distrib. Syst. **25**, 22–32 (2013)
10. Du, S., Zhu, H., Li, X., Ota, K., Dong, M.: MixZone in motion: achieving dynamically cooperative location privacy protection in delay-tolerant networks. IEEE Trans. Veh. Technol. **62**, 4565–4575 (2013)
11. Zhu, H., Lin, X., Rongxing, L., Fan, Y.: SMART: a secure multilayer credit-based incentive scheme for delay-tolerant networks. IEEE Trans. Veh. Technol. **58**, 4628–4639 (2009)
12. Federal Financial Institutions Examination Council, Bank Secrecy Act/ Anti-Money Laundering Examination Manual (2010)
13. Ramjee, R., Towsley, D., Nagarajan, R.: On optimal call admission control in cellular networks. Wirel. Netw. **3**(1), 29–41 (1997)

Infrastructure Deployment and Optimization
for Cloud-Radio Access Networks

Xiang Hou, Bin Lin[✉], Rongxi He, Xudong Wang, and Tao Yu

College of Information Science and Technology,
Dalian Maritime University, Dalian 116026, China
{hou,binlin,hrx,wxd}@dlmu.edu.cn

Abstract. In the mobile Internet and big data era, wireless networks are facing challenges to transmit the huge amount of data effectively, efficiently and reliably. To deploy a network infrastructure with larger capacity, higher data rate, lower transmission delay, higher spectral efficiency and lower energy consumption, an innovative architecture-the Cloud-Radio Access Network (C-RAN) has been proposed. In this paper, we focus on network planning deployment issue based on the Optical Mixed Diet (OMD) technology. Specifically, the ring and spur topology Optimization (RSTO) problem under the C-RAN architecture is investigated. We solve this RSTO problem using Gurobi. A series of case studies are conducted to validate the optimization framework and demonstrate the solvability and scalability of the RSTO problem. Results also show that cost saving can be achieved by taking advantage of Coordinated Multi-Processing (CoMP) technology.

Keywords: C-RAN · Optical mixed diet · Ring and spur · Optimization

1 Introduction

Nowadays the information society has stepped into a new era, in which the mobile Internet, cloud computing [1, 2], big data, and Internet of Things are the leading technologies [3]. Smart mobile terminals, which are widely applied in everyday life, are driving the explosive demands of wireless data services. Recent wireless networks are facing great challenges to transmit the huge amount of data effectively, efficiently and reliably. The future wireless access networks are required to provide larger capacity, higher data rate, lower transmission delay, higher spectral efficiency and lower energy consumption. To deal with these challenges, a new type of the radio access network architecture named Cloud Radio Access Network (C-RAN) has been proposed in [4].

The C-RAN has four 'C' characteristics, i.e., Clean, Centralized processing, Collaborative radio, and real-time Cloud radio access network. C-RAN is viewed as an architecture evolution based on distributed Base Stations (BSs). The C-RAN architecture breaks down the traditional BS into a Base Band Unit (BBU) and Remote Radio Units (RRUs). The BBU is a digital unit that implements the MAC, PHY and Antenna Array System functionality. The BBU is often located in a remote site such as a central office (CO) and thus the energy, real-estate and security costs are minimized. The RRU can be mounted either outdoor or indoor such as on poles, sides of buildings or anywhere power

© Springer International Publishing Switzerland 2015
K. Xu and J. Zhu (Eds.): WASA 2015, LNCS 9204, pp. 201–211, 2015.
DOI: 10.1007/978-3-319-21837-3_20

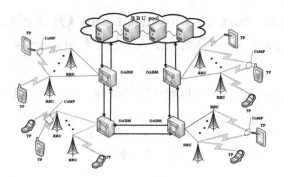

Fig. 1. The C-RAN network model based on ring and spur topology

and a broadband connection exist, making installation less costly and easier. The RRU is typically connected to the BBU using fibers. C-RAN adopts CoMP technology to reduce interference, lower power consumption, and improve spectral efficiency [5, 6].

Due to the requirements of high volume, variety, and non-uniform distribution of the big data in time domain and space domains, wireless access networks must have high survivability. For example, many applications of online banking, mobile payment, and remote business are generated on smart phones. Thus, the networks are required to transmit data with high reliability.

Different from tree and branch topology, the fiber can transmit the signals between the BBU and the Optical Add-Drop Multiplexers (OADMs) bidirectionally in the ring and spur topology as shown in Fig. 1. When one of the fiber interrupts, the other fiber could continue to achieve optical signal transmission. Thus, the ring and spur topology can avoid the network paralysis caused by fiber interruption [7].

Our previous work have studied on the network planning and placement, which have direct influence on the further network deployment and long-term performance [8–12]. In this paper, we focus on the Ring and Spur Topology Optimization (RSTO) problem under the C-RAN architecture. Given an area of interest (AOI) and a set of Potential Sites (PSs) for RRU and OADM placement within the area, the RSTO problem can optimally and simultaneously: (i) minimize the network deploying cost; (ii) identify the locations of RRU and OADM; (iii) identify the association relations between RRUs and OADMs; (iv) satisfy the coverage requirements so as to allow the mobile user access through RRUs. We solve this RSTO problem using Gurobi, which is the newest ILP solver by now. A series of case studies are conducted to validate the optimization framework and demonstrate the solvability and scalability of the RSTO problem.

2   Network Model and Problem Formulation

2.1   Network Model

The C-RAN network model consists of four network entities: BBU, OADM, RRU and Mobile Stations (MSs), as shown Fig. 1. The OADMs and the RRUs are eligible to be

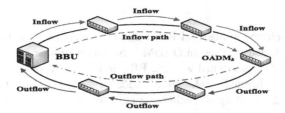

Fig. 2. Flow on the OADM ring

deployed at certain outdoor Potential Sites (PSs) where uninterrupted power supply can be provided [5].

In order to construct the OADM ring, we define the concept of "flow" and related terms as shown in Fig. 2.

Term 1: Inflow: the directed path which represents the flow from BBU to $OADM_k$.
Term 2: Outflow: the directed path which represents the flow from $OADM_k$ to BBU.
Term 3: Inflow path: the path starts from BBU and ends at $OADM_k$.
Term 4: Outflow path: the path starts from $OADM_k$ and ends at the BBU.

Without loss of generality, we assume that the MSs are homogeneously distributed in the AOI, which yields a uniform distribution on the traffic demand in the AOI. We define that a site is covered under the C-RAN architecture if the received radio signal strength at the site is above a given threshold level (receiver sensitivity). Small scale fading is not explicitly included in the system model since a long-term planning and design is targeted. To test the mobile coverage, we define Test Points (TPs) within the AOI. The TPs are also used for testing the received power intensity for MSs from the associated RRU. In Fig. 1, the locations of TPs and PSs for both OADM and RRU are also illustrated.

2.2   Problem Statement

The RSTO problem can be stated as follows. Let $G = (\Omega : E)$, where Ω is the set of the nodes, E is the set of the direct edge/links. The BBU is denoted as the node B. Ω is partitioned into four parts: i.e., the set of TP, the set of OADM, the set of RRU, the set of BBU, which are denoted as Ω_{TP}, Ω_{OADM}, Ω_{RRU}, Ω_B, i.e. $\Omega = \Omega_{TP} \cup \Omega_{RRU} \cup \Omega_{OADM} \cup \Omega_B$.

Given:

(1) The set of fixed TPs, which are the customer premises.
(2) The set of Potential Sites (PSs) for deploying RRUs and OADMs.
(3) The location of the BBU.
(4) The cost per unit length of fiber ($\$/km$)$C^f$, including fiber purchase and deployment cost.
(5) The Manhattan distance between node i and node $j(d_{ij})$.
(6) The cost of RRU (C^R) and OADM (C^O).
(7) The maximal transmit power of a RRU.
(8) The minimal signal-to-noise-ratio (SNR) requirement for an MS.

Variable:

(1) The PS_m is selected to place a RRU if $a_m = 1$, otherwise $a_m = 0$.
(2) The PS_t is selected to place an OADM if $b_t = 1$, otherwise $b_t = 0$.
(3) The MS at TP_n is associated with the RRU at if $z_{mn} = 1$, otherwise $z_{mn} = 0$.
(4) There is a directed link from node $i \in \Omega_B \cup \Omega_{OADM}$ to node $j \in \Omega_B \cup \Omega_{RRU} \cup \Omega_{OADM}$ if $e_{ij} = 1$, otherwise $e_{ij} = 0$.
(5) The TP_n is covered if $q_n = 1$, otherwise $q_n = 0$.
(6) e_{ij} is on the directed flow from the BBU to $OADM_k$ if $g_{ij}^k = 1$, otherwise $g_{ij}^k = 0$.
(7) e_{ij} is on the directed flow from the $OADM_k$ to BBU if $h_{ij}^k = 1$, otherwise $h_{ij}^k = 0$.

Constraints:

(1) The mobile coverage requirement should be satisfied, i.e., the coverage ratio should be larger than a predefined value.
(2) The SNR for an MS located at each TP should be larger than a SNR threshold.
(3) Each TP is covered by at least one RRU.
(4) The OADM- ring consists the BBU and the selected OADMs.
(5) There must be at least a RRU to connect to the selected OADM.
(6) The RRU can coverage the MS with CoMP technology.
(7) The double-flow control is used to establish the mathematical model.
(8) If the PS is selected to place an OADM on the OADM-ring, there must be the input path and output path.

Objective: The objective is to minimize the infrastructure deployment cost of the whole C-RAN network. Table 1 lists important symbols for the problem formulation.

2.3   Problem Formulation

(RSTO) Objective:

$$\text{Minimize } C = C^F + C^{RRU} + C^{OADM} \tag{1.1}$$

where

$$\sum_{i \in \Omega_B} (e_{ij} + e_{ij}) \cdot d_{ij} + C^f \sum_{i \in \Omega_{OADM}} e_{ij} \cdot d_{ij} + C^f \sum_{i \in \Omega_{OADM}} \sum_{j \in \Omega_{RRU}} e_{ij} \cdot d_{ij} \tag{1.1a}$$

$$C^{RRU} = C^R \sum_{m \in \Omega_{RRU}} a_m \tag{1.1b}$$

$$C^{OADM} = C^O \sum_{t \in \Omega_{OADM}} b_t \tag{1.1c}$$

Table 1. Definitions of symbols in the RSTO problem

Symbol	Definition
Ω_B	The set of the BBU
Ω_{OADM}	The set of the OADMs
Ω_{RRU}	The set of the RRUs
Ω_{TP}	The set of the TPs
T	The number of OADMs in network
M	The number of RRUs in network
N	The number of TPs in network
d_{ij}	the distance between node i and node j
P	The maximal transmit power of a RRU
ξ	The average normalized thermal noise in AOI
α	The path loss exponent
s_0	The minimal SNR requirement for each TP
A	The location incidence vector, $A = (a_m)_{1 \times M}$
B	The location incidence vector, $B = (b_t)_{1 \times T}$
Q	A TP coverage incidence vector, $Q = (q_n)_{1 \times N}$
Z	RRU-TP association matrix $Z = (z_{mn})_{M \times N}$
E	BBU-OADM-RRU association matrix, $E = (e_{ij})_{(T+1) \times (M+T)}$
D_{MAX}	The maximal distance of OMD-RRU can be deployed in network
H^K	$OADM_k - BBU$ flow association matrix $H^K = \left(h_{ij}^k\right)_{(1+T) \times (T+M)}$
G^K	$BBU - OADM_k$ flow association matrix $G^K = \left(g_{ij}^k\right)_{(1+T) \times (T+M)}$

Subject to:

$$\sum_{m \in \Omega_{RRU}} z_{mn} \geq 1, \ \forall n \in \Omega_{TP} \tag{1.2}$$

$$z_{mn} \leq a_n, \ \forall m \in \Omega_{RRU}, \ \forall n \in \Omega_{TP} \tag{1.3}$$

$$e_{ij} \leq b_i, \ \forall i \in \Omega_{OADM}, \ \forall j \in \Omega_{RRU} \tag{1.4}$$

$$\sum_{j \in \Omega_{OADM}} e_{ij} = 1, \ \forall i \in \Omega_B \tag{1.5}$$

$$\sum_{i \in \Omega_{OADM}} e_{ij} = 1, \ \forall j \in \Omega_B \tag{1.6}$$

$$\sum_{i \in \Omega_B \cup \Omega_{OADM}} e_{ij} = a_j, \ \forall j \in \Omega_{OADM}, \ i \neq j \tag{1.7}$$

$$\sum_{j \in \Omega_B \cup \Omega_{OADM}} e_{ij} = a_j, \ \forall i \in \Omega_{OADM}, \ i \neq j \tag{1.8}$$

$$\sum\nolimits_{i\in\Omega_{OADM}} e_{ij} = a_j, \ \forall j \in \Omega_{RRU} \tag{1.9}$$

$$\sum\nolimits_{j\in\Omega_{RRU}} e_{ij} \geq b_i, \ \forall i \in \Omega_{OADM} \tag{1.10}$$

$$e_{ij} \cdot d_{ij} \leq D_{\max}, \ \forall i \in \Omega_{OADM}, \ \forall j \in \Omega_{RRU} \tag{1.11}$$

$$g_{ij}^k \leq e_{ij} \ \forall i \in \Omega_B \cup \Omega_{OADM}, \ \forall j \in \Omega_{OADM}, \ k \in \Omega_{OADM}, \ i \neq k \tag{1.12}$$

$$h_{ij}^k \leq e_{ij}, \ \forall i \in \Omega_{OADM}, \ \forall j \in \Omega_B \cup \Omega_{OADM}, \ k \in \Omega_{OADM}, \ j \neq k \tag{1.13}$$

$$g_{ij}^k \leq b_k, \ \forall i \in \Omega_B \cup \Omega_{OADM}, \ \forall j \in \Omega_{OADM}, \ k \in \Omega_{OADM}, \ i \neq k \tag{1.14}$$

$$h_{ij}^k \leq b_k, \ \forall i \in \Omega_{OADM}, \ \forall j \in \Omega_B \cup \Omega_{OADM}, \ k \in \Omega_{OADM}, \ j \neq k \tag{1.15}$$

$$\sum\nolimits_{j\in\Omega_{OADM}} g_{ij}^k = b_k, \ \forall k \in \Omega_{OADM}, \ i \in \Omega_B \tag{1.16}$$

$$\sum\nolimits_{i\in\Omega_{OADM}} h_{ij}^k = b_k, \ \forall k \in \Omega_{OADM}, \ j \in \Omega_B \tag{1.17}$$

$$\sum\nolimits_{i\in\Omega_B \cup \Omega_{OADM}} g_{ik}^k = b_k, \ \forall k \in \Omega_{OADM}, \ i \neq k \tag{1.18}$$

$$\sum\nolimits_{j\in\Omega_B \cup \Omega_{OADM}} h_{kj}^k = b_k, \ \forall k \in \Omega_{OADM}, j \neq k \tag{1.19}$$

$$\sum\nolimits_{j\in\Omega_{OADM}} \sum\nolimits_{k\in\Omega_{OADM}} g_{ij}^k = \sum\nolimits_{k\in\Omega_{OADM}} b_k, \ i \in \Omega_B \tag{1.20}$$

$$\sum\nolimits_{i\in\Omega_{OADM}} \sum\nolimits_{k\in\Omega_{OADM}} h_{ij}^k = \sum\nolimits_{k\in\Omega_{OADM}} b_k, \ j \in \Omega_B \tag{1.21}$$

$$\sum\nolimits_{i\in\Omega_B \cup \Omega_{OADM}} g_{ij}^k = \sum\nolimits_{m\in\Omega_{OADM}} g_{jm}^k, \ \forall j, \ k \in \Omega_{OADM}, \ i \neq j \neq m, \ i \neq j \neq k \tag{1.22}$$

$$\sum\nolimits_{i\in\Omega_{OADM}} h_{ij}^k = \sum\nolimits_{m\in\Omega_B \cup \Omega_{OADM}} h_{jm}^k, \ \forall j, \ k \in \Omega_{OADM}, \ i \neq j \neq m, \ i \neq j \neq k \tag{1.23}$$

$$g_{ij}^k + h_{ij}^k \leq 1, \ \forall i, j, \ k \in \Omega_{OADM}, \ i \neq j \neq k \tag{1.24}$$

$$e_{ij} + e_{ji} \leq 1, \ \forall i \in \Omega_B \cup \Omega_{OADM}, \ \forall j \in \Omega_{OADM}, \ i \neq j \tag{1.25}$$

$$\frac{1}{\xi} \sum\nolimits_{m\in\Omega_{RRU}} \frac{z_{mn} \times P}{d_{mn}^\alpha} \geq s_0, \ \forall n \in \Omega_{TP} \tag{1.26}$$

$$q_n \geq \frac{1}{\sum\nolimits_{m\in\Omega_{RRU}} \frac{P}{\xi d_{mn}^\alpha} - s_0} \left(\sum\nolimits_{m\in\Omega_{RRU}} \frac{P}{\xi d_{mn}^\alpha} - s_0 \right) \tag{1.27}$$

$$1 - q_n \geq \frac{1}{\sum_{m \in \Omega_{RRU} \frac{P}{\xi d_{mn}^{\alpha}}} - s_0} \left(s_0 - \sum_{m \in \Omega_{RRU}} \frac{P}{\xi d_{mn}^{\alpha}} \right) \tag{1.28}$$

$$\frac{1}{N} \sum_{n \in \Omega_{TP}} q_n \geq \eta \times 100\% \tag{1.29}$$

$$a_m \in \{0,1\}, \ \forall m \in \Omega_{RRU}, \ b_t \in \{0,1\}, \ \forall t \in \Omega_{OADM}, \ q_n \in \{0,1\}, \ \forall n \in \Omega_{TP} \tag{1.30}$$

$$z_{mn} \in \{0,1\}, \ \forall m \in \Omega_{RRU}, \ \forall n \in \Omega_{TP} \tag{1.31}$$

$$e_{ij} \in \{0,1\}, \ \forall i \in \Omega_B \cup \Omega_{OADM}, \ \forall j \in \Omega_{OADM} \cup \Omega_{RRU} \tag{1.32}$$

$$g_{ij}^k \in \{0,1\}, \ \forall i \in \Omega_B \cup \Omega_{OADM}, \ \forall j \in \Omega_{OADM}, \ k \in \Omega_{OADM}, \ i \neq k \tag{1.33}$$

$$h_{ij}^k \in \{0,1\}, \ \forall i \in \Omega_{OADM}, \ \forall j \in \Omega_B \cup \Omega_{OADM}, \ k \in \Omega_{OADM}, \ j \neq k \tag{1.34}$$

Equation (1.1) is to minimize the total deployment cost of the C-RAN network, including the cost of fibers, the cost of RRUs, the cost of OADMs. Constraint (1.2) stipulates that each TP is covered by at least one RRU and it ensures the CoMP feature of C-RAN. Constraint (1.3) ensures that the PS is selected to place a RRU if $a_m = 1$. Constraint (1.4) ensures that the PS is selected to place an OADM if $b_i = 1$. Constraints (1.5) and (1.6) ensure that the BBU can be connected to the OADM ring. Constraint (1.5) stipulates the BBU has just only one OADM as BBU's output. Constraint (1.6) stipulates the BBU has just only one OADM as BBU's input. Constraints (1.7) and (1.8) ensure that an OADM can be connected to the OADM-ring. Constraint (1.7) ensures that if the PS is selected to place an OADM on the OADM ring, then anther OADM serves as an output terminal in OADMs ring; Constraint (1.8) ensures that if the PS is selected to place an OADM on the OADM ring, then anther OADM serves as an input terminal in OADMs ring. Constraint (1.9) ensures that if the PS is selected to place an OADM on the OADM ring, then at least one RRU should be connected to the selected OADM, if $a_j = 1$.Constraint (1.10) ensures that RRUs can be connected to the OADM, if $b_i = 1$. Constraint (1.11) sets an upper bound on the fiber length between an OADM and a RRU in C-RAN network. Constraint (1.12) stipulates only when $e_{ij} = 1$, e_{ij} probably exists in the inflow path from BBU to $OADM_k$. Constraint (1.13) stipulates only when $e_{ij} = 1$, e_{ij} probably exists in the outflow path from the BBU to $OADM_k$. Constraints (1.14) and (1.15) ensure only when $OADM_i$ and $OADM_j$ exist firstly, then there probably exists the path between the BBU and $OADM_k$. For all OADMs, constraints (1.16) and (1.17) ensure where inflow path must start from the BBU, and the outflow path must end at the BBU. Constraints (1.18) and (1.19) stipulate for $OADM_k$, its inflow path must end at $OADM_k$, and its outflow must start from $OADM_k$. Constraints (1.20) and (1.21) ensure that only when $OADM_k$ is selected to place on the OADM-ring, then $OADM_k$ has inflow path and outflow path. Constraint (1.22) stipulates that if $OADM_j$ is on the path from BBU to $OADM_k$, then $OADM_j$ has an input path and an output path. Also, there is an inflow path belongs to the path from BBU to $OADM_j$. Constraint (1.23) stipulates that if $OADM_j$ is on the path from BBU to

$OADM_k$, then $OADM_j$ has an input path and an output path. Also, there is an outflow path belongs to the path from BBU to $OADM_k$. For $OADM_k$, constraint (1.24) stipulates the same path cannot exist in the inflow path and outflow path at the same time. Constraint (1.25) stipulates that the path is directional, which means only one direction can be chose. Constraint (1.26) ensures that the TP satisfy the constraint of minimum SNR requirement. Constraints (1.27)–(1.29) stipulate the definition of Q. Constraints (1.30)–(1.34) state the each entry A, B, Q, Z, E, H^K and G^K is binary.

3   Numerical Analysis

3.1   Simulation Settings

We implement the optimization model of Sect. 2.3 and solve the RSTO problem using Gurobi Optimizer [13], which is a state-of-the-art LP solve. Gurobi is designed from the ground up to exploit modern multi-core processors and the performance is proved to be superior to CPLEX. Without loss of generality, the distance of two nodes is used to represent the corresponding edge length of the fiber deployment route, and all the fiber segment links have the same weighted deployment costs.

Tables 2 and 3 show the component cost of C-RAN and experimental parameters, respectively. We define a generic cost unit (gcu) [14] to simplify the evaluation of deployment costs in the case studies.

Table 2. C-RAN component cost

Component	Fiber(/km)	Burying fiber(/km)	RRU	OADM
Cost (gcu)	1	50	16	50

3.2   Validation of the RSTO Formulation

To examine the RSTO formulation, firstly, a relatively small-size network (so-called Scenario 0) is show in Fig. 3a. The coordinates of all the nodes with the area of interest are normalized. It validates that the problem can be solved successfully by ILP solver. We also observe that the ring and spur structure in Fig. 3b and c are maintained correctly with the topological features of connected and directed. The problem size, the optimization gap and the objective values in three scenarios are shown in the Table 4.

To investigate the effect of CoMP in the C-RAN planning strategy, we compare the resulting network layout configuration with and without CoMP technology as shown in Fig. 3b and c. We can obverse the difference between Fig. 3b and c. Table 5 show the

Table 3. Simulation parameter settings

Parameter	α	P	s_0	ξ	D_{MAX}	Scale
Value	2	8 W	29 dB	2 mW	10 km	20 km

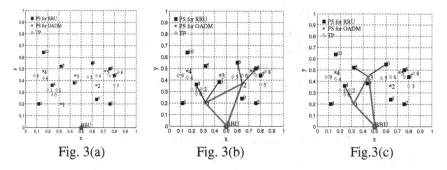

Fig. 3(a)   Fig. 3(b)   Fig.3(c)

Fig. 3. (a) Experimental setup of scenario 0 before optimization (scenario 0 is set for RSTO problem verification.)

Table 4. Optimality gap, objective value in scenario I, II and III

Scenario	Number of nodes			Obj. value (gcu)	Optimality gap
	TP	RRU	OADM		
I	20	20	5	2208.12	0 %
II	40	30	5	2895.03	0 %
III	100	50	5	3890.01	0 %

Table 5. Comparison of RSTO results between with and without CoMP in Scenario 0

	Without CoMP	With CoMP
Selected number of PSs	4 RRUs	3 RRUs
Obj. value (gcu)	1760.8	1543.8
Compute time (s)	0.02	0.03
Optimality gap	0 %	0 %

corresponding computing result of network optimal layout in scenario 0. In other words, the incorporation of CoMP technology can lead to a significant cost reduction for C-RAN.

3.3 Comparison of Tree-and-Branch and Ring-and-Spur Topology

Comparing Tables 6 and 7, we can observe that:

(i) The deployment cost of the ring topology is relatively higher than that of tree topology due to the deployment of bidirectional optical fiber.

(ii) In respect of computing time, the ring topology is shorter than the tree topology. In the tree topology, it needs to make restrictions to every path form the BBU to RRUs, but in the ring topology, it only needs to make restrictions to the path in the OADM-ring.

Table 6. The network scale of scenario IV, V and VI

Scenario	IV	V	VI
PS for OA/OADMs	5	5	5
PS for RRUs	20	30	50
The number of TPs	20	40	100

Table 7. Comparison of the tree and ring topology

Scenario	IV		V		VI	
Scheme	Tree	Ring	Tree	Ring	Tree	Ring
Total cost (unit: gcu)	1834.46	2208.12	2436.54	2895.03	3269.07	3890.01
Computing time	2.09	0.34	5.41	0.87	7.65	1.21

4 Conclusion

In this paper, we formulate the RSTO problem to minimize the total deployment cost of the C-RAN network based on ring and spur topology. We have examined the proposed RSTO problem via extensive case studies in term of its feasibility and scalability. Computational results show that cost savings can be achieved by taking advantage of CoMP in C-RAN. In the future work, a heuristic algorithm will be proposed to solve the problem more efficiently for even larger scale network planning tasks. The proposed optimization frame work is expected to provide a guideline in the future C-RAN network deployment for the operators.

Acknowledgement. This study is sponsored by National Science Foundation of China (NSFC) No. 61371091, No. 61171175 and No. 61301228, the National Science Foundation of Liaoning Province No. 2014025001, and Program for Liaoning Excellent Talents in University (LNET) No. LJQ2013054 and Fundamental Research Funds for Central Universities under grant No. 3132015045.

References

1. Dong, M., Li, H., Ota, K., Yang, L.T., Zhu, H.: Multicloud-based evacuation services for emergency management. IEEE Cloud Comput. 1(4), 50–59 (2014)
2. Wei, L., Zhu, H., Cao, Z., Dong, X., Jia, W., Chen, Y., Vasilakos, A.V.: Security and privacy for storage and computation in cloud computing. Inf. Sci. **258**, 371–386 (2014)
3. Zhang, P., Cui, Q., Hou, Y., Xu, J.: Opportunities and challenges of wireless networks in the era of mobile big data. China Sci. Bull. **60**, 433–438 (2015)
4. Lei, Q., Zhang, Z., Cheng, F.: 5G radio access network architecture based on C-RAN. Telecommun. Sci. J. **1**, 1–10 (2015)
5. Wang, X.: C-RAN: the road towards green RAN. China Commun. J. (2010)
6. Chen, K.: C-RAN White Paper, version 2.5. China Mobile Research Institute, Beijing (2011)

7. Esmail, M.A., Fathallah, H.: Fiber fault management and protection solution for ring-and-spur WDM/TDM long-reach PON. In: 2011 IEEE Global Telecommunications Conference, pp. 1–5 (2011)
8. Lin, B., Lin, L.: Site planning of relay station in green wireless access networks: a genetic algorithm approach. In: Soft Computing and Pattern Recognition (SoCPaR), pp. 167–172. Dalian, China (2011)
9. Lin, B., Ho, P.H., Xie, L., Shen, X., Tapolcai, J.: Optimal relay station placement in broadband wireless access networks. IEEE Trans. Mob. Comput. **9**(2), 259–269 (2010)
10. Lin, B., Tian, Y.: Energy and radiation-aware base station placement in eco-sustainable LTE networks. In: 2nd International Conference on Electronics, in Communication and Control (ICECC2012), pp. 3162–3165 (2012)
11. Lin, B., Lin, L., Ho, P.H.: Cascaded splitter topology optimization in LRPONs. In: International Conference on Communications (ICC), Ottawa, Canada. pp. 3105–3109 (2012)
12. Lin, L., Lin, B., Ho, P.H.: Power-aware optimization modeling for cost-effective LRPON infrastructure deployment. In: 21st International Conference on Software, Telecommunications and Computer Networks (SoftCOM), pp. 1–5 (2013)
13. Gurobi Optimizer 4.6, Gurobi Optimization Inc. (2012)
14. Chaves, D.A.R., Barboza, E.A., Bastos-Filho, C.J.A.: A multi-objective approach to design all-optical and translucent optical networks considering CapEx and QoT. In: 14th International Conference on Transparent Optical Networks (ICTON), pp. 1–4 (2012)

A Cluster Head Rotation Cooperative MIMO Scheme for Wireless Sensor Networks

Huaida Hua, Jian Qiu[✉], Shiwei Song, Xizhe Wang, and Guojun Dai

Institute of Computer Application Technology,
Hangzhou Dianzi University,
Hangzhou, China
qiujian@hdu.edu.cn

Abstract. Energy and communication efficiency are key limitations of wireless sensor networks. Multiple sensor nodes can form virtual antenna array which is called cooperative MIMO that can improve the bandwidth efficiency by using multiple antennas. A typical way of using CMIMO in WSNs is cluster-based, which selects cluster heads for long distance communication between clusters. In this paper, a cluster head rotation scheme is introduced to save energy in re-clustering and balance the energy consumption among different nodes. The simulation results show that the total energy consumption can be reduced and the network can work stably until the prolonged life time goes up.

Keywords: Wireless sensor networks · Cooperative MIMO · Cluster head rotation

1 Introduction

In Wireless Sensor Networks (WSNs), due to the limited capacity of batteries and difficulty to recharge, lifetime maintaining is always a big problem. MIMO technology is introduced to improve communication performance as it has the capability to exploit multipath fading and achieve diversity and spatial multiplexing gain [1].

However, tiny sensor nodes can only carry single antenna. The idea of cooperative MIMO (CMIMO) is introduced, in which multiple sensor nodes cooperate as antenna array. So that data can be cooperatively delivered between transmitters and receivers like traditional MIMO system [2]. Considering both the circuit complexity of nodes with CMIMO and energy consumption of MIMO communication, energy saving can be achieved in large WSNs coverage [3]. Recently, researchers have carried out substantial studies in applying CMIMO to WSNs effectively and efficiently. It's important to determine how to group nodes, select cluster heads (CH) and cooperative nodes (CN) in CMIMO systems [4].

In random distributed schemes, all nodes have equal responsibilities. Main transmitter selects cooperative nodes [5] in neighborhood by using handshaking method to organize virtual MIMO. CHs aggregate data in the intra-cluster communication and

© Springer International Publishing Switzerland 2015
K. Xu and J. Zhu (Eds.): WASA 2015, LNCS 9204, pp. 212–221, 2015.
DOI: 10.1007/978-3-319-21837-3_21

choose cooperative nodes within their own clusters to transmit data to neighbor CHs in inter-cluster communication [6–15].

A simple scheme by combining the cooperative MIMO communication to traditional cluster-based protocol LEACH [6], while a distributed energy-efficient clustering/ routing scheme is proposed for multi-hop CMIMO communication in [7]. In these schemes, each cluster has up to two cluster-heads responsible for traffic between clusters and has the ability to adapt the transmission mode and power level based on inter-cluster handshaking. Variable cluster size for CMIMO-WSNs is applied in [8], in which the cluster size is determined based on the residual energy of CHs. In [9], cooperative nodes are not voted by cluster members, multiple cluster heads of different clusters cooperate to form virtual antenna array so that STBC based MIMO technique can be implemented. An algorithm for optimal inner-cluster cooperative node selection problem is introduced in [10]. In [11], a scheme which can reform clusters dynamically according to remaining energy of cluster heads is proposed; the cooperative node can also be dynamic according to inter-cluster communicating distance.

As the CH nodes consume much more energy than normal nodes, nodes must take turns to be CHs to balance the energy dissipating. Therefore, cluster reformation, cluster head selection and inter-cluster routing construction must be performed periodically, which consume large amount of energy. An alternative way of cluster head replacing is called cluster-head rotation introduced in this paper. In the proposed Cluster Head Rotation Cooperative MIMO (CHR-CMIMO) scheme, cluster members rotate to be cluster heads by inner-cluster selection, which replaces re-clustering. A procedure called "Over-Jump" is applied to alleviate traffic burden of the low energy cluster. Energy consumption balance between and in clusters can both be achieved.

The reminder of this paper is organized as follows: Sect. 2 provides the entire architecture and describes the procedure of the CHR-CMIMO scheme in detail. The energy consumption model and mathematical framework are carried out in Sect. 3. In Sect. 4, the simulation setup is determined and the results are compared. Finally, a conclusion is given to summarize the contents and contributions.

2 System Architecture and Scheme Description

CHR-CMIMO scheme combines cooperative MIMO with energy-driven cluster head rotation, which includes four phases: cluster formation phase, intra-cluster communication phase, inter-cluster communication phase and CH rotation phase.

As shown in Fig. 1, sensors are grouped into clusters at the beginning, which is carried out in a distributed way. After that, every cluster has one or two cluster heads (CHs), which are main CH (mCH) and assistant CH (aCH). During intra-cluster communication, cluster member (CM) nodes transmit sensed data at low power to the mCH or aCH according to the distance and pre-assigned slots. In order to achieve diversity in MIMO system, CHs must encode the data by Space-time block code (STBC). When the CHs aggregate certain amount of data, inter-cluster communications take places. During this phase, CHs of each cluster conduct cooperative MIMO to forward data to next-hop clusters. All packets are forwarded to the sink node eventually through multi-hop routes.

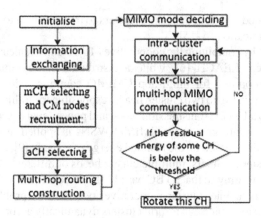

Fig. 1. Schedule of communications and rotation.

After several rounds of intra-cluster and inter-cluster communications, once the residual energy level of a mCH or aCH is lower than a particular threshold, the CH rotation starts. The low energy mCH chooses a node which has most residual energy in the cluster to be the new mCH. The node with second highest energy becomes aCH. After that, the cluster continues intra-cluster and inter-cluster communication. As process continues, once a cluster is in an entire low energy state, in which no nodes can be selected as CHs, the previous hop clusters in the routing path will find another next hop cluster to deliver packets. This process is called "Over-Jump".

In our scheme, it is important to carry out CH rotation as well as Over-Jump such that the average time of every node to be CH can be kept relatively even, which avoids energy waste in re-clustering and topology reconstruction. Consequently, the entire network can keep stable and the lifetime can be extended.

2.1   Cluster Formation Phase

At the beginning, all nodes exchange 'Hello Messages' with neighbors at a fixed low power P_{intra} which contains the node ID, node status and remaining energy. After this step, all nodes store the neighbor information in their neighbor lists.

The criterion of choosing mCH is the nodes' remaining energy. As mCH nodes' procedure is much more complicated than CM nodes, they should have the most residual energy. Every node selects one with most residual energy as mCH according to the neighbor lists. If a node chooses itself as mCH, it broadcasts at power P_{intra} a Cluster Formation (CF) message containing its ID, cluster ID and residual energy. The nodes which do not chose themselves as mCH keep waiting for CF messages. If a node receives a CF message, it becomes a CM node and returns a Join Cluster (JC) message. If a node receives multiple CF messages, it compares the signal strength and joins the nearest mCH. If any nodes are still not clustered, they repeat this step until all nodes either become a mCH or join a cluster. To form virtical antenna array, each mCH chooses an assistant CH (aCH) by comparison of the remaining energy of all nodes within its cluster. The node with most energy is qualified to be the aCH.

The multi-hop routes are constructed by a modified Dijkstra's algorithm using Inter-cluster Controlling Messages much smaller than data packets. The weight of a link is decided by two factors: the link cost, which is affected by communicating distance, channel condition and so on; and the residual energy of the clusters at both ends.

The method of MIMO for inter-cluster communicating should also be carefully chosen. Higher order of MIMO diversity requires more circuit processing power especially in short distance, which causes unnecessary resource dissipating. Considering the results in [3], 2–2 and 2–1 are the proposed MIMO mode according to the inter-cluster communication distance. In certain short distance, SISO system may even be better, which is also applied.

2.2   Intra-Cluster and Inter Cluster Communication Phase

In this phase, CM nodes collect sensed data and forward it to mCH or aCH at Pintra in turns by pre-assigned schedules. They determine the destination according to the signal strength of CF messages received in cluster formation phase. A CM node falls in sleep after transmission until its next slot. After all CM nodes get the chance to transmit for a certain number of rounds, CHs aggregate the data and encode the packets by STBC. All the packets received in this phase are added by two bytes of data about the residual energy of the transmitters, so that the CHs can obtain real-time information of the energy consuming statistics of the nodes in its cluster. Finally, mCH exchanges encoded packets with aCH in the same cluster. CHs compute their threshold for rotating and forward prepared packets hop by hop as descript in Fig. 2.

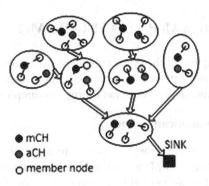

● mCH
◉ aCH
○ member node

SINK

Fig. 2.   Inter-Cluster communication.

2.3   Cluster Head Rotation Phase

For lifetime maintenance, nodes energy consumption should be balanced [12]. Energy-driven cluster head rotation algorithm is introduced to balance the energy consumption of nodes in a cluster. Moreover, an operation named "Over-Jump" is also proposed to keep energy consumption balance between clusters.

After several rounds, the low energy mCH and aCH exchange the neighbor lists to select the node with largest amount of residual energy in the cluster as new mCH and it broadcast an mCH Selection Message contains the information of new mCH. Then it turns to CM mode with aCH. Then, the new mCH replies an ACK and selects the node with second highest energy in the cluster as new aCH by broadcasting an aCH selection message. The CM nodes reply an ACK to decide whether communicate with the new mCH or new aCH. If any CM node cannot receive any control messages from new mCH or new aCH, in other words, it is beyond the intra-cluster communication radius of the power P_{intra}, it will find another cluster to join.

New mCH and aCH compute the energy threshold for next CH rotation. The new CHs exchange Inter-cluster Control Messages with CHs of previous hops and next hop at power Pinter to estimate the channel condition and optimal VMIMO mode, data communications continues. When the new mCH or aCH reaches the threshold, all above steps will be repeated until there is no capable node in the cluster to be CH.

(h) "Over-Jump" operation. The clusters closer to the SINK process more inter-cluster packets relay, which causes faster energy dissipating. In order to counterweigh energy consumption of each cluster, Over-Jump operation is conducted. As shown in Fig. 4, when the residual energy of cluster u is less than the computed threshold, CHs of u transmit a Low Energy Notice Message (LENM) to inform the CHs of previous hop cluster v. The LENM contains CHs ID, cluster ID, etc. CHs of cluster v directly forward data to cluster w which is the next hop of cluster u. The low energy cluster u does not relay packets for upstream clusters but only collecting data and submitting to next hop for itself. Therefore, the connectivity from cluster v to w can be organized and is more efficient.

3   Energy and System Model of CHR-CMIMO

The total energy consumption of the system mainly consists of two components: intra-cluster communication and inter-cluster communication. Each component contains circuit energy consumption and transmission energy consumption [15].

3.1   Intra-Cluster Communication Energy

In this process, each CM node transmits packets to mCH or aCH according to the distances between CHs and itself. It is assumed that there are m_{t1} CM nodes transmit data to mCH and m_{t2} CM nodes to aCH in a cluster.

The intra-cluster transmission energy consumption per bit is given by $E_{intra} = (Ppa + Pc)/Rb$, Where P_{pa} is the transmission power consumption for forwarding a packet, P_c is the circuit power consumption to forward a packet and R_b is the bit rate. P_{pa} is calculated by $P_{pa} = (1 + a)P_{out}$, where a is a factor depending on the drain efficiency of the power amplifier. The total transmission power at the air interface P_{out} is given:

$$P_{out} = \frac{(4\pi d)^2 m_t N_0}{P_b^{-1/m_t} G_r G_t \lambda^2} M_l N_f R_b \tag{1}$$

In which, d is the intra-cluster communicating radius, R_b is the given bit error rate, λ is carrier wave length, G_r, G_t is the transmitter and receiver antenna gain respectively, M_l is link margin, N_f is the receiver noise figure calculated by $N_f = N_r/N_0$ with $N_0 = -171$dBm/Hz the single-sided thermal noise power spectral density (PSD) at room temperature and N_r is the PSD of the total effective noise at receiver input. m_t is the number of transmitters.

The circuit power consumption per packet is departed into P_{tc} which represents transmitting circuit power and P_{rc} which represents receiving circuit power.

$$P_{tc} = P_{DAC} + P_{mix} + P_{filt} + P_{syn} \tag{2}$$

$$P_{rc} = P_{LNA} + P_{mix} + P_{IFA} + P_{filr} + P_{ADC} + P_{syn} \tag{3}$$

where P_{DAC}, P_{ADC} are the power consumption of digital-to-analog converter (DAC) and analog-to-digital converter (ADC), P_{mix} is the power consumption of mixer, P_{filt} and P_{filr} are the power consumption of transmitter and receiver filter, P_{syn} is power consumption of frequency synthesizer, P_{LNA} is the power consumption of low noise amplifier, and P_{IFA} is the power consumption of intermediate frequency amplifier.

3.2 Inter-Cluster Communication Energy

In this procedure, CHs forward packets to next hop with MIMO mode of 2–2, 2–1 or 1–1, which is denoted as M_{tl}-M_{rl}. Similarly, the energy consumption per bit is calculated by $E_{inter} = (P'_{pa} + P'_c)/R_b$, P'_{pa} where P'_{pa} is given as

$$P'_{pa} = (1 + \alpha) \frac{(4\pi D)^2 M_t N_0}{P_b^{-1/M_t} G_r G_t \lambda^2} M_l N_f R_b \tag{4}$$

where D is the inter-cluster MIMO communication distance, M_t and M_r are the number of transmitters and receivers respectively. P'_c can be approximated as

$$P'_c = M_t(P_{DAC} + P_{mix} + P_{filt} + P_{syn}) + M_r \left(P_{LNA} + P_{mix} + P_{IFA} + P_{filr} + P_{ADC} + P_{syn} \right) \tag{5}$$

3.3 System Model

Assuming that n nodes with unequal initial energy $(E_0)i$, $i = 1, 2, 3..., n$, are deployed randomly on an area of $S = a^2$. In order to make every node act as CH about once, the optimal residual energy threshold for CHs rotating should be find.

All nodes transmit data periodicity round after round. In every round of data submission, CM nodes transmit k bits data to the CHs and the CHs perform data fusion/aggregation, we define the energy consumption of this procedure as ε_y. Then the CHs submit the collected data hop by hop to the sink. We define the energy consumption of this procedure as ε_t.

$$\varepsilon_v = \varepsilon_{v\_collect} + \varepsilon_{v\_exchange} = n\left(k' + k\right)\left(P_{tc} + P_{rc} + P_{pa}\right)/R_b \tag{6}$$

$$\varepsilon_c = nk'\left[2(P_{tc} + P_{rc})(h_{average} - 1) + P'_{pa}|_{D=R_{average}}\right]/R_b \tag{7}$$

where $k' = \beta_k$, β is the data fusion coefficient, n is the number of nodes. $R_{average}$ is the average distance from mCHs to the sink, $h_{average}$ is the average hops of clusters to sink, obtained by the sink node after the multi-hop routing construction. So the entire energy consumption of the network is:

$$\varepsilon = \varepsilon_c + \varepsilon_v \tag{8}$$

Accordingly, the largest number of rounds of the whole net is given as:

$$\bar{T} = \left(E_{sum}\right)/\varepsilon = \left[\sum_{i=1}^{n}(E_0)_i\right]/\varepsilon \tag{9}$$

This is the approximate upper bound of network lifetime. Consider one cluster, for example, in cluster j, the k bit energy consumption of CM, aCH, mCH in a round is E_{cm}, E_{mch}, E_{ach}, respectively.

$$Ecm = k(Ptc + Ppa)/Rb \tag{10}$$

$$\begin{aligned} Emch = E_{mch\_intra} + E_{mch\_inter} = &[c_j\eta_1 kP_{rc}/R_b + c_j\eta_1 k'(P_{tc} + P_{pa})/R_b \\ &+ c_j\eta_2 k'P_{rc}/R_b] + [c_j k'(P_{tc} + P'_{pa}/2)/R_b + (P_{rc} + P'_{pa}/2 + P_{tc})/R_b\mu] \end{aligned} \tag{11}$$

$$\begin{aligned} Each = E_{ach\_intra} + E_{ach\_inter} = &[c_j\eta_2 kP_{rc}/R_b + c_j\eta_2 k'(P_{tc} + P_{pa})/R_b \\ &+ c_j\eta_1 k'P_{rc}/R_b] + [c_j k'(P_{tc} + P'_{pa}/2)/R_b + (P_{rc} + P'_{pa}/2 + P_{tc})/R_b\mu] \end{aligned} \tag{12}$$

Where μ is a variable denoting the amount of inter-cluster forwarding for previous hop clusters, η_1, η_2 is the proportion of nodes which communicate with mCH, aCH respectively. c_j is the number of nodes in the cluster j.

For the sake of energy consumption balance, every node in a cluster should act as CH for some time. Assume that node i acts as CH for t_i rounds, $i = 1, 2, 3, \ldots\ldots, c_j$, so when the network dies, the energy consumption of node I can be either (13) or (14) when acting as mCH or aCH:

$$(E_{used})_i = (E_{mch})t_i + E_{cm}(\bar{T} - t_i) = \left[(E_{mch})_i - E_{cm}\right]t_i + E_{cm}\bar{T} \tag{13}$$

$$\left(E_{used}\right)_i = \left[(E_{ach})_i - E_{cm}\right]t_i + E_{cm}\bar{T} \tag{14}$$

$$0 \le (E0)_i - (Eused)i < (E_{mch})_i, 0 \le (E0)_i - (Eused)i < (E_{ach})_i \tag{15}$$

So the time node i acting as CH can be (16) or (17) when acting as mCH or aCH

$$t_i = \left[\left(E_{used}\right)_i - E_{cm}\bar{T}\right] / \left[\left(E_{mch}\right)_i - E_{cm}\right] \tag{16}$$

$$t_i = \left[\left(E_{used}\right)_i - E_{cm}\overline{T}\right] / \left[\left(E_{ach}\right)_i - E_{cm}\right] \quad (17)$$

Accordingly, the remaining energy threshold for cluster head rotation are

$$E_{th} = \max\left[E_{cur} - \left(E_{mch}\right)_i t_i\right] = E_{cur} - \left[(E_0)_i - (E_{mch})_i - E_{cm}\overline{T}\right] / \left[1 - E_{cm}/(E_{mch})_i\right] \quad (18)$$

$$E_{th} = E_{cur} - \left[(E_0)_i - (E_{ach})_i - E_{cm}\overline{T}\right] / \left[1 - E_{cm}/(E_{ach})_i\right] \quad (19)$$

4   Simulation Results

In this section, the performance of energy saving and network lifetime of the proposed CHR-CMIMO scheme is evaluated. The system parameters are shown in Table 1, where s is the packet size, R_{bt} is the times of exchanging routing table each round and R_{ts} is the routing table size.

Table 1. Simulation parameters.

$a = 0.4706$	$R_{bt} = 1$	$\lambda = 0.12$ m	$P_b = 10^{-3}$	$R_b = 10$ kbits/s
$M_l = 40$ dB	$N_f = 10$ dB	$G_r G_t = 5$ dBi	$S = 2000$ bits	$R_{ts} = 10$ bits
$P_{rc} = 112.6$ mw	$P_{tc} = 98.2$ mw	$\sigma^2 = N_0/2 = -134$dBm/Hz		

400 sensor nodes are randomly deployed in a 200 m × 200 m area, and the sink node is in the center with axis (100, 100). Each node begins with initial energy from a range of 95 J–105 J and sends data round by round until the energy is used up. During the simulation, the number of active nodes, the residual energy of whole network, and life-time of every node are tracked.

Figure 3 illustrates the number of active nodes against rounds of procedure. Both SISO and re-clustering based multi-hop CMIMO schemes decrease faster than our scheme, in which most of the nodes are still alive until approximately 750 rounds. At

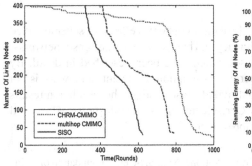

Fig. 3. Number of active nodes over time

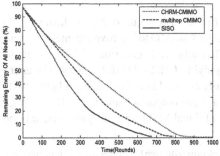

Fig. 4. Total amount of energy over time

that time, almost all the nodes with SISO communication, or more than half of the nodes with re-clustering based multi-hop CMIMO schemes run out of their energy.

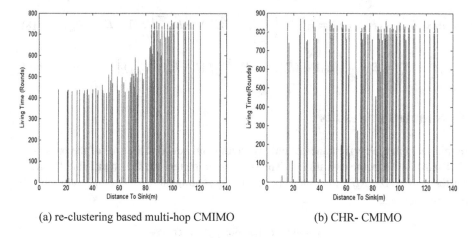

(a) re-clustering based multi-hop CMIMO   (b) CHR- CMIMO

Fig. 5. Living time over distance to sink.

In Fig. 4, the percentage of remaining energy of the entire network over the time is tracked. At the beginning, both CMIMO schemes consume almost the same amount of energy as no re-clustering procedure takes place. After 100 rounds, CHR-CMIMO protocol outperform to the re-clustering based multi-hop MIMO as time goes by. The performance of SISO system is significantly worse than MIMO schemes.

In Fig. 5, the distance to the sink node and active time (rounds) of every node are traced to compare the energy balance effect. It's obvious that in re-clustering multi-hop schemes, the lifetime of nodes closer to the sink is much shorter than those farther to the sink due to heavy packet relay. In CHR-CMIMO protocol, distance to sink is almost not relative to the lifetime of nodes and clusters. This improvement is mainly due to the Over-Jump procedure when a cluster's remaining energy is low. Heavy traffic in low energy clusters is avoided.

5   Conclusion

This paper has introduced a cluster head rotation cooperative MIMO scheme called CHR-CMIMO to improve the energy efficiency and balance in wireless sensor networks. This scheme is constructed by four phases which have been described in detail. By applying CHR-CMIMO scheme, the energy consumption of the entire network is not only reduced but also balanced between different sensor nodes. The simulation results through comparison among CHR-CMIMO, re-clustering based multi-hop CMIMO and traditional SISO schemes prove these improvements.

Acknowledgment. This work is supported by the National Natural Science Foundation of China under Grant No. 61272539 and 61190113.

References

1. Paulraj, A.J., Gore, D.A., Nabar, R.U., Bölcskei, H.: An overview of MIMO communications—a key to gigabit wireless. Proc. IEEE **92**(2), 198–218 (2004)
2. Jayaweera, S.K.: Virtual MIMO-based cooperative communication for energy-constrained wireless sensor networks. IEEE Trans. Wirel. Commun. **5**, 984–989 (2006)
3. Cui, S., Goldsmith, A.J., Bahai, A.: Energy-efficiency of MIMO and cooperative MIMO techniques in sensor networks. IEEE J. Sel. Areas Commun. **22**(6), 1089–1098 (2004)
4. Qu, Q., Milstein, L.B., Vaman, D.R.: Cooperative and constrained MIMO communications in wireless ad hoc/sensor networks. IEEE Trans. Wirel. Commun. **9**(10), 3120–3129 (2010)
5. Boukerche, A., Fei, X.: Energy-efficient multi-hop virtual MIMO wireless sensor network. In: IEEE WCNC Proceedings (2007)
6. Yuan, Y., He, Z., Chen, M.: Virtual MIMO-based cross-layer design for wireless sensor networks. IEEE Trans. Veh. Technol. **55**(3), 856–864 (2006)
7. Siam, M.Z., Krunz, M.: Energy-efficient clustering/routing for cooperative MIMO operation in sensor networks. In: IEEE INFOCOM Proceedings (2009)
8. Ding, J., Liu, D., Wang, X., Wu, H.: An energy-efficient virtual MIMO transmission scheme for cluster-based wireless sensor networks. In: IEEE ICCT (2010)
9. Nguyen, D.N., Krunz, M.: A cooperative clustering protocol for energy constrained networks. In: IEEE Communications Society Conference on Sensor, Mesh and Ad Hoc Communications and Networks (2011)
10. Li, D., Wu, X., Yang, L., Chen, H., Wang, Y., Zhang, X.: Energy-efficient dynamic cooperative virtual MIMO based routing protocol in wireless sensor networks. In: CHINACOM (2013)
11. Gharavi, H., Hu, B.: Cooperative diversity routing and transmission for wireless sensor networks. IET Wirel. Sens. Syst. **3**(4), 277–288 (2013)
12. Wu, Y., Chen, Z., Jing, Q., Wang, Y.C.: LENO: LEast rotation near-optimal cluster head rotation strategy in wireless sensor networks. In: 21st International Conference on Advanced Networking and Applications, AINA 2007, Canada, pp. 195–201 (2007)
13. Li, B., Wang, W.J., Yin, Q.Y., Yang, R., Li, Y.B., Wang, C.: A new cooperative transmission metric in wireless sensor networks to minimize energy consumption per unit transmit distance. IEEE Commun. Lett. **16**(5), 626–629 (2012)
14. Dong, M., Ota, K., Yang, L.T., Chang, S., Zhu, H., Zhou, Z.: Mobile agent-based energy-aware and user-centric data collection in wireless sensor networks. Comput. Netw. **74**, 58–70 (2014)
15. Dong, M., Ota, K., Li, H., Suguo, D., Zhu, H., Guo, S.: ENDEZVOUS: towards fast event detecting in wireless sensor and actor networks. Computing **96**(10), 995–1010 (2014)

A Distributed Game-Theoretic Power Control Mechanism for Device-to-Device Communications Underlaying Cellular Network

Jun Huang[1]([✉]), Yi Sun[1], Cong-Cong Xing[2],
Yanxiao Zhao[3], and Qianbin Chen[1]

[1] School of CIE, Chongqing University of Posts and Telecommunication,
Chongqing 400065, China
xiaoniuadmin@gmail.com
[2] Department of Mathematics and Computer Science,
Nicholls State University, Thibodaux 70310, USA
[3] ECE Department, South Dakota School of Mines and Technology,
Rapid City 57701, USA

Abstract. Although the Device-to-Device (D2D) technology has been extensively studied as an effective means to address the spectrum scarcity and to relieve the overload of base stations in cellular systems, the interference between D2D links and cellular links emerges as an challenging issue that must be dealt with. Among many other techniques to reduce the interference, transmitter power control plays a crucial role. In this paper, we propose a game theoretic model to acquire the compensatory power of D2D link transmitters underlaying the cellular network. This model considers not only interference between cellular links and D2D links but the interference among D2D links themselves as well. Also, it allows the compensatory power for a D2D link to be decided based on the need of this D2D link, leading to a reasonable acquisition/configuration of compensatory powers of all D2D links and an overall improvement of the communication quality. Finally, we developed a distributed compensatory power control mechanism to compute the compensatory power for each D2D link. Simulation results demonstrate the validness and rationality of this mechanism.

Keywords: Device-to-Device · Interference · Power control · Game theory · Distributed algorithm

1 Introduction

Device-to-Device (D2D) technology, as a promising solution to the limited spectrum resources issue by allowing cellular resources to be reused by device terminals, has drawn tremendous amount of research work [1]. While D2D communication technique, as a local-area communication technique with a strong potential, a high capability, and a low cost, is able to effectively reduce the workload and

© Springer International Publishing Switzerland 2015
K. Xu and J. Zhu (Eds.): WASA 2015, LNCS 9204, pp. 222–231, 2015.
DOI: 10.1007/978-3-319-21837-3_22

mitigate the spectrum scarcity issue in cellular networks, it also introduces some problems. When D2D links underlay cellular communications, there are primarily three D2D communication modes: cellular mode, dedicated mode, and reuse mode [2]. As shown in Fig. 1, when a D2D link is in the reuse mode, a cellular link and a D2D link will interfere each other, and two different D2D links may also interfere as well due to the same spectrum being reused. Although the interferences between cellular links and D2D links can be eliminated when a D2D communication is in cellular mode or dedicated mode, the interferences between different D2D links still exists and may even become worse if there are a large number of D2D links underlaying the cellular network. As such, the presence of interferences between different parties imposes a challenge that must be dealt with. Currently, various interference-reducing approaches have been proposed in the literature, which can be classified by: resources allocation [3,4], interference coordination [5], and power control [6,12]. The power control approach refers to the idea of limiting the transmitting powers in D2D links and thereby reducing the interferences that plays an important role.

For power control, extensive researches have been conducted recently. Lee et al. [6] proposed a stochastic geometry model for the D2D-underlaied cellular network, and presented two related algorithms which maximize the number of D2D links underlaying a cellular network by controlling the powers of D2D and cellular users. ElSawy, Hossain, and Alouini [7] analyzed the impact of D2D users on cellular users by constructing a systematic and complete framework. Their work shows that the D2D communication underlaying cellular networks is able to improve the spatial spectrum efficiency and the link spectrum efficiency of the system. Motivated by the power optimization issue when a D2D

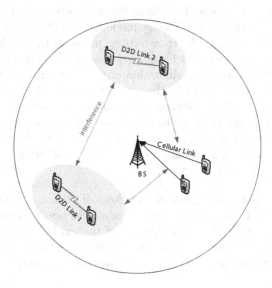

Fig. 1. Interferences between D2D and cellular communications.

user shares the spectrum with a cellular use, Ghazanfari, Tolli, and Pennanen [8] described a joint power control and beamforming algorithm which allows the sum of the D2D link power and the cellular link power to be minimal within their permitted ranges. In [9], a new power control mechanism to avoid the inter-carrier interference was proposed, and in [10], the D2D power control was turned into an optimization problem and a corresponding power control algorithm allowing the maximization of D2D transmission rate was suggested. Fodor and Reider [11] studied a distributed power control scheme for D2D communications which controls the transmitting power by limiting the D2D transmission rate. Although this scheme works well in reducing the interference between cellular and D2D users, it unfortunately also reduces the advantage of D2D communications due to the limitation on the transmission rate, especially in the case when the traffic is heavy. Hoang, Le, and Le-Ngoc [12] studied the uplink subchannel and power allocation problems in the Orthogonal Frequency Division Multiple Access (OFDMA) based D2D-celluar networks. The goal of their power alloca-tion study is to maximize the D2D link throughput while the minimum rate of cellular links is guaranteed. A corresponding iterative algorithm was developed in their work which decouples the bandwidth allocation and the power allocation and improves the object function over iterations.

Although tremendous researches have been done on the power control for D2D underlaying cellular networks, most of the studies assume or stipulate that all D2D links have the same transmitting power at all times. In this paper, we tackle the D2D links power control problem by considering the interference among D2D links themselves leveraging Game Theory. The main contributions of the paper are as follows:

- With the interference among D2D links themselves being included in the con-sideration, we present a Game-Theory model for the D2D power control prob-lem. This model computes the transmitting power of D2D links by consider-ing D2D links own status, which not only reasonably takes the discrepancies among D2D links into the consideration of power controls, but improves the overall communication quality in the network as well. Also, the existence and uniqueness of the Nash equilibrium of the model are proved.
- Based on the involvement of the base station in the process of power controls, a distributed power controlling mechanism is developed. Also, a corresponding distributed algorithm which computes the Nash equilibrium (compensatory) power for each D2D link is devised.

The rest of the paper is organized as follows. Section 2 introduces the SNR-based Game-Theory model for the power control. Section 3 proves the existence and the uniqueness of the Nash equilibrium of the model, and exhibits the dis-tributed power computation mechanisms. Section 4 provides simulation results verifying the distributed power computation mechanisms, and Sect. 5 concludes the paper.

2   Modeling D2D Power Control

2.1   System Model

Throughout this work, we assume that all D2D communications reuse the cellular spectrum resources within a cell. There are several D2D links in such a cellular region each with the initial transmission power. We use h to denote the communication gain of the D2D links; in particular, h_{ii} denotes the gain of link i and h_{ji} denotes the interferential gain of link j by causing an interference to link i. Furthermore, we assume that the transmitter on each D2D communication link may require some extra transmission power in addition to its initial transmission power depending on its own need; these extra transmission powers are called compensatory power and are denoted by $p_1, p_2, \cdots, p_n$. Finally, we assume that when the transmission powers of all D2D links are P_0, the interferences between P2P links can be ignored when compared with other types of interferences.

2.2   Game Theoretic Model and Formulation

For any D2D communication link i, we know its signal-noise ratio is

$$SNR_i = \frac{(P_0 + p_i)h_{ii}}{N_0 + I + \sum_{j \neq i} p_j h_{ji}}, \tag{1}$$

where N_0 is the Gaussian noise, I is the interferences coming from neighboring cells and cellular links, $\sum_{j \neq i} p_j h_{ji}$ is the interference to link i generated by other D2D links. By Shannon Theorem, we have

$$C = B \ln(1 + SNR), \tag{2}$$

where B is the bandwidth of the channel and C is the channel capacity; clearly, a larger SNR will give rise to a larger channel capacity C. Note that formula (Eq. 1) indicates that a larger p_i will lead to a higher SNR_i for link i, but this increase in signal-noise ratio for link i will certainly cause a higher interference to other D2D links. So, interestingly, the relationship among D2D links during the acquisition/allocation of compensatory powers can be characterized as a competition.

We in this paper leverage the Game Theory to model the acquisition/allocation/ competition of the compensatory powers among D2D communication link transmitters. By the discussion above, the utility U_i of the D2D link i can be calculated as follows:

$$U_i = \alpha \frac{p_i(N_0 + I + \sum_{j \neq i} p_j h_{ji})}{h_{ii}} - \beta^{p_i}, \tag{3}$$

where α and β are arithmetic number respectively. In particular, β^{p_i} gives the total negative impact of the compensatory power p_i on the utility of D2D link i.

In (economic) Game Theory, the notion of marginal utility is used to represent the increased amount in utility when a unit amount of product is consumed by the consumer. Here, the marginal utility MU_i of any D2D link i can be computed by using formula (Eq. 3) as follows:

$$MU_i = \frac{\partial U_i}{\partial p_i} = \alpha \frac{(N_0 + I + \sum_{j \neq i} p_j h_{ji})}{h_{ii}} - \beta^{p_i} \ln \beta, \tag{4}$$

which indicates that a larger h_{ii} would result in a smaller MU_i, and a larger $(N_0 + I + \sum_{j \neq i} p_j h_{ji})$ would result in a larger h_{ii}, when other parameters stay unchanged. In other words, in our game-theory modeling of compensatory power allocations, a D2D link that has a smaller gain and suffers a stronger interference from other D2D links will excel in the competition.

Note that the utility function must possess effectiveness and restrictiveness simultaneously. While effectiveness refers to the situation that a larger compensatory power should lead to a higher utility for any D2D links, which is in fact the driving force for various D2D links to compete one another, restrictiveness means the scenario where if the compensatory power is over a certain threshold, then a larger p_i would result in a lower U_i for any D2D link i. The rational for the restrictiveness of the utility function is that if an arbitrary increase in p_i can always result in an increase in U_i, then the increase of p_i will be out of control and will cause immense interferences to other D2D links and cellular users. As such, in order to ensure the effectiveness as well as the restrictiveness, for any D2D link must satisfy the following inequalities.

$$\begin{cases} \frac{\partial^2 U_i}{\partial p_i^2} < 0 \\ \frac{a(N_0 + I + \sum_{j \neq i} p_j h_{ji})}{h_{ii} \ln \beta} > 1 \end{cases} \tag{5}$$

In formula (Eq. 5), Let $h_{\max}$ be the maximal possible gain for D2D links, then it can be inferred that α and β thus must satisfy the following condition

$$\frac{a}{\ln \beta} > \frac{h_{\max}}{N_0 + I}. \tag{6}$$

3   Distributed Game Theoretic Power Control Mechanism

Prior to present the power control mechanism, we would like to first analyze the properties of Nash Equilibrium including the existence and the uniqueness for the developed model, which will provide guidelines to the mechanism design.

3.1   Analysis on Nash Equilibrium

We now discuss the issues of the existence and the uniqueness of the Nash Equilibrium associated with the model we have presented so far. By the Glicksberg-Fan fixed point theorem [14,15], we know that in a game with a finite number

---

Algorithm 1. NE Acquisition Algorithm for the Distributed Mechanism

---

1: initialization $p_1 = p_1^0, p_2 = p_2^0, \cdots, p_n = p_n^0, t = 1$;

2: **for** each p_i **do**

3: $\quad p_i^t = \min \left(p_i' = \log_\beta \left[\dfrac{\alpha(N_0 + I + \sum\limits_{j \neq i} p_j^{t-1} h_{ji})}{h_{ii} \ln \beta} \right], p_{\max} \right)$;

4: $\quad$ **while** $\left(|p_1^t - p_1^{t-1}| > \delta, \cdots, |p_n^t - p_n^{t-1}| > \delta\right)$ **do**

5: $\quad\quad t \leftarrow t + 1$;

6: $\quad\quad p_i^t = \min \left(\log_\beta \left[\dfrac{\alpha h_{ii}}{(N_0 + I + \sum\limits_{j \neq i} p_j^{t-1} h_{ii}) \ln \beta} \right], p_{\max} \right)$;

7: $\quad$ **end while**

8: **end for**

9: $p_1^* = p_1^t, \cdots, p_n^* = p_n^t$;

---

of players, if each players strategy space is a non-empty, closed, and bounded convex set in the Euclidian space, and each players utility function is quasi-concave over its strategy space, then this game has at least one pure strategy Nash equilibrium.

Theorem 1. *The Nash equilibrium of the proposed game exist.*

Proof. Skipped due to the space limitation.

Theorem 2. *The Nash equilibrium of the proposed game is unique.*

Proof. Skipped due to the space limitation.

The game model of the acquisition of compensatory powers for the transmitters in the D2D links can be reformulated as the following to ensure the uniqueness of the Nash equilibrium.

In the following, we present the power control mechanism based on the above two theorems.

3.2 Distributed Power Control Mechanism

Based on the involvement of the base station in the acquisition of the compensatory powers for D2D links, we propose a distributed mechanisms for the acquisition of the Nash equilibrium compensatory powers.

As D2D link i knows its own p_i and h_{ii} only, and it has no way of knowing p_j and h_{ji} for any other D2D link j. From the previous discussions in section, we know that U_i is concave with respect to p_i and that the value of p_i is uniquely determined when p_{-i} is fixed. Thus, the computation of the Nash equilibrium compensatory power for link i is amount to finding the optimal p_i for link i. In other words, we have

$$arg \left\{ \max \left(U_i = \alpha \frac{p_i(N_0 + I + \sum\limits_{j \neq i} p_j h_{ji})}{h_{ii}}) - \beta^{p_i} \right) \right\} = \min(p_i', p_{\max}), \quad (7)$$

where p_i' is the solution of the equation $\frac{\partial U_i}{\partial p_i} = \dfrac{\alpha(N_0 + I + \sum\limits_{j \neq i} p_j h_{ji})}{h_{ii}} - \ln\beta\beta^{p_i} = 0$.
Solving this equation shows that

$$
p_i' = \log_\beta \left[\frac{\alpha(N_0 + I + \sum\limits_{j \neq i} p_j h_{ji})}{h_{ii} \ln \beta} \right]. \tag{8}
$$

Let $(p_1^*, p_2^*, \cdots, p_n^*)$ denote the optimal acquisitions of the compensatory power of the D2D links in the cellular region. By the discussion in this section, $(p_1^*, p_2^*, \cdots, p_n^*)$ can be computed by the following algorithm in the style of distributed computing.

- Each D2D link takes an initial value for its compensatory power. That is, $p_1 = p_1^0, p_2 = p_2^0, \cdots, p_n = p_n^0$, $p_1^0 \in (0, p_{\max}), p_2^0 \in (0, p_{\max}), \cdots, p_n^0 \in (0, p_{\max})$.
- Each D2D link computes its subsequent compensatory powers by formulas (11) and (12), and updates the value of its compensatory power. We use p_i^t to denote the -th computation of the value of compensatory power for link i.
- If $\left| p_i^t - p_i^{t-1} \right| < \delta$ for a predefined threshold at the -th computation, then we terminate the computation of and set $p_i^* = p_i^t$.

By the discussion of uniqueness of the Nash equilibrium in the previous section, we know that $(p_1^*, p_2^*, \cdots, p_n^*)$ must be the value where the Nash equilibrium is reached. The pseudo-code of the algorithm is shown in Algorithm 9.

4   Simulation Results

We in this section verify the validity of the theory discussed in the previous section by conducting simulation experiments. Specifically, we examine the effectiveness and restrictiveness of the utility function and the compensatory power acquisition of the distributed mechanism. Throughout all the experiments, the related parameters are set as shown in Table 1.

4.1   Utility Function Verification

Figure 2 depicts the correlations between the compensatory power of a D2D link i and its utility function as well as signal-noise ratio SNR_i. It can be seen clearly that as p_i increases, U_i increases consistently, but increases to a certain point and then starts decreasing after that point. In other words, at the early stage of the game-playing, a D2D link would try to acquire as much as possible compensatory power to boost its signal-noise ratio and improve its utility. By doing so, link i can avoid the problem of poor communication quality caused by insufficient transmitting power. Meanwhile, the fact that a D2D link i s utility function will decrease when its compensatory power p_i is over a certain amount forces the D2D link i to retain its compensatory power within a certain range (especially when link i is the only D2D link in the cellular region). This will facilitate to alleviate the interferences a link may cause to other D2D links and cellular users.

Table 1. Parameter settings

Parameter	Value
Cell radius	500m
Max D2D communication range	50m
$N_0 + I$	0.4
h_{11}, h_{12}, h_{13}	0.85, 0.1, 0.11
h_{21}, h_{22}, h_{23}	0.09, 0.9, 0.08
h_{31}, h_{32}, h_{33}	0.08, 0.09, 0.95
h_{max}	1
p_{max}	5
p_{min}	0.5
δ	0.005

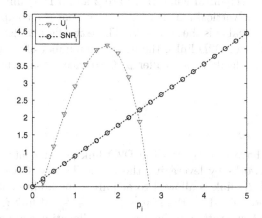

Fig. 2. Correlations between power and utility as well as SNR_i.

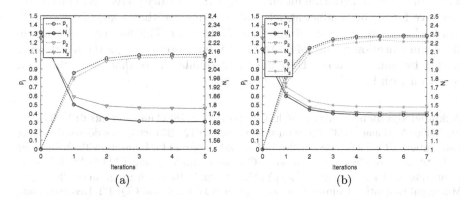

Fig. 3. (a)Compensatory Power Allocation and Link Status for two D2D links. (b)Compensatory Power Allocation and Link Status for three D2D links.

4.2 Compensatory Power Allocation with Distributed Mechanism

Distributed compensatory power allocation/acquisition mechanism can be used when the base station is not involved in the control of the compensatory powers of D2D links. In this case, a D2D link only knows its own compensatory power p_i and link gain h_{ii}, and does not know anything about the compensatory power p_j and the interferential gain for any other D2D link h_{ji}. In order to compare the result of compensatory power allocations for different links, we define the status of a D2D link N_i as follows:

$$N_i = \frac{SNR_i}{P_0 + p_i} = \frac{h_{ii}}{N_0 + I + \sum_{j \neq i} p_j h_{ji}}. \tag{9}$$

with the intention that a larger value of N_i indicates a better status of the link. Figures 3(a) and 3(b), respectively, depict the compensatory power allocation by the distributed mechanism when there are 2 and 3 D2D links in the cellular region, where the left vertical axis is used to represent the compensatory power p_i, and the right vertical axis the status N_i. These two figures clearly suggest that the more the number of D2D links, the more the number of required iterations, and that a larger N_i leads to a smaller p_i (and vice versa) when the iteration terminates.

5 Conclusions

We in this paper have investigated the D2D link power control issue in D2D-cellular mixed networks by leveraging the Game Theory. Given an initial and fixed power, any D2D link is allowed to acquire some additional compensatory power which is determined by the status $N_i = \frac{SNR_i}{P_0 + p_i}$ of link i. In light of the involvement of the base station in the process of allocating compensatory powers for D2D links, a centralized mechanism and a distributed mechanism together with a distributed algorithm for allocating compensatory powers were presented. We have found, by conducting relevant experiments, that a larger value of N_i will lead to a smaller value of p_i for any D2D link i. This fact not only ensures the communication quality of a D2D link i, but also minimizes the interference caused by link i to other D2D links and cellular users that share the same spectrum with link i.

Acknowledgement. This research is supported by NSFC under grants 61309031 and 61272400, National "973" Program under grant 2012CB315803, Postdoctoral Science Foundation of China (Grant No. 2014M551740), Program for Innovation Team Building at Institutions of Higher Education in Chongqing under grant KJTD201310, NSF of Chongqing under grant cstc2013jcyjA40026, S and T Research Program of Chongqing Municipal Education Commission under grant KJ130523, and CQUPT Research Fund for Young Scholars under grant A2012-79.

References

1. Tehrani, M., Uysal, M., Yanikomeroglu, H.: Device-to-Device communication in 5G cellular networks: challenges, solutions, and future directions. IEEE Commun. Mag. **52**(5), 86–92 (2014)
2. Lili, W., Hu, R., Yi, Q., Geng, W.: Enable Device-to-Device communications underlaying cellular networks: challenges and research aspects. IEEE Commun. Mag. **52**(6), 90–96 (2014)
3. Jun, H., Yanxiao, Z., Sohraby, K.: Resource allocation for intercell Device-to-Device communication underlaying cellular network: a game-theoretic approach. In: Proceedings of Computer Communication and Networks (ICCCN), pp. 1–8 (2014)
4. Jun, H., Yanxiao, Z., Sohraby, K.: Game-theoretic resource allocation for intercell Device-to-Device communication underlaying cellular network. In: Proceedings of Wireless Research Collaboration Symposium (NWRCS), pp. 79–83 (2014)
5. Shaoyi, X., Kyung, K.S.: Effective interference coordination for D2D underlaying LTE networks. In: Proceedings of Vehicular Technology Conference (VTC Spring), pp. 1–5 (2014)
6. Namyoon, L., Xingqin, L., Andrews, J., Heath, R.: Power control for D2D underlaid cellular networks: modeling, algorithms, and analysis. IEEE J. Sel. Areas Commun. **33**(1), 1–13 (2015)
7. ElSawy, H., Hossain, E., Alouini, M.: Analytical modeling of mode selection and power control for underlay D2D communication in cellular network. IEEE Trans. Commun. **62**(11), 4147–4161 (2014)
8. Ghazanfari, A., Tolli, A., Pennanen, H.: Sum power minimization for cellular systems with underlay D2D communications. In: Proceedings of Cognitive Radio Oriented Wireless Networks and Communications (CROWNCOM), pp. 45–50 (2014)
9. Hyung, S.J., Hoon, L.D., Jun, H.W., Jin, C.H.: A selective transmission power boosting method for D2D discovery in 3GPP LTE cellular system. In: Proceedings of Information and Communication Technology Convergence (ICTC), pp. 267–268 (2014)
10. Gil-Mo, K., Jaejin, L., Oh-Soon, S.: Power allocation scheme for D2D communications in an OFDM-based cellular system. In: Proceedings of Information Networking (ICOIN), pp. 388–389 (2015)
11. Fodor, G., Reider, N.: A distributed power control scheme for cellular network assisted D2D communications. In: Proceedings of Global Telecommunications Conference (GLOBECOM 2011), pp. 1–6 (2011)
12. Tuong Duc, H., Long Bao, L., Tho, L.: Joint subchannel and power allocation for D2D communications in cellular networks. In: Proceedings of Wireless Communications and Networking Conference (WCNC), pp. 1338–1343 (2014)
13. Hyunkee, M., Jemin, L., Sungsoo, P., Daesik, H.: Capacity enhancement using an interference limited area for Device-to-Device uplink underlaying cellular networks. IEEE Trans. Wirel. Commun. **10**(12), 3995–4000 (2011)
14. Fan, K.: Fixed point and minima theorems in locally convex topological linear spaces. In: Proceedings of National Academy of Sciences, pp. 121–126 (1952)
15. Glecksberg, I.: A further generalization of the kakutani fixed point theorem with application to Nash equilibrium points. In: Proceedings of American Mathematical Society, pp. 170–174 (1952)
16. David, S., Wu, D., Shen, Z.: Handbook of Quantitative Supply Chain Analysis: Modeling in the Ebusiness Era. Kluwer A cademic Publishers, New York (2004)

A Low Overhead and Stable Clustering Scheme for Crossroads in VANETs

Yan Huo[1]([⊠]), Yuejia Liu[1], Xiaoshuang Xing[2],
Xiuzhen Cheng[2], Liran Ma[3], and Tao Jing[1]

[1] School of Electronics and Information Engineering,
Beijing Jiaotong University, Beijing, China
yhuo@bjtu.edu.cn
[2] Department of Computer Science, The George Washington University,
Washington, D.C., WA, USA
[3] Department of Computer Science, Texas Christian University,
Fort Worth, TX, USA

Abstract. In this paper, we study the clustering problem for crossroads in VANETs. We propose a novel Low Overhead and Stable Clustering scheme (LOSC) that considers both the stability of clusters and the communication overhead. In LOSC, a Cluster Head Electing in Advance Mechanism (CHEAM) is developed in order to select a new head for "isolated" vehicles that may not belong to a cluster. Based on CHEAM, a cluster maintenance scheme is proposed so as to reduce the number of isolated vehicles and the communication overhead. Numerical results indicate that the cluster stability and communication overhead can be significantly enhanced by our proposed clustering scheme.

Keywords: VANETs · Cluster formation · Cluster maintenance · Cluster stability · Network overhead

1 Introduction

Communication in Vehicular Ad-hoc Networks (VANETs) becomes an important research topic with the spectrum allocation for Intelligent Transportation System (ITS) and the development of Dedicated Short Range Communication (DSRC) standards. Existing methods that enable communication in Mobile Ad-hoc Networks (MANETs) cannot be directly applied in VANETs due to the following characteristics [1,2]. First, the fast movement of vehicles can lead to a highly dynamic and frequently disconnected network topology. Second, the trajectories of the vehicles in VANETs are strictly restricted by the layout of roads. Clustering based methods that divide vehicles into clusters by taking the advantage of the layout determined trajectories, are considered as effective ways to facilitate communication in VANETs. Stable communication can be achieved in highly dynamic VANETs through cluster based communication where a leader is selected within each cluster to handle intra-cluster and inter-cluster traffic.

© Springer International Publishing Switzerland 2015
K. Xu and J. Zhu (Eds.): WASA 2015, LNCS 9204, pp. 232–242, 2015.
DOI: 10.1007/978-3-319-21837-3_23

Many works have been done to develop effective clustering algorithms for VANETs with most of them focusing on the scenario of highway or straight lanes [2–11]. However, the performance of these schemes turns to be unsatisfactory when it comes to a city scenario with crossroads. This is because a large number of vehicles can become isolated at crossroads. As a result, a considerable amount of communication overhead and congestion can result from the routing discovery processes for the isolated vehicles. To deal with these problems, we propose a novel clustering scheme for the crossroads in VANETs, with the objective to stabilize the clusters, minimize the number of isolated nodes, and reduce the communication overhead. The main contributions of this paper are three folds,

- We propose a novel clustering scheme named Low Overhead and Stable Clustering (LOSC) scheme for crossroads in VANETs, which includes a cluster formation algorithm and a cluster maintenance scheme.
- In the cluster formation algorithm, we introduce a new metric M to describe the capability of a vehicle to be a cluster head by considering both the mobility and the transmission power loss of the vehicle.
- In the cluster maintenance phase, we propose a Cluster Head Electing in Advance Mechanism (CHEAM) to help a cluster member select a new cluster by predicting its stay time. The communication overhead can be significantly reduced via this mechanism.

The rest of the paper is organized as follows. Related works are summarized in Sect. 2. Section 3 depicts our problem formulation and the capability metric for cluster formation. In Sect. 4, we describe the details of cluster formation and maintenance algorithms, respectively. Numerical analysis and simulation results are presented in Sect. 5 to evaluate the performances of our scheme. In the end, the conclusion of this work is provided in Sect. 6.

2 Related Work

Cluster head selection plays an important role in clustering algorithms. Various metrics have been proposed to describe a vehicle's capability of functioning as a cluster head in VANETs. In this section, we briefly review the work related to clustering methods that are based on these different metrics.

In [9], the metric is defined by considering the traffic flow on the lane. A vehicle on the lane with most traffic flow is selected as the cluster head. The clustering algorithm proposed in [10] defines the metric as a function of the path loss. A vehicle with smaller path loss from other vehicles has a higher metric value. It is concluded in [7] that the performance of cluster based communication can be further improved by exploring the geography information for cluster head selection. Based on this conclusion, [6,12] combine the geography information together with the traffic information and the task information to define their metrics.

The aforementioned clustering schemes usually cause frequent re-affiliation and cluster head changes since they do not consider the effects of fast movements of vehicles in VANETs. To solve these problems, mobility-based clustering algorithms are put forward. In [8], Song *et al.* use the moving direction of vehicles together with the location information to design a clustering algorithm. Only the vehicles moving in the same direction can form clusters and the cluster head is selected according to the location information. In [4], Basu *et al.* designs a mobility metric by measuring the fluctuation of a vehicle's received power during successive transmissions. A vehicle with smaller fluctuation is considered as a vehicle with smaller relative speed with others and it is more likely to be selected as a cluster head. The performance of this scheme degrades significantly when the vehicle's speed varies sharply and frequently due to the fact that the vehicle's acceleration is not considered in the mobility metric. [3] solves this problem by designing a mobility metric consisting of both the relative velocity and the relative acceleration to represent a vehicle's ability to be the cluster head.

To the best of our knowledge, these existing schemes [3,4,6–13] consider either the highway scenarios or the straight lane scenarios. None of them considers the complicated and challenging crossroad scenarios where large numbers of vehicles can become isolated, and thus, considerable communication overhead and network congestion can be generated using these existing schemes. In this paper, we will tackle the challenge of designing a low overhead and stable clustering scheme for crossroads in VANETs.

3   Problem Formulation and Capability Metric

3.1   System Model

Our system model is based on a bidirectional multi-lane city road scenario with a crossroad as illustrated in Fig. 1. We assume that all vehicles are equipped with GPS so that each vehicle is aware of its own location (represented by Cartesian coordinates), velocity, and direction (represented by direction vector) at any time. We further assume that the precise time is known and traceable to the Coordinated Universal Time (UTC). We also assume that all vehicles can send packets with a unified transmitting power P_t and decode received packets about the threshold P_r.

As shown in Fig. 1, there exist a number of clusters. Nodes that are in a dashed box belong to the same cluster. The *cluster heads* are red nodes, and the *cluster members* are black ones. In addition, the nodes in grey color are called *hopping cluster members* because they are about to leave the current cluster and hop to a new one. The *undecided nodes* in white color are the isolated nodes. In a cluster, there are one cluster head, several cluster members, and hopping cluster members. The cluster head is responsible for handling the intra-cluster communication and relay the inter-cluster communication among clusters. Note that we use node and vehicle interchangeably in the rest of this paper,

Similar to [8], only those nodes that are moving in the same direction can be clustered together. Once a node joins in a cluster and becomes a cluster member, a timer named *TimerS* that is related to its predicted stay time in the cluster starts. The definition of *TimerS* for member j in cluster i is:

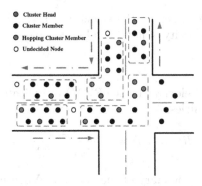

Fig. 1. System model.

$$TimerS(i,j) = T_{j,i}^{stay} - T_f, \tag{1}$$

where $T_{j,i}^{stay}$ is the predicted stay time of member j in cluster i which is detailed in Sect. 4.2. T_f is the ideal time of a cluster formation procedure, which includes the packet transmission cost and capability metric comparison cost.

Because of the dynamic topology of VANETs, a cluster member may change to be a hopping cluster member. When the change happens, the hopping member starts searching for a new cluster head to join even though it may still belong to the current cluster. In addition, the isolated nodes continuously search for clusters to join. Note that if there are too many isolated nodes in a dense network, the total communication overhead increases significantly and can lead to poor network performance. Therefore, it is important to design a clustering algorithm that reduces the number of isolated nodes as much as possible.

3.2   The Capability Metric: M Value

In this subsection, taking into account both the vehicle's mobility and the transmission power loss, we design a metric to measure a vehicle's capability of acting as a cluster head.

Vehicles can obtain their position, velocity, and direction information based on the data derived from GPS. Let $\vec{D}_i = D_{ix}\vec{x} + D_{iy}\vec{y}$ be the direction vector of node i, where $\vec{x}$ and $\vec{y}$ are the unit vectors of X and Y axes. The angle between the direction of two nodes i and j can be calculated as:

$$\theta_{i,j} = \arccos \frac{\vec{D}_i \cdot \vec{D}_j}{\left|\vec{D}_i\right|\left|\vec{D}_j\right|} = \arccos \frac{D_{ix}D_{jx} + D_{iy}D_{jy}}{\sqrt{D_{ix}^2 + D_{iy}^2}\sqrt{D_{jx}^2 + D_{jy}^2}}. \tag{2}$$

We consider node i and node j are moving in the same direction when $\theta \leqslant \pi/4$ and consider they are moving in different directions when $\theta > \pi/4$. In this way, we could avoid mistakenly labeling the vehicle as changing lanes when it is actually turning at the crossroads.

Similarly, let v_i and v_j denote the velocity of nodes i and j obtained from the GPS. The relative velocity of node i and node j can be calculated as follows:

$$v_{i,j}^{rel} = |v_i - v_j|. \tag{3}$$

We use the Relative Velocity Metric (RVM) to indicate the relative mobility between two moving vehicles:

$$RVM(i,j) = \log \frac{v_{max}}{v_{max} - v_{i,j}^{rel}}. \tag{4}$$

Here, v_{max} is the upper boundary of the velocity. When node i has n one-hop (direct) neighbors, the RVM value of node i can be calculated as:

$$RVM(i) = \frac{1}{n} \sum_{j=1}^{n} RVM(i,j) = \frac{1}{n} \sum_{j=1}^{n} \log \frac{v_{max}}{v_{max} - v_{i,j}^{rel}}. \tag{5}$$

Clearly, $RVM(i)$ is not smaller than 1. A smaller $RVM(i)$ indicates that node i's velocity is more similar with that of its direct neighbors'. That is, a node with smaller RVM is more likely to stay with its direct neighbors for a longer time due to their similar velocity. Therefore, a node with lower RVM value is preferred to act as cluster head to make the cluster more stable.

As described in Sect. 3.1, P_t is the unified transmission power of all nodes and $P_r(i,j)$ denotes the received power of node i from node j. We define the transmission Power Loss Metric (PLM) between node i and node j as:

$$PLM(i,j) = \log \frac{P_t}{P_r(i,j)}. \tag{6}$$

When node i has n direct neighbors, the PLM of node i can be presented as:

$$PLM(i) = \frac{1}{n} \sum_{j=1}^{n} \log \frac{P_t}{P_r(i,j)}. \tag{7}$$

$PLM(i)$ is not smaller than 1 that is related to the average channel quality and the sum of distance between a node and its direct neighbors. A node with a smaller PLM value is more likely to have a shorter communication distance and better channel quality with its direct neighbors.

Taking both $RVM(i)$ and $PLM(i)$ into consideration, we define a Capability Metric M to describe the capability of a node to be a cluster head:

$$M(i) = RVM(i) + PLM(i). \tag{8}$$

A node with a smaller M value implies that this node has more similar mobility with its direct neighbors and better channel quality. In other words, a more stable cluster can be formed by selecting a node with smaller M value as the cluster head.

4   Cluster Formation and Maintenance Schemes

Based on the Capability Metric M defined in the previous subsection, we present the LOSC scheme that contains a cluster formation algorithm and a cluster maintenance scheme. For the convenience of description, we assume every node uses its own ID as an identification and the cluster ID is represented by the cluster head's ID.

4.1   Cluster Formation Algorithm

Before forming or changing cluster-based network topology, there are some *unde-cided nodes* or *hopping cluster members* that want to join in a new cluster. For this purpose, these nodes broadcast **HELLO** packets, which contain the position, velocity, and direction information, to their direct neighbors. At the same time, when there are cluster heads in the network, the heads also broadcast their information, called Cluster Head Announcement (**CHA**) packets that contain cluster head's ID, position, velocity, and direction.

Accordingly, when node j receives **HELLO** packets or **CHA** packets, it adds the senders' IDs into its Direct Neighbors List (DNL). Then, it uses (2) to calculate the angle θ between its direction and each direct neighbor's direction. If $\theta > \pi/4$, the corresponding neighbor is considered moving in a different direction and deleted from its DNL. After checking θ and updating DNL, node j computes the M value based on (8) and sends it to other nodes in its DNL.

If there is only one cluster head in node j's DNL, it sends a **ClusterJoin** packet including its ID to the head and becomes a member of the cluster. If there are more than one cluster heads in node j's DNL, it selects the head with the smallest M value and sends a **ClusterJoin** packet to the head. If there is no cluster head in node j's DNL, it compares its M value with its direct neighbors'. When node j finds its M value is smaller than that of any node in its DNL, it will be elected as a cluster head and change its state into *cluster head*. After that, it will broadcast a **ClusterInvite** packet to its direct neighbors which contains the Cluster ID and its M value. Another node in the network who receives this **ClusterInvite** packet will reply a **ClusterJoin** packet to node j if j's M value is smaller than that of any other received **ClusterInvite** packet.

Once a cluster is formed, the cluster head periodically (with the time period being T_c) broadcasts **CHA** packets. Similarly, the cluster members regularly broadcast Cluster Member Announcement (**CMA**) packets containing the cluster member's ID, position, velocity, and direction. Through this way, the cluster head and the cluster members know each other and maintain the cluster. Additionally, because the undecided nodes broadcast **HELLO** packets periodically with T_c until they joins in a cluster, the DNL of all nodes should be updated periodically as well.

The details of cluster formation algorithm are shown in Algorithm 1.

Algorithm 1. Cluster Formation Algorithm

Require: node: j; cluster set: Ω; DNL set: Θ
1: Calculate $M(j)$ for node j
2: Send $M(j)$ to all DNL nodes $\gamma \in \Theta(j)$
3: **if** $\exists$ cluster head $i \in \Theta(j)$ whose M is the smallest of all cluster heads **then**
4:     Add j to $\Omega(i)$
5: **else**
6:     **if** $M(j) \leqslant \forall M(\gamma)$ **then**
7:         j becomes the Cluster Head and sends **ClusterInvite** to $\Theta(j)$
8:     **else**
9:         j receives **ClusterInvite** packets and $M(\gamma)$ is the smallest among senders
10:        Add j to $\Omega(\gamma)$
11:    **end if**
12: **end if**
13: Go To Cluster Maintenance

4.2   Cluster Maintenance Scheme

A cluster should be maintained after cluster formation. In this section, we first introduce the stay time prediction of a member in its current cluster. With the prediction, the cluster maintenance scheme using Cluster Head Electing in Advance Mechanism (CHEAM) is proposed.

Stay Time Prediction. The stay time of a cluster member plays a key role in our cluster maintenance algorithm. Therefore, we study the stay time prediction problem before presenting the cluster maintenance algorithm.

Assuming v_i^{Ins}, v_j^{Ins}, (x_i^{Ins}, y_i^{Ins}), and (x_j^{Ins}, y_i^{Ins}) are the instantaneous velocity and position of the cluster head i and its member j which are contained in the **CHA** and the **CMA** packets respectively. The instantaneous distance between head i and member j can be represented by:

$$D^{Ins} = \sqrt{(x_i^{Ins} - x_j^{Ins})^2 + (y_i^{Ins} - y_j^{Ins})^2}. \tag{9}$$

Comparing the position and the velocity of the head i with those of the member j, four different stay time prediction results of member j in cluster i, $T_{j,i}^{stay}$, can be obtained,

$$T_{j,i}^{stay} = \begin{cases} \frac{R+D^{Ins}}{v_j^{Ins}-v_i^{Ins}} & \text{if head } i \text{ is in front of member } j \text{ and } v_i^{Ins} < v_j^{Ins} \\ \frac{R+D^{Ins}}{v_i^{Ins}-v_j^{Ins}} & \text{if head } i \text{ is in front of member } j \text{ and } v_i^{Ins} > v_j^{Ins} \\ \frac{R-D^{Ins}}{v_j^{Ins}-v_i^{Ins}} & \text{if head } i \text{ is behind member } j \text{ and } v_i^{Ins} < v_j^{Ins} \\ \frac{R-D^{Ins}}{v_i^{Ins}-v_j^{Ins}} & \text{if head } i \text{ is behind member } j \text{ and } v_i^{Ins} > v_j^{Ins}, \end{cases} \tag{10}$$

where R is the communication radius of a mobile node.

Maintenance Scheme. In most cluster schemes, nodes are only allowed to get together when they are moving in the same direction. However, when a cluster member has to leave the current cluster and join in another one, it needs to go through the undecided state. Yet, too many undecided nodes in the network can result in high network overhead, because these nodes employ the formation algorithm continuously. Specially, those traditional schemes may degrade communication performance under the crossroad scenario because of a large number of undecided nodes in the network. Therefore, we propose a novel cluster maintenance scheme to reduce the number of undecided nodes.

As mentioned in Sect. 3.1, the hopping cluster members are ready to handoff from one cluster to another. Once a cluster member changes into a hopping cluster member, it starts the cluster head selection procedure. The maintenance scheme is used for this handoff process.

The main idea of CHEAM, which is the key of proposed cluster maintenance scheme, is to select the most stable (optimal) head for the hopping cluster member as a substitute in advance. In this procedure, the scheme needs to detect the direction and predict the stay time of all members in the cluster. Additionally, the substitute head could be the current head if there are no other candidates with smaller M. Once a substitute is selected, the hopping cluster member hops into the new cluster and becomes a cluster member. Through this way, the number of the undecided nodes can be significantly reduced so that the cluster-based network overhead is minimized.

In addition, as mentioned in Cluster Formation Algorithm, cluster heads, members and undecided nodes broadcast **CHA**, **CMA** and **HELLO** packets periodically if the clusters are formed. After receiving those packets from neighbors, every node in the network recalculates its M value and update its DNL. Once a cluster head's M value is not the smallest among its neighbors, the neighbor node with the smallest M value will become the new cluster head.

Accordingly, the cluster maintenance scheme is introduced in Algorithm 2.

5   Numerical Evaluation

In this section, we carry out an extensive simulation study on MATLAB platform to evaluate the performance of the proposed LOSC scheme in a crossroad scenario. MOBIC clustering algorithm [3] is also implemented as a comparison with our scheme.

The simulation scenario is a two-lane crossroad as shown in Fig. 1. The communication between two vehicles follows the free-space path loss: $FSPL = (\frac{4\pi df}{c})^2$, where f is the signal frequency, c is the speed of light in a vacuum, and d is the distance between the transmitter and the receiver. Without loss of generality, the transmitting and receiving antenna gain are assumed to be 1, and the number of vehicles N_n is 100. Besides, the communication radius is set up from 50 m to 200 m and the vehicle speed is selected randomly between 30 km/h and 50 km/h.

Figure 2 shows the performance of clusters stability that is represented by the average number of cluster head changing per second. Intuitively, we believe

---

Algorithm 2. Cluster Maintenance Scheme via CHEAM

Require: cluster member: j; cluster head: i; undecided node: u; cluster set: Ω; DNL
 set: Θ

1: **for** each i, j and u **do**
2:     Broadcast **CHA**, **CMA** and **HELLO** packets periodically with T_c.
3:     Recalculate M periodically after receiving **CHA**, **CMA** and **HELLO** packets.
4:     **if** $\exists i^{'} \in \Theta(i)$ that $M(i^{'}) > M(i)$ **then**
5:         $i^{'}$ replaces i to become a new cluster head.
6:     **end if**
7:     Each $j \in \Omega(i)$ calculates $T_{j,i}^{stay}$ and starts $TimerS$ as soon as j joins in the
         cluster of i.
8:     **if** $TimerS$ expires or $\theta_{j,i} > \pi/4$ **then**
9:         j becomes a hopping cluster member and executes **Cluster Formation**.
10:     **end if**
11:     **if** j hasn't received any **CHA** packets from i for over $2T_c$ **then**
12:         Delete j from $\Omega(i)$.
13:     **end if**
14:     **if** There is no cluster member in $\Omega(i)$ **then**
15:         i changes its state to *undecided*
16:     **end if**
17: **end for**

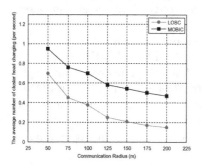

Fig. 2. Clusters stability analysis.

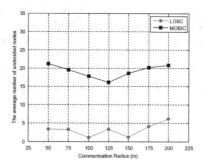

Fig. 3. Undecided nodes analysis.

that the cluster-based network is not stable if this average value is large because
of the frequent head handoff. Depicted in the Fig. 2, the number of head changing in the proposed scheme is lower than that of MOBIC with the various R,
which means the stability of clusters formed by our algorithm is better than that
formed by MOBIC. Besides, it can be also inferred that this average value in
MOBIC is vulnerable to the large communication radius. In other words, compared with MOBIC, the LOSC scheme is more suitable for the crossroad scenario
in VANETs, especially in a large communication radius.

For the purpose of illustrating the communication overhead, we explore the
average number of undecided nodes which is calculated for the duration of periodic broadcasting T_c. During each T_c, every nodes in a cluster broadcasts either

a **CHA** or a **CMA** packet. In contrast to MOBIC, the result in Fig. 3 reports that our scheme achieves great improvements on reducing the average number of undecided node due to the proposed CHEAM. In fact, the congestion and overhead caused by the undecided nodes can be cut down significantly in the crossroad when using the LOSC scheme.

6   Conclusion

In this paper, we propose a low overhead and stable clustering scheme for VANETs that focuses on the cluster stability and network overhead in the crossroad scenario. A new capability metric M, which is related to the relative velocity and the power loss, is introduced to describe a node's capability of being a cluster head. Based on this metric, a cluster formation algorithm and a cluster maintenance algorithm using the Cluster Head Electing in Advance Mechanism are proposed. Compared with the existing MOBIC clustering algorithm, the simulation results show that there are more stable clusters and less isolated nodes in VANETs by using LOSC scheme. For future research, we will consider a enhanced routing protocol based on our scheme in VANETs.

Acknowledgment. The authors would like to thank the support from the National Natural Science Foundation of China (Grant No. 61172074 and 61471028), the Fundamental Research Funds for the Central Universities (2015JBM016), the Specialized Research Fund for the Doctoral Program of Higher Education (Grant No.20130009110015), and the financial support from China Scholarship Council.

References

1. Rawashdeh, Z., Mahmud, S.: A novel algorithm to form stable clusters in vehicular ad hoc networks on highways. EURASIP J. Wirel. Commun. Netw. **2012**(1), 15 (2012)
2. Fan, W., Shi, Y., Chen, S., Zou, L.: A mobility metrics based dynamic clustering algorithm for VANETs. In: IET International Conference on Communication Technology and Application, pp. 752–756, October 2011
3. Basu, P., Khan, N., Little, T.: A mobility based metric for clustering in mobile ad hoc networks. In: International Conference on Distributed Computing Systems Workshop, pp. 413–418, April 2001
4. Gunter, Y., Wiegel, B., Grossmann, H.: Cluster-based medium access scheme for VANETs. In: IEEE Intelligent Transportation Systems Conference, pp. 343–348, September 2007
5. Sood, M., Kanwar, S.: Clustering in MANET and VANET: a survey. In: International Conference on Circuits, Systems, Communication and Information Technology Applications (CSCITA), pp. 375–380, April 2014
6. Song, T., Xia, W., Song, T., Shen, L.: A cluster-based directional routing protocol in VANET. In: IEEE International Conference on Communication Technology (ICCT), pp. 1172–1175, November 2010

7. Harikrishnan, Y., He, J.: Clustering algorithm based on minimal path loss ratio for vehicular communication. In: International Conference on Computing, Networking and Communications (ICNC), pp. 745–749, January 2013
8. Santos, R., Edwards, R., Seed, N.: Using the cluster-based location routing (CBLR) algorithm for exchanging information on a motorway. In: International Workshop on Mobile and Wireless Communications Network, pp. 212–216 (2002)
9. Wang, Z., Liu, L., Zhou, M., Ansari, N.: A position-based clustering technique for ad hoc intervehicle communication. IEEE Trans. Syst. Man Cybern. Part C: Appl. Rev. **38**(2), 201–208 (2008)
10. Souza, E., Nikolaidis, I., Gburzynski, P.: A new aggregate local mobility (ALM) clustering algorithm for VANETs. In: IEEE International Conference on Communications (ICC), pp. 1–5, May 2010
11. Zhou, B., Cao, Z., Gerla, M.: Cluster-based inter-domain routing (CIDR) protocol for MANETs. In: International Conference on Wireless On-Demand Network Systems and Services, WONS 2009, pp. 19–26, February 2009
12. Luo, Y., Zhang, W., Hu, Y.: A new cluster based routing protocol for VANET. In: International Conference on Networks Security Wireless Communications and Trusted Computing (NSWCTC), vol. 1, pp. 176–180, April 2010
13. Almalag, M., Weigle, M.: Using traffic flow for cluster formation in vehicular ad-hoc networks. In: IEEE Conference on Local Computer Networks (LCN), pp. 631–636, October 2010

Online Channel Assignment, Transmission Scheduling, and Transmission Mode Selection in Multi-channel Full-Duplex Wireless LANs

Zhefeng Jiang and Shiwen Mao[✉]

Department of Electrical and Computer Engineering, Auburn University,
Auburn, AL 36849-5201, USA
zzj0007@tigermail.auburn.edu, smao@ieee.org

Abstract. Although full-duplex transmission can be helpful for enhancing wireless link capacity, it may require extra energy to overcome the residual self-interference. In this paper, we investigate the trade-off between energy consumption and delay in a multi-channel full-duplex wireless LAN (WLAN). The goal is to minimize the energy consumption while keeping the packet queues stable. With Lyapunov optimization, we develop an online scheme to achieve the goals with optimized channel assignment, transmission scheduling, and transmission mode selection. We prove the optimality of the proposed algorithm and derive upper bounds for the average queue length and energy consumption, which demonstrate the energy-delay trade-off. The proposed algorithm is validated with simulations.

1 Introduction

Due to the dramatic increase of wireless data demands driven by the wide use of smartphones, tablets and other smart devices, there is an urgent need to improve the spectrum efficiency of existing wireless networks. Through effective self-interference cancellation, full-duplex transmission, i.e., transmitting and receiving simultaneously in the same band, has been successfully demonstrated [1]. With various self-interference cancellation techniques, full-duplex transmission has the potential to increase and even double the wireless link capacity [2].

Combined with RF interference cancellation and digital baseband interference cancellation, antenna cancellation can achieve a sufficient self-interference cancellation for full-duplex transmissions. In [2–4], analog and digital cancellation techniques were investigated. With full-duplex transmissions, various full-duplex links can be formed. For example, in the three-node full-duplex link scenario, one node (e.g., a base station) executes self-interference cancellation to transmit to and receive from two different half-duplex nodes simultaneously [5]. In the two-node link scenario, both nodes are capable of self-interference cancellation and can transmit to and receive from each other simultaneously [6].

Due to imperfect self-interference cancellation, the residual self-interference may still lead to a lower signal-to-interference-plus-noise ratio (SINR) and deteriorate the performance of a full-duplex link [7]. Additional power is needed to

K. Xu and J. Zhu (Eds.): WASA 2015, LNCS 9204, pp. 243–252, 2015.
DOI: 10.1007/978-3-319-21837-3_24

combat the residual self-interference to achieve a suitable SINR. As a result, full-duplex transmission may not always be helpful, and there is a trade-off between the energy cost and delay in the design of full-duplex wireless networks [8]. In [7,8], the extra energy consumption and the limits of full-duplex transmission were investigated. Joint resource allocation and scheduling in wireless networks is a challenging problem, for which Lyapunov optimization has been applied and shown to be effective [9–12]. However, these prior works are all focused on half-duplex wireless networks. Many challenging issues that arise in full-duplex wireless networks have not been adequately addressed.

In this paper, we consider a multi-channel wireless LAN (WLAN) where both the access point (AP) and user equipments (UE) are capable of full-duplex transmission. Since full-duplex is not always more efficient than half-duplex, we aim to jointly consider the problems of channel assignment, transmission scheduling, and transmission mode selection for the AP and UEs. We develop a problem formulation to capture the trade-off between energy consumption and queue length (which is indicative of delay) in the multi-channel full-duplex WLAN, with the objective to minimize the overall energy consumption of the system and stabilize the packet queues at all the nodes. We then develop an effective solution algorithm based on the Lyapunov optimization framework. With the proposed algorithm, the overall optimization problem over the entire time period is first reduced to the minimization of a *drift-plus-penalty* for each node in each time slot. The reduced problem only depends on the queue lengths, wireless link rates, and energy consumptions in the current time slot. We then transform the reduced problem into a maximum weighted matching problem and solve it with the Hungarian Method [13].

The proposed algorithm is an online algorithm since it does not require any past and future information of the WLAN system. We prove that the proposed algorithm maximizes the *drift-plus-penalty* among all possible transmission modes and channel assignment schemes. Furthermore, we derive upper bounds on the average sum queue length and average total energy consumption under the proposed algorithm, which clearly demonstrate the energy-delay trade-off in the multi-channel full-duplex WLAN. The performance of the proposed algorithm is validated with simulations.

The remainder of this paper is organized as follows. The system model and problem formulation are presented in Sect. 2. The proposed scheduling algorithm is developed and analyzed in Sect. 3. A simulation study is presented in Sect. 4. Section 5 concludes this paper.

2   System Model and Problem Statement

2.1   System Model

We consider a WLAN with one AP, a set of UEs denoted as $\mathcal{N} = \{1, 2, ..., N\}$, and a set of orthogonal channels denoted as $\mathcal{S} = \{1, 2, ..., S\}$. The AP determines the channel assignment, transmission schedule, and transmission mode selection for both uplink and downlink transmissions. We assume that data is transmitted via the AP in packets, and there is no direct transmission among the UEs. The packets waiting for transmission are buffered and served in the First In First Out (FIFO) manner. We assume a discrete time system. The uplink queue lengths at the beginning of time slot t are denoted as $\boldsymbol{Q}^u(t) = \{Q_1^u(t), Q_2^u(t), ..., Q_N^u(t)\}$ and the downlink queue lengths are denoted as $\boldsymbol{Q}^d(t) = \{Q_1^d(t), Q_2^d(t), ..., Q_N^d(t)\}$, where $Q_i^u(t)$ is the backlog of the uplink queue maintained at UE i and $Q_i^d(t)$ is the backlog of the downlink virtual queue for UE i maintained at the AP.

At time slot t, the arrivals of packets to the uplink queues are denoted as $\boldsymbol{A}^u(t) = \{A_1^u(t), A_2^u(t), ..., A_N^u(t)\}$. The arrivals of packets to the downlink queues are denoted as $\boldsymbol{A}^d(t) = \{A_1^d(t), A_2^d(t), ..., A_N^d(t)\}$. In addition, we assume that the arrivals of packets, either to the uplink or downlink queues, are i.i.d over time. The expectations, i.e., the average arrival rates, are

$$\boldsymbol{\lambda}^u \triangleq \mathbb{E}\{\boldsymbol{A}^u(t)\} = \{\lambda_1^u, \lambda_2^u, ..., \lambda_N^u\} \text{ and } \boldsymbol{\lambda}^d \triangleq \mathbb{E}\{\boldsymbol{A}^d(t)\} = \{\lambda_1^d, \lambda_2^d, ..., \lambda_N^d\}. \quad (1)$$

Recall that there are $\mathcal{S} = \{1, 2, ..., S\}$ orthogonal channels. During each time slot t, a UE can transmit and/or receive on one of the channels in $\mathcal{S}$. The channel assignment decision is denoted as $\alpha_i(t)$, where $i \in \mathcal{N}$ and $\alpha_i(t) \in \{\mathcal{S} \cup \{0\}\}$ is the channel UE i uses at time slot t. Note that $\alpha_i(t) = 0$ indicates that no channel is assigned to UE i. In addition, each UE can choose from three transmission modes: uplink, downlink, or full-duplex. The transmission mode selection is denoted as $\beta_i(t) \in \{U, D, F\}$, where $\beta_i(t) = U$, $\beta_i(t) = D$, and $\beta_i(t) = F$ indicate that at time slot t, UE i selects half-duplex uplink, half-duplex downlink, and full-duplex transmission, respectively.

With the full-duplex mode, the residual self-interference is treated as interference. Let $C_i^u(t)|_{\alpha_i(t)=s,\beta_i(t)=F}$ and $C_i^d(t)|_{\alpha_i(t)=s,\beta_i(t)=F}$ be the uplink and downlink channel capacity of UE i at time slot t, respectively, given that channel s is assigned to UE i and the full-duplex mode is selected. We have

$$C_i^u(t)|_{\alpha_i(t)=s,\beta_i(t)=F} = B \log_2 \left(1 + \frac{p_i^u(t)|h_s^u|^2}{N_0 + p_i^d \eta_d}\right) \quad (2)$$

$$C_i^d(t)|_{\alpha_i(t)=s,\beta_i(t)=F} = B \log_2 \left(1 + \frac{p_i^d(t)|h_s^d|^2}{N_0 + p_i^u \eta_u}\right), \quad (3)$$

where B is the channel bandwidth; h_s^u and h_s^d are the channel gains between the AP and UE i for the uplink and downlink channel, respectively; $p_i^u(t) > 0$ and $p_i^d(t) > 0$ are the uplink and downlink transmit power, respectively; η_d and η_u are the self-interference cancellation ratio at the AP and a UE, respectively; and N_0 is additive white Gaussian noise power.

For half-duplex uplink transmission, the uplink channel capacity for UE i, given that it is assigned with channel s, is

$$C_i^u(t)|_{\alpha_i(t)=s,\beta_i(t)=U} = B \log_2 \left(1 + \frac{p_i^u(t)|h_s^u|^2}{N_0}\right). \quad (4)$$

In this case, we have $p_i^u(t) > 0$ and $p_i^d(t) = 0$. For half-duplex downlink transmission, the downlink channel capacity for UE i, given that it is assigned with channel s, is

$$C_i^d(t)|_{\alpha_i(t)=s,\beta_i(t)=D} = B\log_2\left(1 + \frac{p_i^d(t)|h_s^d|^2}{N_0}\right). \tag{5}$$

In this case, we have $p_i^u(t) = 0$ and $p_i^d(t) > 0$.

The dynamics of the uplink and downlink queues can be written as

$$Q_i^u(t) = \max\{Q_i^u(t) + A_i^u(t) - B_i^u(t), 0\} \tag{6}$$

$$Q_i^d(t) = \max\{Q_i^d(t) + A_i^d(t) - B_i^d(t), 0\}, \tag{7}$$

where $B_i^u(t) = \frac{T}{L}C_i^u(t)|_{\alpha_i(t), \beta_i(t)}$ and $B_i^d(t) = \frac{T}{L}C_i^d(t)|_{\alpha_i(t), \beta_i(t)}$ are the service rates in packets per time slot at time t for the uplink and downlink queues, respectively, T is the duration of a time slot, and L is the packet length in bits.

2.2   Problem Formulation

As can be seen from (2)–(5), the overall throughput can be enhanced with full-duplex transmissions, but at the cost of higher energy consumption. The energy efficiency maybe degraded due to the residual self-interference. There is a trade-off between the overall queue length (which is indicative of delay) and energy efficiency with different transmission mode selections. Furthermore, both energy efficiency and throughput can be enhanced by transmitting only on good channels. However, there may be the extra delay to wait for the channel condition to be good from a deep fade.

The average total energy consumption of the system can be written as $\bar{P} \triangleq \limsup_{T\to\infty} \frac{1}{T}\sum_{t=0}^{T-1}\sum_{i=1}^{N}\mathbb{E}\{p_i^u(t) + p_i^d(t)|\alpha_i(t),\beta_i(t)\}$. We also define the average queue length as $\bar{Q} \triangleq \limsup_{T\to\infty} \frac{1}{T}\sum_{t=0}^{T-1}\sum_{i=1}^{N}\mathbb{E}\{Q_i^u(t) + Q_i^d(t)\}$. We schedule the uplink and downlink transmissions at the beginning of each time slot. According to the notion of *throughput-optimal* [10], the objective is to minimize the average energy consumption while keeping all the uplink and downlink queues stable. We have the following problem formulation.

$$\min : \bar{P} = \limsup_{T\to\infty} \frac{1}{T}\sum_{t=0}^{T-1}\sum_{i=1}^{N}\mathbb{E}\{p_i^u(t) + p_i^d(t)|\alpha_i(t),\beta_i(t)\} \tag{8}$$

$$\text{s.t.}\quad \alpha_i(t) \neq \alpha_j(t), \text{if } \alpha_i(t) \in \mathcal{S} \text{ or } \alpha_j(t) \in \mathcal{S}, \text{ for all } i \neq j, i,j \in \mathcal{N} \tag{9}$$

$$\bar{Q} < \infty, \text{ for all } \{\boldsymbol{\lambda}^u, \boldsymbol{\lambda}^d\} \in \Lambda, \tag{10}$$

where Λ is the capacity region of the WLAN system. Constraint (9) forbids two nodes accessing the same channel and Constraint (10) ensures that the schedule meets the notion of throughput-optimal.

3   Solution Algorithm and Performance Analysis

3.1   Lyapunov Optimization Based Scheduling Algorithm

Following the Lyapunov optimization framework, we first define the Lyapunov function $L(Q(t))$ as $L(Q(t)) \triangleq \frac{1}{2} \sum_{i=1}^{N} \{\{Q_i^u(t)\}^2 + \{Q_i^d(t)\}^2\}$, where $L(Q(0)) = 0$. Note that $L(Q(t))$ is small if and only if all the queue lengths are small; $L(Q(t))$ will become large if any of the queues is congested. The system is thus stable when $\mathbb{E}\{L(Q(t))\} < \infty$.

We then define the drift $\Delta(L(t))$ as

$$\Delta(L(t)) \triangleq \mathbb{E}\{L(Q(t+1)) - L(Q(t)) \,|\, Q(t)\}. \tag{11}$$

The system is stable when $\mathbb{E}\{L(Q(t))\} = \mathbb{E}\left\{\sum_{k=0}^{t-1}[L(Q(k+1))-L(Q(k))]\right\} = \sum_{k=0}^{t-1} \mathbb{E}\{L(Q(k+1))-L(Q(k))|Q(k)\} = \sum_{k=0}^{t-1} \Delta(L(k)) < \infty$. We can minimize the drift in every time slot t to maintain a finite expectation for $L(Q(t))$.

It follows the queue dynamics (6) and (7) that

$$\begin{aligned}
&\{Q_i^u(t+1)\}^2 + \{Q_i^d(t+1)\}^2 \\
&\leq \{Q_i^u(t) + A_i^u(t) - B_i^u(t)\}^2 + \{Q_i^d(t) + A_i^d(t) - B_i^d(t)\}^2 \\
&= \{Q_i^u(t)\}^2 + \{A_i^u(t) - B_i^u(t)\}^2 + 2Q_i^u(t)(A_i^u(t) - B_i^u(t)) + \\
&\quad \{Q_i^d(t)\}^2 + \{A_i^d(t) - B_i^d(t)\}^2 + 2Q_i^d(t)(A_i^d(t) - B_i^d(t)).
\end{aligned} \tag{12}$$

Substituting (12) into (11), we have

$$\Delta(L(t)) \leq \Phi + \mathbb{E}\left\{\sum_{i=1}^{N}\{Q_i^u(t)(A_i^u(t) - B_i^u(t)) + Q_i^d(t)(A_i^d(t) - B_i^d(t))\}\right\}, \tag{13}$$

where $\Phi = \frac{1}{2}\mathbb{E}\left\{\sum_{i=1}^{N}\{[A_i^u(t) - B_i^u(t)]^2 + [A_i^d(t) - B_i^d(t)]^2\}\right\}$, which is bounded if the arrival rate and service rate of each uplink and downlink queue are bounded. This is true if the arrival rates are within the capacity region of the system.

Defining $P(t) \triangleq \sum_{i=1}^{N} \{p_i^u(t) + p_i^d(t)\}$, we then obtain the *drift-plus-penalty* $\Delta(L(t)) + V\mathbb{E}\{P(t)\}$ as in [12], by incorporating the energy penalty (i.e., the overall energy consumption at time t) with a positive coefficient V. Parameter V indicates the UEs' emphasis on energy consumption. That is, the more emphasis on energy consumption, the greater the value of V. In particular, $V = 0$ indicates that the UEs are not sensitive to energy consumption at all. Based on (13), we can derive an upper bound on the *drift-plus-penalty* as

$$\begin{aligned}
&\Delta(L(t)) + V\mathbb{E}\{P(t)\} \\
&\leq \Phi + \mathbb{E}\left\{\sum_{i=1}^{N}\{Q_i^u(t)(A_i^u(t) - B_i^u(t)) + Q_i^d(t)(A_i^d(t) - B_i^d(t))\} + VP(t)\right\}.
\end{aligned}$$

We minimize the second term on the right-hand-side $\Theta \triangleq \sum_{i=1}^{N} \{Q_i^u(t)(A_i^u(t) - B_i^u(t)) + Q_i^d(t)(A_i^d(t) - B_i^d(t))\} + VP(t)$ at each time slot t in order to minimize the *drift-plus-penalty*. Notice that Θ can be rewritten as $\Theta = \sum_{i=1}^{N} \{Q_i^u(t)A_i^u(t) + Q_i^d(t)A_i^d(t)\} - \sum_{i=1}^{N} \{Q_i^u(t)B_i^u(t) - Vp_i^u(t) + Q_i^d(t)B_i^d(t) - Vp_i^d(t)\}$. Then first term on the right-hand-side, $\sum_{i=1}^{N} \{Q_i^u(t)A_i^u(t) + Q_i^d(t)A_i^d(t)\}$, only depends on the arrival rates and the current queue lengths. Therefore, it doesn't affect the scheduling decision. We only need to maximize the second term of Θ, which is a function of both $\alpha_i(t)$ and $\beta_i(t)$.

Let the channel assignment be $\boldsymbol{\alpha}(t) = \{\alpha_1(t), \alpha_2(t), ..., \alpha_N(t)\}$ and the transmission mode selection be $\boldsymbol{\beta}(t) = \{\beta_1(t), \beta_2(t), ..., \beta_N(t)\}$. We have

$$\Psi(t)|_{\boldsymbol{\alpha}(t),\boldsymbol{\beta}(t)} \triangleq \sum_{i=1}^{N} \{Q_i^u(t)B_i^u(t) - Vp_i^u(t) + Q_i^d(t)B_i^d(t) - Vp_i^d(t)\}|_{\alpha_i(t),\beta_i(t)}$$
$$= \sum_{i=1}^{N} \psi_i(t)|_{\alpha_i(t),\beta_i(t)}, \qquad (14)$$

where $\psi_i(t)|_{\alpha_i(t),\beta_i(t)} = \{Q_i^u(t)B_i^u(t) - Vp_i^u(t) + Q_i^d(t)B_i^d(t) - Vp_i^d(t)\}|_{\alpha_i(t),\beta_i(t)}$. Let the optimal channel assignment be $\boldsymbol{\alpha}^*(t) = \{\alpha_1^*(t), \alpha_2^*(t), ..., \alpha_N^*(t)\}$ and the optimal transmission mode selection be $\boldsymbol{\beta}^*(t) = \{\beta_1^*(t), \beta_2^*(t), ..., \beta_N^*(t)\}$. To find the optimal schedule $\{\boldsymbol{\alpha}^*(t), \boldsymbol{\beta}^*(t)\}$, we first need to identify the transmission mode for a given channel assignment $\alpha_i(t) = s$ for each UE i. That is,

$$\beta_i^*(t)|_{\alpha_i(t)=s} = \underset{\beta_i(t) \in \{U,D,F\}}{\arg \max} \{\psi_i(t)|_{\alpha_i(t)=s,\beta_i(t)}\}. \qquad (15)$$

Note that $\psi_i(t) = 0$ if no transmission is conducted. Therefore we have

$$\psi_i^*(t)|_{\alpha_i(t)=s} = \max\{\psi_i(t)|_{\alpha_i(t)=s,\beta_i^*(t)}, 0\} \qquad (16)$$
$$\boldsymbol{\psi}_i^*(t)|_{\alpha_i(t)} \triangleq \{\psi_i^*(t)|_{\alpha_i(t)=1}, \psi_i^*(t)|_{\alpha_i(t)=2}, ..., \psi_i^*(t)|_{\alpha_i(t)=S}\}. \qquad (17)$$

We need to find the maximum channel assignment $\boldsymbol{\alpha}^*(t)$ based on $\boldsymbol{\psi}_i^*(t)|_{\alpha_i(t)}$, for $i = 1, 2, ..., N$. The channel assignment problem can be transformed into a *maximum weighted bipartite matching problem*. In the bipartite graph $\mathcal{G}$, UEs and the channels represent the two independent sets of vertices: the set of UEs G_1 and the set of channels G_2. In graph $\mathcal{G}$, the weight of the edge between an vertex in G_1 (i.e., a UE i) and another vertex in G_2 (i.e., a channel s) is set to $\psi_i^*(t)|_{\alpha_i(t)=s}$. This way, the maximum weighted bipartite matching of graph $\mathcal{G}$ corresponds to the optimal channel assignment $\boldsymbol{\alpha}^*(t)$. The maximum weighted bipartite matching problem can be solved with the Hungarian Method [13]. The complexity of the Hungarian Method is $O(NS^2)$ if $N > S$, or $O(N^2S)$ if $N \leq S$.

When the optimal channel assignment is derived, the optimal transmission mode $\beta_i^*(t)$ for UE i is readily obtained as in (15), i.e., $\beta_i^*(t) = \beta_i^*(t)|_{\alpha_i^*(t)}$. Now we obtain the optimal schedule $\{\boldsymbol{\alpha}^*(t), \boldsymbol{\beta}^*(t)\}$ as well as the corresponding $\Psi(t)|_{\boldsymbol{\alpha}^*(t),\boldsymbol{\beta}^*(t)}$. Then we can assign the channels and decide the transmission

---

Algorithm 1. Scheduling Algorithm for Channel Assignment and Transmission Mode Selection

---

1 Update all uplink and downlink queues and estimate all channel conditions at the beginning of each time slot t ;
2 For each UE i, find the transmission mode $\beta_i^*(t)|_{\alpha_i(t)=s}$ as in (15) ;
3 Obtain the channel assignment matrix $\{\psi_1^*(t)|_{\alpha_1(t)}^T, \psi_2^*(t)|_{\alpha_2(t)}^T, ..., \psi_N^*(t)|_{\alpha_N(t)}^T\}$;
4 Apply the Hungarian Method and (15) to find the optimal schedule $\{\alpha^*(t), \beta^*(t)\}$;
5 **if** $\psi_i(t)|_{\{\alpha_i^*(t), \beta_i^*(t)\}} > 0$ **then**
6 $\quad$ UE i transmits on channel $\alpha_i^*(t)$ with transmission mode $\beta_i^*(t)$;
7 **end**

---

mode for each UE based on the optimal schedule. Note that $\psi_i(t)|_{\alpha_i^*(t), \beta_i^*(t)} = 0$ if no transmission is scheduled for UE i; so UE i transmits if and only if $\psi_i(t)|_{\alpha_i^*(t), \beta_i^*(t)} > 0$.

The detailed algorithm for deriving the optimum schedule $\{\alpha^*(t), \beta^*(t)\}$ is presented in Algorithm 1, which is executed at the beginning of each time slot.

3.2 Performance Analysis

We have the following theorems for the performance of Algorithm 1. The proofs are omitted for lack of space.

Theorem 1. *The schedule $\{\alpha^*(t), \beta^*(t)\}$ obtained by Algorithm 1 achieves the maximum $\Psi(t)$.*

We also derive the upper bounds for the expectations of average sum queue lengths of all the uplink and downlink queues and the corresponding average total energy consumption as follows.

Theorem 2. *Assume that the arrival rates to the queues λ^u and λ^d are strictly within the system's capacity region, i.e., the system can be stabilized under certain $\{\alpha(t), \beta(t)\}$. Then the upper bounds on the average sum queue lengths and average energy consumption under Algorithm 1 can be derived as*

$$\limsup_{T\to\infty} \frac{1}{T} \sum_{t=1}^{T-1} \sum_{i=1}^{N} \mathbb{E}\{Q_i^u(t) + Q_i^d(t)\} \leq \frac{1}{\epsilon}(\Phi + V\bar{P}) \tag{18}$$

$$\limsup_{T\to\infty} \frac{1}{T} \sum_{t=1}^{T-1} \sum_{i=1}^{N} \mathbb{E}\{p_i^u(t) + p_i^d(t)\} \leq \bar{P}^* + \frac{\Phi}{V}, \tag{19}$$

where $\bar{P}^*$ is the minimum average energy consumption under any stable scheduling strategy, $\bar{P}$ is the average energy consumption under the proposed algorithm, $\epsilon > 0$ is the distance between the arrival rates $\{\lambda^u, \lambda^d\}$ and the system capacity region under the proposed algorithm, and Φ is given in (13).

4 Performance Evaluation

In this section, we evaluate the performance of the proposed algorithm through Matlab simulations. We assume that the maximum transmit power is 46 dBm at the AP and 23 dBm at the UEs. We assume that there is a 110 dB self-interference cancellation in both the uplink and downlink transceivers. For the wireless channels, we adopt the commonly used Okumura-Hata model for small and medium-sized cities. Each channel has a bandwidth of 360 kHz. We assume that there are 12 UEs and 10 channels in the WLAN.

We compare the average energy consumptions and queue lengths of a half-duplex only system and a full-duplex system under different V values. The simulation results are presented in Figs. 1 and 2 for different traffic arrival rates. From the simulations, we find that the full-duplex system always outperforms the half-duplex only system with respect to both average queue length and energy consumption. Moreover, there is a trade-off between the average queue length and energy consumption for the full-duplex system under different V values.

Figure 1 presents the average queue length versus traffic load. When $V = 0$, the scheme only minimizes the drift and does not care about energy consumption. In this case, the average queue length of the half-duplex case is always greater than that of the full-duplex case. Moreover, in the half-duplex only case, the queues cannot be stabilized when the arrival rate exceeds 25. In the full-duplex case, the queues can be stabilized until the arrival rate reaches 38. Clearly, full-duplex transmissions are helpful to keep the queue backlog low and increase the capacity region of the WLAN. It is also interesting to see that for all the full-duplex cases, the queues can be stabilized when the arrival rate is lower than 38, indicating that different V values do not affect the stability of the system. Moreover, the average queue length increases when V is increased, as indicated by the upper bound of average queue length (18) in Theorem 2.

Figure 2 presents the average energy consumption versus traffic load. We find the average energy consumption of the half-duplex only case is smaller than that of the full-duplex cases under heavy load, when the queues become unstable. However, in the stable capacity region of the half-duplex only case (i.e., when the arrival rate is lower than 25), the average energy consumption of the half-duplex only case is greater than that of the full-duplex cases with $V > 50$. This is because when $V > 50$, the energy consumption is more seriously considered (i.e., in the drift-plus-penalty) and the UEs would transmit only when the energy efficiency is high. For the full-duplex case with $V = 0$, the average energy consumption is the highest among all the cases, since the proposed scheme does not consider energy efficiency. Furthermore, the energy consumption drops when the arrival rate is greater than 38. This is due to the unbalanced service rates of the uplink and downlink. When the queues are not stable, more uplink transmissions were made; the uplink transmit power is comparatively smaller than that of the downlink transmissions. Finally, it can be seen that the energy consumption decreases when V is increased, as indicated by the upper bound of average energy consumption (19) in Theorem 2.

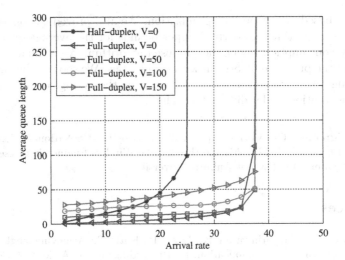

Fig. 1. Average queue lengths achieved by the proposed algorithm: half-duplex only with V=0, full-duplex with V=0, full-duplex with V=50, full-duplex with V=100, and full-duplex with V=150.

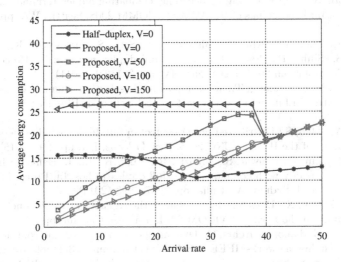

Fig. 2. Average energy consumptions achieved by the proposed algorithm: half-duplex with V=0, full-duplex with V=0, full-duplex with V=50, full-duplex with V=100, and full-duplex with V=150.

5   Conclusion

In this paper, we proposed an online scheduling algorithm to jointly decide the channel assignment, transmission scheduling, half- or full-duplex transmission mode selection for each UE in a multi-channel ful-duplex WLAN. The proposed

scheme was based on Lyapunov optimization. We also proved the optimality of
the proposed algorithm and derived upper bounds for the average queue length
and energy consumption under the proposed algorithm. We evaluated the performance of the proposed algorithm with simulations. We showed that under the
proposed algorithm, there was a trade-off between the average queue length and
energy consumption under different V values.

Acknowledgment. This work is supported in part by the US National Science Foundation under Grant CNS-1247955, and through the Wireless Engineering Research and
Education Center (WEREC) at Auburn University.

References

1. Choi, J.I., Jain, M., Srinivasan, K., Levis, P., Katti, S.: Achieving single channel,
full duplex wireless communication. In: Proceedings of the ACM MobiCom 2010,
Chicago, IL, pp. 1–12 (2010)
2. Bharadia, D., McMilin, E., Katti, S.: Full duplex radios. SIGCOMM Comput.
Commun. Rev. **43**(4), 375–386 (2013)
3. Gollakota, S., Katabi, D.: Zigzag decoding: combating hidden terminals in wireless
networks. In: Proceedings of the ACM SIGCOMM 2008, Seattle, WA, pp. 159–170
(2008)
4. Jain, M., Choi, J.I., Kim, T., Bharadia, D., Seth, S., Srinivasan, K., Levis, P.,
Katti, S., Sinha, P.: Practical, real-time, full duplex wireless: In: Proceedings of
the ACM MobiCom 2011, Las Vegas, NV, pp. 301–312 (2011)
5. Feng, M., Mao, S., Jiang, T.: Joint duplex mode selection, channel allocation, and
power control for full-duplex cognitive femtocell networks. Elsevier Digit. Commun.
Netw. J. **1**(1), 30–44 (2015)
6. Wang, Y., Mao, S.: Distributed power control in full duplex wireless networks. In:
Proceedings of the IEEE WCNC 2015, New Orleans, LA, pp. 1–6 (2015)
7. Goyal, S., Liu, P., Panwar, S., DiFazio, R., Yang, R., Li, J., Bala, E.: Improving
small cell capacity with common-carrier full duplex radios. In: Proceedings of the
IEEE ICC 2014, Sydney, Australia, pp. 4987–4993 (2014)
8. Xie, X., Zhang, X.: Does full-duplex double the capacity of wireless networks? In:
Proceedings of the IEEE INFOCOM 2014, Toronto, Canada, pp. 253–261 (2014)
9. Neely, M., Modiano, E., Rohrs, C.: Dynamic power allocation and routing for time-
varying wireless networks. IEEE J. Sel. Areas Commun. **23**(1), 89–103 (2005)
10. Kar, K., Luo, X., Sarkar, S.: Throughput-optimal scheduling in multichannel access
point networks under infrequent channel measurements. In: Proceedings of the
IEEE INFOCOM 2007, Anchorage, AK, pp. 1640–1648 (2007)
11. Huang, Y., Mao, S., Nelms, R.M.: Adaptive electricity scheduling in microgrids.
IEEE Trans. Smart Grid **5**(1), 270–281 (2014)
12. Neely, M.J.: Stochastic Network Optimization with Application to Communication
and Queueing Systems, 1st edn. Morgan & Claypool Publishers, San Rafael, CA
(2010)
13. Kuhn, H.W.: The Hungarian method for the assignment problem. Nav. Res. Logistics Q. **2**(1/2), 83–97 (1955)

Optimal Preference Detection Based on Golden Section and Genetic Algorithm for Affinity Propagation Clustering

Libin Jiao[1], Guangzhi Zhang[1], Shenling Wang[1(✉)],
Rashid Mehmood[1,2], and Rongfang Bie[1]

[1] College of Information Science and Technology,
Beijing Normal University, Beijing, China
{92xianshen,zgz}@mail.bnu.edu.cn, wangsl0362@163.com, rfbie@bnu.edu.cn
[2] Department of Computer Science and Information Technology,
University of Management Sciences and Information Technology,
Kotli, AJK, Pakistan
gulkhan007@gmail.com

Abstract. Affinity Propagation Clustering Algorithm is a well-known effective clustering algorithm that outperforms other traditional and classical clustering algorithms, and the selection of related sensitive parameters (preference, damping factor) is a popular research topic. In this paper, a feasible detecting procedure "GS/GA-AP" based on Golden Section and Genetic Algorithm is proposed to address the aforementioned issue. As a default option, preference is given based on golden section for Affinity Propagation. Unsatisfactory clustering result is robust with selection of preference with Genetic Algorithm. One simulation dataset and five standard benchmark datasets are utilized to verify effectiveness of algorithm we proposed, and the experiment results show that GS/GA-AP outperforms traditional Affinity Propagation clustering algorithm.

Keywords: Affinity propagation · Golden section · Genetic algorithm · Preference selection · Optimal clustering

1 Introduction

Cluster analysis is a process of separating a set of physical or abstract objects into several classes of similar objects [1]. A cluster is a subset of original objects set and the objects are similar to each other within the same cluster and dissimilar to the objects in other clusters. Plenty of traditional and classical methods have been widely used in a variety of computer science fields, and new methods are emerging in endlessly from research institutes and engineering projects.

In 2007, Affinity Propagation (AP) is proposed in Science by Brendan J. Frey and Delbert Dueck. AP performs well in many fields, such as clustering faces, detecting genes, identifying key sentences and air-travel routing in [2]; the square-error of the clustering result is much less than K-means as well, which has attracted researchers' attention in recent years.

© Springer International Publishing Switzerland 2015
K. Xu and J. Zhu (Eds.): WASA 2015, LNCS 9204, pp. 253–262, 2015.
DOI: 10.1007/978-3-319-21837-3_25

As other traditional and classical clustering algorithms, AP also has two related sensitive parameters, the preference and the damping factor, which affect the number of clusters and iterations, so the selection of preference and damping factor is a popular topic in recent researching papers concerning AP clustering. Therefore, we propose a feasible procedure in this paper to get better clusters, which is called "GS/GA-AP". In "GS-AP" phase, preference is given based on Golden Section for AP, and the fitness function oversees the clustering result. If the clustering result is unsatisfactory compared to traditional AP with median as preference, we use Genetic Algorithm to detect the optimal preference for AP. so the optimal preference and clustering results could be detected automatically.

The rest of this paper is organized as follows. Section 2 related work introduces recent research concerning preference selection in AP. Section 3 presents AP clustering algorithm, Golden Section and Genetic Algorithm. Section 4 describes GS/GA-AP Algorithm. Section 5 presents evaluation experiments and results of traditional AP and GS/GA-AP. Finally Sect. 6 concludes this paper.

2   Related Work

After Brendan J. Frey and Dueck Delbert published AP [2] in Science in 2007, researchers started to improve the algorithm. In 2009, I. E. Givoni and B. J. Frey [3] presented a new much simpler model which was based on a quite different graph model. The new model allowed a easier derivations of message updates for extensions and modifications. In 2010, X. Zhang, et al. [4] proposed an algorithm called K-AP to exploit the immediate results of K clusters by introducing a constraint in the process of message passing. In the same year, D. Tang, et al. [5] designed PoissonAPS incorporating AP and Poisson to overcome the limitations of AP and automatically cluster SAGE data without user-specified parameters.

In 2012 I. E. Givoni, C. Chung, and B. J. Frey [6] extended AP in a principled way to solve the hierarchical clustering problem and applied in a number of domains such as biology and so on. In 2013, C. Wang, et al. [7] proposed Multi-exemplar AP algorithm to provide a solution to multi-topic and multi-exemplar clustering problem, which was a great improvement for AP Clustering Algorithm. [3–5] focused on modifying AP more faster and controllable, [6,7] serve interdiscipline research, but they avoid the optimal selection of preference.

Several research papers concerning preference selection in AP has been published. WANG Kai-jun, et al. [8] presented an adaptive preference selection method to choose the suitable preference. In 2010, Y. He, et al. [9] proposed an adaptive preference selection method that found out the range of preference, then searched the space of preference to find an appropriate value to cluster. And in 2012, H. Sun, et al. [10] proposed an adaptive AP algorithm for semi-supervised hyperspectral band selection and used bisection method to address preference selection. In 2014, Dong-Wei Chen, et al. [11] proposed a new approach based on stability, using NMI measurement to calculate the stability of AP. They used adaptive methods to detect preference, but these preference may not be the optimal one: The algorithm Wang [8] proposed traverses the whole preference space to find the most suitable one violently, which means they sacrifice time to cluster optimally, and The algorithms in [9,10] and [11] proposed traverses the solution space, too.

In recent years, some research work that combining AP and optimization algorithms has emerged, which gave inspiration to other researchers. Xian-hui Wang, et al. [12,13] also used PSO to find the optimal preference of AP. Yi ZHONG, et al. [14] proposed an approach that utilized PSO to detect the optimal preference and the optimal number of clusters in AP. YOU Xiazhu, et al. [15] presented a similar approach to find the preference. it is obvious that [12–14] and [15] have been designed to detect the optimal clustering results, but they sacrifice time complexity to search the optimal solution in the solution space. So a feasible procedure could be proposed to reduce the time complexity at a certain probability, and GS/GA-AP is a feasible method to solve the problem of optimal choice of preference.

3   Background

3.1   Affinity Propagation

Affinity Propagation (AP)[2,16] is a type of partition methods to identify the appropriate exemplar for each data points. Given a dataset $\mathbf{X} = \{x_1, x_2, \cdots, x_n\}$, the algorithm aims at identifying a valid configuration of exemplar labels: $\mathbf{c} = [c_1, c_2, \cdots, c_n]$, where c_i is the exemplar of data point $x_i (i = 1, 2, \cdots, n)$. There are two kinds of message passing in this algorithm: One is called "responsibility" $r(i, k)$, sent from data point i to candidate exemplar point k, reflecting how well-suited data point k is to become an exemplar for data point i; Another is called "availability" $a(i, k)$, sent from candidate exemplar point k to data point i, reflecting the how appropriate data point i chooses data point k as its exemplar. The responsibility and availability are calculated using rules:

$$r(i, k) = s(x_i, x_k) - \max_{j:j \neq k} [s(x_i, x_j) + a(x_i, x_j)] \tag{1}$$

$$a(i, k) = \begin{cases} \sum_{i':i' \neq k} \max(0, r(x_{i'}, x_k)), & \text{for } k = i \\ \min \left[0, r(x_k, x_k) + \sum_{i':i' \notin \{i,k\}} \max(0, r(x_{i'}, x_k)) \right], & \text{for } k \neq i \end{cases} \tag{2}$$

The responsibility and availability are calculated iteratively until convergence, and the exemplar labels $\mathbf{c} = [c_1, c_2, \cdots, c_n]$ are computed as:

$$c_i = \underset{x_k}{\arg\max} [a(i, k) + r(i, k)] \tag{3}$$

Here is the description of AP clustering algorithm:

Algorithm 1. AP Clustering Algorithm (AP)[2]

Input:

$\mathbf{X} = \{x_1, x_2, \cdots, x_n\}$: A dataset.

p: Preference.

λ: Damping factor.

Output:

$Labels = [Cluster(x_1), \cdots, Cluster(x_n)]$: The clustering labels where $Cluster(x_i)$ represents which cluster x_i belongs to.

1: Calculate the similarity measurement $s(i, k)$ between data point x_i and x_k ($i, k = 1, 2, \cdots, n$). All the similarities form the similarity matrix $S = [s(i, k)]_{n \times n}$

2: $p \leftarrow$ preference or $p \leftarrow median([s(i, k)_{n \times n}])$ according to a priori convention.

3: Initial the availability matrix $A = [a(i, k)]_{n \times n}$ as a zero matrix: $a(i, k) = 0$

4: **repeat**

5:     Update the responsible matrix $R = [r(i, k)]_{n \times n}$ using the update rule (1)

6:     Update the availability matrix $A = [a(i, k)]_{n \times n}$ using the updating rule (2)

7:     $R_i \leftarrow (1 - \lambda) \times R_i + \lambda \times R_{i-1}$

8:     $A_i \leftarrow (1 - \lambda) \times A_i + \lambda \times A_{i-1}$

9: **until** R and A converge

10: Calculate the exemplar labels $\mathbf{c} = [c_1, c_2, \cdots, c_n]$ using rule (3)

11: Calculate the cluster labels $Labels = [Cluster(x_1), \cdots, Cluster(x_n)]$ using rule:$Cluster(x_i) = Cluster(c_i)$

3.2   Golden Section

Golden section, also well-known as golden ratio, has a long history in mathematics, arts and architectures. Golden section comes from the partition of a line segment. Partition exhibits a substantial harmony and aesthetics when the ratio of shorter part to the longer one is equal to the ratio of longer part to the whole line segment. The equation of this ratio in mathematics is as follow:

$$\frac{x}{1} = \frac{1 - x}{x} \tag{4}$$

The positive root of equation $x = \frac{\sqrt{5}-1}{2}$ is the famous golden section ratio.

3.3   Genetic Algorithm

Genetic Algorithm (GA) is one of the famous intelligent optimal algorithms, and the original theoretical foundation of GA were proposed by John H. Holland [17] in 1975. GA uses three phases to search the optimal or satisfactory solution: reproduction, crossover, and mutation. In the phase of reproduction, the fitness values are calculated, and individual reproduces the next generation according to its fitness. In the phase of crossover, each two individuals surviving exchange their fragments of genes to generate new species. In the phase of mutation, each individual has a small probability to alter their genes. This reproduction-crossover-mutation cycle is repeated until a stable or satisfactory solution emerges, which is defined as a basic steps of a simple GA. Here is the description of GA [17]:

Algorithm 2. Genetic Algorithm (GA)[17]

Input:
    F:Fitness function for GA.
    Crossover_rate: Crossover rate for GA.
    Mutation_rate: Mutation rate for GA.

Output:
    Solution: Feasible solution.
  1: Generate the initial population randomly, and encode them.
  2: **repeat**
  3:    Calculate the fitness value of each individual using fitness function F.
  4:    Select suitable individuals according to their fitness values.
  5:    Execute crossover between two individuals with *Crossover_rate*
  6:    Execute mutation in individuals with *Mutation_rate*.
  7: **until** individuals stay constant
  8: Output the individual with max fitness value

4   GS/GA-AP Algorithm

In this section, first we introduce the fitness function we use in the GS/GA-AP algorithm, then the description of GS/GA-AP algorithm is exhibited explicitly.

4.1   Fitness Function

Silhouette Coefficient [1] evaluates the quality of the clustering algorithm by taking the compactness and separation into consideration synthetically. Therefore, we select silhouette coefficient as the fitness function of GA in GS/GA-AP.

Suppose a given dataset containing n data points: $\mathbf{X} = \{x_1, x_2, \cdots, x_n\}$, and the separation of $\mathbf{X}$ is a set of k clusters: $\{C_1, C_2, \cdots, C_k\}$. Considering a data point $x \in C_i$, first we calculate the average distance between x and any other data points in C_i as $a(x)$. Similarly, we calculate the minimum of average distance between x and any other data points in any other clusters except C_i as $b(x)$. Here is the formulae of $a(x)$ and $b(x)$:

$$a(x) = \frac{\sum\limits_{x' \in C_i, x' \neq x} dist(x, x')}{|C_i| - 1} \tag{5}$$

$$b(x) = \min_{C_j : i \leqslant j \leqslant k, j \neq i} \left\{ \frac{\sum\limits_{x' \in C_j} dist(x, x')}{|C_j|} \right\} \tag{6}$$

And the silhouette coefficient of x is given by:

$$s(x) = \frac{b(x) - a(x)}{\max\{a(x), b(x)\}} \tag{7}$$

In order to evaluating the quality of clustering, it is necessary to calculate the average of silhouette coefficient of each data points in given dataset. If the average of silhouette coefficient is much closer to 1, it is demonstrated that the cluster containing x is more compact, and it is much further from any other clusters. The average exhibits the quality of the result of clustering. According to the property, it is a suitable fitness function of GA.

4.2 Description of GS/GA-AP Algorithm

GS/GA-AP includes two parts, GS-AP and GA-AP. Firstly, median of similarity and golden section preference could be selected as the input of AP clustering algorithm. If the selection of golden section preference has improved the clustering result to an acceptable evaluation index and the result is a feasible solution, the algorithm could be terminated. This part of procedure can be named GS-AP. Otherwise we use GA to detect the optimal preference for AP, so the result should be improved substantially, and it could be the feasible solution finally.

The description of GS/GA-AP is exhibited as follow:

Algorithm 3. GS/GA-AP

Input:
    $\mathbf{X} = x_1, x_2, \cdots, x_n$:A dataset.
    λ: Damping factor.
    F:Evaluation function and fitness function for GA.
    $Crossover\_rate$: Crossover rate for GA.
    $Mutation\_rate$: Mutation rate for GA.

Output:
    $Labels = [Cluster(x_1), \cdots, Cluster(x_n)]$: The clustering labels where $Cluster(x_i)$ represents which cluster x_i belongs to.
    $Opti\_preference$: The optimal preference.

1: Calculate the similarity measurement $s(i, k)$ between data point x_i and x_k ($i, k = 1, 2, \cdots, n$). All the similarities would form the similarity matrix $S = [s(i, k)]_{n \times n}$
2: Choose median of similarity matrix and golden section preference as preference. Execute AP Clustering algorithm and obtain evaluation value. Golden section preference is calculated as followed:

$$gs\_preference = \frac{\sqrt{5} - 1}{2} \times (minimum + maximum)$$

3: Evaluate these two results with evaluation values, if the golden section result improve the result tremendously, output the result and terminate algorithm.
4: Use GA to find the optimal preference. Input F as fitness function.
5: Output the optimal preference and cluster labels, terminate algorithm.

---

5 Experiments and Results

To evaluate the GS/GA-AP Algorithm, a number of experiments have been done, and the data in experiments contains one artificially generated dataset, and

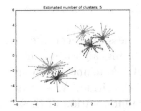 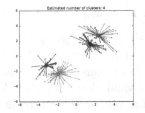 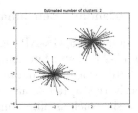

Fig. 1. The clustering result of traditional AP

Fig. 2. The clustering result of GS-AP

Fig. 3. The clustering result of GA-AP

five standard benchmark datasets. Unless mentioned specially, the traditional preference of median of similarities is described as "median", the golden section value of minimum and maximum of similarities is described as "golden section", the distance measurement is the squared Euclidean distance, and the parameters of GA program are set as follows: the solution of GA is coded by real number; the minimum and maximum of searching space are minimum and double value of median of similarities; the default selector of GA is ranking selection, and the default mutation rate is 2 % and the crossover rate is 80 %; the fitness function is silhouette coefficient. The results of experiments are shown as followed.

5.1 Test Randomly Generated Dataset

A two-dimensional dataset has been generated by a random generator in scikit-learn [18] machine learning toolkit. It includes two hundred data points and is separated into two classes where $(2, 2)$ and $(-2, -2)$ are centers of classes respectively . Here the traditional AP clustering algorithm and GS/GA-AP are used to cluster the test dataset, and the result of clustering are shown as Figs. 1, 2, and 3.

From Figs. 1, 2, and 3, we find out that the number of traditional AP clustering result is 5, and the numbers of GS-AP and GA-AP clustering results are 4 and 2, and the result of GS-AP is better than traditional AP, and GA-AP obtains the best result compared to traditional AP and GS-AP. To further verify the effectiveness of these three algorithm, the experiment results is shown in Table 1:

Table 1. The experiment result of AP and GS/GA-AP

Algorithm	Number of clusters	Silhouette coefficient
Traditional AP	5	0.45
GS-AP	4	0.436
GA-AP	2	0.937

5.2 Standard Benchmark Datasets

To evaluate GS/GA-AP algorithm and verify the effectiveness and accurate of GS/GA-AP algorithm compared to traditional AP clustering algorithm, five standard benchmark datasets have been selected from UCI Machine Learning Repository [19] to estimate the validation of GS/GA-AP Algorithm. After pre-processing such as filling missing values, Table 2 shows the information of these five dataset:

Table 2. Information of standard benchmark dataset from UCI

Datasets	Iris	Wine	Glass	Wholesale	SPECTF
#Instances	150	178	214	440	80
#Features	4	13	9	6	44
#Clusters	3	3	6	3	2

Table 3 shows the experiment results of traditional AP clustering algorithm and GS-AP, GA-AP clustering algorithm respectively. The experiment results include the preferences, numbers of clusters, and silhouette coefficients (Sil).

Table 3. The result of traditional AP, GS-AP and GA-AP clustering

Datasets		Iris	Wine	Glass	Wholesale	SPECTF
cluster number		3	3	6	3	2
AP with median	preference	−5.425	−78535.142	−5.446	−264840099.5	−3208.5
	#clusters	7	8	9	17	5
	Sil	0.530	0.713	0.439	0.423	0.113
GS-AP	preference	−31.025	−1215142.599	−89.546	−10279664354.2	−26328.248
	#clusters	3	4	4	5	3
	Sil	0.735	0.703	0.761	0.533	0.569
GA-AP	preference	−36.813	−889239.607	−97.558	−13293775150.7	−31465.564
	#clusters	3	2	4	3	2
	Sil	0.735	0.821	0.761	0.623	0.736

According to Table 3, it is indicated that GS-AP and GA-AP obtain two more accuracy numbers of clusters compared to traditional AP clustering algorithm, and the quality of clustering results are improved due to these higher silhouette coefficient.

Figure 4 shows the accurate of numbers of clusters from traditional AP, GS-AP and GA-AP, it is obvious that GA-AP obtain the most accuracy numbers of clusters substantially, while the results of GS-AP are better than traditional AP clustering algorithm. Figure 5 shows the improvement of silhouette coefficient. Greater silhouette coefficients mean a better quality of clustering result,

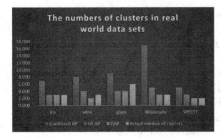

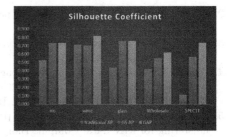

Fig. 4. The number of clusters in standard benchmark datasets

Fig. 5. Silhouette coefficient

so Fig. 5 illustrates the quality of clustering result from GS-AP and GA-AP is always better than traditional AP, and GS/GA-AP could find the optimal clustering result. So it is indicated that GS/GA-AP acquires a great improvement compared to traditional AP, and improves the clustering result of traditional AP clustering algorithm. According to the silhouette coefficient, three results of five datasets have improved to satisfactory evaluation index and the results are feasible solution, so GS/GA-AP could save time at a certain probability.

6 Conclusion

This paper proposes a new feasible procedure called GS/GA-AP. To evaluate the effectiveness of GS/GA-AP, a simulation dataset and five standard benchmark datasets are used to test the traditional AP and GS/GA-AP clustering algorithm. The results of experiments shows that GS/GA-AP is accuracy and effectiveness compared to traditional AP in the six datasets substantially, which means GS/GA-AP improves traditional AP clustering algorithm.

Although GS/GA-AP is more accuracy and effective, the time complexity is a complicated problem to deal with. So it is necessary to find a new approach to reduce the time complexity of GS/GA-AP, and under the condition of guaranteeing the accurate and effectiveness, the algorithm runs more rapidly.

Acknowledgements. This research is sponsored by National Natural Science Foundation of China (No.61171014, 61472044, 11401028) and the Fundamental Research Funds for the Central Universities(No. 2014KJJCB32, 2013NT57, 2012LYB46) and by SRF for ROCS, SEM.

References

1. Han, J., Kamber, M., Pei, J.: Cluster Analysis. In: Data Mining: Concepts and Techniques, Third Edition, pp. 443–444. Elsevier Inc. (2006)

2. Frey, B.J., Dueck, D.: Clustering by passing messages between data points. Sci. **315**(5814), 972–976 (2007)

3. Givoni, I.E., Frey, B.J.: A binary variable model for affinity propagation. Neural comput. **21**(6), 1589–1600 (2009)

4. Zhang, X., Wang, W., Nørvag, K., Sebag, M.: K-AP: generating specified k clusters by efficient affinity propagation. In: 2010 IEEE 10th International Conference on Data Mining (ICDM), pp. 1187–1192. IEEE (2010)

5. Tang, D.M., Zhu, Q.X., Yang, F.: A poisson-based adaptive affinity propagation clustering for sage data. Comput. Biol. Chem. **34**(1), 63–70 (2010)

6. Givoni, I., Chung, C., Frey, B.J.: Hierarchical affinity propagation (2012) . arXiv preprint arXiv:1202.3722

7. Wang, C.-D., Lai, J.-H., Suen, C.Y., Zhu, J.-Y.: Multi-exemplar affinity propagation. IEEE Trans. Pattern Anal. Mach. Intell. **9**, 2223–2237 (2013)

8. Wang, K., Zhang, J., Li, D., Zhang, X., Guo, T.: Adaptive affinity propagation clustering (2008). arXiv preprint arXiv:0805.1096

9. He, Y., Chen, Q., Wang, X., Xu, R., Bai, X., Meng, X.: An adaptive affinity propagation document clustering. In: 2010 The 7th International Conference on Informatics and Systems (INFOS), pp. 1–7. IEEE (2010)

10. Hongjun, S., Sheng, Y., Peijun, D., Liu, K.: Adaptive affinity propagation with spectral angle mapper for semi-supervised hyperspectral band selection. Appl. Opt. **51**(14), 2656–2663 (2012)

11. Chen, D.-W., Sheng, J.-Q., Chen, J.-J., Wang, C.-D.: Stability-based preference selection in affinity propagation. Neural Comput. Appl. **25**(7–8), 1809–1822 (2014)

12. Wang, X., Qin, Z., Zhang, X.: Automatically affinity propagation clustering using particle swarm. J. Comput. **5**(11), 1731–1738 (2010)

13. Wang, X.-H., Zhang, X.-P., Zhuang, C.-X., Chen, Z.-N., Qin, Z.: Automatically determining the number of affinity propagation clustering using particle swarm. In: 2010 the 5th IEEE Conference on Industrial Electronics and Applications (ICIEA), pp. 1526–1530. IEEE (2010)

14. Zhong, Y., Zheng, M., Wu, J., Shen, W., Zhou, Y., Zhou, C.: Search the optimal preference of affinity propagation algorithm. In: 2012 Fifth International Conference on Intelligent Computation Technology and Automation (ICICTA), pp. 304–307. IEEE (2012)

15. Xiazhu, Y., Wenli, D., Liang, Z., Feng, Q.: Energy consumption monitoring of the steam pipe network based on affinity propagation clustering. In: 2012 10th World Congress on Intelligent Control and Automation (WCICA), pp. 3364–3368. IEEE (2012)

16. Frey, B.J., Dueck, D.: Clustering by passing messages between data points. Sci. **315**, 972–976 (2007). Supporting online material

17. Holland, J.H.: Adaptation in Natural and Artificial Systems: An Introductory Analysis with Applications to Biology, Control, and Artificial Intelligence. U Michigan Press, Ann Arbor (1975)

18. scikit-learn. online. http://scikit-learn.org/stable

19. Uci irvine machine learning repository. http://archive.ics.uci.edu/ml/index.html

DRL: A New Mobility Model in Mobile Social Networks

Tao Jing[✉], Yating Zhang[✉], Zhen Li, Qinghe Gao,
Yan Huo, and Wei Zhou

School of Electronics and Information Engineering,
Beijing Jiaotong University, Beijing, China
{tjing,14120178}@bjtu.edu.cn

Abstract. Due to the complexity and variability of mobile social networks, the difficulty of evaluating protocols brings a demand to design a pragmatic mobility model, which can estimate these protocols well. A new mobility model according with the actual situation is proposed in this paper. A new characteristic of a community is defined as Community Attraction to decide the next goal of a certain node. It is related to three factors, that is, the distance between the node and the whole community, the node's relationships with all nodes within this community, and the Location Attraction of the community. Thus, our new mobility model is called DRL (Distance, Relationship, Location). Besides, the abstract people's social relationships as well as the Location Attractions of communities to people are firstly indicated through interaction matrices, which are initialized by the social attributes of relevant people. Finally, the simulations validate that the results of our model fit for the real data. DRL proves to be reasonable and practical for various protocol evaluations.

Keywords: Mobile social networks · Mobility model · Social relationships · Protocol evaluation

1 Introduction

In real life, the relationships among people constitute social networks, which play a very important role in people's daily life. And mobile communication networks have become indispensable in human societies. Particularly, with the rapid development of mobile communication technologies and the great variety of mobile businesses, ubiquitous communication is becoming an emerging reality. As a result, mobile social networks (MSNs), as a kind of mobile communication systems involving the social relationships of the users, have combined the two disciplines and triggered a wave of researches [5,12,13].

The research community of mobile social networks is confronted with many challenges, especially in designing well-performed protocols. However, because of the complexity of mobile social networks, it is difficult to assess protocols in MSNs. In order to solve this problem, we can create a mobility model accurately

© Springer International Publishing Switzerland 2015
K. Xu and J. Zhu (Eds.): WASA 2015, LNCS 9204, pp. 263–273, 2015.
DOI: 10.1007/978-3-319-21837-3_26

simulating the motion characteristics of the people in a mobile social network. As a substitute of the real MSN, the new model is required to accord with the actual situations. Then we can examine the performance of these protocols by loading them on it.

From [2], a comprehensive survey on mobility models, we can make a conclusion that traditional mobility models can be divided into two categories by the number of simulation objects, that is, entity mobility models and group mobility models. Not considering the social relationships among people, these models do not embody the characteristics of the real society. In recent years, new models appeared embracing the motion characteristics of the people in social networks, such as the community/group based model [9], the encounter-based model [6], the time-varying model [4], the working day movement model [3], the SWIM [7], the VSSE [10], and so on. Each of these models actually seizes some of the characteristics of social networks. Nevertheless, not comprehensive enough are they. Except for strong points of them, some new factors are essential to establish a new model based on users' social relationships.

This paper introduces the concepts of Community Attraction, Social Relationship Attributes, Social Relationship Matrix, and Location Attraction. A new model is designed more approximate to the real situations of mobile social networks and simulated on THE ONE simulator. We apply some routing protocols on this mobility model to analyze their performance. Moreover, to verify the reasonableness of the new mobility model, we compare the simulation results with the real data. Our innovations are three folds:

1. We build a new mobility model, integrating some factors mentioned in the previous models, for example, the social relationships among people, the "community weight" and the time-varying characteristics, and so on.
2. When designing the community selection rules of a certain node, we put forward the concept of Community Attraction, which is decided by the distance between the community and the node, the relationships between the node and the nodes in this community, and the Location Attraction of this community. According to these three factors, our new mobility model is named DRL (Distance, Relationship, Location). To the best of our knowledge, this is the first paper that takes Location Attraction into consideration, making the model more comprehensive and more realistic.
3. We initialize the Social Relationship Matrix with Social Relationship Attributes. The actual information of the people in societies is used as the input to the model, which makes it more similar to the real world.

The rest of the paper is organized as follows. Section 2 briefly describes several important related mobility models. Section 3 details the design of DRL. And Sect. 4 reports the simulations and result analysis. Our conclusions are provided in Sect. 5.

2   Related Work

Different from traditional models, a lot of mobility models are based on mobile social networks. To be more specific, the designers take people's social relationships into consideration to various degrees. The following is a brief introduction of several models related to this paper.

Firstly, in the community/group based model [9], the authors express people's social relationships through Interaction Matrix M, by which they distribute the nodes into several communities. All the nodes move according to social-based attraction laws. For any of them, denoted as node i, the next goal is to find a community whose nodes have the closest relationships with node i. Secondly, the encounter-based model [6] mainly focuses on two parameters, the inter-contact time and the contact-duration. The former refers to the time interval between two successive contacts, while the later deals with the duration from meeting to separating of two nodes. They are both power law distributions truncated by an exponential cut-off. Besides, the time-varying model [4] is based on two characteristics observed in mobile social networks: location preference, which means the node prefers to visit the places near to it, and periodical re-appearance of the node at the same location. What's more, founded on the observation of daily life, the SWIM [7] describes the situation that one usually prefers popular and nearby places. The next goal community of any node i is selected by calculating the "community weight" of each community, which is related to the popularity and the distance from the community to node i. Above models are all concerned with the social relationships of people, yet rarely do they take the influence of the location into account. Thus, the correlations of these models and the real society are not tight enough.

3 Design of the New Mobility Model: DRL

This section gives a detailed description of our new mobility model. We integrate some factors mentioned in the previous models, i.e., the social relationships among people, "community weight" and the time-varying characteristics. Using some data taken from the real MSN as the input of our model, we employ the Social Relationship Matrix and the Location Attraction Matrix to present the relationships of nodes to nodes and nodes to locations, respectively. By the way, the Location Attraction Matrix is time-varying. When designing the community selection rules of the nodes, we put forward the new concept named Community Attraction. Its formula is specified to determine the next goal community. Additionally, by analyzing the contact-duration and the contact-number of our model, we make a prediction of their distributions.

3.1 Modeling Social Relationships

(1)Initializing the Social Relationship Matrix with Social Relationship Attributes

We use an $n \times n$ symmetric matrix M, called Social Relationship Matrix, to represent the social relationships among people. n denotes the number of nodes. Correspondingly, both rows and columns of the matrix M are ordered by 1 to n. The generic element $m_{i,j}$ in matrix M represents the relationship between two nodes i and j. The value of $m_{i,j}$ could be 1 or 0. 1 indicates friends and

0 denotes strangers. In order to prevent the influence of the node itself, the diagonal elements are set to 0. A matrix M of 10 nodes is shown in Fig. 1.

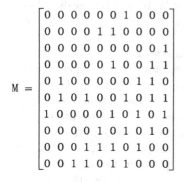

$$M = \begin{bmatrix} 0 & 0 & 0 & 0 & 0 & 0 & 1 & 0 & 0 & 0 \\ 0 & 0 & 0 & 0 & 1 & 1 & 0 & 0 & 0 & 0 \\ 0 & 0 & 0 & 0 & 0 & 0 & 0 & 0 & 0 & 1 \\ 0 & 0 & 0 & 0 & 0 & 1 & 0 & 0 & 1 & 1 \\ 0 & 1 & 0 & 0 & 0 & 0 & 0 & 1 & 1 & 0 \\ 0 & 1 & 0 & 1 & 0 & 0 & 1 & 0 & 1 & 1 \\ 1 & 0 & 0 & 0 & 0 & 1 & 0 & 1 & 0 & 1 \\ 0 & 0 & 0 & 0 & 1 & 0 & 1 & 0 & 1 & 0 \\ 0 & 0 & 1 & 1 & 1 & 0 & 1 & 0 & 0 & 0 \\ 0 & 0 & 1 & 1 & 0 & 1 & 1 & 0 & 0 & 0 \end{bmatrix}$$

Fig. 1. An social relationship matrix of 10 nodes.

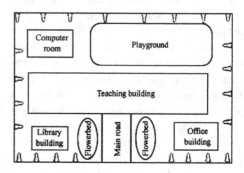

Fig. 2. Division of the simulation area.

Before initializing the Social Relationship Matrix, we need to judge whether two people are friends or strangers by Social Relationship Attributes, e.g., profession, nationality, research area, etc. And different attributes include specific contents, for instance, the profession of a person can be an expert, a teacher or a student, while his nationality may be China, the U.S., Russia, Japan, etc. Take the occasion of conference as an example, first we number the n participators from 1 to n, and then record everyone's Social Relationship Attributes. By comparing them, we can find the similarities of two persons. We assume that the case of two or more attributes with the same contents means friends. For example, participator i and j are both Chinese wireless communications experts, the corresponding elements $m_{i,j}$ and $m_{j,i}$ of the matrix are initialized to 1. On the contrary, no or only one common attribute, they are regarded as strangers and the elements are initialized to 0.

(2) Location Attraction Matrix

We represent the Location Attractions of communities to nodes as a $g \times n$ matrix P, where g and n are the numbers of communities and nodes, respectively. The generic element $p_{i,j} \in [0,1]$ in matrix P means the normalized location appel of community i to node j. Figure 3 shows an example of the matrix P with 6 communities and 10 nodes. It should be emphasized that, the Location Attraction of a community is an inherent attribute of this location, which is independent of the node's subjective consciousness. For example, the Location Attraction of the office in work hours is bigger than other places, but it is hard to say one loves to stay at the office.

In real life, the Location Attraction of one community usually varies at different time. For instance, the Location Attraction of the office is large in working hours, small at lunch time, contrary to the restaurants or canteens. Thus the matrix P is time-varying as it changes several times in a day. Besides, it is generally repeated every day because of the regularity of human activities, e.g., people

$$P = \begin{bmatrix} 0.4550 & 0.4367 & 0.2411 & 0.2262 & 0.9173 & 0.3931 & 0.9995 & 0.1108 & 0.4409 & 0.6916 \\ 0.1273 & 0.4366 & 0.8414 & 0.5368 & 0.1616 & 0.1790 & 0.9810 & 0.4075 & 0.9562 & 0.9790 \\ 0.0086 & 0.0492 & 0.8572 & 0.7621 & 0.7156 & 0.6333 & 0.1270 & 0.8841 & 0.1240 & 0.2833 \\ 0.7271 & 0.0496 & 0.9636 & 0.3476 & 0.5777 & 0.6240 & 0.2322 & 0.5481 & 0.4708 & 0.1338 \\ 0.3541 & 0.0911 & 0.4889 & 0.4612 & 0.4333 & 0.3279 & 0.0236 & 0.3690 & 0.8569 & 0.6853 \\ 0.7804 & 0.5940 & 0.2203 & 0.6393 & 0.8842 & 0.8030 & 0.6074 & 0.2083 & 0.0434 & 0.9095 \end{bmatrix}$$

Fig. 3. An example of location attraction matrix.

mostly go straight home after work and occasionally participate in recreational activities. Like this, the Location Attraction of one's home is viewed the biggest, and the hotels' or the KTVs' are relatively small at this time of day.

3.2   Description of the DRL

(1)Division of the simulation area

The simulation area is divided into blocks according to geographic locations. Each block remarks a community corresponding to a real place, the classroom, the playground, and the library, etc. Figure 2 displays an example of the simulation area division. When a node is initialized, it is randomly distributed in the area and grouped according to its position.

(2)Design of the community selection standard: the Community Attraction $w(c)$

By comparing the attractiveness of all the communities, the node chooses the most desired one to be the next target community. We propose the Community Attraction $w(c)$ to indicate the attractiveness of corresponding communities and take the value of $w(c)$ as the next goal community selection standard.

In real life, the choice of the next destination is often a mixture of multiple aspects. For example, at lunch time, a person most possibly goes to the restaurant instead of the library. When selecting which restaurant to go, he may prefer the one where his friends often go to, but he would also consider whether the restaurant is near enough such that he can get back to the office in time. Based on the above characteristics, we define that, the Community Attraction of a community to a node is decided by three aspects: the distance between the node and the community; the relationships between the node and nodes in the community; the location attraction of the community. The Community Attraction can be calculated as follows.

$$\widetilde{w}(c) = \alpha \cdot distance(d_{C,i}) + (1 - \alpha) \cdot [\beta \cdot isfriend(M) + (1 - \beta) \cdot place(P)] \quad (1)$$

where $distance(d_{C,i})$ represents the influence of the distance between community C and node i. $isfriend(M)$ represents the relationships between node i and the nodes in community C. $place(P)$ denotes the element $p_{C,i}$ in the matrix P.

At last, α and β are constants in the range [0,1]. The following are their specific expressions.

$$\widetilde{distance}(d_{C,i}) = \frac{1}{(1+k\|x-y\|)^2} \tag{2}$$

$$\widetilde{isfriend}(M) = \frac{\sum_{j=1,j\in C}^{z} m_{i,j}}{z} \tag{3}$$

In (2), x is the position of node i and y is the position of the center of community C, $\|x-y\|$ suggests the distance between community C and node i, denoted as $d_{C,i}$. k is a tuning parameter which affects the probability of choosing nearby community. Obviously, $distance(d_{C,i})$ is a power-law decay function of $d_{C,i}$.

In (3), z is the number of nodes in community C. The numerator represents the sum of the elements in matrix M matched with the relationships between node i and all the nodes in community C, that is, the number of node i's friends in community C. This equation represents the proportion of node i's friends in community C.

In addition, $place(P)$ represents the Location Attraction of community C to node i. Noted that the Matrix P is time-varying, the $place(P)$ of the same community to the same node is also changing. By adjusting the values of α and β, we can determine which of the three factors has more impacts on $w(c)$.

(3)The movement pattern of nodes

First, compute and compare the values of $w(c)$ of all the communities. The community corresponding to the maximum $w(c)$ is reckoned as the next destination. Next, let the node move, with a randomly set speed within a given range, following a straight line to the target location. After reaching the destination, the node pauses for a while, then repeats the process.

3.3 Prediction of the Results

Based on the movement characteristics of the people in the MSN and relevant results in previous papers, the distributions of the contact-duration and the contact-number of our model will meet the power-law distribution truncated by an exponential cut-off.

4 Evaluation

Simulations of this paper are mainly carried on THE ONE, a opportunistic network simulator with open source software of JAVA language. Whether classic or new mobility models can be simulated on it to asset different kinds of protocols. Before simulating, simulation parameters should be set in file $defaultsettings.txt$. In our experiment, the number of simulation nodes and the simulation time are 50 and one day, respectively.

Figure 4 intuitively reveals the characteristics of the connections of the 50 nodes. Obviously, the cases of short contact-durations and small contact-numbers are numerous. On the contrary, just a few cases have long contact-durations and big contact-numbers. It is because most of the nodes are strangers, the probability of the cases that the two meeting nodes are friends is small, while only friends have long contact-duration and big contact-number. It can be preliminarily predicted that the distribution of the connections of the nodes conforms to the traits of power-law.

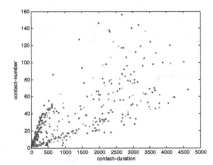

Simulated Scenario	Infocom05	Infocom06	Cambridge
Duration(days)	3	3	11
Devices number	41	78	36
Value of α	0.5	0.5	0.33
Value of β	0.5	0.5	0.5
Value of k	2	2	2

Fig. 4. Distributions of the contact-duration and contact-number.

Fig. 5. Simulated datasets.

4.1   Evaluation of Protocols

We load different routing protocols on DRL to analyze and compare their performance. Figures 6 and 7 show the Packet Delivery Rate and the Overhead of different protocols, respectively. The Packet Delivery Rate is the proportion of successfully received data packets in the total data packets. The higher the Packet Delivery Rate, the more reliable the routing protocol. The Overhead refers to the amount of routing control information during the simulation. Low Overhead indicates high efficiency, low bandwidth and low energy consumption.

From Figs. 6 and 7, it can be seen that we can simulate the routing protocols on DRL. That is to say, the new mobility model can replace the real mobile social network to load routing protocols and analyze their performance. We can see from the figures that as the amount of information increases, the Packet Delivery Rate tends to decrease and the Overhead tends to increase. Specifically, in the same contact duration, the more information is delivered, the more likely are packets lost which causes the decrease of Packet Delivery Rate. Meanwhile, with the increase of the information, more routing control information is needed, leading to a higher Overhead.

As can be seen from the figures, MaxProp has the highest Packet Delivery Rate and the least Overhead. Prophet has a general Packet Delivery Rate and a high Overhead. Spray And Wait protocol has a low Packet Delivery Rate, but the Overhead is very small. MaxProp protocol [1] is a modified version of the traditional flooding protocols, so its Packet Delivery Rate is high. In Max-Prop protocol, nodes don't flood all of the messages throughout the network like

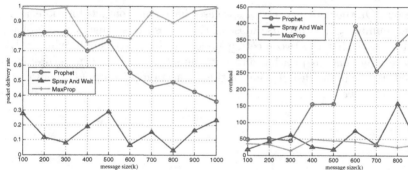

Fig. 6. Packet delivery rate comparison of various protocols under DRL.

Fig. 7. Overhead comparison of various protocols under DRL.

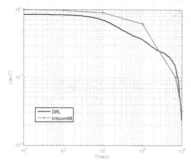

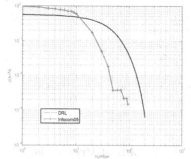

(a) Distributions of the contact-duration in Infocom 05 and in DRL.

(b) Distributions of the contact-number in Infocom 05 and in DRL.

Fig. 8. DRL and Infocom 05

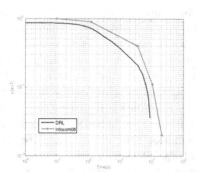

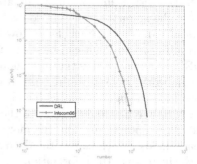

(a) Distributions of the contact-duration in Infocom 06 and in DRL.

(b) Distributions of the contact-number in Infocom 06 and in DRL.

Fig. 9. DRL and Infocom 06

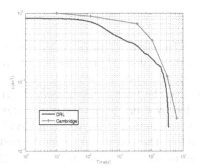
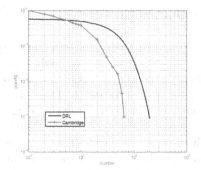

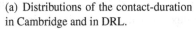

(a) Distributions of the contact-duration in Cambridge and in DRL.

(b) Distributions of the contact-number in Cambridge and in DRL.

Fig. 10. DRL and Cambridge

the traditional flooding protocols, therefore, the Overhead becomes smaller. In Prophet protocol [8], first, the probability of the successful delivery of each chain is calculated, to choose the best chain. Nevertheless, due to the complication of the calculation, we can obtain a relatively high Packet Delivery Rate while the Overhead is large. In Spray and Wait protocol [11], nodes send copies of the messages along binary trees, as a result, this protocol can reduce the flooding overhead. This protocol has two procedures and the value of parameter L in this protocol is difficult to choose. When it is big, the Overhead increases, conversely, when it is small, the Packet Delivery Rate decreases. In our simulation, L is relatively small to ensure low Overhead, so the Packet Delivery Rate is correspondingly reduced. Results shown in Figs. 6 and 7 are consistent with the characteristics of each protocol.

4.2   DRL Vs Real Traces

This section compares our simulation results with the reality records of Infocom 05, Infocom 06 and Cambridge from two facets: the distributions of contact-number and contact-duration. The details of these three traces are shown in Fig. 5. The Infocom 05 recorded the data of connections among 41 students attending the workshop. According to the real situation, we set 41 nodes in DRL and simulate on THE ONE simulator. The distributions of contact-duration and contact-number under Infocom 5 as well as DRL are shown in Fig. 8(a) and (b), respectively. The results of Infocom 06 and Cambridge are show in Figs. 9 and 10.

Figures 8(a), 9(a) and 10(a) depict the distributions of contact-durations of the simulation data and the real data. One can see that the trend of the curve of the simulation data is consistent with the real data. Moreover, it is in line with a power-law distribution, then truncated by an exponential cut-off. We can make a similar conclusion about the distributions of contact-numbers from Figs. 8(b), 9(b) and 10(b). So the new model is rational and practical.

5 Conclusion

In this paper, we design a novel mobility model based on users' social relationships, through which we can predict the next destination of any user in any time. We first distribute the users into different communities according to their current geographical locations. Then, we initialize the Social Relationship Matrix with each element in the matrix being decided by users' social features. Following, we propose the concept of Community Attraction $w(c)$, which is decided by three aspects, namely, the distance between the community and the node, the relationships between the node and the nodes in the community, and the Location Attraction of the community. Finally, we select the community with the maximal Community Attraction as the next destination. In simulation part, we deploy three routing protocols on DRL via THE ONE simulator, to evaluate their performance. Moreover, the comparison results show that the data of our model fit well with the real traces, which verifies the rationality of our mobility model.

Acknowledgements. The authors would like to thank the support from the National Natural Science Foundation of China (Grant No.61471028 and 61371069), the Specialized Research Fund for the Doctoral Program of Higher Education (Grant No.20130009110015), and the financial support from China Scholarship Council.

References

1. Burgess, J., Gallagher, B., Jensen, D., Levine, B.N.: Maxprop: routing for vehicle-based disruption-tolerant networks. In: INFOCOM, vol. 6, pp. 1–11 (2006)
2. Camp, T., Boleng, J., Davies, V.: A survey of mobility models for ad hoc network research. Wirel. Commun. Mob. Comput. **2**(5), 483–502 (2002)
3. Ekman, F., Keränen, A., Karvo, J., Ott, J.: Working day movement model. In: Proceedings of the 1st ACM SIGMOBILE Workshop on Mobility Models, pp. 33–40. ACM (2008)
4. jen Hsu, W., Spyropoulos, T., Psounis, K., Helmy, A.: Modeling time-variant user mobility in wireless mobile networks. In: 26th IEEE International Conference on Computer Communications, INFOCOM 2007, pp. 758–766. IEEE, May 2007
5. Huang, J., Wang, S., Cheng, X., Liu, M., Li, Z., Chen, B.: Mobility-assisted routing in intermittently connected mobile cognitive radio networks. IEEE Trans. Parallel Distrib. Syst. **25**(11), 2956–2968 (2014)
6. Karagiannis, T., Le Boudec, J.Y., Vojnovic, M.: Power law and exponential decay of intercontact times between mobile devices. IEEE Trans. Mob. Comput. **9**(10), 1377–1390 (2010)
7. Kosta, S., Mei, A., Stefa, J.: Small world in motion (swim): modeling communities in ad-hoc mobile networking. In: 2010 7th Annual IEEE Communications Society Conference on Sensor Mesh and Ad Hoc Communications and Networks (SECON), pp. 1–9, June 2010
8. Lindgren, A., Doria, A., Schelén, O.: Probabilistic routing in intermittently connected networks. ACM SIGMOBILE Mob. Comput. Commun. Rev. **7**(3), 19–20 (2003)

9. Musolesi, M., Mascolo, C.: Designing mobility models based on social network theory. ACM SIGMOBILE Mob. Comput. Commun. Rev. **11**, 59–70 (2007)

10. Nazir, F., Prendinger, H., Seneviratne, A.: Participatory mobile social network simulation environment. In: 2010 IEEE International Conference on Communications (ICC), pp. 1–6, May 2010

11. Spyropoulos, T., Psounis, K., Raghavendra, C.S.: Spray and wait: an efficient routing scheme for intermittently connected mobile networks. In: Proceedings of the 2005 ACM SIGCOMM Workshop on Delay-Tolerant Networking, pp. 252–259. ACM (2005)

12. Wang, S., Liu, M., Cheng, X., Li, Z., Huang, J., Chen, B.: Opportunistic routing in intermittently connected mobile p2p networks. IEEE J. Sel. Areas Commun. **31**(9), 369–378 (2013)

13. Wang, S., Liu, M., Cheng, X., Song, M.: Routing in pocket switched networks. IEEE Wirel. Commun. **19**(1), 67–73 (2012)

SGSA: Secure Group Setup and Anonymous Authentication in Platoon-Based Vehicular Cyber-Physical Systems

Chengzhe Lai[1,2]([✉]), Rongxing Lu[3], and Dong Zheng[1]

[1] National Engineering Laboratory for Wireless Security,
Xi'an University of Posts and Telecommunications, Xi'an 710121, China
lcz_xupt@163.com, zhengdong@xupt.edu.cn
[2] State Key Laboratory of Information Security,
Institute of Information Engineering, Chinese Academy of Sciences,
Beijing 100093, China
[3] School of Electrical and Electronics Engineering,
Nanyang Technological University, Singapore, Singapore
rxlu@ntu.edu.sg

Abstract. Recently, the platoon-based vehicular cyber-physical system (VCPS) has attracted significant attention. The members of platoon may change quite dynamically, and vehicles may join or leave the platoon at any time. Therefore, how to securely set up a group and guarantee anonymity of platoon members when performing authentication with road side units (RSUs) along the highway is a challenge. To address this issue, in this paper, we propose a secure group setup and anonymous authentication scheme in the platoon-based VCPS by using a special group signature technique, named SGSA. The proposed SGSA can securely set up a temporary platoon, and flexibly support platoon merging/platoon splitting. Particularly, once a dispute occurs on an access request during the authentication, any platoon member can trace the corresponding vehicle of the disputed access request message. Finally, we also carry out extensive analysis to show the security and efficiency of our proposed SGSA.

Keywords: Vehicular cyber-physical systems · Platoon · Authentication and key agreement · Anonymous

1 Introduction

With the development of automobile industry and urbanization, a growing number of vehicles are on the highway linking adjacent cities. As stated in [8], about 24 % of all miles driven in U.S. use the interstate highway system. China's automobile industry is also experiencing explosive growth, which brings about a series of problems, such as traffic congestion, traffic accidents, energy waste, and environmental pollution. In addition, numerous applications based on modern

K. Xu and J. Zhu (Eds.): WASA 2015, LNCS 9204, pp. 274–283, 2015.
DOI: 10.1007/978-3-319-21837-3_27

transportation systems [7,9] also require the cooperation among vehicle users. For instance, travelers in vehicles often have strong willingness to share their travel experience and exchange information to each other through social networks, such as Facebook and Twitter; or need to cooperatively download/forward a file [6,11]. To address these issues, an effective approach is to change the driving pattern from individual driving to a platoon-based driving [1]. Vehicles on the road with some common interests (e.g., destination, hobby, groups of friends, etc.,) can cooperatively form a platoon-based driving pattern, in which a vehicle follows another one and maintains a small and nearly constant distance to the preceding vehicle. Such a platoon-based driving pattern can significantly improve the road capacity and energy efficiency. In addition, the physical dynamics of vehicles inside the platoon can also affect the performance of VANET. Such a complex system can be considered as a platoon-based vehicular cyber-physical system (VCPS), which has attracted significant attention recently.

In such a platoon-based VCPS, any vehicle can form a temporary platoon and enjoy various services in a platoon-based driving pattern. The members of platoon may change quite dynamically, and vehicles may join or leave the platoon at any time. Therefore, how to securely set up a group and guarantee anonymity of platoon members when performing authentication with RSUs along the highway is a challenge. To address this issue, in this paper, we propose a secure group setup and anonymous authentication scheme in platoon-based vehicular cyber-physical systems by using a new group signature technique [10], named SGSA. To summarize, the main contributions of this paper are three-fold: (1) Firstly, the proposed SGSA can securely set up a temporary platoon by applying any anonymous attribute-based group setup scheme and group key agreement scheme. In addition, SGSA can flexibly support platoon merging/platoon splitting, and update the group key timely; (2) Secondly, the proposed SGSA employs a new group signature scheme to achieve anonymous mutual authentication with RSUs and efficient traceability. Specifically, once a dispute occurs on an access request during the authentication, any platoon member can trace the corresponding vehicle of the disputed access request message; (3) Finally, we also carry out extensive analysis to show the security and efficiency of our proposed SGSA.

The remainder of this paper is organized as follows. In Sect. 2, we formalize the network model, and identify the design goals. In Sect. 3, we present our SGSA in detail, followed by its security analysis and performance evaluation in Sect. 4 and 5, respectively. Finally, we draw our conclusions in Sect. 6.

2   Network Model and Design Goals

In this section, we introduce the network model and identify our design goals.

2.1   Network Model

As shown in Fig. 1, our system model is composed of the following parts: the trust authority (TA), road side units (RSUs), and vehicles. The TA is responsible

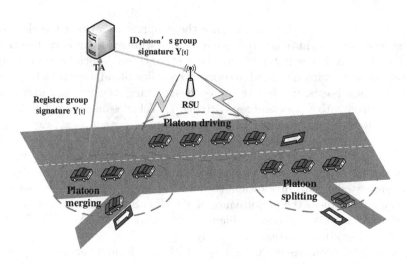

Fig. 1. Network model

for authenticating the group public keys of platoons. After authentication, the TA will issue the corresponding public key certificates. The RSU is responsible for performing access authentication with vehicles in the platoon.

On the highway, any vehicle can initiate a platoon forming procedure. The privacy-preserving attributes matching and group key agreement will be performed among vehicles. Once a platoon has formed, all vehicles can move on the highway in a platoon-based driving pattern. These vehicles can access the core network and enjoy various services (e.g., Internet). In addition, any vehicle can join and leave the platoon at any time.

2.2   Design Goals

Our goal is to propose a secure group setup and anonymous authentication scheme in platoon-based vehicular cyber-physical systems. In particular, the following goals should be achieved.

(1) *Secure and Flexible Group Setup*: The proposed SGSA should securely set up a temporary platoon by applying any anonymous attribute-based group setup scheme and group key agreement scheme. In addition, SGSA must flexibly support platoon merging/ platoon splitting, and update the group key timely.

(2) *Strong Anonymous Access Authentication*: First, the proposed scheme should provide strong anonymous access authentication. Specifically, it requires that authentication messages, which are interacted by the vehicle in the platoon and the RSU, have not been altered during the transmission, i.e., if the adversary $\mathcal{A}$ forges and/or modifies the authentication messages, the malicious operations should be detected. Meanwhile, the identity of the vehicle cannot be revealed to adversary $\mathcal{A}$ or the RSU.

(3) *User Tracking on the Disputed Access Request*: An important and challenging issue is to maintain traceability for all the access messages in the presence of the anonymous access authentication. Without the tracking function, the above anonymous access authentication can only prevent an outside attack, but cannot deal with an inside one. Therefore, once a dispute occurs on an access request during the authentication, any platoon member can trace the corresponding vehicle of the disputed access request message.

3   The Proposed SGSA Scheme

In this section, we present the proposed SGSA scheme, which mainly consists of the following two parts: secure vehicular group setup, and anonymous authentication and key agreement.

3.1   Secure Vehicular Group Setup

3.1.1   System Initialization

Assuming at the beginning, there are n vehicles on the highway, which already have formed a platoon based on their attributes (e.g., destination, hobby, groups of friends, etc.,). For example, we can apply the anonymous attribute-based group setup scheme [5], which uses a novel solution named efficient and anonymous attribute-based encryption (EA-ABE). Our scheme can also work with any anonymous group setup protocol suite that fulfills the security requirements.

Given a cyclic group $\mathbb{G}$ with prime order q and a generator $g \in \mathbb{G}$, where the discrete logarithm assumption holds, let $\mathcal{SPGKA} = (Setup(), Join(), Leave())$ be a secure privacy-preserving group key agreement protocol suite where group members can form a group and agree on a group key with privacy-preservation mechanism, such as [2]. The protocol among n vehicles to set up a platoon proceeds as follows, each vehicle V_i:

- Sets counter value $t = 0$, selects secret signing key $x_{i[0]} \in_R \mathbb{Z}_q$, and computes the corresponding signing public key $z_{i[0]} = g^{x_{i[0]}}$;
- Performs interactive algorithm $\mathcal{SPGKA}.Setup(x_{i[0]}, z_{i[0]})$, and obtains the tracing trapdoor (i.e., group secret key) $\hat{x}_{[0]} \in \mathbb{Z}_q$ and auxiliary information $aux_{i[0]}$ that contains the set of contributions of all vehicles in the platoon, i.e., $Z_{[0]} = \{z_{1[0]},...,z_{n[0]}\}$;
- Computes $\hat{y}_{[0]} = g^{\hat{x}_{[0]}}$, and defines the group public key $Y_{[0]} = (\hat{y}_{[0]}, Z_{[0]})$.

The public output of the system is the group public key $Y_{[0]}$, and the private outputs are $\hat{x}_{[0]}, x_{1[0]},...,x_{n[0]}$.

3.1.2   Platoon Merging

As mentioned above, on the highway, some vehicles may want to join a platoon at any time. We call this platoon merging. When a vehicle joins an existing platoon, the protocol between the platoon and a joining vehicle V_J proceeds as follows. Let t be the current counter value and n be the number of vehicles in the platoon.

- V_J selects a secret signing key $x_{V_J[t+1]} \in_R \mathbb{Z}_q$, and computes the corresponding signing public key $z_{V_J[t+1]} = g^{x_{V_J}[t]}$;
- Vehicles in the platoon and the V_J perform the protocol $\mathcal{SPGKA}.Join()$ by calling the instance $Join()$: i.e., $\mathcal{SPGKA}.Join(x_{V_J[t+1]}, z_{V_J[t+1]})$ is called by the joining vehicle V_J, and outputs the updated $\hat{x}_{[t+1]}$ and $aux_{V_J[t+1]}$;
- Every vehicle in the platoon increases t, and computes $\hat{y}_{[t+1]} = g^{\hat{x}[t+1]}$, and $Y_{[t+1]} = (\hat{y}_{[t+1]}, z_{1[t+1]}, ..., z_{n+1[t+1]})$.

The updated group public key is $Y_{[t+1]}$, and group secret key is $\hat{x}_{[t+1]}$ that is also the tracing trapdoor.

3.1.3   Platoon Splitting

When a vehicle wants to leave a platoon, we call this platoon splitting. The protocol between the remaining vehicles in the platoon after a vehicle V_L has left the platoon proceeds as follows. Let t be the current counter value and n the number of vehicles in the platoon. Every remaining vehicle V_{pi} in the platoon, $i \in [1, n-1]$:

- Performs the interactive algorithm $\mathcal{SPGKA}.Leave((x_{i[t]}, z_{V_J[t]}, aux_{i[t]})$, and obtains the updated $\hat{x}_{[t+1]}$, $aux_{i[t+1]}$ and possibly updated $x_{i[t+1]}$;
- Increases t, and computes $\hat{y}_{[t+1]} = g^{\hat{x}[t+1]}$ and $Y_{[t+1]} = (\hat{y}_{[t+1]}, z_{1[t+1]}, ..., z_{n-1[t+1]})$.

The public output of the system is the updated group public key $Y_{[t+1]}$. The private outputs are $x_{i[t+1]}, , \hat{x}_{[t+1]}$, and $aux_{i[t+1]}$.

3.2   Anonymous Authentication with Traceability

After vehicular group setup, vehicles have formed a platoon-based driving pattern on the highway. When they arrive at the social spot S_j and meets the RSU R_j deployed at S_j; then, any vehicle in the platoon V_{pi} and R_j make the mutual authentication and key agreement, as shown in Fig. 2, and the detailed steps are as follows.

3.2.1   Anonymous Authentication and Key Agreement

When the vehicle V_{pi} in the platoon visits one social spot S_i, it performs the mutual authentication with the RSU R_j at S_j. V_{pi} first picks up the current timestamp TS, and chooses a random number $a \in_R \mathbb{Z}_q^*$ and computes g^a. H is a secure cryptographic hash function. Then, V_{pi} generates a signature on a message $M_{pi} = (ID_{platoon}||TS||g^a)$ as follows.

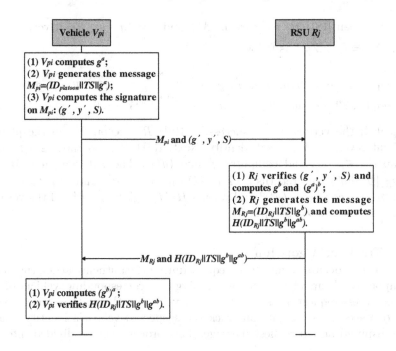

Fig. 2. Anonymous authentication and key agreement between V_{pi} and R_j

- *Step 1:* The vehicle V_{pi} in the platoon selects a random number $r \in_R \mathbb{Z}_q$, and computes

$$g' = g^r, y' = \hat{y}_{[t]}^r z_{i[t]}; \tag{1}$$

- *Step 2:* V_{pi} selects random numbers $r_{u_1}, r_{u_2}, ..., r_{u_n}, r_{v_1}, r_{v_2}, r_{v_3} \in_R \mathbb{Z}_q$, $c_1, c_2, ..., c_{i-1}, c_{i+1}, ..., c_n, \in_R \{0, 1\}^k$;
- *Step 3:* Then, V_{pi} computes

$$u_i = \hat{y}_{[t]}^{r_{u_i}}, v_i = g^{r_{v_i}}, and \ w_i = g^{r_{u_i}}. \tag{2}$$

- *Step 4:* For all $j \neq i$, V_{pi} computes

$$u_j = y'^{c_j} \hat{y}_{[t]}^{r_{u_j}} g^{r_{v_j}}, v_j = z_{j[t]}^{c_j} g^{r_{v_j}}, w_j = g'^{c_j} g^{r_{u_j}}; \tag{3}$$

- *Step 5:* Next, V_{pi} computes

$$c_i = \oplus_{j \neq i}^n c_j \oplus H(g, \hat{y}_{[t]}, g', y', u_1, ..., u_{i-1}, u_i v_i, u_{i+1}, ..., u_n, \atop v_1, ..., v_n, w_1, ..., w_n, M_{pi}); \tag{4}$$

- *Step 6:* V_{pi} computes $s_{u_i} = r_{u_i} - c_i r$, $s_{v_i} = r_{v_i} - c_i x_{i[t]}$; for all $j \neq i$, $s_{u_j} = r_{u_j}, s_{v_j} = r_{v_j}$;
- *Step 7:* Let $S = (c_1, ..., c_n, s_{u_1}, ..., s_{u_n}, s_{v_1}, ..., s_{v_n})$. V_{pi} sends M_{pi} and $\sigma = (g', y', S)$ to RSU R_j;

- **Step 8:** When RSU R_j receives the M_{pi} and $\sigma = (g', y', S)$, it verifies S by using $Y_{[t]} = (\hat{y}_{[t]}, Z_{[t]})$ as follows:

$$c_1 \oplus \ldots \oplus c_n \overset{?}{=} H(g, \hat{y}_{[t]}, g', y', y'^{c_1}\hat{y}_{[t]}^{s_{u1}} g^{s_{v1}}, \ldots, y'^{c_n}\hat{y}_{[t]}^{s_{un}} g^{s_{vn}}, \\ z_{1[t]}^{c_1} g^{s_{v1}}, \ldots, z_{n[t]}^{c_n} g^{s_{vn}}, g'^{c_1} g^{s_{u1}}, \ldots, g'^{c_n} g^{s_{un}}, M_{pi}); \quad (5)$$

- **Step 9:** If the verification is successful, RSU R_j accepts V_{pi} in the platoon without revealing V_{pi}'s real identity. Next, RSU R_j also chooses a random number $b \in_R \mathbb{Z}_q^*$, and computes g^b and $(g^a)^b$. Then, it generates $M_{R_j} = (ID_{R_j}||TS||g^b)$, and returns back $H(ID_{R_j}||TS||g^b||g^{ab})$ and M_{R_j} to V_{pi};
- **Step 10:** V_{pi} computes $(g^b)^a$ and verifies $H(ID_{R_j}||TS||g^b||g^{ab})$. If the verification is successful, V_{pi} accepts R_j.

3.2.2   Tracking Algorithm

Once a dispute occurs on an access request during the authentication, the SGSA is equipped with an algorithm for tracking the corresponding vehicle of the disputed access request message. When any vehicle in the platoon raises doubts about one access request, it can track the suspected vehicle's identity related to the disputed access request message. This process can be divided into two phases:

- *Tracking*: Given a disputed $\sigma = (g', y', S)$, message M_{pi}, the group public key $Y_{[t]} = (\hat{y}_{[t]}, Z_{[t]})$ and the tracing trapdoor $\hat{X}_{[t]}$, any vehicle in the platoon can proceed as follows:
  - checks if the disputed $\sigma = (g', y', S)$ is valid;
  - computes $V_1 = g'^{\hat{x}_{[t]}}$ and $z_{i[t]} = \frac{y'}{V_1}$;
  - checks $z_{i[t]} \overset{?}{\in} Y_{[t]}$;

  If and only if all checks are successful, this phase outputs the suspected vehicle's $z_{i[t]}$ (or its real identity) and a proof (V_1, V_2), where V_2 is the zero-knowledge proof that V_1 equals to the $\hat{y}_{[t]}$-part of y', i.e., $V_1 = \hat{y}_{[t]}^r$; otherwise the algorithm fails.
- *Verifying*: Given a disputed $\sigma = (g', y', S)$, message M_{pi}, the group public key $Y_{[t]} = (\hat{y}_{[t]}, Z_{[t]})$ and the proof (V_1, V_2), any vehicle in the platoon can proceed as follows:
  - checks if the disputed $\sigma = (g', y', S)$ is valid;
  - checks $y' \overset{?}{=} V_1 z_{i[t]}$;
  - verifies V_2.

It outputs 1 if and only if all checks and verifications are successful; otherwise the algorithm fails.

4   Security Analysis

In this section, we analyze the security properties of our proposed SGSA. First, our proposed scheme satisfies the democratic group signature properties. Especially, we are most concerned with the following two security aspects, i.e., how SGSA can achieve anonymous authentication and key agreement, and how SGSA can achieve traceability among platoon members.

- *The proposed SGSA scheme can provide strong anonymous mutual authentication and key agreement*

When the vehicle V_{pi} in the platoon visits one social spot S_i, it performs the mutual authentication with the RSU R_j at S_j. V_{pi} first picks up the current times tamp TS, and chooses a random number $a \in_R \mathbb{Z}_q^*$ and computes g^a. Then, V_{pi} generates a signature on a message $M_{pi} = (ID_{platoon}||TS||g^a)$ as $\sigma = (g', y', S)$. Then, V_{pi} sends M_{pi} and $\sigma = (g', y', S)$ to RSU R_j. When RSU R_j receives the M_{pi} and $\sigma = (g', y', S)$, it verifies the validity of the signature.

If the verification is successful, RSU R_j accepts V_{pi} in the platoon without revealing V_{pi}'s real identity. Next, RSU R_j also chooses a random number $b \in_R \mathbb{Z}_q^*$, and computes g^b and $(g^a)^b$. Then, it generates $M_{R_j} = (ID_{R_j}||TS||g^b)$, and returns back $H(ID_{R_j}||TS||g^b||g^{ab})$ and M_{R_j} to V_{pi}. V_{pi} computes $(g^b)^a$ and verifies $H(ID_{R_j}||TS||g^b||g^{ab})$. If the verification is successful, V_{pi} accepts R_j, and authentication and key agreement finishes. Basically our key agreement is the same as in Diffie-Hellman key exchange. However, MitM attacker is prevented because we design our scheme followed by SIGn-and-MAc (SIGMA) [3], which is a provable secure and efficient DH key exchange approach proposed by Krawczyk. The proposed SGSA scheme can provide anonymous authentication and key agreement, and resist MitM attack by combining the democratic group signatures.

- *The proposed SGSA scheme can provide an efficient user tracking function*

Once a dispute occurs on an access request during the authentication, any vehicle in the platoon can raise doubts about one access request and can track the suspected vehicle's identity related to the disputed access request message. This process have been introduced in Sect. 3.2.2. During *Tracking* phase, the vehicle in the platoon can obtain the suspected vehicle's $z_{i[t]}$ (or its real identity) and the corresponding proof (V_1, V_2). During the *Verifying* phase, by using the suspected vehicle's ID and the corresponding proof (V_1, V_2), the vehicle in the platoon can check

- if the disputed $\sigma = (g', y', S)$ is valid;
- $y' \overset{?}{=} V_1 z_{i[t]}$;
- if V_2 is valid.

If all three verification pass, the suspected vehicle's ID is tracked. However, any other vehicle or RSU without trapdoor information cannot trace the platoon member's real identity.

5   Performance Evaluation

In this section, we simulate the computational cost of our proposed SGSA scheme. The time used for the primitive cryptography operations has been measured by using C/C++ OPENSSL library tested on an Celeron 1.1 GHz processor as an OBU and Dual-Core 2.6 GHz as an RSU in reference [4]: T_H^{OBU}=0.0356 ms; T_H^{RSU}=0.0121 ms. T_{PM}^{OBU} = 1.537 ms; T_{PM}^{RSU}=0.475 ms. T_H and T_{PM} represent time cost of hash and time cost of point multiplication, respectively. Moreover, n represents the number of vehicles.

Table 1. Computational cost (ms)

	OBU side	RSU side
AKA procedure	$13T_{PM}^{OBU}+T_H^{OBU}= 20.02$	$(7n+2)T_{PM}^{RSU}+2T_H^{RSU}=3.325n+0.119$
Tracking	$(7n+5)T_{PM}^{OBU}+T_H^{RSU}=10.795n+7.72$	Null

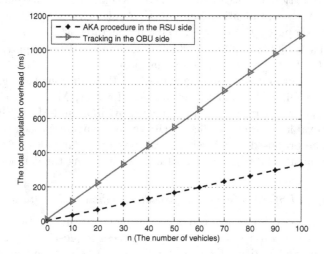

Fig. 3. The computational cost (ms)

The computational cost is shown in Table 1. The computational cost is divided two parts: (1) During authentication and key agreement phase, the OBU needs to compute its own signature, and the RSU needs to verify OBU's signature. In addition, they need to compute the key material for key agreement. The results show that the total computational cost approximately takes 20.02 ms in the OBU side, while takes 3.325n+0.119 ms in the RSU side; (2) During the tracking phase, the OBU needs to take 10.795n+7.72 ms to trace the suspected vehicle's ID. While the RSU does not take any time since it cannot perform tracking procedure. Moreover, we plot Fig. 3 to show that the relationship between computational cost and the number of vehicles in the platoon.

6   Conclusions

In this paper, we have proposed a secure group setup and anonymous authentication scheme in the platoon-based VCPS by using a special group signature technique, named SGSA. The proposed SGSA can securely set up a temporary platoon, and flexibly support platoon merging/platoon splitting. Particularly, once a dispute occurs on an access request during the authentication, any platoon member can trace the corresponding vehicle of the disputed access request message. The security analysis shows that SGSA can achieve anonymous authentication and key agreement, and achieve traceability among platoon members. In our future work, we will study the more efficient and flexible anonymous group setup scheme to support the SGSA.

Acknowledgments. Our research is financially supported by the National Natural Science Foundation of China Research Grant (61272037, 61472472), the International Science and Technology Cooperation and Exchange Plan in Shaanxi Province of China (2015KW-010), and the Natural Science Basic Research Plan in Shaanxi Province of China (2015JQ6236).

References

1. Jia, D., Lu, K., Wang, J., Zhang, X., Shen, X.: A survey on platoon-based vehicular cyber-physical systems. IEEE Communications Surveys & Tutorials, to appear
2. Kim, Y., Perrig, A., Tsudik, G.: Communication-efficient group key agreement. In: Dupuy, M., Paradinas, P. (eds.) Trusted Information. IFIP, pp. 229–244. Springer, Boston (2001)
3. Krawczyk, H.: SIGMA: The 'SIGn-and-MAc' approach to authenticated diffie-hellman and its use in the IKE protocols. In: Boneh, D. (ed.) CRYPTO 2003. LNCS, vol. 2729, pp. 400–425. Springer, Heidelberg (2003)
4. Lai, C., Li, H., Lu, R., Shen, X.S.: SE-AKA: A secure and efficient group authentication and key agreement protocol for LTE networks. Comput. Netw. **57**(17), 3492–3510 (2013)
5. Li, B., Wang, Z., Huang, D.: An efficient and anonymous attribute-based group setup scheme. In: Proceedings of IEEE GLOBECOM, pp. 861–866. IEEE (2013)
6. Lu, R., Lin, X., Shen, X.: Spring: A social-based privacy-preserving packet forwarding protocol for vehicular delay tolerant networks. In: Proceedings of IEEE INFOCOM, pp. 1229–1237 (2010)
7. Lu, R., Lin, X., Zhu, H., Ho, P., Shen, X.: ECPP: Efficient conditional privacy preservation protocol for secure vehicular communications. In: Proceedings of IEEE INFOCOM, pp. 1229–1237 (2008)
8. Luan, T., Shen, X., Bai, F., Sun, L.: Feel bored? join verse! engineering vehicular proximity social network. IEEE Trans. Veh. Technol. **64**(3), 1120–1131 (2015)
9. Luan, T.H., Cai, L.X., Chen, J., Shen, X., Bai, F.: Engineering a distributed infrastructure for large-scale cost-effective content dissemination over urban vehicular networks. IEEE Trans. Veh. Technol. **63**(3), 1419–1435 (2014)
10. Manulis, M.: Democratic group signatures: on an example of joint ventures. In: Proceedings of ASIACCS, pp. 365–365. ACM (2006)
11. Zhou, H., Liu, B., Luan, T.H., Hou, F., Gui, L., Li, Y., Yu, Q., Shen, X.: ChainCluster: engineering a cooperative content distribution framework for highway vehicular communications. IEEE Trans. Intell. Transp. Syst. **15**(6), 2644–2657 (2014)

A Bidder-Oriented Privacy-Preserving VCG Auction Scheme

Maya Larson[1], Ruinian Li[1(✉)], Chunqiang Hu[1], Wei Li[1],
Xiuzhen Cheng[1], and Rongfang Bie[2(✉)]

[1] Department of Computer Science,
The George Washington University, Washington, D.C., USA
{maya_,ruinian,chu,weili,cheng}@gwu.edu
[2] College of Information Science and Technology,
Beijing Normal University, Beijing, China
rfbie@bnu.edu.cn

Abstract. Vickrey-Clarke-Groves (VCG) is a type of sealed-bid auction of multiple items which has good economic properties. However, VCG has security vulnerabilities, e.g. it is vulnerable to auctioneer fraud. To make VCG more practical, bid prices must be well protected. To tackle this challenge, we propose a bidder-oriented, privacy-preserving auction scheme using homomorphic encryption, where the bidders can calculate the results by themselves, and the auctioneer is able to verify the results. Compared to previous research, our scheme is more trustworthy with stronger privacy.

Keywords: Privacy-preserving · Homomorphic encryption · VCG

1 Introduction

Over past years, auctions have been widely applied to real-world applications [1,9,10,12,14,15,21,23], among which VCG is an important auction mechanism which receives a lot of attention. In VCG, bidders submit their sealed bids without knowing other bids, and each bidder is charged its social opportunity cost. It has been proven that VCG has good economic properties of incentive-compatibility, Pareto-efficiency and individual-rationality [11]. Despite its good economic properties, VCG has security vulnerabilities, one of which is auctioneer fraud. For example, if an auctioneer knows the highest bid, he can create a fake bid which is very close to the highest bid, thus gaining more profits.

To tackle this problem, we propose a bidder-oriented privacy-preserving VCG scheme based on homomorphic encryption. In previous work using homomorphic encryption [19,25], the bids are encrypted with the auctioneer's public key, and all the computations are done on the auctioneer's side. This is not secure because the auctioneer has all the information needed to get bidders' information. Different from previous work, we let the bidders calculate the results by themselves, and the auctioneer is only able to verify the results. In our scheme, each bid is

K. Xu and J. Zhu (Eds.): WASA 2015, LNCS 9204, pp. 284–294, 2015.
DOI: 10.1007/978-3-319-21837-3_28

encrypted twice, first by the auctioneer's public key and then a group key. The auctioneer is not able to see the contents of bids without the group key. The computed result can be verified by the auctioneer to make sure that it is correct. Compared to previous work, our scheme provides stronger privacy.

The contribution of this paper can be summarized as follows:

- We propose a bidder-oriented privacy-preserving VCG auction scheme using homomorphic encryption. This scheme achieves high privacy because it does not need a trusted third party. Furthermore, even the auctioneer is not supposed to be trusted in this scheme.
- We analyze the security and privacy protection of our scheme, and discuss how it achieves correctness, confidentiality, and verification.

The remainder of the paper is organized as follows: In Sect. 2, we introduce related work. In Sect. 3, we outline the most important preliminaries. In Sect. 4, we present our scheme in detail. In Sect. 5, we discuss the scheme from the following angles: security analysis, limitations, and how to easily adapt our scheme for a first-price auction. Finally, we give a conclusion in Sect. 6.

2   Related Work

Much work has been done to ensure the security and user privacy of auctions, in which the common cryptographic tools are secret sharing [3,22], homomorphic encryption, and hash functions.

Kobayashi, Morita and Suzuki use hash chains to form a sealed-bid auction [10,23]. H.Kikuchi proposed (m+1)-st price auction with secret sharing, which is a useful cryptographic tool and is utilized in many applications such as body area networks [5,7], attribute-based encryption [6,7], image security [4] and so on. Later, Suzuki and Yokoo combine dynamic programming and secret sharing to build a secure auction scheme [24]. However, the scheme only works in passive adversary models, and the evaluators have to obtain their shares from a third party via a secure channel. Nojoumian et al. applies verifiable secret sharing to construct sealed-bid auctions in [16], but this scheme also requires a secure channel and it can not resist collusion attacks between evaluators and the third parties. Larson et al. [12] present a scheme to secure auctions without an auctioneer via verifiable secret sharing. The scheme can resist passive attacks and collusion attacks and does not require a secure channel. A truthful and privacy preserving auction mechanism called SPRING was proposed in [8], and this scheme introduces a trust-worthy agent to interact with the auctioneer and the bidders. An obvious weakness is that there is a trusted third party in this system.

Leveraging homomorphic encryption to protect bidder's privacy is not a new idea. In [21], Goldwasser-Micali encryption is used to design a new sealed-bid auction. In [1], a secure McAfee double auction scheme is proposed using homomorphic encryption for spectrum auctions. In [20], a new proof technique is explored to improve efficiency and privacy of homomorphic e-auction applications. Larson *et al.* employ homomorphic encryption to protect the security and privacy in first price auctions [13]. There is also some research on leveraging homomorphic encryption to secure VCG, such as [18, 19, 25]. However, in the previous research, all the computations are done on the auctioneer's side, and the auctioneer holds the secret key for decryption. These schemes are not secure unless the auctioneer can be completely trusted.

In this paper, we propose a bidder-oriented privacy-preserving VCG auction scheme using homomorphic encryption. The bidders calculate the final result by themselves, and the auctioneer decrypts this result and broadcasts it to the bidders. During this process, the auctioneer does not need to have the bids, thus the privacy of the bidders is highly protected. Furthermore, the results from the bidders can be verified. The correctness of the scheme is determined by the majority of the bidders.

3   Preliminaries

3.1   Homomorphic Encryption

Homomorphic encryption is an important cryptographic primitive where the computation party can operate on the ciphertext, without seeing the contents of the plaintext. In our scheme, we adopt multiplicative homomorphic encryption, such as pallier cryptosystem [17] and ElGamal cryptosystem [2]. More generally, given an encryption function E, $E(x_1 \cdot x_2) = E(x_1) \cdot E(x_2)$. With this property, encrypted data could be processed without knowing the plaintext. Furthermore, different ciphertexts from the same plaintext are indistinguishable, which means that no one can succeed in distinguishing the corresponding plaintext with a probability much higher than $1/2$. With these properties, Pallier or ElGamal cryptosystem are fit for privacy-preserving systems.

3.2   VCG Auction

In this subsection, we explain the details of VCG auction.

We consider a market with a set of g goods: $G = 1, 2, 3, ...i...g$, and a set of of b bidders: $B = \{1, 2, 3, ...i...b\}$. Consequently, the set of allocations of goods G to bidders in B is denoted as: $S = \{A : B \to G\}$. Suppose the bidder i's evaluation function is b_i where $b_i = S \to Z^+$, then bidder i's bid value for each assignment is denoted as $b_i(A)$. Therefore, $b_i(S)$ represents the set of bid i's bid values for all possible allocations:

$$b_i(S) = \{b_i(S_1), b_i(S_2), b_i(S_3), ..., b_i(S_{|S|})\}, \tag{1}$$

where $|S|$ is the number of allocations in the auction.

At the beginning of the auction, each bidder submits his bid b_i to the auctioneer. Based on the VCG auction mechanism, the auctioneer determines the allocation and the clearing prices by the following procedures:

1. *Finding the maximum sum of bid values:* The auctioneer reveals the sealed bid values and determines the allocation that can achieve the maximum sum of bid values, which is denoted as S^*.
2. *Computation of the clearing prices:* We use p_i to denote the clearing price of bidder i for $1 \leq i \leq b$:

$$p_i = \max \sum_{j \neq i} b_j(S) - \sum_{j \neq i} b_j(S^*), \qquad (2)$$

in which $\max \sum_{j \neq i} b_j(S)$ is the maximum sum of bid values when bidder i does not join the auction, and $\sum_{j \neq i} b_j(S^*)$ is the sum of bid values for allocation S^* without bidder i's value. Note that p_i is the so-called "social opportunity cost".

In VCG, as long as the optimal solution S^* is obtained, incentive-compatibility can be guaranteed; that is, for any bidder, the optimal strategy is bidding its true bid value [11]. Thus, by adopting VCG, we simply assume that each bidder submits its true valuation in the auction.

4 Proposed Scheme

4.1 Requirements

The system for a privacy-preserving auction should meet the following requirements:

1. *Correctness:* The computation result must be correct, and strictly follow the policy of VCG scheme. This should be verifiable.
2. *Confidentiality:* Users' bid values must be encrypted such that neither the auctioneer nor the other bidders can see the original prices.
3. *Verification:* The correctness of the result can be verified, and fake messages from bidders can be detected.

Correctness is the basic requirement, which means that the auction result must strictly follow the policy of VCG. Confidentiality is to guarantee that bidders' privacy is well protected. To achieve this goal, the bids will be encrypted twice with the auctioneer's public key and a group key of the bidders. In this way, the bidders can share their bids for computation, but they still can not see the contents because they are encrypted by the auctioneer's key.

4.2 Basic Idea

We utilize a key generation center (KGC) to assign group key k_g to a group of bidders before the auction itself. The KGC also assigns a pair of asymmetric keys k_p and k_s to the auctioneer, and broadcasts the public key k_p to the group of bidders. Each bidder i will first encrypt his own bid using the auctioneers' public key k_p, then encrypt the bid again using the group key k_g. The encrypted message $E_{k_g}(E_{k_p}(b_i))$ will be shared among this group. Each bidder can decrypt the message received from other bidders, and get $E_{k_p}(b_i)$, but they can not decrypt $E_{k_p}(b_i)$ as they do not know the private key of the auctioneer. Then each bidder is able to perform a computation to find the allocation where the sum of the bidding price is maximized based on the homomorphic property, and sends the result to the auctioneer for decryption. The auctioneer will decrypt the message from the bidders and broadcast the result, S^*. Once the result is received from the auctioneer, the bidders use the maximum allocation S^* to perform another homomorphic computation to find the final allocation according to the VCG scheme. Then the bidders send the encrypted results to the auctioneer for decryption. The auctioneer then decrypts the message and obtains the final allocation result.

During this process, the auctioneer is only responsible for decryption, which is the most complicated and time-consuming step. The key characteristic is that the auctioneer only receives the encrypted results which have been processed, rather than the original bid prices. The bidders are responsible for performing homomorphic computations twice during this process. If we suppose there are n bidders in this system, then there will be n copies of results sent to the auctioneer, thus the auctioneer will be able to verify the correctness of the result by checking that the n copies are consistent. In general, the correctness of the system is guaranteed by the whole group of bidders, not a single trusted individual. We assume there is no collusion between the auctioneer and bidders: In this system, each bidder is bidding his true value, and neither the auctioneer nor the bidder know the other bidder's bids. Thus a bidder should not be willing to risk colluding with the auctioneer.

4.3   Proposed Scheme

System Model. There are three phases: the system initialization, the bidding process, and the computation process. The system model is described in Fig. 1: The KGC constructs a group key and a pair of asymmetric keys. It then sends the secret key k_s to the auctioneer, and sends the public key k_p and the group key k_g to the group of bidders. The bidders in this group share each other's information; all the bidders are able to communicate with the auctioneer.

System Initialization

1. KGC constructs a group key k_g and a pair of asymmetric keys in preparation of an auction. Suppose there are n bidders in an auction.
2. The bidders who want to take part in the auction contact the KGC for a registration, and obtain the the group key k_g .
3. The KGC assigns the secret key k_s to the auctioneer and broadcasts the public key k_p to the group of bidders.
4. The auctioneer publishes the set of possible allocations S.

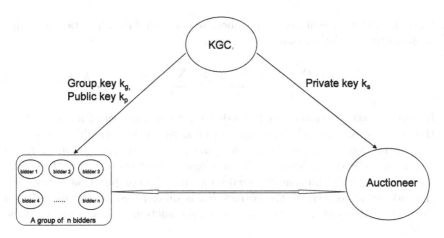

Fig. 1. System Model

Bidding Process

1. Each bidder first applies Pallier or ElGamal method to encrypt his bids using the public key of the auctioneer k_p, then encrypts the bids again using the group keyK_g.

$$E_{k_g}(E_{k_p}(b_i(S))) = E_{k_g}((E_{k_p}(b_i(S_1)), E_{k_p}(b_i(S_2)), E_{k_p}(b_i(S_3)), ...,$$
$$E_{k_g}(b_i(S_{|S|}))), 1 \leq i \leq n \qquad (3)$$

2. The bidders share their encrypted bids with the other bidders in the same group. Then each bidder decrypts the message received from the others using the group key and obtains $E_{k_p}(b_i)$, where

$$E_{k_p}(b_i(S)) = \{(E_{k_p}(b_i(S_1)), E_{k_p}(b_i(S_2)), E_{k_p}(b_i(S_3)), ...,$$
$$E_{k_p}(b_i(S_{|S|})\}, 1 \leq i \leq n \qquad (4)$$

Computation Process

1. Each bidder computes $\prod_{i=1}^{n} E_{k_p}(b_i(S))$, and sends this set to the auctioneer.
2. The auctioneer decrypts the message from the bidders, and obtains:

$$D_{k_s}(\prod_{i=1}^{n} E_{k_p}(b_i(S))) = D_{k_s}(\prod_{i=1}^{n} E_{k_p}(b_i(S_1)), \prod_{i=1}^{n} E_{k_p}(b_i(S_2)), \prod_{i=1}^{n} E_{k_p}(b_i(S_3)), ...,$$
$$\prod_{i=1}^{n} E_{k_p}(b_i(S_{|S|}))$$
$$= (\sum_{i=1}^{n} b_i(S_1), \sum_{i=1}^{n} b_i(S_2), \sum_{i=1}^{n} b_i(S_3), ..., \sum_{i=1}^{n} b_i(S_{|S|}) \qquad (5)$$

3. Once the plaintext is obtained, the auctioneer can find the allocation S^* which achieves the maximum sum of bid values:

$$S^* = argmax\{\sum_{i=1}^{n} b_i(S_1), \sum_{i=1}^{n} b_i(S_2), \sum_{i=1}^{n} b_i(S_3), ..., \sum_{i=1}^{n} b_i(S_{|S|})\} \quad (6)$$

In this step, the auctioneer only needs to decrypt a subset of messages from the group of bidders. The strategy can be designed in a flexible way by the auctioneer; when the auctioneer decrypts a sufficient proportion of the n messages and gets consistent results, it is reasonable to believe that the results are accurate. This solution will guarantee that the computation result from the bidders is correct, as the correctness is determined by the majority of the group. After obtaining the correct S^*, the auctioneer broadcasts it to the bidders.

4. Once the bidders obtain S^*, they will continue computation according to the VCG scheme. Here, we use Δp_i to denote a set of possible prices that the bidder should pay.

$$E_{k_p}(\Delta p_i) = \frac{\prod_{j \neq i} E_{k_p}(b_j(S))}{\prod_{j \neq i} E_{k_p}(b_j(S^*))}$$

$$= (\frac{\prod_{j \neq i} E_{k_p}(b_j(S_1))}{\prod_{j \neq i} E_{k_p}(b_j(S^*))}, \frac{\prod_{j \neq i} E_{k_p}(b_j(S_2))}{\prod_{j \neq i} E_{k_p}(b_j(S^*))}, \frac{\prod_{j \neq i} E_{k_p}(b_j(S_3))}{\prod_{j \neq i} E_{k_p}(b_j(S^*))}, ...,$$

$$\frac{\prod_{j \neq i} E_{k_p}(b_j(S_{|S|}))}{\prod_{j \neq i} E_{k_p}(b_j(S^*))}) \quad (7)$$

Then the computation results from all the bidders will be sent to the auctioneer again for decryption.

5. The auctioneer decrypts the message, and obtains:

$$\Delta p_i = D_{k_s}(\frac{\prod_{j \neq i} E_{k_p}(b_j(S_1))}{\prod_{j \neq i} E_{k_p}(b_j(S^*))}, \frac{\prod_{j \neq i} E_{k_p}(b_j(S_2))}{\prod_{j \neq i} E_{k_p}(b_j(S^*))}, \frac{\prod_{j \neq i} E_{k_p}(b_j(S_3))}{\prod_{j \neq i} E_{k_p}(b_j(S^*))}, ...,$$

$$\frac{\prod_{j \neq i} E_{k_p}(b_j(S_{|S|}))}{\prod_{j \neq i} E_{k_p}(b_j(S^*))})$$

$$= \sum_{j \neq i} b_j(S) - \sum_{j \neq i} b_j(S^*) \quad (8)$$

6. The auctioneer finds the maximum value in this set, which is the price that bidder i would pay:

$$p_i = max\{\Delta p_i\} = max\{\sum_{j \neq i} b_j(S) - \sum_{j \neq i} b_j(S^*)\}$$

$$= max \sum_{j \neq i} b_j(S) - \sum_{j \neq i} b_j(S^*), \qquad (9)$$

7. The auctioneer broadcasts the results. The winners pay the auctioneer and receive the corresponding goods.

5 Discussion

5.1 Correctness

The proposed scheme follows the VCG scheme strictly and the result is correct. In this scheme, the computations are processed on the bidder's side, and the auctioneer is able to decrypt the messages from the bidders and get the result. Unless a large proportion of bidders collude and send the identical wrong results to the auctioneer, the fake result can be detected by the auctioneer. It is reasonable to assume that most of the bidders are honest, and therefore the correctness is guaranteed.

5.2 Security Analysis

Confidentiality. The bidding prices are encrypted twice: first using the auctioneer's public key, and then using the group key. The bidders cannot see the bids of other bidders because they do not have the auctioneer's private key to decrypt the message. The auctioneer cannot see the original contents of the bids because all the messages sent to the auctioneer have been processed. In this way, the confidentiality of the bids is well protected.

Verification. Verification can be achieved in our scheme. As discussed above, the auctioneer can verify the correctness of the computation from the bidders because he receives n copies of results instead of one. Thus the result's correctness is based on the majority of the bidders. Unless the majority of the bidders are cheating in this auction, the correct result will be obtained by the auctioneer.

5.3 First-Price Auction

Our proposed scheme can be easily applied to a first-price auction and still maintains correctness, confidentiality and verification. Notice that the third step of our computation process is to find the allocation S^* which maximizes the sum of bid values. This result indicates the clearing prices for all bidders, as the clearing price of each winner is the amount he bids for the item. Specifically, bidder i will know whether he wins an item and how much he should pay for this auction based on S^*. Furthermore, non-repudiation is easy to achieve in this process.

For example, suppose the final result shows that bidder i should pay 500 dollars for one item, but bidder i denies that he did bid 500 dollars. Then the auctioneer can request the other bidders to reveal this bidder's original bids and check if it is 500 dollars. Intuitively, this system is under surveillance of all the bidders. In this system, a dishonest bidder can be spotted by the auctioneer and proved to be cheating by other bidders. Unless all other bidders help this dishonest bidder, the auctioneer's profit will be protected. Therefore, non-repudiation can be achieved because none of the bidders in the system is able to deny his behavior.

5.4 Limitation

One limitation of our scheme is that it introduces more computations compared to [25], because all the bidders need to perform the computation. However, our scheme offers much higher security levels and brings more trustworthy results to the bidders. This is a trade-off between bidder's privacy and computation efficiency. To alleviate the problem, the bidders could employ a cloud processor to do the computations.

6 Conclusion and Future Work

In this paper, we propose a bidder-oriented privacy-preserving VCG auction scheme using homomorphic encryption. This scheme achieves strong privacy by letting the bidders calculate the auction result. The auctioneer gets the final result and is able to verify the correctness. Furthermore, the correctness of this scheme is based on the majority of the bidders, not a trusted party, and all bidder's information is highly protected. Our future research lies in designing a more efficient mechanism to ensure bidders' privacy and data security in VCG auction, which will work better in practical applications.

Acknowledgment. The authors would like to thank all the reviewers for their helpful comments. This project was supported by the US National Science Foundation (ECCS-1407986, AST-1443858, CNS-1265311, and CNS-1162057), and the National Natural Science Foundation of China (61171014).

References

1. Chen, Z., Huang, L., Li, L., Yang, W., Miao, H., Tian, M., Wang, F.: Ps-trust: provably secure solution for truthful double spectrum auctions. In: 2014 IEEE Proceedings on INFOCOM, pp. 1249–1257. IEEE (2014)
2. El Gamal, T.: A public key cryptosystem and a signature scheme based on discrete logarithms. In: Blakely, G.R., Chaum, D. (eds.) CRYPTO 1984. LNCS, vol. 196, pp. 10–18. Springer, Heidelberg (1985)

3. Hu, C., Liao, X., Cheng, X.: Verifiable multi-secret sharing based on LFSR sequences. Theor. Comput. Sci. **445**, 52–62 (2012)
4. Hu, C., Liao, X., Xiao, D.: Secret image sharing based on chaotic map and Chinese remainder theorem. Int. J. Wavelets Multiresolut. Inf. Process. **10**(03), 1250023 (1–18) (2012)
5. Hu, C., Zhang, F., Cheng, X., Liao, X., Chen, D.: Securing communications between external users and wireless body area networks. In: Proceedings of the 2nd ACM workshop on Hot topics on wireless network security and privacy, pp. 31–36. ACM (2013)
6. Hu, C., Zhang, F., Xiang, T., Li, H., Xiao, X., Huang, G.: A practically optimized implementation of attribute based cryptosystems. In: 2014 IEEE 13th International Conference on Trust, Security and Privacy in Computing and Communications (TrustCom), pp. 197–204. IEEE (2014)
7. Hu, C., Zhang, N., Li, H., Cheng, X., Liao, X.: Body area network security: a fuzzy attribute-based signcryption scheme. IEEE J. Sel. Areas Commun. **31**(9), 37–46 (2013)
8. Huang, Q., Tao, Y., Wu, F.: Spring: a strategy-proof and privacy preserving spectrum auction mechanism. In: 2013 IEEE Proceedings on INFOCOM, pp. 827–835. IEEE (2013)
9. Jing, T., Zhao, C., Xing, X., Huo, Y., Li, W., Cheng, X.: A multi-unit truthful double auction framework for secondary market. In: IEEE ICC (2013)
10. Kobayashi, K., Morita, H., Suzuki, K., Hakuta, M.: Efficient sealed-bid auction by using one-way functions. IEICE Trans. Fundam. Electron. Commun. Comput. Sci. **84**(1), 289–294 (2001)
11. Krishna, V.: Auction theory. Academic press, San Diego (2009)
12. Larson, M., Hu, C., Li, R., Li, W., Cheng, X.: Secure auctions without an auctioneer via verifiable secret sharing. In: Workshop on Privacy-Aware Mobile Computing (PAMCO) 2015 In conjunction with ACM MobiHoc 2015. ACM, pp. 1–6 (2015)
13. Larson, M., Li, W., Hu, C., Li, R., Cheng, X.: A secure multi-unit sealed first-price auction mechanism. In: The 10th International Conference on Wireless Algorithms, Systems, and Applications (WASA 2015), vol. 9204, pp. 295–304. Springer, Heidelberg (2015)
14. Li, W., Cheng, X., Bie, R., Zhao, F.: An extensible and flexible truthful auction framework for heterogeneous spectrum markets. In: ACM MobiHoc, pp. 175–184. Philadelphia, USA, August 2014
15. Li, W., Wang, S., Cheng, X., Bie, R.: Truthful multi-attribute auction with discriminatory pricing in cognitive radio networks. ACM SIGMOBILE Mob. Comput. Commun. Rev. **18**(1), 3–13 (2014)
16. Nojoumian, M., Stinson, D.R.: Efficient sealed-bid auction protocols using verifiable secret sharing. In: Huang, X., Zhou, J. (eds.) ISPEC 2014. LNCS, vol. 8434, pp. 302–317. Springer, Heidelberg (2014)
17. Paillier, P.: Public-key cryptosystems based on composite degree residuosity classes. In: Stern, J. (ed.) EUROCRYPT 1999. LNCS, vol. 1592, pp. 223–238. Springer, Heidelberg (1999)
18. Pan, M., Sun, J., Fang, Y.: Purging the back-room dealing: secure spectrum auction leveraging paillier cryptosystem. IEEE J. Sel. Areas Commun. **29**(4), 866–876 (2011)
19. Pan, M., Zhu, X., Fang, Y.: Using homomorphic encryption to secure the combinatorial spectrum auction without the trustworthy auctioneer. Wirel. Netw. **18**(2), 113–128 (2012)

20. Peng, K.: Efficient proof of bid validity with untrusted verifier in homomorphic e-auction. IET Inf. Secur. **7**(1), 11–21 (2013)
21. Peng, K., Boyd, C., Dawson, E.: A multiplicative homomorphic sealed-bid auction based on goldwasser-micali encryption. In: Zhou, J., López, J., Deng, R.H., Bao, F. (eds.) ISC 2005. LNCS, vol. 3650, pp. 374–388. Springer, Heidelberg (2005)
22. Shamir, A.: How to share a secret. Commun. ACM **22**(11), 612–613 (1979)
23. Suzuki, K., Kobayashi, K., Morita, H.: Efficient sealed-bid auction using hash chain. In: Won, D. (ed.) ICISC 2000. LNCS, vol. 2015, pp. 183–191. Springer, Heidelberg (2001)
24. Suzuki, K., Yokoo, M.: Secure combinatorial auctions by dynamic programming with polynomial secret sharing. In: Blaze, M. (ed.) FC 2002. LNCS, vol. 2357, pp. 44–56. Springer, Heidelberg (2003)
25. Suzuki, K., Yokoo, M.: Secure generalized vickrey auction using homomorphic encryption. In: Wright, R.N. (ed.) FC 2003. LNCS, vol. 2742, pp. 239–249. Springer, Heidelberg (2003)

A Secure Multi-unit Sealed First-Price Auction Mechanism

Maya Larson[1], Wei Li[1]([✉]), Chunqiang Hu[1], Ruinian Li[1],
Xiuzhen Cheng[1], and Rongfang Bie[2]([✉])

[1] Department of Computer Science,
The George Washington University, Washington DC, USA
{maya_,weili,chu,ruinian,cheng}@gwu.edu
[2] College of Information Science and Technology,
Beijing Normal University, Beijing, China
rfbie@bnu.edu.cn

Abstract. Due to the popularity of auction mechanisms in real-world applications and the increase in the awareness of securing private information, auctions are in dire need of bid-privacy protection. In this paper, we deliberately design a secure multi-unit sealed-bid first-price auction scheme, in which the auction is processed on the bidders' encrypted bids by the server and the final output is only known by the auctioneer. As a result, neither the auctioneer nor the server can obtain the full information of the bidders. What's more, the auctioneer can verify whether a winner pays its full payment in the auction. Finally, a comprehensive analysis on the performance of our auction mechanism is conducted.

Keywords: Secure auction · Bid-privacy preserving · Sealed-bid first-price auction · Homomorphic encryption

1 Introduction

In past decades, auction mechanisms have been a particularly successful application of game theory to the real world, with its uses ranging from eBay auctions on personal items, such as phones and laptops, to those which sell treasury bonds, rights to use radio spectrums, and schedule and allocate transportation routes.

Typically, an auction is centrally controlled by an auctioneer and bidders are supposed to faithfully reveal their valuations of the goods in the auction [9,10, 15,16]. However, the true valuations of goods are the private information of the bidders. Therefore, a secure auction must preserve the bid-privacy as once the valuations are revealed to an insincere auctioneer, it may exploit such knowledge for its own benefit either in future auctions or by reneging on the sale [17]. Sealed-bid auctions prevent releasing private information to other bidders, but not the auctioneer, who keeps the information in hand even after the auction. With such information, the auctioneer can commit fraud by overcharging/underpaying the winning buyers/sellers with a forged price for its personal monetary gain.

© Springer International Publishing Switzerland 2015
K. Xu and J. Zhu (Eds.): WASA 2015, LNCS 9204, pp. 295–304, 2015.
DOI: 10.1007/978-3-319-21837-3_29

Therefore, it is critical to design privacy-preserving auctions to protect the bid privacy and secure the auction. For this purpose, a number of secure auctions have been proposed [2,8,11,13,18,20,21,23]. However, there are still some weaknesses in these approaches. For example, in [20], the auctioneer can decrypt all bidder's bids as the bids are encrypted with the auctioneer's public key; in [8], the auctioneer can know the bids of all buyer groups and their ranking order in the auction.

In this paper, we propose a secure multi-unit sealed-bid first-price auction with homogeneous and heterogeneous goods. In our auction framework, a trust-worthy server is brought to compute the auction results for the auctioneer so that the auctioneer only knows the final auction result without awareness of the other bidders' bids. Since the server carries out computation on the encrypted bids, it learns nothing about the bidders' actual bids. In this way, the bidders' bid can be preserved. Moreover, the auctioneer can verify whether a winner pays the full payment for its allocated goods.

The rest of this paper is organized as follows. Section 2 briefly summarizes related work. Section 3 introduces the preliminaries about the sealed-bid first-price auction and the homomorphic cryptosystem. Our auction model and auction scheme are presented in Sects. 4 and 5, respectively. After analyzing the auction performance in Sect. 6, this paper is concluded in Sect. 7.

2   Related Work

In auction mechanisms, bid privacy is mainly protected via cryptographic tools, such as symmetric encryption, homomorphic encryption, and secret sharing [3, 22], etc.

By introducing a trust-worthy party in the auction, [2,8] propose secure McAfee-based double auctions such that no party in the auction has the knowledge to obtain any sensitive information. Their major difference is that [8] employs the order preserving encryption and the oblivious transfer and [2] utilizes the Paillier cryptosystem. In [20,21], the authors mask the bidding prices with a vector of ciphertext, and ensure that the auctioneer can find the maximum value, randomize the bids, and charge the bidders securely based on homomorphic encryption. However, in [20], the auctioneer can decrypt all bidder's bids, because the bids are encrypted with the auctioneer's public key; in [8], the auctioneer can know the bids of all buyer groups and their ranking order in the auctions.

In [11,14,23], the authors hide bidding prices with secret sharing, which is a useful cryptographic tool and is utilized in many applications such as body area networks [5,7], attribute-based encryption [6,7], image security [4] and so on. However, there are two shortcomings in [11]: (i) the scheme can not handle relationships among multiple winners; and (ii) it is not computationally efficient. In [23], the authors hide the bids as the degree of polynomials. However, this scheme is limited to the passive adversary model, and the evaluators have to obtain their shares from a third party via a secure channel, so this scheme can not resist collusion attacks. Therefore, this scheme is not practical. In [18], the authors apply verifiable secret sharing to construct sealed-bid auctions. The scheme provides verification to resist collusion attacks among the evaluators. Because the evaluators obtain their secret shares from a third party via a private secure channel, the scheme is vulnerable to collusion attacks between evaluators and the third party. We present a scheme to secure auctions without an auctioneer via verifiable secret sharing in our pervious work [13], which can resist passive attacks and collusion attacks and not require a secure channel.

3 Preliminaries

3.1 Sealed First-Price Auction

The sealed first-price auction is an efficient auction [1,12]. In a multi-unit sealed auction, all bidders simultaneously submit their sealed bids to the auctioneer in advance of a deadline, without knowledge of any of their opponents' bids. After the deadline, the auctioneer unseals the bids and determines the clearing price at which demand equals supply. Each bidder wins the quantity demanded at the clearing price and pays the payment that he bids for the corresponding units of the goods.

This type of auction is used for refinancing credit and foreign exchange. The U.S. Treasury uses the sealed first-price auction to sell most of the treasury bills, notes, and bonds that finance the national debt of the United States.

3.2 Homomorphic Encryption

Homomorphic encryption is a form of encryption that enables the decrypted result computed on the ciphertext to match the result calculated on the plaintext. In addition, we require that such a homomorphic encryption is randomized and indistinguishable.

- **Paillier Cryptosystem**
  In this paper, we adopt a Paillier cryptosystem [19], (G, E, D), in which G is the key generation algorithm, E is the encryption algorithm, and D is the decryption algorithm. The Paillier cryptosystem works as follows [19]:
  (i) *Key Generation G*: Set $n = pq$ and $\lambda = \text{lcm}(p-1, q-1)$ where p and q are two large primes and lcm represents the least common multiple. Select a random number $g \in \mathbb{Z}_{n^2}^*$, such that $\gcd(L(g^\lambda \bmod n^2), n) = 1$, in which $L(\cdot)$ is function defined as $L(k) = (k-1)/n$. The public and the private keys are (n, g) and (p, q), respectively.
  (ii) *Encryption E*: Let m be the plaintext and $r \in \mathbb{Z}_n^*$ be a random number, the ciphertext c is

  $$c = E(m, r) = g^m \cdot r^n \quad \bmod n^2.$$

  (iii) *Decryption D*: For a ciphertext, the corresponding plaintext can be decrypted as

  $$m = D(c) = \frac{L(c^\lambda \bmod n^2)}{L(g^\lambda \bmod n^2)} \quad \bmod n.$$

The Paillier encryption has randomizability, indistinguishability, and the following *homomorphic properties*:

$$D(E(m_1, r_1)E(m_2, r_2) \mod n^2) = m_1 + m_2 \mod n,$$

where m_1 and m_2 are two plaintexts, and r_1 and r_2 are two random numbers.

– **Encrypted Vector**

For a vector $x_i = (x_{i1}, x_{i2}, \ldots, x_{ik})$, its ciphertext is represented as follows:

$$\mathbf{e}(x_i) = (e_{i1}, e_{i2}, \ldots, e_{im}) = (E(x_{i1}), E(x_{i2}), \ldots, E(x_{ik})).$$

Since E is indistinguishable, we cannot identify the value of x_i without decrypting each element. Accordingly, the component-wise product of $\mathbf{e}(x_1)$ and $\mathbf{e}(x_2)$ is

$$\mathbf{e}(x_1)\mathbf{e}(x_2) = (e_{11}e_{21}, e_{12}e_{22}, \ldots, e_{1k}e_{2k}).$$

For a general case, we have

$$\prod_i \mathbf{e}(x_i) = (\prod_i \mathbf{e}(x_{i1}), \prod_i \mathbf{e}(x_{i2}), \ldots, \prod_i \mathbf{e}(x_{ik}))$$
$$= (\prod_i E(x_{i1}), \prod_i E(x_{i2}), \ldots, \prod_i E(x_{ik})). \tag{1}$$

4   Auction Model

We consider a market with a set of homogeneous goods denoted by $\mathcal{Q}$ ($|\mathcal{Q}| = Q$), in which a set of bidders denoted by $\mathcal{M}$ ($|\mathcal{M}| = M$) bid for the goods, an auctioneer takes charge of the auction process, and a server performs the computations. From the original sealed first-price auction, we can see that the auctioneer can know all bidders' information, which is a risk to bidder's privacy. Thus, to prevent information leakage in the auction, we employ the server to calculate the auction result for the auctioneer.

The homogeneity of all goods means that each individual good is identical and that all goods have the exactly same characteristics. Consequently, bids can be expressed in terms of prices that the bidder is willing to pay for various quantities of units of the homogeneous goods, without indicating the identity of the particular good that is desired. Formally, let $\mathcal{M}^{\mathcal{Q}} = \{A : \mathcal{Q} \longrightarrow \mathcal{M}\}$ be the set of allocations of goods $\mathcal{Q}$ to bidders $\mathcal{M}$.

Suppose that bidder i's evaluation function is $f_i : \mathcal{M}^{\mathcal{Q}} \longrightarrow \mathbb{Z}^+$; that is, for each assignment $A \in \mathcal{M}^{\mathcal{Q}}$, bidder i's bid value is $b_i(A)$. For any bidder i, f_i is private and is not revealed to others. In addition, any bidder i's evaluation function is independent to others, implying that bidder i decides the function f_i by himself without any influence from others.

Different from some previous work that considers the third party is trustworthy, the auctioneer and the server in our model may be adversaries who intend to steal bidders' private information. Therefore, our main idea to preserve privacy is that the auctioneer only knows the winners and their payments, and that the server only processes the calculation without learning bidders' information.

5   Secure Auction Mechanism

In this section, we propose a secure multi-unit sealed first-price auction mechanism, in which there are five major stages: *initiation*, *bidding*, *computation*, *winner determination*, and *payoff*. An overview of our auction mechanism is presented in Fig. 1.

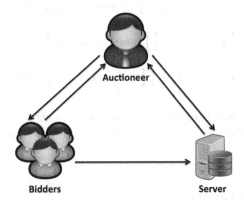

Fig. 1. An overview of the proposed auction mechanism.

As shown in Fig. 1, all necessary information is prepared at the initiation stage. Then, the server receives the encrypted bids from all bidders, computes the auction results, and sends the encrypted results to the auctioneer. Based on the results, the auctioneer determines the winners and assignments. Finally, all winners pays the payments to the auctioneer. In addition, the auctioneer can verify whether a winner pays the full payment with the help of the server. Note that in this paper, we assume that there is no collusion activity among the bidders, the auctioneer, and the server in the auction.

5.1   Initiation

The auctioneer generates its secret and public keys of homomorphic encryption E via G, and publishes the corresponding public key based on E. It also announces the set of possible assignments $\mathcal{M}^Q$ to all buyers.

At the same time, the server also generates its secret key K_s based on RSA public-key cryptosystem, and public key K_p, and announces K_p.

5.2 Bidding

Each bidder i encrypts the bid value $b_i = (b_i(A_1), b_i(A_2), \ldots, b_i(A_{|\mathcal{M}^Q|}))$ by using Paillier encryption E first and then the server's public key K_p, outputs $K_p(\mathbf{e}(b_i))$, and sends $K_p(\mathbf{e}(b_i))$ to the server directly. Since each bid value vector b_i is encrypted twice and there is no collusion between the auctioneer and the server, neither the auctioneer nor the server can learn the actual value of b_i.

5.3 Computation

After receiving the encrypted bid values from all bidders, the server decrypts $K_p(\mathbf{e}(b_i))$ for $1 \leq i \leq M$ with its secret key K_s, gets $\mathbf{e}(b_i)$, and calculates the sum of bid values for each assignment in $\mathcal{M}^Q$ as follows:

$$\prod_i \mathbf{e}(b_i) = (\prod_i \mathbf{e}(b_i(A_1)), \prod_i \mathbf{e}(b_i(A_2)), \ldots, \prod_i \mathbf{e}(b_i(A_{|\mathcal{M}^Q|})))$$

$$= (\prod_i E(b_i(A_1)), \prod_i E(b_i(A_2)), \ldots, \prod_i E(b_i(A_{|\mathcal{M}^Q|}))). \qquad (2)$$

As the server cannot decrypt the homomorphic encryption, it cannot know any information of the result. Then, the server sends the result of $\prod_i \mathbf{e}(b_i)$ to the auctioneer.

5.4 Winner Determination

The auctioneer performs the decryption on $\prod_i \mathbf{e}(b_i)$ and obtains:

$$D(\prod_i \mathbf{e}(b_i) \mod n^2) = (D(\prod_i \mathbf{e}(b_i(A_1)) \mod n^2), \ldots, D(\prod_i \mathbf{e}(b_i(A_{|\mathcal{M}^Q|})) \mod n^2))$$

$$= (\sum_i b_i(A_1) \mod n, \ldots, \sum_i b_i(A_{|\mathcal{M}^Q|}) \mod n)$$

$$= (\sum_i b_i(A_1), \ldots, \sum_i b_i(A_{|\mathcal{M}^Q|})). \qquad (3)$$

According to the decrypted result, the auctioneer selects the maximum value, Sum^*, and the corresponding assignment A^*, i.e.,

$$Sum^* = \max\{\sum_i b_i(A_1), \sum_i b_i(A_2), \ldots, \sum_i b_i(A_{|\mathcal{M}^Q|})\},$$

$$A^* = \arg\max\{\sum_i b_i(A_1), \sum_i b_i(A_2), \ldots, \sum_i b_i(A_{|\mathcal{M}^Q|})\}.$$

That is, Sum^* is the maximum sum of bidders' evaluation values, and goods are sold according to A^* in the auction. Furthermore, based on the allocation A^*, the auctioneer can determine the set of winners, $\mathcal{W}$.

5.5   Payoff

The auctioneer announces the winners and the allocation, and collects the payments from all winners. If bidder i is a winner, it pays a price of $b_i(A^*)$ to the auctioneer; otherwise, it pays nothing.

Since the auctioneer only knows the value of Sum^* rather than $b_i(A^*)$ for all winning bidders, the auctioneer cannot judge whether each winner pays a full payment or not. Denote by p_i the payment of bidder i in the auction. If $Sum^* \neq \sum_{i \in W} p_i$, the auctioneer can utilize the following "*payment checking*" process to check whether p_i is equal to $b_i(A^*)$ or not: the auctioneer sends a request to the server, to get $e(b_i(A^*)) = E(b_i(A^*))$ for all $i \in W$; the server returns all required information to the auctioneer; then, the auctioneer decrypts $E(b_i(A^*))$ and obtains $b_i(A^*)$; and the auctioneer can find out which winner does not pay the full price via a comparison.

Example. We use a simple example to demonstrate our auction mechanism. Suppose $Q = 2$, $\mathcal{M} = \{1, 2\}$, and $\mathcal{M}^Q = \{(0, 2), (1, 1), (2, 0)\}$. Two bidders' bids are $b_1 = (0, 3, 5)$ and $b_2 = (4, 3, 0)$, respectively. At the beginning of the auction, these two bidders submit $K_p(\mathbf{e}(b_1))$ and $K_p(\mathbf{e}(b_2))$ to the server. The server decrypts the bids, carries out a computation on the cipertexts $\mathbf{e}(b_1)$ and $\mathbf{e}(b_2)$, and gets the following result:

$$\mathbf{e}(b_1)\mathbf{e}(b_2) = (e(0)e(4), e(3)e(3), e(5)e(0)).$$

Next, the server returns the result to the auctioneer. The auctioneer decrypts the result and gets a vector of $(4, 6, 5)$. Accordingly, the maximum value is $Sum^* = 6$ and the corresponding assignment is $A^* = A_2$; that is, bidders 1 and 2 can respectively win one unit of the goods. Finally, bider 1 pays 3 and bidder 2 pays 3 to the auctioneer.

5.6   Extension to Heterogeneous Markets

Our proposed secure multi-unit sealed first-price auction can be easily extended to a heterogenous market, in which goods have different characteristics. Thus, the assignment considers not only how many units of the goods, but also which units of goods, leading to a larger set of possible assignments $\mathcal{M}^Q$. Except for this, the auction process is the same as that of the proposed secure multi-unit homogeneous sealed first-price auction.

6   Performance Analysis

6.1   Security

In this subsection, we investigate the security issues of our proposed auction mechanism from the following aspects.

Due to the randomizability and the indistinguishability of the encryption E in the Paillier cryptosystem, the same message can be encrypted into different ciphertexts by using different random blinding factors r, indicating that such an encryption scheme can resist dictionary attacks. In addition, since each bidder's bid is a vector and we separately encrypt every element of the bid vector, any bidder's bid vector can be kept secret unless every encrypted element of the bid vector is revealed.

Neither the auctioneer nor the server can learn the full information of bidders. On one hand, the auctioneer knows the final winners and their bids for the allocated goods (not the bid vectors of winners); on the other hand, the server computes the auction result based on the encrypted bids not the plaintexts. As a result, in the collusion-free market, our proposed auction scheme can secure the information of bidders.

The auctioneer can verify the bids of winners with the help of the server. According to the pricing method of the sealed-bid first-price auction, each winner's payment is the bid value for the allocated goods. When the amount of payments collected from the winners does not equal the calculated auction result, the auctioneer can decrypt the encrypted bids that are requested from the server and check whether each winner pays the full price or not. Therefore, the winners cannot cheat on payments in the auction.

6.2 Efficiency

The communication and the computational complexities of our auction mechanism are analyzed as follows.

- **Communication Complexity**
  At the bidding stage, all bidders report their encrypted bids to the server at the same time and the communication volume of each bidder is $O(|\mathcal{M}^Q|)$, thus the communication volume of this stage is $O(|\mathcal{M}| \cdot |\mathcal{M}^Q|)$, where $|\mathcal{M}|$ is the number of bidders, Q is the number of goods, and $|\mathcal{M}|^Q$ is the number of possible assignments in the auction. At the computation stage, the communication volume between the server and the auctioneer is $O(|\mathcal{M}^Q|)$. Since all winners simultaneously submit their payments to the auctioneer at the payoff stage, the communication volume $O(|\mathcal{W}|)$, in which $|\mathcal{W}|$ is the number of winners. If the auctioneer needs to perform the payment checking process, the corresponding communication volume is $O(1)$.
- **Computational Complexity**
  For each bidder, $|\mathcal{M}^Q|$ bids are computed in the auction, leading to a computational complexity of $O(|\mathcal{M}^Q|)$. The server computes the sum of all bidders' encrypted bids within $O(|\mathcal{M}| \cdot |\mathcal{M}^Q|)$. For the auctioneer, the computational complexity of searching for the maximum value is $O(|\mathcal{M}^Q|)$ and the computational complexity of the payment checking process is $O(|\mathcal{W}|)$.

7   Conclusion

In this paper, we propose a secure multi-unit sealed-bid first-price auction. By employing a server that computes the auction result based on the encrypted bids, our secure auction mechanism can protect the private bids from both the server and the auctioneer. In addition, our auction supports the verification of winners' payments for the auctioneer; that is, the auctioneer can check whether a winner pays its full price for its allocated goods. Finally, we evaluate the performance of our proposed auction scheme in terms of security, communication complexity, and computational complexity.

In our work, the scheme does not consider collusion activity among the bidders, the auctioneer, and the server. In future work, we will consider how to defend against collusion attacks in the auction.

Acknowledgment. The authors would like to thank all the reviewers for their helpful comments. This project was supported by the US National Science Foundation (ECCS-1407986, AST-1443858, CNS-1265311, and CNS-1162057), and the National Natural Science Foundation of China (61171014).

References

1. Ausubel, L.M.: Auction theory for the new economy. In: Jones, D. (ed.) New Economy Handbook, ch. 6. Academic Press, San Diego (2003)
2. Chen, Z., Huang, L., Li, L., Yang, W., Miao, H., Tian, M., Wang, F.: Ps-trust: Provably secure solution for truthful double spectrum auctions. In: IEEE INFOCOM, pp. 1249–1257 (2014)
3. Hu, C., Liao, X., Cheng, X.: Verifiable multi-secret sharing based on LFSR sequences. Theor. Comput. Sci. **445**, 52–62 (2012)
4. Hu, C., Liao, X., Xiao, D.: Secret image sharing based on chaotic map and chinese remainder theorem. Int. J. Wavelets Multiresolut. Inf. Process. **10**(03), 1250023(1–18) (2012)
5. Hu, C., Zhang, F., Cheng, X., Liao, X., Chen, D.: Securing communications between external users and wireless body area networks. In: Proceedings of the 2nd ACM Workshop on Hot Topics on Wireless Network Security and Privacy, pp. 31–36. ACM (2013)
6. Hu, C., Zhang, F., Xiang, T., Li, H., Xiao, X., Huang, G.: A practically optimized implementation of attribute based cryptosystems. In: 2014 IEEE 13th International Conference on Trust, Security and Privacy in Computing and Communications (TrustCom), pp. 197–204. IEEE (2014)
7. Hu, C., Zhang, N., Li, H., Cheng, X., Liao, X.: Body area network security: a fuzzy attribute-based signcryption scheme. IEEE J. Sel. Areas Commun. **31**(9), 37–46 (2013)
8. Huang, Q., Tao, Y., Wu, F.: Spring: a strategy-proof and privacy preserving spectrum auction mechanism. In: IEEE INFOCOM, pp. 851–859, Turin, Italy, April 2013
9. Jing, T., Zhang, F., Ma, L., Li, W., Chen, X., Huo, Y.: Truthful online reverse auction with flexible preemption for access permission transaction in macro-femtocell networks. In: Ren, K., Liu, X., Liang, W., Xu, M., Jia, X., Xing, K. (eds.) WASA 2013. LNCS, vol. 7992, pp. 512–523. Springer, Heidelberg (2013)

10. Jing, T., Zhao, C., Xing, X., Huo, Y., Li, W., Cheng, X.: A multi-unit truthful double auction framework for secondary market. In: IEEE ICC (2013)
11. Kikuchi, H.: (M+1)st-price auction protocol. In: Syverson, P.F. (ed.) FC 2001. LNCS, vol. 2339, pp. 351–363. Springer, Heidelberg (2002)
12. Krishna, V.: Auction Theory, 2nd edn. Elsevier, Burlington (2010)
13. Larson, M., Hu, C., Li, R., Li, W., Cheng, X.: Secure auctions without an auctioneer via verifiable secret sharing. In: Workshop on Privacy-Aware Mobile Computing (PAMCO), 2015 In conjunction with ACM MobiHoc 2015. ACM (2015)
14. Larson, M., Li, R., Hu, C., Li, W., Cheng, X.: A bidder-oriented privacy-preserving vcg auction scheme using homomorphic encryption. In: Xu, K., Zhu, H., Yu, J. (eds.) WASA 2015. LNCS, vol. 9204, pp. 284–294. Springer, Heidelberg (2015)
15. Li, W., Cheng, X., Bie, R., Zhao, F.: An extensible and flexible truthful auction framework for heterogeneous spectrum markets. In: ACM MobiHoc, Philadelphia, USA, pp. 175–184, August 2014
16. Li, W., Wang, S., Cheng, X., Bie, R.: Truthful multi-attribute auction with discriminatory pricing in cognitive radio networks. ACM SIGMOBILE Mob. Comput. Commun. Rev. 18(1), 3–13 (2014)
17. Naor, M., Pinkas, B., Sumner, R.: Privacy preserving auctions and mechanism design. In: The 1st ACM Conference on Electronic Commerce, pp. 129–139 (1999)
18. Nojoumian, M., Stinson, D.R.: Efficient sealed-bid auction protocols using verifiable secret sharing. Inf. Secur. Experience 8434, 302–317 (2014)
19. Paillier, P.: Public-key cryptosystems based on composite degree residuosity classes. In: Stern, J. (ed.) EUROCRYPT 1999. LNCS, vol. 1592, pp. 223–238. Springer, Heidelberg (1999)
20. Pan, M., Sun, J., Fang, Y.: Purging the back-room dealing: Secure spectrum auction leveraging paillier cryptosystem. IEEE J. Sel. Areas Commun. 29(4), 866–876 (2011)
21. Pan, M., Zhu, X., Fang, Y.: Using homomorphic encryption to secure the combinatorial spectrum auction without the trustworthy auctioneer. Wirel. Netw. 18(2), 113–128 (2012)
22. Shamir, A.: How to share a secret. Commun. ACM 22(11), 612–613 (1979)
23. Suzuki, K., Yokoo, M.: Secure combinatorial auctions by dynamic programming with polynomial secret sharing. In: Blaze, M. (ed.) FC 2002. LNCS, vol. 2357, pp. 44–56. Springer, Heidelberg (2003)

Flow-Level Performance of Device-to-Device Overlaid OFDM Cellular Networks

Lei Lei[1][(✉)], Huijian Wang[2], Xuemin (Sherman) Shen[3], Zhangdui Zhong[1], and Kan Zheng[2]

[1] State Key Lab of Rail Traffic Control and Safety,
Beijing Jiaotong University, Beijing, China
leil@bjtu.edu.cn
[2] Beijing University of Posts and Telecommunications, Beijing, China
[3] Department of Electrical and Computer Engineering,
University of Waterloo, Waterloo, Canada

Abstract. Spectrum partition and mode selection are two fundamental issues in D2D overlaid cellular networks, whose performance has been studied at the packet level for a static user population assuming infinite backlogs. In this paper, we aim at the flow-level performance with user dynamics governed by the arrival and completion of random service demands over time. We demonstrate the flow-level performance can be evaluated based on a queuing model with a dispatcher that assigns the service demands to two independent Processor Sharing servers. The queue model provides closed-form expressions for the mean number of users, the mean delay and the mean throughput, based on which the optimal spectrum partition and mode selection parameters can be derived and useful insights for the design principle can be obtained. Finally we perform numerical experiments to validate our model.

Keywords: Flow-level performance · Device-to-device communications

1 Introduction

Device-to-device (D2D) communications commonly refer to a type of technologies that enable devices to communicate directly with each other without the communication infrastructure, e.g., access points (APs) or base stations (BSs). With the emergence of context-aware applications and the accelerating growth of Machine-to-Machine (M2M) applications, D2D function plays an increasingly important role since it facilitates the discovery of geographically close devices, and enables direct communications between these proximate devices so as to increase communication capability and reduce communication delay and power consumption. To seize the emerging market that requires D2D function, the mobile operators and vendors are exploring the possibilities of introducing D2D communications in the cellular networks [1,2], which can work in the licensed band with more controllable interference.

© Springer International Publishing Switzerland 2015
K. Xu and J. Zhu (Eds.): WASA 2015, LNCS 9204, pp. 305–314, 2015.
DOI: 10.1007/978-3-319-21837-3_30

In D2D communications, a pair of D2D user equipments (UEs) can either communicate directly over-the-air using *D2D mode*, or communicate via the BS using *cellular mode*. Specifically, the data between the D2D UEs will be routed along a one-hop route of D2D link (direct over-the-air link) in D2D mode and a two-hop route of cellular links in cellular mode. The question on when a D2D UE pair should use D2D mode and when not is known as *mode selection*. Two resource sharing paradigms are defined for D2D communications: either *overlay* where cellular and D2D links use orthogonal time/frequency resources, or *underlay* where D2D links opportunistically access the time/frequency resources occupied by cellular users.

In this paper, we consider an Orthogonal Frequency Division Multiple (OFDM)-based cellular network with overlay D2D, or equivalently D2D overlaid OFDM cellular networks, where a fraction η of the cellular uplink spectrum is assigned to D2D communications while the other $1 - \eta$ is used for typical cellular uplink communications. We consider distance-based mode selection, which means a pair of D2D UEs uses D2D mode if the distance between the UEs is less than some threshold δ, or else it reverts to cellular mode. The optimal spectrum partition and selection threshold (η^*, δ^*) are studied in [3] to maximize the time-average transmission rate assuming the spatial locations of the UEs satisfy the Poisson point process (PPP) and every UE is saturated with infinite backlog.

Different from [3], we consider stochastic traffic loads with flow-level dynamics, where new file transfers, or equivalently flows, are initiated randomly and leave the system after being served. Under the flow-level traffic model, the number of flows or UEs varies dynamically over time as governed by the arrival/departure process of the flows, and depends on the spectrum partition and selection threshold (η, δ). The interdependence between flow-level performance such as the mean delay and mean throughput of flows and (η, δ) can be very different from those or even cannot be predicted by a saturated model as in [3].

Flow-level performance analysis has been conducted for cellular networks considering opportunistic scheduling, where the system is described by a processor-sharing (PS) server with state-dependent service rate [4–6]. However, the D2D overlaid OFDM cellular networks face the following challenges in flow-level performance analysis: (1) D2D introduces intra-cell interference between the D2D links with resource reuse; (2) the performance of cellular uplink and downlink communications need to be jointly analyzed due to the D2D UE pairs in cellular mode; and (3) the interdependence between cellular and D2D communications due to spectrum partition and mode selection needs to be characterized.

We formulate a flow-level performance model for D2D overlaid OFDM cellular networks that addresses the above challenges. Closed-form expressions for the mean number of flows, the mean delay and the mean throughput as functions of (η, δ) are provided, based on which the (η^*, δ^*) to optimize the flow-level performance can be obtained. *The contributions of this paper mainly lie in the following aspects: (1) we jointly apply stochastic geometry and queuing theory in formulating the performance model, where the service rates of the queues are derived based on the stochastic point processes of the UEs; and (2) the mode selection and spectrum partition problem in D2D communications is modeled as a joint task assignment and resource allocation problem in multi-server queuing system.*

2   System Model

Consider a D2D overlaid OFDM cellular network, where there are multiple D2D UE (DUE) pairs, cellular UEs (CUEs) with uplink communications and CUEs with downlink communications with a BS in a single cell. A DUE pair consists of a source D2D UE (src. DUE) and a destination D2D UE (dest. DUE) within direct over-the-air communication range. The whole uplink spectrum (resp. downlink spectrum) is divided into N_F equal size uplink subchannels (resp. downlink subchannels). The data transmission is performed on a slot-by-slot basis, where all time slots have equal length.

2.1   Traffic Characteristics

We define a dynamic flow model for elastic traffic, where new DUE pairs, new uplink CUEs and new downlink CUEs arrive at the system with finite-size file transmission tasks from the src. DUEs to the dest. DUEs, the uplink CUEs to the BS, and the BS to the downlink CUEs, and leave the system after they finish transmissions. Therefore, we will also use the terms "D2D flow", "uplink cellular flow", and "downlink cellular flow" to refer to "DUE pair", "uplink CUE" and "downlink CUE" in the rest of the paper. Under the dynamic flow model, the number of UEs or flows in the system varies over time due to the arrival and departure processes. Denote by $N_D(t)$, $N_{Cu}(t)$ and $N_{Cd}(t)$ the number of D2D flows, uplink cellular flows and downlink cellular flows at time slot t, respectively. Assume every type of flows arrive to the system as a Poisson process with homogeneous spatial distribution and independent and identically distributed (i.i.d.) flow sizes [4,5]. Specifically, the mean arrival rate at which src. DUEs (resp. uplink CUEs, downlink CUEs) arrive into an area of dx is $\lambda_D dx$ (resp. $\lambda_{Cu} dx$, $\lambda_{Cd} dx$), and the mean flow size is σ_D (resp. σ_{Cu}, σ_{Cd}). We assume the transceiver distance L_D of a typical DUE pair is Rayleigh distributed [3]:

$$f_{L_D}(x) = 2\pi\xi x e^{-\xi\pi x^2}, x \geq 0 \tag{1}$$

Note that (1) implies that a dest. DUE is randomly distributed on the circle centered at its src. DUE according to a two-dimensional Gaussian distribution. The following analysis can be extended to other distributions as well. We assume that the positions of the UEs remain fixed for the duration of the transfer.

2.2   Resource Control

Mode Selection: Under the distance-based mode selection, the probabilities that a D2D flow chooses D2D mode and cellular mode are $\Pr.\{L_D < \delta\} = 1 - e^{-\xi\pi\delta^2}$ and $\Pr.\{L_D \geq \delta\} = e^{-\xi\pi\delta^2}$, respectively. Let the number of D2D flows in D2D mode and in cellular mode at time slot t be represented by $N_{Dd}(t)$ and $N_{Dc}(t)$, respectively, where $N_{Dd}(t) + N_{Dc}(t) = N_D(t)$. Moreover, the D2D flows in cellular mode can be further classified into two categories, i.e., there are $N_{Dc}^{(u)}(t)$ D2D flows with cellular uplink communications and $N_{Dc}^{(d)}(t)$ D2D flows with cellular downlink communications at time slot t, where $N_{\text{Dc}}^{(u)}(t) + N_{\text{Dc}}^{(d)}(t) = N_{\text{Dc}}(t)$. Therefore, the number of D2D links or D2D transmitters/receivers equals $N_{\text{Dd}}(t)$, the number of cellular uplinks or cellular transmitters equals $N_{\text{Ct}}(t) = N_{\text{Cu}}(t) + N_{\text{Dc}}^{(u)}(t)$, and the number of cellular downlinks or cellular receivers equals $N_{\text{Cr}}(t) = N_{\text{Cd}}(t) + N_{\text{Dc}}^{(d)}(t)$. Note that a D2D transmitter (resp. D2D receiver) corresponds to a src. DUE (resp. dest. DUE) in D2D mode. On the other hand, a cellular transmitter can either be an uplink CUE or a src. DUE with cellular uplink communications, while a cellular receiver can either be a downlink CUE or a dest. DUE with cellular downlink communications. Since there are three types of links in our model, i.e., D2D links, cellular uplinks, and cellular downlinks, we use the term "link" to refer to any type of links in the rest of paper.

Resource Allocation: ηN_{F} uplink subchannels are allocated to the cellular uplinks and the rest of the $(1 - \eta)N_{\text{F}}$ uplink subchannels are allocated to D2D links. On the other hand, all the N_{F} downlink subchannels are all allocated to cellular downlinks.

We consider the following two classes of typical local resource allocation policies for the D2D links: (1) *Full Reuse (FR)*: D2D links share the $(1 - \eta)N_{\text{F}}$ uplink subchannels in a full reuse fashion, where all the D2D links perform data transmission simultaneously at each time slot; and (2) *Orthogonal Sharing (OS)*: each of the $(1 - \eta)N_{\text{F}}$ uplink subchannels is assigned to one of the D2D links at each time slot, either in a round robin (RR) fashion or the D2D link with relatively good channel condition is opportunistically selected to exploit the multiuser diversity gain. In the latter case, we assume that the BS splits time/frequency resources evenly among all D2D links, so that a degree of "fairness" is imposed. This can be achieved by opportunistic scheduling algorithms such as Proportional Fair (PF).

On the other hand, only OS is allowed for the local resource allocation of cellular uplinks and cellular downlinks to share the ηN_{F} uplink subchannels and N_{F} downlink subchannels, respectively.

Power Control: Let the random variables (r.v.s) P_{Dd} and L_{Dd} (resp. P_{Ct} and L_{Ct}; P_{Cr} and L_{Cr}) represent the transmit power and link length of D2D links (resp. cellular uplinks, cellular downlinks). We use P and L to represent either P_{Dd} and L_{Dd}, P_{Ct} and L_{Ct} or P_{Cr} and L_{Cr} in the rest of paper for simplicity whenever possible. We consider the following two typical power control policies: (1) *Fixed Power Control (FPC)*: all the D2D links or cellular uplinks/downlinks transmit at a fixed power, e.g., the maximum transmit power of BS or UE; and (2) *Adaptive Power Control (APC)*: a D2D link or cellular uplink/downlink uses channel inversion for power control, i.e., $P = L^{\alpha}$, where $\alpha > 2$ denotes the path-loss exponent.

2.3 Transmission Rate

Denote by $C_{\text{Dd}}(n)$ (resp. $C_{\text{Ct}}(n)$, $C_{\text{Cr}}(n)$) the time-average transmission rate of a typical D2D link (resp. cellular uplink, cellular downlink) when there are n D2D links (resp. cellular uplinks, cellular downlinks) in the system. We use $C(n)$ to represent either $C_{\mathrm{Dd}}(n)$, $C_{\mathrm{Ct}}(n)$ or $C_{\mathrm{Cr}}(n)$ in the rest of paper whenever possible. Since the time-average transmission rate of a link depends on the locations of its corresponding UE(s), and may also depends on the locations of other UEs (in the case of D2D link with *FR*), $C(n)$ indicates the spatially averaged value of the cell.

We use Shannon formula to derive the instantaneous data rate on every subchannel, and the time-average transmission rate of a link can be derived as $C(n) = \zeta N_{\mathrm{F}} B \mathbb{E}[\log(1 + SINR)]$, where $SINR = \frac{W}{N_0 + I}$ is an r.v. representing the Signal to Interference and Noise Ratio (SINR) of the link with W, N_0 and I denoting the signal, noise and interference power, respectively. Since the SINR of a link is determined by both the path loss and multipath fading of the signal path and interference path (if there is any), the expectation in the above formula is taken over both the multipath fading process and the spatial locations of the UEs in the cell. For simplicity we consider Rayleigh flat fading on each subchannel and assume independent fading over space. Moreover, we consider a circular cell with radius R and assume that the D2D transmitters, cellular transmitters and receivers are all uniformly distributed in the cell. B is the bandwidth of a subchannel. ζ denotes the time-frequency resources accessed by a link, which equals $1 - \eta$ and $\frac{1-\eta}{n}$, respectively, when the considered link is a D2D link with FR and OS policy; and equals $\frac{\eta}{n}$ and $\frac{1}{n}$ when the considered link is a cellular uplink and downlink, respectively.

The time-average transmission rate of a link when there is no other links of the same type in the cell depends only on the power control policy, which is given by

$$C(1) = \frac{\zeta N_{\mathrm{F}} B}{R} \int_0^R \int_0^\infty \log(1 + \frac{xPr^{-\alpha}}{N_0}) e^{-x} \mathrm{d}x \mathrm{d}r, \qquad (2)$$

The time-average transmission rate of a link when there are more than one link of the same type in the cell also depends on the local resource allocation policy apart from the power control policy, which are given as follows.

- When RR scheduler is used, we simply have $C(n) = \frac{1}{n}C(1)$.
- When PF scheduler is used, the UE with the maximum power gain determined by multipath fading is scheduled in every time slot, and we have

$$C(n) = \frac{\zeta N_{\mathrm{F}} B}{nR} \int_0^R \int_0^\infty \log(1 + \frac{xPr^{-\alpha}}{N_0}) e^{-x} n(1 - e^{-x})^{n-1} \mathrm{d}x \mathrm{d}r, \quad (3)$$

- When FR is adopted for D2D communications, the SINR value also depends on the channel gains of the interference path. By applying corollary 1 in [3], we have

$$C(n) = \zeta N_{\mathrm{F}} B \int_0^\infty \frac{e^{-N_0 x}}{1 + x} \mathcal{L}_I(x) \mathrm{d}x, \qquad (4)$$

where $\mathcal{L}_I(x) = \mathbb{E}[e^{-xI}]$ denotes the Laplace transform of the interference power I. Since we assume that the D2D transmitters are uniformly distributed and there are $n-1$ interference path, we have

$$\mathcal{L}_I(x) = (\frac{1}{R^2} \int_0^{R^2} \frac{1}{1 + x\mathbb{E}[P_{Dd}]r^{-\frac{\alpha}{2}}} dr)^{n-1}, \tag{5}$$

the proof of which is omitted due to page limit. With APC, $\mathbb{E}[P_{Dd}] = \frac{(\xi\pi)^{-\frac{\alpha}{2}}}{1-e^{-\xi\pi\delta^2}}\gamma(\frac{\alpha}{2}+1, \xi\pi\delta^2)$ [3].

Let $H_{FR}(n)$ and $H_{OS}(n)$ represent the value of $\frac{nC(n)}{C(1)}$ under FR and OS policy, respectively. Note that $\frac{H_{FR}(n)}{n}$ is a factor which quantifies the service impairment of a D2D link due to interference from the other $n-1$ D2D links, while $H_{OS}(n) > 1$ is the multiuser diversity gain under the PF algorithm and $H_{OS}(n) = 1$ under the RR algorithm.

3   Processor Sharing Queuing Model

Since the duration of the time slot is relatively short with respect to the size and arrival frequency of the flows (e.g., the minimum scheduling time unit is 1ms in 3G LTE, while it usually takes at least several seconds to transmit a flow), the flow-level performance can be analyzed in continuous rather than discrete time [4]. The time index t will be a non-negative real number indicating a time instant instead of an integer indicating a time slot in the rest of the paper. Since the channel fading is much faster than the flow number variation speed, the rate fluctuations of a flow almost "averages out" during its transmission period. It can be assumed that a flow is served by a single server with a deterministic service rate, rather than by multiple servers in a time-slotted fashion with random service rate [6].

The flow-level queuing model of the D2D overlaid OFDM cellular system is illustrated in Fig. 1. When the D2D flows arrive at the system, they will be dispatched to two different queues according to the mode selection principle. The D2D flows in D2D mode arrive to the queue q_{Dd} with mean arrival rate $\lambda_{Dd}\pi R^2 = \Pr.\{L_D < \delta\}\lambda_D\pi R^2$, share the server corresponding to the

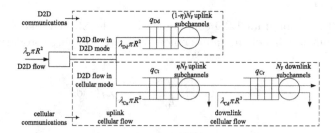

Fig. 1. Flow-level queuing model

$(1 - \eta)N_F$ uplink subchannels, and leave the system after receiving service. On the other hand, the D2D flows in cellular mode and uplink cellular flows arrive to the queue q_{Ct} with mean arrival rate $\lambda_{Dc}\pi R^2 = \text{Pr.}\{L_D \geq \delta\}\lambda_D\pi R^2$ and $\lambda_{Cu}\pi R^2$, respectively, and share the server corresponding to the ηN_F uplink subchannels. Upon completion of service, the uplink cellular flows leave the system. On the other hand, the D2D flows in cellular mode enter the queue q_{Cr}, at which downlink cellular flows arrive with mean arrival rate $\lambda_{Cd}\pi R^2$; and both type of flows share the server corresponding to the N_F downlink subchannels, and leave the system after receiving service. Note that the queuing model for D2D communications and cellular communications are completely independent after the D2D flows are dispatched to the corresponding queues. We will discuss the two queuing models separately in the following.

The queuing behavior of D2D links can be modeled as a PS system with state-dependent service rate under both FR and OS policies. Let $\frac{1}{\mu_{Dd}} = \frac{\sigma_{Dd}}{C_{Dd}(1)}$ be the mean *normalized service requirement* of a D2D flow in D2D mode, which is the amount of time it would take to complete the flow transfer if it were the only D2D flow in D2D mode in the cell. Define $H_D(n) = \frac{nC_{Dd}(n)}{C_{Dd}(1)}$ as the *service capacity* of D2D links, which equals $H_{FR}(n)$ or $H_{OS}(n)$ depending on the local resource allocation policy. Under the FR policy, when there are n flows in the system, each of them is served at a fraction $\frac{1}{n}$ of the service capacity $H_D(n)$, which has a similar probabilistic fashion as a PS system. Under the OS policy, on the other hand, recall that when there are n D2D links in the cell, we consider every D2D link receives a fraction $\frac{1}{n}$ of the total allocated time-frequency resources for D2D communications. Considering the different time scales of flow dynamics and time slots, it is reasonable to assume that each of the n D2D links is continuously served at a fraction $\frac{1}{n}$ of the service capacity $H_D(n)$ [4]. Note that the service capacity $H_D(n)$ is dependent on the number of D2D flows in D2D mode or the system state n. Define $\mu_{Dd}H_D(n)$ as the *normalized service rate* of D2D flows in D2D mode, which represents the rate at which the D2D flows in D2D mode are served. Therefore, our queuing model is a PS system with state-dependent service rate. Define the *normalized load* of D2D communications as $\rho_{Dd} = \frac{\lambda_{Dd}\pi R^2}{\mu_{Dd}}$.

Similarly, both the cellular uplink and cellular downlink communications can be modeled as a two-class PS system with state-dependent service rate. Specifically, for the PS queue representing cellular uplink (resp. downlink) communications, there are two classes of flows, i.e., D2D flows in cellular mode with uplink (resp. downlink) communications and uplink (resp. downlink) cellular flows. Let $\frac{1}{\mu_{Cu}} = \frac{\sigma_{Cu}}{C_{Ct}(1)}$ and $\frac{1}{\mu_{Dc}^{(u)}} = \frac{\sigma_D}{C_{Ct}(1)}$ (resp. $\frac{1}{\mu_{Cd}} = \frac{\sigma_{Cd}}{C_{Cr}(1)}$ and $\frac{1}{\mu_{Dc}^{(d)}} = \frac{\sigma_D}{C_{Cr}(1)}$) be the mean normalized service requirement of an uplink (resp. downlink) cellular flow and a D2D flow with uplink (resp. downlink) cellular communications. Let $H_C(n)$ be the service capacity for both cellular uplink and downlink communications, which equals $H_{OS}(n)$. Therefore, the queuing system for cellular communications consists of two PS queues with state-dependent service rate and Poisson arrival in tandem, which has product-form solution and the two queues can be analyzed independently [7]. Define the normalized load of D2D flows with cellular uplink (resp. downlink) communications and uplink (resp. downlink) cellular flows as $\rho_{\text{Dc}}^{(u)} = \frac{\lambda_{\text{Dc}}\pi R^2}{\mu_{\text{Dc}}^{(u)}}$ and $\rho_{\text{Cu}} = \frac{\lambda_{\text{Cu}}\pi R^2}{\mu_{\text{Cu}}}$ (resp. $\rho_{\text{Dc}}^{(d)} = \frac{\lambda_{\text{Dc}}\pi R^2}{\mu_{\text{Dc}}^{(d)}}$ and $\rho_{\text{Cd}} = \frac{\lambda_{\text{Cd}}\pi R^2}{\mu_{\text{Cd}}}$). Therefore, the total normalized load of cellular uplink (resp. downlink) communications is given by $\rho_{\text{Ct}} = \rho_{\text{Dc}}^{(u)} + \rho_{\text{Cu}}$ (resp. $\rho_{\text{Cr}} = \rho_{\text{Dc}}^{(d)} + \rho_{\text{Cd}}$).

According to the above discussion, the D2D and cellular uplink/downlink communications can all be modeled as multi-class PS queues with state-dependent service rates. Following from the standard results as given in Appendix 5, i.e., (9), (10), we can derive the mean number, mean delay, and mean throughput of D2D flows in D2D mode (resp. D2D flows with cellular uplink/downlink communications, uplink cellular flows, downlink cellular flows) $\mathbb{E}[N_{\text{Dd}}]$, S_{Dd}, and T_{Dd} (resp. $\mathbb{E}[N_{\text{Dc}}^{(u)}]/\mathbb{E}[N_{\text{Dc}}^{(d)}]$, $S_{\text{Dd}}^{(u)}/S_{\text{Dd}}^{(d)}$, and $T_{\text{Dd}}^{(u)}/T_{\text{Dd}}^{(d)}$; $\mathbb{E}[N_{\text{Cu}}]$, S_{Cu}, and T_{Cu}; $\mathbb{E}[N_{\text{Cd}}]$, S_{Cd}, and T_{Cd}). Since a D2D flow in cellular mode is served by two PS queues in tandem, its mean flow number, end-to-end mean delay and mean throughput is given by

$$\mathbb{E}[N_{\text{Dc}}] = \mathbb{E}[N_{\text{Dc}}^{\text{u}}] + \mathbb{E}[N_{\text{Dc}}^{\text{d}}], \quad S_{\text{Dc}} = S_{\text{Dc}}^{\text{u}} + S_{\text{Dc}}^{\text{d}}, \quad T_{\text{Dc}} = \frac{T_{\text{Dc}}^{\text{u}} T_{\text{Dc}}^{\text{d}}}{T_{\text{Dc}}^{\text{u}} + T_{\text{Dc}}^{\text{d}}}. \quad (6)$$

Finally, the mean number of D2D flows is $\mathbb{E}[N_{\text{D}}] = \mathbb{E}[N_{\text{Dd}}] + \mathbb{E}[N_{\text{Dc}}]$. The mean delay of a D2D flow is given by

$$S_{\text{D}} = S_{\text{Dd}}\text{Pr.}\{L_{\text{D}} < \delta\} + S_{\text{Dc}}\text{Pr.}\{L_{\text{D}} \geq \delta\} = \frac{\mathbb{E}[N_{\text{D}}]}{\lambda_{\text{D}}\pi R^2}, \quad (7)$$

where the second equality is due to $\text{Pr.}\{L_{\text{D}} < \delta\} = \frac{\lambda_{\text{Dd}}}{\lambda_{\text{D}}}$ and $\text{Pr.}\{L_{\text{D}} \geq \delta\} = \frac{\lambda_{\text{Dc}}}{\lambda_{\text{D}}}$. Similarly, the mean throughput of a D2D flow is given by

$$T_{\text{D}} = T_{\text{Dd}}\frac{\lambda_{\text{Dd}}}{\lambda_{\text{D}}} + T_{\text{Dc}}\frac{\lambda_{\text{Dc}}}{\lambda_{\text{D}}}. \quad (8)$$

As a remark, note that (6)–(8), (9) and (10) together provide explicit formulas for the flow-level performance as functions of η and δ, since μ_{Dd} (resp., μ_{Cu} and $\mu_{\text{Dc}}^{(u)}$) is a linear function of $(1 - \eta)$ (resp. η) by (2) and its definition, while $\frac{\lambda_{\text{Dc}}}{\lambda_{\text{D}}} = 1 - \frac{\lambda_{\text{Dd}}}{\lambda_{\text{D}}} = e^{-\xi\pi\delta^2}$. Based on the explicit formulas, the D2D mode selection threshold δ^* and spectrum partition factor η^* can be determined in order to minimize the mean delay or maximum the mean throughput. The above optimization problem is similar to a joint task assignment and resource allocation problem in multi-server queuing system, where two servers share a common resource pool and the service rate of every server grows linearly with the number of allocated resources. Closed-form expressions for (η^*, δ^*) can be derived under some simplified assumptions to generate insights for the design principle. Due to page limit, we omit the detailed discussion on optimizing the spectrum partition and threshold. Interested readers can refer to the extended version of this paper.

4   Numerical Results and Discussions

In this section, we present numerical experiments to demonstrate the analytical results. The cell radius R and the D2D distance parameter ξ are set to 500 m and $10/\pi(500)^2$, respectively. The path loss exponent α is set to 3 and the noise power N_0 is set to $-48\,\mathrm{dBm}$. The mean sizes of all the flows are set to $5\,\mathrm{Mbits}$ and the mean arrival rates $\lambda_D = \lambda_{Cu} = \lambda_{Cd} = \lambda$. The slot duration and the bandwidth of each subchannel ΔW are set to $1\,\mathrm{ms}$ and $180\,\mathrm{kHz}$, respectively, as in LTE system. The available bandwidth of the OFDM system is set to $10\,\mathrm{MHz}$, which are divided into $N_F = 50$ subchannels.

For the power control and local resource allocation methods, we consider both the D2D and cellular uplink communications adopt APC, while the cellular downlink communications adopts FPC with fixed transmit power $46\,\mathrm{dBm}$. Moreover, the D2D communications use FR, while the cellular communications use OS. Specifically, we consider two scenarios, where the RR and PF scheduling algorithms are used in scenarios 1 and 2, respectively.

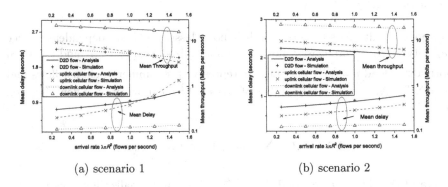

(a) scenario 1   (b) scenario 2

Fig. 2. Mean delay and mean throughput as functions of flow arrival rate

We validate the analytical results, where the spectrum partition factor η and mode selection threshold δ are set to 0.6 and $200\,\mathrm{m}$, respectively. We consider the arrival rate $\lambda\pi R^2$ varies from 0.25 to 1.5 flows/s. The simulations were run for 10^7 time slots. Figure 2(a) and (b) show the mean delay and mean throughput of D2D flows, uplink and downlink cellular flows in scenario 1 and scenario 2, respectively. The mean delay increases and the mean throughput decreases with the increasing arrival rate in both scenarios as expected, and the analytical results match closely with the simulation results. The performance of the downlink cellular flows is better than those of the uplink cellular flows and D2D flows in both scenarios, since the former uses FPC with maximum transmit power while the latter two use APC. In scenario 2, the performance of cellular flows are improved due to the use of PF algorithm. Moreover, the performance of D2D flows is also improved due to the D2D flows in cellular mode.

5   Conclusion

In this paper, we have studied the flow-level performance of D2D overlaid OFDM cellular networks, and derived explicit formulas to characterize the relationships of the mean delay and mean throughput with the spectrum partition and mode selection threshold (η, δ). The formulas can be used to optimize the D2D mode selection threshold δ^* and spectrum partition factor η^* in terms of flow-level performance. Possible extensions of this work include studying the multi-cell scenario with inter-cell interference and the underlay scenario with interference between D2D and cellular links.

Acknowledgments. This work is supported by the National Natural Science Foundation of China (No. 61272168 and No. U1334202), and the State Key Laboratory of Rail Traffic Control and Safety (Contract No. RCS2014ZT10), Beijing Jiaotong University.

Appendix A: Multi-class PS Queue with State-Dependent Service Rate

Consider a multi-class PS queue with K flow classes and state-dependent service capacity $H(n)$, where class-k flows have normalized load $\rho_k = \frac{\lambda_k}{\mu_k}$ and the total normalized load $\rho = \sum_{k=1}^{K} \rho_k$. Let N_k represent the number of class-k flows and $N = \sum_{k=1}^{K} N_k$ be the total number of flows. The mean number of flows is given by [4,7]

$$\mathbb{E}(N) = J^{-1} \sum_{n=1}^{\infty} \frac{n\rho^n}{\phi(n)}, \quad \mathbb{E}(N_k) = \frac{\rho_k}{\rho}\mathbb{E}(N). \tag{9}$$

where $\phi(n) = \prod_{m=1}^{n} H(m)$ and $J = \sum_{n=0}^{\infty} \frac{\rho^n}{\phi(n)}$ is a normalization constant. By Little's law, we obtain the mean delay S_k and mean throughput T_k of a class-k flow as

$$S_k = \frac{\mathbb{E}(N_k)}{\lambda_k}, \quad T_k = \frac{\sigma_k}{S_k}. \tag{10}$$

References

1. Lei, L., Zhong, Z., Lin, C., Shen, X.: Operator controlled device-to-device communications in LTE-advanced networks. IEEE Wirel. Commun. **19**(3), 96–104 (2012)
2. Fodor, G., et al.: Design aspects of network assisted device-to-device communications. IEEE Commun. Mag. **50**(3), 170–177 (2012)
3. Lin, X., Andrews, J.G., Ghosh, A.: Spectrum sharing for device-to-device communication in cellular networks. IEEE Trans. Wirel. Commun. **13**(12), 6727–6740 (2014)
4. Borst, S.C.: User-level performance of channel-aware scheduling algorithms in wireless data networks. Proceedings of IEEE INFOCOM (2003)
5. Bonald, T., Proutiere, A.: Wireless downlink channels: user performance and cell dimensioning, In: Proceedongs of the ACM MobiCom, pp. 339–352 (2003)
6. Lei, L., Lin, C., Cai, J., Shen, X.: Flow-level performance of opportunistic OFDM-TDMA and OFDMA networks. IEEE Trans. Wirel. Commun. **7**(12), 5461–5472 (2008)
7. Cohen, J.W.: The multiple phase service network with generalized processor sharing. Acta Informatica **12**(4), 245–285 (1979)

Bernoulli Sampling Based (epsilon, delta)-Approximate Frequency Query in Mobile Ad Hoc Networks

Ji Li[1]([✉]), Siyao Cheng[2], Zhipeng Cai[1], Qilong Han[3], and Hong Gao[2]

[1] Department of Computer Science, Georgia State University, Atlanta, GA, USA
{jli30,zcai}@gsu.edu
[2] School of Computer Science, Harbin Institute of Technology, Harbin, China
{csy,honggao}@hit.edu.cn
[3] College of Computer Science and Technology,
Harbin Engineering University, Harbin, China
hanqilong@hrbeu.edu.cn

Abstract. A frequency query is to acquire the occurrence frequency of each value in a sensory data set, which is a popular operation in Mobile Ad hoc Networks (MANETs). However, exact frequency results are not easy to obtain due to the unique characteristics of MANETs. Fortunately, approximate frequency results are acceptable in most MANET applications. We study how to process an approximate frequency query in this paper and propose a sampling based method to estimate approximate frequencies. A distributed algorithm to calculate approximate frequency results is introduced. The simulation results show that on the aspects of both energy efficiency and accuracy, the proposed algorithm has high performance.

Keywords: Mobile ad hoc networks · Frequency query · Sampling

1 Introduction

A Mobile Ad hoc Network (MANET) is a continuously self-configuring and infrastructure-less network consisting of mobile nodes. The mobile nodes in a MANET is able to communicate using wireless links. This kind of network can be widely used in many applications such as pollution monitoring, animal surveillance, etc. [1–6]. Many works such as [7,8] and [9] have studied the problem of routing, fuzzy intrusion detection and performance evaluation in MANETs. One of the most important problems is the frequency query aiming at acquiring the frequency of each value in a sensory data set. For example, a frequency query can help with estimating the numbers of the injured persons and survivors in a disaster rescue [10].

Obviously, an exact frequency result can be calculated by collecting all the sensory data and aggregating partial results during the transmission. However, it results in a huge amount of energy consumption. Moreover, because most nodes

© Springer International Publishing Switzerland 2015
K. Xu and J. Zhu (Eds.): WASA 2015, LNCS 9204, pp. 315–324, 2015.
DOI: 10.1007/978-3-319-21837-3_31

in a MANET are moving and each node's communication radius is limited, the isolated nodes cannot send their data immediately. Then a severe delay may be incurred to wait for the isolated nodes to get connected with some other nodes. Therefore, many MANET applications are in favor of approximate results considering the save on energy consumption and delay [11,12]. The works in [13] and [14] propose approximate data aggregation algorithms in Wireless Sensor Networks (WSNs). However, they cannot be employed in MANETs because these algorithms are for stationary networks.

In this paper, we propose a Bernoulli sampling based approximate algorithm to process frequency queries in MANETs. This algorithm is able to return the query result which satisfies the specified precision and failure probability. The simulation results show that on the aspects of both energy efficiency and accuracy, the proposed algorithm has high performance.

2   Problem Definition

Suppose there is a MANET with n mobile nodes. The set of all the mobile nodes in a MANET is denoted by $S = \{s_1, s_2, \ldots, s_n\}$. All the mobile nodes are deployed in a $l \times l$ square uniformly, randomly and independently. All the nodes are moving under the random waypoint model [15]. For each mobile node, the destination, speed and pause time during the movement are chosen in $[0, l)^2$, $[v_{min}, v_{max})$ and $[p_{min}, p_{max})$ uniformly, randomly and independently.

At time t, a frequency query is proposed by query node q located at position $(\frac{l}{2}, \frac{l}{2})$. All the mobile nodes and the query node have communication radius r. For $\forall u, v \in S \cup \{q\}$, let $dis(u, v)$ be the Euclidean distance between u and v. Suppose u and v can communicate if $dis(u, v) \leq r$. Obviously, since all the nodes are moving and r is limited, not all the nodes can communicate with the query node in one or multiple hops. Let S' be the set of nodes which can communicate with the query node in one or multiple hops. We also assume the topology of a MANET changes between different queries while the network topology remains the same during one query even if it needs multiple hops for data transmission.

Suppose a query is proposed at time t. For node v, $d(v, t)$ denotes the sensory data of v at time t. For node set V, $D(V, t)$ is the sensory data set containing all the data of all the nodes in V at time t. We assume all the possible values of the sensory data set distribute uniformly for all the nodes. Spatial and temporal correlations of sensory data are ignored. For a given data set D and value x, the exact frequency of x in D is denoted by $F(D, x) = \frac{|\{d \in D | d = x\}|}{|D|}$. In this paper, we study how to obtain the (ϵ, δ)-approximate frequency. The definition of the (ϵ, δ)-estimator proposed in [13] is given as follows.

Definition 1 ((ϵ, δ)-estimator). *For any ϵ ($\epsilon > 0$) and δ ($0 \leq \delta \leq 1$), $\widehat{I_t}$ is called the (ϵ, δ)-estimator of I_t if $Pr(\frac{|I_t - \widehat{I_t}|}{I_t} \geq \epsilon) \leq \delta$.* ☐

The problem of computing (ϵ, δ)-approximate frequency is defined as follows.

Input: A MANET with n nodes, the sensory data set D_t, ϵ ($\epsilon > 0$) and δ ($0 \leq \delta \leq 1$).

Output: (ϵ, δ)-approximate frequency result.

3   Preliminaries

In this section, some preliminary knowledge regarding how to decide the optimal sampling probability is introduced. $\phi_{\delta/2}$ denotes the $\delta/2$ fractile of the standard normal distribution and $\inf(x)$ denotes the lower bound of value x. Firstly, the definition of unbiased estimator proposed in [13] is given as follows.

Definition 2 (unbiased estimator). $\widehat{I_t}$ *is called the unbiased estimator of* I_t *if* $E(\widehat{I_t}) = I_t$, *where* $E(\widehat{I_t})$ *denotes the mathematical expectation of* I_t. □

Let $B(D,q) = \{b_1, b_2, \ldots, b_{|B(D,q)|}\}$ denote a Bernoulli sample of data set $D = \{d_1, d_2, \ldots, d_{|D|}\}$ with sample probability q. $Count(D) = |D|$ is the exact size of D. Then the estimator of $Count(D)$ is $\widehat{Count}(D) = \frac{|B(D,q)|}{q}$ [14]. Then we have the following theorem proved in [14].

Theorem 1. $\widehat{Count}(D)$ *is an unbiased estimator of* $Count(D)$ *and it is an* (ϵ, δ)-*estimator of* $Count(D)$ *if* $q \geq \frac{\phi_{\delta/2}^2}{\inf(|D|)\epsilon^2 + \phi_{\delta/2}^2}$. □

Let $I(a,b)$ be a variable which satisfies

$$I(a,b) = \begin{cases} 1 & \text{if } a = b \\ 0 & \text{otherwise} \end{cases}$$

Let $Equal(D,x)$ be the number of elements equal to x in D, then we have $Equal(D,x) = \sum_{d_i \in D} I(d_i, x)$. The estimator of $Equal(D,x)$ is $\widehat{Equal}(D,x) = \frac{1}{q}\sum_{d_i \in B(D,q)} I(d_i, x)$. The following two theorems indicates that $\widehat{Equal}(D,x)$ is an unbiased estimator of $Equal(D,x)$, provides the variance of $\widehat{Equal}(D,x)$ and an optional sampling probability to make $\widehat{Equal}(D,x)$ be an (ϵ, δ)-estimator of $Equal(D,x)$. The detailed proof is omitted due to space limitation.

Theorem 2. $\widehat{Equal}(D,x)$ *is an unbiased estimator of* $Equal(D,x)$ *and* $Var(\widehat{Equal}(D,x)) \leq \frac{1-q}{q} Equal(D,x)$. $\widehat{Equal}(D,x)$ *is an* (ϵ, δ)-*estimator of the value* $Equal(D,x)$ *if sampling probability* $q \geq \frac{\phi_{\delta/2}^2}{\epsilon^2 \inf(|D|)\inf(F(D,x)) + \phi_{\delta/2}^2}$. □

The estimator of $F(D,x)$ is defined as $\widehat{F}(D,x) = \frac{\widehat{Equal}(D,x)}{\widehat{Count}(D)}$. Using the similar strategy in [14], it is easy to have the following corollary.

Corollary 1. *If sampling probability* $q < 1$, $\widehat{F}(D,x)$ *is a biased estimator of* $F(D,x)$. *If both* $\widehat{Equal}(D,x)$ *and* $\widehat{Count}(D)$ *are the* $(\frac{\epsilon}{2+\epsilon}, \frac{\delta}{2})$ *estimator of the value* $Equal(D,x)$ *and* $Count(D)$, *then* $\widehat{F}(D,x)$ *is an* (ϵ, δ)-*estimator of* $F(D,x)$. □

However, not all the nodes can communicate with the query node in one or multiple hops. At time t, we can only get the (ϵ, δ)-approximate frequency of $D(S',t)$. Fortunately, $D(S',t)$ can be regarded as a sample of $D(S,t)$ without replacement with sampling ratio $\frac{|D(S',t)|}{|D(S,t)|} = \frac{|S'|}{|S|}$. $F(D(S',t),x)$ can be regarded as an estimator of $F(D(S,t),x)$. According to [16], it is easy to have the following corollary using the similar strategy in the proof of Theorem 2.

Corollary 2. $F(D(S',t),x)$ is an unbiased estimator of $F(D(S,t),x)$. If we have $F(D(S',t),x)$ as an (ϵ,δ)-estimator of $F(D(S,t),x)$, then ϵ and δ satisfy the following formula: $\phi_{\delta/2}^2(\frac{1}{\inf(F(D(S,t),x))} - 1)(\frac{1}{|S'|} - \frac{1}{|S|}) \leq \epsilon^2$. $\qquad\square$

Suppose we have $F(\widehat{D(S',t)},x)$ as an (ϵ_1,δ_1)-estimator of $F(D(S',t),x)$ and $F(D(S',t),x)$ as an (ϵ_2,δ_2)-estimator of $F(D(S,t),x)$ respectively. According to the definition of (ϵ,δ)-estimator, we have the following corollary.

Corollary 3. $F(\widehat{D(S',t)},x)$ is an (ϵ,δ)-estimator of $F(D(S,t),x)$ if $(1-\delta_1)(1-\delta_2) \geq 1-\delta$, $(1+\epsilon_1)(1+\epsilon_2) \leq 1+\epsilon$ and $(1-\epsilon_1)(1-\epsilon_2) \geq 1-\epsilon$. $\qquad\square$

Finally, we have the final methodology to calculate sampling probability q. Firstly, find ϵ_1 and δ_1 satisfying the following condition: $(1-\delta_1)(1-\delta_2) \geq 1-\delta$, $(1+\epsilon_1)(1+\epsilon_2) \leq 1+\epsilon$, $(1-\epsilon_1)(1-\epsilon_2) \geq 1-\epsilon$, $\phi_{\delta_2/2}^2(\frac{1}{\inf(F(D(S,t),x))} - 1)(\frac{1}{|S'|} - \frac{1}{|S|}) \leq \epsilon_2^2$. Secondly, calculate q_1 which makes $Count(\widehat{D(S',t)})$ to be an $(\frac{\epsilon_1}{2+\epsilon_1}, \frac{\delta_1}{2})$-estimator of $Count(D(S',t))$. Thirdly, calculate q_2 which makes $Equal(\widehat{D(S',t)},x)$ to be an $(\frac{\epsilon_1}{2+\epsilon_1}, \frac{\delta_1}{2})$-estimator of $Equal(D(S',t),x)$. Finally, $q = \max(q_1, q_2)$ is the final sampling probability.

4   Network Connectivity

The calculation of sampling probability depends on $|S|$ and $|S'|$. It is reasonable to assume $|S|$ is known [17], but it is almost impossible to know $|S'|$.

This problem can be solved by doing an exact $COUNT$ query on S' before carrying out an approximate frequency query. However, it costs a huge amount of extra energy. Furthermore, the network topology possibly changes during the gap between the exact $COUNT$ query and the approximate frequency query. Another solution is to use a formula to calculate $|S'|$ according to the related variables. However, we have to confine ourselves to simulation results due to the intractability of analysis with the existing mathematical method. Moreover, it is still a hard problem. Therefore, we only present the stimulation results for the lower 0.05 fractile of $|S'|$ denoted by $f_{0.05}(|S'|)$. However, $f_{0.05}(|S'|)$ is not the exact value of $|S'|$. Fortunately, according to the definition of lower 0.05 fractile, this problem can be solved by changing the original δ to a new $\delta' = 1 - \frac{1-\delta}{0.95}$. Due to space limitation, we only present the conclusions. The stimulation results can be downloaded at [18].

The results of the first group of stimulations indicate that if related variables are in the reasonable ranges and $f_{0.05}(|S'|) \geq 0.75n$, $f_{0.05}(|S'|)$ tends to be stable, if $f_{0.05}(|S'|) \geq 0.75n$, $f_{0.05}(|S'|)$ has has much to do with n and r only. The results of the second and third groups of stimulations indicate $f_{0.05}(|S'|) > 0.75n$ if $r > \frac{6l}{5\sqrt{n}}$ and $f_{0.05}(|S'|) > 0.99n$ if $r > \frac{11l}{5\sqrt{n}}$. The results of the forth group of stimulations indicate $f_{0.05}(|S'|)$ is closely mapped to $\frac{1}{4}n\sqrt{1 - n(r - \frac{11}{5\sqrt{n}})^2} +$ 0.74n if $\frac{6l}{5\sqrt{n}} < r \leq \frac{11l}{5\sqrt{n}}$. Finally, we have the following conclusions.

Firstly, $f_{0.05}(|S'|)$ is not stable if $r \leq \frac{6l}{5\sqrt{n}}$m. Secondly, $f_{0.05}(|S'|)$ is closely mapped to $\frac{1}{4}n\sqrt{1 - n(r - \frac{11}{5\sqrt{n}})^2} + 0.74n$ if $\frac{6l}{5\sqrt{n}} < r \leq \frac{11l}{5\sqrt{n}}$. Thirdly, $f_{0.05}(|S'|)$ is greater than $0.99n$ if $r > \frac{11l}{5\sqrt{n}}$.

5 (ϵ, δ)-Approximate Frequency Query Algorithm

To calculate an approximate frequency, the following steps are required. Firstly, determine sampling probability q according to the specified ϵ and δ. Secondly, use a distributed Bernoulli sampling algorithm to sample sensory data. Finally, based on the sampled data, calculate the (ϵ, δ)-approximate frequency.

5.1 The Bernoulli Sampling Algorithm

Although the network topology is dynamic, it is still possible to organize the whole network as a spanning tree using the similar method in [19]. Once a proper sampling probability q is determined, we can design the Bernoulli sampling algorithm as follows. Firstly, the query node broadcasts sampling probability q to each node. Secondly, each node produces a random number $rand$ in range $[0, 1]$. Thirdly, for each node, if $rand \leq q$, it sends its data to its parent node.

5.2 The (ϵ, δ)-Approximate Frequency Algorithm

The basic idea of calculating an approximate frequency is as follows. Firstly, each node in the spanning tree holds Fre and Sub_Count. Secondly, Fre records the number of the occurrences of each value, while Sub_Count records the number of the sensory data items. Finally, the query node calculates the frequency according to the final Fre and Sub_Count.

Algorithm 1. (ϵ, δ)-Approximate Frequency Algorithm

Input: ϵ, δ

Output: (ϵ, δ)-approximate frequency

1: Find ϵ_1 and δ_1 satisfying $(1 - \delta_1)(1 - \delta_2) \geq \frac{1-\delta}{0.95}$, $(1 + \epsilon_1)(1 + \epsilon_2) \leq 1 + \epsilon$, $(1 - \epsilon_1)(1 - \epsilon_2) \geq 1 - \epsilon$ and $\phi_{\delta_2/2}^2 \big(\frac{1}{\inf(F(D(S,t)))} - 1\big)\big(\frac{1}{f_{0.05}(|S'|)} - \frac{1}{|S|}\big) \leq \epsilon_2^2$;

2: $\epsilon_3 = \frac{\epsilon_1}{2+\epsilon_1}$, $\delta_3 = \frac{\delta_1}{2}$;

3: $q_1 = \frac{\phi_{\delta_3/2}^2}{f_{0.05}(|S'|)\epsilon_3^2 + \phi_{\delta_3/2}^2}$, $q_2 = \frac{\phi_{\delta_3/2}^2}{\epsilon_3^2 f_{0.05}(|S'|)\inf(F(D(S',t))) + \phi_{\delta_3/2}^2}$, $q = \max(q_1, q_2)$;

4: Sink node broadcasts q. Call SubData for each node in the spanning tree;

5: Query node holds Fre and Sub_Count, divides each value in Fre by Sub_Count;

6: **return** Fre;

The methodology of aggregating the partial result is as follows. Firstly, $Fre_j = \emptyset$ and $Sub\_Count_j = 0$ for each node j in the spanning tree. Secondly, each leaf node sends its data to its parent with probability q. Finally, each non-leaf node receives and merges data from its children, and adds its own data with probability q, then transfers the result to its parent.

The detailed algorithms are shown in Algorithm 1 and Algorithm 2. c is the number of children for node j in the spanning tree. $|Fre|$ can be regarded as a constant. Using the similar strategy in [14], we have the communication cost and energy cost of the proposed algorithm as $O(\frac{1}{\epsilon_1^2} \ln \frac{1}{\delta_1})$.

Algorithm 2. Submitting-Data Algorithm (SubData)

Output: (Fre, Sub_Count)
1:   $Fre_j = \emptyset$, $Sub\_Count_j = 0$ for all j in the spanning tree;
2:   **for** each leaf node j in the spanning tree, if $rand < q$ **do**
3:     $Fre_j[j.data] = 1$, $Sub\_Count_j = 1$, send (Fre_j, Sub_Count_j) to its parent node;
4:   **for** each non-leaf node j in the spanning tree **do**
5:     Receive $\{(Fre_{jv}, Sub\_Count_{jv}) \mid 1 \le v \le c\}$ from its children;
6:     $Fre_j = \cup_{v=1}^c Fre_{jv}$, $Sub\_Count_j = \sum_{v=1}^c Sub\_Count_{jv}$;
7:     **if** $rand < q$ **then**
8:       $Fre_j[j.data] + +$, $Sub\_Count_j + +$;
9:     **if** j is the query node **then**
10:       **return** (Fre_j, Sub_Count_j);
11:    Send (Fre_j, Sub_Count_j) to its parent node;

---

6   Simulation Results

To evaluate the proposed algorithm, a MANET with 5000 nodes deployed in a 1000m × 1000m square is simulated. All the nodes are moving under the random waypoint model [15]. We set $v_{min} = 0$, $v_{max} = 500m/s$, $p_{min} = 0$, $p_{max} = 0.5s$, and $r = 20m$. The sensory data set is from the AADF Data Traffic Counts Metadata [20]. The energy cost to send and receive one byte of data is set to be 0.0144mJ and 0.0057mJ [21]. The energy cost for calculation is omitted [22].

6.1   Sampling Probability and Energy Cost

The first and second group of simulations is to investigate the relationship among ϵ, δ, the sampling probability and energy consumption. The results are presented in Fig. 1 and Fig. 2 respectively. The results show that the required sampling probability and energy consumption increases with the decrease of ϵ and δ. For example, if $\epsilon = \delta = 0.2$, the energy consumption is 157mJ/Byte. The energy consumption is 173mJ/Byte if $\epsilon = \delta = 0.14$. When $\epsilon = 0.3$ and $\delta = 0.2$, the sampling probability is about 0.5. This means only about half of the nodes need to transfer its data. Therefore, the proposed algorithm saves much energy.

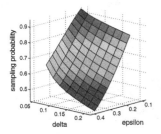

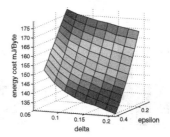

Fig. 1. The relationship among ϵ, δ and the sample size.

Fig. 2. The relationship among ϵ, δ and the energy cost.

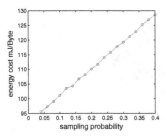

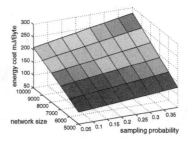

Fig. 3. The relationship between sample probability and energy cost.

Fig. 4. The relationship among ϵ, δ and energy cost.

The third group of simulations is to investigate the relationship between sampling probability q and energy cost. The results are shown in Fig. 3. It can be seen that the energy cost increases with the increase of q. Furthermore, the increase of the energy cost is not proportional to the increase of q. The reason is there is extra energy consumption for broadcasting the sampling probability.

The forth group of simulations is to investigate the relationship among sampling probability, network size and energy cost. The results are shown in Fig. 4. For the same network size, the energy cost increases with the increase of sampling probability. Similarly, the increase of the energy cost is not proportional to the increase of sampling probability. For the same sampling probability, the energy cost increases with the increase of network size.

The fifth group of simulations is to compare the energy cost of our algorithm and that of the naive algorithm. The naive algorithm is to collect all the sensory data in S' and aggregate the partial results during the transmission. The results are shown in Fig. 5. It can be seen that our algorithm has smaller energy consumption. Furthermore, although the naive method collects all the data in S', it only returns the accurate frequency results of $D(S', t)$ rather than $D(S, t)$.

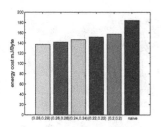

Fig. 5. Energy cost comparison.

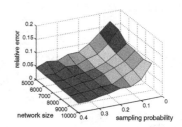

Fig. 6. The relationship among ϵ, δ and relative error.

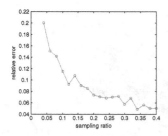

Fig. 7. The relationship between sampling probability and relative error.

Fig. 8. The relationship among sampling probability, network size and relative error.

6.2 Relative Error

The first group of simulations is to investigate the relationship among ϵ, δ and relative error of the final result. The results are shown in Fig. 6. We can see that our algorithm can achieve the specified precision. In most cases, the relative error increases with the increase of ϵ and δ since less sensory data is sampled.

The second simulation is to investigate the relationship between sampling probability and relative error. The results are shown in Fig. 7. We can see that in most cases, the relative error decreases with the increase of the sampling probability, and the precision is still high even the sampling probability is low.

The third simulation is to investigate the relationship among network size, sampling probability and relative error. The results are shown in Fig. 8. Similar to the previous group of simulations, for the same network size, the relative error decreases with the increase of sampling probability. For the same sampling probability, the relative error decreases with the increase of the network size.

7 Related Works

In many areas, a great number of algorithms for frequency query and network connectivity have been proposed, such as [23–27] and [28].

The work in [23] and [24] propose two algorithms for frequency query in large-scale database systems. However, these algorithms are centralized. So they cannot be used in MANETs.

The random geometric graph introduced in [25] is an excellent theoretical model to analyze the network connectivity. But it is only suitable for static networks. The dynamic random geometric graph introduced in [26] can be used in the analysis of connectivity for MANETs. But it only studies the period for a network to be connected or disconnected.

The work in [27] studies the connectivity of MANETs by simulations. The simulation result is the probability of the networks to be connected. But our work focuses on the number of the connected nodes. [28] is like an evaluation of the connectivity of MANETs. The stimulation results for the size of the largest connected component are shown. But [28] does not specify how to calculate the size of the largest connected component. Furthermore, the stimulation results shown in [28] are the average size. This kind of results cannot be applied to our work since it is possible that the actual size is smaller than the average size.

8   Conclusion

An (ϵ, δ)-approximate algorithm to process a frequency query is proposed by the paper. This algorithm is based on Bernoulli sampling, so only a small set of nodes need to transfer data. Furthermore, the sampling probability which can make the final query result to satisfy the specified precision requirement. The stimulation results for the connectivity of MANETs are presented, which can be used in the calculation of sampling probability. Finally, a Bernoulli sampling algorithm is provided and analyzed. The simulation results show that on the aspects of energy efficiency and accuracy, the proposed algorithm has high performance.

Acknowledgement. This paper is partly supported by the NSF 1252292 National Natural Science Foundation of China under Grant No.61370084, 61190115, 61370217, and the Fundamental Research Funds for the Central Universities under grant No.HEUCF100605.

References

1. Mohan, R.S., Sachin, R., Sakthivel, U.: Vehicular ad hoc network based pollution monitoring in urban areas. In: CICN, pp. 214–217 (2012)
2. Cheng, S., Cai, Z., Li, J.: Curve query processing in wireless sensor networks. IEEE Trans. Veh. Technol. (2014)
3. He, Z., Cai, Z., Cheng, S., Wang, X.: Approximate aggregation for tracking quantiles in wireless sensor networks. In: Zhang, Z., Wu, L., Xu, W., Du, D.-Z. (eds.) COCOA 2014. LNCS, vol. 8881, pp. 161–172. Springer, Heidelberg (2014)
4. Li, J., Cheng, S., Gao, H., Cai, Z.: Approximate physical world reconstruction algorithms in sensor networks. IEEE TPDS **25**(12), 3099–3110 (2014)

5. Cai, Z., Goebel, R., Lin, G.: Size-constrained tree partitioning: a story on approximation algorithm design for the multicast k-tree routing problem. In: Du, D.-Z., Hu, X., Pardalos, P.M. (eds.) COCOA 2009. LNCS, vol. 5573, pp. 363–374. Springer, Heidelberg (2009)
6. Guo, L., Li, Y., Cai, Z.: Minimum-latency aggregation scheduling in wireless sensor network. JCO, 1–32 (2014)
7. Fujiwara, S., Ohta, T., Kakuda, Y.: An inter-domain routing for heterogeneous mobile ad hoc networks using packet conversion and address sharing. In: ICDCSW, pp. 349–355 (2012)
8. Chaudhary, A., Tiwari, V., Kumar, A.: Design an anomaly based fuzzy intrusion detection system for packet dropping attack in mobile ad hoc networks. In: IACC, pp. 256–261 (2014)
9. Afroze, T.: Performance evaluation of the hostile environment in mobile ad-hoc network. In: ATNAC, pp. 1–8 (2012)
10. Fajardo, J.T.B., Yasumoto, K., Shibata, N., Sun, W., Ito, M.: Dtn-based data aggregation for timely information collection in disaster areas. In: WiMob, pp. 333–340 (2012)
11. Considine, J., Li, F., Kollios, G., Byers, J.: Approximate aggregation techniques for sensor databases, pp. 449–460 (2004)
12. Nath, S., Gibbons, P.B., Seshan, S., Anderson, Z.R.: Synopsis diffusion for robust aggregation in sensor networks, pp. 250–262 (2004)
13. Cheng, S., Li, J.: Sampling based (epsilon, delta)-approximate aggregation algorithm in sensor networks, pp. 273–280 (2009)
14. Cheng, S., Li, J., Ren, Q., Yu, L.: Bernoulli sampling based (ϵ, δ)-approximate aggregation in large-scale sensor networks, pp. 1181–1189 (2010)
15. Broch, J., Maltz, D.A., Johnson, D.B., Hu, Y.-C., Jetcheva, J.: A performance comparison of multi-hop wireless ad hoc network routing protocols. In: MobiCom, pp. 85–97 (1998)
16. Devore, J.: Probability and Statistics for Engineering and the Sciences
17. Pascoe, M., Gomez, J., Rangel, V., Lopez-Guerrero, M.: An upper bound on network size in mobile ad-hoc networks. In: GLOBECOM, pp. 1–6 (2008)
18. http://www.cs.gsu.edu/jli30/
19. Huang, G., Li, X., He, J.: Dynamic minimal spanning tree routing protocol for large wireless sensor networks, pp. 1–5 (2006)
20. https://www.gov.uk/government/collections/road-traffic-statistics (2013)
21. MPR-Mote Processor Radio Board User's Manual, Crossbow Inc
22. Li, J., Li, J.: Data sampling control, compression and query in sensor networks. IJSNet 2(1), 53–61 (2007)
23. Malik, H.H., Kender, J.R.: Optimizing frequency queries for data mining applications. In: ICDM, pp. 595–600 (2007)
24. Yang, D.-Y., Johar, A., Grama, A., Szpankowski, W.: Summary structures for frequency queries on large transaction sets. In: DCC, pp. 420–429 (2000)
25. Penrose, M.: Random Geometric Graphs, vol. 5. Oxford University Press, Oxford (2003)
26. Díaz, J., Mitsche, D., Pérez-Giménez, X.: Large connectivity for dynamic random geometric graphs. IEEE Trans. Mob. Comput. 8(6), 821–835 (2009)
27. Pitsiladis, G.T., Krokos, A., Panagopoulos, A.D., Constantinou, P.: Connectivity calculation in mobile ad hoc networks: realistic performance simulation. In: ICUMT, pp. 1–5 (2011)
28. Santi, P., Blough, D.M.: An evaluation of connectivity in mobile wireless ad hoc networks. In: DSN, pp. 89–98 (2002)

Secure and Verifiable Multi-owner
Ranked-Keyword Search in Cloud Computing

Jinguo Li[1](✉), Yaping Lin[2], Mi Wen[1], Chunhua Gu[1], and Bo Yin[3]

[1] College of Computer Science and Technology,
Shanghai University of Electric Power, Shanghai 200090, China
lijg@shiep.edu.cn
[2] College of Information Science and Engineering,
Hunan University, Changsha 410082, Hunan, China
[3] College of Computer and Communication Engineering,
Changsha University of Science and Technology, Changsha 410114, Hunan, China

Abstract. To preserve the privacy of cloud data, sensitive files are always encrypted by data owners, which let the keyword search be more difficult to the crucial applications. Thus, a secure and efficient keyword search protocol over encrypted files is required. Most of the prior keyword search works over encrypted cloud files focus on single-data-owner settings. However, there are a large number of data owners involved in real applications. To retrieve user required files, single-owner keyword search schemes need to be repeated several times to search over files encrypted by different unique private keys, which is a very costly way. To achieve high efficiency and privacy preserving in multi-data-owner scenario, we propose a Secure and Verifiable Multi-owner Ranked-keyword Search protocol, named SVMRS, in this paper. Specifically, to preserve privacy and to improve the keyword search precision, we combine a modified asymmetric scalar-product encryption function with the TF$times$IDF rule. Furthermore, to preserve the integrity of search results, we extend the SVMRS based on circular bidirection-linked list, which can make the query result verifiable. Detailed analysis and experiments show that the SVMRS can preserve the file privacy and integrity, and confirms the high efficacy and efficiency of SVMRS.

Keywords: Cloud computing · Keyword search · Privacy preserving · Integrity preserving · Multiple data owners

1 Introduction

Cloud computing provides the on-demand high quality applications and services a shared pool of configurable computing resources [1]. Due to the greatly flexibility and economic savings provided by this computing model, lots of files such as emails, business plans, private videos and photos are outsourced into the cloud server. Usually, these sensitive files are encrypted to preserve the privacy of data owners [3]. However, encrypted files set an obstacle to data utilization service,

© Springer International Publishing Switzerland 2015
K. Xu and J. Zhu (Eds.): WASA 2015, LNCS 9204, pp. 325–334, 2015.
DOI: 10.1007/978-3-319-21837-3_32

such as plaintext keyword search. Most prior related works concerning encrypted keyword search focus on single-owner settings. In reality, there are always more than one data owners contributing files to the cloud in real applications. For example, patients' health records in a centralized health management system are always provided and encrypted by several different hospitals. For security purpose, the system administrator should not know the contents of these health records while they are still searchable by authorized doctors. Therefore, we need to design a secure and efficient keyword search protocol in multi-owner settings.

However, files belonging to different owners are encrypted by different unique private keys, which prevent users from directly searching the files with a single index signal [4,5].Therefore, how to search over these files effectively is a very challenging problem. Prior works [6–9] concerning the secure ranked keyword search have not proposed solutions for this problem.

To address the above problem, in this paper, we propose a Secure and Verifiable Multi-owner Ranked-keyword Search protocol (SVMRS). We focus on ranked key-word search in this paper, since a relevance-ranked result is much more valuable for users than the undifferentiated result derived from large amount of cloud files [4].

Compared with prior ranked keyword search protocols [6–9], our contributions can be summarized as follows:

1. We propose a multi-owner ranked-keyword search protocol called SVMRS to enable users to effectively search the files encrypted by different owners. To improve the search efficiency, a novel trapdoor signal is designed, while in a traditional single-owner method, the original trapdoor needs to be encrypted for several times to search over encrypted files belonging to different owners.
2. SVMRS provides more precise query result than prior secure multi-keyword searches [7,8] by considering the frequencies of keywords. When keyword frequencies are ignored in similarity score calculation [7,8], files with frequent keywords may be excluded in query results (we will analyze it in Sect. 4).
3. SVMRS has achieved the integrity preserving of query results by designing a circular bi-direction-linked list in this paper, which enables users to verify the integrity of query results and detect the misbehaviors of semi-honest cloud server.

Note that, prior works concerning secure keyword search can be divided into single-keyword searches [6,9] and multi-keyword searches [7,8]. We focus on multi-keyword search in this paper, since single-keyword search often yields far too coarse result.

The rest of this paper is organized as follows: Sect. 2 introduces the system and threat models. Section 3 provides the detailed description of our proposed protocol. Section 4 analyze the security and performance of proposed protocol, and experiment it on a real dataset. Section 5 is the conclusion.

2   System and Threat Models

System Model: A widely adopted model for cloud file hosting service is considered in this paper (Fig. 1), which consists of three different entities: *data owners*,

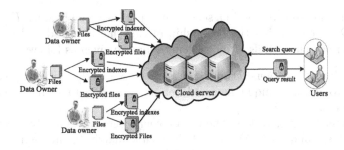

Fig. 1. Architecture for cloud file searching service

data users, and *cloud server*. Each data owner intends to outsource a collection of encrypted files on the cloud server, and still keeps the capability to search through them for effective data utilization reasons. To achieve this goal, for each file, an encrypted searchable index is built from a set of distinct keywords extracted from the file collection. Both the indexes and encrypted files will be sent to the cloud server. To search the file collection for the given keywords, data users firstly translate the search request into several queries, and then send them to the cloud server. Upon receiving the queries from users, the cloud server performs ranked search on the encrypted files with corresponding indexes, and sends back the top-k most relevant files to users.

Threat Model: The security threats faced by cloud file searching-service model primarily come from the cloud server. In our model, data owners and users are trusted, but the cloud server is considered as "semi-honest but curious", which is consistent with prior works [8]. The cloud server would not modify or destroy the files stored on it, but it is "curious" to analyze the owners' encrypted files (including indexes) and the user generated queries. The threat model is considered as follows: the cloud server is aware of the outsourced ciphertext file collection, the searchable indexes and a few backgrounds on the file collection such as related statistical information. File frequency or keyword frequency may be utilized to identify keywords in a query request. Moreover, the cloud server may execute only a fraction of search operates honestly or send back only a fraction of query result honestly.

3   The Proposed SVMRS Protocol

In this section, we describe details of multi-owner privacy-preserving ranked search protocol. The details of our privacy preserving protocol include index generation, trapdoor generation, query processing and integrity preserving of query result which are shown as follows.

Index Generation: Assume there are m data owners $o_1, o_2, ..., o_m$. Each owner o_i first generates plaintext index $v_{i,j}$ for each file $f_{i,j}$ according to the relevance scores of keywords $W = w_1, w_2, ..., w_\varepsilon$. All keywords are agreed by authorized users and data owners. For privacy preserving, o_i encrypts these plaintext index $v_{i,j}$ by an asymmetric scalar-product encryption function, and further splits and extends the result to obtain a secure encrypted searchable index $I'_{i,j}$. Finally, a vector $OS_{i,j}$ concerning the ownership of each file is introduced to support multi-owner search. Details of index generation are given as follows:

Step 1: Keyword set generation. The system scans the total file collection G_{total} to obtain unique keyword set agreed by data owners and users: $W = w_1, w_2, ..., w_\varepsilon$;

Step 2: Secret key generation. The data owner o_i generates a ε bit vector $S_i = s_{i,1}s_{i,2}...s_{i,\varepsilon}$ and a $(\varepsilon + 1) \times (\varepsilon + 1)$ invertible matrix U_i randomly as private keys. S_i is used to indicate the splitting position of indexes or trapdoors and U_i is used to encrypt files. The secret private key is $k_i = S_i, U_i$;

Step 3: Relevance score calculation. o_i calculates the relevance score sc_{i,j,w_x} of each keyword $w_x \in W$ and file $f_{i,j} \in F_{i,coll}$ according to the following TF$times$IDF equation [11], here $F_{i,coll}$ denotes the file collection of o_i. If $f_{i,j}$ does not contain w_x, o_i sets the relevance score to 0.

$$Score(W', f_{i,j}) = \sum_{w_x \in W'} \frac{1}{|f_{i,j}|}(1 + \ln ft_{i,j,w_x}) \ln(1 + \frac{N}{fn_{i,w_x}}) \qquad (1)$$

Here, $(j \in [1, n])$ denotes the term frequency of keyword w_x, and fn_{i,w_x} is the number of files containing w_x; $|f_{i,j}|$ denotes the length of file $f_{i,j}$ and N is the total number of files in the collection.

Step 4: Plaintext index generation. o_i firstly generates a ε vector $v_{i,j} = (sc_{i,j,w_1}, sc_{i,j,w_2}, ..., sc_{i,j,w_\varepsilon})$ as a plaintext index of each file $f_{i,j}$, and then extends $v_{i,j}$ to a $\varepsilon + 1$ vector $v'_{i,j}$, where the $\varepsilon + 1$-th dimension is set to 1;

Step 5: Encrypted searchable index generation. $v'_{i,j}$ is encrypted for security purpose as $I_{i,j} = E_f(v'_{i,j}, U_i) = U_i^T \cdot v'_{i,j} = (e_{i,j_1}, e_{i,j_2}, ..., e_{i,j_{\varepsilon+1}})$, here, E_f is an asymmetric scalar-product encryption function(ASPE) [10];
Then $I_{i,j}$ is spitted and extended to a $2\varepsilon + 1$ vector $I'_{i,j}$ by the following function SE to strengthen the security of searchable index. Thus $I'_{i,j}$ is the encrypted searchable index of file $f_{i,j}$.

$$I'_{i,j} = SE(I_{i,j}) = \begin{cases} (e_{i,j_1}, e_{i,j_2}, ..., e_{i,j_{x_1}}, e_{i,j_{x_2}}, ..., e_{i,j_{\varepsilon+1}}), & if\, s_{i,x} = 1; \\ (e_{i,j_1}, e_{i,j_2}, ..., e_{i,j_x}, e_{i,j_x}, ..., e_{i,j_{\varepsilon+1}}), & if\, s_{i,x} = 0. \end{cases} \qquad (2)$$

Here, $e_{i,j_{x_1}}$ is a random number, $e_{i,j_x} = e_{i,j_{x_1}} + e_{i,j_{x_2}}$;

Step 6: Ownership vector generation. A binary vector $OS_{i,j} = (os_1, os_2, , os_m)$ is generated to indicate the ownership of file $f_{i,j} \cdot os_x = 1$ if and only if $f_{i,j}$ belongs to owner o_x, here, $1 \le x \le m$;

Step 7: File encryption and outsourcing. All files in $F_{i,coll}$ are encrypted by data owner o_i using the secret key k_i and MD5 encryption function. The encrypted file set is $C_{i,coll} = c_{i,1}, c_{i,2}, ..., c_{i,n}$, and it is sent to the cloud with corresponding indexe $I'_{i,j}|OS_{i,j}$.

The above steps show that the index generation function BuildIndex is defined as follows:

$$BuildIndex(f_{i,j}) = I'_{i,j}|OS_{i,j} \qquad (3)$$

Trapdoor Generation: Keyword-search trapdoors are generated by users to search files on the cloud. Their generation procedure is similar to indexes. Users firstly generate the plaintext trapdoor Q with their interested keywords $W'(W' \subseteq W)$. Then Q is extended and scaled as indexes to resist known-plaintext attack [10]. To search the encrypted file, traditional method is encrypting the plaintext trapdoor by each data-owner private key to generate several trapdoor copies, which is indeed costly. In SVMTS, to save the computation and transmission consumption, the keys of data owners are constructed as a vector and the result is further encrypted by a global key U_u, the plaintext trapdoor is encrypted by another U_u^{-1}. The encryption function is an ASPE function which is similar to the index generation. Each pair of U_u and U_u^{-1} are invertible matrixes and are set as the private key components of users. Finally, a vector TS concerning user-interested-owners is introduced. Details are shown as follows:

Step 1: Plaintext trapdoor generation. The user generates a ε bit binary vector $Q = (q_1, q_2, ..., q_\varepsilon)$ as a plaintext trapdoor. $q_x = 1$ if keyword w_x is the user-interested-keyword which is in the search query W', else q_x is set to 0 $(1 \leq x \leq \varepsilon)$;

Step 2: Encrypted trapdoor generation. Similar to index generation, Q is firstly extended and scaled to a $\varepsilon + 1$ bit vector Q' by random numbers a and b: $Q' = (aQ, b), a > 0$. Then Q' is encrypted by the global secret key U_u, and the result is: $T = E_g(Q', U_u) = U_u^T \cdot Q' = (d_1, d_2, ..., d_{\varepsilon+1})$. Here, E_g also denotes an ASPE function. T will be split and extended to a $2\varepsilon + 1$ bit vector T' to strengthen the security of trapdoor.

Step 3: Key vector generation. A key vector consisting of each data-owner-private key is generated as: $GK = (|U_1^{-1}|, |U_2^{-1}|, ..., |U_m^{-1}|)$. $|U_x^{-1}|$ is a $2\varepsilon + 1$ vector computed from the matrix U_x. A global key U_u^{-1} is used to encrypted GK, and the result is: $TK = U_u^{-1} \cdot GK$. The split and extend procedure is similar as in Step 2, and a final result TK' is obtained.

Step 4: Owner vector generation. Generate a binary vector $TS = (ts_1, ts_2, ..., ts_m)$. $ts_i = 1$ if users are interested to files belonging to owner o_i, otherwise $ts_i = 0$. TS is termed an owner vector here;

Step 5: Trapdoor transmitting. Send the encrypted trapdoor $T'|TK'|TS$ to the cloud server for searching through encrypted files.

The above steps show that the trapdoor generation function Trapdoor is defined as follows:

$$Trapdoor(W') = T'|TK'|TS \qquad (4)$$

Query Processing: Upon receiving the encrypted files with indexes and trapdoors, cloud server firstly calculate similarity score $Sco_{i,j}$ of each file $f_{i,j}$, and then sorts all similarity scores. At last, cloud server sends files corresponding to the top-k highest scores to users. Details are given as follows:

Step 1: Similarity score computation: The cloud computes similarity score $Sco_{i,j}$ for each file $f_{i,j} \in G_{total}$ by using the trapdoor $T'|TK'|TS$ and file indexes $I'_{i,j}|OS_{i,j}(1 \leq i \leq n, 1 \leq j \leq n)$. The equation is:

$$Sco_{i,j} = \begin{cases} 0, & if OS_{i,j} \cdot TS^T = 0; \\ I'_{i,j}{}^T \cdot (OS_{i,j} \cdot (TK')^T \times (T')^T), & if OS_{i,j} \cdot TS^T \neq 0. \end{cases} \quad (5)$$

Step 2: Query result: The cloud sorts all similarity scores by the QuikSort algorithm and returns the top-k most relevance files to users.

Integrity Preserving of Query Result: In general, the query result integrity is two-fold. Firstly, the query result is correct, i.e., the result does not include any tampered data; Secondly, the query result is complete, i.e., the result contains all data items satisfying the search query. According to the properties of semi-honest cloud server, it will not tamper the query result intentionally [11], so we just need to consider the completeness of query result as the integrity in this paper.

A linked data structure called the bi-direction-linked list can be used to solve the integrity-preserving problem. The bi-direction-linked list is composed of a set of sequentially linked records called nodes, and each node contains two links that point to the previous and to the next nodes in the sequence. However, when the cloud server does not respond to users, the following two situations cannot be distinguished: (1) There is not any file satisfying the query on the cloud server; (2) The semi-honest cloud server does not return back files satisfying the query. Therefore, a circular bi-direction-linked list is further explored for integrity-preserving. The upper bound S_max of all relevance scores is further inserted into the list, and the last node and the first node are pointed to each other. The details are given as follows.

Embedding: Assume there are encrypted files $c_{i,1}, c_{i,2}, ..., c_{i,x-1}, c_{i,x}, c_{i,x+1}, ..., c_{i,n}$ with corresponding indexes $I'_{i,1}, I'_{i,2}, ..., I'_{i,x-1}, I'_{i,x}, I'_{i,x+1}, ..., I'_{i,n}$ belonging to data owner o_i, S_max is the upper bound of all relevance scores. For each $w_x \in W$, o_i constructs a circular bi-direction-linked list as follows.

Step 1: Sorts all encrypted files according to the relevance scores which are calculated by Eq. 1. Assume $Score(w_x, f_{i,1}) \leq Score(w_x, f_{i,2}) \leq ... \leq Score(w_x, f_{i,x-1}) \leq Score(w_x, f_{i,x}) \leq Score(w_x, f_{i,x+1}) \leq ... \leq Score(w_x, f_{i,n})$.

Step 2: Embeds each index $I'_{i,x}$ as a VO into the previous file $c_{i,x-1}$ and the next file $c_{i,x+1}$ to generate links, here, $1 \leq x \leq n$. There are 3 bits of each letter in a file that can be utilized to embed VOs, since the length of each letter is 8 bits, and we just need 5 bits to distinguish the 26 different letters. The embedding capacity in a 1 KB file is about 3 bytes.

Step 3: Inserts S_max as the last node in the list to generate a circular bi-direction-linked list as shown in Fig. 2. Makes S_max point to the files $c_{i,1}, c_{i,n}$, and makes indexes $I'_{i,1}, I'_{i,n}$ point to S_max.

Step 4: Sends all nodes on the circular bi-direction-linked list to the cloud server for integrity-preserving.

Extracting: Upon receiving the search query, the cloud server returns back top-k most relevant files as query result together with embedded VOs to users. To preserve integrity, users perform the following steps to extract the VOs.

Step 1: Decrypts all files in the query result with a secret key k_i;

Step 2: Extracts VO bits from the letters in these plaintext files. If all VO indexes do not satisfy the query, then the result is complete, otherwise not.

Figure 2 illustrates the process of integrity verification. Assume $c_{i,x}, c_{i,x+1}$ are the files satisfying the query. To verify the integrity, users need to extract corresponding VOs, i.e., $I'_{i,x-1}, I'_{i,x+2}$ from $c_{i,x}, c_{i,x+1}$. If $I'_{i,x-1}$ and $I'_{i,x+2}$ do not satisfy the query, then the query result is complete, otherwise not.

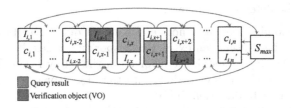

Query result

Verification object (VO)

Fig. 2. An example of integrity verification

4   Analysis and Experiments

In this section, we analyze the security, search precision and performance of proposed SVMRS protocol, and further experiment it on a real dataset. The algorithm security includes file privacy and search-result integrity. The performance includes communication and computation overhead.

4.1   Security Analysis

Privacy analysis: In SVMRS protected cloud computing model, the curious server is not allowed to learn the content of encrypted files (including indexes) sent by owners, and the search queries generated by users. The privacy of indexes and files is preserved since they are encrypted by private secret keys before being outsourced to cloud server, and it is computationally infeasible to compute their actual values. The security of our encryption functions is guaranteed by the matrices-based encryption scheme, which has been proved to be secure and can resist the known-plaintext attack [10]. The index privacy will not be leaked unless the private keys are disclosed. Moreover, statistical attack becomes more difficult when the number of dimensions in a query or index vector increases. This is because the number of possible combinations of keywords appeared in a query or index increases exponentially as the number of keywords becomes larger. Furthermore, different keyword combinations are more difficult to be distinguished statistically when the number of indexes increases. For example, given $I'_{i,j} = SE(I_{i,j}) = SE(U_i^T \cdot v'_{i,j})$, where SE is a splitting and extending function, $I'_{i,j}$ is the encrypted form of index $v'_{i,j}$, U_i is a secret private key. Suppose that the cloud server takes $O(\theta)$ steps to compute $v'_{i,j}$. Recall that the number of encrypted indexes out-sourced from owners is nm. To reveal a keyword value, the cloud server needs to reveal all keyword combinations in indexes. Thus, to reveal keyword, the storage node would take steps $O(nm\theta)$. Here, $\theta = 2^{2\varepsilon+1}$.

Integrity Analysis: The cloud server is semi-honest in SVMRS. It may execute only a fraction of query operates honestly or return back only a fraction of query result honestly, but the files stored on cloud will not be modified or destroyed. To preserve the integrity of query results, all files belonging to the same owner form a circular bi-direction-linked list, which can be verified by users. Misbehaviors of cloud could be detected as follows.

(1) When the cloud server does not send back all query results (for instance, $c_{i,x-1}$ is missing), users can extract corresponding index $I'_{i,x-1}$ from $c_{i,x}$ to detect whether $c_{i,x-1}$ should be involved in the query result. The reason is that, the index $I'_{i,x-1}$ is embedded into the precursor $c_{i,x-2}$ and successor $c_{i,x}$ in a circular bi-direction-linked list;
(2) When none of the query results is sent back, the cloud server is required to return the S_{max} node. Users can extract the smallest index $I'_{i,1}$ and largest index $I'_{i,n}$ from S_{max} to detect whether there is indeed no files satisfying the query request.

4.2   Precision Analysis

The search results in SVMRS are more precise than prior works concerning secure multi-keyword search, for example, MRSE [8]. The reasons are given as follows. SVMRS considers the frequencies of keywords in similarity score calculation to avoid excluding files with frequent keywords in query result while in most prior related works, the similarity score is simply based on the presence/absence of given keywords in files, which is of less precision. For example, assume keyword w_x appears more than once in $f_{i,1}$ and only one time in $f_{i,2}$. According to similarity score definition in SVMRS, $f_{i,1}$ is more relevant than $f_{i,2}$ to the search request $W' = w_x$. However, in MRSE, the similarity sores of both $f_{i,1}$ and $f_{i,2}$ are the same, which indicates that the two files are in the same degree of similarity to W'. Thus when the number of keywords in a search request is more than one, files with frequent keywords may be excluded in query results.

On the other hand, to improve the security and resist statistical attacks, MRSE inserts dummy keywords into index and trapdoor vectors, which make similarity scores of files not accurate. Some real top-k files are excluded in the query result. In SVMRS, although a splitting and extending method is applied to resist statistical attacks and each index or trapdoor vector is split into two sub-vectors randomly, the file similarity scores are not influenced by it. The reason is that, the final result is still the same as that before vector splitting.

4.3   Experiments

To further confirm the efficiency of proposed protocol, SVMRS protocol and MRSEs are implemented on a real-world dataset: the Enron Email Dataset [12].

All protocols are experimented with different number of data owners ranging from 10 to 100. Each owner intends to outsource emails randomly selected from the Enron Email Dataset to generate different datasets ranging from 10 to 1000. All experiments are applied by Java language on a Linux Server with Intel Xeon Processor 2.13 GHz. The experiment results are given as follows.

Trapdoor Generation: Result in Fig. 3(a) shows that time consumption of trap-door generation in SVMRS is nearly linear with the total number of files and data owners. The MRSE schemes have similar characteristics [10]. Other results in Fig. 3(b)–(d) have demonstrated that, the total time consumption of trapdoor generation in SVMRS is much lower than that of MRSE schemes for the same number of keywords in a query (i.e., 10). Since each unique trapdoor needs to derive several copies by different keys of data owners in MRSEs, which is a costly way to realize ranked search. While in SVMRS, a single trapdoor signalling based on decomposition is designed to search through encrypted files efficiently.

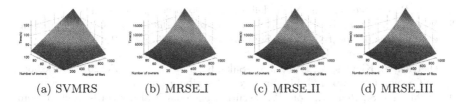

| (a) SVMRS | (b) MRSE_I | (c) MRSE_II | (d) MRSE_III |

Fig. 3. Trapdoor generation cost for the same number (10) of keywords in a query with different number of files

Query Processing: Results in Fig. 4 have demonstrated the query efficiency of SVMRS. The search time consumption MRSEs is greatly affected by the number of data owners, due to the trapdoor copies generated by them.

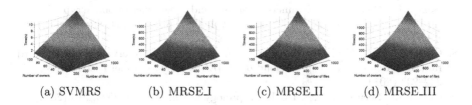

| (a) SVMRS | (b) MRSE_I | (c) MRSE_II | (d) MRSE_III |

Fig. 4. Query cost for the same number (10) of keywords in a query within different number of files

5 Conclusions

In this paper, we address the problem of multi-owner ranked-keyword search over encrypted files by proposing a SVMRS protocol. We firstly apply the

TF*times*IDF rule combining with the modified asymmetric scalar-product encryption function to realize the ranking scheme, and then further extend the protocol based on circular bi-direction-linked list to preserve the integrity of query results. Analysis and experiments show the SVMRS protocol has achieved several security metrics: privacy preserving, integrity preserving, and also has high efficacy and efficiency. In the future, we will further consider the conjunctive keyword search in a more complex cloud service model.

Acknowledgments. This work is partly supported by the Foundation Key Project of Shanghai Science and Technology Committee (No. 12JC1404500, 13JC1403503) and Start-up Fund for Talent Introduction of Shanghai University of Electric Power(No. K2015-008).

References

1. Mell, P., Grance, T.: The NIST definition of cloud computing (2011)
2. Marston, S., Li, Z., Bandyopadhyay, S., Zhang, J., Ghalsasi, A.: Cloud computing-the business perspective. Decis. Support Syst. **51**, 176–189 (2011)
3. Kamara, S., Lauter, K.: Cryptographic cloud storage. In: Sion, R., Curtmola, R., Dietrich, S., Kiayias, A., Miret, J.M., Sako, K., Sebé, F. (eds.) FC 2010 Workshops. LNCS, vol. 6054, pp. 136–149. Springer, Heidelberg (2010)
4. Li, M., Yu, S., Ren, K., Lou, W.: Securing personal health records in cloud computing: patient-centric and fine-grained data access control in multi-owner settings. In: Jajodia, S., Zhou, J. (eds.) SecureComm 2010. LNICST, vol. 50, pp. 89–106. Springer, Heidelberg (2010)
5. Liu, X., Zhang, Y., Wang, B., Yan, J.: Mona: secure multi-owner data sharing for dynamic groups in the cloud. IEEE Trans. Parallel Distrib. Syst. **24**, 1182–1191 (2013)
6. Wang, C., Cao, N., Ren, K., Lou, W.: Enabling secure and efficient ranked keyword search over outsourced cloud data. IEEE Trans. Parallel Distrib. Syst. **23**, 1467–1479 (2012)
7. Boneh, D., Waters, B.: Conjunctive, subset, and range queries on encrypted data. In: Vadhan, S.P. (ed.) TCC 2007. LNCS, vol. 4392, pp. 535–554. Springer, Heidelberg (2007)
8. Cao, N., Wang, C., Li, M., Ren, K., Lou, W.: Privacy-preserving multi-keyword ranked search over encrypted cloud data. IEEE Trans. Parallel Distrib. Syst. **25**, 222–233 (2014)
9. Goh, E.-J.: Secure Indexes. IACR Cryptology ePrint Archive 2003, 216 (2003)
10. Wong, W.K., Cheung, D.W.-l., Kao, B., Mamoulis, N.: Secure kNN computation on encrypted databases. In: Proceedings of the 2009 ACM SIGMOD International Conference on Management of data, pp. 139–152. ACM (2009)
11. Aizawa, A.: An information-theoretic perspective of tfidf measures. Inf. Process. Manage. **39**, 45–65 (2003)
12. Shetty, J., Adibi, J.: The Enron email dataset database schema and brief statistical report. Information Sciences Institute Technical Report, University of Southern California 4 (2004)

A Dynamic Differentiated QoS Based Call Admission Control Service Model for Core Node in Wireless Sensor Network Topology Control

Luqun Li[⊠]

Department of Computer Science and Technology,
Shanghai Normal University, Shanghai, People's Republic of China
liluqun@gmail.com

Abstract. Topology control is a fundamental issue in wireless sensor network, there are a lot of topology control approaches, and however most of them care little about the transmission quality of service of the network. So there is no exception packets lose if a sensor node owns too much neighbor nodes to relay their data packets. Focus on this issue, we build a dynamic call admission control service model for core nodes in wireless sensor network. By analysis, we get the maximum number of core node's neighbor, when some emergent things happen our service model can guarantee QoS for emergent messages transmission and maintain the topology structure unchanged by using a buffered call admission control strategy.

Keywords: Topology control · Wireless sensor network · Call admission control

1 Introduction

As an import part of internet of things (IOT), wireless sensor network (WSN) constitute a major trend in modern networking, which play an indispensable role in environment monitoring, digital content delivery in rural areas with under-developed infrastructure, as well as wildlife and habitat monitoring and so on [1, 3]. However, due to some intrinsic limitations, e.g., the limited available power, weight, and memory size, and also the uncertain ad hoc deployment, may seriously affect a WSN life span and performance [4, 5]. To deal with these problems, network topology control techniques act as a key determinant factor for prolong the lifetime and the performance of WSN.

As for topology control in WSN, by now, there are over thirty network topology control approaches that have been proposed [6, 7], almost in every approaches there are some nodes that act as core nodes (CN) [1] which are nodes in backbone network of WSN, such as, the heads of cluster in low energy adaptive clustering hierarchy (LEACH) topology control which is integrated with clustering and a simple routing protocol in WSN, full function device (FFD) nodes in Zigbee network, or sink nodes in every WSN. These nodes collect packets from their neighbors (e.g. reduced function device node, RFD), and transmit packets to their upstream nodes [7].

© Springer International Publishing Switzerland 2015
K. Xu and J. Zhu (Eds.): WASA 2015, LNCS 9204, pp. 335–344, 2015.
DOI: 10.1007/978-3-319-21837-3_33

However, due to the limited network band width of WSN, packets maybe lose, when too many neighbor nodes send packets to a CN simultaneously, especially in large scale WSN. Focused on this issue, instead of proposing a concrete network topology approach, we will study the fundamental parameters' relationship among link capacity, CNs' neighbor node number and traffic type, and our research achievements will give a reference for CNs' topology control on maximum neighbor nodes number selection under QoS transmission requirements.

2 Problem and Related Works

Topology control is one of the most important techniques used in wireless ad hoc and sensor networks for transmitting data, reducing radio interference and saving energy consumption. Reference [3–11] gave a comprehensive survey of topology control protocols for WSNs.

In each topology approach there are some CNs, they may be head of a WSN cluster or sink node which serve as some irreplaceable roles in WSN, if one of them fail to work, the WSN may be intermitted (See Fig. 1).

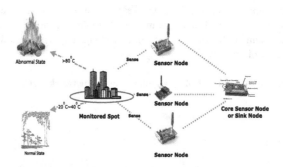

Fig. 1. Core nodes (CNs) in wireless sensor network

Therefore, the CNs selection algorithms in very tricky, for example, cluster head selection in low energy adaptive clustering hierarchy (LEACH) protocol must follow some rules. However, cluster head selection in topology control protocols like LEACH do not consider the traffic situation of nodes and CNs' ability of transmitting packets for their neighbors, for example, under a certain traffic type of nodes, if a cluster head only serves thirty neighbor nodes, it may work good, if it serves two hundred neighbor nodes, the cluster head may fail to work due to the CN's limited ability to process and transmit or the congestion of network traffic. Hence, by analysis the CNs' behavior, we will study that for a given QoS, and how many neighbor nodes can a CN serve. We will study the relationship among these node neighbor number, buffers size, band width and the probability of packets loose.

3   Modeling and Analysis

3.1   Definition of Symbols

In order to facilitate the analysis of this issue, the following symbols are defined as shown in Table 1.

Table 1. Definition of symbols

Symbol	Description
C	Link capacity of a core node or sink node
C_n	Link capacity for transmitting normal message
C_a	Link capacity for transmitting abnormal message
R_n^p	Transmission rate for normal message
ω	The probability to generate normal message
R_a^p	Transmission rate for abnormal message
ζ	The probability to generate abnormal message
p_a	The probability use C_a
p_n	The probability use C_n
α_n	Normal message is in "off"state
α_a	Abnormal message is in "off" state
β_n	Normal message is in "on" state
β_a	Abnormal message is in "on" state
ε_n	Lose probability of normal message
ε_a	Lose probability of abnormal message
N	Total core node's neighbors
N_n^ε	Total core node's neighbors that generate normal message
N_a^ε	Total core node's neighbors that generate abnormal message
x	Buffer size for C_n

3.2   Problem Description

The fundamental topology control issues above can be described as the followings:

Assuming that there are k sensor nodes, each with its own traffic descriptors, to be multiplexed into one network access link of capacity C, if each sensor node requires some specified QoS such as bandwidth, loss probability, delay, how many sensor nodes can be admitted to be as CNs' neighbors?

This issue can be taken as a typical call admission control problem (See Fig. 2).

3.3   Nodal Traffic Types and Transmission Services Requirements

In a WSN, each node will sense environment data and send it to its neighbors (See Fig. 1). Usually, each node can detect two basic states of the monitored spot, one state

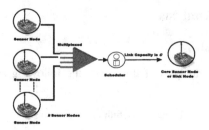

Fig. 2. A typical call admission control issue in wireless sensor network

is in normal state, for example if temperature is between negative 20° and 80°, the node will send normal data messages, data traffic type is R_n^p. The probability that sensor node in this state is ω.

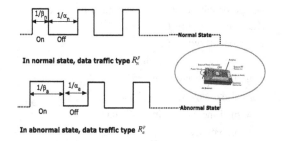

Fig. 3. Traffic types of messages that sensor nodes send

The other state is something maybe wrong with the monitored spot, for example if temperature is above 80°, the data is in abnormal range, it can be deduced that something happed on the monitored spot or fire maybe break out soon (See Fig. 1), and in this state, the node will send much more urgent abnormal messages which include warning and data messages, the corresponding data traffic type is R_a^p. The probability that sensor node in this state is ξ, and $\varpi + \xi = 1$. It means the sensor node can only be in one of the stated of R_n^p and R_a^p. The total link capacity requirement of a sensor node is $\varpi \cdot R_n^p + \xi \cdot R_a^p$.

These two traffic types, R_a^p and R_n^p require differentiated transmission service, R_a^p has much more priority than R_n^p, R_a^p requires reliable transmission, R_a^p usually transmits warning or dangerous information, it has great influences on safety and reliability of the systems, so there is little tolerant for packets lose, while some packets lose of R_n^p will not affect the system too much. Our study will focus on how to dynamically meet the differentiated QoS requirements of R_a^p and R_n^p. To make it simple, we suppose k sensor nodes are homogeneous On/Off sources (See Fig. 3), the probability a source is in the "On" state of R_n^p is p_n, while in the "On" state of R_a^p is p_a,

$$\begin{cases} p_n = \dfrac{\alpha_n}{\alpha_n + \beta_n} \\[2mm] p_a = \dfrac{\alpha_a}{\alpha_a + \beta_a} \end{cases} \tag{1}$$

as for the link capacity each type traffic required need, we assumed that for k sensor nodes of R_n^p need C_n, while R_a^p need C_a, and this can be expressed in Eq. (2).

$$\begin{cases} C = C_n + C_a \\ \varpi + \xi = 1 \\ C_n = \sum_{i=1}^{k} \left(\varpi \cdot p_n^i \cdot R_n^p \right) \\ C_a = \sum_{i=1}^{k} \left(\xi \cdot p_a^i \cdot R_a^p \right) \end{cases} \tag{2}$$

3.4 QoS Requirement Analysis

For a give link capacity C, and $C = C_n + C_a$, if C_n and C_a are predefined, and will not be changed after the WSN' setup, we call it static QoS link capacity strategy. We will address the issue, and get the maximum multiplexing sensor nodes can be gained, under the condition of tolerant packets lose probability ε_n and ε_a, for R_n^p and R_a^p respectively. From the call admission conclusion in [2], we can get maximum multiplexing sensor nodes that send normal messages are N_n^ε in Eq. (3).

$$\begin{cases} k_n = \sqrt{-\ln(2\pi) - 2\ln(\varepsilon_n)} \\[2mm] G_n^\varepsilon = \dfrac{1}{p_n} - \dfrac{1}{p_n} \left\{ k_n \cdot \sqrt{\dfrac{(1-p_n)}{C_n/R_n^p} \left[1 + \dfrac{(k_n)^2(1-p_n)}{4C_n/R_n^p} \right]} - \dfrac{(k_n)^2(1-p_n)}{2C_n/R_n^p} \right\} \\[2mm] N_n^\varepsilon = G_n^\varepsilon \cdot (C_n/R_n^p) \end{cases} \tag{3}$$

For urgent abnormal messages N_a^ε can be got in Eq. (4).

$$\begin{cases} k_a = \sqrt{-\ln(2\pi) - 2\ln(\varepsilon_a)} \\[2mm] G_a^\varepsilon = \dfrac{1}{p_a} - \dfrac{1}{p_a} \left\{ k_a \cdot \sqrt{\dfrac{(1-p_a)}{C_a/R_a^p} \left[1 + \dfrac{(k_a)^2(1-p_a)}{4C_a/R_a^p} \right]} - \dfrac{(k_a)^2(1-p_a)}{2C_a/R_a^p} \right\} \\[2mm] N_a^\varepsilon = G_a^\varepsilon \cdot (C_a/R_a^p) \end{cases} \tag{4}$$

And the total sensor nodes that a CN can serve under the QoS of packets lose probability ε_n and ε_a is N, which is the maximum multiplexing sensor nodes can be gained in Eq. (5),

$$\begin{cases} N = N_n^\varepsilon + N_a^\varepsilon \\ C = N_n^\varepsilon \cdot p_n \cdot R_n^p + N_a^\varepsilon \cdot p_a \cdot R_a^p \end{cases} \tag{5}$$

Simply, if use Eq. (5) in LEACH topology control, by limiting the neighbor nodes of a cluster head node, we can get a QoS-LEACH protocol.

3.5   Numeral Results

For Eqs. (3) and (4) are similar. We only present numeral results for Eq. (3). To demonstrate the relationship among the admission number, packet lose probability, we use the following initial parameters in Table 2.

Table 2. Initial parameters of α, β, C and R_p

α	β	C	R_p
1	10	100	5
1	10	100	7
1	10	100	10

Figure 4 shows that under a certain ratio of C_a/R_a^p or C_n/R_n^p, if the packets lose probability tolerant drop between $[0, 0.025]$ almost vertically.

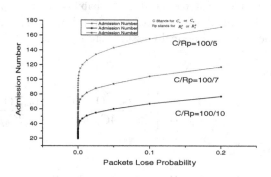

Fig. 4. The relationship between admission number and packets lose probability

4   Dynamic Differentiated QoS Based Call Admission Control

4.1   Analysis and Problem Description

In Eq. (2) for a give link capacity C, and $C_n + C_a = C$, if C_n and C_a are predefined, the probability that sensor node in state of R_a^p is ξ, in state of R_n^p is ω, under the QoS requirements of tolerant packets lose probability ε_n and ε_a the neighbor nodes can be determined by Eq. (5).

If C_n and C_a can be dynamic changed, under the constraint of $C_n + C_a \leq C$, each link capacity can only be allocated in the area of an ellipse (See Fig. 5).

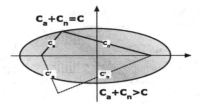

Fig. 5. Link capacity allocation ellipse area

Usually, after a WSN topology architecture formed, a CN's neighbor nodes number will not change during a relative long period, which means N is a constant, $N = N_n^\varepsilon + N_a^\varepsilon$. However, due to the monitored spots event change, the traffic situations of a sensor node may change from time to time. For example, during summer time, there is a relative high probability of forest fire, while in winter the probability of forest fire will drop, if a fire occurs in the monitored spot, some sensor nodes will generate much more urgent abnormal messages and send to their CN, which means ξ will be increased, ω will be decreased, N_a^ε will be increased, N_n^ε will be decreased.

In this scenario, CN must have a high priority service guarantee for urgent abnormal messages transmission, because they are important.

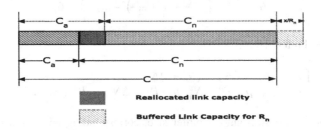

Fig. 6. Some link capacity of C_n be reallocated to C_a

However, because of the difference link capacity requirement for the traffic of R_a^p and R_n^p, usually, $R_a^p > R_n^p$ $p_a > p_n$, if $N = N_n^\varepsilon + N_a^\varepsilon$ is a constant, when N_a^ε increased, though N_n^ε decreased, the total link capacity $C_n + C_a > C$, the total link capacity required will be beyond the area of a ellipse (See Fig. 5), which means some sensor node will lose their link capacity and have no opportunity to send their packets to CN.

Now, to make things simple, the problem is, if $C_n + C_a = C$ is constant, how to guarantee that $N = N_n^\varepsilon + N_a^\varepsilon$ is also a constant. This can be described in Eq. 6

$$\begin{cases} N = (N_n^\varepsilon - \Delta N) + (N_a^\varepsilon + \Delta N) \\ C = (N_n^\varepsilon - \Delta N) \cdot p_n \cdot R_n^p + (N_a^\varepsilon + \Delta N) \cdot p_a \cdot R_a^p \end{cases} \tag{6}$$

where ΔN is the increased sensor nodes which detect and send abnormal message to CN. It is obviously that some link capacity of C_n must be reallocated to C_a (See Fig. 6).

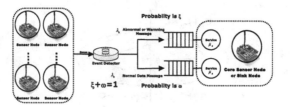

Fig. 7. Two call admission control models

4.2   Model and Analysis

To deal the issue above, we can build two call admission control models (See Fig. 7). The first call admission control model is used for abnormal messages, for abnormal messages must be transmitted with no delay, there is no buffer for this model. This model can be expressed in Eq. (4).The second call admission control model is for normal message. For normal message transmission delay is usually tolerant. We build buffered call admission control model in Eq. (7).

$$
\begin{cases}
k_n = \dfrac{\beta_n x}{R_n^p (1-p_n)\ln(1/\varepsilon_n)} \\
N_n^\varepsilon = R_n^p \cdot \left(\dfrac{1-k_n}{2} + \sqrt{\left(\dfrac{1-k_n}{2}\right)^2 + k_n p_n} \right) \Big/ C_n
\end{cases}
\tag{7}
$$

where, x is the buffer size.

$$
\begin{cases}
N = (N_n^\varepsilon - \Delta N) + (N_a^\varepsilon + \Delta N) \\
C = N_n^\varepsilon \cdot p_n \cdot R_n^p + N_a^\varepsilon \cdot p_a \cdot R_a^p - \Delta N(p_n \cdot R_n^p + p_a \cdot R_a^p)
\end{cases}
\tag{8}
$$

To see the relationship among buffer size, corresponding admission number and packet lose probability in Fig. 8, we give numeral results with the initial parameters in Table 3.

Table 3. Initial parameters of α, β, C, R_p and ε_n in Eq. (7)

α	β	C	R_p	ε_n
1	100	100	5	0.00001
1	100	100	5	0.0001
1	100	100	5	0.001

Figure 8 shows that for a given packet lose probability, additional call admission number will increase with buffer size almost in linear growth.

So we can conclude that under the condition of the constant link capacity of CN $C_n + C_a = C$, and maintain its constant number of neighbors, $N = N_n^\varepsilon + N_a^\varepsilon$, to guarantee increased abnormal message transmission, some link capacity of C_n must be reallocated to C_a, the trade is that CN must allocate some buffers to get buffered link capacity for R_n^p (See Fig. 6).

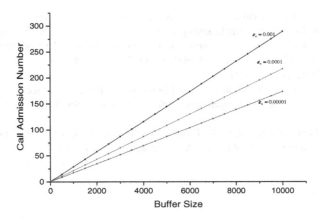

Fig. 8. Numeral result for Eq. 7

5 Conclusion

From the analysis above, we can get the conclusion that if the total link capacity of CN is a constant, to guarantee the QoS for abnormal messages and normal messages transmission, a differential call admission control strategy can be used. When some emergent things happen in the monitored spot, some parts of the link capacity of C_n is reallocated for C_a to handle more abnormal messages, to keep the topology structure unchanged, this strategy can dynamically increase the buffer size to guarantee no backlog in R_n^p for normal messages, and this will lead some tolerant delay for normal messages transmission.

The conclusion give a reference of bound condition for CN's neighbor number for QoS topology control in WSN.

References

1. Li, L., et al.: Analysis on topology control boundary conditions in delay tolerant wireless sensor networks. J. Harbin Inst. Technol. **19**(3), 15–20 (2012)
2. Schwartz, M.: Broadband Integrated Network. Prentice Hall, New Jersey (1998)
3. Akyildiz, I.F., et al.: Wireless sensor networks: a survey. Comput. Netw. **38**(4), 393–422 (2002)
4. Becquaert, M., et al.: Topology control in wireless sensor networks. In: MCC 2008 (2008)
5. Choubey, N., Rao, S.: Topology control in wireless sensor networks. In: Third International Conference on Sensor Technologies and Applications, SENSORCOMM 2009. IEEE (2009)
6. Deshpande, A., et al.: Wireless sensor networks–a comparative study for energy minimization using topology control. In: 2014 Sixth Annual IEEE Green Technologies Conference (GreenTech). IEEE (2014)
7. Gupta, I., et al.: Cluster-head election using fuzzy logic for wireless sensor networks. In: Proceedings of the 3rd Annual Communication Networks and Services Research Conference, 2005. IEEE (2005)

8. Hammoudeh, M., Newman, R.: Adaptive routing in wireless sensor networks: QoS optimisation for enhanced application performance. Inf. Fusion **22**, 3–15 (2015)
9. Handy, M., et al.: Low energy adaptive clustering hierarchy with deterministic cluster-head selection. In: 4th International Workshop on Mobile and Wireless Communications Network, 2002. IEEE (2002)
10. Jameii, S.M., et al.: AMOF: adaptive multi-objective optimization framework for coverage and topology control in heterogeneous wireless sensor networks. Telecommun. Syst., 1–16 (2015)
11. Labrador, M.A., Wightman, P.M.: Topology Control in Wireless Sensor Networks: with a Companion Simulation Tool for Teaching and Research. Springer, The Netherlands (2009)

Secure and Privacy-Preserving Location Proof in Database-Driven Cognitive Radio Networks

Yi Li[1], Lu Zhou[1], Haojin Zhu[1(✉)], and Limin Sun[2]

[1] Shanghai Jiao Tong University, Shanghai 200240, China
{bluely02,zhoulu,zhu-hj}@sjtu.edu.cn
[2] Chinese Academy of Sciences, Beijing 100093, China
sunlimin@iie.ac.cn

Abstract. The latest FCC ruling has enforced database-driven cognitive radio networks (CRNs), in which all secondary users (SUs) can query a database to obtain spectrum available information (SAI). Database-driven CRNs is regarded as a promising approach for dynamic and highly efficient spectrum management paradigm. However, as a typical location-based service (LBS), there is no verification of the queried location, which is very vulnerable to Location Spoofing Attack. This will introduce serious interference to the PUs. In this study, we identify a new kind of attack coined as location cheating attack. To thwart this attack, we propose a novel infrastructure-based approach to provide privacy-preserving location proof. With the proposed solution, the database can verify the locations without knowing the user's accurate location. Experimental results show that our approach, besides providing location proofs effectively, can significantly improve the user's location privacy.

Keywords: Location cheating attack · Location proof verification · Privacy-preserving · Database-driven CRNs

1 Introduction

The rapid advancement of the emerging wireless technology has significantly increased the demand for the wireless spectrum resources. However, most of the spectrum resources have been assigned to the existing systems (e.g. such as Military communications). To address the ever increasing demand for spectrum resources, cognitive radio networks (CRNs) have been proposed to improve the efficiency of spectrum utilization.

In database-driven CRNs, SUs are required to submit a request containing its location to the database to obtain spectrum available information (SAI). As a variant of location-based service (LBS), we focus on the security challenge that the user may cheat about its location when querying for services. Since there is no location verification, this will lead to the unauthorized spectrum access of SUs and introduce serious interferences to PUs. On the other hand, privacy issue

© Springer International Publishing Switzerland 2015
K. Xu and J. Zhu (Eds.): WASA 2015, LNCS 9204, pp. 345–355, 2015.
DOI: 10.1007/978-3-319-21837-3_34

is another important issue in CRNs. Loss of location privacy can expose users to location-based spams, cause social reputation or economic damages. Therefore, location verification in database-driven CRNs is highly desirable.

In this study, we study the problem of location proof in database-driven CRNs without leaking the users' accurate location. A straightforward solution is to enforce the users to provide location proof while querying for services. A location proof is a piece of electronic data that certifies someone's presence at a certain location for some duration. There are several existing works that study the location verification, which can be classified into two categories. In the infrastructure-independent approach [5,9], a user can obtain location claims from neighbors. However, the maximum transmission power may be the bottleneck of this scheme. In the infrastructure-dependent approach [4,12], a set of WiFi access points (APs) exists to produce location proof to the users.

As WiFi APs become increasingly prevalent, using WiFi AP for location proof will be fairly effective, especially in urban areas. Different from the previous researches, we propose a novel hybrid infrastructure-based approach that relies on the existing WiFi AP networks or the cellular networks to provide secure and privacy location proof. In the cases of presence of WiFi APs, the users can prove their locations under the help of WiFi APs. However, in the case of unavailable WiFi APs nearby, the users can tune to the cellular tower to request location proof, since the latter can provide a much larger coverage. To protect their location, we adopt the private proximity testing technology to allow the users to query the database for service without leaking their accurate location.

The contributions of this paper are summarized as below:

- We identify location cheating attack in database-driven CRNs, which allows an attacker to mislead users with a fake location and make them query the database with fake locations, or allows a malicious user to claim a location arbitrarily and query the database for service.
- We propose a novel infrastructure-based approach that relies on the existing WiFi AP network or cellular network to provide guarantees for location cheating prevention and location privacy for the users. The users can choose the location privacy level as he needs, and enable the user to prove his location without leaking his accurate location.
- Our experimental results show that our approach, besides providing location proofs effectively, can significantly improve the user's location privacy.

The rest of the paper is organized as follows. Section 2 gives the background of the database-driven CRNs and identifies two kinds of location cheating attacks. Section 3 introduces the proposed system architecture. Section 4 gives a detailed work flow of the approach and analyses the security of the system. Section 5 discusses the experimental evaluation. Section 6 concludes the paper.

2   Background and Attack Model

2.1   Overview of Database-Driven CRNs Service

The Database-driven CRNs contain three components: primary users (PUs), secondary users (SUs), and the database. The SAI is calculated and stored in the database. The database query process [1] has three phases:

Query Phase: An SU sends a query that contains his current location obtained from his built-in GPS location readings to the database for services.

Response Phase: The database calculates the SAI that contains available channels and corresponding maximum transmission power (MTP) for the SU's locations and sends it back to the SU.

Notify Phase: After receiving the SAI from the database, the SU chooses an available channel from the SAI and registers the chosen channel in database.

2.2   Location Cheating Attacks in Database-Driven CRN

As mentioned above, an SU receives the SAI from the database by sending a query containing its current location. Since this happens completely on the SU side, it is relatively easy to hack. In what follows, we define the attack in two cases as summarized below and present more details about the possible damage.

Active Location Cheating Attack. A malicious SU can simply launch an active location cheating attack by reporting a fake location to the database. His goal is to obtain the SAI for the fake location to gain more advantages.

From the system implementation point of view, there are several ways for a malicious SU to forge a location and make the device believe that it is really in the fake location [11]. In [7], a LocationFaker is developed as a system device to conduct a fake location arbitrarily which can be accepted as a real location

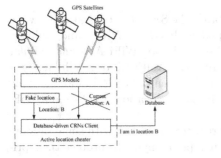   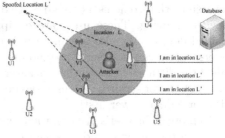

(a) active location cheating   (b) passive location cheating

Fig. 1. (a) Illustration of active location cheating: Location Faker generates location B and makes the device believe it is really in location B. (b) Illustration of passive location cheating: all victims in location L that query the database for services are spoofed to location L'.

by Android device. Figure 1(a) shows the concept of such location cheating. In Fig. 1(a), the attacker obtains the SAI for location B while actually locates at location A. Then, he chooses several channels with better quality and sends a notification message to the database, making the database believe that he is accessing these channels while actually not. This introduces Denial of service (DoS) to other SUs in location B, and also causes service quality loss.

Passive Location Cheating Attack. The attacker is another malicious attacker that is located in the same cell with the victim who is launching a query towards the database for SAI. The attacker's goal is to mislead the victim that he is located in a wrong location and obtain the wrong SAI, which will introduce the interference to the PU.

As pointed out in [9], an attacker can use GPS spoofing device to generate and broadcast fake GPS signals synchronized with the real GPS signals to the target receiver. Then, the fake GPS signals gradually overpower the real GPS signals and make the target receiver lock on them. After replacing the real GPS, the attacker can fool the target receivers to an arbitrary location. If all victims receive the fake signals from the same attacker, they are all spoofed to the same location L' as shown in Fig. 1(b). Then, the attacker can occupy the available channel with better quality for location L as his exclusive channel to achieve better transmission throughput. The SUs who query the database for services with spoofed location L' may also cause interference to the primary users (PUs), since they access the channels that may not be available for location L.

3   System Architecture

In this section, we describe the different entities involved in our system: SUs, a WiFi AP network operator or a cellular network, and the database that contains SAI provider database, location proof server, and certificate authority (CA). Figure 2 depicts the overview of the system we consider.

3.1   The Users

We assume that some users are going to obtain the SAI from the database when they are moving. These users are equipped with GPS-, WiFi-, and cellular-enabled devices. We also assume a unit-disc model for WiFi APs and cellular towers, that means an user can communicate with a WiFi AP or a cellular tower only if the distance between them is lower than a given radius R. Before querying the database for services, the user should obtain the location proof from a WiFi AP or a cellular tower firstly.

To protect the user's privacy, the users register to the CA with some random generated pseudonyms and they can use such pseudonyms to protect their privacy while gaining location proof. A pseudonym contains a public/private key pair (K_{pri}, K_{pub}). We assume that users do not give their pseudonyms to other users, and pseudonyms should not be easy to spoof and clone. While registering, we also assume that the CA can generate other public/private key pairs (PK_{pri}, PK_{pub}), in which PK_{pub} is given to the user and PK_{pri} is kept by the CA.

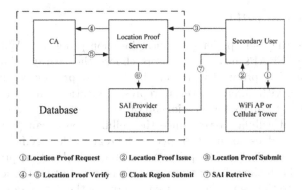

① Location Proof Request   ② Location Proof Issue   ③ Location Proof Submit

④ + ⑤ Location Proof Verify   ⑥ Cloak Region Submit   ⑦ SAI Retreive

Fig. 2. Overview of the system. First, the user obtains location proof from the nearby WiFi AP or cellular tower, then submit it to the location proof server. Second, CA verifies whether the location proof is legitimate. Only if the verification is pass, then SAI provider database provides the SAI to the user.

3.2 WiFi AP Network and Cellular Network

We assume that there are one or multiple WiFi AP networks or cellular networks and each network contains a set of fixed WiFi APs or cellular towers deployed in the area. Each WiFi AP or cellular tower knows its geographic position and its transmission range. Each WiFi AP or cellular tower from the same network shares a public-key group key pairs (GK_{pub}, GK_{pri}). We assume that the WiFi AP network and cellular network are honest but curious, and do not collude with the database.

3.3 Database

We make a little change to the database and divide it into three parts: *Location Proof Server*, *Certification Authority (CA)* and *SAI Provider Database*.

Location Proof Server. *Location Proof Server* directly communicate with the users to collect location proofs.

CA. CA is the only party who knows the mapping between real identity and pseudonym. CA also knows the corresponding secret key PK_{pri}.

SAI Provider Database. The *SAI Provider Database* calculates the SAI and sends it back to the users.

4 The Proposed Privacy Preserving Location Verification Scheme

In this section, we present our approach for privacy-preserving location verification (PPLV) scheme. First, we give an overview of the proposed approach. Subsequently, we present the detailed work flow. Finally, we analysis the security and privacy. Figure 2 shows an overview of the approach and main processes.

4.1 Overview of PPLV

In our scheme, the users prefer to request location proof with WiFi AP; while there are no WiFi APs nearby, the users choose the nearby cellular tower to request for location proof. To protect the location privacy, we adopt a grid reference system with different levels to represent locations, and users can choose appropriate level to query for location proof.

In the case of cellular tower, since the cellular tower can provide a larger coverage, the user does not need to specify the region. He specifies a granularity of level to protect his location privacy, and requests location proof with the cellular tower. Then the cellular tower embeds its coverage to the location proof and sends back to the user. Then the user can query the database for services by submitting the location proof containing the cellular tower's coverage. Finally, the database calculates the SAI for the coverage and sends back to the user.

In the case of WiFi AP, since the WiFi AP's coverage is much smaller than the cell size, the user not only specifies the granularity of level, but also specifies the region. To further protect the location privacy (i.e. enable the user to prove his location without leaking the accurate cell to the database), we adopt private equality testing [2] to determine if two cells match without revealing the exact cell number. The basic idea is that if the user is located at cell a and WiFi AP is located at cell b, CA learns if $a = b$ and nothing else. We will give a detailed work flow in Sect. 4.3.

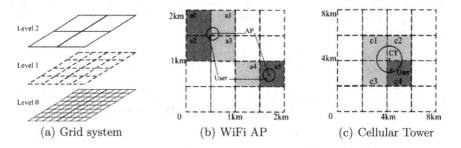

(a) Grid system   (b) WiFi AP   (c) Cellular Tower

Fig. 3. Grid reference system. We assume the grid cell with side length of 250 meters for level 0, the unit-disc communication model with a radius of 25 meters for WiFi APs and of 2 km for cellular towers.

4.2 System Initialization

Global setup. The location of a user can be defined with different granularities. For example, the user may be willing to use fine-grained location information in urban area while using coarse-gained location information in countryside. As show in Fig. 3(a), the system adopts a grid reference system [6] denoted by $\Gamma(l)(l = 0, 1, 2, \cdots)$ to represent locations. For each level l, the grid cell size (i.e. width and height) is fixed and equal. The size at level $l - 1$ is always lower than that at level l. Every grid cell $c \in \Gamma(l)$ is identifiable by an index $id(c) \in \mathbb{N}$ and is fully contained by several grid cells $c \in \Gamma(l - 1)$.

User setup. Let G be a cyclic group of prime order p and g a generator of G. We assume that the Diffie-Hellman problem is hard in G. All users, WiFi APs, and the CA are pre-configured with the same G and g. We will use $\mathbb{Z}_p$ to denote the set $\{0, \cdots, p-1\}$. When the user firstly registers to the CA, the CA generates several public/private key pairs (e.g. CA chooses a random x in $\mathbb{Z}_p$ and computes $h = g^x$, in which h given to the user served as PK_{pub}, and x is kept by the CA served as PK_{pri}). We assume the WiFi APs have the user's public key h.

4.3   System Process

Location Proof Request. The user periodically uses its WiFi module to scan the channels, hearing beacons from the nearby WiFi APs. Upon receiving a beacon, the user extracts the beacon's sequence number to use it in the request for location proof. Sending back to the WiFi AP guarantees the freshness of the request. The location proof request can be denoted as:

$$Request = (P_{user}, n, l, t, R_{user}, C_{loc_{user}}) \tag{1}$$

Here, P_{user} denotes the user's pseudonym; n denotes the beacon's sequence number; l denotes the granularity of level; t denotes the request time. R_{user} is a set of cell *ids* that denotes the region that the user queries for. $C_{loc_{user}}$ encrypted with the public key PK_{pub} contains the user's location information, which can be denoted as

$$C_{loc_{user}} = (g^r, h^{a+r}) \tag{2}$$

Here, r is a random number in $\mathbb{Z}_p$, a is the user's grid cell *id* under level l.

Assume that a user and a WiFi AP use granularity of level 1 in Fig. 3(b). The user specifies the region R_{user}, containing cells $\{a_0, a_2\}$, in which cell a_2 is the user's cell, then he computes an encryption of his location a_2 encoded as h^{a_2} and sends the ciphertext to the WiFi AP. In particular, the user computes

$$C_{loc_{user}} = (g^r, h^{a_2+r}) \tag{3}$$

and embeds it into the request.

Location Proof Issue. Upon receiving the location proof request, the WiFi AP firstly checks whether the number is a current one. We assume that the WiFi AP can accept requests whose sequence number was broadcasted within last 100 milliseconds. Then, the WiFi AP should verify that the region R_{user} is reasonable (i.e. since the user's cell must be in coverage area of the WiFi AP R_{AP}, R_{user} should have intersection with R_{AP}[10]). If the intersection is denoted as $\{b_1, \cdots\}$, then the WiFi AP uses the element of $\{b_1, \cdots\}$ and the ciphertext $C_{loc_{user}} = (g_1, g_2)$ from the user to construct a new encryption message, which can be denoted as

$$C_{loc_{AP}} = (g_1^s g^t, g_2^s h^{(t-s \cdot b_1)}, \cdots) \tag{4}$$

Here, s is a random none-zero number in $\mathbb{Z}_p$, t is a random number in $\mathbb{Z}_p$. Note that setting $w = s \cdot r - t$, we get

$$C_{loc_{AP}} = (u_0, u_1, \cdots) = (g^w, h^{s \cdot (a-b_1)+w}, \cdots) \tag{5}$$

As show in Fig. 3(b), the WiFi AP finds the coverage area $\{a_0, a_1, a_2, a_3\}$, and compares with R_{user}. The intersection grid cells are $\{a_0, a_2\}$. Then, the WiFi AP computes

$$C_{loc_{AP}} = (u_0, u_1, u_2) = (g^w, h^{s \cdot (a_2-a_0)+w}, h^{s \cdot (a_2-a_2)+w}) \tag{6}$$

Then, the WiFi AP embeds its location information into the location proof response that signed with private group key GK_{pri}, and sends back to the user. The location proof response can be denoted as

$$Response = sig_{GK_{pri}}(P_{user}, l, t, R_{user}, C_{loc_{AP}}) \tag{7}$$

Location Proof Verify. To submit a location proof, a user must sign it before transmission. Upon receiving the location proof, the *Location Proof Server* performs four steps. First it checks the user's signature to make sure that the location proof has not been tampered with while submitting. Second, it checks the WiFi AP's signature in the location proof. This step makes sure that the location proof has not been modified by the user. Third, it checks that the user is indeed the recipient of the location proof. Fourth, if these three steps are successful, it forwards P_{user} and $C_{loc_{AP}}$ to the CA for verification. CA searches the corresponding secret key PK_{pri} for P_{user}, and decrypts $C_{loc_{AP}}$, or computes $\{m_1 \leftarrow u_1/u_0^x, m_2 \leftarrow u_2/u_0^x, \cdots\}$. If one of elements is equal to 1, the location proof is considered as legitimate, then the *Location Proof Server* submits R_{user} and l to the *SAI Provider Database*. Otherwise, it is rejected.

SAI Retrieval. When *SAI Provider Database* receives l from *Location Proof Server*, it applies the granularity of level l and calculates the SAI for grid cells in R_{user}. Note that, a channel in the SAI for grid cell a_2 means that the channel is available for all subcells in cell a_2, thus when a user specifies a higher granularity of level, the database may respond with the SAI contains less available channels.

4.4 Security and Privacy Analysis

Malicious User. First, we prevent users from forging the location proofs by using the digital signature GK_{pri}. Moreover, the users can only obtain the valid location proof if they are in transmission range with the WiFi APs or cellular towers. Second, a fake region R_{user} can be verified by the WiFi AP. Third, a fake location a can be verified by the CA. Thus, a malicious user can be detected immediately when he is cheating about his location.

Curious Database. In our scheme, the *Location Proof Server* has access only to location proofs and pseudonyms of the users. It can not know the real identities of the location proofs. Moreover, the location proof verification do not reveal the user's accurate location. By using *Spectrum Utilization based Location Inferring attack*[8], the user can be geo-located to an accurate estimated location. However in our scheme, we can also use different granularity levels to protect the user's location privacy.

Curious WiFi AP Network. Several WiFi APs could collude and track the location of a user based on the collected location proof requests. To thwart this issue, our scheme employs randomized pseudonyms as well as randomized encryption keys. Since WiFi APs only know pseudonym P_{user} and encryption key PK_{pub}, and the user uses a pair of a pseudonym and a public key PK_{pub} each time while requesting location proof, it could not link different location proof requests to a same user, thus it can not track the user's trajectory.

5   Evaluation

In this section, we evaluate the effectiveness and efficiency of the proposed infrastructure-based approach from following aspects: 1) cost of involved three entities; 2) effectiveness of the proposed approach.

5.1   Cost of Involved Entities

We conduct experiments on a 64-bit computer with Intel i5 CPU of 2.5GHz and 4G memory and an android smart phone with Exynos 4412 1.6GHz CPU and 2G RAM, 16G ROM. In the experiment, we evaluate the efficiency of three involved entities under different sizes of prime p as shown in Table 1.

Table 1. Evaluation of the cost of involved three entities on smart phone with Exynos 4412 1.6 GHz CPU and computer with Intel i5 CPU of 2.5 GHz

bit number of p	user	WiFi AP	CA
128	$48 \sim 52\,\mathrm{ms}$	$20 \sim 60\,\mathrm{ms}$	$10 \sim 12\,\mathrm{ms}$
256	$85 \sim 90\,\mathrm{ms}$	$42 \sim 150\,\mathrm{ms}$	$21 \sim 30\,\mathrm{ms}$
512	$185 \sim 190\,\mathrm{ms}$	$82 \sim 250\,\mathrm{ms}$	$41 \sim 50\,\mathrm{ms}$

Cost on User Side. The first metric is the cost of location proof request. The user needs to perform two exponentiations when generating location proof request. Note that, this process could be sped up considerably using pre-computations, which could further reduce the computation latency of location proof request.

Cost on WiFi AP Side. The second metric is the cost of location proof issue. Since computing a product of exponents such as $g_1^s g^t$ is only slightly expensive than computing a single exponent, we count these as a single exponentiation. The best case is to compute two exponentiations while the worst case is to compute five exponentiations.

Cost on CA Side. The last metric is the cost of location proof verification. The cost of location proof verification is to computer $\{u_1/u_0^x, \cdots\}$. Since computing division is much faster than computing exponentiation, the cost of location proof verification for each user is to compute a exponentiation.

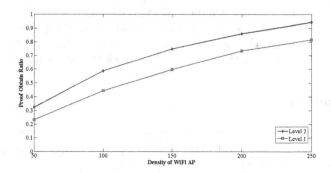

Fig. 4. Location proof obtain ratio under different density of WiFi AP.

5.2   Effectiveness of the Proposed Approach

We evaluate the effectiveness of the proposed approach by setting up simulation environment with several WiFi APs uniformly distributed in a region of $10\,km \times 10\,km$ which is divided into 100×100 cells. For each simulation, we use the Levy walk mobility model to generate trajectory for mobile user and assume the user should update a location proof with certain time interval. A successful location proof is obtained when the user is in the coverage area of a WiFi AP.

Figure 4 shows the location proof obtain ratio under different granularities of level with different densities of WiFi AP. We can see that the location proof obtain ratio reaches 90% when the density of WiFi is $200/km^2$. The higher granularity of level the user specifies, the more location proof obtains.

6   Conclusion

In this paper, we identify a new kind of attack coined as location cheating attack in database-driven CRNs, which can cause interference to PUs. To thwart this attack, we propose a novel infrastructure-based approach that relies on the existing WiFi AP network or cellular network to provide secure and privacy location proof. We use a grid reference system and adopt the private proximity testing technology to further improve the user's location privacy. Simulations well demonstrate the effectiveness and efficiency of the proposed approach.

Acknowledgments. This work is supported by National Science Foundation of China (no. 61272444, U1401253, U1405251, 61411146001).

References

1. Chen, V., Das, S., Zhu, L., et al.: Protocol to Access White-Space (PAWS) Databases. draft-ietf-paws-protocol-10 (work in progress) (2014)
2. Narayanan, Arvind, et al. Location Privacy via Private Proximity Testing. NDSS. (2011)
3. Zhang, L., Fang, C., Li, Y., et al.: Optimal Strategies for Defending Location Inference Attack in Database-driven CRNs. ICC. IEEE (2015)
4. Capkun, S., Buttyan, L., Hubaux, J.-P.: SECTOR: secure tracking of node encounters in multi-hop wireless networks. In: Proceedings of the 1st ACM Workshop on Security of Ad Hoc and Sensor Networks. ACM (2003)
5. Zhu, Z., Cao, G.: Applaus: a privacy-preserving location proof updating system for location-based services. INFOCOM. IEEE (2011)
6. Zheng, Y., Li, M., Lou, W., Hou, Y.T.: SHARP: private proximity test and secure handshake with cheat-proof location tags. In: Foresti, S., Yung, M., Martinelli, F. (eds.) ESORICS 2012. LNCS, vol. 7459, pp. 361–378. Springer, Heidelberg (2012)
7. Li, M., et al.: All your location are belong to us: breaking mobile social networks for automated user location tracking. MOBIHOC. ACM (2014)
8. Gao, Z., et al.: Location privacy in database-driven cognitive radio networks: attacks and countermeasures. INFOCOM. IEEE (2013)
9. Zeng, K., Ramesh, S.K., Yang, Y.: Location spoofing attack and its countermeasures in database-driven cognitive radio networks. In: 2014 IEEE Conference on Communications and Network Security (CNS). IEEE (2014)
10. Siksnys, L., et al.: Private and flexible proximity detection in mobile social networks. MDM. IEEE (2010)
11. He, W., Liu, X., Ren, M.: Location cheating: a security challenge to location-based social network services. ICDCS. IEEE (2011)
12. Pham, A., et al.: Secure and private proofs for location-based activity summaries in urban areas. In: Proceedings of the 2014 ACM International Joint Conference on Pervasive and Ubiquitous Computing. ACM (2014)

SDP: Separate Design Principle for Multichannel Scheduling in Priority-Aware Packet Collection

Feilong Lin[1,2], Cailian Chen[1,2(✉)], Cunqing Hua[3], and Xinping Guan[1,2]

[1] Department of Automation, Shanghai Jiao Tong University, Shanghai, China
[2] Key Laboratory of System Control and Information Processing,
Ministry of Education of China, Shanghai, China
cailianchen@sjtu.edu.cn
[3] School of Information Security Engineering,
Shanghai Jiao Tong University, Shanghai 200240, China

Abstract. Industrial wireless sensor networks (IWSNs) are expected to play a key role in the next generation of Industry Internet, which present a flexible and low-cost way to comprehensively perceive process systems in industrial field. Priority-aware packet collection is of vital importance for IWSNs to gather the data packets according to their differentiated transmission requirements. In multichannel IWSNs, this is still a challenging problem due to the complexity of collision avoidance design and transmission delay optimization. In this paper, we consider the packet collection with two priority classes, and propose a separate design principle (SDP) for multichannel scheduling based on IEEE 802.15.4e protocol. In SDP, we separately design two multichannel superframes for high and low priority sensors, where each superframe fully uses the time slots on all channels. Then, a concession strategy is devised to resolve the possible transmission collisions. Simulation results demonstrate that SDP based multichannel scheduling achieves lower transmission delay to both high and low priority sensors comparing with the IEEE 802.15.4e protocol.

Keywords: Industrial wireless sensor networks · Multichannel scheduling · Priority-aware packet collection

1 Introduction

Industrial wireless sensor networks (IWSNs) are expected to play a key role in the next generation of Industry Internet. It is reported by General Electric Co. that about 46 % of the global economy or \$32.3 trillion in global output can benefit from the Industrial Internet [3]. IWSNs help to perceive comprehensive running states of process systems in industrial field, then to optimize the production control and improve the production efficiency [8]. Generally, in industrial process systems, the IWSNs are required to collect different classes of data packets with different quality of service (QoS) requirements. For example, industrial process monitoring data transmission for online control can only tolerate the latency no more than tens of milliseconds [10]. Thus it requires higher transmission priority

© Springer International Publishing Switzerland 2015
K. Xu and J. Zhu (Eds.): WASA 2015, LNCS 9204, pp. 356–365, 2015.
DOI: 10.1007/978-3-319-21837-3_35

than other monitoring data which may allow long latency. Therefore, Priority-aware packet collection is of vital importance in IWSNs. In multichannel IWSNs, how to efficiently coordinate multiple channel access for Priority-aware packet collection is a fundamental but challenging problem due to the complexity of collision avoidance design and transmission delay optimization.

Many researches have been done for the priority-aware packet transmission in IWSNs. The IEEE Standard 802.15.4, extensively applied in industrial applications, has provided the preliminary solution for packet transmission with different delay constraints [1]. By reserving the guaranteed time slots (GTSs) in contention free period (CFP), the high priority data packets can be transmitted in a collision-free way. Relatively, the low priority data packets are committed to access to radio channel by CSMA-CA approach in contention access period (CAP). Based on IEEE 802.15.4 protocol, an adaptive strategy is proposed in [4] to determine the lengths of CFP and CAP to deal with the dynamics of high and low priority traffics. Compared to reservation transmission for high priority packets, the authors in [7] suggest high priority packets transmitting in CSMA-CA manner while the low priority packets in TDMA manner by allowing high priority packet to hijack the transmission chance of low priority packet. The work [11] proposes a proportional delay model where the mean transmission delays of different data traffics approach a proportional fashion. The above literatures are specified on single channel, which necessitate multichannel access coordination to extend to multichannel IWSNs. To exploit the multichannel diversity, the work [9] proposes a multichannel superframe scheduling mechanism for cluster-tree topology network based on IEEE 802.15.4 protocol. It allocates each cluster with one orthogonal channel to avoid inter-cluster interference. The superframe designed by the cluster head still works on single channel. A fixed priority packet transmission method is proposed in [6] for multichannel multi-hop networks. Multiple channels are scheduled for parallel transmissions over multiple routing paths to reduce the end-to-end delay of packet delivery.

Recently, IEEE 802.15.4e [2] has been released, in which the deterministic and synchronous multichannel extension (DSME) mechanism supports multichannel superframe. Similar to reservation based method in IEEE 802.15.4, priority-aware packet transmission can be implemented by allocating DSME-GTSs in CFP to high priority traffics on multiple channels. Although IEEE 802.15.4e provides the implementation approach for multichannel transmission scheduling, it has not specified any method or algorithm to optimize the packet transmission performance, such as transmission delay, the primary concern in IWSNs. For example, in TDMA scheduling, the distribution of scheduled slots for each sensor would affect its mean packet transmission delay.

In this paper, we introduce a separate design principle (SDP) for multichannel scheduling in priority-aware packet collection. For simplicity but without loss of generality, we consider two classes of sensors in the IWSN, which are denoted as the high and low priority sensors, respectively. The data packets from high priority sensors have the transmission superiority over the packets from low priority sensors. The main idea of SDP is to design multichannel superframes for high and low priority sensors separately, whereby each superframe fully uses the slotted channels. To resolve the collision between two classes of sensors, a concession strategy is then devised by introducing a priority indicator at the beginning of each slot for the high priority sensors. By checking the priority indicators, the low priority sensors can opportunistically utilize the unused slots which have been scheduled to high priority sensors. The main contributions of this work are summarized as follows:

1. The SDP is proposed for multichannel scheduling in Priority-aware packet collection. It not only guarantees the transmission superiority of high priority sensors but also improves the transmission of low priority sensors.
2. Considering the impact of each sensor's scheduling intervals on its mean transmission delay, a greedy multichannel superframe determination (GMSD) algorithm is devised to optimize the multichannel superframe design.
3. The lower bounds of mean packet transmission delays for both high and low priority sensors are obtained based on queueing theory analysis.

The remainder of this paper is organized as follows: Priority-aware multichannel scheduling problem is formulated in Sect. 2. The determination of multichannel superframe is presented in Sect. 3. Section 4 shows the separate design principle. Finally, the performance evaluation is conducted in Sect. 5.

2   Problem Formulation

Consider a classic star-topology IWSN, which consists of one access point (AP) and two classes of sensors with different priorities, i.e., N^H high priority sensors and N^L low priority sensors, respectively. Assume the data packet flows of sensors follow independent Poisson processes with mean rates $\{\lambda_n^H | n = 1, \ldots, N^H\}$ and $\{\lambda_n^L | n = 1, \ldots, N^L\}$. The rates are slowly time-varying. For example, they keep invariable during the production of one batch or one order in industry. The packet size is fixed and normalized to 1. Suppose that there are L channels in the network. The network is synchronized and time is slotted. During each time slot, only one packet can be delivered on each channel. The packet transmission of each sensor follows first-come first-served manner. Each sensor only transmits on a single channel in a slot, but can take per-slot channel hopping if required. AP supports multichannel transmission, which covers all of the L channels. To guarantee the transmission schedulability of the network, the average packet arrival rate in the network should be less than L. Accordingly, the network traffic rate must satisfy $\sum_{n=1}^{N^H} \lambda_n^H + \sum_{n=1}^{N^L} \lambda_n^L < L$.

This paper works towards an optimal multichannel schedule mechanism for priority-aware packet collection based on IEEE 802.15.4e protocol. To this end, the following two sub-problems need to be solved.

Multichannel Superframe Design: It is observed that the schedule of the time slots on multiple channel would affect the packet transmission delay. As demonstrated in Sect. 3, the distribution of scheduled slots for each sensor, in particular the second moment of scheduling intervals, affects the mean packet transmission delay. Hence, the delay optimization needs to be considered in the multichannel superframe design.

Priority-aware Transmission Coordination: In order to meet the differentiated packets collection, a priority-aware transmission coordination mechanism is needed. This coordination mechanism charges to resolve the channel access collision between high and low priority sensors. Further, it is expected to improve the packet transmission performance of low priority sensors to the best.

3 Multichannel Superframe Design

In this section, we present the design of the optimal TDMA based multichannel superframe. Based on IEEE 802.15.4e protocol, the targeted multichannel superframe in this paper relies on TDMA based scheduling in CFP. Particularly, the CAP for CSMA based channel access is not considered.

3.1 TDMA Based Multichannel Superframe Design

Consider a general network consisting of N sensors with Possion-distributed packet arrival at the rates $\{\lambda_n | n = 1, \ldots, N\}$. Denote $\mathbf{A}$ as the multichannel superframe on L channels with period of T slots, which can be represented by a $L \times T$ matrix. Each element $a_{i,j}$ is one *resource block* of the jth slot on the ith channel. All the resource blocks of $\mathbf{A}$ are allocated to sensors in a proportional way. Each sensor is allocated with resource blocks as

$$R_n = \frac{\lambda_n}{U} LT, \tag{1}$$

where $U = \sum_{n=1}^{N} \lambda_n$ is the overall packet rates of all sensors. In implementation, set R_n to an integer number and keep $\sum_{n=1}^{N} R_n = LT$. For simplicity, we assign an integer to each $a_{i,j}$ to represent the resource block allocation in $\mathbf{A}$, e.g., $a_{i,j} = n$ means that j^{th} slot on i^{th} channel is allocated to sensor n. In practice, the whole superframe information is not necessary for each sensor. To save the storage resource, each sensor only needs to store its transmission schedule $\mathbb{A}_n = \{(i,j) | a_{i,j} = n\}$.

3.2 Mean Delay Analysis

Let $\mathbb{J}_n = \{J_{n,k} | k = 1, \ldots, R_n\}$ be the time sequence of resource blocks in $\mathbb{A}_n$. Obviously, $\mathbb{J}_n$ is a strictly increasing sequence of time slot indexes. With respect to the superframe $\mathbf{A}$, the *scheduling interval* for sensor n is defined as

$$s_n^k = \begin{cases} J_{n,k+1} - J_{n,k}, & k = 1, \ldots, R_n - 1, \\ T - J_{n,k+1} + J_{n,1}, & k = R_n. \end{cases} \tag{2}$$

If the sensor delivers data packets according to the superframe periodically, the first and second moments of $\{s_n^k\}$ are

$$\bar{s}_n = \frac{T}{R_n} \text{ and } s_n^{(2)} = \frac{1}{R_n} \sum_{k=1}^{R_n} (s_n^k)^2. \tag{3}$$

The packet transmission of each sensor can be modelled as a queueing process with Poisson arrival. Then the packet transmission follows the general distribution with the mean transmission interval $\bar{s}_n$ and the second moment $s_n^{(2)}$. According to M/G/1 queueing model [5], the mean waiting time of sensor n is

$$W_n = \frac{\lambda_n s_n^{(2)}}{2(1 - \lambda_n \bar{s}_n)}. \tag{4}$$

Note that the minimum $s_n^{(2)}$ is achieved when all slots assigned to the sensor n are equally distributed. In this case, we have $s_n^{(2)} = (\frac{T}{R_n})^2$. Then the lower bound of the mean waiting delay can be obtained as

$$W_n^{\text{LB}} = \frac{\lambda_n T^2}{2R_n^2 - 2\lambda_n T R_n}. \tag{5}$$

As one packet is delivered in one time slot, the lower bound of mean transmission delay (including the waiting slots and the transmission slot) of sensor n is

$$D_n = W_n + 1. \tag{6}$$

As the second moment cannot be easily determined, the lower bound will be used in the following analysis.

3.3 Determination of Multichannel Superframe

From (3) and (4), a good superframe should make second moments of scheduling intervals as small as possible. The optimal $\mathbf{A}$ can be obtained by solving the following optimization problem

$$\mathbf{A}^* = \arg\min\max_{n \in [1,N]} s_n^{(2)}. \tag{7}$$

The optimization problem (7) is an integer programming problem, which normally does not have an analytical solution. In this paper, we employ a greedy multichannel superframe determination (GMSD) algorithm to find the $\mathbf{A}^*$ as shown in Algorithm 1.

The algorithm GMSD includes two steps. The first step is initial scheduling. The resource blocks $\{R_n\}$ are distributed to a one-dimensional sequence, i.e., $\mathbf{B}_{1 \times LT}$ in Algorithm 1. Then, reshape $\mathbf{B}$ to $\mathbf{A}$. The second step is optimal scheduling by a greedy manner. In each iteration, the sensor $\tilde{n}$ with maximal second moment $s_{\max}^{(2)}$ is first selected. Then find the largest scheduling interval of $\tilde{n}$ and its left schedule $a_{i,j}$. Try to exchange $a_{i,j}$ with its neighboring schedules $\{a_{l,j+1} | l = 1, \ldots, L\}$ and record the minimal second moment from the sensors $\{n' | n' = a_{l,j+1}, l = 1, \ldots, L\}$. If this minimal second moment obtained by sensor $n' = a_{l^*,j+1}$ is smaller than $s_{\max}^{(2)}$, confirm the schedule exchange between $\tilde{n}$ and n'. Otherwise, cancel the exchange and end the scheduling.

Algorithm 1. Greedy Multichannel Superframe Determination

1: **Input:** L; T; $\{\lambda_n | n = 1, \ldots, N\}$;
2: **Output: A**;
3: Calculate $\{R_n | n = 1, \ldots, N\}$ according to (1);
4: $\mathbf{B}_{1 \times LT} \leftarrow \mathbf{0}$; $K \leftarrow 0$;
5: **for** $n = 1$ to N **do**
6:     $\mathbf{B}(K + 1 : K + R_n) \leftarrow n$; $K \leftarrow K + R_n$;
7: **end for**
8: Reshape: $\mathbf{A}_{L \times T} \leftarrow \mathbf{B}_{1 \times LT}$;
9: $flag \leftarrow 1$;
10: **while** $flag = 1$ **do**
11:     $s_{\max}^{(2)} \leftarrow \max\{s_n^{(2)}\}$; $\tilde{n} \leftarrow \arg\max\{s_n^{(2)}\}$; $J_{\tilde{n},k} \leftarrow \arg\max\{s_{\tilde{n}}^k\}$;
12:     Select $a_{i,j}$ with $j = J_{\tilde{n},k}, a_{i,j} = \tilde{n}$;
13:     $Temp_{1 \times L} \leftarrow \mathbf{0}$;
14:     **for** $l = 1$ to L **do**
15:         Exchanging $a_{i,j}$ and $a_{l,j+1}$; // Try
16:         $Temp(l) \leftarrow s_{n'}^{(2)} | n' = a_{l,j+1}$;
17:     **end for**
18:     $l^* \leftarrow \arg\min\{Temp(l)\}$;
19:     **if** $Temp(l^*) < s_{\max}^{(2)}$ **then**
20:         Exchanging $a_{i,j}$ and $a_{l^*,j+1}$; // Confirm
21:     **else**
22:         $flag = 0$;
23:     **end if**
24: **end while**

4 Separate Design Principle for Multichannel Scheduling

4.1 Separate Design Principle

Fig. 1 gives the illustration of separate design principle (SDP) for multichannel scheduling. In order to exploit the reuse gain of network resource, the packet transmissions of high and low priority sensors are first separately scheduled with the full use of resource blocks. Although the TDMA based schedules avoid the collisions among the sensors in same priority class, they bring in the possible collisions between the high and low priority sensors. To avoid the collisions, a concession strategy is then devised. The SDP consists of two parts as follows:

Separate Scheduling: According to the multichannel superframe design presented in Subsect. 3.1, for scheduling period T slots on L channels, the number of resource block allocated to each high priority sensor is

$$R_n^H = \frac{\lambda_n^H}{U^H} LT, \ n = 1, 2, \ldots, N^H, \tag{8}$$

where $U^H = \sum_{n=1}^{N^H} \lambda_n^H$ is the total packet rate of high priority sensors. Similarly, the number of slots allocated to each low priority sensor is

$$R_n^L = \frac{\lambda_n^L}{U^L} LT, \ n = 1, 2, \ldots, N^L, \tag{9}$$

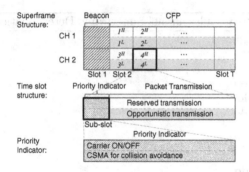

Fig. 1. Illustration of separate design principle for multichannel scheduling.

where $U^L = \sum_{i=n}^{N^L} \lambda_n^L$ is the total packet rate of low priority sensors. For realization, we use the floor and ceil functions to make sure that R_n^H and R_n^L are integers. The multichannel superframes $\mathbf{A}^H$ and $\mathbf{A}^L$ for high and low priority sensors can be obtained by GMSD algorithm independently. As shown in Fig. 1, AP can broadcast the superframe information to sensors in the beacon slot.

Concession Strategy: To deal with the collision between the high and low priority sensors, we introduce a priority indicator. Set a sub-slot at the beginning of each time slot as shown in Fig. 1, which only occupies a small portion of the time slot. If a high priority sensor has packets to transmit on the scheduled resource block, it transmits the carrier signal during the sub-slot to declare the intention to transmit packet. Otherwise, the high priority sensor remains silence. On the other hand, if a low priority sensor has packets to transmit in the scheduled time slot on the specified channel, it should do the carrier sensing in the sub-slot on this channel. If the carrier signal is detected, the low priority sensor has to postpone the packet transmission to the next scheduled slot. Otherwise, the low priority sensor transmits one packet.

4.2   Mean Delay Analysis for SDP Based Scheduling

Substitute the number of allocated slots of each high priority sensor as given by (8) into (5) and (6), the lower bound of the mean packet transmission delay of each high priority sensor is

$$D_n^H = \frac{\rho^{H2}}{2\lambda_n^H(1-\rho^H)} + 1, \tag{10}$$

where $\rho^H = \frac{U^H}{L}$ is the utilization of high priority class.

Following SDP, any low priority sensor has to give up the scheduled time slot if it collides with a high priority sensor. Based on the queueing theory, each slot scheduled to the high priority sensor n^H will be occupied by this high priority sensor with probability

$$\rho_n^H = \lambda_n^H \bar{s}_n^H = \lambda_n^H \frac{T}{R_n^H} = \frac{U^H}{L}. \tag{11}$$

Note that each slot has an identical probability to be occupied by high priority sensor, i.e., ρ^H. As a result, the successful transmission probability for low priority sensor becomes $(1 - \rho^H)$. Let $\bar{s}_n^L$ be the mean scheduling interval of low priority sensor n^L with respect of superframe $\mathbf{A}^L$. Then, the mean transmission interval with the consideration of successful transmission probability is $\frac{\bar{s}_n^L}{1-\rho^H}$, and accordingly, the lower bound of second moment is $(\frac{\bar{s}_n^L}{1-\rho^H})^2$. As a result, the lower bound of mean waiting delay of packet transmission for each low priority sensor can be obtained as

$$W_n^L = \frac{\rho^{L\,2}}{2\lambda_n^L(1 - \rho^H)(1 - \rho^H - \rho^L)}, \tag{12}$$

where $\rho^L = \frac{U^L}{L}$ is the utilization of low priority traffics.

Since the successful transmission probability of a low priority packet is $(1 - \rho^H)$, the mean time slots from the slot for this packet to be transmitted to the slot at which it is successfully transmitted can be given by

$$\Delta_n^L = (1 - \rho^H) \cdot 1 + \sum_{k=1}^{\infty} \rho^{H\,k}(1 - \rho^H)(1 + k\bar{s}_n^L) = 1 + \frac{\rho^H \rho^L}{\lambda_n^L(1 - \rho^H)}. \tag{13}$$

Hence, the lower bound of the mean packet transmission delay of a low priority sensor is

$$D_n^L = \frac{\rho^{L\,2}}{2\lambda_n^L(1 - \rho^H)(1 - \rho^H - \rho^L)} + \frac{\rho^H \rho^L}{\lambda_n^L(1 - \rho^H)} + 1. \tag{14}$$

5   Performance Evaluation

In this section, we first evaluate the mean packet transmission delay of sensors for SDP based multichannel scheduling. The comparison of simulated results and theoretical lower bounds is presented. Then, we provide the comparisons between SDP based and IEEE 802.15.4e based multichannel scheduling (noted by 'SDP-MS' and '15.4e-MS' for simplicity in the following). The network parameters are set as follows: $L = 16$, $N^H = 20$, $N^L = 60$, $T = 16$, $\rho^H = 0.2$ and $\rho^L = 0.5$. For scheduling of IEEE 802.15.4e, high priority sensors are scheduled to transmit in CFP with TDMA manner and low priority sensors are committed to transmit in CAP with CSMA manner. The CFP and CAP are tunable as used in [4]. To guarantee the stability of packets transmission, we have $4 \leq$ CFP ≤ 7 and $9 \leq$ CAP ≤ 12 under our network settings.

Figure 2 shows the mean packet transmission delays of two class sensors based on SDP-MS. The theoretical lower bounds of mean packet transmission delays are also presented. It is shown that the mean packet transmission delay of each high priority sensor is small and close to the theoretical lower bound. On the other hand, The mean transmission delay of each low priority sensor is relatively larger than its lower bound. As the number of low priority sensors and their

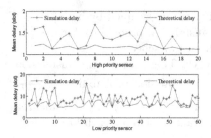

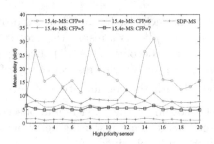

Fig. 2. Mean packet transmission delay based on SDP-MS.

Fig. 3. Mean packet transmission delays of high priority sensors.

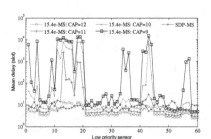

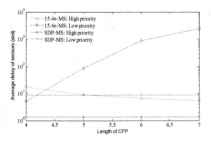

Fig. 4. Mean packet transmission delays of low priority sensors.

Fig. 5. Average delay of all sensors with same priority.

traffic rates are large, it is nontrivial to design perfect multichannel superframe to approach the lower bound of mean transmission delay.

We also present the comparison results between SDP-MS and 15.4e-MS. From Fig. 3, it can be seen that SDP-MS achieves lower mean transmission delay than 15.4e-MS, as 15.4e-MS has to reserve CAP for low priority sensors. For the packet transmission of low priority sensors, the results in Fig. 4 show that low priority sensors obtain low transmission delays based on SDP-MS. The delay level is at 10^1 slots. Based on 15.4e-MS, the delays of sensors vary dramatically with different CAPs. When CAP is short, CAP=7 for example, the delays of some sensors go up to level of 10^4 slots. For longer CAP is long, the delays of sensors become much smaller. In the case of CAP=12, 15.4e-MS can even achieve smaller mean delays than SDP-MS. However, the delays of high priority sensors are larger than the ones of the low priority sensors, which are not expected.

In Fig. 5, we further show the delay performance comparison from the perspective of network level. The average delay is the mean delay of all sensors from the same priority class. From the figure, it can be seen that if the 15.4e-MS has to guarantee the shorter average delay for high priority sensors than low priority sensors, it must satisfy CFP $\geq$ 5. As a result, both the average delays of two classes based on 15.4e-MS are larger than the corresponding ones based on SDP-MS. Therefore, SDP-MS outperforms the 15.4e-MS.

6 Conclusions

In this paper, a separate design principle is proposed for multichannel scheduling in Priority-aware packet collection. The GMSD algorithm is developed to optimize the multichannel superframe and a concession strategy is devised to resolve the channel access collision. Simulation results are provided to show that the SDP based multichannel scheduling reduces the transmission delay of both classes of high and low priority sensors comparing to IEEE 802.15.4e based scheduling.

Acknowledgement. This work was partially supported by NSF of China under the grants 61371085, 61431008, 61221003, 61290322, 61273181.

References

1. Part 15.4: Wireless Medium Access Control (MAC) and Physical Layer (PHY) Specifications for Low-Rate Wireless Personal Area Networks (LR-WPANs). IEEE Standard 802.15.4 (2006)
2. IEEE Standard for Local and Metropolitan Area Networks-Part. 15.4: Low-Rate Wireless Personal Area Networks (LR-WPANs)–Amendament1: MAC Sublayer. IEEE Standard 802.15.4e (2012)
3. Evans, P.C., Annunziata, M.: Industrial internet: pushing the boundaries of minds and machines. General Electric Co. (2012)
4. Gilani, M.H.S., Sarrafi, I., Abbaspour, M.: An adaptive CSMA/TDMA hybrid MAC for energy and throughput improvement of wireless sensor networks. Ad Hoc Netw. **11**(4), 1297–1304 (2013)
5. Ross, S.M.: Introduction to Probability Models. Academic Press, New York (2014)
6. Saifullah, A., Xu, Y., Lu, C., Chen, Y.: End-to-end communication delay analysis in industrial wireless networks. IEEE Trans. Comput. **64**(5), 1361–1374 (2015)
7. Shen, W., Zhang, T., Barac, F., Gidlund, M.: PriorityMAC: a priority-enhanced MAC protocol for critical traffic in industrial wireless sensor and actuator networks. IEEE Trans. Ind. Inform. **10**(1), 824–835 (2014)
8. Stenumgaard, P., Chilo, J., Ferrer-Coll, P., Angskog, P.: Challenges and conditions for wireless machine-to-machine communications in industrial environments. IEEE Commun. Mag. **51**(6), 187–192 (2013)
9. Toscano, E., Lo Bello, L.: Multichannel superframe scheduling for IEEE 802.15. 4 industrial wireless sensor networks. IEEE Trans. Ind. Inform. **8**(2), 337–350 (2012)
10. Willig, A., Uhlemann, E.: Deadline-aware scheduling of cooperative relayers in TDMA-based wireless industrial networks. Wirel. Netw. **20**(1), 73–88 (2014)
11. Zhou, A., Liu, M., Li, Z., Dutkiewicz, E.: Cross-layer design for proportional delay differentiation and network utility maximization in multi-hop wireless networks. IEEE Trans. Wirel. Commun. **11**(4), 1446–1455 (2012)

On Computing Multi-agent Itinerary Planning in Distributed Wireless Sensor Networks

Bo Liu[1(✉)], Jiuxin Cao[1], Jie Yin[1], Wei Yu[2], Benyuan Liu[3],
and Xinwen Fu[3]

[1] School of Computer Science and Engineering,
Southeast University, Nanjing, China
{bliu,jx.cao,jyin}@seu.edu.cn
[2] Department of Computer and Information Sciences,
Towson University, Towson, USA
wyu@towson.edu
[3] Department of Computer Science,
University of Massachusetts Lowell, Lowell, USA
{bliu,xinwenfu}@cs.uml.edu

Abstract. The agent technology has been widely used in wireless sensor networks to perform data fusion and energy balancing. Existing multi-agent itinerary algorithms are either time-consuming, or too complicated to realize in reality. In this paper, we design a routing itinerary planning scheme for the multi-agent itinerary problem by constructing the spanning tree of WSN nodes. First, we build a multi-agent based distributed WSN (DWSN) model. Second, we present a novel routing itinerary algorithm named DMAIP, which can group all the sensor nodes into multiple itineraries for agents. We also extend DMAIP and design DMAIP-E, which can avoid long distance transmission in DMAIP. Our evaluation results demonstrate that our algorithms are better in the aspect of life cycle and energy consumption than the existing DWSN data collecting schemes.

Keywords: Distributed wireless sensor network · Mobile agent · Itinerary planning · Energy efficiency

1 Introduction

Wireless Sensor Networks (WSNs) have been widely used for data collection and situation monitoring in various applications. The raw data collected by sensors can then be forwarded through a number of relay nodes to a remote base station, denoted as the sink node, [5, 6]. In a WSN, sensor nodes with limited energy are often randomly deployed in massive quantities, and each node may act both as a data collector and a traffic relay, as shown in existing research [1].

Agent-based technology has attracted growing attention to improve energy efficiency, scalability, and reliability of a WSN [2–4, 7, 21]. In an agent-based WSN, the main technical challenges include data fusion, energy efficiency, as well as energy balancing. For example, Lin et al. [8] leveraged the agent-based technology to balance energy consumption in data collection process of WSNs.

© Springer International Publishing Switzerland 2015
K. Xu and J. Zhu (Eds.): WASA 2015, LNCS 9204, pp. 366–376, 2015.
DOI: 10.1007/978-3-319-21837-3_36

A critical problem of an agent-based WSN is how to design the itinerary through the WSN for the mobile agent to collect data. Existing approaches for agent itinerary in WSNs can be classified into two categories: (i) single agent itinerary planning based on clustering [9–12], and (ii) multi-agent itinerary planning. For example, Xu et al. [9] investigated static, dynamic, and predictive dynamic schemes to solve the target tracking problem in a WSN. Nonetheless, their work assumes that there is only one target node in the field, and the itinerary is for only one agent. In reality, using a single agent is not practical because of large delay, unbalanced load, and insecurity with large accumulated size [14, 15]. So, multi-agent based WSN and the problem of multi-agent itinerary planning have attracted growing attention [13, 14]. Chen et al. [14] proposed a source-grouping scheme and an iterative algorithm for multi-agent based itinerary planning. They partition source nodes into several sets and use the least number of agents while achieving the required coverage of source nodes. Nonetheless, finding an optimal number of agents is a NP-hard problem and their algorithm is heuristic. Cai et al. [15] applied the genetic algorithm for multiple mobile agents traversing a WSN. Nonetheless, their proposed scheme is complicated and hard to be realized in reality.

Clustering is another important strategy to solve the data fusion and collection problem in WSNs and has been widely adopted. In the typical clustering algorithm called LEACH (Low Energy Adaptive Clustering Hierarchy) [16], the high-energy cluster-head positions are randomly rotated so that the energy consumption of sensors can be balanced. But LEACH assumes a homogeneous distribution of sensor nodes in the given area, which may not be realistic. We will compare our algorithm with clustering based algorithms [21–24].

Existing research efforts on multi-agent routing mainly focus on how to select source nodes to generate itineraries other than how to compute routes. Our work fills this gap. The rest of this paper is organized as follows: In Sect. 2, we present the problem. In Sect. 3, we present the agent routing approach considering energy balancing. In Sect. 4, we present performance evaluation results. Finally, we conclude the paper in Sect. 5.

2 Mobile-Agent Based Wireless Sensor Networks

2.1 Problem Definition

Given a WSN, we utilize mobile agent techniques to accomplish data collection and fusion with less energy consumption and longer life-cycle. A sink node (e.g., base station) is responsible for gathering data from sensor nodes. The objective of our research is to find multiple disjoint paths which cover all sensor nodes in the WSN. The disjoint paths will be assigned to mobile agents.

Our problem is defined as follows: Given an undirected connected graph $G = <V, E>$, where V is the set of nodes and E is the set of edges, the problem is to find k disjoint paths in G to cover all nodes in V, where every edge in these paths can be found in E. It is NP-hard to find optimal number of disjoint paths as we mentioned in Sect. 1. We focus on developing efficient heuristic and polynomial time algorithms to make agents work effectively in a WSN and produce near-optimal itineraries.

2.2 Multi-agent Based WSN

We propose a multi-agent based data collection scheme. As shown in Fig. 1, there are three parts: *remote user, sink node, sensor node* in our scheme. Remote user assigns tasks to sink node. All sensor nodes have operating environment installed for mobile agent. When sink node receives a task from remote user, sink node traversals network topology to generate a spanning tree, then assigns every path to a mobile agent. When a mobile agent moves along its own path to a sensor node, it will do data processing and carry the raw data to the next node. All agents will perform tasks in parallel until they visit all nodes of their paths. Sink node will manipulate data from every path and send back the final results to remote user. Figure 2 shows the detailed workflow.

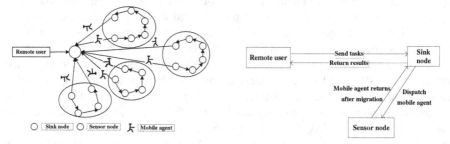

Fig. 1. Multi mobile agent data collection model

Fig. 2. Task flow model

3 Novel Algorithm for Multi-agent Itinerary

In this section, we present a novel DFS based Multi-Agent Itinerary Planning (DMAIP) algorithm in WSNs. Particularly, we first present the DMAIP algorithm that decreases the communication distance between sensor nodes in the agent's migration path. We then present the enhanced DMAIP algorithm, denoted as, DMAIP-E. DMAIP-E changes the process of traversing the network, considering distance between sink node and sensors when generating disjoint paths.

3.1 DMAIP Algorithm

We firstly build a network topology graph from WSN, then generate a spanning tree of the connected graph in the order of increasing weight and finally traverse the spanning tree recursively to find disjoint paths of all the subtrees.

Algorithm 1 introduces how we build the network topology G. We assume that the wireless sensor nodes can locate themselves. They will send position coordinates to the sink node. Accordingly, the sink node will collect position data and compute distances between all the pairs of nodes. If the distance is not larger than the radius, we leave it as what it is. Otherwise, we will mark it inaccessible explicitly by value -1.

Algorithm 1: Build a network topology graph G.

Input: Array c[n][2] and R //c includes n nodes' two-dimension coordinates. R is the communication radius.

Output: Weighted adjacent matrix $M = [d_{u,v}]_{n*n}$ //$d_{u,v}$ is the distance between node u and v.

Algorithm description: Calculate distance between all the pairs of nodes. Assume u and v are two nodes, then their distance is:

$$d_{u,v} = \sqrt{(c[u][0] - c[v][0])^2 + (c[u][1] - c[v][1])^2} \tag{1}$$

If $d_{u,v} \leq R$ or $u = sink$ or $v = sink$, then leave $d_{u,v}$ as what it is, else $d_{u,v} = -1$. If $u = v$, $d_{u,v} = -1$. It is obvious that $d_{u,v} = d_{v,u}$. At last, we get matrix $M = [d_{u,v}]_{n*n}$.

Algorithm 2 generates a spanning tree of the connected graph G. Basically, we traverse weighted adjacent matrix M (the graph) by DFS and generate a spanning tree.

Algorithm 2: Generate a spanning tree of connected graph.

Input: Weighted adjacent matrix $M = [d_{u,v}]_{n*n}$

Output: A connected spanning tree T

Algorithm description: Define an array storing visited states of nodes as $S[i] (1 \leq i \leq n)$. Initialize all values to zero except that $S[sink] = 1$.

Choose u_0 from all sensor nodes where $d_{u_0,sink}$ is minimum, as the initial start node or source node.

Visit node u_0 first. Regard u_0 as u, set its visited state $S[u] = 1$, then find next node v where $d_{u,v}$ is minimum, $d_{u,v} \neq -1$ and $S[v] = 0$. Create an undirected edge from u to v, then set $S[u_1] = 1$ and regard node v as the next node u.

Repeat the process until we cannot find the next node v. At the time, a path is formed from node v to the current node u. Then we go back along the path to find a node from which we can find the nearest node v and we continue to do so using DFS. The visited nodes form a spanning tree. After all nodes are visited, a spanning tree is generated.

In Algorithm 3, we traverse the spanning tree recursively to find disjoint paths of all the subtrees.

Algorithm 3: Generate disjoint paths

Input: A connected spanning tree T

Output: Several disjoint paths $P_1 ... P_k$.

Algorithm description: We will achieve this algorithm by calling function GeneratePath defined as follows with its pseudo code.

```
GeneratePath(TreeNode &rootNode)
Begin
   TreeNode subtreeRootNodes[];
   find the path from rootNode to the left-most node;
   store the path as one disjoint path;
   delete the left-most child of all nodes in the path;
   store all nodes in the path that still have child node(s) in subtreeRootNodes [];
   For every subtreeRootNodes [i]
          GeneratePath(subtreeRootNodes [i]);
   End for;
End
```

3.2   DMAIP-E Algorithm

If the sensor node is far away from the sink node, energy consumption increases and this will reduce the life time of the WSN. Based on DMAIP, we propose an algorithm called DMAIP-E that considers the distance between the sink node and all sensor nodes, as shown in Algorithm 4. We first build network topology graph according to Algorithm 1 of DMAIP to get the distance matrix $M = [d_{u,v}]_{n*n}$. Secondly, we generate multiple paths for agents.

In Algorithm 4, we start from the nearest node A to the sink node, find the next node B that meets these conditions

$$d_{A,sink} < d_{B,sink} \text{ and } d_{A,B} < d_{B,sink} \tag{2}$$

We illustrate the process of choosing appropriate node B in Fig. 3. Node B must be satisfied with Formula (2). So nodes 1, 2 and 3 are being considered. Besides, we require the nearest node to node A. Therefore, node 2 is the node B. Assume node B as the next A and find the next node B. Once there is no more node B to be found, it will form a path from the first node A to the last

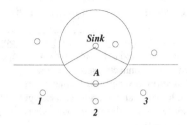

Fig. 3. A process of choosing appropriate node B

node B. Then go back to the sink node and repeat the process above. It will stop when all nodes are included in all generated paths.

Algorithm 4: Generate multiple disjoint paths when traversing.

Input: Weighted adjacent matrix $M = [d_{u,v}]_{n*n}$
Output: A group of disjoint paths $P_1 ... P_k$
Algorithm description: Define an array storing visited states of nodes as S[i]($1 \leq i \leq n$). Initialize all values to 0 except that S[sink] = 1.
step 1) Within M, find the nearest node A_0 to the sink node.
step 2) Regard node A_0 as node A, let S[A] = 1, and find appropriate node B.
step 3) Regard node B as node A, S[B] = 1 let find the next appropriate node B.
step 4) Repeat step 3) until we cannot find the next B. Store the path from the first A to the last B as a new path.
step 5) If there is at least one node u that $S[u] = 1$, go to step 1) else end.

The sink node will dispatch an agent to the farthest node of every disjoint path generated above. When an agent finished its task, it will return from the other end of its path to the sink node, and the sink node will manipulate all data from all paths. In fact, we let the sink node dispatch agents to the outermost location of the path to decrease the distance that the agent loaded with data migrates.

The time complexity of DMAIP algorithm is $O(n^3)$. The time complexity of DMAIP-E algorithm is $O(n^2)$.

4 Performance Evaluation

We implemented the DMAIP and DMAIP-E schemes in the Qualnet environment [20], and compared them with LEACH based algorithms [16, 22, 23]. At last, we present the experimental results of comparing DMAIP, DMAIP-E and LEACH.

4.1 Methodology

We deployed sensor nodes randomly in an area of 200 m × 200 m. Each node was deployed at a fixed position. Sink node is located at (100, 100). Table 1 gives the parameter settings.

We take the following assumptions: (i) wireless sensor network is of large-scale and nodes are distributed randomly, (ii) the initial energy batteries of all the sensor nodes are the same, (iii) The data packet is of the same size, and (iv) all sensor nodes stay in the fixed position.

Table 1. Simulation experimental parameter settings

Parameter Name	Value
Number of nodes	50, 75, 100, 125, 150
Size of the area/m^2	200*200
Location of the base station/m	(100, 100)
Initial energy E_{init}/J	0.5
Energy consumption of transmitting amplifier E_{fs}/(pJ*bit^{-1}*m^{-2})	10
Energy consumption of transmitting amplifier E_{amp}/(pJ*bit^{-1}*m^{-4})	0.0013
Energy consumption of transmitting and receiving circuit E_{elec}/nJ* bit^{-1}	50
Initial size of mobile agent/byte	1024
Length of data packet/byte	2048
IData fusion rate p	0.9
Communication radius/m	40

4.2 Results

We evaluate the performance of our proposed schemes in terms of energy efficiency and life cycle. In the following, we first compare three related algorithms and then show their performance results.

- **Results Generated by three Algorithms**

All LEACH based algorithms use a typically clustering mechanism for data collection, while our proposed DMAIP and DMAIP-E use multi-path methods. The WSN has 100 sensor nodes. In our experiments, the three algorithms run in the same environment. Initially, all sensor nodes are deployed as shown in Figs. 4, 5 and 6.

Itineraries of LEACH Algorithm: In LEACH algorithm, we choose 13 sensor nodes as cluster heads from 100 ones. Ordinary nodes can only communicate with cluster heads, and only cluster heads can communicate with sink nodes. As shown in Fig. 4, according to LEACH strategy, ordinary nodes will choose the nearest cluster head as theirs because of the randomness of deployed sensor nodes and cluster head nodes. Therefore, each cluster head node manages unbalanced number of ordinary nodes within its domain. A cluster head may communicates with many cluster members, and may have long communication distance with the sink node. This phenomenon leads to fast death of some cluster head due to the fast energy consumption. With the increasing number of the sensor nodes in large-scale WSNs, the distance between a cluster head, its cluster member nodes and sink node will be larger and consume much more energy.

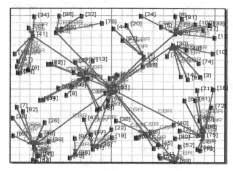

Fig. 4. The branches generated by LEACH   **Fig. 5.** The branches generated by DMAIP

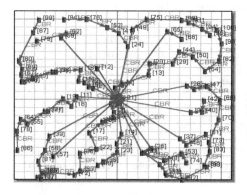

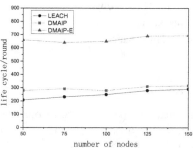

Fig. 6. The branches generated by DMAIP-E   **Fig. 7.** Life cycle with different number of nodes

Itineraries of DMAIP and DMAIP-E Algorithms: Figure 5 illustrates the results for DMAIP. It has 4 paths and the last node along each path consumes the most energy. For example, in Fig. 5, the 70th node, the last node of a path, is far from the sink node and dies fast because of the fast energy consumption. Figure 6 shows the results for DMAIP-E algorithm. Recall that DMAIP-E is the enhanced version of the DMAIP algorithm and considers not only the distance between nodes, but also the distance between the last node of each path and sink node. The sink node dispatches mobile agents to the farther end of each path, and the agent returns to the other end of the path. This reduces the amount of energy consumption to a certain degree and extends the life cycle of the wireless sensor network.

- **Performance Results**

The following three performance metrics are considered in our simulation: life cycle, energy consumption, impact of the number of nodes. Table 2 gives the evaluation metrics.

Table 2. Performance metrics

Evaluation metrics	Descriptions
Round	The whole process from when the sink node dispatch agents for every path for data collection to when all agents return to the sink node
Energy consumption of network nodes	The total energy consumption by sensor nodes when sink node completes one round of data collection
Number of residual nodes	The number of sensor nodes alive in the network
Life cycle	The round number from the beginning of the network to the death of the first node

Life cycle: From Fig. 7, we can see that with different number of nodes, the life cycle of DMAIP -E is much longer than that of DMAIP, and the life time of DMAIP is a little longer than that of LEACH algorithm as the communication distance of DMAIP-E is the smallest, while the distance of LEACH is mostly very large.

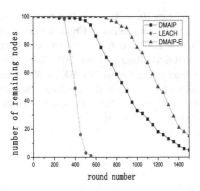
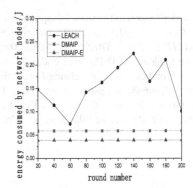

Fig. 8. Changes of residual nodes' number with rounds

Fig. 9. Changes of total energy of nodes with rounds

The Number of Residual Nodes: Figure 8 illustrates results that present the number of remaining nodes versus the number of rounds. As we can see, as the number of rounds increases, some sensor nodes will die. The number of rounds for LEACH, DMAIP and DMAIP-E to have dead nodes are 250, 280 and 650, respectively. DMAIP-E has the largest number of rounds, i.e., the longest life cycle, more than twice rounds of the other two algorithms. The reason why nodes in DMAIP die very early is that it is very far from the end node of some paths to the sink node and therefore transmitting data from the end node to the sink node will consume energy heavily. In addition, all nodes for LEACH die in about 600th round, while for DMAIP and DMAIP-E, nodes will not be all dead until about 1500th round. This is because DMAIP and DMAIP-E adopt a mobile agent model that saves and balances the energy of sensor nodes. Since DMAIP-E outperforms the others.

Energy consumption: Energy consumption is another important performance metric for WSNs [17–19]. This experiment was performed in a network with 100 nodes and the results are shown in Fig. 9. As we can see, the energy consumption of DMAIP and DMAIP-E algorithm is almost the same while the energy consumption of LEACH is not stable. This is because DMAIP and DMAIP-E collect data according to preset paths while LEACH chooses cluster head randomly and changes it every few rounds. Therefore, energy consumption of LEACH varies with rounds. After every round, DMAIP-E algorithm consumes the least energy while LEACH uses the most.

5   Conclusion

The itinerary planning problem is a key issue in distributed WSN. In this paper, we present a multi-agent based paradigm for data collecting in WSN. Since the optimal multi-agent itinerary generation problem is NP-hard, we propose an approximate algorithm called DMAIP-E based on the global topology graph. Our simulation results show that DMAIP-E is appropriate for large-scale WSN and has better performance than the existing clustering based algorithms in terms of life cycle and energy consumption.

Acknowledgment. This work is supported by National Key Basic Research Program of China under Grants No. 2010CB328104, National Natural Science Foundation of China under Grants, No. 61272531, No. 61370208, No. 61320106007, No. 61472081, No. 61402104, China National Key Technology R&D Program under Grants No. 2010BAI88B03 and No. 2011BAK21B02, Jiangsu Provincial Natural Science Foundation of China under Grants No. BK20130634 and No. BK20140648, Jiangsu Provincial Key Laboratory of Network and Information Security under Grants No. BM2003201, and Key Laboratory of Computer Network and Information Integration of Ministry of Education of China under Grants No. 93K-9.

References

1. Wang, F., Wang, D., Liu, J.C.: Traffic-aware relay node deployment for data collection in wireless sensor networks. In: Proceedings of the 6th Annual IEEE Communications Society Conference on Sensor, Mesh and Ad-HoC Communications and Networks, Rome, Italy, pp. 351–359 (2009)
2. Qi, H., Wang, X., Iyengar, S.S., Chakrabarty, K.: Multisensor data fusion in distributed sensor networks using mobile agents. In: Proceedings of the International Conference on Information Fusion, pp. 11–16 (2001)
3. Du, W., Deng, J., Han, Y.S., Varshney, P.K.: A pairwise key pre-distribution scheme for wireless sensor networks. In: Proceedings of the 10th ACM Conference on Computer and Communications Security (CCS 2003), pp. 42–51 (2003)
4. Eschenauer, L., Gligor, V.D.: A key-management scheme for distributed sensor networks. In: Proceedings of the Ninth ACM Conference on Computer and Communications Security (CCS 2002), pp. 41–47 (2002)
5. Wang, F., Wang, D., Liu, J.C.: Traffic-aware relay node deployment for data collection in wireless sensor networks. In: Proceedings of the 6th Annual IEEE Communications Society Conference on Sensor, Mesh and Ad-HoC Communications and Networks, Rome, Italy, pp. 351–359 (2009)
6. Luo, H., Liu, Y., Das, S.K.: Distributed algorithm for en route aggregation decision in wireless sensor networks. IEEE Trans. Mob. Comput. 8(1), 1–13 (2009)
7. Qi, H., Xu, Y., Wang, X.: Mobile-agent-based collaborative signal and information processing in sensor networks. Proc. IEEE 91, 1172–1183 (2003)
8. Lin, K., Chen, M., Zeadally, S., Rodrigues, J.J.P.C.: Balancing energy consumption with mobile agents in wireless sensor networks. Future Gener. Comput. Syst. 28(2), 446–456 (2012)
9. Xu, Y., Qi, H.: Mobile agent migration modeling and design for target tracking in wireless sensor networks. Ad Hoc Netw. 6(1), 1–16 (2008)
10. Chen, M., Yang, L.T., Kwon, T., Zhou, L.: Itinerary planning for energy-efficient agent communications in wireless sensor networks. IEEE Trans. Veh. Technol. 60(7), 3290–3299 (2011)
11. Chen, B., Liu, W.: Mobile agent computing paradigm for building a flexible structural health monitoring sensor network. Comput. Aided Civ. Infrastruct. Eng. 25, 504–516 (2010)
12. Wu, Q., Rao, N.S.V., Barhen, J., et al.: On computing mobile agent routes for data fusion in distributed sensor networks. IEEE Trans. Knowl. Data Eng. 16(6), 740–753 (2004)
13. Wang, X., Chen, M., Kwon, T., Chao, H.C.: Multiple mobile agents' itinerary planning in wireless sensor networks: survey and evaluation. IET Commun. 5(12), 1769–1776 (2011). (Special issue on distributed intelligence and data fusion for sensor systems)
14. Chen, M., Gonzalez, S., Zhang, Y., Leung, V.C.M.: Multi-agent itinerary planning for wireless sensor networks. In: Bartolini, N., Nikoletseas, S., Sinha, P., Cardellini, V., Mahanti, A. (eds.) QShine 2009. LNICST, vol. 22, pp. 584–597. Springer, Heidelberg (2009)
15. Cai, W., Chen, M., Hara, T., Shu, L.: GA-MIP: genetic algorithm based multiple mobile agents itinerary planning in wireless sensor network. In: Proceeding of the 5th Annual International Wireless Internet Conference (WICON), Singapore, Mar 2010
16. Heinzelman, W.R., Chandrakasan, A., Balakrishnan, H.: Energy-efficient communication protocol for wireless microsensor networks. In: IEEE Proceedings of the 33rd Annual Hawaii International Conference on System Sciences (2000)

17. Xiao, Y.K., Shan, X.M., Ren, Y.: Game theory models for IEEE802.11DCF in wireless ad hoc networks. IEEE Radio Commun. **43**, S22–S26 (2005)
18. Tseng, C.-C., Liang, Y.J.: Organizing power efficient cluster-based network architectures for wireless ad hoc networks. In: IEEE Cat No. 07CH37784, pp. 114–118 (2007)
19. Zhi, L., Zhong, C., Wolisz, A.: An integrated data-link energy model for wireless sensor networks. In: IEEE Communication Society, pp. 3777–3783 (2004)
20. Simulator Q N. Scalable Network Technologies Inc (2011). www.qualnet.com
21. Amiri, E., Keshavarz, H., Fahleyani, A.S., Moradzadeh, H., Komaki, S.: New algorithm for leader election in distributed WSN with software agents. In: IEEE International Conference on Space Science and Communication (IconSpace) (2013)
22. Malhotra, R., Aggarwal, R., Monga, S.: Analyzing core migration protocol wireless ad hoc networks by Adopting Multiple Nodes Diverse Test-bed. Int. J. Comput. Appl. 9(3) 35–41 (2010)
23. Nugraheni, C.E.: Formal verification of ring-based leader election protocol using predicate diagrams. IJCSNS Int. J. Comput. Sci. Netw. Secur. **9**(8), 1 (2009)
24. Galstyan, A., Krishnamachari, B., Lerman, K.: Resource allocation and emergent coordination in wireless sensor networks. In: American Association for Artificial Intelligence (2004)

FFDP: A Full-Load File Delivery Protocol in Satellite Network Communication

Chang Liu[✉], Chunqing Wu, Wanrong Yu, Baokang Zhao, and Zhenqian Feng

School of Computer, National University of Defense Technology, Changsha 410073, China
{liuchangnudt,yu.wanrong}@gmail.com,
{wuchunqing,bkzhao,zhqfeng}@nudt.edu.cn

Abstract. Satellite network communication has the features of long propagation delay, high bit error rate (BER) and bandwidth asymmetry [1]. Through analyzing the advantages and disadvantages of existing file delivery protocols, we propose Full-load File Delivery Protocol (FFDP) based on periodically requesting negative acknowledgement and retransmitting lost data packets timely. Theoretical analysis and experimental test reveal that FFDP can effectively utilize link bandwidth to transfer file reliably in the link with a long propagation delay, high BER and bandwidth asymmetry.

Keywords: Satellite network · File delivery protocol · Negative acknowledgement · Efficiency and reliability

1 Introduction

With the development of communication technology and space technology, satellite network communication has been rapidly developed in recent years. At present, satellite network communication has been applied in various fields, such as military investigation, resources observation, weather forecast, environment monitoring and so on.

Compared to traditional terrestrial networks, satellite network communication mainly has the following differences: long propagation delay, high bit error rate (BER), bandwidth asymmetry. It is precisely because satellite network communication has these differences, existing file delivery protocols have a low performance in satellite network communication [2].

In this paper, we first introduce the research status of file delivery protocols, and then we propose a new efficient file delivery protocol—Full-load File Delivery Protocol (FFDP), which can transmit files at a line speed close to the available link bandwidth. Next, we establish a mathematical model of FFDP, analyzing the effects of BER, data packet length and period time on the performance. At last, we test FFDP under different satellite network conditions simulated by the Spirent network impairment emulator and the results prove the validity of our improvement measures.

This work is supported by National Natural Science Foundation of China (NSFC), under agreement no 61103182 and 6137914.

© Springer International Publishing Switzerland 2015
K. Xu and J. Zhu (Eds.): WASA 2015, LNCS 9204, pp. 377–385, 2015.
DOI: 10.1007/978-3-319-21837-3_37

2   Related Works

At present, the main file delivery protocols applied to the satellite network communication include CCSDS File Delivery Protocol (CFDP) and Saratoga protocol [3–6]. CFDP is a new generation of file delivery protocol proposed by the Consultative Committee for Space Data System. It utilizes four kinds of negative acknowledgement mechanism to provide reliable delivery, making it meet the complex requirements of deep space communication. However, CFDP is too complicated for limited memory and processing ability in satellite network communication.

Similarly to CFDP, Saratoga also uses a negative acknowledgment mechanism to provide reliable delivery. And Saratoga is lightweight and more suitable for satellite network communication. However, when the BER is too high, both CFDP and Saratoga need several rounds of retransmission to complete the file transfer. Therefore, the time of the file transfer in the long delay link increases significantly, because each round of retransmission spends at least a round-trip time (RTT) waiting for negative acknowledgement.

Currently, the common optimizing solution to this problem is the introduction of codec algorithms to improve the reliability of point to point transmission, such like DSFTP and PI-CFDP [7–9]. However, both DSFTP and PI-CFDP will bring new problems of decoding threshold, large data storage and complex process. In contrast, improvement measures based on optimizing the transmission mechanism seem more reasonable and feasible.

3   Full-Load File Delivery Protocol

3.1   Basic Principle of FFDP

From the perspective of optimizing the transmission mechanism, we proposed a novel and lightweight file delivery protocol—FFDP, which can effectively utilize the available link bandwidth to transmit files. FFDP depends on periodically requesting negative acknowledgement and retransmitting lost data packets timely.

In FFDP, the file-sender continuously sends data packets at a line rate and periodically sets a flag bit in the data packet, requesting the file-receiver to return status packets. The status packets include negative acknowledgement information if there are some data packets lost during the transmission. On receiving status packets, the file-sender will retransmit those lost data packets and only after having finished retransmission, the file-sender can carry on transmitting new data packets.

The choice of period time is an important factor to FFDP, determining the frequency of negative acknowledgement. A shorter period time can increase the frequency of negative acknowledgement and spur the lost data packets to be retransmitted more timely. However, period time shouldn't be too short for the following two reasons: (i) The bandwidth of backchannel is limited, shorter period time leads to more status packets which may cause congestion. (ii) If period time is smaller than RTT, the retransmitted data packets may haven't arrived the file-receiver when a new status packet is sent out from the file-receiver, bringing a lot of unnecessary retransmissions.

Applying the above transmission mechanism, most of lost data packet are retransmitted among normal data packets, greatly reducing the numbers of lost data packets to be retransmitted in the last several periods, in which there are not any more new data packets. Therefore, the file transmission time is mainly determined by the lost ratio of data packet. In Sect. 4, we will discuss it more carefully.

3.2 Details of FFDP

FFDP is a lightweight file delivery protocol designed for use with UDP protocol and it has four types of packet: request, metadata, data and status. Each type of packet appears as a typical UDP header followed by an octet indicating how the remainder of the packet is to be interpreted.

The formats of data packet and status packet are shown in Fig. 1. Next, we will explain the meanings of some important fields. Flags fields in both data packet and status packet are reserved for future use and now we only set bit 15 of data packet to trigger the file-receiver immediately generate a status packet. Offset in data packet indicates the location where the first byte of this packet's payload is to be written. Payload fields of a series of data packets constitute the actual file data being transferred. Progress Indicator in status packet marks the amount of received file data and when a transfer has completed successfully, this field will contain the length of the file. Immediately following the status packet header is a possible set of "Hole" definitions indicating all the lost packets.

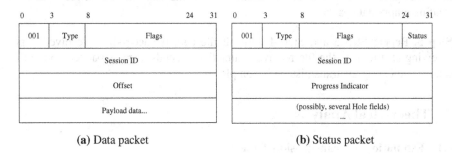

(a) Data packet   (b) Status packet

Fig. 1. Packet formats

Learning of the packet's formats, a transmission procedure of FFDP is shown in Fig. 2. Five steps of the procedure are as follows.

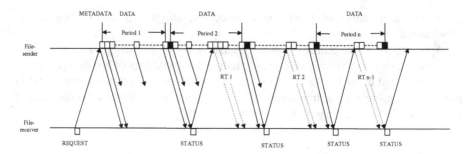

Fig. 2. Transmission procedure of FFDP

Step 1. The file-receiver sends a request packet to the file-sender asking for a specific file and it will repeat sending the request packet until receiving packets from the file-sender.

Step 2. The file-sender first sends the metadata packet and informs the file-receiver beginning of the file transfer. Then it sends data packets at a line speed and periodically sets a flag bit in data packets requesting for negative acknowledgement.

Step 3. The file-receiver checks received data packets and stores correct ones; if the data packet has been set a flag bit, the file-receiver counts the lost data packets and includes this information in a status packet to be sent to the file-sender.

Step 4. The file-sender receives a status packet and judges if there are any data packets should be retransmitted; the file-sender retransmits those lost packets and go on sending new data packets after that. After having sent all file data, the file-sender continues sending empty data packets.

Step 5. Repeat Step 3 and Step 4 until all file data is successfully received. Upon receiving all file data, the file-receiver immediately sends a status packets to the file-sender, indicating the transmission is completed.

4 Theoretical Analysis

4.1 Estimation of Transmission Time

File transmission time is the key indicator of transmission protocol, and it is the time between the file-sender sending data and the file-receiver receiving all file data. Next, the theoretical estimation of the transmission delay of FFDP and the analysis of its impact factors will be given.

As show in Fig. 2, delivery of file in FFDP consists of a series of transmission periods and in each period the last data packets requests the file-receiver to return status packet. Except the first period, all periods include retransmission of lost data packets up-to-date. While, in the last few periods the file-sender only retransmit lost data packets, not sending any new data packets. Estimation of the transmission time is to determine how many periods does the file-sender need to transmit all file data correctly to the file-receiver.

Suppose F is the size of file, B is the available bandwidth of link, T_p is the period time, L_{header} is the length of data packet header, L_{data} is the length of data packet, P_e is the BER of link and P_{data} is the probability of the lost ratio of data packet. In our deduction, we assume that T_p has been chosen as an appropriate value, not causing the two potential problems discussed in Sect. 3.1.

The relationship between P_{data} and P_e is

$$P_{data} = 1 - (1 - P_e)^{L_{data}} \tag{1}$$

N is the total number of data packets, according to the packet format of our design, $L_{header} = 12$ byte, so:

$$N = \frac{F}{L_{data} - L_{header}} = \frac{F}{L_{data} - 12} \tag{2}$$

In each period, the file-sender can transmit N_p data packets depending on the value of B, T_p and L_{data}:

$$N_P = \frac{B \times T_p}{L_{data}} \tag{3}$$

Except the first period, the file-sender will retransmit lost packets in the prior periods. The expected number of lost packets in each period N_L is $N_P \times P_{data}$, so in each period there are only $N_P \times (1 - P_{data})$ new packets sent and the total periods needed to transmit all new data packet is

$$S = \frac{N - N_P}{N_P \times \left(1 - P_{data}\right)} \tag{4}$$

After transmitting all new data packets, the file-sender needs to retransmit all the lost data packets up-to-date successfully in the last few period and until all these lost data packets have been transmitted correctly, the transmission will be ended. We define random variable M as the maximal times needed to transmit these lost data packets. According to literature [10], $E(M)$ can be expressed as a finite summation as follows:

$$E\left(M\right) = \sum_{k=1}^{N_P} \binom{N_P}{k} \frac{P_{data}^k}{1 - P_{data}^k} (-1)^{k+1} \tag{5}$$

So the expected file-delivery time can be expressed as

$$E\left(T_{FFDP}\right) = (S + E(M)) \times T_p$$

$$= (\frac{F \times L_{data}}{(L_{data} - 12) \times (1 - P_e)^{L_{data}}} - \frac{1}{(1 - P_e)^{L_{data}}}$$ (6)

$$+ \sum_{k=1}^{N_P} \binom{N_P}{k} \frac{P_{data}^k}{1 - P_{data}^k} (-1)^{k+1}) \times T_p$$

4.2 Performance Analysis

Let $F = 10$ MB, $B = 1$ Mb/s, we will analyze the effect of BER, data packet length on the performance of FFDP.

(i) Effect of P_e

The relationship between T_{FFDP} and P_e is shown in Fig. 3. As we can see, the greater P_e is, the longer transmission time is, and when $P_e > 1 \times 10^{-5}$, the transmission time increases dramatically. At the same time, the greater L_{data} is, the more obvious of the influence brought by P_e is. This is because the probability of the lost ratio of data packet has an exponential growth rate with L_{data}.

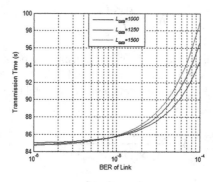

Fig. 3. Relationship between T_{FFDP} and P_e under different L_{data}

(ii) Effect of L_{data}

The relationship between T_{FFDP} and L_{data} is shown in Fig. 4. As we can see, when $P_e = 5 \times 10^{-6}$, the transmission time decreases as L_{data} increases. However, when $P_e = 10^{-5}$, the transmission time firstly decreases and then increases as L_{data} increases, with this trend becoming even more obvious when $P_e = 1.5 \times 10^{-5}$. The reason is that when P_e is relatively small, the probability of the lost ratio of data packet would be negligible and the growth of the length of data packet would reduce the bandwidth wasted in transmitting the data packet headers. While P_e grows larger, the effect of the probability of the lost ratio of data packet becomes more significant.

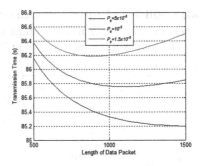

Fig. 4. Relationship between T_{FFDP} and L_{data} under different P_e

From what has been discussed above, we can make a conclusion that when the BER of link is relatively small, we should choose a larger length of data packet to faster the transmission of file and the period time for requesting negative acknowledgment can also be set relatively large as the probability of the lost ratio of data packet is not notable; but when the BER of link is much bigger, we should decrease the length of data packet and the period time to make the transmission time get shorter.

5　Experimental Test

In order to test the performance of FFDP, we used the Spirent network impairment emulator to simulate different satellite network conditions and transferred the same file. As we thought applying our proposed transmission mechanism, the effect of bandwidth asymmetry could be neglected, the main factors we had taken into consideration were only BER of link and the propagation delay—T_{delay}. Parameter utilized in the experiments are listed in Table 1.

Table 1. Experiment parameters

Parameter	Value
F	10 MB
B	1 Mb/s
L_{data}	1000B, 1250B, 1500B
P_e	$1 \times 10^{-6}, 1 \times 10^{-5}, 5 \times 10^{-5}, 1 \times 10^{-4}$
T_{delay}	250 ms, 500 ms, 750 ms, 1000 ms
T_p	$2 \times T_{delay}$

For all kinds of P_e and T_{delay}, we set the period time T_p to be $2 \times T_{delay}$ and the length of data packet to be 1000B, 1250B and 1500B. Under each circumstance we tested 3 times and the calculated out the throughput using average transmission time. The average transmission time and throughput are show shown in Fig. 5.

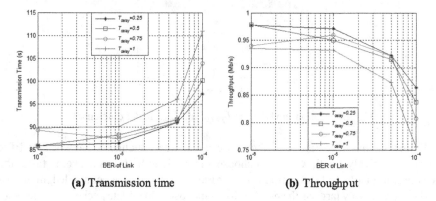

(a) Transmission time   (b) Throughput

Fig. 5. Transmission time and throughput under different circumstances

Through the experiment results in Fig. 5 we can see the real performance of FFDP are very close to our theoretical analysis. With the increase of BER and the propagation delay, the transmission time will increase and the effect of BER is much more obvious than the effect of propagation delay. Furthermore, the effects of BER and propagation delay on the performance of FFDP are within an acceptable range. For $P_e < 1 \times 10^{-5}$, FFDP can utilize more than 90 % of the available link bandwidth to transfer file and in the worst case, FFDP can also utilize more than 75 % of the available link bandwidth.

In general, there are good grounds for believing that FFDP can effectively utilize the available link bandwidth to transfer file reliably in satellite network communication.

6 Conclusions and Future Works

In this paper, we propose a novel protocol called Full-load File Delivery Protocol (FFDP) using the mechanism of negative acknowledgement. In order to shorten the transmission time, the file-sender will periodically request the file-receiver to return status packets. Our theoretical evaluation and experimental test reveal that FFDP can effectively cope with the problems of long propagation delay, high BER and bandwidth asymmetry in satellite network communication.

However, as the file-sender transmit data packets at a line speed, which will not change during the transmission, the available bandwidth of link should be known in advance. Moreover, when there are other applications competing for link capacity simultaneously, FFDP doesn't have any congestion control mechanisms. These are the problems we would like to solve in the future.

References

1. Clare, L.P., Agre, J.R., Yan, T.: Considerations on communications network protocols in deep space. In: Proceedings of the IEEE Aerospace Conference, pp. 943–950 (2001)
2. Aken, O.B., Fang, J.: Performance of TCP protocol in deep space communication networks. J. IEEE Commun. Lett. **6**(11), 478–480 (2002)
3. CCSDS File Delivery Protocol (CFDP), Part 1: Introduction and Overview, CCSDS 720.1-G-1 (2002)
4. CCSDS File Delivery Protocol (CFDP), Part 2: Implementers Guide, CCSDS 720.2-G-1 (2002)
5. CCSDS File Delivery Protocol (CFDP), Recommendation for Space Data System Standards, CCSDS 727.0-B-2 (2002)
6. Wood, L., Eddy, W.M., Ivancic, W., McKim, J., Jackson, C.: Saratoga: a delay-tolerant networking convergence layer with efficient link utilization. In: International Workshop on Satellite and Space Communications, IWSSC 2007, pp. 168–172. IEEE press (2007)
7. De, Cola T., Marchese, M.: Reliable data delivery over deep space networks: benefits of long erasure codes over ARQ strategies. J. IEEE Wirel. Commun. **17**(2), 57–65 (2010)
8. Cheng, M.K., Nakashima, M.A., Moision, B.E.: Optimizations of a hardware decoder for deep-space optical communications. J. IEEE Trans. Circ. Syst. I Fundam. Theor. Appl. **55**(2), 644–658 (2008)
9. Jiao, J., Guo, Q., Zhang, Q.Y.: Packets interleaving CCSDS file delivery protocol in deep space communication. J. IEEE Aerosp. Electron. Syst. Mag. **26**(2), 5–11 (2011)
10. Lee, D.C., Baek, W.: Expected file-delivery time of deferred NAK ARQ in CCSDS file-delivery protocol. J. IEEE Trans. Commun. **52**(8), 1409–1416 (2004)

Energy-Aware Clustering and Routing Scheme in Wireless Sensor Network

Chang Lou, Xiaofeng Gao$^{(\boxtimes)}$, Fan Wu, and Guihai Chen

Department of Computer Science and Engineering,
Shanghai Key Laboratory of Scalable Computing and Systems,
Shanghai Jiao Tong University, Shanghai 200240, China
mcfatealan@sjtu.edu.cn, {gao-xf,fwu,gchen}@cs.sjtu.edu.cn

Abstract. Maximizing the network lifetime is always a main challenge ahead of wireless sensor network (WSN). Clustering and routing has been proved to be energy-efficient strategies for extending the network lifetime. In this paper, we put forward an energy-consumption model for sensors in WSNs and calculate network energy consumption in a short period for any given network configuration, including sensor state scheduling, clustering, and routing information. Then we address an energy-aware optimal planning problem with area coverage and connectivity constraints, seeking for the best sensor scheduling scheme to extend the network lifetime. We formulate it as an Integer Linear Programming (ILP) model, and add some extra constraints to reduce the scale of the model. We use Gurobi to compute this model and compare the basic model, scale-reduced model, with a previous work OPT-ALL-RCC [6]. The simulation results prove that the reduction is necessary and our model have better performance than the previous model.

Keywords: Wireless sensor network · Clustering · Routing · Energy-efficient

1 Introduction

A large collection of densely deployed, spatially distributed, and autonomous devices (or nodes) that communicate via wireless signals and cooperatively monitor physical or environmental conditions is called wireless sensor network (WSN) [1]. In surveillance applications, sensors are deployed in a certain field

This work was supported in part by the State Key Development Program for Basic Research of China (973 project 2012CB316201), in part by China NSF grant 61422208, 61202024, 61472252, 61272443 and 61133006, CCF-Intel Young Faculty Researcher Program and CCF-Tencent Open Fund, the Shanghai NSF grant 12ZR1445000, Shanghai Chenguang Grant 12CG09, Shanghai Pujiang Grant 13PJ1403900, and in part by Jiangsu Future Network Research Project No. BY2013095-1-10. The opinions, findings, conclusions, and recommendations expressed in this paper are those of the authors and do not necessarily reflect the views of the funding agencies or the government.

© Springer International Publishing Switzerland 2015
K. Xu and J. Zhu (Eds.): WASA 2015, LNCS 9204, pp. 386–395, 2015.
DOI: 10.1007/978-3-319-21837-3_38

to detect and report events like presence, movement, or intrusion in the monitored area [2]. Generally speaking, the battery of sensors is unchangeable or the uncertainty of the deployed area makes recharging impossible. In consequence, maximizing the lifetime of WSNs is always a vital issue of this topic. In this paper, we mainly conserve the network energy from the following two steps [2,3]:

1. Energy-efficient scheduling of sensor states (active or sleep);
2. Energy-efficient clustering and routing among sensors;

We assume that the sensor deployment is dense enough that in any certain area there is more than one sensor. That allows sensors take turns to monitor the overlapped area. By scheduling some redundant nodes into sleep states, the network lifetime is extended while the coverage and connectivity is preserved.

Clustering has been admitted as one of the energy-efficient way for WSNs [4, 14–17]. In a cluster-based WSN, some sensors are elected as CHs (cluster head). The duty of CHs is to receive the information collected from non-CHs and send to the sink node (a special node which has infinite energy and all the information feedbacks to this node). One main advantage of clustering is that it could solve some potential problems like bandwidth limits thus increasing the capacity of the system [5]. Furthermore, CHs could function as routers. Since a long-distance transmitting costs much more energy than a short one [7], the nodes from the relatively far location could send the information through a node chain.

Our target is to seek an optimal planning to extend the network lifetime. While maintaining the coverage and connectivity of the whole network, we try to find a synthesize scheme including sensor state scheduling, clustering, and routing to maximize the lifetime of the network. Compared with Chamam's work in [6], a similar design to schedule sensors acting for different roles, we further consider all possible energy consumption in a WSN, and further introduce a reduction method to reduce the problem scale. Thus our designs are more accurate and time-efficient. We also provide various numerical experiments and comparisons to validate the efficiency of our design.

The rest of this paper is organized as follows: In Sect. 2, we introduce some related work about energy-efficient planning of sensor network. In Sect. 3, we give necessary definition, address energy consumption model for single node, put forward the optimal planning problem, and state all assumptions. In Sect. 4, we show how to formulate this model into an integer linear programming problem. In Sect. 5, we describe how to reduce the problem scale to improve the computing efficiency. In Sect. 6, we display the simulation results and comparisons with previous literature. In Sect. 7, we make the conclusion.

2   Related Work

Much progress has been made on the study of sensor state scheduling, clustering, and routing. For sensor state scheduling, Xing et al. [8] proposed Coverage Configuration Protocol (CCP), which can provide different degrees of coverage requested by applications and nodes' states can be alternated according to the

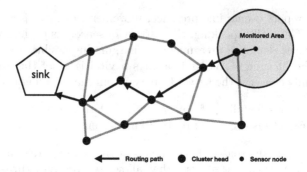

Fig. 1. Multi-hop clustering sensor network

coverage degree. Heinzelman et al. [7] proposed LEACH (Low-Energy Adaptive Clustering Hierarchy), a clustering-based protocol that put forward the concept of cluster head and utilizes randomized rotation of CHs to balance the energy load among the sensors in WSN. The protocol proved to be energy-efficient and convenient to adapt to practical situations. Lindsey et al. [9] proposed PEGASIS (power-efficient gathering in sensor information systems), an improved, near optimal chain-based protocol. In PEGASIS, each node communicates only with a close neighbor and takes turns transmitting to the base station, thus reducing the amount of energy spent per round. However, the transmission distance is limited to only one hop and routing is not considered. Manjeshwar et al. [12,13] proposed TEEN (Threshold-sensitive Energy Efficient sensor Network protocol) and APTEEN (Adaptive Periodic Threshold-sensitive Energy Efficient sensor Network protocol). In TEEN, the data transmission is not transmitted as frequently as sensing activities. A cluster head sensor sends its members the threshold value of the sensed attribute and a small change in the value of the sensed attribute that triggers the node to switch on its transmitter and transmit. Rodoplu et al. [10] proposed Small Minimum Energy Communication Network (MECN). The protocol identifies a relay region for every node, which consisting of nodes in a surrounding area where it is more energy efficient to transmit through those nodes than direct transmission. But still it does not prove its routing strategy is the optimal strategy (Fig. 1).

Most works concentrate on raising new mechanisms or protocols to conserve network's energy, while only a few considered trying to address a linear programming model to formulate the problem and to find the optimal solution. Chamam et al. [6] put forward an optimal configuration problem. The authors classified nodes into three levels (cluster, active, sleep), and set a standard energy constant for each state. The target is to determine the state of each sensor in the next round. Nevertheless, the energy consumption rate in the real situation varies significantly among CHs and active nodes. The number of connected nodes and link ways could largely affect the energy consumption rate, and the communication cost is overly underestimated. The authors suggest that the balance of retained energy among nodes are critical and use balance as the target function of ILP, without giving any proof or reference. Also, the model ensures the existence of the spanning tree but the specific optimal routing scheme is not considered.

3   Problem Statement and Assumptions

3.1   Network Configuration

Consider a cluster-based WSN deployed in a certain flat area, nodes can collect information from the environment, transmit data to others, receive data from others, or sleep. It is important to alternate sensors that are redundant to sleep. According to [3], the power consumption in sleeping mode is generally about 5 % ∼10 % of active mode.

Besides, sensors in our network are divided into clusters. Sensors connect to cluster heads (CHs) to send message to sink. The election of CHs is critical since CHs form the backbone of the network. CHs usually dissipate energy much faster than non-CHs, for its frequent data exchange with others. Thus usually we choose those who have more energy left to become CHs. On the other hand sensors should also choose wisely about which cluster to join. A cluster of more nodes can have more potential CHs but after deaths of some nodes on the border, the whole area could be cut off from the network leaving a coverage hole.

Directly sending data from sensors to sink has been proved inefficient. Instead of simple sink-to-CH communication, we seek some intermediate CHs to act as routers. Message will be transferred from CH to CH and the delivering path follows some rules. Each time there is only a very short distance to pass data so the energy consumption could be lowered. Still there is a tradeoff between transferring times and transferring distance because compared to sending data directly, intermediate CHs need to process this package and spend extra energy. Thus it is unwise to use routers as much as it can. Also, we need to ensure that for each CH there will be a path for it to communicate with sink. To achieve this, there should be a spanning tree in the topology.

Now we give the definition of coverage. We use the basic Disk model to judge if an area is covered by a set of sensors, which means a point can only be covered or not. The covered area is a disk with the sensor as its center. We assume all sensors having the same sensing range. In this article we require the monitored area fully covered.

Definition 1. *Sensor set S covers the area A if and only if ∀ point $P \in A$, ∃ sensor $i \in S$, the distance between P and i is less than the sensing range of sensor i.*

Then we define the connection between sensors. To make sure communication between sensors is stable and reliable, we assume only sensors within safe distance can establish connection.

Definition 2. *Sensor i can reach to sensor j in one hop if and only if the distance between i and j is less than the communication range of sensor i.*

Our optimal solution consisting three layers (state scheduling, clustering, routing) above, and it has to meet the following demands:

1. The energy consumption is minimized.
2. The whole area should be fully covered.

3. Every active sensor is connected to one and only one CH.
4. There must be a spanning tree including all CHs.

We made the following assumptions:

1. All sensors are homogenous and fixed. Sensors can collect data from all directions.
2. The location and energy information of all sensors are known to sink. Each sensor is unique and can be recognized by sink. We do not consider the initial step of the network construction and neither its energy consumption.
3. Sensors are randomly deployed and the network is dense enough.
4. Sensors can function well as long as retained energy is not used up. The lifetime of their components is not considered.
5. Only CHs can act as routers. CHs receive and transmit data to other CHs or sink.
6. The amount of data a sensor collects from the environment in a period is steady. Here we treat the size of message package every sensor needs to pass to sink as a constant.

3.2 Energy Consumption Estimation

We address the SC model to estimate the energy consumption.

In the SC model, we only consider two major energy dissipations: Standalone cost and Communication cost. The standalone cost includes the energy a sensor uses for gathering data from environment and data processing. It is relatively stable and in the most common situation it will not change. While the communication cost relate to the amount of transmitted data and transmitting range. For example, to transmit a k-bit message a distance d needs:

$$E_{Tx}(k, d) = E_{elec} \cdot k + \epsilon_{amp} \cdot k \cdot d^2.$$

E_{elec} and ϵ_{amp} are constants. We assume $E_{elec} = 50nJ/bit$, $\epsilon_{amp} = 100pJ/bit \cdot m^2$ [5]. d means the distance between communicating nodes.

To receive this message, the radio expends:

$$E_{Rx}(k) = E_{elec} \cdot k.$$

During the period δt, the energy a sensor consumes:

$$\delta E = (E_S + \sum kt_j \cdot (E_{elec} + \epsilon_{elec} \cdot d_j^2) + \sum kr_j \cdot E_{elec}) \cdot \delta t.$$

E_S is a constant, which means standalone cost rate. kt and kr mean bits transmitted and received in a time unit.

Now we can calculate the energy consumption of any node in the next period if we already have the sensor scheduling, in other words, clustering and routing scheme for the next round. If a node is active but not a CH in the next period, the energy consumption includes standalone cost and transmitting cost for sending collected data to CH. If a node is a CH, the energy consumption should not only include the above two costs, but also the receiving cost for gathering data from the cluster, the receiving and transmitting cost for being a routing node.

Undoubtedly we want the total sum of δE as small as possible, which means the whole energy consumption is minimized. But this does not necessarily lead to the network lifetime maximization. For example, some sensors die out quickly while others are nearly as healthy as newborns. In this situation the network is becoming equivalently sparse, which leads to the coverage holes and disagrees with our assumption. Keeping the balance of retained energy among the sensors is of vital importance. Thus, instead to minimize total sum of δE, we choose to minimize the sum of ratio between predicted consumed energy and retained energy of sensors $\delta E/E_i$.

4   Modeling and Definitions

Our work is on the basis of research of Chamam et al. [6]. After taking communication costs into consideration, we formulate the optimal planning problem into an integer linear programming problem.

First we define all the sets, constants, variables we will use later in Table 1. Here S, C, d_{ij}, ρ_{ic} are constants, while X_i, Y_i, Z_{ij}, V_{ij}^{kl} are variables we want to compute. The domain of variables i, j, k, l, c is $i, j, k, l \in \{1..N\}, c \in \{1..M\}$.

Table 1. Set table

Symbol	Meaning
S	the set of sensors, $S \in \{1, \cdots, N\}$
C	the set of cells composing the monitored area, $C \in \{1, \cdots, M\}$
d_{ij}	$d_{ij} = 1$ if sensor i can reach sensor j in one hop, otherwise 0
ρ_{ic}	$\rho_{ic} = 1$ if sensor i covers cell c, otherwise 0
X_i	$X_i = 1$ if sensor i is Active, otherwise 0
Y_i	$Y_i = 1$ if sensor i is a CH, otherwise 0
Z_{ij}	$Z_{ij} = 1$ if sensor i is connected to CH j, otherwise 0
V_{ij}^{kl}	$V_{ij}^{kl} = 1$ if flow (i, j) passes through the link kl , otherwise 0

The problem is modeled below. The meaning of the target function has been described in the last section, namely the sum of the predicted consumption rate of all sensors, including standalone cost and communication cost. Constraint (1) is coverage requirement that the monitored area should be fully covered. Constraint (2) means a sensor has to be active if it is a CH. Constraint (3) guarantees that there must be one sensor that can reach the sink (though we did not include sink in the sensor table, we can regard sink as a special node). Constraint (4) guarantees that a sensor has to be active if it is connected to CHs, a sensor has to be a CH if there are other nodes connecting to it and the distance requirement for the connection between CHs, which we talked in the definition of connection. Constraint (5) guarantees that one sensor can only join one cluster to avoid redundancy and disorder, and the CHs have the maximum connection limits taking bandwidth of sensors into consideration. Constraint (6) means this is a 0–1 programming problem. Constraints (7) (8) guarantee that the network contains a spanning tree, which ensures the connectivity of network. However, Constraint (7) is not linearized. Thus we use Constraints (9) to help to linearize it. In the end, we get the linear programming model.

$$min \quad \sum_{i=1}^{|S|} X_i \cdot \frac{E_S}{E_i} + \sum_{i=1}^{|S|} \sum_{j=1}^{|S|} Z_{ij} \cdot \frac{E_{elec} + \epsilon_{elec} \cdot dist_{ij}^2}{E_i}$$

$$+ \sum_{i=1}^{|S|} \sum_{j=1}^{|S|} \left(Z_{ji} \cdot \frac{E_{elec}}{E_i} + \sum_{k=1}^{|S|} \sum_{l=1}^{|S|} (V_{kl}^{ij} \cdot \frac{E_{elec} + \epsilon_{elec} \cdot dist_{ij}^2}{E_i} + V_{kl}^{ji} \cdot \frac{E_{elec}}{E_i}) \right)$$

$$s.t. \quad \forall \, c = 1..|C|, \quad \sum_{i=1}^{|S|} X_i \cdot \rho_{ic} \geq 1 \tag{1}$$

$$\forall \, i = 1..|S|, \; Y_i \leq X_i \tag{2}$$

$$\sum_{i=1}^{|S|} Y_i \cdot d_{i0} \geq 1 \tag{3}$$

$$\forall \, i,j = 1..|S|, \; j \neq i, \; Z_{ij} \leq X_i - Y_i, \; Z_{ij} \leq Y_j, \; Z_{ij} \leq d_{ij} \tag{4}$$

$$\forall \, i = 1..|S|, \quad \sum_{j=1,j\neq i}^{|S|} Z_{ij} + Y_i = X_i, \; Z_{ij} \leq N_{max} \tag{5}$$

$$X, Y \in \{0,1\}^{|S|}, \; Z \in \{0,1\}^{|S|^2}, \; V \in \{0,1\}^{|S|^4} \tag{6}$$

$$\forall \, i,j,k = 1..|S|, \; j \neq i, \; \sum_{l \in |S|, l \neq k} V_{ij}^{kl} - \sum_{l \in |S|, l \neq k} V_{ij}^{lk} = \begin{cases} 0 & \text{if } k \neq i \text{ and } k \neq j \\ Y_i \cdot Y_j & \text{if } k = i \\ -Y_i \cdot Y_j & \text{if } k = j \end{cases} \tag{7}$$

$$\forall \, i,j,k,l = 1..|S|, \; j \neq i, \; k \neq l, \; V_{ij}^{kl} \leq Y_i, \; V_{ij}^{kl} \leq Y_j, \; V_{ij}^{kl} \leq Y_k, \; V_{ij}^{kl} \leq Y_l, \; V_{ij}^{kl} \leq d_{kl} \tag{8}$$

$$\forall \, i,j = 1..|S|, \; Y_i \cdot Y_j \leq Y_i, \; Y_i \cdot Y_j \leq Y_j, \; Y_i \cdot Y_j \geq Y_i + Y_j - 1 \tag{9}$$

5 Problem Scale Reduction

Though the size of the problem grows with the number of sensors in a polynomial speed, for 10^2 sensors there should at least be 10^8 variables to optimize since $V \in \{0,1\}^{|S|^4}$. We can eliminate some computing redundancy to make the problem smaller. For V_{ij}^{kl}, it makes sense only if sensor k and l can reach each other, which is written as : $d_{ij} = 1$.

Also, we can strictly control the use of routing, for example, sensor i,k,l,j should gradually approach the sink in sequence. The constraint is written as:

$$d_{i0} \geq d_{k0} > d_{l0} \geq d_{j0}.$$

6 Simulation Results

We perform our simulation in Gurobi [11], a commercial optimization solver, which has a superior performance dealing with large-scale constraints and variables. For convenience we use "EAS" to refer to our model.

Table 2. Number of variables and constraints vs number of sensors

Sensor num	Reduced		Not reduced	
	Variables	Constraints	Variables	Constraints
10	164	10598	8220	25230
20	2376	24732	144840	268060
30	10039	76223	757860	1395970
40	32899	233293	2435280	4233000
50	74310	519420	6005100	10523050

Table 3. Number of variables and constraints vs communicating ranges

Comm. range	Reduced		Not reduced	
	Variables	Constraints	Variables	Constraints
10	1970	19740	757860	920950
20	5122	41804	757860	1067110
30	10039	76223	757860	1395970
40	10749	81193	757860	1829230
50	19286	140952	757860	1928410

6.1   Performance Evaluation: Impact of Problem Scale Reduction

Variation of the Number of Variables and Constraints with the Number of Sensors: In a settled map, the larger the number of sensors is, the denser the network becomes and the diversity of network structure has more potential. We fix the map size as $100 \cdot 100$, the sensing and communication ranges as 30, and change the number of sensors to see the impact. The result is shown in Table 2. The number of variables and constraints is increasing w.r.t. sensor number, but the reduced model has gained a small-scale advantage and a slower growing speed.

Variation of the Number of Variables and Constraints with the Communicating Ranges: The communicating ranges has a great impression on network planning. A large communicating range means a cluster could potentially contain more nodes, while a small communicating range needs routing technique more. We fix the size of the map as $100 \cdot 100$, the number of sensors as 30. We change the communicating ranges to see the impact. The result is shown in Table 3. Since our reduction technique takes the connecting possibility between nodes into consideration, the communicating ranges affect the degree of reduction and the smaller the communicating ranges become, the better the reduction behaves.

Variation of the computation time with the problem scale: Let us take a closer look at the impact of the problem scale on the computation time. We fix the size of the map as $100 \cdot 100$, the sensing range and communication ranges 50, and change the number of sensors to see the impact. The result is shown in Table 4. We can see that there is a positive correlation between the computation time and the problem scale. Also, when we tried to solve the unreduced model, we run out of memory resources on our machine, which reveals the necessity of reduction.

Variation of Objective Function Values Obtained by Two Models: Objective function values are positively correlate to energy consumption in the whole network. We fix the size of the map as $100 \cdot 100$, the sensing range and communication ranges as 30, and change the number of sensors to see the impact. The result is shown in Table 5. We can see that after reduction, the obtained objective function value will not inevitably cause the decrease of solution quality. On the contrary, it helped to find a near-optimal solution.

Table 4. Variation of the computation time with the problem scale

	Computation time	
Sensor num	Reduced	Not reduced
10	5	5
20	8	141
30	41	406
40	70	1031
50	138	Out of memory

Table 5. Variation of the objective function with the problem scale

	Objective function	
Sensor num	Reduced	Not reduced
10	4.18	6.2
20	0.4	6.158
30	5.92	5.318
40	4.157	5.679
50	3.85	Out of memory

6.2   Comparison Between Reduced OPT-ALL-RCC and EAS

Here we choose to compare our model to the reduced OPT-ALL-RCC(generated by doing the same reduction to OPT-ALL-RCC as to our EAS model) instead of OPT-ALL-RCC for sake of time efficiency. We fix the size of the map as $100 \cdot 100$, the sensing range and communication ranges as 50, and change the number of sensors to see the impact.

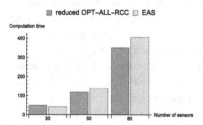

Fig. 2. Computation time using reduced OPT-ALL-RCC and EAS

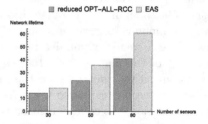

Fig. 3. Network lifetime using reduced OPT-ALL-RCC and EAS

Computation Time: The result is shown in Fig. 2. For the same problem set, the reduced OPT-ALL-RCC and EAS spend similar time to find a near-optimal solution because after reduction these two models have the exact same problem scale. In other words EAS needs to spend less time than the original versional of OPT-ALL-RCC.

Network Lifetime: The result is shown in Fig. 3. There is an obvious network lifetime lift from OPT-ALL-RCC to EAS. Especially when the scale of network gets large, our model could effectively lengthen the network lifetime.

7   Conclusion

In this article we propose a model that based on communication cost estimation to calculate the energy consumption of sensor network. On top of this we put forward a mechanism to find an optimal or near-optimal configuration for sensor network to maintain coverage and connectivity and extend lifetime of sensor network. The simulation shows that our mechanism could prolong the lifetime of network with the computation time remains nearly constant. As future research directions, we plan to further decrease the problem scale and improve the energy consumption model.

References

1. Akyildiz, I.F., Su, W., Sankarasubramaniam, Y., et al.: Wireless sensor networks: a survey. Comput. Netw. **38**(4), 393–422 (2002)
2. Chong, C.Y., Kumar, S.P.: Sensor networks: evolution opportunities, and challenges. Proc. IEEE **91**(8), 1247–1256 (2003)
3. Raghunathan, V., Schurgers, C., Park, S., et al.: Energy-aware wireless microsensor networks. IEEE Signal Process. Mag. **19**(2), 40–50 (2002)
4. Ahmed, A.A., Younis, M.: A survey on clustering algorithms for qireless sensor networks. Comput. Commun. **30**(14), 2826–2841 (2007)
5. Yao, Y., Giannakis, G.B.: Energy-efficient scheduling for wireless sensor networks. IEEE Trans. Commun. **53**(8), 1333–1342 (2005)
6. Chamam, A., Pierre, S.: On the planning of wireless sensor networks: energy-efficient clustering under the joint routing and coverage constraint. IEEE Trans. Mob. Comput. **8**(8), 1077–1086 (2009)
7. Heinzelman, W.R., Chandrakasan, A., Balakrishnan, H.: Energy-efficient communication protocol for wireless microsensor networks. In: IEEE International Conference on System Sciences, vol. 2, pp. 1–10 (2000)
8. Xing, G., Wang, X., Zhang, Y., et al.: Integrated coverage and connectivity configuration for energy conservation in sensor networks. ACM Trans. Sens. Netw. (TOSN) **1**(1), 36–72 (2005)
9. Lindsey, S., Raghavendra, C.S.: PEGASIS: power efficient gathering in sensor information systems. In: IEEE Aerospace Conference Proceedings, vol. 3 (2002)
10. Rodoplu, V., Meng, T.H.: Minimum energy mobile wireless networks. IEEE J. Sel. Areas Commun. **17**(8), 1333–1344 (1999)
11. Gurobi - Wikipedia, the free encyclopedia. http://en.wikipedia.org/wiki/Gurobi
12. Manjeshwar, A., Agarwal, D.P.: TEEN: a routing protocol for enhanced efficiency in wireless sensor networks. In: IEEE Parallel and Distributed Processing Symposium(IPDPS), vol. 3, pp. 30189a–30189a (2001)
13. Manjeshwar, A., Agarwal, D.P.: APTEEN: a hybrid protocol for efficient routing and comprehensive information retrieval in wireless sensor networks. In: IEEE Parallel and Distributed Processing Symposium(IPDPS), pp. 195–202 (2002)
14. Akkaya, K., Younis, M.: A survey of routing protocols in wireless sensor networks. Ad Hoc Netw. **3**(3), 325–349 (2005)
15. Arboleda, L.M.C., Nasser, N.: Comparison of clustering algorithms and protocols for wireless sensor networks. In: IEEE Canadian Conference on Electrical and Computer Engineering(CCECE), pp. 1787–1792 (2006)
16. Younis, M., Munshi, P., Gupta, G., Elsharkawy, S.M.: On efficient clustering of wireless sensor networks. In: IEEE Workshop Dependability and Security in Sensor Networks and Systems, pp. 78–91 (2006)
17. Karl, H., Wiling, A.: Protocols and Architectures for Wireless Sensor Networks. Wiley, New York (2005)

Serial Number Based Encryption and Its Application for Mobile Networks

Rong Ma[1]([⊠]) and Zhenfu Cao[1,2]

[1] Shanghai Jiaotong University, Shanghai, China
marong.sjtu@gmail.com
[2] East China Normal University, Shanghai, China

Abstract. Security and privacy of many mobile applications rely on lightweight cryptographic protocol. In this paper, we develop a lightweight functional public key encryption scheme and demonstrate its applictions for mobile networks. We call such a scheme the Serial Number Based Encryption (SNBE). Our scheme is provable secure base on the DBDH assumption in the standard model, while the ciphertext consists of only three elements. We also discuss some applications of SNBE scheme in the mobile environment.

1 Introduction

We develop a lightweight public key functional encryption scheme and demonstrate its applications for moblie networks. In our system each ciphertext is labeled by the encryptor with a serial number. Each private key is also associated with a serial number that specifies which ciphertexts the key can decrypt. Any party is allowed to generate a public key from a known serial number. A trusted third party, called the central authority, generates the corresponding private keys. As a result, anybody may encrypt messages with no prior distribution of keys between individual participants. This is extremely useful in cases where pre-distribution of authenticated keys are inconvenient or infeasible due to technical restraints, such as the mobile environment. We call such a scheme the Serial Number Based Encryption (SNBE).

1.1 Definition

Formally, a serial number based encryption scheme is specified by a set of probabilistic polynomial time algorithms:

- The setup algorithm **Setup** is run by the central authority, which takes as input a security parameter 1^λ and an initial global counter cnt, outputs the public system parameters pp together with a master (secret) key mk. The system parameters will be publicly known, while the master key will be known only to the key generation algorithm.
- The registration algorithm **Reg** is run by the central authority, simply advances the global counter by $cnt \leftarrow cnt + 1$.

© Springer International Publishing Switzerland 2015
K. Xu and J. Zhu (Eds.): WASA 2015, LNCS 9204, pp. 396–406, 2015.
DOI: 10.1007/978-3-319-21837-3_39

- The key generation algorithm **Gen** is run by the central authority, which takes as input the master secret key mk and a number y, if $y \leq cnt$, outputs a related privated key sk_y.
- The encryption algorithm **Enc** is run by the sender, which takes as input a number x and a message m, outputs a ciphertext ct_x.
- The decryption algorithm **Dec** is run by the receiver, which takes as input a private key sk_x and a valid ciphertext ct_y, returns a plain message m.

These algorithms must satisfy the standard consistency constraint, namely when sk_x is the private key generated by algorithm $Gen(x)$ and when it is given x as the public key, then for each message m,

$$\mathbf{Dec}(sk_x, ct_x) = m, \text{ where } ct_x = \mathbf{Enc}(x, m).$$

At first glance, SNBE and IBE are much alike [2]. SNBE is a kind of function-limited IBE in essence, however, they are different. Firstly, SNBE substitutes serial number for arbitrary string which is used in IBE as the public key. Secondly, central authority keeps a state, which is called global counter cnt when it issues the private key. Central authority is not allowed to issue private keys whose serial numbers are beyond cnt. Except for those differences, the SNBE and IBE have the same function. Since we have already had IBE scheme, which is a mature cryptography primitive, why do we try to limit the function of IBE? Our dominant motive is to change the IBE to make it lightweight in order that simple encryption scheme can be used on the mobile devices without losing high level security.

1.2 Contributions

New Primitive and Construction. The first contribution of our paper is that it defines a new cryptography primitive, which is known as serial number based encryption. Although we can construct SNBE directly from IBE, the design and security analysis of IBE is always complicated that it is difficult to reach the satisfying level in efficiency and security at the same time. In general, highly efficient cryptographic protocols require constant size ciphertexts, constant size public parameters and fewer number of arithmetic operations and pairing on groups. On the other hand, highly security cryptographic protocols require adaptive adversary model, standard assumption and tight reduction. Cryptographic community has devoted a lot of attention to studying IBE and obtained lots of significant achievements [1,6,7]. However, designing an efficient and full security IBE scheme under the most strict demands is still an open question. In comparison to the mainstream results, the efficiency and safety of our scheme can reach their best level at the same time.

New Security Model and Application Scenario. In Sect. 1.3, we have found many useful application scenarios for SNBE, we also define a full security adversary model for SNBE in Sect. 2.1.

New Proof Idea. From the respect of reduction proof, simulator in the security game has many advantages in comparison with IBE proof. The simulator can guess the range of the challenge target t^* of the adversary. The challenge target

Table 1. Comparison.

Scheme	$|pk|$	$|sk|$	$|ct|$	Model	Loss	Assumption	Pairing
BF01 [2]	$2|\mathbb{G}|$	$|\mathbb{G}|$	$|\mathbb{G}|$	RO	$O(q)$	CBDH	Sym
BB04 [8]	$3|\mathbb{G}| + |\mathbb{G}_T|$	$2|\mathbb{G}|$	$2|\mathbb{G}|$	Selective	$O(1)$	DBDH	Sym
Wat05 [1]	$(4+\lambda)|\mathbb{G}|$	$2|\mathbb{G}|$	$2|\mathbb{G}|$	Standard	$O(\lambda q)$	DBDH	Sym
LW10 [3]	$24|\mathbb{G}_1| + |\mathbb{G}_T|$	$6|\mathbb{G}_2|$	$6|\mathbb{G}_1|$	Standard	$O(q)$	2-LIN	Asym
JR13 [6]	$6|\mathbb{G}_1| + |\mathbb{G}_T|$	$5|\mathbb{G}_2|$	$3|\mathbb{G}_1|$	Standard	$O(q)$	2-LIN	Asym
CW13 [7]	$(16\lambda+8)|\mathbb{G}_1| + 2|\mathbb{G}_T|$	$8|\mathbb{G}_2|$	$8|\mathbb{G}_1|$	Standard	$O(\lambda)$	2-LIN	Asym
This paper	$4|\mathbb{G}| + |\mathbb{G}_T|$	$2|\mathbb{G}|$	$2|\mathbb{G}|$	Standard	$O(q)$	DBDH	Sym

t^* can be type I: a serial number within the range of cnt; or t^* can be type II: a serial number out of the range of cnt. In terms of type I, since cnt is polynomial-time bounded, the probability that the simulator guesses the t^* correctly is not negligible. In terms of type II, we can guess the binary length of t^*, call it k, then define the singular point of the hash funciton at k. Taking advantage of the classified discussion above, we simplify an adaptive model proof to a selective model proof. This is the most interesting part of our proof. As far as we know, this skill hasn't been used in IBE scheme before.

1.3 Applications

Serial number can be seen everywhere in daily life. We discuss a few important scenarios of application and study the prospect of SNBE scheme.

– Mobile phone number as the serial number. Most mobile network applications regard mobile phone number as the unique identity of the user. During New Year Festival, Chinese people are used to sending Lucky Red Envelopes (usually not filled with a lot of money) to each other to celebrate the festival and strengthen their relationship. As a software used to pay money, Alipay recognizes users' mobile phone numbers as the default user identity. SNBE can help these apps to encrypt the confidential information by using the receivers' mobile phone numbers as the public key.
– ID number as the serial number. The citizens receive their unique ID numbers from the government. In applications which involves encrypting by a certain ID number, SNBE can play the important role. In addition, electronics engineers will always welcome the lightweight protocol if they want to try integrating cryptographic circuits in smart cards.
– Product ID number as the serial number. The concept of Internet of things originated from connecting all the products with the Internet through RFID. It can realize the intelligent recognition and management because every product is assigned a unique number. These numbers can be used as the public key of the products naturally.
– Time as the serial number. Some cryptographic protocols may involve encrypting by time. For example, revocable identity based encryption, forward secrecy key agreement protocols, etc., in which SNBE can be used as the building block of these high-level cryptographic protocols.

2   Preliminaries

Pairing Group. Let **Gen** be a probabilistic polynomial-time algorithm taking 1^λ as security parameter and outputs $(\mathbb{G}, \mathbb{G}_T, p, g, e)$ where $\mathbb{G}$ and $\mathbb{G}_T$ are groups of prime order p, $2^\lambda < p < 2^{\lambda+1}$, g is a generator of group $\mathbb{G}$ and $e : \mathbb{G} \times \mathbb{G} \to \mathbb{G}_T$ is a non-degenerate efficiently computable bilinear map. See [2] for a description of the properties of such pairings.

DBDH Assumption. Decisional Bilinear Diffie-Hellman (BDDH) problem is to distinguish two distributions $\mathcal{P}_{\text{BDH}} = (g^\alpha, g^\beta, g^\gamma, e(g, g)^{\alpha\beta\gamma})$ and $\mathcal{R}_{\text{BDH}} = (g^\alpha, g^\beta, g^\gamma, R)$ for random α, β, γ and R. To state the assumption asymptotically we rely on the bilinear group generator algorithm **Gen**(1^λ).

Definition 1. *Let **Gen**(1^λ) be a bilinear group generator. The DBDH assumption holds for **Gen**(1^λ) if for all probabilistic polynomial-time algorithm $\mathcal{B}$, its BDDH advantage, denoted by*

$$\boldsymbol{Adv}_{\mathcal{B}}^{DBDH}(\lambda) = \left| \Pr[\mathcal{B}(g^\alpha, g^\beta, g^\gamma, e(g, g)^{\alpha\beta\gamma}) = 1] - \Pr[\mathcal{B}(g^\alpha, g^\beta, g^\gamma, R) = 1] \right|$$

*is a negligible function of λ, where the probability is over $(\mathbb{G}, \mathbb{G}_T, p, g, e) \leftarrow$ **Gen**(1^λ), $\alpha, \beta, \gamma \leftarrow \mathbb{Z}_p^*$, $R \leftarrow \mathbb{G}_T$.*

2.1   Security Model

To capture the semantic security formally, a game between a challenger and an adversary $\mathcal{A}$ is defined as follows:

Setup Phase: The challenger runs **Setup**(1^λ) and sends pp to adversary, keeps mk to itself.

Pre-Challenge Phase: In this phase adversary $\mathcal{A}$ is allowed to make two kinds of qureies:

> – **Register**. The challenger advances the counter by $cnt \leftarrow cnt + 1$.
> – **Reveal**(y). If $y \leq cnt$, the challenger responds the private key of y by sending $\mathcal{A}$ the output of **Ext**(mk, y).

Challenge Phase: Once the adversary decides that Pre-Challenge Phase is over, it submits a number x which is restricted to that he did not reveal and two plaintexts M_0, M_1 on which it wishes to be challenged. The challenger flips a fair binary coin μ and returns **Enc**(pp, x, M_μ) as challenge ciphertext.

Post-Challenge Phase: This phase is repeat of pre-challenge phase. The adversary issues additional adaptive queries with the restriction that he can not reveal private key of x.

Guess Phase: Finally, The adversary $\mathcal{A}$ submits a guess μ' of μ. We say $\mathcal{A}$ wins game if $\mu' = \mu$.

Definition 2 (Semantic Security of SNBE). *A serial number based encryption scheme says semantically secure if for any probabilistic polynomial-time algorithm $\mathcal{A}$, its advantage, denoted by*

$$\boldsymbol{Adv}_{\mathcal{A}}(\lambda) = \left| \Pr[\mu' = \mu] - \frac{1}{2} \right|$$

is a negligible function of λ, where the probability is over the random bits used by the challenger and the adversary.

3   Construction

In this section, we present an efficient SNBE scheme with constant-size ciphertext and public parameters. The design inspiration of our scheme comes from [9] and [8].

Setup(1^λ): On input security parameter 1^λ, the setup algorithm works as follows:

1. Generate $(p, \mathbb{G}, \mathbb{G}_T, g, e) \leftarrow \textbf{Gen}(1^\lambda)$.
2. Randomly sample $a, b \leftarrow \mathbb{Z}_p^*$.
3. Randomly sample $u, v, w \leftarrow \mathbb{G}^*$.
4. Output ab as master key, $(g, u, v, w, e(g, g)^{ab})$ as public parameters.
5. Define $H(x) = u^x v^{\lceil \log x \rceil} w$, since u, v, w is public, $H(x)$ is a pulic computable function.

Ext(mk, y): On input the master key ab, the key extraction algorithm does the following:

1. Check whether $y \leq cnt$. if not, reject to execute the following steps.
2. Randomly choose $r \leftarrow \mathbb{Z}_p^*$.
3. Compute $D \leftarrow g^{ab} H(y)^r$ and $R \leftarrow g^r$.
4. Output (D, R) as the private key of y.

Enc(pp, x, M): Given x and a message $M \in \mathbb{G}$, the encryption algorithm does:

1. Randomly sample $s \leftarrow \mathbb{Z}_p^*$.
2. Compute $S \leftarrow g^s$, $C \leftarrow M \cdot (e(g, g)^{ab})^s$, $T \leftarrow H(x)^s$.
3. Output (C, S, T) as a ciphertext of x.

Dec(ct_x, sk_x): Let ciphertext ct_x be a valid encryption of M under the number x, Then ct_x can be decrypted by sk_x as:

1. Parse ct_x as (C, S, T), sk_x as (D, R).
2. Compute

$$M' = C \cdot \frac{e(T, R)}{e(D, S)}$$

3. Output M' as the plaintext.

Correctness. For any number x, we need to guarantee $M' = M$, where $ct_x \leftarrow$ **Enc**(pp, x, M), $sk_x \leftarrow$ **Ext**(mk, x) and $M' \leftarrow$ **Dec**(ct_x, sk_x). Denoting $ct_x = (E, S, T)$ and $sk_x = (D, R)$, that is clear since

$$M' = C \cdot \frac{e(T, R)}{e(D, S)} = M(e(g, g)^{ab})^s \frac{e(H(x)^s, g^r)}{e(g^{ab}H(x)^r, g^s)} \tag{1}$$

$$= Me(g, g)^{abs} \frac{e(H(x), g)^{sr}}{e(g^{ab}, g^s)e(H(x), g)^{rs}} \tag{2}$$

$$= M \frac{e(g, g)^{abs}}{e(g, g)^{abs}} \tag{3}$$

$$= M. \tag{4}$$

4 Security

We use reduction technique to prove semantic security of our scheme under the DBDH assumption.

Lemma 1. *Suppose there is an adversary $\mathcal{A}$ that can win the security game with advantage $\epsilon(\lambda)$. Then there is a algorithm $\mathcal{B}$ solves the DBDH problem with advantage $\epsilon(\lambda)/(2\lambda + 2q(\lambda))$ where $q(\lambda)$ is the number of register queries made by the adversary.*

Proof. Abbreviate $q(\lambda)$ to q where it is clear from context. We do so by noting an adversary can have two types of challenge ciphertex:

Type I. The adversary chooses a challenge ciphertex with number x greater than $2^{\lceil \log q \rceil}$.

Type II. The adversary chooses a challenge ciphertex with number x less than or equal to $2^{\lceil \log q \rceil}$.

In Lemma 2, we show that a type I adversary can be used to break DBDH with a loss of a q factor in the reduction. In Lemma 3, we show that a type II adversary can be used to break DBDH with a loss of a λ factor in the reduction. This concludes our proof. □

4.1 Type I Adversary

Lemma 2. *Suppose there is a type II adversary $\mathcal{A}$ that can win the security game with the advantage $\epsilon(\lambda)$. Then there is a algorithm $\mathcal{B}$ solves the DBDH problem with the advantage $\epsilon(\lambda)/(2q)$.*

Proof. Given a tuple $(g_\alpha, g_\beta, g_\gamma, Z)$, that is either sampled from $\mathcal{P}_{\text{BDH}}$ or from $\mathcal{R}_{\text{BDH}}$. The simulator $\mathcal{B}$ interacts with adversary $\mathcal{A}$ as follows:

Setup Phase. $\mathcal{B}$ works as follows:

1. Randomly samples an integer k in the range from cnt to $q + cnt$. This represents a guess that the adversary will challenge on number x such that $k = x$.
2. Randomly samples $\tilde{u}, \tilde{v}, \tilde{w} \leftarrow \mathbb{Z}_p^*$, computes $u \leftarrow g_\alpha g^{\tilde{u}}$, $v \leftarrow g^{\tilde{v}}$. $w \leftarrow g_\alpha^{-k} g^{\tilde{w}}$
3. Outputs public parameter as $(g, u, v, w, e(g_\alpha, g_\beta))$.

Pre-Challenge Phase.

- **Register.** $\mathcal{B}$ simply advances the counter by $cnt \leftarrow cnt + 1$.
- **Reveal**(y). On $\mathcal{A}$ issuing a secret key for y, $\mathcal{B}$:

    1. randomly samples $\tilde{r} \leftarrow \mathbb{Z}_p^*$,
    2. computes

    $$\tau \leftarrow \tilde{u}y + \tilde{v}\lceil \log y \rceil + \tilde{w},$$
    $$\psi \leftarrow y - k,$$

    3. computes

    $$D \leftarrow g_\beta^{-\tau/\psi} g^{\tilde{r}},$$
    $$R \leftarrow g_\beta^{-1/\psi} g^{\tilde{r}},$$

    4. returns (D, R) as y's private key.

Correctness of Simulation. Denote $r = -\beta/\psi + \tilde{r}$, we argue that (D, R) is always a proper private key corresponding to y since

$$
\begin{aligned}
H(y) &= u^y v^{\lceil \log y \rceil} w \\
&= (g_\alpha g^{\tilde{u}})^y (g^{\tilde{v}})^{\lceil \log y \rceil} g_\alpha^{-k} g^{\tilde{w}} \\
&= g_\alpha^{y-k} g^{\tilde{u}y + \tilde{v}\lceil \log y \rceil + \tilde{w}} \\
&= g_\alpha^\psi g^\tau,
\end{aligned}
$$

and

$$
\begin{aligned}
g^{\alpha\beta} H(y)^r &= g^{\alpha\beta} (g_\alpha^\psi g^\tau)^{-\beta/\psi + \tilde{r}} \\
&= g^{\alpha\beta} g_\alpha^{-\beta} g_\beta^{-\tau/\psi} g^{\tilde{r}} \\
&= D.
\end{aligned}
$$

Challenge Phase. When $\mathcal{A}$ decides Pre-Challenge Phase is over, it outputs the challenge target x and two message M_0 and M_1 on which it wishes to be challenged. Algorithm $\mathcal{B}$:

1. if $k \neq x$, $\mathcal{B}$ aborts the game, else:
2. picks a random bit $\mu \leftarrow \{0, 1\}$
3. computes

$$\delta \leftarrow \tilde{u}x + \tilde{v}\lceil \log x \rceil + \tilde{w}$$

4. computes

$$C \leftarrow M_\mu \cdot Z, \quad S \leftarrow g_\gamma, \quad T \leftarrow g_\gamma^\delta$$

5. responds with the challenge ciphertext as (C, S, T)

Correctness of Simulation. If $k = x$, (C, S, T) is idenitcal to the ciphertext generated from $\mathbf{Enc}(pp, x, M_\mu)$ since

$$
\begin{aligned}
H(x)^\gamma &= (u^x v^{\lceil \log x \rceil} w)^\gamma \\
&= ((g_\alpha g^{\tilde{u}})^x (g^{\tilde{v}})^{\lceil \log x \rceil} g_\alpha^{-k} g^{\tilde{w}})^\gamma \\
&= (g_\alpha^{x-k} g^{\tilde{u}x + \tilde{v}\lceil \log x \rceil + \tilde{w}})^\gamma \\
&= g_\gamma^{\tilde{u}x + \tilde{v}\lceil \log x \rceil + \tilde{w}} \\
&= T.
\end{aligned}
$$

Post-Challenge Phase. $\mathcal{B}$ responds as before in pre-challenge phase.

Guess Phase. Finally $\mathcal{A}$ outputs a guess μ' of μ. $\mathcal{B}$ concludes its own game by outputting a guess as follows. if $\mu' = \mu$, $\mathcal{B}$ returns 1, else returns 0.

Probability Analysis. Fristly suppose $\mathcal{B}$ does not abort in the game. If $(g_\alpha, g_\beta, g_\gamma, Z)$ is a correct DBDH combination, the adversary will respond with $\mu' = \mu$ with probability $1/2 + \epsilon(\lambda)$ and the simulator will respond with "yes" correctly, thus solving DBDH. If Z was random, then the adversary will give a random answer with probability $1/2$ and the simulator will answer correctly in half of the cases. To summarize, if $\mathcal{B}$ does not abort in the game, the probability of solving DBDH is:

$$
\begin{aligned}
&\Pr[\mu' = \mu | Z = e(g_\alpha, g_\beta)^\gamma] \cdot \Pr[Z = e(g_\alpha, g_\beta)^\gamma] \\
&+ \frac{1}{2} \cdot \Pr[Z \neq e(g_\alpha, g_\beta)^\gamma] \\
&= (\frac{1}{2} + \epsilon(\lambda))\frac{1}{2} + \frac{1}{4} = \frac{1}{2}\epsilon(\lambda) + \frac{1}{2}.
\end{aligned}
$$

If $\mathcal{B}$ aborts the game, the probability of solving DBDH is $1/2$, notice that the probability $\mathcal{B}$ need not to abort is $1/q$, so the probability of $\mathcal{B}$ solves the DBDH problem is

$$
\frac{1}{q}\left(\frac{\epsilon(\lambda)}{2} + \frac{1}{2}\right) + \frac{1-q}{q}\frac{1}{2} = \frac{\epsilon(\lambda)}{2q} + \frac{1}{2}.
$$

4.2   Type II Adversary

Lemma 3. *Suppose there is a type II adversary $\mathcal{A}$ that can win the security game with the advantage $\epsilon(\lambda)$. Then there is a algorithm $\mathcal{B}$ solves the DBDH problem with the advantage $\epsilon(\lambda)/(2\lambda)$.*

Proof. Given a tuple $(g_\alpha, g_\beta, g_\gamma, Z)$, that is either sampled from $\mathcal{P}_{\mathrm{BDH}}$ or from $\mathcal{R}_{\mathrm{BDH}}$. The simulator $\mathcal{B}$ interacts with adversary $\mathcal{A}$ as follows:

Setup Phase. $\mathcal{B}$ works as follows:

1. Randomly samples an integer k in the range from 1 to λ. This represents a guess that the adversary will challenge on number x such that $k = \lceil \log x \rceil$.
2. Randomly samples $\tilde{u}, \tilde{v}, \tilde{w} \leftarrow \mathbb{Z}_p^*$, computes $u \leftarrow g^{\tilde{u}}$, $v \leftarrow g_\alpha g^{\tilde{v}}$. $w \leftarrow g_\alpha^{-k} g^{\tilde{w}}$
3. Outputs public parameter as $(g, u, v, w, e(g_\alpha, g_\beta))$.

Pre-Challenge Phase.

- **Register.** $\mathcal{B}$ simply advances the counter by $cnt \leftarrow cnt + 1$.
- **Reveal(y).** On $\mathcal{A}$ issuing a secret key for y, $\mathcal{B}$:

    1. randomly samples $\tilde{r} \leftarrow \mathbb{Z}_p^*$,
    2. computes

$$\tau \leftarrow \tilde{u}y + \tilde{v}\lceil \log y \rceil + \tilde{w},$$
$$\psi \leftarrow \lceil \log y \rceil - k,$$

    3. computes

$$D \leftarrow g_\beta^{-\tau/\psi} g^{\tilde{r}},$$
$$R \leftarrow g_\beta^{-1/\psi} g^{\tilde{r}},$$

    4. returns (D, R) as y's private key.

Correctness of simulation. Denote $r = -\beta/\psi + \tilde{r}$, we argue that (D, R) is always a proper private key corresponding to y since

$$\begin{aligned} H(y) &= u^y v^{\lceil \log y \rceil} w \\ &= g^{\tilde{u}y} (g_\alpha g^{\tilde{v}})^{\lceil \log y \rceil} g_\alpha^{-k} g^{\tilde{w}} \\ &= g_\alpha^{\lceil \log y \rceil - k} g^{\tilde{u}y + \tilde{v}\lceil \log y \rceil + \tilde{w}} \\ &= g_\alpha^\psi g^\tau, \end{aligned}$$

and

$$\begin{aligned} g^{\alpha\beta} H(y)^r &= g^{\alpha\beta} (g_\alpha^\psi g^\tau)^{-\beta/\psi + \tilde{r}} \\ &= g^{\alpha\beta} g_\alpha^{-\beta} g_\beta^{-\tau/\psi} g^{\tilde{r}} \\ &= D. \end{aligned}$$

Challenge Phase. When $\mathcal{A}$ decides Pre-Challenge Phase is over, it outputs the challenge target x and two message M_0 and M_1 on which it wishes to be challenged. Algorithm $\mathcal{B}$:

1. if $k \neq \lceil \log x \rceil$, $\mathcal{B}$ aborts the game, else:
2. picks a random bit $\mu \leftarrow \{0, 1\}$
3. computes

$$\delta \leftarrow \tilde{u}x + \tilde{v}\lceil \log x \rceil + \tilde{w}$$

4. computes
$$C \leftarrow M_\mu \cdot Z, \quad S \leftarrow g_\gamma, \quad T \leftarrow g_\gamma^\delta$$

5. responds with the challenge ciphertext as (C, S, T)

Correctness of Simulation. If $k = \lceil \log x \rceil$, (C, S, T) is idenitcal to the ciphertext generated from $\mathbf{Enc}(pp, x, M_\mu)$ since

$$
\begin{aligned}
H(x)^\gamma &= (u^x v^{\lceil \log x \rceil} w)^\gamma \\
&= (g^{\tilde{u}x}(g_\alpha g^{\tilde{v}})^{\lceil \log x \rceil} g_\alpha^{-k} g^{\tilde{w}})^\gamma \\
&= (g_\alpha^{\lceil \log x \rceil - k} g^{\tilde{u}x + \tilde{v}\lceil \log x \rceil + \tilde{w}})^\gamma \\
&= g_\gamma^{\tilde{u}x + \tilde{v}\lceil \log x \rceil + \tilde{w}} \\
&= T.
\end{aligned}
$$

Post-Challenge Phase. $\mathcal{B}$ responds as before in pre-challenge phase.

Guess Phase. Finally $\mathcal{A}$ outputs a guess μ' of μ. $\mathcal{B}$ concludes its own game by outputting a guess as follows. if $\mu' = \mu$, $\mathcal{B}$ returns 1, else returns 0.

Probability Analysis. Fristly suppose $\mathcal{B}$ does not abort in the game. If $(g_\alpha, g_\beta, g_\gamma, Z)$ is a correct DBDH combination, the adversary will respond with $\mu' = \mu$ with probability $1/2 + \epsilon(\lambda)$ and the simulator will respond with "yes" correctly, thus solving DBDH. If Z was random, then the adversary will give a random answer with probability $1/2$ and the simulator will answer correctly in half of the cases. To summarize, if $\mathcal{B}$ does not abort in the game, the probability of solving DBDH is:

$$
\begin{aligned}
&\Pr[\mu' = \mu | Z = e(g_\alpha, g_\beta)^\gamma] \cdot \Pr[Z = e(g_\alpha, g_\beta)^\gamma] \\
&+ \frac{1}{2} \cdot \Pr[Z \neq e(g_\alpha, g_\beta)^\gamma] \\
&= (\frac{1}{2} + \epsilon(\lambda))\frac{1}{2} + \frac{1}{4} = \frac{1}{2}\epsilon(\lambda) + \frac{1}{2}.
\end{aligned}
$$

If $\mathcal{B}$ aborts the game, the probability of solving DBDH is $1/2$, notice that the probability $\mathcal{B}$ need not to abort is $1/\lambda$, so the probability of $\mathcal{B}$ solves the DBDH problem is

$$
\frac{1}{\lambda}\left(\frac{\epsilon(\lambda)}{2} + \frac{1}{2}\right) + \frac{1 - \lambda}{\lambda}\frac{1}{2} = \frac{\epsilon(\lambda)}{2\lambda} + \frac{1}{2}.
$$

5 Conclusion

In this article, we have discussed the problem of encryption by serial number in asymmetric setting. An interesting open problem is to construct SNBE schemes for other classes of functions. A possible starting point is to consider simple functionalities, such as wildcard [4] and inner-product testing [5]. Another fascinating open problem is to design a SNBE scheme which is secure without pairing.

Acknowledgements. This work is supported by the National Natural Science Foundation of China (Grant No. 61411146001, 61373154 and 61371083) and the Prioritized Development Projects of the Specialized Research Fund for the Doctoral Program of Higher Education of China (Grant No. 20130073130004).

References

1. Waters, B.: Efficient identity-based encryption without random oracles. In: Cramer, R. (ed.) EUROCRYPT 2005. LNCS, vol. 3494, pp. 114–127. Springer, Heidelberg (2005)
2. Boneh, D., Franklin, M.K.: Identity-based encryption from the weil pairing. SIAM J. Comput. **32**(3), 586–615 (2003)
3. Lewko, A., Waters, B.: New techniques for dual system encryption and fully secure HIBE with short ciphertexts. In: Micciancio, D. (ed.) TCC 2010. LNCS, vol. 5978, pp. 455–479. Springer, Heidelberg (2010)
4. Abdalla, M., Birkett, J., Catalano, D., Dent, A.W., Malone-Lee, J., Neven, G., Schuldt, J.C.N., Smart, N.P.: Wildcarded identity-based encryption. J. Cryptology **24**(1), 42–82 (2011)
5. Katz, J., Sahai, A., Waters, B.: Predicate encryption supporting disjunctions, polynomial equations, and inner products. J. Cryptology **26**(2), 191–224 (2013)
6. Jutla, C.S., Roy, A.: Shorter quasi-adaptive NIZK proofs for linear subspaces. In: Sako, K., Sarkar, P. (eds.) ASIACRYPT 2013, Part I. LNCS, vol. 8269, pp. 1–20. Springer, Heidelberg (2013)
7. Chen, J., Wee, H.: Fully, (Almost) tightly secure IBE and dual system groups. In: Canetti, R., Garay, J.A. (eds.) CRYPTO 2013, Part II. LNCS, vol. 8043, pp. 435–460. Springer, Heidelberg (2013)
8. Boneh, D., Boyen, X.: Efficient selective identity-based encryption without random oracles. J. Cryptology **24**(4), 659–693 (2011)
9. Hohenberger, S., Waters, B.: Realizing hash-and-sign signatures under standard assumptions. In: Joux, A. (ed.) EUROCRYPT 2009. LNCS, vol. 5479, pp. 333–350. Springer, Heidelberg (2009)

Fine-Grained Searchable Encryption over Encrypted Data in Multi-clouds

Yinbin Miao[1], Jiajia Liu[2(✉)], and Jianfeng Ma[2,3]

[1] School of Telecommunication Engineering, Xidian University, Xi'an, China
ybmiao@stu.xidian.edu.cn
[2] School of Cyber Engineering, Xidian University, Xi'an, China
liujiajia@xidian.edu.cn
[3] School of Computer Science and Technology, Xidian University, Xi'an, China
jfma@mail.xidian.edu.cn

Abstract. Cloud computing has increased rapidly due to its abundant benefits in terms of low cost and accessability of data. Privacy protection and data security are two issues in cloud computing, as users often outsource sensitive information to honest-but-curious cloud storage providers (CSP). While encryption seriously obsoletes the traditional information retrieval over plaintext. Therefore, searchable encryption (SE) technology which allows the users to securely search over ciphertext through keywords and selectively retrieve files of interest becomes important. Dealing with single CSP is predicted to become less popular with cloud customers for fear of risks of single-point failure threat and potential malicious insiders. To tackle above problems, two schemes based on Identity-Based Encryption (IBE) and Key-Policy Attribute-Based Encryption (KP-ABE) are proposed in multi-clouds environment, respectively. Through rigorous security and performance analysis, both schemes can ensure security and reliability, and greatly reduce computational burden.

Keywords: Cloud computing · Multi-clouds · SE · IBE · KP-ABE

1 Introduction

Cloud computing is growing exponentially and posses abundant advantages including flexible resource management, quick deployment, decreased costs and easy access. In spite of cheaper data storage and computation in cloud computing, cloud clients lose direct control over sensitive data and face more privacy

This work is supported by National High Technology Research and Development Program (863 Program) (No. 2015AA011704), Major Nature Science Foundation of China (No. 61370078), Fundamental Research Funds for the Center Universities (No. JY10000903001).

K. Xu and J. Zhu (Eds.): WASA 2015, LNCS 9204, pp. 407–416, 2015.
DOI: 10.1007/978-3-319-21837-3_40

preservation problems. Privacy protection and data security are two issues in cloud computing [1], as users often outsource sensitive information to honest-but-curious cloud storage providers(CSP). Therefore, developing an efficient and secure searchable encryption which allows user to securely search over cipher-text through keywords and selectively retrieve files of interest is of paramount importance.

Although there has been much work focusing on improving the efficiency and security, existing schemes just concentrate on reliability of single CSP, which has some other limitations, such as data corruption, lack of availability and privacy protection. Traditional data replication on multi-clouds is the most straightforward but least cost-efficient approach. Therefore, the focus of searchable encryption has turned to multi-clouds, inter-clouds or cloud-of-cloud. In this paper, we explore the fine-grained searchable encryption technology in multi-clouds [2,3] and define two schemes as basic scheme and enhanced scheme, respectively. Through Identity-Based Encryption (IBE) scheme [4] the basic scheme can supports single keyword searching in multi-clouds environment, and the enhanced scheme based on Attribute-Based Encryption scheme [5] can achieve a fine-grained access control and allow to perform expressive searching over encrypted data. To avoid time delay and improve efficiency, both schemes can be further extended with Shamir's (t,n) secret sharing scheme [6] to gain functions of availability and robustness.

The rest of this article is organized as follows. Section 2 begins with the related works. Section 3 introduces some definitions associated with our schemes. Section 4 gives the system model and threat model of both schemes. Section 5 demonstrates our proposed schemes in detail. Section 6 presents the security and performance analysis. Section 7 draws a conclusion.

2   Related Work

Searchable encryption is a cryptographic primitive which allows user to securely search over ciphertext through keywords and selectively retrieve files of interest. Since Song et al. [7] first proposed symmetric key-based scheme for retrieving encrypted data according to IBE scheme, vast subsequent searchable encryption schemes [8,9] have been proposed to improve the efficiency and security using vector space model, edit distance or multi-way trie-tree. However, these schemes cannot support expressive search like boolean search or non-monotone search. The concept of attribute-based encryption(ABE) was first proposed by Sahai et al. [5]. According to the access policy, ABE schemes can be roughly categorized into KP-ABE(i.e. the key is associated with access policy and ciphertext is embedded with attribute) or CP-ABE(contrary to KP-ABE), only there is a match between attributes and access policy data users can decrypt encrypted data. With abundant ABE schemes [10], we can extend them to searchable encryption schemes to achieve fine-grained access control so as to support expressive searching.

3 Preliminaries

In this section we give some definitions associated with our proposed schemes.

Definition 1. Composite order bilinear groups [11] Given a security parameter k, the bilinear group generator $\mathcal{G}(\cdot)$ outputs two cyclic groups G_1, G_2 of order q. Where $q = q_1 q_2 q_3 q_4$ (q_1, q_2, q_3, q_4 are distinct primes), $e : G_1 \times G_1 \rightarrow G_2$ is the bilinear map. And $G_{q_1}, G_{q_2}, G_{q_3}, G_{q_4}$ are the subgroup of order q_1, q_2, q_3, q_4. The following features will be satisfied:

1. Bilinear: $\forall g, h \in G_1$, $a, b \in \mathbb{Z}_q$, $e(g^a, h^b) = e(g, h)^{ab}$.
2. Non-degenerate: $\exists g \in G_1$ such that $e(g, g)$ has order q in G_2.
3. Orthogonality: $\forall h_i \in G_{q_i}$ and $\forall h_j \in G_{q_j}$, $i \neq j$, $e(h_i, h_j) = 1$, where 1 is the identity element in G_2.

4 System and Threat Models

We consider a cryptographic cloud storage system supporting both information retrieval and fine-grained access control over encrypted records. There are four

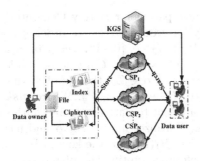

Fig. 1. Framework of our scheme

entries contained in these schemes, namely data owner, data user, key generator server(KGS) and N CSPs. Where data owner uploads ciphertext and index to each CSP, KGS manages master key and transmits secret key to data owner and users, and CSP stores the ciphertext and index and performs search operation for data users. The framework of our scheme is shown in Fig. 1.

In this paper, suppose the data owner and authorized data user are trusted, while the CSP is honest-but-curious. Specifically, the CSP honestly follows established protocols, but it is still anxious to sensitive or crucial information. The most frequent threat is that the vicious CSP may collude with other CSPs to analyze and deduce the paintext of data files or keywords. To ensure the security and robustness of our schemes, we employ Shamir's secret sharing scheme to enhance the availability and privacy of our proposed schemes.

5   Constructions of Our Schemes

With the increasing attacks and intrusions, maintaining the security of CSP becomes increasing difficult. The natural solution is to encrypt outsourced data in order to reduce the vulnerability on the case that CSP is compromised. Therefore, it is necessary to resolve the previous challenges and ensure the robust even when certain CSP crashes in distributed system. In the multi-cloud model, certain CSP may collute with other CSPs to analyze and deduce sensitive information. To preserve the data privacy and security against above threats, our basic scheme can tackle these problems and is appropriate for common applications. In actual scenarios, in order to accurately locate the relevant files so as to reduce unnecessary computation burden, data users need to submit several keywords. Therefore, in our enhanced scheme based on KP-ABE we can make up the flaws of basic scheme and achieve expressive searching.

5.1   Basic Scheme

In our basic scheme in which the ciphertext is encrypted based on single keyword, collusion attack can be effectively avoided in multi-clouds model. The specific construction of basic scheme is shown as follows:

- Setup(1^k): Given secure parameter k, Key Generator Server(KGS) outputs two multiplication cyclic groups G_1, G_2 of order q and two hash functions $H_1 : \{0,1\}^* \to G_1, H_2 : G_2 \to \{0,1\}^n$. Let g be a generator of G_1 and e be the bilinear map, $e: G_1 \times G_1 \to G_2$. Choose random elements $r_j \in \mathbb{Z}_q (1 \leq j \leq N)$ and master secret $\alpha \in \mathbb{Z}_q$, then publish the system parameters as $Params = (G_1, G_2, H_1, H_2, e, g, g_1 = g^\alpha)$. Where $msk = \{\alpha\}$ is only owned by KGS, $\{r_1, ..., r_N\}$ are sent to data owner and authorized data users.
- KeyGen(w, α, H_1): KGS utilizes master key α and hash function H_1 to generate the secret key $sk = H_1(w)^\alpha$ for the keyword w submitted by data user.
- Enc(f_i, H_1, g_1, w_i): Before encrypting the plaintext $f_i \in \{0,1\}^n$, data owner first divides f_i into N chunks $f_i = \{f_{i,1}, ... f_{i,N}\}$, which each chunk has the same length as file f_i, such that $f_i = f_{i,1} \oplus ... \oplus f_{i,N}$. Next he or she selects random $r_j \in \mathbb{Z}_q$ for each CSP and computers $g_w = e(H_1(w_i), g_1)$, $c_{i,j} = \langle g^{r_j}, f_{i,j} \oplus H_2(g_w^{r_j}) \rangle, I_{i,j} = H_1(w_i)^{r_j}$, finally $c_{i,j}$ and $I_{i,j}$ are outsourced to the j-th($1 \leq j \leq N$) CSP. Where w_i is extracted from file f_i.
- Search($w', H_1, r_j, c_{i,j}, I$): When wanting to retrieval files containing keyword w', data user first performs an interaction with KGS and gains sk, then generates the trapdoor $T_{w'} = sk^{r_j}$ of keyword w', finally submits it to the j-th CSP. After receiving the trapdoor $T_{w'}$, the j-th CSP verifies whether the equation $e(T_{w'}, g) = e(g_1, I_{i,j})$ holds.
  If $w_i = w'$, then the equation holds and returns the ciphertext $c_{i,j} = \langle A, B \rangle$ to data user. Otherwise $\perp$.
- Dec($c_{i,j}, pk$): Data user decrypts the ciphertext $c_{i,j}$ through using secret key. $f_{i,j} = B \oplus H_2(e(sk, A))$

Discuss 1: With the basic scheme, we can easily solve the problems of single-point failure and collusion attack. As the ciphertext stored in every CSP uses different parameter r_j, even though several CSPs collaborate each other they cannot decrypt the ciphertext. Therefore, we can ensure the security and availability in basic scheme. However, one shortcoming of basic scheme is that it cannot be applied in practical applications and achieve fine-grained access control. To address the above drawbacks, we define an enhanced scheme based on Key-Policy Attribute-Based Encryption(KP-ABE).

5.2   Enhanced Scheme

Though there are many searchable encryption schemes focusing on multi-keyword or boolean search [12–14], the need of expressive search schemes is still urgent in practical applications. The ciphertext in the enhanced scheme is defined by a set of attributes, while the private key is described by an access matrix [15]. As a result, our enhanced scheme can effectively avoid vicious collusion attack and support expressive search even though the access structure [5] is leaked to malicious CSPs.

- Setup($1^k, \mathcal{U}$): Given secret parameter k, KGS outputs parameters $G_1, G_2, e, G_{q_1}, G_{q_2}, G_{q_3}, G_{q_4}$. Where G_1, G_2 are two cyclic groups of order q, e: $G_1 \times G_1 \to G_2$, $q = q_1 q_2 q_3 q_4$, and G_{q_i} is the subgroup of order q_i in G_1 . Let $\mathcal{U} = \{1, ..., n\}$ be an attribute set , for each attribute $i \in \mathcal{U}$, randomly choose $t_i \in \mathbb{Z}_q$. And select random numbers $\alpha \in \mathbb{Z}_q, g_1, \nu_1 \in G_{q_1}, g_4, \nu_4 \in G_{q_4}$, where g_1, g_4 are the generators of G_{q_1}, G_{q_4}, respectively, $\mu = \nu_1 \nu_4$. Then it chooses random $s_j \in \mathbb{Z}_q, (1 \leq j \leq N)$ for each CSP, finally pk, msk are defined as $pk = \{q, g_1, g_4, e(g_1, g_1)^\alpha, \mu, \beta_i = g_1^{t_i}, \forall i\}, msk = \{\nu_1, \alpha\}$. Where $\{s_1, ..., s_N\}$ are sent to data owner and authorized data users.
- Enc(f_i, s_j, pk, W): Unlike the file chunk in basic scheme, each file chunk $f_{i,j}$ contains m keyword fields, namely $W = \{w_1, ..., w_m\}$. Data owner chooses $\eta_1, \eta_2 \in G_{q_4}$, then takes the keyword set as attributes to encrypt file $f_{i,j}$. The ciphertext is computed as $c_{i,j} = \{c = f_{i,j} e(g_1, g_1)^{\alpha s_j}, c_0 = g_1^{s_j} \eta_1, c_r = (\mu \beta_r)^{s_j} \eta_2, \forall w_r \in W, 1 \leq r \leq m\}$. Then the ciphertext $(c_{i,j}, 1 \leq j \leq N)$ is sent to the j-th CSP.
- Trapdoor($\mathbb{A}, \rho, pk, msk$): An access matrix will be derived from submitted keyword set $W' = \{w_1, ..., w_{l|l \leq m}\}$ before data user performing search requirements. Suppose $\mathbb{A}$ be the $m \times n$ access matrix, each row $\mathbb{A}_{\rho(i)}$ represents a keyword field, where ρ is a function from $\{1, ..., l\}$ to $\{1, ..., m\}$, $i \in \{1, ..., l\}$. Data user first selects a random vector $V \in \mathbb{Z}_q^n$ such that $1 \cdot V = \alpha$, where $1 = (1, 0, ..., 0)$. Then he or she randomly chooses $\theta_{\rho(i)} \in \mathbb{Z}_q, \varphi_{\rho(i),1}, \varphi_{\rho(i),2} \in G_{q_3}$, and computes the trapdoor as $T = \{T_{\rho(i)}^1 = g_1^{\mathbb{A}_{\rho(i)} V} (\nu_1 \beta_{\rho(i)})^{\theta_{\rho(i)}} \varphi_{\rho(i),1}, T_{\rho(i)}^2 = g_1^{\theta_{\rho(i)}} \varphi_{\rho(i),2}\}$.
- Test($c_{i,j}, pk, T$): If the keyword set W embedded in ciphertext satisfies the access matrix of data user, CSP chooses a constant $\omega_{\rho(i)}$, such that

$\sum_{\mathbb{A}_{\rho(i)} \in W'} (\omega_{\rho(i)} \mathbb{A}_{\rho(i)}) = 1$. Then CSP computers the following equation:

$$\prod_{\mathbb{A}_{\rho(i)} \in W'} \frac{e(c_0, T^1_{\rho(i)})^{\omega_{\rho(i)}}}{e(c_{\rho(i)}, T^2_{\rho(i)})^{\omega_{\rho(i)}}} = \prod_{\mathbb{A}_{\rho(i)} \in W'} \frac{e(g_1, g_1)^{s_j \mathbb{A}_{\rho(i)} V \omega_{\rho(i)}} e(g_1, \nu_1 \beta_{\rho(i)})^{s_j \theta_{\rho(i)} \omega_{\rho(i)}}}{e(\nu_1 \beta_{\rho(i)}, g_1)^{s_j \theta_{\rho(i)} \omega_{\rho(i)}}}$$

$$= \prod_{\mathbb{A}_{\rho(i)} \in W'} e(g_1, g_1)^{s_j \mathbb{A}_{\rho(i)} V \omega_{\rho(i)}}$$

$$= e(g_1, g_1)^{s_j \alpha}$$

Finally, the plaintext is returned as $f_{i,j} = \frac{c}{e(g_1, g_1)^{s_j \alpha}}$.

5.3   Extension

In our proposed schemes, until N file slices have been gained from CSPs, the data user can reconstruct the original file. However, in actual applications data user cannot restore the whole file f_i because of single-point failure of CSP. Furthermore, searching all file chunks inevitably leads to time delay, which seriously impacts the availability and robustness of our schemes. To settle this problem, the Shamir's secret sharing scheme can be adopted to improve the efficiency and reliability of our schemes, Namely, the each file chunk will be encrypted with a (t-1)-order polynomial before re-encrypted by data owners. Specific steps are shown as follows:

- After file f_i has been divided into N chunks, a random $(t\text{-}1)$-order function will be chosen by data owner for each file as follows:

$$\mathcal{F}_i(x) = c_{t-1} x^{t-1} + c_{t-2} x^{t-2} + \dots + c_1 x^1 + f_i$$

- Before encrypting file chunk $f_{i,j}$, data owner first preprocess each file chunk as follows:

$$\mathcal{F}_{i,1}(f_{i,1}) = c_{t-1} f^{t-1}_{i,1} + c_{t-2} f^{t-2}_{i,1} + \dots + c_1 f^1_{i,1} + f_i$$
$$\mathcal{F}_{i,2}(f_{i,2}) = c_{t-1} f^{t-1}_{i,2} + c_{t-2} f^{t-2}_{i,2} + \dots + c_1 f^1_{i,2} + f_i$$

$$\vdots$$

$$\mathcal{F}_{i,N}(f_{i,1}) = c_{t-1} f^{t-1}_{i,N} + c_{t-2} f^{t-2}_{i,N} + \dots + c_1 f^1_{i,N} + f_i$$

- Data user can employ any t plaintext gained from N CSPs to reconstruct the original file.

Based on the efficient and secure multiple CSPs mechanism, data user can reconstruct the original file even though the $\{n - t\}$ CSPs have been compromised, where the t is the predefined threshold value. However, the search pattern may be leaked when more than t CSPs collude with each other. Therefore, the proposed schemes combined with Shamir's secret sharing ensure the security and privacy of data to some extent.

Table 1. Performance analysis

	Enc	Trap	Test
J Lai's scheme	$2(m+2)e$	$4me$	$2mp+me$
Z Lv's scheme	$(m+2)e+p$	$4me$	$me+3mp$
Basic scheme	$h_1+p+N(h_2+e)$	h_1+Ne	$2Np$
Enhanced scheme	$N(m+2)e$	$3me$	Ne

6 Security and Performance Analysis

6.1 Security Analysis

As chosen ciphertext security(IND-CPA) is the standard acceptable notion of security of public key searchable encryption scheme, our basic scheme is required to satisfy this strong notion of security. So we can say the proposed basic scheme is semantically secure against IND-CPA attack if no polynomially bounded adversary $\mathcal{A}$ has a non-negligible advantage against the challenger in the IND-CPA game as follows.

- **Setup:** Given a security parameter k, the challenger runs the *Setup* algorithm and sends the resulting parameters to adversary $\mathcal{A}$, while the msk is owned by himself.
- **Phase 1:** The adversary issues queries $q_1, ..., q_n$ where query q_i is: – KeyGen $\langle w_i \rangle$. The challenger runs the *KeyGen* algorithm and generates the private key pk_i corresponding to w_i, then he or she sends the private keys to adversary. As these queries may be asked adaptively, namely, each query q_i may depend on the replies to $q_1, ..., q_{i-1}$.
- **Challenge:** After the Phase 1 is over, the adversary outputs two equal length files $f_0, f_1 \in \mathbf{F}$ and keywords w_0, w_1 on which he or she wishes to be challenged. The only constraint is that keywords w_0, w_1 did not appear in Phase 1. The challenger picks a random bit $b \in \{0, 1\}$ and sends $c_b \in \mathbf{C}$ to adversary.
- **Phase 1:** The adversary issues more queries $q_{n+1}, ..., q_m$, where each q_i is: – KeyGen $\langle w_i \rangle$. The challenger responds as in Phase 1, where $w_0, w_1 \neq w_i$.
- **Guess:** Finally, the adversary outputs a guess $b' \in \{0, 1\}$ and wins the game if $b' = b$.

We call this adversary $\mathcal{A}$ as an IND-CPA adversary, and the advantage of the adversary in successfully attacking the basic scheme (BS) is given as follows:

$$Adv_{BS,\mathcal{A}}(k) = |Pr[b = b'] - \frac{1}{2}|$$

Theorem 1: Suppose the hash function H_1, H_2 are random oracles, then our basic scheme is IND-CPA security if the BDH Problem is hard.

Theorem 2: If the assumptions in [15] hold, our enhanced scheme is secure and anonymous. Due to space constraints, the detailed proofs can refer to full paper.

6.2   Performance Analysis

The computational complexity mainly depends on pairing operation(p), exponentiation operation(e) and hash operations(h_1, h_2) in the Encryption(Enc), Trapdoor(Trap) and Test algorithms, where h_1 maps a string to the point in G_1, h_2 maps the point in G_2 to a string.

Where the values of m, N represent the keyword fields and the number of CSP, respectively. The theoretical analysis of computational complexity is shown in Table 1.

In order to intuitively show the superior performance in Fig. 2, we use the Type A curves defined within the PBC library. Regarding on the computational cost of above operations, we set $p = 5.811ms, e = 3.85ms, h_1 = 12.418ms, h_2 = 0.947ms$, and the specific parameters are shown in literature [16].

Considering the practical applications, we set m,N $\in$ [1,10]. From the subgraph Fig. 2(a) we notice that the computational cost of Enc algorithm in basic scheme is limited to the range $(23.026ms, 66.199ms)$, and our enhanced scheme has less computational cost than other schemes when N=1. However, with the increased N $\geq$ 2, the Enc algorithm of enhanced scheme will have biggest computational overhead as it needs to compute N ciphertext for N CSPs. In Fig. 2(b) the Trap algorithm in enhanced scheme has the least computational cost, which is superior to other schemes [15,17]. And the performance of basic scheme is still better than previous schemes within certain range. In Fig. 2(c) the Test algorithm of our enhanced scheme almost has the lowest computational cost, and the basic scheme is also has less computational overhead under certain conditions. Next we will give an example in Fig. 3 to show performance superiority of our schemes, in which we set m=5,N=3. In conclusion, the computational complexity of our proposed schemes are lower than previous schemes, especially

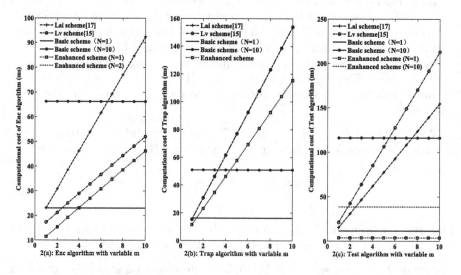

Fig. 2. Performance analysis of different schemes

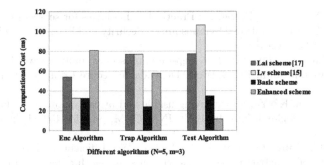

Fig. 3. An example of performance comparison

in the single CSP setting. Although the computational cost of Enc operation in enhanced scheme is larger than other schemes, our enhanced scheme can be applied to multiple CSPs setting so that the problems of single-point failure and collusion attack can be avoided.

7 Conclusion

In this paper, we design two searchable encryption technologies in multi-clouds model. Our proposed schemes can avoid single-point failure threat and potential collusion attack. However, searching all file chunks inevitably leads to time delay, which seriously impacts the availability and robustness of our schemes. Through using Shamir's secret sharing scheme we can improve the efficiency and reliability of our schemes. Compared with existing searchable encryption schemes in single-cloud model, our schemes can achieve availability and security at the same time without increasing computational burden.

References

1. Wei, L., Zhu, H., Cao, Z., et al.: Security and privacy of storage and computation in cloud computing. Inf. Sci. **258**, 371–386 (2014)
2. Zhu, Y., Hu, H., Ahn, G.J.: Cooperative provable data poession for integrity verification in multicloud storage. IEEE Transa. Parallel Distrib. Syst. **23**(12), 2231–2244 (2012)
3. Alzain, M.A., Pardede, E., Soh, B.: Cloud computing security From single to multi-clouds. International Conference on System Science. IEEE Computer Society Press, Manoa (2012)
4. Boneh, D., Franklin, M.: Identity-based encryption from the weil pairing. In: Kilian, J. (ed.) CRYPTO 2001. LNCS, vol. 2139, pp. 213–229. Springer, Heidelberg (2001)
5. Goyal, V., Pandey, O., Sahai, A., et al.: Attribute-based encryption for fine-grained access control of encrypted data. In: 13th ACM Conference on Computer and Communication Security, pp. 89–98. ACM Press, New York (2006)
6. Shamir, A.: How to share a secret. Commun. ACM **22**, 612–613 (1979)

7. Song, D., Wagner, D., Perrig, A.: Practical technologies for searches on encrypted data. In: IEEE International Symposium on Security and Privacy, pp. 44–55. IEEE Press, New York (2010)

8. Yu, J., Lu, P., Zhu, Y.: Two-step-ranking secure multi-keyword seach over encrypted cloud data. IEEE Trans. Dependable Secure Comput. **10**(4), 239–250 (2013)

9. Wang, C., Ren, K., Yu, S.: Achieving usable and privacy-assured similarity search over outsourced cloud data. In: IEEE INFOCOM, pp. 451–459. IEEE Press, New York (2012)

10. Ibraimi, L., Tang, Q., Hartel, P., Jonker, W.: Efficient and provable secure ciphertext-policy attribute-based encryption schemes. In: Bao, F., Li, H., Wang, G. (eds.) ISPEC 2009. LNCS, vol. 5451, pp. 1–12. Springer, Heidelberg (2009)

11. Boneh, D., Goh, E.-J., Nissim, K.: Evaluating 2-DNF formulas on ciphertexts. In: Kilian, J. (ed.) TCC 2005. LNCS, vol. 3378, pp. 325–341. Springer, Heidelberg (2005)

12. Hwang, Y.-H., Lee, P.J.: Public key encryption with conjunctive keyword search and its extension to a multi-user system. In: Takagi, T., Okamoto, E., Okamoto, T., Okamoto, T. (eds.) Pairing 2007. LNCS, vol. 4575, pp. 2–22. Springer, Heidelberg (2007)

13. Moataz, T., Shikfa, A.: Boolean symmetric searchable encryption. In: 8th ACM SIGSAC Symposium on Information, Computer and Communication Security, pp. 265–276. ACM Press, New York (2013)

14. Cash, D., Jarecki, S., Julta, C., Roşu, M.-C., Steiner, M.: Highly-scalable searchable symmetric encryption with support for boolean queries. In: Canetti, R., Garay, J.A. (eds.) Advances in Cryptology – CRYPTO 2013. LNCS, vol. 8042, pp. 353–373. Springer, Heidelberg (2013)

15. Lv, Z., Hong, C., Zhang, M., Feng, D.: Expressive and Secure searchable encryption in the public key setting. In: Chow, S.S.M., Camenisch, J., Hui, L.C.K., Yiu, S.M. (eds.) ISC 2014. LNCS, vol. 8783, pp. 364–376. Springer, Heidelberg (2014)

16. Kilinc, H.H., Yanik, T.: A survey of SIP authentication and key agreement schemes. IEEE Commun. Surv. Tutorials **16**(2), 1005–1023 (2014)

17. Lai, J., Zhou, X., Deng, R.: Expressive search over encrypted data. In: 8th ACM SIGSAC Symposium on Information, Computer and Communication Security, pp. 243–252. ACM Press, New York (2013)

Big-Little-Cell Based "Handprint" Positioning System

Zhonghong Ou[✉], Jun Wu, and Antti Ylä-Jääski

Aalto University, Espoo, Finland
{zhonghong.ou,jun.wu,antti.yla-jaaski}@aalto.fi

Abstract. Mobile computing has been a hot research field in the past decade. Although the computation capability of mainstream smartphones are several orders of magnitude better than desktops twenty years ago, the capacity of battery does not increase at the same pace. Thus, the gap between battery life and the demand from applications increases. To save energy, certain recent work tries to schedule network traffic according to signal strength variations. To achieve this goal, a platform that is used for collecting signal strength traces is essential. We first design and implement a platform to collect cellular network information, including cell ID and signal strength. We then deploy the platform and collect signal strength information in one area of Finland. After a set of carefully designed experiments, we make several interesting observations: (1) the density of base stations is much higher than expectation; (2) small cells account for a large portion in the overall cells; (3) in the same location a device may connect to different base stations, which is also applicable to different devices. Based on the observations, we design a novel energy-efficient positioning system called "Handprint", which utilizes fingerprint information from neighbouring devices to assist positioning. Performance evaluation demonstrates that, compared with Google Geolocation API and other existing work, our Handprint system can improve positioning accuracy by more than 20 %.

Keywords: Handprint · Positioning system · Energy-efficient

1 Introduction

Energy-efficiency has been a prominent issue for battery-powered mobile devices in recent years. Despite the latest advancements of battery capacity, the battery life of mobile devices, on the contrary, is decreasing. The culprit of the decrease is the ever-increasing number of power-hungry applications available on mobile devices. Amongst them, location-based services (LBS) are the salient representative, which heavily relies on the notoriously power-hungry global positioning system (GPS) module. From our own experiments [5,6], the power consumption of GPS module varies from 200 mW to 300 mW, depending on the phone model. Furthermore, unlike other network interfaces, e.g., Wi-Fi and cellular, which can be switched into low-power idle mode if no traffic is going on for

© Springer International Publishing Switzerland 2015
K. Xu and J. Zhu (Eds.): WASA 2015, LNCS 9204, pp. 417–426, 2015.
DOI: 10.1007/978-3-319-21837-3_41

a period, power consumption of GPS module remains continuously high once the module is turned on, until it is turned off explicitly. The inherent feature of GPS, together with the increasing popularity of LBS applications, makes improving energy-efficiency of GPS based applications a hot topic in the past years.

Towards that direction, two threads of research work have been conducted in the literature. One thread is to minimize the fraction of time while the GPS module is switched on to save energy, which is referred to as `intermittent GPS` in this paper. The other thread is to avoid GPS module completely and use other energy-friendly techniques instead, which is referred to as `GPS-free`. For the `intermittent GPS` based scheme, [5,7,8] are representatives, which usually utilize historical signal traces, i.e., **fingerprinting**, of the end user. The problem with this approach is that it still needs involvement from GPS intermittently. Thus, it inherits partially the same weaknesses from GPS, e.g., slow initialisation and low positioning accuracy when the line-of-sight-view is blocked from the satellites. For the `GPS-free` approach, triangular-based cellular positioning system is a representative. Typical techniques include time of arrival, angle of arrival, and time difference of arrival. Compared with the `intermittent GPS` scheme, this approach has better positioning accuracy. Nevertheless, the main drawback of this approach is that it requires extra infrastructure, which inevitably limits its usage.

In this paper, we strive to achieve the benefits from both approaches mentioned above, meanwhile to avoid the drawbacks from neither of them. Specifically, we are trying to achieve the same positioning accuracy as the `GPS free` scheme, while to be as lightweight as the `intermittent GPS` approach from energy-efficiency perspective. Our scheme is inspired from several interesting **observations** we make through realistic experiments:

1. The coverage of cells varies significantly, ranging from a few hundred meters to several kilometres. The coverage difference holds true even for neighbouring cells. The small cells are potential to be used as stoppers for the accumulated positioning errors. (**Observation 1**).
2. The density of cell towers is remarkably high in the areas we have investigated, which indicates that it is time to revisit and re-evaluate the cell-ID based approach for positioning. (**Observation 2**)
3. Mobile devices may connect to different cell towers even at the same location, which makes it potential to utilize fingerprint information from neighboring devices to decrease positioning errors. (**Observation 3**)

Based on the observations, we propose to utilize **fingerprint** information from (potentially multiple) neighbouring devices for positioning. We thus name the system "Handprint" to vividly describe the analogy from multiple "fingerprint". The fingerprint information consists of cell-ID and signal strength. Before the real positioning process, we propose to utilize crowdsourcing to build a signal map ahead of time, which includes cell-ID, signal strength, and geographical coordinates. For the real-time positioning, besides the mobile device that requests positioning, the fingerprint information from neighbouring devices are also collected through a peer-to-peer fashion. By doing this, we can effectively narrow down the search space, which is especially useful for large cells.

To summarise, we make the following key contributions in this paper:

1. Through experiments from real networks, we make several interesting observations (refer to **Observations**);
2. Based on the observations, we propose a novel positioning scheme, i.e., Handprint system, which utilizes fingerprint information from multiple neighbouring devices to improve positioning accuracy;
3. We design and implement Handprint on real Android devices; evaluation results demonstrate that, compared with Google Geolocation API and other existing work, our Handprint system can improve positioning accuracy by more than 20 %.

2   Related Work

As stated previously, because of the high power consumption from GPS based systems, two approaches have been used in the literature to improve energy-efficiency of outdoor positioning systems: `GPS-free` and `intermittent GPS`.

GPS-free Positioning Systems. There are two approaches with this category. The first one is based on `triangle algorithms`. According to the metric for distance estimate, they can further be classified as time of arrival (ToA) [9] method, angle of arrival (AoA) [3] method, and time difference of arrival method (TDOA) [2]. Existing observed time difference (E-OTD) [11] is one of the TDOA methods that becomes the de facto standard for U.S. Federal Communications Commission (FCC)'s enhanced 911 (E911) service. The accuracy of E-OTD ranges from 50 to 125 m, but the response delay is relatively long. In certain cases, it can be as long as 5 s. Triangle algorithm based positioning systems face certain challenges: (1) compared with GPS, the accuracy of this approach is still low; (2) in most cases, extra infrastructure is needed. The second approach is based on `cell-ID`, which is recommended by the 3rd Generation Partnership Project (3GPP) [12]. The idea is to simply retrieve and exploit cell sector information. This method does not require extra infrastructure and modification in software. But the weakness is also obvious. The accuracy of cell-ID based method is strictly based on the size of cell sectors. On the other hand, the cell-ID based approach is much more energy-efficient than the other approaches in general. Thus, it is possible to trade-off accuracy to gain energy-efficiency.

Intermittent GPS Systems. To improve the positioning accuracy of the cell-ID based systems, researchers proposed to combine the cell-ID based approach with occasional support from GPS. Namely, when the positioning error is higher than certain threshold, GPS is turned on to eliminate the accumulated positioning error. The representative of this approach includes [4,5,8,10]. Among them, Ou et al. [5] and Bartendr [8] mostly leverage signal strength variations to schedule network traffic efficiently to save energy. Nguyen et al. [4] proposed a cell-ID sequence matching scheme to estimate location and velocity of buses. Takenga et al. [10] proposed a system that considers the signal strength of nearby base stations as fingerprint. Nevertheless, none of these work mentioned above considers fingerprint information from neighbouring devices.

The most relevant work to our Handprint system is from Paek et al. [7], which proposed a Cell-ID Aided Positioning System (CAPS). CAPS uses a cell-ID sequence matching technique to estimate position based on historical cell-ID and GPS sequence records. Nonetheless, CAPS still needs to turn on GPS for intermittent calibration. In this paper, we strive to avoid the GPS calibration completely by utilizing the small cells to eliminate the accumulated positioning error. Furthermore, we propose to use fingerprint information from neighbouring devices to improve positioning accuracy.

3   Observations

To investigate how dense base stations are deployed nowadays, we develop an Android application to collect signal information. We collect data in Espoo area (Finland) through walking and taking public transportations. The dataset we collect covers most major streets and pedestrian routes of Otaniemi and Tapiola areas. Furthermore, a portion of the bus routes in Espoo area are also covered. Based on the cellular information collected in this area, we observe several interesting phenomena. Due to space limit, we only present the observations here, without detailed analysis. Firstly, the area we investigated is approximately 2 km in diameter, nevertheless, we detect more than 67 different cell-IDs. Thus, the density of cell towers is much higher than expected. Secondly, there exists big and small cells in the same area. While the big cell covers more than 1000 records in our database, the small cell may cover less than 50 records. Lastly, at different time, the same mobile phone might connect to different cell towers. The probability is very high. These observations give positive implications to the cell-ID based positioning systems, which motivate us to design the system in the subsequent section.

4   Handprint Positioning System

4.1   Principles

From the previous section, we know that as the new generations of telecommunications technology roll out quickly, the density of cell towers increases significantly; oppositely, the coverage of each cell tower decreases fast. This two phenomena together makes it promising to utilize the small cells as the stopper to eliminate accumulated positioning errors. Furthermore, since it is likely that different devices (or even the same device at different time) will connect to different cell towers at the same location, it makes sense to utilize fingerprint information from neighbouring users to collectively determine the position. We name the system "Handprint" to mimic multiple "fingerprint" information. Handprint has high potential because the cell-ID aided positioning systems are primarily designed for urban areas. In such areas there are usually many devices surround a specific user, e.g., when waiting for or taking public transportation, or walking with friends.

The operation process of Handprint system consists of two steps: (1) acquire the shared fingerprint from nearby devices; (2) send the combined Handprint information to the server and acquire positioning. Accordingly, the implementation of the prototype faces two major challenges: (1) how to share fingerprint information; (2) how to estimate position with the fingerprints acquired.

4.2   How to Share Fingerprint Information

The mainstream smartphones nowadays usually integrate multiple short-range communication interfaces, including Bluetooth Low Energy (BLE), Wi-Fi, and Near Field Communication (NFC). NFC is not an appropriate option because of its limited communications range, which is typically a distance of 10 cm or less.

At a first glance, BLE seems to be more suitable for Handprint due to the proper communication range and low power consumption. Nevertheless, there are several weaknesses with BLE that makes it inappropriate for our purpose. First, the device discovering time, which is usually higher than 10 s, is too long for our Handprint system. Second, the master/slave operational mode makes it difficult to share information instantly between more than two devices. The last and fatal weakness is that it defines a mandatory pairing process for authentication. It is cumbersome to ask verification code from strangers for a simple positioning purpose.

Thus, we choose Wi-Fi Direct to share fingerprint information with neighbouring devices. Compared with BLE, the setup time of Wi-Fi Direct is short, which is less than 1 s. Nonetheless, it still shares a similar feature with BLE, i.e., requiring a pairing process before exchanging information. To address the pairing problem, we utilize an indirect approach to share cellular information. At the beginning, every smartphone equipped with Handprint client maintains a connection with the Handprint server. After the connection is set up, the smartphone periodically broadcasts a Wi-Fi Direct service beacon. If a device needs to estimate its position, it can discover nearby devices by extracting the MAC addresses from the beacons received. Then it will send a request that contains the MAC address list to the Handprint server, which is responsible for positioning the device. By this design, we effectively avoid the pairing process. Furthermore, the event-driven approach is energy-efficiency because it keeps the radio on idle state when there is no positioning request going on.

4.3   How to Estimate Position

Handprint system adopts an iterative algorithm to estimate the position. Due to factors like multipath propagation, signal strength of a moving device is not as stable as that from a static one. Occasionally, the variation can become as large as 10 dBm. Thus, we introduce a tolerance parameter, i.e., eps, to reflect this fact. When the server receives a positioning request, it will first look for potential positions for each device in range $[ss - eps, ss + eps]$. After that, it will check the number of points belonging to the intersection of all sets. If the number of points is larger than certain threshold C, the algorithm will decrease eps and calculate again. When the loop ends, the estimated position will be returned by calculating the weighted average value of all intersection points. The detailed algorithm is presented in Algorithm 1.

Furthermore, if Set_i is an empty set, Handprint will drop it to increase robustness. The logic is that if there is no knowledge about this position (no one has uploaded it before), we ignore it accordingly to avoid unwanted noise. Thus, if there is only one valid device in the area, Handprint will fall back to a generic cell-ID and signal strength based solution.

Data: Cellular information list $[model_i, cid_i, ss_i]$
Result: Estimated position
Set threshold eps and C;
while *size of $Set_{int} > C$* **do**
    | $Set_i = \{position$ that satisfies $cid = cid_i$ and $ss_i - eps < ss < ss_i + eps\}$;
    | $Set_{int} =$ intersection of all Set_i;
    | $eps = eps/2$;
end
Calculate weighted average value of coordinates in Set_{int};

Algorithm 1. Handprint positioning algorithm.

---

5   Performance Evaluation

In this section, we evaluate our Handprint system in comparison with two existing cell-ID aided positioning systems. The first reference system is CAPS [7], a cell-ID aided positioning system that leverages historical fingerprint information, as stated previously. The second reference positioning system is Google Geolocation API (GGA) [1]. GGA is integrated into the contemporary Android smartphones. It uses a fused method that combines fingerprint from Wi-Fi and Bluetooth, location of cell towers, and positioning result from GPS. It supports two modes: GPS-enabled and GPS-disabled. Undoubtedly, GPS positioning has the highest accuracy. Thus, to provide a fair comparison with the Handprint system, all the experiments using GGA are conducted with GPS disabled.

5.1   Experiment Scenarios

In the experiment, we assume a user is taking a bus from Westendin asema to Leppavaara, Espoo. The Handprint system is used for positioning, while GPS is enabled and used as the ground truth to calculate positioning error for the Handprint system. This area is a suburban area that has medium population density. Thus, experiments on this route can be considered as a lower bound for urban areas, because the density of base stations is expected to be much higher in those areas.

All the data with Handprint are collected with two smart phones (Samsung Galaxy S4 and Galaxy S2), which is a minimal requirement of this system. Otherwise the Handprint system falls back to the generic cell-ID based scheme, as mentioned before. In principle, the more devices participating in the Handprint system, the more accurate positioning can be achieved. Thus, we can consider the following experimental results as the lower bounds for the Handprint system.

5.2 Comparison with CAPS

We use one Samsung Galaxy S4 and one Samsung Galaxy S2 as the testing devices. In the 20 min journey, requests are sent per five seconds. The positioning errors are listed in Table 1. From the table, we can see that, in general, more than 90 % of requests receive valid responses. The positioning error of more than 60 % of samples is less than 100 m on both devices.

Table 1. Positioning errors of Handprint on bus No. 550 in Espoo

Model	Direction	Samples	Valid	< 100 m	Average Error
S2	S → N	160	153	63.3 %	112.94 m
S2	N → S	160	157	66.24 %	121.00 m
S4	S → N	177	172	62.79 %	105.72 m
S4	N → S	163	138	76.81 %	89.73 m

CAPS does not provide an open-source implementation; thus, we are not able to evaluate it directly on the same route. However, we can compare Handprint with the published results from CAPS [7]. Figure 1 depicts the Cumulative Distribution Function (CDF) graphs of Handprint and CAPS. The data of CAPS is collected at Los Altos in the US, which is similar to the testing route for Handprint. They share similar length and driving speed. From Fig. 1, we can see that although the median error of Handprint system (68.61 m) is close to that of CAPS (79 m), the 80th percentile error of Handprint decreases by 26.4 % compared with CAPS, i.e., decreasing from 197 m to 145.25 m. Furthermore, CAPS needs involvement from GPS for around 0.9 % of time, while Handprint gets rid of GPS completely. Even though the percentage of GPS involvement is not high for CAPS, nevertheless, it is still cumbersome to have two positioning systems running at the same time. Additionally, note that the red curve on the right figure represents the positioning error of pure cell-ID based approach, which demonstrates much higher positioning error than both CAPS and Handprint.

5.3 Comparison with Google Geolocation API

We repeat the same experiment using Google Geolocation API (GGA) on the route mentioned above. As stated previously, GPS was disabled to provide a fair comparison with Handprint. The average error of GGA is 239 m while the median error is 174.42 m. Both of the two numbers are significantly higher than those from the Handprint system (cf. left subfigure of Fig. 1).

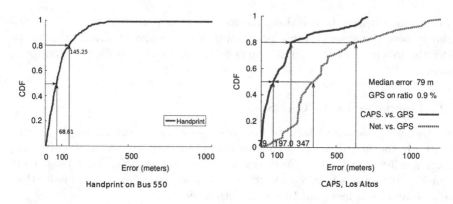

Fig. 1. Comparison between Handprint (left) and CAPS (right).

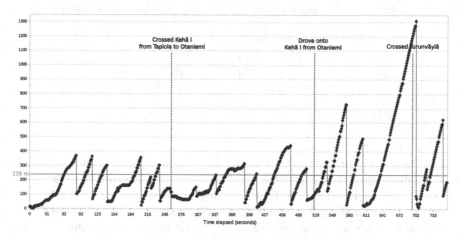

Fig. 2. Positioning error of Google Geolocation API.

To analyse the variations of positioning error from GGA, we plot the error per one second in Fig. 2. From the figure, we can see that in certain locations the error jumps to more than 1000 m. This can be explained by a large cell tower in that location. Furthermore, we also observe that the updating frequency of GGA is much lower than requested (once per second). This is because GGA does not update the position until it obtains changes; while in certain cases, the cellular information barely changes in a short period of time (e.g., tens of seconds) from our experiments.

5.4   Converging Speed

Another important factor that needs to be taken into account is the converging speed. Namely, how much data are needed to make Handprint work efficiently? To answer this question, we choose another route for analysis. The new route is a freeway with similar length. Supposedly, the new route is different from the one tested in the previous sections, which is an arterial road.

One Samsung Galaxy S4 and one Samsung Galaxy S3 are used to collect cellular information along this road. The two phones use cellular services from two different operators. One is from Elisa, while the other is from DNA (a Finnish operator). In the experiment, we collect 10 traces for each smartphone. Each time a pair of new traces are uploaded, we simulate the real behaviours of taking a bus with two phones, i.e., sending positioning requests per one second and acquiring positioning.

Figure 3 illustrates the distribution of the response types. "Invalid" response means there are no corresponding data, so Handprint can not estimate the location. "One phone" means the estimated position is calculated with information from one device. "Two phones" means the result is calculated from the intersection of two devices. Based on the definitions, the percentages acquired by "Two phones" represent the state of Handprint. We can see from the figure that after ten traces are uploaded from each device, Handprint is able to answer 90 % of the requests (excluding the `invalid` ones), and 60 % of the responses are returned by the Handprint algorithm. As a short summary, 10 traces are enough to make Handprint system work decently.

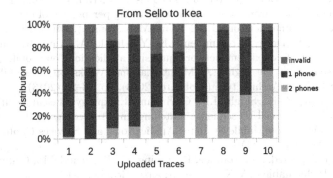

Fig. 3. Distribution of response

6   Conclusion

In this paper, we revisited cell tower deployment in a suburban area, and investigated utilizing fingerprint information from neighbouring devices for positioning, which we named Handprint system. Towards that direction, we conducted extensive experiments and developed a prototype to evaluate the feasibility of Handprint. The key contributions are summarised as follows: (1) We designed and implemented a crowd-sourcing platform that can be used to collect cellular information such as cell-ID and signal strength. The platform is extensible and has good flexibility. (2) Using the platform, we collected data in the Espoo area and observed there interesting phenomena of existing cellular networks. Namely, the density of cell towers and number of "small cells" account for a large portion; furthermore, most areas are covered by more than one cell tower. (3) Inspired by the observations mentioned above, we designed an innovative cell-ID aided positioning system named "Handprint". It achieves good performance comparing with the state-of-the-art. In the future, we will design protocols to facilitate exchanging information among neighboring devices. Furthermore, we will also conduct experiments in urban areas to verify the observations made in this paper.

References

1. The Google Maps Geolocation API. https://developers.google.com/maps/documentation/business/geolocation/ (2015). Online Accessed 20 April 2015
2. Huang, B., Xie, L., Yang, Z.: TDOA-based source localization with distance-dependent noises. IEEE Trans. Wireless Commun. **14**(1), 468–480 (2015)
3. Malajner, M., Gleich, D., Planinsic, P.: Angle of arrival measurement using multiple static monopole antennas. IEEE Sens. J. **PP**(99), 1–10 (2015)
4. Nguyen, H., Ho, T.M., Dinh, T.B.: Localization and velocity estimation on bus with Cell-ID. In: Huynh, V.N., Denoeux, T., Tran, D.H., Le, A.C., Pham, B.S. (eds.) KSE 2013, Part I. AISC, vol. 244, pp. 259–270. Springer, Heidelberg (2014)
5. Ou, Z., Dong, J., Dong, S., Wu, J., Ylä-Jääski, A., Hui, P., Wang, R., Min, A.: Utilize signal traces from others? a crowdsourcing perspective of energy saving in cellular data communication. IEEE Trans. Mob. Comput. **14**(1), 194–207 (2015)
6. Ou, Z., Dong, S., Dong, J., Nurminen, J.K., Ylä-Jääski, A., Wang, R.: Characterize energy impact of concurrent network-intensive applications on mobile platforms. In: Proceedings of the Eighth ACM International Workshop on Mobility in the Evolving Internet Architecture (MobiArch 2013), pp. 23–28 (2013)
7. Paek, J., Kim, K.-H., Singh, J.P., Govindan, R.: Energy-efficient positioning for smartphones using cell-ID sequence matching. In: Proceedings of the 9th International Conference on Mobile Systems, Applications, and Services (MobiSys 2011), pp. 293–306. ACM (2011)
8. Schulman, A., Navda, V., Ramjee, R., Spring, N., Deshpande, P., Grunewald, C., Jain, K., Padmanabhan, V.N.: Bartendr: a practical approach to energy-aware cellular data scheduling. In: Proceedings of the Sixteenth Annual International Conferenceon Mobile Computing and Networking (Mobicom 2010), pp. 85–96. ACM (2010)
9. Sharp, I., Yu, K.: Indoor TOA error measurement, modeling, and analysis. IEEE Trans. Instrum. Meas. **63**(9), 2129–2144 (2014)
10. Takenga, C., Kyamakya, K.: A low-cost fingerprint positioning system in cellular networks. In: Second International Conference on Communications and Networking in China (CHINACOM 2007), pp. 915–920 (2007)
11. Tekinay, S.: Wireless geolocation systems and services. IEEE Commun. Mag. **36**(4), 28–28 (1998)
12. Zhao, Y.: Standardization of mobile phone positioning for 3G systems. IEEE Commun. Mag. **40**(7), 108–116 (2002)

Spectrum Sublet Game Among Secondary Users in Cognitive Radio Networks

Deming Pang[✉], Ming Zhu, Gang Hu, and Ming Xu

Department of Network Engineering, Computer Science Editorial,
National University of Defense Technology, Changsha, China
{pang3724,hugang,xuming}@nudt.edu.cn

Abstract. Dynamic spectrum sharing can improve the efficiency of spectrum utilization. Spectrum trading between primary users (PUs) and secondary users (SUs) is a popular and efficient way to fulfill this kind of spectrum sharing. In this paper we present a novel spectrum trading mechanism which operate among secondary users. More specifically, some secondary users which has leased spectrum from PUs can sublet it to other SUs to reduce their own leasing cost. Then all of the SUs can share these spectrum bands to conduct data transmission respectively. This leads to a new multi-leader multi-follower (MLMF) game which is different from existing works. The existence of Nash equilibrium of this formulated game is proven by redefining it as a shared MLMF constraint game. A decentralized algorithm is then proposed to find Nash equilibrium of this two tiers game with only local information. Simulations are provided to illustrate the convergence and effectiveness of the proposed algorithm.

Keywords: Spectrum sublet · Game · Nash equilibrium · Decentralized algorithm

1 Introduction

Wireless spectrum can be shared by primary users (PUs) and secondary users (SUs) through dynamic trading in cognitive radio networks (CRNs) to achieve more efficient spectrum utilization [1]. PU dynamically trade the usage right of temporarily unused part of its licensed spectrum to SUs in exchange for monetary compensation. SUs are price takers who lease the licensed spectrum for their own data transmissions. Various spectrum trading mechanisms have been proposed along this direction in literature. The common mode of these works assume that each SU occupies the leased bands alone regardless of the behaviors of owners so long as it's under the interference constraint. PU sells its spectrum bands to SUs and charge them respectively without considering who buys its channel.

However, wireless spectrum is often considered as scarce resource, thus the rent of spectrum could be very high for SUs even they only lease them temporarily. Existing works deal with the spectrum trading of separate purchase mode in

© Springer International Publishing Switzerland 2015
K. Xu and J. Zhu (Eds.): WASA 2015, LNCS 9204, pp. 427–436, 2015.
DOI: 10.1007/978-3-319-21837-3_42

which each SU buys a channel independently and is charged separately, which may restrict the spectrum market. Multiple SUs form a group purchasing the same spectrum band together could reduce the burden of everyone. There could be two schemes to enforce this kind of spectrum trading. One is that a group of SUs purchase the same spectrum band with PU concurrently and joint funding the trade. Another one is that one SU buy a spectrum band at first, and then it sublets it to others and share it with them. We focus on the latter one in this paper, and the former will be left as our future work.

We call the users that can't afford the spectrum alone but still need frequency bands as hungry users (HUs). The users who have bought spectrum and want to share the leasing cost by subletting spectrum to HUs are called full users (FUs). The spectrum trade between FU and PU is called primary market, while the spectrum trade between HU and FU is called secondary market. FU needs to make leasing and pricing decision in primary market based on its own demand and the demand from secondary market to maximize its payoff which is the sum of its own data rate and sublet profits. After perceiving the prices of FUs, each HU sets appropriate communication power on the channel of the selected FU and pay the rent. So they need deal with FU selection and power allocation problem jointly. We focus on the interaction in secondary market in this paper, where FU and HUs share the same channel and interfere with each other. On the FU's side, more HUs purchasing with itself, lower cost it will pay for its leased channel, but higher interference from HUs would lead to lower data rate. More FUs coexisting in the network will complicate this problem due to the competition among these FUs, which makes the pricing strategy more challenging.

This paper studies the spectrum sublet problem in the secondary market and model the interaction between FUs and HUs as a multi-leader multi-follower (MLMF) game. A similar problem related to the joint price decision of leader and resource selection of follower has been addressed in CRNs and femtocell networks. All these works consider the problem of spectrum trade between PU and SU in primary market, not the trade among different SUs. These two kinds of trade have much in common, but there are specific features in the later one and can not be solved using existing schemes.

There exists a rich body of related literature on spectrum trading in primary market. [2,3] tackled the problem of pricing strategy of PUs and power allocation of SUs by model it as a stackelberg game. These works only consider interference among SUs which are charged with fixed price. In [4,5], a single PU prices interference power from SUs under the interference power constraint, so the communication rate is not influenced by the strategies of SUs. All SUs works on the same single channel based on CDMA, and the channel selection is not considered in this paper. In [6], authors studied the trade between macrocell base station and femtocell users. The former controls the received interference from femtocell users through pricing the interference from later. However, all of above works resolve the two-tier resource trading with single leader multiple followers game, while the problem considered in this paper is a MLMF scenario.

Competition of multiple wireless providers to sell spectrum is studied in related works, which uses MLMF game to model the two stages decision problem.

Reference [7] considered multiple-seller and multiple-buyer spectrum trading in CRNs using MLMF game, where PUs compete by setting price to attract SUs. The profit of each PU is the product of price and number of users who purchase spectrum with it. There is no interference between PU and SU. More SUs making trade with it produce higher profits in this model. Reference [8] studied spectrum leasing from owners and trading with end users for two secondary operators whose profits are functions of bandwidths sold to users. The operators profit from a price discrepancy when they buy spectrum from owners and sell it to end users.

All of these works above do not consider how spectrum is exploited and only treat it as ordinary commodity. A seller doesn't care about whom it sells the spectrum resource to, only care about how much sold. However, in the secondary market where spectrum is shared by FUs and HUs, interference plays a more important role. FUs hope to sublet spectrum to the harmless HUs who produce minimum interference. This interference aware spectrum sublet in secondary market has not been studied before. This problem is challenging when there is competition among FUs in the first stage and among HUs in the second stage, especially the optimal decision of these users are made dynamically.

The key results and contributions of this paper are summarized as follows.

- We proposed a novel spectrum trading mechanism which is conducted among secondary users. The two kinds of secondary users can improve their payoff by spectrum sublet. The interaction of SUs is formulated as a MLMF game with a new defined utility function.
- Due to the challenge that there is no closed form best response function of the leader optimization problem in the MLMF game, we present a new method to prove the existence of the Nash equilibrium.
- We provide a distributed algorithm that results in an equilibrium of the spectrum sublet game. The participants only need local information during the execution of this algorithm.

We organize the paper as follows. In Sect. 2, we present the system model and formulate the problem into a multi-leader multi-follower game. In Sect. 3, we analyze the properties of the NE. In Sect. 4, we provide our main algorithm and its convergence properties. We present simulation results in Sect. 5 and conclude the paper in Sect. 6.

2 System Model and Problem Formulation

Suppose there are a set $F = \{1, ..., M\}$ of FUs and a set $H = \{1, ..., N\}$ of HUs in CRNs. Each user (a FU or HU) consists of a transmitter and receiver forming a data link. FU j has leased a channel from primary user with bandwidth of size B_j and it would like to sublet the leased channel to HUs to share cost. Each HU can access multiple channels of FUs simultaneously. Assume that the channels of each FU are orthogonal. A FU and the HUs purchased with it share the channel equally and take the interference caused by others as noises.

There are two levels of competition in this multiple-seller multiple-buyer secondary market. The competition in the first level is among FUs to conduct price war. FU j charges HU μ_j per unit interference power and all the price are set simultaneously. Lower price could make a FU attract more HUs thus boost its profits, but the increased interference will reduce its own transmission rate. In the second level, after perceiving the price vector $\{\mu_j\}_{j \in F}$, HUs allocate power to all channels to maximize their own utility. In this case, if many HUs choose to buy channel offered by the same FU or put more power on this it, the corresponding channel becomes congested, which may result in an increased spectrum price and/or performance degradation.

Let p_{ij} represent the amount of power HU i transmits on the channel of FU j when it purchases with j. $p_{ij} = 0$ means i doesn't purchase with j. Let $p_i = (p_{i1}, ..., p_{iM})$ denotes the power profile of HU i and p_{-i} be the joint power profiles of all the HUs other than i. The power profiles of the HUs must also satisfy the following two constraints: (1) Total power constraints: $\sum_{j=1}^{M} p_{ij} \leq \bar{p}_i$, $\forall i \in H$, where $\bar{p}_i$ is the power limit for HU i; (2) Positivity constraints: $p_{ij} \geq 0$.

The aggregated received transmission power of FU j on its own channel is $I_j = \sum_{i=1}^{N} |h_{ji}|^2 p_{ij}$, where h_{ji} is the channel gain of the transmitter of HU i to the receiver of FU j. We assume that the link gains will be fixed for the duration of the sublet game as [6,9]. This indicates that the fading rate of the channel is slow in comparison to the rate of power control algorithm.

The FUs objective is to maximize its utility obtained from selling the interference quota to femtocell users and its own transmission rate. Mathematically, the utility function of FU j can be defined as

$$U_j(\mu_j, \mu_{-j}, P) = \beta_j B_j \log(1 + \frac{|h_j|^2 p_j}{w + I_j}) + \mu_j I_j - \varphi(B_j) \tag{1}$$

where p_j is the transmission power of FU j, w is the variance of noise, β_i is predefined coefficient that transforms the ith FUs transmission rate to a monetary utility. We refer to β_i as the preference factor of FU j. If FU j prefers to achieve higher data rate, it can set β_i to a large value. $\varphi(B_j)$ is the cost of spectrum leasing from PU. B_j is a constant in this paper since we focus on the interaction of users in secondary market. $P = p_1, ..., p_N$ is the power profile of all HUs, which is actually a function of (μ_j, μ_{-j}) under the stackelberg game formulation. This indicates that the amount of the interference quota that the HUs are willing to buy is dependent on the interference price. Each FU j has to find the optimal interference price μ_j to maximize its utility.

At the second competition level, the aggregated received transmission power of HU i on the channel of FU j can be written as

$$I_{ij} = \sum_{k=1, k \neq i}^{N} |h_{ki}(j)|^2 p_{kj} + |h_{ji}|^2 p_j \tag{2}$$

where $h_{ki}(j)$ is the channel gain from k to i on the channel of FU j, h_{ji} is the channel gain from j to i. Then the utility of HU i can be defined as

$$U_i(p_i, p_{-i}, \mu) = \sum_{j=1}^{M} [\beta_i B_j \log(1 + \frac{|h_{ij}|^2 p_{ij}}{w + I_{ij}}) - \mu_j |h_{ji}|^2 p_{ij}] \tag{3}$$

where h_{ij} is the channel gain of HU i on FU jth channel, $\mu = (\mu_i, ..., \mu_M)$. It is observed from (3) that the utility function of HU consist of two parts: profit and cost. If the HU increases its transmit power, the transmission rate will increase, and thus the profit will increase. On the other hand, with the increasing of the transmit power, the HU will definitely cause more interference to FUs. Then, it has to buy more interference quota from FUs, and this will increase the cost. Therefore, power allocation strategies are needed at the HUs to maximize their utilities. Mathematically, for each user i, the problem can be formulated as

$$\max_{p_i} U_i(p_i, p_{-i}, \mu)$$
$$s.t. \sum_{j=1}^{M} p_{ij} \leq \bar{p}_i, p_{ij} \geq 0, \forall i \in H \tag{4}$$

where $\bar{p}_i$ is the maximum allowable transmission power. Based on the discussion above, we are now ready to define a multi-leader stackelberg game $\Gamma = (F, H, \{\mu_j\}_{j \in F}, \{P_i\}_{i \in H}, \{U_j\}, \{U_i\})$ The utility functions of leader U_i and U_j are given in (1) and (3). The objective of such a Stackelberg game is to find the subgame perfect equilibrium (SPE) point(s) where neither the leader (FUs) nor the followers (HUs) have incentive to deviate unilaterally from that point(s). More specifically, the point (μ^*, p^*) is a SPE for the proposed Stackelberg game if for any (μ, p), the following conditions are satisfied:

$$U_j(\mu_j^*, \mu_{-j}^*, p^*) \geq U_j(\mu_j, \mu_{-j}^*, p^*)$$
$$U_i(p_i^*, p_{-i}^*, \mu^*) \geq U_i(p_i, p_{-i}^*, \mu^*) \tag{5}$$

3   Property of the Sublet Game

A common approach of analyzing multiple layers game is backward induction to characterize the subgame perfect equilibrium. We start with the second stage game and analyze the HUs' behaviors given the FUs' pricing decisions. In order to maximize its utility, each HU competes with each other to allocates limited power to the channels with lower price and little interference. We prove this subgame among HUs has only one NE by showing that it belong to a potential game, which is defined as

Definition 1. *(Potential Game [10]): A game is called a potential game if it admits a potential function $\Phi(x)$ such that for every $i \in H$ and p_{-i},*

$$\Phi(p_i^*, p_{-i}, \mu) - \Phi(p_i, p_{-i}, \mu) = U_i(p_i^*, p_{-i}, \mu) - U_i(p_i, p_{-i}, \mu) \tag{6}$$

Based on this definition, we can give the conclusion as follows.

Theorem 1. *Given any pricing strategy μ, the low-tier game among HUs is a potential game and there is only one NE p^* which is the maximum of the potential function, i.e., $p^* \in \arg\max\limits_{p \in P} \Phi(p, \mu)$. The upper-tier game among FUs also possess at least one pure strategy Nash equilibrium.*

Proof. The potential function of subgame among HUs is

$$\Phi(p_i, p_{-i}, \mu) = \sum_{j=1}^{M} [\beta_i B_j \log(w + \sum_{i=1}^{N} |h_{ij}|^2 p_{ij} + |h_{ji}|^2 p_j) - \sum_{i=1}^{N} \mu_j |h_{ji}|^2 p_{ij}] \quad (7)$$

We can readily observe that the following identity is true for all $i \in H$:

$$\begin{aligned}
&\Phi(p_i, p_{-i}, \mu) - \Phi(p_i', p_{-i}, \mu) \\
&= \sum_{j=1}^{M} [\beta_i B_j \log(\frac{w + |h_{ji}|^2 p_j + \sum_{i=1}^{N} |h_{ij}|^2 p_{ij}}{w + |h_{ji}|^2 p_j + \sum_{i=1}^{N} |h_{ij}|^2 p_{ij}'}) - \sum_{i=1}^{N} \mu_j |h_{ij}|^2 (p_{ij} - p_{ij}')] \\
&= U_i(p_i, p_{-i}, \mu) - U_i(p_i', p_{-i}, \mu)
\end{aligned} \quad (8)$$

Thus, based on Definition 1 we can get that $\Phi(p_i, p_{-i}, \mu)$ is a potential function and the subgame posses a pure-strategy NE. Observing that $\Phi(p, \mu)$ is concave and the domain of which is convex, thus there is only one extreme value which corresponding to the unique NE of the subgame.

The competition among FUs belongs to equilibrium problem with equilibrium constraints (EPECs) in which a collection of FUs compete in a game constrained by the equilibrium conditions of another Nash game amongst the HUs. The resulting equilibrium problem is complicated by nonconvex constrainted deduced by the follower game, thus the Kakutani's fixed point theorems can't be used to prove the existence of NE of the up tier game. In this paper we adopt another method to bypass this challenge. Note that the low-tier game among HUs is potential game and the NE of it is the maximization of potential function (8), then we can redefine the optimization problem of each FU as follows:

$$\begin{aligned}
&\max_{\mu_j, p_j} U_j(\mu_j, p_j; \mu_{-j}) \\
&s.t. p_j \in \arg\max_{p_i} = \Phi(p_i, p_{-i}, \mu) \\
&\mu_j \geq 0, for\ \forall j \in F
\end{aligned} \quad (9)$$

where p_j is conjecture about HU's equilibria seen by FU j, which could be different from p_{-j} if there are multiple NE in the low-tier game. The constraint of each FU's optimization problem is identical since the function Φ is the same to each one. Based on discussion above, there is unique extreme value of Φ. In another word, FUs as leaders of the two level game share all equilibrium constraints. This lead to that the new defined optimization problem of FUs belong to shared constraint EPECs and based on the Theorem 4.4 of [11], we can deduce that the up tire game possess at least one pure strategy Nash equilibrium.

4 Iterative Algorithm to Approach Subgame Nush Equilibrium

To obtain the subgame Nash equilibrium of the prices set by the FUs, information on the net utility function of all HUs would be required. Also, the power allocation profile of HUs at the equilibrium would be required. However, these information may not be available in a practical cognitive radio environment. Therefore, we propose that a FU iteratively adjusts the price and observe the received net utility. A FU adjusts the price in a direction that results in a higher payoff. The relationship between the strategies in the current and the future iteration can be expressed as follows:

$$\mu_j(t+1) = \mu_j(t) + \alpha_j \frac{\partial U_j(\mu_j, \mu_{-j}, p)}{\partial \mu_j} \tag{10}$$

where α_j is the speed of adjustment for the spectrum price of FU j. Since the closed form solution of the best response function of FUs can't be obtained, the partial derivative has no closed form neither. But the marginal payoff can be estimated by a FU by observing the variations in utilities for small variation ε in μ_j. That is,

$$\frac{\partial U_j(\mu_j, \mu_{-j}, p)}{\partial \mu_j} \approx \frac{U_j(\mu_j + \varepsilon, \mu_{-j}, p) - U_j(\mu_j - \varepsilon, \mu_{-j}, p)}{2\varepsilon} \tag{11}$$

After the price of each FU is adjusted, the HUs will select the best FU(s) and trade spectrum with it(them). There are multiple factors that influence the decision of each HU. Generally speaking, a HU would like to choose the FU with lower price and furthest distance. It also need to avoid the interference from other HUs which select the same FU, since other HUs could impact received signal and the pricing of FU. We present an iterative algorithm that enables the HUs to distributedly compute the subgame NE among HUs under a given price profile from FUs.

(1) Calculate the best reply power allocation:

$$\Phi_{ij}(\mu_j, I_{ij}) = \max[0, \frac{\beta_i B_j}{\lambda_i + \mu_j |h_{ji}|^2} - \frac{w_j + I_{ij}}{|h_{ji}|^2}] \tag{12}$$

where λ_i ensures $\sum_{j=1}^{M} p_{ij} = \bar{p}_i$, and let $\Phi_i = \{\Phi_{ij}\}_{j \in F}$.

(2) Adjust their power profiles according to:

$$p_{ij}^{t+1}(\mu_j, I_{ij}) = p_{ij}^t(\mu_j, I_{ij}) + \alpha^t \Phi_{ij}(\mu_j, I_{ij}) \tag{13}$$

where the sequence $\{\alpha^t\}_{t=1}^\infty$ satisfy $\alpha^t \in (0,1)$ and:

$$\lim_{t\to\infty} \alpha^t = 0, \ \lim_{T\to\infty} \sum_{t=1}^T \alpha^t = \infty, \ \lim_{T\to\infty} \sum_{t=1}^T (\alpha^t)^2 < \infty$$

Then the HUs' individual power profiles converge to a NE power allocation profile, i.e., $\lim_{t\to\infty} p_{ij}^t(\mu_j, I_{ij}) = p_{ij}^*(\mu_j, I_{ij}), \forall i \in H, j \in F$, where $p_{ij}^*(\mu_j, I_{ij})$ is a NE power allocation of HU i on then channel of FU j given price μ_j.

All HUs are able to decide on their NE power allocation profiles distributedly by running this algorithm. In order to calculate $\Phi_{ij}(\mu_j, I_{ij})$ in each iteration, each HU i only needs to know the sublet rent of channel j and the aggregated interference plus noise contributed by all other HUs and FU j, and this information can be fed back to HU i by FU j.

This algorithm includes two processes of iteration which corresponding to upper-tier inter-FU game and lower-tier inter-HU game respectively. FUs update their pricing decision after the all HUs iterate to reach a equilibrium. The convergence of this algorithm can be proved easily by exploiting the feature of utility functions of users (including HUs and FUs). As it's shown in last section, both tiers of subgame belong to potential game. It means it possess the finite improvement property. The update rule (10) and (13) of each player in this algorithm is also a better response to opponents, thus the convergence can be guaranteed.

5   Numerical Results

5.1   Parameter Setting

We now evaluate the proposed algorithms by simulations. We have the following general settings for the simulation. Consider a cognitive radio environment with three full users (i.e., $M = 3$) and five hungry users (i.e., $N = 5$) which are placed randomly in a $200\,m \times 200\,m$ area. We let d_{ij} denote the distance between user i and user j (including FUs and SUs). We consider a Rayleigh fading channel environment. The channel gain amplitudes $h_{ij} = \varepsilon_{ij}/d_i^{\alpha/2}j$ follow Rayleigh fading, where ε_{ij} is a Rayleigh distributed random variable with parameter 1, and $\alpha = 1.7$. The total bandwidth of each FU is $25\,MHz$ (i.e., $B_j = 25$) and the maximum allowable transmission power $\bar{p}_i$ is $100\,mW$. The cost of spectrum leasing $\varphi(B_j)$ for each FU is assumed to be constant for simplicity. The coefficients β_i that transforms the ith user's transmission rate to a monetary utility is randomly chosen between 1 and 20 for each user.

We first show the results regarding to the convergence of the algorithm with the parameters presented above, as shown in Fig. 1. Each FU updates its price after the low-tier spectrum sharing game converging to subgame nash equilibrium. Thus every iteration in this figure represents a time period for the evolution

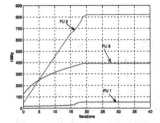

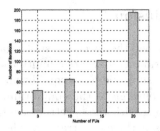

Fig. 1. Dynamics of FUs' sublet game

Fig. 2. Average time of convergence for different numbers of users.

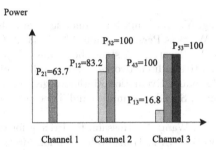

Fig. 3. Spectrum sublet results under different FUs' prefer coefficients

of HUs. However, it is seen that the up-tier pricing game converges to an equilibrium (μ_j^*, μ_{-j}^*) in less than 50 iterations, and no user has the incentive to deviate its channel selection and price decision unilaterally.

In Fig. 2, we compare the average convergence time for different number of users. As its illustrated that as the increase of number of users, more iterations are needed to converge to mixed NE.

To characterize the influence of the prefer coefficient β_j of each FU on the spectrum trading between FUs and HUs, we show the power allocation profiles of each HU at the subgame Nash equilibrium in Fig. 3. The prefer coefficients $\{\beta_j\}_{j \in F}$ are set to satisfy $\beta_1 > \beta_2 > \beta_3$ in this simulation. The three bars in this figure correspond to the channels of three FUs and the height of each bar stands for the amount of power allocated on each channel by HUs. There are two points to be noted about this results. At first, not every HU consumes all of its power at the NE. HU 2 only use 63.7 mW on the channel of FU 1 because the later prefer to achieve higher data rate and would not like to share its channel with other users. Second, the channel selection is not orthogonal due to the price regulation of FUs. HUs balance the profit from higher data rate and the cost of spectrum leasing. These two results are different from related works. Therefore, it's interest and challenging to study the interaction of different kinds of secondary users to improve spectrum sharing efficiency.

6 Conclusion

We have studied the spectrum sublet game among secondary users and modeled this interaction as a two-tier multi-leader multi-follower game. Then we characterized its subgame Nash equilibrium and proposed a decentralized algorithm which can converge to the equilibrium. In the future work, we will study this problem along with the spectrum trading between full user and primary user, which forms a three-tier trading. The competition among PUs and FUs will appear to attract more HUs and the problem will be more challenging.

References

1. Maharjan, S., Zhang, Y., Gjessing, S.: Economic approaches for cognitive radio networks: a survey. Wireless Pers. Commun. **57**(1), 33–51 (2011)
2. Bloem, M., Alpcan, T., Başar, T.: A stackelberg game for power control and channel allocation in cognitive radio networks. In: Proceedings of the 2nd International Conference on Performance Evaluation Methodologies and Tools. ICST (Institute for Computer Sciences, Social-Informatics and Telecommunications Engineering), pp. 4 (2007)
3. Yu, H., Gao, L., Li, Z., Wang, X., Hossain, E.: Pricing for uplink power control in cognitive radio networks. IEEE Trans. Veh. Technol. **59**(4), 1769–1778 (2010)
4. Jiang, L., He, C., et al.: Optimal price-based power control algorithm in cognitive radio networks. IEEE Trans. Wireless Commun. **13**, 5909–5920 (2014)
5. Wang, Z., Jiang, L., He, C.: A novel price-based power control algorithm in cognitive radio networks. IEEE Commun. Lett. **17**(1), 43–46 (2013)
6. Kang, X., Zhang, R., Motani, M.: Price-based resource allocation for spectrum-sharing femtocell networks: a stackelberg game approach. IEEE J. Sel. Areas Commun. **30**(3), 538–549 (2012)
7. Niyato, D., Hossain, E., Han, Z.: Dynamics of multiple-seller and multiple-buyer spectrum trading in cognitive radio networks: a game-theoretic modeling approach. IEEE Trans. Mob. Comput. **8**(8), 1009–1022 (2009)
8. Duan, L., Huang, J., Shou, B.: Duopoly competition in dynamic spectrum leasing and pricing. IEEE Trans. Mob. Comput. **11**(11), 1706–1719 (2012)
9. Zheng, L., Tan, C.W.: Cognitive radio network duality and algorithms for utility maximization. IEEE J. Sel. Areas Commun. **31**(3), 500–513 (2013)
10. Monderer, D., Shapley, L.S.: Potential games. Games Econ. Behav. **14**(1), 124–143 (1996)
11. Kulkarni, A.A., Shanbhag, U.V.: Global equilibria of multi-leader multi-follower games with shared constraints. Arxiv preprint (2012)

Delivering Content with Defined Priorities by Selective Agent and Relay Nodes in Content Centric Mobile Social Networks

Qifan Qi[1], Zhou Su[1(✉)], Qichao Xu[1], Jintian Li[1], Dongfeng Fang[1], and Bo Han[2]

[1] School of Mechatronic Engineering and Automation, Shanghai University,
Shanghai 200444, People's Republic of China
zhousu@ieee.org
[2] Center of Information and Networks, Xi'an Jiaotong University,
Xi'an 710049, People's Republic of China

Abstract. With the rapid advance of mobile communication technologies, to design the next generation mobile social networks with content centric architecture has attracted much attention. However, in such content centric mobile social networks, on one hand, there are a huge number of interest packets to be forwarded. On the other hand, to deliver the content to the destination, the forwarding node and relay node need to be efficiently selected. Therefore, in this paper we present a novel scheme to deal with the above two problems. Firstly, based on the analyses of the degree, capacity and mobility of nodes, methods to select the agent node to forward interest packets and the relay node to transmit the data packets are proposed. Secondly, with the consideration of content popularity and communities properties, the priorities to forward the interest packets and provide the corresponding data packets are defined. Finally, with the defined priorities, we present the scheme to deliver the mobile social content by the selective agent nodes and relay nodes. The simulation results show that the proposal can outperform the conventional schemes with the reduced delay.

Keywords: Mobile social networks · Content centric networks · Content popularity · Community

1 Introduction

With the development of mobile devices, especially the emergence of smart phones, mobile users can access mobile social networks (MSNs) to obtain various mobile services [1, 2]. With the MSNs, mobile social users can share content with each other, without relying on the conventional network infrastructure, but through opportunistic links with the short range wireless technologies. Furthermore, as it can be predicted that both the number of mobile social users and the popularity of social services will be increased in recent years, the MSNs have become one of the most important paradigms in future networks.

Due to the sparse connectivity and mobile users' mobility, how to deliver the content based on different situation of wireless networks is still an unresolved issue [3–5]. As

© Springer International Publishing Switzerland 2015
K. Xu and J. Zhu (Eds.): WASA 2015, LNCS 9204, pp. 437–445, 2015.
DOI: 10.1007/978-3-319-21837-3_43

the current architecture of MSNs is designed based on a host-to-host structure, it is difficult to satisfy the demand of the Internet with some problems (e.g., mobility, flexibility, security etc.) [6–8]. In recent years, the content centric networks (CCNs) have been advocated to deal with the above problems. The CCNs are no longer concerned about where the content is from, but care about what the content is [9–12].

To design the next generation MSNs based on the content centric architecture has been studied by many researchers. In such content centric mobile social networks, there are some expected advantages. (1) By providing content with a name ID, the content is recognized by both interest packet and data packet. When a mobile user requests for the wanted content, he only needs to send the interest, then the corresponding data packet will be provided based on the interest. (2) In the CCNs, there are some nodes which can cache the replicas of content and forward the interest of mobile user, to help the content to be delivered to the destination node.

However, there are some coming challenges as follows: (1) Since the content is requested by the interest, there exist a huge number of interests spreading over the network, how to manage these interests becomes a problem. (2) To deliver content to the destination, it needs an agent node to forward the interest and relay node to transmit data, how to select the agent node and relay node need to be studied (Fig. 1).

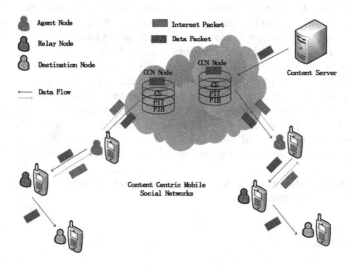

Fig. 1. Schematic diagram of content centric mobile social networks

Therefore, in this paper, we propose a novel scheme to resolve the above problems. Firstly, based on the analyses of the degree, capacity and mobility of mobile nodes, we choose the agent node in each community. The agent node receives user's interest packets and is responsible to forward the interest packets. Next, as there are multiple interests to be forwarded by the agent node, according to users' interest of the packet and the number of the requesters, we define a demand degree to determine the priority of each interest to be forwarded by the agent node. Then, an emergency degree is defined to determine the priority to provide the corresponding data packets of the interest packets. In addition, by comparing the probability that different nodes encounter with each other, a relay node is selected to transmit the data packets. The simulation results show that the proposed scheme can reduce the delay to obtain content when the popularity of content or the number of content requesters is changed.

The rest of this paper is organized as follows. In Sect. 2, the related work is reviewed. The analysis of interest and data packets delivery is presented in Sect. 3. Section 4 shows the simulation results. The conclusion is given in Sect. 5.

2 Related Work

Boldrini et al. [13] propose an evaluating algorithm, which utilizes the users' dynamical social relationship to evaluate each user. The content is transmitted to the highest value node to optimize content availability. Mangili et al. [14] talk about the performance bounds of CCNs and develop an optimization model. Furthermore the authors compare the performance bounds of the CCNs with a traditional IP-based network. Sourlas et al. [15] propose two storage management methods for CCNs. These two methods are used to manage the storage of nodes to reduce the total cost of content transmission and users' charge. Udugama et al. [16] study multi-path content transmission and develop an analytical model to evaluate the performance (round trip times, throughput and download times).

Hu et al. [17] consider the mobility of the providers in CCNs and propose a novel scheme to handle the providers' mobility. In this method when the providers move away, the domain proxies will buffer the interest packets and forward the packets to the providers when they come back to reduce the retrieval time. Asaeda et al. [18] propose a network tool "contrace", which consists of a user program and a forwarding daemon. This tool can be used to investigate the round-trip time of content transmission, the states of nodes' cache and the forwarding path. Fang et al. [19] consider the energy consumption in CCNs and propose a distributed caching scheme. In this scheme, the energy consumption in both content caching and content transmission are used to decide whether to cache the content or not, to reduce the total energy consumption of content distribution.

3 Analysis of Interest and Data Packets Delivery

3.1 Selection of Agent Node to Forward Interest Packets

We consider the sequence of forwarding interest packets in a community, where an agent node is used to forward interest packets and transfer data packets. Each community has a certain number of nodes, the set of $N = \{1, 2, \ldots, N\}$ is the nodes in the community. Firstly, an agent node is selected in the community by evaluating the transmission ability of each node. Here the transmission ability of a node is evaluated according to the number of friends and the rest memory of the node as follows.

$$P_n = \alpha \log\left(1 + \frac{k_n}{N}\right) + (1 - \alpha) \log(1 + \beta \frac{B_{Rn}}{B_R}), \quad \alpha \in (0, 1) \tag{1}$$

where, k_n represents the number of friends of the node n and N is the number of nodes of the community. B_{Rn} denotes the rest memory space of node n while B_R means the rest memory space of all nodes in the community. β is defined as the amplification factor and α is the weight factor. To calculate the transmission ability of each node, the node with the maximum value is chosen as the agent with the above equation.

3.2   Definition of Priority for Interest Packets to be Forwarded

The next is that the agent calculates the demand degree of the interest packets. Assume that there are J different contents. The interest degree of the community can be obtained according to the historical record, where the formula of interest degree is shown as follows.

$$Id_j = \frac{Q_j}{\sum\limits_{j=1}^{J} Q_j} \tag{2}$$

Here, Q_j represents the request times of the community for the content j in past. $\sum_{j=1}^{J} Q_j$ represents the request times of the community for all content in history. Then the agent calculates the demand degree according to the interest degree and the number of requests of the packet. Assume that the agent receives I different interest packets at the moment t, the set of $I = \{1, 2, \dots, I\}$ represents the interest packets. The demand degree can be obtained as follows.

$$DM_i = \gamma \log(1 + Id_i) + (1 - \gamma) \log(1 + \frac{z_i}{N}) \tag{3}$$

where, Id_i represents the interest degree of content for interest packet i. z_i is defined as the number of wanted content with interest packet i at the moment t. γ is the weight factor. Thus at moment t, the agent chooses the forwarding interest packet Ip_r by.

$$Ip_r = \arg\max\{DM_i\}, \quad i \in I \tag{4}$$

3.3   Definition of Priority of Interest Packets to be Provided
with the Corresponding Data Packets

We consider an MSN with M communities. Each community chooses the agent node and forwards the interest packets according to the above procedure. Furthermore each community has different priorities according to the nature of the community. Suppose that the CCN node receives E ($E < I$) interest packets at time t, and the set $E = \{1, 2, \dots, E\}$ represents the interest packets. We define an emergency degree is as follows.

$$ED_e = \varepsilon \log(1 + \frac{CP_m}{\sum\limits_{m=1}^{M} CP_m}) + (1 - \varepsilon) \log(1 + DM_e) \tag{5}$$

where CP_m is an integer belongs to $[1, M]$, which represents the priority level of the community m. DM_e is the demand degree of the interest packet e, which is calculated by Eq. (3). ε is the weight factor. Thus at the moment t, the processing interest packet HIp is chosen by.

$$HIp = \arg\max\{ED_e\}, \quad e \in E \tag{6}$$

3.4 Selection of Relay Node to Transmit Data Packets

After the interest packet has been provided with the corresponding data packet, the data packets will be sent to the agent node of the community. Then the agent node needs to determine the relay node to transmit the data packet to the destination node. Assume that the agent node in the community m receives the data packet and needs to transmit the packet to V destination nodes. The set $V = \{1, 2, \dots V\}$ represents the destination nodes. The communication frequency between nodes is defined as follows.

$$CF_{n,n'} = \frac{NC_{n,n'}}{T} \tag{7}$$

where $NC_{n,n'}$ is the times of communication between node n and node n' during time T. Thus, the relative frequency that node n encounters node n' is obtained by.

$$P_{n,n'} = \frac{CF_{n,n'} - CF_{\min, n'}}{CF_{\max,n'} - CF_{\min, n'}} \tag{8}$$

Here, $CF_{\min,n'}$ represents the minimum communication frequency of all nodes encountering node n' while $CF_{\max,n'}$ represents the maximum communication frequency among all nodes encountering node n'.

The agent node duplicates V data packets after obtaining the data packet. Each duplicate is corresponding to a destination node. For example, the duplicate DP_v will be transmitted to node v. Assume that node n has the duplicate DP_v which needs to be transmitted to node v. When node n encounters node n', the probability that node n transmits the duplicate to node n' is obtained by

$$Pt_{n,n'} = \begin{cases} 1, & p_{n,v} < p_{n',v} \quad or \quad n' = v \\ 0 & others \end{cases} \tag{9}$$

where $p_{n,v}$ and $p_{n',v}$ are the relative frequency of node n and node n' encountering the node v, respectively. Here, $n' = v$ represents that the node n' is the destination node v.

4   Simulation Results

4.1   Simulation Scenario

We choose the following two conventional methods to compare the performances with our proposal. The first one is the method based on community priority. The second is based on the content popularity. Here we define the weighted time of all content transmitted to users as the performance metric, which is shown by the following equation.

$$T = \sum_{j}^{J} ED_j \cdot T_j \tag{10}$$

where, T_j is the time of the content j transmitted to the destination. ED_j is denoted as the emergency degree of content j.

In simulation experiments, we assume that there are three communities and each community has 100 mobile social users, where $\gamma = 0.4$ and $\varepsilon = 0.3$. Here we test the performances under the following different scenarios.

(1) The performance of these three methods under different content popularity. We take three different cases of content popularity: [0.6 0.2 0.2; 0.65 0.2 0.15; 0.7 0.2 0.1]. And the number of requesters in each community is 30. The result of this scenario is shown in Fig. 2.

(2) The performances of these three methods with different number of requesters in communities. We carry out the simulation by the following three different cases with the number of requesters: [80 10 35; 60 50 10; 10 80 30]. And all of the requesters request for the same content. The result of this scenario is shown in Fig. 3.

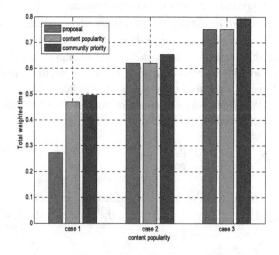

Fig. 2.   The weighted time of three strategies under different content popularity

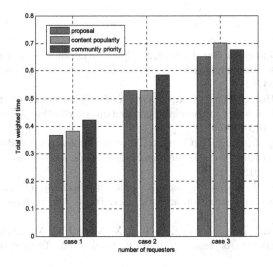

Fig. 3. The weighted time of three strategies under different requesters

4.2 Simulation Results

The simulation results of the weighted time by using the three strategies under different scenarios are shown as follows. Figure 2 shows the performances of the three methods with different content popularity. As the weighted time of our method is lowest compared with the other two cases in this scenario, it shows that our method is the best with the different content popularity. In Fig. 3 we test the performance of these three methods under the scenario with different number of requesters. From Fig. 3 we can find that our method has the lowest weighted time among the three cases. It proves that our method is the best when the number of requesters is changed.

5   Conclusion

In this paper, for the content centric mobile social network, we have proposed a method to determine the agent node to forward the interest packets and the replay node to transmit the data packets. Besides, the priorities to determine the forwarding order of interests and the processing order of the corresponding data packets have also been presented. With simulation results, it proves that our scheme can obtain better performance to deliver mobile content than the conventional methods. About the future work, the analysis of the packet delivery ratio and network traffic will be considered.

Acknowledgement. This work was supported in part by the fundamental key research project of Shanghai Municipal Science and Technology Commission under grant 12JC1404201, the Ministry of Education Research Fund-China Mobile(2012) MCM20121032.

References

1. Xu, Q., Su, Z., Zhang, K., Ren, P., Shen, X.: Epidemic information dissemination in mobile social networks with opportunistic links. IEEE Trans. Emerg. Top. Comput. doi:10.1109/TETC.2015.2414792
2. Xu, Q., Su, Z., Han, B., Fang, D., Xu, Z., Gan, X.: Analytical model with a novel selfishness division of mobile nodes to participate cooperation. Peer-to-Peer Networking Appl. doi:10.1007/s12083-015-0330-6
3. Yang, T., Zheng, Z., Liang, H., Cheng, N., Shen, X.: Green energy and content aware data transmission in maritime wireless communication network. IEEE Trans. Intell. Transp. Syst. 16(2), 751–762 (2015)
4. Yang, T., Liang, H., Cheng, N., Shen, X.: Efficient scheduling for video transmission in maritime wireless communication network. IEEE Trans. Veh. Technol. doi:10.1109/TVT.2014.2361120
5. Cheng, N., Lu, L., Zhang, N., Yang, T., Shen, X., Mark, J.W.: Vehicle-assisted device-to-device data delivery for smart grid. IEEE Trans. Veh. Technol. doi:10.1109/TVT.2015.2415512
6. Wu, G., Ren, P., Du, Q.: Recall-based dynamic spectrum auction with the protection of primary users. IEEE J. Sel. Areas Commun. 30(10), 2070–2081 (2012)
7. Su, Z., Xu, Q., Zhu, H., Wang, Y.: A novel design for content delivery over software defined mobile social networks. IEEE Network 29(4) (2015) (in press)
8. Ren, P., Wang, Y., Du, Q., Xu, J.: A survey on dynamic spectrum access protocols for distributed cognitive wireless networks. EURASIP J. Wirel. Commun. Networking 60, 1–21 (2012)
9. Li, J., Liu, B., Wu, H.: Energy-efficient in-network caching for content-centric networking. IEEE Commun. Lett. 17(4), 797–800 (2013)
10. Su, Z., Xu, Q.: Content distribution over content centric mobile social networks in 5G. IEEE Commun. Mag. 53, 67–72 (2015)
11. Wang, S., Bi, J., Wu, J.: Collaborative caching based on hash-routing for information-centric networking. ACM SIGCOMM Comput. Commun. Rev. 43(4), 535–536 (2013)
12. Su, Z., Fang, D., Han, B.: Caching algorithm with a novel cost model to deliver content and its interest over content centric networks. China Commun. 12(7) 65–72 (2015)
13. Boldrini, C., Conti, M., Passarella, A.: ContentPlace: social-aware data dissemination in opportunistic networks. In: The 11th International Symposium on Modeling, Analysis and Simulation of Wireless and Mobile Systems, pp. 203–210. New York, USA (2008)
14. Mangili, M., Martignon, F., Capone, A.: A comparative study of content-centric and content-distribution networks: performance and bounds. In: 2013 IEEE Global Communications Conference, pp. 1403–1409. Atlanta, USA (2013)
15. Sourlas, V., Gkatzikis, L., Tassiulas, L.: On-line storage management with distributed decision making for content-centric networks. In: 7th EURO-NGI Conference on Next Generation Internet, Kaiserslautern, pp. 1–8. Germany (2011)
16. Udugama, A., Palipana, S., Goerg, C.: Analytical characterisation of multi-path content delivery in content centric networks. In: 2013 Conference on Future Internet Communications, pp. 1–7. Coimbra, Portugal (2013)
17. Hu, B., Li, Z., Zou, S.: Provider mobility management based on domain proxies in content centric networks. In: 2014 14th International Symposium on Communications and Information Technologies, pp. 393–397. Incheon, Korea (2014)

18. Asaeda, H., Matsuzono, K., Turletti, T.: Contrace: a tool for measuring and tracing content-centric networks. IEEE Commun. Mag. **53**(3), 182–188 (2015)
19. Fang, C., Yu, F., Huang, T., Liu, Y.: A game theoretic approach for energy-efficient in-network caching in content-centric networks. China Commun. **11**(11), 135–145 (2014)

Rogue Access Point Detection in Vehicular Environments

Hao Qu[1], Longjiang Guo[1,2(✉)], Weiping Zhang[1],
Jinbao Li[1,2], and Meirui Ren[1,2]

[1] School of Computer Science and Technology,
Heilongjiang University, Harbin 150080, China
[2] Key Laboratory of Database and Parallel Computing, Harbin 150080, China
longjiang_guo@yeah.net

Abstract. The threat of rogue access points (APs) has attracted significant attentions from both industrial and academic researchers. This paper considers a category of rogue APs that are set up in moving vehicles to lure users. Usually, rogue access points are on the moving vehicles that can keep close distance to the users at all time, thus the adversary has more time to expose private information of users. This paper proposes a practical detecting rogue APs algorithm based on received signal strength (RSS), which calculates the distance between the user and the APs to defend against the rogue APs. The paper also develops a relative position algorithm to find the position of AP. If the position of AP is on the road rather than on the road side, the algorithm suspects that the AP is rogue AP. In this paper, we also have implemented the detection algorithm on real vehicular environments and also have evaluated the performance of the proposed algorithm.

Keywords: Rogue access point · Vehicular networks · RSS

1 Introduction

Vehicular networks have gained considerable research interest recently given their potential in improving traffic management and public safety [1–3]. Access points (APs) in public spaces has provided users easy access to the Internet anytime and anywhere. Some researchers also propose the layout of road APs for vehicular networks. In the future we believe vehicular networks must foster a wide range of emerging applications, such as driving safety [4], intelligent transport services [5]. Because the APs may be deployed everywhere on the roadside, the security issue of APs is must be solved as soon as possible. A rogue AP is a malicious AP that wants to steal the sensitive information of client. The adversary can steal the user's private information such as bank account numbers and passwords.

In the vehicular networks, there are two kinds of rogue APs: static rogue APs and mobile rogue APs. The first type is that rogue APs deployed at a fixed place, such as a busy road or downtown business district. Due to this kind

© Springer International Publishing Switzerland 2015
K. Xu and J. Zhu (Eds.): WASA 2015, LNCS 9204, pp. 446–456, 2015.
DOI: 10.1007/978-3-319-21837-3_44

of rogue AP always keep stay at a fixed place for a long time and do not use the different road infrastructure to connect the Internet. So it is comparatively not complex for researchers to defend against them. For these static rogue APs, previous methods have already been proposed to detect them [6–9]

However, there is little research tell us how to detect the mobile rogue APs. In general, these rogue APs are deployed in a moving vehicle and lure users to connect to them. As we know, vehicular environments have very short channel coherence time. Measurements [10, 11] have show that wireless channel coherence time in vehicular environments could be as short as a few hundred microsecond. Hence, we only have very short coherence time to detect the rogue AP. Beyond that, when a user was driving a car on the road, if the user wants to connect a AP, the user must choose a AP that has the strongest received signal strength(RSS), because the moving vehicular rogue AP are close to clients, the users would prefer to connect to them. Furthermore, it is very difficult to prevent the installation of a vehicular rogue AP, because this kind of rogue AP is always moving Thus, the administrator has no chance to find the vehicular rogue AP since the vehicular rogue AP can move to different location before the administrator detect it. Thus, we need a fast and efficient detecting scheme in vehicular environments.

The fundamental issue in this project is to detect the vehicular rogue APs. Considering the above challenges, we propose a practical detection scheme based on RSS. We choose RSS because it is widely available among off-the-shelf 802.11 radios. So our solution can be implemented on existing wireless platforms without hard ware changes. The vehicular client use the GPS of beacons which are broadcasted by APs to calculate the distance between the vehicular client and the APs. If the distance is not match the RSS values, it will be regarded as a rogue AP. Moreover, based on the principle of legitimate AP is on the roadside, we propose a relative position algorithm that can locate the position of AP. If the position of tested AP is on the roadside , we also suspect the AP to be a rogue AP. Contributions of this paper include the following aspects.

- We propose a rogue APs detection scheme based on RSS that only relies on existing networking protocols and can be implemented by the vehicular clients.
- We design a new detecting schemes based on RSS and use these schemes to detect and position vehicular rogue APs. To the best of of our knowledge, we are the first to consider the unstable vehicular environments and propose a practical detection solution.
- Our extensive experiments are conducted using data collected from real world vehicular environments.

The rest of this paper is organized as follows. Section 2 introduces the related work. Our detection algorithm is described in Section 3. Section 4 shows the experimental results. Finally, Section 5 concludes our work.

2   Related Work

Vehicular network has seen tremendous growth and widespread business adoption in the past decade. The security threats of rogue APs have attracted attentions of both commercial and academic researchers. Precious research has been mainly focused on detecting static rogue APs. The general approach relies on wireless sniffers [12,13] scan the spectrum at 2.4 and $5GHz$, they will alert the administrator when they detect any communication information from unauthorized APs. Some commercial products e.g. [14,15] have been invented by this technique. This method always request well controlled infrastructure such as LAN and depends these products possess a variety of identifying characteristics including MAC address, vendor name and so on, which to distinguish whether an AP turns out to be legitimate or not. In [16], where a solution called DAIR is proposed. It uses USB wireless adapters to capture comprehensive traffic. Differ from above schemes, our solution does not depend on sniffers. Because this category suffers always need enough wireless detection cover and extensive deployment cost. In some cases, it is impractical.

In addition to sniffers, the researchers also use the fingerprints [17,18] to identify rogue APs. The previous schemes often leverage the advantage of fingerprints that cannot be easily forged. For example, radio frequency variations [19] and RSS values [20]. In [21], They adopt the clock skew by calculating every AP's clock skew as their fingerprints, if any AP has illegal clock skew, it will be regarded as a rogue AP. Our solution differs from above schemes that need a large fingerprints database. Hence, our detection scheme is more suitable for vehicular network.

Beyond that, [22] is leveraging the characteristics of wireless traffic to defend the presence of rogue APs. In [6], a positive scheme that utilizes the measurement of round trip time of TCP traffic. Work [9] uses the interval of packets to distinguish wireless networks from wired networks, other work by [7] employs the round trip time between the user and the DNS server to independently determine whether an AP is legitimate or not without assistance from the WLAN operator. In our work, we propose a scheme for the new type of rogue AP based on RSS. Our method was proved to be very efficient.

3   Our Solution

3.1   Detecting Rogue APs Based on Ranging

In our model, the roadside APs must to report its GPS location in beacons. If rogue APs wants to induce a client to connect to it. They will choose the maximum TX power. But the adversary could not report its real GPS location. Because the real GPS location of the rogue AP is on the road. Therefor, the adversary has to report a fake GPS location. In this way, when a client is driving a car on the road, after receiving a beacon, the client obtain AP's reported GPS location and a measured RSS. By knowing the reported GPS location as well as its own GPS location, the client is able to know the distance d between the

AP and itself. Then we adopt the proposed ranging algorithm to calculate the distance l by recorded RSS. Generally speaking, if the AP is legitimate, d and l will be almost equal, if d and l are not equal, the AP will be regarded as a rogue AP.

More researchers are interest in applying shadowing [23] model in vehicular environments to calculate the distance by RSS, the theoretical model is given by

$$P_r = A - 10 \cdot n \cdot lg(d) \tag{1}$$

where P_r is the received signal strength and A is the RSS of $1m$. n denotes the path loss exponent. Variable d is the distance between sender and receiver.

We introduce a new ranging method based on RSS, which can be well applied in the vehicular environments. In the shadowing model, the relationship between RSS values and distance values will eventually convert into a one-to-one mapping relationship, which is a distance value map a RSS value. But from the data of real experimental results, we can see that there are several different RSS values under each distance value. So a RSS value not only map a distance value, but a distance range. Using this feature, this section presents a ranging algorithm based on the mapping between RSS values and distance values.

Definition 1 Off-line Data $\Phi(R,l)$. *Every $f \in \Phi$ contains two parts: a series of RSS values R and a distance value l, where r_j represents a element of $R_i (i=1,2...n)$.*

Definition 2 Query Data f_x. *f_x expresses the query data From user, f_x contains two parts: a series of RSS values and the number of occurrences of each RSS value denoted by d.*

The range of RSS is -49~0 in this paper. In order to minimize fluctuate of RSS values of collection, we utilize formula (2) to divide RSS values into 10 levels: 1~10.

$$r' = 11 - \lceil \frac{|r - 1|}{5} \rceil \tag{2}$$

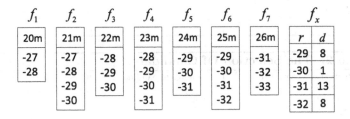

Fig. 1. Off-line data and a query data

I_{-27}	I_{-28}	I_{-29}	I_{-30}	I_{-31}	I_{-32}	I_{-33}
f_1	f_1	f_2	f_2	f_4	f_6	f_7
f_2	f_2	f_3	f_3	f_5	f_7	
	f_3	f_4	f_4	f_6		
	f_4	f_5	f_5	f_7		
		f_6	f_6			

Fig. 2. Inversion of the data collection

where r' is the classification result of RSS value r. For instance, if r = -32, it will be calculated as level 4. Then we can evaluate the similarity value by formula (3).

$$\omega(r_1, r_2) = 1 - |2^{r_1'} - 2^{r_2'}|/2^{10} \tag{3}$$

where $|2^{r_1'}-2^{r_2'}|$ denotes the variances of the two RSS. For instance, $\omega(-23,-25)=1-|2^6-2^5|/2^{10}=1-|64-32|/2^{10}=0.96875$. For two data in Φ, as showed in Figure 1, there are two RSS values -29 and -30 are same between f_2 and f_x. The same values in f_4 and f_x are -29, -30 and -31. So the similarity degree between f_2 and f_x is less than f_4 and f_x. According to this property, we define a similarity value function $S(f_i,f_x)$ between f_i and f_x. The computation formula of $S(f_i,f_x)$ is shown in formula (4).

$$S(f_i, f_x) = \sum d + (\sum \omega)/n \tag{4}$$

In formula (4), $\sum d$ is the sum of d of f_x when RSS values f_i and f_x are same. $\sum \omega$ is the sum of ω of different RSS values between f_i and f_x and all RSS values in f_x.

Algorithm 1. The Inverted Index

Require: RSS-Distance mapping data Φ
Ensure: Inverted index I
1: **for** f in Φ **do**
2:    **for** r in $f.R$ **do**
3:        $r.r'=11-\lceil |r-1|/5 \rceil$
4:        $I_r.add(f)$
5:    **end for**
6: **end for**

Algorithm 2. The Selection Of Candidates

Require: Query f_x, Inverted index I, The number of candidates k and Set t, h
Ensure: Distance l
1: **for** r in $f.R$ **do**
2:    $t.add(I.get(r))$
3: **end for**
4: **for** f in t **do**
5:    $\omega=S(f,f_x)$
6:    $h.add(\omega)$
7: **end for**
8: $I = getDistance(h,k)$
9: **RETURN** l

According to this similarity value model. If we want to know the distance between client and AP. The similarity model will choose some f_i as candidates and exploit these candidates to confirm the final distance. It is very important about the size of the candidates. A simple way is use maximum similarity value to determine the final distance. We can also utilize the top k candidates. The final result is the average of k candidates.

Our ranging method consists two algorithms: Algorithm 1 and Algorithm 2. The basic idea of Algorithm 1 is to scan every f of Φ, create a inverted index for every r in f, expressed as I_r. I_r is a series of f. Figure 2 is a inverted index example of Fig. 1. In Fig. 1, for example, the RSS value -28 is appear in f_1, f_2, f_3 and f_4. Hence, inverted index I_{-28} include f_1, f_2, f_3 and f_4, as show in Fig. 2. Algorithm 3 is to find all f_i which have intersection with f_x in the loop from line 1 to 3, that is $R_i \cap R_x \neq \varnothing$. This process is easy to finish by scanning all $I_r(r \in R_x)$. For all candidates f_i which are chosen from the previous step, we calculate the similarity values by formula (4). After that, this paper use k candidates f_i to obtain the final distance value l.

3.2 Detecting Rogue APs Based on Positioning

A situation is that AP can't report its GPS information. For this condition, this paper proposes a novel detecting rogue APs algorithm based on relative position. This method do not demand every AP broadcast its GPS information in beacons. So this method is more practical in the vehicular environments.

As show in Fig. 3. This paper assumes that a vehicle is driving on the road with uniform straight line motion and the client vehicle is driving on the forward direction of X axis, the speed of the vehicle is v. At the $t_i(i=1,2...)$ moment, the values of RSS is $s_i(i=1,2...)$. We can get a series of sampling values (t_i,s_i). According to the ranging algorithm in the previous section, the values of RSS are transformed into distances $d_i(i=1,2...)$. Then we can use the geometric knowledge to calculate coordinate(a,b) of AP. the distance d can be obtained by

$$d_i = f(s_i) = 10^{\frac{A-s_i}{10n}} \tag{5}$$

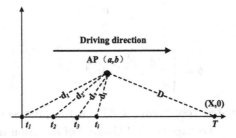

Fig. 3. Illustration of relative location of client and AP

If $t_1=0$, the coordinate of t_i moment is $(t_i \times v, 0)$, we obtain:

$$\Delta_i = t_i \times v \tag{6}$$

So based on the pythagorean theorem, we have:

$$(a - \Delta_i)^2 + b^2 = d_i^2 \tag{7}$$

According to the formula (7), so:

$$d_i^2 = -2a\Delta_i + \Delta_i^2 + a^2 + b^2 \tag{8}$$

Setting:

$$\begin{cases} y_i = d_i^2 - \Delta_i^2 = 10^{\frac{A-s_i}{5n}} - (v \times t_i)^2 \\ x_i = \Delta_i = v \times t_i \\ c = a^2 + b^2 \\ d = -2a \end{cases}$$

Then we can obtain:

$$y_i = \hat{c} + \hat{d}x_i \tag{9}$$

Using maximum likelihood estimation to estimate the parameter $\hat{c}$ and $\hat{d}$. Differentiating y_i and setting it to be zero, the value of $\hat{c}$ and $\hat{d}$ can be derived as follows:

$$\hat{d} = \frac{n\sum_{i=1}^{n} x_i y_i - (\sum_{i=1}^{n} x_i)(\sum_{i=1}^{n} y_i)}{n\sum_{i=1}^{n} x_i^2 - \sum_{i=1}^{n} x_i} \tag{10}$$

$$\hat{c} = \frac{1}{n}\sum_{i=1}^{n} y_i - \frac{\hat{d}}{n}\sum_{i=1}^{n} x_i \tag{11}$$

Thus:

$$\hat{a} = -\frac{\hat{d}}{2} \tag{12}$$

$$\hat{b} = \begin{cases} \sqrt{\hat{c} - \frac{\hat{d}^2}{4}}, \hat{c} - \frac{\hat{d}^2}{4} \geq 0 \\ 0, \hat{c} - \frac{\hat{d}^2}{4} < 0 \end{cases} \tag{13}$$

$(\hat{a}, \hat{b})$ is the estimated coordinate of AP. In the process of calculation, the situation $\hat{c} - \frac{\hat{d}^2}{4} < 0$ may be happened. This kind of situation usually will appear when the AP is in the vehicle's path. Beacuse the legitimate AP is on the road side. So we can use $\hat{c} - \frac{\hat{d}^2}{4} < 0$ to judge the rogue AP.

4   Experiments

In this section, we describe the setup of our experiments and evaluate the proposed methods based on measurement from real vehicular environments. Followed by the experimental results.

4.1   Experimental Environment

The real world vehicular networks experiments have three components: a roadside AP, a vehicular rogue AP and a client. Our deployment uses TelosB [24] motes of Crossbow company. The sensors transmit in $2.4GHz$ with IEEE 802.15.4 protocol.

Client: The client has three parts: a laptop, a base station and a receiver. The receiver sent the received signal to the laptop by the base station. The receiver was fixed on a car. The laptop was running Windows XP and Cygwin. Programming environment was TinyOS2.x.

Roadside AP and **Vehicular Rogue AP:** For this case of setup, the roadside AP is a sender node bound on a fixed stick with height of 1.5 m. We deployed the roadside AP alongside the road. The configuration of our vehicular rogue AP is similar to the roadside AP except that the sender node was mounted on the top of a car. Both road side AP and vehicular AP are the maximum TX power.

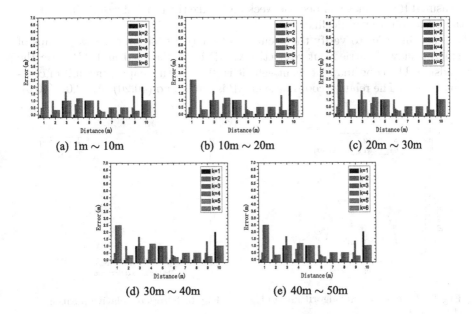

(a) 1m ~ 10m   (b) 10m ~ 20m   (c) 20m ~ 30m

(d) 30m ~ 40m   (e) 40m ~ 50m

Fig. 4. The effect of k

We conducted these experiments in an outdoor parking lot. The roadside AP was put at the parking lot around 15 m away from the road. There were two cars, one was the vehicular client and the other was the vehicular rogue AP. The two cars drove on the road and maintained 10 m from each other.

4.2 Experimental Results

First, in our ranging algorithm, the final distance l is decided by k candidates. We set k from 1 to 6 in the experiments. Figure 4 shows the k's effect on error. As we see, if $k = 1$, over 90 % errors within 1.5 m in the range of 30 m, over 70 % errors within 1.5 m in the range of 30 m $\sim$ 50 m when $k = 6$. So we make 30 m to be an empirical bound, denoted by RSS_{30}. In the practical application, we can collect some sample RSS values in advance, RSS_d is the average of these RSS values. If $RSS_d > RSS_{30}$, we adopt $k = 1$ in our ranging algorithm. If $RSS_d < RSS_{30}$, this paper adopts $k = 6$ to calculate the final distance. This paper also makes a comparison between shadowing model and our ranging algorithm. As shown in Fig. 5, the results of our solution obtain good performance on ranging error.

Second, in order to verify the practicability of our solution. This paper conducted real vehicular experiments, where the roadside AP was static, the vehicular rogue AP and the vehicular client were moving on the road. The experimental results showed that the positive rate of our method is over 95 % when the vehicular client and vehicular rogue AP maintained the distance of 10 m away from each other. When the distance become larger or in heavy traffic conditions, the measured RSS values will become week and make the ranging results inaccuracy, the positive rate will decline.

Last, in order to verify the accuracy of relative positioning. Two groups of experiment was carried out respectively: AP is on the road and AP is on the roadside. The coordinate of client vehicle is (0,0). In this paper, the unit of coordinate is m. The relative coordinate of AP is (40,0) and (40,20). At (0,0), (10,0),

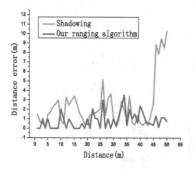

Fig. 5. Errors of our algorithm and shadowing

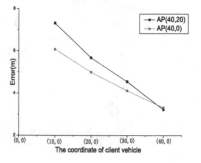

Fig. 6. Errors of relative position

(20,0), (30,0), (40,0), the client vehicle obtain RSS values respectively. The Fig. 6 shows the experimental result, where the x-axis denotes the coordinates of client vehicle and the y-axis presents the errors of relative position. It is true that the errors less than 3.5 m after using maximum likelihood estimation with five pairs of coordinates. So as you can see from the results of the experiment, the errors of relative position is very small. Thus, our solution is able to determine the location of the AP and detect the rogue AP.

5   Conclusion

In this paper, we propose a practical rogue APs detection to prevent the users to connect to the vehicular rogues. And it is suitable for the unstable vehicular environments. The detection identifies potential rogue APs and measures their properties. Then we run the detection algorithms based on RSS to identify rogue APs. We implement our schemes to commercially hardware, and conduct extensive real vehicular experiments to evaluate our solutions.

References

1. Wu, Y., Zhu, Y.: CCR: Capacity-constrained replication for data delivery in vehicular networks. In: INFOCOM, pp. 2580–2588 (2013)
2. Guan, X., Huang, Y., Cai, Z., Ohtsuki, T.: Intersection-based forwarding protocol for vehicular ad hoc networks. Telecommunication Systems. 10.1007/s11235-015-9983-y (2015)
3. Cheng, S., Cai, Z., Li, J.: Curve query processing in wireless sensor networks. IEEE Trans. Veh. Technol., 1–12 (2014)
4. Farnoud, F., Valaee, S.: Reliable broadcast of safety messages in vehicular ad hoc networks. In: INFOCOM, pp. 226–234 (2009)
5. Zhu, H., et al.: ZOOM: Scaling the mobility for fast opportunistic forwarding in vehicular networks. In: INFOCOM, pp. 2832–2840 (2013)
6. Watkins, L., et al.: A passive approach to rogue access point detection. In: GLOBECOM, pp. 355–360 (2007)
7. Han, H., Sheng, B.: A measurement based rogue ap detection scheme. In: INFOCOM, pp. 1593–1601 (2009)
8. Yin, H., Chen, G.: Detecting protected layer-3 rogue aps. In: BROADNEtS, pp. 449–458 (2007)
9. Shetty, S., Song, M.: Rogue access point detection by analyzing network traffic characteristics. In: MILCOM, pp. 1–7 (2007)
10. Cheng, L., et al.: Doppler spread and coherence time of rural and highway vehicle-to-vehicle channels at 5.9 GHz. In: GLOBECOM, pp. 1–6 (2008)
11. Camp, J., et al.: Modulation rate adaptation in urban and vehicular environments: cross-layer implementation and experimental evaluation. IEEE/ACM Trans. Netw. 18(6), 1949–1962 (2010)
12. Liu, C., Yu, J.: Rogue access point based Dos attacks against 802.11 WLANs. In: AICT, pp. 271–276 (2008)
13. Chandra, R., et al.: A location-based management system for enterprise wireless lans. In: NSDI (2007)

14. Air defence. www.airdefence.net
15. Air magnet. www.airmagnet.com
16. Bahl, P., et al.: Enhancing the security of corporate Wi-Fi networks using DAIR. In: MobiSys (2006)
17. Gao, K., et al.: A passive approach to wireless device fingerprinting. In: DSN, pp. 383–392 (2010)
18. Han, H., et al.: Defending against vehicular rogue APs. In: INFOCOM, pp. 1665–1673 (2011)
19. Brik, V., et al.: Wireless device identification with radiometric signatures. In: MOBICOM (2008)
20. Sheng, Y., Tan, K.: Detecting 802.11 MAC layer spoofing using received signal strength. In: INFOCOM, pp. 383–392 (2008)
21. Jana, S., Kasera, S.: On fast and accurate detection of unauthorized wireless access points using clock skews. In: TMC, pp. 449–462 (2010)
22. Ling, Z., et al.: Novel packet size-based covert channel attacks against anonymizer. IEEE Trans. Comput. **62**, 2411–2426 (2013)
23. Long, T., et al.: Optimization of RSSI algorithm in wireless sensor network. In: Computer System Application (2013)
24. TelosB Ddatasheet. http://www.willow.co.uk/html/telosb_mote_platform.html

Information-Centric Resource Management for Air Pollution Monitoring with Multihop Cellular Network Architecture

Pengbo Si[1,2(✉)], Qiuran Li[1], Yanhua Zhang[1], and Yuguang Fang[2]

[1] College of Electronic Information and Control Engineering,
Beijing University of Technology, Beijing 100124, China
{sipengbo,zhangyh}@bjut.edu.cn, liqiuran@emails.bjut.edu.cn
[2] Department of Electrical and Computer Engineering,
University of Florida, Gainesville, FL 32611, USA
fang@ece.ufl.edu

Abstract. Air pollution monitoring systems attract much attention recently due to the increasingly serious health problems caused by the pollutants in the air. In this paper, an Information-Centric Multihop Cellular network for Air pollution Monitoring (IC-MCAM) is introduced for efficient collection of the sensing data. Furthermore, we propose a dynamic radio resource management scheme, by which the physical resource blocks (PRBs) are allocated to the wireless links to minimize the long-term overall energy consumption, taking into account the packet priority, size, delays as well as the wireless channel state. The resource management optimization problem is formulated as a restless bandits model with constraints, which is further reformulated as a restless bandits model for efficient solutions. Extensive simulation results are also presented to demonstrate the significant performance improvement of the proposed scheme.

Keywords: Information-centric network · Resource management · Air pollution monitoring · Multi-hop cellular network

1 Introduction

Air pollution from industries, automobiles, agricultural activities, etc., has been a complex and serious problem since over one hundred years ago, and is becoming much more lethal, especially in recent years in some developing countries such as China and India. It is reported that heavy smog and haze resulted from air pollution kill over 16,000 people a year in Beijing, and affect the health of over 500 million people in northern China [1]. Hence, there is a growing demand for air pollution monitoring systems, to facilitate the governments to make policies, the factories to control pollution, and the people to protect themselves.

Most existing air pollution monitoring systems are composed of the large-size and fixed-location devices with wired network connections for accurate measurement of the major pollutants. However, these systems measure the air quality

© Springer International Publishing Switzerland 2015
K. Xu and J. Zhu (Eds.): WASA 2015, LNCS 9204, pp. 457–466, 2015.
DOI: 10.1007/978-3-319-21837-3_45

at only certain isolated locations, due to the difficulties on device deployment. Fortunately, recent advances on gas/air/particle sensor and wireless sensor network (WSN) technologies enable flexible air quality information collection for comprehensive sensing coverage and high fault tolerance from large amounts of sensors connected by WSNs.

Sensors are usually directly connected for data delivery in traditional WSNs. However, these low-power, low-computational/storage-capacity sensors may not be capable to simultaneously cope with the sensing and data transmission tasks well. To address this problem, more powerful data aggregators, or wireless routers, is introduced to WSNs for data processing and delivery. Besides, the recently promising concept of information-centric network (ICN) could help reducing information delivery delay by in-network caching equipped on the routers [2,3]. This could be very effective due to the fact that the air pollution data does not usually change dramatically and many packets may contain very similar information. In [2], the sensor and actor nodes collaborate without centralized management, to perform data aggregation with data-centric storage system. The information dependency of sensors has been explored to form a community structure of sensor data and been used to develop an information-centric processing methodology in [3]. The authors of [4] have proposed the data-centric routing for wireless sensor networks, considering the energy efficiency and reliability. A pruning scheme is proposed in [5] to reduce the overhead introduced by greedy perimeter stateless routing algorithm in practical data-centric storage sensor networks.

However, as a key issue in wireless communications, the radio resource management problem has not been well addressed in air pollution monitoring networks with information-centric technology. Since spectrum resource is very scarce and valuable [6], how to efficiently utilize the limited radio resources for data transmission merits careful design [7]. In this paper, to address this problem, the Information-Centric Multihop Cellular network for Air pollution Monitoring (IC-MCAM) architecture is introduced, and the dynamic spectrum management scheme for IC-MCAM is proposed. The multihop cellular network architecture is introduced to enable centralized controlling as well as distributed data transmission. The radio resources, i.e., physical resource blocks (PRBs), are optimally managed, with the objective of minimizing the long-term energy consumption in the network. Different delay requirements for different data types are modeled as the constraint, to deal with the problem that some emergency events such as toxic gas leaking need faster data delivery for quick response. The resource management optimization is formulated as a restless bandits problem with constraints (RB-C), and reformulated as a restless bandits problem by converting the constraints to the punishment factor [8].

The rest of this paper is organized as follows. Section 2 discusses the network architecture and the system models. In Sect. 3, the resource management optimization is formulated as an RB-C problem. Section 4 reformulates and solves the RB-C problem. Numerical results are provided and discussed in Sect. 5 and the conclusion is drawn in Sect. 6.

2   System Model

The network architecture and the network and service models are discussed in this section.

2.1   Network Architecture

The current 3G/4G technologies provide high-speed Internet connection and wide coverage, which could be utilized by the air pollution monitoring systems to deliver the collected data to the data centers for storage and processing. However, in some rural areas, the base stations are sparsely distributed so that the low-power sensors or routers may not be able to maintain reliable one-hop connections to the base stations. Therefore, we adopt multihop network architecture in our work. In IC-MCAM, air pollution data is sensed by the sensors and transmitted to the routers within their communication ranges. The routers pre-process the raw data to reduce traffic, and deliver the processed data to the base station in a multihop manner. We assume that all the routers could receive the broadcast signals from the base station, but the base station cannot hear the routers, except the ones that are close enough to have a successful direct connection. Besides, the up-to-date information-centric network architecture is adopted. In-network cache is equipped in each of the routers for temporary data storage. Thus to reduce the traffic, the routers could compare the data to be forwarded with the data in their cache, and deliver the differences only.

2.2   Network Model

We assume that there are N routers, one base station, and L wireless links connecting the routers and the base station. Obviously, $L \leq \binom{N+1}{2}$. The radio resource is divided into blocks by time and frequency, i.e., PRBs. Assume that at each specific time point, the number of PRBs that can be utilized is C. Interference is always one of the key problems in multi-hop wireless networks. In case that $C \geq L$, we do not have to consider the PRB allocation problem because we have sufficient PRBs to allocate to all the links. Thus we focus on the case that $C < L$. Besides, the whole time line is divided into slots, the duration of which is exactly the same as the temporal width of a PRB. Let $[t_k, t_{k+1}), 1 \leq k \leq K$, to denote the kth time slot from the time point t_k to t_{k+1}. Here t_k is the decision time point, at which the PRB allocation decision is made.

   We consider block fading channel, implying that the changing of the channel gain within one time slot can be ignored, but the changing between different time slots should be taken into account. We also ignore the frequency selective effect of wireless channels. The most commonly adopted Rayleigh channel model is used in this paper, of which the probability density function is $f(x) = \frac{x}{\kappa^2} e^{-\frac{x^2}{2\kappa^2}}$, and the cumulative distribution function is $F(x) = 1 - e^{-\frac{x^2}{2\kappa^2}}$. Note that we consider x as the envelope of the channel response. Then its variance and mean are $\frac{(4-\pi)\kappa^2}{2}$ and $\kappa\sqrt{\frac{\pi}{2}}$, respectively. Since the channel state x is a random process, we use $x(l,t)$ to denote the state of link l at time point t_k. The tranceivers are equipped with the channel estimation model, thus $x(l,t)$ can be observed at t_k.

Energy consumption is always a key issue in designing wireless networks, especially in IC-MCAMs where the routers are usually powered by batteries with relatively low capacity. Let q_R represent the receiving power, $q_R = q_T x^2$, where q_T is the transmission power. According to the signal propagation loss equation in [9], we have $\bar{q}_R(l) = q_T M_T M_R / \gamma_P$, where $\bar{q}_R(l)$ is the average receiving signal power, M_T and M_R are the gain of the transmitting and the receiving antenna respectively, and γ_P is the propagation loss, which can be represented as $\gamma_P = (4\pi\alpha(l)/\lambda)^2$. We can easily derive that $\kappa = \sqrt{M_T M_R / \gamma_P}$.

2.3 Service Model

In an IC-MCAM, the sensors are supposed to collect and upload the air quality data periodically. For simplicity, the intervals between two data uploading actions are assumed to be integral multiples of $t_{k+1} - t_k$. Most data is the regular report on the air quality. However, emergency events may require real-time monitoring for immediate response. Thus we consider two types of data packets in the IC-MCAM: regular packets with lower priority and emergency packets with higher priority. Whenever an emergency packet arrives at a router for forwarding, it goes ahead of all regular packets in the sending queue. We use $y(l,k)$ to denote the type of the first packet in the queue at the sender of link l at t_k, where $y(l,k) = 1$ represents the emergency packet and $y(l,k) = 2$ represents the regular one. Let $h(l,k)$ represent the size of the first packet in the queue at the sender of l at t_k, $l \in \mathbb{L}$, where $\mathbb{L}$ is the set of all links. The duration of an emergency is usually larger than one time slot. There has been some work on the duration distribution of events [10]. For simplicity, we use $f_{\tau_e}(\tau_e(l,k))$ to denote the probability distribution function of the emergency duration $\tau_e(l,k)$ of which the emergency packet is transmitted by l at t_k. Furthermore, we model the delay of the first packet at the sender of link l as discrete random processes, which is denoted as $g(l,k)$. The realizations of $g(l,k)$ is the number of time slots for which the packet has been on the way since it is originally generated.

3 Restless Bandits with Constraints Formulation

In this section, the resource management scheme is formulated as a restless bandits problem with constraints.

3.1 System State Space

In the proposed resource allocation scheme, each link is considered as an object to control. The queueing state should be involved as the object state, on which the PRB allocation decision is based. Mathematically, the state of the link l at t_k is formulated as the combination state of the delay, type and size of the first packet in the queue at the sender of l, as well as the channel state of l.

We use the discrete state z instead of the continuous x.

$$z = \begin{cases} \tilde{z}_0, & \text{if } \tilde{x} \leq \epsilon_1, \\ \tilde{z}_i, & \text{if } \epsilon_i \leq \tilde{x} \leq \epsilon_{i+1}, \text{ for } 1 \leq i \leq Z - 2, \\ \tilde{z}_{Z-1}, & \text{if } \tilde{x} > \epsilon_{Z-1}, \end{cases} \tag{1}$$

where $\tilde{z}_i, 0 \leq i \leq Z - 1$ are the realizations of z, and $\epsilon_i, 1 \leq i \leq Z - 1$ are the thresholds. Then the system state is a tuple

$$s(l, k) = \langle g(l, k), y(l, k), h(l, k), z(l, k) \rangle. \tag{2}$$

Let $\tilde{s}$ denote the realization of $s(l, k)$, and $\mathbb{S}$ the system state space, which is the set of all available realizations of $\tilde{s}$.

Similarly, we use $\tilde{g}$, $\tilde{y}$, $\tilde{h}$ and $\tilde{z}$ to denote the realizations of $g(l, k)$, $y(l, k)$, $h(l, k)$ and $z(l, k)$, respectively, and $\mathbb{G}$, $\mathbb{Y}$, $\mathbb{H}$ and $\mathbb{Z}$ the set of all available $\tilde{g}$, $\tilde{y}$, $\tilde{h}$ and $\tilde{z}$, respectively. With the notation G, Y, H and Z as the sizes of $\mathbb{G}$, $\mathbb{Y}$, $\mathbb{H}$ and $\mathbb{Z}$, the size of $\mathbb{S}$ can be written as $|\mathbb{S}| = S = G \times Y \times H \times Z$.

3.2 Actions and Policies

At each decision time point t_k, decisions are made and actions are taken to allocate the C PRBs to the L links. Let $a(l, k)$ denote the action for link l at t_k,

$$a(l, k) = \begin{cases} 0, & \text{if a PRB is allocated to } l \text{ at } t_k, \\ 1, & \text{if no PRB is allocated to } l \text{ at } t_k. \end{cases} \tag{3}$$

Since there are only C PRBs to be allocated to the L links, and $C < L$, we have $\sum_{l \in L} a(l, k) = C$. We call the links with $a(l, k) = 1$ the active objects and the ones with $a(l, k) = 0$ the passive objects.

The policy A is defined as the set of the actions from t_1 to t_K, i.e., $A = \{a(l, k)\}_{k=\{1,2,\ldots,K\}}$. We use $\mathbb{A}$ to denote the set of all available policies. An optimal policy A^* is the policy that achieves the optimum objective of the system.

3.3 One-Step State Transition Probabilities

As we have proven in [11], this channel state can be considered as a Markov random process. According to the cumulative distribution function of the channel, the transition probability of $z(l, k) = \tilde{z}_i$ to $z(l, k + 1) = \tilde{z}_j$ is

$$P_z(i, j) = P(z(l, k + 1) = \tilde{z}_j | z(l, k) = \tilde{z}_i)$$

$$= \begin{cases} \check{F}(\epsilon_1, \tilde{z}_i), & \text{if } j = 0, \\ \check{F}(\epsilon_{j+1}, \tilde{z}_i) - F(\epsilon_j, \tilde{z}_i), & \text{if } 1 \leq j \leq Z - 2, \\ 1 - F(\epsilon_{Z-1}, \tilde{z}_i), & \text{if } j = Z - 1, \end{cases} \tag{4}$$

where $P_z(i, j)$ is short for $P(z(l, k + 1) = \tilde{z}_j | z(l, k) = \tilde{z}_i)$. Obviously, $z(l, k)$ is independent of $a(l, k)$, $h(l, k)$, $y(l, k)$ and $g(l, k)$.

Three substates $h(l, k)$, $y(l, k)$ and $g(l, k)$ denote the size, type and delay of the first packet in the queue at the sender of link l respectively. When $a(l, k) = 0$, no PRB is allocated to the link, thus the packet state may change only if the delay of the first packet is too high and it needs to be dropped. Consequently, we can write the joint transition probability of $y(l, k)$ and $g(l, k)$ as

$$P_{y,g}^0(i,j) = P(y(l, k+1) = \tilde{y}_j, g(l, k+1) = \tilde{g}_j | a(l, k) = 0, y(l, k) = \tilde{y}_i, g(l, k) = \tilde{g}_i)$$

$$= \begin{cases} \left[1 - \bar{P}_{y,1}' + \bar{P}_{y,1}\bar{P}_{y,1}'\right] P_{g,1}(\tilde{g}_j), & \text{if } \tilde{y}_j = \tilde{y}_i = 1, g_i = \hat{g}_{\tilde{y}} \\ \bar{P}_{y,1}'(1 - \bar{P}_{y,1})\bar{P}_{g,2}(\tilde{g}_j), & \text{if } \tilde{y}_j = 2, \tilde{y}_i = 1, g_i = \hat{g}_{\tilde{y}} \\ \bar{P}_{y,1}\bar{P}_{g,1}(\tilde{g}_j), & \text{if } \tilde{y}_j = 1, \tilde{y}_i = 2, g_i = \hat{g}_{\tilde{y}}, \\ (1 - \bar{P}_{y,1})\bar{P}_{g,2}(\tilde{g}_j), & \text{if } \tilde{y}_j = \tilde{y}_i = 2, g_i = \hat{g}_{\tilde{y}}, \\ \bar{P}_{g,\tilde{y}_j}(\tilde{g}_j), & \text{if } \tilde{y}_j = \tilde{y}_i, g_i < \hat{g}_{\tilde{y}}, \\ 0, & \text{if } \tilde{y}_j = \tilde{y}_i, g_i < \hat{g}_{\tilde{y}}, \end{cases} \tag{5}$$

where $\hat{g}_{\tilde{y}}$ is the maximum delay (number of slots) acceptable for type $\tilde{y}$ packets, $\bar{P}_{y,1}$ is the probability of an emergency event happens in one time slot, $\bar{P}_{g,\tilde{y}_j}(\tilde{g}_j)$ is the distribution probability of the delay of the packet of type $\tilde{y}_j$, and $\bar{P}_{y,1}'$ is the probability that the first packet is the last one of a sequence of emergency packets,

$$\bar{P}_{y,1}' = \frac{1}{\left\lfloor \frac{\bar{\tau}_e}{\tau_t} \right\rfloor} = \frac{1}{\left\lfloor \frac{\int_0^\infty \tau_e f_{\tau_e}(\tau_e) \mathrm{d}x}{\tau_t} \right\rfloor}. \tag{6}$$

Here $\lfloor \bullet \rfloor$ denotes the floor function.

With $a(l, k) = 0$, $y(l, k) = \tilde{y}_i$ and $g(l, k) = \tilde{g}_i$ as the conditions, the transition probability of $h(l, k)$ is

$$P_{h|y,g}^0(i,j) = P(h(l, k+1) = \tilde{h}_j, | a(l, k) = 0, h(l, k) = \tilde{h}_i, y(l, k+1) = \tilde{y}_j,$$
$$g(l, k+1) = \tilde{g}_j, y(l, k) = \tilde{y}_i, g(l, k) = \tilde{g}_i)$$

$$= \begin{cases} \bar{P}_h, & \text{if } g_i = \hat{g}_{\tilde{y}}, \\ 1, & \text{if } \tilde{h}_j = \tilde{h}_i, g_i < \hat{g}_{\tilde{y}}, \\ 0, & \text{if } \tilde{h}_j \neq \tilde{h}_i, g_i < \hat{g}_{\tilde{y}}, \end{cases} \tag{7}$$

where $\bar{P}_h$ is the distribution probability of the size of a packet.

When $a(l, k) = 1$, the packet size will change even if $g_i < \hat{g}_{\tilde{y}}$, because the first packet may be transmitted using the allocated PRB. Similarly,

$$P_{y,g}^1(i,j) = P(y(l, k+1) = \tilde{y}_j, g(l, k+1) = \tilde{g}_j | a(l, k) = 1, y(l, k) = \tilde{y}_i, g(l, k) = \tilde{g}_i)$$

$$= \begin{cases} \left[1 - \bar{P}_{y,1}' + \bar{P}_{y,1}\bar{P}_{y,1}'\right] P_{g,1}(\tilde{g}_j), & \text{if } \tilde{y}_j = \tilde{y}_i = 1, \\ \bar{P}_{y,1}'(1 - \bar{P}_{y,1})\bar{P}_{g,2}(\tilde{g}_j), & \text{if } \tilde{y}_j = 2, \tilde{y}_i = 1, \\ \bar{P}_{y,1}\bar{P}_{g,1}(\tilde{g}_j), & \text{if } \tilde{y}_j = 1, \tilde{y}_i = 2, \\ (1 - \bar{P}_{y,1})\bar{P}_{g,2}(\tilde{g}_j), & \text{if } \tilde{y}_j = \tilde{y}_i = 2, \end{cases}$$

and

$$P_{h|y,g}^1(i,j) = \bar{P}_h = P(h(l, k+1) = \tilde{h}_j, | a(l, k) = 1, h(l, k) = \tilde{h}_i, y(l, k+1) = \tilde{y}_j,$$
$$g(l, k+1) = \tilde{g}_j, y(l, k) = \tilde{y}_i, g(l, k) = \tilde{g}_i). \tag{8}$$

Due to the fact that the channel state $z(l, k)$ is independent on other substates, the transition probability of $s(l, k)$ can be represented as $P_s^a(i,j) =$

$P_z(i,j)P^a_{h,y,g}(i,j)$, where $P^a_{h,y,g}(i,j)$ is the joint transition probability of $h(l,k)$, $y(l,k)$ and $g(l,k)$.

$$P^a_{h,y,g}(i,j) = P(h(l,k+1) = P^a_{h|y,g}(i,j)P^a_{y,g}(i,j) = \tilde{h}_j, y(l,k+1) = \tilde{y}_j,$$
$$g(l,k+1) = \tilde{g}_j | a(l,k) = 1, h(l,k) = \tilde{h}_i, y(l,k) = \tilde{y}_i, g(l,k) = \tilde{g}_i)$$
$$= P^a_{h|y,g}(i,j)P^a_{y,g}(i,j). \tag{9}$$

3.4 Energy Consumption

A router always tries to minimize its energy consumption to transmit its queueing packet within one time slot. Assume the length of a time slot to be τ_t. Then to finish transmitting a packet of size $h(l,k)$ within τ_t, the minimum transmitting energy consumption $e^*_t(l,k)$ is

$$e^*_t(l,k) = \min_{0 \le e_t \le \hat{q}_t \tau_t} e_t, \text{ s.t., } \frac{h(l,k)}{W \log(1 + \frac{q_R(l,k)}{\sigma^2})} \le \tau_t, \tag{10}$$

where $\hat{q}_t$ is the maximum transmission power, and $\hat{q}_t \tau_t$ is the maximum transmission energy during one time slot. Deriving the optimal $e^*_t(l,k)$ is straightforward,

$$e^*_t(l,k) = \frac{2\tau_t\sigma^2 \left(2^{\frac{h(l,k)}{\tau_t W}} - 1\right)}{x(l,k)^2}, \tag{11}$$

which depends on both $x(l,k)$ and $h(l,k)$

Energy is consumed for data processing, signal receiving, etc., even when the router is not transmitting, Let e' denote the expected energy consumption within one time slot besides the energy for transmitting signals, then the total energy consumption for l in $[t_k, t_{k+1})$ is

$$e(l,k) = e^*_t(l,k) + e'. \tag{12}$$

3.5 System Reward

The proposed resource management scheme aims to minimize the energy consumption with delay constraints for different types of packets. Thus we use $\hat{q}_t \tau_t - e(l,k)$ as the system reward obtained by the transmission on link l within $[t_k, t_{k+1})$, when $a(l,k) = 1$ and the delay of the transmitted packet is acceptable. The reward $R^a(l,k)$ can be written as

$$R^a(l,k) = \begin{cases} \hat{q}_t \tau_t - e(l,k), & \text{if } a(l,k) = 1, \\ 0, & \text{otherwise.} \end{cases} \tag{13}$$

The total system reward is formulated as

$$R = \sum_{k=1}^{K} \beta^{K-k} \sum_{l \in \mathbb{L}} R^a(l,k), \tag{14}$$

where β is the discount factor. Thus the optimal resource management problem can be represented as a restless bandits problem with constraints.

$$A^* = \underset{A \in \mathbb{A}}{\operatorname{argmax}} R, \tag{15}$$

s.t.,

$$\forall 1 \le k \le K \text{ and } l \in \mathbb{L}, g(l,k), \le \hat{g}_{\tilde{y}},$$

$$\sum_{l \in \mathbb{L}} a(l,k) = C. \tag{16}$$

4   Solving the RB-C Problem

We need to reformulate the above restless bandits problem with constraints as a standard restless bandits problem to utilize the existing algorithms. To deal with the constraints in the RB-C formulation, we introduce the punishment factor V, which is defined as the cost when the system does not satisfy the constraints. In our case, we use $V_{g(l,k)}$ to represent the punishment factor for packets with different type states $\tilde{g}_i$. Consequently, the system reward in the RB-C problem is updated as

$$R'^a(l,k) = \begin{cases} R^a(l,k), & \text{if } g(l,k) \le \hat{g}_{y_i}, \\ -V_{g(l,k)}, & \text{otherwise,} \end{cases} \tag{17}$$

where $V_{g(l,k)}$ is usually set to be a large positive number in the problem. The system sate $s(l,k)$, the actions $a(l,k)$, the one-step transition probabilities $P_s^a(i,j)$ do not have to be revised. To solve this standard restless bandits problem, a hierarchy of increasingly stronger linear programming (LP) relaxations is developed based on the result of LP formulations of Markov Decision Chains (MDCs) [12], the last of which is exact. To reduce the computational complexity, a heuristic algorithm for the stochastic restless bandits problem can be used, utilizing the information contained in optimal primal and dual solutions to the first-order relaxation [12]. The indices of the objects for all the available states can be calculated off-line, while in the on-line stage, the objects determine their indices according to the current system states, and share the indices with each other. The objects with the lowest indices will be selected as the active ones.

5   Simulation Results and Analysis

In our simulation, we assume that $N = 20$ routers are randomly distributed in a $1 \text{ km} \times 1 \text{ km}$ area, with a base station as the sink in the center of this area. There are $C = 16$ PRBs simultaneously available to the wireless links. The length of the time slot $\tau_t = 10 \text{ ms}$. The maximum acceptable delay of emergency and regular packets $\hat{g}_1 = 6$ time slots and $\hat{g}_2 = \hat{g}_1 \times 3$, respectively, and the cost of exceeding $\hat{g}_1$ and $\hat{g}_2$ and dropping the packets $V_1 = 100$ and $V_2 = 20$.

Power consumption is always key to the performance of the whole system. Since we assume that the non-transmission power consumption (in case of receiving, processing and idle) is a constant value for all the routers, we only draw the average transmission power comparison of the routers in the networks, which is shown in Fig. 1a. We can observe that, as the number of routers increases in the network, the average power decreases because more links cannot obtain adequate radio resource for transmission and spend zero transmission power. Our proposed scheme significantly reduces the average power consumption, for the number of router ranging from 12 to 32.

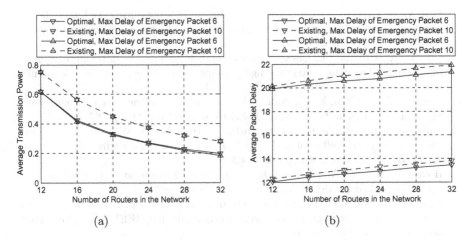

Fig. 1. (a) Average transmission power consumption and (b) average packet drop probability with different numbers of routers.

In Fig. 1b, with different number of routers in the network, our proposed scheme always performs better compared to the existing one that ignores the optimal resource management. Since the packets whose delay exceeds $\hat{g}_{\tilde{y}}$ are discarded, the average delay when $\hat{g}_1 = 6$ is much lower than that when $\hat{g}_1 = 10$ (note that $\hat{g}_2 = \hat{g}_1 \times 3$ and we compare the average packet delay in this figure).

6   Conclusion

In this paper, we have studied the air pollution monitoring systems and proposed a new architecture with both the concepts of information-centric and multi-hop cellular networking. The in-network caching and on-router processing was introduced in the network to reduce the traffic. Furthermore, with the consideration of data packet priority, delay and size, and the Rayleigh fading of the wireless links, we proposed the optimal radio resource management scheme, for minimizing the long-term energy consumption. This optimization problem has been formulated as a restless bandits model with constraints, and we further reformulated it as a standard restless bandits model, whose "indexibility" feature can reduce the on-line computation complexity. As shown in the simulation results, our proposed scheme significantly improves the performance of the networks.

Acknowledgment. This work was jointly supported by the National Natural Science Foundation of China under Grant 61372089 and 61201198, and the Beijing Natural Science Foundation under Grant 4132007. The work of Y. Fang was partially supported by US National Science Foundation under grant CNS-1409797 and CNS-1423165.

References

1. Pan, X., Li, G., Gao, T.: Dangerous breathing-PM2.5: measuring the human health and economic impacts on China's largest cities. Technical report, Greenpeace (2012)
2. Cuevas, A., Urueña, M., Cuevas, R., Romeral, R.: Modelling data-aggregation in multi-replication data centric storage systems for wireless sensor and actor networks. IET Commun. **5**(12), 1669–1681 (2011)
3. Chuang, T.-Y., Chen, K.-C., Poor, H.V.: Information centric sensor network management via community structure. IEEE Commun. Lett. **19**(5), 767–770 (2015)
4. Zabin, F., Misra, S., Woungang, I., Rashvand, H.F., Ma, N.-W., Ali, M.A.: REEP: data-centric, energy-efficient and reliable routing protocol for wireless sensor networks. IET Commun. **2**(8), 995–1008 (2008)
5. Hoang, X., Lee, Y.: An efficient scheme for reducing overhead in data-centric storage sensor networks. IEEE Commun. Lett. **13**(12), 989–991 (2009)
6. Si, P., Ji, H., Yu, F.R., Leung, V.C.: Optimal cooperative internetwork spectrum sharing for cognitive radio systems with spectrum pooling. IEEE Trans. Veh. Technol. **59**(4), 1760–1768 (2010)
7. Si, P., Yu, F.R., Zhang, Y.: Joint cloud and radio resource management for video transmissions in mobile cloud computing networks. In: Proceedings of the IEEE International Conference on Communications (ICC), Sydney, Australia, pp. 2270–2275. IEEE, June 2014
8. Whittle, P.: Restless bandits: activity allocation in a changing world. In: Gani, J. (ed.) A Celebration of Applied Probability. J. Appl. Probab., vol. 25, pp. 287–298. Applied Probability Trust, Sheffield (1988)
9. Sarkar, T.K., Ji, Z., Kim, K., Medouri, A., Salazar-Palma, M.: A survey of various propagation models for mobile communication. IEEE Antennas Propag. Mag. **45**(3), 51–82 (2003)
10. Gusev, A., Chambers, N., Khaitan, P., Khilnani, D., Bethard, S., Jurafsky, D.: Using query patterns to learn the duration of events. In: Proceedings of the Ninth International Conference on Computational Semantics (IWCS), Oxford, UK, pp. 145–154. Association for Computational Linguistics, January 2011
11. Si, P., Yu, F.R., Wang, H., Zhang, Y.: Optimal transmission behaviour policies of secondary users in proactive-optimization cognitive radio networks. China Commun. **10**(8), 1–17 (2013)
12. Bertsimas, D., Niño-Mora, J.: Restless bandits, linear programming relaxations, and a primal-dual index heuristic. Oper. Res. **48**(1), 80–90 (2000)

A Novel Location Privacy Mining Threat in Vehicular Internet Access Service

Yipin Sun[✉], Shuhui Chen, Biao Han, Bofeng Zhang, and Jinshu Su

School of Computer, National University of Defense Technology,
Changsha 410073, Hunan, People's Republic of China
{ypsun,shchen,nudtbill,bfzhang,sjs}@nudt.edu.cn

Abstract. Due to the limited communication range and the unbalance distribution of Wi-Fi access points, the disconnection gap during vehicular Internet access almost depends on the access point distribution along the driving path. In this way, with the vehicle mobility statistics, the service provider of account-based web service (i.e., Email and Weblog) could mine the current access point of an interested account owner by the sequence of disconnection gap. As the first paper to study this issue, we propose a probability algorithm for location mining that can be computed recursively with the length of communication feature sequence. Real map based simulations evaluate the location privacy threat and the relationship with the density of access points and communication feature classes.

Keywords: VANET · Vehicular Internet access · Location privacy mining · Disconnection gap

1 Introduction

Vehicular Ad Hoc Networks (VANET) is a promising network paradigm for facilitating road safety, traffic management, and in-vehicle entertainment. Specially, equipped with a Wi-Fi radio, vehicles could access the Internet by the Roadside Units (RSUs) [1]. According to Dedicated Short Range Communications (DSRC)[2], the data rate of the infrastructure-to-vehicle (I2V) communication could be as high as 27Mbps. In this way, compared with the off-the-shelf cellular networks in terms of cost and bandwidth, vehicular Internet access is regarded as a standard feature of motor vehicles to satisfy the ever-increasing Internet demand of passengers [3].

Attracted by the bride future of Wi-Fi based vehicular Internet access, the evaluation and deployment issues had been well studied over the last decade [4–6]. However, it is worth noting that few works pay attention to the privacy issues in vehicular Internet access. In fact, as a double-edged sword, most of VANET applications brings serious concern on the driver's privacy [7,8]. For example, in safety-related application, the adversary could link the mobility trace according to the spatial and temporal correlation between successive locations [9,10].

© Springer International Publishing Switzerland 2015
K. Xu and J. Zhu (Eds.): WASA 2015, LNCS 9204, pp. 467–476, 2015.
DOI: 10.1007/978-3-319-21837-3_46

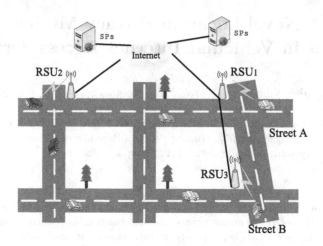

Fig. 1. Vehicular Internet access

Contrasted with other network scenarios, the spatial and temporal correlation of vehicle mobility is regarded as a special lever for location privacy threat in VANET. With the similar opinion, vehicular Internet access seems to be not invulnerable against privacy threat. As shown in Fig. 1, the passengers could use the vehicular Internet access on road. The location of RSUs and the average driving velocity are known by the public. Suppose a passenger who driving along $Street_A$ browses his private web account (e.g., Email account or Facebook account) when passing by RSU_1 and RSU_2. Due to the limited communication range, there is a bounded disconnection gap during Internet accessing. In this way, according to the correlation of the velocity, the disconnection gap time, and the distance between RSUs, the web service provider (SP) could deduce that the account owner travels along $Street_A$ (not $Street_B$) and is in the communication range of RSU_2 (not RSU_3) now.

Generally, the new privacy threat is caused by the following key elements: (1) The SP could link all access actions by the long-term account ID. This is a new capability for the privacy adversary compared with other threat model known by public. (2) RSUs usually refer to the open Wi-Fi access point in vehicular Internet access. Since open Wi-Fi access point is provided by different organizations, the communication features from each RSU would be different, such as IP address, bandwidth, and disconnection gap. (3) The mobility of vehicle accords with certain spatial and temporal statistics. With the mobility statistics, it is possible to evaluate the probability relationship between the driving path and the communication feature sequence observed by the SPs.

To the best of our knowledge, this is the first paper to study the above-mentioned privacy threat in vehicular Internet access. Specially, our contributions are threefold:

- First, we present the system model and threat model for vehicular Internet access, and indicate a new location privacy mining threat that the web SP

could deduce the current access point of an interested account owner based on the communication feature sequence and the vehicle mobility statistics.
- Second, we formalize the location mining threat and further propose a probability algorithm for location mining which could be computed recursively with the length of the communication feature sequence.
- Finally, utilizing the reality road map, extensive simulations evaluate the threat of the accessed RSU problem. The simulations demonstrate that the spatial and temporal correlation of vehicle mobility is a special lever for location privacy threat.

The remainder of the paper is organized as follows. Section 2 presents the system model. Section 3 formalizes the location threat problem and presents the probability algorithm for location mining, following by the threat evaluation in Sect. 4. Section 5 concludes the paper.

2　System Model

As shown in Fig. 1, a typical scenario of vehicular Internet access consists of three entities:

- **SP:** SP is the service provider of account-based web services, i.e., e-mail, and Weblog. With the claimed purpose of auditing or improving service quality, SPs may record the communication features of network visitor, including the time stamp, account id, IP address, network bandwidth, requested resource, session cookies, and so on. Maybe most of SPs are strictly self-discipline, but until now there is no strong technology mechanism to supervise how the logs to be utilized further.
- **RSU:** RSUs act as the infrastructure of VANETs and connect with the SP by wired links. They provide service for information dissemination and Internet access. To reduce the deployment cost, open Wifi access points is widely regarded as the main source of RSUs, especially in the early stage of VANET. In this way, the RSU distribution would be out of layout, and the communication feature of RSUs would be various, such as IP pools, and link bandwidth. Generally, the location and communication features of RSUs are known by public.
- **Passenger:** Passengers travel by the vehicles equipped with OBUs. Through the vehicular Internet access, the passenger could request web service from the SP during the trip. With an increasing demand for Internet data, the passenger may utilize vehicular Internet access as long as passing by RSUs. However, the passengers do not have the priority to adjust driving path for more accessing chance.

3　Location Privacy Threat

To simply the formulation, the following assumptions are adopted: (1) The road maps and traffic statistics are known by the public. Different from traditional

Table 1. Notations

Symbol	Notation
v_i	The i-th intersection
V_G^R	The vertices set with deployed RSUs
$S_{x,y}$	The vertex set on the shortest path from v_x to v_y
$S_{x,y}^R$	The vertices subset with deployed RSUs of $S_{x,y}$
$S_{x,y}^{R^*}$	The vertices subset with accessed RSUs during the trip along $S_{x,y}$
v_*	The vertex where the RSU is accessed currently
v_+	The vertex where the RSU is pre-accessed before v_*
v_-	The vertex where the RSU is accessed firstly during a travel
O^n	The observation sequence

mobile ad hoc networks, the movement of vehicles is restricted on roads. Moreover, the mobility profiles and traffic statistics are published by the government for traffic optimization [11]. (2) Most of RSUs are deployed at road intersections. Otherwise, the RSU position will be regarded as a virtual intersection in the literature. (3) The vehicle prefers the shortest path to the destination.

3.1   Formulation

Let $G =< V_G, V_G^R, E_G >$ denote the simplified road map, i.e., v_i denote the i-th intersection, and $e_{i,j}$ denote the the road segment that connect v_i with v_j. Moreover, the edge weight is valued with the expectant driving time between these two intersections according to the traffic statistics. Let $S_{x,y}$ denote the vertex set of the shortest path from v_x to v_y. In this way, given $v_i \in S_{x,y}$,then $S_{x,y} = S_{x,i} \cup S_{i,y}$. Suppose the popular probability that the vehicles drives from v_x to v_y is known as $\alpha_{x,y}$, and the driving time distribution from v_x to v_j is known as $f_{x,y}(\triangle t)$. Furthermore, $\sum_{v_x,v_y \in V_G} \alpha_{x,y} = 1$, and $\sum_{\triangle t \in [0,\infty]} f_{x,y}(\triangle t) = 1$. Let V_G^R denote the vertices set with deployed RSUs, and $S_{x,y}^R$ denote the vertices subset with deployed RSUs of $S_{x,y}$. Obviously, $V_G^R \subseteq V_G$, and $S_{x,y}^R = V_G^R \cap S_{x,y}$.

According to the above definitions (Table 1), as shown in Fig. 2, it can be seen that $V_G^R = \{v_4, v_5, v_7, v_8, v_{11}, v_{14}\}$, $S_{3,12} = \{v_3, v_7, v_8, v_{11}, v_{12}\}$, and $S_{3,12}^R = \{v_7, v_8, v_{11}\}$.

Suppose the probability that a passenger requesting the service from the SP when passing by a RSU is known as q. Let S^{R^*} denote the vertex set where the RSU is accessed, v_* denote the vertex where the RSU is accessed currently, v_+ denote the vertex where the RSU is pre-accessed before v_*, v_- denote the vertex where the RSU is accessed firstly during a trip. In this way, for a passenger traveling along $S_{x,y}$, given $v_- = v_i$, and $v_* = v_j$, it means that the passenger given up the access chance when passing by the RSU set, i.e., $S_{x,i}^R - \{v_i\}$. Thus, the conditional probability could be computed as:

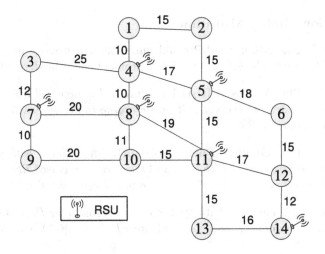

Fig. 2. An formalization instance of street map

$$Pr(v_- = v_i, v_* = v_j \mid S_{x,y}) = \begin{cases} (1-q)^{|S_{x,i}^R|-1} * q^2, v_i, v_j \in S_{x,y}^R \\ \\ 0, otherwise \end{cases} \tag{1}$$

Furthermore, the probability of the situation, $(v_- = v_i, v_* = v_j)$, could be computed as:

$$Pr(v_- = v_i, v_* = v_j) = \sum_{v_x, v_y \in V_G} Pr(v_- = v_i, v_* = v_j \mid S_{x,y}) * \alpha_{x,y} \tag{2}$$

Without loss of generally, $\{S_{x,i}^R\}$ and $\{Pr(v_- = v_i, v_* = v_j)\}$ could be pre-computed. The computation cost is ignored in the following literature.

When a passenger requests service from a SP, the SP will compute the observation log (denoted as o), including the disconnection gap Δt and the candidate RSU set (denoted as C) according with other communication features. If Δt is larger than the threshold δ, the observation log is counted as the first one, i.e., $o_1 = \{\Delta t_1, C_1\}$. Given $v_* = v_j$, the probability to observe o_1 depends on $v_- = v_j \in C_1$, i.e.,

$$Pr(o_1 \mid v_- = v_i, v_* = v_j) = \begin{cases} 1 & v_i = v_j \in C_1 \\ 0 & otherwise \end{cases} \tag{3}$$

Let O^n denote the observation sequence, i.e., $O^n = \{o_1, ..., o_{n-1}, o_n\}$. In this way, given $v_+ = v_i$, $v_* = v_j$, observing o_k means the vehicle is driving from v_+ to v_* with time Δt_k, and the passenger did not request service when passing by the RSUs, i.e., $S_{i,j}^R - \{v_i, v_j\}$. So that the probability could be computed as:

$$Pr(o_k \mid v_+ = v_i, v_* = v_j) = \begin{cases} f_{i,j}(\Delta t_k) * (1-q)^{|S_{i,j}^R|-2} & v_j \in C_k \\ 0 & otherwise \end{cases} \tag{4}$$

3.2   Location Mining Algorithm

Through the formalization, the SP could mine location privacy by probability evaluation. Moveover, the following privacy problem could be derived.

Definition 1 (The Accessed RSU Problem). *The accessed RSU problem is stated to find the current accessed RSU v_* according to the observation sequence O^n, i.e., find $\max Pr(v_*|O^n)$.*

Definition 2 (The Driving Path Problem). *The driving path problem is stated to find the first accessed RSU v_- and the current accessed RSU v_* according to the observation sequence O^n, i.e., find $\max Pr(v_-, v_*|O^n)$.*

According to conditional probability theorem, to find $\max Pr(v_*|O^n)$ equals to find $\max Pr(v_*, O^n)$, and to find $\max Pr(v_-, v_*|O^n)$ equals to find $\max Pr(v_-, v_*, O^n)$.

Moreover, according to the law of total probability, the following relationship is proposed:

$$Pr(v_* = v_j, O^n) = \sum_{v_i, \in V_G^R} Pr(v_- = v_i, v_* = v_j, O^n) \tag{5}$$

$$Pr(v_- = v_i, v_* = v_j, O^n) = Pr(O^n|v_- = v_i, v_* = v_j) * Pr(v_- = v_i, v_* = v_j) \tag{6}$$

Therefore, the key issue to mine location privacy is transformed to compute $Pr(O^n|v_- = v_i, v_* = v_j)$. In this way, utilizing $\{v_+ \in S_{i,j}^R\}$ as a probability partition, and then

$$Pr(O^n|v_- = v_i, v_* = v_j) = \sum_{v_k \in S_{i,j}^R} Pr(v_+ = v_k, O^n|v_- = v_i, v_* = v_j) \tag{7}$$

Furthermore, the event $(v_+ = v_k, O^n|v_- = v_i, v_* = v_j)$ can be divided into the concurrence of two independent events, i.e., $(O^{n-1}|v_- = v_i, v_* = v_k)$, and $(o_n \mid v_+ = v_k, v_* = v_j)$, and then an iterative relationship is proposed:

$$Pr(O^n|v_- = v_i, v_* = v_j) = \sum_{v_k \in S_{i,j}^R} Pr(O^{n-1}|v_- = v_i, v_* = v_k) * Pr(o_n \mid v_+ = v_k, v_* = v_j) \tag{8}$$

In conclusion, the location mining algorithm is listed in Algorithm 1. According to the iterative relationship for $Pr(O^n|v_- = v_i, v_* = v_j)$, the storage cost is $O(|V_G^R|^2)$. Let λ denote the maximum size of $S_{i,j}^R$, i.e., $\lambda = \max |S_{i,j}^R|$, and then the total computation cost of the algorithm is $O(n * \lambda * |V_G^R|^2)$. Moreover, based on the middle result for O^{n-1}, the increment computation cost for O^{n-1} is $O(\lambda * V_G^{R^2})$. Generally, because $n \leqslant \lambda$, and $\lambda \ll |V_G^R|$, and then the increment computation cost is almost as much as $O(|V_G^R|^2)$.

Algorithm 1. [A1] Location Privacy Mining

Data: O^n
Result: $\max Pr(v_*, O^n)$, $\max Pr(v_-, v_*, O^n)$
begin
    for $x \in [1, n]$ **do**
        for *each* $v_i \in V_G^R$ **do**
            for *each* $v_j \in V_G^R$ **do**
                | Compute $Pr(O^x | v_- = v_i, v_* = v_j)$
            end
        end
    end
    for *each* $v_j \in V_G^R$ **do**
        for *each* $v_i \in V_G^R$ **do**
            | Compute $Pr(v_- = v_i, v_* = v_j, O^n)$
        end
        Compute $Pr(v_* = v_j, O^n)$
    end
    return $(\max Pr(v_*, O^n), \max Pr(v_-, v_*, O^n))$
end

---

4   Threat Evaluation

To evaluate our scheme, we select the map of the West University Place and Braeswood Place, Houston, TX, USA from the publicly available TIGER (Topologically Integrated Geographic Encoding and Referencing) database of the U.S. Census Bureau [13]. Excluding few highways in this $5\,km \times 5\,km$ area, there are 1713 intersections(denoted as MAP_{1713}), as shown in Fig. 3(a). For simplicity, we recursively omit the intersections where less than 3 roads are connected. As shown in Fig. 3(b), there are 885 intersections left after the predigestion (denoted as MAP_{885}). Moreover, we simulate mobility traces with SUMO [12], a urban mobility simulator. For each intersection in MAP_{885}, traffic light with the signal period of $94\,s$ is built as same as the simulation with SUMO, and the average waiting time at the intersection is $19\,s$. When a simulation start, the signal period of each traffic light set with a random value in [0s, 47s]. The velocity of each road segment randomly fluctuates in the range $15\,m/s \pm \mu\,\%$. With the average speed of $15\,m/s$, the shortest path between each intersections is computed. Suppose the vehicles prefer the shortest path that the driving time of which is larger than $720\,s$. For each selected shortest path, 1000 simulations run to obtain the driving time distribution $f_{x,y}(\Delta t)$.

Suppose the RSUs are deployed randomly, and let γ denote the deployment density. Given the $\gamma = 0.05$, 0.1 and 0.15, three deployment scenarios are generated with 45, 83, 131 RSUs respectively. Due to the signal attenuation of buildings, the RSU communication coverage is restricted within the road segment connected with RSU intersections directly, and the maximal coverage is less than $300\,m$. To simulate the data mining capability of SPs, suppose the

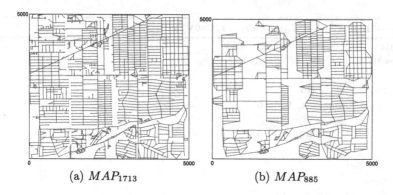

(a) MAP_{1713} (b) MAP_{885}

Fig. 3. West University Place and Braeswood Place, Houston, 5 km × 5 km. (a) Original map with 1713 intersections; (b) 885 intersections left after predigestion.

SP could map the RSUs into ω candidate classes based on the communication features. In other words, the SP could judge which candidate class the current accessed RSU belongs to according to the communication features. The larger the ω is, the stronger the data mining capability of SPs is. Suppose RSUs are divided into ω candidate classes uniformly, and then the packets from the RSUs would take the corresponding tag in the simulations.

In terms of the similarity between the accessed RSU problem and the driving path problem, the following simulations just evaluate the former one. When passing by RSUs, the passenger would request service from the SP, and the SP would try to deduce the accessed RSU according to the proposed algorithm in Sect. 3. The locating ratio is defined as the ratio between the number of success mining and the total number of service requesting, and is adopted as a benchmark to evaluate the location privacy threat. Obviously, the larger the locating ratio is, the more serious the location privacy threat is.

It's worth noting that a simulation scenario in this paper is restricted by three key parameters, i.e., the velocity variance μ, the communication feature based RSU classes number ω and the RSU density γ. Given a simulation scenario, the average locating ratio is computed after 1000 simulations ran.

Figure 4 presents the locating ratios of 18 simulation scenarios, i.e., given the velocity variance $\mu\% = 20\%$ while the RSU classes number $\omega \in [1,6]$, and the RSU density $\gamma \in \{0.05, 0.1, 0.15\}$ (the corresponding RSU number is 45, 83, 131). The location ratios indicate that the location privacy threat in vehicular Internet access should be recognized seriously. For example, the maximal location ratio is almost as large as 0.8. On the other hand, although the minimal location ratio is 0.247, it means the equivalent anonymity size for privacy preservation is 4, which also make the privacy-sensitive passengers stewed. Moreover, it is worth noting that the SP could store all judgement result in long term, and do further mining to amend the failed judgement or assistant the current judgement. In fact, the bypass location information is still efficient to indicate more privacy information, such as identity, and consumption habits.

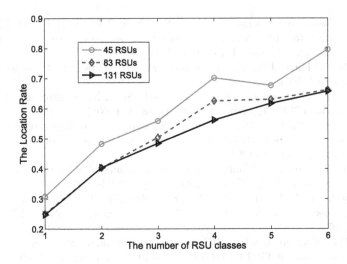

Fig. 4. Location ratio vs RSU density and communication features

5 Conclusions

In this paper, we indicate that passengers may leak location privacy to the web service provider when using vehicular Internet access. According to the proposed probability mining algorithm, real map based simulations demonstrate the fearful location threat. Moreover, our future work will evaluate the location privacy threat and the relationship with the velocity variances, the density of access points, communication feature classes, and the disconnection gap sequences.

Acknowledgements. This work was supported by the National Natural Science Foundation of China under Grant No. 61202482, No. 61303264, No. 61202488, and No. 61379148.

References

1. Ott, J., Kutscher, D.: Drive-thru internet: IEEE 802.11b for automobile users. In: Proceedings of the IEEE INFOCOM, pp. 362–373 (2004)
2. DSRC ITS standards advisory. http://grouper.ieee.org/groups/scc32/dsrc/index. html
3. KPMGs Global Automotive Executive Survey. http://www.kpmg. com/GE/en/IssuesAndInsights/ArticlesPublications/Documents/ Global-automotive-executive-survey-2012.pdf
4. Balasubramanian, A., Mahajan, R., Venkataramani, A., Levine, B.N., Zahorjan, J.: Interactive WiFi connectivity for moving vehicles. In: Proceedings of the ACM SIGCOMM, pp. 427–438 (2008)
5. Zheng, Z., Sinha, P., Kumar, S.: Sparse WiFi deployment for vehicular internet access with bounded interconnection gap. IEEE/ACM Trans. Network. **20**(3), 956–969 (2012)

6. Lu, N., Zhang, N., Cheng, N., Shen, X., Mark, J.W., Bai, F.: Vehicles meet infrastructure: toward capacity-cost tradeoffs for vehicular access networks. IEEE Trans. Intell. Transp. Syst. **14**(3), 1266–1277 (2013)

7. Raya, M., Hubaux, J.P.: Securing vehicular ad hoc networks. J. Comput. Secur. **15**(1), 39–68 (2007)

8. Lin, X., Lu, R., Zhang, C., Zhu, H., Ho, P.-H., Shen, X.: Security in vehicular ad hoc networks. IEEE Commun. Mag. **46**(4), 88–95 (2008)

9. Liu, X., Zhao, H., Pan, M., Yue, H., Li, X., Fang, Y.: Traffic-aware multiple mix zone placement for protecting location privacy. In: Proceedings of the IEEE INFO-COM 2012, pp. 972–980 (2012)

10. Ying, B., Makrakis, D., Mouftah, H.T.: Dynamic mix-zone for location privacy in vehicular networks. IEEE Commun. Lett. **17**(8), 1524–1527 (2013)

11. Sampigethaya, K., Li, M., Huang, L., Poovendran, R.: AMOEBA: robust location privacy scheme for VANET. IEEE J. Sel. Areas Commun. (JSAC) **25**(8), 1569–1589 (2007)

12. Simulation of urban mobility (SUMO). http://sumo.sourceforge.net

13. U.S. Census Bureau: TIGER, TIGER/Line and TIGER-Related Products. http://www.census.gov/geo/www/tiger/

iProtect: Detecting Physical Assault Using Smartphone

Zehao Sun[1], Shaojie Tang[3], He Huang[2]([⊠]), Liusheng Huang[1],
Zhenyu Zhu[1], Hansong Guo[1], and Yu-e Sun[2]

[1] University of Science and Technology of China, Hefei, China
[2] Soochow University, Suzhou, China
huangh@suda.edu.cn
[3] University of Texas at Dallas, Dallas, TX, USA

Abstract. Motivated by the reports about assaults on women, especially college girls, in China, we take the first step to explore possibility of using off-the-shelf smartphone for physical assault detection. The most difficult one among challenges in our design is the extraordinary complexity and diversity of various assault instances, which lead to an extremely hard, if not impossible, to perform fine-grained recognition. To this end, we decide to focus on the characteristics of intensity and irregularity, based on which several features are extracted. Moreover, we proposed a combinatorial classification scheme considering individuality of user's ADLs(Activities of Daily Living) and universality of differences between ADLs and assaults to most people. The data we used for evaluation are collected from simulated assaults which are performed by our volunteers in controlled settings. Our experiment results showed that physical assaults could be distinguished with the majority of ADLs in our proposed feature space, and our proposed system could correctly detect most instances of aggravated assault with low false alarm rate and short delay.

Keywords: Assault detection · Smartphone sensing · Activity recognition · Machine learning

1 Introduction

As smartphones equipped with various sensors are increasingly prevalent, activity recognition is becoming one of the emerging mobile applications in the area of ubiquitous computing [1]. Successful researches have so far focused on many real-life, human-centric tasks such as: healthcare [3], harmful habit [4], socialization [5] and so on. However, few of the existing works has ever explored the possibility of using smartphone to detect or even prevent potential crime. According to the 2013 crime statistics from NIBRS released by FBI [6], there are 1,120,614 incidents of crimes against persons with 1,289,799 victims. Thus we believe that crime detection and prevention using personal mobile devices is another very important research issue that needs more attention from researchers.

© Springer International Publishing Switzerland 2015
K. Xu and J. Zhu (Eds.): WASA 2015, LNCS 9204, pp. 477–486, 2015.
DOI: 10.1007/978-3-319-21837-3_47

Despite the deficiency of researches about personal security against crime offences in the area of ubiquitous computing, there have been a plenty of commercial mobile applications on smartphone for citizen emergency management. For example, EmergenSee [7] could transmit live video, audio, location, etc. of user's incident directly to pre-selected emergency contacts for help by just one tap. iGoSafely [8] is another personal security alarm and emergency contact notification tool which can be activated by simply plugging in headphones. However, in most circumstances, people encountering violence may not have chance to take out their phone and open the app. To this end, a passive and real-time crime detection system is highly desired.

In this paper, for the first time, we propose a non-intrusive and real-time method for detecting ongoing aggravated assault using smart phones. The proposed solution leverages the accelerometer sensor equipped on most off-the-shelf smartphones to capture actions and movements of human body under aggravated assaults, which can accurately identify whether user is being assaulted in real time. The main contributions of this work are as follows:

(1) To distinguish aggravated assaults and ADLs, we extracted several features from raw accelerometer readings, which are demonstrated to be discriminative by our evaluation.
(2) Considering the difficulty of collecting training data of aggravated assaults from users and the imbalance distribution of classes, we designed a combinatorial classification scheme, based on which a probabilistic threshold method is used to make the final judgement about user's status.
(3) To evaluate the performance of our proposed system, we collected sensor data of actions under aggravated assaults by imitating the process of real instances in the surveillance videos. Results of the experiments showed that our proposed system could correctly detect most instances while keeps little false alarm rate and short delay.

2   Background

To acquire knowledge of aggravated assault in aspects of recognizable characteristics, for the first time, we collect and analyze 100 surveillance videos involving aggravated assault. For each video, we extract the duration of the instance and the performed actions of victims and assailants respectively which belongs to a vocabulary we defined to depict the possible actions in the instance of aggravated assault. The vocabulary contains 20 verbs or phrases, and the statistics are presented in Fig. 1.

Although these verbs and phrases covered most actions, it is extremely difficult if not impossible to define aggravated assaults using a simple and common rule. We argued that fine-grained recognition of assaults is particularly hard because: (1) actions of real assault are fast and each action may last for a very short duration leading to the difficulty to find the boundary between actions; (2) the accelerometer reading at every moment is influenced concurrently by

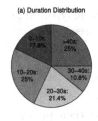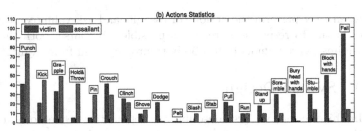

Fig. 1. Statistics of 100 surveillance videos

initiative actions of victim to fight or flee, force from assailant and interference to actions from ambience, which blur the signal unidirectionally and make it impossible to recur the actions reversely. Thus we decide to first extract some coarse-grained and general characteristics of aggravated assault by analyzing our surveillance videos. The characteristics are as follow:

- *Fierceness:* It is obvious that actions of assailant in real situation are always extremely powerful and destructive, and as a result, the victim has to act intensively to fight or flee. Thus, the first characteristic of actions under aggravated assaults is fierce. Of course, there are fierce actions in ADLs as well, such as running, jumping, thus we extracted next characteristic to distinguish such fierce ADLs.
- *Irregularity:* The fierce actions in ADLs are mostly come from sports, such as running and jumping, the shared characteristic of which is that these actions are repetitive. However actions under assaulting are always not repetitive, because the real situation is extremely complex and disordered, where victim act to fight or flee while assailant act to maximize his force on victim, none of them could act in a totally initiative manner.

The base intuitions of our solution are two folds: Firstly, ADLs are not as fierce and irregular simultaneously as actions under aggravated assault. Secondly, although there is diversity among actions of different instances of aggravated assault, they are consistent in aspects of fierceness and irregularity.

3   Data Collection

In order to collect original timestamped accelerometer data for analysis and experiments, we developed an application on Android platform which could keep running in the background. The data of ADLs are collected from volunteers who are asked to install and start our application on their smartphones, and then do whatever they are going to do like nothing have been happened. Since we did not find any existing dataset contains sensor records of smartphones from victims. We decide to obtain these data by imitating the process of real assault instances in our collected surveillance videos. To make our collected data more realistic, we ask volunteers who play the role of assailant to free all inhibitions when they perform the actions of assault, and ask volunteer who play the role of victim to response as really as possible. Of course, both the assailants and victims weared amors of full body to protect them from injury.

4   System Design

In this section, we first describe our segmentation method, and then present the features used to represent segments. After that, we introduce design of the combinatorial classification scheme. Then we introduce the procedure of assault detection.

4.1   Segmentation and Feature Extraction

Given the streaming accelerometer data, interval-based sliding window is used to generate segments with the same time span, which are the inputs of the following procedures. A sliding window is initialized once the system starts and filled by the real-time data until time span of current window reaches the preset interval threshold, then the data of current window will be output as a segment.

In order to distinguish actions under aggravated assaulting with actions of ADLs, for each segment, we extracted a feature vector which contains several features to measure the fierceness and irregularity. All the features are described as follows:

– *Intensity Features.* These features measure the energy level in a segment to reflect the intensity of actions: range and mean of accelerometer values in the segment, zero-crossing rate of the waveform taking the mean as the zero-crossing level, peak amplitude and spectral energy(except DC) in the frequency spectrum of the segment after performing DFT.
– *Irregularity Features.* Irregularity is another discriminative characteristic to distinguish actions under assaults with ADLs, thus we further compute auto-correlation, Lemple-Ziv complexity and sample entropy to extract regularity of a segment.

4.2   Segment Recognition

In this subsection, the design detail of our segment recognition procedure is introduced. The method we used to recognize is supervised classification, which is to construct classifiers by learning the training data and distinguish new coming data by the learned model.

Classification Scheme: To provide general knowledge of difference between ADLs and assaults for better recognition, we proposed *public ADLs and assaults samples database*, which contains data collected from users performing ADLs and victims who are assaulted. Since there is no such database currently, a primary mechanism to initialize and update such a database is introduced in the discussion section. Given the database, a general binary classifier could be learned with an objective to maximize the separation between objects of ADLs and assaults.

The classification scheme we used is a combinator of the individual one-class classifier and the general binary classifier. The former describes the individuality of a user's ADLs, while the later describes the universality of difference between ADLs and assaults to most people. Figure 2 present an example to illustrate the difference of the combinatorial classification scheme with other two schemes. Our proposed combinatorial classifier works as follows:

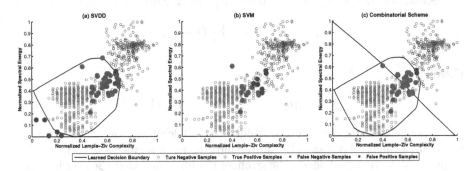

Fig. 2. Example of the combinatorial classification scheme (only two features are used for visualization)

- In the *training phase*, we first use SVDD(support vector data description)[9] to learn an individual one-class classifier C_1 using datasets collected from users. Then the general binary classifier C_2 is learned from *public ADLs and assaults samples database* using SVM. After that, the learned classifiers will be calibrated respectively using Platt scaling manner to enable probabilistic output.
- In the *using phase*, the feature vector F_t of current segment S_t will firstly be processed by the two calibrated classifiers respectively, each of which will generate an output containing a binary classification label $L_{i,t}$(0 for "ADLs" and 1 for "assaults") and a prediction probability $P_{i,t}$(range from 0 to 1). The final output of our combinatorial classification scheme is taken from the two outputs using the max-probability manner, i.e. the one with higher probability will be output as the final recognition result.

Calibration: We have mentioned above that probabilistic output are required to estimate the credibility of classification result, however all one-class classifiers and most binary classifiers could not output probability. The process to transform the outputs of a classifier into a probability distribution over classes is called calibration, and the technology we used to calibrate our classifiers is Platt scaling [10], which works by fitting a sigmoid to classifier's scores. In SVDD, the unthreshold classification score is the distance from an object to the center, while in SVM is the signed distance from an object to the decision hyperplane.

4.3 Assault Detection

Once the recognition result of current segment is generated, the assault detection procedure will than decide whether to trigger the alarm according to the classification labels and prediction probabilities of most recent several segments including the current one. Let $\{(L_{t-k+1}, P_{t-k+1}), (L_{t-k+2}, P_{t-k+2}), ..., (L_t, P_t)\}$ be a sequence of the most recent k recognition results at time t. Then we defined a detection confidence at time t, noted as A_t, which could be calculated as

$$A_t = sgn(\|T\|) - \prod_{j \in T} (1 - P_j),$$

where

$$T = \{j | L_j = 1, t - k + 1 \leq j \leq t\}$$

The formulation indicates the probability that at least one of the recognition results with the label of "assaults" in the most recent k segments is correct. The bigger the detection confidence, the stronger the likelihood that the user is being assaulted. An detection confidence threshold A_θ is used to decide whether alarm or not. Only when the realtime detection confidence A_t exceeds A_θ, is an alarm of being assaulted will generated to activate the related emergency applications.

5 Evaluation

In this section, we present the experiment results for the evaluation of iProctect. Firstly, we introduce the data sets, metrics, and methodology of the evaluation. Then, we study the impact of classifier model complexity on the performance of segments recognition. After that, we evaluate the impact of probability threshold and time-related parameters on the performance of detection and delay.

5.1 Datasets, Metrics and Methodology

We selected 100 surveillance videos of aggravated assaults to be the templets of our imitation, process of all these videos are recurred by 10 *victim volunteers*. Moreover, the data of ADLs of the 10 *victim volunteers* are also collected during their daily livings for 7 days. Since data of ADLs are easy to be obtained, there are another 50 *regular volunteers*, who are not involved in our assaults imitation, but contribute by providing samples of their ADLs which can be used to evaluate the false alarm rate.

We regard assaults as the positive class, and ADLs as negative class. Thus, *false positive* in the segment recognition level means that segments of ADLs are wrongly labeled as assaults, while in the instance detection level it means that false alarm is generated when the user is performing ADLs. On the other hand, *false negative* in the segment level means that segments of real assaults are wrongly labeled as ADls, and in the instance level it means that an instance of assault is not detected. The results of our experiment are reported in terms of false positive rates (FPR) and false negative rates (FNR) [11]. Note that, the FPR in the instance level we used is obtained by averaging the number of false alarms per day, thus, the unit of which is "times per day" rather than percentage used by FPR, FNR in segment level and FNR in instance level.

Besides, delay is also used as a performance metric in the evaluation of instance detection. The method we used to evaluate is cross validation, which works by partitioning the dataset into training and validation subsets, and averaging performance metrics over different partition cases.

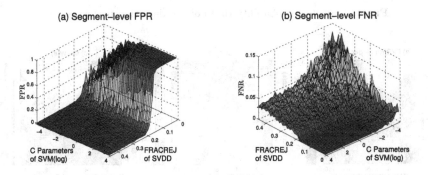

Fig. 3. Impact of model complexity to the performance of segments recognition

5.2   Impact of Model Complexity

Since our classification scheme is a combinator of SVDD and SVM, it is important to evaluate how the parameter choice of the two classifiers will influence the performance. In Fig. 3, we present our experiment results of parameters tuning. The parameter of SVDD we studied is FRACREJ, denoted as F for short, which is a parameter in the implementation by Duwin to tell the learning algorithm how many target objects in the training dataset could be rejected. And the parameter we studied in SVM is C-parameter, which is the penalty factor and could affect the model complexity. From the result, we can find that: (1) F-parameter of SVDD is the key factor of FPR; (2) when FPR takes the minimum value, FNR is accordingly raised to the maximum level, and vice versa; (3) FPR and FNR could be balanced when the F-parameter is around 0.2 and C-parameter is larger than 10^{-2} where both of the two metrics are below 5 %.

5.3   Impact of Probability Threshold

To evaluate the relationship between performance of assault detection and probability threshold, we calculate FPR, FNR, and delay at different probability threshold that ranges from 0.8 to 0.999 with the increment value of 0.001, while other parameters are set to default values. The results are plotted in Fig. 4, where

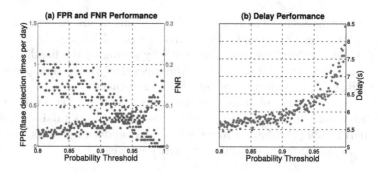

Fig. 4. Impact of probability threshold to detection performance

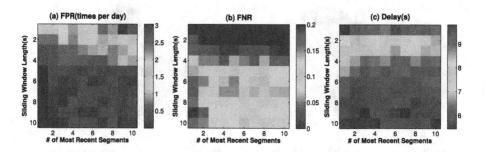

Fig. 5. Impact of time-related parameters to detection performance

we can observed that with the increase of the probability threshold, the FPR decreased from 2 times per day to nearly 0 times per day, and meanwhile the FNR increased from 1 % to above 10 %, which reflects that smaller probability threshold is apt to produce more false alarms, while bigger probability threshold is apt to miss more real assaults. On the other hand, delay is also apparently influenced by the probability threshold, and the the tendency of the delay along with the increase of probability threshold is in the same manner with the FNR, i.e. higher threshold leads to longer delay.

5.4   Impact of Time-Related Parameters

There are two time-related parameters in our system: sliding window length and the number of most recent segments. We evaluate the impact of these two parameters to the performance of assaults detection by fixing other parameters and changing these two parameters respectively. The overall results are presented in Fig. 5, where we can observe that: (1) the FPR could be decreased by shortening the sliding window length which meanwhile leads to the increase of the FNR; (2) the impact of the number of most recent segments to the FPR is not that obvious except when the sliding window length is set to 1 seconds; (3) it is surprising that when the sliding window length and the number of most recent segments are both set to the minimum, the delay reaches to the maximum, which could be explained that the time required to make a credible decision is larger when the information could be used is too little.

6   Related Work

There have been significant amount of prior works on activity recognition, which can be firstly classified according to the human activity domain of interest, most of previous works targeted on recognition of some specific activities, such as activities of daily living [12,13], healthcare [4], and so on. Besides, there are also works to recognize unseen or unspecific activities [14,15] by incorporating human knowledge about the similarity between different activities. These approaches are best fit to the activities with clear and simple pattern, and it cannot be applied to the problem of this paper due to the extremely diversity and complexity of actions under assaults.

In terms of the learning method, most of previous work [4,5,13] used supervised classification [21] approaches which require labeled data for the classifier learning. To lessen the reliance on labeled training data, some work [12,16,17] used semi-supervised learning or un-supervised learning [20]. In addition, active learning is another emerging approach for activity recognition [16,18], which is characterized by actively requesting labels from users when possible and thus avoid the boring training phase before using. The learning method we used is different with previous works due to the particularity of assaults, which is impossible to require user to provide training data of assaults. For this situation, anomaly detection [19] is a natural choice, which is always implemented as one-class classification. However, although one-class classification has the advantage that only data of target class is required for the learning, the performance is extremely susceptible to comprehensiveness of the training data. Based on this consideration, we proposed our combinatorial classification scheme.

7   Conclusion

In this paper, we present *iProtect*, a system using accelerometer equiped in the smartphones to detect aggravated physical assault on users. We analyze the characteristics of actions under assaulting, and propose a practical detection system which process the raw streaming accelerometer data and output the judgement of whether to trigger alarm. We conduct experiments to demonstrate the practicality of our system and evaluate impact of different parameters to the performance. And we will improve our detection system by incorporating acoustic recognition in the future work.

Acknowledgement. This paper is supported by the National Science and Technology Major Project under No. 2012ZX03005-009, National Science Foundation of China under No. U1301256, 61170058, Special Project on IoT of China NDRC (2012-2766), Research Fund for the Doctoral Program of Higher Education of China No. 20123402110019, and joint innovation fund of Jiangsu Provision No. BY2012127.

References

1. Lane, N.D., Miluzzo, E., Lu, H., Peebles, H.: A survey of mobile phone sensing. Commun. Mag. **48**(9), 140–150 (2010)
2. Ladha, C., Hammerla, N.Y., Olivier, P., et al.: ClimbAX: Skill assessment for climbing enthusiasts. In: Ubicomp 2013, ACM, pp 235–244 (2013)
3. Buman, M.P., et al.: Objective light-intensity physical activity associations with rated health in older adults. Am. J. Epidemiol. **172**(10), 1155–1165 (2010)
4. Parate, A., Chiu, M.C., et al.: RisQ: recognizing smoking gestures with inertial sensors on a wristband. In: Mobisys 2014, ACM, pp 149–161 (2014)
5. Hung, H., Englebienne, G., Kools, J.: Classifying social actions with a single accelerometer. In: Ubicomp 2013, ACM, pp 207–21 (2013)
6. NIBRS. http://www.fbi.gov/about-us/cjis/ucr/nibrs
7. EmergenSee. http://emergensee.com
8. iGoSafely. http://www.igosafely.com
9. Tax, D.M., Duin, R.P.: Support vector data description. Mach. Learn. **54**(1), 45–66 (2004)
10. PPlatt, J.: Probabilistic outputs for support vector machines and comparisons to regularized likelihood methods. Advances in large margin classifiers (1999)
11. Ward, J.A., et al.: TIST. Perform. Metrics Act. Recogn. **2**(1), 6 (2011)
12. Gu, T., et al.: An unsupervised approach to activity recognition and segmentation based on object-use fingerprints. Data Knowl. Eng. **69**(6), 533–544 (2010)
13. Kwapisz, J.R., Weiss, G.M., Moore, S.A.: Activity recognition using cell phone accelerometers. ACM SigKDD Explor. Newsl. **12**(2), 74–82 (2011)
14. Kong, Q., Maekawa, T.: Sharing training data among different activity classes. In: Ubicomp 2013, ACM, pp 701–712 (2013)
15. Cheng, H.T., Sun, F.T., et al.: Nuactiv: recognizing unseen new activities using semantic attribute-based learning. In: Mobisys 2013, ACM, pp 361–374 (2013)
16. Stikic, M., Van Laerhoven, K., Schiele, B.: Exploring semi-supervised and active learning for activity recognition. In: ISWC 2008, IEEE, pp 81–88 (2008)
17. Maekawa, T., Watanabe, S.: Unsupervised activity recognition with user's physical characteristics data. In: ISWC 2011, IEEE, pp 89–96 (2011)
18. Bagaveyev, S., Cook, D.J.: Designing and evaluating active learning methods for activity recognition. In: Ubicomp 2014, ACM, pp 469–478 (2014)
19. Yin, J., Yang, Q., Pan, J.J.: Sensor-based abnormal human-activity detection. IEEE Trans. Knowl. Data Eng. **20**(8), 1082–1090 (2008)
20. Zheng, Y., Jeon, B., Xu, D., Wu, Q.J., Zhang, H.: Image segmentation by generalized hierarchical fuzzy C-means algorithm. J. Intell. Fuzzy Syst. **28**(2), 961–973 (2015)
21. Gu, B., Sheng, V.S., Wang, Z., Ho, D., Osman, S., Li, S.: Incremental learning for support vector regression. Neural Netw. **67**, 140–150 (2015)

Enhancing Wireless Security Against Reactive Jamming Attacks: A Game-Theoretical Framework

Xiao Tang$^{(\boxtimes)}$, Pinyi Ren, Qinghe Du, and Li Sun

Department of Information and Communication Engineering,
Xi'an Jiaotong University, Xi'an 710049, China
xiaotang@stu.xjtu.edu.cn,
{pyren,duqinghe,lisun}@mail.xjtu.edu.cn

Abstract. Reactive jamming, which launches jamming attacks when the legitimate transmissions are detected, is one of the most serious security threats in wireless communications. In this paper, we investigate the wireless security issue in the presence of a reactive jammer from a game-theoretical perspective. Specifically, the legitimate user and jammer respectively aim at maximize and minimize the expected legitimate transmission rate, which is formulated as a zero-sum game. For the jammer, we consider the imperfection in detection and analyze the optimal jamming strategy by the joint optimization over detection time and jamming power. For the legitimate user, the transmit power is optimized by achieving the tradeoff between obtained transmission rate and the probability to be accurately detected and thus jammed by its adversary. The Nash equilibrium is characterized by the best-response playing between the legitimate user and reactive jammer. Finally, we present simulation results to verify the effectiveness of our proposed approach.

Keywords: Wireless security · Reactive jamming · Zero-sum game · Nash equilibrium

1 Introduction

The open and shared nature of wireless medium makes wireless communications vulnerable to jamming attacks [1]. Jamming attacks can be easily launched by the malicious nodes in almost any kind of wireless networks while cause significant quality-of-service degradation at the legitimate transmissions [2]. To defend jamming towards secure wireless communications, various approaches have been proposed in the literature, such as frequency hopping [3], direct sequence spread spectrum [4], and so on.

Despite the effectiveness of those existing anti-jamming researches, they mainly target at the general constant jamming, where jamming attacks are

The research work reported in this paper is supported by the the National Natural Science Foundation of China (NSFC) under Grant No. 61431011.

K. Xu and J. Zhu (Eds.): WASA 2015, LNCS 9204, pp. 487–496, 2015.
DOI: 10.1007/978-3-319-21837-3_48

assumed to be conducted all the time [5]. While recently, a different category of jamming attack emerges: the reactive jamming [6]. Under such a policy, the jammer detects the legitimate transmission before taking actions. It launches jamming attacks when the legitimate transmissions are detected, and otherwise, stays idle. The reactive jamming is widely accepted as the most threatening type, to any kind of networks [7]. The reason includes two-folds. On one hand, such attacks are conducted discontinuously, which implies that they are more difficult to be discovered, thus allowing them more easily to avoid the countermeasures. On the other hand, they are conducted based on detection, which makes them more efficient and capable to save energy for long-lasting attacks. Therefore, it is of paramount importance to tackle the reactive jamming challenge for wireless security.

While currently, there are only limited research works targeting at the reactive jamming issue. The existing researches mainly focus on the reactive jamming detection [8] and a few countermeasures are proposed, such as utilization of timing channel [9], protocol design [10], and so on. Despite those inspiring works, there still lacks a precise mathematical model to study the reactive jamming and the details regarding detection-based reactive jamming are not yet clearly specified, which leaves some important questions unresponded. On the other hand, although being reactive makes the jammer smarter, it also induces certain disadvantages, because the jamming attacks are then highly dependent on the preceding detection. Obviously, the detection cannot be guaranteed to be perfect due to the link uncertainties such as pathloss, fading, and noise. The legitimate user can then take advantage of such imperfection to enhance its security. However, to the best of the authors' knowledge, there still lacks research work to tackle those problems currently.

Towards the issues noted above, in this paper, we investigate the reactive jamming problem for wireless security enhancement. We formulate the problem within a zero-sum game framework where the utility function is defined as the expected legitimate transmission rate. Specifically, we present a novel mathematical model for detection-based reactive jamming, where the imperfection in detection is considered. Based on the model, the reactive jammer needs to jointly optimize its detection time and jamming power so as to minimize the utility. Meanwhile, for the legitimate user, it elaborately selects the transmit power to maximize the utility, by achieving the tradeoff between the instantaneous transmission rate and the probability to be accurately detected and jammed. By the best-response playing iterations between them, the Nash equilibrium is reached. Finally, we present simulation results to verify the effectiveness of our proposal.

The reminder of this paper is organized as follows. In Sect. 2, we present the legitimate transmitting vs. jamming system model. In Sect. 3, the problem is formulated as a zero-sum game and the optimization at the legitimate user and jammer are respectively characterized. In Sect. 4, the joint optimization over detection time and jamming power is analyzed for the reactive jamming. In Sect. 5, the optimal strategy of legitimate user is presented. Section 6 highlights the simulation results and Sect. 7 concludes this paper.

2   System Model

We consider a wireless system that a legitimate transmitter-receiver pair[1] are communicating in the presence of a malicious jammer, as shown in Fig. 1(a). The legitimate user aims at improving its transmit rate while on the contrary, the jammer tries to impair the legitimate transmissions by inject noise-like signals at the legitimate receiver's front end. Here, for notation simplicity, we use "T" and "J" to represent the legitimate transmitter and jammer, respectively. The power of legitimate transmission and jamming are denoted by p_T and p_J, respectively. Also, the channel gain of the legitimate transmission and jamming are denoted by h_T and h_J, respectively. If the wireless system is jamming-free, then the legitimate transmission rate is

$$r_1 = \log\left(1 + \frac{p_T h_T}{N_R}\right), \tag{1}$$

according to Shannon's theory, where N_R is the background noise power at the receiver. While if jamming attacks are in the presence of the legitimate transmissions, the legitimate transmission rate becomes

$$r_2 = \log\left(1 + \frac{p_T h_T}{p_J h_J + N_R}\right). \tag{2}$$

Note here, we assume unit bandwidth for the transmissions.

In this work, we consider that in practical wireless scenarios that the transmissions are not conducted all the time. Correspondingly, we here assume that the legitimate transmission is discontinuous, which is represented by a transmission possibility. Specifically, for a certain frame, the legitimate transmission occurs with probability α, and correspondingly, it stays idle with probability $1 - \alpha$.

Because of the discontinuous legitimate transmission, it would be unwise for the jammer to adopt the traditional constant jamming policy, which wastes significant amount of energy, especially when the legitimate transmission occurs with relatively low probability. Instead, the reactive jamming policy is employed, i.e., it detects the legitimate transmission beforehand while starts jamming when the detection returns positive results. Specifically, for whole frame duration T_f, part of it, βT_f, is used for detection, while the remaining part, $(1 - \beta) T_f$, is used for jamming. β is then referred to as the detection time portion. Based on system settings above, the timing of legitimate transmission and malicious jamming are shown in Fig. 1(b).

The reactive jamming policy helps the jammer to save energy, however, it also induces negative effects on jamming. Particularly, in actual wireless systems, due to unpredictable motions of the jamming target as well as stochastic factors such as fading and noise, the detection cannot be perfect. To model such imperfection, we here adopt the probability of detection and false alarm. The probability

---

[1] We also refer to the legitimate pair as legitimate user.

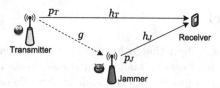

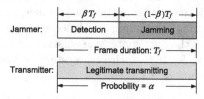

(a) The transmitting-jamming system model.

(b) Timing of the legitimate transmission and detection-based jamming.

Fig. 1. A wireless system that consists of a legitimate transmission pair and a malicious reactive jammer.

of detection, $\mathcal{P}_D$ and the probability of false alarm, $\mathcal{P}_F$. Based on [11], the probability of detection and false alarm can be given by

$$\mathcal{P}_D = Q\left(\left(\frac{\epsilon}{N_J} - \gamma - 1\right)\sqrt{\frac{\beta T_f f_s}{2\gamma + 1}}\right) \tag{3}$$

and

$$\mathcal{P}_F = Q\left(\left(\frac{\epsilon}{N_J} - 1\right)\sqrt{\beta T_f f_s}\right), \tag{4}$$

respectively, where $\gamma = \frac{p_T g}{N_J}$ is the received signal-to-noise ratio (SNR) at the jammer for detection with g being the detection channel gain and N_J being the noise power, ϵ is the detection threshold specified by the jammer, and f_s is the sampling frequency for detection. Also, $Q(\cdot)$ is the complementary distribution function of standard Gaussian, given as,

$$Q(x) = \frac{1}{\sqrt{2\pi}} \int_x^{\infty} \exp\left(-\frac{t^2}{2}\right) \mathrm{d}t. \tag{5}$$

Note that (3) and (4) hold under the assumption that a complex-valued phase-shift keying modulated signal is utilized. For the cases with different signal modulations, similar results on $\mathcal{P}_D$ and $\mathcal{P}_F$ can be given, and the analysis in the reminder of this paper can also be similarly proceeded.

3   Game-Based Problem Formulation

Naturally, the legitimate user and jammer have conflicting interests, both acting selfishly [12], thus it is appropriate to model their interactions within a non-cooperative game framework. In this section, we formulate the legitimate transmitting vs. jamming problem as a zero-sum game, a special category of non-cooperative game, and characterize its Nash equilibrium.

We first consider the case that legitimate transmissions are conducted. The whole frame duration is divided into two slots. In the first slot, the jammer performs detection, thus the utility is the jamming-free transmission rate

$$u_1 = r_1. \tag{6}$$

For the next slot, the legitimate transmission rate depends on the detection results. If the detection result is correct, which happens with probability $\mathcal{P}_D$, then jamming attack takes place, the legitimate transmission rate is then r_2. However, if the detection is not correct, the jammer stays idle and the legitimate transmissions enjoy jamming-free rate r_1. Thus the utility function is the expected legitimate transmission rate from this slot

$$u_2 = \mathcal{P}_D r_2 + (1 - \mathcal{P}_D) r_1. \tag{7}$$

If no legitimate transmission ever happens, the rate is zero and so is the utility. Therefore, the expected utility[2] can be presented by the time-weighted legitimate transmission rate in the two time slot, multiplied by the probability of legitimate transmissions

$$\begin{aligned} U &= \alpha \left[(\beta T_f) u_1 + (1 - \beta) T_f u_2 \right] \\ &= \alpha T_f \left\{ \beta r_1 + (1 - \beta) \left[\mathcal{P}_D r_2 + (1 - \mathcal{P}_D) r_1 \right] \right\}. \end{aligned} \tag{8}$$

Note the utility U is a function of both jamming power and legitimate transmission power as well as the detection time portion, given as $U(p_T, p_J, \beta)$. Since the expression includes Q-function, thus the optimization is rather complex, as we can see below.

For the legitimate user whose goal is to maximize the utility by optimize its transmit power while satisfying the average power consumption constraint P_T^{av}, the problem can be then formulated as

$$\max_{p_T} \quad U = \alpha T_f \left\{ \beta r_1 + (1 - \beta) \left[\mathcal{P}_D r_2 + (1 - \mathcal{P}_D) r_1 \right] \right\} \tag{9a}$$

$$\text{s. t.} \quad \alpha p_T \le P_T^{\mathrm{av}}. \tag{9b}$$

For the malicious reactive jammer, it tries to minimize the utility by jointly design its detection strategy and jamming strategy, i.e., the detection time and jamming power, under the average power consumption constraint. Specifically, the power consumption of jammer can be categorized into two cases. The first is the jamming attack against an actual legitimate transmission, with a probability $\alpha \mathcal{P}_D$. The second corresponds to a false alarm event, with a probability $(1 - \alpha) \mathcal{P}_F$. Note that for the second case, the energy is complete wasted. Then the power constraint can be represented by

$$(1 - \beta) \left[\alpha \mathcal{P}_D p_J + (1 - \alpha) \mathcal{P}_F p_J \right] \le P_J^{\mathrm{av}}. \tag{10}$$

---

[2] We will refer to the expected utility as utility for simplicity hereinafter.

To even strength the power constraint for energy conserving as a reactive jammer is usually motivated by its limited energy support, we impose an extra constraint on the energy that is wasted in a false alarm event. Specifically, we have $\mathcal{P}_F \leq \bar{\mathcal{P}}_F$. Therefore, the optimization problem at the jammer's side can be summarized as

$$\min_{p_J, \beta} \quad U = \alpha T_f \left\{ \beta r_1 + (1 - \beta) \left[\mathcal{P}_D r_2 + (1 - \mathcal{P}_D) r_1 \right] \right\} \tag{11a}$$

$$\text{s. t.} \quad 0 < \beta \leq 1 \tag{11b}$$

$$\mathcal{P}_F \leq \bar{\mathcal{P}}_F \tag{11c}$$

$$(1 - \beta) \left[\alpha \mathcal{P}_D p_J + (1 - \alpha) \mathcal{P}_F p_J \right] \leq P_J^{\mathrm{av}}, \tag{11d}$$

which indicates that the jammer has to determine the detection time portion and jamming power to minimize the utility to its best interests.

Based on the formulation above, the interactions between the legitimate user and reactive jammer can be modeled as a zero-sum game, where the utility function U is the payoff. For the legitimate user, its strategy space is given by $\Phi = \{p_T \,|((9b))$ is satisfied.$\}$. While for the jammer, its strategy space is given by $\Psi = \{\{p_J, \beta\} \,|(11b), (11c), (11d)$ are satisfied.$\}$.

The Nash equilibrium is referred to as the solution to a game model According to [13], Nash equilibrium for our proposed zero-sum game satisfies that

$$\max_{p_T} \min_{p_J, \beta} U = \min_{p_J, \beta} \max_{p_T} U, \tag{12}$$

which indicates that, the Nash equilibrium is a saddle point of the utility.

To achieve the Nash equilibrium, we apply the best-response strategy, which is exactly to solve the problem (9) and (11) at the legitimate user and reactive jammer with the strategy of the adversary fixed, given as

$$p_T^* = \mathsf{BR}_T \left(p_J, \beta \right) \quad \text{and} \quad \{p_J^*, \beta^*\} = \mathsf{BR}_J \left(p_T \right), \tag{13}$$

respectively. From the perspective of the best-response, the Nash equilibrium $\{p_T^*, p_J^*, \beta^*\}$ satisfies that $p_T^* = \mathsf{BR}_T \left(p_J^*, \beta^* \right)$ and $\{p_J^*, \beta^*\} = \mathsf{BR}_J \left(p_T^* \right)$, which implies that we can applies the best-response iteration to obtain the Nash equilibrium for the proposed game model. In the following two sections, we respectively address the optimization problem of for the reactive jammer and legitimate user, i.e., their best-response strategy.

4   Optimal Strategy for the Reactive Jammer

In this section, we investigate the Jammer's optimal jamming strategy with respect to the legitimate transmission power fixed, which is exactly to solve the optimization problem (11). To facilitate the solving procedure, we first characterize a few properties of the problem.

Proposition 1. *The optimization objective U in problem (11) is decreasing and convex with respect to jamming power p_J. Thus when the other parameters are fixed, the optimal is the maximum allowed jamming power.*

Proof. This conclusion is obvious thus the proof is omitted here.

Proposition 2. *The optimal solution to (11) is obtained with the constraints (11c) and (11d) are satisfied with equality.*

Proof. The proof is omitted here for space limitation.

With Proposition 2, the optimization given by (11) can be restated as

$$\min_{p_J, \beta} \quad U = \alpha T_f \left\{ \beta r_1 + (1 - \beta) \left[\mathcal{P}_D r_2 + (1 - \mathcal{P}_D) r_1 \right] \right\} \tag{14a}$$

$$\text{s. t.} \quad 0 < \beta \le 1 \tag{14b}$$

$$(1 - \beta) \left[\alpha \mathcal{P}_D p_J + (1 - \alpha) \bar{\mathcal{P}}_F p_J \right] = P_J^{\text{av}}, \tag{14c}$$

Further, for the problem (14), we have the followings.

Proposition 3. *Suppose that the probability of false alarm satisfies that $\mathcal{P}_F < 0.5$, the utility is convex with respect to the detection time portion β, thus the optimal β exists and is unique.*

Proof. The proof is omitted here for space limitation.

However, the optimization problem (11) is not jointly convex with respect to (β, p_J). To solve for the optimal, a two-step procedure can be performed. First, we calculate the optimal jamming power with detection time fixed. Second, the optimal detection time is obtained by one-dimensional searching. Specifically, for given detection time portion β, the optimal jamming power is the maximum power allowed, which can be obtained by solving the equality (14c). Then, by searching over the interval $[0, 1]$, we can then obtain the optimal time portion β^*. Finally, solving (14c) with β^* provides the optimal jamming power p_J^*.

5 Optimal Strategy for the Legitimate User

In this section, we propose the optimal strategy design for legitimate transmissions. In accordance with previous formulation, the legitimate user needs to deliberately determines the transmit power so as to maximize the expected legitimate transmission rate. Generally, the transmission rate increases with higher transmit power. However, in the presence of a reactive jammer, the relationship is not so straightforward. The increasing transmit power does increase the legitimate transmission rate. While it also enables the jammer more accurately detect the legitimate transmissions, which triggers jamming attacks. Therefore, there exists a tradeoff between the instantaneous legitimate transmission rate and the probability to be detected and jammed. Such a tradeoff is summarized in the optimization problem (9a).

For the problem (9a), we have the following proposition.

Proposition 4. *The utility function is continuous in the interval defined by (9b), thus an the optimal legitimate transmit power exits.*

Proof. This conclusion obviously holds thus the proof is omitted.

The maximization of a continuous function exists either at the extreme point or at the boundary point, while the extreme point can be obtained by $\frac{\partial U}{\partial p_T} = 0$, which can be calculated efficiently by bi-directional search.

6   Simulation Results

In this section, we evaluate our proposed strategy with numeric results to verify the effectiveness. We consider a wireless system as shown in Fig. 1. For the simulation, we simply set the frame duration $T_f = 1$ and the sampling rate $f_s = 1$. Also, the maximum probability of false alarm during the detection at the reactive jammer is $\bar{\mathcal{P}}_F = 0.01$. The background noise power at the front end of the jammer and the legitimate receiver are $N_J = N_R = 0.05$. The legitimate user has a probability of 0.8 to conduct legitimate transmission, i.e., $\alpha = 0.8$. The average power constraints are also the same as $P_T^{\mathrm{av}} = P_J^{\mathrm{av}} = 5$. The other relevant parameters are explained along with respective simulation results.

6.1   Convergence to Nash Equilibrium

We first verify the convergence to the Nash equilibrium of the game by the two players' best-response playing. The result is shown in Fig. 2. It is initialized by setting p_T, p_J, and β to be sufficiently small. Then the legitimate user and reactive jammer iteratively update their strategies by solving the optimal for (9) and (11), respectively. From Fig. 2, we can see that Nash equilibrium is reached rapidly, as only a few iterations are required.

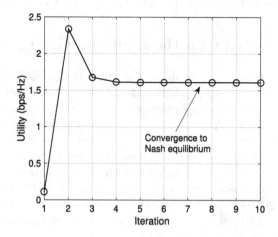

Fig. 2. Convergence to the Nash equilibrium by the best-response playing. ($h_T = h_J = 0.5$ and $g = 0.3$.)

6.2   Performance Evaluation

In this subsection, we evaluate the performance of the proposed strategy for the secure wireless transmissions. For the comparison, we consider the constant jamming policy as the baseline, which can also be modeled as a non-cooperative game. We can easily prove that under the constant jamming settings, the Nash equilibrium is reached when both players transmit with their maximum power. The numerical results are presented in Fig. 3.

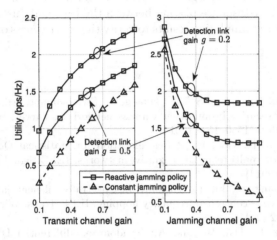

Fig. 3. The utility (expected legitimate transmission rate) with respect to legitimate link gain, jamming link gain, and detection link gain.

As we can see from the figure, the utility increases with improved legitimate transmit channel gain while decreases with better jamming channel gain. Compared with constant jamming case, the legitimate transmission rate is improved under reactive jamming. The reason includes two-folds. On one hand, the legitimate transmission suffers more severe interference under constant jamming because the attacks are conducted all the time. On the other hand, the reactive jamming considers the detection imperfection, which further degrades the jamming performance. While by contrast, the constant jammer is powerful and perfect, which is not as realistic as ours for practical wireless systems.

Also, we investigate the performance of reactive jamming against detection link gain. As we can see, when the detection link improves, the utility decreases. This is because that, with better detection link, the jammer can more accurately detect the legitimate transmissions. On one hand, it provides larger time portion for jamming attacks. On the other hand, the increased detection probability implies that the legitimate transmissions have greater chance to suffer jamming attacks. Therefore, the utility decreases with better detection link.

7   Conclusions

In this paper, we investigated the reactive jamming issue for secure wireless communications. We formulated the problem as a zero-sum game, where the legitimate user and jammer respectively aim at maximizing and minimizing the expected legitimate transmission rate. Specifically, we first established an refined reactive jamming model, based on which the joint optimization over detection time and jamming power was analyzed. Then the optimal legitimate transmission power was analyzed for the legitimate transmissions. The Nash equilibrium is obtained by the best-response playing between the legitimate user and jammer. Finally, we presented simulation results to verify the effectiveness of our proposal.

References

1. Mukherjee, A., Fakoorian, S.A.A., Huang, J., Swindelhurst, A.L.: Principles of physical layer security in multiuser wireless networks: a survey. IEEE Commun. Surv. Tuts. **16**(3), 1550–1573 (2014)
2. Wang, Y., Ren, P., Gao, F.: Power allocation for statistical QoS provisioning in opportunistic multi-relay DF cognitive networks. IEEE Signal Process. Letts. **20**(1), 43–46 (2013)
3. Wang, H., Zhang, L., Li, T., Tugnait, J.: Spectrally efficient jamming mitigation based on code-controlled frequency hopping. IEEE Trans. Wireless Commun. **10**(3), 728–732 (2011)
4. Liu, Y., Ning, P., Dai, H., Liu, A.: Randomized differential DSSS: jamming-resistant wireless broadcast communication. In: 29th IEEE Conference on Computer Communications, pp. 1–5. IEEE Press, New York (2010)
5. Xu, W., Ma, K., Trappe, W., Zhang, Y.: Jamming sensor networks: attack and defense strategies. IEEE Netw. **20**(3), 41–47 (2006)
6. Wilhelm, M., Martinovic, I., Schmitt, J.B., Lenders, V.: Short paper: reactive jamming in wireless networks: how realistic is the threat?. In: 4th ACM Conference on Wireless Network Security, pp. 47–52. ACM, New York (2011)
7. Su, Z., Xu, Q., Zhu, H., Wang, Y.: A novel design for content delivery over software defined mobile social networks. IEEE Netw. **29**(4) (2015)
8. Spuhler, M., Giustiniano, D., Lenders, V., Wilhelm, M., Schmitt, J.B.: Detection of reactive jamming in DSSS-based wireless communications. IEEE Trans. Wirel. Commun. **13**(3), 1593–1603 (2014)
9. D'Oro, S., Galluccio, L., Morabito, G., Palazzo, S., Chen, L., Martignon, F.: Defeating jamming with the power of silence: a game-theoretic analysis. IEEE Trans. Wirel. Commun. **14**(5), 2337–2352 (2015)
10. Richa, A., Scheideler, C., Schmid, S., Zhang, J.: An efficient and fair MAC protocol robust to reactive interference. IEEE/ACM Trans. Netw. **12**(3), 760–771 (2013)
11. Wang, Y., Ren, P., Gao, F., Su, Z.: A hybrid underlay/overlay transmission mode for cognitive radio networks with statistical quality-of-service provisioning. IEEE Trans. Wirel. Commun. **13**(3), 1482–1498 (2014)
12. Xu, Q., Su, Z., Han, B., Fang, D., Xu, Z., Gan, Z.: Analytical model with a novel selfishness division of mobile nodes to participate cooperation. Peer-to-Peer Netw. Appl., 1–9 (2015). doi:10.1007/s12083-015-0330-6
13. Fudenberg, D., Tirole, J.: Game Theory. MIT Press, Cambridge (1991)

A Quasi-Dynamic Inter-Satellite Link Reassignment Method for LEO Satellite Networks

Zhu Tang[1][✉], Zhenqian Feng[1], Wanrong Yu[1], Wei Han[1], Baokang Zhao[1],
Chunqing Wu[1], Xilong Mao[1], and Feng Chen[2]

[1] College of Computer, National University of Defense Technology, Changsha, Hunan, China
{tangzhu,wlyu,bkzhao,wuchunqing,xlmao}@nudt.edu.cn,
z_q_feng@163.com, hanwei_phd@126.com
[2] College of Information System and Management, National University of Defense Technology,
Changsha, Hunan, China
chenfeng@nudt.edu.cn

Abstract. This paper presents a quasi-dynamic inter-satellite link (ISL) reassignment method to optimize the snapshot routing performance for LEO (low Earth orbit) satellite networks. When the snapshot routing tables are switching in all satellites, we propose to reassign the inter-plane ISLs regularly to improve the quality of the next snapshot. Evaluation results indicate that our method can obtain invariable and longer snapshot duration, which is superior to the natural partition method. Meanwhile, compared with the equal partition method, the proposed method can averagely increase 5.95 % on-board transceiver utility ratio. We believe that our method could be practically and effectively applied in future LEO satellite networks.

Keywords: ISL reassignment · Snapshot routing algorithm · Satellite networks

1 Introduction

Compared with the geostationary-earth orbit (GEO) and medium-earth orbit (MEO) satellite networks, LEO satellite networks are more desirable for the global voice and data communication due to shorter transmission latency and lower signal attenuation. However, the rapid movements of LEO satellites lead to frequent handoff on the inter-satellite links and ground-satellite links, making the topologies of satellite networks change acutely. Lots of routing algorithms have been proposed to mask the topological dynamics of satellite networks, e.g. static routing algorithms based on virtual topology [1–4], virtual node [5], and dynamic routing algorithms [6, 13, 14].

In fact, the only operational LEO satellite network Iridium system [7] employs the virtual topology based algorithms - snapshot routing algorithm. Therefore, we also focus on this algorithm for their simplicity and practicability in this paper. The main idea of the snapshot routing algorithm is to cut the orbit period into many time slices Δt_i, and in each slice, the network topology $G_i = (V_i, E_i)$ is considered to be stable, i.e. the connectivity of ISLs are unchanged and the delay of each ISL can be treated as

© Springer International Publishing Switzerland 2015
K. Xu and J. Zhu (Eds.): WASA 2015, LNCS 9204, pp. 497–507, 2015.
DOI: 10.1007/978-3-319-21837-3_49

invariable. Then the two-tuples $< t_i, G_i >$ representing the predicted topology in the time interval Δt_i is called a *snapshot* [4]. Due to the predictability and periodicity of satellite movements, routing tables for each snapshot can be pre-calculated and stored on-board with a precise switch timetable. Thus, the topology dynamics are concealed.

As existing satellite networks adopt the fixed assignment method for organizing ISLs, there are naturally two basic methods to obtain the snapshot sequences:

- **Natural Partition Method:** Gounder [1] proposed that once an ISL is established or broken down depending on the line-of-sight (LOS) visibility or relative angular velocity constraints, a new snapshot begins. Since this method utilizes the natural connectivity property of ISLs, we call it natural partition throughout this paper.
- **Equal Partition Method:** Werner [2] proposed to use the equal time interval for snapshot partition because of its simplicity and ease of administration. The Iridium system employs this method and switches routing tables every 2.5 min [7].

Since the natural partition method adapts the original ISL on/off changes, the on-board transceiver utilization of this method is high. For the equal partition method, the resulting equal snapshot duration can efficiently increase the simplicity and stability of routing algorithm. However, the above two advantages are separated and could not be archived at the same time by either method. According to our analysis, the unavoidable tradeoff of the two methods roots in the inflexibility of existing fixed ISL assignment. For the dynamic ISL reassignment in LEO satellite networks, previous studies mainly proposed to maximize the minimum residual capacity links [3], maximize the transceiver usage [8] and maintain connected, cost-efficient network topology [9]. However, these methods are mainly based on the greedy and other heuristic algorithms, without taking full advantage of the specialty of LEO satellite networks.

In this paper, we propose a quasi-dynamic ISL reassignment method to optimize the snapshot distribution (duration and quantity) of LEO satellite networks. At the end of each snapshot, we reassign ISLs regularly to improve the quality of the following snapshot. Extensive simulations are performed with orbit data obtained from Satellite Tool Kit (STK) and the performance evaluation is carried out in NS2. Results show that our method can obtain invariable and longer snapshot duration, which is superior to the natural partition method. Meanwhile, our method improves the snapshot distribution (snapshot duration and quantity) and on-board transceiver utilization ratio.

The rest of the paper is organized as follows: In Sect. 2, the basic inclined-orbit LEO satellite network model and the feasibility of ISL reassignment for satellite networks are presented. In Sect. 3, we propose the ISL reassignment based snapshot partition method for LEO satellite networks. The proposed method is analyzed and validated by simulations in Sect. 4. Finally, we summarize the paper in Sect. 5.

2 Preliminaries

The LEO satellite networks can be divided into two types according to the inclination angle of orbit planes α (i.e. the angle between the orbit plane and the equator plane, $0 \leq \alpha \leq 180$), such as the polar-orbit satellite network and inclined-orbit satellite network. The inclination angle of the polar-orbit satellite network is near 90°, while the inclination angle of the inclined-orbit satellite network is more general. In this view, the polar-orbit satellite network is a special and simple case of inclined-orbit satellite networks, so we mainly focus on the inclined-orbit satellite network to propose the ISL reassignment method in this paper.

2.1 General LEO Satellite Network Model

Assume that there are N orbit planes, and each plane has M satellites uniformly distributed, thereby the total number of satellites in the network is $N*M$. Each plane is separated in range of 2π by the same angle $\Delta\Omega$, and satellites in the same plane are separated from each other with the angle distance of $\omega = \frac{2\pi}{M}$. Let S_{ij} denote the j_{th} satellite in plane i, $i = 1,...,N$, $j = 1,...,M$, α the inclination of the orbit plane, h the orbit altitude above the ground and T the orbit period of satellites. The phase angle of satellites in adjacent planes is $\omega_f = \frac{2\pi F}{N*M}$, which is determined by the phase factor $F = 0,...,N-1$. Based on the terminologies, the inclined-orbit satellite network can be represented by $\alpha{:}h{:}N*M/M/F$. A typical inclined-orbit satellite network topology based on the Globalstar system is shown in Fig. 1, and it can be represented as $52°{:}1414\ km{:}48/6/1$. Figure 2 illustrates the topology model of the inclined-orbit satellite network which is abstracted from Fig. 1.

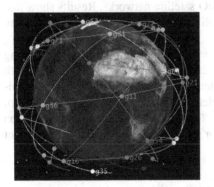
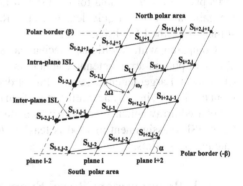

Fig. 1. Inclined-orbit LEO satellite network topology

Fig. 2. Network model of the Inclined-orbit LEO satellite network

Disregarding the unpredictable satellite failures, the ISLs are the main concern for the snapshot partition. Generally, there are two kinds of ISLs in the polar-orbit constellation:

- Intra-Plane ISLs: They connect the immediate up and down satellites in the same plane, such as ISL $(S_{i-2,j}, S_{i-2,j+1})$ in Fig. 2. Since the satellites in the same plane have the same moving direction and speed, their relative positions keep unchanged all the time, so the intra-plane ISLs maintain permanently.

- Inter-Plane ISLs: They connect the neighboring satellites in immediate left and right adjacent planes, such as $(S_{i-2,j}, S_{i-1,j})$ in Fig. 2. The connectivity and latency of these ISLs change periodically with the satellite movements.

As the adjacent orbit planes intersect in high latitude areas, the satellites in adjacent planes will exchange their positions from left to right after crossing the poles. Thus, the relative speed of adjacent satellites will increase sharply when approaching high latitude areas, and the automatic tracking speed of the on-board antennas will exceed the upper limit. Therefore, the inclined-orbit satellite network defines a north and a south polar area for protection (Fig. 2). When satellites are about to enter the polar areas, the inter-plane ISLs assigned on them are closed. Until satellites exit from the polar areas, the inter-plane ISLs can be reestablished. The latitudes of north and south polar area borders are usually equivalent and denoted by β and $-\beta$, respectively. For example in Fig. 2, when $S_{i+1,j+1}$ enters the north polar area, the inter-plane ISL $(S_{i+1,j+1}, S_{i,j+1})$ will be switched off. Until the satellites $S_{i,j+1}$ and $S_{i+1,j+1}$ both have exited from the polar areas, the inter-plane ISL can be established again.

2.2 Feasibility Analysis of ISL Reassignment

The S-band phased-array antenna for ISLs has been tested in Engineering Test Satellite VI (ETS-VI) in 1995 [10]. Recently, many high frequency band phased-array antennas are designed for ISLs. Cowley et al. [11] designed a Ka Band sectorised and a V Band torus phased-array antenna for the ISLs of LEO satellite networks. Results show that the gains and EIRP (Equivalent Isotropic Radiated Power) of the new antennas are sufficient for the LEO ISLs.

Compared with traditional mechanical steering antenna, the electronic steering ability of phased-array antenna can help make larger elevation ($0° \sim 90°$) and azimuth ($0° \sim 360°$). Larger antenna gain for longer distance communication after ISL reassignment can be obtained by activating more feed elements in the phased-array [11]. In sum, the phased-array antenna technology is mature for ISLs, and the phased-array antenna based ISL reassignment method is feasible for LEO satellite networks under current antenna constraints.

3   ISL Reassignment Based Snapshot Partition

To combine the advantages of the natural partition method (i.e. high on-board transceiver utilization ratio) and equal partition method (i.e. simplicity and stability), we propose the ISL reassignment method in this paper. In fact, many adjacent satellites can be used for assigning ISLs, but for the snapshot routing algorithm, it is believed that regular connectivity changes of inter-plane ISLs can lead to the regularity of snapshot distribution. Therefore, we only use the inter-plane ISLs between satellites with certain phase angle, such as oblique ISLs and vertical ISLs as follows:

3.1 Oblique and Vertical ISLs

Firstly, we construct the plane right angle coordinate for each satellite. The coordinate is on the tangent plane of the spherical surface where satellites locate. As is shown in Fig. 3, the Y axis is parallel with the orbit plane, and the positive direction is consistent with the satellite moving direction. The positive direction of the X axis points to the ascending direction of orbital plane numbers.

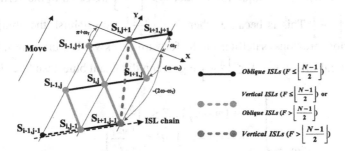

Fig. 3. Oblique and vertical inter-plane ISLs and the ISL chain

Definition 1. Oblique Inter-Plane ISLs (abbr. Oblique ISLs): The inter-plane ISLs between satellites in adjacent planes with angle distance ω_o are called oblique inter-plane ISLs. For the line of sight availability, the phase angle distance ω_o is determined by the phase factor F as follows,

$$\omega_o = \begin{cases} \omega_f, & F \leq \left[\frac{N-1}{2}\right] \\ \pi + \omega_f, & F \leq \left[\frac{N-1}{2}\right] \\ -(\omega - \omega_f), & F > \left[\frac{N-1}{2}\right] \\ \pi - (\omega - \omega_f), & F > \left[\frac{N-1}{2}\right] \end{cases} \tag{1}$$

According to the definition, each satellite can build maximum one oblique ISL with satellites on the forward and backward adjacent plane, because the phase angles between satellites on both adjacent planes equal to ω_f. Normally, when $F \leq \left[\frac{N-1}{2}\right]$, we just connect the satellites based on the ordinary sequence number increment, such as ISLs $(S_{i,j}, S_{i+1,j+F-1})$ and $(S_{N,j}, S_{0,mod(j+F-1, M)})$. For example, the black thin lines in Fig. 3 are also oblique ISLs. However, if $F > \left[\frac{N-1}{2}\right]$, adjacent satellites are far from each other, and ISLs $(S_{i,j}, S_{i+1,j+F-1})$ and $(S_{N,j}, S_{0,mod(j+F-1, M)})$ may be blocked by Earth when the orbit altitude is low, so we connect the posterior satellite in the next plane, or the previous satellite in the last plane compared to the ISLs under $F \leq \left[\frac{N-1}{2}\right]$. For example in Fig. 3, when $F > \left[\frac{N-1}{2}\right]$, the green thick lines are oblique ISLs.

Definition 2. Vertical Inter-Plane ISLs (abbr. Vertical ISLs): The inter-plane ISLs between satellites in adjacent planes with angle distance ω_v are called vertical inter-plane ISLs. The phase angle distance ω_v is also determined by the phase factor F as Eq. (2).

Similar to oblique ISLs, each satellite can also build maximum one vertical ISL with satellites on the forward and backward adjacent plane. Furthermore, as we can see in Eqs. (1) and (2), oblique ISLs under $F > \left[\frac{N-1}{2}\right]$ are equal to the vertical ISLs under $F \le \left[\frac{N-1}{2}\right]$. This is because when $F > \left[\frac{N-1}{2}\right]$, we establish the oblique ISLs with posterior (previous) satellites on the forward (backward) orbit planes, which is just the vertical ISLs when $F \le \left[\frac{N-1}{2}\right]$, e.g. green thick and blue dash lines in Fig. 3.

$$\omega_v = \begin{cases} -\left(\omega - \omega_f\right), & F \le \left[\frac{N-1}{2}\right] \\ \pi - \left(\omega - \omega_f\right), & F \le \left[\frac{N-1}{2}\right] \\ -\left(2 * \omega - \omega_f\right), & F > \left[\frac{N-1}{2}\right] \\ \pi - \left(2 * \omega - \omega_f\right), & F > \left[\frac{N-1}{2}\right] \end{cases} \tag{2}$$

In most inclined-orbit satellite networks, the oblique and vertical ISLs stated above can always be connected outside the polar areas. They normally could not be blocked by Earth and atmosphere because of the consideration of phase angle between satellites. Therefore, both ISLs can be assigned as needed in the non-polar area during the ISL reassignment.

3.2   ISL Chain (IC)

To better describe the ISL reassignment method, we redefine the concept of ISL chain [12] in inclined-orbit constellation as follows:

Definition 3. ISL Chain (abbr. IC): In the inclined-orbit constellation, the set of connected oblique ISLs started from the one just exiting the polar area to the one just about to enter the polar area, is called a ISL chain. The ISLs $(S_{i-1,j-1}, S_{i,j-1})$ and $(S_{i,j-1}, S_{i+1,j-1})$ shown in Fig. 3 are part of an IC in inclined-orbit LEO satellite networks.

According to the connection style of oblique ISLs, if the ISLs are not closed in the polar area, all the oblique ISLs can form a close cycle. And the number of loops for the close cycle surrounding the Earth is determined by the sum of phase angle of all satellites between adjacent planes. Since each ISL loop can be cut by the polar border into two ICs, the number of ICs (i.e. *NIC*) is two times of the number of loops, which is finally determined by the phase factor F as follows,

$$NIC = 2 * \frac{\omega_f * N * M}{2 * \pi} = 2 * \frac{\frac{2*\pi*F}{N*M} * N * M}{2 * \pi} = 2 * F \qquad (3)$$

Let IC^{head} denote the start satellite of IC which just exits the polar area and IC^{tail} denote the end satellite of IC which is about to enter the polar area. Then at any given time t, the ISL reassignment can be executed normally from all IC^{head}s. Single snapshot partition event (i.e. ISLs breakdown event) is applied to gain invariable snapshot duration, which is prior to current natural partition method.

3.3 Proposed ISL Reassignment Method

In this paper, the ISL reassignment method is only based on the ISL breakdown event. This event is triggered by the heads of LCs entering the polar area, and then the ISLs can be reassigned in three steps as follows:

Step 1: Add oblique and vertical ISLs for all IC^{tail}s

Firstly, we calculate the tail satellites for all ICs. Then for each IC_k^{tail} ($k = 0,...,NIC-1$), we assign one oblique ISL for it if available, and record the other end satellite as $IC_k^{tail\_oblique}$. Meanwhile, if the vertical ISL is available, we assign one vertical ISL for it, too. As is shown Fig. 4, since satellite $g_{8,4}$ is the tail satellite, so we add oblique ISL ($g_{8,4}$, $g_{1,5}$) and vertical ISL ($g_{7,5}$, $g_{8,4}$) to it. Meanwhile, the other IC^{tail} $g_{8,1}$ in the example is just behind the Earth.

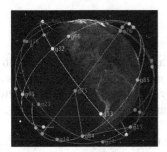 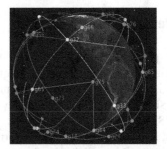

Fig. 4. Oblique and vertical ISLs addition for IC^{tail}s of the Globalstar system ($F = 1$)

Fig. 5. IC construction near the polar area borders of the Globalstar system ($F = 1$)

Step 2: Construct the ICs near the polar area borders

We construct the ICs beginning from each $IC_k^{tail\_oblique}$ ($k = 0,...,NIC-1$) near the polar area borders to form a ISL ring near the polar borders. These ICs would not extend too long, because part of the satellites near the polar area borders are used to construct the vertical ISLs, so after constructing the ICs, they would have no sparse on-board transceivers to extend the IC. Finally, an ISL ring is formed in Fig. 5.

Step 3: Assign ISLs in the middle of the non-polar areas

By now, the satellites in the middle of the non-polar area are not assigned with inter-plane ISLs. Therefore, we start to construct ICs from the following nodes of IC_k^{tail} which is on the same plane and in the non-polar areas. For each following node of IC_k^{tail}, the forward and backward oblique ISLs are tested for assignment. However, if oblique ISLs could not be established on this node and there are still sparse transceivers, we try to assign the vertical ISLs for them. As is shown in Fig. 6, the IC consisting the ISL ($g_{3,6}$, $g_{4,6}$) and the IC consisting the ISL ($g_{3,2}$, $g_{4,2}$) are constructed in this step. Meanwhile, the vertical ISLs ($g_{8,2}$, $g_{7,3}$) and ($g_{7,6}$, $g_{8,5}$) belonging to different ICs are also constructed in this step. Figure 6 shows the final network topology of the Globalstar system after three steps.

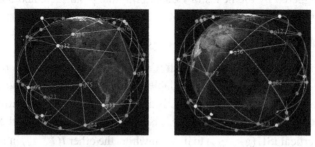

Fig. 6. Final satellite network topology of the Globalstar system ($F = 1$)

4 Performance Evaluation

In this paper, the snapshot distribution and on-board transceiver utilization ratio are evaluated for the natural partition, equal partition and the proposed ISL reassignment method. Since currently only the Iridium system provides the mesh-like satellite network with ISLs, our simulations are mainly carried out on the Globalstar system with simulated ISLs.

Table 1 shows the snapshot information of the Globalstar system under different partition methods, polar border configurations ($\beta = 45°$, $48°$) and phase factor ($F = 1,...,7$). Parameter δ, S and $NISL$ respectively denote the snapshot duration, snapshot number and the average number of inter-plane ISLs in each snapshot. Columns $\widehat{\delta_{reassign}}$, $\widehat{S_{reassign}}$, and $\widehat{NISL_{reassign}}$ are obtained by simulations with ISL reassignment method, while columns $\widehat{\delta_{natural}}$, $\widehat{S_{natural}}$ and $\widehat{NISL_{natural}}$ present the snapshot information using the natural partition method [12]. Meanwhile, two types of snapshot duration time are evaluated for the equal partition method with the name of equal1 and equal2. Columns $\widehat{\delta_{equal1}}\big/\widehat{\delta_{equal2}}$, $\widehat{S_{equal1}}\big/\widehat{S_{equal2}}$ and $\widehat{NISL_{equal1}}\big/\widehat{NISL_{equal2}}$ present the snapshot information using the equal partition method where $\widehat{\delta_{equal1}} = \widehat{\delta_{reassign}} = 142.61$s and $\widehat{\delta_{equal2}} = \frac{\widehat{\delta_{reassign}}}{2} = 71.35$s. Compared with the results of natural and equal partition method, the ISL reassignment method improves the snapshot distribution and on-board transceiver utilization ratio:

Table 1. Snapshot information of the globalstar system by simulations

System	β	F	$\delta_{reassign}$	$NISL_{reassign}$	$S_{reassign}$	$\delta_{natural}$ max	$\delta_{natural}$ min	$NISL_{natural}$ max	$NISL_{natural}$ min	$S_{natural}$	$\delta_{equal1}/\delta_{equal2}$	$NISL_{equal1}/NISL_{equal2}$	S_{equal1}/S_{equal2}
	45°	1	142.61	32	48	140.35	2.26	32	30	96	142.61/71.35	30/30	48/96
		3	142.61	32	48	140.35	2.26	28	26	96	142.61/71.35	26/26	48/96
		5	142.61	32	48	140.35	2.26	28	26	96	142.61/71.35	26/26	48/96
Globalstar		7	142.61	32	48	140.35	2.26	32	30	96	142.61/71.35	30/30	48/96
	48°	2	285.22	32	24	168.37	116.85	32	36	48	142.61/71.35	32/32	48/96
		4	570.43	32	12	402.07	168.36	32	24	24	142.61/71.35	28/28	48/96
		6	285.22	32	24	168.37	116.85	32	36	48	142.61/71.35	32/32	48/96

- Longer and invariable snapshot duration

As is shown in Table 1, the snapshot duration gained by ISL reassignment method is longer and retains invariable when the latitude of polar border and phase factor are given, while the natural partition method divides the orbit period non-uniformly into max and min values according to the polar border latitudes. Some of the min values are as small as 2.26 s that the network could not converge successfully. Actually, the snapshot duration of the ISL reassignment method equals to the sum of max and min snapshot duration of natural partition method. As a result, invariable and longer duration will be more desirable to enhance the stability of routing in satellite networks.

- Half of the snapshot number

The number of snapshots obtained by ISL reassignment method (e.g. 48, 24 and 12) is the half of the number obtained by natural method (e.g. 96, 48 and 24), respectively. While the equal partition method gains fixed snapshot number, such as 48 and 96 for equal1 and equal2 method, respectively. The reduction of snapshot number can decrease the impact of routing table switches, also leading to more stable routing in satellite networks.

- Invariable and normally higher on-board transceiver utilization ratio

The on-board transceiver utilization ratios (U) of the three methods are compared in this paper. The utilization ratio can be calculated as follows,

$$U = \frac{2 * \sum_{i=1}^{S} NISL^i * \delta^i}{2 * N * M * T} \tag{4}$$

where $NISL^i$ denote the number of inter-plane ISLs, δ^i denote the snapshot duration of snapshot i, and S denote the number of snapshots. In Eq. (4), the denominator denotes the available time of all on-board transceivers ignoring whether ISLs are established or not, and the numerator denotes the available time of on-board transceivers currently in use by a specific partition method.

As we can see in Fig. 7, the utilization ratio of on-board transceivers by the ISL reassignment method is constant 66.67 %, and normally higher than the natural and equal partition method except when $F = 2, 6$. The exception is because the single trigger event of ISL breakdown in the ISL reassignment method abandons the ISLs constructed by the ISL establishment event in the natural partition method. Specially, when $F = 2$, the satellites near the polar area border all have established ISLs, thus some of the satellites in the middle of the non-polar area are left over with one transceiver unoccupied. However, if the unoccupied satellites are neighboring in pairs but moving in different direction on adjacent planes, we do not assign ISLs between them in our method, because the satellites might cross or blocked soon and lead to another ISL breakdown event.

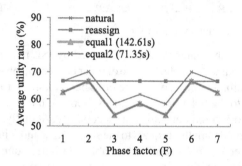

Fig. 7. Average utility ratio of on-board transceivers

For the equal partition method, the utilization ratios of equal1 and equal2 methods are equivalent under all F values, because the number of inter-plane ISLs by these two methods is the same (Table 1). In sum, the ISL reassignment method can increase 2.15 % and 5.95 % utility ratio of on-board transceivers than the natural and equal partition method.

5   Conclusions

In this paper, we propose a novel quasi-dynamic ISL reassignment method to improve the snapshot routing performance of LEO satellite networks. When the ISL breakdown event occurs, we reassign oblique and vertical inter-plane ISLs for a better next snapshot topology by steering the inter-plane ISL antennas. Simulation results show that the ISL reassignment method can obtain invariable and longer snapshots duration, which is superior to the natural partition method, and averagely increases 5.95 % utility ratio of on-board transceivers than the equal partition method.

Acknowledgment. The work described in this paper is supported by the National Natural Science Foundation of China (No.61103182, 61202488, 61272482 and 61379147).

References

1. Gounder, V.V., Prakash, R., Abu-Amara, H.: Routing in LEO-based satellite networks. In: Wireless Communications and Systems, 1999 Emerging Technologies Symposium, pp. 22.1–22.6 (1999)
2. Werner, M.: A dynamic routing concept for ATM-based satellite personal communication networks. IEEE J. Sel. Areas Commun. **15**, 1636–1648 (1997)
3. Chang, H.S., Kim, B.W., Lee, C.G., Min, S.L., Choi, Y., Yang, H.S., Kim, D.N., Kim, C.S.: FSA-based link assignment and routing in low-earth orbit satellite networks. IEEE Trans. Veh. Technol. **47**, 1037–1048 (1998)
4. Fischer, D., Basin, D., Eckstein, K., Engel, T.: Predictable mobile routing for spacecraft networks. IEEE Trans. Mob. Comput. **12**, 1174–1187 (2012)
5. Yong, L., Fuchun, S., Youjian, Z.: Virtual topology for LEO satellite networks based on earth-fixed footprint mode. IEEE Commun. Lett. **17**, 357–360 (2013)
6. Yong, L., et al.: Routing techniques on satellite networks. J. Softw. **25**, 1085–1100 (2014)
7. Evans, J.V.: Satellite systems for personal communications. Proc. IEEE **86**, 1325–1341 (1998)
8. Harathi, K., Krishna, P., Newman-Wolfe, R.E., Chow, R.Y.C.: A fast link assignment algorithm for satellite communication networks. In: Computers and Communications, Twelfth Annual International Phoenix Conference on, pp. 401–408 (1993)
9. Minsu, H., et al.: Topology control for time-evolving and predictable delay-tolerant networks. IEEE Trans. Comput. **62**, 2308–2321 (2013)
10. Samejima, S.: Phased array antenna systems for commercial applications in Japan. In: IEEE International Symposium on Phased Array Systems and Technology, pp. 237–242 (1996)
11. Cowley, W.G., Green, H.E.: Phased-array antennas for inter-satellite links. In: Communications Theory Workshop (AusCTW), Australian, pp. 102–106 (2010)
12. Wang, J., Li, L., Zhou, M.: Topological dynamics characterization for LEO satellite networks. Comput. Netw. **51**, 43–53 (2007)
13. Ma, Y., Wang, X., Su, J., Wu, C., Yu, W., Zhao, B.: A multicast routing algorithm for datagram service in delta LEO satellite constellation networks. J. Netw. **9**, 896–907 (2014)
14. Bai, J., Lu, X., Lu, Z., Peng, W.: A distributed hierarchical routing protocol for non-GEO satellite networks. In: Parallel Processing Workshops, 2004 International Conference on, pp. 148–154 (2004)

Domatic Partition in Homogeneous Wireless Sensor Networks

Chao Wang, Chuanwen Luo, Lili Jia, Qingbo Zhang, and Jiguo Yu[✉]

School of Information Science and Engineering, Qufu Normal University,
Ri-zhao 276826, Shandong, People's Republic of China
jiguoyu@sina.com

Abstract. In wireless sensor networks, for balancing energy consumption of nodes and hence maximizing the lifetime of the networks, an important technique is to rotate dominating sets periodically. This technique can be abstracted as domatic partition (DP) problem, which is the problem of partitioning the set of nodes in networks into disjoint dominating sets. Through rotating each dominating set of DP periodically, the energy consumption of nodes can be greatly balanced and the lifetime of the networks can be prolonged in turn. In this paper, for homogenous wireless sensor networks, we present a Cell Structure which is constructed as follows. Firstly, the network is divided into clusters, and then a clique is constructed in each cluster. Based on the Cell Structure, we propose a centralized nucleus algorithm for DP, which is called centralized nucleus domatic partition (CNDP) algorithm. We show that the algorithm balances the energy consumption by adopting sleep scheduling and maximizes the lifetime of the networks based on the domatic number. Through analysis, the domatic number of the algorithm is $\frac{N}{6}$, where N is the number of nodes in the clique.

Keywords: Wireless Sensor Networks · Domatic Partition(DP) · Clustering

1 Introduction

In wireless sensor networks (WSNs), sensor nodes usually are charged with battery whose energy is limited and placed one-time, which makes it impossible for a second charging. Hence, prolonging the lifetime of networks by reducing the energy consumption of nodes is an important challenge. One common method for saving energy is to find a dominating set for data gathering or a connected dominating set for efficient routing. While there exits a problem that the dominators consume too much extra overheads such as gathering, processing and forwarding data information to consume energy faster than other nodes in the network, which shortens the lifetime of the network. Consequently, it is an important

This work was partially supported by the NNSF of China for contract 61373027, 61472418 and NSF of Shandong Province for contract ZR2012FM023.

© Springer International Publishing Switzerland 2015
K. Xu and J. Zhu (Eds.): WASA 2015, LNCS 9204, pp. 508–517, 2015.
DOI: 10.1007/978-3-319-21837-3_50

challenge to find a mechanism for balancing energy consumption and prolonging the network lifetime.

Sleep scheduling is a standard approach for balancing energy consumption. By this approach, the nodes make local decisions to sleep or to join the dominating set so that they can take turns being dominators. Thus, each node in the network has a chance to become a dominator and then the energy consumption among nodes comes to balance. The problem of rotating the role of being a dominator has been abstracted as the domatic partition problem in [1]. Given a graph $G = (V, E)$ corresponding to a WSN, a dominating set (DS) of G is a subset of vertices V such that each node $v \in V$ is either in D or has a neighbor in D. A domatic partition (DP) is a partition $\mathcal{D} = \{D_1, D_2, \cdots, D_t\}$ of V such that each D_i is a dominating set of G, where t is called the domatic number (DN), which is the number of disjoint DSs. The domatic partition problem seeks a domatic partition with maximal domatic number.

The domatic partition problem has a related problem, the connected domatic partition problem. A connected domatic partition (CDP) is a partition $\mathcal{D} = \{D_1, D_2, \cdots, D_t\}$ of V such that each D_i is a connected dominating set of G, where t is called connected domatic number (CDN), which is the number of disjoint CDSs. Constructing a connected dominating set from a dominating set is straightforward and easy. However, extending a given domatic partition into a connected domatic partition appears to be highly non-trivial. Then, in this paper, we focus on the domatic partition problem. Moreover, the final objective of the domatic partition problem is to maximize the lifetime of the networks, which are similar to the multicast routing problem that is treated as finding a multicast tree in a network, whose objective is to minimize the network cost [2].

To understand the motivation, suppose that $\mathcal{D} = \{D_1, D_2, \cdots, D_t\}$ is a DP of G. Then a simple sleep scheduling is that the nodes in D_1 are activated in a fixed period T, during which the rest of the nodes are asleep, followed by the period T in which nodes in D_2 are active, while the rest of nodes are asleep, and so on. After such one-time sleep scheduling, the period of being active of dominators in each DS is T. The DP has t DSs, the period of one-time scheduling is tT. Therefore maximizing the domatic number t results in maximizing the period of one-time scheduling, in turn maximizing the lifetime of the network.

Clustering is a basic and effective method of sleep scheduling. It is a fundamental mechanism to design scalable sensor network protocols. A clustering algorithm divides the network into disjoint subsets of nodes such that each subset is a cluster. A good clustering imposes a high-level structure on the network. It is easier to design efficient protocols on this high-level structure than at the level of the individual node. Many efficient clustering protocols [3–5] have been proposed.

The main contribution of the paper can be summarized as follows.

1. A Cell Structure is constructed for obtaining DP using only connectivity information, without relying on geometric information.
2. A novel approximation algorithm for domatic partition.

The rest of this paper is organized as follows. Section 2 reviews the existing algorithms for the DP. Section 3 gives the algorithm CNDP with theoretical analysis. Finally, Sect. 4 concludes this paper.

2   Related Works

Graph coloring is an approach which is widely used to solve the domatic partition problem. The nodes in the graph can be divided into different coloring classes such that each color class is a dominating set of a domatic partition. This approach is commonly used in arbitrary graphs.

In [7], in order to achieve energy savings, Cardei et al. proposed a centralized algorithm using graph coloring to generate a number of disjoint dominating sets without providing any bound analysis. To maximize the lifetime of a sensor network, in [8], Islam et al. also used the graph coloring to obtain a domatic partition without any bound analysis. While both of them fail to give any theoretical analysis about the domatic number bound.

In [9], applying the graph coloring theory, Feige et al. proved that each graph with maximum degree Δ and minimum degree δ contains a domatic partition of size $(1 - o(1))(\delta + 1)/\ln \Delta$. They turned this proof into a centralized algorithm that produces a domatic partition of $\Omega(\delta/\ln \Delta)$ sets. In [1], Moscibroda and Wattenhofer defined the domatic partition problem as the maximum cluster-lifetime problem and proposed a randomly distributed algorithm which is an $O(\log n)$-approximation with high probability in arbitrary graphs. This algorithm is the distributed implementation of the centralized algorithm in [9]. Both of them obtain a logarithmic approximation algorithm for domatic partition.

In [10], Mahjoub and Matula showed that simple topology-based graph coloring can solve the domatic partition problem in random geometric graphs (RGGs) and provide up to $(\delta + 1)$ disjoint $(1 - \varepsilon)$ dominating sets on a large range of experimented graphs. Later, they carried the further study in [11] by proposing a practical solution to the distributed $(1 - \varepsilon)$ dominating sets partition problem that is based on localized graph coloring algorithms. While both of them obtain the approximation only by simulation results other than theoretical analysis.

The uniform partition is a new approach used in unit disk graphs (UDGs). By this approach, a constant-factor approximation algorithm can be found on UDGs.

In [12], Pemmaraju and Pirwani first proposed the method of the uniform partition and gave three deterministic distributed algorithms for finding k-domatic partition of size at least a constant fraction of the largest possible $(k - 1)$-domatic partition for $k > 1$. The first algorithm runs in constant time on UDGs assuming that all nodes know their positions in a global coordinate system. The second algorithm runs in $O(\log n)$ time on UDGs assuming that pairwise distances between neighboring nodes are known instead of dropping knowledge of global coordinates. The third algorithm runs in $O(\log(\log n))$ time in growth-bounded graphs dropping all reliance on geometric information, using connectivity information only.

In [13], Pandit et al. first drove a constant-factor distributed algorithm Dom-Part that can be implemented in $O(\log n)$ rounds of communication in the congest model on UDGs.

In [14], Misra and Mandal proposed a domatic partition based scheme for cluserhead rotation on UDGs from the technical application of the uniform partition idea. However, the cluserhead rotation via re-clustering is a global operation which suffers from significant energy overheads when rotation. Later, in [6], Misra and Mandal proposed an efficient rotation scheme using local rotation with the aim of reducing wasteful energy in re-clustering.

3   Cell Structure-Based Centralized Algorithm for DP

3.1   Network Model

Assume that all the sensor nodes are randomly distributed in a monitoring area, and the network has the following properties.

1. The transmission radius R of any node in the network is uniform. Then, the graph corresponding to the network is an unit disk graph (UDG).
2. The network is static. That is, the nodes do not move after deploying.
3. Each node has the same energy, and can not be recharging.
4. Each node has a globally unique identification id.
5. Each node in the network only knows the connection information rather than geometry information. And the connection information contains such as the degree of the nodes in the network and the distance between them. However, the geometry information that we acquire through additional hardware configuration, which inevitably increases the hardware cost and corresponding energy node overhead.

This section presents a Cell Structure-based centralized algorithm for DP, which includes two steps. The first step is the construction of Cell Structure, which contains the formation of clusters and cliques as shown in Sect. 3.2. The second step in Sect. 3.3 obtains a domatic partition using nucleus algorithm.

3.2   The Construction of Cell Structure

The Formation of Cluster. This subsection presents a uniform distributed clustering (UDC) algorithm, which uses the degree of nodes as the main parameter of the clusterhead competition. The formation process is divided into three phases: information collection phase with duration T_1, clusterhead competition phase with duration T_2 and cluster formation phase with duration T_3.

Phase 1. Information Collection Phase

In this phase, each node broadcasts a $Node\_Msg$ message with its id. Meanwhile, each node receives the $Node\_Msg$ from its neighbor nodes. Thus, each node knows its degree d. For each node i, we give the following formula to calculate its waiting time t_i for broadcasting the $Head\_Msg$ message.

$$t_i = \begin{cases} \frac{D-1}{d} \times \frac{T_2}{2} \times \rho & d \geq D \\ \frac{T_2}{2} + (1 - \frac{d}{D-1}) \times \frac{T_2}{2} \times \rho & d < D \end{cases} \qquad (1)$$

where D is the estimated average number of nodes in one disk with radius R, and its value is presented for $\frac{N\pi R^2}{\|\mathcal{A}\|}$, where N is the number of nodes that are distributed in the square field with area $\|\mathcal{A}\|$. ρ is a real value uniformly distributed in $[0.9, 1]$ that is introduced to reduce the probability with which two nodes send $Head\_Msg$ at the same time. It is quite clear that $\frac{D-1}{d} \times \frac{T_2}{2} \times \rho < \frac{T_2}{2} < \frac{T_2}{2} + (1 - \frac{d}{D-1}) \times \frac{T_2}{2} \times \rho$. The first half period t_i ranging form 0 to $\frac{T_2}{2}$ identifies the most clusterheads with larger degree. The last half period t_i ranging form $\frac{T_2}{2}$ to T_2 selects the few clusterheads among the rest of nodes in the uncovered area.

Phase 2. Clusterhead Competition Phase

In this phase, if a node does not receive the $Head\_Msg$ when its waiting timer t_i expires, it broadcasts the $Head\_Msg$ to advertise that it will be a clusterhead. Meanwhile, if a node receives the $Head\_Msg$, it gives up the clusterhead competition.

Phase 3. Cluster Formation Phase

In this phase, each non-clusterhead node may receive $Head\_Msg$ from different clusterheads, and it chooses the nearest clusterhead and sends the $Join\_Msg$ which contains its id and the id of the clusterhead that it joins. After this phase, the formation of the cluster is completed.

It is observed that the UDC algorithm has the following properties.

1. UDC produces the most clusterheads with larger degree in the first half period t_i. This ensures that the nodes with relatively larger degree become the clusterheads and hence contributes to bring more nodes together in each cluster.
2. UDC produces the few clusterheads from the rest of nodes in the last half period t_i. This avoids the generation of isolated nodes to guarantee complete coverage.

Theorem 1. There is no other clusterhead in the coverage of each clusterhead.

Proof. According to formula (1), the waiting time t_i of each node uniformly distributes in the whole duration of T_2. Suppose that when some nodes broadcast a $Head\_Msg$, in duration Δt, all of its neighbor nodes can receive the $Head\_Msg$. Obviously, the node would be the only clusterhead in its coverage if its neighbor nodes do not broadcast the $Head\_Msg$ in the duration Δt. While there would exist multi-clusterheads in the coverage of a clusterhead if multi-nodes broadcast the $Head\_Msg$ at the same time. Now we discuss the probability that there exist multi-clusterheads in the coverage of a clusterhead.

Since the time t_i of each node for broadcasting the $Head\_Msg$ uniformly distributes in the whole duration T_2, the probability that only one node broadcasts the $Head\_Msg$ in its coverage will fulfill the following inequality [15]:

$$P \geq C^0_{n_{exp}-1}(1 - \frac{\Delta t}{T_2})^{n_{exp}-1} \tag{2}$$

In the inequality, n_{exp} is the expectation number of the nodes in the coverage of one node and obviously, $n_{exp} = \lceil \frac{N\pi R^2}{\|\mathcal{A}\|} \rceil$. For a specific wireless sensor network, N and Δt are all constants. For example, assume that $r = 15m$, $\|\mathcal{A}\| = (100 \times 100)m^2$, $N = 100$, $\Delta t = 10ms$, $T_2 = 10s$, then we can obtain $P \geq 0.994$. This means the probability that multi-nodes broadcast the $Head\_Msg$ at the same time is rather low. In addition, by extending the duration T_2 or decreasing the cluster radius, we can further guarantee that there is no other clusterhead in the coverage of each clusterhead.   □

Theorem 2. The region of the clusters with minimum and maximum area is a regular hexagon of side length $\frac{\sqrt{3}}{3}R$ and R, respectively.

Proof. In the following Fig. 1, there are at most six clusterheads (ch_1, ch_2, ch_3, ch_4, ch_5, ch_6) adjacent to the clusterhead A. If we add one clusterhead more, the clusterhead will be covered by one of the cluterheads $ch_1, ch_2, ch_3, ch_4, ch_5, ch_6$. By theorem 1, it is impossible. The distance between the clusterhead A and its adjacent clusterheads is $R + e$, $e \to 0$. If the distance between the clusterhead A and one of its adjacent clusterheads is less than or equal to R, the clusterhead A will be covered by its adjacent clusterhead. By theorem 1, it is impossible. Therefore, the Fig. 1 shows the cluster with minimum area. The sides of the cluster consist of the perpendicular bisectors of the lines from the clusterhead A to its six adjacent clusterheads. It is easy to know that the region of the cluster with minimum area is a regular hexagon of side length $\frac{\sqrt{3}}{3}R$.

In the following Fig. 2, there are at least 6 clusterheads (ch_1, ch_2, ch_3, ch_4, ch_5, ch_6) adjacent to the clusterhead A. If we take out one clusterhead, then the gap area would be produced. The distance between the clusterhead A and its adjacent clusterheads is $\sqrt{3}(R - e)$, where $e \to 0$. If the distance between the clusterhead ch and one of its adjacent clusterheads is larger than R, then

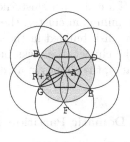

Fig. 1. The cluster with minimum area.

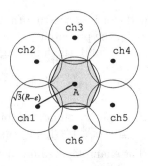

Fig. 2. The cluster with maximum area.

the gap area would be produced. Therefore, the Fig. 2 shows the cluster with maximum area. It is easy to know that the region of the cluster with minimum area is a regular hexagon of side length R.   □

The Formation of Clique. The formation of cluster is followed by the formation of clique with duration T_4. In this phase, each clusterhead broadcasts $Clique\_Msg$ message that contains its id to its cluster members with the perceived radius $\frac{R}{2}$ which is the half of the transmission radius R. If a cluster member receives $Clique\_Msg$ from its clusterhead, it becomes a member of the clique. When T_4 expires, the formation of the clique is completed.

By the process above, in each cluster, we build a disk with the clusterhead as the center and $\frac{R}{2}$ as the radius. For simplicity, the disk is called the nucleus disk or nucleus, and the area of each cluster excluding the disk is called the cytoplasm. Thus, the Cell Structure is constructed. The nodes in each nucleus have two properties as follows.

Theorem 3. The set of nodes in the nucleus form a clique in each cluster.

Proof. Since the distance between any two nodes in the nucleus is at most R, any two nodes in the nucleus are connected by an edge. By the definition of the clique, nodes in the nucleus form a clique.   □

Theorem 4. The cliques in all clusters are pairwise disjoint with each other.

Proof. By Theorem 2, the region of the cluster with minimum area is a regular hexagon of side length $\frac{\sqrt{3}}{3}R$. If a disk with clusterhead ch as the center and $\frac{R}{2}$ as the radius is builded in the minimum cluster, the disk is a inscribed circle of the regular hexagon. Since the disk builded in the cluster with minimum area is not beyond the border of the cluster, the disks builded in all clusters do not intersect with each other. That is, the cliques in all clusters are pairwise disjoint with each other.   □

3.3   Centralized Nucleus Domatic Partition (CNDP)

In this section, we propose a centralized nucleus algorithm. And we locally solve the domatic partition problem for each cluster. If a domatic partition with domatic number t can be found in each cluster, then the union of all domatic partitions is the domatic partition with domatic number t for the whole graph.

We now present the centralized nucleus algorithm as follows.

Centralized Nucleus Domatic Partition (CNDP)

Input: cluster members: the node set A_c inside nucleus and the node set B outside nucleus.
Output: domatic partition $\{A_1, A_2, \cdots, A_k\}$, where each dominating set $A_i \in A_c$.

Initially, $j = 0$.

When $D(A_c)$ can covers B, repetitive execution on the following steps:

1. $A_j = \emptyset, j = j + 1$.

2. For every node $b \in B$, initially, we mark the state $available(b)$ of b is 0. $available = 0$ denotes that the node is not dominated, and $available = 1$ denotes that the node is dominated.

3. While there exists a node $b \in B$, and $available(b) = 0$ **Do**

　　(1) For every node $a \in A \setminus A_j$, compute the number $N(a)$ of nodes in B and $available = 0$ which is dominated by a.

　　(2) For every node $a \in A \setminus A_j$, select a node b which can dominate the maximum number of nodes of B. That is, $N(b) = \max\{N(a) | a \in A \setminus A_j\}$. If there are more than one such nodes, we select one randomly.

　　(3) Add the node b into A_j, and change the state $available$ of the nodes in B which are dominated by b to 1, denoting that the nodes are dominated.

4. $A_c = A_c \setminus A_j$, that is, removing A_j from A_c.

Assume that the algorithm ends when $j = k$. Obviously, $A_1, A_2, \cdots, A_k$ are disjoint subsets of A and each $D(A_j)$ covers B. The following Theorem 5 shows that the domatic number k is at least $\frac{N}{6}$, where N is the number of the nodes in the clique.

Theorem 5. The domatic number returned by the nucleus algorithm is $\Omega(\frac{N}{6})$.

Proof. In the following Fig. 3, the cluster is a regular hexagon of side length R. By Theorem 1, it shows the cluster with maximum area. We use the clusterhead O as the endpoints to draw 6 rays OA, OB, OC, OD, OE and OF in a cluster. The angle of the adjacent two rays is $60°$. The cluster is divided into six cones with equal cone angle and each cone is a equilateral triangle.

The cone in nucleus is A^p, and the cone in cytoplasm is B^p, where $p = 1, 2, 3, 4, 5, 6$. Then, we randomly select six nodes in each cone in the nucleus. Obviously, they can cover all nodes in the cluster since each of them can cover each of the six cones. Therefore, the number of iterations is at least the number of nodes in each cone area. That is, $k \geq \frac{N}{6}$, where N is the number of nodes inside nucleus. Thus, the domatic number returned by the nucleus algorithm is at leat $\frac{N}{6}$. □

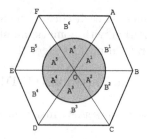

Fig. 3. The partition with equal cone angles in a maximum cluster.

4 Conclusion

In this paper, for homogenous wireless sensor network, based on the proposed Cell structure, we propose a centralized nucleus algorithm CNDP, which is a novel algorithm for DP. Through theoretical analysis, the algorithm prolongs the lifetime of the network and saves the energy. In the future, we will further study the connected domatic partition to balance energy consumption and prolong the lifetime of the network. In addition, we will find a backbone network with k-fault tolerant in a homogenous sensor network and study other fault tolerant mechanism, such as m-connected k-dominating sets partition accordingly.

References

1. Moscibroda, T., Wattenhofer, R.: Maximizing the lifetime of dominating sets. Proc. IEEE IPDPS **4**, 8–15 (2005)
2. Cai, Z., Lin, G., Xue, G.: Improved approximation algorithms for the capacitated multicast routing problem. In: Wang, L. (ed.) COCOON 2005. LNCS, vol. 3595, pp. 136–145. Springer, Heidelberg (2005)
3. Kumar, D., Trilok, C., Patel, R., Eehc, B.: Energy efficient heterogeneous clustered scheme for wireless sensor networks. Comput. Commun. **32**, 662–667 (2009)
4. Chamam, A., Pierre, S.: A distributed energy-efficient clustering protocol for wireless sensor networks. Comput. Electr. Eng. **36**, 303–312 (2010)
5. Yu, J., Qi, Y., Wang, G., Gu, X.: A cluster-based routing protocol for wireless sensor networks with nonuniform node distribution. AEÜ-Int. J. Electr. Commun. **66**, 54–61 (2012)
6. Misra, R., Mandal, C.: Efficient clusterhead rotation via domatic partition in self-organizing sensor networks. Wirel. Commun. Mob. Comput. **9**(8), 1040–1058 (2009)
7. Cardei, M., Maccallum, D., Cheng, M.X., Min, M., Jia, X., Li, D., Du, D.: Wireless sensor networks with energy effcient organization. J. Int. Netw. **3**(3–4), 213–229 (2002)
8. Islam, K., Akl, S.G., Meijer, H.: Maximizing the lifetime of a sensor network through domatic partition. In: Proceedings of IEEE LCN, pp. 436–442 (2009)
9. Feige, U., Halldorsson, M.M., Kortsarz, G., Srinivasan, A.: Approximating the domatic number. SIAM J. Comput. **32**(1), 172–195 (2003)

10. Mahjoub, D., Matula, D.W.: Employing $(1-\varepsilon)$- dominating set partitions as back-bones in wireless sensor networks. In: Proceedings of ALENEX, pp. 98–111 (2010)

11. Mahjoub, D., Matula, D.W.: Building $(1-\epsilon)$ dominating sets partition as back-bones in wireless sensor networks using distributed graph coloring. In: Rajaraman, R., Moscibroda, T., Dunkels, A., Scaglione, A. (eds.) DCOSS 2010. LNCS, vol. 6131, pp. 144–157. Springer, Heidelberg (2010)

12. Pemmaraju, S.V., PirwaniI, A.: Energy conservation via domatic partitions. In: Proceedings of ACM MobiHoc, pp. 143–154 (2006)

13. Pandit, S., Pemmaraju, S.V., Varadarajan, K.: Approximation algorithms for domatic partitions of unit disk graphs. In: Dinur, I., Jansen, K., Naor, J., Rolim, J. (eds.) Approximation, Randomization, and Combinatorial Optimization. LNCS, vol. 5687, pp. 312–325. Springer, Heidelberg (2009)

14. Misra, R., Mandal, C.: ClusterHead Rotation via Domatic Partition in Self-Organizing Sensor Networks. In: Proceedings of COMSWARE, pp. 1–7 (2007)

15. Liu, M., Cao, J., Chen, G., et al.: An energy-aware data gathering protocol for wireless sensor networks. J. Softw. **18**(5), 1092–1109 (2007)

High Performance DDDT-CWT Based Compressed Sensing Recovery of Images via Structured Sparsity

Hai-xu Wang, Shao-hua Wu$^{(\boxtimes)}$, Jing-ran Yang, and Chan-juan Ding

Shenzhen Graduate School, Harbin Institute of Technology, Shenzhen 518055, China
hitwush@hit.edu.cn

Abstract. Due to its low encoding complexity, compressed sensing (CS) has gained wide attention in image processing related areas such as image compression, medical imaging and remote sensing. In existing research on CS based image processing, the commonly used sparse representation scheme for image recovery is the discrete wavelet transform (DWT), which is limited by poor directionality and lack of phase space information. What's more, the structural information of transform-domain coefficients other than pure sparsity is seldom explored. In this paper, to improve the image recovery performance, we propose a new recovery method by adopting the double-density dual-tree complex wavelet transform (DDDT-CWT) as the sparse representation scheme. In addition, the structural characteristics of the DDDT-CWT coefficients are utilized as extra prior knowledge in the recovery process to further improve the recovery quality. Extensive simulation results have been conducted, and the results show that under the same compression ratio, the proposed method has achieved considerable PSNR gain compared with the traditional recovery algorithm.

Keywords: Compressed sensing · Double-density dual-tree complex wavelet transform · Structural prior

1 Introduction

Compressed sensing has gained wide attention in image processing related areas such as image compression, medical imaging and remote sensing. In space communication, image transmission has become great demand. Because of the huge amount of image data, the equipment storage and operation has enormous pressure and there also need much requirement on channel bandwidth. The traditional image compression and transmission technology is unable to break through the constraints of equipment load limited resource. CS [1–3] as new theory provides a solution for the asymmetric resource environment: compress image signal linear on the encoding end and decompress by nonlinear reconstruction algorithm on the decoding end. This method can transfer the complexity from the encoding side to the decoding side and it is conductive to the communication environment which has seriously asymmetric resource and the limited computing power on the encoding side.

Reconstruction algorithm as an important part of CS theory has been more attention. The traditional CS reconstruction algorithm can be divided into three categories:

© Springer International Publishing Switzerland 2015
K. Xu and J. Zhu (Eds.): WASA 2015, LNCS 9204, pp. 518–527, 2015.
DOI: 10.1007/978-3-319-21837-3_51

(1) greedy algorithm: a local optimal solution is selected to approach the original signal in each iteration such as orthogonal matching pursuit [4] (OMP), subspace pursuit [5] (SP), compressive sampling matching pursuit [6] (CoSaMP); (2) convex relaxation method: signal approximation is achieved by converting the non-convex problem into convex problem such as basis pursuit [7] (BP), iteration threshold [8] (IT), gradient pursuit for space reconstruction [9] (GPSR); (3) combination method: this method requires that the signal sampling to support fast reconstruction by group testing.

Traditional CS image compression reconstruction algorithm [10,11] use sparse basis DWT, which is limited by poor directionality and lack of phase space information. What's more, the structural information of transform-domain coefficients other than pure sparsity is seldom explored. In order to improve the image recovery performance, we propose a new recovery method by adopting the double-density dual-tree complex wavelet transform (DDDT-CWT) as the sparse representation scheme. In addition, the structural characteristics of the DDDT-CWT coefficients are utilized as extra prior knowledge in the recovery process to further improve the recovery quality. Extensive simulation results have been conducted, and the results show that under the same compression ratio, compared with traditional recovery algorithm which use DWT basis and does not consider structured characteristic of coefficient, the PSNR of using DDDT-CWT basis and considering structured characteristic can obtain 2.9 ~ 3.2 dB and 0.2 ~ 1.2 dB gain and the two together can obtain more than 3.8 ~ 4.3 dB gain.

This paper is organized as follows. Section 2 provides a briefly review about image compressed sensing. Section 3 presents the DDDT-CWT and wavelet tree model. Section 4 presents the structured compressed sensing recovery algorithm of images based on DDDT-CWT. Section 5 is the simulation results for natural images and performance comparison with the existing research. Section 6 gives the conclusion and proposes the follow-up research.

2   Image Compressed Sensing

Image compressed sensing system is shown in Fig. 1. On the coding end, the process is "vector" the two-dimensional image first. "Vector" operation means:

$$x = vec(X) = \{col_1(X), col_2(X), \dots, col_{N_2}(X)\} \tag{1}$$

then vector $x \in R^{N_1 N_2 \times 1}$ is measured by operation $y = \Phi x$, where $\Phi \in R^{M \times N_1 N_2}$ is a measurement matrix. On the decoding end, the process is recovery $\hat{\alpha}$ from $y = \Phi \Psi \hat{\alpha}$ by recovery algorithm. Here, we use a new recovery algorithm which is DDDT-CWT based compressed sensing recovery of images via structured sparsity to obtain high performance. Then vector $\hat{\alpha}$ formulate signal $\hat{x}$ by wavelet inverse transform, and signal $\hat{x}$ form two-dimension image $\hat{X}$ by "matrix" operation. "Matrix" operation means:

$$\hat{X} = \{\hat{x}(1:N_1); \hat{x}(N_1 + 1:2N_1); \dots; \hat{x}(N_1^2 - N_1 + 1:N_1^2)\} \tag{2}$$

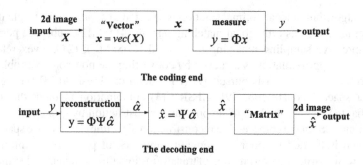

Fig. 1. Image compressed sensing system

Image compressed sensing can avoid wasting large amount of data for the reason that traditional image compression method is first sample then compress, but the CS method can sample and compress the signal at the same time. What's more, the low encoding complexity is more conductive to seriously resource asymmetric and limited computing power coding communication environment.

3   DDDT-CWT and Wavelet Tree Structure Model

3.1   DDDT-CWT

Double-density dual-tree complex DWT [12] can be incorporated into image denoising and image resolution improvement [13, 14] due to its enhancement than traditional DWT. Furthermore, we can use DDDT-CWT as the sparse representation scheme which can have wavelets oriented in sixteen directions.

Both the double-density DWT and the dual-tree complex DWT [15] have their own distinct characteristics and advantages, and as much, it was only natural to combine the two into one transform called the double-density dual-tree complex DWT. To combine the properties of both the double-density and dual-tree complex DWT, we ensure that: (1) one pair of the four wavelets is designed to be offset from the other pair of wavelets so that the integer translates of one wavelet pair fall midway between the integer translates of the other pair, and (2) one wavelet pair is designed to be approximate Hilbert transforms of the other pair of wavelets.

The filter bank structure corresponding to the double-density complex DWT consists of two oversampled iterated filter banks operating in parallel on the same input data. The iterated oversampled filter bank pair, corresponding to the simultaneous implementation of the double-density and dual-tree DWT is illustrated in Fig. 2.

As we can see in Fig. 2, there are two separate filters banks denoted by $\{h_i(n)\}$ and $\{g_i(n)\}$ where $i = 0, 1, 2$. The filter banks $\{h_i(n)\}$ and $\{g_i(n)\}$ are unique and designed in a specific way so the subband signals of the upper DWT can be interpreted as the real part of a complex wavelet transform, and the subband signals of the lower DWT

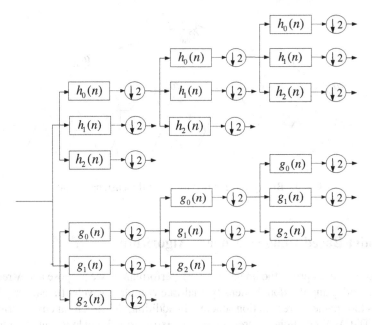

Fig. 2. Iterated filter bank for the DDDT-CWT

can be interpreted as the imaginary part. Equivalently, for specially designed sets of filters, the wavelets associated with the upper DWT can be approximate Hilbert transforms of the wavelets associated with the lower DWT. That is

$$\psi_{h,1}(t) = \psi_{h,2}(t - 0.5), \psi_{g,1}(t) = \psi_{g,2}(t - 0.5), \psi_{g,1}(t) = H\{\psi_{h,1}(t)\}, \psi_{g,2}(t) = H\{\psi_{h,2}(t)\}$$

where $\psi_{h,i}(t)$ and $\psi_{g,i}(t)$ are wavelet function. When designed in this way, the double-density dual-tree complex wavelet transform is expected to outperform in various applications, such as image compression.

3.2 Wavelet Tree Model

Wavelet decompositions have found wide application in the analysis, processing, and compression of smooth and piecewise smooth signals because these signals are K-sparse and compressible, respectively. Moreover, the wavelet coefficients can be naturally organized into a tree structure, and for many kinds of natural and manmade signals the largest coefficients cluster along the branches of this tree. This motivates a connected tree model for the wavelet coefficients in Fig. 3.

Model-based compressed sensing [16] proved that connected tree model of wavelet coefficient can be used in recovery algorithm of CS theory.

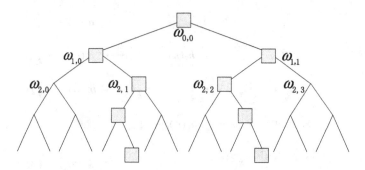

Fig. 3. Binary wavelet tree for a one-dimensional signal

4   Model-Based Image Recovery Algorithm

In this section, to improve the image recovery performance, we propose a new recovery method by adopting the double-density dual-tree complex wavelet transform (DDDT-CWT) as the sparse representation scheme. In addition, the structural characteristics of the DDDT-CWT coefficients are utilized as extra prior knowledge in the recovery process to further improve the recovery quality.

The new recovery method is based on CoSaMP algorithm. Here, we choose to modify the CoSaMP algorithm for three reasons. First, CoSaMP as a greedy algorithm has robust recovery guarantees that are on par with the best convex optimization-based approaches. Second, CoSaMP algorithm has a simple iterative that is easily modified to incorporate a best structured sparse approximation. Third, at the same compression ratio, CoSaMP algorithm can recovery image more accurately and faster.

4.1   DDDT-CWT-Tree-CoSaMP Algorithm

We propose the DDDT-CWT-Tree-CoSaMP algorithm by adopting the double-density dual-tree complex wavelet transform (DDDT-CWT) as the sparse representation scheme. In addition, the structural characteristics of the DDDT-CWT coefficients are utilized as extra prior knowledge in the recovery process to further improve the recovery quality.

Here, we take advantage of CSSA [17] to find the optimal K tree approximation as the extra prior knowledge and then replace the nonlinear approximation in CoSaMP algorithm with it. The new algorithm is shown in Table 1.

Where α represents the original signal, $\hat{\alpha}$ is the estimation signal of α, y is measurement function, l is iteration number, M represents CSSA, K means signal sparsity level, since this parameter is not known as a priori, one method would be to use the number M of measurements to deduce the sparsity level, $K = M/4$ is often sufficient for general images Ω and Γ represent set.

Table 1. DDDT-CWT-Tree-CoSaMP algorithm

Inputs:

Extract DDDT-CWT 16 direction wavelet component form wavelet basises Ψ_i, $i = 1 \sim 16$;

Matrix $\Theta_i = \Phi\Psi_i$, measurement y, sparse K.

Output:

Reconstruction signal $\hat{x}$ 。

Function procedure:

  Loop: $i = 1 \sim 16$;

  Initialize: $(\alpha_i)_0 = 0$, $(r_i)_0 = y$, supports $\Omega_i = \text{supp}((\alpha_i)_0) = \varnothing$, $l = 0$.

  Repeat

  $l = l + 1$

  Step1. Form signal proxy $c_i = \Theta_i^T(r_i)_{l-1}$;

Step2.: prune residual estimate according to structure $\Gamma_i = \text{supp}(M(c_i, K))$, and merge supports

$\Omega_i = \Gamma_i \bigcup \text{supp}((\alpha_i)_{l-1})$;

  Step3.form signal estimate:

  $(s_i)_{\Omega_i} = ((\Theta_i)_{\Omega_i}^T(\Theta_i)_{\Omega_i})^{-1}(\Theta_i)_{\Omega_i}^T y$;

  Step4. Prune signal estimate according to structure $(\alpha_i)_l = M(s_i, K)$;

  Step5. Update measurement residual $(r_i)_l = y - \Theta_i(\alpha_i)_l$;

  Until halting criterion true;

  Signal $\hat{\alpha}_i$ ($i = 1 \sim 16$) after inverse DDDT-CWT get signal $\hat{x}$.

---

5 Simulation and Results

In order to prove the high performance of the proposed algorithm, we take extensive simulation to compare with the traditional algorithm. (a) traditional image CS recovery algorithm named DWT-CoSaMP; (b) DDDT-CWT-CoSaMP algorithm which take DDDT-CWT basis and do not use tree structure knowledge; (c) DWT-Tree-CoSaMP algorithm which take DWT basis and take advantage of tree structure knowledge; (d) DDDT-CWT-Tree-CoSaMP algorithm which take DDDT-CWT basis and take advantage of tree structure knowledge. Compare the recovery performance of these four methods.

The simulation select 8 bit "256*256" gray "Lena", "peppers" and "Barbara" images. We select Gaussian random matrix as the Measurement matrix Φ, sparsity level $K = M/4$, the iteration number are 80, compression ratio is 0.3. And the results are shown in Figs. 4, 5 and 6.

(a)DWT-CoSaMP   (b) DDDT-CWT-CoSaMP

(c)DWT-Tree-CoSaMP   (d)DDDT-CWT-Tree-CoSaMP

Fig. 4. Recovery "Lena" image at 0.3 compression ratio. (a) DWT-CoSaMP(PSNR = 27.45 dB). (b) DDDT-CWT-CoSaMP(PSNR = 31.47 dB). (c) DWT-Tree-CoSaMP(PSNR = 28.16 dB). (d) DDDT-CWT-Tree-CoSaMP(PSNR = 32.44 dB)

(a)DWT-CoSaMP   (b) DDDT-CWT-CoSaMP

(c)DWT-Tree-CoSaMP   (d)DDDT-CWT-Tree-CoSaMP

Fig. 5. Recovery "peppers" image at 0.3 compression ratio. (a) DWT-CoSaMP(PSNR = 30.05 dB). (b) DDDT-CWT-CoSaMP(PSNR = 32.93 dB). (c) DWT-Tree-CoSaMP(PSNR = 30.95 dB). (d) DDDT-CWT-Tree-CoSaMP(PSNR = 33.84 dB)

(a)DWT-CoSaMP   (b) DDDT-CWT-CoSaMP

(c)DWT-Tree-CoSaMP   (d)DDDT-CWT-Tree-CoSaMP

Fig. 6. Recovery "Barbara" image at 0.3 compression ratio. (a) DWT-CoSaMP(PSNR = 27.06 dB). (b) DDDT-CWT-CoSaMP(PSNR = 29.97 dB). (c) DWT-Tree-CoSaMP(PSNR = 28.65 dB). (d) DDDT-CWT-Tree-CoSaMP(PSNR = 32.33 dB)

In order to further prove the proposed algorithm high performance, we compare images peak signal to noise ratio(PSNR) at different compression ratios. Where PSNR represents the peak signal to noise ratio between recovery images and original images. The results are shown in Figs. 7, 8 and 9.

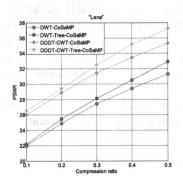

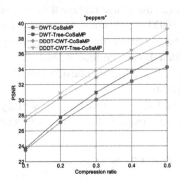

Fig. 7. PSNR of different algorithms   **Fig. 8.** PSNR of different algorithms

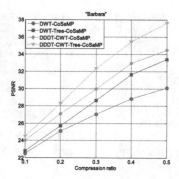

Fig. 9. PSNR of different algorithms

As we can see from Figs. 7, 8 and 9, the results show that under the same compression ratio, the proposed method has achieved considerable PSNR gain compared with the traditional recovery algorithm. In particular, compared with traditional recovery algorithm which use DWT basis and do not consider structured characteristic of coefficient, the PSNR of adopting DDDT-CWT as the sparse representation scheme and considering structured characteristic of coefficients as extra prior knowledge can respectively obtain 3.9 ~ 3.2 dB and 0.2 ~ 1.2 dB gain and the two together can obtain more than 3.8 ~ 4.3 dB gain.

6 Conclusion and Follow-up Research

In this paper, to improve the image recovery performance, we propose a new recovery method by adopting the double-density dual-tree complex wavelet transform (DDDT-CWT) as the sparse representation scheme. In addition, the structural characteristics of the DDDT-CWT coefficients are utilized as extra prior knowledge in the recovery process to further improve the recovery quality. Extensive simulation results have been conducted, and the results show that under the same compression ratio, the proposed method has achieved considerable PSNR gain compared with the traditional recovery algorithm.

The follow-up research, we will try to take advantage of wavelet statistics as extra prior knowledge in the recovery process to further improve the recovery quality.

References

1. Donoho, D.L.: Compressed sensing. IEEE Trans. Inf. Theory **52**, 1289–1306 (2006)
2. Colonnese, S., Rinauro, S., Cusani, R., Scarano, G.: The restricted isometry property of the Radon-like CS matrix. In 2013 IEEE 15th International Workshop on Multimedia Signal Processing, MMSP, pp. 248–253. IEEE, Pula (2013)
3. Hayashi, K., Nagahara, M., Tanaka, T.: A user's guide to compressed sensing for communications systems. IEICE Trans. Commun. **96**, 685–712 (2013)
4. Davenport, M.A., Wakin, M.B.: Analysis of orthogonal matching pursuit using the restricted isometry property. IEEE Trans. Inf. Theory **56**, 4395–4401 (2010)

5. Wang, W., Ni, L.: Multipath subspace pursuit for compressive sensing signal reconstruction. In: 2014 7th International Congress on Image and Signal Processing (CISP), pp. 1141–1145. IEEE (2014)
6. Sathyabama, B., Siva Sankari, S.G., Nayagara, S.: Fusion of satellite images using compressive sampling matching pursuit (CoSaMP) method. In: 2013 Fourth National Conference on Computer Vision, Pattern Recognition, Image Processing and Graphics (NCVPRIPG), pp. 1–4. IEEE (2013)
7. Ekanadham, C., Tranchina, D., Simoncelli, E.P.: Recovery of sparse translation-invariant signals with continuous basis pursuit. IEEE Trans. Sig. Process. **59**, 4735–4744 (2011)
8. Li, J., Shen, Y., Wang, Q.: Stepwise suboptimal iterative hard thresholding algorithm for compressive sensing. In: 2012 IEEE International Instrumentation and Measurement Technology Conference (I2MTC), pp. 1332–1336. IEEE (2012)
9. Lai, L., Wang, Q., Wang, Q.: Research on one kind of improved GPSR algorithm. In: 2012 International Conference on Computer Science and Electronics Engineering (ICCSEE), pp. 715–718 (2012)
10. Duarte, M.F., Davenport, M.A., Takhar, D., Laska, J.N., Sun, T., Kelly, K.F., Baraniuk, R.G.: Single-Pixel imaging via compressive sampling. IEEE Sig. Process. Mag. **25**, 83–91 (2008)
11. Goyal, V.K., Fletcher, A.K., Rangan, S.: Compressive sampling and lossy compression. IEE Sig. Process. Mag. **25**, 48–56 (2008)
12. Selesnick, I.W.: The double-density dual-tree DWT. IEEE Trans. Signal Process. **52**, 1304–1314 (2004)
13. Sarawale, R.K., Chougule, S.R.: Noise removal using double-density dual-tree complex DWT. In: 2013 IEEE Second International Conference on Image Information Processing (ICIIP), pp. 219–224. IEEE (2013)
14. Prasanthi, G., Harini, P.: Robust satellite image resolution enhancement using double density dual tree complex wavelet transform. Int. J. Adv. Trends Comput. Sci. Eng. 223–228 (2014)
15. Selesnick, I.W., Baraniuk, R.G., Kingsbury, N.C.: The dual-tree complex wavelet transform. IEEE Sig. Process. Mag. **22**, 123–151 (2005)
16. Baraniuk, R.G., Cevher, V., Duarte, M.F., Hegde, C.: Model-based compressive sensing. IEEE Trans. Inf. Theory **56**, 1982–2001 (2010)
17. Baraniuk, R.G., De Vore, R.A., Kyriazis, G., Yu, X.M.: Near best tree approximation. Adv. Comput. Math. **16**, 357–373 (2002)

Influential Spatial Facility Prediction over Dynamic Objects

Hongtao Wang[1,2], Qiang Li[1,2], Feng Yi[1,2], Qi Han[3], and Limin Sun[1(✉)]

[1] Beijing Key Laboratory of IOT Information Security,
Institute of Information Engineering, CAS, Beijing 100093, China
sunlimin@iie.ac.cn
[2] University of Chinese Academy of Sciences, Beijing 100093, China
[3] Department of EECS, Colorado School of Mines, Golden, CO 80401, USA

Abstract. Calculating the influence of facilities is an important part of urban computing, which adopts sensing technology to obtain people's movement patterns in urban spaces and then applies this information to discover many hidden issues our cities face today. Influence of facilities is affected by people's daily activities such as work and relax. In this paper, we compute the influence of facilities in real time and predict their future influence under a grid partition method. We Next predict influence changes of facilities over dynamic objects using trajectory based markov model. We conduct evaluation using a real world dataset, including one-month taxi trajectories with 27,000 taxis and 1000 facilities. Experimental results shows that our solution requires computation time close to 0.1 seconds and achieves an accuracy of 85 %.

Keywords: Urban computing · Facility influence · Human mobility

1 Introduction

Along with the rapid progress of urbanization, urban computing [14,15] has emerged to focus on the integration of computing, sensing, and actuation technologies into everyday urban settings and lifestyles. Nowadays, modern urban has a variety of public infrastructures including subway stations, overpasses, office facilities, sports arenas, supermarkets, convention centers, hospitals, and entertainment parks, etc. These facilities [8] support different needs of people's urban lives and serve as a valuable tool for getting a detailed understanding of how a metropolitan area works.

Facilities have varying degrees of influence [3,4] heavily affecting people's lifestyle. In the other hand, moving objects can generate time-varying and dynamic influence(e.g., number of people/cars close by) to nearby facilities. Understanding the dynamic influences of facilities may help urban planners to make more informed decisions. For instance, urban planners can use there massive GPS location data from taxies to help analyzing traffic anomalies [2], area functions [11], travel routes [6], etc.

© Springer International Publishing Switzerland 2015
K. Xu and J. Zhu (Eds.): WASA 2015, LNCS 9204, pp. 528–538, 2015.
DOI: 10.1007/978-3-319-21837-3_52

While the idea of using the count of moving objects gathered to compute and predict the influence of a facility seems simple, several challenges arise in practice. The first challenge is how to *efficiently* calculate the influence of a facility given massive objects and facilities. Naive counting method and index suffer from too much computing overhead. The second challenge is how to predict the future influence of a facility when only current locations of objects are known. Objects always move around and this dynamic nature of movements leads to varying influence of a facility over time.

In this paper, we propose our ideas to address these two challenges based on the following intuitions. Each facility itself has an influence range. When one object stays in the range of one facility, it is added to the facility's influence to reflect this object's impact. In particular, we partition a city into grids and each grid has a uniform influence value to its nearest facility and zero as the inference for other facilities. The grid index maps object location information to a specific cell, and the object count within the cell is added to the influence of the nearest facility. Another intuition, every object has its own trajectory and if two objects have similar trajectories, they will go to the same area in next time slot with a high probability. In particular, we use Trajectory based Markov chain Model, a variation of Markov chain trained by historical movements, to predict new objects' movement and then future influence. Experimental results show that our solutions are effective and efficient in computing and in predicting facility influence.

The rest of the paper is organized as follows. Section 2 presents the problem of facility influence calculation. We then propose a grid partition approach to efficiently compute facility influence in Sect. 3. Trajectory based Markov Model is used to predict people location in the future (Sect. 4). In Sect. 5, we evaluate our solution using a large-scale dataset. Finally, we introduce related work and make concluding remarks.

2 Problem Definition

Influential facility computing was first introduced by [8] in which the influence of facility f is defined as the number of objects that consider f as the nearest site among all objects.

Let $\mathcal{P}$ denote a set of objects and $\mathcal{F}$ a set of facilities. Assume object $p \in \mathcal{P}$ and facility $f \in \mathcal{F}$. We denote influence of a facility f as

$$I_{\mathcal{P}}(f) = \sum_{p \in \mathcal{P}} R_f(p), \tag{1}$$

where function $R_f(p)$ determines whether p is within the range of facility f. Euclidean distance $d(p, f)$ can be used to measure the influence of the facility impacted by the object p.

$$R_f(p) = \begin{cases} 1, \text{ if } d(p,f) \le d(p,f_i), \ f_i \in \mathcal{F} \\ 0, \text{ otherwise} \end{cases} \tag{2}$$

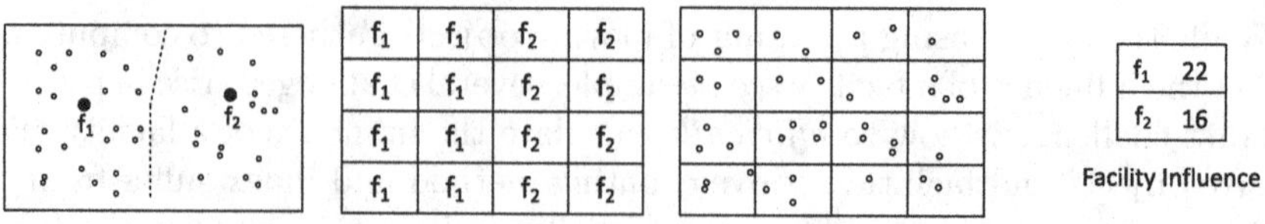

Fig. 1. An example on calculation of facility influence using grids. Left to right: (a)-(d).

With the definition of facility influence, we propose two problems that need to be addressed: (1) How to find out the current top k influential facilities efficiently; and (2) How to predict top k influential facilities in future time under dynamic objects?

3 Fast Computation of Facility Influence

3.1 Grid Partition Method

The computation overhead is exacerbated when people are moving via any transportation methods (e.g., car, bike, or walk) because the distance of every pair need to be recomputed frequently. However, it is unnecessary to calculate the distance for every pair of facility f and object p at every time stamp, as most of them remain invariant within a period of time. We partition a geographic region into equal-sized grids and provide an index for each grid. Since different facilities influence on different scope area, one grid can be viewed as a whole to compute facility influence. For every grid, we store a value which denotes the influence of this grid on the facilities and update it only when the number of objects in this grid change.

Let us use an example (Fig. 1) to walk through this grid-based approach. Two facilities f_1 and f_2 are in the region in Fig. 1(a). Each has a scope associated and each has multiple objects around. The cell influence view (b) shows that every grid cell has a nearest facility and the objects view (c) shows objects in every cell. We can overlay these two views and get all facilities' influence (d) very quickly.

Although the grid-based approach seems simple, one practical issue by ambiguous grids need to be handled. Ambiguous grid which is within the scope of multiple facilities may lead to inaccuracy in calculation of facility influence. Due to the existence of ambiguous cells, we use *Approximate Influence* instead of accurate facility influence. For every facility f in $\mathcal{F}$, the approximate influence of facility f is defined as follows:

$$\hat{I}_{\mathcal{P}}(f) = \sum_{p \in \mathcal{P}} Pr(NN(g) = f | g = H(p)) \tag{3}$$

where $NN(g)$ denotes the nearest facility of grid cell g, $H(p)$ outputs the cell that p is mapped to, $Pr(\cdot)$ is the probability.

Since every object can be mapped to a cell, we separate the objects set $\mathcal{P}$ into two subsets: one is unique cell set $\mathcal{P}'$, and the other is ambiguous cell set $\mathcal{P}''$. If the mapped cell g is a unique cell, then $Pr(NN(g) = f | g = H(p)) = 1$; when the mapped cell g is an ambiguous cell, we design thee methods to compute $Pr(NN(g) = f | g = H(p))$ approximately.

- **Case 1 (Centering):** We use the center of g(denoted by c) representing grid g to compute the probability.
- **Case 2 (Sampling):** We randomly sampling several points in a grid and thus compute every sampling point's nearest neighbor in $\mathcal{F}$. The sampling points are uniformly distributed.
- **Case 3 (Area):** We partition the whole region using Voronoi diagram generated by $\mathcal{F}$, then we compute the proportion related to facility f as the probability.

Centering is the simplest scheme as it uses the center point to represent a grid. If objects' locations mapped to a grid follow uniform distribution, Sampling and Area schemes are recommended. The Area scheme is a generalization of the Sampling scheme and can utilize the information of Voronoi diagram [13] generated by facility set $\mathcal{F}$.

3.2   Facility Influence Computation

After the entire geographic region is divided into cells, we can get a mapping between cells and facilities. Then we use Algorithm 1 to get top k influential facilities.

Algorithm 1. Grid based Top k Facility Influence Computation

Input: objects set $\mathcal{P}$, and facilities set $\mathcal{F}$;
Output: top k facilities set $\mathcal{F}_k$;

1 **foreach** *object p in $\mathcal{P}$* **do**
2   Get current cell gid_c and previous cell gid_p of object p
3   **if** $gid_c \neq gid_p$ **then**
4   Get nearest facility f_c of gid_c and nearest facility f_p of gid_p
5   **if** $f_c \neq f_p$ **then**
6   Update f_c and f_p via Eq.(3).

7 $\mathcal{F}_k \leftarrow$ top k score of facilities
8 **return** $\mathcal{F}_k$

---

4   Influence Prediction

Facility influence is determined by objects gathered around the facility. Intuitively, moving objects' future locations could be predicted from their historical movement patterns. In this section, we present how to use Trajectory based

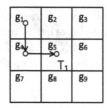 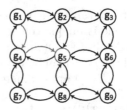

Fig. 2. An example of Trajectory based Markov model. Left to right: (a) grid partition, and (b) 3×3 Markov model.

Markov Model(TMM) to predict objects' location in future time based on their trajectories. Specifically, we first discuss how to construct a Markov model to estimate nodes transition matrix, then present the details of TMM. Finally, we propose an algorithm that predicts future facility influence under TMM.

4.1 Construction of Trajectory Based Markov Model

We utilize the same grid representation as in previous section to predict object's future location. Partitioned grids can be converted to a graph, where each node is one grid and an edge exists between adjacent cells. There are two advantages using a grid partition based approach. First, a grid representation is appropriate for facility influence prediction. Second, a grid based approach can avoid the data sparsity problem when predicting future location.

To further understand the processing of Markov model for trajectories, we use an example to illustrate it. In Fig. 2, the region is partitioned into 3×3 grids. Trajectory T_1 is represented as a sequence of grid cells: g_1, g_4, g_5 (Fig. 2(a)). Each grid is represented a state in Markov model, so T_1 is represented as a sequence of states over time (Fig. 2(b)).

The prediction of objects' future locations consists of two phases: a training phase where the historical trajectories are mined offline to obtain a Markov transition matrix, and an online prediction phase where the historical trajectory of a given object is analyzed and its future locations are predicted.

In the training phase, let S_{ij} denote a travel from g_i to g_j. The transition probability of S_{ij} is denoted by $Pr(S_{ij})$. Note that a trajectory T_{ij} is composed of a set of steps: $T_{ij} = \{S_{i,i+1}, S_{i+1,i+2}, \cdots, S_{i+n,j}\}$. Formally,

$$Pr(S_{ij}) = \frac{|S_{ij}|}{|S_{i\neg}|} \tag{4}$$

where $|S_{i\neg}|$ is the total number of grid needed to travel from g_i to all Neighboring cells. After computing all possible transitions using Eq. (4), we get the transition matrix M.

4.2 Prediction of Future Locations

In this section, we formulate the prediction under trajectory based Markov model. Assume an object has a trajectory T_{ij}, i.e., it started from g_i to g_j

through a certain path. Now the question is how to derive the probability of the object arriving at an adjacent cell g_k in the next time slot, given the knowledge of T_{ij}. This probability can be computed using Bayes rule as follows.

$$Pr(S_{jk}|T_{ij}) \propto Pr(T_{ij}|S_{jk})Pr(S_{jk}) \tag{5}$$

where $Pr(S_{jk})$ can be obtained from transition matrix M. $Pr(T_{ij}|S_{jk})$ denotes the probability of an object traveling from g_i to g_j given that transition steps are from grid j to grid k. It can be computed as follows [9].

$$Pr(T_{ij}|S_{jk}) = \frac{Pr(T_{ij}) \cdot Pr(S_{jk})}{Pr_{i \to k}} \tag{6}$$

where $Pr_{i \to k}$ is the total transition probability of all possible trajectories traveling from g_i to g_k. Combining Eq.(6) and Eq.(5), we have

$$Pr(S_{jk}|T_{ij}) \propto \frac{Pr^2(S_{jk})}{Pr_{i \to k}} \tag{7}$$

In fact, $Pr_{i \to k}$ can also be calculated from M. In general, $M^r(r \in [0, \infty))$ holds the probabilities of transition from one node to another in exactly r steps (i.e., M^r holds r-step transition probabilities). One method to compute $Pr_{i \to k}$ is:

$$Pr_{i \to k} = M_{ik}^{L_{i \to k}} \cdot (M_{ik}^0 + M_{ik}^1 + \cdots + M_{ik}^{L_{de,i \to k}}) \tag{8}$$

where $L_{i \to k}$ denotes l_1 distance (step counts of the shortest path) from g_i to g_k and $L_{de,i \to k}$ denotes the maximal steps which an object may run more paths from g_i to g_k. $L_{de,i \to k}$ is often set to be $0.2L_{i \to k}$ [9].

4.3 Prediction of Future Facility Influence

Predicting future facility influence is feasible using TMM. We assume the speed of object is stable as current speed. Then we can get a set of possible grid cells C which an object could arrive according to current speed. If cell g in C is next to current cell, we can directly use Eq.(7) to compute the probability. After get all possible cells' probability, we can use the highest one as the final prediction result for that object. Algorithm 2 summarizes how prediction of facility influence is done.

Algorithm 2. Facility Influence Prediction

Input: updated trajectory set $\mathcal{T}$ and grid transition Matrix M;
Output: Top k facilities' set $\mathcal{F}_k$ in next time slot;
1 **foreach** *trajectory* $\{T_{ij}\}$ **do**
2   Evaluate all possible cell set C;
3   **foreach** *every cell in C* **do**
4   Compute $Pr(S_{jk}|T_{ij})$ using M and Eq.(7);
5   Identify the cell g with maximal probability;
6   Compute the influence of the facility in grid g;
7 $\{f\} \leftarrow$ Top k score of facilities;
8 **return** $\{f\}$

---

5 Performance Evaluation

5.1 Experiment Setup

Since taxis always give rides to people to different places and taxis' trajectories impact facility influence in the same way, We use taxi mobility to evaluate the performance of our algorithms. The large real world dataset consists of one-month moving trajectories of taxis in Beijing. It contains more than 27,000 taxis over one billion trajectories. Facilities are overpasses, subway stations, tourism destinations, shopping malls, etc., which are extracted from over 1000 Beijing POIs [11].

Our implemented algorithms were run on a desktop machine with Intel Core I5-3380 2.90 GHz dual core CPU and 8 GB of main memory. We first separate every taxi trajectory into sub-trajectories which starts in one grid cell and ends in another. Then we split the sub-trajectory database to two parts, one for training Markov Transition Matrix and the other for testing the effectiveness of our algorithm. We then compute the Markov Transition Matrix M using Eq.(4), and $M^2, M^3, \cdots$ are also derived. When doing online prediction, we put all the matrices into memory, avoiding complex matrix multiplication operations.

5.2 Facility Influence Computing

We evaluate Algorithm 1 by offline training and online prediction. Firstly, grid size l is a key factor affecting offline training both in efficiency and effectiveness. From Fig. 3(a) we see that when we increase grid size, the training time decrease dramatically. However, as we can see in Fig. 4, large grid size would also reduce the accuracy. We suggest to make a trade-off which grid size can range from 100 to 500 meters. Figure 3(b) shows how taxi count affects the response time of online facility influence calculation. We set grid size $l = 100$ and facility count $m = 300$. We see that the response time increases linearly with the increase of taxi count n. Figure 3(c) depicts how facility count affects response time. These results have confirmed that using grid is suitable for calculating facility influence in real time.

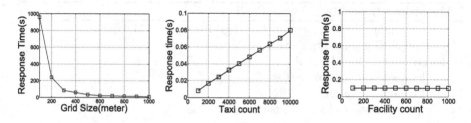

Fig. 3. Overhead. Left to right: (a) Grid Size, (b) Taxi count, and (c) Facility count.

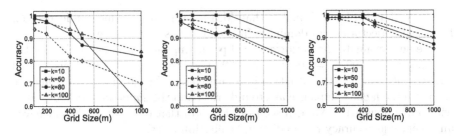

Fig. 4. Accuracy. Left to right: (a) Centering, (b) Sampling, and (c) Area.

We next evaluate the effectiveness of dealing with ambiguous grids. In these experiments, we set facility count $m = 300$ and taxi count $n = 10,000$. From Fig. 4 we find out that the accuracy decreases with the increase of grid size. We suggest to set l between 100 meters and 500 meters according to different surroundings (various facility types). Figure 4 also demonstrates the accuracy with different k values, i.e., finding out top k most influential facilities.

5.3 Prediction Accuracy

We first evaluate location prediction accuracy of our Trajectory based Markov model(TMM). Two factors affect the accuracy: trajectory length and the number of future steps we would predict. Figure 5(a) depicts the impact of trajectory length on location prediction accuracy with assumption of one future step. When the trajectory length is long (10 steps in this case), the accuracy is close to 85 %. When the number of historical steps equals 1, the accuracy is below 70 %. This is reasonable since more historical data will lead to higher accuracy in prediction.

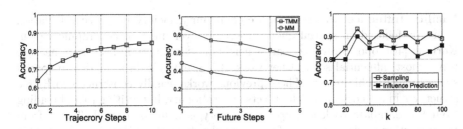

Fig. 5. Facility prediction accuracy. Left to right: (a) Historical step count, (b) Future step count, and (c) Top k facilities.

For future steps, we compare TMM with the naive Markov Model(MM) which is considered as baseline. MM is a common methods in location prediction with normal transition, which directly uses the transition probability of current state to neighbors. The trajectory length used for TMM and MM ranges from 3 to 10. Figure 5(b) depicts impact of future steps on the prediction accuracy. The accuracy of TMM is much higher than MM in every steps, which indicates that historical trajectories can dominate future locations to a large extent.

We next evaluate the performance of predicting facility influence. We set the parameters $l = 500, m = 500, n = 30,000$. The historical steps is bigger than 4 and we only consider the situation in 5 future steps. We use nearest distance to calculate the facility influence as ground-truth and the *sampling* method to deal with ambiguous grids. We can see from Fig. 5(c) that our solution has achieved an acceptable accuracy for predicting facility influence.

6   Related Work

Our work lies at the intersection of urban computing and facility influence query in databases.

Urban Computing. Urban computing is emerging as a concept where every sensor, device, person, vehicle, building, street and so on in urban areas can be used as a component to probe city dynamics and further enable a city-wide computing for serving people and their cities. The increasing availability of GPS-embedded taxicabs provides taxi trajectories in urban computing. Previous work has mainly focused on solving specific issues that urban residents face, such as measuring air pollution of point of interests (POIs) using human mobility in different city regions [11], recommending taxi routes [1,7], or inferring energy consumption of city via the car refueling behavior [12]. These works mostly focus on dynamic locations due to human mobility, but less on facility influence. Previous work has studied taxi trajectories and analyzed traffic anomalies [2], area functions [11], travel routes [6], etc. We also use taxi trajectories; however, we use them to consider how taxis or objects impact facility influence.

Facility Influence. In the database community, facility influence calculation is mainly focused on spatial query processing over different geographic region. Korn al. [4] proposes reverse nearest neighbor as influence indicator to measure top k most influential sets. Other work [3,5,8] extends data queries to spatial space in geographic region. These previous works usually construct two R-tree structures in memory, in which objects are stationary, but writing to and reading from the database to load into the memory is a major cost. Different from these existing works, our work focuses on the dynamic objects in a geographic area. Several previous works [10,13] propose the preprocessing stage to efficiently compute rather than using R-tree. Voronoi-based partition [13] divides scopes of facility into various region-irregular areas and each area represents the scope of a facility. This approach requires to build tree index for Voronoi partition and time cost over query Voronoi index is related to area count. Work [10] adopts adaptive grid partition to find influential locations. Similar to Voronoi-based partition, adaptive grid also requires R-tree indices to identify right grid number to calculate the facility influence.

7 Conclusion

In this paper, we propose to predict the influence of top k facilities in urban computing. A facility supports public services to satisfy needs of people's urban lives and its influence is affected by the count of people/cars gathered around it. We present a grid partition approach to efficiently computing facility influence over dynamic objects. To predict facility influence in future, trajectory based markov model trained by historical trajectories is proposed to predict objects' future movement, which is then used to evaluate future influence of facilities. Experimental results show that our approaches are acceptable in terms of both computing facility influence in real time and predicting future facility influence with high accuracy.

Acknowledgment. This work was supported in part by the National Natural Science Foundation of China (Grant No. 61202066, 61472418), and the "Strategic Priority Research Program" of the Chinese Academy of Sciences (Grant No. XDA06040101).

References

1. Bassoli, A., Brewer, J., Martin, K., Dourish, P., Mainwaring, S.: Underground aesthetics: rethinking urban computing. IEEE Pervasive Comput. **6**(3), 39–45 (2007)
2. Chawla, S., Zheng, Y., Hu, J.: Inferring the root cause in road traffic anomalies. In: 12th IEEE International Conference on Data Mining, ICDM 2012, Brussels, Belgium, December 10–13, 2012, pp. 141–150 (2012)
3. Huang, J., Wen, Z., Qi, J., Zhang, R., Chen, J., He, Z.: Top-k most influential locations selection. In: CIKM, pp. 2377–2380 (2011)
4. Korn, F., Muthukrishnan, S.: Influence sets based on reverse nearest neighbor queries. In: SIGMOD Conference, pp. 201–212 (2000)
5. Liu, J., Yu, G., Sun, H.: Subject-oriented top-k hot region queries in spatial dataset. In: CIKM, pp. 2409–2412 (2011)
6. Wei, L.Y., Peng, W.C., Lee, W.C.: Exploring pattern-aware travel routes for trajectory search. ACM Trans. Intell. Syst. Technol. **4**(3), 48:1–48:25 (2013)
7. Wei, L.Y., Zheng, Y., Peng, W.C.: Constructing popular routes from uncertain trajectories. In: Proceedings of the 18th ACM SIGKDD International Conference on Knowledge Discovery and Data Mining, pp. 195–203. ACM (2012)
8. Xia, T., Zhang, D., Kanoulas, E., Du, Y.: On computing top-t most influential spatial sites. In: VLDB, pp. 946–957 (2005)
9. Xue, A.Y., Zhang, R., Zheng, Y., Xie, X., Huang, J., Xu, Z.: Destination prediction by sub-trajectory synthesis and privacy protection against such prediction. In: 29th IEEE International Conference on Data Engineering, ICDE 2013, Brisbane, Australia, April 8–12, 2013, pp. 254–265 (2013)
10. Yan, D., Wong, R.C.W., Ng, W.: Efficient methods for finding influential locations with adaptive grids. In: CIKM, pp. 1475–1484 (2011)
11. Yuan, J., Zheng, Y., Xie, X.: Discovering regions of different functions in a city using human mobility and pois. In: Proceedings of the 18th ACM SIGKDD International Conference on Knowledge Discovery and Data Mining, pp. 186–194. ACM (2012)

12. Zhang, F., Wilkie, D., Zheng, Y., Xie, X.: Sensing the pulse of urban refueling behavior. In: Proceedings of the 2013 ACM International Joint Conference on Pervasive and Ubiquitous Computing, pp. 13–22. ACM (2013)
13. Zhang, P., Cheng, R., Mamoulis, N., Renz, M., Züfle, A., Tang, Y., Emrich, T.: Voronoi-based nearest neighbor search for multi-dimensional uncertain databases. In: ICDE, pp. 158–169 (2013)
14. Zheng, Y., Capra, L., Wolfson, O., Yang, H.: Urban computing: concepts, methodologies, and applications. ACM Trans. Intell. Syst. Technol. 5(3), 38:1–38:55 (2014)
15. Zheng, Y., Liu, Y., Yuan, J., Xie, X.: Urban computing with taxicabs. In: Proceedings of the 13th International Conference on Ubiquitous Computing, pp. 89–98. ACM (2011)

A Heuristic Stream Order Scheduling Algorithm for Intra-Superframe Power Management in WPANs

Licheng Wang[1]([✉]), Yun Pan[2], Minzheng Jia[3], and Ahmad Haseeb[1]

[1] State Key Laboratory of Networking and Switching Technology,
Beijing University of Posts and Telecommunications,
Beijing 100876, People's Republic of China
wanglc@bupt.edu.cn

[2] School of Computer, Communication University of China,
Beijing 100024, People's Republic of China

[3] Department of Information Engineering,
Beijing Polytechnic College, Beijing 100042, People's Republic of China

Abstract. A wireless personal area network (WPAN) is comprised of battery-powered portable devices that support short-range communications. For saving energy and enlarging WPAN lifetime, one of the key issues in WPANs is to schedule the order of multiple streams among multiple devices so that the idle devices can go to sleep, and the total wakeup times become as small as possible. Guo et al. modeled the stream order scheduling (SOS) problem in WPANs as a Hamilton path problem and concluded that it is difficult to find exact and optimal solutions in general. However, in this paper, we will falsify the aforementioned suggestion by presenting a counterexample. Moreover, we propose a heuristic algorithm for solving the SOS problem in WPANs near to optimal. By carrying out various tests on 935 random graphs, we find that our method achieves the optimal solution with a very high success probability, about 99.5 %.

Keywords: Wireless personal area networks · Multiple-stream scheduling · Heuristic algorithm · Eular path · Hamilton path

1 Introduction

IEEE 802.15.3, as a MAC support for Ultra-Wide Band (UWB), enables a high-speed and lower power wireless connectivity among portable devices within a wireless personal network (WPAN) [1,5]. WPAN has gained a lot of attention due to its great significance for applications such as intelligent home networking.

IEEE 802.15.3 is mainly based on Time Division Multiple Access (TDMA) technology. That is, the time in 802.15.3 is divided into multiple superframes (SF for short). To enlarge the lifetime of WPANs, several power saving modes such as Device Synchronized Power Save (DSPS) have been defined in 802.15.3

© Springer International Publishing Switzerland 2015
K. Xu and J. Zhu (Eds.): WASA 2015, LNCS 9204, pp. 539–549, 2015.
DOI: 10.1007/978-3-319-21837-3_53

standards, and these modes enable the involved devices to sleep for one or more SF. Apparently, these modes schedule the related devices by taking an inter-superframe perspective.

In 2002, Guo et al. [1] firstly addressed the power management of WPANs from an intra-superframe perspective. Within a SF, the TDMA-based Channel Time Allocation Period, shared by multiple streams among multiple devices, is further divided into different time slots, named Channel Time Allocations (CTAs). The pre-selected piconent coordinator (PNC) assigns a CTA for each stream and announces the position and the duration of the CTA in the beacon at the beginning of SF. Since each device knows its CTA position in a SF from the beacon, it can go to sleep during the phase when CTAs are not assigned for its streams and only wake up during the phase when CTAs are assigned for its streams. As a result, the relative positioning of the streams within a TDMA SF might have significant effections on the total number of wakeups. Consider that each transformation between the wakeup phase and the sleeping phase consumes significant amount of power [2], the PNC must have to schedule multiple streams within a SF, so that the number of total wakeup times could be made as small as possible.

Guo et al. [1] proposed that finding the optimal solutions for the problem of stream order scheduling (SOS) within a SF is *equivalent to* solving the Hamilton path problem over the corresponding edge-dual graph. However, the hardness of the Hamilton problem blocked Guo et al's continuous efforts for proceeding in this direction. Instead, they turned to another way: They proposed an algorithm, named as min-degree searching (MDS for short), to find the sub-optimal order of the streams.

MOTIVATION AND CONTRIBUTION. Our start point is just the corner where Guo et al. [1] once stopped. On one hand, we falsify the equivalence of the SOS problem and the Hamilton path problem (see Sect. 2.2 for details). In fact, we find that the existing Hamilton path is merely a sufficient but not necessary condition to lead towards the optimal solutions for the SOS problem. Moreover, we find that the optimal solution of SOS problem can even be derived from some partial Hamilton paths. On the other hand, even if it is theoretically difficult to solve the SOS problem by finding Hamilton paths, we should make more attempts to find nearly optimal solutions by resorting on certain heuristic strategies in practice.

Based on the above considerations, in this paper we propose a heuristic stream order scheduling algorithm for intra-SF power management in WPANs. Our method has the following merits:

- Time efficient. For a given instance of stream scheduling problem with n devices and m streams, the time complexity of our algorithm is $\mathcal{O}(m^2)$.
- Nearly optimal. Based on our simulations over 935 random graphs, we show that our algorithm finds the optimal solutions with the probability about 99.5 %.

– Scalable. Our simulations also present that not only the searching time, but also the quality of the solutions are very stable with increasing the scales of devices and streams.

RELATED WORK. In 2002, Stine and Veciana [3] proposed an energy efficient algorithm for stream scheduling in centrally controlled wireless data networks. But the performance of their algorithm is totally outperformed by Guo et al.'s MDS algorithm that was put forward in 2005 [1]: Based on amount of simulations, Guo et al. presented that the MDS algorithm finds the optimal solutions with a probability more than 95 %. At IS3C 2012, Wang and Wen [5] further studied the performance of MDS algorithm from several aspects such as wakeup times, device and stream scales, as well as stream densities. Their work presented that MDS algorithm also outperforms over the related standards about WPANs [5].

ROADMAP. Related definitions and models about the SOS problem in WPANs are reviewed in Sect. 2. Our main contributions, including a heuristic algorithm for solving the SOS problem, as well as analysis on the time complexity, are presented in Sect. 3. Simulations are organized and evaluated in Sect. 4. Finally, concluding remarks are given in Sect. 5.

2 Stream Order Scheduling Problem in WPANs

2.1 Notations and Models

It is a convenient way to represent the scenario of multiple streams among multiple devices within a TDMA intra-SF as an undirected graph $G = (V, E)$, where each node in V represents a device, and each edge in E indicates a stream between two devices. Suppose $m = |E|$, then any permutation $\pi \in S_m$ is a *schedule* of E. That is, given a schedule π, the streams in E are transmitted according to the following order:

$$e_{\pi(1)} \rightarrow e_{\pi(2)} \rightarrow \cdots \rightarrow e_{\pi(m)}. \tag{1}$$

For two streams $e_1, e_2 \in E$, if we meaningly use the notation $e_1 \cap e_2$ to denote the joint set of the numbers that indicate the devices for defining the streams e_1 and e_2. Now, the *wakeup number* of each stream, denoted by $w(e_{\pi(i)})$, under a schedule π is defined as follows:

$$w(e_{\pi(i)}) = \begin{cases} 2, & i = 1, \\ 2 - |e_{\pi(i)} \cap e_{\pi(i-1)}|, & 2 \le i \le m. \end{cases} \tag{2}$$

Finally, the wakeup number of a schedule π is defined by

$$w(\pi) = \sum_{i=1}^{m} w(e_{\pi(i)}). \tag{3}$$

Then, the objective of stream order scheduling (SOS for short) problem is to find $\pi \in S_m$ such that $w(\pi)$ achieves minimal. That is, the SOS problem can be modeled as

$$\min_{\pi \in S_m} w(\pi). \tag{4}$$

2.2 A Counterexample Towards Guo et al.'s Suggestion

In [1], Guo et al. built connections among the SOS problem with two well-known graph problems: Eular path problem and Hamilton path problem. According to their suggestion, the existence of Eular path in the graph $G = (V, E)$ is a *sufficient but not necessary* condition to get an optimal solution for the SOS problem in a TDMA intra-SF scenario defined by G. Furthermore, they concluded that the existence of Hamilton path in the edge-dual topology G^* is an *equivalent* condition for leading an optimal SOS solution [1], where $G^* = (V^*, E^*)$ is defined according to the following rules:

1. For each edge $(i, j) \in E$, we define a node, labeled as e_{ij}, for V^*;
2. For two distinct edges $e_1, e_2 \in E$, we define an edge, labeled as $e^*_{e_1, e_2}$, for E^* if and only if $e_1 \cap e_2 \neq \emptyset$.

However, we find that the existence of Hamilton paths in G^* is merely a *sufficient but not necessary* condition for deriving the optimal SOS solutions. A counterexample is presented in Fig. 1. We observe that one of the optimal schedules for this SOS instance specified by the original topology Fig. 1 (a) would be

$$e_{12} \to e_{23} \to e_{37} \to e_{38} \to e_{34} \to e_{45} \to e_{67} \to e_{89}, \tag{5}$$

and the corresponding wakeup number of this schedule is 11. But apparently this optimal solution cannot be derived from any Hamilton path. In fact, there is neither Eular path in the original topology (See Fig. 1 (a)), nor Hamilton path in its edge-dual topology (See Fig. 1 (b)).

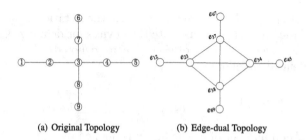

(a) Original Topology   (b) Edge-dual Topology

Fig. 1. A counterexample towards Guo et al.'s suggestion

3 Proposed Algorithm

3.1 Basic Idea

In fact, the NP-hardness results never block people's efforts for finding nearly optimal solutions towards many well-known NP-complete problems, such as the travelling salesman problem, the knapsack problem, the Steiner stree problem, the integer programming problem, etc. Instead, during the past decades, many interesting applications were built successfully based on the capability of solving the related NP-complete problems approximately or intelligently.

This encourages us to resume the efforts that Guo et al. [1] gave up. This is, try to find nearly optimal solutions by using some heuristic strategy. Unlike Guo et al.'s MDS algorithm that works on original topologies, we focus on the corresponding edge-dual topologies. Although Guo et al.'s suggestion about the equivalence between the existence of Hamilton path and the optimal solution of the SOS problem is false, their idea is still instructive. In fact, we find that not only a complete Hamilton path on the edge-dual graph can lead to an optimal SOS solution, but a partial Hamilton path on the edge-dual graph can also easily lead to an optimal SOS solution. For example, as for the original topology presented in Fig. 1 (a), we can find a partial Hamilton path on its edge-dual topology presented in Fig. 1 (b) as follows:

$$e_{12} \rightarrow e_{23} \rightarrow e_{37} \rightarrow e_{34} \rightarrow e_{38} \rightarrow e_{89}.$$

Then, a random arrangement the remaining two nodes e_{45} and e_{67} at the tail of the above Hamilton path, say

$$e_{12} \rightarrow e_{23} \rightarrow e_{37} \rightarrow e_{34} \rightarrow e_{38} \rightarrow e_{89} \rightarrow e_{45} \rightarrow e_{67}$$

will lead to another optimal solution, with a total 11 times wakeup, for the original SOS problem.

Therefore, the only remaining hurdle is how to find partial Hamilton paths that could be as long as possible. Our heuristic strategy is based on two very intuitive rules [4]. The first is: Whenever a node is visited, it is immediately dropped so that it could never be re-visited. The second is: The remaining nodes that have less connections with others must have to be visited as soon as possible.

3.2 Compact Representation of Edges

Considering that in the proposed modeling process, it is required to associate a node and an edge not only with the original topologies, but also with the edge-dual topologies, we would like to introduce a compact mode for representing the edges. In particular, we find that this kind of compact representation can simplify algorithmic descriptions.

In essential, this compact representation method labels not only nodes but also edges as positive integers. Given an undirected graph $G = (V, E)$, at first we label all nodes in V as $|V|$ distinct positive integers. Say, $V = \{\ell_1, \cdots, \ell_{|V|}\}$.

Next, for any integer $N \geq \max V$, we also label all edges in E as $|E|$ distinct positive integers as follows: for each edge $(i, j) \in E$, we associate it with an integer

$$\zeta_N(i, j) \triangleq \min\{i, j\} * N + \max\{i, j\}. \tag{6}$$

In fact, it is easy to observe that the representation has the following reverse representation:

$$\zeta_N^{-1}(z) \triangleq \left(\lfloor \frac{z}{N} \rfloor, z - \lfloor \frac{z}{N} \rfloor \cdot N \right), \tag{7}$$

where $\lfloor x \rfloor$ returns the greatest integer $\leq x$. It is not difficult to observe that for the same N, we have the following identities

$$\zeta_N(i, j) = \zeta_N(j, i), \tag{8}$$
$$\zeta_N(\zeta_N^{-1}(z)) = z, \tag{9}$$
$$\zeta_N^{-1}(\zeta_N(i, j)) = (\min\{i, j\}, \max\{i, j\}). \tag{10}$$

3.3   Algorithm Description

Based on the aforementioned preprocessing, our algorithm is presented below.

Algorithm 1. SOS(V, E)

Input: An undirected graph $G = (V, E)$, where V represents the device set, while E represents the stream set.
Output: A tuple $(find, H)$, where

- $find \in \{0, 1\}$ indicates whether an optimal solution is reached,
- $H = i_1 \cdots i_k$ is a queue that represents the scheduling order of streams.

1: {Building Edge-Dual Topology $G^* = (V^*, E^*)$}
2: $V^* \leftarrow \emptyset$, $E^* \leftarrow \emptyset$;
3: **for all** $(i, j) \in E$ or $(j, i) \in E$ **do**
4:     $z = \zeta_{|V|}(i, j)$;
5:     $V^* \leftarrow V^* \cup \{z\}$;
6:     $deg_z = 0$;
7: **end for**
8: $N = \max V^*$;
9: **for all** $z_1, z_2 \in V^* (z_1 \neq z_2)$ **do**
10:     $(i, j) \leftarrow \zeta_{|V|}^{-1}(z_1)$, $(k, l) \leftarrow \zeta_{|V|}^{-1}(z_2)$,
11:     **if** $\{i, j\} \cap \{k, l\} \neq \emptyset$ **then**
12:         $z \leftarrow \zeta_N(z_1, z_2)$;
13:         $E^* \leftarrow E^* \cup \{z\}$;
14:         $deg_{z_1} \leftarrow deg_{z_1} + 1$, $deg_{z_2} \leftarrow deg_{z_2} + 1$;
15:     **end if**

16: **end for**
17: {Finding a (nearly) optimal scheduling order}
18: Initialize H as an empty queue;
19: Choose i such that the node $i \in V^*$ has minimum degree, i.e., $i = \min_{z \in V^*} deg_z$;
20: Append the node i to the tail of H;
21: **if** $deg_i = 0$ **then**
22:    goto 34;
23: **end if**
24: Choose j such that the node $j \in V^*$ has minimum degree among all nodes that are still connected to the node i, i.e. $j = \min_{\substack{k \in V^* \\ \zeta(i,k) \in E^*}} deg_z$;
25: {Drop all edges in E^* that are associated to i}
26: **for all** $j \in V^*$ **do**
27:    $z = \zeta_N(i, j)$;
28:    **if** $z \in E^*$ **then**
29:       $E^* \leftarrow E^* \setminus \{z\}$;
30:       $deg_i \leftarrow deg_i - 1, \ deg_j \leftarrow deg_j - 1$;
31:    **end if**
32: **end for**
33: $i \leftarrow j$, goto 21;
34: **if** all nodes $z \in V^*$ lie in H **then**
35:    $find = 1$;
36:    Return $(find, H)$;
37: **end if**
38: Assign i as the head of H;
39: $(x, y) = \zeta_{|V|}^{-1}(i)$;
40: {Recover all edges that are once associated with i but not belonging to H}
41: **for all** $j \in V^* \setminus H$ **do**
42:    $(s, t) = \zeta_{|V|}^{-1}(j)$;
43:    **if** $\{x, y\} \cap \{s, t\} \neq \emptyset$ **then**
44:       $E^* \leftarrow E^* \setminus \{\zeta_N(i, j)\}$;
45:       $deg_i \leftarrow deg_i + 1, \ deg_j \leftarrow deg_j + 1$;
46:    **end if**
47: **end for**
48: **if** $deg_i = 0$ **then**
49:    goto 63;
50: **end if**
51: Choose j such that the node $j \in V^*$ has minimum degree among all the nodes that are still connected to the node i, i.e. $j = \min_{\substack{k \in V^* \\ \zeta(i,k) \in E^*}} deg_z$;
52: {Drop all edges in E^* that are associated with i}
53: **for all** $j \in V^*$ **do**
54:    $z = \zeta_N(i, j)$;
55:    **if** $z \in E^*$ **then**
56:       $E^* \leftarrow E^* \setminus \{z\}$;

57:     $deg_i \leftarrow deg_i - 1$, $deg_j \leftarrow deg_j - 1$;
58:     **end if**
59: **end for**
60: $i \leftarrow j$;
61: Insert i at the head of H;
62: Goto 47;
63: **if** all nodes $z \in V^*$ lie in H **then**
64:     $find = 1$;
65:     Return $(find, H)$;
66: **end if**
67: $find = 0$;
68: {Schedule remaining streams by degree ascendant order}
69: $R = V^* \setminus H$;
70: Append R to the tail of H;
71: Return $(find, H)$.

3.4   Complexity Analysis

Theorem 1. *The time complexity of the SOS algorithm is determined by the number of streams. More precisely, for a given SOS instance with m streams, the time complexity of the algorithm SOS, denoted by $T(m)$, is given by*

$$T(m) = \mathcal{O}(m^2). \tag{11}$$

Proof. The algorithm SOS is divided into three stages:

- building edge-dual topology (Step 1 ∼ Step 16),
- finding (near) optimal order (Step 17 ∼ Step 67), and
- scheduling the remaining streams if there are (Step 68 ∼ Step 71).

Since $|V^*| = |E| = m$, it is easy to observe that the complexities of the first stage and the third stage are bounded by $\mathcal{O}(m^2)$ and $\mathcal{O}(m)$, respectively.

As for the second stage, the main complex task is to *iteratively* select a candidate node from $V^* \setminus H$ that could be appended to the tail of H (i.e., Step 19 and Step 24) or inserted at the head of H (i.e., Step 51), while the other steps, including edge dropping (i.e., Steps 25∼32, 52∼59) and edge recovering (i.e., Steps 40∼47), can be clearly finished within the complexity $\mathcal{O}(|V^*|)$. Thus, we need only to discuss the total number of comparisons for selecting the candidates nodes.

Suppose that the sequence of degrees of $G^* = (V^*, E^*)$ is $\{deg_i\}_{i=1}^m$. We at first need $m - 1$ time comparisons for selecting H's head node, while for selecting the $(i+1)^{th}$ node, the required comparison number cannot be more than deg_i. Without loss of generality, let us assume that a node with degree $d_1 > 0$ is finally selected. Then, the total number of comparisons of the SOS algorithm for the candidates selection can be bounded as follows

$$C(m) \leq (m-1) + \sum_{i=2}^{m} d_i$$

$$= (m-1) + \sum_{i=1}^{m} d_i - d_1$$

$$= (m-1) + 2|E^*| - d_1$$

$$< 2(m + |E^*|).$$

Now, considering that $|E^*| = \mathcal{O}(m^{1+\delta})$ for some $0 \leq \delta \leq 1$, we have that $\lim_{m\to\infty} C(m)/m^2 < 4$. This concludes the theorem. $\qquad\square$

Remark 1. Note that our algorithm is essentially different from the minimum degree searching (MDS) algorithm presented in [1]. For each step, MDS algorithm selects an edge in the original graph G so that both of the associated nodes have the "minimum" degree. Here, the notion "minimum" for two nodes is meant to consisting of two steps: First, find all candidate nodes with minimum degree, and then for each of them, along with their adjacent nodes, find one with the minimum degree [1]. However, for each iteration, our algorithm only needs to select a node with minimum degree in the edge-dual graph G^*. The phrase "minimum" in our algorithm is much intuitive and simple. The related process is indeed more efficient than MDS.

4 Simulations and Evaluations

According to Theorem 1 we have that the computational cost of the SOS algorithm is independent to the scale of devices, but determined by the scale of streams. In addition, we notice that both Guo et al.'s work [1] and Wang et al.'s work [5] reported that the edge density has significant effect on the quality (i.e., the probability of achieving the optimal solutions) of the MDS algorithm. Thus, our simulations are organized with respect to two dimensions: the scale of streams and the density of edges.

Up to the time of writing this paper, we have finished simulations towards in total 935 random graphs. These simulations are divided into 8 groups and the results are listed in Table 1 and depicted in Fig. 2.

From Table 1 and Fig. 2, we observe that our algorithm has the following merits:

1. High efficiency. Figure 2 (a) presents the average running time of SOS algorithm with respect to different scale of streams. Clearly, the simulated computational cost is almost linear with respect to the scale of streams. On one hand, linear time complexity is the best one we can expect, since anyway we have to output the streams one by one. On the other hand, our simulated efficiency is ever better than the theoretical results provided by Theorem 1, which says that the time cost should be quadratic with respect to the scale of steams. At present, we have not made clear why the SOS algorithm performs better in simulations than its time complexity in theory

Table 1. Simulations: settings and results

Test group no	Density of edges	Scale of streams	Number of instances	Number of optimal solutions	Total running time (s)
1	0.5	4 ~ 20	10	9	< 10
2	0.3	20 ~ 100	15	15	44
3	0.5	100 ~ 200	92	91	303
4	0.5	200 ~ 500	478	476	34391
5	0.3	500 ~ 1000	10	10	2046
6	0.5	500 ~ 1000	144	144	58420
7	0.5	500 ~ 1000	146	145	53648
8	0.5	500 ~ 1000	40	40	14112
Total	–	–	935	930	–

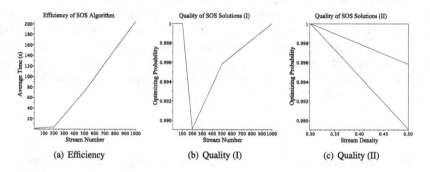

(a) Efficiency   (b) Quality (I)   (c) Quality (II)

Fig. 2. Simulations of SOS algorithm

2. Steady and High quality of solutions. There are in total 930 out of 935 random instances that are solved optimally by the SOS algorithm. That is, our algorithm manifests a very high success probability, $\frac{930}{935} \approx 99.5\%$. Moreover, Fig. 2 (b) and Fig. 2 (c) present that the probability of achieving optimal solution is steady with respect to different stream scales as well as different edge densities, respectively. These results outperform the reported results of the MDS algorithm [1,5].

5   Conclusions

Stream order scheduling problem is one of key issues for power management in WPANs. The standards of IEEE 802.13.5 specify how to do inter-superframe scheduling, but left the ways for intra-superframe scheduling for the vendors. In this paper, a heuristic algorithm for this problem is developed. Simulations manifest that our method efficiently finds optimal solutions with a very high success probability (about 99.5%). The future work is to probe the reason why our algorithm performs better in simulations than its time complexity in theory.

Acknowledgements. This work was supported by the National Natural Science Foundation of China (NSFC) (Nos. 61370194, 61411146001), the Engineering Disciplines Planning Project of the Communication University of China (No. 3132014XNG1445), and the Research Program of Beijing Municipal Commission of Education (No. KM201310853001).

References

1. Guo, Z., Yao, R., Zhu, W., Wang, X., Ren, Y.: Intra-superframe power management for IEEE 802.15.3 WPAN. IEEE Commun. Lett. **9**(3), 228–230 (2005)
2. Li, D., Chou, P., Badherzadeh, N.: Mode selection and mode dependency modeling for power-aware embedded systems. In: Procedeings of the Asia and South Spacific Design Automation Conference, pp. 697–704, Jan 2002
3. Stine, J., Veciana, G.: Improving energy efficiency of centrally controlled wirelss data networks. Wirelss Netw. **8**, 681–700 (2002)
4. Wang, L.: Finding Hamilton paths in random graphs. http://arxiv.org/list/math.Co arxiv.org:1504.nnnnn (to appear)
5. Wang, N.-C., Wen, C.-C.: A performance study for power management schemes in WPANs. In: Proceedings of 2012 Internaltional Symposium on Computer, Consumer and Control, pp. 427–430. IEEE. doi:10.1109/IS3C.2012.14

Minimum-Latency Broadcast and Data Aggregation Scheduling in Secure Wireless Sensor Networks

Lixin Wang[(⊠)], C.P. Abubucker, William Washington, and Katrina Gilmore

Paine College, Augusta, GA 30901, USA
lwang@paine.edu

Abstract. Wireless sensor networks (WSNs) have a wide range of applications such as emergency disaster relief and environmental monitoring. Most of these applications for WSNs are not only time-critical, but also dependent on the secure operations of a sensor network, and have serious consequences if the network is compromised. WSNs are often deployed in hostile environments where communication is monitored. Sensor nodes are subject to be compromised and manipulated by an adversary. On such WSNs, it is vital to provide secure communications among the sensor nodes. Based on the m-composite key pre-distribution schemes in [4], two nodes within each other's transmission range have a secure link if their key rings have at least m common keys. In this paper, we develop short communication schedules for broadcast and data aggregation in *secure* WSNs. Our broadcast scheduling algorithm for secure WSNs outperforms the best known scheduling algorithm for broadcasting in general graphs.

1 Introduction

Multihop wireless sensor networks (WSNs) have a wide range of applications such as emergency disaster relief, environmental monitoring and military surveillance real-time traffic monitoring, building safety monitoring, military sensing and tracking, distributed measurement of seismic activities, real-time pollution monitoring. Most of these applications for WSNs are not only time-critical, but also dependent on the secure operations of a sensor network, and have serious consequences if the network is compromised or disrupted.

WSNs are often deployed in remote and hostile environments where communication is monitored. Sensor nodes are subject to be compromised and manipulated by an adversary. On such WSNs, it is vital that the communications between the sensor nodes are secure. Many mechanisms have been proposed in the literature to provide secure communications between sensors nodes of WSNs [4,6,8,20,23]. One of the popular mechanisms is the m-composite key predistribution schemes proposed by Chan et al. in [4]. Due to the limited capacity

---

This work of Dr. Lixin Wang and Dr. C.P. Abubucker is supported in part by the NNSA cybersecurity grant F1040061-14-09 of U.S. Department of Energy.

© Springer International Publishing Switzerland 2015
K. Xu and J. Zhu (Eds.): WASA 2015, LNCS 9204, pp. 550–560, 2015.
DOI: 10.1007/978-3-319-21837-3_54

and memory resources of the sensor nodes, traditional security schemes and key management algorithms are too complex and not feasible for WSNs. In the m-composite key predistribution scheme, K distinct keys are randomly chosen from the key space to form the key pool. A key ring is a k-element subset of the key pool. Before deployed, each sensor node randomly loads a key ring into its memory. Two nodes within each other's transmission range have a secure link if their key rings have at least m common keys. In secure wireless sensor networks (SWSNs), only secure links can participate in the communication tasks. Hence, if all the nodes have uniform transmission range r, the secure wireless sensor network is the graph in which two nodes have an edge between them if and only if their Euclidean distance is at most r and they have at least m common keys in their key ring. In other words, the connectivity of the secure wireless sensor network can only consider the secure links. A secure WSN is said to be connected if all the networking nodes form a connected network by using the secure links only.

The main objective of this paper is to develop short communication schedules for the following two primitive communication tasks in *secure* WSNs under the protocol interference model with the interference radius equal to the communication radius that is normalized to one (thus the communication topology including both secure and insecure links is a unit-disk graph):

- Broadcast: A distinguished source node sends a common packet to all other nodes.
- Data Aggregation: A distinguished sink node collects the data aggregated from all the packets at the nodes other than the sink node. In other words, every intermediate node combines all received packet with its own packet into a single packet of fixed-size according to some aggregation function such as logical and/or, maximum, or minimum.

Assume that all the communications proceed in synchronous time-slots and each node can transmit at most one packet of a fixed size in each time-slot. A broadcasting schedule assigns a time-slot to every node subject to the constraint that the nodes assigned in each time-slot are interference free, and a node cannot transmit until it has received the broadcast message. The latency of a broadcasting schedule is the number of the time-slots during which at least one transmission occurs. The problem of computing a broadcasting schedule with minimum latency in multihop wireless sensor networks is referred to as Minimum-Latency **B** roadcasting **S** chedule (**MLBS**). Under the assumption that all the communication links are secure, **MLBS** in multihop WSNs has been proved to be NP-hard and extensively studied in the literature [2,3,5,7,10–15,22,26].

A link schedule of an spanning inward arborescence is an assignment of time-slots to all links in this arborescence subject to two constraints: (1) A node can only transmit after all its children complete their transmissions to itself; and (2) all links assigned in a common time-slot are interference free. Thus, an aggregation schedule specifies not only a spanning in-arborescence for routing but also a link schedule of such spanning in-arborescence. The latency of an aggregation schedule is the number of time-slots during which at least one transmission occurs. The problem of computing an aggregation schedule with minimum latency in a multihop WSN is referred to Minimum-Latency Aggregation Schedule (**MLAS**). Under the assumption that all the communication links are secure, **MLBS** in multihop WSNs has been well studied (see [16] and [24] and references therein).

Let V denote the set of all the networking nodes. Denoted by G_u the unit-disk graph over V. Two nodes have a *secure* link between them if and only if their Euclidean distance is at most one and they have at least m common keys in their key rings. Denoted by G_{se} the secure WSN over V. Then, G_{se} is a subgraph of G_u. Note that two nodes in V may not have a secure link between them even if they are very close to each other, and thus they cannot have direct communications on G_{se}. It is well-known that any node of G_u has at most five independent neighbors. But a node of G_{se} may have many independent neighbors. Such a nature of the secure network G_{se} makes both MLBS and MLAS much more challenging than on unit-disk graphs. As a matter of fact, all the existing scheduling algorithms for both MLBS and MLAS based on UDGs are no longer suitable for the secure network G_{se}.

In this paper, we develop efficient approximation algorithms for both **MLBS** and **MLAS** in *secure* WSNs, referred to as **MLBS-Se** and **MLAS-Se**, respectively. To the best of our knowledge, this is the first paper that proposes efficient approximation solutions for both MLBS-Se and MLAS-Se in secure WSNs. The broadcast scheduling algorithm we develop for MLBS-Se outperforms the best known scheduling algorithm for broadcast in general graphs [19]. Under certain conditions, our algorithm proposed for MLBS-Se achieves constant approximation.

The remaining of this paper is organized as follows. In Sect. 2, we give a literature review for related works on broadcast and data aggregation scheduling algorithms. In Sect. 3, we introduce some terms and notations that will be used in both algorithms. In Sect. 4, we develop a broadcasting schedule for MLBS-Se. In Sect. 5, we propose an efficient algorithm for MLAS-Se. Finally, we conclude our paper and discuss some future research directions in Sect. 6.

2   Related Works

MLBS in multihop WSNs has been extensively studied [2,3,5,7,9–14,17–19,22, 29]. In general graphs, the NP-hardness of MLBS was proved in [2]. Cicalese et al. [3] presented an approximation algorithm for MLBS in general graphs which produced a broadcast schedule with latency at most $O(R + \log^3 n / \log \log n)$, where R is the graph radius of the communication topology with respect to the source node s, and n is the number of nodes in the network. The best known approximation algorithm for MLBS in general graphs, proposed by Kowalski et al. [19], has broadcast latency at most $O(R + \log^2 n)$.

For a multihop WSN with all nodes having uniform transmission radius equal to one, its communication topology is a unit-disk graph (UDG). In UDGs, MLBS has also been well studied and its NP-hardness was proved in [11]. Dessmark et al. [7] presented a broadcasting schedule of latency at most $2400R$ for MLBS in UDGs. Gandhi et al. [11] proposed another algorithm to produce a broadcasting schedule of latency at most $648R$. They then improved their algorithm for MLBS in [10] to produce a broadcast schedule of total latency at most $12R$. Wan et al. [15] developed three progressively improved approximation algorithms for MLBS in UDGs, which produce broadcasting schedules with latency at most $24R - 23, 16R - 15$, and $R + O(\log R)$, respectively.

The problem MLAS in UDGs with the interference radius ρ equal to the communication radius is NP-hard [1]. Let n be the number of networking nodes, and s be the sink node of the data aggregation. Both R and $\log n$ are two lower bounds for any optimal aggregation schedule for MLAS even when the interference radius $\rho \geq 1$ is arbitrary. For $\rho = 1$, [1] and [16] proposed respectively two data aggregation schedules of total latency at most $(\Delta - 1)R$ and $23R + \Delta - 18$, where Δ is the maximum degree of the network. For $\rho = 1$, Wan et al. [24] developed three approximation algorithms which produced aggregations schedules of total latency at most $15R + \Delta - 4$, $2R + \Delta + O(\log R)$ and $\left(1 + O\left(\log R/\sqrt[3]{R}\right)\right)R + \Delta$, respectively.

In secure WSNs, connectivity of networks has been well studied in recent years [21,23,28]. Pietro et al. [23] showed that the key pool size can be fixed in such a way that secure WSN is connected with probability approaching to one as the number of sensor nodes $n \to \infty$ even assigning a small constant number of keys to each sensor. Yi et al. [28] proved that if n sensor nodes are distributed uniformly in a unit-area disk or square, and all the nodes have a maximum transmission radius $r_n = \sqrt{\frac{\log n + \xi}{\pi p n}}$ for some constant ξ, then the total number of the isolated nodes is asymptotically Poisson with mean $e^{-\xi}$, where p denotes the probability of two neighboring sensor nodes having a secure link. Mao et al. [21] studied the connectivity of large wireless networks under a generic connection model and implied the following results: if all nodes are distributed on a unit square following a Poisson distribution with density n and have a maximum transmission radius r_n, then the secure network is a.a.s. connected as $n \to \infty$ if and only if it has no isolated nodes.

3 Preliminaries

In this section, we introduce some terms and notations. Let $G = (V, E)$ be an undirected graph with $|V| = n$, and s be a fixed node on G. The subgraph of G induced by a subset $U \subseteq V$ is denoted by $G[U]$. The minimum and maximum degrees of G are denoted by $\delta(G)$ and $\Delta(G)$, respectively. The independent number and chromatic number of G are denoted by $\alpha(G)$ and $\chi(G)$, respectively. The inductivity of G is defined by

$$\delta^*(G) = \max_{U \subseteq V} \delta(G[U]).$$

The square of G, denoted by G^2, is the graph over V in which there is an edge between two nodes u and v if and only if their graph distance on G is at most two. The *depth* of a node v is the hop distance from s to v. The *radius of Gwith respect tos*, denoted by $R(G)$, is the maximum hop distance between s and other nodes in G. They can be computed by conducting a standard breadth-first-search (BFS) on G. For $0 \leq i \leq R(G)$, let L_i denote the set of all the nodes at the i-th layer, i.e., the nodes of depth i.

Given any positive integer k. A subset $U \subseteq V$ is said to be a *k-independent set*(k-IS) of G if the pairwise graph distances of the nodes in U are all at least $k+1$. A *maximal k-independent set* of G is a *k-independent set* U of G such that no proper subset of U is a *k-independent set* of G. Note that U is a (maximal) *k-independent set* of G if and only if U is a (maximal) *independent set* of G^k.

Given any $r > 0$. For any point x on the plane, denote by $D(x, r)$ the disk centered at x with radius r.

4   Broadcast Scheduling

Let s be the source node of the broadcast. In this section, we develop an efficient approximation algorithm for MLBS-Se to compute fast broadcast schedules for a secure wireless sensor network. Let V denote the set of all the networking nodes, G_u the unit-disk graph on V, and G_{se} the *secure* wireless sensor network on V. Note that G_{se} is a subgraph of G_u.

Given $r > 0$ and any point x on the plane. We say that a link $(u, v) \in E(G_u)$ belongs to a disk $D(x, r)$ if and only if both ends u and v of the link are contained in the disk. In this paper, we assume that for any point x on the deployment region, the disk $D(x, \frac{\sqrt{3}}{3})$ contains at most M links in $E(G_u)$ that are not secure, where M is a parameter which will be used in our algorithms.

We begin with a simple geometric lemma that partitions a half disk of radius two into 14 small subregions with diameter at most one, whose proof is omitted due to the space limitation (see the proof of Lemma 1 in [15]).

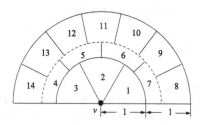

Fig. 1. Partition of the half disk of radius two into 14 small pieces, each of which has diameter at most one.

Lemma 1. *Any half disk with radius equal to two can be partitioned into 14 small subregions, each of which has diameter at most one and is contained in a disk of radius $\frac{\sqrt{3}}{3}$ (see Fig. 1).*

Next in Lemma 2 we give an upper bound on the number of independent nodes in G_{se} that can be contained in any of the 14 small subregions shown in Fig. 1, and an upper bound on the inductivity of the induced subgraph $G_{se}^2[I]$ of the square G_{se}^2 for any independent set I of G_{se} in Lemma 3. The proofs of these two lemmas are omitted due to the space limitation.

Lemma 2. *Let S denote any of the 14 small subregions shown in Fig. 1. For any independent set I of the secure network G_{se}, we have $|S \cap I| \leq M + 1$.*

Lemma 3. *For any independent set I of the secure wireless sensor network G_{se}, we have*

$$\delta^*(G_{se}^2[I]) \leq 14M + 11.$$

Lemma 3 immediately implies the following corollary, whose proof is omitted due to the space limitation.

Corollary 1. *Any independent set I of the secure network G_{se} can be partitioned into at most $(14M + 12)$ 2-independent sets of G_{se}.*

Now we are ready to describe the algorithm to compute a broadcast schedule for the secure wireless sensor network G_{se} (BS-SWSN). We first construct a BFS tree T of the secure network G_{se} rooted at the source node s, and computer the depths of all the nodes in T and the radius $R_{se} = R(G_{se})$ of G_{se}. Then we construct the maximal independent set I of G_{se} induced by the increasing order of the depths in T. Since I is a dominating set of G_{se}, the nodes in I are referred to as *dominators*. The parents of the dominators in T are referred to as *connectors*. The set of all the dominators and connectors forms a connected dominating set of G_{se}. Only the dominators and the connectors are the transmitting nodes. Their transmissions are scheduled layer by layer in the top-down manner. At each layer, transmissions by dominators precede the transmissions by the connectors.

Specifically, for each $0 \leq i \leq R_{se}$, denote by I_i the set of dominators with depth i. Note that $I_0 = \{s\}$ and $I_1 = \varnothing$. For each $2 \leq i \leq R_{se}$, compute a partition of I_i into c_i 2-IS sets I_{ij} for $1 \leq j \leq c_i$. By Corollary 1, $c_i \leq 14M + 12$. For each $1 \leq i \leq R_{se} - 1$ and $1 \leq j \leq c_{i+1}$, denote by W_{ij} the set of parents of nodes in $I_{i+1,j}$ on the tree T. Then, at layer 0, only the source node s transmits as a dominator at the time-slot 0. At layer 1, $I_1 = \varnothing$, and the connectors transmit in the sequence $< W_{11}, W_{12}, \cdots, W_{1c_2} >$. At each layer $2 \leq i \leq R_{se} - 1$, dominators transmit in the sequence $< I_{i1}, I_{i2}, \cdots, I_{ic_i} >$. Immediately afterwards, connectors transmit in the sequence $< W_{i1}, W_{i2}, \cdots, W_{ic_{i+1}} >$. At the last layer R_{se}, there is no connectors and all the dominators transmit in the sequence $< I_{R_{se}1}, I_{R_{se}2}, \cdots, I_{R_{se}c_{R_{se}}} >$.

The next theorem asserts the correctness of the algorithm BS-SWSN and gives an upper bound on the latency of the broadcast schedule produced by the above algorithm BS-SWSN.

Theorem 1. *The algorithm BS-SWSN described above is correct and it produces a broadcast schedule with latency at most* $(28M + 24)R_{se} - 28M - 23$.

Proof. Note that for any 2-IS subset of the nodes in I, the distance between any pair of nodes are at least three hops away on G_{se}. After a dominator in G_{se} transmits, all of its neighbors in G_{se} will receive the broadcast message. Based on the construction of the broadcast tree, each connector is adjacent to some dominator in previous layer or the same layer. Thus, after all the dominators in a layer have transmitted the broadcast message, every connector in the same layer must be informed. On the other hand, after all the connectors in a layer have transmitted the broadcast message, every dominator in the same layer or previous layers must have completed their transmissions. Therefore, after all the dominators in the last layer have completed their transmissions, all the nodes in the networks have been informed. Hence, the algorithm BS-SWSN is correct.

Note that for each $2 \leq i \leq R_{se}$, we have $c_i \leq 14M + 12$. The latency of the broadcast schedule produced by the above algorithm BS-SWSN is given by

$$1 + c_2 + \sum_{i=2}^{R_{se}-1}(c_i + c_{i+1}) + c_{R_{se}}$$
$$= 1 + 2\sum_{i=2}^{R_{se}}c_i$$
$$\leq 1 + 2\sum_{i=2}^{R_{se}}(14M + 12)$$
$$= (28M + 24)R_{se} - 28M - 23.$$

This completes the proof of the theorem. $\qquad\square$

Clearly, R_{se} is a lower bound on the latency of any optimal broadcast schedule for the secure network G_{se}. Therefore, we have the following two corollaries that give the approximation bound for the above algorithm BS-SWSN.

Corollary 2. *The approximation bound of the above algorithm BS-SWSN is at most* $28M + 24$.

Corollary 3. *If M is a constant, then the above broadcast algorithm BS-SWSN achieves constant approximation.*

In general graphs, the best known communication scheduling algorithm for broadcast proposed by Kowalski et al. [19] has latency at most $O(R + \log^2 n)$, where R is the graph radius of the communication network with respect to s, and n is the number of nodes in the network. Our scheduling algorithm BS-SWSN for broadcast developed above has latency at most $(28M + 24)R_{se} - 28M - 23$, which is independent of n. Therefore, our scheduling algorithm BS-SWSN for broadcast outperforms the best known scheduling algorithm for broadcast in general graphs.

5 Data Aggregation Scheduling

Let s be the sink node of the data aggregation. In this section, we use the same notations and assumptions as in Sect. 4. Recall that V denotes the set of all the networking nodes, G_u the unit-disk graph on V, and G_{se} the *secure* wireless sensor network on V. We first construct a Connected Dominating Set (CDS) of the secure network G_{se} that will be used for routing in the data aggregation algorithm, and then develop an efficient approximation algorithm for MLAS-Se to compute a data aggregation schedule for a secure wireless sensor network.

5.1 Connected Dominating Sets

The construction of the CDS follows a general two-phased approach [27]. The first phase selects an MIS U induced by a breadth-first-search (BFS) ordering with respect to the sink node s as the *dominating set*. The second phase selects additional nodes, called connectors, which together with the dominators induce a connected topology. Let $H = G_{se}^2[U]$ and $Rad(H)$ be the radius of H with respect to s. Then, H is connected and $Rad(H) \leq R_{se} - 1$. For each $0 \leq i \leq Rad(H)$, let U_i be the set of dominators of depth i in H. Then, $U_0 = \{s\}$. For each $0 \leq i \leq Rad(H)$, let P_i be the set of nodes adjacent to at least one node in U_i and at least one node in U_{i+1}, and compute a minimal cover $W_i \subseteq P_i$ of U_{i+1}. Let $W = \cup_{i=0}^{Rad(H)-1} W_i$. Then, $G_{se}[U, W]$ is connected and $U \cup W$ forms a CDS of G_{se}. We refer to all nodes in W as *connectors* and all nodes not in the CDS $U \cup W$ as *dominatees*. Clearly, $|W| \leq |U| - 1$. Also, we have

$$Rad(G_{se}[U, W]) = 2Rad(H) \leq 2(R_{se} - 1).$$

The following lemma gives some additional properties of the output CDS which is similar to Lemma 4.1 of [24]. The proof of this lemma is omitted due to the space limitation.

Lemma 4. *The following statements are true for the CDS constructed above: (a) For each $0 \leq i \leq Rad(H)$, each connector in W_i is adjacent to at most $6M + 5$ dominators in U_{i+1}; (b) For each $1 \leq i \leq Rad(H) - 1$, each dominator u in U_i is adjacent to at most $14M + 10$ connectors in W_i; (c) $|W_0| \leq 14M + 11$.*

5.2 Aggregation Scheduling

We adopt the Sequence Aggregation Scheduling algorithm (SAS) proposed in [24] on the secure network G_{se} when the interference radius $\rho = 1$. The algorithm utilizes a CDS for routing, which consisting of a set U of dominators (an MIS induced by a BFS ordering with respect to the sink node s), and a set W of connectors. Thus, $G_{se}[U \cup W]$ is a connected subgraph. Let Δ denote the maximum degree of the secure network G_{se}.

The next theorem gives an upper bound on the latency of the entire aggregation schedule for the secure network G_{se} produced by the algorithm SAS. The proof of this theorem is omitted due to the space limitation.

Theorem 2. *The algorithm SAS proposed in [24] on the secure network G_{se} produces an aggregation schedule with latency at most $\Delta + (20M + 15)R_{se} - 6M - 5$.*

6 Conclusion and Future Work

In this paper, we proposed two efficient approximation algorithms for both MLBS-Se and MLAS-Se in secure WSNs. On a secure WSN, two sensor nodes that are close to each other may not have a secure link between them. Such a nature of secure WSNs makes it much more complicated to develop broadcast and data aggregation scheduling than on UDGs. Our broadcast scheduling algorithm for MLBS-Se in this paper has latency at most $(28M + 24)R_{se} - 28M - 23$, which is independent of n. Therefore, our broadcast scheduling algorithm for MLBS-Se outperforms the best known scheduling algorithm for broadcast in general graphs. When M is a constant, our broadcast scheduling algorithm for MLBS-Se achieves constant approximation.

For future research on these topics, one can put other constraints on the secure WSNs so that the proposed communication scheduling algorithms for either broadcast or data aggregation might achieve constant approximation. One can also develop constant approximation algorithms to compute data gathering schedules or data gossiping schedules that achieve low latency for secure WSNs.

Acknowledgement. This work of Dr. Lixin Wang and Dr. C. P. Abubucker is supported in part by the NNSA cybersecurity grant F1040061-14-09 of U.S. Department of Energy.

References

1. Chen, X., Hu, X., Zhu, J.: Minimum data aggregation time problem in wireless sensor networks. In: Jia, X., Wu, J., He, Y. (eds.) MSN 2005. LNCS, vol. 3794, pp. 133–142. Springer, Heidelberg (2005)
2. Chlamtac, I., Kutten, S.: On broadcasting in radio networks - problem analysis and protocol design. IEEE Trans. Commun. **33**, 1240–1246 (1985)
3. Cicalese, F., Manne, F., Xin, Q.: Faster centralized communication in radio networks. In: Asano, T. (ed.) ISAAC 2006. LNCS, vol. 4288, pp. 339–348. Springer, Heidelberg (2006)
4. Chan, H., Perrig, A., Song, D.: Random key predistribution schemes for sensor networks. In: Proceedings of the 2003 IEEE Symposium on Security and Privacy, pp. 197–213, May 11–14 2003
5. Chen, Z., Qiao, C., Xu, J., and Lee, T.: A constant approximation algorithm for interference aware broadcast in wireless networks. In: Proceedings of IEEE INFOCOM (2007)
6. Du, W., Deng, J., Han, Y. S., Varshney, P.K.: A pairwise key predistribution scheme for wireless sensor networks. In: Proceedings of the 10th ACM Conference on Computer and Communications Security (CCS 2003) (2003)

7. Dessmark, A., Pelc, A.: Tradeoffs between knowledge and time of communication in geometric radio networks. In: Proceedings of the 13th Annual ACM Symposium on Parallel Algorithms and Architectures (SPAA), pp. 59–66 (2001)

8. Eschenauer, L., Gligor, V.D.: A key-management scheme for distributed sensor networks. In: Proceedings of the 9th ACM Conference on Computer and Communications Security, pp. 41–47, Nov 18–22 2002

9. Ephremides, A., Truong, T.V.: Scheduling broadcasts in multihop radio networks. IEEE Trans. Commun. **38**(4), 456–460 (1990)

10. Gandhi, R., Kim, S. L. Y.-A., J. Ryu, Wan, P.-J.: Approximation algorithms for data broadcast in wireless networks. In: IEEE INFOCOM (2009)

11. Gandhi, R., Parthasarathy, S., Mishra, A.: Minimizing broadcast latency and redundancy in ad hoc networks. In: ACM MobiHoc (2003)

12. Huang, S.C.-H., Du, H., Park, E.-K.: Minimum-latency gossiping in multi-hop wireless networks. In: ACM MobiHoc (2008)

13. Huang, S.C.-H., Wan, P.-J., Deng, J., Han, Y.S.: Broadcast scheduling in interference environment. IEEE Trans. Mobile Comput. **7**(11), 1338–1348 (2008)

14. Huang, S.C.-H., Wan, P.-J., Du, H., Park, E.-K.: Minimum latency gossiping in radio networks. IEEE Trans. Parallel Distrib. Syst. **21**(6), 790–800 (2010)

15. Huang, C.-H., Wan, P.-J., Jia, X., Du, H., Shang, W.: Minimum latency broadcast scheduling in wireless ad hoc networks. In: IEEE INFOCOM (2007)

16. Huang, S.C.-H., Wan, P.-J., Vu, C. T., Li, Y., Yao, F.: Nearly constant approximation for data aggregation scheduling in wireless sensor networks. In: IEEE INFOCOM (2007)

17. Jiao, X., Lou, W., Ma, J., Cao, J., Wang, X., Zhou, X.: Minimum latency broadcast scheduling in duty-cycled multihop wireless networks. IEEE Trans. Parallel Distrib. Syst. **23**(1), 110–117 (2012)

18. Jahan, M., Narayanan, L.: Minimum energy broadcast in duty cycled wireless sensor networks. In: IEEE Wireless Communications and Networking Conference (WCNC), pp. 980–985, April 2013

19. Kowalski, D., Pelc, A.: Optimal deterministic broadcasting in known topology radio networks. Distrib. Comput. **19**(3), 185–195 (2007)

20. Liu, D., Ning, P.: Establishing pairwise keys in distributed sensor networks. In: Proceedings of the 10th ACM Conference on Computer and Communications Security (CCS 2003) (2003)

21. Mao, G., Anderson, B.: Connectivity of large wireless networks under a general connection model. IEEE Trans. Inf. Theory **59**(3), 1761–1772 (2013)

22. Mahjourian, R., Chen, F., Tiwari, R.: An approximation algorithm for conflict-aware broadcast scheduling in wireless ad hoc networks. In: ACM MobiHoc (2008)

23. Pietro, R.D., Mancini, L., Mei, A., Panconesi, A., Radhakrishnan, J.: Connectivity properties of secure wireless sensor networks. In: Proceedings of the 2004 ACM Workshop on Security of Ad Hoc and Sensor Networks (SASN 2004), October 25 2004

24. Wan, P.-J., Huang, C.-H., Wang, L., Wan, Z.-Y., Jia, X.: MinimumLatency Aggregation Scheduling in Multihop Wireless Networks. In: ACM MOBIHOC (2009)

25. Wan, P.-J., Wang, Z., Du, H., Huang, S. C.-H., Wan, Z.: First-fit scheduling for beaconing in multihop wireless networks. In: IEEE INFOCOM (2010)

26. Wan, P.-J., Wang, L., Frieder, O.: Fast group communication in multihop wireless networks subject to physical interference. In: IEEE MASS (2009)

27. Wan, P.-J., Wang, L., Yao, F.: Two-phased approximation algorithms for minimum cds in wireless ad hoc networks. In: IEEE ICDCS, pp. 337–344 (2008)

28. Yi, C.-W., Wan, P.-J., Lin, K.-W., Huang, C.-H.: Asymptotic distribution of the number of isolated nodes in wireless ad hoc networks with unreliable nodes and links. In: IEEE GLOBECOM (2006)
29. Zhao, D., Chin, K.W., Raad, R.: Minimizing broadcast latency and redundancy in asynchronous wireless sensor networks. Wireless Netw. **20**(3), 345–360 (2014)

Data-Driven Privacy Analytics: A WeChat Case Study in Location-Based Social Networks

Rongrong Wang[1], Minhui Xue[1,2]([✉]), Kelvin Liu[2], and Haifeng Qian[1]

[1] Department of Computer Science, East China Normal University, Shanghai, China
carmenwang1990@gmail.com, hfqian@cs.ecnu.edu.cn
[2] Department of Computer Science, New York University Shanghai, Pudong, China
{minhuixue,kelvin.liu}@nyu.edu

Abstract. Location-based Social Network (LBSN) services enable people to discover users nearby and establish the communication with them. WeChat as both LBSN and Online Social Network (OSN) application does not impose a real-name policy for usernames, leaving the users to choose how they want to be identified by nearby people. In this paper, we show the feasibility to stalk WeChat users in any city from any place in the world and in parallel examine the anonymity of those users. Based on previous studies, we develop an automated attacking methodology by using fake GPS location, smart phone emulation, task automation, and optical character recognition (OCR). We then study the prevalence and behavior of Anonymous and Identifiable WeChat users and correlate their anonymity with their behavior, especially for those who repeatedly query the *People Nearby* service, a feature that triggers WeChat to discover nearby people. By monitoring Wall Street for 7 days, we gather location information relevant to 3,215 distinct users and finally find that Anonymous users are largely less inhibited to be dynamic participants, as they query more and are more willing to move around in public. To the best of our knowledge, this is the first work that quantifies the relationship between user mobility and user anonymity. We expect our study to motivate better privacy design in WeChat.

Keywords: Location-based social networks · Mobility · Anonymity

1 Introduction

The wide proliferation of both smartphones and ubiquitous location-based services (LBSs) has driven the exponential growth of location-based social networks (LBSNs). LBSNs, a subcategory of LBSs, are designed to enable people to discover nearby users and establish on-the-spot communication. Currently, there is a plethora of popular LBSN applications – applications that help recommend nearby restaurants (e.g. Dianping, Yelp); applications that help find potential nearby candidates for dating, also termed find-and-flirt (e.g. Momo, Tinder); and applications that create anonymous platforms for university students (e.g. Yik Yak).

© Springer International Publishing Switzerland 2015
K. Xu and J. Zhu (Eds.): WASA 2015, LNCS 9204, pp. 561–570, 2015.
DOI: 10.1007/978-3-319-21837-3_55

In addition to LBSNs, many online social networks (OSNs) are also growing rapidly, such as Facebook, Google+, and Twitter. Facebook and Google+ strictly enforce a real-name policy, requiring all users to use their real names for registration. One of the reasons behind implementing a real-name policy is that it can improve the quality of the content and easily regulate the networks. Twitter, on the other hand, does not impose a real-name policy for users, allowing users to provide either real-names or unique pseudonyms when creating accounts. Many users want to remain anonymous and deliberately choose their pseudonyms with no link to their actual names so as to follow sensitive accounts and participate in controversial discussions.

Among all the above-mentioned applications, we focus our study on WeChat. WeChat – characterized as both a LBSN and OSN application – already boasts more than 600 million users globally. Recent work has shown methodologies to pinpoint any target user within a narrow area in both theory and practice [1,2]. In this work, we cast a broad net, attempting to track the locations and mobility traces of a myriad of people on Wall Street. This broad-net approach allows for the surveillance of people working on Wall Street who are involved in suspicious activities. For example, the leadership of the New York Stock Exchange (NYSE) – the world's largest stock exchange by market capitalization of its listed companies – may, by chance, discover a terrorist plot to launch an attach in the vicinity; or investigate their employees' whereabouts during work hours. For our approach, we use 2 probes set on Wall Street to monitor the same users, helping us track their mobility. In order to leverage the combined information and further profile the users, we extract the WeChat usernames and eventually correlate the user anonymity with their mobility behavior.

This paper aims to reveal the ease with which one can be targeted on WeChat, which is already taking measures against this, by adversaries with limited resources and to further show the correlation between a user's name anonymity and mobility. To achieve this, we re-develop an automated attacking methodology by using fake GPS location, smart phone emulation, task automation, and optical character recognition (OCR), without prior knowledge of WeChat's internals or reverse engineering its communication protocols. Specifically, we employ a single machine to collect data from two virtual probes set on Wall Street for a period of 7 days. In total, we collect 8,462 screenshots, 41,874 entries in the form of $< username, distance, timestamp, probe\_coordinate >$, which correspond to 3,215 distinct Latin-Chinese character names. With the help of 5 labmates, these users are then classified into 4 categories: Anonymous, Identifiable, Partially Anonymous, and Unclassifiable. We are eventually able to correlate user anonymity with their mobility behavior.

The contributions of this paper are summarized in two points:

- We develop a generic framework that enables us to bypass existing WeChat privacy protection measures, thus enabling us to detect user mobility and identify their mobility patterns on Wall Street.
- We analyze the anonymity of a large number of WeChat users. Specifically, we leverage 5 labmates to help label the users and classify them as Anonymous,

Identifiable, Partially Anonymous, and Unclassifiable based on the first and last names that appear in their profiles. Through close examination of these datasets, we discover that Identifiable and Anonymous Users exhibit distinctly different behavior with respect to mobility patterns.

The rest of this paper is organized as follows. Section 2 briefly discusses the background of the WeChat application. Section 3 presents our proposed privacy analytics framework and datasets. Section 4 evaluates our real-world experiments in detail. Section 5 surveys related work. Finally, Sect. 6 concludes the paper.

2   Background

We limit our study to one of the most prevalent LBSN applications – WeChat. Since its inception in 2011, it has gained a large number of users both living in China and the United States. Although it was originally designed as a mobile-based free messaging application, WeChat is actively developing many OSN features. In this section, we first showcase the mechanism of *People Nearby* services and then take a look at WeChat's real-name policy for usernames.

2.1   People Nearby Services

The WeChat application provides a *People Nearby* service, which takes as input the current geo-location of a user's mobile device and returns a list of WeChat users in close proximity. When WeChat reports the nearby users, it blurs the location information of the users and does not provide their direction or exact distance for privacy reasons. Rather, it gives the distance in bands of 100 yd. For example, if Alice submits her location to the WeChat server, the server does not provide Bob with her exact location, but instead suggests that she is somewhere in a circular band. In particular, if Alice is 368 yd away from Bob, the WeChat server will only report that she is between 300 and 400 yd away from Bob. We must emphasize that if a WeChat user only uses the application for communication or posting selfies and never triggers the WeChat *People Nearby* service, then the user is not traceable by the methods described in this paper. User mobility is only traceable if a user repeatedly queries WeChat's *People Nearby* service.

WeChat lists the nearby people starting from closest to furthest within different distance ranges. It also employs a complex algorithm to determine the ordering of users within the same distance range. Figure 1 shows a sample image of the *People Nearby* functionality of WeChat. The granularity of distances WeChat reports is non-linear; distances up to 1000 yd are reported in bands of 100 yd, but beyond 1000 yd, the band size increases to 1 mile increments. Additionally, refreshing this list is susceptible to many factors such as synchronization issues. Therefore, we take into account the fact that it is possible for our virtual probes to not always discover a user if he or she is near.

Fig. 1. The screenshot of the WeChat's People Nearby feature

Fig. 2. Fake GPS

2.2 Classifying WeChat Users

We rely on human knowledge to classify WeChat user accounts as Anonymous and Identifiable. We leverage 5 university labmates to help label these accounts (See Fig. 1). Specifically, the labmates are asked to decide whether these user-names contain the following [3]:

- just a first name;
- just a last name;
- both a first name and a last name;
- neither a first nor a last name;
- not sure or other.

We require the labmates to only choose the "neither a first or a last name" or "both a first name and a last name" options if they have full confidence, so as to avoid mislabeling particularly ambiguous user accounts. To take into account human error, each account is labelled by three labmates, and in the case of disagreement, a majority vote is used to decide. If, however, decision still cannot be reached, we (the authors) provide a definitive, final label for the account in question. By exploiting these labels, we define each WeChat user as one of the following:

- Anonymous: A WeChat account containing neither a first nor a last name;
- Identifiable: A WeChat account containing both a first name and a last name;
- Partially Anonymous: A WeChat account containing either a first name or a last name, but not both;
- Unclassifiable: A WeChat account that is neither Anonymous, Identifiable nor Partially Anonymous.

To be sure, WeChat does not support complete anonymity (i.e. accounts that are never associated with any pseudonym). However, in this paper, we use the commonly-employed term *anonymous* in lieu of the term *pseudonymous* which appears frequently in cryptography. We regard the above two terms to be equivalent.

3   Methodology

3.1   Analytics Framework

This paper aims to create a system that places two virtual probes in any location in the world and uses these probes to collect the names of nearby WeChat users and their distance with respect to the probe. Based on a previous study [4], we also exploit available off-the-shelf automation tools, most of which are easily installed on any computer. We then use the *BlueStacks Android Emulator*[1], to run mobile applications on the same computer. The Android emulator runs the WeChat application and another application, named *Fake GPS*[2], to fake the geo-location of the probing account (See Fig. 2). Therefore, a virtual probe is simply a probing account. We use Fake GPS to set the probe's GPS location to any place in the world by inputting the latitude and longitude of corresponding to the desired location. The WeChat application subsequently perceives this spoofed location to be the actual location of the user.

By using the off-the-shelf task automation tool, *Sikuli*[3], we can then automate user interaction with the WeChat application (e.g. tapping buttons, typing text, scrolling up and down, etc.). Sikuli is primarily designed to automate and test graphical user interfaces (GUIs) and can be easily adapted to any change in user interface. We use Sikuli to not only automatically set the locations of the two virtual probes via Fake GPS, but also query WeChat's *People Nearby* feature.

By using a popular commercial optical character recognition (OCR) software, *ABBYY FineReader*[4], we can then extract a textual list of nearby people from WeChat screenshots taken by Sikuli. FineReader is used to turn scanned documents and digital images into searchable and editable formats. For our purposes, FineReader is leveraged to extract usernames and reported distances for each WeChat screenshot.

---

[1] http://www.bluestacks.com.
[2] https://play.google.com/store/apps/details?id=com.lexa.fakegps.
[3] http://www.sikuli.org.
[4] http://finereader.abbyy.com.

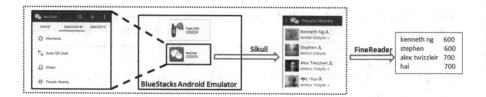

Fig. 3. WeChat analytics framework

As summarized in Fig. 3, the Android emulator runs WeChat and Fake GPS; Sikuli interacts with the applications to set the fake GPS location, get lists of nearby people, and take screenshots of WeChat; FineReader then extracts the usernames and reported distances for each screenshot. Hence, tracking users can be done with all off-the-shelf softwares, rather than highly complex tools.

After obtaining WeChat usernames, we perform a large-scale analysis of these users. Spam users are filtered out, and the users are subsequently classified as either Anonymous, Identifiable, Partially Anonymous, or Unclassifiable based on the criteria described in Sect. 2.2.

3.2 Data Collection

In this paper, we track users with either Latin character or Chinese character screen names (denoted Latin-Chinese character names) on Wall Street. To accomplish this task, we use one desktop located outside New York City to manage two virtual probes. The distance between the two probes is fixed at 100 yd. With this setting, a target user can be tracked from the two virtual probes. Additionally, a reasonable area is covered (based on the assumption that each probe can detect users within 2 miles). After the first probe scans for nearby people, the second probe scans after a random period of time less than 2 min. The first probe is set to scan every 30 min in order to reduce traffic to the WeChat servers.

For each 30-min period, the machine sets the location of the virtual probe by using the Fake GPS application and captures the list of nearby people from the corresponding virtual probe. In general, these lists of nearby people contain 96 users, however only 8 are shown on screen at a time. The machine alternates between taking screenshots of the list and scrolling down, until the bottom of the list is reached. We configured the machine, initiated the 30-min time increments, and collected data from 19 January 2015 to 25 January 2015. After the data collection, we used the OCR tool, FineReader, to extract the textual data as a tuple in the form of $< username, distance, timestamp, probe\_coordinate >$.

The accuracy of OCR is affected by many factors, including image resolution, color contract, character size, etc. To improve accuracy, we pre-processed the screenshots by converting them to grayscale, cropping them, and adjusting the image brightness and contrast. We also developed an algorithm to automatically correct these common misinterpretations in WeChat user screen names. There was no misinterpretation of digits in the reported distances.

3.3 Datasets

We used one machine to collect data from two virtual probes set on Wall Street for 7 days. In total, 8,462 screenshots, 41,874 entries as tuples in the form of $< username, distance, timestamp, probe\_coordinate >$ corresponding to 3,215 distinct Latin-Chinese character names were collected. With the help of 5 labmates, these users were split into 4 datasets, corresponding to Anonymous, Identifiable, Partially Anonymous, and Unclassifiable users. The partitioning of users was done as described in Sect. 2.2

4 Experimental Evaluation

4.1 User Mobility and User Anonymity

The number of distinct users that appear each day is displayed in Fig. 4. We see that the number of users that appear on any given day fluctuates around 800, which guarantees us to have enough distinct user accounts in our datasets, rather than very few users with high query frequencies.

The distribution of our datasets of WeChat users is shown in Table 1. Out of all the 3,215 distinct user accounts, we find 39.5 % of the accounts are Anonymous. Notice that some of the Identifiable users may also include fake usernames and hence actually be anonymous. Therefore, we must emphasize that the anonymity is a crucial feature for WeChat users, and 39.5 % acts as the lower bound of the percentage of Anonymous users found. Furthermore, over 75 % of the WeChat users are semi-anonymous – that is, Partially Anonymous or Anonymous. This indicates that user anonymity plays a significant role in

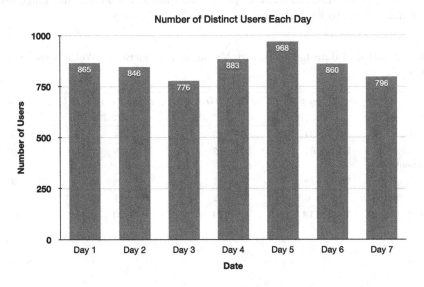

Fig. 4. Number of distinct WeChat users appearing each day

Table 1. Labelled data for quantifying WeChat user anonymity

Label	# of WeChat accounts
Identifiable	631 (19.6%)
Partially anonymous	1211 (37.7%)
Anonymous	1270 (39.5%)
Unclassifiable	103 (3.2%)

Table 2. Labelled data for anonymity of WeChat user appearing in all 7 days

Label	# of WeChat accounts
Identifiable	11 (13.4%)
Partially anonymous	44 (53.7%)
Anonymous	23 (28.0%)
Unclassifiable	4 (4.9%)

WeChat. Giving users a sense of security when querying *People Nearby* and not having a strict real-name policy is probably the best selling point for online social networks. Identifiable users make up 19.6% of the accounts, though an unknown fraction of this group may actually be anonymous. These users are vulnerable to attacks and re-identification.

In order to establish the relationship between user mobility and user anonymity, we specifically screen out users who did not appear in our datasets every day, leaving 82 users. As shown in Table 2, over 80% of these remaining accounts are semi-anonymous, suggesting that unidentifiable users are generally less inhibited to be active participants, as they query WeChat's *People Nearby* feature more often and are more willing to move around in public.

As summarized in Table 3, we can see that most users query *People Nearby* less than 50 times, indicating that a majority of users are always moving around. On the other hand, very few users query *People Nearby* more than 200 times, indicating that only a few users stay in a specific bounded area (in our case, Wall Street). We also find those who often query *People Nearby* tend to belong to either the Partially Anonymous or Anonymous datasets. We then conclude that, regardless of the number of queries, WeChat users who often use *People Nearby* are, in general, Anonymous or at least Partially Anonymous. Thus, user anonymity seems to be correlated to user mobility behavior.

Table 3. Labelled data for anonymity VS number of queries of WeChat user in All 7 days

Label	< 50	50 ≤ # of Queries < 100	100 ≤ # of Queries < 150	150 ≤ # of Queries < 200	200 ≤
Identifiable	595	24	5	4	2
Partially anonymous	1121	61	13	9	9
Anonymous	1218	29	11	8	4
Unclassifiable	99	0	2	1	0
Total	**3033**	**114**	**31**	**22**	**15**

5 Related Work

Location privacy concerns on LBSNs has attracted much attention in recent years. Many researchers have been trying to infer the exact location and mobility trajectory of any given user using only limited location information [4]. By performing a large scale study on user profiles, Chen et al. [5] is able to re-identify many users and reveal their top locations. Srivatsa and Hicks [6] leverage social networks as a side-channel to de-anonymize user mobility trajectories. These works indicate that a large amount of seemingly non-sensitive information may enable an adversary to locate and re-identify potential targets. In this paper, we investigate WeChat users who repeatedly utilize the *People Nearby* service. Their profile information is gathered in order to track their mobility trajectories and identify possible behavioral patterns.

User anonymity is another focus on LBSNs. Peddinti et al. [3] performs a large scale analysis of Twitter in order to study the prevalence and behavior of Anonymous and Identifiable users and found a correlation between content sensitivity and a user's anonymity. In contrast, our study is the first work to investigate the anonymity of WeChat users.

There are many other works that have taken interest in inferring user's trajectory and anonymity [7,8]. However, our study is unique in that we proceed to quantify the relationship between user mobility and user anonymity by re-developing an automated attacking methodology for tracking WeChat users on Wall Street.

6 Conclusions

This paper shows the feasibility of stalking WeChat users in a specific area from any place in the world. By leveraging the *People Nearby* feature in WeChat, we develop an automated attacking methodology by using a fake GPS application, Android emulator, task automation tools, and optical character recognition. In addition, we notice that WeChat users do not necessarily use real names as their usernames. Rather, users are given the option to be either anonymous or identifiable. Based on these findings, we label the users gathered by our system by adopting a voting method and attempt to investigate the relationship between user mobility and anonymity. We find users who queried the most are more likely to be Anonymous or Partially Anonymous. We must emphasize, however, that a person can only be discovered if he or she actually uses the *People Nearby* service. For example, if a WeChat user only uses the application to message friends and post photos, then the user is not locatable and his or her username is not extractable by the methods described in this paper. We also consider usernames as a unique identity to distinguish users, thus different users who have the same usernames may be mistakenly recognized as a single user.

To the best of our knowledge, this is the first detailed case study focused on WeChat that quantifies the relationship between user mobility and user anonymity. We expect our study to motivate better privacy design in WeChat.

Acknowledgments. This work was supported in part by the National Natural Science Foundation of China, under Grant 61172085 and 61021004, in part by the Science and Technology Commission of Shanghai Municipality under Grant 13JC1403500.

References

1. Xue, M., Liu, Y., Ross, K.W., Qian, H.: I know where you are: thwarting privacy protection in location-based social discovery services. In: 2015 IEEE Conference on Computer Communications Workshops (INFOCOM WKSHPS). IEEE (2015)
2. Li, M., Zhu, H., Gao, Z., Chen, S., Yu, L., Hu, S., Ren, K.: All your location are belong to us: breaking mobile social networks for automated user location tracking. In: Proceedings of the 15th ACM International Symposium on Mobile Ad Hoc Networking and Computing, pp. 43–52. ACM (2014)
3. Peddinti, S.T., Ross, K.W., Cappos, J.: On the internet, nobody knows you're a dog: a twitter case study of anonymity in social networks. In: Proceedings of the Second Edition of the ACM Conference on Online Social Networks, pp. 83–94. ACM (2014)
4. Ding, Y., Peddinti, S.T., Ross, K.W.: Stalking beijing from timbuktu: a generic measurement approach for exploiting location-based social discovery. In: Proceedings of the 4th ACM Workshop on Security and Privacy in Smartphones & Mobile Devices, pp. 75–80. ACM (2014)
5. Chen, T., Kaafar, M.A., Boreli, R.: The where and when of finding new friends: analysis of a location-based social discovery network. In: ICWSM (2013)
6. Srivatsa, M., Hicks, M.: Deanonymizing mobility traces: using social network as a side-channel. In: Proceedings of the 2012 ACM Conference on Computer and Communications Security, pp. 628–637. ACM (2012)
7. Zang, H., Bolot, J.: Anonymization of location data does not work: a large-scale measurement study. In: Proceedings of the 17th Annual International Conference on Mobile Computing and Networking, pp. 145–156. ACM (2011)
8. de Montjoye, Y.-A., Hidalgo, C.A., Verleysen, M., Blondel, V.D.: Unique in the crowd: the privacy bounds of human mobility. Sci. Rep. **3**, 1–5 (2013)

A Double Pulse Control Strategy for Misinformation Propagation in Human Mobile Opportunistic Networks

Xiaoming Wang[1]($\boxtimes$), Yaguang Lin[1], Lichen Zhang[1], and Zhipeng Cai[2]

[1] School of Computer Science, Shaanxi Normal University, Xi'an 710119, China
wangxm@snnu.edu.cn
[2] Department of Computer Science, Georgia State University,
Atlanta, GA 30303, USA

Abstract. Mobile Opportunistic Networks (MONs) are effective solutions to uphold communications in the situations where traditional communication networks are unavailable. However, MONs can be abused to disseminate misinformation causing undesirable effects in public. To prevent misinformation from propagating, we first propose a formal model to formulate the process of misinformation propagation based on the ordinary differential equation. Secondly, we explore a general framework to describe the random mobility of nodes, and derive a new contact rate between nodes. Thirdly, we propose a double pulse control strategy of vaccination and treatment for inhibiting misinformation propagation. Moreover, a novel pulse control model of misinformation propagation is developed based on the impulsive differential equation. Finally, through the derivation and stability analysis of a misinformation-free period solution of the proposed model, we obtain a threshold upon which misinformation dies out. The simulation results validate our theoretical analysis.

Keywords: Mobile Opportunistic Network · Misinformation propagation · Contact rate · Pulse control model · Stability analysis

1 Introduction

With the rapid growth of wireless communication and integrated circuit, portal smart devices have been very popular in the real world. A large number of portal smart devices carried by mobile humans may organize themselves into a special Delay-Tolerant Network (DTN) [1]. Similar to traditional mobile ad hoc networks [2], no fixed infrastructures exist in such DTNs, and nodes utilize their encountering opportunities and depend on short-distance wireless links to communicate with each other. Such DTNs are referred as human Mobile Opportunistic Networks (MONs). MONs are applied in many areas, such as disaster emergence relief communications and sociality-aware advertisements [3].

One of the most basic and important services provided by a MON is information (message) propagation [3]. Unfortunately, malicious individuals can utilize

© Springer International Publishing Switzerland 2015
K. Xu and J. Zhu (Eds.): WASA 2015, LNCS 9204, pp. 571–580, 2015.
DOI: 10.1007/978-3-319-21837-3_56

such MONs to distribute misinformation, which is called misinformation propagation [4]. The misinformation is a piece of malicious information intentionally made to cause undesirable effects in the general public [5]. Therefore, it becomes an important and key issue to control misinformation propagation in MONs [6].

As we know, vaccination and treatment are two effective ways to control the diffusion of epidemic deceases in the human population [7]. Vaccination is to forward a positive piece of information correcting misinformation toward the nodes without the misinformation, so that a part of these nodes do not believe in the misinformation permanently or temporarily and will not forward the misinformation. This can minimize the negative effects of the misinformation. Treatment is to forward a positive information correcting the misinformation toward the nodes with the misinformation, so that a part of these nodes change their attitude to the misinformation, no longer believe in the misinformation, and will not forward the misinformation to other nodes. Following this idea, many epidemiology based modeling methods have been suggested to study the laws governing misinformation propagation in networks, such as the SIS models, SIR models, SIRS models, SEIR models, SEIRS models, and SEIQRS models [8].

However, most of the existing strategies for viruses are continuous in time, resulting in serious traffic congestions. Moreover, the continuous strategies incur much network resource consumption. Hence, we suggest a double pulse control strategy to inhibit misinformation propagation in a MON. Our basic idea is to apply vaccinations on a subset of nodes without the misinformation, and treatments on a subset of nodes with the misinformation every τ time units. As a result, the vaccinated or treated nodes acquire a permanent or temporary immunity to the misinformation in a very short time. Compared to the continuous strategies, our impulsive control strategies are easier to be manipulated.

2 System Model

2.1 Network Description

We consider a MON composed of N nodes carried by mobile humans. We assume that all the nodes randomly move inside a square region of area L^2. Each node is equipped with short-range radio capabilities and the communication range is a circle with radius ξ ($\xi \ll L$). MON is a sparse network. Hence, the *store-carry-forward* mechanism is used to transmit information in a multi-hop way.

2.2 Mechanism of Misinformation Propagation

According to our analysis and observation on misinformation propagation, we identify the following facts: (a) when an individual receives misinformation the first time, the individual may doubt it, believe in it with a probability; (b) an individual who initially doubts the misinformation will finally believe in it with a probability when a latency period expires; (c) an individual who believed in the misinformation will no longer believe in it with a probability as the individual receives a positive information from a trusted information source; (d) an individual who does not believe in the misinformation may change her faith to the misinformation when a period of time expires.

In fact, we may regard a node in a MON as an individual in the human population, misinformation may be mapped to an epidemic disease. While a piece of misinformation may propagate to one or more nodes utilizing the short-distance contacts between nodes. Hence, we believe that misinformation propagation is very similar to the epidemic disease spread. Therefore, we may apply the modeling methods of epidemic disease spread to describe misinformation propagation.

For this purpose, we divide the nodes in a human MON into four groups: susceptible nodes (S), latent nodes (L), infected nodes (I), and recovered nodes (R). At any time, each node changes its state according to the following rules: (a) When a susceptible node n_i encounters an infected node n_j, n_j may forward misinformation to n_i, so that n_i enters state L with probability α, or enters state I with probability β, or enters state R with probability γ, or keeps its current state unchanged. (b) A latent node has misinformation in its buffer, but it does not forward to its neighbor nodes for a period of time; however, when the period of time expires, the node may believe in the misinformation, and then enters state I with probability λ; or the node may not believe in the misinformation, and then enters state R with probability θ. (c) An infected node may no longer believe in misinformation, further removes the misinformation from its buffer, and then enters state R with probability ε. (d) A recovered node may lose its immunity to the misinformation, and then enters state S with probability η.

In addition, each node may move out of the MON with probability δ at any time. To keep the total number stable, we assume the nodes in state S are added with rate δ at any time, so that the total number of nodes is a constant N.

To quantify the transition relationships between node states, we use $S(t)$, $L(t)$, $I(t)$, and $R(t)$ to represent the number of the nodes in states S, L, I, and R at any time t, respectively. Then we have $S(t) + L(t) + I(t) + R(t) = N$ and $S(t)/N + L(t)/N + I(t)/N + R(t)/N = 1$. Let $s(t) = S(t)/N$, $l(t) = L(t)/N$, $i(t) = I(t)/N$, and $r(t) = R(t)/N$. We believe that the maximal number of susceptible nodes that each infected node can encounter is $s(t)$. We denote the number of the contacts between each node as μ per time unit, called an effective contact rate. Then, the number of the practical contacting nodes in states S and I is estimated by $\mu s(t)i(t)$. For simplicity, we only consider the speed, direction, movement duration, and pause duration as the mobility properties of nodes in our work. Thus, we can describe the state transition relationships of nodes by a directed weighted graph $G(V, E, D)$ as shown in Fig. 1. Here, $V = \{S, L, I, R\}$ is the set of nodal states, E is the set of the transition relationships between nodal states, D is the set of the weights on edges, and the weight on each edge denotes the number of the nodes transiting from one state to another.

2.3 Description of the Random Mobility of Nodes

Through extracting the common properties of the existing models, we develop a general framework to describe the random mobility of nodes. Our basic idea

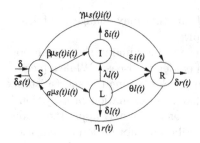

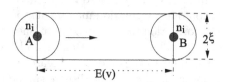

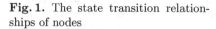

Fig. 1. The state transition relationships of nodes

Fig. 2. The area an infected node scans per unit time.

is to model the random mobility of a node through a group of random variables v, d, m, and h, which are the speed, direction, movement duration, and pause duration, respectively. Considering the real semantics of these random variables in human MONs, we have the following constraints: $v \in [v_{min}, v_{max}]$, $d \in [d_{min}, d_{max}]$, $m \in [m_{min}, m_{max}]$, and $h \in [h_{min}, h_{max}]$, $x \in \{v, d, m, h\}$. In addition, we denote the distribution law of the values of x in the interval $[x_{min}, x_{max}]$ as a probability density function $f_x : [x_{min}, x_{max}] \to [0, 1]$. As such, we can describe the random mobility of nodes by tuple $M = ((v, f_v), (d, f_d), (m, f_m), (h, f_h))$.

2.4   Measure of the Mobility Properties of Nodes

To describe the random uncertainty of the mobility of nodes, we approximately denote the average values of the speed, direction, movement duration, and pause duration of nodes as $E(v)$, $E(d)$, $E(m)$ and $E(h)$. In addition, we describe the mobility difference between nodes by the standard deviation of these random variables as $\rho(v)$, $\rho(d)$, $\rho(m)$ and $\rho(h)$. For a given human MON, we can calculate the number of the susceptible nodes per unit area by $s(t)/L^2$ at time t. Suppose that an infected node n_i moves from location A to location B at speed $E(v)$ in a unit time as shown in Fig. 2. Then the area that n_i scans is $2\xi E(v)$. The number of the susceptible nodes that node n_i may meet per unit time is $\frac{2\xi E(v)}{L^2} s(t)$. The total number of the susceptible nodes that $i(t)$ infected nodes may meet per unit time is $\frac{2\xi E(v)}{L^2} s(t) i(t)$. We call $\varsigma = \frac{2\xi E(v)}{L^2}$ as a basic contact rate between nodes.

To observe whether the mobility properties affect the contact rate between nodes, we conduct two groups of simulations using the Matlab tool in a human MON. From simulation results, we have the following new observations: (a) a larger $E(v)$ or $E(m)$ implies a larger contact rate, and the change of $E(d)$ seldom affects the contact rate, whereas a larger $E(h)$ implies a smaller contact rate; (b) a larger $\rho(v)$, $\rho(d)$, $\rho(m)$, or $\rho(h)$ implies a larger contact rate. To describe the impact of the mobility properties on the basic contact rate, we define factor

$$Q = \frac{log_2^{(1+E(m)\rho(v)\rho(d)\rho(m)\rho(h))}}{log_2^{(1+E(m)\rho(v)\rho(d)\rho(m)\rho(h))(1+E(h))}},$$

where $log_2^{(1+x)}$ used to smooth the values of x to avoid the fluctuation of Q. Combining β' and Q, we define a new contact rate by $\mu = \varsigma Q$. Thus, we have

$$\mu = \frac{2\xi E(v) log_2^{(1+E(m)\rho(v)\rho(a)\rho(m)\rho(h))}}{L^2 log_2^{(1+E(m)\rho(v)\rho(d)\rho(m)\rho(h))(1+E(h)))}}. \tag{1}$$

Obviously, the value of μ increases as the values of $E(v)$, $E(m)$, $\rho(v)$, $\rho(a)$, $\rho(m)$, and $\rho(h)$ increase; whereas the value of μ decreases as the value of $E(h)$ increases.

2.5   A Formal Model of Misinformation Propagation

In this subsection, we develop a mathematical model to formally describe the state transition relationships of nodes shown in Fig. 1. According to the mean-field theory [9], we can derive the rate equations of $s(t), l(t), i(t), r(t)$ as follows.

$$\begin{cases} \frac{ds(t)}{dt} = \delta - (\alpha + \beta + \gamma)\mu s(t)i(t) + \eta r(t) - \delta s(t), \\ \frac{dl(t)}{dt} = \alpha\mu s(t)i(t) - (\lambda + \theta + \delta)l(t), \\ \frac{di(t)}{dt} = \beta\mu s(t)i(t) + \lambda l(t) - (\varepsilon + \delta)i(t), \\ \frac{dr(t)}{dt} = \gamma\mu s(t)i(t) + \theta l(t) + \varepsilon i(t) - (\eta + \delta)r(t). \end{cases} \tag{2}$$

System (2) is an ordinary differential dynamic system, initial values are as follows.

$$i(0) = i_0 \ll 1, l(0) = 0, r(0) = 0, s(0) = s_0 = 1 - i_0. \tag{3}$$

The domain of the solutions of system (2) is $O = \{(s(t), l(t), i(t), r(t)) | s(t) \geq 0, l(t) \geq 0, i(t) \geq 0, r(t) \geq 0, s(t) + l(t) + i(t) + r(t) = 1\}$.

2.6   The Double Pulse Control Strategy of Misinformation Propagation

Our basic idea is to vaccinate a subset of the susceptible nodes with a positive piece of information corresponding to the misinformation every τ unit time, and the vaccination rate is σ_1; a subset of infected nodes are treated with a positive piece of information to correct the misinformation every τ unit time, and the treatment rate is σ_2. $t = k\tau$ is called a pulse control time, where k is a positive integer. As a result, $\sigma_1 s(t)$ nodes in state S and $\sigma_2 i(t)$ nodes in state I enter state R at time kt. Then, the system of misinformation propagation evolves from its new initial state until the same pulse control strategies are applied at the next pulse instant. Our pulse control strategies are formulated as follows.

$$\begin{cases} s(t^+) = (1 - \sigma_1)s(t), l(t^+) = l(t), \\ i(t^+) = (1 - \sigma_2)i(t), r(t^+) = r(t) + \sigma_1 s(t) + \sigma_2 i(t), \end{cases} \tag{4}$$

where t^+ is the time just after the pulse control strategies are conducted. The equation $l(t^+) = l(t)$ shows that the strategies don't affect the latent nodes.

2.7   A Modeling Framework of Misinformation Propagation and Pulse Control

Combining our proposed formal models and pulse control strategies, we develop a novel modeling framework of misinformation propagation and control as follows.

$$
\begin{cases}
\begin{rcases}
\frac{ds(t)}{dt} = \delta - (\alpha + \beta + \gamma)\mu s(t)i(t) + \eta r(t) - \delta s(t), \\
\frac{dl(t)}{dt} = \alpha\mu s(t)i(t) - (\lambda + \theta + \delta)l(t), \\
\frac{di(t)}{dt} = \beta\mu s(t)i(t) + \lambda l(t) - (\varepsilon + \delta)i(t), \\
\frac{dr(t)}{dt} = \gamma\mu s(t)i(t) + \theta l(t) + \varepsilon i(t) - (\eta + \delta)r(t),
\end{rcases} t \neq k\tau, \\
\begin{rcases}
s(t^+) = (1 - \sigma_1)s(t), \\
l(t^+) = l(t), \\
i(t^+) = (1 - \sigma_2)i(t), \\
r(t^+) = r(t) + \sigma_1 s(t) + \sigma_2 i(t).
\end{rcases} t = k\tau.
\end{cases}
\tag{5}
$$

The above modeling framework is a pulse ordinary differential system. Systems (5) and (2) have the same initial conditions and domain of the solutions.

3   Model Analysis

3.1   Existence of a Misinformation-Free τ-Period Solution

For system (5), we have $\frac{di(t)}{dt} \equiv 0$ when $i(t) \equiv 0$ and $l(t) = 0$ for all large t. At this time, system (5) is simplified as the following system:

$$
\begin{cases}
\begin{rcases}
\frac{ds(t)}{dt} = \delta - (\alpha + \beta + \gamma)\mu s(t)i(t) + \eta r(t) - \delta s(t), \\
\frac{dr(t)}{dt} = \gamma\mu s(t)i(t) + \theta l(t) + \varepsilon i(t) - (\eta + \delta)r(t),
\end{rcases} t \neq k\tau, \\
\begin{rcases}
s(t^+) = (1 - \sigma_1)s(t), \\
r(t^+) = r(t) + \sigma_1 s(t) + \sigma_2 i(t).
\end{rcases} t = k\tau.
\end{cases}
\tag{6}
$$

We say that solution $(\widetilde{s}(t), 0, 0, \widetilde{r}(t)) \in O$ is a misinformation-free τ-period solution of system (5) if system (6) has a τ-period solution $(\widetilde{s}(t), \widetilde{r}(t))$. For system (6), we have the following assertion.

Theorem 1. System (6) has a globally asymptotically stable τ-period solution $(\widetilde{s}(t), \widetilde{r}(t))$, where
$\widetilde{r}(t) = \widetilde{y}e^{-(\eta+\delta)(t-k\tau)}$, $\widetilde{s}(t) = 1 - \widetilde{y}e^{-(\eta+\delta)(t-k\tau)}$, $\widetilde{y} = \frac{\sigma_1}{1-(1-\sigma_1)e^{(\delta+\eta)\tau}}$, $k\tau < t \leq (k+1)\tau$, k is a non-negative integer, and τ is a period of time of pulses.

Theorem 2. System (5) has a unique misinformation-free τ-period solution $(\widetilde{s}(t), 0, 0, \widetilde{r}(t))$, where
$\widetilde{r}(t) = \widetilde{y}e^{-(\eta+\delta)(t-k\tau)}$, $\widetilde{s}(t) = 1 - \widetilde{y}e^{-(\eta+\delta)(t-k\tau)}$, $\widetilde{y} = \frac{\sigma_1}{1-(1-\sigma_1)e^{(\delta+\eta)\tau}}$, $k\tau < t \leq (k+1)\tau$, k is a non-negative integer, and τ is a period of time of pulses.

Theorem 2 ensures the existence of the only misinformation-free τ-period solution of system (5). This means that a piece of misinformation may die out.

3.2   Stability of a Misinformation-Free τ-Period Solution

To examine the locally asymptotically stability of the misinformation-free τ-period solution of system (5) $(\tilde{s}(t), 0, 0, \tilde{r}(t))$, suppose $(s(t), l(t), i(t), r(t))$ is any solution of system (5) with the initial value (s_0, l_0, i_0, r_0). Then, let $s(t) = \tilde{s}(t) + z(t), l(t) = 0 + u(t), i(t) = 0 + g(t)$, and $r(t) = \tilde{r}(t) + y(t)$, we have the system

$$
\begin{pmatrix} z(t) \\ y(t) \\ u(t) \\ g(t) \end{pmatrix} = \Phi(t) \begin{pmatrix} z(0) \\ y(0) \\ u(0) \\ g(0) \end{pmatrix},
\tag{7}
$$

where $\Phi(t)$ is a fundamental solution matrix of Eq. (7), and $\Phi(t)$ satisfies

$$
\frac{d\Phi(t)}{dt} = J\Phi(t).
\tag{8}
$$

In Eq. (8), matrix J is a Jcobian matrix of system (5) at the misinformation-free solution $(\tilde{s}(t), 0, 0, \tilde{r}(t))$ when $t \neq k\tau$. Matrix J is defined as follows:

$$
J = \begin{pmatrix} \frac{\partial s(t)}{\partial s} & \frac{\partial s(t)}{\partial r} & \frac{\partial s(t)}{\partial l} & \frac{\partial s(t)}{\partial i} \\ \frac{\partial r(t)}{\partial s} & \frac{\partial r(t)}{\partial r} & \frac{\partial r(t)}{\partial l} & \frac{\partial r(t)}{\partial i} \\ \frac{\partial l(t)}{\partial s} & \frac{\partial l(t)}{\partial r} & \frac{\partial l(t)}{\partial l} & \frac{\partial l(t)}{\partial i} \\ \frac{\partial i(t)}{\partial s} & \frac{\partial i(t)}{\partial r} & \frac{\partial i(t)}{\partial l} & \frac{\partial i(t)}{\partial i} \end{pmatrix}_{(\tilde{s}(t),0,0,\tilde{r}(t))}
$$

$$
= \begin{pmatrix} -\delta & \eta & 0 & -(\alpha + \beta + \gamma)\mu\tilde{s}(t) \\ 0 & -(\eta + \delta) & \theta & \varepsilon + \gamma\mu\tilde{s}(t) \\ 0 & 0 & -(\lambda + \theta + \gamma\mu) & \alpha\mu\tilde{s}(t) \\ 0 & 0 & \lambda & \beta\mu\tilde{s}(t) - \varepsilon - \delta \end{pmatrix}.
$$

When $t = k\tau$, from system (5), we have

$$
\begin{pmatrix} s(t^+) \\ r(t^+) \\ l(t^+) \\ i(t^+) \end{pmatrix} = \begin{pmatrix} 1-\sigma_1 & 0 & 0 & 0 \\ \sigma_1 & 1 & 0 & \sigma_2 \\ 0 & 0 & 1 & 0 \\ 0 & 0 & 0 & 1-\sigma_2 \end{pmatrix} \begin{pmatrix} s(t) \\ r(t) \\ l(t) \\ i(t) \end{pmatrix}.
$$

Let $\Phi(0)$ be a unit matrix, and

$$
W = \begin{pmatrix} 1-\sigma_1 & 0 & 0 & 0 \\ \sigma_1 & 1 & 0 & \sigma_2 \\ 0 & 0 & 1 & 0 \\ 0 & 0 & 0 & 1-\sigma_2 \end{pmatrix} \Phi(\tau).
\tag{9}
$$

For the misinformation-free τ-period solution of system (5) $(\tilde{s}(t), 0, 0, \tilde{r}(t))$, we have the following assertion.

Theorem 3. The misinformation-free τ-period solution of system (5), $(\tilde{s}(t), 0, 0, \tilde{r}(t))$, is locally asymptotically stable if $|\chi_1| < 1$, $|\chi_2| < 1$, $|\chi_3| < 1$, and $|\chi_4| < 1$, where χ_1, χ_2, χ_3, and χ_4 are the eigenvalues of matrix W, $\widetilde{r}(t) = \widetilde{y}e^{-(\eta+\delta)(t-k\tau)}$, $\widetilde{s}(t) = 1 - \widetilde{y}e^{-(\eta+\delta)(t-k\tau)}$, $\widetilde{y} = \frac{\sigma_1}{1-(1-\sigma_1)e^{(\delta+\eta)\tau}}$, $k\tau < t \leq (k+1)\tau$, k is a non-negative integer, and τ is a period of time of pulses.

Theorem 4. The locally asymptotically stability of the misinformation-free τ-period solution of system (5), $(\widetilde{s}(t), 0, 0, \widetilde{r}(t))$, implies that this solution is globally asymptotically stable.

Theorem 4 ensures that misinformation must die out in a given human MON over time when some conditions are satisfied. Hence, ones can check whether a pulse control strategy can ensure misinformation dies out, so that effective pulse control strategies can be designed to remove misinformation propagation.

4 Simulation Results

In this section, we perform numerical studies on both a synthesis network and a real-world network. A MON with 100 nodes (individuals), the network field is 200×200, and the communication radius is 4, $v \in [0, 10]$, $d \in [0, 2\pi]$, $m \in [0, 10]$, and $h \in [0, 10]$. The mobility of individuals follow the random waypoint (RWP) model [9]. We also test our models on the real trace data by groups of users carrying small devices (iMotes) in Conference IEEE Infocom in Grand Hyatt Miami. The numerical results are obtained by the Matlab tool, and the simulation results are obtained by the opportunistic network simulator ONE [10].

4.1 The Impact of the Pulse Control Strategies on the Extinction of Misinformation Propagation

To check the impact of the different pulse control strategies on the extinction of misinformation propagation, we regard the time of the extinction of misinformation propagation as our evaluation metric. For system (5), we assume $\delta = 0.2, \alpha = 0.5, \beta = 0.5, \gamma = 0.1, \eta = 0.5, \lambda = 0.5, \theta = 0.1, \varepsilon = 0.4, \tau = 2$. We conduct the following simulations: (a) $\sigma_1 = 0$ and $\sigma_2 = 0$; the time of the extinction of misinformation propagation is denoted as T_0; (b) $\sigma_1 = 0.3$ and $\sigma_2 = 0$; the time of the extinction of misinformation propagation is denoted as T_{σ_1}; (c) $\sigma_1 = 0$ and $\sigma_2 = 0.3$; the time of the extinction of misinformation propagation is denoted as T_{σ_2}; (d) $\sigma_1 = 0.9$, $\sigma_2 = 0.3$, and the time of the extinction of misinformation propagation is denoted as $T_{\sigma_1 > \sigma_2}$; $\sigma_1 = 0.3$, $\sigma_2 = 0.9$, and the time of the extinction of misinformation propagation is denoted as $T_{\sigma_1 < \sigma_2}$. The results are shown in Fig. 3, we notice that $T_0 > T_{\sigma_1} > T_{\sigma_2} > T_{\sigma_1 > \sigma_2} > T_{\sigma_1 < \sigma_2}$. This implies that our double pulse control strategies can make misinformation propagation to die out in a MON earlier, causing a smaller number of the nodes to be infected. It is worth noting that the trend of the change of the fraction of infected individuals are consistent on the synthesis data and the real trace data. This shows our proposed models are effective.

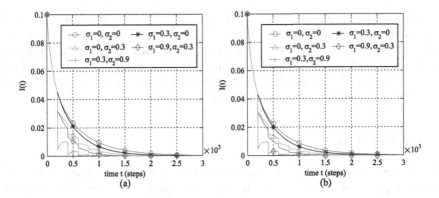

Fig. 3. The impact of the pulse control strategies on the extinction of misinformation propagation.

4.2 The Impact of the Pulse Control Strategies on the Persistence of Misinformation Propagation

To check the impact of different pulse control strategies on the persistence of misinformation propagation, we regard the fraction of the infected nodes $I(t)$ as our evaluation metric when misinformation propagation reaches its stable state. For system (5) we assume $\delta = 0.1, \alpha = 0.5, \beta = 0.9, \gamma = 0.1, \eta = 0.5, \lambda = 0.8, \theta = 0.1, \varepsilon = 0.1, \tau = 2$. We conduct the following simulations: (a)$\sigma_1 = 0$ and $\sigma_2 = 0$; when misinformation propagation reaches its stable state, $I(t)$ is denoted as N_0; (b) $\sigma_1 = 0.1$ and $\sigma_2 = 0$; when misinformation propagation reaches its stable state, $I(t)$ is denoted as N_{σ_1}; (c) $\sigma_1 = 0$ and $\sigma_2 = 0.1$; when misinformation propagation reaches its stable state, $I(t)$ is denoted as N_{σ_2}; (d) $\sigma_1 = 0.2, \sigma_2 = 0.1$, and $I(t)$ is denoted as $N_{\sigma_1 > \sigma_2}$ when misinformation propagation reaches its stable state; $\sigma_1 = 0.1, \sigma_2 = 0.2$, and $I(t)$ is denoted as $N_{\sigma_1 < \sigma_2}$ when misinformation

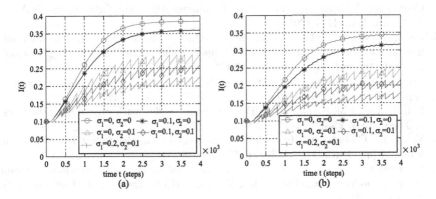

Fig. 4. The impact of the pulse control strategies on the persistence of misinformation propagation.

propagation reaches its stable state. The simulation results are shown in Fig. 4, from where we notice that $N_0 > N_{\sigma_1} > N_{\sigma_2} > N_{\sigma_1 > \sigma_2} > N_{\sigma_1 < \sigma_2}$. This implies that our double pulse control strategies can inhibit misinformation propagation in a human MON more effectively. In particular, the trend of the change of the fraction of infected individuals are consistent on the synthesis data and the real trace data. This shows our proposed models are effective.

5   Conclusions

We propose a directed weighted graph model to describe the mechanism of misinformation propagation. A double pulse control strategy of vaccination and treatment is suggested to inhibit misinformation propagation. Furthermore, a novel modeling framework of misinformation propagation is suggested. We derive a threshold upon which misinformation dies out, which can provide better guidance for the design of strategies to inhibit misinformation propagation.

Acknowledgment. This work is supported by the Natural Science Foundation of China (Grant Nos. 61373083, 61402273), and the Program of Key Science and Technology Innovation Team in Shaanxi Province (No. 2014KTC-18).

References

1. Wang, Y., Chuah, M.C., Chen, Y.: Incentive based data sharing in delay tolerant mobile networks. IEEE Trans. Wirel. Commun. **13**(1), 370–381 (2014)
2. Conti, M., Giordano, S.: Mobile ad hoc networking: milestones, challenges, and new research directions. IEEE Commun. Mag. **52**(1), 85–96 (2014)
3. Teng, J., Zhang, B., Li, X., Bai, X., Xuan, D.: E-shadow: lubricating social interaction using mobile phones. IEEE Trans. Comput. **63**(6), 1422–1433 (2014)
4. Kumar, K.K., Geethakumari, G.: Information diffusion model for spread of misinformation in online social networks. In: Proceedings of the IEEE International Conference Advances in Computing, Communications and Informatics (ICACCI 2013), pp. 1172–1177 (2013)
5. Lewandowsky, S., Ecker, U.K.H., Seifert, C.M., Schwarz, N., Cook, J.: Misinformation and its correction: continued influence and successful debiasing. Psychol. Sci. Pub. Interest **13**(3), 106–131 (2012)
6. Trifunovic, S., Kurant, M., Hummela, K.A., Legendre, F.: Preventing spam in opportunistic networks. Comput. Commun. **41**(15), 31–42 (2014)
7. Liu, X., Takeuchi, Y., Iwami, S.: SVIR epidemic models with vaccination strategies. J. Theor. Biol. **253**(1), 1–11 (2008)
8. Yang, Y.: Global stability of VEISV propagation modeling for network worm attack. Appl. Math. Model. **39**(2), 776–780 (2015)
9. Bettstetter, C., Resta, G., Santi, P.: The node distribution of the random waypoint mobility model for wireless ad hoc networks. IEEE Trans. Mob. Comput. **2**(3), 257–269 (2003)
10. Li, Y., Hui, P., Jin, D., Sheng, C.: Delay-tolerant network protocol testing and evaluation. IEEE Commun. Mag. **53**(1), 258–266 (2015)

Efficient Line K-Coverage
Algorithms in Mobile Sensor Network

Yang Wang, Shuang Wu, Xiaofeng Gao$^{(\boxtimes)}$, Fan Wu, and Guihai Chen

Shanghai Key Laboratory of Scalable Computing and Systems,
Department of Computer Science and Engineering,
Shanghai Jiao Tong University, Shanghai 200240, China
{y_wang,steinsgate}@sjtu.edu.cn,
{gao-xf,fwu,gchen}@cs.sjtu.edu.cn

Abstract. In this paper, we address a new type of coverage problem in mobile sensor network, named Line K-Coverage. It guarantees that any line cutting across a region of interest will be detected by at least K sensors. We aim to schedule an efficient sensor movement to satisfy the line K-coverage while minimize the total sensor movements for energy efficiency, which is named as LK-MinMovs problem. We propose a pioneering layer-based algorithm LLK-MinMovs to solve it in polynomial time. Compared with a MinSum algorithm from previous literature to solve line 1-coverage problem, LLK-MinMovs fixes a critical flaw after finding a counter example for MinSum. We further construct two time-efficient heuristics named LK-KM and LK-KM+ based on the famous Hungarian algorithm. By sacrificing optimality a little bit, these two algorithms runs extremely faster than algorithm LLK-MinMovs. We validate the efficiency of our designs in numerical experiments and compare them under different experiment settings.

1 Introduction

Wireless Sensor Network (WSN) nowadays attracts special attentions from scientific and technological community. Coverage is a fundamental problem among all challenges of WSN. Broadly speaking, coverage is a measure that determines how well a sensor network monitors objectives. Many variations of coverage problem have been proposed for different applications. As an example, the area K-coverage problem requires that each point in the area be covered by at least K sensors.

This work was supported in part by the State Key Development Program for Basic Research of China (973 project 2012CB316201), in part by China NSF grant 61422208, 61202024, 61472252, 61272443 and 61133006, CCF-Intel Young Faculty Researcher Program and CCF-Tencent Open Fund, the Shanghai NSF grant 12ZR1445000, Shanghai Chenguang Grant 12CG09, Shanghai Pujiang Grant 13PJ1403900, and in part by Jiangsu Future Network Research Project No. BY2013095-1-10. The opinions, findings, conclusions, and recommendations expressed in this paper are those of the authors and do not necessarily reflect the views of the funding agencies or the government.

© Springer International Publishing Switzerland 2015
K. Xu and J. Zhu (Eds.): WASA 2015, LNCS 9204, pp. 581–591, 2015.
DOI: 10.1007/978-3-319-21837-3_57

Barrier coverage is more applicable to monitor borders due to exploiting less sensors than area coverage. In front of or surrounding an area, a barrier is a belt-like region in which the sensors are spread. The barrier is said to be K-covered [2,3] if every path that passes through the barrier touches the sensing range of at least K sensors. Many researchers considered line track rather than arbitrary pathes for barrier coverage [4–7], since in reality intruders usually go through a region with a line track. Moreover, intruders do not know any knowledge on distribution of sensors, they cannot figure out a "smart" path to follow. In [16], the authors proposed a MinSum algorithm to build a barrier by scheduling mobile sensors, so that any line intrusion will be detected by at least one sensor. We refer this problem as Line 1-Coverage problem.

In this paper, we consider an advance version of line 1-coverage problem: Line K-Coverage. A line is said to be K-covered if it is detected by at least K sensors. A region is called line K-covered if any line intrusion is K-covered. Usually, sensors at their initial positions may not form a line K-cover for the target region. Thus mobile sensors could move according to some strategy to form a line K-cover. For energy efficiency purpose, we hope that sensors will move with a shortest distance. In all, our optimization object is to minimize the sum of sensor movements to achieve the line K-cover for target region. We refer it as LK-MinMovs problem.

If the initial sensors deployment does not form a line K-cover, the target region will have "gaps" (K-uncovered intervals) against the intrusion. Due to the structural complexity, it is not easy to form line K-cover in one shot. A natural idea is to build line K-cover layer by layer because gaps have different degrees. We first fill up 1-level gaps by twofold overlaps, and then fill up 2-level gaps by threefold overlaps, until K-level gaps are filled. With this idea we propose a layer-based algorithm named LLK-MinMovs. For one layer repairing, a MinSum was proposed in a previous literature [16]. However, although authors in [16] claimed that MinSum outputs the optimal solution, it is not always correct. We illustrate the critical flaw of MinSum by a counter example, and fix the problem in our LLK-MinMovs algorithm. We also construct another two time-efficient heuristics named LK-KM and LK-KM+ based on the famous Hungarian algorithm. By sacrificing optimality a little bit, these two algorithms runs extremely fast with suboptimal results. We analyze the time complexity of them, and then validate their efficiency in numerical experiments under different experiment settings. To the best of our knowledge, we firstly solve the line K-coverage problem in mobile sensor networks, which has both theoretical and practical significance.

The rest of the paper is organized as follows. Section 2 introduces some related works. Section 3 presents the problem statement. Section 4 describes our layer-based algorithm (LLK-MinMovs) and gives its time complexity analysis. A counter example for MinSum is also introduced and corrected. In Sect. 5, we design LK-KM and its enhanced version LK-KM+. Numerical experiments are presented in Sect. 6. Finally, Sect. 7 gives conclusion.

2   Related Works

In the research area of mobile sensor networks, several recent literatures considered the strategy of mobile sensor movement to cover a region of interest, for example [9,10]. Unlike the problem considered in this paper, they aimed to form an area coverage rather than barrier coverage for the region of interest.

Some of the existing works focus on line coverage [8] in a region. Baumgartner et al. [5] proposed the track coverage problem. Their objective is to place a set of sensors in the region such that the chance of detecting the path tracks by at least some given number of sensors is maximized. Other path coverage metrics are defined in [6,7] by analytical expressions for any random deployment in a region. Balister et al. [4] defined a coverage metric called trap coverage which measures the longest distance an intruder can achieve within the region before touching the sensing range of any sensor.

In terms of mobile sensor for barrier, distributed algorithms are proposed in [11] to schedule mobile sensors for forming a barrier. Bar-Noy et al. [12] studied the problem of maximizing the coverage lifetime of a barrier composed by mobile sensors with limited battery powers. How to guide sensor moving to improve the quality of barrier coverage are studied in [13]. All of them consider barrier coverage for path, this is not the objective of this paper. We focus on line K-coverage.

Czyzowicz's work [16] is most related to our objective. The authors proposed MinSum algorithm for line 1-coverage problem which inspired us to design the LLK-MinMovs algorithm. However, MinSum cannot always output an optimal solution. We provide a counter example and correct it in our design, so that LLK-MinMovs could work optimally for arbitrary instance. We also provide numerical experiments to compare LLK-MinMovs with MinSum when $K = 1$.

3   Problem Statement

Assume our region of interest is a rectangle with horizontal length of L (otherwise we can use the minimum bounding rectangle of this region). n sensors $s_1, s_2, ..., s_n$ are randomly deployed in this region. Each sensor s_i has coordinator (x_i, y_i), regarding to left-bottom point $(0,0)$, with same sensing range R. Sensors can move freely in this region, but they are supported by nonrenewable battery powers.

Figure 1 is an example scenario (Assume $K = 3$), where the intrusion direction is vertical against the rectangle. Hence, we could project s_i horizontally as a line segment represented by interval $[x_i - R, x_i + R]$. Then, we just need to consider our problem on line segment $[0, L]$. To better describe our problem, we label sensors with their x-coordinate, and assume each sensor has distinct x_i value in increasing order. Note that we should have "enough" sensors to satisfy a line K-coverage. Thus, initially we have $2Rn \geq KL$ to get a feasible solution.

Easy to see, if we want to form a line K-coverage, every point along the x axis in $[0, L]$ should belong to as least K intervals transformed from sensors.

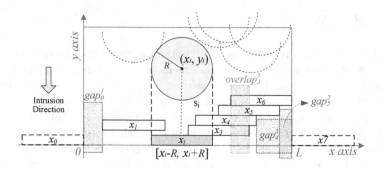

Fig. 1. An example of line coverage transformation ($K=3$).

However, as shown in Fig. 1, there are many intervals on x axis that are covered by less than K sensors, i.e. the interval $[x_4 + R, L]$. We consider such intervals as gaps. Thus, to form a line K-cover is equivalent as to fill up the gaps along x axis after sensor projection. Note that gaps may have different degrees. Some gaps are already covered by several sensors (but less than K), while some other gaps are even bare. To describe a gap rigorously, we have the following definition.

Definition 1 (Line k-Covered Gap). *A line k-covered gap, denoted as gap_i^k, is an interval which starts from the ending point of sensor x_i and ends up to the starting point of sensor x_{i+k}, say, the interval $[x_i + R, x_{i+k} - R]$.*

Easy to see, gap_i^k is covered by $k - 1$ sensors, and $x_{i+k} - x_i > 2R$ (otherwise they will overlap to each other). Three example gaps are shown in Fig. 1, which are line 1-covered gap_0^1, line 2-covered gap_5^2 and line 3-covered gap_4^3. We add two virtual sensors adhesively to the starting point and ending point of the target region. In this example, s_0 locates at $x_0 = -R$, and s_7 locates at $x_7 = L + R$. To illustrate our design, we have another definition for overlap intervals as follow.

Definition 2 (Line k-Covered Overlap). *A line k-covered overlap, denoted as $overlap_i^k$, is an interval which starts from the starting point of sensor x_{i+k} and ends up to the ending point of sensor x_i, say, the interval $[x_{i+k} - R, x_i + R]$.*

Similarly, $overlap_i^k$ is covered by $k+1$ sensors, and $x_{i+k} - x_i < 2R$ (otherwise we cannot find an overlap interval). Thus, some sensors could move to cover other gaps. An example line 3-covered $overlap_3^3$ is shown in Fig. 1, which is covered by sensors x_3, x_4, x_5, and x_6 respectively.

We will move some sensors to fill up all gaps in $[0, L]$. Define the final position of sensor s_i as x_i^f. Then the moving distance d_i of s_i is $|x_i^f - x_i|$. The LK-MinMovs problem is to find the final position for n sensors $s_1, s_2, \cdots, s_n$, so that these sensors will form a line K-cover while the total sensor movements $\sum_{i=1}^{n} |x_i^f - x_i|$ is minimized. We require sensor movement schedule obeying an order preservation restriction given by a Lemma in [16] and sensors cannot move out of $[0, L]$.

In the following sections, we will introduce three algorithms to solve the LK-MinMovs problem.

4 A Layer-Based Algorithm for LK-MinMovs Problem

In our design, we plan to fill up the gaps in an ascending order of their coverage degree. Correspondingly, we fill up line 1-covered gaps first, then line 2-covered gaps, and so forth until filling the line K-covered gaps. During the procedure of filling the line k-covered gaps, we can use the line k-covered overlaps. This strategy is proved to be efficient and better than MinSum by experiments in Sect. 6.

4.1 LLK-MinMovs Algorithm

In our layer-based algorithm, named as LLK-MinMovs algorithm, we try to find the two closest overlaps and select a cheaper one to fill a target gap. Note that such movement process should maintain current coverage level. That means the algorithm will not bring new gaps or downgrade the current coverage quality.

Algorithm 1 is the pseudo-code of LLK-MinMovs. The inputs are an array $X[1 \dots n]$ representing the initial positions of n sensors, the length of the region, L, the coverage degree, K, and the sensor radius, R. It returns an array $X^f[1 \dots n]$ of n elements representing the final positions of sensors.

In Algorithm 1, Line 1 sets two virtual stable sensors to bound the region. Line 2 depicts the layer-based procedure. At each level $k \in [1, K]$, Algorithm 1 finds every line k-covered gap and fills them in a left-right order. The function $isCovered(i, k)$ in Line 4 is a binary function to determine whether the interval $[x_i + R, x_{i+k} - R]$ is line k-covered at current stage. If there exists a gap_i^k, we find its left and right closest overlaps as potential candidates (Line 5-6), compare the cost to use them filling the gap according to cost functions $Lcost(\cdot)$ and $Rcost(\cdot)$, pick up the cheaper one, and move corresponding sensors to fill up gap_i^k according a distance constraint function $Ldist(\cdot)$ and $Rdist(\cdot)$ to keep the current coverage level (Line 7-9). The "while" loop from Line 4 to 9 guarantees that we will fill up all k-covered gaps generated by each x_i.

Algorithm 1. LLK-MinMovs

Input: $X[1 \dots n]$, L, K, R
Output: The final positions $X^f[1 \dots n]$ of n sensors

1 $X[0] = -R$, $X[n+1] = L + R$;
2 **for** $k \leftarrow 1$ *to* K **do**
3   **for** $i \leftarrow 0$ *to* n **do**
4   **while** $isCovered(i, k) = 0$ **do**
5           $l = find(gap_i^k, \text{left})$;   // find the left closest $overlap_l^k$
6           $r = find(gap_i^k, \text{right})$;   // find the right closest $overlap_r^k$
7   **if** $Lcost(i, l, k) \le Rcost(i, r, k)$ **then**
8              $move(l, i, Ldist(l, i, k))$;   // fill gap by its left overlap
9   **else** $move(i, r, -Rdist(i, r, k))$;   // fill gap by its right overlap
10   ;

11 **return** $X^f[1 \dots n]$;

Now, let us define the cost functions and distance constraint functions respectively. At the beginning of every iteration, we say one sensor has *negative shift* if it has moved to left and has *positive shift* if it has moved to right or stays still compared to its initial position. Define $shift_i$ as the shift distance of x_i.

Definition 3 (Left/Right Overlap Cost). *For gap_i^k, the lth to $(l+k)^{th}$ sensors left to x_i form $overlap_l^k$ and the rth to $(r+k)^{th}$ sensors right to x_{i+k} form $overlap_r^k$. Let NS_l^k (PS_l^k) be the set of sensors which have negative (positive) shift among $x_{l+k}, x_{l+2k}, \cdots, x_{l+mk}, \cdots, x_i$ sensors, where $l+mk \leq i$. Let S_r^k be the set of $x_r, x_{r-k}, x_{r-2k}, \cdots, x_{r-mk}, \cdots, x_{i+k}$ sensors, where $r - mk \geq i + k$. Then Eq. (1) computes the left/right overlap costs.*

$$Lcost(l, i, k) = |PS_l^k| - |NS_l^k|, \qquad Rcost(i, r, k) = |S_r^k|. \qquad (1)$$

Definition 4 (Left/Right Overlap Shift Distance). *Easy to know, the size of gap_i^k is $x_{i+k} - x_i - 2R$, the size of $overlap_l^k$ and $overlap_r^k$ are $x_l - x_{l+k} + 2R$ and $x_r - x_{r+k} + 2R$ respectively. Let $MinShift = \min\{|shift_i| \mid x_i \in NS_l^k\}$, which is the effect shift window. Then the left/right shift distance are*

$$\begin{cases} Ldist(l, i, k) = \min\{x_{i+k} - x_i - 2R, x_l - x_{l+k} + 2R, MinShift\}, \\ Rdist(i, r, k) = \min\{x_{i+k} - x_i - 2R, x_r - x_{r+k} + 2R\} \end{cases} \qquad (2)$$

4.2 A Counter Example for MinSum Algorithm

Note that the shifting cost for the left and right overlaps are different. The left shifts for the right overlap only involve sensors whose shift values are zero or negative, while the right shifts for the left overlap involve sensors will all possible shift values. It is due to the left-to-right processing of the gaps. That means right shift will benefit those sensors which have moved left. The authors in [16] also considered the compensation by using similar cost functions for $K = 1$. However, they did not consider the influence of right shift distance to the calculation of $Lcost(\cdot)$. We find that only if the movement strategy considers the shift window effect of the left overlap, the algorithm could work optimally. A counter example is shown in Fig. 2.

In Fig. 2 (a) we give the original positions of 11 sensors. Figure 2 (b) shows the situation when the first 3 gaps are filled, and there is still a gap_7^1 with size g which is greater than *unit* distance a lot. The results are same for our algorithm and MinSum. We can see the left shifts of x_4 and x_6 are very small (Assume x_6 left shift 1 *unit* distance, x_4 left shift 2 *units* distance). Now the cost function $Lcost(1, 7, 1)$ of $overlap_1^1$ equals to $4 - 2 = 2$ because 4 positive shifts ($PS_1^1 = \{x_2, x_3, x_5, x_7\}$) and 2 negative shifts ($PS_1^1 = \{x_4, x_6\}$). The cost function $Rcost(7, 10, 1)$ of $overlap_{10}^1$ equals to 3 ($S_{10}^k = \{x_8, x_9, x_{10}\}$). So $overlap_1^1$ is the cheaper one. Figure 2 (c) shows the result using MinSum which exploits $overlap_1^1$ to fill gap_7^1. Figure 2 (d) shows our algorithm uses the effect moving window. Then $Lcost(1, 7, 1)$ of $overlap_1^1$ is evaluated again since the negative shift of x_6 changes to positive, thus $Lcost(1, 7, 1) = 5 - 1 = 4$.

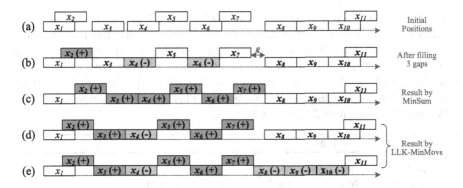

Fig. 2. A counter example to algorithm in [16] ($K=1$).

So $overlap_{10}^1$ is the cheaper one. Figure 2 (e) shows the result after using $overlap_{10}^1$ in our algorithm. MinSum fills gap_7^1 with additional $6 \cdot g - 2 \cdot (2+1) \cdot unit = 6 \cdot g - 5 \cdot unit$ movements while LLK-MinMovs just uses additional $3 \cdot g$ movements. Obviously, Our algorithm is better when $g >> unit$. This is because MinSum does not consider the effect shift window which influences the cost calculation.

4.3   Time Complexity of LLK-MinMovs

For the LLK-MinMovs algorithm, there are K loops to cover each level gaps. For each loop, we consider the total times of movements. There are two types of movements, left-movement and right-movement. In each left-movement, either a gap or a overlap will disappear, thus the total times of left-movements $T_l \leq T_{ol} + T_{gl}$, where T_{ol} is the times of movement where an overlap disappears and T_{gl} is the times of movement where an gap disappears. In each right-movement, a gap or a overlap will disappear or a sensor is moved back to its initial location. Similarly, we have $T_r \leq T_{or} + T_{gr} + T_b$ where T_b is the times of movement where a sensor is moved back. Since in our algorithm, neither a new gap or a new overlap will occur, we have $T_{gl} + T_{gr} = |gaps|$, $T_{ol} + T_{or} \leq |overlaps|$ and $|gaps| + |overlaps| < n$. On the other hand, since any sensor will not move to the left after moving to the right, $T_b \leq n$. Thus we get the total times of movement $T = T_l + T_r < 2n$. For each movement, we will at most move n sensors, thus the time complexity is $O(Kn^2)$.

5   The Design of LK-KM and LK-KM+ Algorithms

We new design another two algorithms for LK-MinMovs problem based on the famous Hungarian Algorithm. They have better time efficiency in spite of sacrificing the optimality a little bit. But their results are still sub-optimal.

The basic idea is to place the sensors to several fixed points evenly distributed on the line segment $[0, L]$. Obviously, it is a perfect Line K-coverage to put K sensors at each virtual fixed points with $2R$ distance between two neighbors.

Then we construct a complete bipartite graph (S, P, E). S represents the sensor set and P represents the virtual fixed point set. Each virtual fixed point has K copies for K-coverage. The edge weight $w(s, p)$ is $L - distance(s, p)$, then the maximum matching for P is the solution of original LK-MinMovs problem. We can use the Kuhn-Munkres algorithm (also known as the famous *Hungarian algorithm*) [14, 15] to compute this matching. This algorithm is referred as LK-KM algorithm shown in Algorithm 2.

Algorithm 2. LK-KM

Input: $X[1 \ldots n]$, L, K, R
Output: The final positions $X^f[1 \ldots n]$ of n sensors

1 Let $S = \{s_1, s_2, \ldots, s_n\}$ and $P = \{d_1, d_2, \ldots, d_{KL/(2R)}\}$ where d_j represents the point in $R + (i(mod)K) \cdot R$
2 Let $w_{i,j} = L - dis(s_i, v_i)$;
3 Using the Hungarian algorithm to compute a matching for (S, P, E);
4 **for** *each $w_{i,j}$ that has been added up* **do**
5 $\quad \lfloor \; X[i] \leftarrow R + (i(mod)K) \cdot R$;
6 **return** $X^f[1 \ldots n]$

Besides, we enhance the LK-KM algorithm with an idea to pull back the sensors which do not need to go so far away from their original positions because the sensor redundance provides the chance. The line K-coverage enhanced KM algorithm, denoted as LK-KM+ uses $PullToLeft(\cdot)$ and $PullToRight(\cdot)$ are added using a function $move(\cdot)$ for movement back of each sensor. We give an example for function call on $move(\cdot)$ in $PullToLeft$, thus is $move(iK + j, iK + j, min(X[iK + j] - X^f[iK + j], X^f[iK + j + 1] - X^f[iK + j], X^f[iK + j] - X^f[iK + j - K])$. It move x_{iK+j} to left in a distance which is shortest one among its shift distance, distance between it and its later neighbor, and distance between it and its K-hops previous neighbor (they should form line K-cover together). The similar procedure in $PullToRight$.

For LK-KM algorithm, the complexity is $O((KL/2R)^2 n)$. And for LK-KM+ algorithm, in spite of adding $move(\cdot)$ steps using only $O(n)$ time, the total complexity of LK-KM+ is also $O((KL/2R)^2 n)$, which is still better than LLK-MinMovs.

6   Numerical Experiments

In experiments, we mainly compare our LLK-MinMovs with MinSum, LK-KM, and LK-KM+. They are all implemented in C++. For each case, we ran each algorithm 100 times at random inputs and calculate the average sum of movement. We define the redundance rate as $\frac{LK}{2Rn}$. First of all, we verify that LLK-MinMovs have the best performance for line 1-coverage, which proves that the MinSum is not optimal. Let $L = 1000, R = 5$ and the results are shown in Fig. 3 (a). LLK-MinMovs is the best and MinSum is better than LK-KM+.

Next, we study the coverage level K. Here we set $K = 1$ to $10, L/R = 20$ and redundance rate be 0.8. We can see LLK-MinMovs and LK-KM+ get more superiority than LK-KM when coverage level K is increasing. Figure 3(b) gives the results. In term of running time, Fig. 3(c) shows LK-KM+ outperforms LLK-MinMovs much more when coverage level K is increasing.

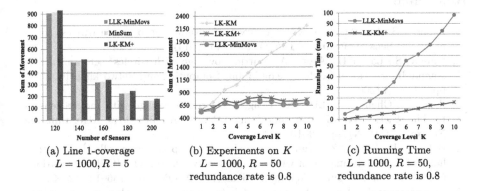

(a) Line 1-coverage
$L = 1000, R = 5$

(b) Experiments on K
$L = 1000, R = 50$
redundance rate is 0.8

(c) Running Time
$L = 1000, R = 50$,
redundance rate is 0.8

Fig. 3. Comparison On LLK-MinMovs, MinSum and LK-KM+(LK-KM)

Then, we study influence on the result with different sensor redundance rate. Besides, we conduct 3 groups of experiments on different $L/R = 10, 20$ and 40. And we set $L = 1000, K = 3$. Figure 4 shows that in all cases LLK-MinMovs has best performance. Three algorithms have the same result at redundance rate 1. Sensors need move less distance when L/R becomes bigger. The LK-KM+ also improves LK-KM very much and is very close to LLK-MinMovs.

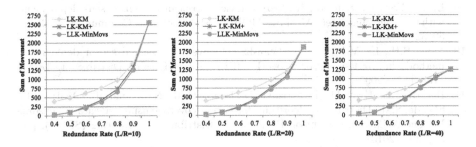

Fig. 4. Experiments on redundance rate and L/R ($L = 1000, K = 3$).

7 Conclusion

In this paper, we address the Line K-coverage problem (LK-MinMovs) in mobile sensor network. We first propose a polynomial time optimal layer-based algorithm LLK-MinMovs. It fixes a critical flaw for the MinSum algorithm designed in [16] for line 1-Coverage problem. We also designed two sub-optimal but faster algorithms, LK-KM and LK-KM+, based on Hungarian algorithm, which have good time complexity $O(\frac{K^2 L^2 n}{R^2})$ in comparison with LLK-MinMovs of $O(Kn^2)$ considering n is significantly bigger than K usually.

References

1. Liang, J.B., Liu, M., Kui, X.Y.: A survey of coverage problems in wireless sensor networks. Sens. Transducers **163**(1), 240–246 (2014)
2. Kumar, S., Lai, T.H., Arora, A.: Barrier coverage with wireless sensors. In: The Annual International Conference on Mobile Computing and Networking (ICMCN), pp. 284–298 (2005)
3. Shen, C., Cheng, W., Liao, X., Peng, S.: Barrier coverage with mobile sensors. In: The IEEE International Symposium on Parallel Architectures, Algorithms and Networks (ISPAN), pp. 99–104 (2008)
4. Balister, P., Zheng, Z., Kumar, S., Sinha, P.: Trap coverage: allowing coverage holes of bounded dimeter in wireless sensor network. In: The IEEE International Conference on Computer Communications (INFOCOM), pp. 136–144 (2009)
5. Baumgartner, K., Ferrari, S.: A geometric transversal approach to analyzing track coverage in sensor networks. IEEE Trans. Comput. **57**(8), 1113–1128 (2008)
6. Harada, J., Shioda, S., Saito, H.: Path coverage properties of randomly deployed sensors with finite data-transmission ranges. Comput. Netw. **53**(7), 1014–1026 (2009)
7. Ram, S.S., Manjunath, D., Iyer, S.K., Yogeshwaran, D.: On the path coverage properties of random sensor networks. IEEE Trans. Mob. Comput. **6**(5), 446–458 (2007)
8. Mondal, D., Kumar, A., Bishnu, A., Mukhopadhyaya, K., Nandy, S.C.: Measuring the quality of surveillance in a wireless sensor network. Int. J. Found. Comput. Sci. **22**(4), 983–998 (2011)
9. Li, X., Frey, H., Santoro, N., Stojmenovic, I.: Localized sensor self- deployment with coverage guarantee. ACM SIGMOBILE Mob. Comput. Commun. Rev. **12**(2), 50–52 (2008)
10. Yang, S.H., Li, M.L., Wu, J.: Scan-based movement-assisted sensor deployment methods in wireless sensor networks. IEEE Trans. Parallel Distrib.Syst. **18**(8), 1108–1121 (2007)
11. Hesari, M.E., Kranakis, E., Krizanc, D., Ponce, O.M., Narayanan, L., Opatrny, J., Shende, S.M.: Distributed algorithms for barrier coverage using relocatable sensors. In: The ACM Symposium on Principles of Distributed Computing (SPDC), pp. 383–392 (2013)
12. Bar-Noy, A., Rawitz, D., Terlecky, P.: Maximizing barrier coverage lifetime with mobile sensors. CoRR, vol. abs/1304.6358 (2013)
13. Saipulla, A., Westphal, C., Liu, B., Wang, J.: Barrier coverage with line-based deployed mobile sensors. Ad Hoc Netw. **11**(4), 1381–1391 (2013)
14. Kuhn, H.W.: The Hungarian method for the assignment problem. Nav. Res. Logist. Q. **2**, 83–97 (1955)
15. Munkres, J.: Algorithms for the assignment and transportation problems. J. Soc. Ind. Appl. Math. **5**(1), 32–38 (1957)

16. Czyzowicz, J., Kranakis, E., Krizanc, D., Lambadaris, I., Narayanan, L., Opatrny, J., Stacho, L., Urrutia, J., Yazdani, M.: On minimizing the sum of sensor movements for barrier coverage of a line segment. In: International Conference on Ad Hoc Networks and Wireless (ADHOC-NOW), 6288: 29–42 (2010)
17. Chen, D.Z., Gu, Y., Li, J., Wang, H.: Algorithms on minimizing the maximum sensor movement for barrier coverage of a linear domain. Discrete Comput. Geom. 50(2), 374–408 (2013)

A Trust Evolution Mechanism for Mobile Social Networks Based on Wright-Fisher

Yingjie Wang[1], Yingshu Li[2]($\boxtimes$), Yang Gao[1], and Xiangrong Tong[1]

[1] School of Computer and Control Engineering, Yantai University,
Yantai 264005, Shandong, China
[2] Department of Computer Science, Georgia State University,
Atlanta, GA 30022, USA
yili@gsu.edu

Abstract. With the development of mobile social networks, the trust problem of networks attracts more and more attentions. According to the existing problems of evolution model, this paper proposes a trust evolution mechanism for mobile social networks based on Wright-Fisher. Combining the evolutionary game theory and Wright-Fisher model, we establish the trust evolution model under white noise environment to analyze and predict the evolution trend of mobile social networks. In addition, in order to solve the free-riding problem in mobile social networks, this paper proposes an incentive strategy based on evolution theory. Through the experiments, we verify the effectiveness and adaptability of the proposed trust evolution mechanism. The proposed incentive strategy can inspire users to select trustful strategy, and improve the trust degree of the whole mobile social networks.

Keywords: Mobile social networks · Trust · Wright-Fisher · Evolutionary game theory · Incentive strategy

1 Introduction

With the development of big data, the study on mobile social networks become more and more important. The popularity of Mobile Social Networks (MSNs) has enhanced the communications between people, and made people's lives convenient [1]. Mobile social networks can be seen as communities connected by the mobile devices, such as PAD, smartphones and so on [2]. Users can share their status anytime and anywhere through mobile social networks more conveniently [3].

In the big data era, the data changes dynamically with high speed in networks. Therefore, it puts forward a high requirement to the response speed of calculation [4,5]. In order to adapt the development of mobile social networks, the concept of *mobile crowdsourcing* emerged at the right moment [6]. The group of users who hold mobile devices contains enormous potential, they can participate task to sense data in order to complete tasks [7]. Therefore, the research on mobile crowdsourcing in mobile social networks has great significance and good

© Springer International Publishing Switzerland 2015
K. Xu and J. Zhu (Eds.): WASA 2015, LNCS 9204, pp. 592–601, 2015.
DOI: 10.1007/978-3-319-21837-3_58

application prospect. With the generation of mobile crowdsourcing, the trust of users in mobile social networks is the foundation and an important condition that can make mobile crowdsourcing systems operate normally [8,9].

Because of the dynamic evolution environment, the mobile social networks are full of complexity and ecology. It is necessary to establish effective methods to control the users' behaviors and selection for the interactive strategies in order to make mobile social networks converge to stable and trustful state. In recent years, scholars have obtained some research achievements in this research field. However, there are still some problems need to be resolved: (1) when establishing evolution model, the noise problem in networks is not considered, which influences the accuracy of prediction results; (2) most of the control mechanisms fail to combine the incentive strategy with the ecology feature of users to resolve the free-riding problem.

According to the above problems, we establish a trust evolution mechanism for mobile social networks through considering the complexity and ecology of mobile social networks. The contributions of this paper are summarized as follows.

1. Combining the evolutionary game theory and Wright-Fisher model, we establish the trust evolution model.
2. We consider the noise problem of networks and multi-strategy selection into the establishment of trust evolution model.
3. We resolve the free-riding problem through designing an incentive strategy based on evolution theory.

The rest of the paper is organized as follows. Section 2 presents the related works. Section 3 introduces the proposed trust evolution mechanism. Section 4 illustrates the simulations, along with the parameter settings, followed by the result analysis and discussions. Finally, Sect. 5 concludes this paper.

2   Related Work

On the aspect of evolution model, the typical methods mainly include the evolution model based on evolutionary game theory and the evolution model based on neural network.

So far, basic evolutionary game thoughts are almost derived from the research results of Taylor, Jonker and Maynard Smith. In replicate dynamic equation, the growth rate of pure strategy is proportional to the fitness of individual. Replicate dynamic equation strengthens dynamic processing for networks complex states. Therefore, it provides strategy foundation for entities trust evolution in network. At present, replicate dynamic equation is widely applied in dynamic models of system evolution, so that its deformations have also been the hot issue of dynamic models [10].

Neural network is widely applied in engineering field and economic research. Utilizing neural network, Siang Yew Chong and Xin Yao [11] researched iterated prisoners dilemma. In addition, they described the trust strategies of entities, and established evolution model. In aspect of evolution, reference [12] introduced neural network into evolutionary game. It simulated learning and adjusting process of bounded rationality gamers, and adopted particle swarm optimization algorithm to train neural network. This research made neural network not only be a powerful analysis tool for system evolution, but also add new method for research of trust evolution model.

However, the present methods fail to consider the real network environment, such as the noise problem and the ecology feature of networks, which leads to the lack of accuracy on the prediction results. In addition, the present methods fail to analyze the multi-strategy game, so that cannot adapt to the complexity feature of networks.

In order to solve the free-riding problem in mobile crowdsourcing systems, a lot of incentive and punishment strategies were proposed.

Many of the incentive mechanisms on crowdsourcing websites rely on monetary rewards in the form of micro-payments [13]. The requester pays workers in the form of cash upon the completion of a task. However, the monetary incentive mechanism possesses several disadvantages which prevent it from being easily deployed on crowdsourcing websites. The first problem associated with the payment system is the absence of associated effective pricing schemes. Due to the heterogeneity in tasks and requesters, the existing pricing scheme often provides competitive advantages to the requesters with high budgets [14]. Secondly, such pricing schemes often deploy auctions to set the price, which may results in high delay and implementation complexity in order to achieve desirable resource allocations and often cause *currency inflation* on the crowdsourcing websites. Moreover, it is also worth nothing that to deploy such pricing schemes usually necessitates the usage of complicated and reliable financial accounting, which is difficult to design and deploy in large-scale online websites.

In order to solve above problems, Zhang et al. [15] proposed a class of incentive protocols based on social norms, which is simple to design and flexible in implementation. They formalized the interactions between workers and requesters using a rigorous repeated game framework to analyze the time-dependency of their current and future behavior. It is the first work that integrates payment and reputation mechanisms in a rigorous manner to design protocols for crowdsourcing applications. However, this incentive mechanism only has one threshold for worker's reputation. Under this condition, once a worker selects the *Distrust* strategy for one time, she will never be selected by the platform forever, *i.e.*, be isolated all the time, which is unfair for the potential trustable workers.

3   The Proposed Trust Evolution Mechanism

In this section, we research the trust evolution model through combining evolutionary game theory and Wright-Fisher model firstly. Then, according to the proposed trust evolution model, the corresponding incentive strategy is proposed based on evolution theory.

3.1   The Trust Evolution Model

In order to analyze and predict the trust evolution trend of mobile social networks more accurately, we research the trust evolution model based on the complexity and ecology features of mobile social networks. Combining evolutionary game theory and Wright-Fisher model, we propose a trust evolution model in this paper.

In the process of sensing data, it is an evolutionary game process when users selects their trust strategies. In order to discuss the gaming process between users, we divide the trust degree into five levels. Firstly, T_i is defined as the trust degree of user i, and $T_i \in [0, 1]$. Therefore, the divided trust degree of users is shown as: $[0.8, 1.0] \rightarrow level_1$, $[0.6, 0.8) \rightarrow level_2$, $[0.4, 0.6) \rightarrow level_3$, $[0.2, 0.4) \rightarrow level_4$ and $[0.0, 0.2) \rightarrow level_5$.

According to two users who participate the same task, their selections for different trust strategies have the game relationship. Because of the selfishness and perception features, the game between users satisfies the Prisoner's Dilemma Game. Therefore, according to the evolutionary characteristic of networks, we utilize iterated prisoner's dilemma game to analyze the gaming process of different trust strategies.

If two users A and B game with each other, they both have five strategies to select. The game matrix for gamer A and gamer B with five trust levels is a symmetric game matrix. $b_{i,j}$ represents the benefit if gamer A select the strategy with trust $level_i$, and gamer B select the strategy with trust $level_j$. In a mobile social networks, users obtain the rewards through sensing the corresponding task. We define $p_{i,j}$ as the payment for user A (or user B), if user A (or user B) selects the trust strategy with $level_i$, and user B (or user A) selects the strategy with trust $level_j$. c_i represents the associated cost that a user selects the strategy with trust $level_i$. Therefore, the calculation of $b_{i,j}$ is shown by Eq. (1).

$$b_{i,j} = p_{i,j} - c_i \qquad (1)$$

The *Wright-Fisher process* has a wide range of application. All of the individuals produce offspring in the same time based on the adaptability of individual. And These offspring individuals generate an offspring set. The updated next generation generates randomly from this offspring set [16]. Therefore, based on the ecology feature of networks, we can establish trust evolution model through combining the evolutionary game theory and Wright-Fisher model. Assume the total number of entities in a mobile social network is N, and the initial numbers of entities with different trust levels are n_1, n_2, n_3, n_4 and n_5 respectively. The corresponding relationships are: $n_1 \rightarrow level_1$, $n_2 \rightarrow level_2$, $n_3 \rightarrow level_3$, $n_4 \rightarrow level_4$ and $n_5 \rightarrow level_5$. Therefore, the adaptability F_i of users who select the strategy with trust $level_i$ is calculated by Eq. (2), where $i, j \in (1, 2, 3, 4, 5)$.

$$F_i = \frac{\left(\sum_{j=1}^{5} b_{i,j} \cdot n_j \right) - b_{i,i}}{N - 1} \qquad (2)$$

The Wright-Fisher process is $n - fold$ Bernoulli trials in the offspring set, so the users obey binomial distribution. Assume $Y_i^{(m)}$ is the number of users with trust $level_i$ in the mth generation, and $Y_i^{(m)} = n_i^{(m)}$. Therefore, the probability, when $Y_i^{(m+1)} = n_i^{(m+1)}$, is shown by Eq. (3), where $i, j \in (1, 2, 3, 4, 5)$.

$$P(Y_i^{(m+1)} = n_i^{(m+1)} | Y_i^{(m)} = n_i^{(m)}) = \binom{N}{n_i^{(m+1)}} \prod_{i=1}^{5} \left(\frac{n_i^{(m)} \cdot F_i}{\sum_{j=1}^{5} n_j^{(m)} F_j} \right)^{n_i^{(m+1)}} \tag{3}$$

The Wright-Fisher process is a synchronous update process, so we utilize $\frac{E(\Delta x)}{\Delta t}$ instead of replicated dynamic equation $\frac{dx}{dt}$ in evolutionary game theory. $E(\Delta x)$ expresses the individual frequency variation of some type of users, and Δt is the update time step. Therefore, $E(\Delta x)$ can be calculated based on Wright-Fisher model. The calculation equation of $E(\Delta x)$ is shown by Eq. (4).

$$\begin{aligned} E(\Delta x) &= \frac{\sum_{n_i^{(m+1)}=0}^{N} (n_i^{(m+1)} - n_i^{(m)}) \cdot P(Y_i^{m+1} = n_i^{(m+1)} | Y_i^m = n_i^{(m)})}{N} \\ &= \frac{n_i^{(m)} \cdot F_i}{\sum_{j=1}^{5} n_i^{(m)} \cdot F_j} - x \end{aligned} \tag{4}$$

Let the proportions of users with different trust levels be:x_1, x_2, x_3, x_4 and x_5. According to the calculation method of $E(\Delta x)$, combining with the replicated dynamic equation $\frac{dx}{dt}$, the trust evolution model is shown by Eq. (5), where $i \in (1, 2, 3, 4, 5)$.

$$dx_i = (\frac{x_i \cdot E_i}{E} - x_i)dt \tag{5}$$

In Eq. (5), E_i represents the expected revenue of users who select the strategy with trust $level_i$, and E indicates the average expected revenue of the whole mobile social networks. The calculation methods of E_i and E are shown by Eq. (6), where $i, j \in (1, 2, 3, 4, 5)$.

$$E_i = \sum_{j=1}^{5} x_j \cdot b_{i,j}, E = \sum_{i=1}^{5} x_i \cdot E_i \tag{6}$$

Therefore, we can predict the trust evolution trend of a mobile social network through Eq. (5). However, in a mobile social network, it is full of complexity and uncertainty. Equation (5) indicates the deterministic trust evolution model, so it fails to express the complexity and uncertainty of a mobile social network. In order to reflect the complexity and uncertainty of a mobile social networks, we introduce white noise into the deterministic trust evolution model. Therefore,

Eq. (5) is extended into random dynamics equation by considering white noise in an evolution process of a mobile social network. The trust evolution model with white noise is shown by Eq. (7), where w indicates one-dimension standard Brown movement. It means that w obeys normal distribution $N(0, t)$ for given time t. And dw obeys normal distribution $N(0, \Delta t)$. Therefore, it is Gaussian White Noise. That is to say, if the noise's amplitude obeys Gaussian distribution, and its power spectral density is evenly distributed, it is called *Gaussian White Noise*.

$$dx_i = (\frac{x_i \cdot E_i}{E} - x_i)dt + \sqrt{x_i \cdot (1 - x_i)}dw \tag{7}$$

Equation (7) is the random dynamics equation, which can reflect the complexity and uncertainty of a mobile social networks. Therefore, this trust evolution model can analyze and predict the trust evolution trend of a mobile social networks more accurately.

3.2 Incentive Strategy Based on Evolution Theory

Because of the complexity and ecology features of mobile social networks, the users are so selfish that do their best to maximize their benefits. In order to maximize their benefits, users intend to select distrust strategy to obtain more benefits. Therefore, the mobile social networks are easy to generate free-riding phenomenon if there is not any control means.

According to the free-riding problem, we design an incentive strategy based on evolution theory. Because of the selective evolution, the users who have higher adaptability can survive in mobile social networks. In order to solve the free-riding problem, the benefit of users who adopt the strategies with high trust level should be increased to improve their adaptability.

Based on the evolution theory, we define an incentive and punishment parameter $\lambda_{i,j}$ to modify the game matrix, and $\lambda_{i,j} \in [0, 1]$. The benefits of users after adding the incentive and punishment parameter is shown by Eq. (8). In addition, the incentive and punishment satisfies the condition: $\lambda_{i,j} = \lambda_{j,i}$, that is to say, parameter $\lambda_{i,j}$ is symmetrical. If $i = j$, parameter $\lambda_{i,j} = 0$.

$$B_{i,j} = \begin{cases} p_{i,j} + \lambda_{i,j} \cdot (p_{i,j} + p_{j,i}) - c_i, & if\, i < j; \\ p_{i,j} - c_i, & if\, i = j; \\ p_{i,j} - \lambda_{i,j} \cdot (p_{i,j} + p_{j,i}) - c_i, & if\, i > j. \end{cases} \tag{8}$$

Based on the social norm, with the increasing of the value of $|i - j|$, the parameter $\lambda_{i,j}$ will increase. The adaptability after adding the incentive strategy is shown by Eq. (9). In order to make sure the trustful strategy be the Nash equilibrium strategy, F^* should satisfies the condition: $F_1^* > F_2^* > F_3^* > F_4^* > F_5^*$. Therefore, through adjusting the payments for users based on evolution theory, the cloud platform can control the trust evolution direction of the whole mobile social network.

$$F_i^* = \frac{\left(\sum\limits_{j=1}^{5} B_{i,j} \cdot n_j\right) - B_{i,i}}{N-1} \tag{9}$$

Because of the ecology feature of users, they intend to maximize their benefits, and have learning ability. Based on this feature, we design the incentive strategy to inspire users to select trustful strategy as their best selection. Through the incentive strategy, the trust degrees of users and the whole mobile social network are both increased in the end.

4   Simulations and Performance Analysis

We conduct two groups of simulations to evaluate the proposed trust evolution mechanism. First of all, we verify the accuracy of the proposed trust evolution model. Then, through the corresponding experiments, the effectiveness of the proposed incentive strategy is verified. All the experiments were run on Windows XP operating system with Intel Core (TM) Duo 2.66 GHz CPU, 12 GB Memory and Matlab 7.0 simulation platform.

In order to verify the effectiveness of the proposed trust evolution model, we compute the initial benefits of different trust strategies based on evolutionary game theory. In this paper, we divide trust degrees of users into five levels. The experimental data is obtained through Eq. (1), and $p_{i,j}$ is determined by the prisoner's dilemma game function, c_i is determined through the function $c_i = 0.2 * (6 - i)$.

Therefore, according to the initial benefits of different trust strategies, we obtain the comparison results of the evolution trends for different trust strategies, which is shown by Fig. 1. From Fig. 1, it can be seen that the strategy with $level_5$ leads the evolution direction of the whole mobile social networks, $i.e.$, users will select distrustful strategy in the end because of the high benefit. However, other four strategies decrease as time goes on because of the low benefit. This experimental result verifies the selfishness of users: a user is willing to select distrustful strategy as their first selection if there is not any incentive strategy. In another word, a mobile social network without any control method, is easy to generate free-riding phenomenon.

In order to improve the accuracy of this trust evolution model, we add white noise into the trust evolution model to reflect the complexity characteristic of mobile social networks. The experimental result is shown on Fig. 2. Because of the complexity of mobile social networks, the trust evolution model with white noise can predict trust evolution trend of a mobile social network more accurately. It can be seen that after considering the effect of white noise, the networks evolution process has slight fluctuations. This situation is more in line with the real evolution process of a network. It is because that the network environment has uncertainties, the evolution process of a mobile social network must perform in an uncertain manner.

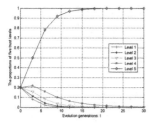
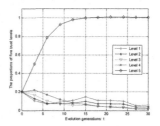

Fig. 1. The evolution trends for different trust strategies.

Fig. 2. The evolution trends for different trust strategies with white noise.

In order to solve the free-riding problem in mobile social networks, we verify the effectiveness of the proposed incentive strategy. In these experiments, the incentive and punishment parameter $\lambda_{i,j}$ is shown by followings.

$$\lambda_{1,2}=\lambda_{2,1}=\lambda_{2,3}=\lambda_{3,2} = \lambda_{3,4}=\lambda_{4,3}=\lambda_{4,5}=\lambda_{5,4} = 0.08,$$
$$\lambda_{1,3}=\lambda_{3,1}=\lambda_{2,4}=\lambda_{4,2}=\lambda_{3,5}=\lambda_{5,3}= 0.16,$$
$$\lambda_{1,4}=\lambda_{4,1}=\lambda_{2,5}=\lambda_{5,2}= 0.24,$$
$$\lambda_{1,5}=\lambda_{5,1}= 0.32$$

Therefore, according to the benefits of different trust strategies with incentive strategy, we obtain the comparison results of the evolution trends for different trust strategies, which is shown by Fig. 3. From Fig. 3, it can be seen that the strategy with $level_1$ leads the evolution direction of the whole mobile social networks, *i.e.*, users will select trustful strategy in the end because of the high benefit. That is to say, the free-riding problem is solved through adding the incentive strategy. Therefore, we can verify the effectiveness of the proposed incentive strategy through this experiment.

We also design the experiment to verify the effectiveness of the proposed incentive strategy under white noise environment, which is shown by Fig. 4. From Fig. 4, it can be seen that there are some small fluctuations in the process of evolution. However, the whole evolution trend is similar with the experimental result of Fig. 3. Because of the uncertainty of mobile social networks, this situation is more in line with the real evolution process of a network.

According to the evolution trends of the average benefits of mobile social network without incentive strategy and with incentive strategy, this paper compare the experimental results for their evolution trends of the average benefits, which is shown by Fig. 5. Trough the comparison result, it can be seen that the average benefit of users increases after adding the proposed incentive strategy. Therefore, the effectiveness of the proposed incentive strategy is verified through these experiments. The proposed incentive strategy can inspire users to select trustful strategy, and improve the trust degree of the whole mobile social network effectively.

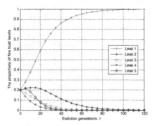
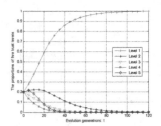

Fig. 3. The evolution trends for different trust strategies with the proposed incentive strategy.

Fig. 4. The evolution trends for different trust strategies with the proposed incentive strategy and white noise.

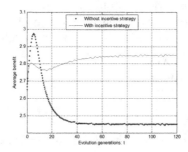

Fig. 5. The average benefit of mobile social network.

5   Conclusions

This paper proposed a trust evolution mechanism for mobile social networks based on Wright-Fisher. According to the complexity and ecology characteristics of mobile social networks, combining the evolutionary game theory and Wright-Fisher model, we established the trust evolution model to analyze and predict the evolution trend of a mobile social network. In addition, we considered white noise into the proposed trust evolution model in order to express the complexity of real mobile social networks. Finally, in order to solve the free-riding problem, we proposed an incentive strategy based on evolution theory. Through the experiments, the effectiveness and adaptability of the proposed trust evolution model were verified in the end. The trust evolution model after adding white noise, can reflect the complexity of real mobile social networks better from the experimental results. In addition, according to the experimental results, it can be seen that the incentive strategy based on evolution theory can inspire users to select trustful strategy, so that improve the trust degree of the whole mobile social networks.

In the future research, we will further research the privacy protection of a user in mobile social networks in order to avoid malicious attacks of malicious users. In addition, the security problem of mobile social networks will be further researched through combining traditional security method with trust management method.

Acknowledgments. This work is supported by the National Natural Science Foundation of China under Grants No.61170224, No.61272186 and No.61472095.

References

1. Cho, J.H., Swami, A., Chen, R.: A survey on trust management for mobile ad hoc networks. IEEE Commun. Surv. Tutorials **13**, 562–583 (2011)
2. Zheng, X., Cai, Z., Li, J., Gao, H.: An application-aware scheduling policy for real-time traffic. In: The 35th IEEE International Conference on Distributed Computing Systems, Columbus, Ohio, USA (2015)
3. Salehan, M., Negahban, A.: Social networking on smartphones: when mobile phones become addictive. Comput. Hum. Behav. **29**, 2632–2639 (2013)
4. Cheng, S., Cai, Z., Li, J., Fang, X.: Drawing dominant dataset from big sensory data in wireless sensor networks. In: The 34rd Annual IEEE International Conference on Computer Communications, Hong Kong, China (2015)
5. Cheng, S., Cai, Z., Li, J.: Curve query processing in wireless sensor networks. IEEE Trans. Veh. Technol. **PP**(99) (2014)
6. Yang, S., Thormann, J.: Poster: crowdsourcing to smartphones: social network based human collaboration. In: The 15th ACM International Symposium on Mobile Ad Hoc Networking and Computing. ACM, New York (2014)
7. Wang, Y., Yin, G., Cai, Z., Dong, Y., Dong, H.: A trust-based probabilistic recommendation model for social networks. J. Netw. Comput. Appl. **55**, 59–67 (2015)
8. Zhang, L., Cai, Z., Lu, J., Wang, X.: Spacial mobility prediction based routing scheme in delay/disruption-tolerant networks. Personal and Ubiquitous Computing (2015)
9. He, Z., Cai, Z., Wang, X.: Modeling propagation dynamics and optimal countermeasures of the social network rumors. In: The 35th IEEE International Conference on Distributed Computing Systems, Columbus, Ohio, USA (2015)
10. Szolnoki, A., Xie, N.G., Ye, Y.: Evolution of emotions on networks leads to the evolution of cooperation in social dilemmas. Phys. Rev. E **87**, 042805 (2013)
11. Chong, S.Y., Yao, X.: Multiple choices and reputation in multiagent interactions. IEEE Trans. Evol. Comput. **11**, 689–711 (2007)
12. Liu, W., Wang, X.: Study on evolutionary games based on PSO-neural networks. Syst. Eng. Electron. **29**, 1282–1284 (2007)
13. Singer, Y., Mittal, M.: Pricing mechanisms for crowdsourcing markets. The 22nd International Conference on World Wide Web, International World Wide Web Conferences Steering Committee, Switzerland (2013)
14. Chen, Y., Ho, T.H., Kim, Y.M.: Knowledge market design: a field experiment at Google answers. J. Public Econ. Theory **12**, 641–664 (2010)
15. Zhang, Y., van der Schaar, M.: Reputation-based incentive protocols in crowdsourcing applications. Proceedings of the IEEE INFOCOM 2012, Orlando, FL, USA (2012)
16. Yin, G., Wang, Y., Dong, Y., Dong, H.: Wright-Fisher multi-strategy trust evolution model with white noise for Internetware. Expert Syst. Appl. **40**, 7367–7380 (2013)

A Localized Channel Allocation Approach for Realtime Reliable and High Throughput Communication in Multi-channel Networks

Wei Li$^{(\boxtimes)}$, Kai Xing, and Jing Xu

School of Computer Science,
University of Science and Technology of China, Hefei 230027, China
{weili011,jxu125}@mail.ustc.edu.cn, kxing@ustc.edu.cn

Abstract. Wireless applications have divergent requirements. For example, safety applications require realtime reliable communications via interference-free channels, while entertainment applications require high throughput via channel competition/coordination. The adoption of interference-free channels may result in low channel utilization and the employment of competition/coordination based channels may result in excessive contentions/oevrhead. To solve this conflict, we propose a fully localized channel allocation scheme in a local neighborhood. Specifically, we divide the whole channel set into three categories at each node's neighborhood: primary channels, competitory channels, and secondary channels. In our analysis, we show that the proposed scheme can exclusively provide interference-free channels to each node for realtime reliable communications, while most of the remaining channels can be fully utilized to achieve high throughput based on an adequate but sophisticated channel competition design.Our experiment study demonstrates that our proposed approach is able to support realtime reliable communications via interference-free channel allocation, while at the same time achieve much better channel utilization than the existing mainstream approaches.

1 Introduction

We propose an adaptive channel allocation scheme to achieve realtime reliable and high throughput communications. Specifically, we divide the entire channel set into three categories: primary channels, competitory channels, and secondary channels at each node's local neighborhood. The primary channels of each node are guaranteed to be interference free for realtime reliable communications, while the competitory channels of each node are used for high throughput. The secondary channels can be used as a competitory channels when there is no conflicting reservation with others in a local neighborhood.Our main contributions can be summarized as follows:our approach provides a fully localized design that enables adequate but sophisticated competition for high throughput while providing the guarantee on latency and reliability through interference-free channels at the same time.

© Springer International Publishing Switzerland 2015
K. Xu and J. Zhu (Eds.): WASA 2015, LNCS 9204, pp. 602–611, 2015.
DOI: 10.1007/978-3-319-21837-3_59

2 Related Work

The static assignment schemes usually assign channels to fixed radios or for long-time duration in [1–5]. TiMesh [1] takes the logical topology, interface assignment, channel allocation, and routing into consideration and tries to find the optimal answer for the joint linear problem with balanced traffic load. However, it is designed for a stationary network, any changes would lead to failure.

Dynamic assignment strategies extend the scope of channel assignment scheme that can be adjusted dynamically with the change of the network environment. Raniwala, Ashish proposed Hyacinth [6], a distributed channel assignment design that can dynamically adapt to traffic loads.The MeshChop scheme in [7], uses a connected component based channel hopping approach to make a centralized assignment.

Both static and dynamic assignment strategies are applied in hybrid channel assignment strategies in [8].

3 Models and Assumptions

3.1 Network Model

In a stationary multi-channel wireless network, the network can be modeled as an undirected graph $G(V, E, X)$, where V denotes the node set and E denotes the edge set. Each node has its own binary vector, and all the vectors can compose a code matrix X with the size of $N \times |V|$, where N denotes the number of orthogonal channels that are labeled as $k_1, k_2, \ldots, k_N$, $V \gg N$. Each column of the X, $\boldsymbol{x_u}$, represents a channel codeword (vector) for the node u. For each node u, $\mathcal{N}_1(u)$ means all the neighbors of node u in one-hop distance and $\mathcal{N}_2(u)$ for the two hops. In this paper, we adopt the protocol interference model: for a node u, the set of its interferers is denoted by $\mathcal{N}(u)$,$\mathcal{N}(u) = \mathcal{N}_2(u)$.

3.2 Channel Model

According to the classification process in [9],we can that all the channels are classified to three kinds for each node: primary channels CH_1, competitory channels CH_2, and secondary channels CH_3. For node u, secondary channels $CH_3(u)$ are all primary channels CH_1 of $\mathcal{N}(u)$, others are $CH_2(u)$. Due to space limitations, see the details in [9]. Moreover, each channel consists of three successive phases: claim phase, competition phase, and transmission phase. The claim phase is used for a node to claim its primary channels whether it is going to use these primary channels or not. The competition phase is used to determine which node could use this channel, where multiple rounds of competition may be required to conclude the phase. The transmission phase is used for the winner node of the channel to transmit data.

When a node u plans to send data, it needs to first determine which channel k_i it should compete/use based on a sophistically designed probability, as shown

Table 1. Basic competition probability table for CH_2

Node	CH_1	CH_2					CH_3
		1	2	3	...	C	
1	1	q	q^2	q^3	...	q^C	p_1
2	1	q^2	q^3	q^4	...	q	p_2
3	1	q^3	q^4	q^5	...	q^2	p_3
...	...	...	...	...	...	...	...
C	1	q^C	q	q^2	...	q^{C-1}	p_C
C+1	1	q	q^2	q^3	...	q^C	p_{C+1}
C+2	1	q^2	q^3	q^4	...	q	p_{C+2}
C+3	1	q^3	q^4	q^5	...	q^2	p_{C+3}
...	...	...	...	...	...	...	...
2C	1	q^C	q	q^2	...	q^{C-1}	p_{2C}
kC+1	1	q	q^2	q^3	...	q^C	p_{kC+1}
kC+2	1	q^2	q^3	q^4	...	q	p_{kC+2}
kC+3	1	q^3	q^4	q^5	...	q^2	p_{kC+3}
...	...	...	...	...	...	...	...
V	1	q^C	q	q^2	...	q^{C-1}	p_V

Note: V is the number of nodes, $C = |Channels|, V = (k+1)C, k \in Z$

in Table 1. We can see from the table that each node chooses its primary channels at the probability of 1, competitory channels at a geometric progression of probability $Q_k(u) = (q, q^2, q^3, \ldots, q^{C-1}, q^C)$ among nodes and channels, where $0 < q < 1$.

If node u chooses a primary channel, it simply sends a bit-length impulse signal in the claim phase. After the claim phase, it can directly use this channel. If node u chooses a secondary channel, it sends a bit-length impulse signal at a randomly picked moment in each round of the competition phase, and competes in a round by round manner. The competitor on the channel k_i that first sends out the bit-length impulse signal could win the channel. After node u wins the channel, it can send data on channel k_i after the competition phase. If node u chooses a secondary channel, it needs to listen to the channel during the claim phase. If there is no impulse signal claiming channel k_i during this phase, node u could compete for this channel with the same strategy adopted for the competitory channels. Otherwise, node u cannot use this channel since it is reserved as a primary channel that is going to be used by its neighbors. Note that the impulse signal has a similar effect of the RTS packet adopted in the RTS/CTS mechanism of 802.11 wireless networks and it is suitable as control signals [10], but the impulse signal can be just bit-length.

In Algorithm 1 when most nodes are idle in the neighborhood of node u, u may apply a dynamic increase on its probabilities in order to more quickly

---

Algorithm 1. Probability Adjustment Function

Require: state indicator C_r,current probability vector Q_k to the channel k
Ensure: new probability vector Q'_k
1: **if** $C_r == 0$ **then**
2:     **for** each element p_i in Q_k **do**
3:         **if** $p_i < q$ **then**
4:             $p_i = \frac{p_i}{q}$
5:         **end if**
6:     **end for**
7: **else**
8:     $Q'_k = (q, q^2, q^3, \dots, q^C)$
9: **end if**

---

use up all the channels since no one is going to use the channel. Specifically, u increases its probability for channel competition by $1/q$ every round, until the probability reaches q. The $Q_k(u)$ will be reset to be the basic vector once node u meets competition from others. The dynamic adjustment mechanism relies on whether most of u's neighbors are idle or not. We use C_r as the indicator in Algorithm 2.

4   Channel Allocation Algorithm

In this section, we present how these channels are used to do different types of transmission according to different characteristics. Our basic idea is trying to make an ingenious allocation for each of the nodes based on the superimposed code. CH_1 channels can be interference-free because of s-disjunct codes' characteristic in [9] which means the node can use the channel as it will and does not need to consider interference. CH_2 channels is partially public, thus we designed an ingenious probability distribution of channel competition. In addition to the fixed basic probability distribution, we make an adjustment algorithm to achieve high channel utilization in some extreme situations. The high competition success rate and low complexity for transmission proves our algorithms' advantages. As a supplement, we release the CH_1 channels for competition as others'CH_3 channels when the owner is out of using and this small change results in a greatly reduction of channel vacancy duration. To be specific, the scheme can be introduced respectively in three parts.

4.1   Channel Allocation Algorithm for CH_1 Channels

In [9] we can know that the CH_1 channel can exist under the condition that $s \geq |\mathcal{N}(u)|$(the proof seen in the Lemma 1 and this condition is easy to satisfy). The channel in $CH_1(u)$ is primary to u and secondary to the $\mathcal{N}(u)$. Therefore, none of the nodes in $\mathcal{N}(u)$ will choose this channel for transmission when u using it (however, it is another circumstance when u is not using the channel). Without the risk of interference, node u can just easily use its $CH_1(u)$ channels to deliver information at its will. It is should be noticed that node u needs to tell its neighbor whether it is using the channels at the beginning of each timeslot for others' convenience.

Lemma 1. *[9] When $s \geq |\mathcal{N}(u)|$ holds for each node u in the network $G(V, E)$, it is guaranteed that every node u has at least one interference free channel, namely $CH_1(u) \neq \emptyset$.*

4.2   Channel Allocation Algorithm for CH_2 Channels

Since $CH_2(u)$ is available to every one in $\mathcal{N}(u)$ and u itself, we try to allocate each node as much channels as needed.

Algorithm 2 shows the complete process of a node u using the $CH(u)$ to send packets. At first, we simplify the process of computing $\mathcal{N}(u)$ from $\mathcal{N}_1(u)$. The parameter $\overrightarrow{Q(u)}$ is the vector of probability u competing for $CH_2(u)$. One of the elements $Q_i(u)$ denotes the probability u taking the channel i. C_r is a indicator which represents whether u is in a crowded environment or competing with others. The algorithm begins with checking u's buffer: an empty buffer results in the end of algorithm, otherwise u will claim the registration of its $CH_1(u)$ channels. Unlike the convenience in CH_1, CH_2 is much more complicated to use legally: u will compete for the channel tch with the probability $Q_{tch}(u)$. Different probability for different aim channel. Even though u takes the channel, one essential step is checking the registration and see wether it has been occupied. If so, u must drop this channel to avoid inferencing with others and, as a result, u will know its neighbors will soon be sending packets. It should be noticed that if the RTS impulse is send by u and v in very short time duration ($< s$, the minimum resolution of radios), it will be taken as a failure. After traversing all the channels in $CH_2(u)$, the obtained channels can be added into $CH'(u)$ for transmission. The last step is to adjust the $Q_k(u)$ for next competition by the Algorithm 1.

4.3   Channel Allocation Algorithm for CH_3 Channels

As for the CH_3 channels, it's the complementary set of CH_1 and CH_2, and sometimes can be a neighbor's CH_1 channel. We try to make the best of the potential in the whole network and noticed that some CH_1 channels' bandwidth will be wasted if the owner isn't using them. CH_3 channels can perfectly solve that problem by reusing all the idle channels. The channel vacancy information can be computed by excluding the channels that have been registered in our algorithm. Node u will check all its $CH_3(u)$ and try to compete the unregistered ones. For a channel c and a node u, if c belongs to N' nodes' CH_3 channels and N'' nodes are in the $\mathcal{N}(u)$, it is apparently u will get this channel with the average probability $\frac{1}{N''}$.

Lemma 2. *If $CH_2(u) \neq \emptyset$ for node u, and u wins a channel k in the competition phase, u's transmission in the transmission phase is interference-free on channel k.*

Algorithm 2. Channel Allocation Algorithm

Require: $CH(u) = [CH_1(u), CH_2(u), CH_3(u)]$,the vector $\overrightarrow{Q(u)}$ of probability for $CH_2(u)$,Buffer,$\mathcal{N}(u)$

Ensure: return the $CH'(u)$ which is the reality channels u using and **TRUE** when transmission done,**FALSE** for the other.

1: $CH'(u) = \emptyset$
2: $C_r = 0$
3: **if** $Buffer.length > 0$ **then**
4:     **if** $CH_1(u) \neq \emptyset$ **then**
5:        u broadcasts its registration of $CH_1(u)$ to $\mathcal{N}(u)$
6:        $CH'(u) \leftarrow CH'(u) \bigcup CH_1(u)$
7:     **end if**
8:     **for** all channel tch in $CH_2(u)$ **do**
9:        **if** $u.comptete(tch, Q_{Tch}(u)) == true$ **then**
10:                  $\triangleright$ u competes the tch channel with a probability of $Q_{Tch}(u)$
11:           **if** $u.check(tch, \mathcal{N}(u)) == true$ **then**
12:                  $\triangleright$ u checks the tch channel whether it is occupied
13:             u adds into tch's registration set
14:             $CH'(u) \leftarrow CH'(u) \bigcup tch$
15:           **else**
16:             $C_r = 1$
17:           **end if**
18:        **end if**
19:     **end for**
20:     $\overrightarrow{Q(u)} = ProGain(\overrightarrow{Q(u)}, C_r)$
21:                         $\triangleright$ the probability vector adjusts value by C_r
22:     **for** all channel tch in $CH_3(u)$ **do**
23:        **if** $u.check(tch, \mathcal{N}(u)) == true$ **then**
24:           **if** $u.comptete(tch, 1) == true$ **then**
25:             u adds into tch's registration set
26:             $CH'(u) \leftarrow CH'(u) \bigcup tch$
27:           **end if**
28:        **end if**
29:     **end for**
30:     **if** $CH'(u) \neq \emptyset$ **then**
31:        u broadcasts all the packets in Buffer away with $CH'(u)$
32:
33:        **return** $CH'(u)$ and **TRUE**
34:     **else**return $\emptyset$ and **FALSE**
35:     **end if**
36: **else**return $CH'(u)$ and **TRUE**
37: **end if**

Proof. According to Algorithm 2, if u is the first one who sends an impulse signal on a channel k in the competition phase, every node will notice the signal and will not use the channel k afterwards, and thus u's transmission on channel k is interference-free in the transmission phase.

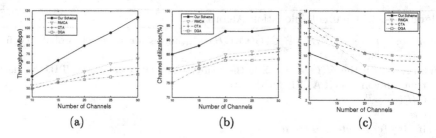

Fig. 1. $k = 40, r = 9$ maintains, the throughput, channel utilization and average time for a successful transmission changes with the increase of total channels number.

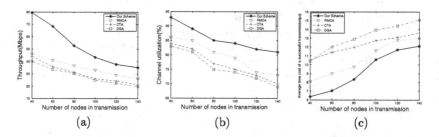

Fig. 2. $C = 20, r = 9$ maintains, throughput, channel utilization and average time for a successful transmission changes with the increase of nodes number need to transmit.

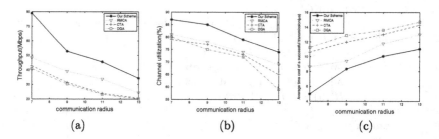

Fig. 3. $C = 20, k = 80$ maintains, the throughput, channel utilization and average time for a successful transmission changes with the change of communication range radius r.

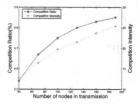

Fig. 4. The competition ratio and competition intensity of our algorithm.

5 Simulation Study

In this section, we present the numerical analysis results in comparison with other approaches, i.e. RMCA [11], CTA and DGA [12]. Both CTA and DGA are based on conflict graph, where CTA is based on a popular heuristic search technique called Tabu search [13], DGA is a greedy approximation algorithm based Max K-cut [14]. RMCA [11] achieves basic connectivity of a network with low interference by assigning fewer resources compared to other protocols. We evaluate how different algorithms affects the network's ability to dynamically respond to changing conditions.

5.1 Settings

In the simulation, 200 nodes are randomly distributed in a 100×100 square area. The communication radius of each node is set to 9. The number of channel is picked from 20. The data transmission speed of each channel is set to 10 Mbps and the size of packets in the network (TCP/IP packet length) is set to 300 Bytes. In the network topology the number of neighbors in 1 hop is 4.24, and in 2 hop is 15.125. Total links are above 400.

The following metrics are used for comparative study:

- Throughput: The amount of data transmitted successfully for each node per unit time.
- Average Time Cost of a Successful Transmission: Average time cost for a node to completely finish a transmission.
- Channel Utilization: The ratio of the number of channels used by node u vs. the number of available channels for u.
- Competition Ratio: The ratio of the number of channels both u and other nodes compete for vs. the number of available channels for u.
- Competition Intensity: The average number of nodes that compete with u for a channel.

5.2 Simulation Results

As shown in Fig. 1(a), when the number of channels increases, the throughput of all four algorithms increases. The throughput of our algorithm increases with a nearly linear speedup as the growth of the number of channels, while the other three algorithm grow much slower. This is mainly because we use a sophisticated competition algorithm trying to make full use of all available channels. In Fig. 1 (b), the channel utilization of our algorithm is significantly higher than the other three algorithms as the growth of the number of channels. This is because the competition mechanism encourages nodes for channel competition while at the same time sophistically reduces contentions, and thus improves channel utilization. In Fig. 1(c), our algorithm exhibits a linear decrease of the time cost for a successful transmission as the growth of the number of channels, while the other three algorithms decrease slower and become stable when the number of channels is large enough. This means that our algorithm could perform better when the number of channels scales.

In Fig. 2(a), we can see that the throughput of all the four algorithms decreases as the number of nodes in transmission grows, but our algorithm always performs at least 30 % better than the other three. This is because our scheme can make full use of the channel resource. In Fig. 2(b), the channel utilization of our algorithm always perform significantly better than the other algorithms and has the ability to achieve 80 % channel utilization even when there are more than 2/3 nodes of one's neighborhood in transmission. In Fig. 2(c), we can see that the time cost for transmission of the four algorithms rises when the number of nodes grows, and our algorithm still has the lowest time cost compared to the others.

In Fig. 3(a), the throughput of all algorithms decreases as the communication radius increases. Our scheme achieves almost 200 % throughput compared with the others among all radii. As shown in Fig. 3(b), channel utilization decreases when the communication radius grows. The channel utilization of our algorithm is much higher than the others because of the imbalanced preference probability resulting in diverse assignment with less contention and better utilization. In Fig. 3(c), the time cost of a successful transmission of our algorithm is lower than the others partially because that the number of the secondary channels grows when the communication radius increases and our approach utilizes them.

Figure 4 may partially explain the reason that our algorithm outperforms the others: with the rise of the nodes in transmission, both the competition rate and the competition intensity increase, which reflects that our algorithm effectively encourages the competition among nodes while at the same time reduce potential contents, and thus raise the channel utilization and throughput.

6   Conclusion

The motivation for this work is to find an effective strategy for channel assignment in a multi-channel network. Such a channel assignment scheme should achieve interference-free and high-throughput. Our work achieves both goals based on sophistically localized channel classification and competition design. Specifically, the classified channels are independently used by users divergent communication requirements and able to complement each other category when necessary. Based on the comparative study on various proposed channel assignment algorithms, our algorithm achieves both goals and provide significantly better throughput, channel utilization and time cost, etc.

References

1. Rad, A.H.M., Wong, V.W.: Joint channel allocation, interface assignment and mac design for multi-channel wireless mesh networks. In: INFOCOM 2007, 26th IEEE International Conference on Computer Communications, pp. 1469–1477. IEEE (2007)

2. Skalli, H., Das, S., Lenzini, L., Conti, M.: Traffic and interference aware channel assignment for multi-radio wireless mesh networks. Technical report, IMT Lucca (2006)

3. Del Re, E., Fantacci, R., Giambene, G.: Handover queuing strategies with dynamic and fixed channel allocation techniques in low earth orbit mobile satellite systems. IEEE Trans. Commun. **47**(1), 89–102 (1999)

4. Das, A.K., Alazemi, H.M., Vijayakumar, R., Roy, S.: Optimization models for fixed channel assignment in wireless mesh networks with multiple radios. In: SECON, pp. 463–474 (2005)

5. Raniwala, A., Gopalan, K., Chiueh, T.-C.: Centralized channel assignment and routing algorithms for multi-channel wireless mesh networks. ACM SIGMOBILE Mobile Comput. Commun. Rev. **8**(2), 50–65 (2004)

6. Raniwala, A., Chiueh, T.-C.: Architecture and algorithms for an IEEE 802.11-based multi-channel wireless mesh network. In: INFOCOM 2005 IEEE Proceedings of 24th Annual Joint Conference of the IEEE Computer and Communications Societies, vol. 3, pp. 2223–2234. IEEE (2005)

7. Agrawal, D., Mishra, A., Springborn, K., Banerjee, S., Ganguly, S.: Dynamic interference adaptation for wireless mesh networks. In: Wireless Mesh Networks: 2nd IEEE Workshop on WiMesh 2006, pp. 33–37, IEEE (2006)

8. Ramachandran, K.N., Belding-Royer, E.M., Almeroth, .C., Buddhikot, M.M.: Interference-aware channel assignment in multi-radio wireless mesh networks. In: INFOCOM, vol. 6, pp. 1–12 (2006)

9. Xing, K., Cheng, X., Ma, L., Liang, Q.: Superimposed code based channel assignment in multi-radio multi-channel wireless mesh networks. In: Proceedings of the 13th Annual ACM International Conference on Mobile Computing and Networking, pp. 15–26. ACM (2007)

10. Cidon, A., Nagaraj, K., Katti, S., Viswanath, P.: Flashback: decoupled lightweight wireless control. ACM SIGCOMM Comput. Commun. Rev. **42**(4), 223–234 (2012)

11. Irwin, R.E., MacKenzie, A.B., DaSilva, L.A.: Resource-minimized channel assignment for multi-transceiver wireless networks. In: Global Telecommunications Conference (GLOBECOM 2011), pp. 1–6. IEEE (2011)

12. Subramanian, A.P., Gupta, H., Das, S.R., Cao, J.: Minimum interference channel assignment in multiradio wireless mesh networks. IEEE Trans. Mobile Comput. **7**(12), 1459–1473 (2008)

13. Hertz, A., de Werra, D.: Using tabu search techniques for graph coloring. Computing **39**(4), 345–351 (1987)

14. Frieze, A., Jerrum, M.: Improved approximation algorithms for max k-cut and max bisection. In: Balas, E., Clausen, J. (eds.) IPCO' 95. LNCS, pp. 1–13. Springer, Heidelberg (1995)

An Efficient and Secure Delegated Multi-authentication Protocol for Mobile Data Owners in Cloud

Lifei Wei[1,2], Lei Zhang[1](✉), Kai Zhang[3], and Mianxiong Dong[4]

[1] College of Information Technology,
Shanghai Ocean University, Shanghai 201306, China
Lzhang@shou.edu.cn
[2] State Key Laboratory of Networking and Switching Technology,
Beijing University of Posts and Telecommunications, Beijing 100081, China
[3] Department of Computer Science and Technology, East China Normal University,
Shanghai 200241, China
[4] Department of Information and Electronic Engineering,
Muroran Institute of Technology, Muroran, Japan

Abstract. Due to plenty of cloud-based applications emerging and booming recently, data owners always store their data in cloud and share them to data consumers through cloud servers. For security equirements, data owners are often asked to provide authentication tags to the corresponding data. Data consumers obtain the authenticated data from the cloud and expect the computation on the authenticated data. However, it is impractical for the mobile data owners to be online all the time and provide the authenticated computing results according to various data consumers' request. To tackle this issue, we propose an efficient and secure delegated multi-authentication protocol for mobile data owners in cloud, which enables the mobile data owners to conditionally delegate signing right to specified cloud servers without exposing the secret signing keys. The cloud servers provide the authentication services when data owners are not available. The security is built on an identity-based multi-proxy signature (IBMPS) scheme, which depends on the cubic residue assumption, equaling to the factorization assumption. Furthermore, our protocol is efficient compared to the pairing based schemes and the overhead is almost independent of the number of cloud servers.

Keywords: Authenticated computing · Mobile data owner · Delegated multi-authentication · Multi-proxy signature · Cloud computing

This work was supported by the National Natural Science Foundation of China (No. 61402282), Shanghai Sailing Program (No. 14YF1410400), Youth Scholars of Shanghai Higher Education Institutions (No. ZZHY14025), Open Foundation of State key Laboratory of Networking and Switching Technology of BUPT (No. SKLNST-2013-1-12), ECNU Fund for Graduate Student's Scientific Research, Innovation, and Practice (No. YJSKC2015-30) and JSPS KAKENHI (No. 26730056, 15K15976), JSPS A3 Foresight Program.

© Springer International Publishing Switzerland 2015
K. Xu and J. Zhu (Eds.): WASA 2015, LNCS 9204, pp. 612–622, 2015.
DOI: 10.1007/978-3-319-21837-3_60

1   Introduction

With the development of cloud computing techniques, a number of cloud-based applications have been emerging and booming recently [1,2]. In particular, applications focusing on the outsourced computation in cloud have been paid much attention due to the powerful computation and storage capability of cloud. Different from the conventional computation in which the users have fully controlled their data, cloud computing enables servers to manage the physical machines and the data on these workstations while the cloud users only retain the control over the virtual machines [3]. As a result, the outsourced computation performed on those untrustworthy cloud has been restricting the further progress of the cloud computing.

In the scenarios, the data owners store their own collected data into cloud servers and share with the data consumers. For the security requirement, the data owners need to provide an authentication tag with the corresponding data to show the valid of the data to the cloud. Related work tried to add authentication tags [4,5] along with the data in order to keep the integrity and authentication in the cloud servers. Signature often provides authenticity and non-repudiation in the communication networks. Data consumers not only want to get the authenticated data from the cloud, but also need to compute on the authenticated data [6] with the help of the powerful computation capability of the cloud servers. In some scenarios, the data owners can not be online all the time such as 24 hours a day due to their mobile characteristics [7]. Moreover, they can not afford the data computation overhead for a large number of the computation request. As a result, they need to delegate the authentication rights (signing rights) to the cloud [8].

There are some straightforward solutions to overcome this obstacle. One solution is that if the data consumers just request the original data, the data owner could pre-store all the authenticated tags in the cloud servers. However, the data owner can not pre-store all kinds of the authenticated data in the cloud before since he/she can not foresee the different data computation requests. In most cases, the demand is that the stored data need to be calculated or taken transforms from the original data according to the data user's requests. Another solution is that all the request must be sent to data owner for further authentication, which leads to lots of computational overhead for the data owners and considerable delay by the offline of the data owners.

To cut down the communication cost and delay, another solution is that the data owners hand out their secret signing keys to the cloud and share them by cloud servers. In this case, the authentication service could be accompanied without the help of the data owners since the cloud servers could finish the data authentication dependently, which achieves the outsourced authentication. However, some of the remote cloud servers may be compromised by the attackers and the secret keys may be revealed, which results in a worse consequence since the data authentication service might be out of control and be misused by malicious cloud servers.

When it comes to the data computation, ordinary signature may not be well available since it violates the existential unforgeable property of signature.

Some essential variations of ordinary digital signature schemes have been proposed. Homomorphic signature [9,10] seems a feasible solution to this problem since homomorphic signature achieves either additional homomorphic or multiply homomorphic. However, for some complicated operation such as data comparison results and SQL based query [11], the homomorphic signature can not achieve the target. In addition, homomorphic signature always bring in considerable extra overhead to the authenticated data.

In this work, we aim to address the above challenges and propose an efficient and secure data delegated multi-authentication protocol for mobile data owners in cloud. Our proposed protocol is feathered by delegated authentication to a number of cloud servers and high efficiency on both the data owner side and the data consumer side. Thanks to the novel identity based multi-proxy signature scheme, the data owners can delegate the signing rights to a number of cloud servers which need to collaborate to carry out the authentication tags generation and aggregation instead of the data owners. Moreover, our protocol allows the data owners to conditionally delegate to the cloud servers and the data consumers could easily verify the authentication tags and alert to the system authority when they find the misusing of the cloud servers. Last but not least, our protocol is quite efficient compared to pairing based protocols.

To the best of our knowledge, this work is the first effort towards considering delegated authentication among mobile data owners and cloud servers in order to provide authentication service for data consumers. The contributions can be briefly summarized:

- Firstly, we propose an identity-based multi-proxy signature scheme which is proved secure under the hardness of integer factorization assumption in the random oracle model.
- Secondly, we propose a secure delegated multi-authentication protocol, based on our efficient multi-proxy signature schemes, to provide authenticated computing results for mobile data owner in cloud environment.
- Thirdly, in contrast to previous solutions, our protocol achieves a conditional delegation with traceability that is malicious cloud servers can be caught and accused of misusing by data consumers.

The rest of the paper is organized as follows. Section 2 describes our system architecture, security models, designed goals, and formal definition of framework for identity-based multi-proxy signature scheme. Section 3 introduces some necessary mathematic preliminaries. In Sect. 4, we propose a detail construction, which is proven secure in the random oracle model in Sect. 5. Section 6 sees the performance comparison of the related work. Finally, Sect. 7 makes a conclusion.

2   System Architecture and Design Goals

2.1   System Architecture

As shown in Fig. 1, we consider a general cloud system, which is composed of four major entities: *system authority*, *cloud servers*, *data owners* and *data consumers*.

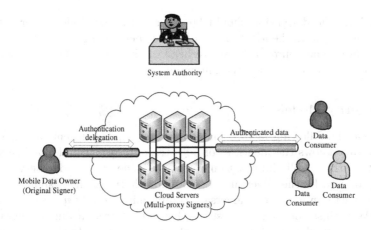

Fig. 1. A delegated multi-server authentication architecture in Cloud.

- **System Authority (SA).** In our scenario, the system authority is the administrator of the system and independent with other roles, which is in charge of system initialization and secret key generation of each parties in the system. We also assume that the system authority can not be compromised by the adversary.
- **Cloud Servers (CSs).** The cloud system is constituted of a number of cloud servers, named as $S_1, S_2, ..., S_n$, with plenty of computation resources and storage resources and controlled by cloud service provider, like the general cloud model. The cloud servers provide the data storage and data computation service and response to the data consumers' requests.
- **Data Owners (DOs).** The mobile data owners obtain the data through the wireless collecting devices and store them into the cloud when the data owners encounter to connect to the networks. We assume that the data owners are not always online (ex. 24-hours) due to the mobile characteristic. For the security requirement, the data owners add the tags to the data. The tags should be unforgeable achieved by digital signature. Thus, the data owners upload the data as well as the tags.
- **Data Consumers (DCs).** Each data consumers queries the data and asks for the data computation from cloud servers. For the security requirement, the data consumers need get the data and authenticated tags for keeping the authenticity of the source.

2.2 Design Goals

The protocol is expected to achieve the following goals:

- **Authentication Delegation.** The data owners can conditionally delegate the signing rights to cloud servers without leaking its own secret keys.
- **Data Authentication.** The data consumers can get the authenticated data from the cloud servers which can not forge such authentication tags.

- **Security.** The delegation should be secure that the cloud servers can not forge the invalid authentication tags without being caught.
- **Efficiency.** The computational overhead of the scheme should be at a low level and be better to meet the minimum.

2.3 Security Models

We assume the following factors that may impact data authentication. Firstly, the adversary knows the identities of both the data owner and cloud servers as well as the other public information. Secondly, some of the cloud servers might be compromised by the adversary. To maximize harm to the system, we model an extreme case in which the adversary compromises totally $n-1$ cloud servers and works against one single honest cloud server to forge invalid authentication tags and find out the secret key of the data owners. In addition, we assume that there is no secure channels between cloud servers and data owners.

2.4 Framework of IBMPS

In an IBMPS scheme [12,13], there exists an original signer $\mathcal{O}$ and a group of proxy signers $\mathcal{P}_1, \mathcal{P}_2, ..., \mathcal{P}_n$ who provide the signing service delegated by original signer. We denote the identity of the original signer as $ID_{\mathcal{O}}$ and the proxy signer $\mathcal{P}_i$ as $ID_{\mathcal{P}_i}$, respectively.

Definition 1 (Framework). *Our delegated authentication protocol is a collection of the following algorithm based on an identity-based multi-proxy signature scheme: **Setup, Extract, Sign, Verify, MPGen, MPSign, and MPVerify.***

3 Preliminaries

To further explain our schemes, we introduce the necessary concepts in our scheme construction and security proof.

3.1 Mathematical Preliminaries

We introduce the definition of *cubic residue* and the following lemma [14,15].

Definition 2. *For an integer $N \equiv 1 \pmod 3$, $a \in \mathbb{Z}_N^*$ is a cubic residue modulo N if $X^3 \equiv a \pmod N$ for some $X \in \mathbb{Z}_N^*$.*

Lemma 1. *The integer factoring problem becomes easy if we find two different cubic roots s_1, s_2 of a cubic residue a modulo N, where $s_1^3 \equiv s_2^3 \equiv a \pmod N$ and $s_1 \neq \pm s_2 \pmod N$.*

Note that the 3-th root pairs satisfying $s_1 \equiv \pm s_2 \pmod N$ do not help to factor N.

4   Protocol Construction

We construct our delegated authentication protocol based on our designed identity-based proxy multi-signature scheme. Our protocol consists of five phases: *System initialization, Tag generation and verification, Authentication delegation, Multi-server authentication, Verification.*

4.1   System Initialization

The system initialization phase is to set up globe parameters and generate each entity's secret key.

Setup. Taking the security parameters λ, this algorithm can be done as follows.

(1). **SA** generates two random secure prime numbers p, q such that $p \equiv 2$ (mod 3) and $q \equiv 4$ (mod 9) or $q \equiv 7$ (mod 9) and computes their product $N = p \cdot q$.

(2). **SA** computes $\eta = [q - 1 \pmod 9]/3$, $\lambda = \eta \pmod 2 + 1$, and $\beta = (q-1)/3$.

(3). **SA** chooses a non-cubic residue a such that $\left(\frac{a}{q}\right) = -1$ and sets $\xi = a^{\eta\beta}$ (mod q).

(4). **SA** picks up five hash functions H_1, H_2, H_3, H_4, H_5, where $H_1, H_4 : \{0,1\}^* \rightarrow \mathbb{Z}_N^*$, $H_2, H_3, H_5 : \{0,1\}^* \rightarrow \{0,1\}^\ell$.

Finally, **SA** finishes **Setup** algorithm by outputting master secret keys $msk = (p, q, \beta)$ and public parameter $pp = (N, H_1, H_2, H_3, H_4, H_5, a, \eta, \lambda)$. **SA** keeps msk secretly.

Key Generation. For each entity in the system , on input the identity ID, **SA** computes the corresponding private key d as follows.

(1). **SA** computes $\omega = h_1(ID)^{\lambda\beta} \pmod q$.

(2). **SA** computes

$$c = \begin{cases} 0, \text{ if } \omega = 1 \\ 1, \text{ if } \omega = \xi \\ 2, \text{ if } \omega = \xi^2 \end{cases}$$

and sets $H(ID) = a^c \cdot H_1(ID) \pmod N$. It is easy to show that $H(ID) \in \mathbb{CR}_N$.

(3). **SA** computes

$$d_{ID} = H(ID)^{\frac{2^{\eta-1}(p-1)(q-1)-3}{9}} \pmod N \tag{1}$$

and sends the secret key d_{ID} to entity with a tag c through a secure channel. Note that $d_{ID}^3 \cdot H(ID) \equiv 1 \pmod N$. After that, every entity can compute $H(ID)$ since the ID and c are in public.

4.2   Tag Generation and Verification

Tag Generation. The data owner could generate the authentication tags for the data m as follows.

1. The data owner $\mathcal{O}$ chooses a random number $r \in \mathbb{Z}_N^*$ and computes $R = r^3$ (mod N).
2. $\mathcal{O}$ obtains the hash value $h_2 = H_2(m||R)$ and computes $V = r \cdot d_o^{h_2}$ using its secret key d_o.

Finally, the authentication tag $tag = (R, V)$ combined with the data m are sent to the cloud servers $\mathcal{P}_1, \mathcal{P}_2, ..., \mathcal{P}_n$.

Tag Verification. When the cloud servers receives the data m and the corresponding authentication tag, they should verify the tag by checking the Eq. (2).

$$V^3 \cdot H(ID_o)^{h_2} \stackrel{?}{=} R, \tag{2}$$

where $h_2 = H_2(m||R)$. The cloud server accepts the data if it has a valid authentication tag. Otherwise, it requests a new valid authentication tag from data owners, or terminates the protocol.

4.3   Authentication Delegation

To delegate the signing capability to the cloud servers as proxy signers $\mathcal{P}_1, \mathcal{P}_2, ..., \mathcal{P}_n$, the data owners, as a original signer $\mathcal{O}$, does the following *three* steps to make the valid warrant ω, which specifies the necessary delegation details, such as the identity of the data owners and the cloud servers (the original signers and the proxy signer), the expiry time of delegation, etc.

Delegation Generation. The data owner confirms the warrant ω by signing it.

1. The data owner $\mathcal{O}$ chooses a random number $r_o \in \mathbb{Z}_N^*$ and computes $R_o = r_o^3$.
2. $\mathcal{O}$ obtains the hash value $h_2 = H_2(\omega||R_o)$ and computes $V_o = r_o \cdot d_o^{h_2}$ using its secret key d_o.
3. $\mathcal{O}$ broadcasts the delegation information $\sigma = (\omega, R_o, V_o)$ to the cloud servers $\mathcal{P}_1, \mathcal{P}_2, ..., \mathcal{P}_n$.

Delegation Verification. After receiving the delegation requests, every cloud server $\mathcal{P}_i$ first confirms $\sigma = (\omega, R_o, V_o)$ by checking the Eq. (3).

$$V_o^3 \cdot H(ID_o)^{h_2} \stackrel{?}{=} R_o, \tag{3}$$

where $h_2 = H_2(\omega||R_o)$. Every cloud server accepts the delegation if it is a valid delegation; otherwise, it requests a new valid delegation from $\mathcal{O}$, or terminates the protocol.

Proxy Signing Key Generation. After accepting the delegations, every cloud server computes its new proxy signer key by Eq. (4).

$$sk_{p_i} = V_o \cdot d_{p_i}^{h_3}, \tag{4}$$

where $h_3 = H_3(\omega \| R_o)$.

4.4 Multi-server Authentication Generation

Each cloud server $\mathcal{P}_i$ signs the message m under ω on behalf of the data owner $\mathcal{O}$ as follows:

(1). $\mathcal{P}_i$ chooses a random number $r_i \in \mathbb{Z}_N$ and computes $R_i = r_i^3$. $\mathcal{P}_i$ computes $t_i = H_4(R_i)$ and broadcasts t_i to other cloud servers.

(2). After receiving t_i, $\mathcal{P}_i$ broadcasts R_i to other cloud servers.

(3). After receiving R_i, $\mathcal{P}_i$ check each $t_i \overset{?}{=} H_4(R_i)$. If any of above equation does not satisfy, the algorithm aborts. $\mathcal{P}_i$ computes $R = \prod_{i=1}^{n} R_i$ and gets the hash $h_5 = H_5(\omega \| m \| R)$ and computes $v_i = r_i \cdot sk_{p_i}^{h_5}$ and broadcasts v_i to other proxy signers.

(4). After receiving v_i from other cloud servers, $\mathcal{P}_i$ first checks each Eq. (5).

$$v_i^3 \cdot H(ID_{p_i})^{h_3 h_5} \overset{?}{=} R_i \cdot V_o^{h_5}, \tag{5}$$

where $h_3 = H_3(\omega \| R_o)$ and $h_5 = H_5(\omega \| m \| R)$. If any of above equation does not satisfy, the algorithm abort. After that, $\mathcal{P}_i$ computes $V = \prod_{i=1}^{n} v_i$.

Once all partial signatures are correct, the multi-server authentication of message m can be generated as $p\sigma = (\omega, V_o, V, R)$

4.5 Authentication Verification

After receiving the message m and the multi-authentication tag $p\sigma = (\omega, V_o, V, R)$, the data consumer operates as follows:

(1). checks whether or not the message m conforms to the warrant ω.

(2). checks whether or not the n cloud servers $\mathcal{P}_1, \mathcal{P}_2, ..., \mathcal{P}_n$ are authorized by the data owner $\mathcal{O}$ in the warrant ω.

(3). accepts the multi-server authentication tag if and only of the following Eq. (6) holds:

$$V^3 \cdot H(ID_o)^{h_2 h_5} \cdot \prod_{i=1}^{n} H(ID_{p_i})^{h_3 h_5} \overset{?}{=} R \cdot V_o^{h_5} \tag{6}$$

where $h_3 = H_3(\omega \| R_o)$ and $h_5 = H_5(\omega \| m \| R)$.

5   Security Analysis

5.1   Correctness

The delegated multi-authentication protocol is correct since

$$V \equiv \prod_{i=1}^{n} v_i \equiv \prod_{i=1}^{n} r_i \cdot sk_{p_i}^{h_5} \equiv \prod_{i=1}^{n} r_i \cdot (V_o \cdot d_{p_i}^{h_3})^{h_5}$$

$$\equiv \prod_{i=1}^{n} r_i \cdot (r_o \cdot d_o^{h_2})^{h_5} \cdot d_{p_i}^{h_3 h_5} \equiv \prod_{i=1}^{n} r_i \cdot r_o^{h_5} \cdot d_o^{h_2 h_5} \cdot d_{p_i}^{h_3 h_5} \quad (\text{mod } N). \quad (7)$$

Thus, we have

$$V^3 \equiv \prod_{i=1}^{n} R_i \cdot V_o^{h_5} \cdot (d_o^3)^{h_2 h_5} \cdot (d_{p_i}^3)^{h_3 h_5} \equiv R \cdot V_o^{h_5} \cdot (d_o^3)^{h_2 h_5} \cdot \prod_{i=1}^{n} (d_{p_i}^3)^{h_3 h_5}$$

$$\equiv R \cdot V_o^{h_5} \cdot (H(ID_o)^{-1})^{h_2 h_5} \cdot \prod_{i=1}^{n} (H(ID_{p_i})^{-1})^{h_3 h_5} \quad (\text{mod } N). \quad (8)$$

From Eq. (8), we can find out the correctness proof since

$$V^3 \cdot H(ID_o)^{h_2 h_5} \cdot \prod_{i=1}^{n} H(ID_{p_i})^{h_3 h_5} \equiv R \cdot V_o^{h_5} \quad (\text{mod } N). \quad (9)$$

5.2   Security Proof

Theorem 1 (Main Theorem). *Our scheme is $(t, q_E, q_S, q_H, n, \epsilon)$-secure against existential forgery on the adaptively chosen message attack and chosen identity attack in the random oracle model if the factoring problem is hard.*

Due to space, we refer the reader to the full version for the proof of this theorem.

6   Performance Comparison

In this section, we compare our protocol with related work, which are provable security based on different hardness assumptions in the oracle model. From [16], we can find the major operation times for one bilinear pairing operation ($P, 20.01\ ms$), map-to-point hash operation ($H, 3.04\ ms$), modular-exponentiation ($E, 11.20\ ms$), normal scale multiplication ($M, 0.83\ ms$), pairing based scalar multiplication ($Psm, 6.38\ ms$). Though every large integer multiplication takes little time, considering the number of cloud servers n, it is necessary to add a reasonable time in **MPSign** and **MPVerify** algorithm.

From the Table 1, it is obvious that our protocol is quite efficient since we do not use the bilinear pairing technique compared to [12,13,17].

Table 1. Comparison of computation cost and running time.

Schemec	MPGen	Time	MPSign	Time	MPVerify	Time	Assumption
LC05 [17]	$3P+6Psm$	103.71	$3P+1E+3Psm$	84.57	$4P+1E+3Psm$	78.19	CDH
CC09 [12]	$3P+2H+3Psm$	85.34	$P+3H+1E+2Psm$	127.39	$4P+2H+3Psm$	99.0	CDH
SP15 [13]	$2P+5Psm$	71.98	$P+5Psm$	71.98	$2P+4Psm$	65.6	CD
Ours	$3E+7M$	39.41	$3E+(n+6)M$	38.58*	$3E+(n+4)M$	36.92*	Factorization

7 Conclusion

In this paper, we have built an efficient and secure delegated multi-authentication protocol in cloud, which enables the mobile data owners to conditionally delegate the signing right to multiple cloud servers without exposing the signing keys. The security of our protocol is based on an identity-based multi-proxy signature scheme, which depends on the factorization assumption.

In our future work, we consider three aspects to improve efficiency and security. Firstly, our protocol needs three round interactions in the multi-proxy signature generation, which leads to considerable communication overhead. We suggest to reduce the interactive rounds by constructing commitment schemes under cubic residue assumptions like that in [18]. Secondly, it is possible to propose general constructions of identity based signature schemes under cubic residues and even higher residues such as 2^k-th power residues [19]. Thirdly, we suggest to consider reliability of the cloud system and design a threshold multi-proxy signature scheme which allows authentication service not stopping even though a part of the cloud servers have been compromised.

References

1. Dong, M., Li, H., Ota, K., Zhu, H.: Hvsto: efficient privacy preserving hybrid storage in cloud data center. In: IEEE Conference on Computer Communications Workshops (INFOCOM WKSHPS 2014), pp. 529–534 (2014)
2. Dong, M., Li, H., Ota, K., Yang, L.T., Zhu, H.: Multicloud-based evacuation services for emergency management. IEEE Cloud Comput. **1**(4), 50–59 (2014)
3. Wei, L., Zhu, H., Cao, Z., Dong, X., Jia, W., Chen, Y., Vasilakos, A.V.: Security and privacy for storage and computation in cloud computing. Inf. Sci. **258**, 371–386 (2014)
4. Wang, C., Chow, S.S., Wang, Q., Ren, K., Lou, W.: Privacy-preserving public auditing for secure cloud storage. IEEE Trans. Comput. **62**(2), 362–375 (2013)
5. Yuan, J., Yu, S.: Efficient public integrity checking for cloud data sharing with multi-user modification. In: INFOCOM 2014, pp. 2121–2129 (2014)
6. Ahn, J.H., Boneh, D., Camenisch, J., Hohenberger, S., shelat, A., Waters, B.: Computing on authenticated data. In: Cramer, R. (ed.) TCC 2012. LNCS, vol. 7194, pp. 1–20. Springer, Heidelberg (2012)
7. Jia, W., Zhu, H., Cao, Z., Wei, L., Lin, X.: SDSM: a secure data service mechanism in mobile cloud computing. In: IEEE Conference on Computer Communications Workshops (INFOCOM WKSHPS 2011), pp. 1060–1065 (2011)

8. Boldyreva, A., Palacio, A., Warinschi, B.: Secure proxy signature schemes for delegation of signing rights. J. Cryptology **25**(1), 57–115 (2012)
9. Johnson, R., Molnar, D., Song, D., Wagner, D.: Homomorphic signature schemes. In: Preneel, B. (ed.) CT-RSA 2002. LNCS, vol. 2271, pp. 244–262. Springer, Heidelberg (2002)
10. Wang, Z., Sun, G., Chen, D.: A new definition of homomorphic signature for identity management in mobile cloud computing. J. Comput. Syst. Sci. **80**(3), 546–553 (2014)
11. Yuan, J., Yu, S.: Flexible and publicly verifiable aggregation query for outsourced databases in cloud. In: IEEE CNS 2013, pp. 520–524 (2013)
12. Cao, F., Cao, Z.: A secure identity-based multi-proxy signature scheme. Comput. Electr. Eng. **35**(1), 86–95 (2009)
13. Sahu, R.A., Padhye, S.: Provable secure identity-based multi-proxy signature scheme. Int. J. Commun. Syst. **28**(3), 497–512 (2015)
14. Shoup, V.: A Computational Introduction to Number Theory and Algebra. Cambridge University Press, Cambridge (2009)
15. Wang, Z., Wang, L., Zheng, S., Yang, Y., Hu, Z.: Provably secure and efficient identity-based signature scheme based on cubic residues. Int. J. Netw. Secur. **14**(1), 33–38 (2012)
16. He, D., Chen, J., Zhang, R.: An efficient and provably-secure certificateless signature scheme without bilinear pairings. Int. J. Commun. Syst. **25**(11), 1432–1442 (2012)
17. Li, X., Chen, K.: Id-based multi-proxy signature, proxy multi-signature and multi-proxy multi-signature schemes from bilinear pairings. Appl. Math. Comput. **169**(1), 437–450 (2005)
18. Bagherzandi, A., Jarecki, S.: Identity-based aggregate and multi-signature schemes based on RSA. In: Nguyen, P.Q., Pointcheval, D. (eds.) PKC 2010. LNCS, vol. 6056, pp. 480–498. Springer, Heidelberg (2010)
19. Joye, M., Libert, B.: Efficient cryptosystems from 2^k-th power residue symbols. In: Johansson, T., Nguyen, P.Q. (eds.) EUROCRYPT 2013. LNCS, vol. 7881, pp. 76–92. Springer, Heidelberg (2013)

Cooperative Spectrum and Infrastructure Leasing on TV Bands

Xiaoshuang Xing[1][(✉)], Hang Liu[2], Xiuzhen Cheng[1],
Wei Zhou[3], and Dechang Chen[4]

[1] Computer Science, The George Washington University, Washington, D.C., USA
{xing,cheng}@gwu.edu
[2] Electrical Engineering and Computer Science,
The Catholic University of America, Washington, D.C., USA
liuh@cua.edu
[3] Electronics and Information Engineering,
Beijing Jiaotong University, Beijing, China
11111032@bjtu.edu.cn
[4] Department of Preventive Medicine and Biometrics,
Uniformed Services University of the Health Sciences, Bethesda, USA
dechang.chen@usuhs.edu

Abstract. In this paper, we propose a cooperative wireless infrastructure and spectrum leasing framework for sharing unused TV spectrum, in which the ownership of network infrastructure and spectrum is decoupled, and each can be leased and delivered as a service on demand. An incumbent TV spectrum owner (TSO) can lease a share of the infrastructure from a network infrastructure owner (NIO) with a pay-per-use model, to provide new services to its end users. On the other hand, the TSO can rent a portion of its unused spectrum to the NIO for revenue such that the NIO can obtain access to the TV spectrum to serve the NIO's customers. This proposed framework creates a win-win situation by allowing TSO and NIO to lease spectrum and infrastructure from each other for providing services and earning profits. We analyze the interplay between the spectrum owner (TSO) and infrastructure owner (NIO) by formulating a multi-stage Stackelberg game, where TSO and NIO determine the infrastructure leasing price, the amount of infrastructure to lease, the spectrum leasing price, and the amount of spectrum to lease sequentially to maximize their utilities. The best strategies that will be taken by TSO and NIO under different situations are obtained through backward induction. The formed cooperative structure, the network throughput, and the two entities' utilities are theoretically analyzed when TSO has different levels of idle bandwidth supply.

1 Introduction

There is abundant unused TV band spectrum left by the termination of analog TV. Currently, these TV white spaces either become idle or are used by the secondary users for free. The secondary users equipped with cognitive radios

© Springer International Publishing Switzerland 2015
K. Xu and J. Zhu (Eds.): WASA 2015, LNCS 9204, pp. 623–633, 2015.
DOI: 10.1007/978-3-319-21837-3_61

can dynamically access the TV white space spectrum only if their transmission will not cause interference to the primary users (TV broadcasters or other TV band licensees/owners). Various mechanisms for dynamic access to the unused TV spectrum based on sensing and database have been proposed [1–4]. However this model is totally transparent to the primary users and does not have any motivation to the original TV spectrum owners/operators (TSOs). The TSOs may want to provide new services such as interactive TV, social networking of viewers, Internet access, etc. to their customers on their spectrum to earn extra profits. To achieve this goal, new network infrastructure will be necessary. However, it is very expensive for the TSOs to deploy and operate new data networks, considering the installation and operation cost of cell sites and towers, base stations, backhaul network, and gateways. Such heavy budgetary burden of upgrading infrastructures is one of the main reasons to prevent them from the further exploration of their TV bands.

On the other hand, a third party may deploy a network, for example, a small cell network (SCN) infrastructure in a metropolitan area, campus, stadium, or shopping mall. If the network operates as a secondary user in the TV band, it has to guarantee no interference to the primary users, i.e. immediately switching to the other channels whenever a primary transmission, for example, a local TV broadcasting or a microphone signal used by TV news crews, occurs. In addition, it has to deal with the co-existence and interference from other secondary users, just like operating on the unlicensed band. This will not only increase the complexity of the secondary systems but also make it difficult for the secondary networks to ensure the quality of service to their users. In this context, it is important to design more flexible and cost-effective infrastructure and spectrum sharing mechanisms that can improve spectrum utilization, enable new services, reduce operator cost, and boost network capacity.

In this paper, motivated by the success of Infrastructure as a Service (IaaS) in cloud computing, we propose the ownership of network infrastructure and spectrum is decoupled, and each of them can be treated as a shared pool of resources and leased as a service on demand. Then based on this principal, we design a new network infrastructure and spectrum leasing framework for sharing TV white space spectrum, in which an independent entity with interests to earn profits by providing infrastructure service can build a programmable small cell network (SCN) and then lease the SCN infrastructure to other entities to generate revenue (*infrastructure as a service*), although it does not own any spectrum. An incumbent spectrum owner, e.g. a TSO, does not need to build its own network infrastructure. It can dynamically lease a share of the infrastructure from the network infrastructure owners (NIOs) with a pay-per-use model according to its needs, to provide new services to its customers, which reduces its capital and operational cost and saves its service deployment time. On the other hand, a legacy TSO can lease a portion of its unused spectrum to the NIO (*spectrum as a service*) to get revenue such that the NIO can obtain bulk access to the spectrum and provide communication service to its end users. This cooperation can create a win-win situation, allowing both TSO and NIO to provide new services and to improve their utilities in terms of user data throughput and payment/revenue. Note that we consider the SCN infrastructure because the concept of SCNs has been considered as a promising way to achieve higher per-user data rate and total network capacity [5–7].

To solve the cooperative spectrum and infrastructure leasing problem, there are several main challenges: 1) how to motivate the NIO to lease infrastructure (i.e., small cells) to the TSO, and how to determine the infrastructure leasing price and the infrastructure leasing amount. 2) how to motivate the TSO to lease spectrum to the NIO, and how to determine the spectrum leasing price and the spectrum leasing amount. The whole process is modeled as a four-stage Stackelberg game and the best strategies taken by the TSO and NIO are obtained through backward induction. In this paper, our main contributions are three folds.

- First, we propose a new framework for sharing unused TV spectrum, in which the ownership of network infrastructure and spectrum is decoupled, and each can be leased and delivered as a service on demand. A TSO and a NIO can cooperate by leasing spectrum and infrastructure from one another to provide network services to their end users. This novel cooperative leasing framework can achieve significant spectrum utilization and wireless network capacity gains.
- Second, we formulate the cooperative spectrum and infrastructure leasing problem into a four-stage Stackelberg game where the TSO and NIO determine the infrastructure leasing price, amount of infrastructure to lease, spectrum leasing price, and amount of spectrum to lease sequentially to maximize their utilities.
- Third, we analyze the cooperative structure and the performance of the cooperative leasing mechanism under different amount of TSO bandwidth.

The rest of this paper is organized as follows. In Sect. 2, we introduce the system model considered in this paper, describe the problem to be solved, and formulate the problem into a four-stage stackelberg game. In Sect. 3, we analyze the four-stage Stackelberg game by exploiting the subgame perfect equilibrium via backward induction. We analyze the cooperative structure and the performance of the cooperative leasing mechanism under different amount of TSO bandwidth in Sect. 4. Finally, we conclude the paper and point out some future research directions in Sect. 5.

2   System Model and Problem Formulation

In this paper, we consider a scenario that a TSO coexists with a NIO. The TSO is the TV band spectrum license owner who has abundant idle spectrum with bandwidth Ω resulting from the termination of analog TV. It wants to earn extra profits by providing new services to users and leasing spectrum to other entities. The NIO is an entity that deploys N small cells in the expectation of earning profits from providing infrastructure leasing service to the TSO and providing communication service to the customers.

Considering the fact that the TSO and the NIO own no infrastructure and no spectrum respectively, they are motivated to conduct a cooperative infrastructure and spectrum leasing process to lease infrastructure and spectrum from each other. A four-stage Stackelberg game is formulated to realize the cooperative leasing process. In the game, the TSO needs to decide the number of small cells N_L to be leased from the NIO, the maximum spectrum supply $W_L \leq \Omega$ for the NIO, and set the the price p_s for selling each unit spectrum. While the NIO needs to set the price p_i for selling each small cell and decide the spectrum bandwidth $W_S \leq W_L$ to be leased from the TSO. Specifically, we detail the four-stages of the game as follows.

- **Stage I:** NIO decides price p_i for selling each small cell infrastructure (namely the price for leasing each small cell basestation).
- **Stage II:** TSO decides N_L the number of small cell basestations to be leases from the NIO. Then the number of small cell basestations left to NIO is $N_S = N - N_L$ with N being the total number of small cells maintained by the NIO. TSO also decides the maximum spectrum supply for the NIO, denoted by W_L. That is, the amount of spectrum that is leased to NIO will no more than W_L. Therefore, the amount of spectrum that TSO would keep for those small cells that it leases from NIO will be $\Omega - W_L$.
- **Stage III:** TSO decides the price p_s for selling each unit spectrum to NIO.
- **Stage IV:** NIO decides W_S, the amount of spectrum it wants to lease from TSO.

Next we analyze the four-stage Stackelberg game by exploiting the subgame perfect equilibrium. A general technique for determining the subgame perfect equilibrium is the backward induction which captures the sequential dependence of decisions in all stages [8–10]. We will start with Stage IV and finally proceed to Stage I in next section.

3   Backward Induction of the Four-Stage Stackelberg Game

3.1   NIO's Decision on W_S in Stage IV

During a time slot of unit length, the customers within a small cell access the spectrum in a time-divided manner. That is, the transmission time of each customer i is $\frac{1}{C}$ with C being the number of customers located within each small cell. When the amount of spectrum leased from the TSO is W_S, the down-link throughput (in nats) of a customer i within a small cell is:

$$r_i = \frac{1}{C} W_M ln(1 + \frac{g}{W_M}) \tag{1}$$

Here, $W_M = \frac{W_S}{N_S}$ is the bandwidth allocated to each small cell basestation; $g = \frac{Ph}{n_0}$; P is the transmission power of the small cell basestation; $h = \frac{1}{d^\alpha}$ is the average path loss from the small cell basestation to a customer, with d being the average distance between a customer and the small cell basestation; n_0 is the noise power per unit bandwidth. In small cells, the distance between customers and small basestations are naturally short, therefore, h is big and the signal to noise ratio (SNR) $\frac{g}{W_M}$ is high. In such a case, the achievable throughput of customer i can be approximated as $r_i = \frac{1}{C} W_M \ln(\frac{g}{W_M})$. The throughput provided by a small cell to NIO's customers is

$$r_S = \sum_{i=1}^{C} r_i = W_M \ln(\frac{g}{W_M}) \tag{2}$$

and the utility of the NIO can be given by

$$U_S(p_i, W_S) = p_t N_S r_S + p_i N_L - p_s W_S \tag{3}$$

It should be noted that in our paper we assume the profits earned by TSO and NIO from serving their users/customers are functions of the provided throughput. One reasonable function is $f(r) = p_t * r$ with r being the provided throughput and p_t being the price for a unit of throughput. Therefore, the item $p_t N_S r_S$ in (3) is the profit earned by NIO from providing a throughput of $N_S r_S$ to its customers.

Obviously, U_S is a concave function in W_S. The utility of NIO can be maximized when $\frac{\partial U_S(p_i, W_S)}{\partial W_S} = 0$. Therefore, we get the optimal W_S as

$$W_S^* = N_S g e^{(-1-\frac{p_s}{p_t})} \tag{4}$$

3.2 TSO's Decision on p_s in Stage III

Let $S_L = W_L$ denote the spectrum provided by TSO for leasing, that is, the total bandwidth supply from TSO to NIO is $S_L = W_L$. Let $D_S = W_S^*$ denote the total demand of the NIO. Then, the utility of TSO can be given as

$$U_L(N_L, W_L, p_s) = p_s \cdot \min(S_L, D_S) + p_t N_L r_L - p_i N_L \tag{5}$$

Here, r_L denotes the throughput provided by a small cell to TSO's users. Considering the fact that N_L and W_L have been decided in Stage II, the objective of TSO in Stage III is to find the optimal price p_s^* that maximizes function $p_s \cdot \min(S_L, D_S)$. That is,

$$p_s^* = \arg \max_{p_s \geq 0} p_s \cdot \min(S_L, D_S) \tag{6}$$

As the demand of the NIO $D_S = N_S g e^{(-1-\frac{p_s}{p_t})}$ is a decreasing function of p_s, the maximum value of D_S is $D_S^{max} = D_S(p_s = 0) = \frac{N_S g}{e}$. With the increase of p_s, the value of D_S gradually approaches 0. When TSO provides a positive supply to the NIO, that is, $S_L > 0$, there will be two different cases relative to the comparison between S_L and D_S:

- Comparison I: $S_L \geq D_S^{max}$
- Comparison II: $0 \leq S_L < D_S^{max}$

In Comparison I, $S_L \geq D_S^{max}$, that is, $W_L \geq \frac{N_Sg}{e}$. The objective of TSO is to get the optimal p_s^* from the following problem,

$$p_c^{I^*} = \underset{p_c \geq 0}{\arg \max} \, p_s D_S \tag{7}$$

Let $f = p_s N_S g e^{(-1-\frac{p_s}{p_t})}$,

$$\frac{\partial f}{\partial p_s} = (1 - \frac{p_s}{p_t}) N_S g e^{(-1-\frac{p_s}{p_t})} \tag{8}$$

It is obvious that f is an increasing function of p_s when $0 \leq p_s < p_t$ and a decreasing function of p_s when $p_s > p_t$. f will get the maximum value when $\frac{\partial f}{\partial p_s} = 0$. That is, $p_s^{I^*} = p_t$.

In Comparison II, $0 \leq S_L < D_S^{max}$, that is $0 \leq W_L < \frac{N_Sg}{e}$. There will be a specific $p_s = p_t \ln \frac{N_Sg}{W_L} - p_t$ such that $S_L = D_S$. We have $S_L \leq D_S$ if $0 \leq p_s \leq p_t \ln \frac{N_Sg}{W_L} - p_t$ and $S_L \geq D_S$ if $p_s \geq p_t \ln \frac{N_Sg}{W_L} - p_t$. Therefore, Comparison II can be further divided into two cases:

- Case I: $0 \leq p_s \leq p_t \ln \frac{N_Sg}{W_L} - p_t$

$$p_s^{II-I^*} = \underset{p_s \geq 0}{\arg \max} \, p_s S_L \tag{9}$$

It is obvious that the objective function is increasing with p_s. Therefore, $p_s^{II-I^*} = p_t \ln \frac{N_Sg}{W_L} - p_t$.
- Case II: $p_s \geq p_t \ln \frac{N_Sg}{W_L} - p_t$

$$p_s^{II-II^*} = \underset{s_c \geq 0}{\arg \max} \, p_s D_S \tag{10}$$

According to the analysis of (7), we get

$$p_s^{II-II^*} = \begin{cases} p_t & \text{if } \ln \frac{N_Sg}{W_L} < 2 \\ p_t \ln \frac{N_Sg}{W_L} - p_t & \text{if } \ln \frac{N_Sg}{W_L} \geq 2 \end{cases} \tag{11}$$

Combining Case I and Case II, the optimal p_s^* in Comparison II can be obtained as

$$p_s^{II^*} = \begin{cases} p_t & \text{if } \frac{N_Sg}{e^2} \leq W_L < \frac{N_Sg}{e} \\ p_t \ln \frac{N_Sg}{W_L} - p_t & \text{if } 0 \leq W_L \leq \frac{N_Sg}{e^2} \end{cases} \tag{12}$$

Summarizing the analyses, we obtain the optimal decision on p_s^* as

$$p_s^*(W_L \geq \frac{N_Sg}{e^2}) = p_t \tag{13}$$

$$p_s^*(0 \leq W_L \leq \frac{N_Sg}{e^2}) = p_t \ln \frac{N_Sg}{W_L} - p_t \tag{14}$$

3.3   TSO's Decision on W_L, N_L in Stage II

According to (13) and (14), we consider two cases with regard to the value range of W_L.

- Case I: $W_L \geq \frac{N_S g}{e^2}$, $U_L(N_L, W_L) = \frac{p_t N_S g}{e^2} + p_t N_L r_L - p_i N_L$.
- Case II: $0 \leq W_L \leq \frac{N_S g}{e^2}$, $U_L(N_L, W_L) = p_t W_L (\ln \frac{N_S g}{W_L} - 1) + p_t N_L r_L - p_i N_L$

Similar to the analysis in Subsect. 3.1, we obtain that

$$r_L = \left(\frac{(\Omega - W_L)}{N_L} \right) \ln \left(\frac{g}{\frac{(\Omega - W_L)}{N_L}} \right) \tag{15}$$

with Ω being the total bandwidth of the TSO. As defined in Sect. 2, $N = N_S + N_L$ is the total number of small cells maintained by the NIO.

In Case I,

$$U_L^I(N_L, W_L) = \frac{p_t(N - N_L)g}{e^2} + p_t N_L r_L - p_i N_L \tag{16}$$

Obviously, $U_L^I(N_L, W_L)$ is a concave function of W_L. When $\frac{\partial U_L^I(N_L, W_L)}{\partial W_L} = 0$, $U_L^I(N_L, W_L)$ obtains the maximum value. Therefore, $W_L^{I^*} = \Omega - \frac{N_L g}{e}$.

$$U_L^I(N_L) = \frac{(N - N_L)p_t g}{e^2} + \frac{N_L p_t g}{e} - p_i N_L \tag{17}$$

Taking the value range of $W_L^I \geq \frac{N_S g}{e^2}$ into consideration, we get the value range of N_L in Case I as $N_L \leq \frac{e^2 \Omega - Ng}{(e-1)g}$. If $\Omega < \frac{Ng}{e^2}$, we have $N_L \leq \frac{e^2 \Omega - Ng}{(e-1)g} < 0$. Case I is infeasible in such a case. When $\Omega \geq \frac{Ng}{e^2}$, we get the optimal value of N_L in Case I as

$$N_L^{I^*} = \begin{cases} \min(\frac{e^2 \Omega - Ng}{(e-1)g}, N) & \text{if } 0 \leq p_i \leq \frac{p_t(e-1)g}{e^2} \\ 0 & \text{if } p_i > \frac{p_t(e-1)g}{e^2} \end{cases} \tag{18}$$

It should be noted that N_L can take any integer value within the range of $[0, \min(\frac{e^2 \Omega - Ng}{(e-1)g}, N)]$ when $p_i = \frac{p_t(e-1)g}{e^2}$. Without loss of generality, we set $N_L^{I^*} = \min(\frac{e^2 \Omega - Ng}{(e-1)g}, N)$ for $p_i = \frac{p_t(e-1)g}{e^2}$ in our analyses.

In Case II,

$$U_L^{II}(N_L, W_L) = p_t W_L (\ln \frac{N_S g}{W_L} - 1) + p_t N_L r_L - p_i N_L \tag{19}$$

U_L^{II} is also a concave function in W_L, and the optimal W_L is $W_L^{II^*} = \frac{N - N_L}{N + N_L e - N_L} \Omega$. Therefore, we get

$$U_L^{II}(N_L) = p_t \Omega \ln \left(\frac{(N + N_L e - N_L)g}{\Omega} \right) - p_t \Omega - p_i N_L \tag{20}$$

Table 1. TSO's decisions on W_L and N_L in Stage II

Value range of Ω	Value range of p_i	N_L^*	W_L^*
$\Omega \geq \frac{Ng}{e}$	$p_i > \frac{p_t(e-1)g}{e^2}$	0	Ω
	$0 \leq p_i \leq \frac{p_t(e-1)g}{e^2}$	N	$\Omega - \frac{Ng}{e}$
$\frac{Ng}{e^2} < \Omega < \frac{Ng}{e}$	$p_i > \frac{p_t(e-1)g}{e^2}$	0	Ω
	$\frac{p_t(e-1)\Omega}{eN} < p_i \leq \frac{p_t(e-1)g}{e^2}$	$\frac{p_t\Omega}{p_i} - \frac{N}{e-1}$	$\frac{p_i eN - (e-1)p_t\Omega}{(e-1)^2 p_t}$
	$0 \leq p_i \leq \frac{p_t(e-1)\Omega}{eN}$	N	0
$\Omega \leq \frac{Ng}{e^2}$	$p_i > \frac{p_t(e-1)\Omega}{N}$	0	Ω
	$\frac{p_t(e-1)\Omega}{eN} < p_i \leq \frac{p_t(e-1)\Omega}{N}$	$\frac{p_t\Omega}{p_i} - \frac{N}{e-1}$	$\frac{p_i eN - (e-1)p_t\Omega}{(e-1)^2 p_t}$
	$0 \leq p_i \leq \frac{p_t(e-1)\Omega}{eN}$	N	0

Obviously, U_L^{II} is a concave function of N_L. When $N_L = \frac{p_t\Omega}{p_i} - \frac{N}{e-1}$, we have $\frac{\partial U_L^{II}(N_L)}{\partial N_L} = 0$. Considering that $0 \leq W_L \leq \frac{N_S g}{e^2}$ in Case II, we get the value range of N_L in Case II as $\frac{e^2\Omega - Ng}{(e-1)g} \leq N_L \leq N$. Comparing the value of $\frac{e^2\Omega - Ng}{(e-1)g}$, $\frac{p_t\Omega}{p_i} - \frac{N}{e-1}$, and N we could get the possible solutions of N_L and W_L in Case II. Taking the values of $U_L(\Omega)$ in both cases into consideration, we finally get the TSO's optimal decisions on N_L and W_L in stage II, which are given in Table 1.

3.4 NIO's Decision on p_i in Stage I

For each value range of Ω in Table 1, NIO should decide an optimal p_i that maximizes its utility.

For $\Omega \geq \frac{Ng}{e}$,

– When $p_i > \frac{p_t(e-1)g}{e^2}$,

$$U_S(p_i) = U_S^{11} = \frac{Np_t g}{e^2} \tag{21}$$

– When $0 \leq p_i \leq \frac{p_t(e-1)g}{e^2}$,

$$U_S(p_i) = U_S^{12} = p_i N \tag{22}$$

U_S^{12} is an increasing function of p_i which reaches the maximum value $\max U_S^{12}$ when $p_i = \frac{p_t(e-1)g}{e^2}$. It can be obtained that $\max U_S^{12} = \frac{(e-1)Np_t g}{e^2} > U_S^{11}$. Therefore, when $\Omega > \frac{Ng}{e}$, the optimal value of p_i that maximizes the NIO's utility is

$$p_i^*(\Omega \geq \frac{Ng}{e}) = \frac{p_t(e-1)g}{e^2} \tag{23}$$

For $\frac{Ng}{e^2} < \Omega < \frac{Ng}{e}$,

– When $p_i > \frac{p_t(e-1)g}{e^2}$,

$$U_S(p_i) = U_S^{21} = \frac{Np_t g}{e^2} \tag{24}$$

– When $\frac{p_t(e-1)\Omega}{eN} < p_i \le \frac{p_t(e-1)g}{e^2}$,

$$U_S(p_i) = U_S^{22} = \frac{p_i N}{(e-1)^2} + \frac{(e-2)p_t\Omega}{e-1} \tag{25}$$

– When $0 \le p_i \le \frac{p_t(e-1)\Omega}{eN}$,

$$U_S(p_i) = U_S^{23} = p_i N \tag{26}$$

U_S^{22} and U_S^{23} are increasing functions of p_i which get the maximum value when $p_i = \frac{p_t(e-1)g}{e^2}$ and $p_i = \frac{p_t(e-1)\Omega}{eN}$, respectively. And,

$$\max U_S^{22} = p_t\Omega + \frac{1}{e^2}\frac{Np_tg}{e-1} - \frac{p_t\Omega}{e-1} \tag{27}$$

$$\max U_S^{23} = p_t\Omega - \frac{p_t\Omega}{e} \tag{28}$$

Since $\max U_S^{22} \ge \max U_S^{23}$ and $\max U_S^{22} \ge U_S^{21}$, we obtain the optimal value of p_i as

$$p_i^*\left(\frac{Ng}{e^2} < \Omega < \frac{Ng}{e}\right) = \frac{p_t(e-1)g}{e^2} \tag{29}$$

For $\Omega \le \frac{Ng}{e^2}$,

– When $p_i > \frac{p_t(e-1)\Omega}{N}$,

$$U_S(p_i) = U_S^{31} = p_t\Omega \tag{30}$$

– When $\frac{p_t(e-1)\Omega}{eN} < p_i \le \frac{p_t(e-1)\Omega}{N}$,

$$U_S(p_i) = U_S^{32} = \frac{p_i N}{(e-1)^2} + \frac{(e-2)p_t\Omega}{e-1} \tag{31}$$

– When $0 \le p_i \le \frac{p_t(e-1)\Omega}{eN}$,

$$U_S(p_i) = U_S^{33} = p_i N \tag{32}$$

U_S^{31} is a constant while U_S^{32} and U_S^{33} are increasing functions of p_i. When $p_i = \frac{p_t(e-1)\Omega}{N}$ and $p_i = \frac{p_t(e-1)\Omega}{eN}$, it can be obtained respectively

$$\max U_S^{32} = p_t\Omega \tag{33}$$

$$\max U_S^{33} = p_t\Omega - \frac{p_t\Omega}{e} \tag{34}$$

Obviously, $\max U_S^{32} = U_S^{31} > \max U_S^{33}$. Without loss of generality, the NIO could take the optimal value of p_i as

$$p_i^*\left(\Omega \le \frac{Ng}{e^2}\right) = \frac{p_t(e-1)\Omega}{N} \tag{35}$$

Table 2. Decision summarization of the four-stage stackelberg game

Value range of Ω	Stage I	Stage II	Stage III		Stage IV
	p_i^*	N_L^*	W_L^*	p_s^*	W_S^*
$\Omega \geq \frac{Ng}{e}$	$\frac{p_t(e-1)g}{e^2}$	N	$\Omega - \frac{Ng}{e}$	N/A	N/A
$\frac{Ng}{e^2} < \Omega < \frac{Ng}{e}$	$\frac{p_t(e-1)g}{e^2}$	$\frac{e^2\Omega - Ng}{(e-1)g}$	$\frac{Ng-e\Omega}{e(e-1)}$	p_t	$\frac{Ng-e\Omega}{e(e-1)}$
$\Omega \leq \frac{Ng}{e^2}$	$\frac{(e^2-1)W}{N}$	0	W	$p_t \ln(\frac{Ng}{W}) - p_t$	W

4   Analysis of the Four-Stage Stackelberg Game

As a summarization of the backward induction described in Sect. 3, Table 2 lists the optimal decisions and the corresponding utilities of the TSO and the NIO for different ranges of Ω. Based on Table 2, we analyze the formed cooperative structure and the network throughput under different amount of TSO bandwidth (i.e. different value range of Ω).

When $\Omega \geq \frac{Ng}{e}$, the NIO will lease all its small cells to the TSO. No small cell will be available for the NIO's customers, and the NIO will not lease spectrum from the TSO. In this situation, the Stackelberg game will end on Stage II as shown in the third row of Table 2. Since all the small cells are used to serve TSO's users, the network throughput gained from this cooperative process is equal to the throughput gained by all the TSO's users, that is

$$R_{Net}^{\Omega \geq \frac{Ng}{e}} = N_L r_L = \frac{Ng}{e} \tag{36}$$

When $\frac{Ng}{e^2} < \Omega^* < W$, the TSO will lease spectrum to the NIO and also lease infrastructure from the NIO. While the NIO will lease a portion of its small cells to the TSO and equip the other small cells with the leased spectrum to serve its own customers. In such a case, both the TSO's users and the NIO's customers gain throughput from the cooperative process. The obtained network throughput is

$$R_{Net}^{\frac{Ng}{e^2} < \Omega^* < W} = N_L r_L + N_S r_S = \frac{Ng + (e^2 - 2e)\Omega}{e(e-1)} \tag{37}$$

When $W < \frac{Ng}{e^2}$, TSO will lease all its idle spectrum to the NIO while not leasing any infrastructure from it. NIO will equip all its small sells with the leased spectrum to serve its customers. Since all the idle spectrum is used to serve NIO's customers, the network throughput gained from this cooperative process is equal to the throughput gained by all the NIO's customers, that is

$$R_{Net}^{W < \frac{Ng}{e^2}} = N_S r_S = W \ln(\frac{Ng}{W}) \tag{38}$$

5 Conclusion and Future Work

In this paper, we present a cooperative spectrum and infrastructure leasing mechanism for small cells working on TV bands. In the mechanism, the TSO and the NIO respectively provide spectrum and network infrastructure as service to each other. A four-stage Stackelberg game is formulated and backword induction is applied to derive the best decisions of the TSO and the NIO in each stage. The strategies that will be taken by TSO and NIO under different situations are concluded according to our derivation. The formed cooperative structure, the network throughput, and the two entities' utilities are analyzed and summarized when TSO has different levels of idle bandwidth supply. In our future work, we will try to study a new decision model when there are multiple competitive TSOs/NIOs in the network.

Disclaimer: The views expressed are those of the author(s) and do not necessarily reflect the official views of the Uniformed Services University of the Health Sciences or the Department of Defense.

Acknowledgment. The authors would like to thank the support from the National Science Foundation of the US (AST-1443858, AST-1443773, AST-1443916, ECCS-1407986, CNS-1265311, and CNS-1162057).

References

1. Fadda, M., Popescu, V., Murroni, M., Angueira, P., Morgade, J.: On the feasibility of unlicensed communications in the tv white space: field measurements in the uhf band. IJDMB **2015**, 1–8 (2015)
2. Jiang, T., Wang, Z., Zhang, L., Qu, D., Liang, Y.-C.: Efficient spectrum utilization on tv band for cognitive radio based high speed vehicle network. IEEE TWC **13**(10), 5319–5329 (2014)
3. Um, J.-S., Kim, S., Jung, H., Pak, J., Jeong, B.: Development and performance improvement of cognitive radio testbed on tv white space. In: IEEE WCNC, pp. 3254–3259, April 2014
4. Kim, H., Shin, K.G.: Asymmetry-aware real-time distributed joint resource allocation in ieee 802.22 wrans. In: IEEE INFOCOM, pp. 543–551 (2010)
5. Nakamura, T., Nagata, S., Benjebbour, A., Kishiyama, Y., Hai, T., Xiaodong, S., Ning, Y., Nan, L.: Trends in small cell enhancements in lte advanced. IEEE Commun. Mag. **51**(2), 98–105 (2013)
6. RWS-120029, "Views on lte rel-12 and beyond," 3GPP, CMCC, June 2012
7. RWS-120010, "Requirements, candidate solutions and technology roadmap for lte rel-12 onward," 3GPP, NTT DOCOMO, June 2012
8. Yin, J., Sun, G., Wang, X.: Spectrum trading in cognitive radio network: A two-stage market based on contract and stackelberg game. In: IEEE WCNC, pp. 1679–1684, April 2013
9. Cao, X., Chen, Y., Liu, K.: Spectrum trading in heterogeneous cognitive radio networks. In: IEEE GlobalSIP, pp. 1150–1154, December 2014
10. Duan, L., Huang, J., Shou, B.: Cognitive mobile virtual network operator: Investment and pricing with supply uncertainty. In: IEEE INFOCOM, pp. 1–9, March 2010

Information Security Enhancement with Actual Access Statuses of Users in the Multi-User System

Datong Xu[1,2], Pinyi Ren[2](✉), Qinghe Du[2], and Li Sun[2]

[1] Key Laboratory of Cognitive Radio and Information Processing,
Guilin University of Electronic Technology, Ministry of Education,
Guilin 541004, Guangxi, China
xdtstc@stu.xjtu.edu.cn

[2] Department of Information and Communications Engineering,
Xi'an Jiaotong University, Xi'an 710049, Shaanxi, China
{pyren,duqinghe,lisun}@mail.xjtu.edu.cn

Abstract. In the new generation wireless communication systems, when multiple users are served, information security among them should be considered to protect each user's privacy. In this case, physical layer security techniques can be adopted for this mutual confidence problem. Unlike other traditional physical layer security methods, the proposed scheme improves secrecy rate with the information of users' access statuses (i.e., being served or idle), and it is denoted as SRT-AS. In the SRT-AS, appropriate parameters expressing users' actual access statuses are introduced, and an adaptive transmitter and receiver design strategy is used to increase security. It can be found that no iterative process is included in the SRT-AS, moreover, performance analysis and simulation results illustrate that the SRT-AS is feasible for the multi-user system.

Keywords: Physical layer security · Access status · Adaptive transmitter and receiver design

1 Introduction

Nowadays, the ever-increasing communication requirements of wireless communication users make the new generation systems [1–5] being researched. These systems provide diverse services and guarantee the high efficiency, continuous reliability and security of these services. In this case, when multiple users are served, the information privacy among them should be considered.

The research reported in this paper was supported in part by the National Natural Science Foundation of China (NSFC) under Grant No. 61431011, and the Opening Project of Key Laboratory of Cognitive Radio and Information Processing (Guilin University of Electronic Technology), Ministry of Education, under Grant No. 2013KF04.

K. Xu and J. Zhu (Eds.): WASA 2015, LNCS 9204, pp. 654–663, 2015.
DOI: 10.1007/978-3-319-21837-3_62

It is well known that the theoretical demonstration of cryptographic techniques' security has not been provided [6] and they may be affected by several direct attacks [7]. Therefore, here, the physical layer security technologies [6,8] are mainly investigated, and the feasibilities of which have been demonstrated in information theory [6]. Based on this premise, several schemes for multiple users' mutual confidences (without pure attackers/eavesdroppers) have been proposed [9–12], which can increase each user's secrecy rate in secrecy capacity region [13]. We find that the common assumption of these schemes is that when one user receives signals, the others can collude to eavesdrop this user's signals. However, when multiple users need services, if one user is being served, he/she does ordinarily not collude with others for his/her own security. That is to say, each user's actual access status (i.e., being served or idle) should be included for physical layer security improvement.

According to the aforementioned explanations, a novel scheme for mutual confidences of multiple users is proposed, which improves secrecy rate with the information of users' access statuses (i.e., being served or idle) and is called as SRT-AS. In the SRT-AS, an adaptive transmitter and receiver design strategy where the proper parameters for users' access statuses are introduced is adopted. By adjusting these parameters, the concrete content of this transmitter and receiver design approach can be varied to adapt the multi-user system, and the information of distance between each user and the base station (BS) is also considered. Note that the SRT-AS is different from the above schemes and does not contain any iterative process. Furthermore, performance analysis and simulation results show that the SRT-AS is feasible for the mutual confidence problem in the aforementioned multi-user scenario.

The rest of this paper is organized as follows: system model is described in Sect. 2. In Sect. 3, the SRT-AS is proposed. Section 4 gives the performance analysis for SRT-AS. The simulation results are depicted in Sect. 5, while Sect. 6 concludes this paper.

This paper uses the following notations: $\mathbf{A}$ is a matrix, $\mathbf{a}$ is a vector, while a and A denote scalars; $\mathbf{A}^H$ is the conjugate transpose of $\mathbf{A}$, and $\|\mathbf{A}\|_F$ is the Frobenius norm of $\mathbf{A}$; in addition, $\mathbf{I}$ is an identity matrix, $\mathbb{E}$ denotes expectation, and $\mathcal{CN}(\mu, \mathbf{C})$ is the cyclic symmetric complex Gaussian distribution with mean μ and covariance matrix $\mathbf{C}$.

2   System Model

Multi-user system [1,5,8] is depicted in Fig. 1. As the discussion given in Sect. 1, there are not pure external or internal attackers/eavesdroppers in this system. The distances between diverse users and the BS can not be always the same, and may change during signal transmission process. Here, for the sake of simplicity, we assume that the distance between each user and the BS is constant in a transmission time interval (TTI), but changes independently between consecutive TTIs. In this case, the channel from the BS to each user is a block-fading channel, which contains the information of large-scale and small-scale path losses. Moreover, it is worth to indicate that we assume each user is not always served

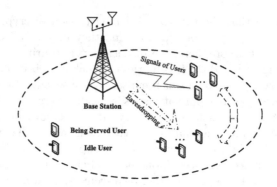

Fig. 1. The schematic figure of multi-user system, where the signals of being served users may be eavesdropped by idle users. The dotted line, double sided arrow denotes that the being served and idle users can transform into each other (this transformation is referred to each user).

in a TTI, while there is not a permanently idle user in this system. Note that the scenario in Fig. 1 is a single cell, however, it can be extended to multiple cells with coordinated multi-point (CoMP) techniques [1,14]. This operation is beyond the scope of this paper and will be considered in our future work.

At present, we describe the configuration of this system. We assume that the BS is equipped with T^b antennas. There are M users within the scope of BS in each TTI, and the mth user is equipped with R_m^b antennas ($m \in \{1, \ldots, M\}$). In addition, for simplicity, the channel between the BS and user m can be expressed as $\mathbf{H}_m^b = \sqrt{(d_m^b)^{-\alpha_m}} \, \bar{\mathbf{H}}_m^b$, where $\bar{\mathbf{H}}_m^b \sim \mathcal{CN}(0, \mathbf{I})$, d_m^b is the distance between the BS and user m, and α_m represents the path loss exponent. Here, we consider that the rich scattering environment makes this channel model achievable, and users can send pilot signals to the BS by time division duplex (TDD) mode for channel acquisition without quantization (the BS obtains these channels satisfying channel reciprocity). According to these definitions, the desired signal vector operated by receiver at each user m can be written as

$$
\mathbf{y}_m^b(t) = \begin{cases} \boldsymbol{\Phi}_m^{bH}\left(\mathbf{H}_m^b \mathbf{W}_m^b \mathbf{s}_m^b(t) + \sum_{k=1, k \neq m}^{M} \mu_k^b \mathbf{H}_m^b \mathbf{W}_m^b \mathbf{s}_m^b(t) + \mathbf{n}_m^b(t)\right), & t \in S_{\tau_m^b} \\ \boldsymbol{\Phi}_m^{bH}\left(\sum_{k=1, k \neq m}^{M} \mu_k^b \mathbf{H}_m^b \mathbf{W}_m^b \mathbf{s}_m^b(t) + \mathbf{n}_m^b(t)\right), & t \notin S_{\tau_m^b} \end{cases}
\tag{1}
$$

In (1), $\boldsymbol{\Phi}_m^b$ is the receiver of user m; $\mathbf{W}_m^b$ is the transmitter from the BS to user m; $\mathbf{s}_m^b(t)$ denotes the signal vector transmitted to user m, meeting $\mathbb{E}(\mathbf{s}_m^b(t)\,\mathbf{s}_m^{bH}(t)) = \mathbf{I}, \forall m$ and $\mathbb{E}(\mathbf{s}_{m_1}^b(t)\,\mathbf{s}_{m_2}^{bH}(t)) = \mathbf{0}, \forall m_1 \neq m_2$; $\mathbf{n}_m^b(t)$ represents the additive white Gaussian noise (AWGN) vector with $\mathbf{n}_m^b(t) \sim \mathcal{CN}(0, N_0 \mathbf{I})$ (N_0 is the noise power spectral density). In addition, We define that the length of each TTI is T, τ_m^b denotes the total access time of user m in a TTI. $S_{\tau_m^b}$ is the set of time corresponding to τ_m^b; t denotes the time symbol. We can find that $E_{\tau_m^b} \subseteq S_T$ (S_T is the set of time corresponding to T). Here, for simplicity, the special access strategy for each user is not involved, which will be considered in future. Hence, we focus on the manipulations after we acquire the information of users' access statuses. In this case, the related parameter can be expressed as

$$\mu_m^b = \begin{cases} 1, t \in S_{\tau_m^b} \\ 0, t \notin S_{\tau_m^b} \end{cases}, m \in \{1, \ldots, M\} \tag{2}$$

which means when user m is served, the corresponding parameter is set as 1; otherwise, it is set as 0.

3   Information Security Enhancement: SRT-AS

In this section, we give the SRT-AS. Here, the BS will not assist any user to wiretap, therefore, the optimization objective for each user m can be shown as

$$\max R_{sm}^b = \left(R_m^b - R_{em}^b, 0\right)^+, \forall m \tag{3}$$
$$s.t.\ p_m^b \le p_{0m}^b$$

where $(a, 0)^+$ means that the larger value of a or 0 is chosen; R_{sm}^b is the secrecy rate; R_m^b is the transmission rate; R_{em}^b is the eavesdropping rate; p_m^b is the transmit power to user m; p_{0m}^b is the power threshold. Based on the users' actual access statuses, the expressions of R_m^b and R_{em}^b can be written as

$$R_m^b = \log \det \left(\mathbf{I} + \frac{\boldsymbol{\Phi}_m^{bH} \mathbf{H}_m^b \mathbf{W}_m^b \mathbf{W}_m^{bH} \mathbf{H}_m^{bH} \boldsymbol{\Phi}_m^b}{\sum\limits_{k=1,k\neq m}^{M} \mu_k^b \boldsymbol{\Phi}_m^{bH} \mathbf{H}_m^b \mathbf{W}_k^b \mathbf{W}_k^{bH} \mathbf{H}_m^{bH} \boldsymbol{\Phi}_m^b + N_0 \boldsymbol{\Phi}_m^{bH} \boldsymbol{\Phi}_m^b} \right) \tag{4}$$

$$R_{em}^b = \log \det \left(\mathbf{I} + \frac{\bar{\mathbf{H}}_m^b \mathbf{W}_m^b \mathbf{W}_m^{bH} \bar{\mathbf{H}}_m^{bH}}{\sum\limits_{k=1,k\neq m}^{M} \mu_k^b \bar{\mathbf{H}}_m^b \mathbf{W}_k^b \mathbf{W}_k^{bH} \bar{\mathbf{H}}_m^{bH} + N_0 \mathbf{D}_m^b} \right) \tag{5}$$

where $\bar{\mathbf{H}}_m^b = \bar{\boldsymbol{\Phi}}_m^{bH} \left[\bar{\mu}_1^b \mathbf{H}_1^{bH}, \ldots, \bar{\mu}_{m-1}^b \mathbf{H}_{m-1}^{bH}, \bar{\mu}_{m+1}^b \mathbf{H}_{m+1}^{bH}, \ldots, \bar{\mu}_M^b \mathbf{H}_M^{bH} \right]^H$, and when $t \in S_{\tau_k^b}$, $\bar{\mu}_k^b = 0$; otherwise, $\bar{\mu}_k^b = 1$. In addition, $\mathbf{D}_m^b = \bar{\boldsymbol{\Phi}}_m^{bH} \bar{\boldsymbol{\Phi}}_m^b$, and $\bar{\boldsymbol{\Phi}}_m^b$ is the receiver applied by potential eavesdroppers. We consider that (4) and (5) includes the impacts of receivers [15]. Moreover, all idle users may collude with each other to eavesdrop the mth user's signals. This is the worst case for user m. That is to say, we should increase the security for user m when this worst case arises. We can also show that when these potential eavesdroppers focus on user m, the other being served users' signals are the interferences to them. This is a reasonable definition for this multi-user scenario.

It is seen that there are multiple transmitters and receivers contained in (3), and jointly optimizing all of them are difficult. Hence, an alternative approach is utilized. It is also indicated that two aspects such as mitigating interference and combating eavesdropping should be included in the SRT-AS.

3.1   Mitigating Inter-user Interference

Here, the inter-user interference is mitigated. First, the dimension compression for each channel is executed as

$$\tilde{\mathbf{H}}_m^b = \mathbf{A}_{m(s_m^b)}^{bH}\mathbf{H}_m^b, \forall m \tag{6}$$

where s_m^b denotes the the number of the mth user's data streams, and $\mathbf{A}_{m(s_m^b)}^b$ is an arbitrary full column rank matrix in which there are s_m^b column vectors.

Afterwards, we define the integrated channel as

$$\bar{\bar{\mathbf{H}}}_m^b = \left[\mu_1^b\tilde{\mathbf{H}}_1^{bH}, \ldots, \mu_{m-1}^b\tilde{\mathbf{H}}_{m-1}^{bH}, \mu_{m+1}^b\tilde{\mathbf{H}}_{m+1}^{bH}, \ldots, \mu_M^b\tilde{\mathbf{H}}_M^{bH}\right]^H \tag{7}$$

Note that (8) includes all of the objects which can be interfered by user m. In this case, the eigenvalue decomposition (EVD) is implemented as

$$\bar{\bar{\mathbf{H}}}_m^{bH}\bar{\bar{\mathbf{H}}}_m^b = \bar{\mathbf{U}}_m^b\bar{\bar{\mathbf{\Sigma}}}_m^b\bar{\mathbf{U}}_m^{bH} \tag{8}$$

where $\bar{\mathbf{U}}_m^b$ is an unitary matrix and $\bar{\bar{\mathbf{\Sigma}}}_m^b$ is a diagonal matrix. Since it is obviously found that $\sum_{m=1}^M \mu_m^b s_m^b \leq T^b$, we can devise that

$$\mathbf{F}_m^b = \mathbf{I} - \bar{\mathbf{U}}_m^{b\left(1:\sum\limits_{k=1,k\neq m}^M \mu_k^b s_k^b\right)}\bar{\mathbf{U}}_m^{b\left(1:\sum\limits_{k=1,k\neq m}^M \mu_k^b s_k^b\right)H} \tag{9}$$

where $\bar{\mathbf{U}}_m^{b(1:a)}$ is composed by the column vectors of $\bar{\mathbf{U}}_m^b$ from 1 to a (from left to right). Here, the eigenvalues in $\bar{\bar{\mathbf{\Sigma}}}_m^b$ are in the descending order. According to the properties of matrix [16], if $\mathbf{F}_m^b$ is adopted, the signals of user m leaked to the other users are effectively restrained. In other words, inter-user interference can be efficiently mitigated with $\mathbf{F}_m^b$. It should be explained that the contents of (7)-(8) can be varied without changing the structures of them by only adjusting the values of all $\mu_k^m, \forall k$. Hence, this mitigating interference method is adaptive.

3.2   Combating Eavesdropping

Based on the results of mitigating inter-user interference process, we implement the method for combating eavesdropping. First, we define that

$$\rho_n^b = \left(d_n^b\right)^{-\alpha_n}, n \in \Phi_0^b \tag{10}$$

where Φ_0^b is a set of users in which each μ_n^b satisfies $\mu_n^b = 0$. According to this parameter, a ratio is given as

$$r_{nm}^b = \rho_n^b\|\mathbf{H}_n^b\|_F^2 \Big/ \left(d_m^b\right)^{-\alpha_m}\|\mathbf{H}_m^b\|_F^2 \tag{11}$$

which indicates the gap between the channel conditions of each idle user and user m. Then two cases should be evaluated as:

(1) $r_{nm}^b \geq \eta_m^b$, where η_m^b is a predetermined threshold for user m. It implies that user n may have more possibility to eavesdrop the signals of user m.

(2) $r_{nm}^b < \eta_m^b$. In the circumstances, user n is less possible to successfully eavesdrop the signals of user m due to his/her terrible channel quality.

After judging each user n with these two cases, Φ_0^b can be compressed as $\tilde{\Phi}_m^b$, in which each user q meets $r_{qm}^b \geq \eta_m^b$. Therefore, the users in $\tilde{\Phi}_m^b$ can be considered as the potential eavesdroppers. This judgement can reduce the computational complexity of following operation.

Afterwards, the optimization objective of combating eavesdropping for user m should be provided. Here, we denote that the total number of users in $\tilde{\Phi}_m^b$ is Q, so the worst case for user m is the Q users collude with each other. As the above discussion, the optimization objective for maximizing the difference of signal power between user m and eavesdroppers is shown as

$$Y_m^b = \arg\max_{\mathbf{P}_m^b} \mathbb{E}\left\|\tilde{\mathbf{H}}_m^b \mathbf{F}_m^b \mathbf{P}_m^b \mathbf{s}_m^b(t)\right\|_F^2 - \mathbb{E}\left\|\hat{\mathbf{H}}_m^b \mathbf{F}_m^b \mathbf{P}_m^b \mathbf{s}_m^b(t)\right\|_F^2 \quad (12)$$

where $\mathbf{P}_m^b$ is the result we want to obtain. Furthermore, the compound channel $\hat{\mathbf{H}}_m^b$ for all potential eavesdroppers is defined as $\hat{\mathbf{H}}_m^b = \left[\mathbf{H}_{q_1}^{bH}, \ldots, \mathbf{H}_{q_Q}^{bH}\right]^H$ $(q_1, \ldots, q_Q \in \tilde{\Phi}_m^b)$. According to (12), we can get the solution by EVD as [16]

$$\mathbf{P}_m^b = \mathrm{eig}_{(s_m^b)}^{\max}\left(\tilde{\mathbf{Q}}_m^b - \hat{\mathbf{Q}}_m^b\right) \quad (13)$$

where $\tilde{\mathbf{Q}}_m^b = \mathbf{F}_m^{bH}\tilde{\mathbf{H}}_m^{bH}\tilde{\mathbf{H}}_m^b\mathbf{F}_m^b$, $\hat{\mathbf{Q}}_m^b = \mathbf{F}_m^{bH}\hat{\mathbf{H}}_m^{bH}\hat{\mathbf{H}}_m^b\mathbf{F}_m^b$, and $\mathrm{eig}_{(s_m^b)}^{\max}$ denotes that $\mathbf{P}_m^b$ is constituted by the s_m^b left eigenvectors of matrix $\left(\tilde{\mathbf{Q}}_m^b - \hat{\mathbf{Q}}_m^b\right)$. Note that this combating eavesdropping process is based on the users' access statuses, this design method is also adaptive. Synthesizing the results of above two processes, we can have that $\mathbf{W}_m^b = \mathbf{F}_m^b \mathbf{P}_m^b$. It is worth to indicate that the power of BS is equally allocated, i.e., sophisticated power allocation methods do not included here and will be involved in future.

After the transmitter design process, the receiving strategy based on minimum mean square error (MMSE) criterion can be written as

$$\mathbf{K}_m^b = \left(\tilde{\mathbf{H}}_m^b \mathbf{W}_m^b \mathbf{W}_m^{bH} \tilde{\mathbf{H}}_m^{bH} + \bar{\mathbf{Q}}_m^b\right)^{-1} \left(\tilde{\mathbf{H}}_m^b \mathbf{W}_m^b\right) \quad (14)$$

where $\bar{\mathbf{Q}}_m^b = \sum_{k=1, k\neq m}^M \mu_k^b \tilde{\mathbf{H}}_m^b \mathbf{W}_k^b \mathbf{W}_k^{bH} \tilde{\mathbf{H}}_m^{bH} + N_0\mathbf{I}$. Therefore, this strategy is still an adaptive one. In this way, we can get that $\Phi_m^{bH} = \mathbf{K}_m^{bH} \mathbf{A}_{m(s_m^b)}^{bH}$. We can find that there is not any iteration in this process, so it can be used for the multi-user system without much delay and exorbitant overheard.

4   Performance Analysis

In this section, we give some performance analyses on the SRT-AS. We mainly focus on the computational complexity and robustness of SRT-AS for observing the feasibility of it in this multi-user system.

4.1   Computational Complexity Analysis

Here, we compare the SRT-AS to the traditional scheme, i.e., when one user is served, all of the others collude with each other. We call this traditional scheme as fully coordinated eavesdropping scheme (FCES). We evaluate complexity in terms of the floating point operations (flops) [17], which are calculated according to the number of complex additions and multiplications. Furthermore, for the sake of simplicity, we assume that $R_m^b = R^b, \forall m$ and $s_m^b = s^b, \forall m$.

At first, we evaluate the computational complexity of FCES. We can get the transmitter for user m as

$$\mathbf{W}_m^b = \mathrm{eig}_{(s^b)}^{\max} \left(\mathbf{H}_m^{bH} \mathbf{H}_m^b - \mathbf{Q}_{\bar{m}}^b \right) \tag{15}$$

where $\mathbf{Q}_{\bar{m}}^b = \sum_{k=1, k \neq m}^{M} \mathbf{H}_k^{bH} \mathbf{H}_k^b$. In addition, the receiver $\mathbf{\Phi}_m^b$ is devised by MMSE criterion without access status parameters. Hence, we have

- Generate $\mathbf{W}_m^b, \forall m$: $MO\left\{ (T^b)^2 R^b \right\} + MO\left\{ (T^b)^2 ((M-1) R^b) \right\} + MO\left\{ (T^b)^3 \right\}$.
- Calculate $\mathbf{\Phi}_m^b, \forall m$: $MO\left\{ MT^b R^b s^b \right\} + MO\left\{ (R^b)^2 s^b \right\} + MO\left\{ (R^b)^3 \right\}$.

The total complexity is the sum of above ones.

Afterwards, we assess the complexity of SRT-AS. We consider the scenario that all users may be simultaneously served for some time, while each user may also be eavesdropped by the other ones for some other time. This is the possible scenario where the complexity of SRT-AS is the highest. In this case, we get

- Transmitter design method: $MO\left\{ (T^b)^2 R^b \right\} + MO\left\{ M(T^b)^2 s^b \right\} + 2MO\left\{ (T^b)^3 \right\}$.
- Receiver design method: $MO\left\{ MT^b (s^b)^2 \right\} + 2MO\left\{ (s^b)^3 \right\}$.

The total complexity is the sum of above ones.

At present, we compare the two complexities by an example. For simplicity, we assume that $M = 4$, $T^b = 8$, $R^b = 4$ and $s^b = 2$. Hence, the total complexity of FCES approximately is 7522, while the total complexity of SRT-AS approximately is 7744. It can be seen that these complexities are in the same order of magnitude. This conclusion can be extended to other scenarios, so the complexity of SRT-AS is acceptable in this multi-user system.

4.2   Robustness Analysis

In this subsection, the robustness of SRT-AS is analyzed. When channel estimation error exists in the TDD mode, each channel can be expressed as [18]

$$\mathbf{H}_m^b = \mathbf{E}_m^b + \mathbf{\Delta}_m^b, \forall m \tag{16}$$

where $\mathbf{E}_m^b$ is the estimated channel, and $\mathbf{\Delta}_m^b$ is the additional error component.

It can be seen that the actual information of each error component is difficult to be acquired, so the statistical information of each component is employed to take place of the precise one. In the circumstances, for the sake of simplicity, we assume that $\Delta_m^b \sim \mathcal{CN}(0, (d_m^b)^{-\alpha_m} \sigma_e^2 \mathbf{I})$, where the value of σ_e^2 is the statistical information and denotes the estimation error level. In this way, when one operation in the SRT-AS with respect to the accurate estimation error components, each accurate error component should be replaced by the statistical average one with the information of σ_e^2 (the similar mathematical manipulations can be found in [18], here, we neglect the concrete process due to the limited space of this paper). It can be predicted that introducing these statistical information is achievable and improves the robustness of SRT-AS.

5   Simulation Results

The simulation results are illustrated in this section. Here, we assume that the coverage of this cell is $500m$ and the transmit power of BS is 46dBm [19]. In addition, for simplicity, we set that $M = 8$, $T^b = 8$, $R^b = 4$ and $s^b = 2$, meanwhile, we also set that $\tau_m^b = 0.5T, \forall m$. In each TTI, we assume that each d_m^b is an arbitrary value between $50m$ and $450m$, all $d_m^b, \forall m$ are mutual independent, and each path loss exponent is equal to 3.8 [19]. We get the final simulation results by averaging the ones over 20000 TTIs, therefore, our results can evaluate the effect of SRT-AS in this changeable system. In addition, the eavesdroppers are also utilize linear MMSE receivers, since they want to reliably eavesdrop signals and the operational capabilities and energy of them are limited.

In Fig. 2, we observe the effects of SRT-AS with different predetermined thresholds. It is already known that the value of threshold affects the combating eavesdropping process. From this figure, we can see that when the threshold is too high (i.e., $\eta_m^b = 0.1$ or $\eta_m^b = 0.05$), the potential eavesdroppers are not sufficiently involved, so the performances of these cases are lower. Contrarily, when the threshold is much reduced (i.e., $\eta_m^b = 0.005$ or $\eta_m^b = 0.001$), the secrecy

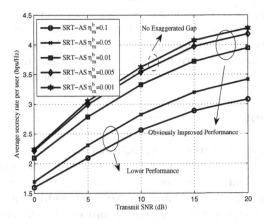

Fig. 2. Comparison of average secrecy rate with different thresholds and $\sigma_e^2 = 0$.

rates are evidently increased with efficient combating eavesdropping. However, the improvement of performance is not obvious when the threshold is reduced at a certain level, meanwhile, decreasing this threshold implies increasing computational complexity. Therefore, how to select a proper threshold is important and should will be researched in future.

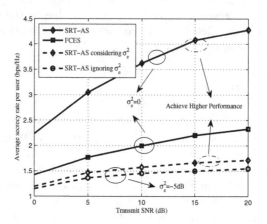

Fig. 3. Comparison of average secrecy rate with different schemes and values of σ_e^2.

In Fig. 3, we first compare the effects of SRT-AS and FCES without channel estimation error (here, $\eta_m^b = 0.001$). In order to guarantee fairness, the secrecy rates with different schemes are uniformly calculated by (3)-(5). It can be seen that the performance of SRT-AS is much better than that of FCES since the SRT-AS considers the users' actual access statuses in this system and adapts this practical multi-user scenario. In addition, if channel estimation error is terrible (i.e., $\sigma_e^2 = -5$dB), we compare the SRT-AS considering this error (i.e., SRT-AS considering σ_e^2, referred to Subsect. 4.2) with the SRT-AS ignoring this error (i.e., SRT-AS ignoring σ_e^2). We can find that the serious channel estimation error can evidently affect the average secrecy rate. Nevertheless, if we introduce the statistical information of this error into the SRT-AS, robustness can be improved. Synthesizing the above results, the SRT-AS is feasible in this multi-user system.

6   Conclusions

In this paper, we have proposed a novel adaptive transmitter and receiver design scheme for improving the physical layer security in the multi-user system, called SRT-AS. In this scheme, the secrecy rate of each user can be improved by the mitigating inter-user interference and combating eavesdropping. It can be noted that the SRT-AS does not need any iterative process. Furthermore, performance analysis and simulation results indicate that the SRT-AS is feasible in the multi-user system where being served users and idle users may coexist.

References

1. 3GPP (v 0.0.6).: Overview of 3GPP Release 13 (2014)
2. Zhu, H.J., Du, S.G., Gao, Z.Y., Dong, M.X., Cao, Z.F.: A probabilistic misbehavior detection scheme toward efficient trust establishment in delay-tolerant networks. IEEE Trans. Parallel Distrib. Syst. **25**(1), 22–32 (2014)
3. Xu, Q.C., Su, Z., Han, B., Fang, D.F., Xu, Z.J., Gan, X.Y.: Analytical model with a novel selfishness division of mobile nodes to participate cooperation. Peer-to-Peer Netw. Appl. (2015). doi:10.1007/s12083-015-0330-6
4. Su, Z., Xu, Q.C., Zhu, H.J., Wang, Y.: A novel design for content delivery over software defined mobile social networks. IEEE Netw. **29**(4) (2015)
5. Calabuig, J., Monserrat, J.F., Gomez-Barquero, D.: 5th generation mobile networks: a new opportunity for the convergence of mobile broadband and broadcast services. IEEE Commun. Mag. **53**(2), 198–205 (2015)
6. Mukherjee, A., Fakoorian, S.A.A., Huang, J., Swindlehurst, A.L.: Principles of physical layer security in multiuser wireless networks: a survey. IEEE Commun. Surv. Tutorials **16**(3), 1550–1573 (2014)
7. Barenghi, A., Breveglieri, L., Koren, I., Naccache, D.: Fault injection attacks on cryptographic devices: theory, practice, and countermeasures. proc. ieee. **100**(11), 3056–3076 (2012)
8. Yang, N., Wang, L., Geraci, G., Elkashlan, M., Yuan, J., Renzo, M.D.: Safeguarding 5G wireless communication networks using physical layer security. IEEE Commun. Mag. **53**(4), 20–27 (2015)
9. Zhang, J., Yuen, C., Wen, C.K., Jin, S., Gao, X.: Ergodic secrecy sum-rate for multiuser downlink transmission via regularized channel inversion: large system analysis. IEEE Commun. Lett. **18**(9), 1627–1630 (2014)
10. Fakoorian, S.A.A., Swindlehurst, A.L.: On the optimality of linear precoding for secrecy in the MIMO broadcast channel. IEEE J. Sel. Areas Commun. **31**(9), 1701–1713 (2013)
11. Geraci, G., Couillet, R., Yuan, J., Debbah, M., Collings, I.B.: Large system analysis of linear precoding in MISO broadcast channels with confidential messages. IEEE J. Sel. Areas Commun. **31**(9), 1660–1671 (2013)
12. Geraci, G., Egan, M., Yuan, J., Razi, A., Collings, I.B.: Secrecy sumrates for multi-user MIMO regularized channel inversion precoding. IEEE Trans. Commun. **60**(11), 3472–3482 (2012)
13. Liu, R., Liu, T., Poor, H.V., Shamai, S.: Multiple-input multiple-output Gaussian broadcast channels with confidential messages. IEEE Trans. Inf. Theory **56**(9), 4215–4227 (2010)
14. Jungnickel, V., Manolakis, K., Zirwas, W., et al.: The role of small cells, coordinated multipoint, and massive MIMO in 5G. IEEE Commun. Mag. **52**(5), 44–51 (2014)
15. Ho, W.W.L., Quek, T.Q.S., Sun, S., Heath, R.W.: Decentralized precoding for multicell MIMO downlink. IEEE Trans. Wirel. Commun. **10**(6), 1798–1809 (2011)
16. Lutkepohl, H.: Handbook of Matrixes. Wiley, Chichester (1997)
17. Golub, G.H., Loan, C.F.V.: Matrix Computations, 3rd edn. The John Hopkins University Press, Baltimore (1996)
18. Li, Q., Yang, Y., Ma, W.K., Lin, M., Ge, J.H., Lin, J.R.: Robust cooperative beamforming and artificial noise design for physical-layer secrecy in AF multiantenna multi-relay networks. IEEE Trans. Signal Process. **63**(1), 206–220 (2015)
19. 3GPP TS 36.104 (v11.3.0).: Evolved universal terrestrial radio access (E-UTRA); Base station (BS) radio transmission and reception. Release 11 (2012)

Joint Secure Beamforming and User Selection for Multi-user MISO Systems with Confidential Messages

Dongyang Xu[1,2], Pinyi Ren[1,2]($\boxtimes$), Qinghe Du[1,2], and Li Sun[1,2]

[1] Department of Information and Communications Engineering,
Xi'an Jiaotong University, Xi'an 710049, China
xudongyang@stu.xjtu.edu.cn
[2] School of Electronic and Information Engineering,
Xi'an Jiaotong University, Xi'an 710049, China
{pyren,duqinghe,lisun}@mail.xjtu.edu.cn

Abstract. In this paper, we propose a joint secure beamforming and user selection (J-SBS) scheme to improve the secrecy sum rate in multi-user multiple-input-single-output (MISO) broadcast channels with confidential messages (BCC). The user selection mechanism can bring about multi-user diversity which may be also exploited by eavesdroppers in multi-user MISO sysytem. We show how the system secrecy sum rate under the semi-orthogonal user selection (SUS) algorithm will be limited if users collude with each other. To solve this problem, based on the prediction that selected users have mutual orthogonal beamformers, we characterize a new expression of the secrecy rate. By optimizing the secrecy rate we then derive a corresponding suboptimal secrecy beamformer for each user to reduce the interference and information leakage. Moreover, we apply SUS to select suitable beamformers matching with the prediction. Simulation results show the effectiveness of our proposed method.

Keywords: Multi-user · MISO · broadcast channel · Secrecy beamforming · User selection · Physical layer security · Secrecy rate

1 Introduction

Security is a vital issue due to the broadcast nature of wireless transmissions. The communication over the wireless channel is often vulnerable to signal interception or eavesdropping by unauthorized receivers. Traditionally, security has been achieved through cryptographic encryption and decryption methods and relies on the computational hardness of decrypting the message when the secret

The research work reported in this paper was supported by the National Natural Science Foundation of China (NSFC) under Grant No. 61431011.

© Springer International Publishing Switzerland 2015
K. Xu and J. Zhu (Eds.): WASA 2015, LNCS 9204, pp. 644–653, 2015.
DOI: 10.1007/978-3-319-21837-3_63

key is not available, which may be impossible in the future. Unlike the conventional cryptographic methods, physical layer techniques can better secure the communication channel by exploiting the fast channel variations and the broadcast nature of the wireless channel.

Much work on the physical security has studied the secrecy capacity from the view of information theory [1–3]. In [1], a three-terminal network having a transceiver pair and a extra eavesdropper, known as the wiretap channel, was considered. It was shown in [2,3] that a non-zero secrecy capacity can be achieved for the source-destination pair if the desire receiver has better channel conditions than the eavesdropper(s). However, these approaches were based on the perfect channel knowledge and undesirable coding complexity, which may not be possible. Departing from the above research efforts, many coding and signal processing techniques have been developed to support and to further enhance security especially in some specific networks [4,5]. It was shown in [6] that, by exploiting the temporal variations of the channel, the system can achieve a positive secrecy rate even when the average channel to the destination is of lower quality than that to the eavesdropper.

An extension from the wiretap channel model to the multiuser channel model with multiple intended users and an eavesdropper is considered in [7,8]. However, the secrecy capacity region for multiuser networks where any number of intended users are potentially eavesdropping remains an open problem. Moreover, [9] studies the secrecy sum-rate for multiuser multiple-input-multiple-output (MIMO) system with regularized channel inversion (RCI) precoding by considering a worst-case scene where malicious users collude with each other and act as an eavesdropper to decode a certain user for obtaining its confidential message. The author obtains a deterministic approximation for the achievable secrecy sum-rate with a fixed ratio of the user number to the transmit antenna number in the large-system regime. However, the method is based on the assumption that the system with a large number of antennas communicates with users simultaneously without user selection, which may be impossible in practical systems with limited transmit antenna number and the necessary user selection and scheduling mechanism for some business requirements such as the user fairness.

Meanwhile, the user selection mechanism for the multi-user system has been widely studied in the past years. In MIMO systems with M transmit antennas and $K \geq M$ single antenna users, the full multiplexing gain M can be achieved. Specifically, it was shown that when channel state information at the transmitter (CSIT) is known ideally, the system capacity grows like $M \log \log K$ in a larger user regime $K \gg M$ due to multiuser diversity [10]. The scheme based on Zero-forcing beamforming (ZFBF) or zero-forcing dirty-paper coding (ZF-DPC) has been proposed to reach this growth rate [11] with low complexity. However, the multi-user diversity may also be exploited by malicious users which jointly act as an eavesdropper and decode the confidential messages for intended users. Worst of all, for an intended user, all the other users always tend to collude with each other for obtaining its message, whether the user selection is performed or not at the transmitter. Thus, the conventional user selection such as SUS will be limited in the respect of system secrecy sum rate.

In this paper, we consider the downlink multi-user MISO system with a transmitter performing user selection and multiple single-antenna users each of which potentially eavesdrops on each other. Owing to the channel broadcast nature, the confidential message for a intended user can be eavesdropped by all the surrounding users, although the transmitter merely selects a few users from all users. Worst of all, for the intended user, we consider all the other users can cooperate and jointly decode its confidential message in a genie-aided way. Then, we show that the conventional ZFBF-SUS scheme can not increase the secrecy sum rate as the signal to noise ratio (SNR) increases if the selected user number is smaller than the total user number. To solve this problem, we formulate an optimization problem for each user by assuming that other selected users streams are transmitted along vectors isotropically distributed in the null space of the conjugate transpose its beamformer. Then, we solve the optimization problem by applying the *generalized singular value decomposition* (GSVD) method and obtain a corresponding suboptimal beamformer for each user. Moreover, we construct the selected user group with mutual orthogonal beamformers by applying the SUS method to beamformers. Simulation results show that our proposed scheme can efficiently improve the secrecy sum rate as compared to ZFBF-SUS scheme.

The remainder of this paper is organized as follows: In Sect. 2, we present the system model overview. Section 3 introduces the existing ZFBF-SUS algorithm. In Sect. 4, a joint secure beamforming and user selection scheme is proposed. Simulation results are presented in Sect. 5. Finally, we conclude our work in Sect. 6.

Notation: Boldface is used for matrixes $\mathbf{A}$ and vectors $\mathbf{a}$. $\mathbf{A}^H$ denotes the conjugate transpose of the matrix $\mathbf{A}$. $\otimes$ is Kronecker matrix product and $\mathrm{E}\{\cdot\}$ is the expectation operator. $|\mathcal{A}|$ denotes the size of a set $\mathcal{A}$.

2   System Model

We consider a downlink multi-user MISO BCC system with a transmitter having M antennas and K users each of which has single antenna, as is shown in Fig. 1. Let $\Psi \triangleq \{1, \ldots, K\}$ and Ω denote the set of all the users in the system and the set of selected users respectively. In this model, the transmitter transmits S independent confidential messages to S users over the block Rayleigh fading channel, where S satisfies $S = |\Omega|, \Omega \in \Psi \triangleq \{1, \ldots, K\}$. S is predetermined by the transmitter in the previous slot or block according to a certain principle which is not our focus in this paper. The transmitted signal is $\mathbf{x} = [x_{i \in \Omega}]^T, x_i \sim \mathcal{CN}(0, 1)$. Then the received signal can be given by

$$\mathbf{y} = \mathbf{HTx} + \mathbf{n} \tag{1}$$

where $\mathbf{H}$ is the $S \times M$ channel matrix between the BS and selected users. The received signal at k-th user is obtained as

$$y_k = \mathbf{h}_k \mathbf{t}_k x_k + \mathbf{h}_k \sum_{i \neq k, i \in \Omega} \mathbf{t}_i x_i + n_k \tag{2}$$

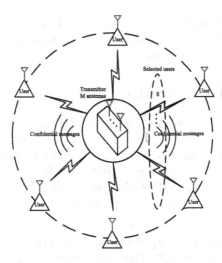

Fig. 1. Multi-user MISO broadcast channels with BCC between the transmitter and multiple users, each of which has single antenna and potentially act as a eavesdropper collusive with other users.

where $\mathbf{h}_k \in C^{1 \times M}$ is complex channel vector of the user k with each element assumed to be identically and independently distributed as zero-mean, circularly symmetric complex Gaussian (ZMCSCG) random variable with unit variance, and $n_k \sim \mathcal{CN}\left(0, \sigma^2\right)$ is the additive white complex-Gaussian noise variable. We assume perfect CSIs are known at the transmitter. The basic idea of zero-forcing (ZF) is to nullify inter-user interference. The precoding matrix $\mathbf{T}$ is designed such that

$$\mathbf{T} = \tilde{\mathbf{T}}\mathrm{diag}\left(\mathbf{P}\right) = \left[\tilde{\mathbf{t}}_{i\in\Omega}\right]\mathrm{diag}\left(\mathbf{P}\right) \tag{3}$$

where $\tilde{\mathbf{t}}_{i\in\Omega}$ is the beamforming vector for each user with unit norm and the power allocation vector $\mathbf{P}$ satisfies $\mathbf{P} = [p_{i\in\Omega}]$. We adopt the equal power distribution across different users, such as $p_i = \sqrt{P/S}, i \in \Omega$.

In our model, we assume a worst-case scenario where for each intended receiver k the remaining $K - 1$ users can cooperate to jointly eavesdrop on the confidential message x_k. There are always $K - 1$ users which can be seen as a equivalent eavesdropper, denoted by k^*, with $K - 1$ receive antennas for each user k to decode the message x_k, although the transmitter in fact just select S users to perform data transmission at in one block fading channel realization. Thus the signals observed by the user k^* can be given by

$$\mathbf{y}_{k^*} = \mathbf{H}_{k^*}\mathbf{t}_k x_k + \mathbf{H}_{k^*}\sum_{\substack{i \neq k}}^{K}\mathbf{t}_i x_i + \mathbf{n}_{k^*} \tag{4}$$

where the channel matrix $\mathbf{H}_{k^*}$ is the channel of the equivalent eavesdropper k^* and $\mathbf{n}_{k^*}$ is the additive white complex-Gaussian noise vector each element of which has zero-mean and variance σ^2.

3   Existing ZFBF-SUS Algorithm

To exploit the multi-user diversity sufficiently, [12] adopts a zero-forcing beamforming (ZFBF) strategy with semi-orthogonal user selection (SUS) where the system can achieve the same asymptotic sum capacity as that dirty paper coding (DPC), as the number of users goes to infinity. By using SUS algorithm, the transmitter selects user group Ω with semiorthogonal channels and relatively large multi-user gain. For convenience, we review the SUS algorithm as follows:

(1) Initialization: $\mathcal{X}_1 = \{1, \cdots, K\}$, $S_0 = \phi$, $i = 1$;
(2) The transmitter calculates $\mathbf{r}_k$, which is the component of the beamforming vector $\mathbf{h}_k$ of each user k in $\mathcal{X}_i$. The component is orthogonal to the subspace spanned by $\{\mathbf{r}_1, \ldots, \mathbf{r}_{i-1}\}$.

$$\mathbf{r}_k = \mathbf{h}_k - \sum_{j=1}^{i-1} \frac{\mathbf{h}_k \mathbf{r}_j^H}{\|\mathbf{r}_j\|^2} \mathbf{r}_j \tag{5}$$

if $i = 1$, $\mathbf{r}_k = \mathbf{h}_k$
(3) In this step, we update the user group as follows:

$$\pi(i) = \arg \max_{k \in \mathcal{X}_i} \|\mathbf{r}_k\|$$
$$S_0 \leftarrow S_0 \cup \{\pi(i)\}, \mathbf{h}_i = \mathbf{h}_{\pi(i)}, \mathbf{r}_i = \mathbf{r}_{\pi(i)} \tag{6}$$

(4) If $|S_0| \leq S$, we calculate $\mathcal{X}_{i+1}$ and go to step (2), otherwise, the algorithm is finished.

$$\mathcal{X}_{i+1} = \left\{ k \in \mathcal{X}_i, k \neq \pi(i), \frac{\mathbf{h}_k \mathbf{r}_i^H}{\|\mathbf{h}_k\| \|\mathbf{r}_i\|} < \alpha \right\}, i = i + 1 \tag{7}$$

where α is a positive constant.

When the user selection has been done, for selected user group Ω, each beamforming column vector of the precoding matrix $\tilde{\mathbf{T}}$ thus can be expressed as

$$\tilde{\mathbf{t}}_i = \frac{\mathbf{w}_i}{\sqrt{\text{trace}(\mathbf{w}_i^H \mathbf{w}_i)}} \tag{8}$$

where $\mathbf{w}_i$ satisfies $[\mathbf{w}_{i \in \Omega}] = \mathbf{H}^H (\mathbf{H}\mathbf{H}^H)^{-1}$.

However, when considering the scene where the eavesdropper k^* composed of multiple collusive users decodes the confidential message x_k, the system secrecy sum rate will be limited even reduced. Although adopting ZFBF to reduce the confidential message obtained by the other selected users for an intended collusive users, the transmitter does not adopt any technique to suppress the the confidential message leakage caused by the unselected collusive users in the MISO BCC system.

4 Proposed J-SBS Scheme

In this section, we will interpret our proposed scheme in detail.

4.1 Achievable Secrecy Sum-Rate

As is shown in [9], if the transmitter uses independent codebooks for each user, where each codebook is a code for the scalar wiretap channel, an achievable secrecy sum rate with the transmitter sending S independent confidential messages to S users simultaneously, can be given by

$$R_s = \sum_{k=1}^{S} R_{s,k} \tag{9}$$

$$= \sum_{k=1}^{S} [\log_2 (1 + \text{SINR}_k) - \log_2 (1 + \text{SINR}_{k^*})]^+ \tag{10}$$

where SINR_k and SINR_{k^*} respectively denote the signal to interference plus noise ratios for message x_k at the user k and the eavesdropper k^*, which are given by

$$\text{SINR}_k = \frac{|\mathbf{h}_k \mathbf{t}_k|^2}{1 + \sum_{i \in \Omega, i \neq k} |\mathbf{h}_k \mathbf{t}_i|^2} \tag{11}$$

and

$$\text{SINR}_{k^*} = \|\mathbf{H}_{k^*} \mathbf{t}_k\|^2 \tag{12}$$

4.2 Secrecy Precoding Design

In this subsection, we derive an corresponding secrecy beamformer for each selected user in the multi-user MISO downlink system. A set of users will be selected by adopting SUS algorithm contributing to the consequent precoding design at the transmitter. By exploiting the orthogonality between the selected beamformers, we can formulate an optimization problem about the secrecy rate of each user k, with $k \in \Psi$ and simplify the problem by assuming that other selected users streams are transmitted along vectors isotropically distributed in the null space of $\tilde{\mathbf{t}}_i^H$. Then we obtain a closed-form solution for the optimization problem.

Firstly, When considering the user k accompanied with the eavesdropper k^*, the achievable secrecy rate for the user k can be given by

$$R_{s,k} = \left[\max_{\tilde{\mathbf{t}}_k : \|\tilde{\mathbf{t}}_k\|^2 = 1} \log_2 \left(\frac{1 + \frac{\frac{P}{\sigma^2 S} \mathbf{h}_k \tilde{\mathbf{t}}_k \tilde{\mathbf{t}}_k^H \mathbf{h}_k^H}{1 + \frac{P}{\sigma^2 S} \mathbf{h}_k \sum_{i \in \Omega, i \neq k} \tilde{\mathbf{t}}_i \tilde{\mathbf{t}}_i^H \mathbf{h}_k^H}}{1 + \frac{P}{\sigma^2 S} \tilde{\mathbf{t}}_k^H \mathbf{H}_{k^*}^H \mathbf{H}_{k^*} \tilde{\mathbf{t}}_k} \right) \right]^+, k \in \Psi \tag{13}$$

From the above, the optimal beamforming $\tilde{\mathbf{t}}_k$ can be found by maximizing the ratio inside the logarithm. Obviously, we need to obtain the covariance matrix of the interference. However, since the transmit precoders employed for the selected users are unknown, the user employs an expected covariance matrix of the interference.

Lemma 1. *For a given user k with channel $\mathbf{h}_k$, the expected covariance matrix of the interference whose streams are distributed in the null space of $\tilde{\mathbf{t}}_k^H$ can be computed as*

$$E\left[\mathbf{h}_k \sum_{i \in \Omega, i \neq k} \tilde{\mathbf{t}}_i \tilde{\mathbf{t}}_i^H \mathbf{h}_k^H\right] = \frac{S-1}{M-1} \mathbf{h}_k \mathbf{T}_\perp \mathbf{h}_k^H \tag{14}$$

where $\mathbf{T}_\perp$ satisfies $\mathbf{T}_\perp = \mathbf{I}_M - \tilde{\mathbf{t}}_k \tilde{\mathbf{t}}_k^H$. Thus, we obtain a lower bound on the SINR for the user k

$$\text{SINR}_k^{\text{Lower}} = \frac{\frac{P}{\sigma^2 S} \mathbf{h}_k \tilde{\mathbf{t}}_k \tilde{\mathbf{t}}_k^H \mathbf{h}_k^H}{1 + \frac{P}{\sigma^2 S} \frac{S-1}{M-1} \mathbf{h}_k \left(\mathbf{I}_M - \tilde{\mathbf{t}}_k \tilde{\mathbf{t}}_k^H\right) \mathbf{h}_k^H} \tag{15}$$

Secondly, according to the above principle, the secrecy rate for each user with user selection can be updated as

$$R_{s,k} = \left[\max_{\tilde{\mathbf{t}}_k : \|\tilde{\mathbf{t}}_k\|^2 = 1} \log_2 \left(\frac{1 + \frac{\frac{P}{\sigma^2 S} \mathbf{h}_k \tilde{\mathbf{t}}_k \tilde{\mathbf{t}}_k^H \mathbf{h}_k^H}{1 + \frac{P}{\sigma^2 S} \frac{S-1}{M-1} \mathbf{h}_k (\mathbf{I}_M - \tilde{\mathbf{t}}_k \tilde{\mathbf{t}}_k^H) \mathbf{h}_k^H}}{1 + \frac{P}{\sigma^2 S} \tilde{\mathbf{t}}_k^H \mathbf{H}_{k*}^H \mathbf{H}_{k*} \tilde{\mathbf{t}}_k}\right)\right]^+ \tag{16}$$

$$= \left[\max_{\tilde{\mathbf{t}}_k : \|\tilde{\mathbf{t}}_k\|^2 = 1} \log_2 \left(\frac{\tilde{\mathbf{t}}_k^H \mathbf{A} \tilde{\mathbf{t}}_k}{\tilde{\mathbf{t}}_k^H \mathbf{B} \tilde{\mathbf{t}}_k}\right)\right]^+, k \in \Psi \tag{17}$$

where

$$\mathbf{A} = \left(1 + \frac{P}{\sigma^2 S} \frac{S-1}{M-1} \mathbf{h}_k \mathbf{h}_k^H\right) \otimes \mathbf{I}_M + \frac{P}{\sigma^2 S} \frac{M-S}{M-1} \mathbf{h}_k^H \mathbf{h}_k \tag{18}$$

and

$$\mathbf{B} = \left(\left(1 + \frac{P}{\sigma^2 S} \frac{S-1}{M-1} \mathbf{h}_k \mathbf{h}_k^H\right) \otimes \mathbf{I}_M - \frac{P}{\sigma^2 S} \frac{S-1}{M-1} \mathbf{h}_k^H \mathbf{h}_k\right) \left(\mathbf{I}_M + \frac{P}{\sigma^2 S} \mathbf{H}_{k*}^H \mathbf{H}_{k*}\right) \tag{19}$$

To solve the above optimization, we maximize the ratio inside the logarithm by applying the GSVD method [13].

Theorem 1. *Given that the selected users in group Ω has mutually orthogonal beamformers, the maximum secrecy rate achievable for the user k belonging to Ω can be given by*

$$R_{s,k} = \left[\log_2 \lambda_{\max}\left(\mathbf{A}, \mathbf{B}\right)\right]^+, k \in \Omega \tag{20}$$

where $\mathbf{A}$ and $\mathbf{B}$ can be obtained from equation (18) and equation (19), respectively. $\lambda_{\max}(\mathbf{A}, \mathbf{B})$ is the maximum generalized eigenvalue of the matrix pair $(\mathbf{A}, \mathbf{B})$. The corresponding optimal precoding matrix is given by

$$\mathbf{T} = \left[\tilde{\mathbf{t}}_{k \in \Omega}^{\Delta}\right] \operatorname{diag}(\mathbf{P}), \tilde{\mathbf{t}}_k^{\Delta} = \psi_{\max}(\mathbf{A}, \mathbf{B}), k \in \Omega \tag{21}$$

where $\psi_{\max}(\mathbf{A}, \mathbf{B})$ is the generalized eigenvector corresponding to the maximum generalized eigenvalue $\lambda_{\max}(\mathbf{A}, \mathbf{B})$.

The k-th beamforming vectors obtained in the above is suboptimal for the problem (13). When obtaining suboptimal beamforming vectors for all users, the transmitter performs SUS algorithm to constitute a selected user group Ω^*, with $|\Omega^*| = S^* \leq S$. Thus for the user k, the true secrecy rate using beamforming vector $\tilde{\mathbf{t}}_k^{\Delta}$ can be given by

$$R_{s,k}^{\mathrm{True}} = \left[\log_2\left(\frac{1 + \frac{\frac{P}{\sigma^2 S} \mathbf{h}_k \tilde{\mathbf{t}}_k^{\Delta} (\tilde{\mathbf{t}}_k^{\Delta})^H \mathbf{h}_k^H}{1 + \frac{P}{\sigma^2 S} \mathbf{h}_k \sum_{i \in \Omega, i \neq k} \tilde{\mathbf{t}}_i^{\Delta} (\tilde{\mathbf{t}}_i^{\Delta})^H \mathbf{h}_k^H}}{1 + \frac{P}{\sigma^2 S} (\tilde{\mathbf{t}}_k^{\Delta})^H \mathbf{H}_{k^*}^H \mathbf{H}_{k^*} \tilde{\mathbf{t}}_k^{\Delta}}\right)\right]^+, k \in \Omega^* \tag{22}$$

5 Simulation Results

In this section, we compare the numerical results of the proposed scheme J-SBS with the conventional ZF-SUS scheme in respect of the secrecy sum rate. All simulation results are obtained by averaging over 5000 independent quasi-static flat Rayleigh fading channel realizations. We consider that the system has a transmitter equipped with $M = 10, 20$ antennas and different total user number K, where each user has single antenna in a certain region. We set SNR $= P/\sigma^2$ and the true secrecy sum rate $R_s = \sum_{i \in \Omega^*} R_{s,i}^{\mathrm{True}}$.

In Fig. 2, we compare the secrecy sum rate of the proposed J-SBS scheme to that of the ZFBF-SUS scheme versus K under different total user number K but with fixed transmit antenna number, selected user number and SNR such as $M = 10$, $S = 4$, SNR $= 10$ dB. We observe that when we increase K, the secrecy sum rate of J-SBS will outperform that of the ZFBF-SUS algorithm. In particular, when $K = 10$, the former is 8 bit/s/Hz larger than the latter in the respect of secrecy sum rate. That is because these suboptimal beamformers of selected users can better tackle with the multiuser diversity and the confidential message security jointly. Intuitively, we can better direct the beams of selected users into a suitable region achieving a relatively high system sum rate, while suppressing the confidential message leakage to the unselected collusive users to a certain extent. With a relatively small K such as $S \leq K \leq 6$, the secrecy sum rate will increase with K. However, if K increases, the tradeoff between the system sum rate and the security of the confidential messages will be difficult. It is shown that when K increases to a relatively large value, the secrecy sum rate of the J-SBS and ZFBF-SUS algorithm will be close to zero. That is due

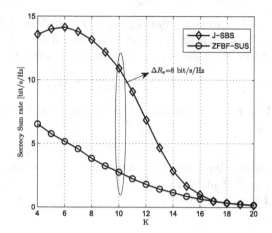

Fig. 2. Secrecy sum rate versus K with $M = 10$, $S = 4$ and SNR = 10 dB.

to the fact that when the number of different users is increasing, the number of different channel directions will be increasing, thus disturbing the beam design.

Figure 3 shows that the secrecy sun rate versus SNR under different selected user number such as $S = 2, 3, 4, 5, 10$ with $K = 10$, $M = 20$. It is shown that our proposed scheme J-SBS outperforms the ZFBF-SUS in the respect of the secrecy sun rate under all the above system configurations. That is because our proposed scheme can better tackle with the tradeoff between multi-user diversity and the secrecy sum rate, while the ZFBF-SUS scheme usually only pay attention to the multi-user diversity. When increasing the selected user number, the system has increased secrecy sun rate. That is because the more alternative users there are in the system, the more users with semi-orthogonal beamformer there will be, which make the proposed beamformers more accurate. In particular, when

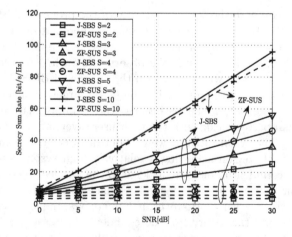

Fig. 3. Secrecy sum rate versus SNR under different selected user number S.

$S = K$, the limit of secrecy sum rate of ZFBF-SUS scheme will be broken. That is due to the fact that if the transmitter performs ZFBF for all the users, the confidential leakage will be well reduced thus improving the secrecy sum rate.

6 Conclusions

We have proposed a joint secure beamforming and user selection (J-SBS) scheme for multi-user MISO system. In this scheme, the transmitter performs user selection and beamforming for multiple single-antenna users each of which potentially eavesdrops on each other. Owing to the uncertainty of the user selection, for the intended user, the transmitter assumes that other selected users streams are transmitted along vectors isotropically distributed in the null space of the conjugate transpose of its beamformer. To keep the accuracy of each beamformer, SUS is performed at the transmitter. The numerical results verify the efficiency of the proposed scheme with respect to ZFBF-SUS scheme in the respect of the secrecy sum rate under different K and selected user number S.

References

1. Wyner, A.D.: The wire-tap channel. Bell. Syst. Tech. J. **54**(8), 1334–1387 (1975)
2. Csiszar, I., Korner, J.: Broadcast channels with confidential messages. IEEE Trans. Inf. Theory **24**(3), 339–348 (1978)
3. Bloch, M., Barros, J., Rodrigues, M., McLaughlin, M.: Wireless information-theoretic security. IEEE Trans. Inf. Theory **54**(6), 2515–2534 (2008)
4. Xu, Q., Su, Z., Han, B., Fang, D., Xu, Z., Gan, X.: Analytical model with a novel selfishness division of mobile nodes to participate cooperation. Peer-to-Peer Netw. Appl. (2015). doi:10.1007/s12083-015-0330-6
5. Su, Z., Xu, Q., Zhu, H., Wang, Y.: A novel design for content delivery over software defined mobile social networks. IEEE Network **29**(4) (2015)
6. Liang, Y., Poor, H.V., Shamai, S.: Secure communication over fading channels. IEEE Trans. Inf. Theory **54**(6), 2470–2492 (2008)
7. Ekrem, E., Ulukus, S.: The secrecy capacity region of the Gaussian MIMO multi-receiver wiretap channel. IEEE Trans. Inf. Theory **57**(4), 2083–2114 (2011)
8. Liu, R., Liu, T., Poor, H.V., Shamai, S.: Multiple-input multiple-output Gaussian broadcast channels with confidential messages. IEEE Trans. Inf. Theory **56**(9), 4215–4227 (2010)
9. Geraci, G., Egan, M., Yuan, J., Razi, A., Collings, I.B.: Secrecy sum-rates for multi-user MIMO regularized channel inversion precoding. IEEE Trans. Commun. **60**(11), 3472–3482 (2012)
10. Viswanath, P., Tse, D.N.C., Laroia, R.: Opportunistic beamforming using dumb antennas. IEEE Trans. Inf. Theory **48**(6), 1277–1294 (2002)
11. Hochwald, B.M., Peel, C.B., Swindlehurst, A.L.: A vector-perturbation technique for near-capacity multiantenna multiuser communication - Part II: Perturbation. IEEE Trans. Commun. **53**(3), 537–544 (2005)
12. Yoo, T., Goldsmith, A.: On the optimality of multiantenna broadcast scheduling using zero-forcing beamforming. IEEE J. Sel. Areas Commun. **24**(3), 528–541 (2006)
13. Paige, C., Saunders, M.A.: Towards a generalized singular value decomposition. SIAM J. Numer. Anal. **18**(3), 398–405 (1981)

Network Reachability Analysis on Temporally Varying Interaction Networks

Zhonghu Xu$^{(\boxtimes)}$ and Kai Xing

School of Computer Science, University of Science and Technology of China,
Hefei 230027, China
xzhh@mail.ustc.edu.cn, kxing@ustc.edu.cn

Abstract. Tremendous effort has been made in understanding the network connectivity and reachability in the spacial domain in the past decades. However, few of them focuses on time-varying the network connectivity and reachability problem in the time domain, which nevertheless exists in the most popular interactive networks, e.g., interactive forums, websites, tweeter-like online social applications, and etc. In this paper, we formulate the reachability problem in such interactive networks, and provide a novel way of quantitatively analyzing the reachability problem via the reverse chronological order. Based on real data, we further demonstrate the analytical power of our theoretical design and show that such reachability problem can be further modeled in a random digraph and a Markov process where time intervals obey exponential distribution $\mathbb{D}$ with the appearance of interaction edges following a Poisson process. In the extensive experiment study, we collect all the interaction behaviors such as reply and forward in recent 10 years from the largest forums in China (specifically, Tianya) with more than 3 million of daily active users. The experiment results show that there is a good match between the theoretical results and the real data.

Keywords: Reachability · Social network · Temporally varying interaction network

1 Introduction

The Internet has become one of the most important elements in our daily lives. There are plenty of interactive applications available for billions of users that can provide different kinds of interactions among the users. These user interactions may form an intermittently connected network for information propagation. In such networks, e.g., interactive forum, website, and tweeter-like online social applications, user behavior generally exhibits temporally varying features due to the extensive temporal-spatial diversity and sparsity among user interactions (such as users' online/offline activities). It is easy to see that at any time and area, any pair of users in a temporally varying interaction network are not necessarily connected since there may not exist such a path between them. Usually

© Springer International Publishing Switzerland 2015
K. Xu and J. Zhu (Eds.): WASA 2015, LNCS 9204, pp. 654–663, 2015.
DOI: 10.1007/978-3-319-21837-3_64

each piece of information between them is transmitted intermittently at different discrete time series, and thus, form a path in a chronological order.

Although lots of effort has been made on understanding such interaction networks, e.g., social networks. However, few of them focuses on the temporally varying features and their impacts on the network connectivity and reachability in the time domain according to literature. According to [2], the temporally varying user interaction behavior may lead to significant changes of the network reachability. Hence, it is important to be able to solve the conflict between the limited understanding of the reachability of temporally varying interaction networks and the ever-increasing usage and popularity of such networks.

By observing the temporally varying features, and the diversity and sparsity of user interactions, we propose a novel theoretical framework and a series of tools for quantitatively modeling and analyzing the network reachability in temporally varying interaction networks. Specifically, we adopt a digraph model to describe the information flow in the temporally varying interaction network. Then we apply the reverse chronological order to reformulate the reachability problem in an equivalent state space. In our theoretical framework, we show that the newly formulated problem can be further fit into a random digraph model and a Markov process where time intervals obey an exponential distribution the appearance of interaction edges following a Poisson process.

Our main contributions can be summarized as follows:

– Different from traditional approaches that consider the network reachability in space domain, we propose a novel view on the network reachability in time domain. Our proposed approach provides a novel theoretical framework that includes a novel theoretical modeling method with a series of modeling tools to study the temporally varying interaction networks. In addition, we develop a new quantitative analysis method with a series of analysis tools such as reverse chronological order mapping to quantitatively analyze the network reachability in a given network.
– Both our theoretical analysis and experimental study well match each other. Moreover, we reveal that the time intervals between user interactions obey an exponential distribution with the appearance of interaction edges following a Poisson process.

2   Models, Assumptions and Problem Formulation

2.1   Network Model

Plenty of websites, forums, tweeter-like online social applications are available for billions of Internet users providing various information flows among their interactions. Such interactions within a site (abstracted for websites, forums, tweeter-like online applications, etc.) naturally form an interaction network. In such an interaction network, information usually successively propagates among a finite number of nodes with directions. Therefore, we model the interaction network as a directed graph $G = (V, E)$, where V denotes the user set of size n,

E denotes the edge set in which an arc $(u, v) \in E$ is a directed edge from u to v. Specifically, if a piece of information successively propagates from u to v at time t, there generates a directed edge (u, v, t) indicating the information flow direction.

Note that whether an edge (u, v, t) exists depends on the propagation behavior of u and v. And each user's behavior is independent and may follow certain pattern along time, location, user mood, etc. From the unitary view of the whole site in temporal and spacial domain, the appearance of the edges may follow a certain distribution. Given V, the digraph $G = (V, E)$ belongs to a finite space $\mathcal{G}$. Each element of the space is a subgraph of a complete digraph $\tilde{G}$ and it's generated by selecting each edge following a certain distribution.

By studying the interaction behaviors, e.g., reply, forward, etc., collected in 10 years from the largest forum in China, Tianya, with more than 3 million of daily active users, we find that this distribution could be approximated by a poisson distribution. By sorting the interaction behavior by time order and computing the time interval between each adjacent related behavior (e.g., reply, forward), we draw a scatter diagram of the probability density function of time intervals, as shown in Fig. 1. It is interesting to observe that this curve can be well fitted via exponential function with the goodness of fit 0.98, which is large enough to convince us that the time intervals of responses obeys exponential distribution.

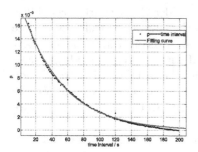

Fig. 1. The distribution of the time intervals of user interactions in Tianya

Besides, since each user's behavior is independent of each other, the time interval is memoryless, which further indicates that the appearance of interaction edges may be formulated as a Poisson process. In other words, the interaction graph model can be further formulated as a Markov process where time intervals obey exponential distribution $\mathbb{D}$ with and the appearance of interaction edges follows a Poisson process (According to Fig. 1, the user interaction intensity $\lambda = 0.0289$).

2.2   Problem Formulation

At the very beginning of information propagation in an interaction network, all the nodes are isolated in the digraph $G = (V, E)$, where $E = \varnothing$. At each time $t_i \in \mathbb{T}$, there may generate a directed edge labelled with t_i from $n(n - 1)/2$ node pairs, where $\mathbb{T}$ denotes a discrete time $t_1, t_2, \ldots$ during time T and the time intervals follows a certain distribution $\mathbb{D}$.

Therefore, we can further model the interaction network as a random digraph, with each edge (u, v, t) following a poisson distribution. Let s and d be vertices in G. If there is a directed path from s to d, $\{(s, a_1, t_0), (a_1, a_2, t_1), \ldots, (a_i, d, t_i)\}$ where $t_0 < t_1 < t_2 < \ldots < t_i$ and $t_0, t_1, \ldots t_i \in T$, we say that d is reachable from s. Once given information propagation behavior, we focus on the problem that how long will the network take in order to generate such a path from s to d. Specifically, we use the appearance of the largest transitive closure of G, the giant component to estimate the probability that a path exists between any pair of nodes in the network.

Specifically, we formulate the reachability problem as the reachability probability estimation problem in random digraph $G = (V, E, T)$ where each edge $e_1, e_2, \ldots \in E$ occurs at discrete time $t_1, t_2, \ldots \in T$ following Poisson distribution, and time intervals Δt of T follow $P(\Delta t) = \lambda e^{-\lambda(e)\Delta t}(sgn(\Delta t) + 1)/2$, where $\lambda(e)$ is the interaction intensity of an edge e.

In $G = (V, E, T)$, each edge $e_1, e_2, \ldots \in E$ is labeled with time $t_1, t_2 \ldots \in T$ respectively. Taking a snapshot at any time $t \in T$, $G_t = (V, E, T)$ is a sub-graph of $G = (V, E, T)$ with edge labeled with time less than t. Given a start time $t = 0$ and T, after time T the cardinal number of the edge set E can be estimated based on the distribution of the elements in space $\mathbb{T}$. After a time duration Δt, let $P(k|\Delta t)$ denote the probability on which there generate k edges. Then we have $P(card(E_{\Delta t=T}) - card(E_{\Delta t=0}) = k) = P(k|T)$ where $card(E_{\Delta t=0}) = 0$. Obviously k is non-decreasing as T increases.

When k is large enough to form a giant component in the network, there probably appears a path between an arbitrary pair of nodes in the network at a probability $P(k|T)$. Therefore, in this paper we mainly focus on the reachability probability $P(k|T)$ given the snapshot G_t of $G = (V, E, T)$ $(T = \infty)$ and study how $P(k|T)$ changes with T and n given the distribution D.

3   Network Reachability Analysis

In this section, we focus on the information reachability problem that an interaction network takes to generate a path between an arbitrary pair of nodes.

3.1   Reverse Chronological Order

Though there are already some results on reachability of random graphs and random digraphs, most of them fail to consider the problem in time domain, i.e., the time of appearance and the time order of the edges.

To solve this problem, we consider reachability in reverse chronological order, which is equivalent to the problem. Specifically, we apply reverse chronological order to reformulate the problem.

Lemma 1. *In random digragph G with time labels, if edges are randomly selected based on a Markov process* **MP** *in time duration T, it is equivalent to following the process* **MP** *to select the same edges in reverse chronological order.*

Proof. We suppose that time starts at 0. In condition $C1$ assuming there are k edges are selected in total during time T, $e_1, e_2, \ldots, e_k$ at time $0 < t_1 < t_2 < \ldots < t_k \leq T$. And in reverse chronological order we select edges $e_k, e_{k-1}, \ldots, e_1$ at time $T - t_k, T - t_{k-1}, ..., T - t_1$ in condition $\mathcal{C}2$. According to the assumption of the Markov process **MP**, we have that $card(E_{t=t'_2}) - card(E_{t=t'_1})$ and $card(E_{t=t'_4}) - card(E_{t=t'_3})$ $(0 < t'_1 < t'_2 < t'_3 < t'_4 < T)$ are independent and $P(card(E_{t=t'}) - card(E_{t=t'+\tau}) = k) = P(k|\tau)$ in $\mathcal{C}1$. In $\mathcal{C}2$ $card(E'_{t=t'_2}) - card(E'_{t=t'_1})$ and $card(E'_{t=t'_4}) - card(E'_{t=t'_3})$ $(0 < t'_1 < t'_2 < t'_3 < t'_4 < T)$ are independent as $card(E'_{t=T-t'_1}) - card(E'_{t=T-t'_2})$ and $card(E'_{t=T-t'_3}) - card(E'_{t=T-t'_4})$ $(0 < T - t'_4 < T - t'_3 < T - t'_2 < T - t'_1 < T)$ are independent. What's more, $P(card(E'_{t=t'}) - card(E'_{t=t'+\tau}) = k) = P(card(E_{t=T-(t'+\tau)}) - card(E_{t=T-t'}) = k) = P(k|\tau)$. By definition the behavior in $\mathcal{C}2$ follows the Markov process **MP** as well.

Corollary 1. *There is a one-to-one mapping relationship of the elements in $\mathcal{G}_T$ and $\tilde{\mathcal{G}}_T$.*

Corollary 2. *Let p_{G_T} denote the probability on which G_T is selected from the space $\mathcal{G}_T$, $p_{\tilde{G}_T}$ representing the probability on which $\tilde{G}_T$ is selected from the space $\tilde{\mathcal{G}}_T$, $p_{G_T} = p_{\tilde{G}_T}$.*

3.2   Reachability Analysis in the Interaction Network

According to our network model and problem formulation, we can see that the edges in G are considered randomly selected with the probability $p(n)$ following a poission distribution at discrete time in the time duration T, in which the interval of the interaction follows the exponential distribution $\mathbb{D}$. Given the random digraph space $\mathcal{G}$ and the discrete time space $\mathcal{T}$, we construct a new space based on Lemma 1.

$$\mathcal{G} = \{G = (V,E) | |V| = n, \forall e \in E, label(e) \in \{1, 2, ..., |E|\},$$
$$label(e_1) \neq label(e_2) \; \forall \; e_1, e_2 \in E, e_1 \neq e_2)\}$$
$$\mathcal{T} = \{(t_1, t_2, ..., t_k) | 0 < t_1 < t_2 < \; ... \; < t_k \leq T, \Delta t \sim \mathbb{D}\}$$
$$\mathcal{G}_T = \{G = (V, E, TS) | G = (V, E) \in \mathcal{G}, TS \in \mathcal{T}, |E| = |TS|,$$
$$for \; e_1, ..., e_{|E|} \in E \; and \; t_1, ..., t_{|TS|} \in TS, \; e_i \; is \; labeled \; with \; t_i\}$$

From $\mathcal{G}_t$, we construct $\tilde{\mathcal{G}}_T$ in reverse chronological order.

$$\tilde{\mathcal{G}}_T = \{G = (V, E, TS) | G = (V, E') \in \mathcal{G}, TS' \in \mathcal{T}, |E'| = |TS'|,$$
$$for \; e'_1, ..., e'_{|E'|} \in E' \; and \; t'_1, ..., t'_{|TS'|} \in TS' \; E = \{e_i | \; e_i = e'_{|E'|+1-i}\}$$
$$TS = \{t_i | t_i = t'_{|TS|+1-i}\}, 1 \leq i \leq |E'|$$
$$for \; e_1, ..., e_{|E|} \in E \; and \; t_1, ..., t_{|TS|} \in TS, \; e_i \; is \; labeled \; with \; t_i\}$$

Lemma 2. *$\forall a, b \in V, a \neq b$, b is reachable from a in G_T if and only if a is reachable from b in corresponding $\tilde{G}_T$*

Proof. According to the one-to-one mapping relationship between G_T and $\tilde{G}_T$, if there is a path in time order $(s, a_1), (s_1, a_2), ..., (a_k, d)$ in G_T, there must exist a path on which all the edges are selected in reverse chronological order in $\tilde{G}_T$. In the same way, reachability in $\tilde{G}_T$ can infers that in G_T as well.

According to Corollarys 1 and 2, we have $p_{G_T} = p_{\tilde{G}_T}$ and $\forall a, b \in V, a \neq b$, a is reachable to b in G_T if and only if a is reachable to b in corresponding $\tilde{G}_T$.

Then we can see the reachability problem in $\mathcal{G}_T$ is equivalent to the reachability problem in $\tilde{\mathcal{G}}_T$: When k becomes large enough to form a giant component in $\mathcal{G}_T$, there will be an exactly same giant component formed $\tilde{\mathcal{G}}_T$, and vice versa. Therefore we can compute $P(k|T)$ in $\tilde{\mathcal{G}}_T$ instead of computing $P(k|T)$ in $\mathcal{G}_T$.

Theorem 1. *In G_T, the expected number of distinct edges is*

$$E(|\mathcal{E}_T|) = \sum_{k=0}^{\infty} k \sum_{x=k}^{\infty} P(x|T) \frac{C_{n(n-1)}^k \sum_{\substack{a_1,\dots,a_k \geq 1 \\ \sum a_k = x}} \frac{x!}{a_1! a_2! \dots a_k!}}{(n(n-1))^x} \tag{1}$$

Proof. Note that the edge emerging behavior is a Markov process and their time intervals obeys distribution $\mathbb{D}$. According to Corollary 2, the reachability probability $P(k|T)$ in G_T is equivalent to the reachability probability $P(k|T)$ given the snapshot G_t of $\tilde{G}_T$. Therefore after time duration T, the number of distinct edges in the random digraph $\tilde{G}_T$ is

$$P(|\mathcal{E}_T| = k) = \sum_{x=k}^{\infty} P(x|T) \frac{C_{n(n-1)}^k \sum_{\substack{a_1,\dots,a_k \geq 1 \\ \sum a_k = x}} \frac{x!}{a_1! a_2! \dots a_k!}}{(n(n-1))^x} \tag{2}$$

According to [1], it can be further given by $E(|\mathcal{E}_T|) = \sum_{k=0}^{\infty} k P(|\mathcal{E}_T| = k)$.

According to Theorem 1, the expected probability of an edge $e(s, d)$ occurs during T is $p(e) = E(|\mathcal{E}_T|)/n(n-1)$. Let $R_T(s, d)$ denote the path appearance probability that there appears at least one path from s to d ($\neq s$) after time duration T, and $R_T(m)(s, d)$ denote the conditional path appearance probability that there appears at least one path from s to d ($\neq s$) under the condition that there is a specified set of m vertices (other than s and d) which are known to be unreachable from s (where other vertices may or may not be reachable from s) in the above random digraph G_T. Specifically, $R_T(m)$ is independent of the choice of s and d. And (s, d) may be omitted from $R_n(T, m)(s, d)$, we have $R_T(m) = R_T$ (*if $m = 0$*).

Theorem 2. *The path appearance probability $R(T)$ that there appears at least one path from s to d ($\neq s$) after time duration T is*

$$R(T) = 1 - q(T) \sum_{i=0}^{n} \left[\binom{n}{i} p(e)^i q(T)^{n-i} \pi_i^{(n+1)}(T) \right] \quad (n \geq 5) \tag{3}$$

where $q(T) \equiv 1 - p(e)$ and $\pi_i^n(T) = \prod_{k=0}^{i-1}(1 - R_T(k))^1$

Theorem 3. *Let $R_{T,n}^U$ and $R_{T,n}^L$ denote the upper and lower bounds of R_T given n nodes in the network, respectively. The $R_{T,n}^U$ and $R_{T,n}^L$ can be given by a recursively formula*

---

[1] $\pi_i(T)$ is provide in [1].

$$\begin{cases} R_{T,2}^U = R_{T,2}^L = p(e) \\ R_{T,n}^U = 1 - (1 - p(e))(1 - p(e) \cdot R_{T,n-1}^U)^{n-2} \quad (n > 2) \\ R_{T,n}^L = 1 - (1 - p(e))\{(1 - R_{T,n-1}^L) \\ \qquad\quad + R_{T,n-1}^L(1 - p(e))^{n-2}\} \quad (n > 2) \end{cases}$$

Proof. According to the definition of $R_{T,n}$ and $R_{T,n}(m)$,

$$\begin{aligned} R_{T,n} &= 1 - (1 - p(e)) \sum_{i=0}^{n-2} [\binom{n-2}{i} p(e)^i q(T)^{n-2-i} \pi_i^{(n-1)}(T)] \\ &\le 1 - (1 - p(e)) \sum_{i=0}^{n-2} \left[\binom{n-2}{i} p(e)^i q(T)^{n-2-i}(1 - R_{T,n-1})^i\right] \\ &= 1 - (1 - p(e))(1 - p(e)R_{T,n-1})^{n-2} \\ &= R_{T,n}^U \end{aligned}$$

Similarly

$$\begin{aligned} R_{T,n} &= 1 - (1 - p(e)\left[(1 - p(e))^{n-2} + \sum_{i=1}^{n-2}\left\{\binom{n-2}{i} p(e)^i q(T)^{n-2-i} \pi_i^{(n-1)}(T)\right\}\right] \\ &\ge 1 - (1 - p(e))\left[(1 - p(e)^{n-2}(1 - R_{T,n-1}) + (1 - p(e))^{n-2} R_{T,n-1}\right. \\ &\quad + \left.\sum_{i=1}^{n-2}[\binom{n-2}{i} p(e)^i q(T)^{n-2-i}(1 - R_{T,n-1})]\right\}\right] \\ &= 1 - (1 - p(e))\{(1 - R_{T,n-1}^L) + R_{T,n-1}^L(1 - p(e))^{n-2}\} \\ &= R_{T,n}^L \end{aligned}$$

4   Theoretical Analysis

According to the analysis in Sect. 2.1, the time intervals in the time series $\mathbb{T}$ obeys the distribution $\mathbb{D}$, with each edge appears as a Poisson process with intensity λ. Since the edge selecting behavior can be modeled as a Markov process, after time duration T we have

$$P(card(E_{\Delta t=T}) - card(E_{\Delta t=0}) = k) = \frac{e^{-\lambda T}(\lambda T)^k}{k!} \tag{4}$$

The cardinality of the edge set E after time duration T is

$$P(|\mathcal{E}_T| = k) = \sum_{x=k}^{\infty} \frac{e^{-\lambda T}(\lambda T)^x}{x!} \cdot \frac{C_{n(n-1)}^k \sum_{\substack{a_1,\dots a_k \ge 1 \\ \sum a_k = x}} \frac{x!}{a_1! a_2! \dots a_k!}}{(n(n-1))^x}$$

According to 4 and 5, the expected number of distinct edges after time duration T is

$$E(|\mathcal{E}_T|) = \sum_{k=0}^{\infty} k \sum_{x=k}^{\infty} \frac{e^{-\lambda T}(\lambda T)^x}{x!} \cdot \frac{C_{n(n-1)}^k \sum_{\substack{a_1,\dots a_k \ge 1 \\ \sum a_k = x}} \frac{x!}{a_1! a_2! \dots a_k!}}{(n(n-1))^x}$$

Since $E(E_{\Delta t=T}) = \sum_{k=0}^{\infty} k \frac{e^{-\lambda T}(\lambda T)^k}{k!} = \lambda T$,

$$E(|\mathcal{E}_T|) \approx \lambda T \sum_{i=0}^{\infty} iP(|\mathcal{E}| = i \mid |E| = \lambda T) = \lambda T \sum_{i=0}^{M} \frac{C_{n(n-1)}^i \sum_{\substack{a_1,\dots\ a_i \geq 1 \\ \sum a_i = \lambda T}} \frac{(\lambda T)!}{a_1! a_2! \dots\ a_i!}}{(n(n-1))^{\lambda T}}$$
(5)

where M represents $max\{\lambda T,\ n(n-1)\}$

It is worth noting that $\sum_{\substack{a_1,\dots\ a_k \geq 1 \\ \sum a_k = x}} \frac{x!}{a_1! a_2! \dots\ a_k!} = \sum_{i=0}^{k}(-1)^i C_k^{k-i}(k-i)^x$. When $\lambda T \neq n(n-1)/10$, Eq. 5 approximately equals to λT. Then we can see $E(|\mathcal{E}_T|)$ exhibits a linear growth of time duration T.

For simplicity, we replace n by $n+2$. Let $f(p) = \gamma_{n+2,p}$, then we have

$$f(p) = 1 - (1-p)\sum_{i=0}^{n}\left[\binom{n}{i}p^i(1-p)^{n-i}\prod_{j=0}^{i-1}(1-\gamma_{n+1,p}^{(-j)})\right] \quad (n \geq 5) \qquad (6)$$

Theorem 4. $R_{T,n}$ *is approximatively a Sigmoid Curve.*

Proof. Let $H(p) = \sqrt[i]{\prod_{m=0}^{i-1}(1 - R_{T,n+1}(m))}$, then Eq. 6 can be rewritten as

$$R_T \approx 1 - (1-p(e))\sum_{i=0}^{n}\left[\binom{n}{i}p(e)^i(1-p(e))^{n-i}H(T)^i\right]$$
$$= 1 - (1-p(e))(1-(1-H(T))p(e)))^n \quad (n \geq 5) \qquad (7)$$

where $H(T)$ is the geometric average of $1 - R_{T,n+1}(m))$, $m = 0 \to i-1$.

Note that $R_{T,n+1}(m)$ represents the path appearance probability from an arbitrary node pair s and d under the condition that there is a specified set of m vertices (other than s and d) which are known to be unreachable from s (where other vertices may or may not be reachable from s), $R_{T,n+1}(m)$ increases as the growth of T. Thus $L(T) = (1 - H(T))$ is an increasing function. Then $R_{T,n} = 1 - (1-p(e))(1 - L(T)p(e)))^n$. Therefore $R_n(T)$ is approximatively a Sigmoid Curve.

Note that the first derivative of $R_{T,n}$ has a unique maximum value globally, the second derivative of $R_{T,n}$ is greater than zero when T is small and later goes down to negative as T increases.

Corollary 3. *The first derivative of $R_{T,n}$ has a unique maximum value globally with positive kurtosis, and thus $R_{T,n}$ exhibits a sudden increase, where the peak of the first derivative of $R_{T,n}$ can be used to estimate the time duration when there appears a giant component in G_T.*

Corollary 4. *$R_{T,n}$ has a unique maximum value globally with positive kurtosis, and thus $R_{T,n}$ exhibits a sudden increase, where the peak of the first derivative of $R_{T,n}$ can be used to estimate the time duration when there appears a giant component in G_T.*

5   Experiment

In the experiment, we study the interaction behavior (e.g., reply, forward, and etc.) collected in last 10 years from the largest forum in China, namely Tianya, with more than 3 million of daily active users. Specifically, we verify our theoretical analysis of the tendency of the reachability by comparing with the real data. All the results are averaged over 1000 runs.

5.1 Reachability Evaluation

To evaluate our theoretical analysis, we compute the path appearance probability between arbitrary pairs of nodes with the known distributions given in Fig. 1. Then, we compare it with the tendency of the reachability based on real data.

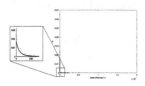

Fig. 2. The reachability as T increases

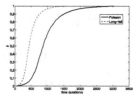

Fig. 3. The reachability vs. the number of users

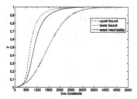

Fig. 4. The user interaction behaviors in the entertainment forum

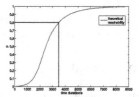

Fig. 5. The reachability of different user interaction behaviors

As shown in Fig. 2, both the theoretical results and the experimental results are similar to each other and approximate to a Sigmoid Curve, which validates our analysis in Sect. 4. Notice that the path appearance probability is always larger than that of the experiment. The reason is because of a scaling approximation in our derivation. In Eq. 5, we approximate λT as the expected cardinality of distinct edges. In practice, the expectation must be smaller than or equal to λT as there exists a certain probability that same edges are selected from the whole set. At the very beginning the gap is negligibly small. As time duration T increases, the gap becomes larger due to the scaling effect of our approximation. However, since the reachability is approximately a Sigmoid Curve, the gap will become smaller and converge to 0 again eventually.

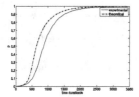

Fig. 6. The upper and lower bounds of the reachability

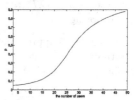

Fig. 7. The reachability when intensity is 0.01724

Figure 6 shows the upper bound and the lower bound of the reachability. It is shown that the reachability curve is closer to the upper bound and exhibits a sharp increase. It means that the giant component in the interaction network appears quickly when the time duration T passes a specific moment.

We apply our theoretical results to predict the reachability in another forum of 1000 active users in Tianya. The user interaction intensity λ is 0.01724, which means that the users in this forum are less active than those in the former one. Based on our theoretical analysis, if a message is required to be transmitted to at least 80 users in the interaction network, it will take about 3400 seconds as shown in Fig. 7.

5.2 Impact Factors of Reachability

In both the theoretical analysis and the experiment study, we have shown that the time duration is a key factor of the network reachability. There are two additional key factors: the interaction behavior and the number of users.

In the same site, we explore the reachability changing along the number of active users. By fixing the intensity of user interaction behavior, the reachability increases as the number of users grows, as shown in Fig. 3. It is interesting to see that the curve is still a Sigmoid Curve.

There are many different forums in Tianya, such as economics forum and entertainment forum, which attract special groups of users. Users of different types show diverse behavior due to the difference in age, avocation, education, and etc. This phenomenon results in different user interaction intensities in different forums. In the entertainment forum, there are more active and diverse users. The time intervals of related adjacent interaction behavior obey a long-tailed distribution as shown in Fig. 4. In the experiment, we compare the reachability of this forum and that under the condition that users' interactions follow a Poisson process in Fig. 5. The interaction intensities are close but the reachability on entertainment forum increases more rapidly due to the difference of the interaction distribution.

6   Conclusion

In this paper, we study the network reachability of temporally varying interaction networks in the time domain. We propose a novel theoretical framework to model the problem via the random digraph and a Markov process with the reverse chronological order, and provide a new quantitative analysis method with a series of tools so as to quantitatively analyze the network reachability in a given network. Moreover, the theoretical analysis and the experimental study well match each other, and reveal interesting observations: The time intervals between user interactions may obey an exponential distribution with the appearance of interaction edges following a Poisson process.

References

1. Uno, Y., Ibaraki, T.: Reachability problems of random digraphs. IEICE Trans. Fundam. Electron. Commun. Comput. Sci. **E81−A**(12), 2694–2702 (1998)
2. Whitbeck, J., de Amorim, M.D., Conan, V., Guillaume, J-L.: Temporal reachability graphs. In: Proceedings of the 18th Annual International Conference on Mobile Computing and Networking (2012)

Performance of Target Tracking in Radar Network System Under Deception Attack

Chaoqun Yang[1], Heng Zhang[2], Fengzhong Qu[1], and Zhiguo Shi[1]($\boxtimes$)

[1] Zhejiang University, Hangzhou, China
{chaoqunyang,jimqufz,shizg}@zju.edu.cn
[2] Huaihai Institute of Technology, Lianyungang, China
ezhangheng@gmail.com

Abstract. This paper studies security issue of target tracking in radar network system. We first derive the analytical result for the attack's effect on the performance of target tracking when one radar station is under deception attack. Based on this, by extending to radar network system, we find the relationship between the performance of target tracking and attack parameter. Simulation is presented to demonstrate the effectiveness of our results.

Keywords: Target tracking · Deception attack · Radar network system · Data fusion

1 Introduction

In recent years, target tracking technique has been substantially developed and used in various important fields, such as traffic monitoring [1], battlefield surveillance [2], mobile robots [3], etc. With the advancement of sensor network technology, multiple sensor system is introduced into target tracking to improve tracking accuracy and monitor extensive areas. Considering data processing capabilities and energy limited of sensors, data fusion center is essential to target tracking system. By gathering and fusing information from different sensors, the fusion center will get more precise target trajectory than any sensor.

Radar network system, as a typical multi-sensor target tracking system, which plays an important role in both civilian and military application [4], consists of multiple radars which are appropriately deployed in different geographic positions [5]. It is known that it can achieve better target tracking performance by fusing data obtained from multiple spatially-separated radars.

However, multi-sensor target tracking system, especially radar network system is vulnerable to various attacks. Researchers have studied some security issues in target tracking in the past years [6–8]. Alma et al. proposed a secure and reliable target tracking protocol that considers security and target tracking tasks simultaneously [6]. Chang et al. explored the topic of security in the context of Bayesian tracking for sensor network [7]. Pozzobon et al. described

© Springer International Publishing Switzerland 2015
K. Xu and J. Zhu (Eds.): WASA 2015, LNCS 9204, pp. 664–673, 2015.
DOI: 10.1007/978-3-319-21837-3_65

a secure framework for tracking application that uses the Galileo signal authentication services [8]. However, these literatures are all based on WSN, and do not consider data fusion scheme. Very few work studied multi-sensor target tracking in radar network system.

Motivated by this, we study the effect of attack on target tracking in radar network system. Specifically, we analyze the performance of target tracking when radar network system is under deception attack. The main contribution of this paper can be summarized as follows:

- We provide the analytical result for the attack's effect on the performance of target tracking for one radar station under deception attack.
- We find the relationship between the performance of target tracking and attack parameter for radar network system. The existing of the maximum performance degradation caused by deception attack is also revealed.

The rest of the paper is organized as follows: Sect. 2 describes the problem formulation. Section 3 analyzes the performance of target tracking when radar network system is under deception attack. Section 4 presents the simulation result. Finally Sect. 5 concludes the whole paper.

2   Problem Formulation

As illustrated in Fig. 1, several radars are appropriately deployed in different geographic positions. The target information from each single radar in the radar network system can be sent to the data fusion center. In our scenario, the data fusion scheme is a centralized fusion scheme in which all measurements are used simultaneously. By obtaining and fusing the detection information from different radars, the fusion center will obtain the position and velocity information of the target. Without loss of generality, we assume that the data fusion center runs probabilistic data association (PDA) algorithm and Kalman filter in this paper.

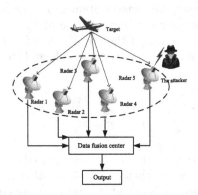

Fig. 1. The basic model of radar network system under deception attack

2.1   Target Dynamics and Measurement Equation

Similar to [9], we assume that the point target dynamics are modeled in Cartesian coordinate by

$$x_{k+1} = Fx_k + v_k, \quad x_k \in \mathbb{R}^{n_x}, \tag{1}$$

where x_k is the target state vector at time k, F is the transition matrix and v_k is zero-mean, white Gaussian noise with covariance Q.

It is assumed that the radar network system is composed of n radars. The target measurement for i-th radar is denoted as

$$y_{k+1}^i = H_i x_k + w_k^i, \quad i \in [1, n], \tag{2}$$

where H_i is the measurement matrix of i-th radar, and w_k^i is Gaussian noise with zero-mean and covariance R^i.

2.2   Kalman Filter and Probabilistic Data Association

Kalman filter is widely used for target tracking. The Kalman filter can be described as follows [10]:

$$x_{k+1|k} = Fx_{k|k}, \tag{3}$$

$$P_{k+1|k} = FP_{k|k}F^T + Q, \tag{4}$$

$$K_k = P_{k|k-1}H^T(HP_{k|k-1}H^T + R)^{-1}, \tag{5}$$

$$x_{k|k} = x_{k|k-1} + K_k(y_k - Hx_{k|k-1}), \tag{6}$$

$$P_{k|k} = P_{k|k-1} - K_kHP_{k|k-1}, \tag{7}$$

where $x_{k|k}$ represents state MMSE estimation, $x_{k+1|k}$ represents one step predicted statement estimation, $P_{k|k}$ is the covariance of the estimation error, $P_{k+1|k}$ is the covariance of one step predicted statement estimation, and K_k is the gain at each time k. F^T stands for the transposition of F.

It is known that the gain and the covariance of the estimation error will converge exponentially if the system is detectable and steady [11,12]. Hence, we can define

$$P = \lim_{k \to \infty} P_{k|k}, \tag{8}$$

$$K = \lim_{k \to \infty} K_k. \tag{9}$$

For radar network system, the fusion center needs to fuse data sent by all radar stations at each time and then runs Kalman filter to gain more precise trajectory. Since PDA algorithm is one of the most fundamental fusion algorithms, we choose PDA algorithm to analyze in this paper.

In our scenario, the fusion center utilizes its predicted state estimation at time $k - 1$, $x_{k|k-1}$ as one-step predicted value in validation region. Then it assigns the weighted coefficient to each radar's data at time k which is in validation region [13]. The PDA algorithm can be described as follows [14]:

$$x_{k|k} = Fx_{k-1|k-1} + K_k \sum_{i=1}^{n} \beta_k^i u_k^i, \tag{10}$$

$$u_k^i = y_k^i - H_i F x_{k-1|k-1}, \tag{11}$$

$$\beta_k^i = \frac{N[u_k^i; 0, S_k]}{b + \sum_{j=1}^{n} N[u_k^j; 0, S_k]}, \tag{12}$$

$$\beta_k^0 = \frac{b}{b + \sum_{j=1}^{n} N[u_k^j; 0, S_k]}, \tag{13}$$

$$P_{k|k} = P_{k|k-1}\beta^0 + (I - \beta^0)(I - K_k H)P_{k|k-1} + \tilde{P}_k, \tag{14}$$

$$\tilde{P}_k = K_k[\sum_{j=1}^{n} \beta_k^i u_k^i u_k^{iT} - (\sum_{j=1}^{n} \beta_k^i u_k^i)(\sum_{j=1}^{n} \beta_k^i u_k^i)^T)]K_k^T, \tag{15}$$

where b is a constant number, $N[u_k^i; 0, S_k]$ represents that the residues u_k^i is Gaussian distributed with zero mean and covariance S_k. β_k^i is the data association probability representing the weighted coefficient of the i-th radar's measurement. K_k and $P_{k|k-1}$ is given by (5) and (4), respectively.

Since the gain and the covariance of the estimation error will converge if the system is detectable [14], it can be seen that (8) and (9) are still true.

2.3   Attack Model

The deception attack, attacker can send false information from sensors by compromising sensors or manipulating program codes to degrade the system performance without being detected. It is ubiquitous in security field [15].

In our scenario, deception attacker aims to degrade the estimation performance of the moving target and deviate the target tracking by sending false data to the fusion center without being detected. The attacker can hijack several or one radar, observe and record their data simultaneously. While carrying out attack, the attacker compromises their data and sends to data fusion center. For easy to analyze the issue, we focus on the scenario that only one radar is under deception attack in the radar network system, but the result can be extend to multiple attacked radars. Without loss of generality, we assume that only the n-th radar is hijacked. Since the estimation error will converge exponentially, we also assume the state estimation is steady before attacker action implements. If the attack occurs at time k, we can obtain

$$y_k^{ai} = \begin{cases} y_k^i, & i \in [1, n-1], \\ y_k^{ai}, & i = n. \end{cases} \tag{16}$$

3 Performance Analysis of Target Tracking Under Deception Attack

In this section, we analyze the performance of target tracking when radar system is under deception attack. As a basis, we first consider only one radar station's performance of target tracking.

At time k, the attacker takes action, and the measurement of the radar y_k is compromised to y_k^a.

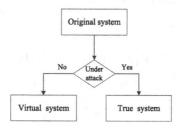

Fig. 2. The virtual system hypothesis

We have to study K_k firstly. According to (5), it is obvious that the attack does not influence K_k. It is no doubt that the system under deception attack is no more the same as the original system. For example, the gain K_k is not optimal any more. However, because the fusion center does not realize the existing of the attack, it will work as usual. For easy to understand, we construct a virtual system which is not under attack, as shown Fig. 2.

Secondly, we study $P_{k|k}$ and $P_{k+1|k}$. From (7), since K_k and $P_{k|k-1}$ do not change, we can see that $P_{k|k}$ is the same as those in the virtual system. From (4), it can be seen that $P_{k+1|k}$ does also not change under attack. Let K_k^a, $P_{k|k}^a$ and $P_{k+1|k}^a$ represent the gain, the covariance of the estimation error and the covariance of one step predicted in true attacked system, respectively. From (4), (5) and (7), It can be seen that $K_k^a = K_k$, $P_{k|k}^a = P_{k|k}$, $P_{k+1|k}^a = P_{k+1|k}$.

Thirdly, we investigate $x_{k+1|k+1}$ after the attack. Let $\Delta y_k = y_k^a - y_k$, where Δy_k represents the deviation applied by the attacker at time k. We also can take Δy_k as a parameter which represents the attack strength. The state estimation of the true attacked system at time $k + 1$ is $x_{k+1|k+1}^a$. Δx_{k+1}, represents the performance degradation on state estimation caused by the attack at time $k+1$, where $\Delta x_{k+1} = x_{k+1|k+1}^a - x_{k+1|k+1}$.

Theorem 1. *If the attacker compromises the radar's measurement y_k to y_k^a, The performance degradation on state estimation caused by the attack at time $k + 1$ is*

$$\Delta x_{k+1} = M\Delta x_k + K\Delta y_k, \tag{17}$$

where $M = (I - KH)F$.

Proof. According to (3) and (6), we have

$$x_{k|k} = (I - K_k H)F x_{k-1|k-1} + K_k y_k. \tag{18}$$

For true system, the state estimate at time $k + 1$ is

$$x_{k+1|k+1}^a = (I - K_{k+1}^a H)F x_{k|k}^a + K_{k+1}^a y_k^a. \tag{19}$$

Similarly, state estimate at time $k + 1$ for virtual system is

$$x_{k+1|k+1} = (I - K_{k+1}H)F x_{k|k} + K_{k+1} y_k. \tag{20}$$

Since $K_{k+1}^a = K_{k+1}$, we can see that

$$x_{k+1|k+1}^a - x_{k+1|k+1} = (I - K_{k+1}H)F(x_{k|k}^a - x_{k|k}) + K_{k+1}(y_k^a - y_k). \tag{21}$$

The true attacked system and the virtual system will be steady after finite steps [14]. From (9), it can be seen that

$$\Delta x_{k+1} = M \Delta x_k + K \Delta y_k. \tag{22}$$

We can see that Δx_{k+1} can measure the performance degradation of target tracking caused by the attack. Now we consider a special case, i.e., the attacker compromises a constant deviation Δy to the real data of the radar.

Theorem 2. *If the attacker applies a deviation Δy to the radar's measurement, then the limitation of performance degradation on state estimation caused by the attack is*

$$\lim_{l \to \infty} \Delta x_l = -(M - I)^{-1} K \Delta y. \tag{23}$$

Proof. From Theorem 1, we have

$$\Delta x_{k+1} = M \Delta x_k + K \Delta y. \tag{24}$$

From (24), it can be seen that

$$\Delta x_l = M^{l-k}[\Delta x_k + (M - I)^{-1} K \Delta y] - (M - I)^{-1} K \Delta y. \tag{25}$$

Since the system is steady, Δx_l will converge to a steady value. As a result, we can obtain (23) when l converges to infinite.

From Theorem 2, we can see the limitation of Δx_l approaches linearly to Δy. Thus, if the attacker wants more serious performance degradation on the system, he just needs to make more deviation to the true measurement.

Now we analyze the performance of target tracking in radar network system with data fusion scheme under deception attack. According to (10), (11), we have

$$x_{k|k} = F x_{k-1|k-1} + K_k \Big(\sum_{i=1}^{n} \beta_k^i y_k^i - \sum_{i=1}^{n} \beta_k^i H_i F x_{k-1|k-1} \Big). \tag{26}$$

Since we have assumed that all radars' measurement is in validation region, then b is 0 and $\sum_{i=1}^{n} \beta_k^i = 1$, according to (12), (13). For easy to deduction, it is assumed that $H_i = H$ for $\forall$ i. We have

$$x_{k|k} = (I - K_k H) F x_{k-1|k-1} + K_k \sum_{i=1}^{n} \beta_k^i y_k^i. \qquad (27)$$

Now let's study K_k when the system is under deception attack at time k. It can be seen that K_k will not change at time k. However, from (10) and (11), the n-th radar's residue u_k^n will change to u_k^{an}, which causes the data association probability β_k^i, the covariance $P_{k|k}$, $P_{k+1|k}$ to change. Then we can see that the true system's gain and covariance will not be the same as the virtual system's gain and covariance. Furthermore, we can also see that the true system will be steady after finite steps. As mentioned above, we also have $K = \lim_{k \to \infty} K_k$, $K^a = \lim_{k \to \infty} K_k^a$.

It can be seen that the state estimate for true system is

$$x_{t+1|t+1}^a = (I - K^a H) F x_{t|t}^a + K^a \Big(\sum_{i=1}^{n-1} \beta_{t+1}^{ai} y_{t+1}^i + \beta_{t+1}^{an} y_{t+1}^{an} \Big). \qquad (28)$$

Similarly, for virtual system we have

$$x_{t+1|t+1} = (I - KH) F x_{t|t} + K \Big(\sum_{i=1}^{n-1} \beta_{t+1}^i y_{t+1}^i + \beta_{t+1}^n y_{t+1}^n \Big). \qquad (29)$$

Let's also define $\Delta x_{t+1} = x_{t+1|t+1}^a - x_{t+1|t+1}$, $\Delta y_{t+1}^n = y_{t+1}^{an} - y_{t+1}^n$.

By iterating (28) and (29), we can obtain the relationship between Δx_{t+1} and Δy_{t+1}^n. However, since it is a challenging work to derive the theoretical result, we study the relationship between Δx_{t+1} and Δy_{t+1}^n by simulating in Sect. 4.

4   Simulation

In this section, we provide the simulation results when the radar network system is under deception attack, and we study the relationship between Δx_{t+1} and Δy_{t+1}^n.

Considering a radar network system with 3 radars and 1 data fusion center which keeps surveillance of a two-dimensional region. One target starts at location $[20\,\text{m}, 10\,\text{m}]$ and its initial velocity is $[2\,\text{m/s}, 1\,\text{m/s}]$. The target dynamic model follows (1) with the Gaussian noise Q being 0, and the transition matrix

$$F = \begin{bmatrix} 1 & 0 & T & 0 \\ 0 & 1 & 0 & T \\ 0 & 0 & 1 & 0 \\ 0 & 0 & 0 & 1 \end{bmatrix}, \qquad (30)$$

where $T = 1$ is the sample period. The state x_k consists of position and velocity in two-dimensional Cartesian coordinate.

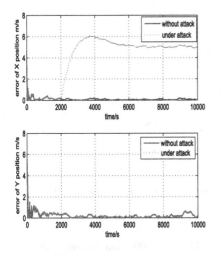

Fig. 3. The position error in one radar station.

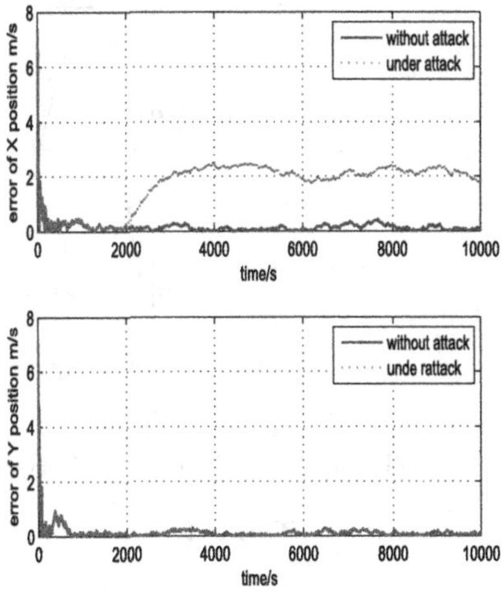

Fig. 4. The position error in radar network system.

The measurement matrix is

$$H_i = H = \begin{bmatrix} 1 & 0 & 0 & 0 \\ 0 & 0 & 1 & 0 \end{bmatrix}. \tag{31}$$

The measurement error covariance matrix is

$$R = \begin{bmatrix} r & 0 \\ 0 & r \end{bmatrix}, \tag{32}$$

where $r = 25$ m.

Firstly, we evaluate the performance of target tracking without attack. As the solid curve shown in Figs. 3 and 4. The attack is carried out at time 2000 s and the compromised deviation is

$$\Delta y_k = \begin{bmatrix} 10 & 0 \\ 0 & 0 \end{bmatrix}, \tag{33}$$

which means the attacker only compromises the measurement of X position.

Secondly, we present one radar station's performance of target tracking under the attack. As the dotted curve shown in Fig. 3, the X position error increases dramatically after time 2000 s and converges to a steady value. Since the attacker only compromises the measurement of X position, the estimation of Y position is still accurate. The performance degradation on target tracking in the system caused by the attack is Δx_k, which is the gap between red solid curve and dotted curve. The numerical value of Δx_k is 4.9973 m at time 10000 s. Using (20) from Theorem 2, the limitation of Δx_k is 5.0000 m. Table 1 shows that Δx_k approaches to its limitation with time increasing.

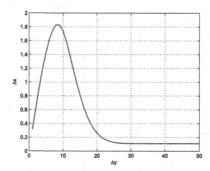

Fig. 5. The relationship between Δx and Δy under deception attack

Table 1. The value of Δx_k under deception attack

Simulation time(s)	6000	7000	8000	9000	10000	Limitation of Δx_k
Δx_k (m)		5.1270	5.0128	4.9900	4.9927	4.9973	5.000

Thirdly, given the same Δy_k to $\Delta y_k{}^n$, we study the relationship between Δx_{t+1} and $\Delta y_k{}^n_{t+1}$ in the radar network system. Figure 4 shows the performance of target tracking in radar network system. It is obvious that Δx_{t+1} converges after finite steps when Δy^n is given. Let's define that the steady value of Δx_{t+1} is Δx.

We investigates the performance of target tracking with different $\Delta y^n{}_{t+1}$. Figure 5 shows the the nonlinear relationship between Δx and $\Delta y^n{}_{t+1}$. As we can see, When Δy^n_{t+1} is very small, which means the attacker gives a very small deviation to the n-th radar' measurement, the effect is very small. When Δy^n_{t+1} is quite large, the effect will be very small too. The reason is that from (12), (28), the weighted coefficient of n-th radar's measurement β^{ai}_{t+1} is very small. There is a peak value of the curve representing the maximum of Δx. The existing of the maximum value means the existing of the largest performance degradation of the system caused by the deception attack. It also means the maximal effectiveness of the attack.

5   Conclusion

In this paper, we analyze the performance of target tracking when radar network system is under deception attack. After formulating problem, We first analyze the performance of target tracking when one radar station is under deception attack. Then the analytical result for the attack's effect on the performance of target tracking is derived. Based on this, by extending the issue to radar network system, we reveal the relationship between the performance of target tracking and attack parameter for radar network system. We show that it is highly necessary to design detection and defence scheme for target tracking in radar network system.

Acknowledgment. This paper is supported by NSFC (61171149,71401060), Zhejiang Province Commonware Technology Projects (2014C33103), Huaihai Institute of Technology Doctoral Research Funding (KQ15007), Lianyungang Science and Technology Projects (CK1331, SH1310).

References

1. Zheng, Y., Shi, Z., Lu, R., Hong, S., Shen, X.: An efficient data-driven particle PHD filter for multitarget tracking. IEEE Trans. Ind. Inf. **9**(4), 2318–2326 (2013)
2. Pannetier, B., Dezert, J., Sella, G.: Multiple targets tracking with wireless sensor network for ground battlefield surveillance. In: Proceedings of International Conference on Radar, pp. 1–8 (2014)
3. Lee, S., Cho, Y., Hwang-Bo, M.: A stable target-tracking control for unicycle mobile robots. In: Proceedings of International Conference on Intelligent Robots and Systems, pp. 1822–1827 (2000)
4. Hong, S., Wang, L., Shi, Z., Chen, K.: Simplified particle PHD filter for multiple-target tracking: algorithm and architecture. Prog. Electromagnet. Res. **120**, 481–498 (2011)
5. Zheng, G., Zheng, Y.: Radar netting technology and its development. In: IEEE CIE International Conference on Radar, pp. 933–937 (2011)
6. Oracevic, A., Akbas, S., Ozdemir, S.: Secure target detection and tracking in mission critical wireless sensor networks. In: Proceedings of International Conference on Anti-counterfeiting, Security, and Identification, pp. 1–5 (2014)
7. Chang, G., Snyder, W.E., Wang, C.: Secure tracking in sensor networks. In: Proceedings of International Conference on Communications, pp. 3082–3087 (2007)
8. Pozzobon, O., Wullems, C., Kubik, K.: Secure tracking using trusted GNSS receivers and galileo authentication services. J. Glob. Position. Syst. Position. **1**(08), 200–207 (2004)
9. Lee, E., Musicki, D., Song, T.: Multi-sensor distributed fusion based on integrated probabilistic data association. In: Proceedings of International Conference on Information Fusion, pp. 1–7(2014)
10. Mo, Y., Sinopoli, B.: Secure control against replay attacks. In: Proceedings of Annual Allerton Conference on Communication, Control, and Computing, pp. 911–918 (2009)
11. Zhang, H., Cheng, P., Shi, L., Chen, J.: Optimal DoS attack policy against remote state estimation. In: Proceedings of IEEE CDC (2013)
12. Zhang, H., Cheng, P., Shi, L., Chen ,J.: Optimal DoS attack policy with energy constraint. IEEE Trans. Autom. Control (2015)
13. Guo, H.D., Zhang, X.H.: Distributed fusion of multisensory data based on probabilistic data fusion. Control and Decision **19**(12), 1359–1363 (2004)
14. He, Y.: Radar Data Processing With Application, 3rd edn. Electronics Industry Press, Beijing (2013)
15. Zhang, H., Cheng, P., Wu, J., Shi, L., Chen, J.: Online deception attack against remote state estimation. In: Proceedings of World Congress of the International Federation of Automatic Control (2014)

Resource Allocation in Cooperative Cognitive Maritime Wireless Mesh/Ad Hoc Networks: An Game Theory View

Tingting Yang[1,2,3](✉), Chengming Yang[1,2,3], Zhonghua Sun[1,2,3], Hailong Feng[1,2,3], Jiadong Yang[1,2,3], Fan Sun[1,2,3], and Ruilong Deng[1,2,3]

[1] Navigation College, Dalian Maritime University,
1 Linghai Road, Dalian, Liaoning, China
yangtingting820523@163.com
[2] School of Naval Architecture, Ocean and Civil Engineering,
Shanghai Jiao Tong University, Shanghai, China
[3] School of Electrical and Electronic Engineering,
Nanyang Technological University, Singapore, Singapore

Abstract. In this paper, an innovative paradigm cooperative cognitive maritime wireless mesh/ad hoc networks (CCMWMAN) is proposed to provide high-speed and low-cost communications for maritime environment. The framework of CCMWMAN is exploited firstly, as well as the analysis of available white space at sea as well as the regulation requirement and standards relatively, to efficiently use the limited frequency resource. Specially, game theory method is applied within the cooperative SUs. An symmetrical system model is constructed, and a price game based on a payoff function is proposed. Then we describe the game theory process to converge to Nash equilibrium, which is verified the results effectiveness of proposed scheme. The simulation results show that the strategy can effectively increases the payoffs of the system.

Keywords: Cooperative cognitive maritime wireless mesh/ad hoc networks · Game theory · Symmetrical model

1 Introduction

There has been proliferation interest in the emerging maritime wideband communication networks, which could be a low-cost alternative for current maritime satellite system. It is envisioned that building up a "maritime highway" system will greatly contribute to the maritime communication services with different priority of distress, urgency, safety and general and so that promote a myriad of glamorous applications with respect to monitoring, safety etc. It is envisaged that maritime wideband communication networks could refashion the navigation traffic more energetic, as well as expand wideband communications to the ocean with lower cost. Recent years, a plenty of wireless technologies have been exploited to achieve maritime data transmission. Adopting Worldwide Interoperability for Microwave Access (WiMAX) technology, wireless-broadband-access

© Springer International Publishing Switzerland 2015
K. Xu and J. Zhu (Eds.): WASA 2015, LNCS 9204, pp. 674–684, 2015.
DOI: 10.1007/978-3-319-21837-3_66

for Seaport (WISEPORT) project in Singapore could achieve broadband data access, with data rate up to 5 Mbps [1]. In addition, cognitive technology has been applied to maritime mesh/ad hoc networks [2], to mitigate the scarcity of dedicated operation spectrums due to the existing overcrowded frequency bandwidth resources. It is envisioned that a cognitive mesh/ad hoc network could explore the connection between neighboring ships, sea farm, oil/gas platform, as well as marine beacons and buoys, to form an attractive network and connect to the land-based network.

However, the notable inherent characteristics of maritime communication are long distance requirement and occasionally deteriorated wireless channel due to the obstacles such as sea clutters. Hence the communication coverage range is still short for the advanced land-based technology to implement on the sea. Cooperative technology is a communication technology developing rapidly in recent years. It can get diversity gain through cooperation between users, which bases on relay transmission principle [3]. It serves to confront the decadence of wireless channel, enhance the reliability of communication, enlarge the coverage and lower transmitting power effectively.

The state-of-the-art cooperative and cognitive technology are combined to construct an innovative maritime communication network paradigm in this paper, i.e., cooperative cognitive maritime wireless mesh/ad hoc network, to efficient exploiting White Space (WS) on the sea, and address the limited transmission range and distorted signal transmission simultaneously. Although the research on maritime scenario is still in the early stage, the counterparts on land-based network could provide a solid foundation for our work [4–7]. In cognitive system, not only the secondary users could cooperate with primary users, but also the secondary users themselves could cooperate with each other. Generally speaking, in the research of cooperative system, it always assume relays would like to help source to transmit information. However a challenge in practice maritime communication system is how to effectively build up a cooperative system in limited transmitter power level on the sea. And nodes are independent selfish individuals and they are not voluntary to help other nodes. So the user must pay fee to buy resource to attain corresponding help. Then the other user calculate payoff of itself to decide to join or not the cooperative communication. Therefore, its inevitable to consume resources such as power and rate helping other nodes to transmit, rational nodes are not obligatory to involve in this cooperate activity. Game theory is a good mathematic method to research effective cooperative condition and requirement. In [8], the authors investigated multi-channel assignment in wireless sensor networks utilizing the game theoretic approach. In [9] the author proposed adjustable price and rate algorithm based on cooperative stimulating method in Ad hoc networks. In [10], cooperative spectrum access of primary and secondary users, as well as MAC protocol for multi-channel cognitive radio networks is developed. In [11] authors discussed a non-symmetrical cooperative three-node model. But in practice, the two users are all likely the potential relay which is better accordant with fairness of network. In this paper, game theory method and price mechanism are applied into the cooperative cognitive mesh/ad hoc maritime network to formulate when to cooperate. An symmetrical system model is constructed, and a price game based on a payoff function is proposed. The idea of this paper is that source node can get relevant help just when it pay for to purchase corresponding resource, and relay node determine whether to involve into the cooperative communication according to profit in this action.

In this paper, an innovative paradigm cooperative cognitive maritime wireless mesh/ad hoc networks (CCMWMAN) is proposed to provide high-speed and low-cost communications for maritime environment. The framework of CCMWMAN is exploited firstly, as well as the analysis of available white space, regulation requirement and standards, to efficiently use the limited frequency resource. Specially, game theory method is applied within the cooperative SUs. An symmetrical system model is constructed, and a price game based on a payoff function is proposed. Then we will describe the game theory process to converge to Nash equilibrium. The remainder of this paper is organized as follows. System model and WS analysis are illustrated in Sect. 2 and problem formulation is shown in Sect. 3. Section 4 describes the game theory based resource allocation of symmetrical cooperative three-node model, as well as the proof of value boundary of some parameters. In Sect. 5, simulation results validate the performance of our scheme. Finally, conclusions and references end this paper.

2   System Model and WS Analysis

This section presents the details of the system model as well as the analysis of WS on the sea.

2.1   System Model

We consider the scenario that an innovative paradigm cooperative cognitive maritime wireless mesh/ad hoc networks (CCMWMAN) could be formed by exploring the connection between neighboring ships, sea farm, oil/gas platform, maritime security/safe monitors as well as marine beacons and buoys. Depending to the node mobility, the network close to shore could be the combination of the classed two network: (1) immobile marine infrastructure mesh network; (2) mobile ship-to-ship/shore mesh/ad hoc network. The nodes are equipped with a mesh/ad hoc module that is capable of implementing cognitive radio functions. The cognitive nodes which sense or collect data regularly, could be the relay to deliver traffic. And then, the immobile or mobile nodes could connect to the land-based network via shore-based base station easily. In this cognitive system, primary users could be the radio devices installed near the coastal region such as authorities on land, or licensed vessels. Thereby, the secondary users could be the devices on the sea, such as the unlicensed vessels neighboring, sea farm, oil/gas platform, as well as marine beacons and buoys. And they could cooperate with each other, and form a cluster to cooperate with primary users further to strive for transmission opportunities. Therefore, the unlicensed users could utilize the unused frequency spectrum resources opportunistically. And the sensed data or monitoring data by the mesh/ad hoc nodes could be transmitted to the land-based administrative agencies through wireline/wireless network on

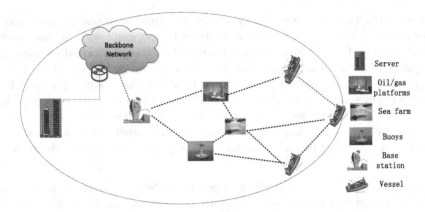

Fig. 1. System model.

land dynamically adopting the unused frequency channels by the primary users. Therefore, this network could provide high-speed and low-cost communications for maritime environment. Network topologies are shown in Fig. 1.

2.2 The Analysis of WS on the Sea

There is nor TV broadcasting frequency neither cellular signal frequently adopted at sea currently. Therefore, there is prosperity TVWS and cellular WS at sea nowadays, especially the open ocean. Furthermore, the state-of-the-art maritime communication system, christened as Global Maritime Distress and Safety System, comprises of terrestrial and satellite systems [12]. The frequency bands of GMDSS system utilized scattered across very high frequency (VHF, 30–300 MHz), medium frequency band (MF, 300 kHz-3 MHz), high frequency band (HF, 3–30 MHz) as well as Microwave bands such as ultra high frequency (UHF, 300 MHz) adopted by satellite communications. Hence, the frequency bands utilized at sea are highly fragmented, and they are not employed efficiently. In the literature [2], it is noted that the channels of 156–174 MHz in VHF band provide attractive opportunistic access for high-speed communications. The unused bands aforementioned dedicated for maritime communication are called "Maritime WS".

Moreover, the utilization rule of maritime WS should be: (1) The primary users like authorities or licensed vessels should be solidly protected, and avoid harmful interference [13]; (2) The priority of communication at sea should be subordinated restricted; (3) The cognitive nodes at sea should have the capability to sense the "Maritime WS" spectrum, wherever they go across the world.

3   Problem Formulation

Some research focused on the resource allocation between primary users and secondary users in cognitive mesh/ad hoc network. Although the cooperation between secondary users are equally significant. And the secondary users could cooperate with each other, and form a cluster to cooperate with primary users further to strive for transmission opportunities. However, the secondary users are independent selfish individuals and they are not voluntary to help other nodes. So the user must pay fee to buy resource to attain corresponding help. Then the other user calculate payoff of itself to decide to join or not the cooperative communication. Therefore, its inevitable to consume resources such as power and rate helping other nodes to transmit. In this paper, we will discuss the cooperative scheme between secondary users, especially the symmetric model.

Game Theory Model. Firstly, its need to confirm the participant element (playersstrategy space, payoffs) to establish game theory model. In this cooperative symmetrical network of triple nodes, we define the source node s and the destination node d, which the status of two is equal. The source nodedestination node d and the relay node r are players. Strategies space are inspirit price μ and ν, which are the price paid to the partner of source node and relay node, and the speed R_{rs} and R_{sr}, which are helping partner to tranmit data. Payoff function is defined as the margin of utility function and price function when adopt the strategies as $Payoff = U - P$, here U denotes utility function and P is price function.

- **Utility Function:** Here we employ a common utility function expressed by received data when consuming one unit energy the same as literature [14] . So the definition of Utility function is unit throughout utility multiply throughout. The unit throughout of local operation is defined as 1/bit. The following expression R_s and ber_{sd} are respectively the transmitting speed and bit error rate(BER) of source nodewhich is in the local operation. R_r and ber_{rd} are respectively the transmitting speed and BER of source node which is in the local operation. T is transmitting time.
  The utility of non-cooperative source node is:

$$U_{s\_non} = 1 \cdot Throughput = R_s \cdot T \cdot (1 - ber_{sd}) \tag{1}$$

  The utility of cooperative source node is:

$$U_{s\_coop} = 1 \cdot Throughput_{local} + 1 \cdot Throughput_{relay} \tag{2}$$

  The utility of non-cooperative relay node is:

$$U_{r\_non} = 1 \cdot Throughput = R_r \cdot T \cdot (1 - ber_{rd}) \tag{3}$$

  The utility of cooperative relay node is:

$$U_{r\_coop} = 1 \cdot Throughput = (R_r - R_{rs}) \cdot T \cdot (1 - ber_{rd}) + R_{sr} T \cdot (1 - ber_{sr}) \tag{4}$$

- **Price Function:** The service price is defined as $\lambda_i = \lambda_0 \frac{R_i}{R_{max}}$, here λ_0 is criterion price. R_i and R_{max} respectively indicate transmitting rate and maximum rate supported by this system. λ_s denotes source unit price of local service; λ_r denotes relays unit price of local service; λ_{rs} denotes unit price of relay helping source to transmit; λ_{sr} denotes unit price of source helping relay to transmit; μ and ν are respectively stimulating price of source and relay; λ_{r-rs} is unit price of relay node when cooperation; λ_{s-sr} is unit price of source node when cooperation.

The price function of non-cooperative source node is:

$$P_{s-non} = \lambda_s \cdot R_s \cdot T \cdot (1 - ber_{sd}) \tag{5}$$

The price function of cooperative source node is:

$$P_{s-coop} = \lambda_{s-sr} \cdot (R_s - R_{sr}) \cdot T \cdot (1 - ber_{sd}) + (\mu + \lambda_{rs}) \cdot R_{rs} \cdot T \cdot (1 - ber_{rs})$$
$$- \nu \cdot R_{sr} \cdot T \cdot (1 - ber_{sr}) \tag{6}$$

The price function of non-cooperative relay node is:

$$P_{r-non} = \lambda_r \cdot R_r \cdot T \cdot (1 - ber_{rd}) \tag{7}$$

The price function of cooperative relay node is:

$$P_{r-coop} = \lambda_{r-rs} \cdot (R_r - R_{rs}) \cdot T \cdot (1 - ber_{rd}) + (\nu + \lambda_{sr}) \cdot R_{sr} \cdot T \cdot (1 - ber_{sr})$$
$$- \mu \cdot R_{rs} \cdot T \cdot (1 - ber_{rs}) \tag{8}$$

- **Payoff Function:** Payoff function is defined as difference of utility function and price function adopting strategies, i.e., $Payoff = U - P$. (U denotes utility function, P is price function)

The payoff function of non-cooperative source node is:

$$payoff_{s-non} = (1 - \lambda_s) \cdot R_s \cdot T \cdot (1 - ber_{sd}) \tag{9}$$

The payoff function of cooperative source node is:

$$payoff_{s-coop} = (1 - \lambda_{s-sr}) \cdot (R_s - R_{sr}) \cdot T \cdot (1 - ber_{sd}) +$$
$$\nu \cdot R_{sr} \cdot T \cdot (1 - ber_{sr}) + (1 - \mu - \lambda_{rs}) \cdot R_{rs} \cdot T \cdot (1 - ber_{rs}) \tag{10}$$

The payoff function of non-cooperative relay node is:

$$payoff_{r-non} = (1 - \lambda_r) \cdot R_r \cdot T \cdot (1 - ber_{rd}) \tag{11}$$

The payoff function of cooperative relay node is:

$$payoff_{r-coop} = (1 - \lambda_{r-rs}) \cdot (R_r - R_{rs}) \cdot T \cdot (1 - ber_{rd}) + \mu \cdot R_{rs} \cdot T \cdot (1 - ber_{rs})$$
$$+ (1 - \nu - \lambda_{sr}) \cdot R_{sr} \cdot T \cdot (1 - ber_{sr}) \tag{12}$$

4 Game Theory Based Resource Allocation

In this section, we described the game theory process to converge to Nash equilibrium by the iteration algorithm. Firstly, the value boundary of u and v are given. Exploiting the same rules, the value boundary of relaying rate R_{rs} and R_{sr} could be obtained easily.

4.1 Value Boundary Analysis

Lemma 1. *Using game theory to converge to Nash equilibrium, the stimulating price of source and relay u and v, as well as the are achieved.*

Proof.

– **Value boundary of u and v:**

When cooperation, according to $Payoff_{s\_coop} - Payoff_{s\_non} \geq 0$ and $Payoff_{r\_coop} - Payoff_{r\_non} \geq 0$, we could get,

$$u \leq 1 - \lambda_s +$$
$$\frac{vR_{rs}(1 - ber_{sr}) + \lambda_s \cdot R_s(1 - ber_{sd}) - R_{sr}(1 - ber_{sd}) - \lambda_{s-sr}(R_s - R_{sr})(1 - ber_{sd})}{R_{rs}(1 - ber_{rs})} \quad (13)$$

$$u \geq \frac{[R_{rs} + \lambda_{r-rs}(R_r - R_{rs})](1 - ber_{rd}) + (v + \lambda_{sr} - 1)R_{sr}(1 - ber_{sr})}{R_{sr}(1 - ber_{sr})} \quad (14)$$

$$v \leq \frac{[\lambda_r - R_{rs} - \lambda_{r-rs}(R_r - R_{rs})](1 - ber_{rd}) + \mu R_{rs}(1 - ber_{rs})}{R_{sr}(1 - ber_{sr})} + 1 - \lambda_{sr} \quad (15)$$

$$v \geq [R_{sr} + \lambda_{s-sr}(R_s - R_{sr}) - \lambda_s R_s](1 - ber_{sd}) - (1 - u - \lambda_s)R_{rs}(1 - ber_{rs}) \quad (16)$$

Jointing the formulas [13]-[16], we could get the value which satisfy the value of $\mu_{\min}$ and $\nu_{\min}$ simultaneously.

– **Value boundary of R_{rs} and R_{sr}:**

$payoff_{r-coop}$ is a quadratic function regarding to R_{rs}. When u is fixed, we can get the extreme value of R_{rs}^* calculating the first order partial derivative of R_{rs}.

$$\frac{\partial payoff_{r-coop}}{\partial R_{rs}} = -T(1 - ber_{rd}) + \frac{2\lambda_0(R_r - R_{rs})T(1 - ber_{rd})}{R_{\max}} + uT(1 - ber_{rs}) \quad (17)$$

When $\frac{\partial payoff_{r-coop}}{\partial R_{rs}} = 0$, we can get

$$R_{rs}^* = R_r - R_{rs\,\max}[\frac{1}{2\lambda_0} - \frac{\mu(1 - r_{rs})}{2\lambda_0(1 - ber_{rd})}] \quad (18)$$

Here, we suppose the calculating method of service price are $\lambda_{r-rs} = \lambda_r - \lambda_{rs}$ and $\lambda_{s-sr} = \lambda_s - \lambda_{sr}$.

Similarly, $payoff_{s-coop}$ is a quadratic function regarding to R_{sr}. When ν is fixed, we can get the extreme value of R_{sr}^* calculating the first order partial derivative of R_{sr}.

$$\frac{\partial payoff_{s-coop}}{\partial R_{sr}} = (R_s - R_{sr})T(1 - ber_{sd}) - \frac{\lambda_0}{R_{\max}}(R_s - R_{sr})^2 T(1 - ber_{sd})$$
$$+ (1 - \mu - \lambda_s)R_s T(1 - ber_{rs}) + \nu R_{sr}T(1 - ber_{sr}) \quad (19)$$

When $\frac{\partial payoff_{s-coop}}{\partial R_{sr}} = 0$, we could get

$$R_{sr}^* = R_s - R_{sr\,max}[\frac{1}{2\lambda_0} - \frac{\nu(1 - r_{sr})}{2\lambda_0(1 - ber_{sd})}] \qquad (20)$$

Hence, we find that R_{rs}^* is just relating to μ but not ν; R_{sr}^* is just relating to ν but not μ.

4.2 Game Theory Process Description

This is two-parties game existing priority decision, so its absolutely information dynamic game. According to the above derivation, $payoff_{s-coop}$ is a monotonous decrease progressively function regarding to μ and monotonous increase progressively function regarding to ν. $payoff_{r-coop}$ is a monotonous decrease progressively function regarding to ν and monotonous increase progressively function regarding to μ. So as to say, the two parties hope the simulating price of opposite side is higher, and the price given to opposite side is lower. So when starting cooperation, they are certain to select μ_{min} and ν_{min}.

Then we can get the cooperation transmitting rate given to opposite side calculating by formulation [18]-[20]. If they are lower than maximum transmitting rate, the game theory process finished and cooperation process started. If they not fit the requirement, it need revalue minimum from the value range to game and repeat the above process.

$$payoff_{total-coop} = payoff_s + payoff_r + payoff_{BS}$$
$$= payoff_s + payoff_r + P_{total}$$
$$= payoff_s + payoff + P_s + P_r = (U_s - P_s) + (U_r - P_r)$$
$$+ P_s + P_r = U_s + U_r \qquad (21)$$

$$payoff_{total-non} = (1 - \lambda_s)R_sT(1 - ber_{sd}) + (1 - \lambda_r)R_rT(1 - ber_{rd}) \qquad (22)$$

$$payoff_{total-coop} = (1 - \lambda_{s-sr})(R_s - R_{sr})T(1 - ber_{sd})$$
$$+ (1 - \mu - \lambda_s)R_{rs}T(1 - ber_{rs}) + \nu R_{sr}T(1 - ber_{sr})$$
$$+ (1 - \lambda_{r-rs})(R_r - R_{rs})T(1 - ber_{rd}) +$$
$$(1 - \nu - \lambda_{sr})R_{sr}T(1 - ber_{sr}) + \mu R_{rs}T(1 - ber_{rs})$$
$$= (1 - \lambda_s)R_{rs}T(1 - ber_{rs}) + (1 - \lambda_{sr})R_{sr}T(1 - ber_{sr})$$
$$+ (1 - \lambda_{s-sr})(R_s - R_{sr})T(1 - ber_{sd})$$
$$+ (1 - \lambda_{r-rs})(R_r - R_{rs})T(1 - ber_{rd}) \qquad (23)$$

We suppose $r_r = r_{rs}$ and $r_s = r_{sr}$, the above formulation can similar to

$$payoff_{total-coop} = (\lambda_{r-rs} - \lambda_s)R_{rs}T(1 - ber_{rd}) + (\lambda_{s-sr} - \lambda_{sr})R_{sr}T(1 - ber_{sd})$$
$$+ (1 - \lambda_{s-sr})R_sT(1 - ber_{sd}) + (1 - \lambda_{r-rs})R_rT(1 - ber_{rd}) \qquad (24)$$

when $\lambda_{r-rs} - \lambda_s > 0$ and $\lambda_{s-sr} - \lambda_{sr} > 0$, then the Nash equilibrium result $(R_{rs\,max}^*, \mu_{min})$, $(R_{sr\,max}^*, \nu_{min})$ can satisfy Pareto optimum following the increase of R_{rs} and R_{sr} thus the whole network could achieve optimum status.

5   Simulation Results

In the simulation, we consider the VHF band as the WS. The coordination of destination is $(0,0)$, source is $(4,0)$. Here, the unit coordinates are all nautical mile. Easy to observe, we select relay (xx, yy) and the horizontal coordination and vertical coordination are varied in the scope of $(1, 10)$.The transmitting time T is 10msthe λ_0 criterion price is 0.1.The local services transmitting rate of source and relay are all 320 Mb/S.

Simulation results are the comparison of payoff of system , source and relay when axis X and Y respective indicating horizontal and vertical coordination, as shown in Fig. 2, respectively. We can see that the cooperative system pay-off are distinctive increased than non-cooperative. And the distinction between relay and destination is increased, the payoff is larger, the desire is stronger, efficiency is better. But the payoffs of source are nearly when cooperation and non-cooperation. It explains that it does not obtain the best offset from fee. The payoff of source can increase if value of μ is larger.

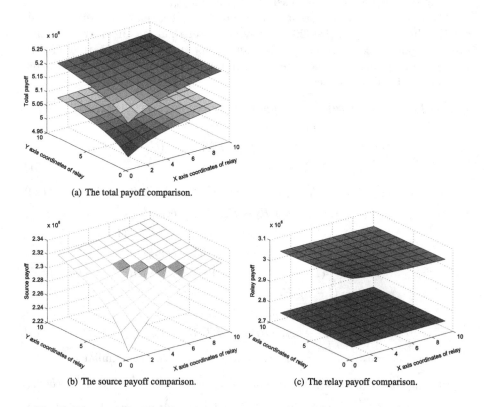

(a) The total payoff comparison.

(b) The source payoff comparison.

(c) The relay payoff comparison.

Fig. 2. The payoff comparison between cooperative and non-cooperative system.

6 Conclusion

In this paper, an innovative paradigm cooperative cognitive maritime wireless mesh/ad hoc networks (CCMWMAN) is proposed to provide high-speed and low-cost communications for maritime environment. The framework is developed, as well as the analysis of available white space at sea to efficiently use the limited frequency resource. Moreover, game theory method is applied within the cooperative SUs. An symmetrical system model is constructed, and a price game based on a payoff function is proposed. Then the game theory process to converge to Nash equilibrium is described. Simulation results indicate that our propose scheme is desirable with regards to performance of total system, source node and relay node. For future work, we plan to research the design of MAC layer and resource allocation issue between primary user and secondary users. Moreover, the security of secondary users could be considered further.

Acknowledgments. This work was supported in part by China Postdoctoral Science Foundation under Grants 2013M530900, Natural Science Foundation of China under Grant 61401057, Science and technology research program of Liaoning under Grants L2014213, NSERC, Canada, Research Funds for the Central Universities 3132015201, China Postdoctoral International Academic Exchange Fund, and also supported by Scientific Research Foundation for the Returned Overseas Chinese Scholars from Ministry of Human Resources and Social Security.

References

1. Cellular-news, Maritime WiMAX Network Launched in Singapore (2008). http://www.cellular-news.com/story/29749.php
2. Zhou, M.T., Harada, H.: Cognitive maritime wireless mesh/ad hoc networks. J. Netw. Comput. Appl. **35**(2), 518–526 (2012)
3. Chen, C., Yan, J., Lu, N., Wang, Y., Yang, X., Guan, X.: Ubiquitous monitoring for industrial cyber-physical systems over relay assisted wireless sensor networks. IEEE Trans. Emerg. Topics Comput. doi:10.1109/TETC.2014.2386615
4. Xu, Q., Su, Z., Han, B., Fang, D., Xu, Z., Gan, X.: Analytical model with a novel selfishness division of mobile nodes to participate cooperation. Peer-to-Peer Netw. Appl. doi:10.1007/s12083-015-0330-6
5. Su, Z., Xu, Q., Zhu, H., Wang, Y.: A novel design for content delivery over software defined mobile social networks. IEEE Netw. **29**(4), 1332–1346 (2015)
6. Liu, S., Zhu, H., Du, R., Chen, C., Guan, X.: Location privacy preserving dynamic spectrum auction in cognitive radio network. In: IEEE ICDCS, pp. 256-265 (2013)
7. Gao, Z., Zhu, H., Liu, Y., Li, M., Cao, Z.: Location privacy in database-driven cognitive radio networks: attacks and countermeasures. In: IEEE INFOCOM, pp. 2751-2759 (2013)
8. Yu, Q., Chen, J., Fan, Y., (Sherman) Shen, X., Sun, Y.: Multi-channel assignment in wireless sensor networks: a game theoretic approach. In: IEEE INFOCOM, USA (2010)
9. Shastry, N., Adve, R.S.: Stimulating cooperative diversity in wireless ad hoc networks through Pricing. In: IEEE ICC, pp. 3747-3752 (2006)

10. Zhang, N., et al.: Risk-aware cooperative spectrum access for multi-channel cognitive radio networks. IEEE J. Sel. Areas Commun. **32**(3), 516C527 (2014)
11. Chen, F., Yang, Y., Wang, Z.: Novel resource allocation for cooperative MB-OFDM UWB Systems. In: IEEE WiCom (2009)
12. Maglogiannis, I., et al.: Next generation maritime communication systems. Int. J. Mob. Commun. **3**(3), 231–248 (2005)
13. Gao, Z., Zhu, H., Li, S., Du, S., Li, X.: Security and privacy of collaborative spectrum sensing in cognitive radio networks. IEEE Wire. Commun. **19**(6), 106–112 (2012)
14. Menghan, W.: Cooperative resource management of wireless multi-medial based on game theory. TN929.53 (2007)

Security and Privacy Issues of Fog Computing: A Survey

Shanhe Yi$^{(\boxtimes)}$, Zhengrui Qin, and Qun Li

College of William and Mary, Williamsburg, VA, USA
{syi,zhengrui,liqun}@cs.wm.edu

Abstract. Fog computing is a promising computing paradigm that extends cloud computing to the edge of networks. Similar to cloud computing but with distinct characteristics, fog computing faces new security and privacy challenges besides those inherited from cloud computing. In this paper, we have surveyed these challenges and corresponding solutions in a brief manner.

Keywords: Fog computing · Cloud/mobile computing · Security · Privacy

1 Introduction

The prevalence of ubiquitously connected smart devices are shaping the main factor of computing. Rapid development of wearable computing, smart metering, smart home/city, connected vehicles and large-scale wireless sensor network are making everything connected and smarter, termed the Internet of Things (IoT). IDC (International Data Corporation) has predicted that in the year of 2015, "the IoT will continue to rapidly expand the traditional IT industry" up 14 % from 2014 [14]. As we know, smart devices usually face challenges rooted from computation power, battery, storage and bandwidth, which in return hinder quality of services (QoS) and user experience. To alleviate the burden of limited resources on smart devices, cloud computing is considered as a promising computing paradigm, which can deliver services to end users in terms of infrastructure, platform and software, and supply applications with elastic resources at low cost.

Cloud computing, however, is not a "one-size-fit-all" solution. There are still problems unsolved since IoT applications usually require mobility support, geo-distribution, location-awareness and low latency. *Fog computing*, a.k.a edge computing, is proposed to enable computing directly at the edge of the network, which can deliver new applications and services for billions of connected devices [2]. Fog devices are usually set-top-boxes, access points, road side units, cellular base stations, etc. End devices, fog and cloud are forming a three layer hierarchical service delivery model, supporting a range of applications such as web content delivery [48], augmented reality [15], and big data analysis [46]. A typical conceptual architecture of fog/cloud infrastructure is shown in Fig. 1.

© Springer International Publishing Switzerland 2015
K. Xu and J. Zhu (Eds.): WASA 2015, LNCS 9204, pp. 685–695, 2015.
DOI: 10.1007/978-3-319-21837-3_67

Fig. 1. An example of fog/cloud architecture

Since fog is deemed as a non-trivial extension of cloud, some security and privacy issues in the context of cloud computing [35], can be foreseen to unavoidably impact fog computing. Security and privacy issues will lag the promotion of fog computing if not well addressed, according to the fact that 74 % of IT Executives and Chief Information Officers reject cloud in term of the risks in security and privacy [49]. As fog computing is still in its infant stage, there is little work on security and privacy issues. Since fog computing is proposed in the context of Internet of Things (IoT), and originated from cloud computing, security and privacy issues of cloud are inherited in fog computing. While some issues can be addressed using existing schemes, there are other issues facing new challenges, due to the distinct characteristics of fog computing, such as heterogeneity in fog node and fog network, requirement of mobility support, massive scale geo-distributed nodes, location-awareness and low latency.

In this paper, we will discuss secur ity and privacy issues in fog computing by reviewing existing work of fog computing and related work in underlying domains, and identify new security and privacy problems.

2   Fog Computing Overview

In this section, we briefly give an overview of fog computing. We prefer not to discuss the cloud computing or mobile cloud computing, and readers can refer to extensive existing surveys if interested [8,47].

Definition. As a new paradigm of computing, fog computing is still not a full-fledged concept in the community. In the position paper [2], fog computing is considered as an extension of the cloud computing to the edge of the network, which is a highly virtualized platform of resource pool that provides computation, storage, and networking services to nearby end users. In the perspective of work [38], they have defined fog computing as *"a scenario where a huge number of heterogeneous (wireless and sometimes autonomous) ubiquitous and decentralised devices communicate and potentially cooperate among them and with the network to perform storage and processing tasks without the intervention of third parties. These tasks can be for supporting basic network functions or new services and applications that run in a sandboxed environment. Users leasing part of* *their devices to host these services get incentives for doing so.*" Although those definitions are still debatable before, fog computing is no longer a buzzword.

Characterization. Fog computing has its advantages due to its edge location, and therefore is able to support applications (e.g. gaming, augmented reality, real time video stream processing) with low latency requirements. This edge location can also provide rich network context information, such as local network condition, traffic statistics and client status information, which can be used by fog applications to offer context-aware optimization. Another interesting characteristic is the location-awareness; not only can the geo-distributed fog node infer its own location but also the fog node can track end user devices to support mobility, which may be a game changing factor for location-based services and applications. Furthermore, the interplays between fog and fog, fog and cloud become important since fog can easily gets local overview while the global coverage can only be achieved at a higher layer.

Fog Node. The ubiquity of smart devices and rapid development of standard virtualization and cloud technology make several fog node implementation available. *Resource-poor fog node* This kind of fog nodes is usually built on existing network devices. ParaDrop [42] is a new fog computing architecture on gateway (WiFi access point or home set-top box), which is an ideal fog node choice due to its capabilities to provide service and its proximity at network edge. Given the fact that typical home environment gateways are resource-limited, the authors implement the ParaDrop using Linux Container (LXC) abstraction which is more lightweight than traditional virtual machines. *Resource-rich fog node* Resource-rich fog nodes are usually specific high-end servers with powerful CPU, larger memory and storage. Cloudlet [29,30], like a "second-class data center", is able to provide elastic resources to nearby mobile devices, with low latency and large bandwidth. With cloud techniques, Cloudlet is easy to upgrade and replace.

Service Delivery and Deployment Models. Similar to cloud computing, we can anticipate that the service delivery models in fog computing can be grouped into three categories: software as a service (SaaS), platform as a service (PaaS), and infrastructure as a service (IaaS). We may also expect the following deployment models: private fog, community fog, public fog and hybrid fog.

Similar Concept. Mobile cloud computing (MCC) and mobile-edge computing (MEC) are similar to fog computing. MCC refers to an infrastructure in which both the data storage and the data processing happen outside of the mobile devices [8]. MEC focus on resource-rich fog servers like cloudlets running at the edge of mobile networks [11]. Fog computing distinguishes itself as a more generalized computing paradigm especially in the context of Internet of Things.

3 Security and Privacy Issues

We admit that security and privacy should be addressed in every layer in designing fog computing system. Here we ask ourselves "what is new about fog computing security and privacy?". Due to the characteristics of fog computing, we may need future work to tackle those problems.

3.1 Trust and Authentication

In cloud computing deployment, data centers are usually owned by cloud service providers. However, fog service providers can be different parties due to different deployment choices: (1) Internet service providers or wireless carriers, who have control of home gateways or cellular base stations, may build fog with their existing infrastructures; (2) Cloud service providers, who want to expand their cloud services to the edge of the network, may also build fog infrastructures; (3) End users, who own a local private cloud and want to reduce the cost of ownership, would like to turn the local private cloud into fog and lease spare resources on the local private cloud. This flexibility complicates the trust situation of fog.

Trust Model. Reputation based trust model [18] has been successful in eCommerce, peer-to-peer (P2P), user reviews and online social networks. Damiani et al. [7] proposed a robust reputation system for resource selection in P2P networks using a distributed polling algorithm to assess the reliability of a resource before downloading. In designing a fog computing reputation-based reputation system, we may need to tackle issues such as (1) how to achieve persistent, unique, and distinct identity, (2) how to treat intentional and accidental misbehavior, (3) how to conduct punishment and redemption of reputation. There are also trusting models based on special hardware such as Secure Element (SE), Trusted Execution Environment (TEE), or Trusted Platform Module (TPM), which can provide trust utility in fog computing applications.

Rogue Fog Node. A rogue fog node would be a fog device or fog instance that pretends to be legitimate and coaxes end users to connect to it. For example, in an insider attack, a fog administrator may be authorized to manage fog instances, but may instantiate a rogue fog instance rather than a legitimate one. Work [34] has demonstrated the feasibility of man-in-the-middle attack in fog computing, before which the gateway should be either compromised or replaced by a fake one. Once connected, the adversary can manipulate the incoming and outgoing requests from end users or cloud, collect or tamper user data stealthily, and easily launch further attacks. The existing of fake fog node will be a big threat to user data security and privacy. This problem is hard to address in fog computing due to several reasons (1) complex trust situation calls for different trust management schemes, (2) dynamic creating, deleting of virtual machine instance make it hard to maintain a blacklist of rogue nodes. Han et al. [16,17] have proposed a measurement-based method which enables a client to avoid connecting rogue access point (AP). Their approach leverages the round-trip time between end users and the DNS server to detect rogue AP at the client side.

Authentication. Authentication is an important issue for the security of fog computing since services are offered to massive-scale end users by front fog nodes. Stojmenovic et al. [34] have considered the main security issue of fog computing as the authentication at different levels of fog nodes. Traditional PKI-based authentication is not efficient and has poor scalability. Balfanz et al. [1] have proposed a cheap, secure and user-friendly solution to the authentication problem in local ad-hoc wireless network, relying on a physical contact for pre-authentication in a location-limited channel. Similarly, NFC can also be used to simplify the authentication procedure in the case of cloudlet [3]. As the emergence of biometric authentication in mobile computing and cloud computing, such as fingerprint authentication, face authentication, touch-based or keystroke-based authentication, etc., it will be beneficial to apply biometric-based authentication in fog computing.

3.2 Network Security

Due to the predominance of wireless in fog networking, wireless network security is big concern to fog networking. Example attacks are jamming attacks, sniffer attacks, etc. Those attacks can be addressed in the research domain of wireless network, which is not in the scope of this survey. Normally, in network, we have to trust the configurations manually generated by a network administrator and isolate network management traffic from regular data traffic [36]. However, fog nodes are deployed at the edge of Internet, which definitely bring heavy burden to the network management, imagining the cost of maintaining massive scale cloud servers which are distributed all over the network edge without easy access for maintenance. The employment of SDN can ease the implementation and management, and increase network scalability and reduce costs, in many aspects of fog computing. We also argue that applying SDN technique in fog computing will bring fog networking security new challenges and opportunities.

How can SDN help the fog network security? (1) Network Monitoring and Intrusion Detection System (IDS): CloudWatch [32] can leverage OpenFlow [21] to route traffic for security monitoring applications or IDS. (2) Traffic Isolation and Prioritization: Traffic isolation and prioritization can be used to prevent an attack from congesting the network or dominating shared resources such as CPU or disk I/O. SDN can easily use VLAN ID/tag to isolate traffic in VLAN group and segregate malicious traffic. (3) Network Resource Access Control: Klaedtke et al. [19] have proposed an access control scheme on a SDN controller based on OpenFlow, (4) Network Sharing: Fog-enhanced router in home network can be opened to guests, if the network sharing to guests is carefully designed with security concerns. Work [44] has proposed OpenWiFi, in which the guest WiFi authentication is shifted to the cloud to establish guest identity; access is independently provided for guests; and accounting is enforced to delegate responsibility of guests.

3.3 Secure Data Storage

In fog computing, user data is outsourced and user's control over data is handed over to fog node, which introduces same security threats as it is in cloud computing. First, it is hard to ensure data integrity, since the outsourced data could be lost or incorrectly modified. Second, the uploaded data could be abused by unauthorized parties for other interests.

To address these threats, auditable data storage service has been proposed in the context of cloud computing to protect the data. Techniques such as homomorphic encryption and searchable encryption are combined to provide integrity, confidentiality and verifiability for cloud storage system to allow a client to check its data stored on untrusted servers. Want et al. [40] have proposed privacy-preserving public auditing for data stored in cloud, which relies on a third-party auditor (TPA), using homomorphic authenticator and random mask technique to protect privacy against TPA. To ensure data storage reliability, prior storage systems use erasure codes or network coding to deal with data corruption detection and data repair, while Cao et al. [5] have proposed a scheme using LT code, which provides less storage cost, much faster data retrieval, and comparable communication cost. Yang et al. [43] have provided a good overview of existing work towards data storage auditing service in cloud computing.

In fog computing, there are new challenges in designing secure storage system to achieve low-latency, support dynamic operation and deal with interplay between fog and cloud.

3.4 Secure and Private Data Computation

Another important issue in fog computing is to achieve secure and privacy-preserving computation outsourced to fog nodes.

Verifiable Computing. Verifiable computing enables a computing device to offload the computation of a function to other perhaps untrusted servers, while maintaining verifiable results. The other servers evaluate the function and return the result with a proof that the computation of the function was carried out correctly. The term verifiable computing was formalized in [13]. In fog computing, to instill confidence in the computation offloaded to the fog node, the fog user should be able to verify the correctness of the computation.

Below are some existing methods to fulfill verifiable computing. Gennaro et al. [13] have proposed a verifiable computing protocol that allows the server to return a computationally-sound, non-interactive proof that can be verified by the client. The protocol can provide (at no additional cost) input and output privacy for the client such that the server does not learn any information about the input and output. Parno and Gentry have built a system, called *Pinocchio*, such that the client can verify general computations done by a server while relying only on cryptographic assumptions [25]. With Pinocchio, the client creates a public evaluation key to describe her computation, and the server then evaluates the computation and uses the evaluation key to produce a proof of correctness.

Data Search. To protect data privacy, sensitive data from end users have to be encrypted before outsourced to the fog node, making effective data utilization services challenging. One of the most important services is keyword search, i.e., keyword search among encrypted data files. Researchers have developed several searchable encryption schemes that allow a user to securely search over encrypted data through keywords without decryption. In [33], the authors proposed the first ever scheme for searches on encrypted data, which provides provable secrecy for encryption, query isolation, controlled searching, and support of hidden query. Later, many other schemes have been developed, such as [6,39].

3.5   Privacy

The leakage of private information, such as data, location or usage, are gaining attentions when end users are using services like cloud computing, wireless network, IoT. There are also challenges for preserving such privacy in fog computing, because fog nodes are in vicinity of end users and can collect more sensitive information than the remote cloud lying in the core network. Privacy-preserving techniques have been proposed in many scenarios including cloud [4], smart grid [28], wireless network [27], and online social network [24].

Data Privacy. In the fog network, privacy-preserving algorithms can be running in between the fog and cloud while those algorithms are usually resource-prohibited at the end devices. Fog node at the edge usually collects sensitive data generated by sensors and end devices. Techniques such as homomorphic encryption can be utilized to allow privacy-preserving aggregation at the local gateways without decryption [20]. *Differential privacy* [10] can be utilized to ensure non-disclosure of privacy of an arbitrary single entry in the data set in case of statistical queries,.

Usage Privacy. Another privacy issue is the usage pattern with which a fog client utilizes the fog services. For example in smart grid, the reading of the smart meter will disclose lots of information of a household, such as at what time there is no person at home, and at what time the TV is turned on, which absolutely breaches user's privacy. Although privacy-preserving mechanisms have been proposed in smart metering [22,28], they cannot be applied in fog computing directly, due to the lack of a trusted third party (i.e., a smart meter in smart grid) or no counterpart device like a battery. The fog node which can easily collect statistics of end user usage. One possible naive solution is that the fog client creates dummy tasks and offloads them to multiple fog nodes, hiding its real tasks among the dummy ones. However, this solution will increase the fog client's payment and waste resources and energy. Another solution would be designing a smart way of partitioning the application to make sure the offloaded resource usages do not disclose privacy information.

Location Privacy. In fog computing, the location privacy mainly refers to the location privacy of the fog clients. As a fog client usually offloads its tasks to the nearest fog node, the fog node, to whom the tasks are offloaded, can infer that the fog client is nearby and farther from other nodes. Furthermore, if a fog client utilizes multiple fog services at multiple locations, it may disclose its path trajectory to the fog nodes, assuming the fog nodes collude. As long as such a fog client is attached on a person or an important object, the location privacy of the person or the object is at risk.

If a fog client always strictly chooses its nearest fog server, the fog node can definitely knows that the fog client that is utilizing its computing resources is nearby. The only way to preserve the location privacy is through identity obfuscation such that even though the fog node knows a fog client is nearby it cannot identify the fog client. There are many methods for identity obfuscation; for example, in [41], the authors use a trusted third party to generate fake ID for each end user. In reality, a fog client does not necessarily choose the nearest fog node but chooses at will one of the fog nodes it can reach according some criteria, such as latency, reputation, load balance, etc. In this case, the fog node can only know the rough location of the fog client but cannot do so precisely. However, once the fog client utilizes computing resources from multiple fog nodes in an area, its location can boil down to a small region, since its location must be in the intersection of the multiple fog nodes' coverages. To preserve the location privacy in such scenario, one can utilize the method used in [12].

3.6   Access Control

Access control has been a reliable tool to ensure the security of the system and preserving of privacy of user. Traditional access control is usually addressed in a same trust domain. While due to the outsource nature of cloud computing, the access control in cloud computing is usually cryptographically implemented for outsourced data. Symmetric key based solution is not scalable in key management. Several public key based solutions are proposed trying to achieve fine-grained access control. Yu et al. [45] have proposed a fine-grained data access control scheme constructed on attribute-based encryption (ABE). Work [9] proposes a policy-based resource access control in fog computing, to support secure collaboration and interoperability between heterogeneous resources. In fog computing, how to design access control spanning client-fog-cloud, at the same time meet the designing goals and resource constraints will be challenging.

3.7   Intrusion Detection

Intrusion detection techniques are widely deployed in cloud system to mitigate attacks such as insider attack, flooding attack, port scanning, attacks on VM and hypervisor [23], or in smart grid system to monitor power meter measurements and detects abnormal measurements that could have been compromised by attackers [26,37]. In fog computing, IDS can be deployed on fog node system side to detect intrusive behavior by monitoring and analyzing log file, access control policies and user login information. They can also be deployed at the fog network side to detect malicious attacks such as denial-of-service (DoS), port scanning, etc. In fog computing, it provides new opportunities to investigate how fog computing can help with intrusion detection on both client side and the centralized cloud side. Work [31] has presented a cloudlet mesh based security framework which can detection intrusion to distance cloud, securing communication among mobile devices, cloudlet and cloud. There are also challenges such as implementing intrusion detection in geo-distributed, large-scale, high-mobility fog computing environ men to meet the low-latency requirement.

4   Conclusion

This paper discusses several security and privacy issues in the context of fog computing, which is a new computing paradigm to provide elastic resources at the edge of network to nearby end users. In the paper, we discuss security issues such as secure data storage, secure computation and network security. We also highlight privacy issues in data privacy, usage privacy, and location privacy, which may need new think to adapt new challenges and changes.

References

1. Balfanz, D., Smetters, D.K., Stewart, P., Wong, H.C.: Talking to strangers: authentication in ad-hoc wireless networks. In: NDSS (2002)
2. Bonomi, F., Milito, R., Zhu, J., Addepalli, S.: Fog computing and its role in the internet of things. In: Workshop on Mobile Cloud Computing. ACM (2012)
3. Bouzefrane, S., Mostefa, A.F.B., Houacine, F., Cagnon, H.: Cloudlets authentication in nfc-based mobile computing. In: MobileCloud. IEEE (2014)
4. Cao, N., Wang, C., Li, M., Ren, K., Lou, W.: Privacy-preserving multi-keyword ranked search over encrypted cloud data. TPDS **25**(1), 222–233 (2014)
5. Cao, N., Yu, S., Yang, Z., Lou, W., Hou, Y.T.: Lt codes-based secure and reliable cloud storage service. In: INFOCOM. IEEE (2012)
6. Cash, D., et al.: Dynamic searchable encryption in very-large databases: data structures and implementation. In: NDSS, vol. 14 (2014)
7. Damiani, E., et al.: A reputation-based approach for choosing reliable resources in peer-to-peer networks. In: CCS. ACM (2002)
8. Dinh, H.T., Lee, C., Niyato, D., Wang, P.: A survey of mobile cloud computing: architecture, applications, and approaches. WCMC **13**(18), 1587–1611 (2013)
9. Dsouza, C., Ahn, G.J., Taguinod, M.: Policy-driven security management for fog computing: preliminary framework and a case study. In: IRI. IEEE (2014)
10. Dwork, C.: Differential privacy. In: van Tilborg, H.C.A., Jajodia, S. (eds.) Encyclopedia of Cryptography and Security. LNCS, vol. 2011. Springer, Heidelberg (2011)
11. ETSI: Mobile-edge computing (2014). http://goo.gl/7NwTLE
12. Gao, Z., Zhu, H., Liu, Y., Li, M., Cao, Z.: Location privacy in database-driven cognitive radio networks: Attacks and countermeasures. In: INFOCOM. IEEE (2013)
13. Gennaro, R., Gentry, C., Parno, B.: Non-interactive verifiable computing: outsourcing computation to untrusted workers. In: Rabin, T. (ed.) CRYPTO 2010. LNCS, vol. 6223, pp. 465–482. Springer, Heidelberg (2010)
14. Gil Press: Idc: Top 10 technology predictions (2015). http://goo.gl/zFujnE
15. Ha, K., Chen, Z., Hu, W., Richter, W., Pillai, P., Satyanarayanan, M.: Towards wearable cognitive assistance. In: Mobisys. ACM (2014)
16. Han, H., Sheng, B., Tan, C.C., Li, Q., Lu, S.: A measurement based rogue ap detection scheme. In: INFOCOM. IEEE (2009)
17. Han, H., Sheng, B., Tan, C.C., Li, Q., Lu, S.: A timing-based scheme for rogue ap detection. TPDS **22**(11), 1912–1925 (2011)
18. Jøsang, A., Ismail, R., Boyd, C.: A survey of trust and reputation systems for online service provision. Decis. Support Syst. **43**(2), 618–644 (2007)
19. Klaedtke, F., Karame, G.O., Bifulco, R., Cui, H.: Access control for sdn controllers. In: HotSDN, vol. 14 (2014)

20. Lu, R., et al.: Eppa: an efficient and privacy-preserving aggregation scheme for secure smart grid communications. TPDS **23**(9), 1621–1631 (2012)
21. McKeown, N., et al.: Openflow: enabling innovation in campus networks. ACM SIGCOMM CCR **38**(2), 69–74 (2008)
22. McLaughlin, S., McDaniel, P., Aiello, W.: Protecting consumer privacy from electric load monitoring. In: CCS. ACM (2011)
23. Modi, C., et al.: A survey of intrusion detection techniques in cloud. J. Netw. Comput. Appl. **36**(1), 42–57 (2013)
24. Novak, E., Li, Q.: Near-pri: Private, proximity based location sharing. In: INFOCOM. IEEE (2014)
25. Parno, B., Howell, J., Gentry, C., Raykova, M.: Pinocchio: nearly practical verifiable computation. In: Security and Privacy. IEEE (2013)
26. Qin, Z., Li, Q., Chuah, M.C.: Defending against unidentifiable attacks in electric power grids. TPDS **24**(10), 1961–1971 (2013)
27. Qin, Z., Yi, S., Li, Q., Zamkov, D.: Preserving secondary users' privacy in cognitive radio networks. In: INFOCOM, 2014 Proceedings IEEE. IEEE (2014)
28. Rial, A., Danezis, G.: Privacy-preserving smart metering. In: Proceedings of the 10th Annual ACM Workshop on Privacy in the Electronic Society. ACM (2011)
29. Satyanarayanan, M., Bahl, P., Caceres, R., Davies, N.: The case for vm-based cloudlets in mobile computing. Perv. Comput. **8**(4), 14–23 (2009)
30. Satyanarayanan, M., et al.: An open ecosystem for mobile-cloud convergence. Commun. Mag. **53**(3), 63–70 (2015)
31. Shi, Y., Abhilash, S., Hwang, K.: Cloudlet mesh for securing mobile clouds from intrusions and network attacks. In: Mobile Cloud 2015)
32. Shin, S., Gu, G.: Cloudwatcher: network security monitoring using openflow in dynamic cloud networks. In: ICNP. IEEE (2012)
33. Song, D.X., Wagner, D., Perrig, A.: Practical techniques for searches on encrypted data. In: Security and Privacy. IEEE (2000)
34. Stojmenovic, I., Wen, S.: The fog computing paradigm: scenarios and security issues. In: FedCSIS. IEEE (2014)
35. Takabi, H., Joshi, J.B., Ahn, G.J.: Security and privacy challenges in cloud computing environments. IEEE Secur. Priv. **8**(6), 24–31 (2010)
36. Tsugawa, M., et al.: Cloud computing security: what changes with software-defined networking? In: Jajodia, S., Kant, K., Samarati, P., Singhal, A., Swarup, V., Wang, C. (eds.) Secure Cloud Computing. LNCS. Springer, Heidelberg (2014)
37. Valenzuela, J., Wang, J., Bissinger, N.: Real-time intrusion detection in power system operations. IEEE Trans. Pow. Syst. **28**(2), 1052–1062 (2013)
38. Vaquero, L.M., Rodero-Merino, L.: Finding your way in the fog: towards a comprehensive definition of fog computing. ACM SIGCOMM CCR **44**(5), 27–32 (2014)
39. Wang, C., Cao, N., Ren, K., Lou, W.: Enabling secure and efficient ranked keyword search over outsourced cloud data. TPDS **23**(8), 1467–1479 (2012)
40. Wang, C., Wang, Q., Ren, K., Lou, W.: Privacy-preserving public auditing for data storage security in cloud computing. In: INFOCOM. IEEE (2010)
41. Wei, W., Xu, F., Li, Q.: Mobishare: Flexible privacy-preserving location sharing in mobile online social networks. In: INFOCOM. IEEE (2012)
42. Willis, D.F., Dasgupta, A., Banerjee, S.: Paradrop: a multi-tenant platform for dynamically installed third party services on home gateways. In: SIGCOMM Workshop on Distributed Cloud Computing. ACM (2014)
43. Yang, K., Jia, X.: Data storage auditing service in cloud computing: challenges, methods and opportunities. World Wide Web **15**(4), 409–428 (2012)

44. Yap, K.K., et al.: Separating authentication, access and accounting: a case study with openwifi. Technical report, Open Networking Foundation (2011)
45. Yu, S., Wang, C., Ren, K., Lou, W.: Achieving secure, scalable, and fine-grained data access control in cloud computing. In: INFOCOM. IEEE (2010)
46. Zao, J.K., et al.: Pervasive brain monitoring and data sharing based on multi-tier distributed computing and linked data technology. Frontiers in Human Neuroscience 8 (2014)
47. Zhang, Q., Cheng, L., Boutaba, R.: Cloud computing: state-of-the-art and research challenges. J. Internet Serv. Appl. 1(1), 7–18 (2010)
48. Zhu, J., et al.: Improving web sites performance using edge servers in fog computing architecture. In: SOSE. IEEE (2013)
49. Zissis, D., Lekkas, D.: Addressing cloud computing security issues. Future Gener. Comput. Syst. 28(3), 583–592 (2012)

Mobile Data Gathering with Time-Constraints in Wireless Sensor Networks

Xuming Yin[1,2,3], Jinghua Zhu[1,2,3]([✉]), Yingshu Li[1,2,3], and Zhiqiang Wu[1,2,3]

[1] School of Computer Science and Technology, Heilongjiang University,
Harbin 150080, Heilongjiang, China
zhujinghua@hit.edu.cn
[2] Key Laboratory of Database and Parallel Computing of Heilongjiang Province,
Harbin, Heilongjiang, China
[3] Georgia State University, Atlanta, GA, USA

Abstract. Recent research shows that significant energy can be saved by using mobile elements (ME)for data gathering in wireless sensor networks. The major drawback of this approach is the low movement speed of MEs which limits them to gather data from all sensor nodes with time constraints. This paper presents a data gathering algorithm called Minimum Mobile Elements Routing with Deadline (M2ERD). The goal of M2ERD is to find a set of minimum cost trajectories whilst satisfying deadline constraint. A genetic algorithm is presented to determine the feasible trajectories. The effectiveness and efficiency of M2ERD are verified through extensive simulations.The presented results show that M2ERD not only can provide substantial energy saving compared with traditional data gathering algorithm, but also can reduce the cost of mobile elements compared with ME-based data gathering algorithm.

Keywords: Wireless sensor network · Data gathering algorithm · Mobile elements · Genetic algorithm

1 Introduction

In recent years Wireless Sensor Networks (WSNs) have been widely deployed for a large number of applications, ranging from monitoring to event detection and target tracking [1–5]. WSNs in these applications often produce high-bandwidth sensor data that need to be gathered under stringent deadline constraints. Traditional routing algorithm for data gathering is energy-inefficient due to a large amount of multi-hop transmissions. Recent work have exploited the use of mobile elements(MEs) for data collection. In this approach, MEs move within the sensing fields,collect data from sensors and carry them back to Base Station(BS). Significant network energy saving can be achieved due to reducing the expensive multi-hop wireless transmissions. However, the major drawback of this approach is the low movement speed of MEs which limits them to gather data from all sensor nodes within given deadline. Multiple mobile elements methods can decrease the network latency, however, this method will incur higher travel cost

© Springer International Publishing Switzerland 2015
K. Xu and J. Zhu (Eds.): WASA 2015, LNCS 9204, pp. 696–705, 2015.
DOI: 10.1007/978-3-319-21837-3_68

and few work takes consideration of minimizing the total travel cost of mobile elements.In many scenarios, deadline constraint, energy saving and travel cost of mobile elements need to be balanced at the same time.

In this paper, a new data gathering algorithm called Minimum Mobile Elements Routing with Deadline (M2ERD) is presented. The goal of the M2ERD algorithm is to maximize network lifetime by finding a set of optimal trajectories for mobile elements whilst satisfying their deadline constraint. In order to minimize the network energy consumption, the mobile elements are required to visit all the source nodes along constraint paths. This problem is related to the Travel Salesman Problem(TSP) and Vehicle Routing Problem(VRP) which are well known NP-hard problems. We formulate the problem and present a genetic algorithm to determine the minimal cost trajectories of mobile elements. We first adapt Prins' Splitting algorithm [6] to initialize the populations (mobile elements' trajectories), then we reproduce and hybridize the populations by crossover and mutation. The output of the genetic algorithm is a set of minimal cost trajectories satisfying deadline constraint. In order to balance energy saving and travel cost, we perform a clustering phase before the genetic algorithm. Mobile elements gather data from Cluster Heads (CH) instead of source nodes. The optimal trajectories are a set of sequence of CH nodes as shown in Fig. 1.

We analyzed the impact of deadline constraints, network scale, movement speed on energy consumption through extensive simulations. Simulation results showed that M2ERD outperformed them in terms of energy saving, travel cost and deadline misses.

The rest of this paper is organized as follows. Section 2 reviews related work. Section 3 formulates the problem and makes some assumptions. The M2ERD algorithm is given in Sect. 4. Simulation results algorithm are discussed in Sect. 5. Finally, the conclusion and future work are drawn in Sect. 6.

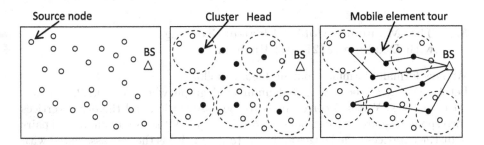

Fig. 1. Examples on sensor nodes distribution with one base station(left) and sensor node clustering(middle) and two tours passing through all cluster heads(right)

2 Related Works

MARIO and SAJAL [1] presents a comprehensive literature survey on WSNs with Mobile Elements. Yao [7] presented a residual energy aware mobile data gathering method. Zhao [8] considered the load balance problem and proposed a dual data gathering method.Several heuristics [9] are proposed to schedule the movement of MEs such that the source nodes can be visited before buffer over-flow. Xing et al. [10] presents a Rendez-vous Data Collection (RDC) approach jointly considering the motion control of an ME. Several mobility patterns are considered, depending on whether the ME can move freely or not. The authors in [11] present a Connectivity-Based Data Collection (CBDC) algorithm. The CBDC algorithm utilizes the connectivity between sensor nodes so as to deter-mine the trajectory of the mobile sink whilst satisfying its path constraint and minimizing the number of multi-hop communications.

Although there are a number of work considering the energy efficient data gathering in mobility-assisted WSN, little work consider energy saving,travel cost and time constraint simultaneously. The M2ERD algorithm proposed in this paper aims at gathering sensing data energy-efficiently under time constraint and minimizing the travel cost of mobile elements at the same time.

3   Problem Definition

3.1   Assumptions

We make the following assumptions in this paper.

- Sensor nodes are randomly and uniform distributed in the sensing field.
- Sensor nodes and mobile elements are aware of their physical locations by GPS.
- Each source node generates a chunk of data at a period of D and data must be delivered to BS within time D.
- Nodes located within the range of the ME can send its data directly to ME.

3.2   The Minimum Mobile Element Routing with Deadline (M2ERD) Problem

We now formally formulate our problem as follows.

Let G=(V, E, C) be a weighted undirected graph where V={0,1,2,...n} is a set of vertices. Vertex 0 corresponds to the base station and the other vertices correspond to source sensor nodes. $E = \{(i,j)|i,j \in V\}$ is a set of unordered pairs of distinct vertices called edges and $C = \{c_{ij}|i,j \in V\}$ is the cost associated with each edge. Let c_{ij} be the travel time from senor node i to j. A trajectory T is a sequence of nodes $T = (i_1, i_2, ...i_k)$ such that $(i_j, i_{j+1}) \in E$ for all $1 \leq j \leq k-1$. Assume that T_i is a feasible route then the total travel time for T_i can be calculated as follows:

$$C(T_i) = c_{0,i_1} + \sum_{j=2}^{k} c_{i_{j-1},i_j} + c_{i_k,0} \qquad (1)$$

Let D be the common deadline for each trajectory and v_m be the maximum speed of each mobile element. Then $L = D \cdot v_m$ represents the maximum tour length for each mobile element. A solution S is a collection of trajectories $S = \{T_1, T_2, ..., T_m\}$, such that each source sensor node can be covered by exactly one trajectory whose length no more than L.

The Minimum Mobile Element Routing with Deadline Problem (M2ERD) can be formulated as the following optimization problem:

$$S = \arg\min \sum_{T_i \in S} C(T_i) \tag{2}$$

We have the following theorem regarding the complexity of the M2ERD problem.

Theorem 1. The M2ERD problem is NP-hard.

4   The Proposed Algorithm

The goal of the M2ERD problem is to minimize the network energy consumption by finding a set of minimum cost trajectories to cover all the source nodes in WSN. However, due to time constraint, sometimes it is not possible to cover all the source nodes by a limited number of feasible trajectories in a large scale WSN. Therefore, a clustering phase is needed to reduce the visiting nodes in the M2ERD problem. Then we present a genetic algorithm to determine optimal trajectories in the second phase. If the number of trajectories beyond a given threshold, we apply a tour reduction procedure to combine tours.

4.1   Nodes Clustering Phase

In this phase, sensor nodes are grouped into M clusters based on its connectivity to each other. Every node can communicate with all the other nodes in the same cluster via one-hop communication. Let G_k represent a set of nodes, such that $G_k = \{i \in V | \forall j \in V, w_{ij} = 1 \wedge i \neq j\}$, $w_{ij} = 1$ if nodes i and j are one-hop connected, otherwise $w_{ij} = 0$. N_k denotes the number of sensor in cluster G_k. The centroid point of each cluster is computed as the cluster head (CH) node. The cluster member nodes transmit their data to their CH. MEs collect data from CH nodes along specific tours.

4.2   Tour Determination Phase

As already mentioned, the primary task of the mobile elements is to collect data from all the cluster head nodes along specific tours. The tours' length of the mobile elements is restricted due to the limited energy resources and the buffer constraints of sensors.Therefore, the mobile elements must follow specified tours with time constraint and minimize total cost of MEs. In this paper, we adapt Prins' algorithm [6] to handle the optimal tour determination. It is based on a genetic algorithm. We will describe the genetic algorithm in details in the following sections.

(1) Chromosomes and Initial Population. A chromosome T is a permutation of n positive integers and each integer is corresponding a sensor node. The chromosome represents the tour of mobile elements. The following splitting algorithm can break one tour into several different tours and get the best partition of a given tour. The main idea of the splitting algorithm can be described as follows. Let $T = (1, 2, ..., n)$ be a given chromosome, consider an auxiliary graph $G' = (V', E')$ where $V' = (0, 1, 2, ..., n)$. An arc $(i, j) \in E'$ if

$$C_{ij} = c_{0,i} + \sum_{k=i+1}^{j-1} C_{k,k+1} + c_{j,0} \leq L \qquad (3)$$

Here C_{ij} is the total travel cost for the tour $T_{ij} = (i, i+1, ..., j)$. An optimal split of T corresponds to the shortest paths from Base Station(node 0) to n in G'.

The following example demonstrates the evaluation of a chromosome. The left graph in Fig. 2 shows a sequence T=(a,b,c,d,e,f). The number on each edger is the travel cost(time). Let us assume that the deadline is 60 in this example. The middle graph in Fig. 2 is a auxiliary graph G'. The edge with weight 50 corresponds to tour (0,a,b,0). The weight associated with other edges are similar defined. The shortest tour from BS to node f is (0,a,b,0,c,0,d,e,f,0) with minimum travel time 170. The right graph in Fig. 2 are the final optimal three tours each of which satisfies the deadline 60.

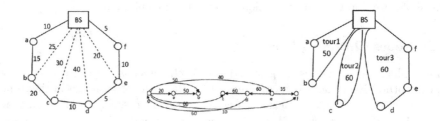

Fig. 2. An example of tour splitting

In practice, we do not have to construct the auxiliary graph. It can be done by a label and split procedure. Two labels C_i and P_i are computed for each vertex in $T = (1, 2, 3, ...n)$, C_i is the cost of the shortest path from Base Station to node i, P_i is predecessor of node i in this path. The minimum cost is given at the end by C_n. The Splitting Algorithm is described as follows.

(2) Crossover. A crossover operation is performed on the selected chromosome in order to reproduce the population. First, two chromosomes P_1 and P_2 are randomly selected in the initial populations and the least cost chromosome becomes the first parent P_1. Then we randomly choose two cutting points i and j in P_1.

Algorithm 1. Splitting_Algorithm

Input: (1) T=(1,2,3,...n) be a given chromosome
(2) L be the maximum length of a tour
Output: The optimal partition paths set

1: $C := 0$;
2: **for** i=1 to n **do**
3:     $C_i = \infty$;
4: **for** i=1 to n **do**
5:     cost:=0; j:=i;
6:     **while** $(j \leq n$) and (cost $\leq L$)) **do**
7:         **if** i==j **then**
8:             cost $= c_{0,s_j} + c_{s_j,0}$;
9:         **else**
10:            cost $=$ cost $- c_{s_{j-1},0} + c_{s_{j-1},s_j} + c_{sj,0}$;
11:        **if** cost $\leq L$ **then**
12:            **if** $(C_{i-1}+$cost $< C_j)$ **then**
13:                $C_j= C_{i-1}+$cost;
14:                $P_j= i - 1$;
15:            j:=j+1;
16: **return** C_n;

Then the substring $P1(i)...P1(j)$ is copied to $C(i)...C(j)$. Finally complete the missing nodes in C using P_2 from $j+1$ circularly. In this way, the initial populations can be reproduced.

(3) Mutation. In classic genetic algorithm, the mutation procedure is used to hybrid the chromosomes. Let C be the chromosome produced by crossover, it can be improved by local search at a fix mutation probability pm which stand for the impact of the mutation on C. For all every pair of distinct node (u,v), x and y be the successor's of u and v in their tours. We follow several rules to create new chromosome in the mutation process.

R1: Remove u from C and insert it after v, the new sequence is $(....v,u,.....)$
R2: Remove (u,x) from C and insert them after v, the new sequence is $(.....v,u,x)$
R3: Swap u and v, the new sequence is $(.....,v...,u...)$
R4: Swap (u,x) and (v,y), the new sequence is $(...v,y,.......u,x.....)$

Let C' be a new chromosome generated by mutation, if C' is better than the worst one in the current population, then C' will be added into the current population and the worst chromosome will be removed. If C' is better than the current best chromosome, we regard the current mutation process as a reproductive mutation.

4.3 Tours Reduction Phase

The presented genetic algorithm minimizes the total travel costs for all mobile elements with deadline constraint. The optimal trajectories start from the Base

Station, pass through all cluster heads and end up with the Base Station. Visiting all clusters in the network perhaps need a large number of mobile elements that exceeds the threshold constraint. In order to minimize the number of mobile elements, a path reduction mechanism should be used. Minimizing the number of MEs is achieved by removing one or more tours from the optimal tours set obtained by the genetic algorithm in Sect. 4.2. We repeatedly remove one tour and insert the clusters belong to this tour into the cheapest cost feasible tours. The insertion must guarantee that all the tours length satisfy the deadline constraint. This process continued until the number of tours constraint is satisfied or no more insertions are feasible. The clusters that could not find a feasible insertion point transfer their data to the nearby cluster through multi-hop routing.

The following algorithm describes the procedure of M2ERD. S is the min-cost feasible route set generated by the genetic algorithm, m is the max number of mobile elements in network.

Algorithm 2. M2ERD_Algorithm

1: Divide the sensors into clusters;
2: Apply GA algorithm to get the optimal feasible route set S;
3: **while** $|S| > m$ **do**
4:     Apply routes reduction procedure
5: Start Data Gathering;

---

5   Performance Evaluation

5.1   Experiments Setup

In this simulation, sensor nodes are randomly and uniformly deployed within 400×400 meter square area. Transmission rate of all sensor nodes including gateway nodes is set to 200 Kbps. The movement speed of MEs varies from 0.2 m/s to 1 m/s. A source generates and stores a data sample of 2 bytes every second. It sends all the accumulated data (20 K bits) to the BS every 20 min (i.e., the deadline is 20 min). Thus the tour length L must not longer than 1200 meters.

We compare the performance of M2ERD, RDC and NET. RDC is a Rendezvous-based Data Collection protocol [10]. NET represents the multi-hop transmission without any mobile elements.

5.2   Scalability of Sensor Nodes

The scalability of our algorithm is evaluated by testing the algorithm at varying number of sensor nodes (from 200 to 1000 nodes). The simulation is repeated for mobile elements of different deadline constraints (i.e., L = 800, 1000, 1200 and 1400 m). The main difference between our algorithm and RDC is that we

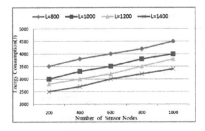

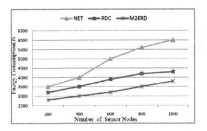

Fig. 3. The impact of number of nodes on energy consumption for different deadline constraints

Fig. 4. The impact of number of nodes on energy consumption for different algorithms

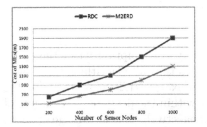

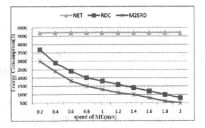

Fig. 5. The impact of number of nodes on ME's cost for different algorithms

Fig. 6. The impact of movement speed on energy consumption for different algorithms

minimize the total cost (distance,time) of the mobile elements' tours which is not considered in RDC. The results are shown in Figs. 3-5 respectively.

Generally speaking, when the number of sensor nodes increased, larger number of clusters is formulated. This, in turn, leads to increase the number of multi-hop nodes and therefore the network energy consumption increased as shown in Fig. 3. It is also clear that the increase of the mobile element path constraint leads to less energy consumption of sensor nodes. This is due to the reason that increasing the path constraint allowed the mobile elements to travel larger area of the sensor field and hence reduced the number multi-hop sensor nodes.

Figure 4 shows that all algorithm yield larger energy consumption when increasing the number of nodes. The NET algorithm incurred the most energy consumption because the multi-hop transmissions increase a lot with the larger number of nodes. Since our algorithm first group all the sensor nodes into clusters, the number of multi-hop nodes increases slowly compared with RDC algorithm. Therefore our algorithm has the least energy consumption.

From Fig. 5 we can see that the movement cost(total distance) varies with the number of nodes. In order to cover more nodes, the mobile elements must travel a longer path which leads to the increase of ME's cost. In contrast, RDC protocol did not take consider of the cost of mobile element.

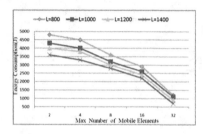

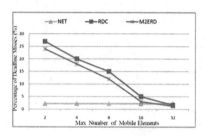

Fig. 7. The impact of max number of MEs on energy consumption for different deadline

Fig. 8. The impact of max number of MEs on percentage of deadline misses for different algorithms

5.3 Impact of Movement Speed

In this section, we evaluate the network energy consumption when the speed of MEs varies from 0.1 to 2 m/s. Figure 6 shows that all algorithms yield lower energy consumption when the MEs move faster except NET. This is because the MEs are able to collect data on a longer tour within the deadline. The results of this simulation show that our algorithms can effectively take advantage of speed increase of the ME.

5.4 Impact of Number of ME

In this section, we evaluate the performance in terms of energy consumption and percentage of deadline misses by varying the mobile elements number constraint. From Fig. 7 we can see that the network energy consumption decreases when the maximum mobile element number increase. This is due to the more mobile element, the less multi-hop transmissions. Figure 8 shows that the percentage of deadline misses decrease when increase the mobile elements number. This is due to the more mobile elements, the more sensor nodes would be covered within deadline. The NET algorithm dose not use any mobile element, therefore the deadline misses would not be affected by the number of MEs.

6 Conclusions

In this paper, we present a minimum movement cost data gathering algorithm that utilizes mobile elements to collect data under deadline constraint. We refer this algorithm to M2ERD and proof that M2ERD is a NP-hard problem. We design a genetic algorithm to determine the minimum cost movement tours satisfying deadline constraint. In order to reduce the number of mobile elements, we apply a tour reduction procedure when the mobile elements number beyond a given threshold.Simulation results showed that M2ERD outperformed the existing algorithm in terms of energy saving, movement cost and deadline misses.

Acknowledgment. This work was supported by the National Science Foundation of China(61100048, 61370222), the Science and technology project of Heilongjiang Provincial Education Department(12531498), and the Heilongjiang province university science and technology innovation team project(2013TD102).

References

1. Mario, D.F., Sajal, K.: Data collection in wireless sensor networks with mobile elements: a survey. ACM Trans. Sens. Netw. **8**(1), 1–34 (2011). Article 7
2. Cai, Z., Chen, Z., Lin, G.: A 3.4713-approximation algorithm for the capacitated multicast tree routing problem. Theor. Comput. Sci. **410**(52), 5415–5424 (2009)
3. Cheng, S., Cai, Z., Li, J.: Curve query processing in wireless sensor networks. IEEE Transactions on Vehicular Technology
4. Cheng, S., Cai, Z., Li, J., Fang, X.: Drawing dominant dataset from big sensory data in wireless sensor networks. In: The 34rd Annual IEEE International Conference on Computer Communications (INFOCOM) (2015)
5. He, Z., Cai, Z., Cheng, S., Wang, X.: Approximate Aggregation for Tracking Quantiles in Wireless Sensor Networks. Theoretical Computer Science
6. Christian, P.: A simple and effective evolutionary algorithm for the vehicle routing problem. Comput. Oper. Res. **31**, 1985–2002 (2004)
7. Yao, X., Huang, H., Tang, J., et al.: Residual energy aware mobile data gathering in wireless sensor networks. Telecomun. Syst. **59**(148), 1–11 (2015)
8. Zhao, M., Yang, Y., Wang, C.: Mobile data gathering with load balanced clustering and dual data uploading in wireless sensor networks. IEEE Trans. Mob. Comput. **14**(04), 770–785 (2015)
9. Somasundara, A., Ramamoorthy, A., Srivastava, M.B.: Mobile element scheduling with dynamic deadlines. IEEE Trans. Mob. Comput. **6**(4), 395–410 (2007)
10. Xing, G., Wang, T., Jia, W., Li, M.: Efficient rendezvous algorithms for mobility-enabled wireless sensor networks. IEEE Trans. Mob. Comput. **11**, 47–60 (2012)
11. Abdullah, A.I., Khaled, K.D., Alasha'ary, H.A., Al-Qadi, Z.A.: Connectivity-based data gathering with path-constrained mobile sink in wireless sensor networks. Wirel. Sens. Netw. **6**, 118–128 (2014)

A Poisson Distribution Based Topology Control Algorithm for Wireless Sensor Networks Under SINR Model

Kan Yu[1], Zhi Li[2,3], Qiang Li[2,3], and Jiguo Yu[1]([✉])

[1] School of Information Science and Engineering,
Qufu Normal University, Rizhao 276826, Shandong, China
jiguoyu@sina.com
[2] Beijing Key Laboratory of IOT Information Security Technology, Beijing, China
[3] Institute of Information Engineering, CAS, Beijing 100093, China

Abstract. Topology control is a fundamental problem in wireless sensor networks. Most of the existing results on topology control focused on how to reduce energy consumption, improve the effectiveness of networks, and prolong lifetime. Though some algorithms considered the time delay, the effects of interference have been neglected. In this paper, we introduce an efficient delay model, and propose a novel topology control algorithm MLTC based on Poisson distribution, along with communication interference considered. We prove that the communication complexity and time complexity are $O(N_u)$ and $O(eN_u^2)$, respectively by theoretical analysis, where N_u is the *neighborlist* of node u, and e is the number of the set of the edges.

Keywords: Wireless sensor networks · Topology control · Poisson distribution · Communication interference

1 Introduction

Wireless sensor networks have broad applications, such as national security, space exploration, environmental monitoring, data management and so on [1]. Topology control is one of the most important technologies in wireless sensor networks. In the network topology, there exists an topological edge between two nodes that can communicate directly. Without topology control, all nodes will work at the maximum transmission power. Under the circumstances, on one hand, the limited energy of nodes will be rapidly consumed by communication components, at the same time, the wireless signal of each node may cover many other nodes, which causes signals conflict frequently, influences the communication quality of nodes, and reduces the throughput of network. On the other hand, there exist lots of edges in the generated network topology, this produces a large amount

This work was partially supported by the NNSF of China for contract 61373027, 61472418 and NSF of Shandong Province for contract ZR2012FM023.

K. Xu and J. Zhu (Eds.): WASA 2015, LNCS 9204, pp. 706–714, 2015.
DOI: 10.1007/978-3-319-21837-3_69

of information and the complexity of routing computation, wasting precious computing resource. Topology control is to improve network throughput, reduce network interference and prolong network lifetime, while maintain some global properties of the topology.

A good network topology can improve the efficiency of MAC, routing and broadcast protocols [2]. In general, if the transmitting ranges of nodes are relatively short, many nodes can transmit simultaneously without interfering with each other, and the network capacity is increased. Hence, topology control not only reduces energy consumption but also has positive effect of reducing contention when accessing the wireless channel.

In this paper, we focus mainly on reducing network delay and energy consumption when the interference is taken into consideration. Xu et al. [3] considered the topology control problem for delay-constraint data collection using only the number of hops, since delay is related closely to location of nodes, this metric may not be accurate. Based on the approaches to measure delay, we put forward a solution for topology control under SINR model, and design a stochastic Poisson distributed based algorithm, where radio follows log-distance path loss model which can be regard as log-normal shadowing model.

The rest of this paper is organized as follows. In Sect. 2, we review the related work. We introduce a detailed description and analysis of the algorithm proposed in this paper in Sect. 3 which is followed by the conclusion section mentioned in Sect. 4.

2 Related Works

In [4], Trung et al. studied the delay of using multiple access control protocols, which decreases end-to-end delay but does not take interference between links into consideration. In [5], Behzad and Rubin proposed a graph-based scheduling algorithm, and provided a probabilistic analysis for the throughput performance of the algorithms. In addition, they also showed in many scenarios, a significant portion of transmissions scheduled based on the protocol interference model result in unacceptable SINR at intended receivers. In [6], Hajiahayi et al. introduced a 2-connectivity heuristic approach which keeps network connecting. It first calculates a minimum spanning tree over the network, and then transforms 1-connectivity minimum spanning tree to 2-connectivity network graph. In [7], Grönkvist et al. studied the average delay and network throughput, they considered two methods of generating traffic controlled reuse schedules decreasing delay and developed algorithms without considering interference. In [8], Li and Hou considered how to reduce the power consumption and improved the network capacity, and provided a minimum spanning tree algorithm using uniform power assignment. In [9], Sethu and Gerety presented a simple distributed topology control algorithm STC (Step Topology Control) without using any location-based information. Simulation results show that STC can reduce energy consumption and interference, but a higher communication or computational complexity was achieved. In [10], Jeng and Jam proposed an adjustable structure, named

r-neighborhood graph, to construct the network topology. Energy is the most crucial resource in wireless sensor networks, many topology control algorithms can greatly reduce power consumption, but the algorithms usually lead to higher communication delay, and do not take interference between links in reality environment into account. In fact, communication interference may results in delay, the more interference, the longer delay.

In [11], Chen *et al.* studied topology control problem which is related to delay. In [3], Xu *et al.* imported and defined the topology control problem for delay-constraint data collection, In [12], Shiu *et al.* designed an energy-efficient topology control algorithm, which considers topology construction and count infinity problem. However, time delay only is measured by hops from source node to destination node.

In the seminal work [13], Gupta and Kumar analyzed the capacity of wireless network under SINR model and protocol interference model. In protocol interference model, transmissions were successful between nodes if and only if there is no other links transmitting at the same time in a circle which is centered by u and transmission range is r, whereas it must consider cumulative interference. In [14], Moscibroda *et al.* took first to analyze topology control under SINR model. In [15], Gui and Liu studied link delay by a new topology control algorithm, which has a respectively low delay and an acceptable energy consumption level but slightly more computation overhead.

3   Description of Algorithms

3.1   Problem Definition

The network has the following assumptions.

1. The nodes are deployed in a two-dimensional plane, each node has a unique ID.
2. The topology graph is a directed graph and path loss between nodes satisfies log-normal shadowing model in the network.
3. All nodes can control power, that is, each node can adjust it transmission power within a given range.
4. In physical interference model SINR, background noise N is a small random number ε.

Definition 1. *Minimum time delay path* A path that has the minimum sum of edge time delay weight from node u to node v, denoted as $L_{min}(u, v)$.

Definition 2. *Log-normal shadowing model* For the same transmission distance and different receivers, the received signal strength follows Gaussian distribution.

3.2   Sensor Node Deployment Model

Given a fixed region Ω, the probability that sensor nodes randomly distributed in the object region $D(D \subseteq \Omega)$ is $P_D = \frac{S_D}{S_\Omega}$. S_D and S_Ω denote the area of the object region and given region, respectively. The location of the nodes can be obtained by GPS. Consider n sensor nodes are deployed in region Ω, then the probability that m nodes distributed in region D is $P(X = m) = C_n^m P^m (1 - P)^{n-m}$. The average density of sensor nodes distributed in region Ω is $\lambda = \frac{n}{S_\Omega}$, when the number of sensor nodes n tends to infinity, we have

$$
\begin{aligned}
&\lim_{n\to\infty} P(X = m) \\
&= \lim_{n\to\infty} \frac{n!}{m!(n-m)!} \cdot \left(\frac{\lambda \cdot S_D}{m!}\right)^m \cdot \left(1 - \frac{\lambda \cdot S_D}{m!}\right)^{n-m} \\
&= \lim_{n\to\infty} \frac{n(n-1)(n-2)\ldots(n-m+1)}{n^m} \frac{(\lambda \cdot S_D)^m}{m!} \cdot \left(1 - \frac{\lambda \cdot S_D}{m!}\right)^n \cdot \left(1 - \frac{\lambda \cdot S_D}{m!}\right)^{-m} \\
&= \lim_{n\to\infty} \left(1 - \frac{1}{n}\right) \cdot \left(1 - \frac{2}{n}\right)\ldots \cdot \left(1 - \frac{m}{n}\right) \cdot \frac{(\lambda \cdot S_D)^m}{m!} \cdot \left(1 - \frac{\lambda \cdot S_D}{m!}\right)^n \cdot \left(1 - \frac{\lambda \cdot S_D}{m!}\right)^{-m} \\
&= \frac{(\lambda \cdot S_D)^m}{m!} \cdot e^{-\lambda \cdot S_D}.
\end{aligned}
$$

Assumed that sensor nodes are randomly and independently distributed, thus, we can approximately regard the distribution of sensor nodes as a Poisson distribution, that is, $n \sim p(\lambda \cdot S_D)$.

Table 1. Some notations used in the paper are listed in the Table 1.

n	The number of nodes	N_u	The number of node u's neighbors
N	Background noise	E_{th}	Residual energy threshold of node
e	The number of links	RSS	Received signal sensitivity
$L_{\min}(u,v)$	Minimum path between node u and v	$D_{u,v}$	The cost of link between node u and v
S_Ω	Area of node deployed regional	ω	Weight of power, $\omega \in (0,1)$
λ	Density of nodes distribution	θ	Weight of time delay, $\theta \in (0,1)$
$\overline{P_{loss}}$	The average of link energy loss	M	The length of data frame for a data packet
d	The distance between sender and receiver	t_z	Time of data package forwarding
d_0	Reference distance (generally $1m$)	$P_{t,\min}$	Minimum transmission power
α	Path loss exponent, $\alpha \in (2,6)$	$P_{\max}$	Maximum transmission power
P_t	Transmission power	γ	The weight of power
$P_x(d)$	Received power	$E_{u,\min}$	The set of directed weighted links
E_{left}^u	Rest energy of sensor node	T_{wait}	Given waiting time

3.3   Path Loss Model

In wireless sensor networks, the average of received power of signal decreases exponentially with the increase of the distance. This phenomenon is universal indoors or outdoors. Usually, the average path loss $\overline{P_{loss}}$ is directly proportion to distance d^α in wireless sensor networks. Thus, the average path loss of received power is denoted $\overline{P_{loss}}(d) = \overline{P_{loss}}(d_0) + 10\alpha \log(\frac{d}{d_0}) + X_\sigma$, where α is the path loss exponent, d_0 is reference distance, d is the distance between the sender and the receiver, $X_\sigma \sim (0, \sigma^2)$ denotes the Gaussian variable with even value 0 and the standard deviation σ is [2, 8]. Generally, the value of α is 2 in open space whereas α is 4 in buildings.

Note that if the distance between a sender and two different receivers is equal, the signal strength received from a common sender may be different. When the transmission power is P_t, we can get the received power $P_r(d)$ satisfying $P_r(d) = P_t(d) - \overline{P_{loss}}(d) + X_\sigma$ after path loss $\overline{P_{loss}}$.

We can use parameters d_0, α, σ to describe the path loss model with specific transmission distance. When the transmission power of node u is P_t, the received power of v is

$$P_r = P_t / \max\left\{(d/d_0)^\alpha, 1\right\} + X_\sigma. \tag{1}$$

3.4   Interference Model

Whether a transmission is successful or not depends on two factors: received signal strength (RSS) and the signal to interference and noise ratio $(SINR)$. Specifically, let RSS be the critical value of the receiver to correctly decode the received signal, and the critical value of $SINR$ be β. A signal that can be successfully received and decoded need to satisfy the following two formulas.

$$P_r(i,j) = P_t(i,j) / \max\left\{(d_{i,j}/d_0)^\alpha, 1\right\} + X_\sigma \geq RSS \tag{2}$$

$$SINR_{i,j} = \frac{g_{i,j} \cdot P_t(i) \cdot d_{i,j}^{-\alpha}}{N + I_j} \geq \beta, \tag{3}$$

where N is ambient noise, I_j is the interference at receiver v_j, $g_{i,j}$ is channel gain. From formula (2), we can calculate the minimum transmitting power which sends signal to a receiver with distance $d_{i,j}$. Assumed that all nodes are homogeneous, independent and have the same maximum power level $P_{\max}$, the critical value of $SINR$ and the receiver signal sensitivity.

We combine the physical model with the path loss model, the signal from node u to node v can be correctly decoded if and only if

$$\frac{\frac{P_t(u)}{\max\{(d_{u,v}/d_0)^\alpha, 1\}}}{N + \sum_{\omega \in V} \frac{P_t(\omega)}{\max\{(d(\omega,v)/d_0)^\alpha, 1\}}} \geq \beta$$

is satisfied.

3.5   Delay Model

In most of existing work, the delay is measured by hops, due to the limitation of some factors, it is imperfect to measure it only by hops. Therefore, we build a communication time model to estimate the delay from a sender to a receiver.

We use the formula $f(\gamma_j) = (1 - e^{-0.5\gamma_j})^M$ to calculate the success rate of frames [15]. Here, M is the length of the frame for given data packet. These packets transmission lead to the interference, and γ_j denotes the sum of interference.

Let t_z denote the time delivering the packets. Since the link delay is in inversely proportional to the successful probability of frame, and is in direct proportional to the time delivering the packets, we give the following link delay model. That is,

$$t_s = \frac{t_z}{1 - e^{-0.5\gamma_j}}.$$

The following model denotes the cost of each link which can be measured by delay and energy.

$$
\begin{aligned}
D_{u,v} &= \omega p_{loss} + \theta t_s \\
&= \frac{1}{2} p_{loss} + \frac{1}{2} t_s \\
&= \frac{1}{2}\left((P_{t,\min} - \frac{P_{t,\min}}{\max\{(d/d_0)^\alpha, 1\}} - X_\sigma) + \frac{t_z}{(1 - e^{-0.5\gamma_j})M}\right).
\end{aligned}
\tag{4}
$$

Where ω is the weight of power, θ is the weight of delay, ω, $\theta \in (0,1)$ and $\omega + \theta = 1$. $P_{t,\min}$ is the minimum sending power of two nodes that successfully transmit the information. In the paper, assume that $\omega = \theta = 0.5$, P_{loss} is energy consumption, t_s is delay. Let γ_j be the approximate value of random number from 1 to 1.5, the length of the packet is the random number from 5 to 10. We use the formula (4) solving the minimum cost of any edge.

3.6 Topology Control Algorithm

We propose a novel topology control algorithm to construct a network topology, with consideration for the delay and energy consumption. Note that the distributed algorithm runs locally, when all nodes execute this algorithm, we obtain a new network topology, where every communication path has approximate minimum cost. This algorithm can be divided into the following several steps.

Step 1. Determine the residual energy
In the initial stage, sink nodes send message to wake up the neighbor nodes, then sensor nodes decide whether the residual energy is greater than given threshold (e.g. $3dB$). If residual energy is smaller than $3dB$, the neighbor nodes deal with the data produced by itself, and do not forward any data.

Step 2. Information exchange, constructing the initial network topology.
The nodes with the residual energy is greater than threshold send $HelloMsg$ to other nodes with transmission power $P_{\max}$ which mainly involves the ID of transmitter, received signal strength RSS_u, residual energy and maximum transmission power $P_{\max}$ and position coordinates (x_u, y_u) obtained by GPS. The nodes which receive $HelloMsg$ decide this message, if the received power is greater than or equal to RSS_u, then the receivers add the sender to $neighborlist$, including the ID, residual energy and the cost of links.

Step 3. Network topology optimization
Every node determines the transmission power according to the information of receiver under the path loss model, then it decides whether the node v receives

successfully the information sent by node u or not according to SINR model. Assume that only neighbor nodes can interfere the transmission, and interference received from other nodes can be ignored. If node v can receive the message that sent by node u, then it adds the node u to *neighborlist* of v otherwise it discards the message.

Step 4. Approximate optimal topology construction based on the cost of edges We present the calculation model for cost of edges in topology control graph. The minimum cost value can regarded as the of the weight of edges by invoking function of every link. We find the optimal path of arbitrary node pair by using *Dijkstra* algorithm. The topology graph generated by topology control algorithm is $G_{u,\min} = (V, E_{u,\min})$, where $E_{u,\min}$ is the set of directed weighted links. The weight of arbitrary link $u \to v$ in $E_{u,\min}$ is $D_{u,v}$. A possible result is shown in Fig. 1.

Algorithm 1. Minimum Link Cost Topology Control (MLTC)

> **Begin**
> 1. **if** u receives a $WakeupMsg$ **then**
> 2.   **if** $E^u_{left} \geq E_{th}$ **then**
> 3. u broadcasts a $WakeupMsg$ with P_{max}
> 4.   **end if**
> 5. **end if**
> 6. **while** $t < T_{wait}$ **do**
> 7.   **if** u receives a $HelloMsg$ and $p_r \geq RSS_u$ **then**
> 8. u updates its neighbor list
> 9.   **end if**
> 10. **end while**
> 11. Calculate $SINR_{u,v}$
> 12. **for all** $v \in neighborlist_u$ **do**
> 13.   **if** $SINR_{u,v} < \beta$ **then**
> 14.   Remove v from the *neighborlist* of u
> 15.   **end if**
> 16. **end for**
> 17. **for all** $v \in neighborlist_u$ **do**
> 18.   Calculate p_{send}
> 19. **end for**
> 20. **for all** $v \in neighborlist_u$ **do**
> 21.   Calculate $D_{u,v}$
> 22. **end for**
> 23.   Capture the approximate optimal path from u to v by *Dijkstra* algorithm
> **End**

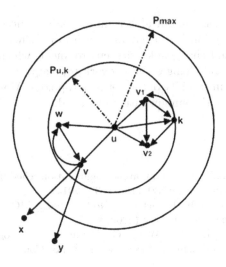

Fig. 1. A possible result after running algorithm

In algorithm 1, the node u gets *neighborlist* by running lines $6 - 8$. SINR is determined and *neighborlist* is updated by running lines $11 - 14$. In lines $17 - 19$, we obtain the corresponding transmission power and adjust the range of transmission power in final neighbor topology. In lines $20 - 22$, we obtain the minimum cost between u and all neighbor nodes. In line 23, we can choose the optimal path of every node pair by executing *Dijkstra* algorithm.

Theorem 1. *The neighborlist of node u communicating with maximum transmission power is denoted by N_u, the message complexity of MLTC algorithm by node u is $O(N_u)$.*

Proof. For arbitrary node u, the time complexity of receiving $WakeupMsg$ message is $O(1)$, the communication complexity of broadcasting $HelloMsg$ message is $O(1)$. In the *while* loop, the communication complexity of node u receiving $helloMsg$ is $O(N_u)$. Thus the communication complexity is $O(N_u)$.

Theorem 2. *Node u communicates with the maximum transmission power, then the time complexity of MLTC algorithm is $o(eN_u^2)$, e denotes the number of the set of edges.*

Proof. For arbitrary node u, we can calculate the minimum edges cost by using the formula (4), the time complexity of using the formula (4) is $O(e)$, the time complexity of determining SINR is $O(N_u)$, the time complexity of running *Dijkstra* algorithm is $O(N_u^2)$, thus the whole time complexity is $O(eN_u^2)$.

4   Conclusion

This paper studies topology control based on SINR model, and proposes a distributed network topology construction algorithm MLTC, which considers both delay and energy. In general, our algorithm not only reduces link delay but also lowers power consumption in theory. In future work, since a wireless networks may be instability and changeable with environment, which may lead to some nodes being disable and changes the network topology, we will design effective algorithms to maintain stability of the network topology. Moreover, we will lower the time complexity and communication overhead.

References

1. Guo, L., Li, Y., Cai, Z.: Minimum-latency aggregation scheduling in wireless sensor network. J. Commun. Optim. **30**(114), 1–32 (2014)
2. Johnson, T.: Networks. In: Klouche, T., Noll, T. (eds.) MCM 2007. CCIS, vol. 37, pp. 311–317. Springer, Heidelberg (2009)
3. Xu, H., Huang, L., Liu, W., Wang, G., Wang, Y.: Topology control for delay-constraint data collection in wireless sensor networks. Comput. Commun. **32**, 1820–1828 (2009)
4. Trung, M., Mo, J.H.: A multichannel TDMA MAC protocol to reduce end-to-end delay in wireless mesh networks. ETRI J. **32**, 819–822 (2010)
5. Behzad, A., Rubin, I.: On the performance of graph based scheduling algorithms for packet radio networks. Proc. IEEE GLOBECOM **6**, 3432–3436 (2003)
6. Hajiaghayi, M., Immorlica, N., Mirrokni, V.S.: Power optimization in fault tolerant topology control algorithm for wireless multi-hop networks. IEEE/ACM Trans. Netw. **15**, 1345–1358 (2007)
7. Grönkvist, J., Hansson, A.: Comparison between graph-based and interference based STDMA scheduling. In: Proceedings of ACM MobiHoc, pp. 255–258 (2001)
8. Li, N., Hou, J.: Localized topology control algorithms for heterogeneous wireless networks. IEEE/ACM Trans. Netw. **13**, 1313–1324 (2005)
9. Sethu, H., Gerety, T.: A new distributed topology control algorithm for wireless environments with non-uniform path loss and multipath propagation. Ad Hoc Netw. **8**(3), 280–294 (2010)
10. Jeng, A.K., Jan, R.: The r-neighborhood graph: an adjustable structure for topology control in wireless ad hoc networks. IEEE Trans. Parallel Distrib. Syst. **18**, 536–549 (2007)
11. Siyuan, C., Ying, Z., Yu, W.: Topology control for time-evolving and predictable delay-tolerant networks. In: Proceedings of IEEE MASS, pp. 82–91 (2011)
12. Shiu, L., Lin, F., Lee, C., Yang C.: An energy-efficient topology construction algorithm in wireless sensor network. In Proceedings of IMLCS, pp. 25–26 (2013)
13. Gupta, P., Kumar, P.R.: The capacity of wireless networks. IEEE Trans. Inf. theory **46**, 388–404 (2000)
14. Moscibroda, T., Wattenhofer, R., Zollinger, A.: Topology control meets SINR: the scheduling complexity of arbitrary topologies. In: Proceedings of ACM MobiHoc, pp. 310–321 (2006)
15. Gui, J., Liu, A.: A new distributed topology control algorithm based on optimization of delay and energy in wireless networks. J. Parallel Distrib. Comput. **72**, 1032–1044 (2012)

PPSSER: Privacy-Preserving Based Scheduling Scheme for Emergency Response in Medical Social Networks

Wenbin Yu, Cailian Chen$^{(\boxtimes)}$, Bo Yang, and Xinping Guan

Department of Automation, Shanghai Jiao Tong University, Shanghai, China
{yuwenbin,cailianchen,bo.yang,xpguan}@sjtu.edu.cn

Abstract. Mobile health monitoring, which can monitor the medical users' real-time physiology parameters, has been expected as an effective way to improve medical service quality and make response to the emergency. Unfortunately, it also risks the information privacy of both the medical users and the healthcare service providers when they upload their information. This paper is to propose a privacy-preserving based scheduling scheme for emergency response (PPSSER) to protect the privacy of the involved users when an emergency occurs. Moreover, the multi-dimensional region query method is introduced to conseal the personal health information and homomorphic encryption is used to protect the location and attribute privacy of the users. Finally, the simulation demonstrates the effectiveness and feasibility of the proposed scheme.

Keywords: Emergency scheduling · Privacy-preserving · MDRQs · Bilinear Pairing · Homomorphic encryption

1 Introduction

In our aging society, Mobile Healthcare System (MHS) has been forseen as an effective way to improve healthcare quality and save lives [4]. With the rapid development of Wireless Body Area Networks (WBANs), the Personal Healthcare Information (PHI) of medical users can be online monitored. The obtained PHI are required to be assembled to the coordinator of the network and then transmitted to the base station [1], which is frequently shown up as the cloud server. Moreover, the WBANs are required to provide efficient treatment when an emergency occurs. A recent study shows that 75 % Americans consider the privacy of their health information important or very important [6]. It has also been reported that patients' willingness to get involved in health monitoring program could be severely lowered when people are concerned with the privacy breach in their voluntarily submitted health data [3].

Former academics have researched in the area of security and privacy preserving methods and have obtained many achievements. Reference [2] designed an event-driven security forwarding protocol, which assumed that the patients

© Springer International Publishing Switzerland 2015
K. Xu and J. Zhu (Eds.): WASA 2015, LNCS 9204, pp. 715–724, 2015.
DOI: 10.1007/978-3-319-21837-3_70

with the same illness would participate in the same activity (illness-related activity) with high probability. Reference [7] designed a privacy-preserving relay filter scheme in delay tolerant network, which could prevent strong and weak privacy-curious users stealing information. The former method can be used in our scheme but they do not take the whole system into consideration and lack emergency scheduling method.

Furthermore, some researchers have studied the Emergency Response Support System (ERSS). Reference [8] proposed a secure and privacy-preserving opportunistic framework, for healthcare emergency. They did not mention the privacy of location and attribute for the healthcare staffs. Reference [10] addressed the conflicting privacy issues from the functional requirements, which took location privacy into consideration but did not pay attention to attribute privacy.

Above all, the function of current emergency response systems are inadequate and the defense for collusion attack is far from satisfactory. The privacy-preserving methods for the ERSS do not guarantee the privacy of all the information (e.g. the PHI and users' attributes) and how to defend collusion attack is a great challenging. Furthermore, how to improve the system efficiency while not compromising the privacy-preserving function is still a challenging problem. Aiming at the disadvantages of existed systems, the contributions are:

- This paper proposes a privacy-preserving based scheduling scheme for emergency response (PPSSER), which can guarantee both efficiency and privacy when dealing with an emergency in MHS.
- We take medical users and healthcare staffs' locations and attributes into account to find the nearest first aider providers. The perfect HSP is selected by the compromise of the upper two factors without revealing the privacy.
- The computing burdens on the medical users, healthcare staffs and other involved parties are calculated to show that the system can balance the privacy and efficiency.

The rest of the paper is organized as follows. Preliminaries are introduced in Sect. 2. The system model and privacy requirements are introduced in Sect. 3. The scheduling scheme is introduced in Sect. 4. The simulation is shown in Sect. 5 and we conclude the paper in Sect. 6.

2   Preliminaries

Multi-dimensional Range Query (MDRQ) scheme was first introduced and applied in database querying and then further used in reputation-based encryption scheme. In MDRQ, the sender encrypts message in interval $[r_1, r_2]$ or with θ-bit data d and then a receiver can decrypt the message if falling into the interval or private key of data d.

In the proposed scheme, MDRQ is used to determine whether the measured physiological values by BAN are in the abnormal range for the detection of emergencies.

Definition 1. *Bilinear Pairing: Let* $\mathbb{G}$ *be a q-order addictive group and* $\mathbb{G}_T$ *be a q-order multiplicative group, in which q is prime and g is a random generator of* $\mathbb{G}$. *An admissible Bilinear Pairing* e: $\mathbb{G} \times \mathbb{G} \to \mathbb{G}_T$ *will satisfy the three principles as following.*

1. *Bilinear:* $e(g^a, h^b) = e(g, h)^{ab}$, $\forall g, h \in \mathbb{G}$ *and* $\forall a, b \in \mathbb{Z}_q$;
2. *Nondegeneration:* $\exists g, h \in \mathbb{G}_{\mathbb{K}}$ *such that* $e(g, g) \neq 1$;
3. *Computable: there exists algorithm with polynomial time complexity to get* $e(g, h)$, $\forall g, h \in \mathbb{G}$.

3   System Structure and Privacy Requirements

Based on cloud computing, Emergency Response Scheduling System (ERSS) is designed to guarantee privacy. The system structure is shown as in Fig. 1.

The system is composed by four parts: Cloud Server (CS), Trusted Agent (TA), Medical Users (MUs) and Healthcare Service Providers (HSPs). The TA, which is totally trusted, takes charge of the whole ERSS. MUs send their PHI, locations and individual attributes to the CS via PDAs or smart phones in the mode of ciphertext. HSPs are medical service providers. The CS monitors MUs' encrypted PHI. When the emergency occurs, it selects the nearest and best matched HSP for first aid.

Because of its large storage and fast computation, the CS is used to store medical data and provide services of inquiry, computation and access. However, the CS is inclined to be attacked by illegal invaders and is honest but curious [5]. In this paper the following privacy requirements are considered.

1. Physiological Data Privacy: The CS must not obtain or infer the MUs' PHI.
2. Location Privacy: The CS must not obtain or infer the MUs or HSPs' locations.

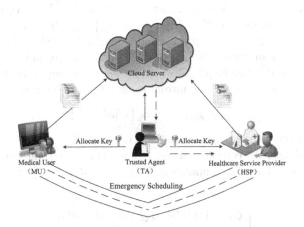

Fig. 1. System architecture of ERSS

3. Personal Attribute Privacy: The CS must not obtain or infer the MUs or HSPs' attribute information.
4. Defence of Collusion Attack: The CS must not obtain any of the former information even it colludes with MUs or HSPs.

4 Privacy Preserving Scheduling Method

4.1 Initialization

As a trusted department, the TA initializes, allocates and manages the key for the system by Algorithm 1.

Algorithm 1. Initialization of the TA

Require: System Security Parameter κ
1: Generates Bilinear Pairing Parameters $(q, g, \mathbb{G}, \mathbb{G}_\mathbb{T}, e)$ using $\mathcal{G}en(\kappa)$;
2: Choose three hash functions $H_1 : \{0,1\}^* \to \mathbb{G}$, $H_2 : \mathbb{G}_\mathbb{T} \to \{0,1\}^*$, $H_3 : \{0,1\}^* \to \{0,1\}^*$;
3: Choose three random numbers $(a, b, r) \in \mathbb{Z}_q^*$, and compute $A = g^a, B = g^b, T = e(g, g)^a$;
4: Generate $P^{3 \times 3}$ and $Q^{m \times m}$ and compute P^{-1}, Q^{-1}, where m is the length of the attribute vector;
5: Generate homomorphic encryption public key PK_{TA}, private key SK_{TA}. Allocate corresponding PK_{MU}, SK_{MU} and PK_{HSP}, SK_{HSP} for MUs and HSPs.
6: Generate the Master Key (MK) and Public Parameter (PP):

$$MK = (a, b, r, P, Q, SK_{TA})$$
$$PP = (q, g, \mathbb{G}, \mathbb{G}_\mathbb{T}, e, H_1, H_2, H_3, A, B, T, PK_{TA})$$

Assume that there are n parameters of PHI for the MU to be monitored, which are denoted by $H = \{h_1, h_2, \cdots, h_n\}$ and the relative indexes are $I_i (1 \leq i \leq n)$. For any $h_i \in H$, the normal range is denoted by $[th_{i1}, th_{i2}]$. The TA generates random numerals $\delta_i (1 \leq i \leq n)$ via pseudorandom function and conceals the normal range to $[th_{i1} + \delta_i, th_{i2} + \delta_i]$. By using MDRQ method, the smallest node set who covers the normal range of parameters is expressed as:

$$S_{[th_{i1}+\delta_i, th_{i2}+\delta_i]} = \{id | id \in S_i\} \tag{1}$$

where id is the elements of the smallest node set S_i.

For convenience, the complement set S_i' (covering abnormal range) is used to detect emergency. The TA computes each element id in set $S_i' (1 \leq i \leq n)$ using its MK:

$$\begin{cases} C_1 = EMC \oplus H_2(e(H_1(id)^a, g^r)) \\ C_2 = H_3(r \parallel id \parallel EMC) \\ C_3 = g^{\frac{a}{C_1+C_2+b}} \end{cases} \tag{2}$$

where EMC is the emergency signal. Afterwards, the TA sends data as follows:

1.
$$TA \rightarrow CS : C = (C_1, C_2, C_3), I_i$$

2.
$$TA \rightarrow MU : E_{PK_{MU}}(r), E_{PK_{MU}}(\delta_i), E_{PK_{MU}}(P^{-1}), E_{PK_{MU}}(Q^{-1})$$

3.
$$TA \rightarrow HSP : E_{PK_{TA}}(P), E_{PK_{TA}}(Q)$$

where $E_{PK_{MU}}(\cdot)$ is encrypted data with PK_{MU}.

4.2 Emergency Detection

After receiving the data from the TA, the MU decrypts $r, \delta_i (1 \leq i \leq n), P^{-1}, Q^{-1}$ using private key and compute:

$$H' = \{h_1 + \delta_1, h_2 + \delta_2, \cdots, h_n + \delta_n\} = \{h'_1, h'_2, \cdots, h'_n\} \tag{3}$$

For $h'_i \in H'$, the MU sets up a binary tree using MDRQ method. The set path S_{path_i} which is between root node and relative leaf node is chosen to denote h'_i as shown in (4).

$$S_{h'_i} = \{id' | id' \in S_{path_i}\} \tag{4}$$

For elements id' in set $S_{h'_i}$, the MU will generate a random numeral β as private key for communication and compute public key $PK_s = g^\beta$ and perform:

$$\begin{cases} C'_1 = H_1(id')^r \\ C'_2 = g^{\frac{1}{C'_1+\beta}} \end{cases} \tag{5}$$

Afterwards, the MU sends encrypted data to the CS as:

$$MU \rightarrow CS : C' = (C'_1, C'_2), I_i$$

When $h'_i \notin [th_{i1} + \delta_i, th_{i2} + \delta_i]$, the CS can decrypt the EMC by:

$$\begin{aligned} C_1 \oplus H_2(e(C'_1, A)) &= C_1 \oplus H_2(e(H_1(id')^r, g^a)) = C_1 \oplus H_2(e(H_1(id'), g)^{ra}) \\ &= EMC \oplus H_2(e(H_1(id), g)^{ra}) \oplus H_2(e(H_1(id'), g)^{ra}) = EMC \end{aligned} \tag{6}$$

4.3 Secure Distance Computation

When the CS detects the EMC, the nearby HSPs are required to be found out.

The location of the MU is denoted by $L_u = (x_1, x_2, x_3)$ and each HSP is denoted by $L_s = (y_1, y_2, y_3)$. The Euclidean distance between them is:

$$d = |L_u - L_s| = \sqrt{\sum_{i=1}^{3}(x_i - y_i)^2} \tag{7}$$

The MU, HSPs and CS will participate in the distance computation.

For the MU:

- **Step 1:** Conceal its location by: $C_{L_u} = P^{-1}L_u$
- **Step 2:** Encrypt the location with homomorphic encryption as: $E_{L_u} = E_{PK_{TA}}(\sum_{i=1}^{3} x_i^2)$
- **Step 3:** $MU \to CS : C_{L_u}, E_{L_u}, E_{PK_{TA}}(L_u)$

Similarly, for each HSP:

- **Step 1:** Conceal the location by: $C_{L_{si}} = \prod_{j=1}^{3} E_{PK_{TA}}^{y_j}(p_{ji})$
- **Step 2:** Encrypt $C_{L_s}(C_{L_{s1}}, C_{L_{s2}}, C_{L_{s3}})$ by: $E_{L_s} = E_{PK_{TA}}(\sum_{i=1}^{3} y_i^2)$
- **Step 3:** $HSP \to CS : C_{L_s}, E_{L_s}$

After receiving data from the MU and HSPs, for the CS:

- **Step 1:** Compute $E_{PK_{TA}}(L_u \cdot L_s)$ by:

$$E_{PK_{TA}}(L_u \cdot L_s) = \prod_{j=1}^{3} \prod_{i=1}^{3} E_{PK_{TA}}^{p_{ij}x_j}(y_1 p_{1i} + y_2 p_{2i} + y_3 p_{3i})$$
$$= E_{PK_{TA}}(L_u \cdot P \cdot P^{-1} \cdot L_s) = E_{PK_{TA}}(\sum_{k=1}^{3}(x_k y_k))$$

- **Step 2:** The distance is obtained by:

$$E_{L_u} \cdot E_{L_s} \cdot E_{PK_{TA}}^{-2}(L_u \cdot L_s) = E_{PK_{TA}}(\sum_{i=1}^{3} x_i^2) \cdot E_{PK_{TA}}(\sum_{i=1}^{3} y_i^2)$$
$$\cdot E_{PK_{TA}}^{-2}(\sum_{k=1}^{3}(x_k y_k)) = E_{PK_{TA}}(\sum_{i=1}^{3}(x_i - y_i)^2)$$
$$= E_{PK_{TA}}(|L_u - L_s|^2) = E_{PK_{TA}}(d^2)$$

4.4 Secure Attribute Matching Computation

The attribute similarity is also taken into account when choosing the best HSP. Assume that the vector length of both MU and HSP is m. The MU and HSP's attributes vectors are respectively expressed as: $U_u = (u_1, u_2, \cdots, u_m)$ and $V_s = (v_1, v_2, \cdots, v_m)$. The Manhattan distance d_m between the two vectors is:

$$S = d(U_u, V_s) = \sum_{i=1}^{m} |u_i - v_i| \tag{8}$$

For the MU,

- **Step 1:** Conceal attributes by: $C_{U_u} = Q^{-1}U_u$.
- **Step 2:** Encrypt attributes by: $E_{U_u} = E_{PK_{TA}}(\sum_{i=1}^{m} u_i^2)$
- **Step 3:** $MU \to CS : C_{U_u}, E_{U_u}$

Similarly, for the HSP:

- **Step 1:** Conceal attributes by: $C_{V_{si}} = \prod_{j=1}^{m} E_{PK_{TA}}^{v_j}(q_{ji})$ $(1 \leq i \leq m)$
- **Step 2:** Encrypt attributes by: $E_{V_s} = E_{PK_{TA}}(\sum_{i=1}^{m} v_i^2)$.
- **Step 3:** $HSP \to CS : C_{V_s}, E_{V_s}$

After receiving data from the MU and HSPs, for the CS:

- **Step 1:** Compute $E_{PK_{TA}}(U_u \cdot V_s)$ by:

$E_{PK_{TA}}(U_u \cdot V_s) = \prod_{j=1}^{m} \prod_{i=1}^{m} E_{PK_{TA}}^{q_{ij}u_j}(\sum_{k=1}^{m} v_k \cdot q_{ki})$
$= E_{PK_{TA}}(U_u \cdot Q \cdot Q^{-1} \cdot V_s) = E_{PK_{TA}}(\sum_{k=1}^{m}(u_k v_k))$

- **Step 2:** Compute the attribute similarity by:

$E_{U_u} \cdot E_{V_s} \cdot E_{PK_{TA}}^{-2}(U_u \cdot V_s) = E_{PK_{TA}}(\sum_{i=1}^{m} u_i^2) \cdot E_{PK_{TA}}(\sum_{i=1}^{m} v_i^2) \cdot$
$E_{PK_{TA}}^{-2}(\sum_{k=1}^{m}(u_k v_k))$
$= E_{PK_{TA}}(\sum_{i=1}^{m}(u_i - v_i)^2) = E_{PK_{TA}}(|U_u - V_s|^2) = E_{PK_{TA}}(S^2)$

4.5 Scheduling Algorithm

In order to guarantee the efficiency for the proposed scheme, both distance and attribute similarity are taken into consideration. To simplify the computation, the scheduling function F_s is designed proportionately. Considering the property of homomorphic encryption, the scheduling function is shown in (9).

$$F_s = S^2 + d^2 \tag{9}$$

To guarantee the security of scheduling, the algorithm is designed as shown in Algorithm 2.

Algorithm 2. Scheduling Algorithm

1: The CS computes the scheduling functions:
$E_{PK_{TA}}(F_s) = E_{PK_{TA}}(S^2) \cdot E_{PK_{TA}}(d^2) = E_{PK_{TA}}(S^2 + d^2)$
2: The CS sends data to the TA including the MU's faked user ID $PUID$,
$E_{PK_{TA}}(L_u)$ and $E_{PK_{TA}}(F_s)$.
3: The TA decrypts the MU's location L_u and scheduling function value of every HSP by SK_{TA}
$$L_u = D_{SK_{TA}}(E_{PK_{TA}}(L_u))$$
$$F_s = D_{SK_{TA}}(E_{PK_{TA}}(F_s))$$
4: The TA chooses the HSP which has the smallest value of scheduling function and sends $E_{PK_{HSP}}(PUID)$, $E_{PK_{HSP}}(L_u)$ to corresponding HSP.
5: The HSP decrypts the location of the MU with its own homomorphic encryption private key: $L_u = D_{SK_{HSP}}(E_{PK_{HSP}}(L_u))$

---

5 Simulations

To assess the proposed scheme, based on the GMP [11] and the PBC library [9], we conduct the experiments on a linux system platform with a 2.93 GHz processor with a 3 GB of RAM.

5.1   Performance of Operation Time

Figure 2(a) and (b) denote the offline operation time of the TA. The operation time increases with the increment of θ, n and m. That's because during the system initialization process, the TA should perform (2) for each id, and then perform homomorphic encryption for each element in matrix P, Q.

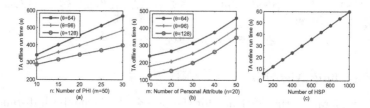

Fig. 2. TA's operation time (a)(b) TA's offline operation time (c) TA's online operation time

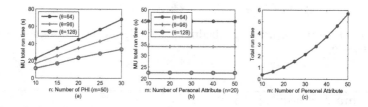

Fig. 3. (a)(b) MU's operation time (c) HSP's operation time

Figure 2(c) denotes the online operation time of the TA. The TA computes the scheduling function values between the MU and each HSP, hence operation time in this part is only related with the quantity of HSPs. When the quantity of HSPs is 1000, the overall time needed for encryption is only 1 min. Figure 2(a) and (b) show that the TA can perform computation offline in the initialization process, which will greatly reduce the online operation time.

Total operation time for the MU is illustrated in Fig. 3(a) and (b). Figure 3(a) denotes that when m is constant MU's computing time becomes longer with the increasing of θ and n, which is because we need to figure out C' for $n\theta$ times repeatedly. When n is constant, Fig. 3(b) shows that the MU's operation time hardly changes with different values of m. This is because the MU needs only m^2 times multiplication calculation of 1024 bits to compute C_{U_u}, which takes only 7.1×10^{-4} ms and can totally be ignored. Hence, MU's overall operation time is mainly decided by the quantity of HSP and parameters of PHI.

Figure 3(c) is overall operation time of the HSP. In our proposed system, two times of homomorphism encryptions, $3^2 + m^2$ times of exponent operations and $m^2 - m + 6$ times of 2048-bit multiplication calculations are needed. Figure 3(c) shows the HSP can upload data in several seconds, which can guarantee real-time monitoring.

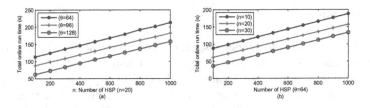

Fig. 4. Emergency detection time

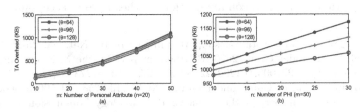

Fig. 5. TA's communication overhead

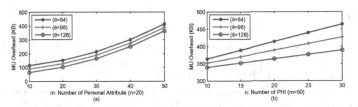

Fig. 6. MU's communication overhead

Figure 4 denotes the overall online operation time. The overall time consumption is affected by both n, θ and the quantity of HSPs.

5.2 Communication Overhead

Figure 5 denotes the communication overhead of the TA. The TA has more communication overhead with bigger θ, n, m. This is because during the initialization process, the data size for the TA to send to the CS is $2n\theta C$. In our simulation, the sizes of elements in set $\mathbb{G}$, $\mathbb{G}_T$ and homomorphic encryption text are relatively 160 bits, 1024 bits and 2048 bits. The size of the TA's total communication overhead is $2 \cdot 480n\theta + 2048(2m^2 + 19 + n)$ and Fig. 5 shows that the overall communication overhead is less then 2 MB. Furthermore, these data need to be sent only once during initialization process.

Figure 6 denotes the communication overhead of the MU. The MU needs to send $C', C_{L_u}, E_{L_u}, C_{U_u}$ and E_{U_u} to the CS. The size of the communication overhead is $320n\theta + 1024(9 + m^2) + 2 \cdot 2048$. C', C_{L_u} and E_{L_u} are supposed to be transmitted in real time. Figure 6 shows that the MU communication overhead is about 0.5 MB.

6 Conclusion

This paper proposes an emergency response scheduling scheme, which guarantees the precision and privacy for emergency detection using the MDRQ and Bilinear Pairing and also protects the location and attributes privacy of the MU and HSP by designing a distance privacy and attributes matching algorithm based on homomorphic encryption. And finally a security scheduling algorithm is proposed to guarantee the scheduling's feasibility and effectiveness. The simulation shows that the operation time and communication overhead are in acceptable range.

Acknowledgment. This work was supported in part by the National Basic Research Program of China under Grant 2010CB731803, in part by the NSF of China under Grants U1405251, 61221003, 61290322, 61174127, and 61273181, in part by the Ministry of Education of China under Grants NCET-13-0358, 20110073130005, and 20110073120025, and in part by the Science and Technology Commission of Shanghai Municipality (STCSM), China under Grant 13QA1401900.

References

1. Alam, M.M., Berder, O., Menard, D., Sentieys, O.: TAD-MAC: traffic-aware dynamic MAC protocol for wireless body area sensor networks. IEEE J. Emerg. Sel. Top. Circuits Syst. **2**(1), 109–119 (2012)
2. Chen, L., Cao, Z., Lu, R., Liang, X., Shen, X.: EPF: An event-aided packet forwarding protocol for privacy-preserving mobile healthcare social networks. In: IEEE GLOBECOM, Houston, TX, USA, pp. 1–5 (2011)
3. Dhukaram, A., Baber, C., Elloumi, L., van Beijnum, B.J., De Stefanis, P.: End-user perception towards pervasive cardiac healthcare services: benefits, acceptance, adoption, risks, security, privacy and trust. In: International Conference on Pervasive Computing Technologies for Healthcare, pp. 478–484, May 2011
4. Feng, D., Kim, J., Khadra, M., Hudson, D., Roux, C.: Guest editorial: telehealth systems and applications. IEEE J. Biomed. Health Inform. **19**(1), 81 (2015)
5. Guo, L., Zhang, C., Sun, J., Fang, Y.: A privacy-preserving attribute-based authentication system for mobile health networks. IEEE Trans. Mob. Comput. **13**(9), 1927–1941 (2014)
6. Lin, H., Shao, J., Zhang, C., Fang, Y.: CAM: cloud-assisted privacy preserving mobile health monitoring. IEEE Trans. Inf. Forensics Secur. **8**(6), 985–997 (2013)
7. Lu, R., Lin, X., Luan, T., Liang, X., Li, X., Chen, L., Shen, X.: Prefilter: an efficient privacy-preserving relay filtering scheme for delay tolerant networks. In: Proceedings IEEE INFOCOM, pp. 1395–1403, March 2012
8. Lu, R., Lin, X., Shen, X.: SPOC: a secure and privacy-preserving opportunistic computing framework for mobile-healthcare emergency. IEEE Trans. Parallel Distrib. Syst. **24**(3), 614–624 (2013)
9. Lynn, B.: The pairing-based cryptography (PBC) library (2012). http://crypto.stanford.edu/pbc
10. Sun, J., Zhu, X., Fang, Y.: Preserving privacy in emergency response based on wireless body sensor networks. In: IEEE GLOBECOM, pp. 1–6, December 2010
11. Gmp library. http://gmplib.org

Secrecy-Oriented Adaptive Clustering Scheme in Device-to-Device Communications

Luke Zhang[1], Li Wang[1($\boxtimes$)], and Xiaojiang Du[2]

[1] School of Electronic Engineering,
Beijing University of Posts and Telecommunications, Beijing, China
[2] Department of Computer and Information Sciences,
Temple University, Philadelphia, USA
kurong5@sina.com, liwang@bupt.edu.cn, dxj@ieee.org

Abstract. This paper proposes a novel clustering scheme by considering both physical and social relationships among handheld terminals in device-to-device (D2D) communications. As social network activities grows explosively, social trust among mobile users based on their daily interactions has had an increasingly significant effect on behaviors and secrecy of D2D cluster communications. We modify the well-known K-means algorithm to characterize the formation of our D2D clusters by taking both physical distance and social trust among nodes into account. Numerical results demonstrate the advantages of our proposed scheme over other existing schemes in terms of system secrecy contribution.

Keywords: Device-to-Device communication · Clustering · Social trust · K-means algorithm

1 Introduction

Device-to-Device (D2D) communications have been proven to significantly improve the performance of wireless networks, which brings a number of advantages, such as improved spectrum utilization, higher throughput, and reduced power consumption. Respectively, there are many works which have studied these perspectives, such as spectrum resource allocation [1], mode selection between cellular and D2D communication [2], D2D clustering [3], and so on.

In D2D communication, the users in close proximity usually form a D2D cluster to share files with each other. However,these works have simply described D2D clusters are composed of users in close proximity [4,5]. As a matter of fact, more and more people are deeply engaged in social networks, which leads to an extensive broadening and significant enhancement of social relationships between people [6]. The authors in [7] have exploited social trust and social reciprocity in human social networks to enhance cooperative D2D communications between devices. Thus, due to its significant influence on people's behaviors [8], social interaction has become an important factor in D2D communication [9], therefore the existing works also lack consideration of intracluster communication secrecy.

© Springer International Publishing Switzerland 2015
K. Xu and J. Zhu (Eds.): WASA 2015, LNCS 9204, pp. 725–734, 2015.
DOI: 10.1007/978-3-319-21837-3_71

The K-means algorithm is a static data analysis method, which has been used widely in Data Mining and Pattern Recognition due to its rapidity and simplicity [10]. With the development of wireless communication, K-means has been extended to deal with distances in some special fields. For example, the authors in [11] adapted the K-means algorithm to form clusters and then selected their cluster heads in the wireless sensor network, improving the energy efficiency of the whole system.

Since the K-means algorithm has been proved to be a practical tool to improve the system's energy efficiency, we can learn from it to model D2D users clustering. The existing works have not given a specific analysis of the performance of intracluster communication secrecy brought by D2D clustering, so we will provide the improvement analysis of D2D clustering.

The rest of this paper is organized as follows. In Sect. 2, we describe the system model. In Sect. 3, we present a modified D2D clustering scheme based on the K-means algorithm. The simulation results and performance evaluation of the proposed D2D clustering scheme are provided in Sect. 4. Section 5 gives conclusion remarks.

2   System Model

As shown in Fig. 1, we consider a single cell environment where there are N users. The users can communicate with each other in D2D mode or seek help from BS in cellular mode. One advantage of D2D clustering is that users in the same D2D cluster can share file resources among them through D2D communication instead of BS, which can improve the throughput and reduce the energy consumption. However, the existing works are not considerate about the outstanding impact of social trust on peoples' behaviors, only taking physical distance into account

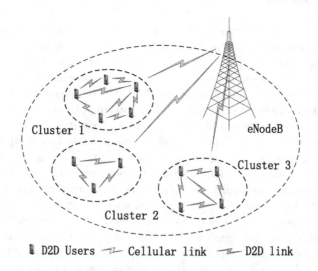

Fig. 1. System model for D2D communication in cellular networks

during the D2D clustering. In some secrecy scene, cluster members will only share their private files to trustworthy users, and whether a user in the same cluster is a trustworthy user or not depends in large part on their past interaction records, which we usually define as social trust. Since the secrecy degree of different users for file resource sharing is different, how to divide the users into D2D clusters to enhance the performance is very important.

We assume the channels from BS to users follow a large-scale path-loss model, and the D2D user channels are independent and identically distributed (i.i.d.) and in flat fading. The noise is additive white Gaussian noise (AWGN). We assume that the file sharing between two users takes no bandwidth overhead.

We denote the maximum D2D communication distance by D_{max}, which can guarantee the quality of communication between D2D users, and the social trust between user m and n by $S_{m,n}$. N_U is the total number of D2D users. Accordingly, C_i is the set of users in the ith cluster, and N_C is the number cluster. P_C and P_D are respectively the transmit powers of cellular and D2D users.

3 Proposed Clustering Scheme

3.1 Traditional K-means

The K-means algorithm is one of the simplest but most popular algorithms to be used extensively to divide data points into clusters. The result of directly appling the K-means algorithm is shown in Fig. 2, in which we decide to divide 50 users randomly distributed in a $100 * 100 \, \mathrm{m}^2$ square into 5 groups.

According to the Fig. 2, we could find two shortcoming of the traditional K-means algorithm. Firstly, some distances between user nodes in the same cluster exceed the maximum of D2D communicating distance. Secondly, using the K-means algorithm directly requires us to decide the number of clusters in advance. Since the location of D2D users is random, the traditional K-means algorithm lacks flexibility and adaptability. We propose a modified K-means algorithm named D-K-means to overcome the shortcomings.

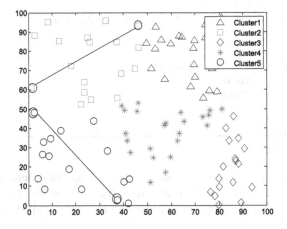

Fig. 2. Traditional K-means clustering case

3.2   D-K-means Clustering Scheme

The main cause of the two shortcomings we find above is that the algorithm simply joints the remaining points into a temporary group that has the closest centroid, leading to two user nodes exceeding their qualified communication range. So we set D_{max} mentioned in the system model as a limitation in the temporary cluster division.

Algorithm 1. D-K-means clustering scheme

U_i: the ith user of the system C_i: the head of ith cluster
N_U: the total number of users N_C: the total number of cluster heads
CH_1: the current cluster heads list CH_2: the updated cluster heads list
1   $L_{i,j}$: the distance between i_{th} user and j_{th} cluster head
D_{max}: the maxmum distance between D2D users to achieve a desired threshold
        of SNR
[A B]: add B to the end of list A
2 **begin**
3 | **Step 1**: Initialize the cluster heads list;
4 | $CH_1 = U_1$
5 | **Step 2**: Judge the belonging and cluster
6 | **for** $i = 1; i < N_U; i + +$ **do**
7 | **for** $j = 1; j < N_C; j + +$
8 | $L_{min} = min[L_{i,j}]$;
9 | **if** $L_{min} < D_{max}$**then**
10 | assign U_i into corresponding cluster;
11 | **else**
12 | $CH_1 = [CH_1\ U_i]$;
13 | $N_C = N_C + 1$;
14 | **end**
15 | **end**
16 | **end**
17 | **Step 3**: Recalculate the cluster heads
18 | **for** $i = 1; i < N_C; i + +$ **do**
19 | $C_i = Centroid(X, Y) = (\frac{1}{N_C} \sum_{i=1}^{N_C} x_i, \frac{1}{N_C} \sum_{i=1}^{N_C} y_i)$;
20 | $CH_2 = [CH_2\ C_i]$;
21 | **end**
22 | **Step 4**: Execute until convergence
23 | **if** $CH_1 \neq CH_2$ **then**
24 | | Go to **step 2** and **step 3**;
25 | **end**
26 **end**

Since Algorithm 1 only takes users' physical location into consideration, ignoring the social trust among users, it is hard to apply in a real scenario. Under this situation, we propose an improved algorithm called SD-K-means to meet a real need.

3.3 SD-K-means Clustering Scheme

An Example. Since some users after clustering are so close to cluster heads that they are difficult to be removed out of cluster, we only focus on cluster margin users whose affiliation are not so stable. Just like what we show in Fig. 3, user 1 is in cluster margin, where the distance between the user and the cluster head satisfy: $L_b * D_{max} <= distance1 <= D_{max}$, L_b is a lower bound coefficient.

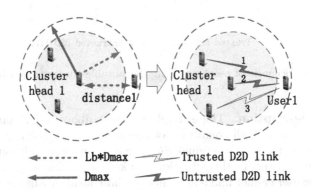

◄······· Lb*Dmax —⚡—Trusted D2D link

◄———— Dmax —⚡—Untrusted D2D link

Fig. 3. Scenario of user1 in the cluster1's margin with weak signal

Under this condition, we have to think about whether the user 1 is suitable to continue staying in the original cluster or not. As we all know, each user has different social trust with other cluster members, and we use a threshold V_S to judge whether the D2D link between two nodes is trusted or not: if the social trust $S >= V_S$, we think that link is trusted, and vice versa. Here we assume that there are two untrusted D2D links and one trusted D2D link.

The capacity of the ith D2D link can be calculated as:

$$C_i = log_2(1 + SNR_i) \tag{1}$$

Then we define a secrecy contribution that user i can provide to the whole cluster, named SC_{Pi}. For the right part of Fig. 3, we have:

$$SC_{P1} = C_3 - C_1 - C_2 \tag{2}$$

If SC_{Pi} is positive, it means that user i is helpful for the improvement of the whole cluster's secrecy circumstance, otherwise it should be expelled or rejected from the cluster.

Assuming that SC_{P1} is negative, the user starts to check adjacent clusters to find in which one the signal is not so weak and is fit for joining. It needs the distance between the user and adjacent cluster head to be satisfied: $distance2 < U_b * D_{max}$, U_b is an upper bound coefficient.

Then we calculate the SC_{P1} to cluster 2, as shown in Fig. 4:

$$SC_{P1} = C_1 + C_3 + C_4 - C_2 \tag{3}$$

if the SC_{P1} is positive, we assign user 1 into the cluster 2.

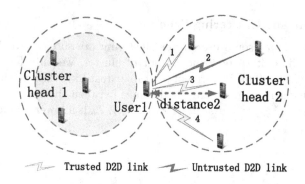

Fig. 4. Scenario of user1 searching the suitable cluster to join in

Algorithm Description. The example we show above is just one situation where the user satisfies all conditions of handover, so we assign it to another cluster. However, the user's original SC_{Pi} may be positive, although it is at the edge of the cluster. In this situation, we keep it in the original cluster. In addition, if the user cannot find a new cluster whose head satisfies distance need, or for the adjacent cluster the user is not so trusted, we expel it from its original cluster and regard it as a single node which can only communicate with other nodes in cellular mode. The detailed algorithm is described as follows.

4 Simulation Results and Evaluation

In this section, the results of the two different clustering schemes proposed above are provided to further analyze the performance of intracluster communication secrecy. In our simulation, we assume the number of users $N = 50$, and that they are uniformly distributed in the square region with a side of 100 m. Meanwhile, the social trust value between users is uniformly distributed between 0 and 1, and $V_S = 0.5$ is to judge whether links among users are trusted or not. What's more, we set a distance limitation, $Dmax = 40\,m$, and correspondingly $L_b = 0.8$ and $U_b = 1.2$. The results are shown as follows.

Comparing (b) with (a) in Fig. 5, we could clearly see a significant change with the six user nodes expelled from clusters independently labeled as cellular users with black "*", and maybe in some secrecy sense, these nodes further become a potential eavesdropper or a so-called outcast user. In addition, there are also some subtle changes about user nodes, which are located at the edge of clusters. For instance, at the bottom left of (a) and (b) in Fig. 5, a user node first belongs to cluster 5, then is assigned to cluster 1. We assume the large scale path-loss exponent between the D2D users $\beta = 4$. We set the noise of AWGN channels $\sigma^2 = -60\,dBm$.

The random clustering scheme is also used as a comparison with our proposed scheme. Then we show the improvement of our proposed scheme in two parts.

Algorithm 2. SD-K-means clustering scheme

U_i: the ith user of the system C_j: the head of ith cluster
N_U: the total number of users N_C: the total number of cluster
L_b: lower bound coefficient U_b: upper bound coefficient
L_{iORG}: the distance between ith user and its original cluster head
L_{iADJ}: the distance between ith user and its adjacent cluster head

1 D_{max}: the maximum distance between D2D users to achieve desired SNR
SC_{P1i}: the secrecy contribution the user i can provide to its original cluster
SC_{P2i}: the secrecy contribution the user i can provide to its adjacent cluster
$List_C$: the list of users who are expelled from clusters
$[A \ B]$: add B to the end of list A

2 **Input**: Result of D-K-means clustering scheme;
3 **begin**
4   **for** $i = 1; i < N_U; i + +$ **do**
5   **if** $L_{iORG} > L_b * D_{max}$**then**
6   **if** $SC_{P1i} < 0$**then**
7   **if** $L_{iADJ} < U_b * D_{max}$**then**
8   **if** $SC_{P2i} > 0$**then**
9   Assign U_i to its adjacent cluster;
10   **else**
11               $List_C = [List_C \ U_i]$;
12   **end**
13   **else**
14             $List_C = [List_C \ U_i]$;
15   **end**
16   **end**
17   **end**
18   **end**
19 **end**

4.1 Power Consumption

First, we divide the way of communication among all user nodes into two categories. When two user nodes are close, they communicate with each other in D2D mode. We denote signal to noise ratio of the receiver by SNR, correspondingly the transmitting power of ith D2D link is P_{Di}. There we have

$$SNR = \frac{P_{Di} \|h_i\|^2}{\sigma^2} \tag{4}$$

So the P_{Di} can be expressed as

$$P_{Di} = \frac{SNR\sigma^2}{\|h_i\|^2} \tag{5}$$

And when the physical distance between two user nodes D_i is longer than $2 * D_{max}$, we determine the user nodes completely cannot communicate in D2D

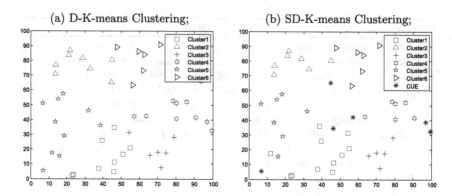

Fig. 5. Simulation result of two different clustering scheme

mode; they can only communicate in cellular mode. We define the power consumption needed as P_C, for the reason that communicating in cellular mode has two steps:

(1) source node to eNodeB; (2) eNodeB to destination node;
the P_C can be expressed

$$P_C = 2 \lim_{D_i \to D_{max}} P_{Di} \tag{6}$$

So for the ith user node which has m D2D links and n cellular links, the average power consumption is written

$$\overline{P_i} = \frac{\sum_{j=1}^{m} P_{Dj} + \sum_{k=1}^{n} P_{Ck}}{m + n} \tag{7}$$

Then the total power consumption is

$$P_{SUM} = \sum_{i=1}^{N_U} \overline{P_i} \tag{8}$$

4.2   Secrecy Contribution

Under the condition that the ith user node wants to share some private files with other cluster members, these user nodes will be divided into two subsets. One contains all the nodes whose social trust with the source nodes is more than 0.5, in which the source is willing to share. We denote it by Set_{i1}, having N_{S1i} users. Another is correspondingly less than 0.5, which means the source does not want to share, denoted it by Set_{i2}, having N_{S2i} users. The capacity of ith link in the same cluster is written

$$C_i = log_2(1 + \frac{P_i \|h_i\|^2}{\sigma^2}) \tag{9}$$

Then the secrecy contribution provided by the ith user node can be expressed as

$$SC_{Pi} = \sum_{j=1}^{N_{S1i}} C_j - \sum_{k=1}^{N_{S2i}} C_k \tag{10}$$

We assume the Kth cluster has N_K user nodes, and there are N_C clusters in total. The whole intracluster secrecy contribution is

$$SC_{SUM} = \sum_{k=1}^{N_C} \sum_{i=1}^{N_K} SC_{Pi} \tag{11}$$

(a) Power Consumption ;   (b) Secrecy Contribution ;

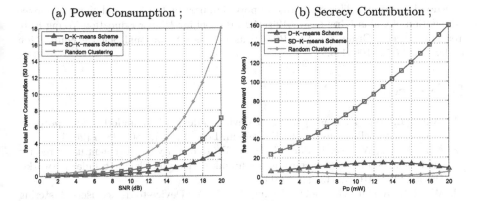

Fig. 6. Performance improvement for the 50 users' system

In items of power consumption, which we show in Fig. 6(a), we could point out that the two clustering scheme we proposed cost far less power than the random way. It fits the fact that our proposed schemes make more users in close proximity to communicate in D2D mode directly. Because of the single cellular users expelled from SD-K-means algorithm, it is to be slightly inferior to the D-K-means algorithm. Meanwhile, just as what we show in Fig. 6(b), the secrecy contribution brought by the SD-K-means algorithm is significant to the other two schemes. The tendency of D-K-means and the random scheme is almost the same, near to zero. This can also prove the validity of our simulation. Combining (a) with (b) in Fig. 6, we can draw a conclusion that our proposed SD-K-means clustering scheme has improvements on both power consumption and secrecy contribution. Besides, compared with the D-K-means scheme, which only takes physical location into consideration, the SD-K-means clustering scheme has an obvious advantage of secrecy contribution, consuming extremely little extra power.

5   Conclusion

In this paper, we have proposed a novel clustering scheme by considering both physical location and social trust among users for D2D communications. Due to the significant impact of social interaction on the feasibility of D2D clustering communications, we have jointly considered both the physical and the social relationship among nodes, and have modified the K-means algorithm to characterize the formation of our D2D link-based clusters. Furthermore, we have presented the performance improvements of our proposed scheme compared with clustering based on random and physical distance only. Numerical results have demonstrated the merits of our proposed scheme in terms of system power consumption, as well as secrecy contribution.

Acknowledgment. This work was supported in part by the National Natural Science Foundation of China (Grant No. 61201150), the Beijing Higher Education Young Elite Teacher Project (Grant No. YETP0442) as well as US National Science Foundation under grant CNS-1065444.

References

1. Wang, L., Wu, H.: Fast pairing of device-to-device link underlay for spectrum sharing with cellular users. IEEE Commu. Lett. **18**(10), 1803–1806 (2014)
2. Min, H., Seo, W., Lee, J., Park, S., Hong, D.: Reliability improvement using receive mode selection in the device-to-device uplink period underlaying cellular networks. IEEE ITWC **10**(2), 413–418 (2011)
3. Wang, L., Araniti, G., Cao, C., Wang, W., Liu, Y.: Device-to-device users clustering based on physical and social characteristics. IEEE JDSN (2015)
4. Wen, S., Zhu, X., Lin, Z., Zhang, X., Yang, D.: Energy efficient power allocation schemes for device-to-device (D2D) communication. In: IEEE VTC Fall, Las Vegas, USA, pp. 1–5, September 2013
5. Tang, H., Ding, Z., Yoo, S.J.B., Hamalainen, J.: Outage constrained joint precoding for D2D underlay cellular networks. In: IEEE GLOBECOM, Atlanta, USA, pp. 3540–3545, December 2013
6. Wang, L., Tang, H., Ciemy, M.: Device-to-device link admission policy based on social interaction information. IEEE TVT **10**(99), 1–7 (2014)
7. Chen, X., Ian Proulx, B., Gong, X., Zhang, J.: Social trust and social reciprocity based cooperative D2D communications. In: ACM MobiHoc, Bangalore, India, pp. 187–196, July 2013
8. Wang, Y., Wu, J.: Social-tie-based information dissemination in mobile opportunistic social networks. In: WWMMN, Madrid, Spain, pp. 1–6, June 2013
9. Chen, K.-C., Chiang, M., Poor, V.: From technological networks to social networks. IEEE JSAC **31**(9), 548–572 (2013)
10. Gupta, U., Ranganathan, N.: A game theoretic approach for simultaneous compaction and equipartitioning of spatial data sets. IEEE TKDE **22**(4), 465–478 (2010)
11. Park, G.Y., Kim, H., Jeong, H.W., Youn, H.Y.: A novel cluster head selection method based on k-means algorithm for energy efficient wireless sensor network. In: IEEE ICAINAW, Barcelona, Spain, pp. 910–915, March 2013

Cooperative Beamforming and Artificial Noise Design for Secure Multi-pair Communications in Wireless Two-Way Relay Networks

Yizhen Zhang, Guobing Li$^{(\boxtimes)}$, Guomei Zhang, and Gangming Lyu

School of Electronics and Information Engineering,
Xi'an Jiaotong University, Xi'an, China
{gbli,zhanggm,gmlv}@mail.xjtu.edu.cn, zhangyizhen210@126.com

Abstract. In this paper, a secure cooperative beamforming and artificial noise design scheme is developed for multi-pair two-way relay networks. We derive the secrecy sum rate for multi-pair two-way relaying, where each communication pair exchanges information through multiple friendly and cooperating relays while under the interception of multiple passive eavesdroppers. We formulate the secrecy sum rate maximization problem and show its non-convexity. We then propose a beamforming and artificial noise design scheme by transforming this problem into a series of convex problems by a tight semidefinite relaxation (SDR) and Taylor approximation. Simulations show that the proposed method converges fast with a high secure sum rate.

Keywords: Physical-layer security · Two-way relay · Multi-pair communications · Secrecy sum rate

1 Introduction

Explosive and versatile wireless applications urges diverse demands on wireless transmissions. Besides instantaneous and statistical requirements on Quality of Service (QoS) including transmission rate and delay [1–4], security and privacy also become a necessity for the design of wireless communications systems to against network- or physical-layer interception [5]. For physical-layer security, secrecy sum rate is a well-recognized performance metric to balance transmission rate and security. To improve secrecy sum rate, user cooperation and relaying are proposed to improved the secure performance for one source-destination pair in the presence of one or more eavesdroppers [6, 7]. Based on the cooperative beamforming (CB), the amplify-and-forward (AF) has lower implementation complexity comparing with the decode-and-forward (DF). In [8], a suboptimal scheme

G. Li – This work was supported by the National Natural Science Foundation of China under Grant No. 61401350, 61102079 and the National 863 Program of China under Grant No. 2014AA01A707.

of secure communications is proposed for a two-hop AF multiple-input multiple-output (MIMO) wireless relay network. Other state-of-the-art studies for secure communications in one-way relay networks can be found in [9,10] and so on.

The above studies all focus on the one-way relay networks. With the development of secure communications, the network scenario is extended to the two-way relay network for high spectral efficiency. In [11], two suboptimal schemes for secure communications in a two-way relay network are developed. One is null-space cooperative beamforming when the eavesdropper's channel state information (CSI) is fully available; the other is adopting the artificial noise scheme while eavesdropper's CSI is unavailable. As an extension of [11,12] focuses on the design of a general approach to find the optimal null space beamforming and the two sources' transmitting power for secure communications in two-way relay networks. Moreover, the objective function is secrecy sum rate in [12] instead of the sum rate. The work in [13] investigates the joint design of CB and AN in the two-way AF relay network with a suboptimal method. In [14], a cooperative jamming scheme for the three-phase two-way relaying system with an untrustworthy relay node is proposed to enhance the secure communications. However, the three-phase two-way relaying will decrease the spectral efficiency in some extent, and the algorithm proposed by [14] is only to minimize jamming signal power at each source node. Moreover, the researches above all address one-pair legitimate user which has no inter-pair interference during the data transmission. However, in practice, there could be more legitimate user pairs in two-way relay networks for high spectral efficiency and transmission rate. In [15], multi-pair users communicating with a friendly jammer in two-way relay is considered. However, the problem in [15] is only used to allocate the total jamming power to improve physical-layer security in a distributed manner. The optimal secrecy sum rate of the two-way relay network with multi-pair users still remains an open problem.

The main contribution of this paper is the design of cooperative beamforming vector and artificial noise to improve the secrecy sum rate of multi-pair two-way AF relaying networks. We formulate the secrecy sum rate maximization problem and show its non-convexity. By semidefinite relaxation and Taylor approximation, we first transform the original non-convex problem into a series of convex problems, and eventually obtain a high-rate cooperative beamforming and artificial noise design scheme by iteratively solving the successive convex problems. The proposed scheme is shown to achieve high secrecy sum rate with fast convergence by simulations.

The rest of the paper is organized as follows: Sect. 2 describes the system model; Sect. 3 formulates the secrecy sum rate maximization problem, then reformulates and relaxes this non-convex problem into a difference of convex programming problem; Sect. 4 presents the simulation results to demonstrate the performance of the proposed algorithm; Finally, we conclude the paper in Sect. 5.

Notations: Lower-case and upper-case denote vectors and matrices, respectively. Superscripts $(\cdot)^*$, $(\cdot)^T$ and $(\cdot)^H$ stand for complex conjugate, transpose, and conjugate transpose, respectively. $\mathbf{I}_N$ is a $N \times N$ identity matrix. $\text{tr}(\cdot)$ and $\text{rank}(\cdot)$ denote the trace and the rank of a matrix, respectively. $|\cdot|$ denotes the absolute value of a scalar or vector, and $[\cdot]_{i,j}$ means the (i,j)th entry of a matrix. $\mathbf{X} \succ \mathbf{0}$ indicates that $\mathbf{X}$ is Hermitian positive definite. Similarly, $\mathbf{X} \succeq \mathbf{0}$ denotes that $\mathbf{X}$ is Hermitian positive semidefinite. diag$\{\,\cdot\,\}$ represents diagonal matrix with main diagonal$\{\,\cdot\,\}$. $\Re e\{\,\cdot\,\}$ stands for the real part of a complex. $\|\cdot\|$ is the Frobenius norm of a vector or matrix. $\log(\,\cdot\,)$ denotes the natural logarithmic function. $E\{\cdot\}$ is the expectation operator.

2 System Model

We consider a wireless two-way relay network with K-pair communication users, N relays and M passive eavesdroppers, as is depicted in Fig. 1. For each user pair $k, k = 1, 2, ..., K$, user UT_{2k-1} and UT_{2k} exchange information with the help of trusted relays $R_n, n = 1, 2, ..., N$, meanwhile under the interception of eavesdroppers $E_m, m = 1, 2, ..., M$. The users, relays and eavesdroppers are all equipped with single antenna, operate in half-duplex mode and distributed manner. We denote the vector of channel coefficients from the l-th, $l = 1, 2, ..., 2K$, user to the relays as $\mathbf{f}_l \in \mathbb{C}^N$. Similarly, the vector of channel coefficients between the l-th, $l = 1, 2, ..., 2K$, user to the eavesdroppers is denoted as $\mathbf{g}_l \in \mathbb{C}^M$. $\mathbf{h}_m \in \mathbb{C}^N$ denotes the channel vector from the eavesdropper E_m to the relays. In addition, considering two-way relaying naturally works in time division mode, we assume the whole transmission is time-divided hence the channels can be assumed reciprocal during the transmission.

The transmission is performed in two phases. In the phase I, all users transmit messages to the relays at the same time. The signal received at the relays can be written by

$$\mathbf{r} = \sum_{k=1}^{2K} \sqrt{P_k} \mathbf{f}_k s_k + \mathbf{n}_R, \tag{1}$$

where P_k is the transmitting power of the k-th user, s_k is the transmitting symbol of the k-th user with $E\left[|s_k|^2\right] = 1$, and $\mathbf{n}_R$ denotes zero-mean circularly symmetric complex Gaussian noise with $E\left\{\mathbf{n}_R \mathbf{n}_R^H\right\} = \sigma_R^2 \mathbf{I}_N$ at the relays.

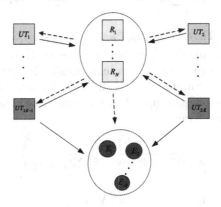

Fig. 1. The system model of two-way relay networks with multi-pair users.

Similarly, in the first phase, the received signal at the eavesdropper E_m is

$$y_{E_m}^{(1)} = \sum_{k=1}^{2K} \left(\sqrt{P_k} g_{k,m} s_k \right) + n_m^{(1)}, \tag{2}$$

where $g_{k,m}$ denotes channel coefficient from the k-th user to the m-th eavesdropper, $n_m^{(1)}$ is the additive white gaussian noise at the eavesdropper E_m with zero mean and variance σ_m^2.

In the phase II, the mixed signals at the relays received at the first phase are amplified and broadcast with manipulated artificial noise (AN) and cooperative beamforming (CB). The transmitting signals can be expressed by

$$\bar{\mathbf{r}} = \mathbf{W}\mathbf{r} + \mathbf{n}_a, \tag{3}$$

where $\mathbf{W} = \mathrm{diag}([w_1^*, w_2^*, ..., w_N^*])$ is the beamforming matrix in which $w_n, n = 1, ..., N$ denotes the weighted value for each relay, $\mathbf{n}_a$ responds to the AN vector, where $\mathbf{n}_a \sim \mathcal{CN}(\mathbf{0}, \boldsymbol{\Sigma})$ with $\boldsymbol{\Sigma} \succeq 0$ standing for the covariance matrix of $\mathbf{n}_a$.

In the second phase, the relays broadcast $\bar{\mathbf{r}}$, the desired signal at the k-th pair users can be obtained after self-interference cancellation, which can be written as

$$\begin{aligned} y_{2k-1} =& \sqrt{P_{2k}} \mathbf{w}^H \mathbf{F}_{2k-1} \mathbf{f}_{2k} s_{2k} + \mathbf{w}^H \mathbf{F}_{2k-1} \sum_{l \neq 2k, 2k-1}^{2K} \sqrt{P_l} \mathbf{f}_l s_l \\ &+ \mathbf{w}^H \mathbf{F}_{2k-1} \mathbf{n}_R + \mathbf{f}_{2k-1}^T \mathbf{n}_a + n_{2k-1}, \end{aligned} \tag{4}$$

$$\begin{aligned} y_{2k} =& \sqrt{P_{2k-1}} \mathbf{w}^H \mathbf{F}_{2k} \mathbf{f}_{2k-1} s_{2k-1} + \mathbf{w}^H \mathbf{F}_{2k} \sum_{l \neq 2k, 2k-1}^{2K} \sqrt{P_l} \mathbf{f}_l s_l \\ &+ \mathbf{w}^H \mathbf{F}_{2k} \mathbf{n}_R + \mathbf{f}_{2k}^T \mathbf{n}_a + n_{2k} \end{aligned} \tag{5}$$

Similarly, the received signal at the m-th eavesdropper during the second phase is

$$y_{E_m}^{(2)} = \mathbf{w}^H \mathbf{H}_m \sum_{k=1}^{2K} \sqrt{P_k} \mathbf{f}_k s_k + \mathbf{w}^H \mathbf{H}_m \mathbf{n}_R + \mathbf{h}_m^T \mathbf{n}_a + n_m^{(2)} \tag{6}$$

where $\mathbf{F}_k = \mathrm{diag}\{\mathbf{f}_k\}$, $\mathbf{H}_m = \mathrm{diag}\{\mathbf{h}_m\}$ and $\mathbf{w} = [w_1, w_2, ..., w_N]^T$. The variance of n_{2k-1}, n_{2k} and $n_m^{(2)}$ are σ_{2k-1}^2, σ_{2k}^2 and σ_m^2, respectively.

Consequently, with (4) and (5), we can obtain the achievable information rate of each user pair. Similarly, with (2) and (6), we obtain the achievable information rate of the eavesdropper E_m. For clarity, we express the information rate for in the following form:

$$I_{UT_k} = \frac{1}{2} \log_2 \left(1 + \frac{\mathbf{w}^H \mathbf{B}_k \mathbf{w}}{\mathbf{w}^H (\mathbf{D}_k + \mathbf{E}_k) \mathbf{w} + \mathbf{f}_{2k}^T \boldsymbol{\Sigma} \mathbf{f}_k^* + \sigma_k^2} \right), k = 1, 2, ..., 2K \tag{7}$$

$$I_{E_m} = \frac{1}{2} \log_2 \left(1 + \frac{\alpha_k}{\beta_k} + \frac{\mathbf{w}^H \mathbf{V}_k \mathbf{w}}{\sigma_m^2 + \mathbf{h}_m^T \boldsymbol{\Sigma} \mathbf{h}_m^* + \mathbf{w}^H \mathbf{U}_k \mathbf{w}} \right), m = 1, 2, ..., M \tag{8}$$

where

$$\mathbf{B}_{2k-1} = P_{2k}\mathbf{F}_{2k-1}\mathbf{f}_{2k}\mathbf{f}_{2k}^H\mathbf{F}_{2k-1}^H, \mathbf{B}_{2k} = P_{2k-1}\mathbf{F}_{2k}\mathbf{f}_{2k-1}\mathbf{f}_{2k-1}^H\mathbf{F}_{2k}^H,$$

$$\mathbf{D}_{2k-1} = \mathbf{F}_{2k-1}\left(\sum_{l\neq 2k,2k-1}^{2K} P_l\mathbf{f}_l\mathbf{f}_l^H\right)\mathbf{F}_{2k-1}^H, \mathbf{D}_{2k} = \mathbf{F}_{2k}\left(\sum_{l\neq 2k,2k-1}^{2K} P_l\mathbf{f}_l\mathbf{f}_l^H\right)\mathbf{F}_{2k}^H,$$

$$\mathbf{E}_{2k} = \sigma_R^2\mathbf{F}_{2k}\mathbf{F}_{2k}^H, \mathbf{E}_{2k-1} = \sigma_R^2\mathbf{F}_{2k-1}\mathbf{F}_{2k-1}^H,$$

$$\alpha_k = P_{2k-1}|g_{2k-1,m}|^2 + P_{2k}|g_{2k,m}|^2, \beta_k = \sigma_m^2 + \sum_{l\neq 2k,2k-1}^{2K} P_l|g_{l,m}|^2$$

$$\mathbf{U}_k = \sigma_R^2\mathbf{H}_m\mathbf{H}_m^H + \sum_{l\neq 2k,2k-1}^{2K} P_l\mathbf{H}_m\mathbf{f}_l\mathbf{f}_l^H\mathbf{H}_m^H,$$

and

$$\mathbf{V}_k = \frac{P_{2k}P_{2k-1}}{\beta_k}[|g_{2k-1,m}|^2\mathbf{H}_m\mathbf{f}_{2k}\mathbf{f}_{2k}^H\mathbf{H}_m^H + |g_{2k,m}|^2\mathbf{H}_m\mathbf{f}_{2k-1}\mathbf{f}_{2k-1}^H\mathbf{H}_m^H$$
$$- 2\Re e\left(g_{2k-1,m}^*g_{2k,m}\mathbf{H}_m\mathbf{f}_{2k-1}\mathbf{f}_{2k}^H\mathbf{H}_m^H\right)]$$
$$+ P_{2k-1}\mathbf{H}_m\mathbf{f}_{2k-1}\mathbf{f}_{2k-1}^H\mathbf{H}_m^H + P_{2k}\mathbf{H}_m\mathbf{f}_{2k}\mathbf{f}_{2k}^H\mathbf{H}_m^H.$$

3   Secrecy Sum-Rate Maximization

In this section, we consider the secrecy problem of two-way relay network. Here we adopt the criteria of making the achievable secrecy sum rate maximization by designing cooperative beamforming matrix and artificial noise covariance matrix.

Define the achievable secrecy sum rate of the system with multi-pair users as the sum of each pair users' maximal achievable secrecy rate. The achievable secrecy sum rate of the system with multi-pair users can be expressed as

$$R_{sum} = \sum_{k=1}^{K}\left(I_{UT_{2k-1}} + I_{UT_{2k}} - \max_{m\in M} I_{E_m}\right)^+. \tag{9}$$

where $[a]^+ := \max(0, a)$.

Therefore, according to the definition in above, to achieve the optimal secrecy sum rate, the optimization problem with individual power constraint of each relay can be formulated as

$$P1 : \max_{\mathbf{W},\mathbf{\Sigma}}\left\{\sum_{k=1}^{K}\left(I_{UT_{2k-1}} + I_{UT_{2k}} - \max_{m\in M} I_{E_m}\right)\right\}$$
$$\text{s.t. } [E\{\bar{\mathbf{r}}\bar{\mathbf{r}}^H\}]_{n,n} \leq P_{R_n}, \forall n.$$

where P_{R_n} is the power of n-th relay. In addition, we can readily determine the power of the relays which can be expressed as $E\left[\bar{\mathbf{r}}\bar{\mathbf{r}}^H\right] = \mathbf{W}\boldsymbol{\Gamma}\mathbf{W}^H + \boldsymbol{\Sigma}$, where $\boldsymbol{\Gamma} = \sum_{k=1}^{2K} P_k\mathbf{F}_k\mathbf{F}_k^H + \sigma_R^2\mathbf{I}_N$.

By substituting Eqs. (7), (8) and (9) into P1, removing $\log_2$ and setting $\mathbf{C}_{2k-1} = \mathbf{D}_{2k-1} + \mathbf{E}_{2k-1}$, $\mathbf{C}_{2k} = \mathbf{D}_{2k} + \mathbf{E}_{2k}$, $\mathbf{A}_{2k-1} = \mathbf{B}_{2k-1} + \mathbf{C}_{2k-1}$, $\mathbf{A}_{2k} = \mathbf{B}_{2k} + \mathbf{C}_{2k}$, $\mathbf{T}_k = (\alpha_k + \beta_k)\mathbf{U}_k + \mathbf{V}_k$, $\delta_{2k-1} = \mathbf{f}_{2k-1}^T\boldsymbol{\Sigma}\mathbf{f}_{2k-1}^* + \sigma_{2k-1}^2$, $\delta_{2k} = \mathbf{f}_{2k}^T\boldsymbol{\Sigma}\mathbf{f}_{2k}^* + \sigma_{2k}^2$, $\delta_m = \sigma_m^2 + \mathbf{h}_m^T\boldsymbol{\Sigma}\mathbf{h}_m^*$, the problem P1 can be reformulated into a min-max problem by taking account the worst case of eavesdropping

$$\text{P2}: \max_{\boldsymbol{\Sigma},\mathbf{w},m}\min \prod_{k=1}^K \left\{ \frac{\mathbf{w}^H\mathbf{A}_{2k-1}\mathbf{w}+\delta_{2k-1}}{\mathbf{w}^H\mathbf{C}_{2k-1}\mathbf{w}+\delta_{2k-1}} \; \frac{\mathbf{w}^H\mathbf{A}_{2k}\mathbf{w}+\delta_{2k}}{\mathbf{w}^H\mathbf{C}_{2k}\mathbf{w}+\delta_{2k}} \; \frac{\beta_k(\mathbf{w}^H\mathbf{U}_k\mathbf{w}+\delta_m)}{\mathbf{w}^H\mathbf{T}_k\mathbf{w}+(\alpha_k+\beta_k)\delta_m} \right\}$$

s.t. $\left[\boldsymbol{\Gamma}\mathbf{w}\mathbf{w}^H+\boldsymbol{\Sigma}\right]_{n,n} \leq P_{R_n}, \forall n.$

It is difficult to obtain the closed-form solution for P2. Therefore, we develop a suboptimal algorithm for the optimization problem. Here we apply the semidefinite relaxation which is proposed in [16] by letting $\mathbf{X} = \mathbf{w}\mathbf{w}^H$ and then substituting it into the optimization problem P2 with the constraint rank$\{\mathbf{X}\} = 1$. Therefore, P2 can be further rewritten as

$$\text{P3}: \max_{\boldsymbol{\Sigma},\mathbf{X},m\in M}\min \prod_{k=1}^K \left\{ \frac{\text{tr}\,(\mathbf{A}_{2k-1}\mathbf{X})+\delta_{2k-1}}{\text{tr}\,(\mathbf{C}_{2k-1}\mathbf{X})+\delta_{2k-1}} \; \frac{\text{tr}\,(\mathbf{A}_{2k}\mathbf{X})+\delta_{2k}}{\text{tr}\,(\mathbf{C}_{2k}\mathbf{X})+\delta_{2k}} \; \frac{\beta_k\,(\text{tr}\,(\mathbf{U}_k\mathbf{X})+\delta_m)}{\text{tr}\,(\mathbf{T}_k\mathbf{X})+(\alpha_k+\beta_k)\,\delta_m} \right\}$$

s.t. $\left[\boldsymbol{\Gamma}\mathbf{X} + \boldsymbol{\Sigma}\right]_{n,n} \leq P_{R_n}, \forall n,$

rank $(\mathbf{X}) = 1, \mathbf{X} \succeq \mathbf{0}.$

We can see that the optimal problem P3 is non-convex thus complicated for the optimal solution. In order to solve the optimization problem, we take the natural logarithm for the objective function. Therefore, P3 can be formulated as

$$\text{P4}: \max_{\boldsymbol{\Sigma},\mathbf{X},m}\min \left\{ \sum_{i=1}^{3K}\log(\hat{\alpha}_i) - \sum_{i=1}^{3K}\log\left(\hat{\beta}_i\right) \right\}$$

s.t. $\left[\boldsymbol{\Gamma}\mathbf{X} + \boldsymbol{\Sigma}\right]_{n,n} \leq P_{R_n}, \forall n,$

rank $(\mathbf{X}) = 1, \mathbf{X} \succeq \mathbf{0},$

$\hat{\alpha}_i = \text{tr}\,(\mathbf{A}_i\mathbf{X}) + \delta_i, \hat{\beta}_i = \text{tr}\,(\mathbf{C}_i\mathbf{X}) + \delta_i, \forall i = 1, ..., 2K,$

$\hat{\alpha}_i = \beta_j\,(\text{tr}\,(\mathbf{U}_j\mathbf{X}) + \delta_m), \forall i = 2K + j, j = 1, ..., K,$

$\hat{\beta}_i = \text{tr}\,(\mathbf{T}_j\mathbf{X}) + (\alpha_j + \beta_j)\,\delta_m, \forall i = 2K + j, j = 1, ..., K.$

The objective function of P4 is the difference of two convex function, and it is still non-convex. To remove the non-convex part, we approximate $\log(\hat{\beta}_i)$ by the first order Taylor polynomial expansion, $\log(\hat{\beta}_{i,0}) + \frac{1}{\hat{\beta}_{i,0}}(\hat{\beta}_i - \hat{\beta}_{i,0}), \forall i$, where $\hat{\beta}_{i,0}$ is a const value.

We continue to remove the rank-1 constraint in P4 by semidefinite relaxation. It can be proved that the optimal $\mathbf{X}$ satisfies rank$(\mathbf{X}) = 1$, i.e., the SDR is tight.

We reformulate the optimization problem as

$$P5 : \max_{\Sigma,\mathbf{X},m} \min \left\{ \sum_{i=1}^{3K} \log\left(\hat{\alpha}_i\right) - \sum_{i=1}^{3K} t_i \right\}$$

$$\text{s.t. } [\mathbf{\Gamma X} + \mathbf{\Sigma}]_{n,n} \le P_{R_n}, \forall n, \mathbf{X} \succeq \mathbf{0}, \tag{10}$$

$$\hat{\alpha}_i = \text{tr}\left(\mathbf{A}_i \mathbf{X}\right) + \delta_i, \hat{\beta}_i = \text{tr}\left(\mathbf{C}_i \mathbf{X}\right) + \delta_i, \forall i = 1, ..., 2K, \tag{11}$$

$$\hat{\alpha}_i = \beta_j \left(\text{tr}\left(\mathbf{U}_j \mathbf{X}\right) + \delta_m\right), \forall i = 2K + j, j = 1, ..., K, \tag{12}$$

$$\hat{\beta}_i = \text{tr}\left(\mathbf{T}_j \mathbf{X}\right) + \left(\alpha_j + \beta_j\right)\delta_m, \forall i = 2K + j, j = 1, ..., K. \tag{13}$$

$$\log\left(\hat{\beta}_{i,0}\right) + \frac{1}{\hat{\beta}_{i,0}}\left(\hat{\beta}_i - \hat{\beta}_{i,0}\right) \le t_i, \forall i = 1, 2, ..., 3K. \tag{14}$$

Since the optimal problem P5 is a max-min problem, we alternatively consider the following problem

$$P6 : \min_{\Sigma,\mathbf{X},m} \tau$$

$$\text{s.t. } \max_{m \in M} \left(-\sum_{i=1}^{3K} \log\left(\hat{\alpha}_i\right) + \sum_{i=1}^{3K} t_i \right) \le \tau,$$

$$(10) - (14)$$

The problem P6 is an SDP problem and its global optimal solution can be efficiently obtained by optimization tools such as CVX [14]. Therefore, we can use an iterative algorithm similar to our previous work in [18] to obtain the optimal $\mathbf{X}$, namely $\mathbf{X}_{opt}$. Once $\mathbf{X}_{opt}$ is obtained, the beamforming matrix $\mathbf{W}$ and its corresponding secrecy sum rate can be achieved.

4 Simulation Results

In the simulation, the power of the k-th pair users are $P_{2k-1} = P_{2k} = P$ for $k = 1, 2, ..., K$ and $P_{R_n} = P_R/N$ for $n = 1, 2, ..., N$, where P_R is the total power of all the relays. Without loss of generality, the variances of the noise are set to $\sigma_R^2 = \sigma_{2k-1}^2 = \sigma_{2k}^2 = \sigma_m^2 = 1$. All the channel coefficients are Gaussian random vectors with zero-mean and unit covariance.

Figure 2 shows the secrecy sum rate for the different relays' power P_R with $K = 2$ and $P = 10\,\text{dBW}$. Clearly, we can see that the secrecy sum rate is increasing with the power of relays P_R. In addition, we can also obtain that the secrecy sum rate will be better when the number of relays is larger. Furthermore, the proposed algorithm with joint CB and AN has slight difference for the algorithm only with CB for $N = 12$ and $M = 3$ when the power P_R is smaller; nonetheless, the difference will become larger as the power P_R increasing.

In order to reveal the convergence of the proposed algorithm, Fig. 3 illustrates the convergence performance of the proposed algorithm for N when the power $P_R = P = 10\,\text{dBW}$, $M = 3$ eavesdroppers and $K = 2$ pair users. It can be observed in Fig. 3 that, with one channel realization, the proposed method will

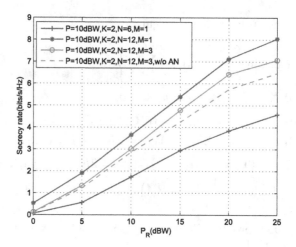

Fig. 2. Secrecy sum rate in different relays power P_R.

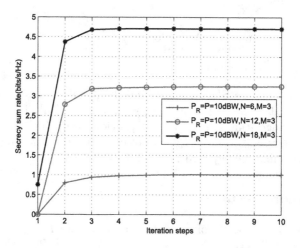

Fig. 3. Secrecy sum rate in different iteration number for $K = 2$.

achieve the optimal secrecy sum rate in a few steps which no more than 4 times. Actually, after three iterations, the secrecy sum rate changes slightly with the number of iteration. Therefore, in practice the proposed algorithm can stop early to save time and computation cost with an acceptable performance. In addition, we can also obtain that when the number of the eavesdroppers, the power of the relays and the users are fixed, the system with more relays will have a higher secrecy performance than that with less relays.

Figure 4 demonstrates the secrecy sum rate vs. the number of user-pair K with $N = 6$ relays and $M = 3$ eavesdroppers. As depicted in the Fig. 4, the secrecy sum rate is larger with more user-pair K which can be understood easily. When $P = 10\,\mathrm{dBW}$, the secrecy sum rate of the system with $P_R = 30\,\mathrm{dBW}$ is

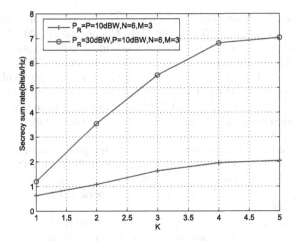

Fig. 4. Secrecy sum rate in different user-pair K.

significantly better than that with $P_R = 10\,\mathrm{dBW}$. Moreover, the secrecy sum rate will become a constant when the K is enough bigger which is resulted by the power of relays P_R which not enough to provide the power to the relays. Also, although so far there is no comparable algorithms for multi-pair networks ($K \geq 2$) available, we can find that, when $K = 1$, the simulation result agree well with the result in [18], implies the proposed scheme also works well for one-pair two way networks.

5   Conclusion

In this paper, the joint cooperative beamforming and artificial noise design to enhance the secure communications has been investigated in wireless multi-pair two-way relay networks. We formulate the secrecy sum rate maximization problem and transform it into a series of solvable convex problems with tight semidefinite relaxation and Taylor approximation. The proposed cooperative beamforming and artificial noise design scheme is shown to achieve high secrecy sum-rate and fast convergence speed.

References

1. Mohapatra, P., Li, J., Gui, C.: QoS in mobile ad hoc networks. IEEE Wirel. Commun. **10**(3), 44–53 (2003)
2. Du, Q., Zhang, X.: QoS-aware base-station selections for distributed MIMO links in broadband wireless networks. IEEE J. Sel. Area Commun. **29**(6), 1123–1138 (2011)
3. Wang, Y., Ren, P., Gao, F., Su, Z.: A hybrid underlay/overlay transmission mode for cognitive radio networks with statistical Quality-of-Service provisioning. IEEE Trans. Wirel. Commun. **13**(3), 1482–1498 (2014)

4. Du, Q., Zhang, X.: Statistical QoS provisionings for wireless unicast/multicast of multi-layer video streams. IEEE J. Sel. Area Comm. **28**(3), 420–433 (2010)

5. Khan, S., Pathan, A.S.K.: Wireless Networks and Security: Issues, Challenges and Research Trends[M]. Springer Science and Business Media (2013)

6. Dong, L., Han, Z., Petropulu, A.P., et al.: Improving wireless physical layer security via cooperating relays. IEEE Trans. Signal Process. **58**(3), 1875–1888 (2010)

7. Wang, H.-M., Yin, Q., Xia, X.-G.: Hybrid opportunistic relaying and jamming with power allocation for secure cooperative networks. IEEE Trans. Wirel. Commun. **PP**(99), 1 (2014)

8. Wang, C., Wang, H.-M.: Robust joint beamforming and jamming for secure AF networks: low complexity design. IEEE Trans. Veh. Technol. **PP**(99), 1 (2014)

9. Yang, Y., Li, Q., Ma, W.-K., Ge, J., Ching, P.C.: Cooperative secure beamforming for AF relay networks with multiple eavesdroppers. IEEE Signal Process. Lett. **20**(1), 35–38 (2013)

10. Sun, L., Zhang, T., Li, Y., Niu, H.: Performance study of two-hop amplify-and-forward systems with untrustworthy relay nodes. IEEE Trans. Veh. Technol. **61**(8), 3801–3807 (2012)

11. Wang, H.-M., Yin, Q., Xia, X.-G.: Distributed beamforming for physical-layer security of two-way relay networks. IEEE Trans. Signal Process. **60**(7), 3532–3545 (2012)

12. Yang, Y., Sun, C., Zhao, H., et al.: Algorithms for secrecy guarantee with null space beamforming in two-way relay networks. IEEE Trans. Signal Process. **62**(8), 2111–2126 (2014)

13. Lin, M., Ge, J., Yang, Y., et al.: Joint cooperative beamforming and artificial noise design for secrecy sum rate maximization in two-way AF relay networks. IEEE Commun. Lett. **18**(2), 1–4 (2014)

14. Long, H., Wei, X., Zhang, X., Wang, J., Wang, W.: Cooperative jamming and power allocation in three-phase two-way relaying system with untrusty relay node. In: Proceedings, pp. 1–4. IEEE URSI GASS, Beijing, Aug. 2014

15. Wang, A., Cai, Y., Guan, X., Wang, S.: Physical layer security for multiuser two-way relay using distributed auction game. In: Proceedings, pp. 1202–1207. IEEE ICIST, Yangzhou, Mar. 2013

16. Luo, Z.-Q., Ma, W.-K., So, A.M.-C., et al.: Semidefinite relaxation of quadratic optimization problems. IEEE Signal Process. Mag. **27**(3), 20–34 (2010)

17. Grant, M.C., Boyd, S.P.: The CVX Users Guide Release 2.0 (beta). CVX Research Inc, Mar. 2013

18. Zhang, Y., Li, G., Du, Q., et al.: High-Rate Cooperative Beamforming for Physical Layer Security in Wireless Cyber-Physical Systems. IEEE ICC2015 workshop 22, to appear

On the Stable Throughput in Wireless LANs

Qinglin Zhao[1]($\boxtimes$), Taka Sakurai[2], Jiguo Yu[3], and Limin Sun[4]

[1] Faculty of Information Technology, Macau University of Science and Technology,
Avenida Wei Long, Macau, Taipa, China
qlzhao@must.edu.mo
[2] Department of Electrical and Electronic Engineering,
The University of Melbourne, Melbourne 3010, Australia
tsakurai@ieee.org
[3] School of Information Science and Engineering, Qufu Normal University,
Rizhao 276826, Shandong, China
jiguoyu@sina.com
[4] Beijing Key Laboratory of IOT Information Security Technology,
Institute of Information Engineering CAS, Beijing 100093, China
sunlimin@iie.ac.cn

Abstract. The throughput stability is concerned with how much traffic load can be sustained in a network, and has been a research hotspot. Recent studies on the stability in 802.11 networks have arrived at contradictory conclusions. This paper delves into the reasons behind these contradictions. Our study manifests that the maximum stable-throughput is not simply larger than, less than, or equal to the saturation throughput as argued in previous works. Instead, there exists two intervals, over which the maximum stable-throughput follows different rules: over one interval, it may be far larger than the saturated throughput; over the other, it is tightly bounded by the saturated throughput. Most existing related research fails to differentiate the two intervals, implying that the derived results are inaccurate or hold true partially. Finally, we verify our study results via extensive simulations.

Keywords: Stable throughput · Saturation throughput · 802.11

1 Introduction

The stability of CSMA networks is a notorious problem due to their distributed, random-access nature. From Aloha [3] to IEEE 802.11 Wi-Fi networks [1], we cannot even answer a very simple problem: what is the maximum stable-throughput (i.e., the network throughput equalling the aggregate input traffic

This work is partially supported by the Macao Science and Technology Development Fund under Grant (No. 081/2012/A3, No. 104/2014/A3, and No. 013/2014/A1), NNSF of China for Contract 61373027, NSF of Shandong Province for Contract ZR2012FM023, and Strategic Priority Research Program of the Chinese Academy of Sciences (No. XDA06040101). Qinglin Zhao is the corresponding author.

© Springer International Publishing Switzerland 2015
K. Xu and J. Zhu (Eds.): WASA 2015, LNCS 9204, pp. 745–755, 2015.
DOI: 10.1007/978-3-319-21837-3_73

load). For example, even for the simplest network version (such as buffered aloha networks), the throughput stability is still in discussion [7]. Therefore, this problem has attracted a great deal of attention such as [7–9, 12, 14, 16, 18].

Recent studies [8, 13, 17, 18] considered the throughput stability problem in a one-hop 802.11 DCF network, and arrived at contradictory conclusions. In [17], the authors asserted that (a) the maximum stable throughput can only be achieved in the nonsaturation regime (where nodes do not always have packets to transmit), and that (b) it can be much higher than the saturation throughput while providing satisfactory quality of service (QoS). In [13], the authors also observed that the stable throughput may rise higher than the saturation throughput before the network is saturated. However, in [18], the authors argued that to ensure stability, the throughput should not be allowed to exceed the level of the saturation throughput. They recommended operating a DCF network far below the saturation load to achieve stable throughput and to avoid unbounded mean packet delay and delay jitter. Finally, the research results in [8] indicated that the maximum stable throughput in a DCF network is approximately the same as the saturation throughput.

In this paper, we investigate this contradictory in general IEEE 802.11 EDCA [1] wireless LANs. 802.11 DCF (that provides a uniform channel contention access) is a special case of 802.11 EDCA (that provides a prioritized channel contention access). Compared with DCF, EDCA can support quality of service for real-time applications and therefore has received continuing attention [11, 15]. In EDCA, nodes belonging to high-priority (HP) access categories (ACs) are configured with a maximum contention window (CW) as small as 16, while nodes belonging to low-priority (LP) ACs are configured with a maximum CW as large as 1024. Such configurations enable HP nodes to enjoy a high opportunity to access the channel. In this paper, we consider an EDCA network with one HP AC and one LP AC (note that when the LP AC does not exist, the EDCA system reduces to the DCF system). Each AC behaves like a DCF network, and has two configurable CWs: the minimum and maximum CWs (i.e., Wmin and Wmax). For simplicity, we assume that Wmin = Wmax; [5] showed that the 802.11 system with such a configuration is similar to the slotted p-persistent CSMA system and can successfully emulate the 802.11 system with Wmin $\neq$ Wmax.

Our study manifests that the maximum stable throughput is not simply larger than, less than, or equal to the saturation throughput as argued in [8, 13, 17, 18]. We show that given the node number, there exists a unique optimal HP CW. The HP throughput is only achieved at the optimal HP CW in the saturation regime. The optimal HP CW partitions the whole HP CW range into two intervals: over one interval, the maximum stable HP throughput may be significantly higher than the saturation throughput; over the other, the maximum stable HP throughput is tightly bounded by the saturation throughput. Most existing related research fails to differentiate the two intervals, implying that the derived results are inaccurate or hold true partially. This study helps utilize the system resources fully; in particular, it shows that the HP AC can acquire more bandwidth allocations even when it coexists with the LP AC.

The rest of this paper is organized as follows. Section 2 models the exact and asymptotic HP throughput. Section 3 investigates the maximum stable HP throughput. Section 4 illustrates the maximum stable HP throughput and verifies our augments via simulation. Section 6 concludes this paper.

2   HP Throughput

The considered EDCA system, running in the basic mode and ideal channel conditions, consists of one HP AC and one LP AC. Each node has an infinite buffer size. All data packets from HP and LP nodes are transmitted to the AP, and the AP acts purely as the receiver of data packets.

The LP AC has n_0 nodes. Each LP node has the same packet size L_0 and always generates a random backoff count uniformly distributed in $[0, W_0]$ for each new transmission or retransmission, where $W_0 > 1$. We assume that each LP node is in saturation operation (i.e., the node always has packets to transmit) because here we study the maximum stable throughput that the HP AC can achieve, regardless of how the LP offered load varies.

The HP AC has n nodes. Each HP node has the same packet size L and packet arrival rate λ, and always generates a random backoff count uniformly distributed in $[0, W]$ for each new transmission or retransmission, where $W > 1$.

When $n_0 = 0$, the considered EDCA system reduces to a DCF system without a backoff mechanism.

2.1   Exact HP Throughput

We now express the total throughput of HP nodes.

Let $\beta_0 \in (0, 1)$ be the saturated attempt rate (i.e., the number of transmission attempts per slot) for each LP node and then we have $\beta_0 = 2/(W_0 + 1)$ from [4]. Let $C_0 = (1 - \beta_0)^{n_0}$ be the probability that none of the n_0 LP nodes transmits packets.

Let $\beta \in (0, 1)$ be the general (i.e., saturated or nonsaturated) attempt rate for each HP node. Let Ω be the mean time that elapses for one decrement of the backoff counter. Then, we have

$$\Omega = P_e \sigma + P_b T_b + P_{b_0} T_{b_0} + P_c T_c, \tag{1}$$

$$\text{where } P_e = (1 - \beta)^n C_0,$$

$$P_b = [1 - (1 - \beta)^n] C_0,$$

$$P_{b_0} = (1 - \beta)^n [1 - C_0],$$

$$P_c = 1 - P_e - P_b - P_{b_0}.$$

In (1), P_e is the probability of an idle slot; P_b (P_{b_0}) is the probability that at least one of the n HP (n_0 LP) nodes transmits when none of the n_0 LP (n HP) nodes transmits packets; P_c is the probability of a collision involving both

Table 1. Parameters for 802.11b basic mode.

SIFS	10 μs	IP	=	40 bytes
Slot	20 ms	MAC	=	30 bytes
DIFS	50 μs	T_{ack}	=	(PHY+14) × 8/R_{basic}
R_{data}	11 Mbps	$T_{data}(L)$	=	PHY × 8/R_{basic} + (IP+MAC+L) × 8/R_{data}
R_{basic}	1 Mbps	$T_{pkt}(L)$	=	DIFS + $T_{data}(L)$ + SIFS + T_{ack}
PHY	24 bytes			

HP and LP nodes. $\sigma = 1$ slot. T_b (T_{b_0}) $\gg \sigma$ is the mean time of a successful transmission for each HP (LP) node and is assumed to equal the mean time of a collision involving HP (LP) nodes only; we adopt this assumption for simplifying the analysis and this assumption can be removed easily [20]; T_b (T_{b_0}) can be calculated by $T_{pkt}(L)$ in Table 1, where L denotes the packet size of HP or LP nodes. T_c ($= \max(T_b, T_{b_0})$) is the mean time for a collision involving both HP and LP nodes.

Exact HP Throughput: Given the HP node number n and the general HP attempt rate β, the total HP throughput, $\Gamma(n, \beta)$, is defined to be the number of bits transmitted successfully by HP nodes in the time interval of Ω. Then $\Gamma(n, \beta)$ is expressed as

$$\Gamma(n, \beta) = \frac{P_s L}{\Omega}, \tag{2}$$

where $P_s = n\beta(1 - \beta)^{n-1}C_0$ is the probability of a successful transmission from any of the n HP nodes, when none of the n_0 LP nodes transmits packets.

Saturated HP Throughput: Let β_s be the saturated HP attempt rate, which is equal to $\beta_s = 2/(W + 1)$ from [4]. We then call $\Gamma(n, \beta_s)$ the saturated HP throughput.

2.2 Asymptotic HP Throughput

We call $k \triangleq n\beta \in [0, \infty)$ the total HP attempt rate and define a constant η as follows:

$$\eta \triangleq -\frac{(T_{b_0} - T_c) + C_0(\sigma - T_b - T_{b_0} + T_c)}{T_c + C_0(T_b - T_c)}. \tag{3}$$

Asymptotic HP Throughput: Let $\Gamma(k) \triangleq \lim_{n \to \infty} \Gamma(n, \beta)$ be the asymptotic HP throughput. Theorem 1 below expresses $\Gamma(k)$ and shows that $\Gamma(k)$ has a unique maximum value $\Gamma(k_{opt})$, where $k_{opt} = \text{argmax}_{k \in [0, \infty)} \Gamma(k)$ is called the optimal total HP attempt rate.

Theorem 1. *(a)* $\Gamma(k) \geq 0$ *is continuous in* $[0, \infty)$ *and is given by*

$$\Gamma(k) = \frac{k}{e^k - \eta} \frac{C_0 L}{T_c + C_0(T_b - T_c)}, \tag{4}$$

where $\eta \in (0, 1)$.

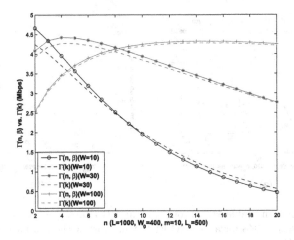

Fig. 1. $\Gamma(n,\beta)$ and $\Gamma(k)$ as n and W vary, where $k = n\beta$ and $\beta = 1/(W+1)$.

(b) $\Gamma(k)$ is increasing in $[0, k_{opt}]$ and is decreasing (k_{opt}, ∞), where

$$k_{opt} = \mathscr{W}_0(\frac{-\eta}{e}) + 1, \tag{5}$$

where $W_0(\cdot)$ is one branch of the Lambert $W(z)$ function [6], $W(z)e^{W(z)} = z$, for any complex number z.
   Proof: Please refer to the Appendix.

In general, $\Gamma(k)$ can well approximate $\Gamma(n,\beta)$ as shown in Fig. 1. Hereafter, we use $\Gamma(k)$ as a theoretical proxy for $\Gamma(n,\beta)$. The dashed circle curve in Fig. 1 illustrates $\Gamma(k)$. Note that (i) when $k = k_s \triangleq n\beta_s$, we call $\Gamma(k_s)$ the asymptotic saturated HP throughput and have $\Gamma(k_s) \leq \Gamma(k_{opt})$ obviously, and (ii) when $C_0 = 1$ and $T_b = T_{b_0}$ (i.e., no LP nodes exist), k_{opt} reduces to the solution to (10) in [10].

3   Maximum Stable HP Throughput

Let us define the stable HP throughput first.

Stable HP throughput: The HP throughput $\Gamma(k)$ is said to be stable if for a given aggregate input traffic load, $n\lambda L$, (a) there exists a theoretical $k > 0$ so that the total HP throughput $\Gamma(k) = n\lambda L$, and (b) the theoretical k is achievable, namely, all HP nodes are able to jointly and spontaneously tune their respective CWs to produce such a k.

Remarks: (i) The statement that k is achievable implies $\Gamma(k) = n\lambda L$, but the converse is not true; the difference is that the k in the original statement represents a realistic value while the k in the converse statement would represent a theoretical value. (ii) We give an example where k is unachievable. Consider

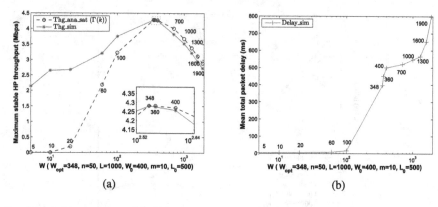

Fig. 2. (a) Maximum stable HP throughput and (b) total packet delay in ms when W varies and $W_{opt} = 348$ for a two-AC EDCA network without a backoff mechanism. Note that $W < W_{opt}$ corresponds to $k > k_{opt}$.

the settings $n = 50$, $W = 5$ and $L = 1000$, as shown in Fig. 2. We have $k_s = 2n/(W + 1) \approx 16.7 > k_{opt} = 0.2866$. Theoretically, k may assume the value k_{opt} since $k \in [0, k_s] = [0, k_{opt}] \cup (k_{opt}, k_s]$. However, $k = k_{opt}$ is unachievable, because the throughput is increasing in $k \in [0, k_{opt}]$ and the simulated maximum stable throughput is about 2.18 Mbps, which is far less than 4.3 Mbps corresponding to $k = k_{opt}$. (iii) The statement that k is achievable implies that the nodes can produce such a k, but not vice versa, because producing a k (say, $k = 0.2866$) possibly requires that the offered load should be far larger than the throughput $\Gamma(k)$.

Proposition 1 below presents a conjecture about the achievable interval of k.

Proposition 1: there exists a $k_{\max} \in (0, k_{opt}] \cap (0, k_s]$ so that $k \in [0, k_{\max})$ is achievable, $k = k_{\max}$ is not necessarily achievable, and $k \in (k_{\max}, k_s]$ is unachievable.

From Proposition 1, $\Gamma(k_{\max})$ is a tight upper bound on the stable HP throughput, namely, any traffic load below $\Gamma(k_{\max})$ is stable. Note that (i) the throughput $\Gamma(k_{\max})$ might be unstable, meaning that we possibly need to inject a much higher traffic load than $\Gamma(k_{\max})$ in order to attain $\Gamma(k_{\max})$; (ii) $\Gamma(k_{\max}) \leq \Gamma(k_{opt})$ and $\Gamma(k_{\max})$ is different from $\Gamma(k_s)$, but they might be equal sometimes, for example, when $(0, k_s] \subset (0, k_{opt}]$, which will explained later. In the following, we investigate $\Gamma(k_{\max})$ when the HP CW is either statically configured or dynamically adjustable.

3.1   Two Cases of Maximum Stable HP Throughput

From Theorem 1, given n, there exists an optimal attempt rate, $\beta_{opt} = k_{opt}/n$, where k_{opt} is given by (5). Further, we can calculate the optimal contention window, W_{opt}, as follows.

$$W_{opt} = \frac{2}{\beta_{opt}} - 1 = \frac{2n}{k_{opt}} - 1.$$

We point out that W_{opt} partitions the whole contention window range into two intervals: $[1, W_{opt})$ and (W_{opt}, ∞); for $W \in [1, W_{opt})$, the maximum stable HP throughput $\Gamma(k_{\max})$ may be significantly higher than the saturation throughput, while for (W_{opt}, ∞), the maximum stable HP throughput $\Gamma(k_{\max})$ is tightly bounded by the saturation throughput.

We now explain our arguments as follow. Given n and W, the per-node and total saturated attempt rates are $\beta_s = 2/(W + 1)$ and $k_s = n\beta_s$, respectively. $\Gamma(k_{\max})$ varies depending on the relationship between k_s and k_{opt}.

The Case of $k_s \leq k_{opt}$. When $k_s \leq k_{opt}$, we conjecture $\Gamma(k_{\max}) = \Gamma(k_s)$ because (i) $\Gamma(k) \leq \Gamma(k_s)$ for any $k \leq k_s$ from Theorem 1 (b), and (ii) any HP node can really transmit packets at the attempt rate of β_s in saturated operation.

The Case of $k_s > k_{opt}$. When $k_s > k_{opt}$, there exists $k_0 \in [0, k_{opt}]$ such that $\Gamma(k_0) = \Gamma(k_s)$ from the intermediate value theorem, since $\Gamma(k) \geq 0$ is continuous and $0 \leq \Gamma(k_s) \leq \Gamma(k_{opt})$. Consequently, we have $\Gamma(k) \geq \Gamma(k_0) = \Gamma(k_s)$ for any $k \in [k_0, k_{opt}] \subset [0, k_s]$ since $\Gamma(k)$ is increasing over $[k_0, k_{opt}]$.

Consider the possible situation where $k_{\max} \in [k_0, k_{opt}]$. This would imply that $\Gamma(k_{\max}) \geq \Gamma(k_s)$ and that $\Gamma(k_{\max})$ would appear before the saturation operation since $k_{\max} \leq k_s$. Such a phenomenon has been observed in Fig. 5 in our previous paper [20] and such a maximum throughput is called the "presaturation throughput peak" in [18].

However, contrary to the opinion expressed in [18] that such a presaturation throughput peak might not be sustainable and therefore the traffic load should be maintained far below the saturation load for DCF with a backoff mechanism, our simulation results show that for some CW settings, such a presaturation throughput peak is sustainable. Furthermore, it can be far above the saturation load, while the total packet delay can be very low. For example, as illustrated in Fig. 2, when CW = 20 (which is a case of $k_s > k_{opt}$), the simulated maximum stable throughput = 2.65 Mbps is far larger than the saturation throughput of 0.24 Mbps, while the mean total packet delay is only about 2 ms.

An intuitive explanation is as follows. A very large attempt rate such as that required for saturated operation can cause too many collisions and lead to a reduced throughput. By limiting the attempt rate, we can potentially achieve a higher throughput than the saturated throughput, whilst maintaining stability. Nevertheless, finding $\Gamma(k_{\max})$ is a challenging task in the case when $k_s > k_{opt}$ and we leave this topic for future research.

4   Model Verification

In this section, we validate the effectiveness of the prediction of the maximum stable HP throughput. We use the TU-Berlin 802.11e simulator [2] in ns2 version 2.28 as a validation tool. In the 802.11e simulator, we disable the binary exponential backoff algorithm by letting the maximum CW be equal to the minimum CW (i.e., Wmax = Wmin), set the retry limit to 7 (setting a larger retry limit, say 100, just produces a negligible impact on the simulation results by our experiments), and use the DumbAgent routing protocol, whose header is 40 bytes. The other protocol parameter settings are listed in Table 1. In addition, we set $W_0 = 400$, $n_0 = 10$, and $L_0 = 500$ bytes for the LP AC unless otherwise specified.

The target of the simulation is to obtain the maximum stable throughput as the CW varies. In simulation, the HP throughput $\Gamma(k)$ is said to be stable if the error between the input traffic load $n\lambda L$ and the obtained throughput $\Gamma(k)$ is less than 1%, namely,

$$\frac{|\Gamma(k) - n\lambda L|}{n\lambda L} < 1\%. \tag{6}$$

For each simulation value, the running time is 200 seconds when $k \leq k_{opt}$, whereas it is 1000 seconds otherwise to exclude the phenomenon that the system once evolves to saturation operation and will never get out of it again, as explained in Fig. 6 in [18]. Note, however, that we do not observe a distinct change in simulation results when the simulation time is set to 1000 seconds, in comparison with 200 seconds. In addition, for readability, we only plot the theoretical saturated throughput in Fig. 2, but its accuracy has been widely validated in [4,19,20].

We ran two experiments to verify our augments. We now explain the two experiments.

Experiment 1 to illustrate the error between $\Gamma(k)$ and $\Gamma(n, \beta)$: In the first experiment, we demonstrate that the asymptotic throughput $\Gamma(k)$ can well approximate the exact throughput $\Gamma(n, \beta)$. Theoretically, the approximation condition is $n \gg \beta$. In practise, the approximation is already good when n is moderately larger than β, which is readily satisfied. Figure 1 plots $\Gamma(k)$ and $\Gamma(n, \beta)$ for a two-AC wireless LAN when $n = 2, 3, \ldots, 20$, $W = 10, 30, 100$ and $L = 1000$ bytes, where $k = n\beta = 2n/(W + 1)$. From this figure, we can see that the $\Gamma(k)$ curve closely matches the $\Gamma(n, \beta)$ curve for each W even when $n = 2$. For example, for $n = 2$, $\beta = 0.1818, 0.0645$, and 0.0198, and the approximation error = 9%, 4%, and 1.5% when $W = 10, 30, 100$, respectively. This indicates that (i) the approximation condition is not restrictive and (ii) the approximation accuracy increases as W increases.

Experiment 2 to illustrate the relationship between the maximum stable throughput and the saturation throughput: In the second experiment, we consider Poisson arrivals and demonstrate the maximum stable HP throughput and the mean total packet delay when the HP CW is statically configured. In this experiment, we set $n = 50$ and $L = 1000$ bytes. The optimal total HP attempt rate k_{opt} is 0.2866 and therefore the optimal per-node HP CW is $W_{opt} = 348$. Figure 2(a) plots the saturated HP throughput and the simulated maximum stable HP throughput, while Fig. 2(b) plots the corresponding total packet delay, when $W = 5, 10, 20, 60, 100, 348, 360, 400, 700, 1000, 1300, 1600$, and 1900. In two subfigure, we plot W on a log-scale for readability, but we label the corresponding W value in linear units near the curve points. Note that since $k_s = 2n/(W+1)$, $W < W_{opt}$ implies $k_s > k_{opt}$ and, conversely, $W > W_{opt}$ implies $k_s < k_{opt}$. We now explain how the experiment was conducted and discuss its result.

- When $W \geq 348$, for each W, we increase the input offered load according to $(0.9 + j0.05)\Gamma(k)$ Mbps as j increases from 1 to 3, and then find the maximum stable throughput and the corresponding total delay. From the figure, we see that when W increases from 348 to 1900, the simulated maximum stable HP throughput decreases while the corresponding delay increases quickly. The simulation curve of the maximum stable throughput is slightly below the theoretical curve of the saturation throughput, confirming that the saturation throughput is a tight upper bound on the stable throughput.
- When $W < 348$, for each W, we increase the input offered load according to $j\Gamma(k_{opt})/8$ Mbps as j increases from 1 to 8, and then find the maximum stable throughput and the corresponding total delay. From the figure, we see that when W increases from 5 to 100, the simulated throughput increases from 2.1 Mbps to 3.8 Mbps while the corresponding delay increases from 2 ms to 16 ms. In contrast, the theoretical saturation throughput underestimates the simulation result, especially when W is small. For example, when $W = 20$, the predicted throughput value is 0.19 Mbsp while the simulated throughput is 2.68 Mbps and the simulated delay is 3.8 ms only. This observation suggests that for some CW settings, the recommendation in [18] calling for operating a wireless LAN far below the saturation load might be too conservative.

The recommended settings for voice transmission in EDCA are backoff factor = 2, Wmin = 8, and Wmax = 16. As a result, the corresponding mean CW is less than 20. Even if we were to adopt such Wmin and Wmax settings (including a backoff mechanism) for HP nodes in our simulations, we can safely deduce that the saturation throughput will still significantly underestimate the maximum stable throughput, from the huge gap between the simulated stable throughput and the theoretical saturation throughput when $W \leq 20$ in Fig. 2.

5 Conclusion

In this paper, we investigate the throughput stability in 802.11 networks, and point out the reasons behinds existing contradictory results. This study provides new insights on the unsaturation performance and helps utilize the system resources fully.

6 Appendix

Proof of Theorem 1: We first prove that $0 < \eta < 1$. Note that $T_c = \max(T_b, T_{b_0}) \gg \sigma$ and $0 < C_0 < 1$. If $T_b \geq T_{b_0}$, then $0 < \eta = \frac{(T_b - T_{b_0}) + C_0(T_{b_0} - \sigma)}{T_b} < \frac{T_b - \sigma}{T_b} < 1$.

If $T_b < T_{b_0}$, then $0 < \eta = \frac{C_0(T_b - \sigma)}{(1-C_0)T_{b_0}+C_0T_b} < \frac{C_0T_b}{(1-C_0)T_{b_0}+C_0T_b} < 1$. Next we prove (a) and (b).

(a) When $n \to \infty$, noting $k = \lim_{n\to\infty}(n-1)\beta$ if k exists, and applying the Poisson distribution to approximate the binomial distributions in (1), we have

$$\lim_{n\to\infty} P_e = e^{-k}C_0, \quad \lim_{n\to\infty} P_s = ke^{-k}C_0,$$

$$\lim_{n\to\infty} P_b = (1 - e^{-k})C_0, \quad \lim_{n\to\infty} P_{b_0} = e^{-k}(1 - C_0),$$

$$\lim_{n\to\infty} P_c = (1 - C_0)(1 - e^{-k}),$$

$$\lim_{n\to\infty} \Omega = T_c + C_0(T_b - T_c) + \frac{C_0(\sigma - T_b) + (1 - C_0)(T_{b_0} - T_c)}{e^k}.$$

Then, (4) is derived from $\Gamma(k) = \lim_{n\to\infty} P_s L/\Omega$.

(b) To maximize $\Gamma(k)$, we set the first derivative of $\Gamma(k)$ to zero and have $k = 1 - \eta e^{-k}$, and hence $(k - 1)e^{k-1} = -\eta e^{-1}$. Then $k - 1 = \mathcal{W}_0(-\eta e^{-1})$ or $\mathcal{W}_{-1}(\frac{-\eta}{e})$. We have $k_{opt} = \mathcal{W}_0(-\eta e^{-1}) + 1 \geq 0$, since only $\mathcal{W}_0(-\eta e^{-1}) > -1$ for $-\eta e^{-1} \in (-1/e, 0)$. ∎

References

1. IEEE Std. 802.11-2007, Part 11: Wireless LAN Medium Access Control (MAC) and Physical Layer (PHY) Specifications, June 2007
2. http://www.tkn.tu-berlinde/research/802.11e_ns2/
3. Abramson, N.: The aloha system c another alternative for computer communication. In: Proceedings of the Fall Joint Computer Conference, AFIP Conference 44, pp. 281–285 (1970)
4. Bianchi, G.: Performance analysis of the IEEE 802.11 distributed coordination function. IEEE J. Sel. Areas Commun. **18**(3), 535–547 (2000)
5. Cali, F., Conti, M., Gregori, E.: Dynamic tuning of the ieee 802.11 protocol to achieve a theoretical throughput limit. IEEE/ACM Trans. Networking **8**(6), 785–799 (2000)
6. Corlessa, R.M., Gonnet, G.H., Hare, D.E.G., Jeffrey, D.J., Knuth, D.E.: On the lambert w function. Adv. Comput. Math. **5**, 329–359 (1996)
7. Dai, L.: Stability and delay analysis of buffered aloha networks. IEEE Trans. Wirel. Commun. **11**(8), 2707–2719 (2012)
8. Dai, L., Sun, X.: A unified analysis of ieee 802.11 dcf networks: Stability, throughput and delay. IEEE Trans. Mobile Comput. **12**(8), 1558–1572 (2013)
9. Fayolle, G., Gelenbe, E., Labetoulle, J.: Stability and optimal control of the packet switching broadcast channel. J. Assoc. Comput. Mach. **24**(3), 375–386 (1977)
10. Heusse, M., Rousseau, F., Guillier, R., Duda, A.: Idle sense: an optimal access method for high throughput and fairness in rate diverse wireless lans. In: Proceedings of ACM Sigcomm (2005)
11. Javed, Y., Baig, A., Maqbool, M.: Enhanced quality of service support for triple play services in ieee 802.11 wlans. EURASIP J. Wirel. Commun. Networking **2015**(1), 1–14 (2015)
12. Kwak, B.J., Song, N.O., Miller, L.E.: Performance analysis of exponential backoff. IEEE/ACM Trans. Networking **13**(2), 343–355 (2005)

13. Malone, D., Duffy, K., Leith, D.: Modeling the 802.11 distributed coordination function in non-saturated heterogeneous conditions. IEEE/ACM Trans. Networking 15(1), 159–172 (2007)

14. Rosenkrantz, W.A., Towsley, D.: On the instability of the slotted aloha multiaccess algorithm. IEEE Trans. Automat. Contr. 28(10), 994–996 (1983)

15. Yao, X., Wang, W., Yang, S., Cen, Y., Yao, X., Pan, T.: Ipb-frame adaptive mapping mechanism for video transmission over ieee 802.11e wlans. Comput. Commun. Rev. 44(2), 5–12 (2014)

16. Zhai, H., Chen, X., Fang, Y.: How well can the ieee 802.11 wireless lan support quality of service? IEEE Trans. Wirel. Commun. 4(6), 3084–3094 (2005)

17. Zhai, H., Kwon, Y., Fang, Y.: Performance analysis of ieee 802.11 mac protocols in wireless lans. Wirel. Commun. Mobile Comput. 4(8), 917–931 (2004)

18. Zhang, Y.J., Liew, S.C., Chen, D.R.: Sustainable throughput of wireless LANs with multipacket reception capability under bounded delay-moment requirements. IEEE Trans. Mobile Comput. 9(9), 1226–1241 (2010)

19. Zhao, Q.L., Tsang, D.H.K., Sakurai, T.: A simple critical-offered-load-based CAC scheme for IEEE 802.11 DCF networks. IEEE/ACM Trans. Networking 19(5), 1485–1498 (2011)

20. Zhao, Q.L., Tsang, D.H.K., Sakurai, T.: Modeling nonsaturated IEEE 802.11 DCF networks under arbitrary buffer size. IEEE Trans. Mobile Comput. 10(9), 1248–1263 (2011)

Antenna Selection in Large-Scale Multiple Antenna Systems

Zhongyuan Zhao[1], Mugen Peng[1]([✉]), Li Wang[1], Wenqi Cai[2], Yong Li[1],
and Hsiao-Hwa Chen[3]

[1] Key Laboratory of Universal Wireless Communication, Ministry of Education,
Beijing University of Posts and Telecommunications, Beijing 100876, China
{zyzhao,pmg,liwang,yongli}@bupt.edu.cn
[2] China Academy of Information and Communications Technology,
Beijing 100191, China
caiwenqi@caict.ac
[3] Department of Engineering Science, National Cheng Kung University,
1 Da-Hsueh Road, Tainan City 70101, Taiwan
hshwchen@mail.ncku.edu.tw

Abstract. Keeping a balance between performance and complexity is a well-known dilemma in large-scale multiple antenna systems. In this paper, the system complexity and the outage probability are evaluated for a large-scale multiple-input-single-output (MISO) system. To obtain the explicit analysis results, the cumulative distribution function (CDF) of the sum of the K-largest order statistics of N independent exponential random variables is first developed. Then the complexity and the outage performance are evaluated with perfect and imperfect channel statement information (CSI). The asymptotic analysis are conducted to give some insights for the design of such a system. Finally, numerical results are provided to verify the accuracy of the developed theoretic results, and show that it is not necessary to always use all antennas to transmit.

Keywords: Large-scale MIMO · Outage probability · Cooperative transmission

1 Introduction

The large-scale antenna technique has been considered as a potential method to significantly improve the system throughput [1], and the performance analysis of large-scale antennas systems also draws a lot of attention recently [2–4]. Due to the conventional view without considering the complexity of system design, such as channel estimation and receiver design, it encourages all the antennas to transmit so that the performance gains can be maximized. However, employing the antennas overly will cause serious delay and intractable complexity, which even suppresses the performance gains in practical large-scale antennas systems. Motivated by finding a solution for such a dilemma, we studied the tradeoff of the performance and the complexity in large-scale multiple-input-single-output

© Springer International Publishing Switzerland 2015
K. Xu and J. Zhu (Eds.): WASA 2015, LNCS 9204, pp. 756–766, 2015.
DOI: 10.1007/978-3-319-21837-3_74

(MISO) systems in this paper, and the main contribution can be summarized as follows:

First, the cumulative distribution function (CDF) of the sum of the K largest out of N independent exponential random variables is obtained, which helps us to obtain the distribution of the receive signal-to-noise ratio (SNR). Secondly, the expected number of employed antennas at the source and the outage probability, which can depict the system complexity and the transmission reliability, respectively, are derived for both case with perfect and imperfect channel statement information (CSI). The derived results show that it is not necessary to always use all the antennas to achieve the best outage performance. Based on the analytical results, the asymptotic results are also given, which provides a simple relationship between the threshold of the equipped antennas at the source to accomplish the transmission successfully and the specific transmission circumstance. Finally, the numerical results are shown to demonstrate the accuracy of the developed analytical results.

Notations and Special Functions: σ^2 denotes the variance of additive white Gaussian noise at each antenna. $\Gamma(i)$ denotes the Gamma function with an argument i, and $\gamma(a, x)$ is the lower incomplete Gamma function with parameters a and x. All special functions follow the form given in [10].

2 System Model and Protocol Description

Consider a scenario where a source S with multiple antennas transmits a message x to a single-antenna destination D. The distance between S and D is defined as d. The number of antennas at S is set as N. The channel coefficients are modeled to captures path loss, shadow fading and flat Rayleigh fading [5,7]. In particular, the channel coefficient for the link from the i-th antenna of S to D can be expressed as

$$h_i = \frac{g_i}{\sqrt{d_i^\alpha}}, \tag{1}$$

where d_i denotes the distance between the i-th antenna of S and D, α describes the path loss exponent, and g_i characterizes the flat Rayleigh fading. Since d is far larger than the distance between either two antennas of S, d_i can be approximated as $d_i \approx d$. Therefore, all the channel coefficients are independently and identically distributed, i.e., $h_i \sim \mathscr{CN}(0, 1/d^\alpha)$, $i = 1, \ldots, N$.

To accomplish the transmission performance with the lowest complexity, K antennas with the best transmission circumstance are selected to transmit, which is the smallest number of antennas can ensure the received signal-to-noise ratio (SNR) larger than a given threshold. Without loss of generality, we assume that $|h_1| \leqslant \cdots \leqslant |h_N|$, and thus the $(N-K+1)$-th, $\ldots$, N-th antennas are chosen to transmit. Then the received SNR can be expressed as follows by using maximum-ratio-transmission (MRT)

$$\gamma_K = \left(\sum_{k=N-K+1}^{N} |h_k|^2 \right) \rho, \tag{2}$$

where $\rho = P/\sigma^2$ denotes the average SNR.

3 How Many Antennas to Transmit?

As discussed in Section II, the number of employed antennas is an important parameter to indicate the cooperation complexity. In this section, we first derive the CDF of the sum of K largest exponential order statistics, which helps us to characterize the system complexity by analyzing the excepted number of employed antennas with/without channel estimation errors, and the outage probability is also provided.

3.1 CDF of the Summation of K Largest Exponential Order Statistics

Lemma 1. *Let $X_1, \cdots, X_N$ be N independent and identically distributed random variables, each of which follows an exponential distribution with a parameter λ, and let $X_{(1)}, \cdots, X_{(N)}$ denote an ordered sequence of $X_1, \cdots, X_N$, $X_{(1)} \leqslant \cdots \leqslant X_{(N)}$. The CDF of $\bar{X} = \sum_{k=N-K+1}^{N} X_{(k)}$, which is the sum of K largest order statistics, can be expressed as*

$$\mathscr{G}\big(\bar{x}, \lambda, K, N\big) = \frac{1}{\Gamma(K)} \gamma\big(K, \lambda \bar{x}\big) - \sum_{i=1}^{N-K} \frac{c_i^K}{\Gamma(K)} \mathscr{J}\big(K, \lambda, \bar{x}\big), \qquad (3)$$

where $a_i^K = \frac{K}{N-i+1}$, $c_i^K = \frac{(a_i^K)^{N-K-1}}{\prod_{m \neq i}^{N-K}(a_i^K - a_m^K)}$ and $\mathscr{J}(K, \lambda, \bar{x})$ is given as

$$\mathscr{J}\big(K, \lambda, \bar{x}\big) = \left[\sum_{k=0}^{K-1} \frac{(-1)^k \binom{K-1}{k} \Gamma(k)}{(b_i^K)^{k+1}} \big(\lambda \bar{x}\big)^{K-k-1} \right] e^{-\lambda \bar{x}}, \qquad (4)$$

with b_i is defined as $b_i^K = \frac{1}{a_i^K} - 1$.

Proof. Due to Eq. (2.2.3) in [9], the joint probability distribution function (PDF) of order statistics $X_{(1)}, \cdots, X_{(N)}$ can be expressed as

$$f_{X_{(1)}, \cdots, X_{(N)}}(x_{(1)}, \cdots, x_{(N)}) = N! \lambda^N e^{-\lambda \sum_{i=1}^{N} x_{(i)}}, 0 \leqslant x_{(1)} \leqslant \cdots \leqslant x_{(N)}. \quad (5)$$

Then we focus on the exponent part in (5), which can be further derived as $\sum_{i=1}^{N} x_{(i)} = \sum_{i=1}^{N} (N-i+1)(x_{(i)} - x_{(i-1)})$. Denoting that $Y_i = (N-i+1)(X_{(i)} - X_{(i-1)})$, (5) can be shown as

$$f_{Y_1, \cdots, Y_N}(y_1, \cdots, y_N) = \lambda^N e^{-\lambda \sum_{i=1}^{N} y_i} = \prod_{i=1}^{N} F_{Y_i}(y_i). \qquad (6)$$

Therefore, $Y_1, \cdots, Y_N$ are N independent exponential variables with a common parameter λ [9], and thus $\bar{X}$ can be shown as

$$\bar{X} = \sum_{k=N-K+1}^{N} X_{(k)} = \sum_{i=1}^{N-K} \frac{K}{N-i+1} Y_i + \sum_{j=N-K+1}^{N} Y_j. \qquad (7)$$

Denoting that $Z_1 = \sum_{i=1}^{N} a_i^K Y_i$, where $a_i^K = \frac{K}{N-i+1}$, its PDF can be obtained by deriving the moment generating function (MFG) $M_{Y_i}(t) = \frac{1}{1-(t/\lambda)}, i = 1, \cdots, N$. Then the MFG of Z_1 can be derived as

$$M_{Z_1}(t) = \prod_{i=1}^{N-K} M_{Y_i}(a_i^K t) = \sum_{i=1}^{N-K} \frac{c_i^K}{1 - (a_i^K/\lambda)t}, \tag{8}$$

where $c_i^K = \frac{(a_i^K)^{N-K-1}}{\prod_{m\neq i}^{N-K}(a_i^K - a_m^K)}$ can be obtained by applying partial fraction expansion on $M_{Z_1}(t)$. Thus $M_{Z_1}(t)$ can be expressed as a summation of $N - K$ exponential distributed variables' MFGs, and the PDF of Z_1 can be shown as

$$f_{Z_1}(z_1) = \sum_{i=1}^{N-K} \frac{\lambda c_i^K}{a_i^K} e^{-\frac{\lambda}{a_i^K} z_1}, \quad z_1 \geqslant 0. \tag{9}$$

We can denote $Z_2 = \sum_{j=N-K+1}^{N} Y_j$, which is a Gamma distributed variable, and its PDF can be given as $f_{Z_2}(z_2) = \frac{\lambda^K}{\Gamma(K)} z_2^{K-1} e^{-\lambda z_2}$, $z_2 \geqslant 0$. Recalling (7), $\bar{X}$ is a summation of two independent variants Z_1 and Z_2, and thus its CDF can be obtained as follows:

$$F(\bar{x}, \lambda, K, N) = \Pr\{Z_1 + Z_2 \leqslant \bar{x}\} = \frac{1}{\Gamma(K)}\gamma(K, \lambda\bar{x}) - \sum_{i=1}^{N-K} \frac{c_i^K}{\Gamma(K)} \mathscr{J}(K, \lambda, \bar{x}), \tag{10}$$

where $\mathscr{J}(K, \lambda, \bar{x}) = \left[\sum_{k=0}^{K-1} \frac{(-1)^k \binom{K-1}{k}\Gamma(k)}{(b_i^K)^{k+1}}(\lambda\bar{x})^{K-k+1} \right] e^{-\lambda\bar{x}}$, and the lemma is proved.

Based on Lemma 1, the performance and the complexity achieved of the studied scenario can be analyzed, which will be shown in the following subsections.

3.2   When Perfect CSI is Available

Since the complexity increases with the number of employed antennas, the key idea of the studied scheme is to use the minimal number of antennas given the constraint of the predefined user quality of service, such as the targeted data rate. Therefore the number of employed antennas is decided opportunistically according to the instantaneous channel conditions, which can be defined as follows when CSI is perfect,

$$\bar{K} = \sum_{K=1}^{N} K \Pr\{\gamma_{K-1} \leqslant \gamma_{\text{th}}, \ \gamma_K \geqslant \gamma_{\text{th}}\}$$

$$= \sum_{K=1}^{N} (\Pr\{\gamma_{K-1} \leqslant \gamma_{\text{th}}\} - \Pr\{\gamma_K \leqslant \gamma_{\text{th}}\})K, \tag{11}$$

where γ_{th} is a given targeted SNR. For notational simplicity, we let $\Pr\{\gamma_0 \leqslant \gamma_{th}\} = 1$ and $\Pr\{\gamma_N \leqslant \gamma_{th}\} = 0$. The expected number of employed antennas can be obtained, as given in the following corollary.

Corollary 1. *When perfect CSI is available, the expected number of employed antennas, which can characterizes the system complexity, can be expressed as*

$$\bar{K} = \sum_{K=1}^{N} \left[\mathscr{G}\left(\frac{\gamma_{th}}{\rho}, d^\alpha, K-1, N\right) - \mathscr{G}\left(\frac{\gamma_{th}}{\rho}, d_{RD}^\beta, K, N\right) \right] K, \qquad (12)$$

where $\mathscr{G}\left(\frac{\gamma_{th}}{\rho}, d^\alpha, K-1, N\right)$ and $\mathscr{G}\left(\frac{\gamma_{th}}{\rho}, d^\alpha, K, N\right)$ follows the definition given in (3) of Lemma 1, $\mathscr{G}\left(\frac{\gamma_{th}}{\rho}, d^\alpha, 0, N\right) = 1$ and $\mathscr{G}\left(\frac{\gamma_{th}}{\rho}, d^\alpha, N, N\right) = 0$.

Then we study the outage probability of proposed scheme, which captures the reception reliability by evaluating the probability that the received SNR fails to achieve a threshold. The explicit expression of outage probability can be provided in the following theorem when CSI is perfect.

Corollary 2. *When perfect CSI is available, the outage probability of the studied scheme can be expressed as*

$$P_{out} = \frac{1}{\Gamma(N)} \gamma\left(N, \frac{\gamma_{th}}{\rho} d^\alpha\right). \qquad (13)$$

Proof. Our studied scheme can achieve the same outage probability as that when all the antennas are applied. Then the outage probability can be derived as

$$P_{out} = \Pr\{\gamma_N \leqslant \gamma_{th}\} = \Pr\left\{ \sum_{k=1}^{N} |h_k|^2 \leqslant \frac{\gamma_{th}}{\rho} \right\}, \qquad (14)$$

where $u = \sum_{k=1}^{N} |h_k|^2$ follows Gamma distribution, and its CDF can be given as

$$G(u) = \frac{1}{\Gamma(N)} \gamma(N, d^\alpha u). \qquad (15)$$

The proof can be finished by substituting $u = \frac{\gamma_{th}}{\rho}$ into (15).

3.3 Impact of Channel Estimation Error

Based on the perfect CSI assumption, we have evaluated the performance and the system complexity in the addressed scenario. However, channel estimation error is commonly found in practical wireless systems, and the channel estimation error can be modeled as follows,

$$h_i = \hat{h}_i + e_i = \frac{\hat{g}_i}{\sqrt{d_i^\alpha}} + \frac{\hat{e}_i}{\sqrt{d_i^\alpha}}, \quad i = 1, \ldots, N, \qquad (16)$$

where $\hat{h}_i$ is an estimate of h_i, and e_i is the channel estimation error. We assume that $\hat{e}_i$ is Gaussian distributed with a common variance ε, which is independent to $\hat{h}_i$. Following the derivations of the signal-to-interference-plus-noise ratio (SINR) given in [6], the SINR at D can be given as

$$\tau_K = \frac{\left(\sum_{k=N-K+1}^{N} |\hat{h}_k|^2\right)\rho}{\rho(\varepsilon/d^\alpha) + 1}, \tag{17}$$

where (17) follows the fact that $\mathbb{E}\{|e_i|^2\} = \varepsilon/d^\alpha$ and $\mathbb{E}\{e_{g_i} e_j\} = 0$, $(i \neq j)$.

Based on (17), we can evaluate the performance and the system complexity of the studied scheme with channel estimation error. In particular, the expected number of employed antennas can be given in the following theorem.

Theorem 1. *Assume that channel estimation error exists with mean square error defined as ε/d^α. The expected number of the employed antennas is given by*

$$\bar{\mathscr{K}} = \sum_{K=1}^{N} \left\{ \mathscr{G}\left(\frac{\gamma_{th}\varepsilon}{d^\alpha} + \frac{\gamma_{th}}{\rho}, \frac{d^\alpha}{1-\varepsilon}, K-1, N\right) - \mathscr{G}\left(\frac{\gamma_{th}\varepsilon}{d^\alpha} + \frac{\gamma_{th}}{\rho}, \frac{d^\alpha}{1-\varepsilon}, K, N\right) \right\} K. \tag{18}$$

Proof. Similar to (11), $\bar{\mathscr{K}}$ can be expressed as

$$\bar{\mathscr{K}} = \sum_{K=1}^{N} \left(\Pr\{\tau_{K-1} \leqslant \gamma_{th}\} - \Pr\{\tau_K \leqslant \gamma_{th}\} \right) K. \tag{19}$$

Due to (17), $\Pr\{\tau_{K-1} \leqslant \gamma_{th}\}$ can be derived as

$$\Pr\{\tau_{K-1} \leqslant \gamma_{th}\} = \Pr\left\{ \sum_{k=N-K+1}^{N} |\hat{h}_k|^2 \leqslant \frac{\gamma_{th}\varepsilon}{d^\alpha} + \frac{\gamma_{th}}{\rho} \right\}$$

$$= \mathscr{G}\left(\frac{\gamma_{th}\varepsilon}{d^\alpha} + \frac{\gamma_{th}}{\rho}, \frac{d^\alpha}{1-\varepsilon}, K, N\right), \tag{20}$$

where (20) follows the fact that $|\hat{h}_k|^2$ is exponential distributed with a parameter $\frac{d^\alpha}{1-\varepsilon}$, and the CDF of the summation of K-largest such order statistics is given in Lemma 1. Then the proof can be finished by substituting (20) into (19). $\blacksquare$

Next we focus on the outage probability when channel estimation error exists. Recalling (14) and (17), the outage probability can be expressed as

$$\mathscr{P}_{out} = \Pr\left\{ \sum_{k=1}^{N} |\hat{h}_k|^2 \leqslant \frac{\gamma_{th}\varepsilon}{d^\alpha} + \frac{\gamma_{th}}{\rho} \right\}. \tag{21}$$

Similar to (15), $\hat{u} = \sum_{k=1}^{N} |\hat{h}_k|^2$ also follows gamma distribution. Then the explicit expression of $\mathscr{P}_{out}$ can be shown in the following corollary.

Corollary 3. *Assume that channel estimation error exists with mean square error defined as ε/d^α. The outage probability can be expressed as*

$$\mathscr{P}_{out} = \frac{1}{\Gamma(N)} \gamma\left[N, \frac{d^\alpha}{1-\varepsilon}\left(\frac{\gamma_{th}\varepsilon}{d^\alpha} + \frac{\gamma_{th}}{\rho}\right)\right]. \tag{22}$$

Unlike the conventional schemes that only concerns performance or complexity partially, such as relay selection and all the antennas employed to transmit, our study shows that it is not necessary to always use all the antennas.

4 Asymptotic Analysis When Large-Scale Antennas Are Equipped at Source

In Section III, the explicit form expressions of the expected number of employed antennas and outage probability are provided, respectively. When S is with a large number of antennas, they can be further simplified, and provide insight for the design of the system. In particular, we focus on a general case when channel estimation error exists, and the main results are given as follows.

Theorem 2. *When the number of antennas at S is large, the asymptotic analysis results can be classified into three cases due to the different settings of N and ρ. In particular, we denote N_{th} as a threshold of N as follows,*

$$N_{\text{th}} = \frac{d^\alpha}{1-\varepsilon}\left(\frac{\gamma_{\text{th}}\varepsilon}{d^\alpha} + \frac{\gamma_{\text{th}}}{\rho}\right). \tag{23}$$

The asymptotic analysis results can be given as

1. *When ρ is fixed, antennas selection is applied.*
2. *When $\rho \to 0$ and $N < N_{\text{th}}$, all the antennas tends to be utilized, and the transmission can hardly accomplished for this case.*
3. *When $\rho \to 0$ and $N \geqslant N_{\text{th}}$, the asymptotic analysis results can be given as*

$$\lim_{\substack{N,K\to\infty,\\ \rho\to 0}} \bar{\mathscr{K}} = \sum_{K=1}^{N_{\text{th}}} \left\{\mathscr{G}\left(\frac{\gamma_{\text{th}}\varepsilon}{d^\alpha} + \frac{\gamma_{\text{th}}}{\rho}, \frac{d^\alpha}{1-\varepsilon}, K-1, N\right) - \mathscr{G}\left(\frac{\gamma_{\text{th}}\varepsilon}{d^\alpha} + \frac{\gamma_{\text{th}}}{\rho}, \frac{d^\alpha}{1-\varepsilon}, K, N\right)\right\}K,$$

$$\lim_{\substack{N,K\to\infty,\\ \rho\to 0}} \mathscr{P}_{\text{out}} = 0. \tag{24}$$

Proof. In this proof, the asymptotic analysis results for three different cases are demonstrated accordingly.

(1) When the relay transmit power is fixed: When $N \to \infty$, the outage probability of antennas selection can be asymptotically expressed as follows,

$$\lim_{N\to\infty} \Pr\{\tau_1 \leqslant \gamma_{\text{th}}\} = \lim_{N\to\infty}\left[1 - e^{-\frac{d^\alpha}{1-\varepsilon}\left(\frac{\gamma_{\text{th}}\varepsilon}{d^\alpha} + \frac{\gamma_{\text{th}}}{\rho}\right)}\right]^N = 0. \tag{25}$$

Such a result shows that antenna selection can accomplish the transmission for this case, and the asymptotic analysis results can be given as

$$\lim_{L\to\infty} \bar{\mathscr{K}} = 1, \text{ and } \lim_{L\to\infty} \mathscr{P}_{\text{out}} = 0. \tag{26}$$

(2) When $\rho \to 0$ and $N < N_{th}$: When the number of employed antennas $K < \infty$, the probability that $\Pr\{\tau_k \leqslant \gamma_{th}\}$ can be analyzed as follows asymptotically,

$$\lim_{\substack{N \to \infty \\ \rho \to 0}} \Pr\{\tau_K \leqslant \gamma_{th}\} \stackrel{(a)}{=} \frac{\gamma(K, \infty)}{\Gamma(K)} - \lim_{\substack{N \to \infty, \\ \rho \to 0}} \sum_{i=1}^{N-K} \frac{a_i^K c_i^K e^{-\mu\theta}}{\Gamma(K)} (\mu q)^{K-1} e^{-\frac{\mu\gamma_{th}}{\rho}}$$

$$\stackrel{(b)}{=} 1 - \lim_{\substack{N \to \infty, \\ \rho \to 0}} \frac{K e^{-\mu\theta} (\mu q)^{K-1}}{N\Gamma(K)} e^{-\frac{\mu\gamma_{th}}{\rho}} = 1, \qquad (27)$$

where $\theta = \frac{\gamma_{th}\varepsilon}{d^\alpha}$ and $\mu = \frac{d^\alpha}{1-\varepsilon}$, equation (a) in (27) is obtained by using L'Hôpital's rule on $\mathscr{G}(K, \mu, \theta)$ given in (10), and (b) in (27) follows the fact that $\lim_{N \to \infty} \frac{a_i^K}{K/N} = 1$ and $\sum_{i=1}^{N-K} c_i^K = 1$. (27) shows that K also goes infinity to accomplish the transmission. Following the notations in (7), $\mathscr{G}(q, \mu, K, N)$ can be expressed as the CDF of a linear combination of N independent exponential variables,

$$\lim_{\substack{N,K \to \infty, \\ \rho \to 0}} \mathscr{G}(q, \mu, K, N) = \lim_{\substack{N,K \to \infty, \\ \rho \to 0}} \Pr\left(\sum_{k=N-K+1}^{N} |\hat{h}_k|^2 = Z_1 + Z_2 \leqslant q \right). \quad (28)$$

Based on the law of large numbers, the value of Z_2 tends to stay as a constant, which can be given as

$$\lim_{N,K \to \infty} Z_2 = \lim_{N,K \to \infty} \left(\sum_{j=N-K+1}^{N} Y_j \right) = \frac{K}{\mu}. \quad (29)$$

Substituting (29) into (28), it can be simplified as

$$\lim_{\substack{N,K \to \infty, \\ \rho \to 0}} \mathscr{G}(q, \mu, K, N) = \lim_{\substack{N,K \to \infty, \\ \rho \to 0}} \Pr\left(Z_1 \leqslant q - \frac{K}{\mu} \right)$$

$$\geqslant \lim_{\substack{N,K \to \infty, \\ \rho \to 0}} \sum_{i=1}^{N-K} c_i^K \left[1 - e^{-\frac{\mu}{a_i^K}\left(q - \frac{N_{th}}{\mu}\right)} \right] = 1, \quad (30)$$

(30) demonstrates that all the antennas tends to be applied for this case. Since the received SNR can hardly beyond the threshold, the asymptotic analysis results shows that the transmission will fail when $N < N_{th}$.

(3) When $\rho \to 0$ and $N \geqslant N_{th}$: Recalling (30), the outage probability can be approximated as follows when the N_{th} best antennas are employed,

$$\lim_{\substack{N,K \to \infty, \\ \rho \to 0}} \mathscr{P}_{out} = \lim_{\substack{N,K \to \infty, \\ \rho \to 0}} \mathscr{G}(q, \mu, N_{th}, N) = \lim_{\substack{N,K \to \infty, \\ \rho \to 0}} \Pr\left(Z_1 \leqslant 0 \right) = 0. \quad (31)$$

Due to the proof of case (2, N_{th} is the largest number of employed antennas to transmit the message successfully). The proof is finished.

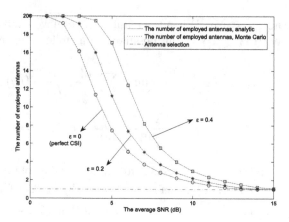

Fig. 1. The number of employed antennas vs. SNR, $N = 20$.

5   Numerical Results

In Fig. 1, the expected number of employed antennas is plotted. As shown in this figure, simulation results match well with the analytic results given in (12) of Corollary 2 and (18) in Theorem 4, respectively. To combat the impact of channel estimation error, more antennas are required to transmit as ε increases. When SNR is high enough, antenna selection tends to be applied. In Fig. 2, the outage performance is plotted, which also verifies the analytical results. The numerical results show that it is not necessary to always use all the antennas to achieve the best outage performance.

To show the performance with different settings of N, Fig. 3 is provided, where the average SNR is set as $\rho = 0$ dB. To better evaluate the performance, the scheme that transmit with fixed number of antennas is selected as a com-

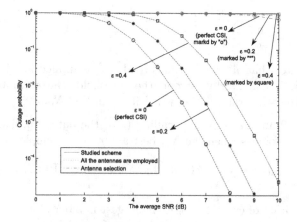

Fig. 2. Outage probability vs. SNR, $N = 20$.

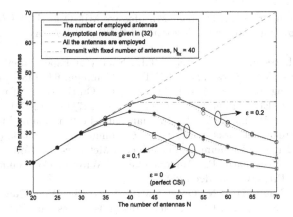

Fig. 3. The number of employed antennas when N is large at S.

parable scheme, and the fixed number of employed antennas is $N_{\text{fix}} = 40$. In Fig. 3, the expected number of employed antennas is plotted. When N is not large enough, all the antennas are employed to accomplish the transmission. As N increases, the expected number of employed antennas begins to decrease, and it matches with the asymptotic result given in (24).

6 Conclusion

In this paper, the complexity and the outage performance of large-scale MISO systems are analyzed. By using the density function of the sum of the K largest order statistics, the explicit analytical results have been provided when perfect and imperfect CSI are available. The asymptotic analysis has been taken to show some insights of designing such a system. In particular, a closed-form threshold has been derived for the number of antennas that can accomplish the transmission successfully when the transmit power approaches to zero. Finally, the numerical results have been provided to verify the analytical results, and show that it is not necessary to always use all antennas to transmit. The research method and results presented in this paper can be implied in the future cloud radio access networks or other massive multiple antenna systems.

References

1. Rusek, F., Persson, D., Lau, B.K., Larsson, E.G., Marzetta, T.L., Edfors, O., Tufvesson, F.: Scaling up MIMO: opportunities and challenges with very large arrays. IEEE Sig. Proc. Mag. **30**, 40–60 (2013)
2. Zhang, J., Wen, C.-K., Jin, S., Gao, X., Wong, K.-K.: On capacity of large-scale MIMO multiple access channels with distributed sets of correlated antennas. IEEE J. Sel. Areas Commun. **31**, 133–148 (2013)

3. Hoydis, J., ten Brink, S., Debbah, M.: Massive MIMO in the UL/DL of cellular networks: how many antennas do we need? IEEE J. Sel. Areas Commun. **31**, 160–171 (2013)
4. Ngo, H.Q., Larsson, E.G., Marzetta, T.L.: Energy and spectral efficiency of very large multiuser MIMO systems. IEEE Trans. Commun. **61**, 1436–1449 (2013)
5. Ding, Z., Leung, K., Goeckel, D.L., Towsley, D.: On the study of network coding with diversity. IEEE Trans. Wirel. Commun. **8**, 1247–1259 (2009)
6. Gao, F., Zhang, R., Liang, Y.-C.: Optimal channel estimation and training design for two-way relay networks. IEEE Trans. Commun. **57**, 3024–3033 (2009)
7. Proakis, J.: Digital Communications, 4th edn. McGraw-Hill, New York (2000)
8. Tse, D.N.C., Viswanath, P.: Fundamentals of Wireless Communications. Cambridge Univ. Press, Cambridge (2005)
9. David, H.A., Nagaraja, H.N.: Order Statistics, 3rd edn. Wiley, New York (2003)
10. Gradshteyn, I.S., Ryzhik, I.M.: Table of Integrals, Series, and Products, 6th edn. Academic Press, New York (2000)

Energy-Balanced Backpressure Routing for Stochastic Energy Harvesting WSNs

Zheng Liu[1], Xinyu Yang[1], Peng Zhao[1(✉)], and Wei Yu[2]

[1] Department of Computer Science and Technology,
Xi'an Jiaotong University, Xi'an 710049, People's Republic of China
sssliu@stu.xjtu.edu.cn, {yxyphd,p.zhao}@mail.xjtu.edu.cn
[2] Department of Computer and Information Sciences,
Towson University, Towson, MD 21252, USA
wyu@towson.edu

Abstract. In Energy Harvesting Wireless Sensor Networks (EHWSNs), energy imbalance among sensor nodes is detrimental to network performance and battery life. Particularly, nodes that are closer to a data sink or have less energy replenishment tend to exhaust their energy earlier, leading to some sub-regions of the environment being left unmonitored. Existing research efforts focus on energy management based on the assumption that the energy harvesting process is predictable. Unfortunately, such an assumption is not practicable in real-world energy harvesting systems. With the consideration of the unpredictability of the harvestable energy, in this paper we adopt the stochastic Lyapunov optimization framework to jointly manage energy and make routing decision, which could help mitigate the energy imbalance problem. We develop an online policies, Energy-balanced Backpressure Routing Algorithm (EBRA) for lossless networks. EBRA is distributed, queuing stable and do not require explicit knowledge of the statistics of the energy harvesting. The simulation data shows that EBRA could achieve significantly higher performance in terms of energy balance than the existing scheme Original Backpressure Algorithm (OBRA).

1 Introduction

Harvesting energy from environment provides a promising solution to address the issues arising from energy scarcity in Wireless Sensor Networks (WSNs). There have been a number of energy harvesting technologies, including solar energy harvester [12], wind turbine [13], piezoelectric transducers [21], thermoelectric generators [4], mechanical vibration energy [3] and so on. These energy harvesting technologies are particularly useful for autonomous sensor networks (e.g., WSNs) that perform monitoring tasks in dangerous areas, or wireless devices that works at locations that are hard to reach, etc.

Although energy harvesting technologies provide numerous extra energy for nodes, they also pose challenges in balancing energy among nodes. Not only nodes closer to a data sink but also nodes having less energy replenishment

K. Xu and J. Zhu (Eds.): WASA 2015, LNCS 9204, pp. 767–777, 2015.
DOI: 10.1007/978-3-319-21837-3_75

tend to run out their energy at an earlier stage. Although those nodes can be available again after harvesting enough energy from the environment, traffic congestion caused by energy exhaustion will occur, making some subregions of the environment being left unmonitored.

Existing research such as [7,10,14,16,23] mainly focused on developing energy management algorithms for EHWSNs with predictable energy. Nonetheless, a number of energy harvesting processes cannot be accurately predicted in real-world energy harvesting systems (e.g., stochastic harvesting process and partially-predictable energy profile [10]). In addition, the overhead of executing an energy prediction algorithm should be taken into account in resource-limited WSNs. Although some existing works such as [8,11,15] have already proposed energy management schemes for ENWSNs with stochastic energy harvesting, the network utility or throughput maximization were focused.

In this paper, with the consideration of the energy profile as a stochastic process, we jointly design the energy management and routing process to mitigate the energy imbalance problem [1,5,6] (also called hot-spots problem in [1,5]). We tackle this problem by using the Lyapunov optimization approach developed in [19,20]. The main idea of this technique is to integrate a penalty and utility information into queue backlog gradients that decrease towards the sink. Using information about queue backlogs, residual energy and link states, nodes can make packet routing, power allocation and forwarding decisions independently. Based on this idea, we first develop an online algorithm, called the Energy-balanced Backpressure Routing Algorithm (EBRA) for lossless networks. In EBRA, greedy decisions are made in every time slot based on the queue backlog and residual energy information of one-hop neighbors. Our experimental data demonstrates that EBRA can significantly improve performance in energy balance while guaranteeing network stability. The major contributions of our work are summarized as follows:

- We model a queue based network system and define reasonable penalty functions for links. We show how to incorporate the penalty minimization into the backpressure framework and overcome the energy imbalance problem.
- We propose the EBRA for a lossless network. EBRA is a low-cost distributed routing algorithm based on the Lyapunov optimization framework. This algorithm tries to balance energy among nodes meanwhile stabilizing the network.
- Through simulations, we show that EBRA indeed significantly improve performance in energy balance while guaranteeing network stability.

The rest of this paper is organized as follows. In Sect. 2, we present the network model and the problem formulation. In Sect. 3, we present EBRA, respectively. In Section 4, we show the performance evaluation and results. Finally, we conclude the paper in Sect. 5.

2   Network Model and Problem Formalization

A wireless multi-hop sensor network for data collection can be formalized as a directed graph $(\mathcal{N}, \mathcal{L})$, where $\mathcal{N} = \{1, 2, \cdots, N\}$ is the set of vertices that represent sensor nodes, and $\mathcal{L} = \{(n, m), n, m \in \mathcal{N}\}$ is the set of edges that represent communication links. Denote $\mathcal{N}_n$ as the set of one-hop neighboring nodes of n and node n itself. Denote $\mathcal{N}_n^{out}$ as the set of nodes m with $(n, m) \in \mathcal{L}$ and $\mathcal{N}_n^{in}$ be the set of nodes m with $(m, n) \in \mathcal{L}$. Notice that the network model in this paper is different from the one in [9, 18]. We assume that there is only one commodity in the network, which is the data collection commodity for the sink.

2.1   Traffic and Transmission Models

In this paper, we consider that time is divided into identical discrete time slots. In each slot, the network decides the number of packets to admit, which is denoted as $\lambda_n(t)$. We also assume that $0 \le \lambda_n(t) \le \lambda_{max}$ for all nodes $n \in \mathcal{N}$ with some finite value λ_{max} at all time. Denote $\mathbf{S}(t)$ as the network channel state vector, and denote $s_{n,m}(t)$ as the link (channel) state between node n and m at slot t. We assume that $\mathbf{S}(t)$ is Independent and Identically Distributed (i.i.d.) and is in some finite set $\mathcal{S}$. The number of packets sent from node n to m at slot t is denoted as $\mu_{n,m}(t)$, and the power allocated to transmit and receive those pockets are $p_{n,m}(t) = p_{n,m}(s_{n,m}(t), \mu_{n,m}(t))$ and $p_{n,m}^r(t) = p_{n,m}^r(s_{n,m}(t), \mu_{n,m}(t))$, respectively. We also assume that $\mu_{n,m}(t)$, $p_{n,m}(t)$, and $p_{n,m}^r(t)$ satisfy constraints, including $0 \le \mu_{n,m}(t) \le \mu_{max}$, $0 \le p_{n,m}(t) \le p_{max}$ and $0 \le p_{n,m}^r(t) \le p_{max}^r$ for some finite values μ_{max}, p_{max} and p_{max}^r. In addition, p and p^r have the following properties:

For any link $(n, m), (n, m') \in \mathcal{L}$, if the link state $s_{n,m}$ is better than $s_{n,m'}$, we have $p_{n,m}(s_{n,m}, \mu_{n,m}) \le p_{n,m'}(s_{n,m'}, \mu_{n,m'})$ and $p_{n,m}^r(s_{n,m}, \mu_{n,m}) \le p_{n,m'}^r(s_{n,m'}, \mu_{n,m})$. In addition, $p_{n,m}(s_{n,m}, \mu_{n,m})$ and $p_{n,m}^r(s_{n,m}, \mu_{n,m})$ are non-decreasing functions of $\mu_{n,m}$.

2.2   Energy Model

In this paper, we assume that each node in the network has a finite energy buffer. The residual energy of node n at slot t is denoted as $E_n(t)$ and $E_n(t)$ is in $[0, E_{max}]$ for all $n \in \mathcal{N}$ and $t \in \mathbb{N}_+$, where E_{max} represents the max energy buffer size. We use $\mathbf{E}(t) = (E_1(t), E_2(t), \cdots, E_n(t))$ to denote the residual energy vector of the network. Denote $h_n(t)$ as the energy harvested in slot t by node n and denote $\mathbf{H}(t) = (h_1(t), h_2(t), \cdots, h_n(t))$ as the energy harvesting vector. In addition, $h_n(t)$ is in $[0, h_{max}]$, where h_{max} is a finite value. For the sake of simplicity, we assume that energy is only consumed during data transmissions. Therefore, in every slot t, we have:

$$\sum_{m \in \mathcal{N}_n^{out}} p_{n,m}(t) + \sum_{m \in \mathcal{N}_n^{in}} p_{m,n}^r(t) \le E_n(t) + h_n(t).$$

The inequality above means that the energy consumed by node n must be no more than the available energy of n. Considering that $h_n(t)$ varies over time, it is hard to know the available energy exactly. To make sure that node n will not run out of its energy at slot t, we consider the available energy constraint as follows:

$$\sum_{m \in \mathcal{N}_n^{out}} p_{n,m}(t) + \sum_{m \in \mathcal{N}_n^{in}} p_{m,n}^r(t) \leq E_n(t). \tag{1}$$

In addition, the residual energy of node n at slot $t+1$ can be represented by:

$$
E_n(t+1) = min[E_n(t) - \sum_{m \in \mathcal{N}_n^{out}} p_{n,m}(t) -
$$
$$
\sum_{m \in \mathcal{N}_n^{in}} p_{m,n}^r(t)] + h_n(t), E_{max}]. \tag{2}
$$

2.3 Date Queue Model

Denote $Q_n(t)$ as the data queue length of node n at slot t and denote $\mathbf{Q}(t) = (Q_1(t), Q_2(t), \cdot, Q_N(t))$ as the data queue vector of the network. Then, we have the data queue length of node n at slot $t+1$:

$$Q_n(t+1) \leq [Q_n(t) - \sum_{m \in \mathcal{N}_n^{out}} \mu_{n,m}(t)]^+ + \sum_{m \in \mathcal{N}_n^{in}} \mu_{m,n}(t) + \lambda_n(t), \tag{3}$$

where $[x]^+ = max[x, 0]$. Equation (3) is inequality rather than an equality because $\sum_{m \in \mathcal{N}_n^{in}} \mu_{m,n}(t)$ may be more than the number of actual endogenous arrivals to the node n at slot t[1]. We consider a network with a queue backlogs $\mathbf{Q}(t)$ is stable if the following constraint is satisfied:

$$\limsup_{t \to \infty} \frac{1}{t} \sum_{r=0}^{t-1} \sum_{n=1}^{N} \mathbb{E}[Q_n(r)] < \infty. \tag{4}$$

2.4 Problem Formulation

Our design goal is to design a joint energy management and routing decision scheme so that the energy imbalance problem can be addressed. The basic idea of our approach is based on the Lyapunov optimization approach developed in [19, 20].

Denote $\mathcal{A}$ as the set of all possible control actions (i.e., routing and energy management actions). For a control action $a(t) \in \mathcal{A}$, we define $g = g(a(t))$ as the penalty function of $a(t)$ and $\bar{g}$ as the long time average penalty of $a(t)$.

---

[1] When node m does not have enough data to forward, idle-fill may be used. The actual endogenous arrivals to node n are none idle packets received by node n.

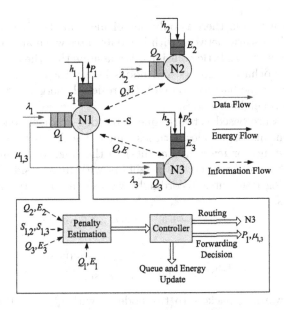

Fig. 1. Overview of EBRA.

Our objective is to find a control action $a(t)$ to minimize $\bar{g}$ while meeting the energy available constraint (1) and the queue stability constraint (4):

$$min : \bar{g}$$
$$s.t.(1),(2),(3),(4), \forall m, n \in \mathcal{N}. \tag{5}$$

3 Design of Energy Balance Routing Scheme

In this section, we first give an overview of our approach. We then present EBRA for the energy-imbalanced problem in lossless networks. EBRA uses energy information and queue length of one-hop neighboring nodes to make routing and forwarding decisions.

Figure 1 shows the detail of our approach. As we can see, when a node needs to send packets, it will first check its queue backlog length and residual energy and make penalty estimations for every link based on the information collected from the network (e.g., channel states, residual energy and queue backlog of neighbors). Notice that the channel states can be obtained through mechanisms such as Link Metric Estimation in BCP, and the energy and queue backlog information can be obtained by adding information in a packet head field for disseminating the information or by broadcasting beacons. Then, the controller will make the routing decision and the forwarding decision based on these penalty estimations. The queue backlog and energy information will also be updated after that.

In a lossless network, there is only one element in the channel state set $\mathcal{S}$. This can occur in a static network with low date rates when all links are in good qualities and network has little collisions. We assume that the energy harvesting process $\mathcal{H}$ is a stochastic process and nodes knows their own residual energy (e.g., by measuring the battery voltage), the residual energy, and queue backlog length of one-hop neighbor nodes.

In a backpressure based network, queue backlog gradients decrease towards the sink. This means that nodes with less queue backlog is closer (i.e., smaller geographical distance or fewer hop counts) to the sink. To balance the energy among nodes, it is better to choose neighbors with more residual energy[2] and less queue backlog gradients. Accordingly, we use the penalty function of link (n,m) as follows:

$$f_{n,m} = E_{max} - 1_{\Delta Q_{n,m}} \cdot E_m, \tag{6}$$

where

$$1_{\Delta Q_{n,m}} = \begin{cases} 1 & if \ \Delta Q_{n,m} > 0, \\ 0 & otherwise. \end{cases}$$

Notice that forwarding packets to the node m with $Q_{n,m} \leq 0$ may result in routing loops. Thus, the penalty function sets the penalty of link (n,m) to the maximum (i.e., E_{max}) when $Q_{n,m} \leq 0$. Otherwise, $f_{n,m}$ decreases when E_m increases.

To incorporate the penalty function minimization into the backpressure framework, we formalize the following optimization problem:

$$min : g = \sum_{n\in\mathcal{N}} \sum_{m\in\mathcal{N}_n^{out}} \mu_{n,m}(t) \cdot f_{n,m}(t)$$
$$s.t.(1),(2),(3),(4), \forall m, n \in \mathcal{N}. \tag{7}$$

Then, we define the Lyapunov function as follows:

$$L(t) \triangleq \frac{1}{2} \sum_{n\in\mathcal{N}} [Q_n(t)]^2. \tag{8}$$

Denote $\mathbf{Z}(t)$ as $\mathbf{Z}(t) = (\mathbf{Q}(t), \mathbf{E}(t))$, and define the one-slot conditional Lyapunov drift as follows:

$$\Delta(t) \triangleq \mathbb{E}\{L(t+1) - L(t)|\mathbf{Z}(t)\}. \tag{9}$$

Then, we have following lemma:

---

[2] Nodes with more residual energy are usually with better energy replenishment or lower traffic loads.

Lemma 1. *Under any routing and scheduling action and feasible power allocation that satisfies constraint* (1) *at slot* t, *we have:*

$$\Delta(t) + V \cdot \mathbb{E}\{\sum_{n \in \mathcal{N}} \sum_{m \in \mathcal{N}_n^{out}} \mu_{n,m}(t) \cdot f_{n,m}(t) | \mathbf{Z}(t)\}$$

$$\leq B - \mathbb{E}\{\sum_{n \in \mathcal{N}} \sum_{m \in \mathcal{N}_n^{out}} \mu_{n,m}(t) \cdot [\Delta Q_{n,m}(t) \qquad (10)$$

$$+ V \cdot (1_{\Delta Q_{n,m}(t)} \cdot E_m(t) - E_{max})] | \mathbf{Z}(t)\},$$

where $B = N^2 \cdot (\mu_{max}^2 + \frac{1}{2}\lambda_{max}^2 + \frac{1}{2}\lambda_{max}^2 \cdot \mu_{max})$ and V is a constant that trades system queue occupancy for penalty minimization.

Proof. The proof is similar to [2,9], and we omit it here for brevity.

Define the weight per outgoing link as follows:

$$W_{n,m}(t) = \Delta Q_{n,m}(t) + V \cdot (1_{\Delta Q_{n,m}(t)} \cdot E_m(t) - E_{max}). \qquad (11)$$

Then, we present the EBRA. The algorithm is to minimize the right-hand side (RHS) of (10) subject to constraint (1)[3].

Energy-balanced Backpressure Routing Algorithm (EBRA): At the beginning of every slot t, every node n observe $Q_m(t)$ and $E_m(t)$ of all nodes $m \in \mathcal{N}_n^{out}$, and do:

- **Routing Decision:** It computes weights for every neighbor m using Eq. (11) and finds the link (n, m^*) with the highest weight as the outgoing link.
- **Forwarding Decision:** If $W_{n,m^*}(t) > 0$, it forwards as many packets as the link (n, m^*) can admit; otherwise, the packets are held until the metric is recomputed.
- **Queue and Energy Update:** It updates $Q_n(t+1)$ according to Eq. (3) and computes $E_n(t+1)$ (e.g., by using Analog-to-Digital Converters of the node).

The routing decision maximizes $\Delta Q_{n,m}(t) + V \cdot (1_{\Delta Q_{n,m}(t)} \cdot E_m(t) - E_{max})$ in the RHS of (10), and the forwarding decision will find a suitable $\mu_{n,m^*}(t)$ to minimize the RHS of (10). If $W_{n,m^*}(t) > 0$, the maximum value of $\mu_{n,m^*}(t)$ will be computed under the constraint (3) and $\mu_{n,m^*}(t) \leq \mu_{max}$. Otherwise, $\mu_{n,m^*}(t) = 0$. Notice that data transmissions only occur when $\Delta Q_{n,m}(t) > 0$, node n simply only needs to compute weights for those neighbors who have less queue backlog than node n. If the length of a slot time is carefully selected and

---

[3] To minimize the time average penalty while stabilizing the network, algorithms based on the Lyapunov optimization framework can be designed to greedily minimize a bound (i.e., RHS of (10)) on the drift-plus-penalty expression (i.e., LHS of (10)) on each slot t.

only one packet can be transmitted per slot (e.g., as in BCP [17]), the forwarding decision could also be simplified further. Every forwarding node n only needs to check whether there is enough energy for it and the receiver m^* to send and receive a packet instead of calculating the maximal value of $\mu_{n,m^*}(t)$.

4   Performance Evaluation

In this section, we provide simulation results of our algorithms. We consider a data collection wireless network with 4×4 nodes showed in Fig. 2. All the links in the network is bidirectional. Node 1 is the sink node while the others sense data and forward it to the sink. The energy buffer size of node 1 is set to $+\infty$ while the others is set to 2000 units. Each unit of energy can be used to send a packet and a retransmission also cost one unit of energy. For the sake of simplicity, we assume that the reception power p^r is negligible. The initial energy of the sink is also set to $+\infty$ and the others are set to 1000 units. We also assume that nodes can forward at most one packet per time slot.

We assume that for every node n, the energy harvested at slot t (i.e., $h_n(t)$) is i.i.d and equally distributed in $[0, 2\overline{h}_n]$, where $\overline{h}_n$ is initialized to a random value in $[0, 1]$. The data collection rate $r(t)$ (i.e., the packets generated at slot t) is a random value and equally distributed in $[0, 2r]$.

We run our EBRA and the Original Backpressure Routing Algorithm (OBRA) [22] for 2×10^5 slots respectively under different date rates. The results are showed in Figs. 3, 4 and Table 1. Figure 3 shows the average queue length under different data collection rates with the step size 0.005. We can observe that the average queue length[4] of both EBRA and OBRA is slightly larger than 0 when $r \leq 0.075$. This is because the network must maintain queue sizes to provide a gradient for data flow. Meanwhile, there is no traffic congestion caused by running out of energy in all nodes. Due to the lack of energy in some nodes, the average queue length begins to increase as the data sensing rate r increasing when $r > 0.08$. Figure 3 shows that the average queue length of EBRA is smaller than that of OBRA with the same r[5]. Figure 4 shows the simulation results of the lowest node energy, i.e., $E_n(t) = \min_{i \in \mathcal{N}} E_i(t)$ with $t = 2 \times 10^5$. We can observe that some node is running out energy in OBRA with $r \geq 0.065$ while with $r \geq 0.095$ in EBRA. This means that EBRA allows a higher data rate than OBRA while experiencing no energy exhaustion. Table 1 shows the number of failed nodes in OBRA and EBRA. From Table 1, we can observe that node failure only occurs when $r \geq 0.095$ in EBRA while three nodes fail when $r = 0.07$ in OBRA. This is mainly because EBRA always tries to avoid forwarding packets to nodes with

---

[4] We denote the average queue length $\overline{Q} = \frac{1}{N} \sum_{n=1}^{N} Q_n(t)$ with $t = 2 \times 10^5$. If the queue is stable, the time average queue length is approximately equal to $N \cdot \overline{Q}$. Otherwise, the time average queue length is approximately proportional to $\overline{Q}$ according the setting of our experiments. We evaluate $\overline{Q}$ instead of time average queue length here.

[5] According to [11,17], a smaller average queue size is related to a better performance of packet delay.

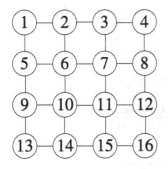

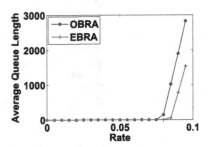

Fig. 2. A 4x4 data collection network

Fig. 3. The average queue size of OBRA and EBRA

Table 1. The Number of failed nodes in lossless networks

Scheme	The Number of Failed Nodes			
	$r \leq 0.06$	r=0.065	$0.07 \leq r \leq 0.09$	r=0.095
OBRA	0	1	3	3
EBRA	0	0	0	3

less residual energy and EBRA also can reduce unnecessary energy consumption caused by a routing loop.

Figure 5 shows the relationship between the variable V and the average queue length. Considering that the trend of different rates is almost the same, we only plot curves for $r = 0.07$, $r = 0.08$ and $r = 0.09$. We can see that the average queue length increases as V becomes larger. Figure 6 shows the relationship between the lowest node energy and V. We only plot curves for $r = 0.085, 0.09$ and 0.095 as all the energy buffers is almost full when $r \leq 0.08$. The lowest node energy increases as V becomes larger. The results showed in Figs. 5 and 6 show V can be seen as a parameter trading system queue occupancy for the penalty minimization.

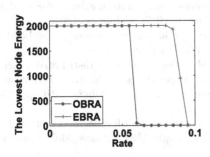

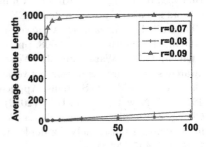

Fig. 4. The lowest node energy of OBRA and EBRA

Fig. 5. Average queue length versus V

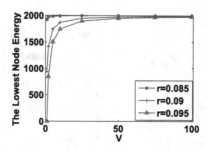

Fig. 6. The lowest node energy vs V

5   Conclusion

In this paper, we addressed the energy imbalance among sensor nodes in EHWSNs and presented the Energy-aware Backpressure Routing Algorithm (EBRA) for energy balance in EH-WSNs. EBRA is a distributed online algorithm and does not need to know the harvestable energy process. We show that EBRA achieves a better performance in both the time average network congestion and energy balance than that of the Original Backpressure Routing Algorithm (OBRA), while guaranteeing the network stability.

Acknowledgment. This work was supported in part by the following funds: Fundamental Research Funds for the Central Universities (xjj2015065) and China Post doctoral Science Foundation (2015M570836).

References

1. Abdulla, A.E.A.A., Hiroki, N., Nei, K.: Extending the lifetime of wireless sensor networks: a hybrid routing algorithm. Comput. Commun. **35**(9), 1056–1063 (2012)
2. Alresaini, M., Sathiamoorthy, M., Krishnamachari, B., Neely, M.: Backpressure with adaptive redundancy (bwar). In: 2012 IEEE Proceedings INFOCOM, pp. 2300–2308 (2012)
3. Bhuiyan, R., Dougal, R., Ali, M.: A miniature energy harvesting device for wireless sensors in electric power system. IEEE Sens. J. **10**(7), 1249–1258 (2010)
4. Chalasani, S., Conrad, J.: A survey of energy harvesting sources for embedded systems. In: Southeastcon, 2008, pp. 442–447. IEEE, April 2008
5. Challen, G.W., Waterman, J., Welsh, M.: Idea: integrated distributed energy awareness for wireless sensor networks. In: Proceedings of the 8th International Conference on Mobile Systems, Applications, and Services, MobiSys 2010, pp. 35–48. ACM, New York, NY, USA (2010)
6. Cheng, Z., Perillo, M., Heinzelman, W.: General network lifetime and cost models for evaluating sensor network deployment strategies. IEEE Trans. Mob. Comput. **7**(4), 484–497 (2008)
7. Chetto, M.: Optimal scheduling for real-time jobs in energy harvesting computing systems. IEEE Trans. Emerg. Top. Comput. **2**(2), 122–133 (2014)

8. Gatzianas, M., Georgiadis, L., Tassiulas, L.: Control of wireless networks with rechargeable batteries [transactions papers]. IEEE Trans. Wirel. Commun. **9**(2), 581–593 (2010)
9. Georgiadis, L., Neely, M.J., Tassiulas, L.: Resource allocation andcross-layer control in wireless networks. Found. Trends Networking **1**(1), 1–144 (2006)
10. Gorlatova, M., Wallwater, A., Zussman, G.: Networking low-power energy harvesting devices: measurements and algorithms. IEEE Trans. Mob. Comput. **12**(9), 1853–1865 (2013)
11. Huang, L., Neely, M.: Utility optimal scheduling in energy-harvesting networks. IEEE/ACM Trans. Networking **21**(4), 1117–1130 (2013)
12. Kansal, A., Hsu, J., Zahedi, S., Srivastava, M.B.: Power management in energy harvesting sensor networks. ACM Trans. Embed. Comput. Syst. **6**(4), (2007)
13. Krishnan, S., Ezhilarasi, D., Uma, G., Umapathy, M.: Pyroelectric-based solar and wind energy harvesting system. IEEE Trans. Sustain. Energ. **5**(1), 73–81 (2014)
14. Longbi, L., Shroff, N.B., Srikant, R.: Energy-aware routing in sensor networks: a large system approach. Ad Hoc Netw. **5**(6), 818–831 (2007)
15. Mao, Z., Koksal, C., Shroff, N.: Near optimal power and rate control of multi-hop sensor networks with energy replenishment: Basic limitations with finite energy and data storage. IEEE Trans. Autom. Control **57**(4), 815–829 (2012)
16. Martinez, G., Li, S., Zhou, C.: Wastage-aware routing in energy-harvesting wireless sensor networks. IEEE Sens. J. **14**(9), 2967–2974 (2014)
17. Moeller, S., Sridharan, A., Krishnamachari, B., Gnawali, O.: Routing without routes: the backpressure collection protocol. In: Proceedings of the 9th ACM/IEEE International Conference on Information Processing in Sensor Networks, IPSN 2010, pp. 279–290. ACM, New York, NY, USA (2010)
18. Neely, M.: Energy optimal control for time-varying wireless networks. IEEE Trans. Inf. Theory **52**(7), 2915–2934 (2006)
19. Neely, M.J.: Stochastic network optimization with application to communication and queueing systems. Synth. Lect. Commun. Netw. **3**(1), 1–211 (2010)
20. Li, C.P., Neely, M.: Network utility maximization over partially observable markovian channels. In: 2011 International Symposium on Modeling and Optimization in Mobile, Ad Hoc and Wireless Networks (WiOpt), pp. 17–24, May 2011
21. Romani, A., Filippi, M., Tartagni, M.: Micropower design of a fully autonomous energy harvesting circuit for arrays of piezoelectric transducers. IEEE Trans. Power Electron. **29**(2), 729–739 (2014)
22. Tassiulas, L., Ephremides, A.: Stability properties of constrained queueing systems and scheduling policies for maximum throughput in multihop radio networks. IEEE Trans. Autom. Control **37**(12), 1936–1948 (1992)
23. Yang, S., Mccann, J.A.: Distributed optimal lexicographic max-min rate allocation in solar-powered wireless sensor networks. ACM Trans. Sen. Netw. **11**(1), 9:1–9:35 (2014)

Motion Recognition by Using a Stacked Autoencoder-Based Deep Learning Algorithm with Smart Phones

Xi Zhou, Junqi Guo$^{(\boxtimes)}$, and Shenling Wang

College of Information Science and Technology,
Beijing Normal University, Beijing, China
zhouxi@mail.bnu.edu.cn,
{guojunqi,slwang}@bnu.edu.cn

Abstract. Due to the increasing machine learning applications in mobile health and security monitoring scenarios, human motion recognition by sensor devices has received remarkable attention from both academic and engineering fields. In this paper, we propose a motion recognition scheme by using a stacked autoencoder based deep learning algorithm with smart phones. Since common sensors such as gravity sensors, accelerometers, gyroscopes, linear accelerometers and magnetometers have been already equipped in Android or iOS based smart phones, the sensor data can be easily recorded by the smart phone that an experimenter carries around. A stacked autoencoder based deep learning algorithm is employed here for data classification so as to precisely recognize several basic motions that are standing, walking, sitting, running, going upstairs and going downstairs, respectively. Experimental results indicate that the stacked autoencoder based deep learning algorithm achieves higher accuracy for human motion recognition than traditional neural network methods.

Keywords: Motion recognition · Stacked autoencoder · Deep learning · Smart phones

1 Introduction

Human motion recognition is a growing problem both in China and around the world. The understanding of human activity is vital to support various kinds of related applications such as mobile health (m-health), patient rehabilitation monitoring, fitness guide, prison management and enterprise security [2]. Although human motions contain a great number of categories, we are more concerned with only several basic ones such as walking, sitting, running, going upstairs in a clinical monitoring scenario for example. Different motions have different characteristics which provide researchers new possibilities for recognizing and distinguishing them. One of the researches decides the body motion states by using sensors on limbs and achieves an adaptive reconstruction of human

© Springer International Publishing Switzerland 2015
K. Xu and J. Zhu (Eds.): WASA 2015, LNCS 9204, pp. 778–787, 2015.
DOI: 10.1007/978-3-319-21837-3_76

motion according to different body characteristics [3]. Another research investigates the applicability of Gaussian processes classification for recognition of articulated and deformable human motions from image sequences [19].

In order to acquire real-time human motion data, great attention has recently been paid to sensor based techniques [5,6,8,12–15]. One kind of representative works [12] implements a wearable sensor system for human motion analysis. Authors in [15] propose a method for arm flexion/extension angles measurement by using a wireless ultrasonic sensor network. The studies in [8] and [13] use wearable 3D acceleration sensors and several other sensors to estimate human walking motion and joint angle respectively. In [14], Takezono etc. use omni-directional vision sensors for tracking human movements. However, all the methods above deploy multiple sensors on human body, which leads to inconvenience for the person under guardianship. With the development of smart phones, many current researches apply sensors in smart phones to collect and analyze human motion data. Since common sensors such as gravity sensors, accelerometers, gyroscopes and so on have been already equipped in Android or iOS based smart phones, the sensor data can be easily recorded by only one smart phone that an experimenter carries around. For example, there is a research on motion recognition with smart phone which has been embedded a 3-axis accelerometer sensor [5]. Besides, the recognition system proposed in [6] uses a smart phone to record users' motion.

Currently, deep learning is an extremely hot research topic in machine learning and pattern recognition field. It has gained theoretical successes in the field of speech recognition, natural language processing and computer vision [4]. Meanwhile, deep learning has been already used in a broad area of practical applications. For example, [17] studies the effectiveness of accomplishing high-level tasks for medical images and achieves good performance. In [10], the authors apply deep learning in decision-making and assessment of healthcare delivery and obtain good results. Besides, there are also many researches on human motion recognition based on deep learning algorithms. One of the researches employs a deep sparse autoencoder to extract low-dimensional features, and enables higher recognition accuracy [11]. A research presents a sparse representation based human activity modeling and recognition approach by using wearable motion sensors, and the experiment achieves a better recognition performance compared to conventional motion primitive-based approach [18]. Another research develops a novel 3D convolution neural network model for action recognition according to airport surveillance videos in a real-world environment, and this work achieves superior performance in comparison to baseline methods [9].

In this paper, we employ a stacked autoencoder (SAE)–based deep learning algorithm to recognize several basic human motions under the circumstance that an experimenter carries only one smart phone on his body for convenience in a real-world environment. First, we develop by ourselves an application on an Android platform to collect and read real-time data from the sensors such as accelerometers, magnetometers and gyroscopes that have been equipped in the smart phone. Then we employ the SAE to classify human motion dataset into six types that are respectively standing, sitting, walking, running, going upstairs and going downstairs, so that different motions can be recognized with a good accuracy. Simulation results demonstrate that the proposed scheme achieves good performance with an accuracy about 93.8 % and outperforms the traditional neural network (NN) algorithm, which obtains an accuracy about 82.37 %.

The rest of this paper is organized as follows. Section 2 describes the principle of the stacked autoencoder-based deep learning, as well as the proposed human motion recognition scheme by using the sensors embedded in a smart phone. In Sect. 3, experiment setting and simulation performance comparison are given for the purpose of verifying efficiency and accuracy of the proposed scheme. Finally, some conclusions are drawn in Sect. 4.

2   Methodology

2.1   Data Collecting and Preprocessing

In our research, we apply sensors that are embedded in smart phones which consist of accelerometers, linear accelerometers, magnetometers, gravity sensors and gyroscopes. Considering the convenience of data acquisition, we develop by ourselves an APP on Android platform to collect and read raw sensor data with the sampling frequency 25 Hz. We collect data according to different positions of a smart phone where it is placed. We consider two locations (in coat pocket and in trouser pocket). Each location has four orientations of the smart phone (horizontal inward, horizontal outward, vertical inward, and vertical outward). For every pair of location and orientation, we collect data for several minutes in a real-world environment. The Fig. 1 shows the four orientations of the smart phone placed in the pocket. Also, the APP interface is shown in Fig. 2.

For each sensor, we get data of X,Y,Z-axis, respectively, which are then sent to a server database periodically by cellular networks. Figures 3, 4, 5, 6, 7, 8 show the first 50 points of 3-axis data of different sensors when the human motion is chosen as going upstairs. Figures 3, 4, 5, 6, 7 exhibit the data collected by accelerometer, gyroscope, magnetometer, linear accelerometer and gravity sensor, respectively, while Fig. 8 shows the orientation data computed by an Android API [1].

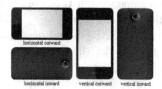

Fig. 1. Four orientations of a smart phone

Fig. 2. APP interface

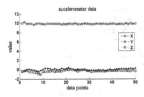

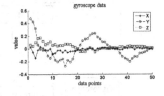

Fig. 3. Accelerometer data   **Fig. 4.** Gyroscope data

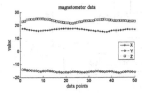

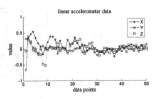

Fig. 5. Magnetometer data   **Fig. 6.** Linear accelerometer data

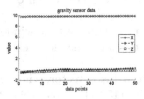

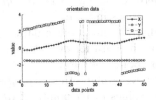

Fig. 7. Gravity sensor data   **Fig. 8.** Orientation data

After getting the sensor data, we implement data preprocessing, the procedure of which is as shown in Fig. 9.

First of all, , we introduce a rotation matrix R by using an Android API [1] to transform a mobile coordinate system to an earth coordinate system. For each data collection, we get 6 groups of data as shown in Figs. 3, 4, 5, 6, 7, 8, and each group contains 3-axis data. Therefore, every collection has 18 coordinate values. In order to get more precision acceleration data Lg, we let accelerometer data marked as acc minus gravity data marked as $gravity$, that is

$$Lg = acc - gravity \tag{1}$$

We need to transform gyroscope data marked as $gyro$ and acceleration data marked as Lg from a mobile coordinate system to an earth coordinate system by using the rotation matrix R.

$$Lg\_earth = Lg \cdot R \tag{2}$$

$$gyro\_earth = gyro \cdot R \tag{3}$$

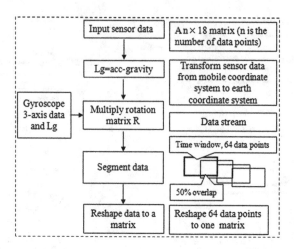

Fig. 9. Data preprocessing procedure

We select accelerometer data, magnetometer data, orientation data, linear accelerometer data, Lg_earth and $gyro\_earth$ as useful data which contains 18 coordinate values in total.

Secondly, we implement a data segmentation by sliding a time window, that is, segment the data for every 2.56 s with 50 % overlap. Therefore, each section contains 64 points of data.

Thirdly, we reshape the 64 points of data to a $1 \times n$ vector, where n is the number of values of 64 points of data, which is 1152 ($18 \times 64 = 1152$). This vector is considered as a sample which is regarded as the input vector of a stacked autoencoder.

2.2   Deep Learning Algorithm—Stacked Autoencoders

One of the deep learning algorithms, stacked autoencoders, has been widely used in many fields. An autoencoder is a three-layer network including an encoder and a decoder [16]. which is shown in Fig. 10. We can obtain a stacked autoencoder

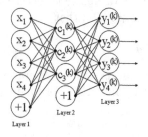

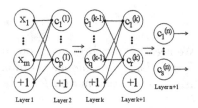

Fig. 10. A model of an autoencoder

Fig. 11. A model of stacked autoencoders

network by stacking several autoencoders for high feature learning, which aims to learn a compressed representation of data with a minimum reconstruction loss. Figure 11 exhibits a model of stacked autoencoders.

The autoencoder is a three-layer network, the Layer 1 is the input layer, its units are input vector $\mathbf{x}$. The Layer 2 is a coding layer or an encoder which is a hidden layer and equal to a feature extractor and the output of the layer is the code of input vector $\mathbf{x}$. The Layer 3 is the decoding layer or the output layer. The encoder maps the input vector $\mathbf{x}$ to the coding layer with an active function.

$$\mathbf{C}^k = f(\mathbf{W}^{(k,1)}\mathbf{x} + \mathbf{b}^{(k,1)}) \tag{4}$$

where $f(.)$ is an active function which we chose the sigmoid function here. $\mathbf{W}$ and $\mathbf{b}$ are parameters, and $\mathbf{W}$ is the weight, $\mathbf{b}$ is the bias, where k means the k-th autoencoder. $\mathbf{W}^{(k,1)}$ is the weight between Layer 1 and Layer 2, $\mathbf{b}^{(k,1)}$ is the bias of Layer 1, $\mathbf{C}^k$ is the output of coding layer, which is indeed a code of $\mathbf{x}$. The decoder maps the coding layer to the output layer which has the same number of units with input layer.

$$\mathbf{y}^k = f(\mathbf{W}^{(k,2)}\mathbf{C}^k + \mathbf{b}^{(k,2)}) \tag{5}$$

where $\mathbf{W}^{(k,2)}$ is the weight between Layer 2 and Layer 3, $\mathbf{b}^{(k,2)}$ is the bias of Layer 2. We define parameter set $\theta = \{\mathbf{W}^{(k,1)}, \mathbf{b}^{(k,1)}, \mathbf{W}^{(k,2)}, \mathbf{b}^{(k,2)}\}$ and $\mathbf{y}$ is the output of the decoding layer, which is used to decode the code $\mathbf{C}^k$ obtained from coding layer. The $\mathbf{y}$ is indeed a reconstruction of $\mathbf{x}$. In order to reconstruct the input from the output layer, the training is performed by minimizing the reconstruction error, that is to say, optimizing the parameter set. In the standard autoencoder model, the reconstruction error is defined as the Minimize Square Error (MSE) between the input vector $\mathbf{x}$ and the output vector $\mathbf{y}$. So, the reconstruction loss function can be defined as follow:

$$L(\mathbf{y}, \mathbf{x}) = \|\mathbf{y} - \mathbf{x}\|^2 \tag{6}$$

In this case, the autoencoder model is similar to the Principle Component Analysis (PCA). However, when the active function $f(.)$ is non-linear, we can use negative logarithmic likelihood function to replace the MSE criteria.

$$J(\theta) = -log\, p(\mathbf{x}|\mathbf{C}) \tag{7}$$

The training aims to minimize the reconstruction loss, and we can achieve the purpose by minimizing the function $J(.)$ or maximizing the probability $p(\mathbf{x}|\mathbf{C})$.

The stacked autoencoder network stacked by several autoencoders lets the first autoencoder's output of the coding layer as the input vector of the next autoencoder. Assume that there is a stacked autoencoder network. The encoding steps for the stacked autoencoder are given by running the encoding step of each layer in forward order.

$$\mathbf{C}^k = f(\mathbf{z})^k \tag{8}$$

where $\mathbf{z}^k$ is defined as

$$\mathbf{z}^k = \mathbf{W}^{(k,1)}\mathbf{C}^{k-1} + \mathbf{b}^{(k,1)} \tag{9}$$

The decoding steps are given by running the decoding stack of each autoencoder in reverse order.

$$\mathbf{y}^l = f(\mathbf{z}^l) \tag{10}$$

where $\mathbf{z}^l$ is defined as

$$\mathbf{z}^l = \mathbf{W}^{(l,2)}\mathbf{C}^l + \mathbf{b}^{(l,2)} \tag{11}$$

The $\mathbf{C}^n$ which is the activation of the deepest layer of hidden units or the final result of encoding steps contains the information of interest. The vector gives us a representation of the input in terms of higher-order features.

A good way to obtain good parameters for a stacked autoencoder network is to use greedy layer-wise training [7]. To do this, first of all, we need train the first layer on raw input to obtain parameters set $\{\mathbf{W}^{(1,1)}, \mathbf{b}^{(1,1)}, \mathbf{W}^{(1,2)}, \mathbf{b}^{(1,2)}\}$. Then, use the first layer to transform the raw input into a vector $\mathbf{C}$, consisting of activation of the hidden units. Next, train the second layer on this vector $\mathbf{C}$ to obtain parameters set $\{\mathbf{W}^{(2,1)}, \mathbf{b}^{(2,1)}, \mathbf{W}^{(2,2)}, \mathbf{b}^{(2,2)}\}$. Repeat for subsequent layers, using the output of each layer as input for subsequent layer.

The method we presented trains parameters of each layer individually while fixes other parameters of the model. To achieve better results, we can apply fine-tuning using backpropagation to improve the results which changes parameters of all layers simultaneously. The training steps are summarized in Table 1.

Table 1. Training steps of the stacked autoencoders

	Training steps of stacked autoencoders
1.	Train the first layer as an autoencoder model, minimize the reconstruction loss, and obtain parameters;
2.	Put the hidden units of the autoencoder as the input of the next layer;
3.	Iterate and initialize parameters of each layer according to the step 2;
4.	Apply the output of the last hidden layer as input to a output layer, and initialize its parameters;
5.	Fine-tune parameters of all layers, and stack all autoencoders into a stacked autoencoder network.

3   Experiment

In this experiment, we use Android smart phones Samsung GALAXY Note3 equipped with common sensors providing a real-time sensor data acquisition. Raw sensor data contains all varieties of human motion data. The purpose of our experiment is to recognize each type of human motion data from all obtained sensor data. To evaluate feasibility and efficiency of the proposed scheme, we compare the stacked autoencoder based deep learning algorithm with a machine learning algorithm, Neural Network (NN).

3.1   Experimental Setting

A. Data Setting. In our experiment, we select trouser dataset, coat dataset and 9 different sizes of the total dataset respectively to train a stacked autoencoder network as a classifier and testify the performance of the classifier through independent test set. The training set and test set respectively account for 70 % and 30 % of total dataset. For every sample, there are 1152 values as well as a corresponding label that indicates its motion type. So our training set or test set can be presented as (x^i, y^i); $i = 1, 2, \cdots, n$, where n is the number of samples. $y^i = 1$ means corresponding motion type is active namely motion type of sample x^i is the type where its corresponding label value is $y^i = 1$.

B. Algorithms for Comparison. We compare the following learning algorithms in our experiment: Stacked Autoencoders (SAE), Neural Network (NN), in which SAE is a deep learning algorithms, while NN is a traditional machine learning algorithm performing well on various classification problems.

3.2   Experimental Results

We use the accuracy as an evaluation indicator to evaluate the performance of our experiment. Classification accuracy reflects the percentage of correctly predicted samples in the whole test set. We conduct the experiment on three training data sets of different position (coat data set, trouser data set and data set that contains both) and 9 different sizes of training data set. Comparing classification accuracy between 2 different algorithms, the results are presented in Table 2 and Fig. 12.

As is shown in Table 2, there is a clear difference between 2 groups of prediction accuracy values of 2 different algorithms. In the case that the size of training set is 3810, the SAE algorithm using coat data set to train SAE achieves an accuracy about 92.47 %. While the training/test data set are from trouser data set, the accuracy is approximately 93.8 %. We mix the coat and trouser data set, and obtain an accuracy nearly 91.58 %. When applying NN algorithm, the accuracy are 85.67 %, 80.25 %, 81.73 % corresponding to coat data set, trouser data set and mixed data set, respectively. We find that SAE algorithm achieves better performance than NN. This is due to the advantage of feature extraction by applying deep learning.

As is shown in Fig. 12, the prediction accuracy of every algorithm on test set gradually rises and becomes stable with a slight fluctuation. With the growth

Table 2. Comparison of classification accuracy

	SAE	NN
Coat data set	92.47 %	85.67 %
Trouser data set	93.8 %	80.25 %
Mixed data set	91.58 %	81.73 %

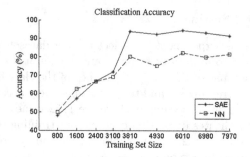

Fig. 12. Comparison of classification accuracy

of training set size, the accuracy of SAE reaches 93.8 % and is fluctuating near 92 % when the training set size is greater than 3810. However, the accuracy of NN achieves 82.37 % and varies near 80 % when the training set size is greater than 3810. It is obvious that SAE is more suitable for human motion recognition since it achieves better performance on classification accuracy compared with NN. This is due to the advantage of feature extraction by applying deep learning.

4   Conclusion

In this paper, we apply the deep learning algorithm–Stacked Autoencoders (SAE) for human motion recognition with the help of smart phones. The SAE algorithm is employed here to train a stacked autoencoder network so as to recognize six types of basic motions. The feasibility and effectiveness of the proposed scheme have been verified by theoretical analysis and experimental simulation in this paper. Simulation results show that the proposed scheme performs well in human motion recognition, compared with traditional neural network methods.

Acknowledgment. This research is sponsored by National Natural Science Foundation of China (No.61401029, 61171014, 61272475, 61472044, 61472403, 61371185, 11401016, 11401028) and the Fundamental Research Funds for the Central Universities (No.2012LYB46, 2014KJJCB32, 2013NT57) and by SRF for ROCS, SEM.

References

1. Android: public abstract class sensormanager extends object. http://developer. android.com/reference/android/hardware/SensorManager.html
2. Bai, L., Pepper, M., Yana, Y., Spurgeon, S., Sakel, M.: Application of low cost inertial sensors to human motion analysis. In: 2012 IEEE International Instrumentation and Measurement Technology Conference (I2MTC), pp. 1280–1285, May 2012
3. Chen, S.Y., Lee, W.T., Chao, H.C., Huang, Y.M., Lai, C.F.: Adaptive reconstruction of human motion on wireless body sensor networks. In: 2011 International Conference on Wireless Communications and Signal Processing (WCSP), pp. 1–5, November 2011

4. Chen, X.W., Lin, X.: Big data deep learning: challenges and perspectives. IEEE Access **2**, 514–525 (2014)
5. Cho, H., Kim, S., Baek, J., Fisher, P.: Motion recognition with smart phone embedded 3-axis accelerometer sensor. In: 2012 IEEE International Conference on Systems, Man, and Cybernetics (SMC), pp. 919–924, October 2012
6. Chu, H.C., Cheng, Y.C., Tsai, H.Y.: A study of motion recognition system using a smart phone. In: 2011 IEEE International Conference on Systems, Man, and Cybernetics (SMC), pp. 3409–3414, October 2011
7. Hinton, G., Osindero, S., Teh, Y.: A fast learning algorithm for deep belief nets. Neural Comput. **18**(7), 1527–1554 (2006)
8. Ito, T.: Walking motion analysis using 3d acceleration sensors. In: Second UKSIM European Symposium on Computer Modeling and Simulation, EMS 2008, pp. 123–128, September 2008
9. Ji, S., Xu, W., Yang, M., Yu, K.: 3D convolutional neural networks for human action recognition. IEEE Trans. Pattern Anal. Mach. Intell. **35**(1), 221–231 (2013)
10. Liang, Z., Zhang, G., Huang, J., Hu, Q.: Deep learning for healthcare decision making with emrs. In: 2014 IEEE International Conference on Bioinformatics and Biomedicine (BIBM), pp. 556–559, November 2014
11. Liu, H., Taniguchi, T.: Feature extraction and pattern recognition for human motion by a deep sparse autoencoder. In: 2014 IEEE International Conference on Computer and Information Technology (CIT), pp. 173–181, September 2014
12. Liu, T., Inoue, Y., Shibata, K.: A wearable sensor system for human motion analysis and humanoid robot control. In: IEEE International Conference on Robotics and Biomimetics ROBIO 2006, pp. 43–48, December 2006
13. Liu, T., Inoue, Y., Shibata, K.: Measurement of muscle motion for improving accuracy of body-mounted motion sensor. In: 2008 IEEE/ASME International Conference on Advanced Intelligent Mechatronics AIM 2008, pp. 1325–1330, July 2008
14. Nishimura, T., Sogo, T., Oka, R., Ishiguro, H.: Recognition of human motion behaviors using multiple omni-directional vision sensors. In: 2000 26th Annual Conference of the IEEE Industrial Electronics Society IECON 2000, vol. 4, pp. 2553–2558 (2000)
15. Qi, Y., Soh, C.B., Gunawan, E., Low, K.S.: A wearable wireless ultrasonic sensor network for human arm motion tracking. In: 2014 36th Annual International Conference of the IEEE Engineering in Medicine and Biology Society (EMBC), pp. 5960–5963, August 2014
16. Qi, Y., Wang, Y., Zheng, X., Wu, Z.: Robust feature learning by stacked autoencoder with maximum correntropy criterion. In: 2014 IEEE International Conference on Acoustics, Speech and Signal Processing (ICASSP), pp. 6716–6720, May 2014
17. Xu, Y., Mo, T., Feng, Q., Zhong, P., Lai, M., Chang, E.C.: Deep learning of feature representation with multiple instance learning for medical image analysis. In: 2014 IEEE International Conference on Acoustics, Speech and Signal Processing (ICASSP), pp. 1626–1630, May 2014
18. Zhang, M., Xu, W., Sawchuk, A., Sarrafzadeh, M.: Sparse representation for motion primitive-based human activity modeling and recognition using wearable sensors. In: 2012 21st International Conference on Pattern Recognition (ICPR), pp. 1807–1810, November 2012
19. Zhou, H., Wang, L., Suter, D.: Human motion recognition using gaussian processes classification. In: 2008 19th International Conference on Pattern Recognition ICPR 2008, pp. 1–4, December 2008

SDN-Based Routing for Efficient Message Propagation in VANET

Ming Zhu[1,2]([⊠]), Jiannong Cao[2], Deming Pang[1], Zongjian He[2], and Ming Xu[1]

[1] College of Computer, National University of Defense Technology,
Changsha 410073, Hu'nan, China
{zhuming,pangdeming,xuming}@nudt.edu.cn
[2] Department of Computing, The Hong Kong Polytechnic University,
Kowloon, Hong Kong
{csmzhu,csjcao,cszhe}@comp.polyu.edu.hk

Abstract. Vehicular Ad hoc Network (VANET) is an intermittently connected mobile network in which message propagation is quite challenging. Conventional routing protocols proposed for VANET are usually in greedy or optimum fashion. Geographical forwarding only uses local information to make the routing decision which may lead to long packet delay, while link-based forwarding has better performance but requires much more overheads. To disseminate message efficiently in VANET, a routing protocol which has both short delivery delay time and low routing overhead is required. In this paper, we proposed a SDN-based routing framework for efficiently message propagation in VANET. Software-Defined Networking (SDN) is an emerging technology that decouples the control plane from the data forwarding plane in switches and collects all the control planes into a central controller. In SDN-based routing framework, the central controller gathers network information from switches and computes optimal routing paths for switches based on the global network information. Since switches don't need to exchange routing information with each other, the routing overhead is much lower. This paper is the first to propose a SDN-based routing framework for efficiently message propagation in VANET. A new algorithm is developed to find the global optimal route from the source to the destination in VANET with dynamic network density. We demonstrate, through the simulation results, that our proposed framework significantly outperforms the related protocols in terms of both delivery delay time and routing overhead.

Keywords: Software-Defined Networking · Vehicular ad hoc networks · Routing · Delay tolerant networks

1 Introduction

Vehicular Ad hoc Network (VANET) is expected to support a large spectrum of applications including traffic information dissemination, p2p file sharing and

© Springer International Publishing Switzerland 2015
K. Xu and J. Zhu (Eds.): WASA 2015, LNCS 9204, pp. 788–797, 2015.
DOI: 10.1007/978-3-319-21837-3_77

gaming. These applications requires either short delivery delay time or high network throughput. However, VANET is an intermittently connected mobile network. Due to the high mobility of vehicles, network topology changes frequently and network partition often happens. In this context, routing messages with both short delivery delay time and low routing overhead is quite challenging [3].

Conventional routing protocols in VANET are usually topology-based routing or geographical-based routing [2]. Topology based routing protocols (e.g. AODV [10] and OLSR [1]) use links information that exists in the network to perform packet forwarding. However, links can breakdown so frequently in VAENT that it is very hard to find a multi-hop route to the destination. Besides, network topology changes so frequently that maintaining network topology can cause a huge routing overhead. Geographical-based forwarding (e.g. GPSR [5]) only uses local information to make the routing decision and local optimal routing decision may lead to long packet delay. Since they don't need to maintain network topology, the routing overhead is quite low. Due to the low routing overhead, geographical position based forwarding method is currently the most common scheme for source-destination routing in VANET. However, the heuristic method they used to choose next hops depends on local neighborhood information which can lead to local optimization and causes long end-to-end packet delay.

Recently, Software-Defined Networking (SDN) [8] has been introduced to wired computer networks. There are two main principles in SDN: one is to depart software from simple forwarding hardware in switches; the other one is to collect all the softwares together into a logical centralized controller. By doing this, SDN can simplify the architecture of network devices and enhance the feasibility of network devices's utilization [4,11]. Openflow is an open communications protocol that gives access to the forwarding plane of a network switch or router over the network [7]. There are some benefits of introducing SDN technology to VANET:

(1) In SDN-based VANET, the central controller can gather network information from vehicles and compute optimal packet routing paths for vehicles based on the global network information. Since vehicles don't need to exchange routing information with each other, the routing overhead is much lower.
(2) In SDN-based VANET, the central controller is made aware of the connections between vehicles.

The emerging SDN technology can be utilized to improve the efficiency of message propagation in VANET, where vehicles and a remote server on the Internet be traded as switches and the central controller. However, SDN is proposed for wired computer networks with the assumption that there is a secure channel between every switch and the controller. Fortunately, many vehicles today are equipped with both vehicle-to-vehicle communication devices (e.g. DSRC and Wifi) and vehicle-to-base-station network devices (e.g. 2G/3G and WiMax)[6]. And nowadays cellular networks can provide Internet access service to mobile devices in most urban places. Hence, we can assume that vehicles can access the central controller via cellular networks. Consequently, the SDN technology could be extended to VANET.

In this paper, we proposed a SDN-based routing framework for message propagation in VANET. The routing framework can route messages from source vehicle to destination vehicle with short delivery delay time and generate quite low routing overhead. To our best knowledge, this paper is the first to propose a SDN-based routing framework for efficiently message propagation in VANET. To adapt to dynamic network density in VANET, we proposed a new metric named "minimum optimistic time" based on which our proposed routing protocol can automatically switch between multi-hop forwarding and carry-and-forward models according to the network density. We implemented our proposed routing framework in ns-3 and compared the performance with other protocols. Simulation results in urban settings show that our proposed routing framework significantly outperforms the related protocols in terms of both delivery delay time and routing overhead.

The rest of the paper is organized as follows: Sect. 2 describes the proposed architecture of SDN-based routing framework for VANET and the centralized routing protocol; We discussed our simulation results in Sect. 3 and concluded our work in Sect. 4.

2   SDN-Based Routing Framework for VANET

In this section, we will firstly present the architecture of SDN-based routing framework of VANET and then describe operation details of this framework including the centralized routing protocol and the minimum optimistic time based routing algorithm.

2.1   Architecture of SDN-Based Routing Framework for VANET

In order to improve the routing efficiency, we firstly implement SDN to VANET. However, vehicles must be able to connect to a central controller. We found that many vehicles are equipped with both vehicle-to-vehicle network devices and vehicle-to-base-station network devices. Besides, cellular networks can provide Internet access service to mobile devices in most urban places. So in this paper, we assume that vehicles have at least two network devices, one of which can support vehicle-to-vehicle communication and another one can be used to access the central controller which is connected to the Internet.

The architecture of SDN-based routing framework in VANET is shown in Fig. 1. In this architecture, there is a remote central controller connected to the Internet and a routing server application running on it. Vehicles are equipped with both Wifi and WiMax network devices and established a routing client application to deal with packet sending out event. The routing client utilizes Wifi network device to transmit data to other vehicles and when there is no route entry for the destination, it will query route from routing server via WiMax network device. We have also proposed a centralized routing protocol(CRP) to enable routing query and reply between routing client and routing server. The proposed routing protocol will be described in details in the next subsection.

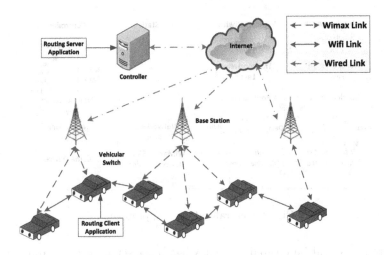

Fig. 1. The architecture of SDN-based routing framework

2.2   Centralized Routing Protocol

In order to explain the centralized routing protocol clearly, we draw the protocol stack in vehicular switch, base station and the central controller, as shown in Fig. 2.

In CRP, the routing client periodically updates the vehicle's state in the routing server by transmitting a "State Update" message to the routing server. The "State Update" messages contains current location and speed of the vehicle. Location can be got by vehicular GPS and speed can be got by vehicular speed sensor. The message will be send out via WiMax network device and forward by the base-station and finally got to the routing server. When routing server received the "State Update" message, it will update the network state vector and record it to the vehicle's history trace database.

When vehicles receive a packet or generate a packet, the routing client will firstly check whether their is a routing trace to the destination in its routing table. If there is one, it will send the packet out according to the trace. Otherwise, it will send a "Route Query" message to the routing server. The message contains the vehicle's ID and destination's IP address.

When routing server receives a "Route Query" message, it will call minimum optimistic time based routing algorithm and the routing algorithm will compute a shortest distance routing path from current vehicle to the destination vehicle using global network state vector and digital map. After that, the routing server will send a "Route Reply" message to the routing client which contains the next hop node ID.

When routing client receives the "Route Reply" message, it will generate a route entry based on the received message and insert the route entry to the routing table. Then the data will be send out according to the new route entry. The route entry will stay alive for a certain length of time, after this time,

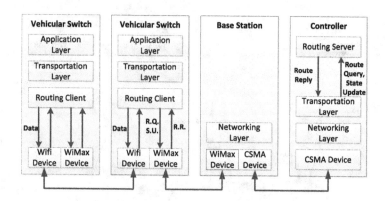

Fig. 2. Centralized routing protocol

the route entry will be deleted so that when a packet need to be route to the destination again, a new best next hop will be generated. This alive-timeout length is important to make the centralized routing protocol adaptive to the dynamic network topology.

2.3 Minimum Optimistic Time Based Routing Algorithm

Previous section has pointed out that SDN-based routing framework can provide a global view of network state. The challenge here is how to use this global network state information to chose the best next hop. When the network is well connected and there is at least a path from source node to the destination, this task can be easily done by utilizing any single-source shortest path algorithm (e.g. Dijkstra Algorithm) to compute a shortest Euclidean distance multi-hop route. However, when network partition happens and there is not any straight multi-hop route between source node and destination, it will be a difficult prob-

---

Algorithm 1. Minimum Optimistic Time Based Routing

Input: N, State[N], R, L, src, dest
  // N is the number of vehicles, State[N] is the current state of vehicles, R is the communication range, L is the road length, src is the source vehicle ID, dest is the destination vehicle ID
Output: NextHop
1: Initially: $MOT[N][N] \leftarrow \Phi$;
  // The minimum-optimistic-time array is initially empty.
2: Initially: $Route[N] \leftarrow \Phi$;
  // The shortest route is initially empty.
3: **for** each pair of vehicles (i,j) **do**
4:    $MOT[i][j] \leftarrow ComputeMOT(i, j, State, R, L)$;
5: **end for**
6: $Route \leftarrow DijkstraAlgorithm(N, MOT, src, dest)$;
7: $NextHop \leftarrow Route[0]$;

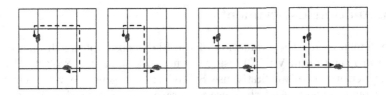

Fig. 3. Four conditions in computing minimum optimistic Time

lem to choose the best next hop node. Because we don't know how vehicles will move in the future.

In this paper, we firstly proposed a new metric named "Minimum Optimistic Time(MOT)" to measure the minimum time for any vehicle to transmit a packet to another one under the assumption that vehicles are moving along the best route to transmit the packet in the future. Based on MOT, we utilize a classical single-source shortest path algorithm to compute a shortest route from source node to the destination as shown in Algorithm 1.

To simplify the computation of MOT, we assume that the road map is a grid with same edge length and vehicles can just turn around at traffic junctions. We also assume that vehicles will move at the same speed. We divide this problem into four conditions according to the position and direction of vehicles as shown in Fig. 3. From this figure, we can find that the shortest route for vehicles are firstly move to the first traffic junction in ahead and then go along two vertical road which is just as long as the manhattan-distance between two traffic junctions. The algorithm of compute MOT for two vehicles are shown in Algorithm 2.

Algorithm 2. ComputeMOT
___
Input: n1, n2, State[N], R, L
Output: mot
1: Initially: $C \leftarrow 10^{-3}$;
   // The multi-hop time const C is initially 0.001.
2: $dist \leftarrow EuclideanDistance(State[n1].pos, State[n2].pos)$;
3: **if** $dist <= R$ **then**
4:   $mot \leftarrow (dist/R)*C$;
5: **else**
6:   $tjPos1 \leftarrow TrafficJunctionAhead(n1).pos$;
7:   $tjPos2 \leftarrow TrafficJunctionAhead(n2).pos$;
8:   $d1 \leftarrow EuclideanDistance(State[n1].pos, tjPos1)$;
9:   $d2 \leftarrow EuclideanDistance(State[n2].pos, tjPos2)$;
10:   $d3 \leftarrow ManhattanDistance(tjPos1, tjPos2)$;
11:   $mot \leftarrow (d1+d2+d3-R)/(State[n1].speed + State[n2].speed)$;
12: **end if**
___

3   Simulation Experiments

This section presents the evaluation of the SDN-based routing framework for message propagation in VAENT using the network simulator NS-3 [9]. To evaluate the performance, we firstly use SUMO [12] to generate vehicular traces in urban environment. And then use the trace as test scenarios. We compare CRP with three existing VANET routing protocols: AODV, OLSR and GPSR. In the following, we will present the metrics for comparing the protocols, and the analysis of the simulation results.

3.1   Simulation Setup

The simulation scenario is a 1000 m 1000 m area that was extracted from the OpenStreetMap of the US NewYork. We used the open source, highly portable, microscopic and continuous road traffic simulation package SUMO to generate the movements of the vehicle nodes. We input the map extracted from the OpenStreetMap into SUMO and specify the speeds limits.

We change the number of vehicles to vary the network density. Simulation parameter is shown in Table 1.

Table 1. Simulation parameter

Parameter	Value
Simulation time	150 s
No. of Nodes	10–100
Traffic type	CBR
Packet size	1024 byte
Interval	0.1 s
MAC protocol	802.11
Mobility model	SUMO Trace

3.2   Metrics

The performance of the routing protocols was evaluated by varying the network density. The metrics to assess the performance are given as follows.

Delivery Delay Time. This metric is defined as the time used to successfully deliver a certain number of data packets to the destinations from the sources. The delivery delay time shows the efficiency of routing protocols to successfully transfer data on an end-to-end basis.

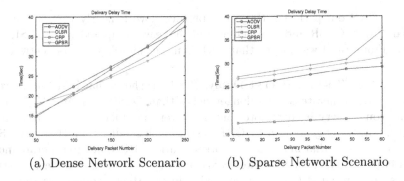

(a) Dense Network Scenario   (b) Sparse Network Scenario

Fig. 4. Delivery delay time

Average End-To-End Packet Delay. This metric is defined as the average delay for all data packets that successfully delivered from source node to the destination. The average end-to-end packet delay show the latency generated by the routing protocol. There are two main possible reasons to generate long end-to-end packet delay. One is that the route chosen by the routing protocol is not the best one. The other one is that the routing protocol needs more time to deal with the packet on the forwarding nodes.

Routing Overhead. This metric is defined as the bytes of extra routing packets per unit bytes of data packets that were received at destinations. The overhead measures the additional traffic that the routing protocol generated for packets that were successfully delivered.

3.3 Simulation Results

Delivery Delay Time. Figure 4 (a) shows that in dense network scenario CRP gains similar performance with OLSR and GPSR. GPSR performs little better than other protocols in this scenario. Figure 4 (b) shows that in sparse network

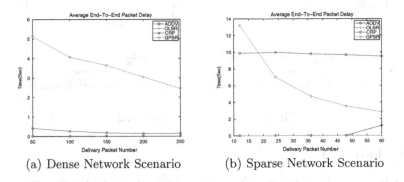

(a) Dense Network Scenario   (b) Sparse Network Scenario

Fig. 5. End-to-end packet delay

scenario, CRP out-performs the other protocols, with nearly a 50 % increase compared with OLSR and as much as 40 % increase compared with GPSR and AODV. From Fig. 4 we can see that CRP is more suitable in sparse networks.

Average End-To-End Packet Delay. Fig. 5 (a) shows that in dense network scenario CRP generate a little longer delay than OLSR and AODV. That is because route query from remote routing server may take some external time. However, the delay generated by CRP is still much smaller than that of GPSR. Figure 5 (b) shows that in sparse network scenario, CRP seems to generate much higher latency. In fact the high latency is caused by intermittent connect between vehicles. Just because CRP can deal with intermittent connections there are some packets get to the destination with long delay. However, OLSR, AODV can not deal with such connections and their deliveries packets are always got short latency. So in average, CRP will generate higher end-toend packet delay.

Routing Overhead. Figure 6 (a) shows that in dense network scenario CRP gains much better performance than other protocols. It saves more than 50 % routing overhead than OLSR and as much as 40 % routing overhead than AODV and GPSR. Besides, all these overhead will not effect data propagation on vehicle's Wifi network device. Because these routing overhead occupy WiMax channel. So in fact, the routing overhead in CRP is zero. Figure 6 (b) shows that in sparse network scenario, CRP's routing overhead is as same as AODV and GPSR. That's because the number of delivered packets is much more than other protocols and it will need more routing packets to serve forwarding nodes. From Fig. 6 we could say that the SDN-based routing framework is really efficient for saving routing overhead which can provide vehicles with more bandwidth to disseminate important information to other vehicles.

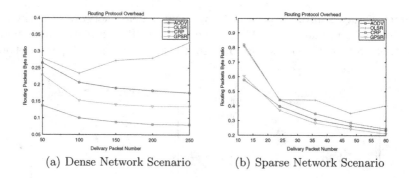

(a) Dense Network Scenario   (b) Sparse Network Scenario

Fig. 6. Routing protocol overhead

4   Conclusion

In this paper, we proposed a SDN-based routing framework for message propagation in VANET for the first time. The proposed routing framework compute globally optimized routing paths for vehicles while just generate quite low routing overhead. To adapt to the dynamic network density of VANET, we proposed a new metric named "minimum optimistic time". Based on the new metric the proposed routing protocol can automatically switch between multi-hop forwarding model and carry-and-forward model. We implemented our proposed routing framework in ns-3 and compared with existing routing protocols in VANET. Simulation result show that CRP can dramatically outperform with other routing protocols in terms of both the packet delivery delay time and routing overhead.

In future work, we plan to investigate more network functions to the controller such as load balancing, that can fulfill and take advantage of SDN architecture to improve the performance of VANET.

References

1. Clausen, T., Jacquet, P.: Optimized link state routing protocol (OLSR). RFC 3626, October (2003)
2. Daraghmi, Y.A., Yi, C.W., Stojmenovic, I., Arabia, S.: Forwarding methods in data dissemination and routing protocols for vehicular ad hoc networks. In: IEEE Network Magazine, pp. 74–79, 11(December), November 2013
3. Hartenstein, H., Laberteaux, K.P.: VANET : Vehicular Applications and Inter-Networking Technologies. John Wiley & Sons Ltd., Chichester (2010)
4. Jain, S., Zhu, M., Zolla, J., Hölzle, U., Stuart, S., Vahdat, A., Kumar, A., Mandal, S., Ong, J., Poutievski, L., Singh, A., Venkata, S., Wanderer, J., Zhou, J.: B4: Experience with a globally-deployed software definedWA. In: Proceedings of the ACM SIGCOMM 2013, pp. 3–14, August 2013
5. Karp, B., Kung, H.T.: GPSR: Greedy perimeter stateless routing for wireless networks. In: Proceedings of MobiCom 2000, pp.243–254, August 2000
6. Khilar, P.M., Bhoi, S.K.: Vehicular communication: a survey. IET. Networks 3(3), 204–217 (2014)
7. Limoncelli, T.A.: OpenFlow: a radical new idea in networking. ACM Commun. 10(6), 1–7 (2012)
8. McKeown, N., Anderson, T.: OpenFlow: enabling innovation in campus networks. ACM SIGCOMM Comput. Commun. Rev. 38(2), 69–74 (2008)
9. NS-3. http://www.nsnam.org/
10. Perkins, C., Royer, E.: Ad-hoc on-demand distance vector routing. In: Proceedings of the 2nd IEEE Workshop on Mobile Computing Systems and Applications, WMCSA 1999, pp. 99–100 (1999)
11. Qazi, Z.A., Tu, C.C., Chiang, L., Miao, R., Sekar, V., Yu, M.: SIMPLE-fying middlebox policy enforcement using SDN. In: Proceedings of the ACM SIGCOMM 2013 Conference on SIGCOMM, pp. 27–38 (2013)
12. SUMO. http://sumo-sim.org/

Critical Point Aware Data Acquisition Algorithm in Sensor Networks

Tongxin Zhu[1], Xinrui Wang[1], Siyao Cheng[1(✉)], Zhipeng Cai[2],
and Jianzhong Li[1]

[1] School of Computer Science and Technology,
Harbin Institute of Technology, Harbin, China
{zhutongxinhit,wangxinruihit}@126.com, {csy,lijzh}@hit.edu.cn
[2] Department of Computer Science, Georgia State University, Atlanta, GA, USA
zcai@gsu.edu

Abstract. With the development and widespread application of wireless sensor networks (WSNs), the objects monitored by WSNs and the query requirements given by users become more and more complicated. For example, most applications require the critical points, including extremum and inflection points, in order to analyze and make decision. However, the traditional query processing and sensory data acquisition algorithm cannot satisfy such requirement since the sensor data considered by them are discrete. Due to this reason, the critical point aware data acquisition algorithm will be studied in this paper. First, we formally defined the concept of δ-approximate critical points. Then, a data acquisition algorithm based on numerical analysis and Lagrange interpolation is proposed to acquire the critical points. The extensive theoretical analysis and simulation results are provided, which show that the proposed algorithm can achieve high accuracy for retrieving the δ-approximate critical points from the monitored physical world.

Keywords: Wireless sensor networks · Adaptive sampling · Critical points

1 Introduction

The appearance of wireless sensor networks (WSNs) makes it possible to observe the complicated physical world with low cost. Nowadays, WSNs are widely used in many applications, including military defense, environment monitoring, traffic monitoring, structural health monitoring, etc. In most of these applications, the sensor nodes sense and sample the data from the monitored environment with equal-sampling-frequency, and the sensory data generated by WSNs are regarded as a set of the discrete values. Under such assumptions, a great number of query processing techniques on discrete sensory data have been proposed, including curve query processing algorithms [1], the aggregation query processing algorithms [2–4], top-k query processing algorithms [5], skyline [6] and quantilen [7] query processing algorithms etc.

© Springer International Publishing Switzerland 2015
K. Xu and J. Zhu (Eds.): WASA 2015, LNCS 9204, pp. 798–808, 2015.
DOI: 10.1007/978-3-319-21837-3_78

However, since the monitored objects are more and more complicated, the query requirements given by users become harder to be dealt with. The above simple queries on discrete sensory data cannot meet the current requirements of users. For example, in the air pollution monitoring application, the users want to estimate the extremum pollution values and obtain the period when these values appear. In the climate monitoring system, the users may want to know the convexity of the wind velocity or rainfall curve, and acquire the inflection points of such curves. The above query requirements cannot be satisfied by existing query processing techniques which only consider the discrete sensory data due to the following reasons. First, as pointed out by [8,9], the monitored physical world varies continuously, and the discrete sensory dataset omits many critical points, so critical points cannot be answered since they do not belong to the discrete sensory dataset. Second, to answer the queries about the convexity, monotonicity or the positions of critical points, the original data should have the continuous first and second derivatives, which cannot be met as well. To overcome the above problems, In [9] proposed an adaptive data acquisition algorithm to reconstruct physical world as much as possible. Besides, [10] proposed an algorithm finding a small data set to represent vast sensory data sampled by WSNs. However, they do not suit critical data acquisition.

Due to the above reasons, we will study the problem of retrieving the critical points, including the extremum and inflection points, in the sensor networks. In this paper, a novel sensory data acquisition algorithm is proposed based on numerical analysis techniques [11] and Lagrange interpolation [12] in order to retrieve the critical points approximately. Such algorithm can adjust the sampling frequency of sensors adaptively according to the variation of physical world. Furthermore, to evaluate the error of approximate critical points, the formal definitions of δ-approximate extremum point and δ-approximate inflection point are firstly provided, where δ denotes the relative error between the approximate critical point and the exact one. The correctness of the algorithm is proved. In summary, the contributions of this paper are as follows.

1. The formal definitions of δ-approximate extremum point and δ-approximate inflection point are firstly proposed. The problem of acquiring critical points from the monitored physical world is also defined.
2. Two critical point aware data acquisition algorithms are proposed based on numerical analysis [11] and Lagrange interpolation [12] techniques. The algorithms can adjust the sampling frequency of the sensors automatically according to variation of the physical world. The correctness of the algorithms is proved and the complexities of the algorithms are analyzed.
3. The extensive simulations on the real data set are carried out. The experimental results show that both of the precision and recall rate of our proposed algorithms are quite high to retrieve δ-approximate extremum point and δ-approximate inflection point from the monitored physical world.

The organization of the paper is as follows. Section 2 gives the problem definition. Section 3 provides the mathematical foundations of the algorithms. Section 4 proposes two critical point aware data acquisition algorithms, to retrieve the δ-*approximate extremum point* and δ-*approximate inflection point* respectively. Section 5 shows the experimental results. Section 6 discusses the related work of the paper. Finally, Section 7 concludes the whole paper.

2 Problem Definition

Let N denote the number of sensor nodes in a given WSN, and $V = \{1, 2, \cdots, N\}$ be the set of sensor nodes, where i ($1 \leq i \leq N$) denotes the ID of a sensor node. Suppose that t_s and t_f denote the start and final time in monitoring the physical world by a WSN respectively. Therefore, the variation of the physical world monitored by sensor node i can be regarded as a curve, which is denoted by S_i. According to the discussion in [9], the physical world always varies continuously and S_i is smooth enough to have continuous fourth-order derivative.

In this paper, the critical points considered by us are extremum points and inflection points of the physical curve S_i. The extremum points of S_i in range $[t_s, t_f]$ can be denoted by $\{x | S_i^{(1)}(x) = 0 \bigwedge x \in [t_s, t_f]\}$, similarly, the inflection points can be denoted by $\{x | S_i^{(2)}(x) = 0 \bigwedge x \in [t_s, t_f]\}$.

Since when the critical points will appear in the future is unknown, it requires that the sampling frequency is infinite to obtain all the critical points of S_i exactly, which is almost impossible. Thus, we will study the sensory data acquisition algorithm to retrieve the critical points, approximately. To evaluate the relative error between the approximate critical points and the exact critical points, the δ-*approximate extremum point* and δ-*approximate inflection point* are defined as follows.

Definition 1 (δ-*approximate extremum points*). $\widehat{x}_i$ from $\widehat{S}_i$ is called as an δ-approximate extremum point if and only if $\exists x_i \in [t_s, t_f]$ satisfying $\frac{|\widehat{x}_i - x_i|}{x_i} \leq \delta$ and $S_i^{(1)}(x_i) = 0$.

Definition 2 (δ-*approximate inflection points*). $\widehat{x}_i$ is called as an δ-approximate inflection point if and only if $\exists x_i \in [t_s, t_f]$ satisfying that $S_i^{(2)}(x_i) = 0$ and $\frac{|\widehat{x}_i - x_i|}{x_i} \leq \delta$.

The intuition of our algorithm is to forecast the first and second derivatives of S_i using the current collected sensory data. If the first or second derivative is close to 0, then the sampling frequency increases. Otherwise, we reduce the sampling frequency in order to save energy. Since the physical world varies continuously, it is acceptable to use the history sensory data to forecast the future.

3 Mathematical Foundations

Let t_c denote the current sampling time, t_{c-1} denote the last sampling time before t_c, and $t_{\frac{2c-1}{2}}$ be the median of t_c and t_{c-1}. For each sensor node i ($1 \leq i \leq N$), $S_i(t_{\frac{2c-1}{2}})$ should always be sampled besides $S_i(t_{c-1})$ and $S_i(t_c)$ in $[t_{c-1}, t_c]$.

Based on such operation and Three Point Central Difference Formula [11], the first and second derivatives of S_i at $t_{\frac{2c-1}{2}}$ can be estimated by the following two formulas.

$$\widehat{S}_i^{(1)}(t_{\frac{2c-1}{2}}) = \frac{S_i(t_c) - S_i(t_{c-1})}{2h} - \frac{h^2}{6}S_i^{(3)}(t_{\frac{2c-1}{2}}) \tag{1}$$

$$\widehat{S}_i^{(2)}(t_{\frac{2c-1}{2}}) = \frac{S_i(t_c) - 2S_i(t_{\frac{2c-1}{2}}) + S_i(t_{c-1})}{h^2} - \frac{h^2}{12}S_i^{(4)}(t_{\frac{2c-1}{2}}) \tag{2}$$

where $h = t_{\frac{2c-1}{2}} - t_{c-1} = t_c - t_{\frac{2c-1}{2}}$ denotes the half length of the sampling interval.

The following theorem guarantees that the difference between $\widehat{S}_i^{(1)}(t_{\frac{2c-1}{2}})$ and $S_i^{(1)}(t_{\frac{2c-1}{2}})$ is determined by h^2. The proof of Theorems 1 and 2 is in our technique report [13].

Theorem 1. $|S_i^{(1)}(t_{\frac{2i-1}{2}}) - \widehat{S}_i^{(1)}(t_{\frac{2c-1}{2}})| = |\frac{h^2}{6}\{S_i^{(3)}(t_{\frac{2c-1}{2}}) - S_i^{(3)}(\xi)\}|$, where $\xi \in [t_{c-1}, t_c]$. □

Theorem 2. $|S_i^{(2)}(t_{\frac{2c-1}{2}}) - \widehat{S}_i^{(2)}(t_{\frac{2c-1}{2}})| = |\frac{h^2}{12}(S_i^{(4)}(t_{\frac{2c-1}{2}}) - S_i^{(4)}(\xi))|$, where $\xi \in [t_{c-1}, t_c]$. □

These two theorems indicate that the difference between the exact critical points and the approximate ones calculated by Formulas (1) and (2) can be arbitrarily small with the decline of h.

In Theorems 1 and 2, $S_i^{(3)}(t_{\frac{2c-1}{2}})$ and $S_i^{(4)}(t_{\frac{2c-1}{2}})$ can be estimated by Lagrange interpolation. The sensory values collected by sensor node i in last and current sampling intervals, i.e. $S_i(t_{c-2})$, $S_i(t_{\frac{2c-3}{2}})$, $S_i(t_{c-1})$, $S_i(t_{\frac{2c-1}{2}})$ and $S_i(t_c)$, are used.

Let $L_1(t)$ and $L_2(t)$ denote the Lagrange interpolation polynomials to estimate $S_i^{(3)}(t_{\frac{2c-1}{2}})$ and $S_i^{(4)}(t_{\frac{2c-1}{2}})$ respectively. The construction of $L_1(t)$ is as follows. First, let $l_{1k}(t)$ be a k-polynomial of t for $0 \leq k \leq 3$, which satisfies $l_{1k}(t) = \prod_{j=0, j \neq k}^{3} \frac{(t - t_{\frac{2c-3+j}{2}})}{(t_{\frac{2c-3+k}{2}} - t_{\frac{2c-3+j}{2}})}$. Therefore, $L_1(t) = S_i(t_{\frac{2c-3}{2}})l_{10}(t) + S_i(t_{c-1})l_{11}(t) + S_i(t_{\frac{2c-1}{2}})l_{12}(t) + S_i(t_c)l_{13}(t)$, so that $S_i^{(3)}(t)$ can be estimated by the following formula, where $t \in [t_{\frac{2c-3}{2}}, t_c]$.

$$S_i^{(3)}(t) \approx L_1^{(3)}(t) \tag{3}$$

Similarly, a fourth-order interpolation Lagrange polynomial $L_2(t)$ can be calculated by the same method. Therefore, $S_i^{(4)}(t)$ can be estimated by the following formula.

$$S_i^{(4)}(t) \approx L_2^{(4)}(t) \tag{4}$$

The error of such estimation is bounded by the following Theorem 3, which is very small in practice. The proof is in our technique report [13].

Theorem 3. The errors generated by Formulas (3) and (4) equal to $\gamma_1(t) = \frac{S_i^{(4)}(\xi)}{4}[4t - (t_{\frac{2c-3}{2}} + t_{c-1} + t_{\frac{2c-1}{2}} + t_c)]$ and $\gamma_2(t) = \frac{S_i^{(5)}(\xi)}{5}[5t - (t_{c-2} + t_{\frac{2c-3}{2}} + t_{c-1} + t_{\frac{2c-1}{2}} + t_c)]$, respectively.   □

4   Critical Point Aware Data Acquisition Algorithm

According to the analysis and symbols in Sect. 3, the whole critical point aware data acquisition algorithm can be divided into two phases. The first one is the initial phase, the sampling frequency in such phase is set to be f_{max} in order not to omit any critical points, where f_{max} is the maximum sampling frequency that a sensor node can achieve. The second one is the maintenance phase, the sampling frequency in such phase is determined according to the variation of physical world. Since the variation of the monitored physical world in the future is unknown, the posterior estimation is adopted, that is, the history sensory data collected in the current time will be used to estimate the variation of the monitored physical world in the future. Because the physical world always varies continuously, such estimation is acceptable and can achieve high precision.

The detailed critical point aware adaptive data acquisition algorithm is shown in Algorithm 1.

Algorithm 1. Critical Point Aware Data Acquisition Algorithm

Input: $t_0(= t_s)$, f_{max}, t', The decrease factor α.
Output: The set of extremum points X_1 and the set of inflection points X_2
1 $c \leftarrow 2$, $h \leftarrow \frac{1}{f_{max}}$
2 Sample sensory values at $\{t_{j/2}|0 \leq j \leq 2 \bigwedge t_{j/2} - t_{(j-1)/2} = 1/f_{max}\}$;
3 **while** $t_c < t_f$ **do**
4 | Sample sensory values at $t_{\frac{2c-1}{2}}$, t_c;
5 | Estimate $S_i^{(3)}(t)$ ($t \in [t_{\frac{2c-3}{2}}, t_c]$) according to Formula (3);
6 | Estimate $S_i^{(4)}(t)$ ($t \in [t_{c-2}, t_c]$) according to Formula (4);
7 | (y_1, h_1)=**EPRA** $(S_i(t_{c-1}), S_i(t_{\frac{2c-1}{2}}), S_i(t_c), h, S_i^{(3)}(t), S_i^{(4)}(t))$;
8 | (y_2, h_2)=**IPRA** $(S_i(t_{c-1}), S_i(t_{\frac{2c-1}{2}}), S_i(t_c), h, S_i^{(3)}(t), S_i^{(4)}(t))$;
9 | $X_1 = X_1 \bigcup y_1$, $X_2 = X_2 \bigcup y_2$, $h = \min\{h_1, h_2\}$;
10 | $t_{\frac{2c+1}{2}} = t_c + h$, $t_{c+1} = t_c + 2h$, $c \leftarrow c + 1$;
11 Return X_1 and X_2

4.1   Extremum Point Retrieving Algorithm (EPRA)

The extremum point retrieving algorithm has four steps.

Step 1. Sensor i estimates the first derivative $\widehat{S}_i^{(1)}(t_{\frac{2c-1}{2}})$ and the second derivative $\widehat{S}_i^{(2)}(t_{\frac{2c-1}{2}})$ based on Formulas (1) and (2). If $\widehat{S}_i^{(1)}(t_{\frac{2c-1}{2}}) = 0$, then return $t_{\frac{2c-1}{2}}$.

Step 2. Compare $\widehat{S}_i^{(1)}(t_{\frac{2c-1}{2}})$ and $\widehat{S}_i^{(1)}(t_{\frac{2c-3}{2}})$ calculated in last loop to find omissive the extremum point in $[t_{\frac{2c-3}{2}}, t_{\frac{2c-1}{2}}]$.

Step 3. There exists three cases that need to be considered when determining the length of the next sampling interval.

1. If $\widehat{S}_i^{(2)}(t_{\frac{2c-1}{2}}) \times \widehat{S}_i^{(1)}(t_{\frac{2c-1}{2}}) > 0$, which means that the first derivative of the physical world increases or decreases monotonously, so that the length of the next sampling interval h_1 can be increased with t' in order to save energy, where t' is a given constant to denote the step size increment.

2. If $\widehat{S}_i^{(2)}(t_{\frac{2c-1}{2}}) \times \widehat{S}_i^{(1)}(t_{\frac{2c-1}{2}}) < 0$ and $|\widehat{S}_i^{(2)}(t_{\frac{2c-1}{2}})| \times 2h > |\widehat{S}_i^{(1)}(t_{\frac{2c-1}{2}})|$, which means that the next extremum point is more likely to be included in the next sampling interval, thus, we decrease the length of sampling interval in order to catch the extremum point. Therefore, $h_1 = max\{\frac{1}{f_{max}}, \alpha h\}$, where $0 < \alpha \leq 1$.

3. Otherwise, the ratio between $|\widehat{S}_i^{(2)}(t_{\frac{2c-1}{2}})|$ and $|\widehat{S}_i^{(1)}(t_{\frac{2c-1}{2}})|$ will be considered, if $|\widehat{S}_i^{(1)}(t_{\frac{2c-1}{2}})| \geq (2h+t') \times |\widehat{S}_i^{(2)}(t_{\frac{2c-1}{2}})|$, $h_1 = h+t'$. In other situations, h_1 maintains the last sampling interval h.

Step 4. Return h_1 and the extremum point.
The detailed algorithm is shown in Algorithm 2.

4.2   Inflection Point Retrieving Algorithm (IPRA)

The inflection point retrieving algorithm can be constructed by similar method shown in above section and is shown in Algorithm 3.

In each sampling interval, the complexity of the above algorithm is $O(1)$ since it only needs to sample two sensory values and the first and second derivatives can be calculated in $O(1)$. Therefore, the total complexity of Algorithm 1 is determined by the number of sampling interval it includes. In the best case, the half length of sampling interval, h, increases t' every loop. Therefore, the sampling interval and the minimum complexity of the above algorithm are both $O(\sqrt{\frac{t_f - t_s}{t'}})$. In the worst case, the sampling frequency is always f_{max}, so that the maximum complexity of the above algorithm is $O(f_{max}(t_f - t_s))$. However, the worst case requires that there exists lots of critical points in $[t_s, t_f]$, which is rarely happened.

5   Experiment Result

5.1   Experiment Setting

We use a simulated network with 200 sensor nodes to evaluate the performance of our sensory data acquisition algorithms. The network is deployed into a rectangular region with $200m \times 200m$ size. The transmission range of each sensor node is set to be $25m$.

Algorithm 2. Extremum Point Retrieving Algorithm (EPRA)

Input: f_{max}, t', α, $S_i(t_c)$, $S_i(t_{\frac{2c-1}{2}})$, $S_i(t_{c-1})$, h, $S_i^{(3)}(t_{\frac{2c-1}{2}})$, $S_i^{(4)}(t_{\frac{2c-1}{2}})$

Output: h_1, y_1

1 $\widehat{S}_i^{(1)}(t_{\frac{2c-1}{2}}) = \frac{S(t_c) - S(t_{c-1})}{2h} - \frac{h^2}{6} S^{(3)}(t_{\frac{2c-1}{2}})$;

2 $\widehat{S}_i^{(2)}(t_{\frac{2c-1}{2}}) = \dfrac{S(t_c) - 2S(t_{\frac{2c-1}{2}}) + S(t_{c-1})}{h^2} - \frac{h^2}{12} S^{(4)}(t_{\frac{2c-1}{2}})$;

3 $y_1 = \emptyset$; $h_1 = h$;

4 **if** $\widehat{S}_i^{(1)}(t_{\frac{2c-1}{2}}) \times \widehat{S}_i^{(1)}(t_{\frac{2c-3}{2}}) < 0$ **then**

5 $\quad$ Then y_1 is determined by curve tessellation techniques [14] in $[t_{\frac{2c-3}{2}}, t_{\frac{2c-1}{2}}]$;

6 **if** $\widehat{S}_i^{(1)}(t_{\frac{2c-1}{2}}) == 0$ **then**

7 $\quad$ $y_1 = \{t_{\frac{2c-1}{2}}\}$;

8 **if** $\widehat{S}_i^{(2)}(t_{\frac{2c-1}{2}}) \times \widehat{S}_i^{(1)}(t_{\frac{2c-1}{2}}) > 0$ **then**

9 $\quad$ $h_1 = h + t'$;

10 **else**

11 $\quad$ **if** $|\widehat{S}_i^{(2)}(t_{\frac{2c-1}{2}})| \times 2h > |\widehat{S}_i^{(1)}(t_{\frac{2c-1}{2}})|$ **then**

12 $\quad\quad$ $h_1 = max\{\frac{1}{f_{max}}, \alpha h\}$;

13 $\quad$ **else**

14 $\quad\quad$ **if** $|\widehat{S}_i^{(1)}(t_{\frac{2c-1}{2}})| \geq (2h + t') \times |\widehat{S}_i^{(2)}(t_{\frac{2c-1}{2}})|$ **then**

15 $\quad\quad\quad$ $h_1 = h + t'$;

16 Return h_1 and y_1;

The sensory data of the network comes from a real sensor system, where the TelosB mote [15] is used to acquire indoor temperature, humidity and light intensity continuously with the frequency 1 Hz, and the light intensity is adopted in our experiments.

5.2 The Performance of the Algorithm

The first group of experiments is going to evaluate the recall rate and precision of our algorithm for retrieving δ-approximate extremum and inflection points. The recall rate equals to the fraction of the exact δ-approximate critical points that are returned. The precision is the fraction of the returned results that are the exact δ-approximate critical points. In the following experiments, the recall rate and the precision of our algorithm were computed respectively while δ increases from 0.005 to 0.025, $\alpha = 0.5$ and $t' = 0.5$. The experimental results are presented in Fig. 1. From Fig. 1(a) and (b), we can see that the recall rate and precision of δ-approximate extremum points increase with the growth of δ, and both of them are close to 1 even when δ is quite small. The results in Fig. 1(c) and (d) show that the recall rate and precision of δ-approximate inflection points are also close to 1 even when δ is very small. In summary, our algorithms achieve high accuracy in practice.

Algorithm 3. Inflection Point Retrieving Algorithm (IPRA)

Input: f_{max}, t', α, $S_i(t_c)$, $S_i(t_{\frac{2c-1}{2}})$, $S_i(t_{c-1})$, h, $S_i^{(3)}(t_{\frac{2c-1}{2}})$, $S_i^{(4)}(t_{\frac{2c-1}{2}})$

Output: h_1, y_1

1   $\widehat{S_i}^{(2)}(t_{\frac{2c-1}{2}}) = \dfrac{S(t_c) - 2S(t_{\frac{2c-1}{2}}) + S(t_{c-1})}{h^2} - \dfrac{h^2}{12} S^{(4)}(t_{\frac{2c-1}{2}})$;

2   $y_2 = \emptyset$; $h_2 = h$;

3   **if** $\widehat{S_i}^{(2)}(t_{\frac{2c-1}{2}}) \times \widehat{S_i}^{(2)}(t_{\frac{2c-3}{2}}) < 0$ **then**

4 | Then y_2 is determined by curve tessellation techniques [14] in $[t_{\frac{2c-3}{2}}, t_{\frac{2c-1}{2}}]$;

5   **if** $\widehat{S_i}^{(2)}(t_{\frac{2c-1}{2}}) == 0$ **then**

6 | $y_2 = \{t_{\frac{2c-1}{2}}\}$;

7   **if** $S_i^{(3)}(t_{\frac{2c-1}{2}}) \times \widehat{S_i}^{(2)}(t_{\frac{2c-1}{2}}) > 0$ **then**

8 | $h_2 = h + t'$;

9   **else**

10 | **if** $|S_i^{(3)}(t_{\frac{2c-1}{2}})| \times 2h > |\widehat{S_i}^{(2)}(t_{\frac{2c-1}{2}})|$ **then**

11 | | $h_2 = max\{\frac{1}{f_{max}}, \alpha h\}$;

12 | **else**

13 | | **if** $|\widehat{S_i}^{(2)}(t_{\frac{2c-1}{2}})| \geq (2h + t') \times |S^{(3)}(t_{\frac{2c-1}{2}})|$ **then**

14 | | | $h_2 = h + t'$;

15   Return h_2 and y_2;

The second group of experiments is to investigate the impact of α on the performance of our algorithm. In the following experiments, the recall rate and the precision of the first and second derivatives generated by our algorithm were computed respectively while α increased from 0 to 1, $\delta = 0.015$ and $t' = 0.5$. The experimental results are presented in Fig. 2(a) and (b). They show the the the recall rate and precision of δ-approximate extremum and inflection points. The recall rate and precision of δ-approximate inflection points decrease with the growth of α, which is because the larger α will omit more inflection points. Besides, the recall rate and precision of δ-approximate inflection points are still every high even when α is not very small. At the mean time, the recall and precision rate of δ-approximate extremum points keep stable and high enough in practice with the variation of α.

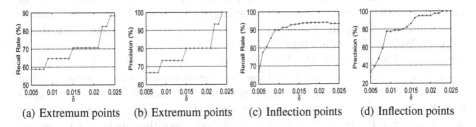

(a) Extremum points   (b) Extremum points   (c) Inflection points   (d) Inflection points

Fig. 1. The relationship among recall rate, the precision and δ

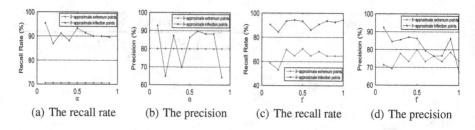

(a) The recall rate   (b) The precision   (c) The recall rate   (d) The precision

Fig. 2. The impact of α and t' in recall rate and precision

The third group of experiments is to investigate the impact of t' on the performance of our algorithm. In the experiments, the recall rate and the precision of the first and second derivatives generated by our algorithm were calculated while t' increases from 0.1 to 1, $\alpha = 0.5$ and $\delta = 0.015$. The experimental results are presented in Fig. 2(c) and (d). They show that the recall rate of δ-approximate inflection points is around 90 % and the precision of δ-approximate inflection points decreases with the growth of t', since more δ-approximate inflection points will be omitted when t' is larger. Although the recall rate and the precision of δ-approximate extremum points are lower than δ-approximate inflection points, they still capture a large portion of extremum points.

6   Related Works

Currently, there exists few published works considering the adaptive sampling in sensor networks. Moreover, none of them could support the requirement of retrieving the critical points from the monitored physical world.

Some adaptive sampling algorithms are proposed for particular applications. For example, the algorithm in [16] is designed for target tracking. Each sensor uses sensory values sensed by its neighbours and itself to predict the target position and adjusts the sampling frequency adaptively. And [17] introduced an energy efficient algorithm to adjust the sampling frequency in the abnormal event detecting applications. It applies Fourier Transform to predict the events and to adjust sampling frequency automatically. Since they are designed for particular applications, they have limitation in applying.

Most of works on adaptive sampling apply prediction models to estimate sensory values instead of sampling them. In [18] uses Kalman Filter based prediction model to predict sensory values, if the estimations beyond the acceptable range, they will adjust sampling frequency. However, the prediction ability of Kalman Filter is limited, the estimation error may be large. The prediction method in [19] is Box-Jenkins approach. The main idea of the work is to skip samplings from equal-sampling-frequency and use the forecast ones, which can adjust the sampling frequency adaptively. However, since the method is based on equal-sampling-frequency, its accuracy is even worse than the EFS method. The work in [20] proposed a heuristic adaptive sampling algorithm for a glacial sensor network. Each sensor locally adjusts its sensing frequency based on the linear regression forecasting model. Such method reduces the energy cost of acquiring sensory data since the forecasting model is sufficiently utilized. However, the forecasting ability of the linear regression model is limited, and it do not consider the problem of retrieving the critical points, either.

7 Conclusion

This paper studies the critical point aware data acquisition algorithm to obtain δ-approximate extremum and inflection points from the physical world. We firstly provide the formal definition of δ-approximate extremum and inflection points. Then, a data acquisition algorithm is proposed based on numerical analysis and Lagrange interpolation. Such algorithm can adjust the sampling frequency of each sensor node adaptively according to the variation of physical world. The correctness of the algorithm is proved and the its complexity is analyzed in detail. Finally, the extensive simulations are carried out, which show that our algorithm can achieve high accuracy of retrieving δ-approximate extremum and inflection points from physical world.

Acknowledgment. This work was supported in part by the National Basic Research Program of China (973 Program) under Grant No. 2012CB316200, the National Natural Science Foundation of China (NSFC) under Grant No. 61190115, 61370217, the Fundamental Research Funds for the Central Universities under grant No. HIT.KISTP201415, the National Science Foundation (NSF) under Grants No. CNS-1152001, CNS-1252292, the Research Fund for the Doctoral Program of Higher Education of China under grant No.20132302120045, and the Natural Scientific Research Innovation Foundation in Harbin Institute of Technology under grant No.HIT.NSRIF.2014070.

References

1. Cheng, S., Cai, Z., Li, J.: Curve query processing in wireless sensor networks. IEEE Trans. Veh. Technol. **99**, 1 (2014)
2. Li, J., Cheng, S.: (ϵ, δ)-approximate aggregation algorithms in dynamic sensor networks. IEEE Trans. Parallel Distrib. Syst. **23**(3), 385–396 (2012)
3. Cheng, S., Li, J.: Sampling based (ϵ, δ)-approximate aggregation algorithm in sensor networks. In: ICDCS, pp. 273–280 (2009)
4. Cheng, S., Li, J., Ren, Q., Yu, L.: Bernoulli sampling based (ϵ, δ)-approximate aggregation in large-scale sensor networks. In: Proceedings of the 29th Conference on Information Communications, pp. 1181–1189 (2010)
5. Cheng, S., Li, J., Yu, L.: Location aware peak value query in sensor networks. In: INFOCOM, pp. 486–494 (2012)
6. Su, I.-F., Chung, Y.-C., Lee, C., Lin, Y.-Y.: Efficient skyline query processing in wireless sensor networks. J. Parallel Distrib. Comput. **70**(6), 680–698 (2010)
7. Huang, Z., Wang, L., Yi, K., Liu, Y.: Sampling based algorithms for quantile computation in sensor networks. In: Proceedings of the 2011 ACM SIGMOD International Conference on Management of Data, pp. 745–756. ACM (2011)

8. Li, J., Cheng, S., Gao, H., Cai, Z.: Approximate physical world reconstruction algorithms in sensor networks. IEEE Trans. Parallel Distrib. Syst. **12**, 3099–3110 (2014)

9. Cheng, S., Li, J., Cai, Z.: "o (ϵ)-approximation to physical world by sensor networks. In: Proceedings of IEEE INFOCOM, pp. 3084–3092 (2013)

10. Cheng, S., Cai, Z., Li, J., Fang, X.: Drawing dominant dataset from big sensory data in wireless sensor networks. In: The 34th Annual IEEE International Conference on Computer Communications (INFOCOM 2015). IEEE (2015)

11. Froberg, C.-E., Frhoberg, C.E.: Introduction to Numerical Analysis. Addison-Wesley Reading, Boston (1969)

12. Powell, M.J.D.: Approximation Theory and Methods. Cambridge University Press, Cambridge (1981)

13. http://www.cs.gsu.edu/zcai/reports/2015/WASACPA.pdf

14. Lindgren, T., Sanchez, J., Hall, J.: Curve tessellation criteria through sampling. In: Graphics Gems III, pp. 262–265(1992)

15. http://www.xbow.com/pdf/telos_pr.pdf

16. Rahimi, M., Safabakhsh, R.: Adaptation of sampling in target tracking sensor networks. In: 2010 IEEE International Conference on Wireless Communications, Networking and Information Security (WCNIS), pp. 301–305. IEEE (2010)

17. Alippi, C., Anastasi, G., Francesco, D., Roveri, M.: An adaptive sampling algorithm for effective energy management in wireless sensor networks with energy-hungry sensors. IEEE Trans. Instrum. Meas. **59**(2), 335–344 (2010)

18. Jain, A., Chang, E.Y.: Adaptive sampling for sensor networks. In: Proceeedings of the 1st International Workshop on Data Management for Sensor Networks: in Conjunction with VLDB 2004, pp. 10–16. ACM (2004)

19. Law, Y.W., Chatterjea, S., Jin, J., Hanselmann, T., Palaniswami, M.: Energy-efficient data acquisition by adaptive sampling for wireless sensor networks. In: Proceedings of the 2009 International Conference on Wireless Communications and Mobile Computing: Connecting the World Wirelessly, pp. 1146–1151. ACM (2009)

20. Padhy, P., Dash, R.K., Martinez, K., Jennings, N.R.: A utility-based sensing and communication model for a glacial sensor network. In: Proceedings of the Fifth International Joint Conference on Autonomous Agents and Multiagent Systems, pp. 1353–1360. ACM (2006)

Constructing Virtual Backbone with Bounded Diameters in Cognitive Radio Networks

Wenchao Li[1], Jiguo Yu[1（✉）], Dongxiao Yu[2], and Baogui Huang[1]

[1] School of Information Science and Engineering, Qufu Normal University,
Rizhao 276826, Shandong, People's Republic of China
li_wenchao1314@126.com, jiguoyu@sina.com, hjbaogui@163.com
[2] Department of Computer Science, The University of Hong Kong,
Pokfulam, Hong Kong, People's Republic of China
dxyu@cs.hku.hk

Abstract. Cognitive radio networks (CRNs) have been recognized as a promising communication paradigm to permit cognitive users (CUs) to access spectrum bands, which are allocated to primary users (PUs). Virtual backbones have brought about many benefits for routing and data transmission in traditional wireless networks, which also have been studied broadly. Virtual backbones also play an important role in CRNs, which would help increase the efficiency of routing and data transmission. The smaller virtual backbones require less maintenance cost. Unfortunately, computing the minimum virtual backbone is NP-hard, meanwhile, in CRNs, due to the stochastic activities of PUs, the links between CUs are unstable. Therefore, there exists a large probability that the virtual backbone becomes invalid, which incurs many works on CRNs concerning about the maximum lifetimes of virtual backbones. However, people neglect other important metrics of the network, such as diameter and average hop distances between two communication nodes. In this paper, we construct the virtual backbone with bounded diameter in CRNs, which constrains the length of the paths on which messages travel. The virtual backbones with bounded diameters save energy of the network and decrease the probability of packet loss and error. We present a centralized algorithm based on the idea of BFS tree to construct a virtual backbone with bounded diameter. To the best of our knowledge, this is the first work to address a virtual backbone satisfying bounded diameter in CRNs.

Keywords: Cognitive radio networks · Virtual backbone · Diameter · BFS tree

1 Introduction

Wireless radio spectrum is one of the most precious resources in wireless communications, which has been divided into small range of licensed spectrums and

---

This work was partially supported by the NNSF of China for contract 61373027 and NSF of Shandong Province for contract ZR2012FM023.

K. Xu and J. Zhu (Eds.): WASA 2015, LNCS 9204, pp. 809–819, 2015.
DOI: 10.1007/978-3-319-21837-3_79

unlicensed spectrums (also called channels) by traditional spectrum allocation policy. With the rapid growing requirement on the rare wireless radio spectrum and the services provided by mobile devices being everywhere, it poses great pressure to the already crowded spectrum bands. On the other hand, Federal Communication Committee reported that the large part of licensed spectrums are under-utilized in time and space due to current static spectrum management policy. The inefficiency of limited spectrum resources prompts spectrum regulatory bodies to review their policy-static spectrum allocation, and start to find new communication technique, which can use more intelligent and convenient way to utilize wireless spectrum. They present the concept of Cognitive Radio (CR) to address the spectrum under-utilization problem. In recent years, CR has drawn more and more attention, since it endows each user an ability, which permits users adjusting their operation parameters optimally according to their communication with surrounding environment. CR admits unlicensed users accessing licensed spectrum bands which are not being occupied by licensed users temporarily. CR achieves opportunistic spectrum access on licensed spectrum, which is a promising technique to alleviate the absence of spectrum and improve the efficiency of the spectrum.

CRNs contain two kinds of users, namely, primary users (PUs, or licensed users) and cognitive users (CUs, or secondary users). PUs pay for specific spectrum band authority while other users in the same area called CUs need not pay for it. Each CU equipped with CR detects whether there exist any idle licensed channels. If do, CUs can access the idle channels without causing interferences to PUs. CUs must vacate all the channels which are related to PUs to avoid interference when CUs detect active PUs. Therefore, if channels CUs operate on are reclaimed by PUs, many CUs in CRN must stop their data transmission or switch to another channel to transfer the data which is not being occupied at present. Thus, the appearance of one or more active PUs may cause disconnection of the CRN, especially during the time in which spectrum transformation, and result in the loss and delay of data packet of CUs. CRNs consist of a number of wireless nodes, which are easy to be deployed for an application field. However, the shortcomings of CRNs also limit network performance. Wireless nodes have limited energy, which greatly affect network lifetime. Nodes possess a relatively short transmission range. Therefore, a signal generated by a source can reach only the nodes that are within the maximum transmission range of the source. There is no predefined physical backbone infrastructure for topology control in CRNs, which makes routing-related tasks more complicated to be accomplished. This drawback motivates a virtual backbone to be employed in a CRN. Conceptually, a virtual backbone is a set of nodes that can be benefit to routing. Any non-backbone nodes can send a message to another destination node through simply forwarding the message directly to a neighboring backbone node. Virtual backbone brings several benefits to network routing and management. The routing path search space can be reduced to the set of backbone nodes. Virtual backbones have many important applications in wireless networks, such as data collection [1]. The network topology of CRN changes unpredictably due to the stochastic activities of PUs. In order to decreasing the loss and error of messages and increasing channel utility prompt us to construct virtual backbone with bounded diameters in CRNs.

Theoretically, computing a minimum virtual backbone problem can be formalized into a minimum connected dominating set (CDS) problem [2]. There have been a large amount of algorithms on constructing backbones in traditional networks, which are not suitable for CRNs. There are two reasons why traditional backbone algorithms are not suitable for CRNs. Firstly, the algorithms do not adapt to the channel dynamics in CRNs. For example, in non−CRNs, the available channel set of each node is same. In other words, every channel is available to every node. However, in CRNs, the available channel set of each node changes with the level of PU activities, time and location, which poses new challenges in CRNs to construct virtual backbones. Secondly, the algorithms may not achieve objectives specific to CRNs. For instance, a common channel may not be established due to the lack of underutilized channels. Currently, Lin et al. presented a new algorithm for CDS construction in CRNs, which concentrated on the lifetime of a CDS [3]. Yi et al. presented a fault-tolerant virtual backbone construction algorithm in CRNs, which considered the fault-tolerance of the virtual backbone [4]. However, in addition to lifetime and fault-tolerance, there still exist other important metrics need to be considered. In this paper, we not only consider the size and the lifetime of the virtual backbone, but also take diameter as a metric to analyze the constructed CDS. The diameter of a given connected graph is the length of the longest shortest paths between a pair of nodes in the graph. In fact, for a wireless network, when a message is sent through a longer path (i.e., more intermediate nodes), the probability of messages transmission failure often increases, which illustrates that the CDS with smaller diameter is better. In this paper, we present a new CDS construction algorithm with bounded diameter, which considers available common channel set to prolong the lifetime of the network and decreases the probability of message error and loss.

The rest of this paper is organized as follows: in Sect. 2, we introduce the related works. Section 3 presents the model and definitions. In Sect. 4, we present a CDS construction algorithm with bounded diameter. Finally, Sect. 5 concludes this paper.

2   Related Work

For CDS construction, there have been an abundance of work. Due to space restriction, we have to review some results closely related to our work. For more other work, one can refer to [5] and [6].

Lin et al. presents a new CDS construction algorithm in CRNs [3]. In their work, given a set of available channels between each pair of CUs, the expected lifetime of the communication link between them is computed, from which an edge weighted communication graph is obtained. Then, a CDS computation algorithm is executed over the induced graph to find a CDS. Yi et al. observed the

CDSs constructed in this way have one drawback. The CDSs can suffer from sudden service disruption if the activities of CUs are highly deviated from the expected idle time of the CUs. Based on this observation, Yi et al. presented fault tolerance virtual backbones in CRNs by designing k-connect m-dominating DS extending edge connectivity [4]. Dai et al. proposed a novel approach for constructing virtual backbones in CRNs. This approach first utilizes the geographical information to let the nodes of a CRN self-organize into cells, forming into clusters. Next, the leader is elected in each cell and the a part of leaders form the virtual backbone [7]. Baddour et al. applied affinity propagation (AP) message-passing technique to form clusters in cognitive radio ad hoc networks [8]. This work assumes that the network topology does not change during the procedure of cluster formulation. That is, the nodes are static or move with relatively low speeds and the available channels of every node do not change. Under these foundation, they presented a new approach for constructing clusters in CRNs-affinity propagation message-passing technique. Cai et al. [9] proposed an efficient distributed opportunistic routing protocols for multi-hop multi-channel CRNs. They aim to construct a cross-layer distributed opportunistic routing protocol and consider the channel sensing strategy, which improves end-to-end delay.

There exists few work concentrating on the CDS with bounded diameter. DSs with bounded diameters are convenient to fast communications between pairs of nodes. Kim et al. considers size, diameter and Average Backbone Path Length (ABPL) of CDS in order to constructing a CDS with better quality [10], which has approximation ratios for both CDS size and diameter for the first time.

3   Model and Definition

We consider $M(M \geq 1)$ PUs and coexist with $n(n \geq 2)$ CUs in the same area. PUs are licensed to use fixed spectrums, which can be divided into $[1, 2, ..., M]$ non-overlap licensed spectrums. For convenience, licensed spectrum of each $PU_k(1 \leq k \leq M)$ is denoted by channel c_k, that is, the underlying whole available channel set can be denoted as $C = \{c_1, c_2, ..., c_M\}$. If CUs do not cause interference to PUs which are transmitting, then CUs can access corresponding licensed spectrum.

We use an undirected graph $G = (V, E)$ to represent a CRN, where $V = \{v_1, v_2, ..., v_n\}$ is the set of CUs in the network and E denotes the edge set of corresponding communication links. $(u, v) \in E$ is the transmission link between nodes u and v, which implies both nodes u and v are within the transmission range of each other, and there exists at least one common channel between u and v. Assume that all the nodes are homogeneous (i.e., they have the same transmission range), and thus G is a UDG.

Multiple rendezvous control channel (MRCC) allocates control channel according to random or predetermined channel hopping sequence. The primary goal of this design is to diversify control channel allocation over spectrum and time spaces to minimize the effect of PU activity. Since CUs may use different hopping sequences, different adjacent pairs in a neighborhood may communicate on different control channels. In the MRCC design, the channel hopping sequence is the key factor for dynamic channel access. One can refer to [11] for more detailed content about adaptive MRCC-based construction of hopping sequence. In this paper, we do not assume channel hopping sequence in advance, while change channel hopping sequence with time. We adopt neighbor discovery protocol which is proposed by Loukas et al. [12] to let nodes know the network topology. Namely, assume a time-slotted system for communication, to agree on a common set of control channels in each neighborhood, CUs must discover the network topology and exchange relevant information such as spectrum availability. This can be typically achieved during the neighbor discovery phase. One can refer to [12] to get more detailed information about neighbor discovery. Some notations are listed in the Table 1.

Table 1. Notations

r	a root node
$|N_i|$	the degree of node i
e_i	the energy level of node i
ID_i	the unique identifier of node i
C_i	the available channel set sensed by node i
$W(|C_i|, e_i, |N_i|, ID_i)$	a weight function to evaluate the importance of node i
Hopdist(i, j)	the hop distance from node i to j on the shortest path between them
Diam(D)	the diameter of the subgraph $G[D]$ induced by a CDS D, which is equal to the maximum Hopdist (i, j)

A *dominating set* (DS) of a graph $G = (V, E)$ is a set of nodes D, where $\forall (v, w) \in E$, $v \in D$ or $w \in D$. A *connected dominating set* (CDS) of a graph $G = (V, E)$ is a DS D such that the subgraph $G[D]$ induced by D is connected. We call the nodes in the CDS the dominators and otherwise the dominatees. The size of a CDS is the number of the dominators in the CDS. The diameter of a CDS is the maximum distance between any two nodes of the CDS.

Weight Function: Given two 4−tuple variables $(|C_i|, e_i, |N_i|, ID_i)$ and $(|C_j|, e_j, |N_j|, ID_j)$, the weight function $W(|C|, e, |N|, ID) \rightarrow R$ satisfies $W(|C_i|, e_i, |N_i|, ID_i) > W(|C_j|, e_j, |N_j|, ID_j)$ if any of the following conditions is true:

(1)$|C_i| > |C_j|$, or (2)$|C_i| = |C_j|$ and $e_i > e_j$, or (3)$|C_i| = |C_j|$, $e_i = e_j$ and $|N_i| > |N_j|$, or (4)$|C_i| = |C_j|$, $e_i = e_j$, $|N_i| = |N_j|$ and $ID_i > ID_j$.

Two nodes u and v are brothers if they are adjacent and Hopdist$(r, u) =$ Hopdist(r, v). A node u is a parent node of v, and v is the child node of u if nodes u and v are adjacent and Hopdist$(r, u) + 1 =$ Hopdist(r, v). If a CDS node (black node) does not have a child CDS node, the CDS node is a terminal node. If a terminal node does not have brother CDS node, the terminal node is an edge node. Figure 1 shows an example for these terminologies.

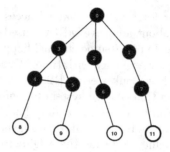

Fig. 1. Nodes 4, 5, 6, and 7 are terminal nodes. Node 6, 7 are also edge nodes.

4   The CDS Construction Algorithm

The fundamental idea of the proposed algorithm is constructing a BFS tree. During the execution procedure of the centralized algorithm, if PUs reclaim the channels occupied by CUs, then corresponding CUs must vacate the channels and transfer into another available channel. Therefore, until a pair of communication nodes transfer into the same channel, do they receive messages.

4.1   How to Successfully Transfer in a Channel

We adopted the success probability of self-organization process of [7] to illustrate how to successfully transfer into a channel. We utilize the idea of Algorithm 1 in [13] to select the spare communication channel when the channel is unavailable which is being used by the node at present.

If the channel being used by node i is reclaimed by PUs, node i needs to choose another available channel again. Assume that the number of channels which is available to the communication pairs at present is m among the $|C|$ channels, where $|C|$ denotes the number of total channels. Let u_k and v_k denote the mean busy and idle durations on the kth channel of the $|C|$ channels respectively. Let $X_k = 1$ or 0 denote whether the kth channel is available or not. X_k follows the Bernoulli distribution with parameter $\frac{v_k}{u_k+v_k}$. Assume that the PUs activities on different channels are independent. If $v_k = v$ and $u_k = u$ for all channels k, then $m = \sum_{k=1}^{|C|} X_k$ follows the Binomial distribution with parameters $\frac{v}{u+v}$ and $|C|$. Furthermore, not every channel is available to every node among the m channels due to the spacial diversity of channel availability. Therefore, when node i transfers into channel k, the other node j of the communication pair may not transfer into channel k. Let p denote the probability that a channel among the available channels is chosen by a node as a spare communication channel. Given m and p, we can analyze the success probability of transferring into the same channel.

Lemma 4.1. Let Z_{ik} denote the event that node i selects the kth channel among the m channels as its spare communication channel. Then the probability of Z_{ik}, denoted as β, is given as $\beta = Pr(Z_{ik}) = \frac{1}{m}(1 - (1-p)^m)$.

Note that β only depends on the m and p. Let node i be a sender and node j be a receiver. Let γ denote the probability that node j can meet the node i in the m available channels. We have the following theorem.

Theorem 4.1. $\gamma = m\beta p$.

Proof. The probability that node j can meet node i on $k^{th}(1 \leq k \leq m)$ channel among the m available channels is βp, i.e., if node i selects the kth channel as spare communication channel and the kth channel is available to node i. The total probability that node i meets node j in any of the m channels is $\sum_{k=1}^{m} \beta p = m\beta p$.

The value of γ is presented in Fig. 2.

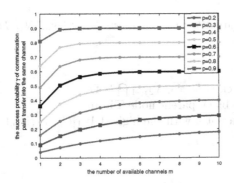

Fig. 2. The probability of communication nodes transfer into the same channel.

After node i choosing channel k, the node j listens to the same channel with probability γ. If they choose the same channel, the transmission will be successful. Any communication node pairs can transfer into the same channel through the same process.

4.2 A Centralized Algorithm for CDS with Bounded Diameter (CDS-BD)

In this section, we utilize the idea of [12] to construct a CDS with bounded diameter in CRNs.

The pseudo codes of CDS-BD algorithm are shown in Algorithm 1.

Algorithm 1. CDS-BD
suppose all nodes in $G(V, E)$ are white initially.

---

1. Choose a node with largest weight function value as a root $r \in V$ (e.g., using a leader selection algorithm)
2. Compute the hop distance from r to each node (e.g., using breadth first search)
3. Let $V_k = \{y \in V | \text{Hopdist(r, y)} = k\}$ and k_{max} be the maximum k

4. For all even k, find an MIS I_k of G_k, the subgraph of G induced by V_k

5. Let $I = \bigcup_{even k} I_k$

6. Color every node in I black and all nodes adjacent to the black nodes grey

7. While a white node $x \in V$ exists **Do**

8.   Color x black and all of its white neighbors in grey

9. end While

10. Denote B as the set of black nodes in V

11. Let $i^* = \lceil k_{max}/2 \rceil$

12. For $j = 1$ to i^* **Do**

13.   **For** every black node $x \in V_{2j} \cap B$ **Do**

14.   If y is $x's$ parent with the highest $W(|C_y|, e_y, |N_y|, ID_y)$ **Then**

15.   color y black.

16.   **end If**

17.   If z is $y's$ parent with the highest $W(|C_z|, e_y, |N_z|, ID_z)$ **Then**

18.   color z black

19.   **end If**

20.   **end For**

21.   **For** every black node $x \in V_{2j-1} \cap B$ **Do**

22.   If x has no black parent node **Then**

23.   color its parent y with the highest $W(|C_y|, e_y, |N_y|, ID_y)$ black

24.   **end If**

25.   **end For**

26. end For

27. Add all the black nodes into D

28. Return D

Theorem 4.2. D returned by CDS-BD is a CDS.

Proof. After line 10 of Algorithm 1, all nodes are black or grey. All black nodes (set B) form a DS. Now, we need to prove that the subgraph $G[D]$ induced by set D through adding more black nodes to set B is connected. If $G[D]$ is connected, there exists a path between any black node to root r except root r. Therefore, we utilize induction to prove D connected by proving that there exists a path which only contains black nodes between every black node $x \in D \setminus r$ and r.

Let x be a black node in V_{2i}. When $i = 1$, from line 14 to line 18, we know that x is connected to r since r is the only parent node of x. Suppose that $i = k$, all black nodes connect to r. For a black node $x \in V_{2(k+1)}$, we color $y \in V_{2k+1}$ and $z \in V_{2k}$ black. Then z is in D or one of its neighbors is in D. Therefore, for all i, black node $x \in V_{2i}$ is connected to r.

Furthermore, for any isolated black node $x \in V_{2i-1}$, according to line 10 to line 21 of Algorithm 1, does not have black parent node, then colors parent node $y \in V_{2i-2}$ with maximum $W(|C_y|, e_y, |N_y|, ID_y)$ black. If y is not black, then one neighbor of node y must be black and it connects to r. If y has been a black node and it has already connected to root r. Therefore isolated black node x connects to r, therefore, black node set D is a CDS.

Theorem 4.3. Every black node in V_k is away from root r within a distance of at most T_k, where $T_i = \begin{cases} \frac{3}{2}i - \frac{1}{2} & i \in (1, 3, 5...) \\ \frac{3}{2}i - 1 & i \in (2, 4, 6...) \end{cases}$

Proof. Let D_i be the distance of a node in V_i to root r. According to line 14 to line 18 of Algorithm 1, if k is even, then we need to color at most two nodes black. Assume nodes y and z are the two nodes to connect the black node to root r. Therefore, the distance between a node at level k to a node at level $k - 2$ is at most 3, i.e., we have

$$D_2 = 2, \; D_4 \le D_2 + 3, \; ..., \; D_k \le D_{k-2} + 3$$

Thus, we have $D_k \le 3(\frac{k}{2} - 1) + D_2$. From lines 19 to 21, if k is an odd number, we only need to add one node in level $k - 1$. Therefore, $D_k \le D_{k-1} + 2 = \frac{3}{2}k - \frac{1}{2}$. Since T_i is the maximum D_i, the theorem is true.

Theorem 4.4. Let D be the CDS obtained from the CDS-BD algorithm. Then, $|D| \le 10.2918opt + 12.4555$, where opt is the size of any optimal CDS of G, and $Diam(D) \le 3D_{opt} + 22.879$, where D_{opt} is the diameter of any optimal CDS of G.

Proof. Let P denote the longest shortest path from a node u to a node v in the original graph G. The length p of path P equals the diameter $Diam$ of graph G, according to the definition of diameter. It is obvious $Diam \ge k_{max}$ since we construct a BFS tree firstly. Suppose that there exists a path P' between node u and node v, which only contains the nodes in the set D except for u and v. The length p' of path P' is not smaller than the diameter of graph G. If nodes u and v are dominates, then $Diam(G[D]) < |p' - 2|$. Therefore, $D_{opt} \ge |p'| - 2 \ge D - 2 \ge k_{max} - 2$.

From [14], the size of an MIS of graph G is $|B| \le 3.4306opt + 4.8185$. We let all nodes in I be connectted by adding at most $2(|I| - 1)$ nodes. Therefore, $|D| \le 3|B| - 2 = 10.2918opt + 12.4555$. As shown above, $k_{max} - 2 \le D_{opt}$. The maximum distance from any edge node to r is $\frac{3}{2}k_{max} - \frac{1}{2}$ according to Theorem 4.3. Hence, $Diam(D) \le 2(\frac{3}{2}k_{max} - \frac{1}{2}) = 3k_{max} - 1 = 3(k_{max} - 2) + 5 \le 3D_{opt} + 5$.

Theorem 4.5. The time complexity of CDS-BD is $O(n^2)$.

Proof. Algorithm 1 finds root r (e.g., utilizing leader election algorithm) at first, then uses BFS algorithm to layer all nodes in the network. In worst case, BFS tree must find the path of all nodes. Thus, the time complexity in the worst case is $O(n^2)$. For all even k to find an MIS, the time complexity of the worst case is $O(n \log n)$. The operation of node coloring can be done within constant time. Hence, line 1 to line 11 at most consume $O(n^2)$ time. Line 12 starts adding other black nodes to B to connect nodes in B, forming D. We analyze every line of codes. Every black node needs to check all its neighbors and chooses the node with largest weight function W as its parent, which is colored black. The whole process consume time $O(n)$. Since every black node need to check at most n nodes, namely at most loop n times. Hence, the time complexity of the algorithm is $O(n^2)$.

5 Conclusion

In this paper, we study the problem of constructing a virtual backbone with bounded diameter in CRNs, which decreases the consumption of energy efficiently and prolongs the lifetime of the network. This is the first work to investigate virtual backbones with bounded diameters in CRNs. We proposed a centralized algorithm satisfying specific constant performance ratio on the size and the diameter of the CDS. The performance ratio is still inefficient compared to the one of the virtual backbone in the traditional wireless network. We can further optimize the performance ratio and study the compromise between the size and the diameter of the CDS in the future work. We also consider constructing a CDS satisfying other requirements in CRNs simultaneously, such as fault tolerance, self-stabilizing and load-balanced.

References

1. Ji, S., Li, Y., Jia, X.: Capacity of dual-radio multi-channel wireless sensor networks for continuous data collection. In: Proceedings of IEEE INFOCOM, pp. 1062–1070 (2011)
2. Sudipto, G., Samir, K.: Approximation algorithms for connected dominating sets. Algorithmica 20(4), 374–387 (1998)
3. Lin, Z., Liu, H., Chu, X., Leung, Y.-W., Stojmenovic, I.: Maximizing lifetime of connected-dominating-set in cognitive radio networks. In: Bestak, R., Kencl, L., Li, L.E., Widmer, J., Yin, H. (eds.) Networking 2012, part ii. LNCS, vol. 7290, pp. 316–330. Springer, Heidelberg (2012)
4. Yi, H., Kim, D., Li, D., Zhong, J., Tokuta, A. O.: On computing resilient virtual backbone in CRNs. In: Proceedongs of IEEE ICISA, pp. 1–4 (2014)
5. Du, D., Wan, P.: Connected Dominating Set: Theory and Applications. Springer, Heidelberg (2012)
6. Yu, J., Wang, N., Wang, G., Yu, D.: Connected dominating sets in wireless ad hoc and sensor networks - a comprehensive survey. Comput. Commun. 36(2), 121–134 (2013)
7. Dai, Y., Wu, J., Xin, C. S.: Virtual backbone construction for cognitive radio networks without common control channel. In: Proceedings of IEEE INFOCOM, pp. 1456–1464 (2013)
8. Kareem, E.B., Üreten, O., Willink, T.J.: A distributed message-passing approach for clustering cognitive radio networks. Wirel. Pers. Commun. 57(1), 119–133 (2011)
9. Cai, Z., Duan, Y., Bourgeois, A.: Delay efficient opportunistic in asynchronous multi-channel cognitive radio networks. J. Comb. Optim. 29(4), 815–835 (2013)
10. Donghyun, K., Wu, Y., Li, Y., Zou, F., Du, D.: Constructing minimum connected dominating sets with bounded diameters in wireless networks. IEEE Trans. Paralell Distrib. Syst. 20(2), 147–157 (2009)
11. Claudia, C., Kaushik, R.C.: Common control channel design for cognitive radio wireless ad hoc networks using adaptive frequency hopping. Ad Hoc Netw. 8(4), 430–438 (2010)
12. Loukas, L., Liu, S., Krunz, M.: Spectrum opportunity-based control channel assignment in cognitive radio networks. In: Proceedings of IEEE SECON, pp. 1–9 (2009)

13. Xin, C., Song, M., Ma, L., Shen, C.C.: Performance analysis of a control-free dynamic spectrum access scheme. IEEE Trans. Wirel. Commun. **10**(12), 4316–4323 (2011)
14. Li, M., Wan, P., Yao, F.: Tighter approximation bounds for minimum CDS in unit disk graphs. Algorithmica **61**(4), 1000–1021 (2011)

A Simplified Attack-Defense Game Model for NSSA

Xueyan Sun, Xiaowu Liu$^{(\boxtimes)}$, and Shuwen Zhang

School of Computer Science and Engineering, Qufu Normal University,
Rizhao 276826, Shandong, People's Republic of China
{s_xy1209,zhangshuwen_happy}@126.com
liuxw@mail.qfnu.edu.cn

Abstract. Most of the existing traditional network security situation assessment methods tend to consider the attacker and defender separately and the mechanisms mainly focus on the theory analysis which are difficult to be applied into the real network environment. In view of the above-mentioned problems, this paper proposes a simplified attack-defense game model for NSSA firstly. Secondly, a hierarchical indicators system is established in order to evaluate the awareness ability of our model and methods. Thirdly, we adopt the improved fuzzy analytic hierarchy process to carry out our quantitative method according to the indicator system. Finally, we executed the simulation experiments and the results show that the model is feasible and effective.

Keywords: Network security situation awareness · Attack-defense game model · Fuzzy analytic hierarchy process

1 Introduction

With the rapid development of network and communication technology, computer network security problems are exposing increasingly. As a result, various network crimes are emerging continuously. The network security is facing with the great threats and challenges. Using the new network attack techniques and tools, attacks appear the random, diversity and hidden features [1]. Some evaluation methods based on rules or scanning tools can only assess the security states of partial network, although many evaluation models have been proposed [2,3]. The attacker and the defender are regarded as two basic components in the network security administration and the zero-sum non-cooperative game is applied into the process of threat evaluation [4]. A complex threat propagation model for network security is proposed and the Markov Game method is adopted to analyze the threat, the administrators' and ordinary users' behavior [5]. According to the models mentioned above, the game security models are becoming a novel method to deal with the problems of network security. However,most of the

We should thank the Shandong Province Higher Educational Science and Technology Plan (Grant No. J11LG09) for its support for this work.

K. Xu and J. Zhu (Eds.): WASA 2015, LNCS 9204, pp. 820–828, 2015.
DOI: 10.1007/978-3-319-21837-3_80

existing models are static and too simple to be used in a complex network. This leads to the fact that these models are difficult to reflect the dynamic changing of the attack-defense and achieve real-time evaluation in the realistic environment.

In this paper, we proposed a simplified attack-defense game model for Network Security Situation Awareness(NSSA). This model can define the situation indicators and describe the relationship of attack-defense which provides an effective expression for network behavior.

2   Simplified Attack-Defense Game Model

According to the game theory and the study of NSSA, a situation awareness framework based on simplified ADGM is constructed as shown in Fig. 1. The framework is composed of four components including the indicators extraction, quantification of indicators, the ADGM analysis and the security situation evaluation.

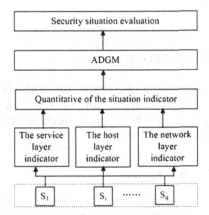

Fig. 1. NSSA framework based on ADGM

The bottom of the model contains many different types of sensors which are used to collect state information in the running network system. The indicator extraction component is used to collect the key indicators according to the all kinds of sensors setup in the network environment. The Network Security Situation Indicator(NSSI) system is divided into the three layers and Fuzzy Analytic Hierarchy Process(FAHP) is adopt to quantify the indicators in every layer. The ADGM component is used to determine the target node and executes the game analysis for network system. The security situation is evaluated by using the outputs of ADGM component. Lastly, the security situation component is the highest part of our framework and is regarded as a reference for the administrator to make a right and real-time decision which can improve the security level of network under monitored.

The most important part in our framework is ADGM. The simplified ADGM is described as a three tuples and represented by G, $G = (P, S, U)$. In this paper, only the attacker and the defender are taken into consideration. That is to say, $P = (P^1, P^2)$ is a vector and consists of the attacker and the defender in the game. $S = (S^1, S^2)$ is a vector which includes strategies of both sides. Similarly, utility function of both sides is also a vector, $U = (U^1, U^2)$. Simplified model for network attack-defense based on game theory shown in Fig. 2. Under this condition, our simplified ADGM model can be demonstrated using Fig. 2 and formalized as $ADGM = ((P^1, P^2), (S^1, S^2), (U^1, U^2))$.

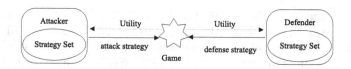

Fig. 2. The simplified ADGM

3   NSSA Indicator System

The determination and obtaining of NSSI is one of the key parts to NSSA. It helps the analysts to understand the factors of NSSA and is an indispensable component in our simplified ADGM. So, a hierarchical NSSI system is adopted in order to analyze different threat factors.

3.1   Parameters of NSSI System

The running state of the service layer, the host layer and the network layer are different aspects to reflect the security status of the whole network system. Firstly, the basic function of the service layer is to provide different services for certain application and this layer is equipped with various types of sensors to collect alarm and vulnerability information. In this paper, we choose the response time, the number of half connections, the frequency of attacks and the type of attacks as the original service data. Besides, the NSSI of service layer also includes the software failure,the application bug number and so on. Secondly, the NSSI of host layer is mainly comprised of the CPU occupancy ratio, the memory utilization ratio, the process status and the disk utilization ratio. Thirdly, the NSSI of network layer is composed of the transmission delay, the packet loss rate, the transmission rate, the bandwidth utilization rate and so on.

3.2   Analysis and quantification of NSSI

We employ the improved FAHP method [6] to obtain relative objective decision for the indicators in different NSSI system layers. This method transforms the priority relation matrix into fuzzy consistent matrix that it satisfies the consistency condition without the need to carry out the consistency test and it can greatly reduce the number of iterations to improve the convergence rate. The specific steps are described as follows.

(1) Priority Relation Matrix. Establishing priority relation matrix $F = (f_{ij})_{n*n}$, where f_{ij} is defined as Eq. (1). In which $c(i)$ and $c(j)$ are the relative importance degree of the indicators f_i and f_j. Then, we adopt FAHP method to sum up f_{ij} according to row i of F and obtain q_i, $q_i = \sum_{j=1}^{n} f_{ij}$. And the fuzzy matrix $Q = (q_{ij})_{n*n}$ is formed using Eq. (2).

$$f_{ij} = \begin{cases} 0 & c(i) < c(j) \\ 0.5 & c(i) = c(j) \\ 1 & c(i) > c(j) \end{cases} \tag{1}$$

$$q_{ij} = \frac{q_i - q_j}{2n} + 0.5 \tag{2}$$

(2) Weight Vector. We utilize the sum-row normalizing method to generate the weight vector. The weight vector is calculated by Eq. (3), where h_i indicates the importance of ith indicator of current layer. So, we can get each normalized indicator weight under the help of Eq. (4). Then the weight vector $\omega^0 = (\omega_1, \omega_2, \ldots, \omega_n)^T$ is obtained.

$$h_i = \sum_{j=1}^{n} q_{ij} - 0.5 \qquad (i = 1, 2, \ldots, n) \tag{3}$$

$$\omega_i = h_i / \sum_{i}^{n} h_i \tag{4}$$

(3) Comprehensive Evaluation. In this step, the most advanced indicators are assessed with the aim of achieving comprehensive evaluation using Eq. (5) in which A is the comprehensive evaluation of the most advanced indicator, R is the fuzzy evaluation matrix.

$$A = \omega \circ R \tag{5}$$

4   Situation evaluation based on ADGM

In the game process,the attacker and defender desire to maximize their own benefits by the optimal strategy, so we assume that he attacker and defender are rational enough and the conflicts between them can be regarded as a type of strategic game. Thereby, we can obtain the attack intention and the optimal defense strategy through the calculation of Nash Equilibrium(NE).

4.1   Quantitative Analysis of ADGM

In the study of NSSA, the attacker generally refers to all kinds of potential attacks and intrusions in network system. the defender indicates the security softwares and safety operations. Nevertheless, the defender is to take security mechanism into effect for assuring the normal operation of network system with the aim of preventing the network from being attacked or compromised. The strategy spaces, the utility functions and the NE of both sides will be described below.

(1) Strategies Space. The attacker's strategy set of P^1 is classified into five categories: $S^1 = (s_1^1, s_2^1, s_3^1, s_4^1, s_5^1)$, which includes the Root, the User, the Data,the DOS and the other categories. The defender's strategy set S^2 of P^2 is divided into two types marked as defensive measures d and the measures ϕ (empty strategy), that is $S^2 = (d, \phi)$.

(2) Utility Function. In the ADGM, We assume that only one attack and defense strategy is adopted at a moment. Firstly, the utility function of attacker is designed using Eq. (6).

$$U_1(s^1, s^2) = \sum_{i=1}^{n_1} wei_i * AV_N * per_N * AS_i \tag{6}$$

In Eq. (6), n_1 is the number of strategies of the P^1, AV_N and per_N indicate the availability and performance of the network, wei_i is the importance weight of attack strategy, AS_i represents the attack severity (AS). The availability of network is confirmed by computing resources which directly effect the performance of network system. It includes the CPU utilization ratio, the memory utilization ratio and so on. Then the network availability can be obtained using Eq. (7) where AV_i is the ith kind of availability of network computing resources, ω_i is the indicator weight of all kinds of computing resources. The network performance is composed of the response time, the transmission delay and so on. The performance of network system can be depicted using Eq. (8) where per_i is the changes of the ith factors after the invasions, ω_i indicates the importance weight of the indicators in the network performance.

$$AV_N = 1 - \Pi_{i=1}^3 (1 - AV_i * \omega_i) \tag{7}$$

$$per_N = \sum_{i=1}^3 per_i * \omega_i \tag{8}$$

Secondly, we formalize the utility function of the P^2 as shown in Eq. (9), where n_2 is the number of defense strategies, k_i is the false detection rate of the defender, wei_i implies the importance weight of the strategy for defending the intrusion.

$$U_2(s^1, s^2) = \sum_{i=1}^{n_2} (1 - k_i) * wei_i \tag{9}$$

(3) NE. We define the mixed strategy NE [7] as the optimal mixed strategy of two-player. The optimal mixed strategy is to maximize the expected utilities of the players. We adopted the maximum payment method [8]. Then, the expected benefits of both sides can be described as $\pi_1(p_1, p_2) = \sum_{i=1}^{m} p_{1i} \sum_{j=1}^{n} p_{2j} U_1$ and $\pi_2(p_1, p_2) = \sum_{j=1}^{n} p_{2j} \sum_{i=1}^{m} p_{1i} U_2$. p_1 and p_2 are the probability distributions of the mixed strategies of both sides. m and n are the number of strategies of both sides. U_1 and U_2 are the utilities of them. $\pi_1(p_1, p_2)$ and $\pi_2(p_1, p_2)$ are the expected benefits of both sides. We can calculate the NE according to the aforementioned π_1 and π_2.

5   Simulation Experiments and Analysis

In order to verify the validity of our proposed model, a network topology is designed and shown in Fig. 3. The following will describe the configuration of the simulation network. The attacker has Root permissions to a host and it can launch an attack freely. The vulnerability analysis of the target system is executed using the scanning software. And the host information, the attack vulnerability information and the corresponding AS values are shown in Table 1.

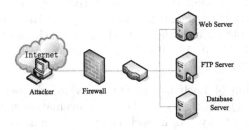

Fig. 3. The network organization simulation structure

Table 1. Vulnerabilities of the server

Host	vuls	Value(AS)
Web server	Apache Chunked Enc	1.0
FTP server	Wu-Ftpd SockPrintf()	1.0
	Ftp.rhost overwrite	0.5
Database server	Oracle TNS Listener	1.0
	Local buffer overflow	1.0

5.1   Situation Indicators Analysis

(1) Weight Vector. In order to make the calculation more simple, the hierarchical NSSI quantitative analysis is labeled as $N = S(I_1, I_2, I_3) =$

$S(D(I_{11}, I_{12}, I_{13}, I_{14}), D(I_{21}, I_{22}, I_{23}, I_{24}), D(I_{31}, I_{32}, I_{33}, I_{34}))$. N is the security situation of the system, S and D represent the overall network system and the each layer of the comprehensive evaluation function. I_1, I_2 and I_3 denote the sets of quantitative indicators of three layers respectively. We construct the priority relation matrix for quantitative indicators of each layer at first. Taking the I_3 (the network layer) as an example, we can build the priority relation matrix based on the experience of the experts as shown in Table 2.

Table 2. Priority relation matrix of I_3

I_3	I_{31}	I_{32}	I_{33}	I_{34}
I_{31}	0.5	1.0	1.0	0.5
I_{32}	0.0	0.5	0.0	0.0
I_{33}	0.0	1.0	0.5	0.0
I_{34}	0.5	1.0	1.0	0.5

Then, the weight vector ω_{I_3} of I_3 indicator can be obtained as following in the network layer of the indicator system, $\omega_{I_3} = (0.3333 \quad 0.125 \quad 0.2083 \quad 0.3333)$ according to Eqs. (2–4). Similarly, the quantitative indicators weight vectors of other layers (the service layer and the host layer) and the comprehensive evaluation can also be obtained as the network layer which can be represented as $\omega_{I_1} = (0.2083 \quad 0.1667 \quad 0.250 \quad 0.375)$, $\omega_{I_2} = (0.25 \quad 0.25 \quad 0.2916 \quad 0.2083)$, $\omega_N = (0.4167 \quad 0.3333 \quad 0.25)$.

(2) Fuzzy Evaluation of Each Layer. The fuzzy matrix can be expressed as $R = (R_{I_1}, R_{I_2}, R_{I_3})$, which R_{I_i} is the fuzzy evaluation matrix of the indicators in the I_i. The fuzzy sets in each layer are formulated and the security grades are configured to five levels, $Level = \{Very\ security, Security, Warning, Dangerous, Very\ dangerous\}$. We can gain the quantization indicators of fuzzy matrix in each layer. Take R_{I_3} as an example and the indicators are shown in Table 3.

Table 3. Hierarchical fuzzy matrix

Fuzzy matrix R	Indicators	Level of fuzzy comprehensive evaluation				
		Very security	Security	Warning	Dangerous	Very dangerous
R_{I_3}	I_{31}	0.2	0.3	0.3	0.2	0.0
	I_{32}	0.4	0.4	0.1	0.1	0.0
	I_{33}	0.1	0.4	0.4	0.1	0.0
	I_{34}	0.2	0.5	0.2	0.1	0.0

Then, the indicators of service layer and host layer can be calculated similar to R_{I_3} and the NSSI is constructed by three vectors, $R_{I_1} = (0.2958\ 0.3147\ 0.2875\ 0.0750\ 0)$, $R_{I_2} = (0.1542\ 0.3791\ 0.3916\ 0.0750\ 0)$ and $R_{I_3} = (0.2042\ 0.4000\ 0.2625\ 0.1333\ 0)$. The most advanced comprehensive evaluation results can be calculated using Eq. (5), $N = (0.2257\,0.3687\,0.3156\,0.0896\,0)$. The performance and availability indicators which obtained by the network monitoring software are different in deeper extent after the network system was attacked. We produce the evolution curve of network availability and show it in Fig. 4 through analyzing and processing the relevant characteristic indicators in attacked network system. From this figure, we can conclude that the availability is declined gradually along with the attack carried on.

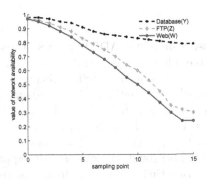

Fig. 4. Value of availability

5.2   Results Analysis of ADGM

According to calculation and analysis of the NSSI in Sect. 5.1, we should calculate the benefits of both sides under the help of Eqs. (6–9) and generate the evolution view of NSSA by adopting the ADGM. In other words, we can obtain the utilities of the both sides at the moment of sampling points. We demonstrate the simulation evolution view in Fig. 5.

When the experiment was carried out to the sampling point 7 or 15, the benefit of the attacker was declined. It is due to the defender has taken the security tools or measures and accomplished the detection of the attacks. In the final of our experiments, the benefit of network attacker was increased to 0.5 while the defender's benefit was dropped to 0.3. It lied in that the security means

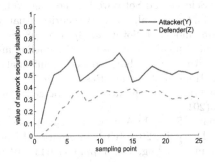

Fig. 5. Simulation evolution view

that the defender adopted took into effect against the malicious intrusion behaviors. After the comprehensive analysis, the simplified ADGM takes the security behavior and the network system configuration into consideration.eventually, ADGM adopts the values of utility functions of both sides to reflect the current network security situation. Compared with the existing models, our model can make administrators to perceive the security degree of the network system more intuitively and concretely.

6   Conclusion

In this paper,we propose a simplified ADGM for NSSA firstly. We also establish the NSSI system in three different layers and adopt the improved FAHP-based method to quantify the indicators in NSSI. Moreover, we discuss a network quantitative method based on game theory in accordance with the viewpoint of network attack-defense, it can get the benefits of both sides in order to accomplish the NSSA analysis. The NSSI system can portray the characteristics of the monitored network and the quantification game analysis can perceive the network state dynamically. This provides a novel security approach for the analysts to monitor and administrate their networks. Simulation results verify the feasibility and effectiveness of the proposed model and methods. However, our current research only take two sides including attacker and defender into account. We will devote ourselves to considering more than one attacker and applying our model into more complex network environment.

References

1. An, B., Tambe, M.: Game theory for security: an important challenge for multiagent systems. In: Cossentino, M., Kaisers, M., Tuyls, K., Weiss, G. (eds.) EUMAS 2011. LNCS, vol. 7541, pp. 17–30. Springer, Heidelberg (2012)
2. Rass, S.: On game-theoretic network security provisioning. J. Netw. Syst. Manage. **21**(1), 47–64 (2013)
3. Nuan, L.X., Yang, X.: Game theory for network security. IEEE Commun.Surv. Tutor. **15**(1), 472–486 (2013)
4. Wei, H., He, X.C., Quan, W.H. et al.: A game theoretical attack-defense model oriented to network security situation assessment. In: 2008 IEEE International Conference on Computer Science and Software Engineering, Vol. 3, pp. 498–504 (2008)
5. Yong, Z., Bin, T.X., Lin, C.X., et al.: Network security situation awareness approach based on Markov Game model. J. Softw. **22**(3), 495–508 (2011)
6. Ying, L.: Service-oriented mission critical formal modeling and analysis of the network system security situation. Harbin engineering university (2009)
7. Qun, L.W., Hui, W., Hong, L.J., et al.: Research on active defense technology in network security based on non-cooperative dynamic game theory. J. Comput. Res. Dev. **48**(2), 306–316 (2011)
8. Yi, W.B., Cai, J., Zhang, S. et al.: A network security assessment model based on attack-defense game theory. In: 2010 IEEE International Conference on Computer Application and System Modeling, Vol. 3, pp. 639–643 (2010)

Hadoop-Based Analysis for Large-Scale Click-Through Patterns in 4G Network

Shuqiang Wang[1]($\boxtimes$), Yanyan Shen[1], Jinxing Hu[1], Zhe Xuan[2], and Zhe Lu[1]

[1] Shenzhen Institutes of Advanced Technology,
Chinese Academy of Sciences, Shenzhen, China
{sq.wang,yy.shen,jx.hu,zhe.lu}@siat.ac.cn
[2] Huawei Central Research Institute, Shenzhen, China
David.zhe1@gmail.com

Abstract. In this work, we focus on understanding what happens under the hood of HTTP traffic. We proposed a systematic approach to reconstruct users click-through patterns in web starting from raw network data. We validated the proposed method using a synthesized network traffic data set and a real-world 4G network traffic data set. The precision calculated by the proposed model is 93.7 % and the recall is 91.6 %. The experiment results on the real-world 4G network traffic data show that the click-through stream of 4G network is more deeper than that of 3G network.

Keywords: Click-through pattern · Big data · 4G network · Users request

1 Introduction

Over the last decade, the web has evolved from simple text content from one server to a complex ecosystem with different types of content from servers spread across several administrative domains. Originally used to host text and images, web pages now include several content types, ranging from videos to scripts executed on the clients device to rich" media such as Flash and Silver-light. Besides, a website today fetches content not only from servers hosted by its providers but also from a range of third party services such as advertising agencies, content distribution networks, and analytic services [1–3]. Understanding these changes is important for overall system design. For example, analyzing end-user browsing behavior can lead to a Web traffic model, which in turn can be used to generate a synthetic workload for benchmark or simulation. Most prior work on web measurement focuses on characterizing the Web graph [4,5], analyzing the network footprint of Web traffic [6–10]. While these have contributed to a better understanding of web usage, they do not analyze what happens under the hood of HTTP traffic and users click through behavior.

HTTP is the new IP in the Web 2.0 world, and traffic analysis methods need to adapt to this new reality. First, web browsers are being used as the

© Springer International Publishing Switzerland 2015
K. Xu and J. Zhu (Eds.): WASA 2015, LNCS 9204, pp. 829–835, 2015.
DOI: 10.1007/978-3-319-21837-3_81

ubiquitous interface to a large number of services and applications, such as Email, gaming, file sharing, video streaming, and social networking sites. Second, today HTTP is the most widely used protocol, contributing up to 80 % of the traffic on some networks [11]. Given the above trends, it is increasingly important for network administrators to monitor and characterize web traffic for operational and security purposes. The more information administrators have about the traffic, the more effectively they can manage the network, identify anomalies and prevent attacks. Besides, analyzing web traffic is important for researchers that want to study modern websites and understand their evolution [1,2,12].

In the present work, we propose a systematic approach to recognize users click-through activity using the raw 3G network data. We employ the head request and embedded request to describe the users click-through pattern. The classification rules extracted from both prior knowledge and labeled data sets are applied to distinguish between the head request and embedded request. Experimental results on a real-world 3G network traffic data set show the effectiveness of the proposed method.

2   Problem Formulation

The principal problem we address is the following. Given web traffic collected at a network link, we want to be able to look under the hood and recognize users click-through patterns. The details of our problem can described as: (1) what websites are explicitly requested by a user as opposed to being accessed automatically in the background? (2) what are the typical users click-through patterns?

Addressing the above questions is challenging even when HTTP headers and payloads are not encrypted. First, users often browse multiple websites at the same time, which causes flows and HTTP requests to intermingle. Second, modern web pages are fairly complex which often render a single page generating many HTTP requests towards different web servers. Besides, another challenge involved in large-scale analysis is the big data problem [13,14]. Take the 4G Web data for example, the raw data of each day is about 3 10 TB in a medium-scale city, China. Distributed computing is indispensable for large-scale data analysis. In this work, Hadoop is employed to analyze users click-through pattern from 4G network. In the next section, we will discuss how to group HTTP transactions into user requests and analyze the users click through pattern using Hadoop.

3   Methods for Reconstructing Web-Surfing Activity

The goal of reconstructing users web surfing activity is to group HTTP transactions into users requests. The logic behind the method of reconstructing web surfing activity is illustrated in Fig. 1(b). The proposed approach mainly includes two parts. First, the head HTTP requests are identified by using different features from each web transaction. The employed features include: the type of the object, the size of the web-object, the timing between successive requests, and others. Second, the referring relationships are used to assign the embedded transactions to the corresponding head requests.

To identify the head requests, the following characteristics are exploited. First, the head requests are HTML or XML objects and they have very few incoming edges and many outgoing edges in the referrer graph. At the same time, the nodes in the same user request are very close together in time. On the other hand, HTTP transaction from different user requests are further away from each other in time. Finally, head requests are connected with only one edge, if there is referring relationship among them. In more detail, head request candidates can be detected according to following rules: (a) The content-type of the candidate should be one of following: text/html, text/xhtml, text/shtml and text/xml. (b) Candidates should include at leat K embedded objects. (c) The size of candidates should be larger than V bytes. (d) Candidates URL should not contain the keywords: adserver, ads, widget, and banner. (e) The time gap between candidates and their referrers should be larger than a predefined threshold T.

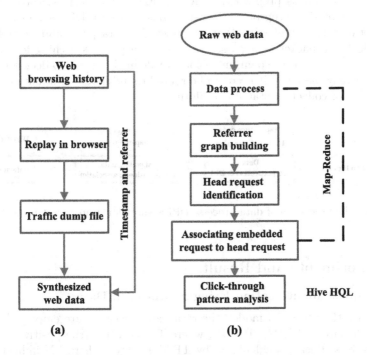

Fig. 1. (a) The diagram shows the steps we take to generate synthesized web traffic by replaying volunteers' browsing history. (b) The framework of reconstructing users' click-through pattern

To train and test the proposed model, A data trace generated in a controlled environment is employed as the benchmark. The web traffic data can be generated by replaying a users browsing history. In this work, the web browsing history from 200 volunteers were employed to generate the synthetic traces. First, the referrer, time-stamp and URL field of each visit from volunteers' browsing history were extracted. Second, each visit were replayed according to the procedure illustrated in Fig. 1(a). The replay of a URL works as follows. The browser was remotely instructed to open each URL separately. Meanwhile, a packet capturing software (tcpdump) was used to collect all the traffic on TCP port 80, 443, 8000 and 8080. the browser closed after 60 seconds and the collected traffic data was saved to an individual file. Finally, the time stamps and referrer fields were artificially adjusted to simulate how the traffic would be like if it came directly from the users surfing activity. Both the referrer relationships and timing information are directly extracted from volunteers' browsing history records (see Fig. 1(a)). After replaying all visits, we merge all these individual files to obtain a complete traffic trace. Since each user activity was collected and stored separately, we get the ground truth for each HTTP request in the trace. Note that the raw web traffic data is of pcap form and signaling data association is necessary. Data preprocess is needed before reconstructing the users web surfing activity. The procedure of data preprocess is given in Fig. 2. The deep packet inspection (DPI) is employed to preprocess the raw web traffic data. DPI is a form of computer network packet filtering that examines the data part (and possibly also the header) of a packet as it passes an inspection point, searching for protocol non-compliance, viruses, spam, intrusions, or defined criteria to decide whether the packet may pass or if it needs to be routed to a different destination, or, for the purpose of collecting statistical information.

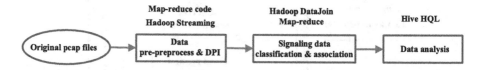

Fig. 2. The procedure of data process (DPI is short for deep packet inspection)

4   Experiments and Results

4.1   Request Identification Using Synthesized Data

To evaluate the proposed model, the recall and precision are employed. Precision is calculated by $TP/(TP+FP)$, where TP indicates true positives and FP false positives. Recall is calculated by $TP/(TP+FN)$, where FN indicated the false negatives. The classification result of head request is shown in Fig. 3. The precision calculated by the proposed model is 93.7% and the recall is 91.6%.

Different classification rule contributes differently to the identification of requests, as shown in Fig. 4. From Fig. 4, it can be found that the content-type of the candidate is the most significant feature for identifying the head request while the time gap between candidates and their referrers is the least important feature.

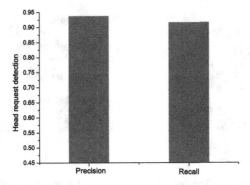

Fig. 3. The precision and recall using the synthesized data collected in a controlled environment

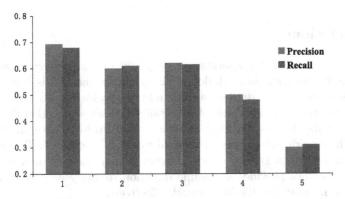

Fig. 4. The precision and recall using different classification rule. The classification rule from 1 to 5 is content-type, amount of embedded objects, the size of candidates, keyword and the threshold of the time gap, in sequence

4.2 Use-Click Pattern Analysis

The real-world data trace is collected from 4G mobile service provider in the Shenzhen city. The vast majority of the traffic is generated by the applications on smart-phones and tablets. The data-collection lasts a week. The raw data is about 48.2 TB and the amount of collected mobile terminal is about 2.15 million. Setting the time-slot of click-through stream as 15 min, the user-click analysis for the above data trace is shown in Fig. 5(b). To analyze the user-click, we also employ the data trace from 3G mobile service from the same area and the analysis result is shown in Fig. 5(b). It can be found that the click-through stream of 4G network is more deeper than that of 3G network. In a click-through stream, 27.3% users browsed 2 websites and 9.2% users browsed 3 websites or over in 4G network while 19.7% users browsed 2 websites and only 5.1% users browsed 3 websites or over in 3G network.

834   S. Wang et al.

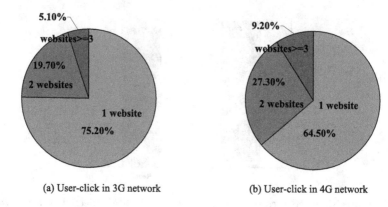

(a) User-click in 3G network   (b) User-click in 4G network

Fig. 5. User-click analysis in a real-world network

5   Conclusions

In this work, a systematic approach is proposed to study users click-through patterns in 4G network using Hadoop. The proposed method is first validated by synthesized web traffic data set and then by the real-world 4G network traffic data. The experiment on synthesized web traffic data set reveals that the content-type of the candidate is the most significant feature for identifying the head request. The experiment results on the real-world 4G network traffic data show that the click-through stream of 4G network is more deeper than that of 3G network. This work provides a possible direction to study modern web traffic, as well as to manage the 4G/5G network effectively.

Acknowledgment. This work was supported in part by China Postdoctoral Science Foundation (Grant No. 2014M562223), Shenzhen Basic Research Project (Grant No. JCYJ20140610151856729), and Natural Science Foundation of Guangdong Province (Grant No. 2014A030310154).

References

1. Erman, J., Gerber, A., Sen, S.: HTTP in the home: it Is not just about PCs. In: ACM SIGCOMM (2011)
2. Ihm, S., Pai, V.: Towards understanding modern web traffic. In: ACM IMC (2011)
3. Butkiewicz, M., Madhyastha, H., Sekar, V.: Understanding website complexity: measurements, metrics, and implications. In: ACM IMC (2011)
4. Maier, G., Feldmann, A., Paxson, V., Allman, M.: On dominant characteristics of residential broadband internet traffic. In: Proceedings of the Internet Measurement Conference, Chicago, Illinois (2009)
5. Broder, A., et al.: Graph structure in the web. Comput. Netw. **33**(1), 309–320 (2000)
6. Gill, P., Arlitt, M., Carlsson, N., Mahanti, A., Williamson, C.: Characterizing organizational use of web-based services: methodology, challenges, observations, and insights. ACM TWEB **5**(4), 1–23 (2011)

7. Schneider, F., Feldmann, A., Krishnamurthy, B., Willinger, W.: Understanding online social network usage from a network perspective. In: Proceedings of the IMC (2009)

8. Nazir, A., Raza, S., Gupta, D., Chuah, C.-N., Krishnamurthy, B.: Network level footprints of facebook applications. In: Proceedings of the IMC (2009)

9. Schneider, F., Agarwal, S., Alpcan, T., Feldmann, A.: The new web: characterizing AJAX traffic. In: Claypool, M., Uhlig, S. (eds.) PAM 2008. LNCS, vol. 4979, pp. 31–40. Springer, Heidelberg (2008)

10. Nah, F.: A study on tolerable waiting yime: how long are web users willing to wait? Behav. Inf. Technol. 23(3), 153–163 (2004)

11. Labovitz, C., Lekel-Johnson, S., Oberheide, J., Jahanian, F.: Internet inter-domain traffic. In: ACM SIGCOMM (2010)

12. Belson, D.: Akamai state of the internet report. SIGOPS Oper. Syst. Rev. 44(3), 27–C37 (2010)

13. Crescenzi, V, Mecca, G., Merialdo, P.: RoadRunner: towards automatic data extraction from large web sites. In: VLDB, pp. 109–118 (2001)

14. Fetterly, D., Manasse, M., Najork, M., et al.: A large-scale study of the evolution of web pages. Softw. Pract. Experience Spec. Issue Web Technol. 34(2), 213–237 (2004)

Detecting Targets Based on a Realistic Detection and Decision Model in Wireless Sensor Networks

Tian Wang[1]([✉]), Zhen Peng[1], Junbin Liang[2], Yiqiao Cai[1], Yonghong Chen[1], Hui Tian[1], and Bineng Zhong[1]

[1] College of Computer Science and Technology, Huaqiao University, Xiamen, Fujian, China
wsnman@gmail.com
[2] School of Computer, Electronics and Information, Guangxi University, Nanning, Guangxi, China

Abstract. Target detection applications in Wireless sensor networks (WSNs) need to detect whether the target is present or not. For accurate detection, sensors need to collaborate with each other to determine the target's presence. However, most of existing works use the "simple disk model" and the "majority rule" to model sensed signal and to make the final decision, respectively, which may not obtain the true judgment. In this work, we utilize a realistic signal model and a probabilistic decision model to describe the sensing process of sensors as well as to make the final decision. Moreover, we propose a realistic decision algorithm in which local signal measurements of sensors are converted to corresponding local detection probabilities in order to make a rational final decision. The effectiveness of the proposed model and algorithm are both validated by simulation results, which show high detection probabilities and acceptable false alarm probabilities.

1 Introduction

In recent years, wireless sensor networks (WSNs) have growing number of applications such as target tracking, object localization, data transmission and so on. Among them, target detection has been a typical use of WSNs [2]. A traditional target detection scenario usually consists of an area of interest where many sensors are deployed. The goal of target detection is to detect the presence of the target/event accurately, namely, achieving high detection probability [7] and low false alarm probability [13]. For doing this, sensors in the area usually need to complete two things: (1) sensing the environment situation and (2) determine whether the target is present or not.

This work is supported by the National Natural Science Foundation (NSF) of China, under grant 61202468, 61370007, 61302094, 61202299 and 61305085, and the Natural Science Foundation of Fujian Province of China, under grant 2014J01240 and 2015J01257.

For a single sensor, sensing the environment situation is largely related to its sensing ability. Generally, sensing radius is an essential character to measure the sensing ability. In some literatures, researchers regard the sensing radius as a boundary that only if a target is within the radius distance can it be detected [3]. This kind of detection model is called a disk model, which is too idealistic. First, since the signal emitted from the target is continuously attenuated with the increasing in distance, it's hard to choose the appropriate radius to get a binary decision. Second, as there are background noises, the sensing radius cannot be a constant. In this paper, we utilize a more realistic signal attenuation model to describe the sensing process. In this model, the signal measured by sensors attenuates continuously with the increase in distance and the influence of noise is also considered. Therefore, signal measurements of sensors can be realistically described rather than a simple binary value.

Moreover, although a single sensor can detect whether a target is present in its vicinity, it is better to aggregate several sensors' decisions. Generally, a single sensor's decision is called a local decision. A fusion center in the network collects local decisions and then makes a global/final decision about the target's presence [6]. Therefore, how to make the global decision is a critical issue for target detection. One of the widespread fusion methods is "majority rule". As its name suggests, the majority rule leans to choose the same decision with the majority part of all local decisions. For example, if more than a half of sensors decide that some target is present, the fusion center will correspondingly decide that the target is present. However, there are a couple of problems for the majority rule. The first is how to set a threshold for all sensors. A uniform threshold is not reasonable as a faraway sensor can hardly get the same signal strength as that of a near one from the target. It can be described as the saying that the absolute fairness is unfair. Second, if faraway sensors make up the majority, the final decision is likely to be 0 even if some adjacent sensors to the target indeed detect it. This kind of situation can be called the *dilemma of democracy*. In this paper, we propose a realistic decision model based on local probabilities to improve the fusion process. In this model, every sensor has its own measurement threshold which is related to its location. The measurement values detected by sensors are transformed to corresponding local detection probabilities. Based on the model, we also propose a detection algorithm, in which we use local detection probabilities to estimate the presence probability of the target.

Therefore, our main contributions in this work are as follows:

1. We propose a more realistic decision model to make decision fusion, which is based on a realistic detection model for sensors.
2. Based on the new model, we design a new target detection algorithm to improve detection quality. The detection quality can be guaranteed even if there are few close sensors to the target
3. The proposed model and algorithm are validated by simulations which are implemented in NS-2 simulator. The results demonstrate high detection probabilities and acceptable false alarm probabilities.

The rest of the paper is organized as follows. Section 2 reviews related work. Section 3 introduces the system model and the problem definition. Section 4 presents the decision model and the solution for target detection. Simulation results are demonstrated in Sect. 5. Section 6 concludes this paper.

2   Related Work

Target detection is an important application in WSNs and attracts a large number of scholars to conduct research in recent years. In earlier research, the disk model of sensors is widely employed, which means the sensing field of a sensor is like a disk around it and the sensor can detect a target only if the distance between them is less than the radius of the disk. Brass [3] discuss and analyze search strategies and target detection capabilities of networks from other literatures in various models of sensors and targets. It can be seen that all these detection strategies use the Boolean sensing model with a constant sensing radius. Lazos et al. [7] map the target detection problem to a line-set intersection problem, and employ an adjusted disk model that the sensing range of sensors can be changed within the limitation of perimeter.

As WSNs for target detection get further studied, scholars gradually adopt more realistic sensing model rather than disk model according to sensors' features. Zhou et al. [15] investigate the detection performance and hope to find a few critical positions to deploy additional sensors so that the freedom of targets can be limited. Therefore, their detection rule is simple that any sensor who has detected the target can indicate its presence. Tan et al. [9] exploit reactive mobility to improve the target detection performance. The detection consensus is based on a positive system decision when not less than a half of sensors in the group all make their positive local decisions. Yi et al. [14] propose a hierarchical decision fusion scheme to improve network wide detection probability. The fusion method is based on the number of positive decisions and higher level decision is based on that of lower level. The problem for these strategies is that the final decision is always based on a certain number, such as one or a half of the total, of positive local decisions made by sensors. In fact, there are times when even only a fewer number of positive local decisions should lead to a positive global decision. Therefore, some more reasonably realistic indicators, rather than only a fixed number, should be set as the benchmark for making decisions.

In this paper, sensors detect the target through a realistic attenuation signal model and can make a more reasonable decision about the presence of target based on a probabilistic decision model as well. In the decision model, the measurement threshold of each sensor is adaptive and the measurement values from sensors are transformed to reasonable probabilistic value. Therefore, the fusion center can rationally estimate the presence probability of the target and then make a final decision.

3 System and Problem Statements

3.1 Detection Model

We use the detection model based on the detection probability similar to literature [9,12]. The target itself emits a signal, e.g., acoustic signal. A sensor can detect the target by measuring its energy. Meanwhile, the measurements of sensors are contaminated by background noise which is modeled as additive Gaussian noise. Assume that H_0 represents the hypothesis that the target is absent and that H_1 represents the other hypothesis that the target is present. Thus the energy measurement e_i of sensor i is given by

$$H_0 : \quad e_i = e_n \tag{1a}$$

$$H_1 : \quad e_i = e_s(d_i) + e_n \ . \tag{1b}$$

Among them, e_n is the energy of noise to which sensor i is exposed; $e_s(d_i)$ is the attenuated signal energy at the position of sensor i, and d_i is the Euclidean distance between sensor i and the target. The $e_s(d_i)$ attenuates with the increasing of d_i and can be expressed as

$$e_s(d_i) = \begin{cases} \dfrac{S_0}{(d_i/d_0)^k} & if\ d_i > d_0 \\ S_0 & if\ d_i \le d_0 \ . \end{cases} \tag{2}$$

Among them, d_0 is a constant as a reference factor, and S_0 is the signal energy measured within the distance d_0 to the source. k is an attenuation factor which is typically from 2 to 5. The noise energy e_n approximately satisfies the Gaussian distribution with mean equal to μ and variance equal to σ^2. Therefore, the total signal energy value measured by sensor i follows a Gaussian distribution, which is given by

$$H_0 : \quad e_i \sim \mathcal{N}(\mu, \sigma^2) \tag{3a}$$

$$H_1 : \quad e_i \sim \mathcal{N}(\mu + e_s(d_i), \sigma^2). \tag{3b}$$

3.2 Network Model and Detection Problem

Network Model. The sensor network consists of a number of fixed sensor nodes, which are randomly deployed in an 2-dimension area of interest. All sensors know their own position and have synchronized clocks [8]. We assume that targets appear at some particular physical locations in this area with certain probabilities. These locations are referred to as target spots. The locations of target spots are known for two reasons: (1) for most situations, the intruders, as targets, only appear in some specific locations such as the entrance or door [10], and (2) after operating for a certain amount of time, the sensor network can identify some target spots where targets are likely to appear based on detection history [9]. After target spots are identified, the network is organized into clusters that each cluster monitors a target spot. The clusters can be dynamically formed [4] when the network is initialized or when the target spots are changed. We note that any suitable clustering protocol can be utilized here and no particular clustering method will be discussed in this paper. In fact, as every cluster performs detection separately with identical process, we narrow down our discussion to one cluster and target spot hereafter.

Problem Definition. There are N sensors randomly deployed in a 2-dimension $L \times L$ plane detection area. The target appears or disappears at the target spot and its signal sensed by sensors is modeled in Sect. 3.1. These sensors are required to detect the target when it is present. Our goal is to develop a method to improve the detection accuracy as much as possible, that is, to improve the detection probability and reduce the false alarm probability. The formula of detection probability and false alarm probability are given in following Sect. 4.2.

4 Target Detection Algorithm Based on a Probabilistic Decision Model

4.1 Probabilistic Decision Model

This section introduces the method for detecting the target. According to (3), the probability of getting the measurement e_i for sensor i is expressed as

$$H_0: \quad p_f(e_i) = \frac{1}{\sqrt{2\pi}\sigma} \exp\left(-\frac{(e_i - \mu)^2}{2\sigma^2}\right) \tag{4a}$$

$$H_1: \quad p_d(e_i) = \frac{1}{\sqrt{2\pi}\sigma} \exp\left(-\frac{(e_i - \mu - e_s(d_i))^2}{2\sigma^2}\right). \tag{4b}$$

At first, the local decisions are generated by every single sensor. Traditionally, the decision rule is based on Likelihood Ratio Test [1,11]. That is, according to the measured value in Sect. 3.1, sensor i compares its signal energy measurement with its threshold λ_i which is equal to $e_s(d_i) + \mu - \sigma^2$. If it is greater than λ_i, the sensor decides 1 which means it detects the target, otherwise it decides 0 which means it doesn't. Generally, the probability of making a positive decision when the target is actually absent is called the false alarm probability, and the probability of making a positive decision when the target is indeed present is called the detection probability [11]. Let P_F^i and P_D^i respectively represent the local false alarm probability and the detection probability of sensor i. According to (4), they can be expressed as

$$P_F^i = \Pr(e_i \geq \lambda_i \mid H_0) = \int_{\lambda_i}^{\infty} p_f(e_i) de_i \tag{5}$$

$$P_D^i = \Pr(e_i \geq \lambda_i \mid H_1) = \int_{\lambda_i}^{\infty} p_d(e_i) de_i \tag{6}$$

where $\Pr(\cdot)$ is the probability function. It shows that sensors closer to the target can lead to higher detection probability. In order to make a final decision [11], a fusion center collects all local decisions in order to make a fusion.

4.2   Probabilistic Decision Method

In the following, we introduce a new decision method. This method fully utilizes the signal value sensed by sensors and extracts the useful information to make decisions. Let A stands for the event that the target is present. The events that the measurement values sensed by n sensors are greater or equal than $\lambda_1, \lambda_2, \ldots, \lambda_n$ are denoted by $B_1, B_2, \ldots, B_n$ respectively. In other words, event B_i means sensor i detects a target. Therefore, the joint probability of B_i where $i = 1, 2, \ldots, n$ can be used to estimate the odds of A's occurrence. In our model, the estimation probability Q which is given by

$$Q = P(A \mid B_1 B_2 \ldots B_n) \tag{7}$$

which denotes the probability of A with the occurrence of $B_1 B_2 \ldots B_n$. According to Bayes' theorem, it can be represented as

$$Q = \frac{P(A B_1 B_2 \ldots B_n)}{P(B_1 B_2 \ldots B_n)}$$

$$= \frac{P(A) P(B_1 B_2 \ldots B_n \mid A)}{P(B_1 B_2 \ldots B_n \mid A) P(A) + P(B_1 B_2 \ldots B_n \mid \overline{A}) P(\overline{A})}. \tag{8}$$

Since events $B_1, B_2, \ldots, B_n$ are independent, the items in the denominator can be represented by $P(B_1 \mid A) P(B_2 \mid A) \ldots P(B_n \mid A)$ and $P(B_1 \mid \overline{A}) P(B_2 \mid \overline{A}) \ldots P(B_n \mid \overline{A})$, respectively, which can be obtained from (6) and (5), respectively. Moreover, $P(\overline{A})$ is equal to $1 - P(A)$, and $P(A)$ can be estimated by historical event information [9]. With this formula, we can compute the probability according to the signals sensed by multiple sensors. If this probability is not less than a threshold ϕ, the target is detected. Therefore, the system false alarm probability and the detection probability, denoted by P_F and P_D, respectively, are expressed as

$$P_F = \Pr(Q \geq \phi \mid H_0) \tag{9}$$

$$P_D = \Pr(Q \geq \phi \mid H_1). \tag{10}$$

We propose our target detection algorithm presented as Algorithm 1. When the network is initialized or when the target spot is changed, sensors around the target spot form a cluster around the spot and a cluster head C_H is selected as the fusion center. According to location information, sensors calculate their own measurement thresholds. Sensors work in detection cycles, which are related to their operating frequency. In every detection cycle, a sensor collects its background signal to detect whether a target is present. If it detects a target as its measurement e_i is hard enough, it will send its λ_i and d_i to C_H. As the sensor's operating frequency is quite high, the detection delay can be ignored. According to (8) and the properties of normal distribution, the C_H calculates the probability Q in order to make a final decision. If Q is not less than the threshold ϕ, C_H decides 1, which means a target is present; Otherwise, C_H decides 0 to indicate the absence of a target. In general, the threshold ϕ can be set 50 % for average estimation. It can be analyzed that, the time complexity for C_H to get Q is $O(n)$ in a single detection cycle. Therefore, the whole time complexity of the algorithm is $O(RDn)$, where R is the cluster round number and D is the detection cycle number.

Algorithm 1. Target Detection Algorithm based on *Probabilistic Decision Model*

1: Sensors around the target spot form a cluster;
2: **for** every sensor i **do**
3:       $\lambda_i := e_s(d_i) + \mu - \sigma^2$
4: **end for**
5: **for** every cluster round **do**
6:       A cluster head C_H is selected; /* It can be any existing method, such as [5]. */
7:       Sensors in a cluster exchange their location information;
8:       **for** every detection cycle **do**
9:             **for** sensor i in the cluster **do**
10:                   **if** $e_i \geq \lambda$ **then**
11:                         i sends λ_i and d_i to C_H;
12:                   **end if**
13:             **end for**
14:             C_H calculates the probability Q using (8)
15:             **if** $Q \geq \phi$ **then**
16:                   C_H outputs the final decision 1;
17:             **else**
18:                   C_H outputs the final decision 0;
19:             **end if**
20:       **end for**
21: **end for**

---

5 Performance Evaluation

In order to verify the effectiveness of our proposed model and algorithm, we conduct simulations with NS-2. In the simulation scenario, sensors are randomly deployed in an area of interest, which is $30\times30\mathrm{m}^2$. The probability of target's presence is 5%, and S_0 is 5 dB with d_0 as 5m. For noise, μ is 0.01 dB and σ^2 is equal to 2μ.

For comparison, we conduct two other target detection algorithms. The first is majority-rule-based algorithm, whose fusion decision rule is the majority rule. The second is the method without fusion, that is, the closest sensor to targets makes the final decision as same as its local decision. In our simulation, *PD* refers to our proposed algorithm, *MD* represents the majority-rule-based one and *CD* stands for the closest-based one.

In the first part, we deploy sensors within $3d_0$ from the target spot. Figure 1 shows how the system detection probabilities are achieved by *PD*, *MD* and *CD* respectively when the number of sensors increases from 2 to 6. Obviously, *PD* achieves the best performance among these three algorithms. When the number of sensors increases, *PD* gradually achieves 100% in detection probability. To the contrary, the performance of *MD* tends to slide down. For *CD* method, it has more opportunity to choose a better sensor when the number of sensors increases, so its performance improves in some degree. When the number of sensors is 6, detection probability achieved by *PD* outperforms *MD* and *CD* by 100% and 45%, respectively.

In Fig. 2, the results of false alarm probability of these three algorithm are presented. It can be seen that *PD* achieves a relatively high false alarm probability. Note that although *PD* has the highest false alarm probability, the probability itself is tiny with the unit ‰and the largest value is even less than 1‰.

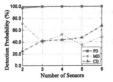 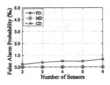 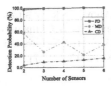 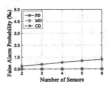

Fig. 1. Detection probability performance within $3d_0$ range.

Fig. 2. False alarm probability perfor-mance within 3d0 range.

Fig. 3. Detection probability performance within $1d_0$ to $3d_0$ range.

Fig. 4. False alarm probability performance within $1d_0$ to $3d_0$ range.

With this little bit of sacrifice in false alarm probability, PD can achieve a large boost in detection probability as showed in Fig. 1, which is valuable.

In the second part, we deploy sensors within $1d_0$ to $3d_0$ from the target spot. This experiment simulates the scenario where there are few sensors in the vicinity of the target. In this situation, the collaborative fusion between sensors is even more important. Figure 3 shows how PD, MD and CD perform with less adjacent sensors to the target spot. It can be seen that PD is hardly affected and its detection probability is still very high. However, those two others algorithm suffer from the change more or less. When there are 6 sensors, PD's performance is over 150 % and 400 % higher than that of MD and CD, respectively.

In Fig. 4, it can be seen that less adjacent sensors also have influences on PD to some extent. As more faraway sensors take part in the detection and fusion process, the false alarm probability of PD increases a little. However, this influence is pretty limited as the value of probability is still very little, which is acceptable.

6   Conclusion

In this paper, we discuss our improvement for target detection solutions in sensing and fusion aspects. First, rather than using simple disk model, we utilize a realistic signal model to describe the sensing process of sensors. After that, we analyze the defects of majority rule which is widely used in decision fusion methods. We propose a probabilistic decision model to make the final decision, in which local signal measurements are converted to corresponding final decision and even those faraway sensors can make contribution to target detection process. Based on these improved models, we propose a realistic detection algorithm to detect target more reasonably. Simulation results show that our proposed algorithm can perform a high detection probability even with lack of adjacent sensors to the target. Although the algorithm produces a little bit of false alarm probability, the influence is quite limited and acceptable in real applications. In the future, we plan to improve our method with some new prospective and introduce mobile sensor nodes to join the detection.

Acknowledgment. Above work was supported in part by grants from the National Natural Science Foundation (NSF) of China under Grant No. 61202468, 61370007, 61302094, 61202299 and 61305085 and the Natural Science Foundation of Fujian Province of China (No. 2014J01240 and No. 2015J01257).

References

1. Addison, L.S.: Statistical Signal Processing: Detection, Estimation, and Time Series Analysis. Addison-Wesley, Reading (1991)
2. Arora, A., Dutta, P., Bapat, S., Kulathumani, V., Zhang, H., Naik, V., Mittal, V., Cao, H., Demirbas, M., Gouda, M., et al.: A line in the sand: a wireless sensor network for target detection, classification, and tracking. Comput. Netw. **46**(5), 605–634 (2004)
3. Brass, P.: Bounds on coverage and target detection capabilities for models of networks of mobile sensors. ACM Trans. Sens. Netw. (TOSN) **3**(2), 9–27 (2007)
4. Chen, W.P., Hou, J.C., Sha, L.: Dynamic clustering for acoustic target tracking in wireless sensor networks. IEEE Trans. Mob. Comput. **3**(3), 258–271 (2004)
5. Chen, W.P., Hou, J.C., Sha, L.: Dynamic clustering for acoustic target tracking in wireless sensor networks. IEEE Trans. Mob. Comput. **3**(3), 258–271 (2004)
6. Clouqueur, T., Saluja, K.K., Ramanathan, P.: Fault tolerance in collaborative sensor networks for target detection. IEEE Trans. Comput. **53**(3), 320–333 (2004)
7. Lazos, L., Poovendran, R., Ritcey, J.A.: Probabilistic detection of mobile targets in heterogeneous sensor networks. In: Proceedings of the 6th International Conference on Information Processing in Sensor Networks, pp. 519–528. ACM (2007)
8. Li, Q., Rus, D.: Global clock synchronization in sensor networks. IEEE Trans. Comput. **55**(2), 214–226 (2006)
9. Tan, R., Xing, G., Wang, J., So, H.C.: Exploiting reactive mobility for collaborative target detection in wireless sensor networks. IEEE Trans. Mob. Comput. **9**(3), 317–332 (2010)
10. Varano, V.: Alarm system activated by buzzers, uS Patent 4,520,349, 28 May 1985
11. Varshney, P.K.: Distributed Detection and Data Fusion. Springer, New York (1996)
12. Wang, T., Peng, Z., Chen, Y., Cai, Y., Tian, H.: Continuous tracking for mobile targets with mobility nodes in wsns. In: 2014 International Conference on Smart Computing (SMARTCOMP), pp. 261–268. IEEE (2014)
13. Wang, W., Srinivasan, V., Chua, K.C., Wang, B.: Energy-efficient coverage for target detection in wireless sensor networks. In: Proceedings of the 6th International Conference on Information Processing in Sensor Networks, pp. 313–322. ACM (2007)
14. Yi, L., Deng, X., Ding, D., Zou, Z., Wang, W.: Dcdf: a distributed clustered decision fusion scheme for target detection in wireless sensor networks. In: 2014 IEEE 17th International Conference on Computational Science and Engineering (CSE), pp. 483–486. IEEE (2014)
15. Zhou, S., Wu, M.Y., Shu, W.: Improving mobile target detection on randomly deployed sensor networks. Int. J. Sens. Netw. **6**(2), 115–128 (2009)

Ant Colony-Based Energy Control Routing Protocol for Mobile Ad Hoc Networks

Jipeng Zhou$^{(\boxtimes)}$, Xuefeng Wang, Haisheng Tan, and Yuhui Deng

Department of Computer Science, Jinan University,
Guang Zhou 510632, People's Republic of China
tjpzhou@jnu.edu.cn

Abstract. The energy of nodes is limited in mobile ad hoc networks (MANETs). In order to extend the lifetime of networks, how to select the best route is the critical issue for routing protocol in MANETs. In this paper, Ant Colony-based Energy Control Routing (ACECR) Protocol is proposed for MANETs. The goal of the proposed protocol is to find an optimized route by using the positive feedback character of Ant Colony optimization (ACO). In ACECR protocol, the route choice is dependent on not only hops between nodes and the energy of nodes, but also the average energy and the minimum energy of the routes to find the route with more energy. Simulation results show that ACECR protocol has better performance than existing protocols in balanced energy use and network lifetime.

Keywords: Mobile ad hoc network · Routing protocols · Ant colony optimization · Energy

1 Introduction

A MANET is self-organizing, dynamic topology network, which enables wireless communication between mobile devices without relying on a fixed infrastructure. Due to limited resources such as power, bandwidth, processing capability and storage space at the nodes as well as mobility, it is important to reduce routing overheads in MANETs, while ensuring a high rate of packet delivery. Since the battery of nodes is limited, the energy of nodes and the life time of network is a critical problem in MANETs. ACO [1] is one computational model of swarm intelligence which provides efficient solutions to several optimization problems. In ACO routing algorithms, multiple ants created by a node traverse the network to search paths between two nodes. If the ant finds a path, it lays down pheromone on the path, the amount of pheromone depends on quality of the path such as its number of hops, delay, energy and etc. A data packet is transmitted on a link with probability based on the amount of pheromone. ACO routing algorithm

This work is supported by NSFC(61373125,61272073), GDNSF(S2013020012865) and GDSTP(2013B010401016).

© Springer International Publishing Switzerland 2015
K. Xu and J. Zhu (Eds.): WASA 2015, LNCS 9204, pp. 845–853, 2015.
DOI: 10.1007/978-3-319-21837-3_83

exhibits interesting properties for MANETs; it works in a fully distributed way and provides multi-path routing.

Routing algorithms for MANETs based on ACO have been proposed in [2–8]. AntHocNet [2] is a hybrid multi-path algorithm with the principle of ACO-based routing in MANETs. It uses FANT to find routes and BANT to build routes from source node to destination node. In recent years, the power problem in MANETs has been receiving significant attention due to power limited batteries in mobile nodes. Power management schemes have two objectives [3], that is to minimize the total network consumption and to minimize the power consumption per node. The first method targets to extend the overall network lifetime and the later aims to extend individual node's lifetime. The overall power consumption reduction can be achieved by two different approaches. An ant-based on-demand energy route (AOER) protocol is proposed for mesh network [4]. Compared to other ant-based route protocols, AOER needs less memory storages and lower processing capabilities for the structures of ants can be simplified by the specific inverse pheromone table. An Energy-Aware Ant-Based Routing(EAAR) protocol is proposed in [5]. It takes into account the various factors such as the power consumed in transmitting a packet and the residual battery capacity of a node to increase the battery life of the nodes by reducing the repetitive use of a selection of these nodes. The minimum battery energy remaining from the weakest node of the route and the hop-count of the route are used the metric for path discovery. An ant-based energy efficient routing protocol (AEERP) is proposed in MANETs [6], the route choice is dependent on not only hops between nodes, but also the energy consumed in transmitting packets and the residual energy of nodes to increase the battery lifetime of the nodes by reducing the repetitive use of a selection of these nodes. AEERP can balance the energy consumption of nodes in the network and extends the network lifetime. This paper is organized as follows. In Sect. 2, we propose Ant Colony-based Energy Control Routing protocol ACECR. In Sect. 3, we give some simulation results; Sect. 4 concludes the paper.

2   Ant Colony-Based Energy Control Routing Protocol

The efficient foraging behavior of naturally occurring small-sized and energy-constrained ants is studied and resulted in the theory of ACO [1]. ACO uses the concept of artificial ants, which is analogous to the natural ants that behave as packets in MANETs. In ACO-based routing algorithms, pheromone content is used to choose the best paths out of a given network. It can be used to forward data stochastically, data for the same destination can be spread over multiple paths, with more data going towards higher quality paths, this results in load balancing. ACO-based routing algorithms perform better in many ways due to their proactive and iterative behavior. The ACO-based route algorithms reduce variability and errors in networks by choosing trusted path which have behaved well for quite some time.

2.1 Data Structures of Ants

In this section, we propose an ant colony-based energy control routing protocol ACECR. In ACECR, when source node wants to send data packet to destination node, source node checks its pheromone table and finds the next node. If pheromone table does not have next node to the destination node, source node will start path discovery process. Source node sends request packet, which called Fant (Forward ant). When a node receives Fant, the node will update the node list and record the node which Fant has passed. Each node in networks forwards the Fant packet until it reaches the destination. When Fant arrives destination node, it will create a new packet which is called Bant (Backward ant). The destination will send the Bant back to the source node along the reverse route. Structures of Fant and Bant are shown in Tables 1 and 2, where SID: source ID; DID: destination ID; Seq: the sequence number of the forward ant(backward ant); HOP: the hops from the source node to the current node for Fant or the hops from the destination node to the current node for Bant; Path: the listed node ID of routing path; E_{min}: the minimum residual energy of nodes in Path; E_{sum}: the summation of residual energy of nodes in Path; TTL: the living time of the ant.

Table 1. Structure of Fant

SID	DID	Seq	HOP	Path	TTL

Table 2. Structure of Bant

SID	DID	Seq	HOP	Path	E_{min}	E_{sum}

To maintain the amount of pheromone on a link, each node has a pheromone table that maintains the amount of pheromone on each incident link. The pheromone table, as shown in Table 3, is a two-dimensional array, in which the row and the column denote neighboring nodes and destination nodes respectively. A value ϕ_{nd} in pheromone table of node u is the amount of pheromone on a link (u, n) in paths to destination d. Thus, the amount ϕ_{nd} of pheromone represents how good the link (u, n) is to transmit a data packet to the destination d. The notations used in this paper are shown in Table 4.

2.2 Route Discovery Process

To establish a path from a source s to a destination d, source s creates a Fant and broadcasts it to all neighbors of s. The aim of Fant is to search a path from source s to destination d, by traversing the network and establishes the pheromone track to the source node. Node i forwards a Fant according to Procedure sendFant(i), if node i has routing information available for d, the node i will forward it to next node j with probability $P_i(j) = \frac{(\phi_{jd})^{\beta}}{\sum_{s \in N_i} (\phi_{sd})^{\beta}}$, where N_i is the neighbor node set

Table 3. Structure of Pheromone Table at Node u

	destination nodes				
neighbor	d_1	d_2		d_i	d_n
n_1	$\phi_{n_1 d_1}$	$\phi_{n_1 d_2}$	...	$\phi_{n_1 d_i}$	$\phi_{n_1 d_n}$
n_2	$\phi_{n_2 d_1}$	$\phi_{n_2 d_2}$	...	$\phi_{n_2 d_i}$	$\phi_{n_2 d_n}$
...	...	...	...	...	
n_k	$\phi_{n_k d_1}$	$\phi_{n_k d_2}$	...	$\phi_{n_k d_i}$	$\phi_{n_k d_n}$

Table 4. Notations Used in This Paper

Symbol	Comments
Fant:	forward ant
Bant:	Backward ant
ϕ	pheromone of nodes
E_{avg}	the average energy of a path
E_{sum}	the summary energy of a path
E_{min}	the minimum energy of a path
$E_{max}(v)$	the maximum energy of node v
$E_{cur}(v)$	the residual energy of node v
$N(v)$	the neighbor node set of node v
HOP	hop count of a path
$S_{Fant}(v)$	set of received Fants of node v

of node i, β is a constant parameter. If i has no pheromone for the destination d (i.e., $\forall j \in N_i, \phi_{jd} = 0$), Fant is broadcasted to all neighbors of node i.

/* Node i sends a Fant*/

Procedure sendFant(i)

1. if i is not a destination, then
2.   if there is an entry for destination d in pheromone table, then
3.   it selects a next node j with maximum probability $P_i(j)$
       and it sends Fant to node j
       else
4.   Broadcast Fant;
       endif
     else
5.   sendBant(i)
     endif
endProcedure

During the route request phase, when a node receives a Fant, the operations are done according to Procedure recvFant. It first checks whether the Fant is in the received S_{Fant} set of node i. If the Fant is in S_{Fant}, it denotes that the Fant has arrived at node i, it does not do anything; If the Fant is not in S_{Fant}, it adds its node ID to Fant.Path, then it checks the DID to determine whether the entry is its own ID. If a node is the destination, it will create a Bant to the source node along the discovered path and initialize some parameters such as $E_{min} = E_{sum} = 0$ and $HOP = 0$. If the node is not the destination, it forwards Fant according to sendFant procedure continually.

/* Node i receives a Fant*/

Procedure recvFant(i)

1. if Fant.ID is in $S_{Fant}(i)$, then return endif
2. it adds node i to Fant.Path and Fant.ID to $S_{Fant}(i)$
3. If i is the destination d, then
4.   node i creates a Bant, Bant.$E_{sum}(i) = 0$,
5.   Bant.$E_{min}(i) = 0$, Bant.$HOP = 0$, Bant.Path=Reverse(Fant.Path)
   else
6.   sendFant(i)
   endif
endProcedure

When a Fant reaches the destination d, node d creates a Bant as shown in Table 2. The task of the Bant is returning to the source node s along the path that was followed by the Fant and establishes the pheromone track to the destination node. Each node forwards Bant according to procedure sendBant. When a Bant arrives at the node i from its neighbor j, it updates corresponding parameters for path discovered by the Bant according to Procedure recvBant, $HOP = HOP+1$, $E_{min} = min\{E_{min}, E_{cur(i)}\}$, $E_{sum} = E_{sum} + E_{cur(i)}$, $E_{avg} = E_{sum}/(HOP+1)$, $\phi_{id} = \frac{E_{avg}*E_{min}}{HOP+1}$. The pheromone of a node is the maximum pheromone of all paths at this node. When a Bant arrives a node, it updates all parameters, the node forwards Bant to next node in the Path. When a Bant arrives the source node, multi-paths have been built and path discovery process is finished.

/* Node i sends a Bant*/

Procedure sendBant(i)

1. If i is not the source, then
2.   it selects a next node j in Bant.Path
3.   it sends Bant to j
   endif
endProcedure

/* Node i receives a Bant from node j*/

Procedure recvBant(i)

1. update parameters of Bant
   Bant.HOP=Bant.$HOP + 1$,
   Bant.E_{min} = min{Bant.E_{min}, $E_{cur}(i)$}, Bant.E_{sum}=Bant.$E_{sum} + E_{cur}(i)$,
   $E_{avg} = \frac{Bant.E_{sum}}{Bant.HOP}$, Bant.$\phi_{id} = \frac{E_{avg}*Bant.E_{min}}{Bant.HOP}$,
2. $\phi_{jd} = max\{$Bant.$\phi_{jd}, \phi_{jd}\}$

3. If v is not the source, then
4.   sendBant(i)
   else
5.   start data transmission
   endif
   endProcedure

2.3   Data Transmission and Route Maintenance

When routes are discovered, the data packets can be sent through one of them. When a node i receives a data packet for a destination d, node i sends the data packet to a neighbor j, which is selected with probability $P_i(j)$. If i has no pheromone for the destination d in its pheromone table, i sends the data packet to a neighbor j, which is selected randomly. If node i has no neighbor, the data packet is discarded. In order to maintain the path and keep alive, the ACECR should update pheromone value dynamically. The traversal of each data packet increases the pheromone value of each link by $\phi_{id} = \phi_{id} * (1 + \Delta_{id})$, where $\Delta_{id} = (E_{cur}(i))^\beta$ and β is a constant, generally we set $\beta = 0.1$. To adapt dynamic network change in the ACO routing algorithm, each node evaporates a amount of pheromone at regular time intervals as $\phi_{id} = \phi_{id} * (1 - \theta_{id})$, $\theta_{id} \in (0, 1)$ is evaporation rate.

In order to explain the proposed ACECR protocol, an example network topology is shown in Fig. 1. There are 11 nodes in the network, each node has its energy. We assume that node 1 is source and node 10 is destination. When source 1 broadcasts a Fant packet to find the route paths, there are many return ants from destination 10, when Bants arrive source 1, many paths are discovered with pheromone to the path listed at node 1 in Table 5. According to Table 5, a route table and route selection probability can be obtained by using RecvBant Procedure and probability calculation formula as shown in Table 6. The multiple paths can be used to forward data packet according to selected probability.

Table 5. Discovered Paths from 1 to 10 with Pheromone at Node 1

Paths	Pheromone
1-2-3-5-8-9-10	14.3
1-2-3-5-8-11-10	14.7
1-6-7-11-10	15.5
1-4-5-8-9-10	2.1
1-4-5-8-11-10	2.6

3   Simulation and Performance Evaluation

In this section, we compare the performance of our proposed protocol ACECR to other two protocols AODV [7] and EAAR [5]. AODV is the typical protocol

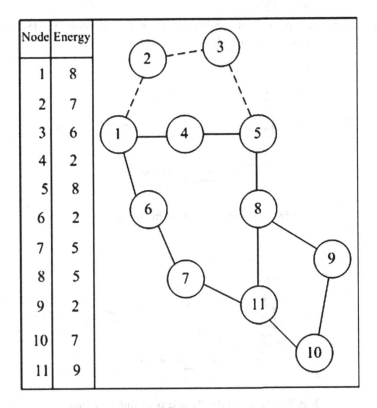

Node	Energy
1	8
2	7
3	6
4	2
5	8
6	2
7	5
8	5
9	2
10	7
11	9

Fig. 1. Network topology and energy distribution

Table 6. Routing Table and Selection Probability at Node 1

Destination	Next hop	Pheromone	Probability
10	2	41.7	0.69
10	6	15.5	0.26
10	4	2.6	0.95

in ad hoc networks and EAAR is based on ACO and use min-max energy to calculate pheromone value. NS-2 simulator is used to evaluate the performance of different protocols. There are 120 nodes in a network, which move around over a square $1000m * 1000m$ flat space. Node's MAC layer uses IEEE-802.11 DCF media access control protocol, the radio transmission range and the interference range of nodes are all set to be 200 meter. Each node has a total energy of $100J$. Mobile nodes are assumed to move randomly according to the random waypoint model [8]. The speed of nodes is set to be $5\,m/s$, each node starts moving from a randomly selected initial position to a target position, which is also selected randomly in the simulation. Each packet size is 512-bytes, 5 CBR flows are generated randomly at a rate of 10 packets per second for 1800 seconds to test the performance of protocols.

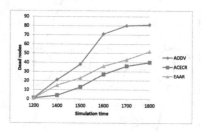

Fig. 2. Energy consumed in the network

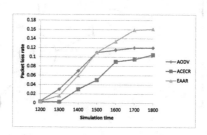

Fig. 3. The loss rate of packets at different time

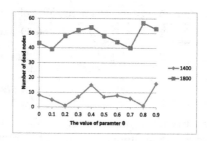

Fig. 4. Energy consumed with different value of evaporation rate θ

Figure 2 shows the number of dead nodes for AODV, EAAR and ACECR protocols at different simulation time. In Fig. 2, the longer the simulation time is, the more there is dead nodes in the network, the number of dead nodes of ACECR protocol is less AODV and EAAR protocols, since both average energy and minimum energy of a path is considered in ACECR, it can select a path with more residual energy on global view, EAAR only considers the residual energy of nodes instead of paths, AODV does not deal with energy balancing problem. Figure 3 shows the packet loss rate for AODV, EAAR and ACECR protocols at different simulation time. Because ACECR protocol forwards data packets with more residual energy path, the packet loss rate will less other two protocols. Figure 4 shows the impact of different value of evaporation rate parameter θ on the performance of networks. In Fig. 4, the number of dead nodes at 1800 second is more than that at 1400 second, this means that the longer the simulation time is, the more there is dead nodes in the network. There is not regular pattern for value selection of evaporation rate θ, the simulation results shows that the performance of the network is better when $\theta = 0.1, 0.5, 0.7$.

4   Conclusion

In this paper, we propose an ant colony-based energy control routing protocol ACECR for MANETs. In the ACECR protocol, the routing protocol will find the better route which has more energy than other routes through the analysis of average energy and minimum energy of paths. Simulation results show that ACECR is better performance than AODV and EAAR in the number of dead node, packet loss rate, this means that ACECR can extend the life time of network. In the future, we plan to test ant colony-based routing protocol for different mobility models in MANETs.

References

1. Dorigo, M., Stuetzle, T.: Ant Colony Optimation. Prentice Hall, Upper Saddle River (2004)
2. Caro, G.D., Ducatelle, F., Gambardella, L.M.: AntHocNet: an adaptive nature-inspired algorithm for routing in mobile Ad Hoc networks. Eur. Trans. Telecommun. **16**(5), 443–455 (2005)
3. Liang, C., Bourgeois, A.G., Yu, B.H.: Power management in wireless Ad Hoc networks using AODV. SNPD/SAWN **2005**(5), 436–443 (2005)
4. Shuang, B., Li, Z.B., Chen, J.P.: An ant-based on-demand energy route protocol for IEEE 802.15.4 mesh network. Int. J. Wirel. Inf. Netw. **16**(4), 225–236 (2009)
5. Misra, S., Dhurandher, S.K., Obaidat, M.S., et al.: An ant swarm-inspired energy-aware routing protocol for wireless Ad Hoc networks. J. Syst. Soft. **83**, 2188–2199 (2010)
6. Zhou, J.P., Lu, J.Z., Li, J.: Ant-based balancing energy routing protocol for mobile Ad Hoc networks. J. Internet Technol. **14**(5), 835–842 (2013)
7. Abedi, O., Fathy, M., Taghiloo, J.: Enhancing AODV routing protocol using mobility parameters in vanet: computer systems and applications. In: Proceedings of IEEE/ACS International Conference on Computer Systems and applications, (AICCSA 2008), pp. 229–235 (2008)
8. Lee, S.J., Su, W., Hsu, J., Gerla, M., Gagrodia, R.: A performance comparison study of Ad Hoc wireless multicast protocols. Proc. IEEE Infocom **2000**(2), 565–574 (2000)

Author Index

Printed in the United States
By Bookmasters